Pro Oracle Spatial for Oracle Database 11*g*

Ravi Kothuri, Albert Godfrind, and Euro Beinat

Apress®

Pro Oracle Spatial for Oracle Database 11*g*

ISBN-13 (hc): 978-1-59059-899-3 [*Originally published as a hardcover first edition on October 29, 2007.*]

ISBN-13 (pbk): 978-1-4302-4287-1

ISBN-13 (electronic): 978-1-4302-4288-8

President and Publisher: Paul Manning
Lead Editor: Jonathan Gennick
Technical Reviewer: Carel-Jan Engel
Editorial Board: Steve Anglin, Mark Beckner, Ewan Buckingham, Gary Cornell, Morgan Ertel, Jonathan Gennick, Jonathan Hassell, Robert Hutchinson, Michelle Lowman, James Markham, Matthew Moodie, Jeff Olson, Jeffrey Pepper, Douglas Pundick, Ben Renow-Clarke, Dominic Shakeshaft, Gwenan Spearing, Matt Wade, Tom Welsh
Coordinating Editor: Kylie Johnston
Copy Editor: Kim Wimpsett
Compositor: Kinetic Publishing Services, LLC
Indexer: BIM Indexing & Proofreading Services
Artist: Kinetic Publishing Services, LLC
Cover Designer: Anna Ishchenko

Distributed to the book trade worldwide by Springer Science+Business Media New York, 233 Spring Street, 6th Floor, New York, NY 10013. Phone 1-800-SPRINGER, fax (201) 348-4505, e-mail `orders-ny@springer-sbm.com`, or visit `www.springeronline.com`.

For information on translations, please e-mail `rights@apress.com`, or visit `www.apress.com`.

Apress and friends of ED books may be purchased in bulk for academic, corporate, or promotional use. eBook versions and licenses are also available for most titles. For more information, reference our Special Bulk Sales–eBook Licensing web page at `www.apress.com/bulk-sales`.

Any source code or other supplementary materials referenced by the author in this text is available to readers at `www.apress.com`. For detailed information about how to locate your book's source code, go to `www.apress.com/source-code/`.

Contents at a Glance

PART 5 ■ ■ ■ Spatial in Applications

PART 6 ■ ■ ■ Appendixes

Contents

PART 2 Basic Spatial

PART 3 ■■■ Spatial and Network Analysis

PART 6 Appendixes

About the Authors

RAVI KOTHURI has a PhD in computer science from the University of California, Santa Barbara, and has been an active researcher and developer in the spatial and multimedia areas for the past 15 years. Currently, he serves as project lead and software architect in the spatial development team of Oracle Corporation. He has more than 20 patents on specific Oracle technology and has authored numerous articles for database conferences and journals. Other activities include teaching database courses (most recently at Boston University), presenting at panel meetings and conferences, and reviewing of research articles for spatial and database conferences. Ravi enjoys music, movies, and playing with his children.

ALBERT GODFRIND has more than 25 years of experience in designing, developing, and deploying IT applications. His interest and enthusiasm for spatial information and geographical information systems started at Oracle when he discovered the spatial extensions of the Oracle database in 1998. Ever since, Albert has been "evangelizing" the use of spatial information both to GIS and IT communities across Europe, consulting with partners and customers, speaking at conferences, and designing and delivering in-depth technical training. Prior to joining Oracle Corporation, Albert held several positions in database engineering at Digital Equipment Corporation (DEC), where he worked on the development of the Rdb database system.

EURO BEINAT has a PhD in economics and a master's degree in electronics and systems engineering. He has been involved in consultancy for more than 10 years in evaluation and strategic advice in sectors ranging from IT, government, the oil industry, and large corporations. Currently, he is the managing director of Geodan Mobile Solutions and holds a chair on Location Services at the Vrije Universiteit of Amsterdam and at the University of Salzburg. His main skills combine geo-IT and the Internet, with an extensive competence in decision analysis and strategy.

About the Technical Reviewer

CAREL-JAN ENGEL is a member of the OakTable Network, lives in the Netherlands, and works as a freelancer. He has been working in IT since 1982, and he started to work with Oracle version 4 in 1985. Fastforms (Forms 1.3) didn't meet the requirements of the software project he was on, and he joined the team that was developing "better" programming tools and applications in C, based on the HLI, now known as the OCI. In 1992, he founded the Dutch software company Ease Automation, which he headed for almost ten years. Some of his projects during this time related to airports and had an important high-availability aspect to them, which inspired him to develop several techniques for standby databases, often pushing Oracle technology to its limits. In 1998, he won the Chamber of Commerce of Rotterdam's Entrepreneur of the Year award. In 2002, he decided to continue his career as a freelancer. He has been a regular author for several (Dutch) Oracle-related magazines since 1998.

Acknowledgments

Many people contributed to this book in numerous and important ways while remaining in the background. Together they have made it possible for us to complete this project and we hope publish a good book.

We would like to thank the team at Apress, in particular Tony Davis for his role in initiating this project and Jonathan Gennick for spearheading the revision. We also like to thank the project manager, Kylie Johnston; the copyeditor, Kim Wimpsett; and the production editor, Ellie Fountain, for their great job editing and proofreading the book as well as for their patience with shifting schedules, flexible submission times, and above all their willingness to consider at any moment improvements, changes, and adaptations that could make the book better.

We acknowledge the efforts of Daniel Abugov, Daniel Geringer, Siva Ravada, James Steiner, Jayant Sharma, Steven Serra, Jay Banerjee, and Steven Hagan at Oracle Corporation for their help in getting this book off the ground. Once we started writing the book, many other Oracle Spatial development team members, including John Herring, Baris Kazar, Bruce Blackwell, Jeffrey Xie, Jack Wang, and Richard Pitts, contributed with reviews of the chapters that fell in their respective areas of expertise. The reviews of these multiple Oracle experts (in addition to those from Apress reviewers) had a tangible effect on the quality of the text, its structure, and its completeness. Among these reviewers, special thanks go to Daniel Abugov and Siva Ravada for their multiple reviews of a majority of the chapters. Dan's comprehensive reviews and valuable suggestions have greatly enhanced the professional quality of the content. Finally, this book would not have been a reality if it were not for the cooperation and flexibility in work schedules extended by the Oracle Spatial management team (Siva Ravada and Steven Serra).

Consultants and application developers at Geodan Mobile Solutions provided a large amount of material for the case studies and reviewed several sections of the book. We would like to thank in particular Evert van Kootwijk and Valik Solorzano Barboza for their contributions regarding implementations of Oracle Spatial. We are also grateful for the contribution of Prof. Henk Scholten, who advised us on a number of sections of the book.

The team of eSpatial has also provided major inputs for the case studies. We would like to thank Matthew Bafford, Paul Baynham, David Miller, and Paul Saunders for their high-quality input, timely revisions, and continuous support. The book has also been reviewed by several independent external experts. We would like to thank in particular Carel-Jan Engel for his meticulous and sometimes very critical comments. We wished, occasionally, to be given an easier ride, but his comments have had a major impact on the book structure and content. They made a tangible and positive contribution to the overall quality of the book.

Several parties helped us collect the material necessary to compile the case studies. We would like to thank all organizations involved for their willingness to share with us their experiences in some important Oracle Spatial implementations. We are grateful to Transport for London (London Buses), the Dutch Ministry of the Interior and the ISC (ICT service association for the Dutch police), the Dutch Ministry of Environment and Spatial Planning and RIVM, the U.S. Department of Defense, and the U.S. Geological Survey.

Finally, we are indebted to our families for their patience and endurance during the book writing process. It is indeed difficult to understand why SQL, geometries, or long-distance conference calls have priority over holidays, birthdays, or weekends. Nonetheless, we had a great time writing this book, thanks to our families who managed to keep us on track while handling diverse priorities.

Ravi Kothuri
Albert Godfrind
Euro Beinat

Introduction

Organizations are discovering with increasing frequency that the vast majority of their information assets have a spatial component, for example, the location of customers, shipments, facilities, personnel, competitors, and so on. The ability to use this information properly is fundamental to reducing operational costs, optimizing production efficiency, and increasing the quality of service. Evidence of the benefits that can be achieved by exploiting spatial information is plentiful, and many organizations are looking at ways of harvesting these benefits.

We have been professionally involved in a variety of projects that introduced spatial information management into public and private organizations. The idea of writing this book came from these projects and from discussing spatial information management with the software developers and architects involved in them. We noticed a clear gap between the knowledge and skills necessary for successful spatial information management projects and the common background of the technical personnel usually involved in large IT and database developments.

The vast majority of these staff members had backgrounds in such diverse areas as database technology, Java, C++, PL/SQL, data models, security, availability, and scalability. However, only a small number had some experience with spatial data—for most, working with spatial data was completely new. It was easy to discover that spatial objects, geocoding, and map projections, for example, were foreign terms to most (and, of course, spatial information management is not about processing signals from space probes). Tools such as Google Maps and Google Earth have introduced few of these concepts to a large audience, but the majority of spatial technology still remains an esoteric subject.

It appears that this lack of knowledge of spatial technology is a common situation. Even within the extensive community of Oracle experts, Oracle Spatial skills are relatively new to many. For those of us who work at the interface between ICT, spatial informatics, management, and the traditional world of geography and mapping, the realization of this gap was especially revealing, and it presents a clear barrier to the diffusion of spatial information management through private and government organizations, where the demand for spatial applications is steadily growing. Furthermore, while Geographical Information Systems (GIS) are extensively used to manage spatial data, often as stand-alone systems, the vast majority of spatial data resides in corporate databases. It is by adding spatial intelligence to these databases that we probably disclose one of the largest untapped reservoirs of added value to organizations.

Oracle Spatial has grown to be one of the most established solutions for providing spatial intelligence to databases. Besides the extensive installed base of Oracle databases, Oracle Spatial manages spatial data just like any other data type, making it in principle easy for experienced database developers and architects to extend their scope into spatial information management. Using MapViewer technology, Oracle Spatial also makes it easy to create and integrate maps in business applications.

Despite the plethora of available books on spatial information management and GIS, we still encounter a lack of suitable material for Oracle developers or architects who do not have any spatial background. This leads to simplistic uses of Oracle Spatial and suboptimal implementations that frequently ignore the extensive list of Oracle Spatial capabilities. Besides the reference user guides, most knowledge about Oracle Spatial is scattered around in technical papers or—even worse—in the heads of those who have developed expertise and mastered the tool.

Our motivation for writing this book was to provide developers and architects with a reference source to master Oracle Spatial and take their skills to a professional level. This book does not replace the technical references. Instead, it presents concepts, examples, case studies, and tips to guide you toward a full understanding of the potential of Oracle Spatial and how to use it at an advanced level. We do not want to just familiarize you with Oracle Spatial; we want you to become an expert in Oracle Spatial.

What Does This Book Cover?

This book covers spatial information management in the Oracle database. In particular:

- It introduces the main concepts of spatial information management and how they relate to database concepts and tools.
- It describes the tools provided by Oracle Spatial to store, retrieve, analyze, and visualize spatial information.
- It presents examples, applications, and case studies that will help you facilitate the incorporation of these concepts and tools into your applications.

While most conceptual discussions will be of general validity, this book is about Oracle Spatial 11*g*, the newest release of the Oracle database product.

The focus of the chapters in this book is the application of Oracle Spatial technology to general e-business applications. All of the features that are relevant to such applications are discussed in full detail, with working examples based on the sample data supplied with the book. In the appendixes, we cover the topics that are more relevant to highly specialized GIS applications. These provide a more general overview of each topic and reference the Oracle documentation for full details.

The following list contains a chapter-by-chapter breakdown summarizing the key topics covered:

- *Setting Up*: The next section of this book, after this introduction, describes how to set up Oracle Spatial and the example schema required to run the code examples in this book. It then describes the specific e-business application and related dataset that are used for most examples in this book. The data used includes mapping data (for example, state boundaries, rivers, built-up areas), geocoding data (for example, lists of addresses with their x,y coordinates), network data (for example, road networks for computing travel distance and providing navigation instructions), and application-specific data (in this case, a set of tables with customers, stores/branches, and competitors). The data covers parts of the United States, such as the cities of Washington, D.C., and San Francisco, and uses typical U.S. terms and notations (for example, counties, interstates, and so on). This does not imply any loss of generality—the same examples can be made for any other similar dataset.
- *Chapter 1: Spatial Information Management*: In this chapter, we describe how spatial information is used in different industry segments and cover the typical functionality required for managing spatial/location information. We use a site-location example to illustrate different aspects of spatial information management: representation and storage using appropriate types, and analysis functionality for stored spatial data. We then discuss the systems that enable spatial information management, such as GIS, and their evolution. We finally look at the benefits of spatial information management using Oracle Spatial.
- *Chapter 2: Overview of Oracle Spatial*: The Oracle Spatial technology suite enables spatial information management inside Oracle. This chapter provides an overview of this suite, its architecture, and its functionality. The overview includes a concise description of the different features of Oracle Spatial, including storage using SDO_GEOMETRY, analysis using spatial operators, and visualization using Oracle MapViewer. We also illustrate how this functionality is productized into the components that are shipped with different editions of Oracle. Finally, we explain what to expect during and in a typical Oracle Spatial installation.

- *Chapter 3: Location-Enabling Your Applications*: In this chapter, we consider how to augment existing application tables with location information. We introduce an e-business application for this purpose, which we use in examples throughout the rest of the book. We also describe several design choices to consider while storing geographic data in Oracle tables. Location-enabling an application requires populating appropriate metadata tables to enable spatial processing on spatial tables. In the last part of the chapter, we look at the details of populating such metadata.
- *Chapter 4: The SDO_GEOMETRY Data Type*: This chapter focuses on the storage and modeling of location information using the SDO_GEOMETRY data type in Oracle. The type can store a wide variety of spatial data, including points, line strings, polygons, surfaces, and solid geometries. We take a detailed look at the structure of SDO_GEOMETRY and at the different attributes and the values it can take to store different types of geometric data. We then show how to construct SDO_GEOMETRY objects for geometries to model roads, property boundaries, and city buildings.
- *Chapter 5: Loading, Transporting, and Validating Spatial Data*: In this chapter, we describe different ways to populate Oracle tables that contain SDO_GEOMETRY columns. These tables could be part of an e-business application or could be tables in CAD/CAM, GIS, GPS, wireless, or telematics applications. We explain how to import the data that comes with this book using the Oracle Import utility. We also describe other utilities and functions/procedures for transferring data between Oracle databases and/or external formats. Finally, we look at how to validate the loaded SDO_GEOMETRY objects and how to correct some invalid objects.
- *Chapter 6: Geocoding*: In this chapter, we cover the functionality of the geocoder in Oracle Spatial. We first introduce geocoding concepts and the geocoding process to provide an understanding of how the conversion from addresses to SDO_GEOMETRY objects takes place. We then discuss how to set up a data catalog to enable geocoding in your application. This catalog is used to determine and extrapolate the location for a specified address. Finally, we describe how to add location columns to application data. We illustrate this using different functions/APIs of the geocoder in Oracle that serve this purpose.
- *Chapter 7: Manipulating SDO_GEOMETRY in Application Programs*: Advanced application developers often need to access and manipulate spatial objects in their applications. In this chapter, we look at how to manipulate SDO_GEOMETRY types in programming languages such as PL/SQL and Java. We also briefly cover C and Pro*C. We examine how to read, decode, construct, and write geometries, providing extensive code examples throughout.
- *Chapter 8: Spatial Indexes and Operators*: In this chapter and in the next chapter, we describe how to use spatial information to perform proximity analysis. In this chapter, we focus on spatial indexes and spatial operators. Spatial indexes ensure effective response times for queries that perform proximity analysis. The chapter introduces the concepts of spatial indexes and their creation. We then describe different spatial operators that Oracle Spatial supports for performing spatial analysis for indexed tables. We give an overview of their syntax and semantics and describe in detail various operators. We also suggest tips that can ensure a faster evaluation of spatial operators. In the final part of the chapter, we address some advanced spatial indexing features that are useful for large spatial repositories.
- *Chapter 9: Geometry Processing Functions*: In this chapter, we discuss geometry processing functions, simply referred to as spatial functions. In contrast to the spatial operators, these geometry processing functions do not require a spatial index, provide more detailed analyses than the spatial operators associated with a spatial index, and can appear in the SELECT list as well as in the WHERE clause of a SQL statement. We discuss each of the spatial functions in turn, including tips for their use.

- *Chapter 10: Network Modeling*: In this chapter, we introduce another way of modeling spatial data based on the concept of the network. A network is a useful way to model information when we need to compute, for instance, routes, travel distances, or proximity based on travel time. We describe the general concepts and terminology for setting up networks, and then we discuss the Oracle Network Data Model and its data structures. We then specify how to set up a network in Oracle and how to perform network analysis.
- *Chapter 11: The Routing Engine*: In this chapter, we introduce Oracle's Routing Engine. Among other things, you'll learn how to use the Oracle Routing Engine to get turn-by-turn directions from a starting address to a destination address.
- *Chapter 12: Defining Maps Using MapViewer*: MapViewer is the tool available in Oracle to visualize spatial information stored in a spatial database. The tool is part of Oracle Application Server. In this chapter, we describe MapViewer and introduce the basic mapping concepts, such as themes, style rules, and user controls. We look at how to install, deploy, and configure MapViewer, as well as how to construct maps and store them in the database using the Map Builder definition tool.
- *Chapter 13: Using Maps in Your Applications*: In this chapter, we show how to integrate maps created from spatial data in business applications. We also show how to support a seamless browsing experience and improve the performance of mapping applications using the recently introduced Oracle Maps technology.
- *Chapter 14: Sample Applications*: In this chapter, we use most of the techniques and tools illustrated so far in the book to create a simple application that integrates spatial analysis and visualization. This chapter presents and dissects such an application. The application includes map and data display, map functionality (zoom, pan, and so on), geocoding, spatial analysis, and routing. We look at how the application was designed and coded, and we review some of the source code that implements the major features of the application. The complete source code is provided for download from the Apress website (`www.apress.com`); see the upcoming "Setting Up" section for more details.
- *Chapter 15: Case Studies*: This chapter describes five case studies that illustrate how to use Oracle Spatial for storing, analyzing, visualizing, and integrating spatial data in business and government applications. The BusNet case study illustrates how to use Oracle Spatial for managing the bus network of the city of London. The P-Info case study describes a system to provide location-enabled information access to police officers operating in the field. The case study on the Dutch Risk Repository for Hazardous Substances shows how to use Oracle Spatial to spatially enable a repository for (bio)chemical risks and effects. The USGS National Land Cover Visualization and Analysis Tool illustrates how to use Oracle Spatial to provide access to the raster land-cover data of the United States. The MilitaryHOMEFRONT case study illustrates how to use Oracle Spatial for storing and accessing points of interest, geocoding, and routing.
- *Chapter 16: Tips, Common Mistakes, and Common Errors*: In this chapter, we describe some useful tips in location-enabling your application. We also discuss some of the mistakes most application developers make that can be easily avoided. Finally, we address some common errors that you may encounter in location-enabling your application and the actions to take to sort out these errors.
- *Appendix A: Additional Spatial Analysis Functions*: In this appendix, we describe analysis functions that are provided, in addition to those described in Chapters 8 and 9, to cater to specific business analysis needs. These functions enable tiling-based analysis, neighborhood analysis, and clustering analysis.

- *Appendix B: Linear Referencing*: Linear referencing is widely used in the transportation and utility industries. It uses one parameter (measure) to identify an object position along a linear feature with respect to some known point (such as its start point). This appendix introduces the concept of linear referencing and its most common operations. It then discusses the `SDO_LRS` package that contains all functions that manipulate linear-referenced geometries.
- *Appendix C: Topology Data Model in Oracle*: In some applications, such as land management, sharing and updating of boundaries between multiple spatial objects is common. This process may cause data inconsistency problems because of updates of underlying shared boundaries. In this appendix, we describe an alternate model, the Topology Data Model, for effective management of shared geometry features. We introduce topology modeling in Oracle Spatial and the functionality to operate on the Topology Data Model.
- *Appendix D: Storing Raster Data in Oracle*: In this appendix, we briefly discuss how to store raster objects in Oracle Spatial. This appendix introduces the `SDO_GEORASTER` data type and explores how raster data is stored in an Oracle database. The chapter also describes how to manipulate GeoRaster objects.
- *Appendix E: Three-Dimensional Modeling Using Point Clouds and TINs in Oracle*: In this appendix, we briefly discuss how to store large point sets, which typically result from laser scanning, in Oracle Spatial. The appendix introduces a new data type called `SDO_POINT_CLOUD` for efficient storage and retrieval of such large point sets. Later, it describes the `SDO_TIN` data type to create triangulated irregular networks for such point sets.

This book is not meant to repeat the content of user and installation guides. It is highly recommended that you have those guides available when reading this book, and especially when running the examples. In several cases, we refer you to the user or installation guide for details. The complete documentation for Oracle Database and Oracle Application Server is available online on the Oracle Technology Network website at `www.oracle.com/technology/documentation`. The Oracle 11*g* manuals relevant to this book are as follows:

- *Oracle Spatial User's Guide and Reference*
- *Oracle Application Server, MapViewer User's Guide*
- *Oracle Spatial Topology and Network Data Models Developer's Guide*
- *Oracle Spatial GeoRaster Developer's Guide*
- *Oracle Spatial Java API Reference*

Who Should Read This Book?

The primary audience for this book is application developers who are familiar with Oracle technologies and want to enhance their applications with spatial information. They typically know about database design, PL/SQL, Java, and so on, but they do not know much (if anything) about spatial data or geographical information systems.

The book will also appeal to the more general technical user of Oracle who is interested in the advanced features of database technology. The book introduces the world of spatial information gradually and guides the reader from the basic concepts to sophisticated analysis and case studies. It has a hands-on style, with extensive examples and practical information.

The book should open up new application domains to developers and prompt them to incorporate spatial aspects to existing applications. However, the book should also attract GIS programmers or users, if only because this is the first book that addresses Oracle Spatial in its entirety. In spite of its title, this book does in fact cover the full spectrum of geospatial technologies at Oracle—that is, the database (Oracle Spatial and Locator) and also Oracle Application Server (MapViewer and Router).

If you're new to PL/SQL and database technology, then we suggest taking some time to get familiar with the language and the main concepts of object-relational databases before tackling this book. It's not intended for the total beginner. On the other hand, we do not assume any previous knowledge of spatial information management.

Once you're up and running, we're certain that you'll find our book an invaluable guide for creating robust spatially enhanced applications that perform well.

Copyrights and Disclaimer

Oracle is a registered trademark, and Oracle9*i*, 10*g*, 11*g*, Oracle iAS (Application Server), and Oracle Spatial are trademarks of Oracle Corporation.

All other company and product names mentioned in the book are used for identification purposes only and may be trademarks of their respective owners.

The data used in this book is provided exclusively to illustrate the concepts in this book and is not authorized for use in any other way. The datasets cannot be transferred, changed, or modified in full or in part without the written consent of the authors. In particular, we refer you to the End User License Agreement for the sample data provided by NAVTEQ and used in this book. This agreement is accessible at `www.navteq.com/oracle-download/end_user_terms.pdf`. By installing and using the data provided with this book, you implicitly agree to the terms of this agreement.

The authors, the publishers, and the companies that originally sourced code and data cannot be liable for any damages incurred by using the data shipped with this book. The authors and the publishers do not guarantee that the data is complete, up to date, or accurate.

Most of the figures in the book were generated using Oracle MapViewer based on data from NAVTEQ and DCW. The data is copyright of the respective owners.

Setting Up

To be able to work through all the content and examples of this book, you need to set up some software and download some data and code. Specifically:

- You need to have Oracle Database 11g and Oracle Spatial installed and configured.
- You need to have Oracle MapViewer (part of Oracle Application Server) installed and configured. The instructions for installing and configuring MapViewer are in Chapter 12.
- You need to download data and scripts for this book from the Apress website (`www.apress.com`).

The Oracle software (Database 11g, Application Server, and MapViewer) is available for download from the Oracle Technology Network website at `www.oracle.com/technology/products`. Note that any software you download from the Oracle Technology Network site is for evaluation purposes only.

Downloads

Data, code, and links to software are provided for this book in the Downloads section of the Apress website (`www.apress.com`). Here you will find a compressed file that contains the following:

- An HTML file with a hierarchical folder structure that contain links to the following:
    - The code and the examples shown in the book chapters
    - The datasets used for these examples and described briefly
    - The download areas of the software tools used in the book, such as OC4J
- The files containing the example code and the data files. You can access all files from the hyperlinks in the HTML file.
- A `readme.txt` file that contains all information needed to use this material.

Note Please read the `readme.txt` file. It contains the most relevant information regarding the code, data, and links provided in support of this book. This information is not provided in the book itself.

Setting Up Oracle Spatial and MapViewer

If you already have a recent version of an Oracle database up and running, you most probably do not need to do anything specific to set up Oracle Spatial. Oracle Spatial technology is automatically installed with the Standard or Enterprise Edition of an Oracle database server. As long as you are using version 10.1.0.2 or newer, you should be able to work through the examples in the book.

Note that the Database Server license includes only a few of the functions described in the book (the so-called Locator suite). To be able to work through all examples and explore the entire functionality of Oracle Spatial, you need to obtain a separate product license for the Spatial option. Chapter 2 includes detailed information on how to set up Oracle Spatial for this book.

MapViewer serves to create mapping applications. You can deploy MapViewer either within a full Oracle Application Server environment or as a stand-alone installation of the Oracle Application Server Containers for J2EE (OC4J). Both MapViewer and OC4J are available for download from the Oracle Technology Network website (see the links in the support material for this book). The instructions to deploy MapViewer within Application Server are provided in Chapter 11, where we use MapViewer for the first time.

The Example Data

Once you have your Oracle 11*g* database up and running, to run the examples in this book you first need to do the following:

1. Create a user `spatial` with the password `spatial`.
2. Grant `resource`, `connect`, and `unlimited tablespace` privileges to the `spatial` user.
3. Create a tablespace called `users`, and make it the default tablespace for the `spatial` schema. This tablespace should have at least 100MB of space.

For each chapter, you should re-create the `spatial` schema and import appropriate datasets listed at the beginning of the chapter using the Oracle Import utility. Starting from Chapter 2, every chapter that requires code or data to be downloaded from the Apress site will clearly specify this. You will find a checklist of all data, scripts, and code that you need to download to be able to run the examples in the chapter, as well as any particular operation that needs to be carried out to prepare for that.

We do not expect that you are using any specific tool for programming or for SQL, which means you should be able to run all examples using your preferred tools.

The data used in the examples for this book comes from several sources. The detailed street-level data is derived from a sample made available by NAVTEQ to Oracle users. (The original sample is available for download at `www.navteq.com/oracle-download`.) This data includes detailed information on San Francisco and Washington, D.C., as separate files. For the purposes of this book, we merged the data and extracted a relevant subset.

The other sources of data are the U.S. Census Bureau and the GIS Data Depot. The GIS Data Depot (`http://data.geocomm.com`) is a central distribution point for free and public domain data.

As noted, we provide the example data as a set of Oracle dump files, which you can import into your database using the standard import (`imp`) tool. The following is a brief overview of what each dump file contains.

app_data.dmp

Source: NAVTEQ
Size: 640KB
Tables: `BRANCHES`, `CUSTOMERS`, and `COMPETITORS`
Description: This file contains the definitions of our "application" tables: `branches`, `customers`, and `competitors`.

app_data_with_loc.dmp

Source: NAVTEQ
Size: 640KB
Tables: `BRANCHES`, `CUSTOMERS`, and `COMPETITORS`
Description: This file is identical to the `app_data.dmp` file described earlier. The only difference is that all the tables (`branches`, `customers`, and `competitors`) have an additional column called `location` of type `SDO_GEOMETRY` to store the location of the corresponding entities.

citybldgs.dmp

Source: Oracle synthetic data
Size: 4MB
Tables: building_footprints, city_buildings, trip_route
Description: This file contains the three-dimensional structures of a few hypothetical buildings and their two-dimensional footprints.

map_large.dmp

Source: Digital Chart of the World
Size: 34.2MB
Tables: US_STATES, US_COUNTIES, US_CITIES, US_INTERSTATES, US_PARKS, US_RIVERS, WORLD_CONTINENTS, and WORLD_COUNTRIES
Description: This file contains the boundaries of states and counties in the United States, as well as the locations of major cities, national parks, rivers, and interstates. It also contains the boundaries of world continents and countries. In addition to the boundaries stored as SDO_GEOMETRY columns, some of the tables have demographic information such as population density or area.

map_detailed.dmp

Source: NAVTEQ
Size: 3.1MB
Tables: MAP_MAJOR_HIGHWAYS, MAP_SEC_HIGHWAYS, MAP_MAJOR_ROADS, MAP_STREETS, MAP_PARKFACILITY_POINTS, and US_RESTAURANTS
Description: This file contains the detailed definition of streets for San Francisco and Washington, D.C.

gc.dmp

Source: NAVTEQ
Size: 9.2MB
Tables: GC_COUNTRY_PROFILE, GC_PARSER_PROFILEAFS, GC_PARSER_PROFILES, GC_AREA_US, GC_INTERSECTION_US, GC_POI_US, GC_POSTAL_CODE_US, GC_ROAD_SEGMENT_US, and GC_ROAD_US
Description: This file contains the geocoding data for two cities in the United States: Washington, D.C., and San Francisco.

net.dmp

Source: NAVTEQ
Size: 5.2MB
Tables: NET_LINKS_SF, NET_NODES_SF, and MY_NETWORK_METADATA
Description: This file contains the description of the street network for San Francisco.

styles.dmp

Source: Oracle
Size: 400KB
Tables: MY_MAPS, MY_THEMES, and MY_STYLES
Description: This file contains a set of map, theme, and style definitions for use by MapViewer.

zip.dmp

Source: U.S. Census Bureau
Size: 24KB
Table: ZIP5_DC
Description: This file contains the boundaries of the zip codes areas in Washington, D.C., with some attributes (area, perimeter, and population).

PART 1

Overview

CHAPTER 1

Spatial Information Management

Location is an inherent part of business data: organizations maintain customer address lists, own property, ship goods from and to warehouses, manage transport flows among their workforce, and perform many other activities. A majority of these activities entail managing locations of different types of entities, including customers, property, goods, and employees. Those locations need not be static—in fact, they may continually change over time. For instance, goods are manufactured, packaged, and channeled to warehouses and retail/customer destinations. They may have different locations at various stages of the distribution network.

Let's consider an example of parcel services to illustrate how location is used. We have become increasingly accustomed to monitoring the status of parcel deliveries on the Web by locating our shipment within the distribution channel of our chosen service supplier. The simplicity and usefulness of this service is the result of a very complex underlying information system. The system relies on the ability to locate the parcel as it moves across different stages of the distribution network. Many information systems share location information in this process, which can be used to estimate, for instance, transit or delivery times. Systems such as RFID[1] are used to automatically record the movements of parcels along the distribution chain. Aircraft, trains, container ships, or trucks that move goods between distribution hubs use systems such as Global Positioning System (GPS) to locate their positions in real time. Even the "last mile"—that is, the delivery of an individual parcel to the end customer—is based on the geographical optimization of the delivery schedule as well as on the ability to locate the truck drivers in real time, to guide them to their destinations, and to estimate delivery times.

All of this location information is stored, analyzed, and exchanged between multiple systems and is the basis for making the entire operation cheaper, faster, and more reliable. Most of these systems are connected to each other through the Internet. The end user also uses the Internet to access the system and to query the current status of his parcel. By analyzing the system in its entirety, you can recognize that the added value is the result of the integration of various systems, of their interoperability, and of the pervasive role of spatial information across the entire process. Spatial information plays a crucial role in enabling the systems and processes to run smoothly and efficiently.

This example illustrates the pervasiveness of location or spatial information in day-to-day business. In fact, market research estimates that the majority of the data handled by organizations—perhaps as much as 80 percent of all data—has a spatial dimension.[2] The ability to properly manage the "where," or the spatial information, is key to the efficiency of organizations and could translate to substantial costs savings and commercial competitiveness. For instance, healthcare, telecommunications, and local government organizations depend on spatial information to run their daily business. Other

1. RFID stands for Radio Frequency IDentification, a technology to exchange data between tags and readers over a short range. See *RFID Essentials* (O'Reilly Media, 2006).

2. See Daratech Inc.'s analysis titled "Geographical Information Systems: Markets and Opportunities" (`www.daratech.com/research/index.php`).

organizations in the fields of retail, distribution, and marketing use spatial information for strategic decision making—for example, choosing store locations, making investment decisions, examining market segmentation, and supporting clients.

At one point in time, the Internet seemed to have made location irrelevant. The Web emerged as a locationless cloud, where we could contact anybody around the world instantly and shop anywhere without the usual constraints of geography. It seemed that the worlds of transport, logistics, and location received a critical blow. Of course, that thinking was naive. The Internet has made geography even more relevant and has bound digital and physical worlds closer than ever. It is now possible to do business over much farther distances, and tracking the locations of different components of a business and analyzing them have become all the more important.

The emergence of wireless and location services promises to add location to every information item that we use or process. Technologies such as RFID have the potential to radically alter the retail and distribution worlds, making it possible to cheaply locate and track individual items, however small they are. With these new developments, the relevance of location has grown, and this is why it has become increasingly important to master the tools that handle spatial information.

Software tools for spatial information management have been traditionally known under the name of Geographical Information Systems (GIS). These systems are specialized applications for storing, processing, analyzing, and displaying spatial data. They have been used in a variety of applications, such as land-use planning, geomarketing, logistics, distribution, network and utility management, and transportation.[3] However, until recently GIS have employed specific spatial data models and proprietary development languages, which held them separate from the main corporate databases. This has represented a barrier for the full deployment of the added value of spatial data in organizations.

As the use of GIS in enterprises and in the public sector has grown in popularity, some of the limitations of GIS have become apparent. Organizations often have to deal with multiple and incompatible standards for storing spatial data, and they have to use different languages and interfaces to analyze the data. Furthermore, systems such as Customer Relationship Management (CRM) and Enterprise Resource Planning (ERP) or the systems used in logistics increasingly rely on the integration of spatial information with all other types of information. This has often been an operational and technical challenge that in some cases was solved by manually extracting information from one system and loading it into another to perform the necessary spatial analysis.

Oracle Spatial has an important role in changing this situation. Once the spatial data is stored in an Oracle database, it can be processed, retrieved, and related to all the other data stored in the database: spatial information, or location, is just another attribute of a business object. This eliminates both the need for coordinating multiple data sources because of an application's dependence on special data structures and using different languages to query the data. Relevant features of Oracle Spatial are the ability to access spatial data through SQL statements, just like any other database content, and support for industry standards for spatial information (SQL and Open Geospatial[4]). Above all, Oracle Spatial facilitates leveraging the full added value of spatial information, which becomes an integral part of the information assets of organizations.

Given this overview of what location information is and how it can be used, in this chapter we will elaborate on the following topics:

---

3. For an introduction to GIS and its applications, see *An Introduction to Geographical Information Systems, Third Edition* (Prentice Hall, 2006).

4. See `www.opengeospatial.org`.

- First, we describe how location information is used in different industry segments. Chances are that this will relate to your application and give you a head start putting spatial information to good use.
- Next, we describe different sources for spatial data. The data could be location information from different applications, or it could be geographical data representing, for instance, political boundaries.
- We then describe typical functionality required for managing spatial/location information. This functionality involves storing and analyzing the spatial data. We look at a specific example to illustrate the different components of such spatial processing.
- Finally, we discuss the systems that enable spatial information management, such as GIS, and their evolution. We consider an out-of-the-box approach to spatial information and the Oracle Spatial approach that integrates spatial data with other data in an Oracle database. We elaborate on this comparison and highlight the benefits of using Oracle Spatial.

Using Spatial Information in Various Industries

Let's now consider a simple business application example. The database for this application contains data about available products (a `Products` table), customers (a `Customers` table), suppliers (a `Suppliers` table), delivery sites (a `Delivery` table), and competitors (a `Competitors` table). The tables for customers, suppliers, delivery sites, and competitors contain information on the location of each item in the table. For instance, the `Customers` table contains the address of each customer and also the x,y coordinates of the address.

Notice that only the address is usually known, but for many spatial analyses, such as the calculation of the distance between a customer's location and delivery sites, you need to know the x,y coordinates of this address. The conversion of address fields to x,y coordinates is one of the most fundamental spatial operations described in this book, called *geocoding*. It serves to translate a text string such as "Abbey Road, 3, London NW8" into something like "longitude = –0.1784; latitude = 51.5320," which is the information used to relate spatial information items to each other.

With this information available, we might want to conduct valuable business analyses that can help determine new marketing campaigns, opening of new stores, and discontinuation of poorly located stores, as well as identify more efficient home-delivery schedules, changes in the stores' product portfolios, and so on. Consider the following options:

- Identify customers that are close to a competitor store (say less than 5 kilometers). To prevent them from switching stores, you could design a specific marketing campaign proposing special discounts for these customers.
- Optimize the distribution network. By counting the number of customers who are located within a certain distance from a distribution center, you could see whether some centers are overloaded or underutilized. This may lead to a redesign of the distribution network.
- Identify routes from delivery sites to customer locations, and cluster goods in such a way that the same delivery can serve multiple customers and save money. Note that this analysis requires additional data, such as the road network.
- Superimpose the location of stores on a population map, and check whether the store locations are appropriate. If some areas are underserved, this would alert you to opportunities for new outlets. Note that additional demographic data is often useful for this analysis.
- Visualize table data and analysis results as maps (such as customer maps, delivery site maps, and so on) and produce rich visual material better suited for communication and decision making.
- Integrate these maps with existing applications, such as a CRM system, so that location information and analysis can promote effective customer relations.

To perform these types of analyses, you need to store location information for customers, delivery sites, and competitors. In practice, this will mean augmenting the corresponding tables with additional columns for storing location information. You also need to store additional information, such as street networks, rivers, city and state boundaries, and so on, to use in visualization and analysis.

The preceding analyses are representative of a vast class of uses for spatial information. The following list summarizes some of the main uses of spatial data, analysis, and visualization in various industries:

- *Banking and finance*: These industries use location data for analysis of retail networks and for market intelligence. The customer database combined with demographics and wealth information helps banks define an optimal retail network and define the best product mix to offer at each branch.
- *Telecommunications*: Location analysis helps telecom operators and carriers improve their competitive position. Spatial data is used for network planning, site location, maintenance organization, call-center and customer support, marketing, and engineering.
- *Local and central government*: Spatial information is heavily used by all government agencies, since they manage a multitude of assets distributed over large territories. Uses include natural resource management or land-use planning, road maintenance, housing stock maintenance, emergency management, and social services.
- *Law Enforcement*: Spatial information helps officers in operational duties, as well as in crime analysis and prevention. Location information is used by field officers to locate places and other resources in the field in real time. Investigators use spatial data for crime analysis. Spatial patterns of crime are used to better locate police resources and improve prevention.
- *Real estate and property management*: Geographic data and demographics are used to identify and assess locations for outlets, housing, or facilities. Land-use, transport, and utility networks are used to site industrial and production facilities.
- *Retail*: Location data serves as a basis for operational and strategic decisions. It can be used to identify the profile of the best customers and help reach similar prospects. Spatial data can increase the relevance and focus of marketing campaigns and find the best layout of a distribution network for maximum profit.
- *Utilities*: Many different utility systems can be found under almost every street. Utility companies use spatial information to design these underground systems, plan and monitor groundwork, and maintain their cable and pipe networks.
- *Communications, media, and advertising*: Location data are frequently used for increasing the return of communications campaigns. Segmentation and location-based targeting help companies finesse the timing and appropriateness of marketing campaigns, thereby increasing their expectation of success.
- *Wireless data services*: Wireless data services increasingly use location data to enrich the user experience and provide valuable services. Uses include personal navigation systems, friend finders, roadside emergency, location-based yellow page searches, and the like. Wireless location services are necessary for fast returns on investments made on third-generation telecom networks.

Sources of Spatial Data

In the previous section we described the uses of spatial information in applications and in various industries, and we introduced the distinction between application data and spatial data. The simplest example is that of address lists collected as text items and subsequently enhanced by associating geographical (longitude, latitude) coordinates to each address. This association makes it possible to analyze the address information from the spatial perspective, an otherwise impossible operation based on the original address list.

In general, the association between nonspatial objects and their corresponding geometry makes it possible to relate the objects based on spatial concepts (close, far, overlap, joined, and so on). Very often the tables derive their spatial dimension from some primarily spatial data sources. In the case of address geocoding, for instance, postal data provides the locations of individual addresses in the form of a reference address list with the associated coordinates.

This is only one of the multitudes of spatial datasets and sources used in practice. Some datasets, such as cadastral data, land-use data, road network data, administrative boundary data, rivers and lakes data, and so on, are almost always present in spatial analysis and visualization. This data is collected, updated, and distributed by public bodies or by companies (the latter is the case, for instance, for the road networks for car navigation). All these datasets are first of all spatial, because the geographic component of the data content defines the usefulness and relevance of the entire dataset, and they are often used as reference layers.

The vast majority of these datasets are dynamic, at least to some extent. However, there are several cases in which the reason for using spatial data is specifically because of their dynamics. For example, use of *real-time location* is increasingly common, thanks to the widespread use of GPS and the growing use of location systems such as Wi-Fi location or RFID tagging, to locate people or objects.

GPS receivers can be located with high accuracy and can feed a database with the real-time location of a moving person/object (a field engineer, a car, a truck, a container, and so on). Note that there are also many commercial GPS applications, such as car navigators, that use real-time location within closed applications that support a specific purpose (such as door-to-door navigation) without connection to corporate data infrastructures. However, in most cases, it is the ability to feed the enterprise databases with the location of the mobile users or assets of an organization that allows planning, scheduling, and logistics improvements.

This is increasingly becoming the case in the retail and distribution industries, where the use of RFID, instead of bar codes, makes it possible to track vast amounts of goods automatically while they travel through the distribution chain from supplier to end user. RFID tagging can be implemented at the level of single items, products, or even documents. With RFID, goods can be followed precisely—for instance, within a warehouse—and this information can be used to minimize inventory, optimize supply schedules, and create a unique opportunity to link logistics with administrative, CRM, and ERP systems. It is likely that these areas, often referred to as *location-based* or *sensor-based* systems and services, will stimulate a rapid increase in the use of spatial information in the near future.

Managing and Analyzing Spatial Data

In this section, we will examine how to manage spatial data and what the typical analysis functions on spatial data are. Note that a variety of spatial processing systems such as GIS and spatial-enabled databases can provide this functionality using their own types and functions. We first describe spatial processing using generic terminology without referring to any specific solution (such as Oracle Spatial).

Spatial operations typically include, but are not limited to, the following:

- *Storage of spatial data*: In most cases, this involves the following:
    - Storing the data in an appropriate form in the database. For instance, the database system could have a *geometry* type to store spatial information as points, lines, polygons, and other types of vector representations. The system may also have a *network* type for modeling road networks.[5]
    - Inserting, deleting, and updating these types of spatial data in the database.
- *Analysis of vector spatial data*: This typically includes the following analysis functionality:
    - *Within-distance*: This operation identifies all spatial data within a specified distance of a query location.
    - *Contains*: This operation identifies all spatial data that contain a specified query location (geometry). Functions to detect other types of relationships may also be defined.
    - *Nearest-neighbor*: This operation identifies all spatial data closest to a query location.
    - *Distance*: This operation computes the distance between two spatial objects.
    - *Buffer*: This operation constructs buffer zones around spatial data.
    - *Overlay*: This operation overlays different layers of spatial data.
    - *Visualization*: This operation presents spatial data using maps.
- *Analysis of network data*: Typically, most spatial data, such as road networks, can also be represented as network data (in addition to vector data). We can perform the preceding analysis on such data using network proximity rather than spatial proximity.

The subjects of spatial analysis and management have filled dozens of books and hundreds of university courses. Our goal here is not to repeat all this—the references at the end of this chapter will provide you with a good background on these topics. Here, we will illustrate spatial analysis and management by describing how you can apply them to solve a common problem in the retail industry: site selection.

The consideration of location in Figure 1-1 streamlines the selection of candidate sites for a shopping mall. The process involves limiting the choice to those locations that are the following:

- Included in areas where construction is allowed
- On sale and of a suitable size
- Not exposed to natural risks, such as floods
- Close to main roads to ensure good accessibility

5. Oracle Spatial includes an additional data type called raster, which is used for images and grid data. We cover raster data and the raster data model in Appendix D.

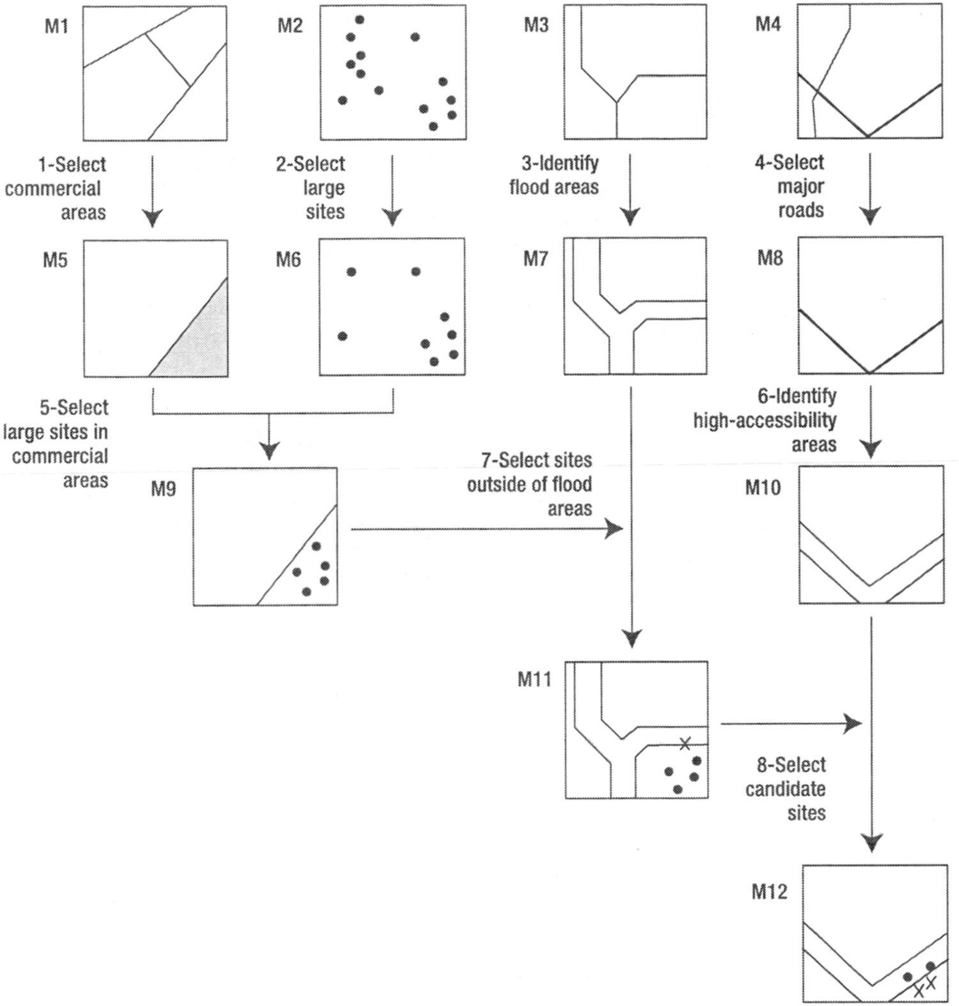

Figure 1-1. *Spatial data and spatial analysis for choosing a site for a shopping mall*

For the selection of suitable sites, we use spatial information and spatial analysis. To keep the example simple, however, we ignore demographic issues.

The main steps of the analysis are as follows:

1. From the land-use map (provided by a public organization), we first select areas for which we can obtain permits to build commercial sites. These areas are labeled as "commercial" and denote sites where new commercial activities can be located.

2. From a map that contains sites for sale (provided by a large real-estate agency), we restrict the choice to sites that are sufficiently large for a shopping mall.

3. On the basis of a risk map, which indicates safety buffer areas around rivers, we eliminate those sites that may be subject to floods.

4. Finally, of the remaining sites, only those close to main roads are deemed suitable for accessibility reasons.

Figure 1-1 shows the sequence of steps, the data used, and the spatial operations involved in this process. Note that the maps are numbered M1–M12 and the steps are numbered 1–8.

The combination of the first two steps leads to five candidate sites. One of them is excluded because of high flood risk, and two additional ones are excluded because they are located too far away from the main roads. This narrows the results to two suitable candidate sites.

Table 1-1 details the steps in this process. Note that the usual way of representing the data used in this example is through maps, as in Figure 1-1. Note also that the description can be easily translated into database and SQL terms. The various "maps" correspond to one or more database tables. The data objects (points, polygons, lines, grids, and so on) and their attributes are table records, while the analysis is performed with SQL statements. It is clear that some SQL extensions are needed to handle spatial and nonspatial objects simultaneously. The rest of this book will essentially deal with the models and tools available in Oracle Spatial for storing and processing this type of data for types of analysis like this one.

Table 1-1. *Steps, Data, and Analysis for Choosing a Site for a Shopping Mall*

Step	Data	Analysis	Result
1. Select commercial areas.	M1: Land use map. Collection of polygons, described by an attribute "land-use type."	Select polygons where the attribute is "commercial."	M5: Commercial areas. A set of polygons with the "commercial" attribute.
2. Select large sites.	M2: Sites for sale. Locations described by price, plot size, etc.	Select points where the size is larger than a certain value.	M6: Large sites. A selection of points corresponding to large sites for sale.
3. Identify flood areas.	M3: River map.	Create a buffer around the riverbed (e.g., 1 km) that is at risk of floods.	M7: Flood risk areas.
4. Select major roads.	M4: Road network map. Road segment attributes are "road type," "max speed," etc.	Select road segments where the attribute is "major roads."	M8: Major roads.
5. Select large sites in commercial areas.	M5 and M6.	Overlay M5 and M6. Select "large" points within "commercial" polygons.	M9: A selection of points corresponding to large sites within commercial areas.
6. Identify high-accessibility zones.	M8.	Create a buffer of 500 meters on each side of a major road.	M10: High accessibility zones.
7. Select sites outside of flood areas.	M9 and M7.	Overlay M9 and M7, and eliminate sites in the flood areas.	M11: Points corresponding to large siteswithin commercial areas not subject to flood risks.
8. Select candidate sites.	M10 and M11.	Select safe sites within high–accessibility zones.	M12: Large sites in commercial areas that are not subject to floods and are highly accessible.

For simplicity, in the example we have assumed that a new map is created at the end of every step. This is certainly a possibility, but it is not necessarily the best option. Later in this book, we will discuss data modeling and how to optimize the sequence of operations. In particular, Chapters 8 and 9 cover spatial operators and functions that make it possible to cluster some of the steps in the example into single queries, making the process much simpler and more efficient.

Storing Spatial Data in a Database

Looking at vector data, we usually distinguish between the following:

- *Points* (for example, the plots for sale in Figure 1-1), whose spatial description requires only x,y coordinates (or x,y,z if 3D is considered)
- *Lines* (for example, roads), whose spatial description requires a start coordinate, an end coordinate, and a certain number of intermediate coordinates
- *Polygons* (for example, a residential area), which are described by closed lines

Figure 1-2 shows an example containing point, line, and polygon data. The figure corresponds to a small portion of the area used in the previous site selection example. The vector representation, here simplified for convenience, shows a point (the stadium), three lines (the roads), and four polygons (the built-up areas, clipped at the picture borders, and the sports complex).

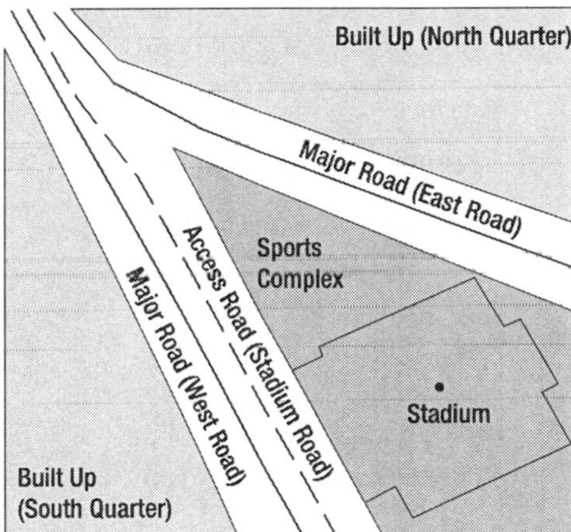

Figure 1-2. *Vector representation of the spatial objects in the picture*

The vector data in Figure 1-2 could be stored in one or multiple tables. The most natural way of looking at this data is to identify *data layers*—sets of data that share common attributes—that become data tables. Most spatial databases use a special data type to store spatial data in a database. Let's refer to this type as the *geometry*. Users can add columns of type *geometry* to a database table in order to store spatial objects.

In this case, the choice of tables would be rather simple with three main data layers present: "Road infrastructures," "Land use," and "Points of interest." These three layers contain objects that share common attributes, as shown in the three tables later in this section. The same objects could have been aggregated into different data layers, if desired. For instance, we could have stored major and minor roads in different tables, or we could have put roads and land use in the same table. The latter would make sense if the only attributes of relevance for roads and land-use areas were the same, for instance, the province name and the city name. It is also worth stressing that every *geometry* column can contain any mix of valid spatial object (points, lines, polygons) and also that every table can contain one or more *geometry* columns.

Structuring spatial data into tables and defining the right table structure are the first logical activities of any spatial analysis. Fortunately, in most cases there is an intuitive correspondence between the data and the table structure used to store them. However, in several cases you may find that the spatial database design can be a complex activity. Proper designs may facilitate analysis enormously, while poor data structures may make the analysis complex and slow. These issues are addressed in various places in the book but in particular in Chapter 3.

Table 1-2 shows the road infrastructure table of Figure 1-2. This table contains three records corresponding to the east road, the west road, and the stadium road. All of them are represented as lines using the *geometry* type. Each road is described by three types of attributes: the road type (one column containing either "major," "local," or "access" road), the road name (a column containing the name of the road as used in postal addresses), and the area attributes (two columns containing the name of the province and city where the road is located).

Table 1-2. *Road Infrastructure Table*

ID	Province	City	Road Name	Road Type	Road Geometry
1	Province name	City name	West road	Major road	
2	Province name	City name	East road	Major road	
3	Province name	City name	Stadium road	Access road	

Table 1-3 shows the land-use table. It contains three records corresponding to the north quarter, the south quarter, and the sports complex. In this case, all spatial objects are polygons. Each object has three types of attributes: the surface of the area (in square meters), the name of the area, and the area location (province and city names).

Table 1-3. *Land Use Table*

ID	Province	City	Area Name	Surface (Square Meters)	Area Geometry
1	Province name	City name	North quarter	10,000	
2	Province name	City name	South quarter	24,000	
3	Province name	City name	Sports complex	4,000	

Table 1-4 shows the points of interest (POI) in the area. It contains two records: a point (in this case, the center of the stadium complex) and a polygon (in this case, the contour of the stadium complex). Attributes include the type of POI from a classification list, the POI name, and the province and city where they are located.

Table 1-4. *Points of Interest Table*

ID	Province	City	POI Name	Type of POI	POI Geometry
1	Province name	City name	Olympic stadium	Sports location	●
2	Province name	City name	Olympic stadium	Sports infrastructure	

In the Table 1-4, we use two records to describe the same object with two different geometries. Another option for storing the same information is presented in Table 1-5, where we use two columns of type *geometry* to store two different spatial features of the same object. The first *geometry* column stores the POI location, while the second stores the outline of the complex. Under the assumption that all other nonspatial attributes are the same, Table 1-5 is a more efficient use of table space than Table 1-4.

Table 1-5. *Points of Interest Table: Two* Geometry *Columns*

ID	Province	City	POI Name	Location (POI) Geometry	Infrastructure Geometry
1	Province name	City name	Olympic stadium	●	

The objects in the preceding tables are represented with different line styles and fill patterns. This information is added for clarity, but in practice it is not stored in the *geometry* object. In Oracle Spatial, the *geometry* data are physically stored in a specific way (which we will describe in Chapters 3 and 4) that does not have a direct relationship to the visual representation of the data. Chapter 12, which describes the Oracle Application Server MapViewer, shows how symbology and styling rules are used for rendering *geometry* instances in Oracle.

Geometry models in the SQL/MM and Open Geospatial (OGC) specifications describe in detail the technical features of the *geometry* type and how points, lines, and polygons are modeled using this type.

Spatial Analysis

Once data is stored in the appropriate form in a database, spatial analysis makes it possible to derive meaningful information from it. Let's return to the site selection example and look again at the three types of spatial operations that we used:

- *Select*, used in the following:
  - Step 1 (to select areas where the attribute was a certain value)
  - Step 2 (to select large sites from the sites for sale)
  - Step 4 (to select major roads from the road network)
- *Overlay*, used in the following:
  - Step 5 (large sites in commercial areas)
  - Step 7 (sites away from risk areas)
  - Step 8 (sites within highly accessible areas)
- *Buffer*, used in the following:
  - Step 3 (areas subject to flood risk)
  - Step 6 (high accessibility areas)

Returning to our example, assuming we have the data stored in a database, we can use the following eight pseudo-SQL statements to perform the eight operations listed previously. Please note that for the sake of the example, we have assumed certain table structures and column names. For instance, we have assumed that M1 contains the columns `LAND_USE_TYPE`, `AREA_NAME`, and `AREA_GEOMETRY`.

1. Use

   ```
   SELECT AREA_NAME, AREA_GEOMETRY
   FROM M1
   WHERE LAND_USE_TYPE='COMMERCIAL'
   ```

   to identify available plots of land for which a construction permit can be obtained for a shopping mall.

2. Use

   ```
   SELECT SITE_NAME, SITE_GEOMETRY
   FROM M2
   WHERE SITE_PLOT_AREA > <some value>
   ```

   to identify available sites whose size is larger than a certain value.

3. Use

```
SELECT BUFFER(RIVER_GEOMETRY, 1,  'unit=km')
FROM M3
WHERE RIVER_NAME= <river_in_question>
```

to create a buffer of 1 kilometer around the named river.

4. Use

```
SELECT ROAD_NAME, ROAD_GEOMETRY
FROM M4
WHERE ROAD_TYPE='MAJOR ROAD'
```

to identify major roads.

5. Use the *contains* operator to identify the sites selected in step 2 that are within areas selected in step 1. You could also achieve this in one step starting directly from M1 and M2:

```
SELECT SITE_NAME, SITE_GEOMETRY
FROM M2 S, M1 L
WHERE CONTAINS(L.AREA_GEOMETRY, S.SITE_GEOMETRY)='TRUE'
  AND L.LAND_USE_TYPE= 'COMMERCIAL'
  AND S.SITE_AREA > <some value>;.
```

6. As in step 3, use the *buffer* function to create a buffer of a certain size around the major roads.
7. Use *contains* to identify sites selected in step 5 that are outside the flood-prone areas identified in step 3.
8. Use *contains* to identify safe sites selected in step 7 that are within the zones of easy accessibility created in step 6.

Oracle Spatial contains a much wider spectrum of SQL operators and functions (see Chapters 8 and 9). As you might also suspect, the preceding list of steps and choice of operators is not optimal. By redesigning the query structures, changing operators, and nesting queries, it is possible to drastically reduce the number of intermediate tables and the queries. M11, for instance, could be created starting from M9 and M3 directly by using the *nearest-neighbor* and *distance* operations together. They would select the nearest neighbor and verify whether the distance is larger than a certain value.

Benefits of Oracle Spatial

The functionality described in the previous section has been the main bread and butter for GIS for decades. In the past five to ten years, database vendors such as Oracle have also moved into this space. Specifically, Oracle introduced the *Oracle Spatial* suite of technology to support spatial processing inside an Oracle database.

Since GIS have been around for several years, you may wonder why Oracle has introduced yet another tool for carrying out the same operations. After all, we can already do spatial analysis with existing tools.

The answer lies in the evolution of spatial information technology and in the role of spatial data in mainstream IT solutions. GIS have extensive capabilities for spatial analysis, but they have historically developed as stand-alone information systems. Most systems still employ some form of dual architecture, with some data storage dedicated to spatial objects (usually based on proprietary formats) and some for their attributes (usually a database). This choice was legitimate when mainstream databases were unable to efficiently handle the spatial data. However, it has resulted in the proliferation of proprietary data formats that are so common in the spatial information industry.

Undesired consequences were the isolation of GIS from mainstream IT and the creation of automation islands dedicated to spatial processing, frequently disconnected from the central IT function of organizations. Although the capabilities of GIS are now very impressive, spatial data may still be underutilized, inaccessible, or not shared.

Two main developments have changed this situation: the introduction of open standards for spatial data and the availability of Oracle Spatial. Two of the most relevant open standards are the Open Geospatial Simple Feature Specification[6] and SQL/MM Part 3.[7] The purpose of these specifications is to define a standard SQL schema that supports the storage, retrieval, query, and update of spatial data via an application programming interface (API). Through these mechanisms, any other Open Geospatial–compliant or SQL/MM-compliant system can retrieve data from a database based on the specifications. Oracle Spatial provides an implementation for these standards[8] and offers a simple and effective way of storing and analyzing spatial data from within the same database used for any other data type.

The combination of these two developments means that spatial data can be processed, retrieved, and related to all other data stored in corporate databases and across multiple sources. This removed the isolation of spatial data from the mainstream information processes of an organization. It is now easy to add location intelligence to applications, to relate location with other information, and to manage all information assets in the same way. Figures 1-3 and 1-4 summarize this paradigm shift.

Figure 1-3 illustrates the industrywide shift from monolithic/proprietary GIS to open, universal, spatially enabled architectures.

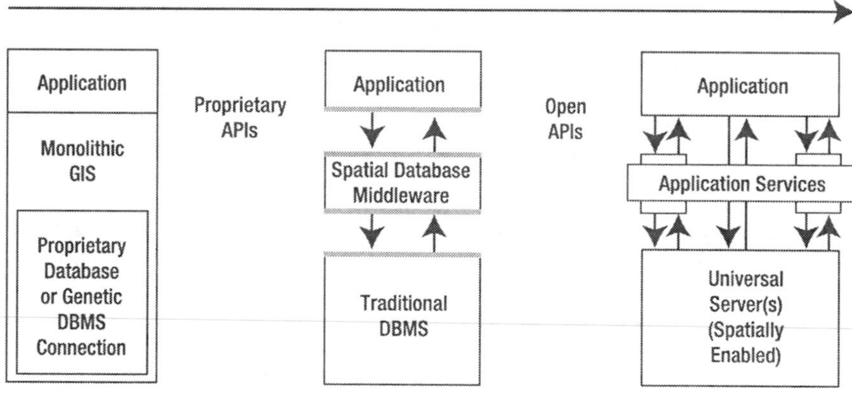

Figure 1-3. *From monolithic/proprietary GIS to universal, spatially enabled servers (Source: UNIGIS-UNIPHORM project. See* `www.unigis.org`*)*

Figure 1-4 emphasizes the shift from geo-centric processing to information-centric processing, where the added value is not in the sophistication of the spatial analysis but in the benefits it delivers. Traditional geoinformation management tools emphasize geodata processing while separating geodata storage from attribute data storage (see the emphasis on *Geography* in "Gis" in the figure).

6. See `www.opengeospatial.org` for information on approved standards, for an overview of ongoing standardization initiatives for spatial information data and systems, and for an up-to-date list of compliant products.
7. See ISO/IEC 13249-3:2003, "Information technology - Database languages - SQL multimedia and application packages - Part 3: Spatial" (`www.iso.org/iso/en/CatalogueDetailPage.CatalogueDetail?CSNUMBER=31369`).
8. The `ST_Geometry` of Oracle Spatial is fully compliant with the OGC Simple Feature specification for the object model.

Oracle Spatial makes it possible to process geodata within the same information platform used for all other data types (see the emphasis on *Information Systems* in "gIS" in the figure).

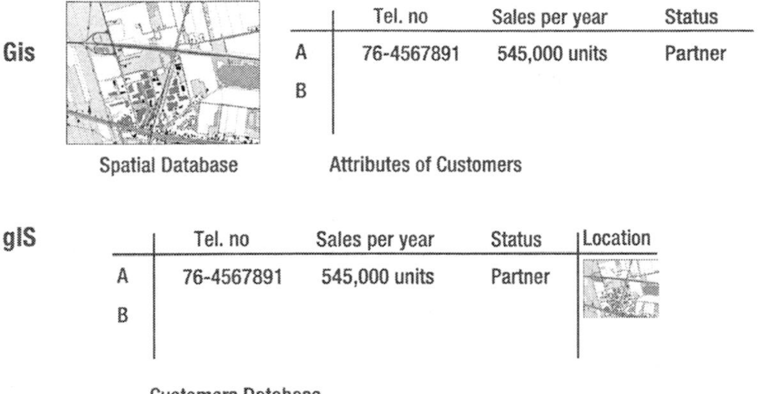

Figure 1-4. *From Gis to gIS*

The benefits of using Oracle Spatial can be summarized as follows:

- It eliminates the need for dual architectures, because all data can be stored in the same way. A unified data storage means that all types of data (text, maps, and multimedia) are stored together, instead of each type being stored separately.
- It uses SQL, a standard language for accessing relational databases, thus removing the need for specific languages to handle spatial data.
- It defines the `SDO_GEOMETRY` data type, which is essentially equivalent to the spatial types in the OGC and SQL/MM standards.
- It implements SQL/MM "well-known" formats for specifying spatial data. This implies that any solution that adheres to the SQL/MM specifications can easily store the data in Oracle Spatial, and vice versa, without the need for third-party converters.
- It is the de facto standard for storing and accessing data in Oracle and is fully supported by the world's leading geospatial data, tools, and applications vendors, including NAVTEQ, Tele Atlas, Digital Globe, 1Spatial, Autodesk, Bentley, eSpatial, ESRI, GE Energy/Smallworld, Intergraph, Leica Geosystems, Manifold, PCI Geomatics, Pitney/Bowes/MapInfo, Safe Software, Skyline, and many others.[9]
- It provides scalability, integrity, security, recoverability, and advanced user management features for handling spatial data that are the norm in Oracle databases but are not necessarily so in other spatial management tools.
- It removes the need for separate organizations to maintain a spatial data infrastructure (hardware, software, support, and so on), and it eliminates the need for specific tools and skills for operating spatial data.
- Through the application server, it allows almost any application to benefit from the availability of spatial information and intelligence, reducing the costs and complexity of spatial applications.

---

9. For a list of partners, visit `http://otn.oracle.com/products/spatial/index.html`, and click the Partners link (in the Oracle Spatial and Locator Resources section).

- It introduces the benefits of grid computing to spatial databases. For large organizations that manage very large data assets, such as clearinghouses, cadastres, or utilities, the flexibility and scalability of the grid can mean substantial cost savings and easier maintenance of the database structures.
- It introduces powerful visualization of spatial data, eliminating the need to rely on separate visualization tools for many applications.

Summary

This first chapter provided an introduction to spatial information management, its importance in business applications, and how it can be implemented in practice. The example of situating a shopping mall illustrated the relationship between the logical operations necessary to make a proper choice and the spatial data and analysis tools that can be used to support it.

After describing the example, we discussed how database vendors such as Oracle enable spatial functionality. We enumerated the benefits of a database approach, specifically that of Oracle Spatial. We observed that the most basic and essential feature of Oracle Spatial is that of eliminating the separation between spatial and nonspatial information in a database. This separation was mainly the result of technology choices and technology limitations, but it does not have any conceptual ground or practical justification. On the contrary, all evidence points toward the need to integrate spatial and nonspatial information to be able to use the spatial dimension in business operations and decision making.

We have also made the explicit choice of emphasizing the relevance of adding the spatial dimension to mainstream database technology, thereby introducing spatial information starting from the database. A GIS specialist, a geographer, or an urban planner would have probably described the same examples with a different emphasis—for instance, highlighting the features and specific nature of spatial data and analysis. This would have been a perfectly legitimate standpoint and is one very common in literature and well served by the selected titles in the "References" section.

In the next chapter, we will give a brief overview of the functionality of Oracle Spatial. The subsequent chapters in the book present an in-depth tour of the different features and functionality of Oracle Spatial and how you can implement them in applications.

References

Glover and Bhatt, *RFID Essentials*, Cambridge: O'Reilly Media, 2006.

Grimshaw, David J. *Bringing Geographical Information Systems into Business, Second Edition*. New York: John Wiley & Sons, 1999.

Haining, Robert. *Spatial Data Analysis: Theory and Practice*. Cambridge: Cambridge University Press, 2003.

Heywood, Ian, Sarah Cornelius, and Steve Carver. *An Introduction to Geographical Information Systems*. New Jersey: Prentice Hall, 2006.

Korte, George B. *The GIS Book, 5th Edition*. Clifton Park, NY: OnWord Press, 2000.

Longley, Paul A., Michael F. Goodchild, David J. Maguire, and David W. Rhind, eds. *Geographical Information Systems and Science*. New York: John Wiley & Sons, 2005.

CHAPTER 2

Overview of Oracle Spatial

To run the examples in this chapter, you need to load three datasets in the spatial schema as follows. Please refer to the introduction for instructions on creating the spatial schema and other setup details.

```
imp spatial/spatial file=gc.dmp ignore=y full=y
imp spatial/spatial file=map_large.dmp tables=us_interstates
imp spatial/spatial file=map_detailed.dmp tables=us_restaurants
```

In Chapter 1, you observed that spatial information can add value to a range of applications. You examined the benefits of storing spatial information with other data in the database.

The Spatial technology suite in Oracle enables storage of spatial data in the database and facilitates different types of analyses on spatial data. This chapter provides an overview of the Spatial technology suite and covers the following topics:

- An overview of the Oracle Spatial architecture and technology.
- An examination of the *functionality* of different components of this Spatial technology suite in Oracle. This includes a brief introduction to the data type that stores spatial data (SDO_GEOMETRY), the query predicates for performing spatial query and analysis, and additional functionality to perform visualization.
- A description of how this functionality is *packaged* into different products that are shipped with different editions of Oracle software. We will discuss the relative merits of each product in turn.
- What to expect in a typical install of Oracle Spatial. This knowledge should get you off to a smooth start in spatially enabling your application.

Technology and Architecture Overview

Oracle Spatial technology is spread across two tiers: the Database Server and the Application Server. Figure 2-1 depicts the various components that comprise Oracle's Spatial technology stack and indicates the distribution of the components across the Database Server and Application Server tiers. Basic components that are provided as part of Oracle Database Server 11*g* include the storage model, query and analysis tools, and location-enabling/loading utilities. The MapViewer component is provided in Oracle Application Server 10g.

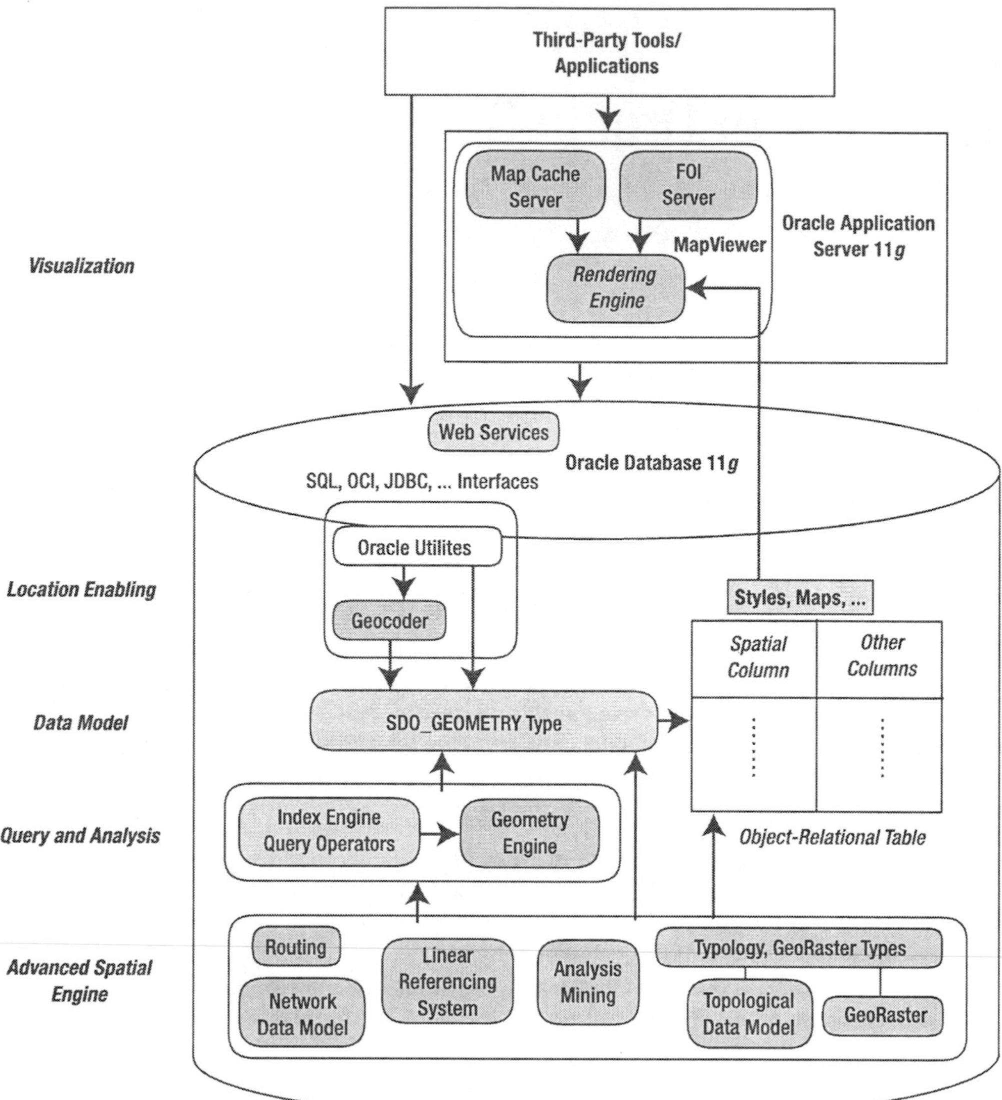

Figure 2-1. *Oracle Spatial technology components*

The basic components from Figure 2-1 can be described as follows:

- *Data model*: Oracle Spatial uses a SQL data type, `SDO_GEOMETRY`, to store spatial data in an Oracle database. Users can define tables containing columns of type `SDO_GEOMETRY` to store the locations of customers, stores, restaurants, and so on, or the locations and spatial extents of geographic entities such as roads, interstates, parks, and land parcels. We describe this data type in detail in Chapter 4.

- *Location-enabling*: Users can add SDO_GEOMETRY columns to application tables. We describe this process in detail in Chapter 3. Users can populate the tables with SDO_GEOMETRY data using standard Oracle utilities such as SQL*Loader, Import, and Export. We describe this process in Chapter 5. Alternatively, users can convert implicit spatial information, such as street addresses, into SDO_GEOMETRY columns using the geocoder component of Oracle Spatial, as described in Chapter 6.
- *Spatial query and analysis*: Users can query and manipulate the SDO_GEOMETRY data using the query and analysis component, comprising the Index Engine and Geometry Engine. We give full details of this process in Chapters 8 and 9.
- *Advanced Spatial Engine*: This component comprises several components that cater to sophisticated spatial applications, such as Geographical Information Systems (GIS) and bioinformatics. This includes the network analysis and the Routing Engine, which are covered in detail in Chapters 10 and 11. The Advanced Spatial Engine also consists of other specialized components such as the GeoRaster that allows storage of spatial objects using images (groups of pixels) rather than points, lines, and vertices. We cover these components in Appendixes A through E.
- *Visualization*: The Application Server components of Oracle's Spatial technology include the means to visualize spatial data via the MapViewer tool. MapViewer renders the spatial data that is stored in SDO_GEOMETRY columns of Oracle tables as displayable maps. In recent releases, Oracle also provides the Oracle Maps suite of technologies to enhance the functionality of the MapViewer. The Oracle Maps suite enables fast map-browsing experience using a map cache server that pregenerates and caches image tiles for a map and a feature-of-interest (FOI) server that renders dynamic application content using a combination of images and geometric themes. We describe these features in detail in Chapters 12 and 13.

In Figure 2-1, observe that third-party tools can access spatial data through the Application Server, directly from the database using SQL, or via programmatic interfaces such as OCI and JDBC. We describe how to program with spatial data via these APIs in Chapter 7. Recent additions to the list of interfaces to Oracle Spatial are the Spatial Web Services. Using the Spatial Web Services infrastructure, users can perform the following spatial functions: geocoding, routing, and feature selection using spatial and nonspatial predicates. Spatial Web Services will not be covered in much detail in this book, but you can find all necessary information in the *Oracle Spatial User's Guide*.

Note The core subset of this functionality (known as the Locator component) is included for free in all editions of the database (essentially, the SDO_GEOMETRY data type and the Index Engine). The rest of the components, along with the data type and the Index Engine, are packaged in a priced option of the Enterprise Edition of the database (known as the Spatial option). We discuss this in more detail later in this chapter.

In the following sections, we'll preview these components and introduce you to some (very basic) SQL to create a table that stores spatial data, to populate that data, and to perform simple proximity analysis. We cover all of these topics in full detail in subsequent chapters, as described previously, but this should serve as a useful introduction to the technology and help you to get started.

Getting Started with Oracle Spatial

Oracle Spatial technology is automatically installed with the Standard or Enterprise Edition of an Oracle database server. So, as long as you have one of these editions of version 10.1.0.2 or newer, you should be able to work through the simple examples in the coming sections. If you encounter any problems, you can refer to the "What to Expect in an Oracle Spatial Install" section later in this chapter. Note that the Database Server license includes only a few of the functions described in this section. To use the rest of the functionality, you should obtain a separate product license for the Spatial option.

Data Model: Storing Spatial Data

In Chapter 1, we briefly discussed the idea that spatial information is specified using two components: a *location* with respect to some origin and a geometric *shape*.

- *Location* specifies where the data is located with respect to a two-, three-, or four-dimensional coordinate space. For instance, the center of San Francisco is located at coordinates (–122.436, 37.719) in the two-dimensional "latitude, longitude" space.
- *Shape* specifies the geometric structure of the data. Point, line, and polygon are examples of possible shapes. For instance, the center of San Francisco is located at coordinates (–122.436, .37.719) in the two-dimensional "latitude, longitude" space and is a *point* shape. Note that point specifies both a location and a default shape. Alternately, shape could specify a *line* or a *polygon* connecting multiple points (specified by their locations). For instance, the city boundary of San Francisco could be a *polygon* connecting multiple *points*.

  In some applications, the shapes could be more complex and could have multiple polygons and/or polygons containing holes. For instance, the state boundaries for Texas and California include multiple polygons and some with islands. In general, spatial information, occurring in GIS, CAD/CAM, or simple location-enabled applications, could be arbitrarily complex.

The SDO_GEOMETRY data type captures the *location* and *shape* information of data rows in a table. This data type is internally represented as an Oracle object data type. It can model different shapes such as points, lines, polygons, and appropriate combinations of each of these. In short, it can model spatial data occurring in most spatial applications and is conformant with the Open GIS Consortium (OGC) Geometry model.[1]

Chapter 4 provides details about what types of spatial data SDO_GEOMETRY can model and what it cannot, and it also covers the structure of SDO_GEOMETRY and the tools to construct, validate, and debug SDO_GEOMETRY objects. For now, it is sufficient to understand that you can create tables with SDO_GEOMETRY columns to store the locations of objects.

Location-Enabling

You can create tables with the SDO_GEOMETRY columns to store locations. For instance, you can create the us_restaurants_new[2] table as shown in Listing 2-1.

---

1. Open GIS Consortium, Inc., "OpenGIS Simple Features Specification for SQL, Revision 1.1," http://www.opengis.org/docs/99-049.pdf, May 5, 1999.
2. Note that the us_restaurants table already exists. So, name this new table as us_restaurants_new.

Listing 2-1. *Creating the* us_restaurants_new *Table*

```
SQL> CREATE TABLE  us_restaurants_new
(
  id                     NUMBER,
  poi_name         VARCHAR2(32),
  location           SDO_GEOMETRY    -- New column to store locations
);
```

Now that you know basically how to create tables to store locations, we'll briefly cover the tools to populate such tables. Since SDO_GEOMETRY is an object type, just like any other object type, you can populate an SDO_GEOMETRY column using the corresponding object constructor. For example, you can insert a location of (–87, 38) for a Pizza Hut restaurant into the us_restaurants table, as shown in Listing 2-2.

Listing 2-2. *Inserting a Value for the* SDO_GEOMETRY *Column in an Oracle Table*

```
SQL> INSERT INTO  us_restaurants_new  VALUES
(
  1,
  'PIZZA HUT',
  SDO_GEOMETRY
  (
    2001,  -- SDO_GTYPE attribute: "2" in 2001 specifies dimensionality is 2.
    NULL,    -- other fields are set to NULL.
    SDO_POINT_TYPE  -- Specifies the coordinates of the point
    (
      -87,  -- first ordinate, i.e., value in longitude dimension
      38,  -- second ordinate, i.e., value in latitude dimension
      NULL  -- third ordinate, if any
    ),
    NULL,
    NULL
  )
);
```

The SDO_GEOMETRY object is instantiated using the object constructor. In this constructor, the first argument, 2001, specifies that it is a two-dimensional point geometry (a line would be represented by 2002, a polygon by 2003, and a collection by 2004).

The fourth argument stores the location of this point in the SDO_POINT attribute using the SDO_POINT_TYPE constructor. Here, we store the geographic coordinates (–87, 38). In this example, the remaining arguments are set to NULL.

■ **Note** In Chapter 4, we examine the structure of the SDO_GEOMETRY type in detail and describe how to choose appropriate values for each field of the SDO_GEOMETRY type.

Note that the preceding example shows a single SQL INSERT statement. Data loading can also be performed in bulk using Oracle utilities such as SQL*Loader and Import/Export or using programmatic interfaces such as OCI, OCCI, and JDBC. These utilities and interfaces come in handy when populating data from GIS vendors or data suppliers.

In some applications, spatial information is not explicitly available as coordinates. Instead, the address data of objects is usually the only spatial information available. You can convert such address data into an SDO_GEOMETRY object using the geocoder component (provided with the Spatial option). The geocoder takes a postal address, consults an internal countrywide database of addresses and locations, and computes the longitude and latitude coordinates for the specified address. This process is referred to as *geocoding* in spatial terminology. The address/location database is usually provided by third-party data vendors. For the United States, Canada, and Europe, NAVTEQ and Tele Atlas provide such data.

Listing 2-3 shows how to use the geocoder to obtain the coordinates in the form of an SDO_GEOMETRY object for the address '3746 CONNECTICUT AVE NW' in Washington, D.C.

Listing 2-3. *Converting Address Data (Implicit Spatial Information) to the* SDO_GEOMETRY *(Explicit Spatial Information) Object*

```
SQL> SELECT
SDO_GCDR.GEOCODE_AS_GEOMETRY
(
   'SPATIAL',                  -- Spatial schema storing the geocoder data
   SDO_KEYWORDARRAY            -- Object combining different address components
   (
     '3746  CONNECTICUT AVE NW',
     'WASHINGTON, DC 20008'
   ),
   'US'                        -- Name of the country
) geom
FROM DUAL ;

GEOM(SDO_GTYPE, SDO_SRID, SDO_POINT(X, Y, Z), SDO_ELEM_INFO, SDO_ORDINATES)
--------------------------------------------------------------------
SDO_GEOMETRY
(
   2001,
   8307,
   SDO_POINT_TYPE(-77.060283, 38.9387083, NULL),
   NULL,
   NULL
)
```

This geocoding function, geocode_as_geometry, takes three arguments. The first argument is the schema. This example uses the 'spatial' schema. The second argument specifies an SDO_KEYWORDARRAY object, composed from different components of an address. In this example, SDO_KEYWORDARRAY is constructed out of the street component '3746 Connecticut Ave NW' and the city/ZIP code component 'Washington, DC 20008'. The third argument to the geocoding function specifies the 'US' dataset that is being used to geocode the specified street address. The function returns an SDO_GEOMETRY type with the longitude set to –77.060283 and the latitude set to 38.9387083.

The geocoder can also perform fuzzy matching (via tolerance parameters, which we'll cover in the next chapter). In the same way that search engines can search on related words as well as exact words, Oracle can perform fuzzy matching on the street names and so on. So, for example, suppose the address field in the preceding example was misspelled as 'CONNETICUT AVE'. The geocoder could perform approximate matching to match the misspelled fields with those in the database.

Note that the SDO_GEOMETRY data type is just like any other object type in the database. Users can view the data and examine and modify the attributes. In contrast, several GIS data vendors and partners have their own proprietary binary formats for representing spatial information. These vendors usually provide tools for loading the data or converting the data into standard Oracle formats. Discussion of these tools, however, is beyond the scope of this book.

Query and Analysis

Now that you've seen how to define SDO_GEOMETRY for storing spatial data in Oracle and how to populate Spatial tables with data, the next topic to look at is how to query and analyze this SDO_GEOMETRY data.

The query and analysis component provides the core functionality for querying and analyzing spatial geometries. This component has two subcomponents: a Geometry Engine and an Index Engine. It is via these components that you perform your spatial queries and analysis, for example, to identify the five nearest restaurants along Interstate 795 or the five nearest hospitals to a construction site.

The Geometry Engine

The Geometry Engine provides functions to analyze, compare, and manipulate geometries. For instance, you could use the Geometry Engine functionality to identify the nearest five restaurants on I-795 in the greater Washington, D.C., area. This involves computing the distance between I-795 and all the restaurants in the us_restaurants table, sorting them in order of increasing distance, and returning the top five restaurants. The SQL in Listing 2-4 illustrates this operation.

Listing 2-4. *Finding the Five Nearest Restaurants on I-795*

```
SQL> SELECT poi_name
FROM
  (
    SELECT poi_name,
      SDO_GEOM.SDO_DISTANCE(P.location, I.geom, 0.5) distance
    FROM us_interstates  I, us_restaurants  P
    WHERE I.interstate = 'I795'
      ORDER BY distance
  )
WHERE ROWNUM <= 5;

POI_NAME
-----------------------------------
PIZZA BOLI'S
BLAIR MANSION INN DINNER THEATER
KFC
CHINA HUT
PIZZA HUT

5 rows selected.
```

Observe that the inner SELECT clause computes the distance between I-795 (which is not a major highway) and each restaurant row of the us_restaurants table using the Geometry Engine function SDO_GEOM.SDO_DISTANCE. Also, note that the ORDER BY clause sorts the results in ascending order of distance. The outer SELECT statement selects the first five rows, or the five nearest restaurants.

In the preceding query, the location of the I-795 highway is compared with every restaurant row of the table, irrespective of how far the restaurant is from I-795. This could mean considerable time is spent processing rows for restaurants that are too far from the I-795 highway and hence are irrelevant to the query. To speed up query processing by minimizing the processing overhead, you need to create *indexes* on the location of the restaurants.

The Index Engine

Oracle Spatial provides the spatial Index Engine for this purpose. Listing 2-5 shows an example of how to create an index on the locations of restaurants.

Listing 2-5. *Creating an Index on Locations (*SDO_GEOMETRY *Column) of Restaurants*

```
SQL> DROP INDEX us_restaurants_sidx;
SQL> CREATE INDEX us_restaurants_sidx ON us_restaurants(location)
INDEXTYPE IS mdsys.spatial_index;
```

Listing 2-5 first drops the index that exists. In the second and third lines, it shows the SQL for creating the spatial index. Note that the clause INDEXTYPE tells the database to create a spatial index on the location (SDO_GEOMETRY) column of the us_restaurants table. This index is a specialized index to cater to the SDO_GEOMETRY data. Using such an index, the Index Engine in Oracle Spatial prunes faraway rows from query processing and thus speeds up the query for most applications. The Index Engine provides equivalent functions, referred to as *operators*, for identifying rows of the table that satisfy a specified proximity predicate such as closeness to I-795. You can rewrite the preceding query to find the five nearest restaurants to I-795 using such *index-based operators*. Listing 2-6 shows the resulting query.

Listing 2-6. *Finding the Five Nearest Restaurants on I-795 Using the Spatial Index*

```
SQL> SELECT  poi_name
FROM us_interstates  I,  us_restaurants  P
WHERE I.interstate = 'I795'
  AND SDO_NN(P.location, I.geom) ='TRUE'
  AND ROWNUM <= 5;
POI_NAME
-----------------------------------
PIZZA BOLI'S
BLAIR MANSION INN DINNER THEATER
KFC
CHINA HUT
PIZZA HUT

5 rows selected.
```

Note that this query returns the same five rows as Listing 2-4. However, this query has a simpler structure with no subqueries. It uses only a new index-based operator called SDO_NN, with NN being short for *nearest neighbor*. This index-based operator returns rows of the us_restaurants table whenever the location column is close to the I-795 highway geometry. The SDO_NN operator returns these rows in order of proximity to the I-795 geometry. So, the row with the closest location is returned first, the next closest next, and so on. The ROWNUM predicate determines how many close restaurants need to be returned in the query. The query uses a spatial index and examines only those rows that are likely to be close to the location of I-795. Consequently, it is likely to execute faster than the query in Listing 2-4.

As a variation on this, suppose that instead of having to find the five nearest restaurants on I-795, you want to identify all restaurants within 50 kilometers of I-795. One way to accomplish this is to construct a buffer around the I-795 highway and determine all businesses inside this buffer geometry. Figure 2-2 shows an example: I-795 appears in black, the 50 km buffer is shown with the gray oval around it, and the restaurants inside this buffer are shown by *x* marks.

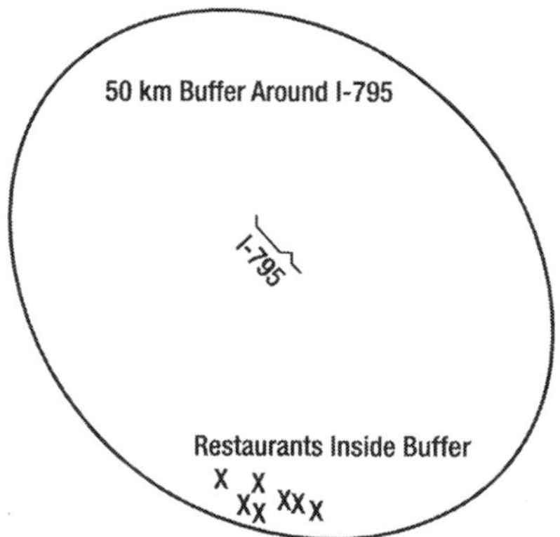

Figure 2-2. *Restaurants in the 50 km buffer around I-795*

Listing 2-7 shows the corresponding SQL query and the results.

Listing 2-7. *Identifying All Restaurants in a 50 km Radius Around I-795*

```
SQL> SELECT POI_NAME
FROM us_interstates I,  us_restaurants P
WHERE
  SDO_ANYINTERACT
  (
    P.location,
    SDO_GEOM.SDO_BUFFER(I.geom, 50, 0.5, 'UNIT=KM')
  ) ='TRUE'
  AND I.interstate='I795' ;
POI_NAME
-----------------------------------
SPICY DELIGHT
PHILLY'S STEAK EXPRESS
EL TAMARINDO
MCDONALD'S
PIZZA HUT
CHINA HUT
KFC
BLAIR MANSION INN DINNER THEATER
PIZZA BOLI'S

9 rows selected.
```

The function SDO_ANYINTERACT is an index-based operator just like the SDO_NN operator in Listing 2-6. This operator identifies all rows of us_restaurants where the locations intersect with the geometry passed in as the second parameter. The second parameter, in this case, is the result returned by an SDO_BUFFER function. The SDO_BUFFER function generates and returns a 50 km buffer around the I-795 geometry. This SDO_BUFFER function is part of the Geometry Engine, which also provides additional functions to facilitate more complex analysis and manipulation of spatial information.

Note that the number of restaurants returned in Listing 2-7 is nine, as opposed to five in Listings 2-4 and 2-6. This means you may not know the cardinality of the result set when you use a query buffer. With an SDO_ANYINTERACT operator, you may get more answers than you expect, or fewer answers. The cardinality of the result set depends on distribution of the data (in other words, the restaurants). In general, when you know how far to search (for example, a 50 km radius, as in Listing 2-7), you can use the SDO_BUFFER and SDO_ANYINTERACT functions.[3] Alternatively, if you know how many results you want to return, then you should use the SDO_NN function, as described in Listing 2-6. In Chapters 8 and 9, we will describe in greater detail the different operators and functions in the Index Engine and Geometry Engine.

Visualizing Spatial Data

How do you visualize the results of spatial queries? Oracle technology includes the MapViewer component to facilitate the generation of maps from spatial data. Each map is associated with a set of *themes*. Each theme denotes spatial data from a specific table and is associated with a *rendering style*. For instance, you can specify that the interstates theme (data from the INTERSTATES table) should be rendered as thick blue lines. Oracle Spatial provides appropriate dictionary views—USER_SDO_MAPS, USER_SDO_THEMES, and USER_SDO_STYLES—to define new maps, to associate them with themes, and to specify rendering styles for the themes in the database, respectively.

---

3. In Chapter 8, we will describe a better alternative using the SDO_WITHIN_DISTANCE operator.

CHAPTER 2

Overview of Oracle Spatial

To run the examples in this chapter, you need to load three datasets in the spatial schema as follows. Please refer to the introduction for instructions on creating the spatial schema and other setup details.

```
imp spatial/spatial file=gc.dmp ignore=y full=y
imp spatial/spatial file=map_large.dmp tables=us_interstates
imp spatial/spatial file=map_detailed.dmp tables=us_restaurants
```

In Chapter 1, you observed that spatial information can add value to a range of applications. You examined the benefits of storing spatial information with other data in the database.

The Spatial technology suite in Oracle enables storage of spatial data in the database and facilitates different types of analyses on spatial data. This chapter provides an overview of the Spatial technology suite and covers the following topics:

- An overview of the Oracle Spatial architecture and technology.
- An examination of the *functionality* of different components of this Spatial technology suite in Oracle. This includes a brief introduction to the data type that stores spatial data (SDO_GEOMETRY), the query predicates for performing spatial query and analysis, and additional functionality to perform visualization.
- A description of how this functionality is *packaged* into different products that are shipped with different editions of Oracle software. We will discuss the relative merits of each product in turn.
- What to expect in a typical install of Oracle Spatial. This knowledge should get you off to a smooth start in spatially enabling your application.

Technology and Architecture Overview

Oracle Spatial technology is spread across two tiers: the Database Server and the Application Server. Figure 2-1 depicts the various components that comprise Oracle's Spatial technology stack and indicates the distribution of the components across the Database Server and Application Server tiers. Basic components that are provided as part of Oracle Database Server 11g include the storage model, query and analysis tools, and location-enabling/loading utilities. The MapViewer component is provided in Oracle Application Server 10g.

is now called Oracle Maps. In addition to a rendering engine, Oracle Maps consists of a map cache server that pregenerates and caches neighboring tiled images of a displayed base map image. Oracle Maps also consists of an FOI server that renders dynamic content for spatially enabled tables (customers, for example) detailing their geographic locations and associated (nonspatial) attribute information. Together, the cached base maps (from the map cache server) and the dynamic FOIs (from the FOI server) enable users to build efficient mapping applications.

Advanced Spatial Engine

The Advanced Spatial Engine has several subcomponents that cater to the complex analysis and manipulation of spatial data that is required in traditional GIS applications.

Note Our focus in this book is the applicability of Oracle Spatial to Oracle business applications, so we do not cover most of these advanced options, with the exception of the Network Data Model and the Routing Engine, in great detail. However, we provide a good overview of these topics in the appendixes, with references for further details.

Internally, each of these additional components uses the underlying geometry data type and Index Engine and Geometry Engine functionality.

- The *Network Data Model* provides a data model for storing networks in the Oracle database. Network elements (links and nodes) can be associated with costs and limits, for example, to model speed limits for road segments. Other functionality includes computation of the shortest path between two locations given a network of road segments, finding the *N* nearest nodes, and so on. The Network Data Model is useful in routing applications. Typical routing applications include web services such as MapQuest and Yahoo! Maps or navigation applications for roaming users using Global Positioning System (GPS) technology. We cover more details about this component in Chapters 10 and 11.
- The *Linear Referencing System* (LRS) facilitates the translation of mile markers on a highway (or any other linear feature) to geographic coordinate space, and vice versa. This component allows users to address different segments of a linear geometry, such as a highway, without actually referring to the coordinates of the segment. This functionality is useful in transportation and utility applications, such as gas pipeline management.
- The *Spatial Analysis and Mining Engine* provides basic functionality for combining demographic and spatial analysis. This functionality is useful in identifying prospective sites for starting new stores based on customer density and income. These tools can also be used to materialize the influence of the neighborhood, which in turn can be used in improving the efficacy and predictive power of the Oracle Data Mining Engine.
- *GeoRaster* facilitates the storage and retrieval of georeferenced images using their spatial footprints and the associated metadata. GeoRaster defines a new data type for storing raster images of geographically referenced objects. This functionality is useful in the management of satellite imagery.
- The *Topology Data Model* supports detailed analysis and manipulation of spatial geometry data using finer topological elements such as nodes and edges. In some land management applications, geometries share boundaries, as in the case of a property boundary and the road on which the property is situated. Oracle Spatial defines a new data type to represent topological elements (such as the shared "road segment") that can be shared between different spatial objects. Updates to shared elements implicitly define updates to the sharing geometry objects. In general, this component allows for the editing and manipulation of nodes and edges without disturbing the topological semantics of the application.

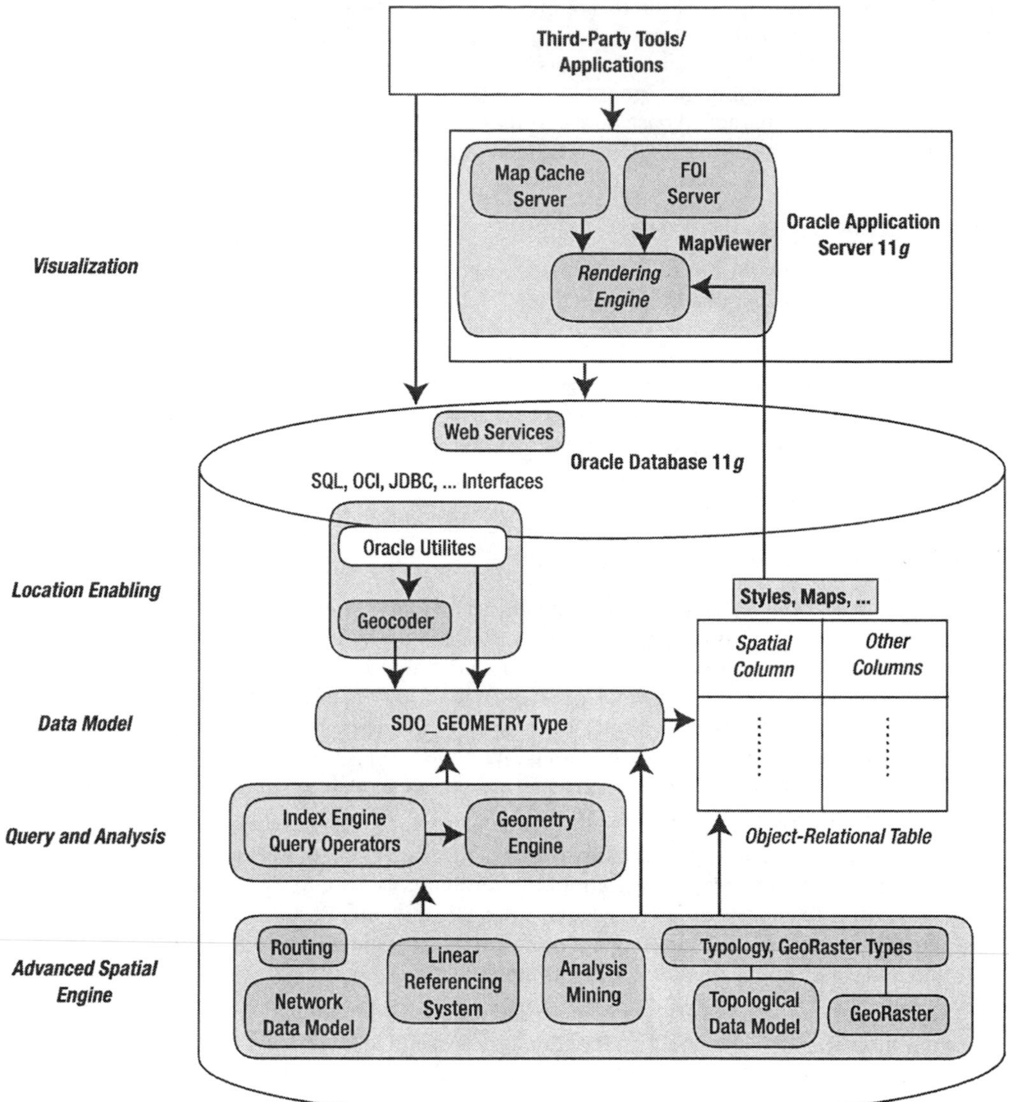

Figure 2-1. *Oracle Spatial technology components*

The basic components from Figure 2-1 can be described as follows:

- *Data model*: Oracle Spatial uses a SQL data type, `SDO_GEOMETRY`, to store spatial data in an Oracle database. Users can define tables containing columns of type `SDO_GEOMETRY` to store the locations of customers, stores, restaurants, and so on, or the locations and spatial extents of geographic entities such as roads, interstates, parks, and land parcels. We describe this data type in detail in Chapter 4.

Listing 2-5 first drops the index that exists. In the second and third lines, it shows the SQL for creating the spatial index. Note that the clause INDEXTYPE tells the database to create a spatial index on the location (SDO_GEOMETRY) column of the us_restaurants table. This index is a specialized index to cater to the SDO_GEOMETRY data. Using such an index, the Index Engine in Oracle Spatial prunes faraway rows from query processing and thus speeds up the query for most applications. The Index Engine provides equivalent functions, referred to as *operators*, for identifying rows of the table that satisfy a specified proximity predicate such as closeness to I-795. You can rewrite the preceding query to find the five nearest restaurants to I-795 using such *index-based operators*. Listing 2-6 shows the resulting query.

Listing 2-6. *Finding the Five Nearest Restaurants on I-795 Using the Spatial Index*

```
SQL> SELECT  poi_name
FROM us_interstates  I,  us_restaurants  P
WHERE I.interstate = 'I795'
  AND SDO_NN(P.location, I.geom) ='TRUE'
  AND ROWNUM <= 5;
POI_NAME
-----------------------------------
PIZZA BOLI'S
BLAIR MANSION INN DINNER THEATER
KFC
CHINA HUT
PIZZA HUT

5 rows selected.
```

Note that this query returns the same five rows as Listing 2-4. However, this query has a simpler structure with no subqueries. It uses only a new index-based operator called SDO_NN, with NN being short for *nearest neighbor*. This index-based operator returns rows of the us_restaurants table whenever the location column is close to the I-795 highway geometry. The SDO_NN operator returns these rows in order of proximity to the I-795 geometry. So, the row with the closest location is returned first, the next closest next, and so on. The ROWNUM predicate determines how many close restaurants need to be returned in the query. The query uses a spatial index and examines only those rows that are likely to be close to the location of I-795. Consequently, it is likely to execute faster than the query in Listing 2-4.

As a variation on this, suppose that instead of having to find the five nearest restaurants on I-795, you want to identify all restaurants within 50 kilometers of I-795. One way to accomplish this is to construct a buffer around the I-795 highway and determine all businesses inside this buffer geometry. Figure 2-2 shows an example: I-795 appears in black, the 50 km buffer is shown with the gray oval around it, and the restaurants inside this buffer are shown by *x* marks.

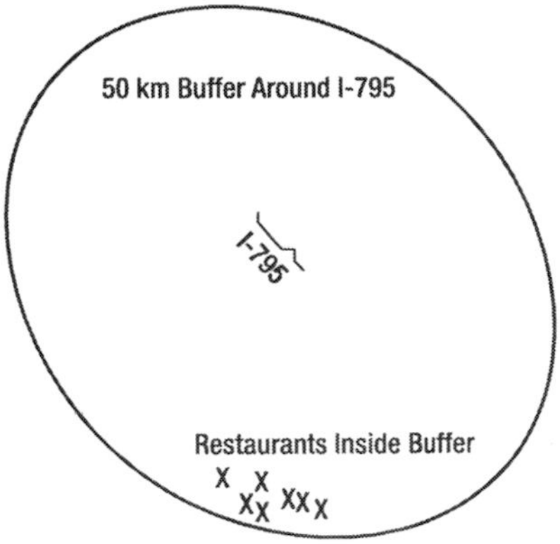

Figure 2-2. *Restaurants in the 50 km buffer around I-795*

- *Simple GIS applications*, which may just work with geographic data such as state, city, or property boundaries and index-based query using associated spatial operators. Typically, though, most GIS applications may need the Geometry Engine functionality (which is not supported in Locator).
- *Simple business applications*, where the spatial data is obtained from third-party vendors. As you will see in Chapter 8, the index-based operators supported in Locator can perform a great deal of analysis in business applications.
- *CAD/CAM and similar applications*, where the spatial data does not refer to locations on the surface of the earth. For instance, in CAD/CAM applications, the data represents the structure/shapes of different parts of an automobile. In this case, the data is inherently in the two- or three-dimensional coordinate space—that is, there is no need to convert nonspatial columns (such as addresses) to obtain spatial information. Typical examples include printed circuit board layouts that are two-dimensional layout mappings. Another example is the storage of city models where three-dimensional building representations are managed. The query operations that are needed for such applications are the index-based proximity analysis operators such as identifying all circuits within specified region in the PCB-layout examples and identifying all buildings within a specified distance of a point or a building or a helicopter trajectory in the city model example.

To summarize, Locator offers a *core subset* of Spatial technology. If you want to exploit the full feature set of Spatial technology, you will need to purchase the Spatial option in the Enterprise Edition of Oracle Database.

Spatial Option

The Spatial option is a priced option of the Enterprise Edition of Oracle Database Server. This option includes all the components of the Spatial technology referred to in Figure 2-4 and is a superset of Locator. Figure 2-5 shows the functionality of the Spatial option in gray. Note that the Spatial option does not include the MapViewer component (shown in black) of Spatial technology. The Spatial option consists of the following:

- *Storage data model using* `SDO_GEOMETRY` *data type*: This includes the storing of all types of geometries (points, lines, polygons, and so on).
- *Query and analysis using the Index Engine*: This includes creating spatial indexes and querying using associated spatial operators such as `SDO_NN`. The functionality also supports three-dimensional geometries such as surfaces and solids that model buildings and other architectural elements in three-dimensional city-modeling applications.
- *Query and analysis using the Geometry Engine*: This supports different analysis functions for individual geometries, pairs of geometries, or a set of geometries. Typical operations include length, area for two-dimensional geometries and length, and area and volume for three-dimensional geometries.
- *Location-enabling using the geocoder*: This facilitates the conversion of address data into `SDO_GEOMETRY` data.
- *Advanced Spatial Engine functionality*: This includes routing and network analysis.

A wide variety of applications can use the full set of functionality provided in the Spatial option.

By now, you should have a good idea of how Oracle Spatial functionality is packaged. This understanding is helpful when determining whether your application needs to license the full set of spatial functionality using the Spatial option. For the remainder of this book, we will not differentiate or explicitly refer to Locator and Spatial option products. Instead, we will refer to the entire set of functionality as Oracle Spatial technology or simply as Oracle Spatial.

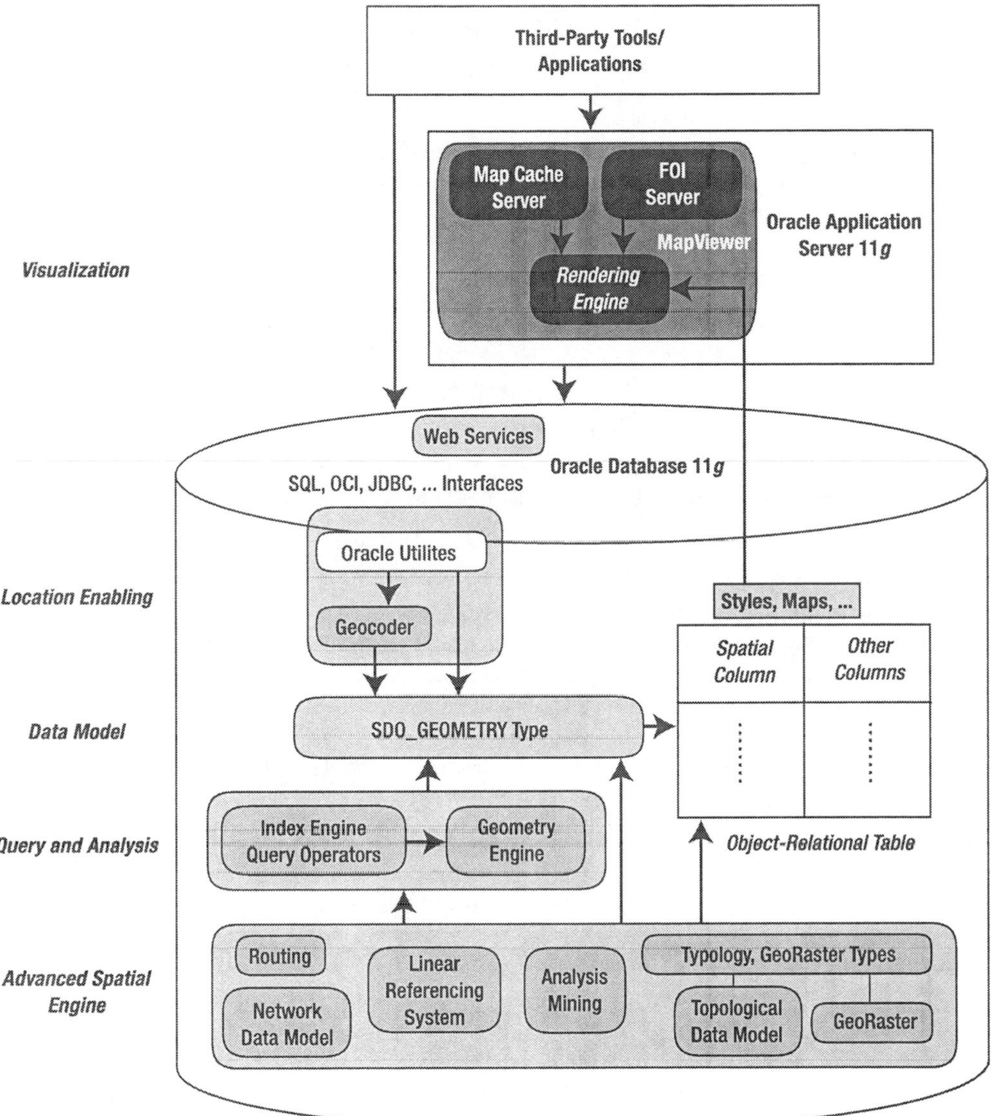

Figure 2-5. *The functionality of the Spatial option is shown in gray.*

What to Expect in an Oracle Spatial Install

In the following sections, we discuss what to expect during or after you install Oracle Spatial technology inside the Oracle Database Server. We describe how to install the MapViewer component, which is part of Oracle Application Server 10g, in Chapter 12.

Installing Oracle Spatial in the Database

As noted previously, Oracle Spatial is automatically installed with the Standard Edition or Enterprise Edition of an Oracle Database Server. All Spatial data types, views, packages, and functions are installed as part of a schema called MDSYS.

To verify that Spatial has been installed properly, you first have to check that the MDSYS account exists. If it does not, then Spatial is not installed. Otherwise, you can execute the SQL in Listing 2-8 after connecting through your SYS (SYSDBA) account.

Listing 2-8. *Verifying That a Spatial Install Is Successful*

```
SQL> SELECT COMP_NAME, STATUS
FROM DBA_REGISTRY
WHERE COMP_NAME = 'Spatial';
COMP_NAME                          STATUS
------------------------------     -----------
Spatial                            VALID
```

After a successful installation, the status will be set to VALID or LOADED.

Upgrades

To understand upgrades properly, let's look at how Spatial technology evolved between different versions of Oracle. Figure 2-6 shows the progression from Oracle 7.2 to Oracle 11g.[5] Note that the figure shows the evolution only of the Spatial components in Oracle Database Server (MapViewer and Oracle Maps, which are part of Oracle Application Server, are not shown).

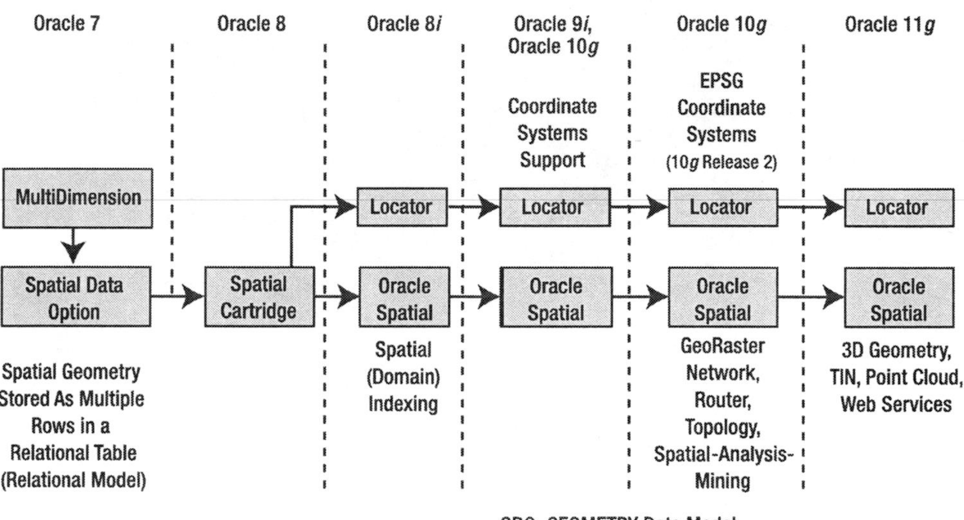

Figure 2-6. *Evolution of Spatial technology in Oracle*

5. Unless otherwise mentioned, Oracle 11g means the Oracle Database 11g in the rest of the book.

Spatial technology was first introduced in Oracle 7.2 under the name Oracle MultiDimension (MD). Later, the product name changed to Oracle Spatial Data Option (SDO) and to Spatial Data Cartridge in Oracle 8. Since objects were not supported in these releases, the coordinates of a geometry were stored as multiple rows in an associated table. Managing spatial (geometry) data in these prior versions was inefficient and cumbersome.

Starting with Oracle 8*i*, the `SDO_GEOMETRY` data type was introduced to store spatial data. Even in the latest versions (Oracle 11*g*, Oracle 10*g*, and Oracle 9*i*), the same `SDO_GEOMETRY` model is used to store spatial data in Oracle. In Oracle 9*i* (and Oracle 10*g*), the geometry data also included support for coordinate systems information specified using the `SRID` attribute in the `SDO_GEOMETRY` data type. In Oracle 10*g*, additional functionality (that exists in the Advanced Spatial Engine) such as the Network Data Model is introduced in the Spatial option of Oracle. In Oracle 10*g* Release 2, the EPSG Coordinate Systems model was added to the Locator option. In Oracle 11*g*, several new features such as 3D geometry support and Spatial Web Services were introduced. You will learn about each of these features in subsequent chapters and appendixes.

Since the prior versions are named MD and SDO, you will see the prefixes `MD` and `SDO` for the files and schemas that install Spatial technology. The name of the spatial install schema is `MDSYS` in all versions of Oracle.

Despite the evolution of Spatial technology with each release, upgrading to the latest version, Oracle 10*g*, is not difficult. *Spatial technology is automatically upgraded with the upgrade of Oracle Database Server.* The upgrade may not need your intervention at all.[6] However, if you are upgrading from pre-8*i* releases, you need to additionally migrate your geometry data from the pre-8*i* format to the `SDO_GEOMETRY` data model. Oracle Spatial provides the `SDO_MIGRATE` package to migrate the data from pre-8*i* models to the current `SDO_GEOMETRY` data model. We discuss this migration package's functionality in Chapter 5.

Understanding a Spatial Install

In this section, we cover where to find appropriate spatial files and how to perform some preliminary investigation when an installation or upgrade fails.

To view all the spatial files, you can go to the `$ORACLE_HOME/md/admin` directory. In this directory, you will find all files relevant to Oracle Spatial. You will observe that a majority of the files have a prefix of either `SDO` or `PRVT`. In other words, the files are of the form `sdoxxxx.sql` or `prvtxxxx.plb`. The `SDO` files, in most cases, contain package definitions for different components of Spatial technology. The `PRVT` files, on the other hand, are binary files and define the package bodies and so on.[7] You should not tamper with these `SDO` and `PRVT` files at any time.

During the creation of the database,[8] the `MDSYS` account is created with appropriate privileges (see scripts `mdinst.sql` and `mdprivs.sql` for more details), and the `catmd.sql` file is loaded into the `MDSYS` schema. This file loads all the `SDO` and `PRVT` files in an appropriate order that resolves all dependencies between all the Spatial packages. In the case of Locator, `catmdloc.sql` (instead of `catmd.sql`) is loaded. Likewise, appropriate files in this directory such as `sdodbmig.sql` (upgrades), `sdopatch.sql` (patches), and `sdoe*.sql` (downgrades) are loaded/executed at the time of upgrades, patches, and downgrades.

During some installations or upgrades, you may find that several package dependencies are unresolved and hence invalid. You can check for such invalid packages or other objects in your Spatial installation by running the SQL in Listing 2-9.

---

6. Note that some spatial components such as GeoRaster have dependencies on other Oracle components such as interMedia and XML. You need to ensure that these components are also upgraded properly or installed if they do not exist in a custom install.

7. Most functions in these package bodies are linked to C/Java libraries that are included with the Oracle kernel.

8. The database can be created either at install time or using a variety of Oracle tools such as DBCA.

Listing 2-9. *Checking for Invalid Objects in a Spatial Installation*

```
SQL> SELECT OBJECT_NAME, OBJECT_TYPE, STATUS
FROM ALL_OBJECTS
WHERE OWNER='MDSYS'  AND STATUS <> 'VALID'
ORDER BY OBJECT_NAME;
```

If Listing 2-9 returns any rows, you should contact Oracle Support for troubleshooting help.

Checking the Version of a Spatial Install

If you have paid for Oracle's Spatial option, you can get the version of the Spatial install by executing the query shown in Listing 2-10. For a Locator install, which is the free functionality of Spatial found in all editions of Oracle, the query returns NULL.

Listing 2-10. *Checking for the Version of a Spatial Install*

```
SQL> SELECT SDO_VERSION FROM DUAL;
```

Summary

This chapter provided a brief overview of the various components of Oracle Spatial technology. First you examined the functionality provided in Oracle Spatial. This functionality included a SQL-level data type for storing spatial data, new operators and functions to perform spatial query and analysis, MapViewer and Oracle Maps technology for visualizing spatial data, and advanced components to perform more sophisticated analysis such as routing or network analysis. We then described how this functionality is packaged in the Database Server and Application Server. Finally, we described what to expect in a typical Spatial installation and where to find appropriate Spatial files.

Starting with the next chapter, we will cover Oracle Spatial functionality in more detail. Specifically in Chapter 3, we describe how to location-enable your application.

CHAPTER 3

Location-Enabling Your Applications

To run the examples in this chapter, you need to import a dataset in the `spatial` schema as follows. Please refer to the "Setting Up" section in the introduction of this book for instructions on creating the `spatial` schema and other setup details.

```
imp spatial/spatial file=gc.dmp ignore=y full=y
```

Consider a business application that stores information about its branches (or stores), customers, competitors, suppliers, and so on. If you location-enable such a business application, you can perform the following types of analysis:

- *Spatial query and analysis*: Identify the number of customers in different sales territories of a branch of this business or a competitor.
- *Network/routing analysis*: Compute the route between a branch and the nearest customer or supplier.
- *Visualization*: Display the results of spatial query or network analysis on a map and integrate this map in other components of the business application.

To exploit the benefits of these types of analysis in a business application, you will first need to location-enable your application. In this chapter, we describe how to augment existing application tables with location information. This location information is usually derived from the address components in application tables such as customers, branches, and competitors and is stored as point locations in these tables. Such location-enabling of the application tables allows simple spatial analysis. We describe such analysis in Chapter 8.

You can augment this analysis, as described in Chapters 8 and 9, by combining the application data with geographic data such as street networks, city boundaries, and so on. The street networks and city boundaries are more complex than the location information in application tables. Such street networks and city boundaries (that is, the geographic data) need to be stored as lines, polygons, and other complex geometry types. We describe several design choices to consider while storing such geographic data in Oracle tables. This geographic data will aid in a more comprehensive analysis for a business application.

After setting up the application and geographic data tables, we show how to insert spatial-specific metadata to location-enable these tables for subsequent analysis. Finally, we discuss how to populate this metadata into appropriate dictionary views for each table that contains spatial data.

Adding Location Information to Tables

Most application data can be categorized into two sets of tables:

- *Application-specific tables*: These contain information that is specific to the application (product and customer information, and so on). Application tables will use standard normalization techniques to arrive at an appropriate set of tables to store the data. These tables might not contain explicit spatial data. However, these tables may have implicit spatial information in the form of addresses.
- *Geographic tables*: Geographic data is independent of the application and contains columns to store explicit spatial information for street networks, city boundaries, and so on. This data may be used as a value-add in the application.

Figure 3-1 shows an example of these two sets of tables for a sample business application. We will use this application along with the associated tables to illustrate all the concepts in this book. Appendix D has appropriate instructions for loading these data.

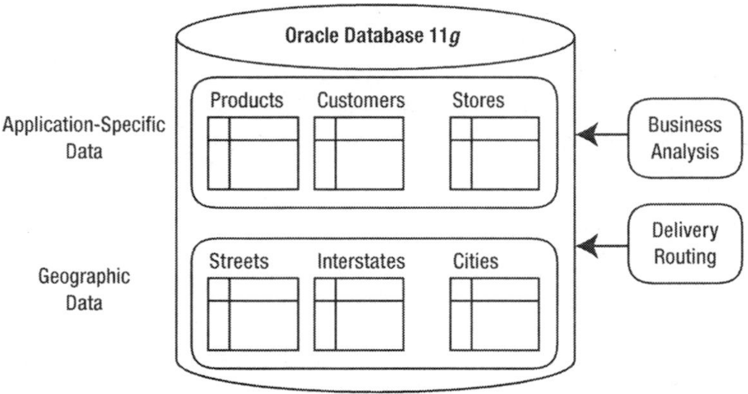

Figure 3-1. *Data for the sample application*

Application-Specific Data

As discussed earlier, for application-specific data, you can employ standard normalization rules to design a set of application tables best suited to the needs of the application. Let's assume that, via this design process, you arrive at the following set of tables for the application layer:

- A `products` table to hold information about all available products
- A `customers` table to hold information about customers
- A `suppliers` table to hold information about suppliers
- A `branches` table to hold information about different branch locations of a business franchise (corresponding to the business application)
- A `competitors` table to hold information about competitors of the business franchise

These tables can be created with appropriate attributes. Listing 3-1 shows the sample SQL for creating the `customers` table. Other tables such as `branches`, `competitors`, and `products` may likewise be created. Note that the `customers` table does not, at this stage, have an explicit column that stores spatial information. The same may apply to other tables in the application that store application-specific data.

Listing 3-1. *Creating the* `customers` *Table*

```
SQL> CREATE TABLE customers
(
  id                              NUMBER,
  datasrc_id                      NUMBER,
  name                            VARCHAR2(35),
  category                        VARCHAR2(30),
  street_number                   VARCHAR2(5),
  street_name                     VARCHAR2(60),
  city                            VARCHAR2(32),
  postal_code                     VARCHAR2(16),
  state                           VARCHAR2(32),
  phone_number                    VARCHAR2(15),
  customer_grade                  VARCHAR2(15)
);
```

These tables can be populated using SQL `INSERT` statements or other loading tools such as SQL*Loader. Listing 3-2 shows an example.

Listing 3-2. *Populating the* `customers` *Table*

```
SQL> INSERT INTO customers VALUES
(
  1,                              -- id
  1,                              -- datasrc_id
  'Pizza Hut' ,                   -- name
  'Restaurant',                   -- restaurant
  '134',                          -- street_number
  '12TH STREET',                  -- street_name
  'WASHINGTON',                   -- city
  '20003',                        -- postal_code
  'DC',                           -- state
  NULL,                           -- phone_number
  'GOLD'                          -- customer_grade
);
```

Adding Location to Application-Specific Data

At a fundamental level, to location-enable the previous business application, you need to store location information for customers, branches, competitors, and so on. This means you need to augment the corresponding tables with an additional column for the storing location. This basic location information is stored as a point using the `SDO_GEOMETRY` type.

For example, to add location information to the `customers` table, you simply alter it as shown in Listing 3-3.

Listing 3-3. *Adding a* `location` *Column to the* `customers` *Table*

```
SQL> ALTER TABLE customers  ADD (location SDO_GEOMETRY);
```

This, by itself, does not populate the `location` column. If you select the `location` column in the table, you will observe that it contains only NULL values.

The most common way to populate the `location` columns in the application tables is by *geocoding* the appropriate address columns. Figure 3-2 illustrates the geocoding process. A variety of tools from different vendors support this geocoding.

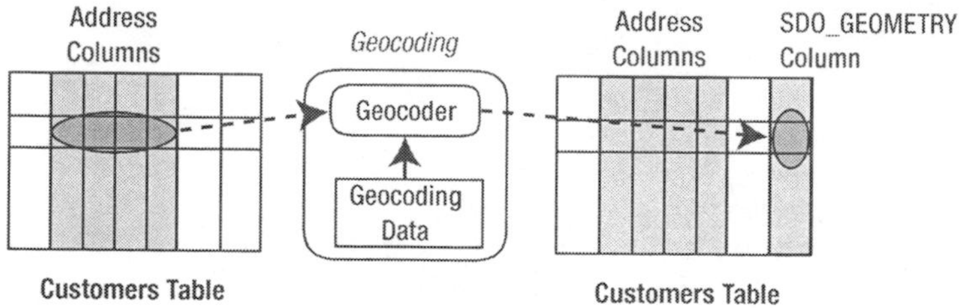

Figure 3-2. *Geocoding application data to populate* SDO_GEOMETRY *columns*

As shown in Figure 3-2, these tools consult an internal database to determine the longitude and latitude values for a specified address. These <longitude, latitude> pairs can then be stored as a point geometry using the SDO_GEOMETRY data type. Oracle Spatial provides a built-in geocoding tool for translating addresses (implicit spatial information) into SDO_GEOMETRY objects.

For instance, let's say the customers, suppliers, branches, and competitors tables store address information. This address is typically stored using the attributes street_number (or Apt#), street_name, city, and postal_code, all of the VARCHAR2 data type. Listing 3-4 shows the address information from the customers table for a specific customer.

Listing 3-4. *Sample Address for a Specific Customer in the* customers *Table*

```
SQL> SELECT street_number, street_name, city, state, postal_code
FROM customers
WHERE id = 1;
134    12TH ST SE    WASHINGTON  DC  20003
```

Oracle Spatial allows you to convert this address (street_number, street_name, city, and postal_code) into a two-dimensional point location on the surface of the earth. The specific function you need is called sdo_gcdr.geocode_as_geometry. This function takes the schema name and the geocoding dataset name as the first and last arguments. The second argument is an sdo_keywordarray object constructed out of the address components street_number, street_name, city, and postal_code. You will learn more about the details of this function in Chapter 6. For now, it is sufficient to note that the simple SQL statement in Listing 3-5 will do the trick. Notice that the sdo_keywordarray object concatenates the street_number and street_name components. Additional whitespace helps in easy identification of the two components.

Listing 3-5. *Geocoding Addresses to Obtain Explicit Spatial Information*

```
SQL> UPDATE customers
  SET location =
  SDO_GCDR.GEOCODE_AS_GEOMETRY
  (
    'SPATIAL',
    SDO_KEYWORDARRAY
    (
      street_number || ` ` || street_name,
    -- add whitespace to separate out street_number and street_name
      city  || `, ` || state || ` `  || postal_code
    ),
    'US'
  ) ;
```

You can now examine what the location information looks like. We will simply select the location column from the customers table. Listing 3-6 shows the SQL to do this.

Listing 3-6. *Geocoded* location *Column in the* customers *Table*

```
SQL> SELECT location
FROM customers
WHERE id=1;

LOCATION(SDO_GTYPE, SDO_SRID, SDO_POINT(X, Y, Z), SDO_ELEM_INFO, SDO_ORDINATES)
---------------------------------------------------------------------
SDO_GEOMETRY(2001, 8307, SDO_POINT_TYPE(-76.99022, 38.888654,  NULL), NULL, NULL)
```

Notice that the specified address (street_number='134', street_name='12th ST SE', city='WASHINGTON', and postal_code='20003') translates to an SDO_GEOMETRY object with longitude and latitude values of –76.99022 and 38.888654 in the sdo_point attribute (instantiated using the SDO_POINT_TYPE object). The sdo_gtype value of 2001 indicates that the location is a *two*-dimensional (*2* in *2*001) point (*1* in 200*1*) location. You will look at other attributes of the location column in the next chapter.

■ **Caution** Coordinate positions are commonly referred to as *latitude/longitude*. However, in Oracle Spatial, the coordinates are stored as longitude followed by latitude.

Once an SDO_GEOMETRY object is constructed, you can insert it, update it, and query it just like any other column in an Oracle table. For instance, you can update the location column directly by constructing a geometry object using an SDO_GEOMETRY constructor, as shown in Listing 3-7.

Listing 3-7. *Updating a* location *Column Using an* SDO_GEOMETRY *Constructor*

```
SQL> UPDATE customers
SET location =
  SDO_GEOMETRY
  (
    2001,                                -- Specify that location is a point
    8307,                                -- Specify coordinate system id
    SDO_POINT_TYPE(-77.06, 38.94, NULL), -- Specify coordinates here
    NULL,
    NULL
  )
WHERE id=1;
```

Once you have basic location data for the application tables, such as customers, branches, and suppliers, you can perform some basic proximity analysis (using SQL-level queries on SDO_GEOMETRY columns; this is covered in Chapters 8 and 9). For instance, you can identify the following:

- Customers close to (for example, within a quarter mile of) a competitor store. For all such customers, you can do some promotion to wean them from your competitor or retain them.
- How many customers are within a quarter-mile of each store or delivery site. Some store sites may be overloaded, and you need to start new store sites at appropriate places.

Design Considerations for Application-Specific Data

As noted, the organization of application-specific data into appropriate tables will be application dependent and will probably involve standard design techniques such as normalization, entity-relationship (ER) diagram-based modeling, and so on. Oracle Spatial does not have any specific recommendations or restrictions for how the application data is to be organized.

One point we can emphasize here, though, is that you should strongly consider table partitioning when table data runs into millions of rows. Consider, for example, the `customers` data for an entire country. These customers share the same attributes. As a result, normalization and other modeling techniques may recommend storing all customers in a single table. However, for spatial applications, the number of customers may be high, running into tens of millions or billions.

In such cases, where the access patterns for the table in question can be tied to a nonspatial attribute (such as `city` or `postal_code`), then partitioning the `customers` table based on the `city` or `postal_code` attribute can ensure good performance and at the same time present a single table on which to operate.

■ **Note** Table partitioning in Oracle is a priced option in the Enterprise Edition of Oracle; it is not available in the Standard Edition.

Partitioning may help in effective and efficient management of large tables. Users can add, split, or modify partitions while continuing to query other unrelated partitions. Partitioning is a convenient mechanism to minimize the impact due to maintenance operations on a table. Whenever possible, partitioned tables are also processed in parallel leading to better create, query, and update times. In addition, partitioning may also improve the efficiency of spatial analysis operations by using partition pruning whenever the partition key is specified in the SQL query. You will look at such analysis examples with partitioned tables in Chapter 8.

Geographic Data

To perform more sophisticated analysis such as routing between two locations or visualization using regional maps, you need to store more than just locations of customers and branches. You may need geographic data such as street networks, city boundaries, and so on. For example, to identify routes from delivery sites to customer locations, you need to store additional information that describes the street network. Likewise, if you want to be able to accurately visualize the locations stored in application tables on a map, then you need to display the boundaries of not just streets and cities but also of rivers, national parks, and so on.

Obtaining the Geographic Data

Geographic data is usually available from a variety of sources, including commercial Geographical Information Systems (GIS) vendors and national mapping agencies. NAVTEQ and Tele Atlas are two such vendors, and both sell geographic data for the United States and Europe. The Ordnance Survey is the national mapping agency for Great Britain: it supplies a highly detailed coverage of Great Britain called MapsterMap. The U.S. Census Bureau is a similar organization serving the United States. Appendix D has details for loading different components of this geographic data to enable network analysis, geocoding, and map-based visualization. In the following sections, we describe the general guidelines for storing and modeling the geographic data in the database.

To enable effective integration and analysis, the geographic data, just like the application-specific data, needs to be stored in the database. This means you need to be able to store a range of different types of data. For example, a street network might be represented by a set of lines connecting different two-dimensional points. Likewise, a city boundary might be represented by a polygon connected by lines. You can represent these types of spatial data using the same `SDO_GEOMETRY` data type that is also used to represent the customer locations (point data) in the application-specific tables. Using a single data type to store all sorts of spatial data ensures a seamless integration and analysis of spatial data in business applications.

Design Considerations for Geographic Data

The next question that arises is how to best store the geographic data. We will illustrate the concepts using typical geographic data (the actual tables used in the book will be directly loaded by importing the appropriate `.dmp` files as discussed in the "Setting Up" section in the introduction of this book). Each type of geographic data can have the following attributes:

- *States*: Attributes can include the state name, the abbreviation of the state name, the population of the state, the average household income, and the boundary of the state (the latter of these being stored in an `SDO_GEOMETRY` object).
- *Counties*: Attributes can include the county name, the state name in which the county belongs, the land area, the population per square mile, and an `SDO_GEOMETRY` object to store the boundary of the county.
- *Interstates*: Attributes can include the name and an `SDO_GEOMETRY` object to store the linear shape of the interstate.
- *Streets*: Attributes can include the name, the city, the state, and an `SDO_GEOMETRY` object to store the linear shape of the street.

Storing streets, interstates, counties, and states in a single table is likely to be inefficient (it may slow down subsequent analysis) and should be avoided. You should store this data in different tables, based on the following general criteria:

- *Separate spatial data that does not share the same attributes*: This is similar to normalization techniques used for regular data. For instance, the `states` data will have different attributes from the `counties`, `streets`, or `interstates` data.
- *Separate coarser data from finer data*: Streets and interstates both represent linear shapes. Sometimes they may even share the same set of attributes. But interstates tend to go across multiple states, whereas streets tend to be localized to a specific city or region. Since the number of streets is likely to be much larger than the number of interstates, storing streets and interstates in the same table may cause performance problems when you want to access just the interstate data. Conversely, the large size of the interstates may pose performance problems when you query for the street data.
- *Separate based on the shape of the geometry*: If you separate spatial data based on the geometric shape—in other words, based on whether it is a point, a line, or a polygon—then you can use the type-checking mechanisms provided by Oracle Spatial indexes at insertion time. For example, if you created a spatial index and specified that a table had only points, the index would raise an error if it encountered nonpoint geometry in the table. Spatial indexes can perform better if they know what type of geometry to expect in a table. We will discuss these features of spatial indexes in Chapter 5.
- *Partition localized data*: Consider the street data for an entire country. The streets share the same attributes and are also at the same resolution level. Based on the previous three criteria, we might store all the streets in the same table. However, because of the large number of the rows in this table, the application may benefit from partitioning this table. We discuss the actual benefits in Chapter 8.

Based on the preceding criteria, you can divide the geographic data, discussed at the beginning of this section, into multiple tables. First, since states have different attributes from other geometries (the first criterion), you can create a separate us_states table as shown in Listing 3-8.

Listing 3-8. *Creating the* us_states *Table*

```
SQL> CREATE TABLE us_states
(
  state                              VARCHAR2(26),
  state_abrv                         VARCHAR2(2),
  totpop                             NUMBER,
  landsqmi                           NUMBER,
  poppssqmi                          NUMBER,
  medage                             NUMBER,
  medhhinc                           NUMBER,
  avghhinc                           NUMBER,
  geom                               SDO_GEOMETRY
);
```

Likewise, you can separate the county data from the rest, as shown in Listing 3-9.

Listing 3-9. *Creating the* us_counties *Table*

```
SQL> CREATE TABLE us_counties
(
  id                                 NUMBER NOT NULL,
  county                             VARCHAR2(31),
  state                              VARCHAR2(30),
  state_abrv                         VARCHAR2(2),
  landsqmi                           NUMBER,
  totpop                             NUMBER,
  poppsqmi                           NUMBER,
  geom                               SDO_GEOMETRY
);
```

Now you have the streets and the interstates, both of which have the same attributes. However, based on the second criterion, you can store them as separate tables, as shown in Listing 3-10.

Listing 3-10. *Creating the* us_interstates *Table*

```
SQL> CREATE TABLE us_interstates
(
  id                                 NUMBER,
  interstate                         VARCHAR2(35),
  geom                               SDO_GEOMETRY
);
SQL> CREATE TABLE us_streets
(
  id                                 NUMBER,
  street_name                        VARCHAR2(35),
  city                               VARCHAR2(32),
  state                              VARCHAR2(32),
  geom                               SDO_GEOMETRY
);
```

Until now, we have described how to location-enable the application-specific tables. We have also discussed how to set up geographic data as regular Oracle tables. This involved creating appropriate tables with a column of the SDO_GEOMETRY type to store associated spatial information. We can populate these tables by either geocoding address data, as we will discuss in Chapter 6, or by using appropriate loading tools, as we will discuss in Chapter 5.

In addition to separating the application-specific data and geographic data into appropriate tables, we also need to specify additional information called *metadata* to location-enable the application. This metadata is used in a variety of spatial functions, such as validation, indexing, and querying of spatial data (as you will see in subsequent chapters).

Metadata for Spatial Tables

Spatial treats all the objects in a single SDO_GEOMETRY column of a table as a *spatial layer*. For instance, the geometry objects stored in the location column of the customers table are treated as a spatial layer.

To perform validation, index creation, and querying with respect to each spatial layer (in other words, all the geometry objects in a specific SDO_GEOMETRY column of a table), you need to specify the appropriate metadata for each layer. This will include the following information:

- The number of dimensions
- The bounds for each dimension
- The tolerance for each dimension (which will be explained later)
- The coordinate system (which will also be explained later)

This information for each spatial layer is populated in the USER_SDO_GEOM_METADATA dictionary view.

Dictionary View for Spatial Metadata

Oracle Spatial provides the USER_SDO_GEOM_METADATA *updatable* view to store metadata for spatial layers. This metadata view has the structure shown in Listing 3-11.

Listing 3-11. *The* USER_SDO_GEOM_METADATA *View*

```
SQL> DESCRIBE USER_SDO_GEOM_METADATA;
Name                                     Null?      Type
 -------------------------------------- ---------- ------------------
TABLE_NAME                               NOT NULL   VARCHAR2(32)
COLUMN_NAME                              NOT NULL   VARCHAR2(1024)
DIMINFO                                             MDSYS.SDO_DIM_ARRAY
SRID                                                NUMBER
```

Together, the TABLE_NAME and COLUMN_NAME columns uniquely identify each spatial layer. For the identified layer, the metadata stores information about the individual dimensions for the layer in the DIMINFO attribute. The information about the coordinate system of the geometry data is stored in the SRID attribute. We will discuss how to choose the SRID attribute in more detail in Chapter 4, but we will briefly describe it here before moving on to examine the DIMINFO attribute.

Note The TABLE_NAME and COLUMN_NAME values are always converted to uppercase when you insert them into the USER_SDO_GEOM_METADATA view.

SRID Attribute

This attribute specifies the *coordinate system* in which the data in the spatial layer is stored. The coordinate system could be one of the following:

- *Geodetic*: Angular coordinates, expressed in terms of "longitude, latitude" with respect to the earth's surface.
- *Projected*: Cartesian coordinates that result from performing a mathematical mapping from an area on the earth's surface to a plane.
- *Local*: Cartesian coordinate systems with no link to the earth's surface and sometimes specific to an application. These are used in CAD/CAM and other applications where the spatial data does not pertain to locations on the earth.

Different geodetic and projected coordinate systems are devised to maximize the accuracy (of distances and other spatial relationship calculations) for different parts/regions of the world. We will describe coordinate systems in detail in Chapter 4.

In the case of geodetic coordinate systems, you can consult the `CS_SRS`[1] table for possible values by selecting rows where the `WKTEXT` column[2] starts with a prefix of `'GEOGCS'`. Listing 3-12 shows the SQL.

Listing 3-12. *Selecting SRIDs of Geodetic Coordinate Systems*

```
SQL> SELECT SRID
FROM MDSYS.CS_SRS
WHERE WKTEXT LIKE 'GEOGCS%';
```

As shown in Listing 3-13, you can select the `SRID`s for the projected coordinate system from the `MDSYS.CS_SRS` table by searching for rows where the `WKTEXT` column starts with `'PROJCS'`. Analogously, you can find the `SRID`s for local coordinate systems by searching for the prefix `'LOCAL_CS'` in the `WKTEXT` column of the `MDSYS.CS_SRS` table.

Listing 3-13. *Selecting SRIDs of Projected Coordinate Systems*

```
SQL> SELECT SRID
FROM MDSYS.CS_SRS
WHERE WKTEXT LIKE 'PROJCS%';
```

In most cases, you don't have to choose the coordinate system. Instead, you obtain the geometry data from a third-party vendor, and the `SRID` is already populated in these geometries.

Caution If the coordinate system is geodetic (in other words, the SRID corresponds to one of the values in the `MDSYS.GEODETIC_SRIDS` table), then the dimensions in the `DIMINFO` attribute are always longitude and latitude. The first element in the `DIMINFO` attribute should always specify the dimension information for the longitude column, and the second element should always specify the information for the latitude dimension.

Starting in Oracle 10*g* Release 2, coordinate systems in Oracle are based on, but not entirely identical to, the European Petroleum Standards Group (EPSG) data model and data set. The EPSG

1. The actual table is `MDSYS.CS_SRS`. In Oracle 10g and Oracle 11g, a synonym is created so that you can access the `CS_SRS` table in the `MDSYS` schema directly by referring to `CS_SRS`. In prior versions of Oracle, you may need to access the table explicitly as `MDSYS.CS_SRS`.
2. The `wktext` column stores the "well-known text" for a coordinate system. This is explained in detail in Chapter 4.

model is a widely accepted standard for coordinate system data representation and provides flexibility in specifying transformations between different coordinate systems. This model extends support to vertical, two-dimensional, and three-dimensional coordinate systems. Users can browse coordinate system information by selecting from the SDO_COORD_REF_SYSTEM table. Oracle has additional tables, views, and functions to support the various operations in the EPSG model. We will cover the EPSG model in more detail in Chapter 4.

DIMINFO Attribute

Spatial data is multidimensional in nature. For example, the location column in the customers table of our business application has two dimensions: longitude and latitude (see Listing 3-3). The DIMINFO attribute in USER_SDO_GEOM_METADATA specifies information about each dimension of the specified layer. The DIMINFO attribute is of type MDSYS.SDO_DIM_ARRAY. Listing 3-14 shows this structure.

Listing 3-14. *The* SDO_DIM_ARRAY *Structure*

```
SQL> DESCRIBE SDO_DIM_ARRAY;
 SDO_DIM_ARRAY VARRAY(4) OF MDSYS.SDO_DIM_ELEMENT
 Name                       Null?       Type
 -----------------------  -----------  --------------
SDO_DIMNAME                             VARCHAR2(64)
SDO_LB                                  NUMBER
SDO_UB                                  NUMBER
SDO_TOLERANCE                           NUMBER
```

Note that SDO_DIM_ARRAY is a variable-length array (VARRAY) of type SDO_DIM_ELEMENT. Each SDO_DIM_ARRAY is sized according to the number of dimensions (so for a two-dimensional geometry, the DIMINFO attribute will contain two SDO_DIM_ELEMENT types, and so on).

Each SDO_DIM_ELEMENT type stores information for a specific dimension and consists of the following fields:

- SDO_DIMNAME: This field stores the name of dimension. For instance, you can set it to 'Longitude' or 'Latitude' to indicate that the dimension represents the longitude or latitude dimension. The name you specify here is not interpreted by Spatial. You can specify 'X' for the longitude dimension and 'Y' for the latitude dimension.
- SDO_LB and SDO_UB: These two numbers define the lower bound and the upper bound limits for the values in a specific dimension. For instance, values in the longitude dimension range from –180 to 180. So, you can set SDO_LB to –180 and SDO_UB to 180. Likewise, for the latitude dimension, you can set SDO_LB and SDO_UB to –90 and 90, respectively. Note that these bounds are application specific. For instance, in a CAD/CAM application, the values in a specific dimension may range from 0 to 100, and the bounds will be set accordingly.
- SDO_TOLERANCE: An SDO_TOLERANCE value, or simply a *tolerance* value, is used to specify a degree of precision for spatial data. It essentially specifies the distance that two values must be apart to be considered different. For example, if the tolerance is specified as 0.5 and the distance between two points A and B is less than 0.5, then points A and B are considered to be at the same location.

  By default, the tolerance value is in the same units as the SDO_LB and SDO_UB values (in other words, in the same units as the ordinates in a dimension). However, in geodetic coordinate systems, the tolerance value is always in meters (whereas the SDO_LB, SDO_UB bounds are in degrees). Oracle additionally requires that the tolerance be the same value in all dimensions (that is, in all SDO_DIM_ELEMENTs).

In the following sections, we will describe the tolerance field in more detail and examine its potential impact on different spatial functions and how to set the tolerance appropriately in an application.

Understanding Tolerance

As discussed, tolerance is specified as a field of the DIMINFO attribute in the USER_SDO_GEOM_METADATA view. The spatial indexes and other spatial layer–level operations use the DIMINFO attribute and the associated tolerance from this view.

A second usage of tolerance is in spatial functions described in Chapters 5, 8, and 9. The majority of these spatial functions do not read the USER_SDO_GEOM_METADATA view and instead expect the tolerance to be passed in as an input parameter. You will see such uses of tolerance in spatial validation or the analysis functions that are described in Chapters 5, 8, and 9. In this section, we will first discuss what tolerance is and then how to set it properly for your application.

Setting incorrect tolerance values can cause incorrect and unexpected results in a variety of functions. Let's illustrate this with an example, as shown in Figure 3-3.

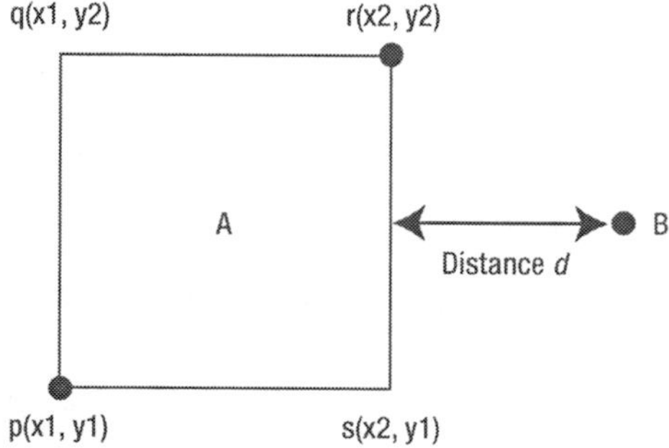

Figure 3-3. *Tolerance and its impact on the validity and relationship of two objects, A and B*

Figure 3-3 shows two objects, A and B. Object A is a rectangle with four vertices: *p*, *q*, *r*, and *s*. The lower-left vertex *p* is at coordinates (x1, y1), and the upper-right vertex *r* is at coordinates (x2, y2). The distance between objects A and B is *d*. The spatial relationship between objects A and B, and whether object A is considered a valid or invalid geometry, will vary depending on how you set the tolerance value.

- *Relationship between A and B*: If the distance *d* < tolerance, then B is considered to be on the outer boundary of A. In other words, object A is considered to be intersecting object B.

  If the distance *d* >= tolerance, then A and B are considered to be *disjoint* or, in other words, nonintersecting.

- *Validation check for object A*: If the distance between *p* and *s* is less than the tolerance value—that is, (x2 – x1) < tolerance—then *p* and *s* are considered duplicate points/vertices. Likewise, *q* and *r* will be considered duplicate vertices. Oracle Spatial does not allow duplicate points in the specification of a geometry, so geometry object A would be considered invalid. The same holds true if the distance (y2 – y1) between *p* and *q* is less than the tolerance.

  If the preceding distances are greater than or equal to the tolerance, then the vertices are considered distinct and geometry object A is considered a valid Oracle Spatial geometry.

From this example, you can understand that tolerance plays an important role in your application. Setting it appropriately is an important step in location-enabling your application.

Choosing the Tolerance Value

As a general rule, the *tolerance value should be set to the smallest distinguishable distance in your application.* In most applications, this distance corresponds to half the difference between two individual coordinate values. For example, if the closest points in your application have the values 0.1 and 0.2 in a specific dimension, you can set the tolerance to (0.2 – 0.1)/2 = 0.05. This will ensure that the two points (and all other points in the application data) are treated as distinct. Note that the tolerance is specified in the same units as the coordinate values.

This technique can be applied directly when the geometry data refers to local coordinate systems (as in CAD/CAM and other applications) or for projected coordinate systems. However, for locations on the surface of the earth modeled using geodetic coordinate systems, the difference in the longitude or latitude values of two locations does not correspond to the actual distance between them. In these cases (that is, in a geodetic coordinate system), the ordinates are interpreted to be in *degrees* and the tolerance in *meters.*

From this discussion, it is clear that specifying an appropriate value for the tolerance depends on the coordinate system (that is, the `SRID` attribute that specifies the coordinate system). In Table 3-1, we describe some recommendations for different coordinate systems.

Table 3-1. *Suggested Values for Tolerance Based on SRID for Applications*

Coordinate System	SRID Values	Tolerance	Units
Geodetic coordinate system (such as 8265, 8307)	Select `SRID` from `MDSYS.CS_SRS`, where `WKTEXT` is like `'GEOGCS%'`.	0.5 (should not be less than 0.05)	Meters for tolerance; degrees for longitude, latitude dimensions.
Projected coordinate system (such as 32774)	Select `SRID` from `MDSYS.CS_SRS`, where `WKTEXT` is like `'PROJCS%'`.	Half of the smallest difference between any two values in a dimension	Units for tolerance are the same as the units for the ordinates in the dimensions.
Local coordinate system	Select `SRID` from `MDSYS.CS_SRS`, where `WKTEXT` is like `'LOCAL_CS%'`.	Half of the smallest difference between any two values in a dimension	Units for tolerance are the same as the units for the ordinates in the dimensions.
No specific coordinate syst	`NULL`.	Half of the smallest difference between any two values in a dimension	Units for tolerance are the same as the units for the ordinates in the dimensions.

Populating Spatial Metadata for Your Application

Given this background on the different attributes in the `USER_SDO_GEOM_METADATA` view, we can now populate the tables in our sample application with metadata.

Since we are dealing with locations on the earth and mostly for the continental United States, we choose the `SRID` of 8307. This `SRID` is used in a majority of navigation systems that use Global Positioning Systems (GPS). The tolerance value for this geodetic coordinate system can be set to 0.5 meters. Using this value, we insert a row in the `USER_SDO_GEOM_METADATA` view for the spatial layer corresponding to the `location` column of the `customers` table. Listing 3-15 shows the corresponding SQL.

Listing 3-15. *Inserting Metadata for the Spatial Layer Corresponding to the* `location` *Column of the* `customers` *Table*

```
SQL> INSERT INTO  USER_SDO_GEOM_METADATA  VALUES
(
  'CUSTOMERS',       -- TABLE_NAME
  'LOCATION',        -- COLUMN_NAME
  SDO_DIM_ARRAY      -- DIMINFO attribute for storing dimension bounds, tolerance
  (
    SDO_DIM_ELEMENT
    (
      'LONGITUDE',   -- DIMENSION NAME for first dimension
      -180,          -- SDO_LB for the dimension
      180,           -- SDO_UB for the dimension
      0.5            -- Tolerance of 0.5 meters
    ),
    SDO_DIM_ELEMENT
    (
      'LATITUDE',    -- DIMENSION NAME for second dimension
      -90,           -- SDO_LB for the dimension
      90,            -- SDO_UB for the dimension
      0.5            -- Tolerance of 0.5 meters
    )
  ),
  8307               -- SRID value for specifying a geodetic coordinate system
);
```

Note that the `SRID` of 8307 specifies that the data in the corresponding spatial layer are in a geodetic coordinate system. There are specific restrictions when specifying the metadata for geodetic coordinate systems:

- The first dimension in `SDO_DIM_ARRAY` should correspond to the longitude dimension. The bounds should always be set to –180 and 180.
- The second dimension in `SDO_DIM_ARRAY` should correspond to the latitude dimension. The bounds should always be set to –90 and 90.
- The tolerance for the dimensions must always be specified in meters. Meters are the "units" of distance in all geodetic coordinate systems in Oracle.

Inserting incorrect metadata that does not conform to the preceding guidelines for geodetic coordinate systems is one of the most common mistakes that Oracle developers make. To ensure accurate distance calculations, you are advised to memorize the preceding three rules, because in most applications you will use a geodetic coordinate system (specified by your data vendor).

In the earlier example, we constructed the metadata for the spatial layer corresponding to the `location` column of the `customers` table and inserted it into the `USER_SDO_GEOM_METADATA` view. Likewise, you have to insert rows into `USER_SDO_GEOM_METADATA` for other spatial layers such as the `location` column in the `branches` table and the `geom` column in the `us_interstates` table.

Additional Information for Visualization and Network Analysis

In the preceding sections, we discussed how to insert metadata for a spatial layer. This metadata will enable validation, spatial indexing, and spatial query and analysis operations, which are discussed in Chapters 5, 8, and 9.

In addition to such spatial analysis, you may want to enable your application with additional functionality such as map-based visualization and network/routing analysis. To enable these types of functionality, you will need to specify additional information in appropriate updatable dictionary views. We discuss the details of this process in Chapters 10 and 11.

Summary

In this chapter, we covered the main steps required to location-enable your business applications, namely, the following:

- Designing and creating tables to store application-specific data
- Designing and creating tables to store geographic data
- Defining metadata for each spatial layer both in the application-specific and the geographic tables

Both the spatial application data and the geographic data are stored using an `SDO_GEOMETRY` object. It is time to move on and discuss this object in detail.

PART 2

Basic Spatial

CHAPTER 4

The SDO_GEOMETRY Data Type

In the previous chapter, we discussed how to location-enable application data and how to organize geographic data into multiple tables, each containing SDO_GEOMETRY columns. In this chapter, we focus on storing and modeling different types of location information using the SDO_GEOMETRY data type in Oracle. The SDO_GEOMETRY type can store a wide variety of spatial data, including the following:

- A *point*, which can be used to store the coordinate location of, for example, a customer site, a store location, a delivery address, and so on
- A *line string*, which can be used to store the location and shape of a road segment
- A *polygon*, which can be used to store city boundaries, business regions, and so on
- Complex geometries, such as multiple polygons, which can be used to store boundaries for states such as Texas, Hawaii, and California

First, we explain the structure of SDO_GEOMETRY, including the different attributes and the values it can take to store the different types of geometric data listed.

After this, we cover how to actually construct SDO_GEOMETRY objects for simple geometries such as points, lines, and polygons (as an application developer, you'll mostly be working with such simple geometries).

Finally, we show how to construct more complex geometries, such as multipolygons. This knowledge is useful in defining spatial regions of interest on the fly. In Chapters 8 and 9, you'll see how to use such constructed geometries to perform spatial analysis in an application. Throughout this chapter, we illustrate potential uses for these different SDO_GEOMETRY data objects with examples applicable to a typical business application.

The SDO_GEOMETRY examples that are constructed in this chapter are stored in the geometry_examples table. You can create this table as shown in Listing 4-1.

Listing 4-1. *Creating a Table to Store All Geometry Examples*

```
SQL> CREATE TABLE geometry_examples
(
  name            VARCHAR2(100),
  description     VARCHAR2(100),
  geom            SDO_GEOMETRY
);
```

The geometry_examples table contains a description of the name and a description of the geometry and the corresponding SDO_GEOMETRY object. You can use this table as a quick reference to construct geometries of appropriate types on the fly. For simple types, you may just have to modify the ordinates in the geom column.

Types of Spatial Geometries in Oracle

Let's take a closer look at the types of spatial data that SDO_GEOMETRY can store. Figure 4-1 illustrates some of these types, categorizing them into both types supported in two and three dimensions and types supported in only three dimensions.

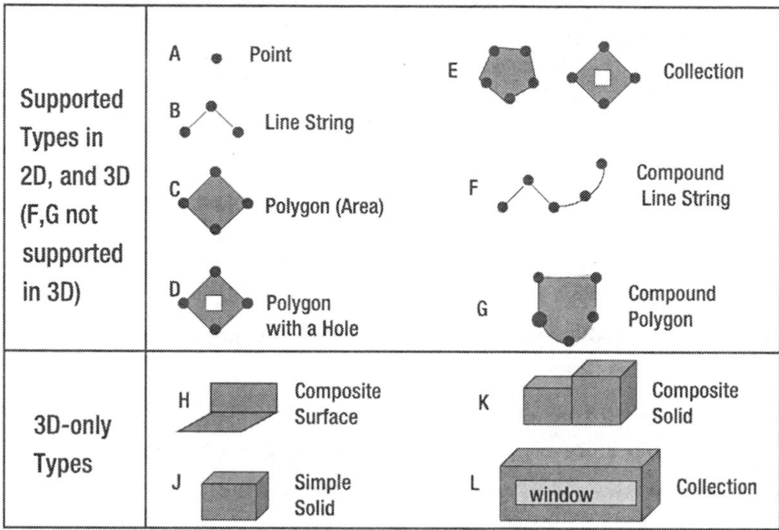

Figure 4-1. *Examples of spatial data that* SDO_GEOMETRY *can represent*

In the sections that follow, we'll take a closer look at the geometry types in Figure 4-1.

Points

The simplest geometry is a *point*, which you have used in previous chapters. A *point* can represent the location of a customer, a delivery site, or a competitor store. Object A in Figure 4-1 is an example of a point geometry.

Line Strings

A *line string* connects multiple points (or *vertices* as they are sometimes called). In general, roads, transportation networks, utility lines, and pipelines are represented as a line string type of SDO_GEOMETRY. If the line string is closed, then it is a *ring*. Otherwise, it is just a *line*. A line string connects two or more points by the following:

- *Straight lines*: We refer to this simply as a *straight-line* line string or as a *line string* when there is no ambiguity. Object B in Figure 4-1 is an example of straight-line line string.
- *Circular arcs*: We refer to this as an *arc string*.[1]
- *A combination of straight lines and circular arcs*: We refer to this as a *compound* line string (curve). Object F in Figure 4-1 is an example of such a compound line string.

1. Oracle supports only circular arcs. From now on, we refer to circular arcs simply as *arcs*.

Polygons and Surfaces

A *polygon* is specified by one or more rings (closed line strings) and is associated with an area. Object C in Figure 4-1 is a polygonal area bounded by straight lines connecting four points (the shaded area in Figure 4-1). In this example, object C is shaped like a diamond, but in general a polygon can have any arbitrary shape. A polygon could represent a city boundary, a ZIP code area, or a buffer zone around a store site. A polygon has the following properties:

- The boundary of a polygon consists of one or more rings (a closed line string). Special cases for the polygon boundary that can be specified easily in SDO_GEOMETRY include rectangles and circles.
- A polygon, unlike a line string, is associated with an *area* enclosed by the boundary. The area has to be *contiguous*—that is, you should be able to travel in the interior of the polygon without crossing the boundary. This means the digit 8 cannot be a valid polygon. (However, the digit 8 can be modeled as a multipolygon or collection geometry, as described later.) Object C in Figure 4-1 is an example of a (valid) polygon. In Chapter 5, you will learn the criterion for determining the *validity* of polygons.
- The ring specifying the boundary or collection of a polygon can be composed of straight lines, arcs, or a combination of arcs and lines. If it is a combination of arcs and lines, we refer to the polygon as a *compound* polygon. Object G in Figure 4-1 is an example of such a compound polygon, because its boundary is connected by straight lines and arcs.
- The area covered by a polygon can be expressed using one *outer* ring and any number (zero or more) of *inner* rings. The inner rings are referred to as *holes* or *voids* because they void out (subtract) the area covered by the outer ring. Object D in Figure 4-1 shows a polygon with one outer ring and one inner ring (void). The inner ring in this example is a rectangle. The area covered by this polygon is the shaded region between the two rings.

Until now we were assuming the example data is in a two-dimensional space. For three-dimensional data, the polygons are in three-dimensional planes and hence are referred to as (planar) *polygonal surfaces*, or surfaces when there is no ambiguity. Note that all vertices of a polygonal surface have to be in a single plane. You can “stitch” one or more polygonal surfaces (each being in a different plane) to constitute an arbitrary three-dimensional (but contiguous) *composite surface*. Object H in Figure 4-1 is an example of such a composite surface. A surface geometry in general can be a single polygonal surface or a composite surface consisting of contiguous polygonal surfaces. Note that a surface can have still have an associated area but is not associated with a volume even if the surface forming the boundary is closed, that is, defines a solid. Examples of three-dimensional surfaces include the exteriors of buildings and soil surfaces.

Solids

A *simple solid* is specified by one outer surface and zero or more inner composite surfaces. Together, the outer and inner composite surfaces define the boundary (or limits) of the simple solid. Unlike a surface, a solid has both an area and a volume. Object J in Figure 4-1 is an example of a simple solid. You can use the solid type to model buildings and other architectural entities in a city-modeling application.

In some cases, buildings may consist of one or more attached components. You can model such buildings either as a simple solid or as a *composite solid* consisting of multiple simple solids that have a single volume. If it is represented as a combination, then it is referred to as a *composite solid*. Object K in Figure 4-1 is an example of a composite solid. Storing different components as components of a composite solid is advantageous if your application intends to access each component of the solid separately. (We will look at functions for accessing components of a surface or a solid in Chapter 7.) Such composite solids come in handy in CAD-type applications, where you may attach a nut to a bolt to make a single composite solid.

Collections

A *collection* has multiple geometry elements. A collection could be *heterogeneous*—that is, it could be any combination of points, lines, and polygons. Alternatively, a collection could be *homogeneous*—that is, it could consist of elements of a single type. Specific types of such homogeneous collections are multipoint, multiline, multipolygon/multisurface, or multisolid collections.

Object E in Figure 4-1 has two polygons, a pentagon-shaped polygon and a polygon with a void, and is an example of a multipolygon collection. The shaded regions in the figure show the area covered by this geometry. The boundaries for some states, such as Texas and California, are represented as collections of polygons, where noncontiguous elements (islands) are stored as separate polygons. Likewise, the digit 8 can also be stored as a collection geometry with two polygons. Object L in Figure 4-1 models a building as a collection of a solid and a surface, with the solid representing the actual building and the surface representing the window.

Logical Implementation of SDO_GEOMETRY

In general, the shape of spatial objects can be quite complex, requiring a large number of connected points (or *vertices*). For instance, the Amazon River may have thousands of vertices. State boundaries, which are modeled as polygons, could also have a large number of vertices. Any data type that models spatial data should be able to represent the wide variety of shapes—from complex road segments to an arbitrarily shaped city and property boundaries.

To represent such complex geometric shapes, the SDO_GEOMETRY type is logically implemented using an array of elements, as shown in Figure 4-2.

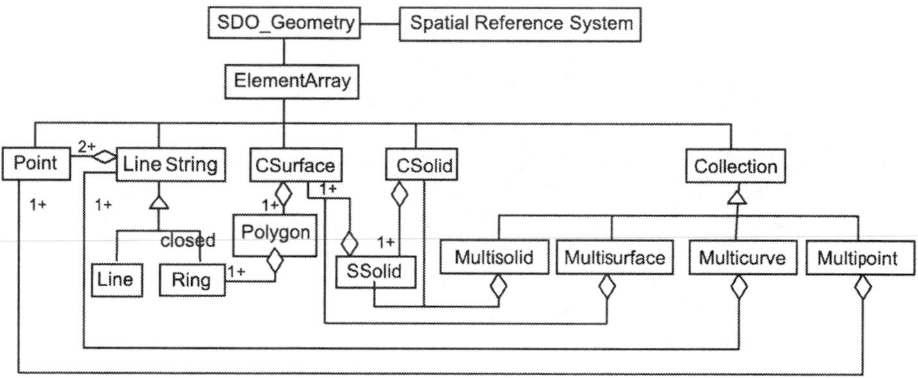

Notation: △ denotes *is-a* relationship
◇ denotes *many-to-1* relationship

CSurface is short for *Composite Surface*
CSolid is short for *Composite Solid*
SSolid is short for *Simple Solid*

Figure 4-2. *Conceptual class diagram of the* SDO_GEOMETRY *data type*

The SDO_GEOMETRY data type has two logical components: the spatial reference system (also called the *coordinate system*) of the geometry and the ElementArray.

■Note The coordinate system specifies the reference frame in which the coordinates of the geometry are represented. Different coordinate systems exist to model the surface of the earth. Alternatively, a coordinate system may refer to a nonearth surface. You will learn more about different coordinate systems in the next section.

The `ElementArray`, or the array of elements, describes the shape and location of the `SDO_GEOMETRY` object (with reference to the specified coordinate system). This array of elements constitutes (or makes up) the `SDO_GEOMETRY` object. The array of elements represents any of the different types of spatial data represented in Figure 4-1: point, line string, polygon, or collection-type geometry. This is depicted in Figure 4-2 by the *is-a* relationship, illustrated by the triangle symbol between these types and the `ElementArray`. Note that the diamond symbol shows a *many-to-one* relationship between different types. For instance, a diamond between a point and a line string indicates that "many" points make up "one" line string. Note that the "2+" next to the diamond symbol indicates the minimum number. For example, at least two or more points make up a line string. Likewise, observe that one or more rings constitute a polygon, and note that one or more polygons constitute a *composite surface* (called a composite if more than one polygon and the surface are connected). One outer composite surface and zero or more inner composite surfaces (represented as one or more in Figure 4-2) form a *simple solid* (SSolid in Figure 4-2) if the surfaces are closed. One or more adjacent (sharing a face) simple solids form a *composite solid* (referred to as CSolid in Figure 4-2). The collection types are formed as one or more elements of the appropriate type (for example, one or more points form a multipoint, one or more solids form a multisolid, and so on).

Spatial Data in SQL/MM and OGC

SQL/MM is the ISO/IEC international standard for "Text, Spatial, Still Images, and Data Mining." SQL/MM Part 3[2] specifically deals with spatial user-defined types and associated routines to store, manage, and retrieve two-dimensional spatial data. This standard specifies the `ST_Geometry` type to store two-dimensional spatial data. This type has subtypes such as `ST_Point`, `ST_LineString`, and `ST_Polygon` to model different types of spatial geometries. This standard also includes a well-known text format for specifying geometries. For instance, the string `'POINT( 1 1)'` indicates a point geometry with coordinates at (1, 1).

The Open GIS Consortium (OGC) has the Simple Features Specification[3] for storing, retrieving, querying, and updating simple geospatial (two-dimensional) features. This specification defines a `Geometry` type with appropriate subtypes to model two-dimensional points, line strings, polygons, and so on. The types represented are a subset of those defined by SQL/MM. For three-dimensional data, the GML 3.0 specification of OGC defines an extensive set of three-dimensional types.

Oracle Spatial explicitly supports `ST_Geometry` and its specific subtypes (`ST_CircularString`, `ST_CompoundCurve`, `ST_Curve`, `ST_CurvePolygon`, `ST_GeomCollection`, `ST_LineString`, `ST_MultiCurve`, `ST_MultiLineString`, `ST_MultiPoint`, `ST_MultiPolygon`, `ST_MultiSurface`, `ST_Point`, and `ST_Polygon`) that are defined in the SQL/MM standard. These types and Oracle Spatial's `SDO_GEOMETRY` data type are essentially interoperable. In other words, you can create `ST_Geometry` from an `SDO_Geometry` type, and vice versa. In addition, Oracle also implements relationship functions defined on `ST_Geometry` and its subtypes in the SQL/MM standard (these are discussed in Chapter 8). In short, Oracle Spatial conforms to the OGC Simple Features Specification (the `ST_Geometry` implementation is compliant with the OGC Simple Features Specification *for Object Model*) and the equivalent

2. ISO/IEC 13249-3:2003, "Information technology – Database languages – SQL multimedia and application packages – Part 3: Spatial," `http://www.iso.org/iso/en/CatalogueDetailPage.CatalogueDetail?CSNUMBER=31369`.

3. Open GIS Consortium, "OpenGIS Simple Features Specification for SQL Revision 1.1," `http://www.opengis.org/docs/99-049.pdf`, May 5, 1999.

sections of SQL/MM Part 3. In this chapter, we illustrate how to construct various types of geometries using the *native* SDO_GEOMETRY data type. For the construction of these geometries using an ST_Geometry type, you can consult the *Oracle Spatial's User Guide and Reference* or use the SDO_GEOMETRY-ST_GEOMETRY conversion functions described in Chapter 5.

For three-dimensional data, Oracle can store and model the majority of the types in the GML 3.0 specification with the exception of parametric curve types (arcs, splines, and so on). In addition, Oracle Spatial provides constructors for converting data between the SDO_GEOMETRY data type and the well-known text (WKT) and well-known binary (WKB) notations of SQL/MM for two-dimensional data and between SDO_GEOMETRY and GML 3.0 types for three-dimensional data. We describe these converters in Chapter 5.

In the next section, we take a closer look at the SDO_GEOMETRY data type. In the subsequent sections, we describe how to construct SDO_GEOMETRY objects to store different types of spatial data.

SDO_GEOMETRY Type, Attributes, and Values

Now that you know what an SDO_GEOMETRY can represent and how it is internally constituted, let's examine its structure in Oracle. Listing 4-2 describes the SDO_GEOMETRY data type.

Listing 4-2. SDO_GEOMETRY *Data Type in Oracle*

```
SQL> DESCRIBE SDO_GEOMETRY
 Name                          Null?    Type
 ----------------------------- -------- --------------------
 SDO_GTYPE                              NUMBER
 SDO_SRID                               NUMBER
 SDO_POINT                              SDO_POINT_TYPE
 SDO_ELEM_INFO                          SDO_ELEM_INFO_ARRAY
 SDO_ORDINATES                          SDO_ORDINATE_ARRAY
```

Let's look at the purpose served by each attribute of SDO_GEOMETRY:

- The SDO_GTYPE attribute specifies the type of shape (point, line, polygon, collection, multipoint, multiline, or multipolygon) that the geometry actually represents. Although the SDO_GTYPE attribute captures what type of geometry is being represented, it does not specify the actual coordinates.
- The SDO_SRID attribute specifies the ID of the spatial reference system (coordinate system) in which the location/shape of the geometry is specified.

In Figure 4-2, we noted that a geometry consists of an element array (that is, one or more elements make up a geometry). How do you specify the coordinates of the elements? You can do it in one of the following ways:

- If the geometry is a point (for example, the location of customers), then you can store the coordinates in the SDO_POINT attribute of SDO_GEOMETRY.
- If the geometry is an arbitrary shape (for example, a street network or city boundaries), then you can store the coordinates using the SDO_ORDINATES and SDO_ELEM_INFO array attributes:
    - The SDO_ORDINATES attribute stores the coordinates of all elements of the geometry.
    - The SDO_ELEM_INFO attribute specifies where in the SDO_ORDINATES array a new element starts, how it is connected (by straight lines or arcs), and whether it is a point (although we recommend you use SDO_POINT for the storage and performance reasons listed later in the chapter), a line, or a polygon.

Let's look at each of these attributes in more detail.

SDO_GTYPE Attribute

This attribute describes the type of geometric shape modeled in the object. It reflects roughly the top levels in the class hierarchy of Figure 4-2. Specifically, it has a distinct value to indicate whether the geometry is a point, a line string, a polygon, a multipoint, a multipolygon, a multiline, or an arbitrary collection. You can think of this attribute as a high-level description of the geometry object. The geometry object may itself be a combination of multiple elements, each of a different shape. But this attribute specifies the general type for the *entire object* (with all elements it is composed of).

The SDO_GTYPE attribute is a four-digit number structured as follows: DOOT. The first and the last digits take different values based on the dimensionality and shape of the geometry, as described in Table 4-1. The second and third digits are always set to 0.

■ **Note** For a linear-referenced geometry, SDO_GTYPE is structured as DLOT. The second digit, L, in that case refers to the dimension number (3 or 4) to use for the measure values in a linear-referenced geometry. In Oracle 11*g* Release 1, linear referenced geometries can have only x,y and measure dimensions and not x,y,z and measure dimensions. You will learn about linear-referenced geometries in Appendix C.

Table 4-1. *Values for* D *and* T *in the* DOOT *Format of the* SDO_GTYPE *Attribute of* SDO_GEOMETRY

Digit	Values
D (dimension of the geometry)	2 = Two-dimensional, 3 = Three-dimensional, 4 = Four-dimensional
T (shape/type of the geometry)	0 = Uninterpreted type, 1 = Point, 5 = Multipoint, 2 = Line, 6 = Multiline, 3 = Polygon/surface, 7 = Multipolygon/ multisurface, 4 = Collection, 8 = Solid, 9 = Multisolid

The D in the DOOT representation of the SDO_GTYPE is used to store the dimensionality of (each vertex in the shape of) the geometry object. Spatial can work with two- to four-dimensional geometries. If the geometry is two-dimensional, then it has two ordinates for each vertex in the geometric shape. If the geometry is three-dimensional, then each vertex has three ordinates, and so on. These ordinates for vertices of the geometry are stored in the SDO_ORDINATES (or SDO_POINT) attribute, which we discuss later.

The T in the SDO_GTYPE specifies the type/shape of the geometry. Let's go over the values. For simple types, such as points, lines, and polygons, T is in the range of 1 to 3. For multiple-item geometries, T is simple_type + 4. For instance, T for a point is 1, and for a multipoint it is 1 + 4 = 5. Likewise, T for a line is 2, and for multiline string it is 2 + 4 = 6, and so on.

The value of T (in SDO_GTYPE) is 1 if the geometry consists of a single point, and it is 5 if the geometry has multiple points. For example, for object A in Figure 4-1, the value of T is 1, and the SDO_GTYPE value is 2001. Listing 4-3 shows the SDO_GTYPE for a point geometry from the customers table. Note that to retrieve the SDO_GTYPE attribute of the location column, you need a table alias.

Listing 4-3. *Example of the* SDO_GTYPE *in the* location *Column of the* customers *Table*

```
SQL> SELECT ct.location.sdo_gtype FROM customers ct WHERE id=1;
SDO_GTYPE
------------------
2001
```

The value of T is 2 if the geometry represents a line string. This line could be a simple line connecting any number of points by straight lines or arcs. Alternatively, this line could be a combination of multiple parts specifying straight-line segments and arc segments. Note that the line is still contiguous. If the geometry consists of multiple line segments that are not connected, then the type is 6 (multiline). For objects B and F in Figure 4-1, the value of T is 2, and SDO_GTYPE is 2002. Listing 4-4 shows an example.

Listing 4-4. *Example of* SDO_GTYPE *in the* geom *Column of the* us_interstates *Table*

```
SQL> SELECT i.geom.sdo_gtype FROM us_interstates  i WHERE rownum=1;
SDO_GTYPE
------------------
2002
```

The type T is 3 if the geometry represents an area bounded by a closed line string (also referred to as *ring*) of edges. Listing 4-5 shows an example. The boundary may be connected by lines, arcs, or a combination of both. The polygon can contain one or more inner rings called *voids*. In such cases, the area of the polygon is computed by subtracting the areas of the voids. The area covered by a geometry that has T equal to 3 should be contiguous. Objects C, D, and G are examples. Note that object D has one outer ring and one inner ring (rectangle), but there is still only one single "contiguous" area shown by the shaded region. So, this is considered a single polygon with type T set to 3.

Listing 4-5. *Example of* SDO_GTYPE *in the* location *Column of the* us_states *Table*

```
SQL> SELECT s.geom.sdo_gtype FROM us_states s WHERE state_abrv='NH';
SDO_GTYPE
------------------
2003
```

If there is more than one (nonvoid) polygon in the geometry (that is, if the area of the geometry is not contiguous), then it is a multipolygon geometry and the type is 7. Object E in Figure 4-1 is an example of this.

If the geometry is a collection of points, lines, and/or polygons, the geometry is a collection geometry. The value of T for this geometry is 4. For object E, which has two polygons (one with a void), you can set the type to 7, a multipolygon. Alternatively, you can set it to the more generic description of a collection. The type T in this case will be 4. Listing 4-6 shows an example when T is 7.

Listing 4-6. *Example of* SDO_GTYPE *in the* location *Column of the* us_states *Table*

```
SQL> SELECT c.geom.sdo_gtype FROM us_cities c WHERE state_abrv='TX';
SDO_GTYPE
------------------
2007
```

Note that most of the shapes represent only two-dimensional geometries. How do you specify three-dimensional (or four-dimensional) geometries? Just set the D in DOOT for SDO_GTYPE to 3 (or 4). Oracle Spatial then allows you to store three (or four) ordinates for each vertex of the geometry. So if you have two points, (1, 1, 4) and (2, 2, 5), you have to specify the SDO_GTYPE to be 3002 (line).

In some applications, the third or fourth dimension holds additional information that can be stored with each vertex of the geometry. This additional dimension may not pertain to the shape of the geometry but may specify a "measure value" that is application-related. For example, the third dimension could model the height of each vertex point in the geometry. In transportation applications, the third ordinate for each vertex in a road segment is used to store the mile marker. To denote that a dimension as a measure dimension, you can use the L digit in SDO_GTYPE. If L is set to 3, then the third dimension is the measure dimension; if L is set to 4, then the fourth dimension is treated as the measure dimension.

Tip Since the geometry has a provision to store four-dimensional ordinates (as specified by D in SDO_GTYPE), even if you model a two- or three-dimensional geometry, you can store additional information such as the elevation, mile marker, time stamp, or speed limit as the third or fourth dimension.

So, Oracle Spatial does not interpret the measure dimension values by default. Oracle Spatial does provide some functions to operate on the measure dimension for specific applications. You will learn about one such application in Appendix B.

SDO_SRID Attribute

This attribute specifies the spatial reference system, or coordinate system, for the geometry. To understand what a coordinate system is, consider the example in Figure 4-3. Recall that we briefly discussed coordinate systems in Chapter 3. Here, we continue that discussion in more detail.

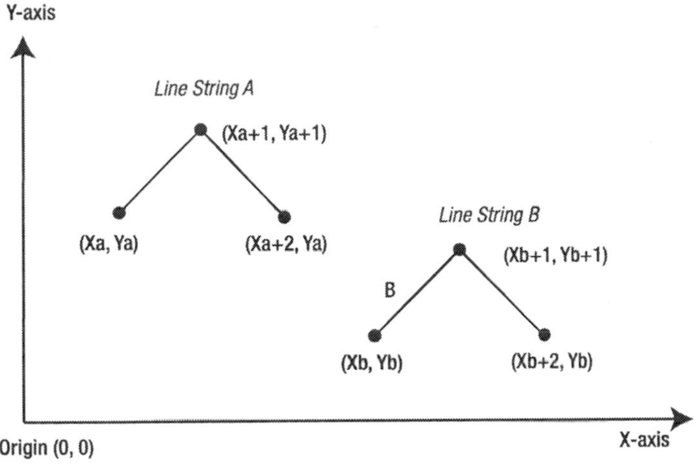

Figure 4-3. *Coordinate systems example*

Note that in Figure 4-3, the locations of two line string objects, A and B, are specified with respect to the origin and using the coordinates in the orthogonal x- and y-axes. Note that both A and B have the same shape; however, their positioning (in other words, location) with respect to the origin is different. If you change the origin, the absolute locations (coordinates) of the two line string objects change. Such a frame of reference using the x- and y-axes is termed the *Cartesian system*. This system is popular in representing two-dimensional data in CAD/CAM applications. But how good is it for representing customer locations and delivery sites on the surface of the earth?

To answer this question, let's examine the surface of the earth. The earth is approximately ellipsoidal in shape. Location has traditionally been specified using the longitude and latitude lines on the earth. Flattening the surface of the earth to a two-dimensional plane loses *spatial proximity* and distorts the shape. Figure 4-4 shows a map of the countries of the world. In Figure 4-4, by dividing the surface of the earth at the dateline meridian, California and Japan appear to be farther apart than they actually are. Also, countries at the North and South Poles, such as Antarctica and Greenland, are distorted in shape.

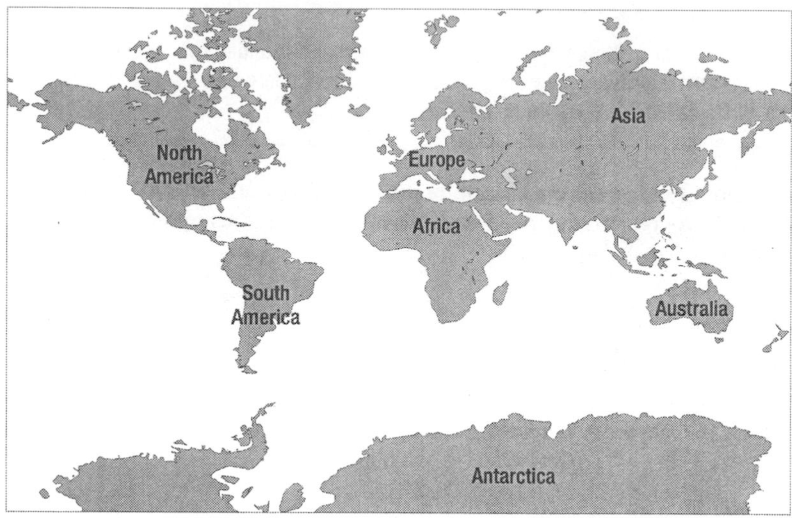

Figure 4-4. *Example map of the world, with countries and distances distorted*

How do you represent locations on the surface of the earth without inaccuracies and distortions? This has been a challenge to many geographers, mathematicians, and inventors for centuries. Several books have dealt with this topic in great detail.[4] There are two general techniques to model the data on the earth's surface. The first is to model the earth using three-dimensional ellipsoidal surfaces. The second is to project the data into a two-dimensional plane. Let's look at each of these in turn. Note that in most cases, an application developer may not need to know much about different coordinate systems. All that is required is to choose an appropriate coordinate system as described in the section "Choosing an Appropriate Coordinate System." The casual reader may skip the discussion in the next three sections.

Geodetic Coordinate Systems

If you model the surface of the earth as a regular three-dimensional ellipsoid, you can measure distance relationships between objects by computing the distances of the locations on the corresponding ellipsoid. Unfortunately, the earth is not a perfect ellipsoid, and therefore a single ellipsoid cannot accurately model the earth in all areas. This led geographers to define multiple ellipsoids to suit their needs. Oracle Spatial supplies commonly used reference ellipsoids in the `MDSYS.SDO_ELLIPSOIDS` table.

Sometimes in your model, you will need to shift the center of the earth and rotate the axes to better suit the curvature at the local region. For this, you can create models referred to as *datums* by shifting and rotating specific ellipsoids to better suit the earth's curvature at different regions. You can examine the different three-dimensional models by looking at the datums in the `MDSYS.SDO_DATUMS` table. Positioning data on the surface of the earth by referring to the coordinates (longitude and latitude) on a specific datum is known as a *geodetic coordinate system* (or *geodetic spatial reference system*).

4. For example, refer to John P. Snyder's *Flattening the Earth: Two Thousand Years of Map Projections* (University of Chicago Press, 1997).

Projected Coordinate Systems

In most applications, data are concentrated within a small region of the earth. Projecting such data to a two-dimensional plane may be a simpler representation and may also be more accurate for the application needs. How do you project data on the earth's surface to a two-dimensional flat plane? First, you start with a three-dimensional model (datum) of the earth. Then, using one of a variety of projection techniques, the three-dimensional data on the reference model is transformed to two-dimensional data on a flat plane.

Why have different projection techniques? Well, there is no single technique that can project from three-dimensional to two-dimensional while preserving the distances between objects, the areas of large objects, the directions, and so on. For example, in the Mercator cylindrical projection, data are projected from the sphere to a cylindrical surface, and the cylindrical surface is unwrapped to result in a two-dimensional plane. It preserves direction and has been used in marine navigation for centuries. However, it does not preserve the area of objects. So, the Mercator cylindrical projection would not be useful in applications that need to compute land area (spatial object area, in other words).

Alternate types of projections include *conic* projections (projecting to a conic surface) and *azimuthal* projections (projecting from the center of a region to a tangential plane). Examples of these projections include Lambert Azimuthal Equal-Area, Azimuthal Equidistant, Albers Equal-Area Conic, and Equidistant Conic projections.

The equal-area projections preserve areas of the objects (unlike the Mercator) but distort direction and distance. The equidistant projections are good for measuring the distance from the center of the projection area (say, New York City) to distant locations, such as San Diego, California, and Seattle, Washington. However, such a projection cannot be used to compute distances between San Diego and Seattle, two locations that are far off from the center of the projection. In short, the specific projection that is to be used depends on which of the following parameters are to be preserved: direction, distance, and area. You can examine the different projections that can be applied to a specific datum by looking at the table `MDSYS.SDO_PROJECTIONS`.

To summarize, by choosing a projection and a three-dimensional reference datum, locations on the surface of the earth can be represented in a two-dimensional plane. Such referencing using a specific datum and an appropriate projection is referred to as a *projected coordinate system* or a *projected spatial reference system*.

Georeferenced, Local Coordinate Systems

Coordinate systems pertaining to locations on the earth (that is, projected and geodetic coordinate systems) are called *georeferenced*. All other coordinate systems, such as those in CAD/CAM, are referred to as *local* or *nongeoreferenced*.

Choosing an Appropriate Coordinate System

You choose the coordinate system by setting an appropriate value for the `SDO_SRID` attribute. Next, we will describe how to determine the appropriate values for projected, geodetic, and local coordinate systems.

If the geometry does not refer to a location on the earth's surface but instead refers to layout in CAD/CAM or other applications, then you can set it either to `NULL` or to a value specified by your data vendor.

Otherwise, if the geometry refers to a location on the earth's surface, you can set `SDO_SRID` to a value corresponding to either a *projected* coordinate system or a *geodetic* coordinate system. Projected coordinate systems are used whenever all the data are located in a small region of the earth. Projected coordinate systems are useful to suit application needs such as preserving the distances between locations, shapes, or areas of geometry objects (such as city boundaries) and other appropriate geometric properties. Geodetic coordinate systems are useful if the data are located in a much larger portion on the surface of the earth and slight inaccuracies in some geometric properties such as distances, areas, and so on, can be tolerated. For example, when dealing with data fully concentrated in southern Texas, you can use a state-plane projection appropriate for southern Texas. However, when dealing with the United States as a whole, you can use a geodetic coordinate system. You can look up the SDO_SRIDs for the geodetic or projected coordinate systems in the MDSYS.CS_SRS table. Listing 4-7 shows the columns in this table.

Listing 4-7. MDSYS.CS_SRS *Table*

```
SQL> DESCRIBE MDSYS.CS_SRS

 Name                                      Null?      Type
 ----------------------------------------- --------   ---------------
 CS_NAME                                              VARCHAR2(68)
 SRID                                      NOT NULL   NUMBER(38)
 AUTH_SRID                                            NUMBER(38)
 AUTH_NAME                                            VARCHAR2(256)
 WKTEXT                                               VARCHAR2(2046)
 CS_BOUNDS                                            SDO_GEOMETRY
```

The MDSYS.CS_SRS table has the following columns:

- CS_NAME: This specifies the name of the coordinate system.
- SRID: This is short for *spatial reference system ID*. This is a unique ID for the spatial reference or coordinate system.
- AUTH_SRID and AUTH_NAME: These refer to the values assigned by the originator of this coordinate system.
- WKTEXT: This is short for *well-known text*. This field provides a detailed description of the coordinate system. For geodetic coordinate systems, the WKTEXT field starts with a prefix of GEOGCS For projected systems, it starts with 'PROJCS'. You can use this information to search for an appropriate coordinate system for your application's needs.
- CS_BOUNDS: This specifies a geometry where the coordinate system is valid. Storing data beyond the bounds may lead to inaccurate results. Currently, set to NULL.

As an application developer, chances are you will be interested only in how to choose the coordinate system (you are not likely to have to populate these rows in the MDSYS.CS_SRS table). You might be able to do this by examining the coordinate system description in the WKTEXT field. For example, to identify a projected coordinate system for southern Texas, you can execute the SQL in Listing 4-8. Note that the ROWNUM=1 predicate displays only one out of three rows for southern Texas.

Listing 4-8. *Selecting an SRID for the Southern Texas Region from the* MDSYS.CS_SRS *Table*

```
SQL> SELECT cs_name, srid, wktext
FROM  MDSYS.CS_SRS
WHERE WKTEXT LIKE 'PROJCS%'
  AND CS_NAME LIKE '%Texas%Southern%'
      AND ROWNUM=1;

CS_NAME
------------------------------
Texas 4205, Southern Zone (1927)
```

```
SRID
-----
41155

WKTEXT
--------------------------------------------
PROJCS
  [
  "Texas 4205, Southern Zone (1927)",
  GEOGCS
  [
    "NAD 27 (Continental US)",
    DATUM
    [
      "NAD 27 (Continental US)",
      SPHEROID ["Clarke 1866", 6378206.4, 294.9786982]
    ] ,
    PRIMEM [ "Greenwich", 0.000000 ],
    UNIT ["Decimal Degree", 0.01745329251994330]
  ],
  PROJECTION ["Lambert Conformal Conic"],
  PARAMETER ["Standard_Parallel_1", 26.166667],
  PARAMETER ["Standard_Parallel_2", 27.833333],
  PARAMETER ["Central_Meridian", -98.500000],
  PARAMETER ["Latitude_Of_Origin", 25.666667],
  PARAMETER ["False_Easting",   2000000.0000],
  UNIT ["U.S. Foot", 0.3048006096012]
]
```

The query returns a projected coordinate system for southern Texas. This coordinate system is formed using the Lambert Conformal Conic projection technique on a datum formed using the NAD 27 (continental United States) reference ellipsoid. You can use the corresponding SRID of 41155 to specify a geometry in this coordinate system.

For most business applications that have location data spread over the entire United States, you can choose one of the widely used geodetic systems for North America, such as WGS84 (SRID=8307) or NAD83 (SRID=8265). For applications in other countries, you can choose either an appropriate geodetic system or a projected system, depending on how widely distributed the location data are. Note that Oracle supports approximately 1,000 coordinate systems that cover almost all countries/regions of the world. These coordinate systems are all described in the MDSYS.CS_SRS table. All you have to do is choose one of them (the SRID field) by searching for the region/country in the WKTEXT field.

Note All geometries in a specific column of a table (for example, the location column of the customers table) should have the same SDO_SRID value.

Note that the previous coordinate systems may or may not be suited for all applications. To obtain more accurate coordinate systems, users can define new coordinate reference systems by appropriately defining new entries in the MDSYS.CS_SRS table.

Coordinate systems enable accurate representation of the data based on the user's region as well as more accurate transformations when converting from data in one coordinate system to another (using the SDO_CS.TRANSFORM function call). Starting in Oracle 10*g* Release 2, Spatial supports the EPSG model for coordinate systems. We'll briefly describe this model because of its popularity. The more casual reader can skip the next section.

The EPSG Coordinate System Model for Two-Dimensional and Three-Dimensional Data in Oracle Spatial

The European Petroleum Standards Group (EPSG) model supports a rich set of predefined one-dimensional, two-dimensional (projected, geodetic, or local), and three-dimensional coordinate systems in addition to providing more flexibility in transformations across coordinate systems. We'll first cover the different types of coordinate systems.

Types of EPSG Coordinate Systems

You can determine the different types of supported two-dimensional and three-dimensional coordinate systems by querying the SDO_COORD_REF_SYS table, as shown in Listing 4-9.

Listing 4-9. *Determining the Different Kinds of EPSG Coordinate Systems*

```
SQL> SELECT DISTINCT coord_ref_sys_kind FROM  SDO_COORD_REF_SYS;
COORD_REF_SYS_KIND
------------------------
PROJECTED
GEOCENTRIC
GEOGRAPHIC2D
VERTICAL
ENGINEERING
COMPOUND
GEOGRAPHIC3D

7 rows selected.
```

Which one of these systems should you use for your data? The answer will depend on your specific application. You can classify the previous seven types of EPSG coordinate systems into one-dimensional (1D), two-dimensional (2D), three-dimensional (3D), or local coordinate systems, as described here:

- *1D coordinate systems*:
  - *Vertical*: These coordinate systems are typically used to model height information above the earth's surface. The height can be either *geoidal height*, which is the height above the earth's geoid (the geoid represents the physical surface of the earth and is highly irregular), or *ellipsoidal height*, which is the height above the ellipsoid that is used to approximate the surface of the earth in a reference coordinate system.
- *2D coordinate systems*:
  - *Geographic2D*: This type of coordinate system specifies the longitude and latitude on the surface of the earth approximated by a reference ellipsoid (usually referred to as *datum*). This type is also referred to as the *Geodetic* coordinate systems (as in earlier sections).
  - *Projected*: This type of coordinate system specifies how to project longitude and latitude values on a reference Geographic2D system to a two-dimensional Euclidean coordinate system. As discussed in the prior section "Projected Coordinate Systems," you can use various types of projection techniques such as equal-area (to preserve areas of projected geometries) or equidistant projections (to preserve distances to objects from projection center).

- *3D coordinate systems*:
    - *Geographic3D*: This type of coordinate system specifies latitude and longitude and ellipsoidal height based on a geodetic datum (ellipsoid).
    - *Geocentric*: This type of coordinate system specifies the x,y,z values with reference to the center of the earth (as opposed to the surface ellipsoid as in a Geographic3D).
    - *Compound*: This type of coordinate system combines either a Geographic2D (latitude, longitude) or a Projected (2D) coordinate system with a vertical coordinate system specifying height based on gravity, above a mean sea level, and so on.
- *Local coordinate systems*:
    - *Engineering*: These coordinate systems are application-specific coordinate systems. They may or may not refer to data on earth's surface, but the data are usually treated as if they are in Euclidean coordinate axes.

As mentioned in the previous section, you can obtain all relevant information about 2D coordinate systems from the CS_SRS table. However, for 3D coordinate systems, the CS_SRS table contains only partial information (this is likely to change in versions after Oracle 11*g*[5]; after such changes, you may be able to get all relevant information in the CS_SRS table itself). In Oracle 11*g*, you have to consult other tables such as SDO_COORD_REF_SYS and SDO_CRS_VERTICAL to obtain detailed information about 3D or 1D coordinate systems. For instance, assume you want to identify the 3D compound coordinate system for the Texas region. You can select the coordinate system ID (SRID), its name (COORD_REF_SYS_NAME), and the horizontal (CMPD_HORIZ_SRID) and vertical coordinate systems (CMPD_VERT_SRID) that make up the compound system from the SDO_COORD_REF_SYS table by specifying the COORD_REF_SYS_KIND to be 'COMPOUND'. Listing 4-10 shows how to find this information about a compound coordinate system for the Texas region.

Listing 4-10. *Searching for a Compound Coordinate System for the Texas Region*

```
SQL> SELECT srid, coord_ref_sys_name name,
            cmpd_horiz_srid hsrid,  cmpd_vert_srid vsrid
            FROM sdo_coord_ref_sys
            WHERE coord_ref_sys_name like '%Texas%'
            AND  coord_ref_sys_kind='COMPOUND';

SRID       NAME                                        HSRID     VSRID
-------    ------------------------------------------  --------  -------
7407       NAD27 / Texas North + NGVD29                32037     5702
```

Observe that the SQL returns the SRID of the compound coordinate system as 7407 and that the compound system is made up of a horizontal coordinate system whose SRID is 32037 and a vertical coordinate system whose SRID is 5702. The horizontal coordinate system typically pertains to the x,y or longitude/latitude dimensions, and the vertical coordinate system usually refers to the height from the surface of the earth. As shown in Listing 4-11, you can look up information on the horizontal coordinate system using the CS_SRS table. From the wktext string returned in Listing 4-11, you can notice that this (SRID=32037) horizontal coordinate system is a Lambert-Conformal Conic projection using the NAD27 (North American Datum 1927) datum, and the default UNIT in this coordinate system is U.S. FOOT (search for PROJECTION and UNIT substrings in the wktext value that is returned).

5. Unless otherwise mentioned, all references to Oracle 11*g* in the book mean Oracle Database 11*g*.

Listing 4-11. *Looking Up Details for Horizontal Coordinate System ID 32037*

```
SQL> SELECT cs_name, wktext FROM CS_SRS WHERE SRID=32037;

CS_NAME                                                          WKTEXT
------------------------------------------------------------     ------------------
NAD27 / Texas North

PROJCS[
  "NAD27 / Texas North",
  GEOGCS [
    "NAD27",
    DATUM [
      "North American Datum 1927 (EPSG ID 6267)",
      SPHEROID ["Clarke 1866 (EPSG ID 7008)", 6378206.4,
                          294.978698213905820761610537123195175418],
      -3, 142, 183, 0, 0, 0, 0],
    PRIMEM [ "Greenwich", 0.000000 ],
    UNIT ["Decimal Degree", 0.01745329251994328]
 ],
 PROJECTION ["Lambert Conformal Conic"], PARAMETER ["Latitude_Of_Origin", 34],
    PARAMETER ["Central_Meridian", -101.5],
    PARAMETER ["Standard_Parallel_1", 34.65],
    PARAMETER ["Standard_Parallel_2", 36.1833333333333333333333333333333333333],
    PARAMETER ["False_Easting", 2000000], PARAMETER ["False_Northing", 0],
    UNIT ["U.S. Foot", .3048006096012192024384048768097536195072]
]
```

Next you want to look up the details of the vertical coordinate system whose SRID is 5702. You can try the CS_SRS table, as shown in Listing 4-12.

Listing 4-12. *Looking Up Details for Vertical Coordinate System ID 5702 in the* CS_SRS *Table*[6]

```
SQL> SELECT cs_name, wktext FROM CS_SRS WHERE SRID=5702;

CS_NAME                                                          WKTEXT
------------------------------------------------------------     -----------------
National Geodetic Vertical Datum of 1929
```

The query returns the name as "National Geodetic Vertical Datum of 1929." The query, however, does not return any value for the wktext field. In that case, how do you identify the reference datum on which this vertical coordinate system is based or what the default units for this vertical coordinate system are? You can query the SDO_CRS_VERTICAL and SDO_COORD_SYS tables as in Listing 4-13. You can observe from the value for the COORD_SYS_NAME that the unit of measure (UoM) is ftUS (in other words, the same as U.S. Foot).

Listing 4-13. *Looking Up Details for Vertical Coordinate System ID 5702 in Appropriate Tables*

```
SQL> SELECT cs.COORD_SYS_NAME
FROM SDO_CRS_VERTICAL v, SDO_COORD_SYS cs
WHERE v.SRID=5702 and cs.COORD_SYS_ID = v.COORD_SYS_ID;

COORD_SYS_NAME
--------------------------------------------------------------------------------
Gravity-related CS. Axis: height (H). Orientation: up.  UoM: ftUS.
```

6. National Geodetic Vertical Datum of 1929

Now that you understand how to look up information about the rich set of 1D, 2D, 3D, or local coordinate systems in EPSG, you'll now focus on the second salient feature of the EPSG model: specifying a user-preferred transformation between two coordinate systems.

Specifying a Preferred Transformation Path Between Coordinate Systems

The EPSG model defines more diverse transformation methods and allows chained concatenations of these methods in transformations. Here is an example of defining a transformation from, say, the projected SRID 41155 (obtained in Listing 4-8) to SRID 4269 (NAD83). For this you need to perform the following steps:

1. First, determine the EPSG-equivalent coordinate system (SRID) for SRID 41155 using the SQL in Listing 4-14.

   Listing 4-14. *Finding an EPSG Equivalent for SRID 41155*

```
SQL > SELECT sdo_cs.find_proj_crs(41155, 'FALSE') epsg_srid FROM DUAL;
   EPSG_SRID
   --------------
      32041
```

2. Since SRID 41155 is equivalent to the EPSG SRID 32041, you can identify the source geographic coordinate system on which this projected coordinate system is based on by querying the SDO_COORD_REF_SYS table as in Listing 4-15.

   Listing 4-15. *Finding the Source Geographic SRID and the* projection_conversion *ID for SRID 41155 (EPSG 32041)*

```
SQL> SELECT projection_conv_id cid, source_geog_srid src_srid FROM
SDO_COORD_REF_SYS
WHERE srid=32041;
cid                src_srid
--------         ------------
14205                4267
```

3. Now you can define a preferred transformation from 41155 to 4269 by entering the transformation using the SQL in Listing 4-16. The transformation from the source SRID 41155 (projected) to target SRID 4269 (NAD83) is accomplished as a concatenation of two conversions using the SDO_TFM_CHAIN procedure call. The first conversion is from source SRID 41155 to the geog_srid 4267 using conversion_id 14205. The second conversion is from SRID 4267 to target SRID 4269 using the NADCON conversion (the corresponding conversion_id ID 1241 can be obtained by querying the SDO_COORD_OPS table).

   Listing 4-16. *Creating a Preferred Transformation Path Between 41155 (Projection-Based on NAD27) and 4269 (NAD83)*

```
SQL > call sdo_cs.create_pref_concatenated_op(
    10000,               -- any unique id of the operation,
    TFM_PLAN(
    SDO_TFM_CHAIN(
         41155,          -- source srid
         14205, 4267,    -- convid  14205 from srid 41155 (32041) to srid 4267
         1241,  4269     -- convid 1241 from 4267 to 4269
      ),
      NULL);
```

After you specify the previous transformation path between coordinate system 41155 and coordinate system 4267, whenever you explicitly (or implicitly) invoke the SDO_CS.TRANSFORM function to transform an SDO_GEOMETRY in the coordinate system 41155 to the coordinate system 4267, Oracle Spatial will implicitly invoke your preferred transformation path defined in Listings 4-14 to 4-16.

In addition to defining preferred transformation paths, you can also define your own coordinate systems by inserting appropriate information into the SDO_COORD_REF_SYSTEM[7] and other appropriate tables. For more details, you will have to refer to the *Spatial User's Guide and Documentation.*

SDO_POINT Attribute

Now that we have finished discussing the SDO_SRID attribute of the SDO_GEOMETRY, let's move on to the next attribute: SDO_POINT. This attribute specifies the location of a point geometry, such as the location of a customer. Notice that this attribute is of type SDO_POINT_TYPE, which is another object type. Listing 4-17 shows the structure of this type.

Listing 4-17. SDO_POINT_TYPE *Data Type*

```
SQL> DESCRIBE SDO_POINT_TYPE
 Name                    Null?    Type
 ----------------------- -------- --------------
 X                                     NUMBER
 Y                                     NUMBER
 Z                                     NUMBER
```

The SDO_GTYPE for a point geometry is set to D001. Consider point A in Figure 4-5, identified by coordinates X_A and Y_A representing a customer location.

A ●

(X_A, Y_A)

Figure 4-5. *Example of a point at coordinates X_A and Y_A*

Listing 4-18 shows how to populate the SDO_GEOMETRY object in the geometry_examples table to represent point A (substitute (–79, 37) with actual coordinates).

Listing 4-18. *Point Data in* geometry_examples

```
SQL> INSERT INTO geometry_examples (name, description, geom) VALUES
(
  'POINT',
  '2-dimensional Point at coordinates (-79,37)  with srid set to 8307',
  SDO_GEOMETRY
  (
    2001,     -- SDO_GTYPE format: DOOT. Set to 2001 for a 2-dimensional point
    8307,     -- SDO_SRID (geodetic)
    SDO_POINT_TYPE
    (
```

7. Note that this is different from the SDO_COORD_REF_SYS table.

```
      -79,    -- ordinate value for Longitude
      37,     -- ordinate value Latitude
      NULL    -- no third dimension (only 2 dimensions)
    ),
    NULL,
    NULL
  )
);
```

Caution Oracle Spatial requires that the longitude ordinates be entered as the first dimension and that the latitude ordinates be entered as the second dimension.

The notation for specifying the geometry column may seem obscure, but it is logical. Objects in Oracle are instantiated using the corresponding object constructors. The `geom` column is an object of type `SDO_GEOMETRY` and is instantiated as shown. The fields of this object are populated as follows:

- `SDO_GTYPE`: The format is `DOOT`, where `D` is 2 and `T` is 1 for two-dimensional `POINT`.
- `SDO_SRID`: This is set to 8307.
- `SDO_POINT`: This sets the x,y coordinates in `SDO_POINT_TYPE` to (–79, 37) in the example. The z coordinate is set to `NULL`.
- `SDO_ELEM_INFO`: This is not used; it is set to `NULL`.
- `SDO_ORDINATES`: This is not used; it is set to `NULL`.

An alternate mechanism to construct a point geometry is by using the *well-known text* (`WKT`) description of the point geometry as referenced in SQL/MM Part 3. Oracle Spatial provides an `SDO_GEOMETRY` constructor that takes the `WKT` and an `SRID` as arguments to construct an `SDO_GEOMETRY` object. Listing 4-19 shows an example.

Listing 4-19. *Constructing a Point Geometry Using Well-Known Text (SQL/MM)*

```
SQL> SELECT SDO_GEOMETRY(' POINT(-79 37) ', 8307) geom FROM DUAL;
GEOM
---------------------------------------------------------------------------
SDO_GEOMETRY(2001, 8307, SDO_POINT_TYPE(-79, 37, NULL), NULL, NULL)
```

Caution The ordinates of a vertex are separated by a space rather than by a comma in a `WKT`. Commas separate multiple vertices, if any, in the WKT. Refer to ISO IEC 12349 (`www.iso.org/iso/en/CatalogueDetailPage.CatalogueDetail?CSNUMBER=31369`) for details on how to construct the well-known text for different types of geometries.

The constructed `SDO_GEOMETRY` object can be passed in anywhere an `SDO_GEOMETRY` object can be used—to insert into the `geom` column of `geometry_examples` as in Listing 4-18, to update the `geom` column value, or in spatial query operators and functions (you will see examples of these in later chapters).

Note that the `SDO_POINT` can store only three ordinates (x, y, and z). This representation is suitable if your data have three or fewer dimensions. For four-dimensional points, you have to use the `SDO_ELEM_INFO` and `SDO_ORDINATES` attributes.

SDO_ELEM_INFO and SDO_ORDINATES Attributes

In the previous example, you saw how to store a point element in the SDO_GEOMETRY using the SDO_POINT attribute. Obviously, you may want to store elements more complex than points; you may also want to store lines and polygons, which may need a large number of vertices. To store such complex elements, you will use the other two structures in the SDO_GEOMETRY type, the SDO_ORDINATES and SDO_ELEM_INFO attributes. Together these attributes allow you to specify different *elements* that compose a geometry: SDO_ORDINATES stores the coordinates of the vertices in all elements of a geometry, and SDO_ELEM_INFO specifies the type of elements and where they start in the SDO_ORDINATES.

First you should understand how to represent elements using the SDO_ELEM_INFO and SDO_ORDINATES attributes. You will learn about the different *element-types* that are supported in Oracle in subsequent sections.

SDO_ORDINATES Attribute

We'll start with the SDO_ORDINATES attribute. This attribute stores the ordinates in all dimensions of all elements of a geometry. The SDO_ORDINATES attribute is of type SDO_ORDINATE_ARRAY, which, as you can see in the following snippet, is a collection of type VARRAY (variable-length array) of numbers. The VARRAY is useful for storing the points that describe a geometric shape in the proper order so that no explicit processing is needed when fetching that shape. If the data dimensionality is D, then every consecutive D number in the SDO_ORDINATES specifies the coordinates of a vertex. For example, if you want to model a line connecting point A that has coordinates (Xa, Ya) with point B that has coordinates (Xb, Yb), then the SDO_ORDINATES will contain the numbers Xa, Ya, Xb, and Yb, in that order. The size of this array attribute is set to 1048576. This large size limit provides enough room to store the vertices of large and complex geometries.

```
SQL> DESCRIBE SDO_ORDINATE_ARRAY
 SDO_ORDINATE_ARRAY VARRAY(1048576) OF NUMBER
```

If the SDO_ORDINATES attribute specifies the ordinates (in all dimensions) of all elements of a geometry object, how are these ordinates interpreted and separated to represent different elements that make up the geometry? The information that is needed to interpret and separate the ordinates into elements is specified in the SDO_ELEM_INFO attribute. We will look at that next.

VARRAYS

A VARRAY is an ordered set of data elements, all of the same data type. It can vary in size up to a specified maximum number of elements. Each element in the array has an *index*, which is a number corresponding to the element's position in the array and can be fetched directly using the index. The index starts at 1.

A VARRAY requires only the exact[8] storage space needed to store the required number of elements, and it can be expanded to accommodate new elements at the end of the array. Note that VARRAYs can be made of complex types (that is, object types), which themselves can contain other VARRAYs. This is a powerful mechanism that enables you to construct complex structures.

8. This is excluding the additional overhead to store information such as the size of the VARRAY.

SDO_ELEM_INFO Attribute

The SDO_ELEM_INFO attribute is of type SDO_ELEM_INFO_ARRAY, which is also a VARRAY of numbers with a maximum size of 1,048,576 numbers. Every three consecutive numbers in the SDO_ELEM_INFO are grouped into a *descriptor triplet*, describing an element or a part of an element. So, logically, the SDO_ELEM_INFO attribute is an array of triplets (three numbers). This means the size of this array attribute is always a multiple of 3.

Each descriptor triplet is associated with an element of the geometry. The triplet is of the form *<offset, element-type, interpretation>*. The *offset* specifies the *starting index* in the SDO_ORDINATES array where the ordinates of the element are stored. The other two numbers, *element-type* (*etype* for short) and *interpretation*, take different values depending on whether the associated element represents a point, a line, or a polygon and whether the boundaries are connected by straight lines, arcs, or both.

Let's first look at SDO_ELEM_INFO values for the data that application developers are most likely to construct. For instance, in our business application, the geometries that we construct could be as follows:

- Points representing location of customers, competitors, and so on
- Line strings representing streets and highways
- Polygons representing city boundaries

In most cases, these geometries have *at most one element descriptor triplet and represent at most one element of a point, line string, or polygon type*. We refer to such elements and geometries as *simple* elements and *simple* geometries. In those cases, the descriptor triplet has the following values:

- *Offset*: This is always set to 1, because there is only one element in the SDO_ORDINATES field.
- *Element-type*: This has a direct correspondence with the type T value in the SDO_GTYPE for the geometry.
    - For points, the *element-type* is 1 (the T value in SDO_GTYPE is 1).
    - For lines, the *element-type* is 2 (the T value in SDO_GTYPE is also 2).
    - For polygons, the *element-type* is 1003 (the T value in SDO_GTYPE is 3).
- *Interpretation*: This is the only subtle information an element contains.
    - For a point, *interpretation* is 1.
    - For line strings and polygons, the *interpretation* is 1 if the connectivity is by straight lines, and the interpretation is 2 if the connectivity is by arcs. For instance, a line string connected by straight lines has the SDO_ELEM_INFO set to (1, 2, 1), in other words, a starting *offset* of 1, an *element-type* of 2, and an *interpretation* of 1.
    - For polygons, you could have *interpretation* set to 3 to indicate that the polygon is a rectangle.
    - Likewise, for polygons you could have *interpretation* set to 4 to indicate that the polygon is a circle.

Table 4-2 summarizes the possible values for the SDO_ELEM_INFO array (and the SDO_ORDINATES array) based on the type of the element. Using these values, you can construct an SDO_GEOMETRY by additionally populating the SDO_GTYPE and SDO_SRID fields appropriately. In the next section, we present detailed examples for such *simple* two-dimensional geometries. In the subsequent section, we describe more complex two-dimensional geometries with more than one element descriptor triplet. Examples of such data would be a street that has both straight lines and arcs. Such geometries are referred to as *complex* geometries. Note that the majority of the 3D types such as composite surfaces and solids need more than one element descriptor triplet. We describe the three-dimensional elements separately in the "Three-Dimensional Geometry Examples" section.

Table 4-2. *Values for* SDO_ELEM_INFO *(and* SDO_ORDINATES*) for Simple Geometries*

Name	Element-Type (Etype)	Interpretation	SDO_ELEM_INFO: (1, Etype, Interpretation)	SDO_ORDINATES	Illustration
Point (for example, customer location)	1	*N*, where *N* is the number of points. 1 is for a single point; >1 is for a point cluster.	(1, 1, 1)	(Xa, Ya)	A (XA, YA)
Line string (for example, streets, highways)	2	1 = Connected by straight lines	(1, 2, 1)	(Xa, Ya, Xb, Yb, Xc, Yc)	B (Xb, Yb) A (Xa, Ya) C (Xc, Yc)
		2 = Connected by arcs	(1, 2, 2)	(Xa, Ya, Xb, Yb, Xc, Yc)	
Polygon (for example, city boundary, buffer zone)	1003	1 = Polygon boundary connected by straight lines	(1,1003, 1)	(Xa, Ya, Xb,Yb, Xc, Yc, Xd, Yd, Xa, Ya)	D (Xd, Yd) C (Xc, Yc) A (Xa, Ya) B (Xb, Yb)
		3 = Rectangle polygon (only specify lower-left and upper-right corners)	(1, 1003, 3)	(Xa, Ya, Xc, Yc)	D (Xd, Yd) C (Xc, Yc) (Xa, Ya) A (Xb, Yb) B
		4 = Circle polygon (specify three points on boundary of circle)	(1, 1003, 4)	(Xa, Ya, Xb, Yb, Xc, Yc)	C (Xc, Yc) (Xb, Yb) B A (Xa, Ya)

Simple Two-Dimensional Geometry Examples

A simple geometry consists of only *one element descriptor triplet and represents a point, line string, or polygon.* The ordinates for the geometry are always stored at a starting offset of 1 (because there is only one element). This means the SDO_ELEM_INFO is always of the form (1, x, y). Let's look at each simple geometry type next.

Point

In Listing 4-19, you saw how to represent a two-dimensional point using the SDO_POINT attribute of SDO_GEOMETRY. An alternate (but not recommended) mechanism is to store the point coordinates in the SDO_ORDINATES array. Listing 4-20 shows the example.

Listing 4-20. *Storing the Point Coordinates in the* SDO_ORDINATES *Array Instead of* SDO_POINT

```
SQL> INSERT INTO geometry_examples VALUES
(
  '2-D POINT stored in SDO_ORDINATES',
  '2-dimensional Point at coordinates (-79, 37) with srid set to 8307',
  SDO_GEOMETRY
```

```
    (
      2001,  -- SDO_GTYPE format: DOOT. Set to 2001 for as a 2-dimensional point
      8307,  -- SDO_SRID
      NULL,  -- SDO_POINT attribute set to NULL
      SDO_ELEM_INFO_ARRAY  -- SDO_ELEM_INFO attribute (see Table 4-2 for values)
      (
        1,   -- Offset is 1
        1,   -- Element-type is 1 for a point
        1    -- Interpretation specifies # of points. In this case 1.
      ),
     SDO_ORDINATE_ARRAY   -- SDO_ORDINATES attribute
     (
        -79, -- Ordinate value for Longitude
        37   -- Ordinate value for Latitude
      )
    )
);
```

In Listing 4-20, note that the SDO_GEOMETRY object is instantiated using the object constructor with all the appropriate attributes for this type. Likewise, the SDO_ORDINATES and SDO_ELEM_INFO attributes are VARRAYs, and they are instantiated using the corresponding types, SDO_ELEM_INFO_ARRAY and SDO_ORDINATE_ARRAY, respectively.

Tip Never store the coordinates of a two- or three-dimensional point in the SDO_ORDINATES attribute (as in Listing 4-20). Always store them in the SDO_POINT attribute (as in Listing 4-19). The latter representation is storage efficient as well as better performing during fetches.

Since SDO_POINT can store only three numbers, this attribute cannot store four-dimensional points. Examples of such points include locations that store temperature and height. For such four-dimensional points, you need to use the SDO_ELEM_INFO and SDO_ORDINATES attributes of SDO_GEOMETRY. Let (Xa, Ya, Za, La) be the ordinates of the four-dimensional point. The SDO_GEOMETRY is populated as shown in Listing 4-21. Note that the only change in the geom column, as compared to Listing 4-21, is that the SDO_ORDINATES attribute has four numbers (corresponding to the four dimensions), as opposed to two in Listing 4-20.

Listing 4-21. *Four-Dimensional Point Example*

```
INSERT INTO geometry_examples VALUES
(
  '4-D POINT',
  '4-dimensional Point at (Xa=>2, Ya=>2, Za=>2, La=>2) with srid set to NULL',
  SDO_GEOMETRY
  (
    4001, -- SDO_GTYPE: DOOT. Set to 4001 as it is a 4-dimensional point
    NULL, -- SDO_SRID
    NULL, -- SDO_POINT_TYPE is null
    SDO_ELEM_INFO_ARRAY(1,1,1),  -- Indicates a point element
    SDO_ORDINATE_ARRAY(2,2,2,2)  -- Store the four ordinates here
  )
);
```

Line String: Connected by Straight Lines

Let's return to two-dimensional data again and look at line geometries that could represent streets and highways. Consider the three points A, B, and C shown in Figure 4-6. How do you represent a line connecting these three points? Will the connection be using straight lines or arcs? First, let's consider straight lines.

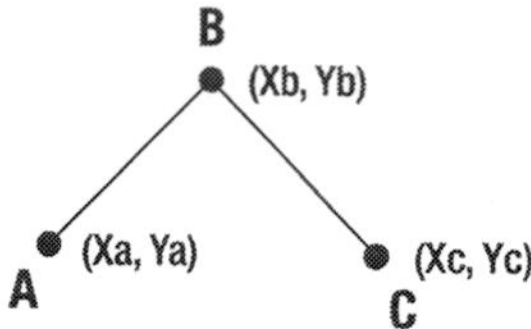

Figure 4-6. *Example of a line string connected by straight lines*

The SDO_GEOMETRY object can be populated as shown in Listing 4-22.

Listing 4-22. *Two-Dimensional Line String Example*

```
SQL> INSERT INTO geometry_examples VALUES
(
  'LINE STRING',
  '2-D line string connecting A(Xa=>1,Ya=>1),B(Xb=>2, Yb=>2), C(Xc=>2,Yc=>1)',
  SDO_GEOMETRY
  (
    2002,   -- SDO_GTYPE: DOOT. Set to 2002 as it is a 2-dimensional line string
    32774,  -- SDO_SRID
    NULL,   -- SDO_POINT_TYPE is null
    SDO_ELEM_INFO_ARRAY  -- SDO_ELEM_INFO attribute (see Table 4-2 for values)
    (
      1,    -- Offset is 1
      2,    -- Element-type is 2 for a LINE STRING
      1     -- Interpretation is 1 if line string is connected by straight lines.
    ),
    SDO_ORDINATE_ARRAY   -- SDO_ORDINATES attribute
    (
      1,1,  -- Xa, Ya values
      2,2,  -- Xb, Yb values
      2,1   -- Xc, Yc values
    )
  )
);
```

Since the geometry is a line string connected by straight lines, the SDO_ELEM_INFO attribute is set to the triplet (1, 2, 1), as described in Table 4-2. The SDO_ORDINATES attribute is then populated with the ordinates of each of the three vertices A, B, and C in the order they appear in the line string.

Observe that all the line segments are contiguous (in other words, they share vertices). If you want to store lines that do not share vertices, you can model them using multiline string geometries. We discuss these later in the chapter.

What happens if there are not just three points but *N* points with coordinates (X1, Y1) . . . (XN, YN) and all of them need to be connected by straight lines in the order (X1, Y1), (X2, Y2), . . . , (XN, YN)? All you have to do is store these vertices in the SDO_ORDINATES attribute (in the order in which they need to be connected). Nothing else needs to change. The geometry constructor looks as follows:

```
SDO_GEOMETRY
(
  2002, 32774, NULL,
  SDO_ELEM_INFO_ARRAY(1,2,1),
  SDO_ORDINATE_ARRAY(X1, Y1, X2, Y2, ...., XN, YN)
)
```

Note All lines joining successive vertices in a simple (that is, noncompound) element use the same *interpretation*—that is, they are connected by straight lines (or by arcs).

Line String: Connected by Arcs

The example in Figure 4-7 stores a line string composed of three points. However, those same three points could actually represent a very different shape: a circular arc that passes through those three points.

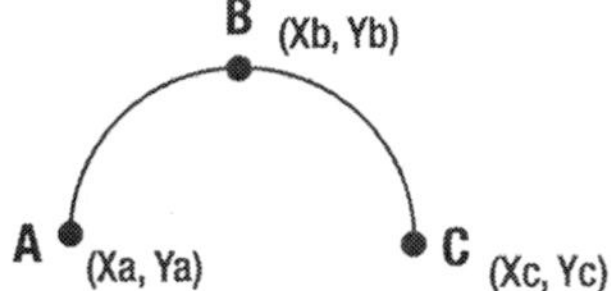

Figure 4-7. *Example of a line string connected by arcs*

How do you do that? Simply change the *interpretation* in SDO_ELEM_INFO to 2 (arc). SDO_ELEM_INFO then changes from (1, 2, 1) to (1, 2, 2), as shown in Listing 4-23.

Listing 4-23. *Two-Dimensional Line String Connected by Arcs*

```
SQL> INSERT INTO geometry_examples VALUES
(
  'ARCSTRING',
  '2-D arc connecting A(Xa=>1,Ya=>1),B(Xb=>2, Yb=>2), C(Xc=>2,Yc=>1)',
  SDO_GEOMETRY
  (
    2002,  --  SDO_GTYPE: DOOT. Set to 2002 as it is a 2-dimensional line string
    32774, -- SDO_SRID
    NULL,  -- SDO_POINT_TYPE is null
    SDO_ELEM_INFO_ARRAY  -- SDO_ELEM_INFO attribute (see Table 4-2 for values)
    (
      1,    -- Offset is 1
      2,    -- Element-type is 2 for a LINE STRING
      2     -- Interpretation is 2 if line string is connected by ARCs.
    ),
    SDO_ORDINATE_ARRAY   -- SDO_ORDINATES attribute
    (
      1,1, -- Xa, Ya values
      2,2, -- Xb, Yb values
      2,1  -- Xc, Yc values
      )
    )
);
```

If you compare this representation with that of the example in Listing 4-22, you will notice that the only difference is the *interpretation* (the third argument in SDO_ELEM_INFO_ARRAY), which is now set to 2. The result is a line string formed using a circular arc instead of a straight line.

Again, what if the line string has more than three points? Since an arc is defined by three points at a time, the line string should have an odd number of vertices. An arc is constructed with the three points starting at every *odd* vertex (except the last vertex). So if there are the five points A, B, C, D, and E, there will be two arcs: arc ABC at vertex A and arc CDE at vertex C, as shown in Figure 4-8.

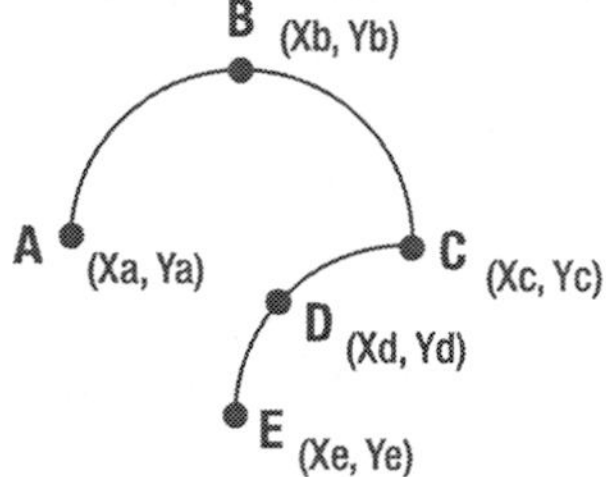

Figure 4-8. *Example of a line string with multiple arcs*

The constructor for this geometry is as follows:

```
SDO_GEOMETRY
(
  2002, 32774, null,
  SDO_ELEM_INFO_ARRAY(1,2,2),
  SDO_ORDINATE_ARRAY(Xa, Ya, Xb, Yb, Xc, Yc, Xd, Yd, Xe, Ye)
)
```

■ **Note** In Oracle Spatial, every arc is specified by three points: a starting vertex, any distinct middle vertex, and an ending vertex (for example, A, B, C). As a consequence, an arc-based line string (arc string) should always have an odd number of vertices. The individual arcs are always contiguous and always start at the odd-numbered vertices.

If you want to model arcs that are not contiguous, these are considered multiline/curve geometries. We describe them later.

What happens if the line string ends at the starting vertex? This causes a loop or a ring. Can it be considered a polygon? The answer is no. To be considered a polygon, the *element-type* in the SDO_ELEM_INFO attribute needs to be 1003 (or 2003).

Polygon: Ring (Boundary) Connected by Straight Lines

Next let's look at another type of geometry: the polygon. The polygon boundary (ring) can be connected by lines, connected by arcs, or specified as a rectangle or as a circle. Let's look at examples for each of these in turn.

In this section, we will consider simple geometries. We will consider more complex polygons (those with voids and so on) later in the "Complex Geometry Examples" section. Figure 4-9 shows an example polygon where the boundary is connected by lines.

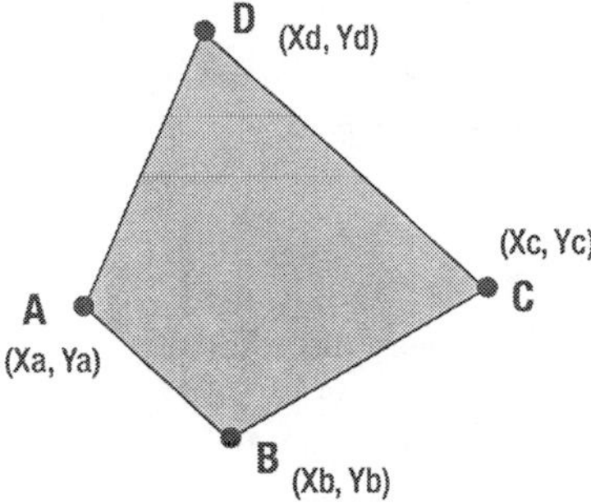

Figure 4-9. *Example of a polygon boundary connected by lines*

Listing 4-24 shows how to insert the polygon into the geometry_examples table.

Listing 4-24. *Example of a Simple Polygon Connected by Lines*

```
SQL> INSERT INTO geometry_examples VALUES
(
  'POLYGON',
  '2-D polygon connecting  A(Xa, Ya), B(Xb, Yb),  C(Xc, Yc), D(Xd, Yd)',
  SDO_GEOMETRY
  (
    2003,     -- SDO_GTYPE: DOOT. Set to 2003 as it is a 2-dimensional polygon
    32774,    -- SDO_SRID
    NULL,     -- SDO_POINT_TYPE is null
    SDO_ELEM_INFO_ARRAY  -- SDO_ELEM_INFO attribute (see Table 4-2 for values)
    (
      1,      -- Offset is 1
      1003,   -- Element-type is 1003 for an outer POLYGON element
      1       -- Interpretation is 1 if boundary is connected by straight lines.
    ),
    SDO_ORDINATE_ARRAY   -- SDO_ORDINATES attribute
    (
      1,1,    -- Xa, Ya values
      2,-1,   -- Xb, Yb values
      3,1,    -- Xc, Yc values
      2,2,    -- Xd, Yd values
      1,1     -- Xa, Ya values : Repeat first vertex to close the ring
      )
    )
  );
```

Compared to the previous examples, the main points to note in this example are as follows:

- The SDO_GTYPE is set to 2003 (two-dimensional polygon).
- The *element-type* in the SDO_ELEM_INFO attribute is set to 1003 to indicate it is an outer polygon, and the *interpretation* is set to 1 to indicate a polygon element connected by straight lines (see Table 4-2 for reference).
- The ordinates of the polygon are stored in the SDO_ORDINATES attribute. Note that the first vertex (Xa, Ya) is repeated as the last vertex (to close the boundary). Also note that the vertices are specified in counterclockwise order. This is a requirement in Oracle Spatial.

Caution The vertices in an outer ring of a polygon need to be specified in counterclockwise order. The vertices for the inner rings, if any, are specified in clockwise order. This is a convention of Oracle Spatial.

Polygon: Ring (Boundary) Connected by Arcs

The previous example can be easily modified to model a polygon where every three consecutive vertices are connected by an arc by simply changing the *interpretation* in the SDO_ELEM_INFO attribute to 2. For this to be valid, you need an odd number of vertices. However, such circular polygons are rarely used in representing spatial data.

Rectangle Polygon

Another popular shape to consider is the rectangle. A rectangle can be modeled as a polygon with four vertices connected by straight lines as in the previous example. However, a simplified representation is possible by specifying 3 instead of 1 for the *interpretation* in SDO_ELEM_INFO. Figure 4-10 shows an example rectangle.

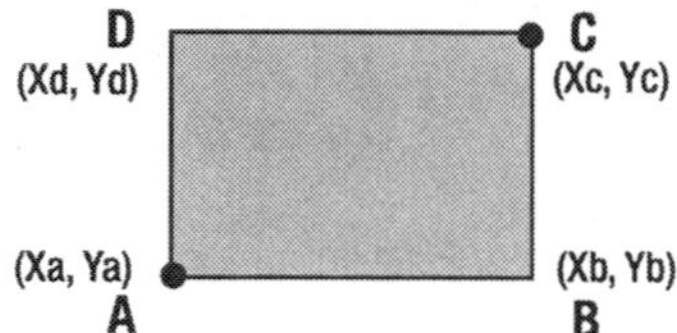

Figure 4-10. *Example of a rectangular polygon*

How is this rectangle different from the polygon in Figure 4-9? The rectangle needs only two vertices to be specified instead of all four (that is, a much more compact representation); Oracle Spatial uses the lower-left and upper-right corner vertices (that is, it specifies only the corresponding ordinates).

- The *lower-left* corner vertex has the minimum values for the ordinates in x- and y-dimensions. In Figure 4-10, A is the lower-left corner vertex.
- The *upper-right* corner vertex has the maximum values for the ordinates in x- and y-dimensions. In Figure 4-10, C is the upper-right corner vertex.

Note Always specify the lower-left corner before the upper-right corner for a two-dimensional rectangle polygon. This holds true even if the rectangle polygon is an inner ring (void) of an outer two-dimensional polygon (see Figure 4-16 later in this chapter).

Listing 4-25 shows how to insert the rectangular polygon into the geometry_examples table using the lower-left and upper-right vertices.

Listing 4-25. *Rectangular Polygon Example*

```
SQL> INSERT INTO geometry_examples VALUES
(
  'RECTANGLE POLYGON',
```

```
  '2-D rectangle polygon with corner points A(Xa, Ya),  C (Xc, Yc)',
  SDO_GEOMETRY
  (
    2003,    -- SDO_GTYPE: DOOT. Set to 2003 as it is a 2-dimensional polygon
    32774,   -- SDO_SRID
    null,    -- SDO_POINT_TYPE is null
    SDO_ELEM_INFO_ARRAY  -- SDO_ELEM_INFO attribute (see Table 4-2 for values)
    (
      1,     -- Offset is 1
      1003,  -- Element-type is 1003 for (an outer) POLYGON
      3      -- Interpretation is 3 if polygon is a RECTANGLE
    ),
    SDO_ORDINATE_ARRAY   -- SDO_ORDINATES attribute
    (
      1,1,   -- Xa, Ya values
      2,2    -- Xc, Yc values
    )
  )
);
```

Once again, note that the *interpretation* is set to 3 in the SDO_ELEM_INFO attribute. Listing 4-25 specifies only two corner vertices in the SDO_ORDINATES attribute. You can appropriately modify these ordinates to store your own rectangle.

What is a rectangle in three dimensions? A cuboid. Can the same values for SDO_ELEM_INFO be used to represent a three-dimensional cuboid (or its four-dimensional equivalent)? Yes. If you have a cuboid with the lower-left corner vertex at (Xa, Ya, Za) (the minimum value ordinates in x-, y-, and z-dimensions) and the upper-right corner vertex (the maximum value ordinates in x-, y-, and z-dimensions) at (Xc, Yc, Zc), then the geometry looks like the following. Note the SDO_GTYPE has changed to 3003 from 2003. The changes from the two-dimensional rectangle are in bold. You can construct the SDO_GEOMETRY for the rectangle equivalent in four dimensions analogously.

```
SDO_GEOMETRY
(
  3003,         -- SDO_GTYPE set 3003 to indicate 3-dimensional polygon.
  32774,
  NULL,
  SDO_ELEM_INFO_ARRAY(1, 1003,3),
  SDO_ORDINATE_ARRAY(Xa, Ya, Za, Xc, Yc, Zc)
)
```

Circle Polygon

Next, let's look at another regular structure: the circle. Figure 4-11 shows an example. Just like rectangles, circles are different from linear polygons/arc polygons only in the *interpretation* in the SDO_ELEM_INFO attribute and the number of ordinates in the SDO_ORDINATES array. The *interpretation* is set to 4, and the ordinate array stores any three distinct points on the circumference of the circle.

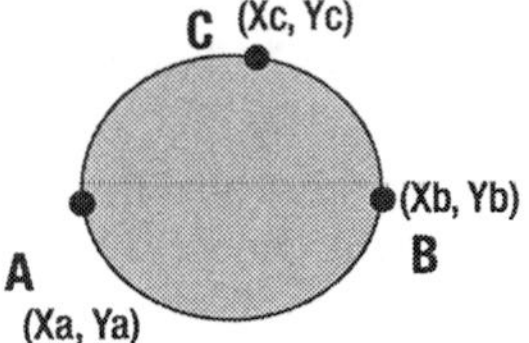

Figure 4-11. *Example of a circular polygon*

Listing 4-26 shows how to insert the circular polygon into the geometry_examples table.

Listing 4-26. *Circular Polygon Example*

```
SQL> INSERT INTO geometry_examples VALUES
(
  'CIRCLE POLYGON',
  '2-D circle polygon with 3 boundary points A(Xa,Ya), B(Xb,Yb), C(Xc,Yc)',
  SDO_GEOMETRY
  (
    2003,     -- SDO_GTYPE: DOOT. Set to 2003 as it is a 2-dimensional polygon
    32774,    -- SDO_SRID
    NULL,     -- SDO_POINT_TYPE is null
    SDO_ELEM_INFO_ARRAY  -- SDO_ELEM_INFO attribute (see Table 4-2 for values)
    (
      1,      -- Offset is 1
      1003,   -- Element-type is 1003 for (an outer) POLYGON
      4       -- Interpretation is 4 if polygon is a CIRCLE
    ),
    SDO_ORDINATE_ARRAY   -- SDO_ORDINATES attribute
    (
      1,1,    -- Xa, Ya values
      3,1,    -- Xb, Yb values
      2,2     -- Xc, Yc values
    )
  )
);
```

■ **Caution** You cannot specify circles and arcs if the SRID corresponds to a geodetic coordinate system. Circles and arcs are valid only in projected and local coordinate systems. In geodetic coordinate systems, "densify" the circumference of the circle with many points and represent the points a linear polygon using the sdo_util.arc_densify function.

Can you specify a circle by its center and radius? Yes. In Chapter 7, we will look at some functions that take the x and y ordinates of the center and a radius and return an SDO_GEOMETRY.

Complex Two-Dimensional Geometry Examples

So far, we have described how to represent simple geometries. These geometries are composed of a *simple* element—an element with just one descriptor triplet. In contrast, *complex* geometries have more than one element descriptor triplet for an element. A complex geometry can be any of the following:

- *A compound line string or a compound polygon*: In such a geometry, the boundary is connected by both straight lines and circular arcs. For instance, streets that have both straight-line segments and arcs (to denote connecting roads) can be stored as a compound line string geometry. Objects F and G in Figure 4-1 are examples of such a compound line string element and a compound polygon geometry, respectively.
- *A voided polygon*: This geometry has an outer ring and one or more inner rings. The outer and inner ring polygon elements are specified as *simple* polygon elements. Object D in Figure 4-1 is an example of a voided polygon geometry. Lakes and other bodies of water that have islands can be stored as voided polygons. Note that the area of the interior rings is not considered part of these geometries.

- *A collection*: This geometry is a collection of multiple elements such as points, lines, and/or polygons. Object E in Figure 4-1 is an example of such a collection. The state boundaries for Texas and California have one or more islands and can be stored as collection geometries.

Constructing Complex Geometries

You can construct complex geometries using the following steps:

1. The SDO_ELEM_INFO triplets of the simple elements constituting the complex geometry are concatenated in the appropriate order.
2. The SDO_ORDINATES values are also concatenated. (Duplication of any shared vertices in contiguous elements is removed.)
3. As a result of the concatenation of the SDO_ORDINATES, the offsets in the SDO_ELEM_INFO attribute for each simple element are adjusted to reflect the correct start of the element in the SDO_ORDINATES array.
4. For *compound* (line string or polygon) elements, additional triplets are added to SDO_ELEM_INFO to specify the combination of subsequent simple elements. Table 4-3 presents the possible values for the *element-type* for these additional triplets.
5. The SDO_GTYPE is set to reflect the resulting geometry.

Let's examine the *compound* geometries and *voided-polygon* geometries. We will consider *collection* geometries in the last part of the section. First we will illustrate how to construct the SDO_ELEM_INFO attributes (that is, the corresponding element descriptor triplets) for these geometries. Table 4-3 shows the SDO_ELEM_INFO values for the compound geometries and the voided-polygon geometries.

Table 4-3. *Values for* <Element-Type, Interpretation> *in an Element Descriptor Triplet for Compound/Voided-Polygon Geometries*

Name	Element-Type (Etype)	Interpretation
Voided polygon	1003 = Outer polygon 2003 = Interior polygon (hole)	1 = Polygon boundary connected by straight lines. 2 = Polygon boundary connected by circular arcs. 3 = Rectangle polygon. The lower_left and upper_right corner vertices of the rectangle are specified in the SDO_ORDINATES array. 4 = Circular polygon. Any three vertices on the boundary of the circle are specified in the SDO_ORDINATES array.
Compound line string	4	*N* = Specifies the number of subelements that constitute the compound line string. The *N* triplets for these *N* subelements follow the current (header) triplet.
Compound polygon	1005 = Outer polygon 2005 = Interior polygon	*N* = Specifies the number of straight-line and circular-arc subelements that constitute the polygon boundary. The *N* triplets for these *N* subelements follow this triplet.

SDO_ELEM_INFO for Compound Elements

If the compound element has *N* subelements, then there will be *N* + 1 descriptor triplets: one *header* triplet specifying that it is a compound element, followed by *N* triplets, one for each subelement. The *N* subelements have to be simple elements, and their descriptor triplets will be constructed as specified previously for simple elements. The header triplet has the following form:

- The *offset* specifies the starting offset for the compound element in the SDO_ORDINATES array.
- The *element-type* specifies one of the following:
  - A compound line string (*element-type* = 4).
  - A compound polygon (*element-type* = 1005 or 2005). The *element-type* will be 1005 if the compound element is used an outer polygon ring, and it will be 2005 if it is used an inner ring (void).
- The *interpretation* for the header triplet specifies the number of subelements that make up this compound element.

For example, for the compound line string object F in Figure 4-1, the *element-type* for the header triplet will be 4, and *interpretation* will be 2 since it has two subelements. The next two triplets in the SDO_ELEM_INFO array will have the description for these subelements. Both elements are lines and have an *element-type* of 2, but one subelement will have an *interpretation* of 1, indicating straight-line connectivity, and another element will have an *interpretation* of 2, indicating arc-based connectivity.[9] The SDO_ELEM_INFO will have the triplets in the following order:

- (1, 4, 2) for the header triplet specifying the compound line string
- (1, 2, 1) for the first subelement triplet connected by straight lines
- (5, 2, 2) for the next subelement triplet representing the arc

Listing 4-27 shows the full SQL for constructing a compound line string corresponding to object F in Figure 4-1. The first subelement connects vertices A, B, and C by a line, whereas the second subelement connects C, D, and E by a circular arc. Note that the shared vertex C is represented only once. Since the second subelement starts at C, the offset for that subelement is set to 5.

Listing 4-27. *Compound Line String Example*

```
SQL> INSERT INTO geometry_examples VALUES
(
  'COMPOUND LINE STRING',
  '2-D Compound Line String connecting A,B, C by a line and C, D, E by an arc
  SDO_GEOMETRY
  (
    2002,     -- SDO_GTYPE: DOOT. Set to 2002 as it is a 2-dimensional Line String
    32774,    -- SDO_SRID
    NULL,     -- SDO_POINT_TYPE is null
    SDO_ELEM_INFO_ARRAY  -- SDO_ELEM_INFO attribute (see Table 4-2 for values)
    (
      1,      -- Offset is 1
      4,      -- Element-type is 4 for Compound Line String
      2,      -- Interpretation is 2 representing number of subelements
        1, 2, 1  -- Triplet for first subelement connected by line
        5, 2, 2 - Triplet for second subelement connected by arc; offset is 5
```

9. Recall that Oracle supports only circular arcs. Arcs in this chapter always refers to *circular arcs*.

```
    ),
    SDO_ORDINATE_ARRAY     -- SDO_ORDINATES attribute
    (
      1,1,     -- Xa, Ya values for vertex A
      2,3,     -- Xb, Yb values for vertex B
      3,1,      -- Xc, Yc values for vertex C
           4,2,     -- Xd, Yd values  for vertex D
            5, 3  -- Xe, Ye values for vertex E
    )
  )
);
```

SDO_ELEM_INFO for Voided Polygon Element

If the voided polygon has *N* void (inner ring) subelements and one outer ring subelement, then there will be at least *N* + 1 descriptor triplets. The first triplet will specify the descriptor triplet for the outer ring. This will be followed by descriptor triplets for each of the *N* void subelements. If all the subelements are simple elements, then there will be exactly *N* + 1 descriptor triplets. Otherwise, the size will reflect the descriptors for any compound subelements.

For example, the voided-polygon object D in Figure 4-1 has two descriptor triplets. The first triplet represents the outer polygon ring and has an *element-type* of 1003. The second triplet represents the rectangular void and has an *element-type* of 2003.

Next let's look at some examples of such complex shapes and how to represent them using the `SDO_GEOMETRY` data type in Oracle.

Compound Line String Example

Most road segments are connected by straight lines. However, there are some segments where the road takes a sharp circular turn. How do you model roads that have a combination of straight-line segments and circular segments? Figure 4-12 shows an example.

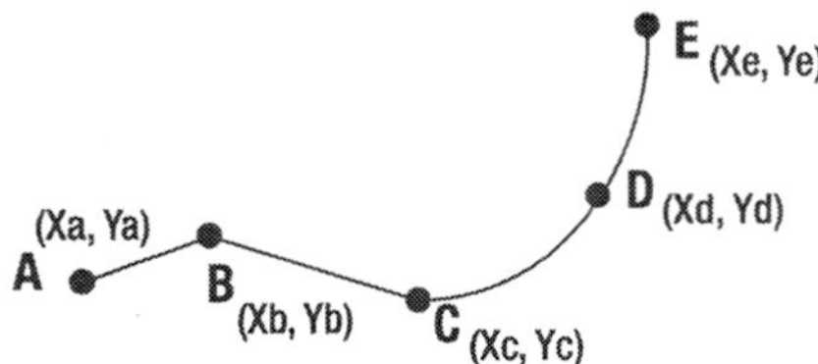

Figure 4-12. *Example of a compound line string connected by lines and arcs*

Line segment ABC is connected by straight lines, and CDE is connected by arcs. How do you represent this compound line? The answer is to construct a compound element by specifying a header triplet followed by simple element triplets for the `SDO_ELEM_INFO` attribute, as described in Table 4-3.

- *Header triplet*: The number of subelements is 2 and the starting offset is 1, so the header triplet is (1, 4, 2). The 4 specifies that it is a header triplet for a compound line string, and the 2 specifies that the number of simple elements is two.
- *The triplet for line ABC*: Since this is the first simple element in the compound, the offset in `SDO_ORDINATES` will still be 1. The *element-type* is set to 2 (line string), and the *interpretation* is set to 1 to indicate straight-line connectivity. This triplet is thus (1, 2, 1). The six ordinates for this element are the first to be stored in the `SDO_ORDINATES` array.

- *The triplet for arc CDE*: Also, this element shares the vertex C with the previous element ABC, so the ordinates for vertex C need not be repeated. Since this element (CDE) starts at vertex C, which is stored at offset 5, the starting offset is set to 5. The *element-type* is set to 2 (line string), and the *interpretation* is set to 2 to indicate arc-based connectivity. The triplet therefore is (5, 2, 2).

Since the geometry has only two-dimensional lines, the SDO_GTYPE is set to 2002.
This representation is described using the SDO_GEOMETRY elements in Figure 4-13.

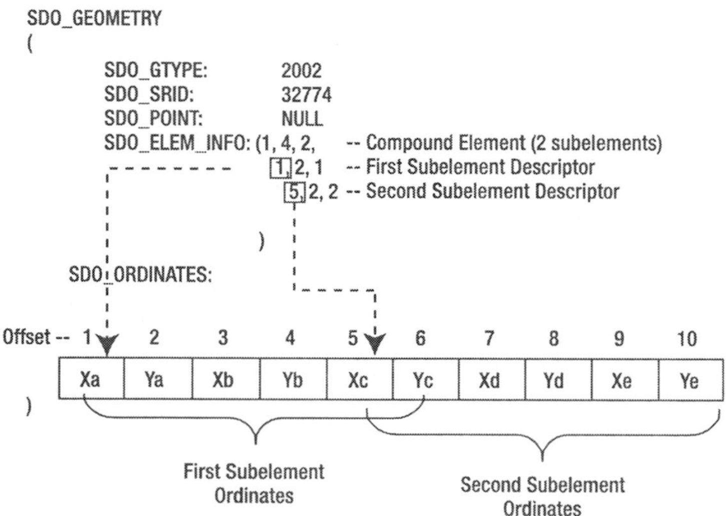

Figure 4-13. *Storing a compound line string as an* SDO_GEOMETRY

■ **Note** Compound line strings should be contiguous (that is, they should share a vertex). In Figure 4-13, the vertex (Xc, Yc) is shared by both the first and second elements. Also, note that a compound line string (or elements with the *element-type* set to 4) can have only line string subelements (that is, subelements of *element-type* = 2).

Compound Polygon Example

If you connect vertex E to vertex A in Figure 4-12, it becomes a closed line as shown in Figure 4-14.

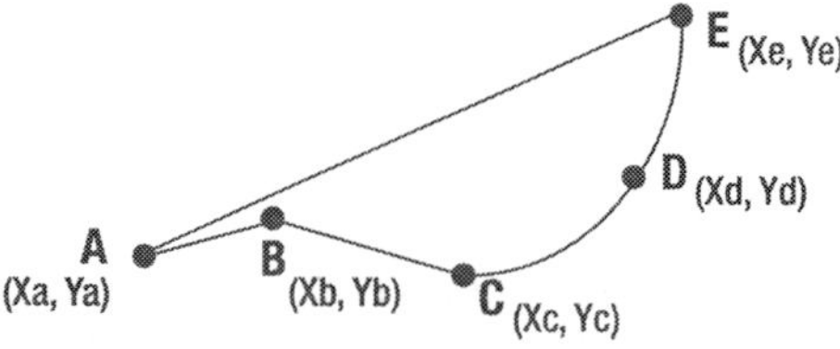

Figure 4-14. *Example of a "closed" compound line string connected by lines and arcs*

You can use this closed compound line string to be the boundary of a polygon by appropriately modifying the SDO_GTYPE (and the *element-types*). Figure 4-15 shows the elements for SDO_GEOMETRY.

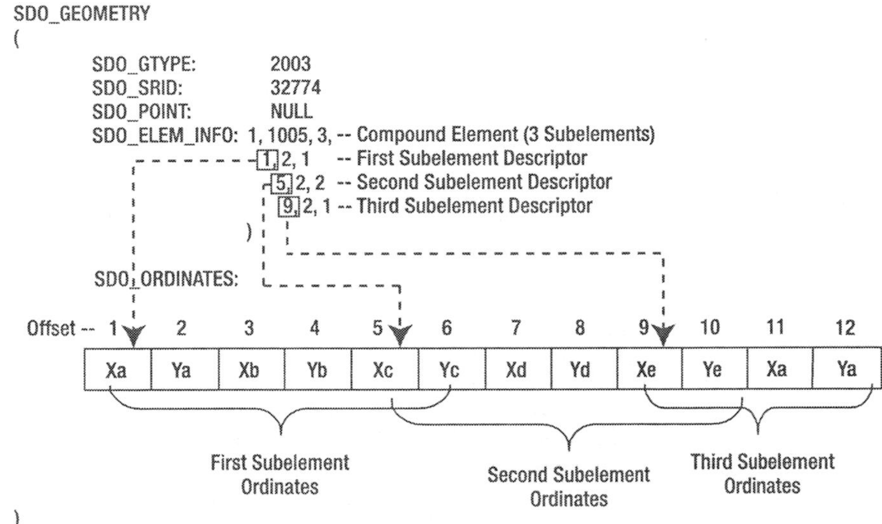

Figure 4-15. *Storing a compound polygon as* SDO_GEOMETRY

Here we note the following changes:

- SDO_GTYPE is set to 2003.
- For the compound element header triplet, the *element-type* is set to 1005 (compound polygon) instead of 4, and the number of subelements changes to three from two.
- A new subelement represents the straight line connecting E to A. This subelement has SDO_ELEM_INFO set to (9, 2, 1) where 9 represents the starting offset for the ordinates of E, 2 indicates it is a line, and 1 indicates connectivity by straight line.
- The ordinates of vertex A are repeated at the end in the SDO_ORDINATES array.

Remember that except for the header triplet, all other subelement triplets still have an *element-type* of 2 (line), because these elements are representing only lines. The header triplet that signifies the compound has an *element-type* of 1005.

■ **Caution** A compound polygon (or elements of *element-type* = 5) can be made up only of line string subelements (that is, subelements of *element-type* = 2).

Polygon with a Void

What about oceans that have islands? How do you represent the area occupied by such large bodies of water? Polygons with voids will help here. Figure 4-16 shows a diamond-shaped polygon with vertices A, B, C, and D. Inside this polygon is a rectangle polygon with corners at E and F. This rectangle polygon serves as a *void*—that is, an area not covered by the outer ABCD polygon. How do you represent this polygon with the void?

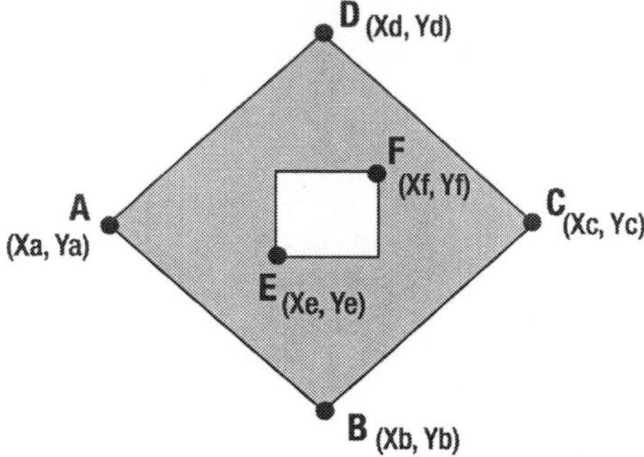

Figure 4-16. *Example of a polygon with a void*

First let's examine the constructors for the two polygons in Figure 4-16 separately. Polygon ABCD (without the void) is a simple polygon whose boundary is connected by straight lines. The constructor looks like this:

```
SDO_GEOMETRY
(
  2003, 32774, NULL,
  SDO_ELEM_INFO(1, 1003,1),
  SDO_ORDINATE_ARRAY(Xa, Ya, Xb, Yb, Xc, Yc, Xd, Yd, Xa, Ya)
)
```

Assuming that the rectangular polygon EF is not inside ABCD, the constructor looks as follows:

```
SDO_GEOMETRY
(
  2003, 32774, NULL,
  SDO_ELEM_INFO(1, 1003, 3),
  SDO_ORDINATE_ARRAY(Xe, Ye, Xf, Yf)
)
```

Using these two constructors, you can combine the two polygons to represent a polygon with a void as shown in Figure 4-17. In this figure, the outer element descriptor describes the outer polygon, and the inner element descriptor describes the inner polygon.

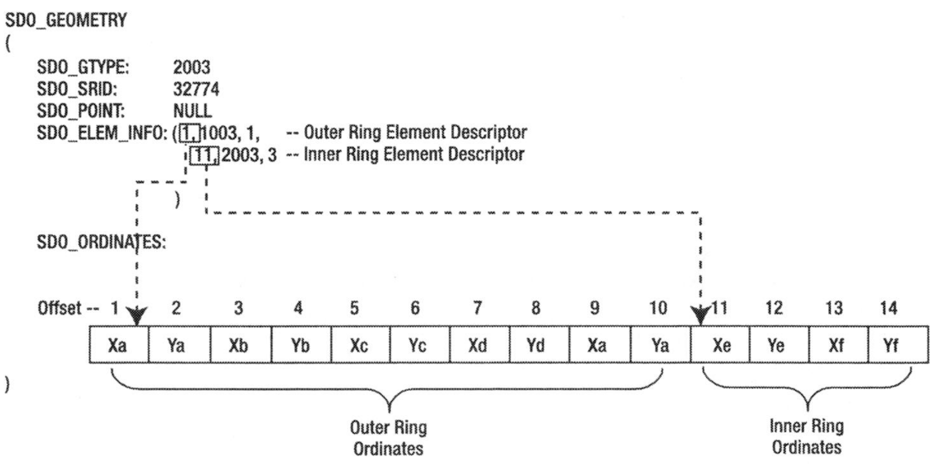

Figure 4-17. *Storing a polygon with a void as an* SDO_GEOMETRY

In this example, the combined polygon has two elements: an outer polygon and an inner polygon. You need to specify these elements as follows:

- The element triplets for the outer polygon are specified first, followed by that for the inner polygon (that is, the void). The outer polygon ring should have the *element-type* set to 1003, and the inner polygon ring should have the *element-type* set to 2003. (If there is more than one inner polygon, these are specified in any order after the outer polygon is specified.)
- Likewise, the ordinates of the outer polygon are specified first, followed by those of the inner polygon.
- The starting offset for the ordinates of the inner polygon are adjusted from 1 to 11 (because they are preceded by the ordinates of the outer polygon).

Note Unlike in a compound (line or polygon) geometry (see Figures 4-13 and 4-15), there is no header triplet for constructing a polygon with a void. All inner elements (that is, triplets with an *element-type* of 2003 or 2005) that follow an outer element (that is, triplets with an *element-type* of 1003 or 1005) are considered to be voids of (that is, inside) the outer element.

Can you have a polygon inside the void (that is, inside the inner ring)? Yes, you can, but that will be treated as a multipolygon geometry (the SDO_GTYPE is 7). The reason is that the area represented by the resulting polygon is not *contiguous*.

Collections

Next, we come to the last geometry type: the collection. Collections can be *homogeneous*, as in a multipoint, multiline, multipolygon collection. Or they can be *heterogeneous*, containing a combination of point, line, and/or polygon geometries. In Table 4-1 you saw that multipoint, multiline, multipolygon, and heterogeneous collections each have a different SDO_GTYPE. Now you will see how to represent these geometries using the SDO_GEOEMTRY data type. At the end of this section, you will learn about a function that appends two geometries. A collection of *N* geometries can be constructed simply by calling this function *N* – 1 times.

Note that collections are created in much the same way as other "complex" geometries. See "Guidelines for Constructing Complex Geometries" later in this chapter.

Multipoint Collection Example

Earlier in the chapter, you learned how to model a single point using the SDO_POINT attribute in the SDO_GEOMETRY type. Here we will model multiple points as a *single* collection geometry—that is, we will store all three points A, B, and C in Figure 4-18 as subelements of a single multipoint geometry.

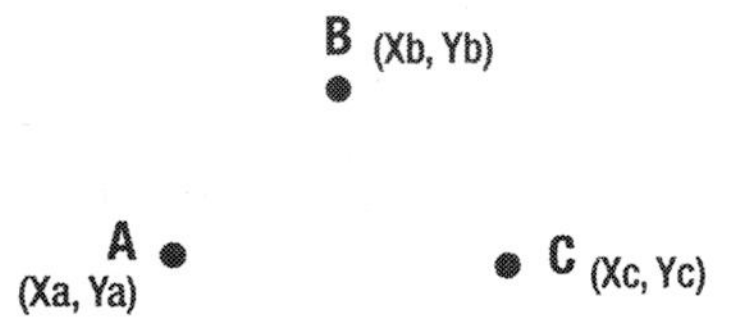

Figure 4-18. *Example of a multipoint collection*

How do you store this geometry? You first construct SDO_GEOMETRY objects for the individual points and combine them using the guidelines described in the beginning of this section:

1. Set SDO_GTYPE to 5 (multipoint).
2. Combine the SDO_ORDINATES attributes of the three point SDO_GEOMETRY objects.
3. Combine the corresponding SDO_ELEM_INFO attributes of the three point objects. The offset in the resulting SDO_ELEM_INFO is adjusted to reflect the offset in the SDO_ORDINATES attribute for each point.

The resulting SDO_GEOMETRY will look like this:

```
SDO_GEOMETRY
(
  2005, 32774, NULL,
  SDO_ELEM_INFO_ARRAY   -- SDO_ELEM_INFO: multiple elements each with 1 pt
  (
    1,1,1,              -- triplet for first "point" element
    3,1,1,              -- triplet for second "point" element
    5,1,1               -- triplet for third "point" element
  ),
  SDO_ORDINATE_ARRAY
  (
    Xa, Ya,             -- coordinates of first point
    Xb, Yb,             -- coordinates of second point
    Xc, Yc              -- coordinates of third point
  )
)
```

In this example, the three points are represented as three elements. Oracle, however, has a much simpler representation: you can represent the three points as a *single* element (and store all the ordinates in the SDO_ORDINATES attribute). The element will have a descriptor triplet of the form (1, 1, *N*) where *N* represents the number of points (if *N* = 1, then the element has just one point). The corresponding constructor is as follows, and the changes are in bold:

```
SDO_GEOMETRY
(
  2005, 32774, NULL,
  SDO_ELEM_INFO_ARRAY   -- SDO_ELEM_INFO attribute
  (
    1, 1, 3             -- "Point cluster" element with 3 points
  ),
  SDO_ORDINATE_ARRAY
  (
    Xa, Ya,             -- coordinates of first point
    Xb, Yb,             -- coordinates of second point
    Xc, Yc              -- coordinates of third point
  )
)
```

We recommend using a single element of *N* points instead of an array of point elements. This representation is more storage efficient and helps in performance.

Multiline String

Multiline string geometry consists of multiple line strings. Figure 4-19 shows an example. The triplets in SDO_ELEM_INFO are used to denote and demarcate each line segment.

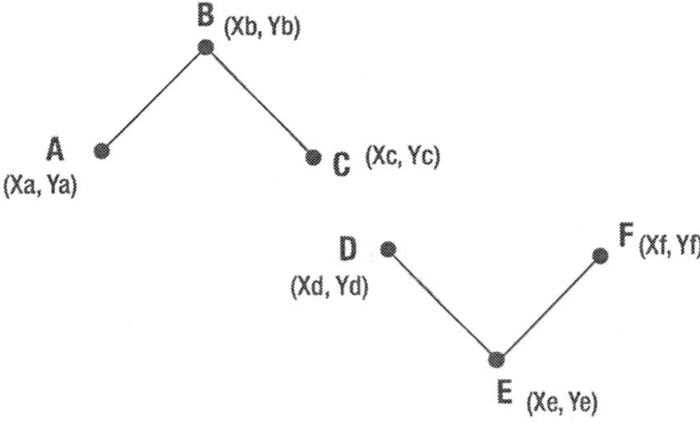

Figure 4-19. *Example of a multiline string*

We will use one triplet in the SDO_ELEM_INFO array to represent each of the elements in our geometry. The offset in each triplet points to the first element in the SDO_ORDINATES array where the first point of the geometric primitive starts. Figure 4-20 shows the resulting SDO_GEOMETRY constructor for a multiline string.

- The first line string (ABC) starts at offset 1 and ends at offset 6 (that is, there are two ordinates for each of the three points).
- The second line string (DEF) starts at offset 7 and ends at offset 12 (that is, there are two ordinates for each of the three points).

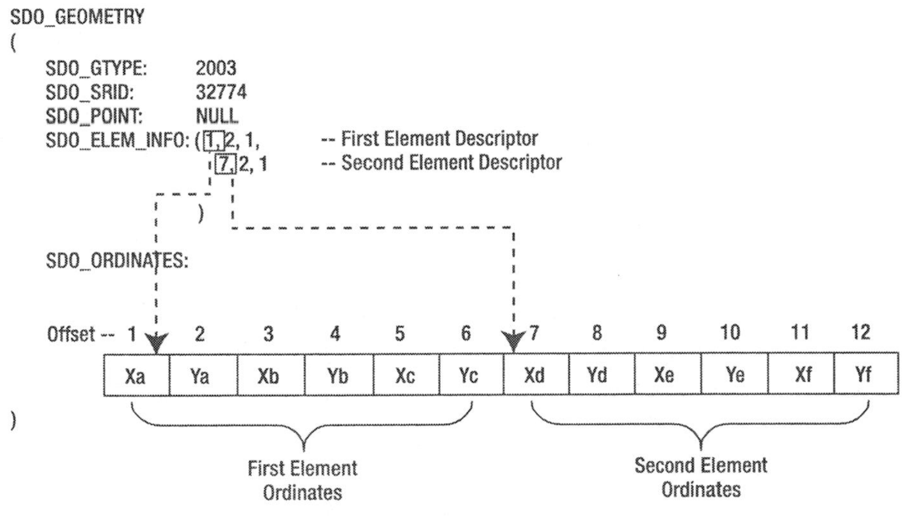

Figure 4-20. *Storing a multiline string in* SDO_GEOMETRY

Note that the two geometry elements could have different interpretations: one could be a straight line, and the other could be a circular arc. Note also that if the geometry were three-dimensional, the offsets (other than the first) would be different.

Multipolygon and Heterogenous Collections

Just as in the case of multipoint and multiline string geometry collections, the triplets in the SDO_ELEM_INFO structure are used to describe each element of the collection. SDO_GTYPE is set to the appropriate value for the collection. The ordinates of each collection element are stored in the SDO_ORDINATES array, and the starting offsets are recorded in the corresponding SDO_ELEM_INFO triplet for each collection element. We leave it as an exercise to the reader to come up with examples of multipolygon and heterogeneous collections by consulting Tables 4-2 and 4-3 and previous examples. You can compare your answers with the collections created using an alternate mechanism. This mechanism is described next.

Creating Collections: The Easy Way

The function SDO_UTIL.APPEND takes in two nonoverlapping geometries and returns an appended geometry. For example, if you invoke APPEND using two polygons, you get a multipolygon geometry as the result. Listing 4-28 shows an example.

Listing 4-28. *Appending Two Geometries*

```
SQL> SELECT SDO_UTIL.APPEND
(
  SDO_GEOMETRY
  (
    2003, 32774, null,
    SDO_ELEM_INFO_ARRAY(1,1003, 3),
    SDO_ORDINATE_ARRAY(1,1, 2,2)
  ),
  SDO_GEOMETRY
  (
    2003, 32774, NULL,
    SDO_ELEM_INFO_ARRAY(1, 1003, 3),
    SDO_ORDINATE_ARRAY(2,3, 4,5)
  )
)
FROM dual;

SDO_UTIL.APPEND(SDO_GEOMETRY(2003,32774,NULL,...
-----------------------------------------------------------------
SDO_GEOMETRY
(
  2007,  -- SDO_GTYPE=  Multi-polygon
  32774, NULL,
  SDO_ELEM_INFO_ARRAY(1, 1003, 3, 5, 1003, 3),
  SDO_ORDINATE_ARRAY(1, 1, 2, 2, 2, 3, 4, 5)
)
```

■ Caution If the input geometries in an APPEND function are polygons that overlap or touch each other, this function will return an invalid geometry.

If you pass in a line and a polygon, you get a heterogeneous collection (SDO_GTYPE =2007) geometry, as shown in Listing 4-29.

Listing 4-29. *Creating a Heterogenous Collection Using* SDO_UTIL.APPEND

```
SQL> SELECT SDO_UTIL.APPEND
(
  SDO_GEOMETRY
  (
    2003, 32774, null,
    SDO_ELEM_INFO_ARRAY(1,1003, 3),
    SDO_ORDINATE_ARRAY(1,1, 2,2)
  ),
  SDO_GEOMETRY
  (
    2002, 32774, NULL,
    SDO_ELEM_INFO_ARRAY(1, 2, 2),
    SDO_ORDINATE_ARRAY(2,3, 3,3,4,2)
  )
)
FROM dual;

SDO_UTIL.APPEND(SDO_GEOMETRY(2003,32774,NULL,...
--------------------------------------------------------------------------------
SDO_GEOMETRY
(
  2004,  -- SDO_GTYPE =(Heterogenous) Collection
  32774, NULL,
  SDO_ELEM_INFO_ARRAY(1, 1003, 3, 5, 2, 2),
  SDO_ORDINATE_ARRAY(1, 1, 2, 2, 2, 3, 3, 3, 4, 2)
)
```

Three-Dimensional Examples

So far, you've seen examples of geometries in two-dimensional spaces. In Oracle Database 11g,[10] you can store in the SDO_GEOMETRY type different three-dimensional shapes that appear in a variety of applications such as city modeling, CAD/CAM, virtual reality, and medical imaging. In Chapter 5, you will learn about importing directly from emerging standard formats such as CityGML into an SDO_GEOMETRY format. In this section, you will learn about how to construct three-dimensional geometries manually.

Table 4-4 shows the list of three-dimensional types (SDO_GTYPEs) supported in Oracle and the corresponding three-dimensional objects. You can trivially extend two-dimensional points, line strings, and polygons to three-dimensional by adding the third dimensional ordinates as shown in Figures 4-21 to 4-23. In addition to these basic types, you can also store in an SDO_GEOMETRY the following additional types:

10. Unless otherwise mentioned, Oracle 11*g* refers to the Oracle Database Server 11*g* (because the majority of Spatial functionality is part of Oracle Database Server).

- Surface geometry, represented by a *composite surface* element. A composite surface is composed of nonoverlapping polygons as shown in Figure 4-25. All surfaces, whether they are simple or composite, define a single contiguous area in three-dimensional space.
- Solid geometry, represented using either a *simple solid* element or a *composite solid* element. The boundary of a simple solid is specified using one outer composite surface and zero or more inner composite surfaces. A composite solid element is an array of nonoverlapping simple solids. Figure 4-29 shows an example of a composite solid. All solids, whether they are simple or composite, define a single contiguous volume in three-dimensional space.
- Collections of either heterogeneous types or homogenous types (multipoint, multiline, multisurface, or multisolid). Figure 4-31 shows an example of a typical building modeled as a heterogeneous collection of solids (for building structure) and surfaces (for windows and doors).

Table 4-4. *Types of Three-Dimensional Data That Can Be Stored in Oracle's* SDO_GEOMETRY

Type of Three-Dimensional Data	SDO_GTYPE Value	Type Description	Top-Level Elements of the Geometry
Point	3001	Point specified in 3D domain.	The top-level element for a point-type geometry is a point. Figure 4-21 shows an example.
Line string	3002	Line string connects two or more distinct points. Connectivity is by straight lines (no arcs). The line string is contiguous (no gaps). Does not have any area or volume.	The top-level element for a line string is a straight-line connected line. Figure 4-22 shows an example.
Surface (can be either a *polygon* or a *composite surface*)	3003	Surface geometry bounds a *single contiguous* area. Does not have any volume.	The top-level element for a surface geometry can be either a polygon or a composite surface. The composite surface is an array of nonoverlapping polygons. Figures 4-23 and 4-24 give examples of a surface geometry constructed with a polygon element or a composite surface element, respectively.
Solid (can be either a *simple solid* or a *composite solid*)	3008	Solid geometry defines a *single contiguous* volume.	The top-level element for a solid geometry can be either a simple solid or a composite solid. A composite solid is an array of nonoverlapping simple solids. Figures 4-25 and 4-26 show examples.
Collection	3005: Multipoint 3006: Multiline 3007: Multisurface 3009: Multisolid 3004: Heterogenous	All elements of the collection are line strings. All elements of the collection are surfaces. All elements of the collection are solids. Elements can be any of the previous geometry types. All elements of the collection are points.	The top-level elements can be any element type for heterogeneous collection. For homogenous collections of a specific type (for example, multipoint, multiline, multisurface, multisolid), the top-level elements have to be of the specified type. Figure 4-30 shows an example of a multi-solid.

Note that the supported list of three-dimensional types matches closely the three-dimensional types in the GML 3 specification with the exception of parametric types (such as circular arcs).

■ **Caution** All the lines joining three-dimensional objects (line strings, polygons, surfaces, solids) are assumed to be straight-line segments. Circular arcs and other parametric curves are not supported.

Let's next examine how to construct each of the three-dimensional objects in Table 4-4 as an SDO_GEOMETRY. First we will start with the simple ones: the points, lines, and polygons that are trivial extensions of the 2D counterparts. Then we will move on to more complex types.

Three-Dimensional Points, Lines, and Polygons

In what way do the three-dimensional points, lines, and polygons differ from the two-dimensional counterparts? The only differences are the specification of the dimensionality D as 3 (instead of 2) in the SDO_GTYPE and the specification of the third ordinate for each point. Listings 4-21 to 4-23 show the SQL for storing the three-dimensional point, a three-dimensional line string, and a three-dimensional polygon by highlighting just these differences.

Three-Dimensional Point

Figure 4-21 shows an example of a three-dimensional point. Listing 4-30 shows how to populate the SDO_GEOMETRY object in the `geometry_examples` table to represent three-dimensional point in Figure 4-21 (substitute (2,0,2) with actual coordinates). Note that compared to the two-dimensional point of Listing 4-18, the three-dimensional point is specified by three ordinate values, one for each of the three dimensions.

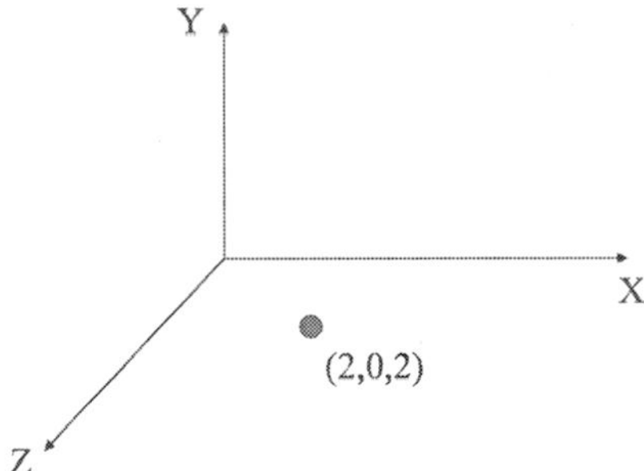

Figure 4-21. *Three-dimensional point example*

Listing 4-30. *Three-Dimensional Point Geometry Example*

```
SQL> INSERT INTO geometry_examples (name, description, geom) VALUES
(
  '3-D POINT',
  '3-dimensional Point at coordinates (2,0,2) ',
  SDO_GEOMETRY
  (
    3001,    -- SDO_GTYPE format: DOOT. Set to 3001 for a 3-dimensional point
    NULL,    -- No coordinate system
    SDO_POINT_TYPE
    (
```

```
      2,   -- ordinate value for first dimension
      0    -- ordinate value for second dimension
      2   -- ordinate value for  third dimension
    ),
    NULL,  -- SDO_ELEM_INFO is not needed as SDO_POINT field is populated
    NULL   -- SDO_ORDINATES is not needed as SDO_POINT field is populated
  )
);
```

Three-Dimensional Line String

You can construct a three-dimensional line string by connecting distinct three-dimensional points by straight lines (no arcs). Figure 4-22 shows an example. Listing 4-31 shows how to populate the SDO_GEOMETRY object in the geometry_examples table to represent the three-dimensional line string in Figure 4-22.

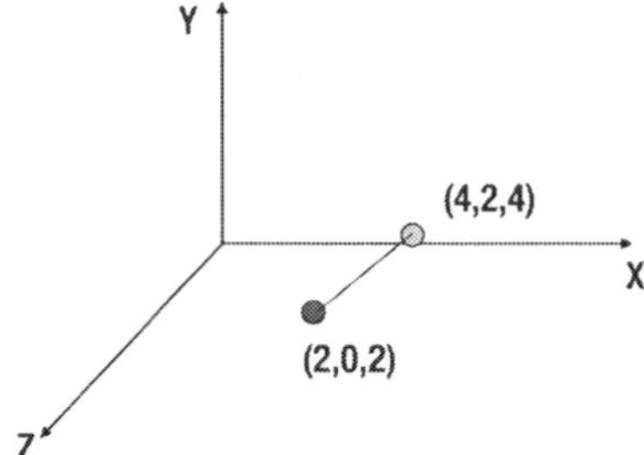

Figure 4-22. *Three-dimensional line string example*

Listing 4-31. *Three-Dimensional Line String Geometry Example*

```
SQL> INSERT INTO geometry_examples (name, description, geom) VALUES
(
  '3-D LineString,
  '3-dimensional LineString  from coordinates (2,0,2) to (4,2,4) ',
  SDO_GEOMETRY
  (
    3002,    -- SDO_GTYPE format: DOOT. Set to 3002 for a 3-dimensional line
    NULL,    -- No coordinate system
     NULL, --- No data in SDO_POINT attribute
     SDO_ELEM_INFO_ARRAY(
          1, -- Offset for ordinates in SDO_ORDINATE_ARRAY
          2,   -- Line String typ
          1,   -- Connected by straight lines
                                                     ),
    SDO_ORDINATES_ARRAY
    (
      2,   -- ordinate value for first dimension for first point
      0,   -- ordinate value for second dimension for first point
      2,   -- ordinate value for  third dimension  for first point
      4,   -- ordinate value for first dimension for second point
      2,   -- ordinate value for second dimension for second point
      4    -- ordinate value for  third dimension  for second point
    )
  )
);
```

■ **Caution** The connectivity between two adjacent three-dimensional points should always be set to straight lines (interpretation value of 1 in the SDO_ELEM_INFO attribute). Oracle Spatial does not support three-dimensional arcs or any other three-dimensional parametric curves.

Note that Listing 4-31 shows a line string connecting just two points. You can extend the example to a line string of an arbitrary number of points by simply adding the ordinates of the points to the SDO_ORDINATES array.

Three-Dimensional Polygon

You can construct a three-dimensional polygon by creating an outer ring followed by 0 or more inner rings. Vertices of the rings have to be coplanar (that is, all vertices on the same plane). Figure 4-23 shows an example of a three-dimensional polygon with and without an inner ring. Note that the edges on the ring are always connected by straight lines (Oracle Spatial does not support connectivity by arcs in Oracle 11g).

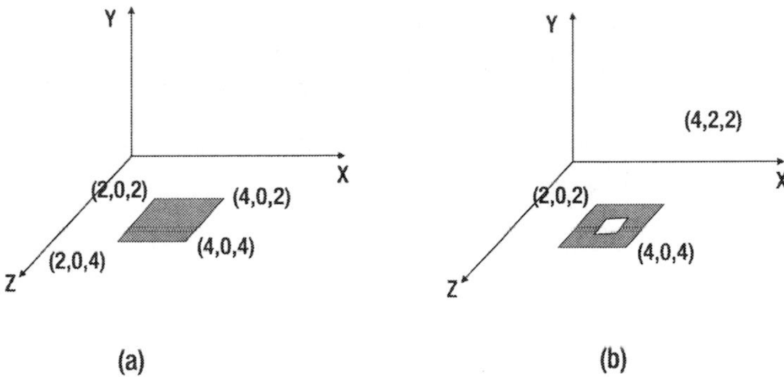

Figure 4-23. *Examples of a (a) three-dimensional polygon and (b) three-dimensional polygon with inner ring (hole)*

Consider the polygon in Figure 4-23 (a). This polygon has one exterior ring specified by the points A, B, C, and D. Listing 4-32 shows the constructor for such a simple polygon geometry.

Listing 4-32. *SQL for Three-Dimensional Polygon in Figure 4-23 (a)*

```
SQL> INSERT INTO geometry_examples (name, description, geom) VALUES
(
  '3-D Polygon',
  '3-dimensional Polygon  from coordinates (2,0,2) to (4,0, 4) ',
  SDO_GEOMETRY
  (
    3003,    -- SDO_GTYPE format: DOOT. Set to 3003 for a 3-dimensional line
    NULL,    -- No coordinate system
     NULL, --- No data in SDO_POINT attribute
     SDO_ELEM_INFO_ARRAY(
          1,  -- Offset for ordinates in SDO_ORDINATE_ARRAY
          3,   -- Polygon type
          1,   -- Connected by straight lines
      ),
```

```
    SDO_ORDINATES_ARRAY
    (
      2, 0, 2,   -- coordinate values for first point
      2, 0, 4   -- coordinate values for second point
      4, 0, 4,   -- coordinate values for third point
      4, 0, 2,   -- coordinate values for fourth point
      2, 0, 2    -- coordinate values for first point
    )
  )
);
```

Recall that for two-dimensional data, we had rules that the order of the vertices should be specified in counterclockwise order for exterior rings and clockwise for interior rings. Do you need any such restrictions for three-dimensional polygons? It's nothing that Oracle stipulates. But the order of the vertices specified implicitly defines the *surface normal* using the "right-hand thumb" rule. If the fingers curl along the order of the specification of the vertices, the outward thumb is the direction of the surface normal for the polygon. Figure 4-24 shows the direction of the surface normal (along the positive Y-axis) for the polygon specification in Listing 4-32.

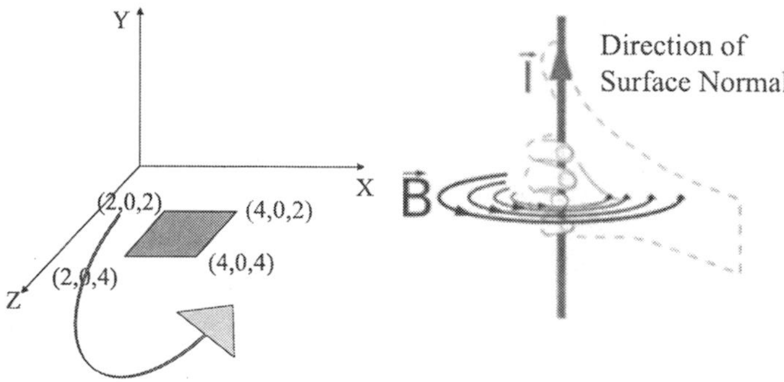

Figure 4-24. *Direction of surface normal for a polygon*

Note that although Oracle does not stipulate a specific order for vertices of a three-dimensional polygon (that is, no restrictions on the direction for a surface normal for the polygon), the surface normal is needed for properly specifying solids. For solids, Oracle stipulates that the surface normals for all the composing polygons have to point *outward* from the solid.

The polygon in Figure 4-23 (a) is aligned with the x-, y-, and z-axes. Instead of specifying all the vertices, it can be represented as a *rectangle* by specifying just the two corners corresponding to the minimum ordinate values and the maximum ordinate values for the x-, y-, and z-dimensions. We refer to these corners as *min-corner* and *max-corner*, respectively. The interpretation value in the element descriptor triplet (in the SDO_ELEM_INFO attribute) for the polygon element is set to 3 (rectangle). Listing 4-33 shows the corresponding SQL.

Listing 4-33. *Three-Dimensional Rectangle Representation for Polygon of Figure 4-23 (a)*

```
SQL> INSERT INTO geometry_examples (name, description, geom) VALUES
(
  '3-D Rectangle Polygon',
  '3-dimensional Polygon  from coordinates (2,0,2) to (4,0, 4) ',
  SDO_GEOMETRY
  (
    3003,    -- SDO_GTYPE format: DOOT. Set to 3003 for a 3-dimensional polygon
```

```
      NULL,     -- No coordinate system
       NULL,  --- No data in SDO_POINT attribute
       SDO_ELEM_INFO_ARRAY(
          1,  -- Offset for ordinates of the Exterior Ring in SDO_ORDINATE_ARRAY
          1003,   -- ETYPE for Exterior ring
           3,   -- Connected by straight lines
           ),
      SDO_ORDINATES_ARRAY
      (
        2, 0,  2,    -- coordinates for min-corner of Exterior ring
        4, 0,  4     -- coordinates  for max-corner of Exterior ring
      )
    )
);
```

What is the direction of the surface normal for the previous rectangle? It depends on whether the rectangle is parallel to the XY, YZ, or XZ plane and the order of specification of the min-corner and max-corner in SDO_ORDINATES_ARRAY. Table 4-5 lists all the possible combinations along with the direction of the surface normal. Note that with the <min-corner, max-corner> order for a rectangle parallel to the XY, YZ, or XZ plane, the surface normal is along the positive perpendicular third dimension (Z-, X-, or Y-axis). On the other hand, if the rectangle is specified as < max-corner, min-corner>, the surface normal is along the negative perpendicular third dimension.

Table 4-5. *Direction of Surface Normal for a Rectangle Polygon Parallel to One of XY, YZ, or XZ Plane*

Plane to Which Rectangle Is Parallel	Order of Specification of (Coordinates of) the Corners	Direction of the Surface Normal
XY	Min-corner, max-corner	Positive Z-axis
YZ	Min-corner, max-corner	Positive X-axis
XZ	Min-corner, max-corner	Positive Y-axis
XY	Max-corner, min-corner	Negative Z-axis
YZ	Max-corner, min-corner	Negative X-axis
XZ	Max-corner, min-corner	Negative Y-axis

Using the information in Table 4-5, you can now determine the direction of the surface normal for the rectangle in Listing 4-33. Since min-corner (2,0,2) is specified before max-corner (4,0,4) and the rectangle is parallel to the XZ plane, the surface normal will be in the direction of the positive Y-axis.

Note that the previous polygons have only one exterior ring and no inner rings. Just as in the case of two-dimensional data, three-dimensional polygons can have zero or more inner rings. This is illustrated in Figure 4-23 (b). Interior rings have an ETYPE of 2003 in contrast to exterior rings that have an ETYPE of 1003. Interior rings should be oriented in the reverse order as the exterior ring. If the outer and inner rings are *rectangles* and the outer ring is specified as <min-corner, max-corner>, the inner ring should be specified in reverse order, as in <max-corner, min-corner> (and vice versa). (Note that this is a deviation from the two-dimensional rectangle where the vertices are specified always as <min-corner, max-corner> irrespective of whether the ring is inner or outer.) Using this information, you can construct SDO_GEOMETRY for Figure 4-23 (b), as shown in Listing 4-34.

Listing 4-34. *SQL for Polygon with Hole in Figure 4-23 (b)*

```
SQL> INSERT INTO geometry_examples (name, description, geom) VALUES
(
  '3-D Rectangle Polygon with Hole',
  '3-dimensional Polygon ',
  SDO_GEOMETRY
  (
    3003,     -- SDO_GTYPE format: DOOT. Set to 3003 for a 3-dimensional polygon
    NULL,     -- No coordinate system
     NULL,  --- No data in SDO_POINT attribute
     SDO_ELEM_INFO_ARRAY(
        1,  -- Offset for ordinates in SDO_ORDINATE_ARRAY
        1003,    -- Exterior ring etype
        3,    -- Rectangle
           7, -- Offset for interior ring ordinates in SDO_ORDINATE_ARRAY
           2003,    -- ETYPE for Interior ring
           3,    -- Rectangle
           ),
    SDO_ORDINATES_ARRAY
    (
      2, 0, 2,      -- coordinates for min-corner of  Exterior ring
      4, 0, 4,      -- coordinates for max-corner of  Exterior ring
      3.5, 0, 3.5, -- coordinates of  max-corner of  Interior ring
      3, 0, 3      -- coordinates of min-corner of  Interior ring
    )
  )
);
```

Caution For a three-dimensional rectangle modeling an inner ring of a three-dimensional polygon, the order of vertex specification should always be the reverse of the order in the outer polygon.

Composite Surfaces

Note that a polygon can have only one exterior ring. What if you want multiple rings composing a contiguous surface? Such a geometry that is constituted from multiple three-dimensional polygons but still constitutes a single contiguous area is referred to as a *composite surface*. Figure 4-25 (a) shows some examples. Observe that in Figure 4-25 (a), the composite surface is composed of two polygons, with one in the XY plane and another in the XZ plane.

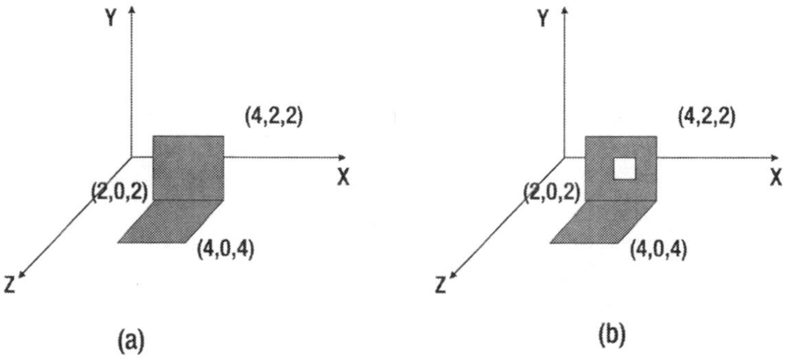

Figure 4-25. *Examples of (a) a composite surface and (b) a closed composite surface*

You can store that as a composite surface. Let's look at how to construct the SDO_ELEM_INFO and SDO_ORDINATES attributes because they are no longer trivial.

A composite surface element is specified by a header triplet of the form <offset, etype=1006, N> where offset specifies the offset of the element in the SDO_ORDINATES array and N specifies the number of polygonal surfaces that make up the composite surface. The element specification for each of the planar polygonal surfaces follows this header triplet. Listing 4-35 shows the SQL for the composite surface in Figure 4-25 (a). Note that SDO_GTYPE is 3003, the same for a three-dimensional polygon and a three-dimensional surface.

Listing 4-35. *SQL for Composite Surface in Figure 4-25 (a)*

```
SQL> INSERT INTO geometry_examples (name, description, geom) VALUES
(
  '3-D Composite Surface',
  '3-dimensional Composite with 2 rectangle polygons  ',


  SDO_GEOMETRY
  (
    3003,    -- SDO_GTYPE format: DOOT. Set to 3003 for a 3-dimensional Surface
    NULL,    -- No coordinate system
    NULL,  --- No data in SDO_POINT attribute
    SDO_ELEM_INFO_ARRAY(
         1,   -- Offset of composite element
         1006,  --- Etype for composite surface element
         2,  -- Number of composing polygons
           1,  -- Offset for ordinates in SDO_ORDINATE_ARRAY
           1003,   -- Etype for Exterior (outer) ring of FIRST polygon
           3,    --  Polygon is an axis-aligned rectangle
             7,  -- Offset for second exterior polygon
             1003,  -- Etype for  exterior Ring of SECOND  polygon
             3   --  Polygon is an axis-aligned rectangle
              ),
    SDO_ORDINATES_ARRAY
    (
       2, 0,2, -- min-corner for exterior ring of first polygon,
       4,2,2,  -- max-corner for exterior ring of first polygon
       2,0, 2, -- min-corner for second element  rectangle
       4,0,4   -- max-corner for second element rectangle
    )
  )
);
```

Note that the polygon elements are in different planes (the first in z=2 plane and the second in the y=0 plane). You can also construct composite surfaces that are on the same plane. The only restriction is that all the elements together should constitute a single "contiguous" area (that is, the interiors of all the elements of a composite surface are connected). The polygons can also have holes, that is, inner (or interior) rings. For example, in Figure 4-25 (b) the polygon in the XY plane has not only an outer (or exterior) ring but also an inner ring. The composite surface then represents the gray area in the polygons in the XY and XZ planes. Listing 4-36 shows the SQL for specifying such a composite surface.

Listing 4-36. *SQL for Composite Surface in Figure 4-25 (b)*

```
SQL> INSERT INTO geometry_examples (name, description, geom) VALUES
(
  '3-D Composite Surface with hole polygons',
  '3-dimensional Composite with 2 rectangle polygons one of which has a hole  ',
  SDO_GEOMETRY
  (
    3003,    -- SDO_GTYPE format: DOOT. Set to 3003 for a 3-dimensional Surface
    NULL,    -- No coordinate system
    NULL,  --- No data in SDO_POINT attribute
    SDO_ELEM_INFO_ARRAY(
          1,   -- Offset of composite element
          1006,  --- Etype for composite surface element
          2,  -- Number of composing Polygons
            1,  -- Offset for ordinates in SDO_ORDINATE_ARRAY
            1003,   -- Etype for Exterior (outer) ring of FIRST polygon
            3,   --  Polygon is an axis-aligned rectangle
              7,  -- Offset for ordinates in SDO_ORDINATE_ARRAY
              2003,   -- Etype for Interior (inner) ring of FIRST polygon
              3,   --  Polygon is an axis-aligned rectangle
                13,  -- Offset for second exterior polygon
                1003,  -- Etype for  exterior Ring of SECOND  polygon
                3   --  Polygon is an axis-aligned rectangle
                                                 ),
    SDO_ORDINATES_ARRAY
    (
      2, 0,2, -- min-corner for exterior ring of first polygon,
       4,2,2,  -- max-corner for exterior ring of first polygon
           3,     1,     2, -- min-corner for interior ring of first polygon
           3.5,  1.5, 2,   -- max-corner for interior ring of first polygon
              2,0, 2,    -- min-corner for second element  rectangle
              4,0,4    -- max-corner for second element rectangle
    )
  )
);
```

Note that a surface geometry only has an area but never a volume. This is true even if the surface is closed, as shown in Figure 4-26. The composite surface consists of the six sides of the cube (note that the faces are not shown in gray). Listing 4-37 shows the SQL for such a surface geometry.

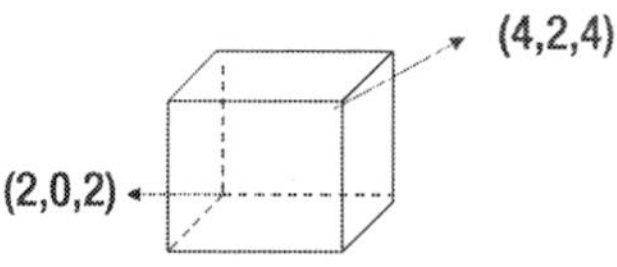

Figure 4-26. *Example of a closed composite surface*

Listing 4-37. *SQL for Composite Surface in Figure 4-26*

```
SQL> INSERT INTO geometry_examples (name, description, geom) VALUES
(
  '3-D Composite Surface2',
  '3-dimensional Composite with 6 rectangle polygons  ',
  SDO_GEOMETRY
  (
```

```
    3003,     -- SDO_GTYPE format: DOOT. Set to 3003 for a 3-dimensional Surface
    NULL,     -- No coordinate system
    NULL,  --- No data in SDO_POINT attribute
    SDO_ELEM_INFO_ARRAY(
         1,   -- Offset of composite element
         1006,  --- Etype for composite surface element
         6,  -- Number of composing polygons; element triplets for each follow
           1, 1003,3 --Axis-aligned Rectangle element descriptor
           7,  1003,3, --Axis-aligned Rectangle element descriptor
           13,1003,3 , --Axis-aligned Rectangle element descriptor
           19, 1003,3, -- Axis-aligned Rectangle element descriptor
           25,  1003,3, --Axis-aligned Rectangle element descriptor
           31,1003,3  --Axis-aligned Rectangle element descriptor
                                            ),
    SDO_ORDINATES_ARRAY
    (
      2, 0,2,  4,2,2,     -- min-, max- corners for  Back face,
      2,0,4,   4,2,4,     -- min-, max- corners for  Front face,
      4,0,2,   4,2,4 ,    -- min-, max- corners for  Right side face,
      2.0.2,   2,2,4,     -- min-, max- corners for  Left side face,
      4,0,4,   2,0,2,     -- min-, max- corners for  Bottom face,
      4,2,4,   2,2,2      -- min-, max- corners for  Top face
    )
  )
);
```

Caution The composing elements of a composite surface element can only be polygonal surface elements (i.e., cannot be composite surfaces themselves). Together, the composing polygonal elements should define a single contiguous area.

Caution A surface-type geometry (that is, SDO_GTYPE=3003) can have at most only one composite surface as the exterior (that is, ETYPE=1006). You cannot have any inner composite surfaces (that is, ETYPE=2006). The individual polygon elements in the surface, however, can have both exterior (ETYPE=1003) and inner (ETYPE=2003) rings.

To associate a volume with the object of Figure 4-26, you need to denote it as a solid. How do you make the surface geometry in Figure 4-26 a solid? You need to specify additional information in the SDO_ELEM_INFO attribute as described next.

Simple Solid

A *simple solid* has one exterior composite surface and zero or more inner composite surfaces. A simple solid element is denoted by the ETYPE of 1007. A simple solid is described using the following sequence of descriptor triplets in the SDO_ELEM_INFO attribute:

- A header triplet for the solid element with an ETYPE of 1007
- A header triplet for exterior composite surface (with an ETYPE of 1006)
- Element descriptor triplets for each composing element of exterior surface
- Zero or more occurrences of the following:
    - Header triplet for an inner composite surface (with Etype=2006)
    - Element descriptor triplets for each composing element of the inner surface

---

Caution For all solids, simple or composite (described in the next section), the following two restrictions hold in Oracle: First, the surface normal for each polygon in the solid specification should always point outside from the solid. The surface normal is implicitly derived from the order of the vertex specification using the "right-hand thumb" rule as illustrated in Figure 4-24. Second, the polygons in the composite surfaces (of a solid) cannot have any inner rings; that is, polygons cannot be like the polygon in the XY plane in Figure 4-25 (b) that has an inner ring.

Consider the simple solids in Figure 4-27. Both of them are bounded by one exterior composite surface. The solid in Figure 4-27 (b) has an additional interior surface to represent the hole.

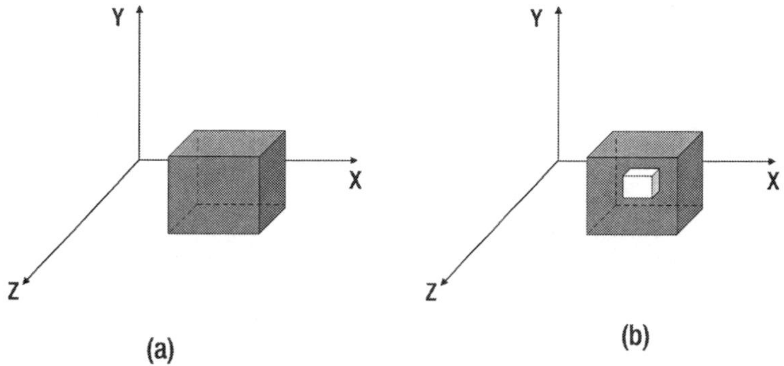

Figure 4-27. *Examples of (a) simple solid and (b) a simple solid with a hole inside*

You can construct the SQL for the simple solid of Figure 4-27 (a), as shown in Listing 4-38. The changes from Listing 4-39 are in bold. Observe that the only differences compared to Listing 4-27 are the addition of the solid element triplet <1, 1007, 1>, the rearranging of the vertices orders for the rectangles so that their surface normals point outside from the solid, and the changing the SDO_GTYPE to 3008.

Listing 4-38. *SQL for Simple Solid in Figure 4-27 (a)*

```
SQL> INSERT INTO geometry_examples (name, description, geom) VALUES
(
  '3-D Simple Solid',
  '3-dimensional Solid with 6 rectangle polygons as its boundary  ',
  SDO_GEOMETRY
  (
    3008,     -- SDO_GTYPE format: DOOT. Set to 3008 for a 3-dimensional Solid
    NULL,     -- No coordinate system
    NULL,   --- No data in SDO_POINT attribute
    SDO_ELEM_INFO_ARRAY(
       1,    -- Offset of a Simple solid element
       1007,   --- Etype for a Simple solid
       1,  -- Indicates all surfaces are specified explicitly
         1,    -- Offset of composite element
         1006,  --- Etype for composite surface element
          6,  -- Number of composing elements;
               -- element triplets for each element follow
          1, 1003,3, --Axis-aligned Rectangle element descriptor
          7,  1003,3, --Axis-aligned Rectangle element descriptor
```

```
        13, 1003,3 , --Axis-aligned Rectangle element descriptor
        19, 1003,3, -- Axis-aligned Rectangle element descriptor
        25,  1003,3, -Axis-aligned Rectangle element descriptor
        31, 1003,3  --Axis-aligned Rectangle element descriptor
        ),
    SDO_ORDINATES_ARRAY
    (
      4,2,2,    2,0,2, -- max-, min- corners for  Back face (normal: -ve Z-axis)
      2,0,4,    4,2,4, -- min-, max- corners for  Front face (normal:  +ve Z axis)
      4,0,2,    4,2,4, -- min-, max- corners for  Right face (normal: +ve X axis)
      2,2,4,    2,0,2, -- min-, max- corners for  Left  face (normal: -ve X axis)
      4,0,4,    2,0,2, -- max-, min-  for  Bottom face (normal:  -ve  Y axis)
      2,2,2,    4,2,4  -- min-, max- corners for  Top face (normal: +ve Y axis)
    )
  )
);
```

Caution The polygons (in the composite surface) of a simple solid cannot have inner rings.

Since the solid in Figure 4-27 (a) is aligned with the X-, Y-, Z-axes, you can simplify the SQL by specifying it as a solid box with a specific etype of 3 and using only the min-corner (the minimum ordinate values in x-, y-, z-dimensions) and the max-corner (the maximum ordinate value in x-, y-, z-dimensions). Listing 4-39 shows the SQL, using a box element and only two corners for the solid.

Listing 4-39. *SQL for Simple Solid in Figure 4-27 (a)*

```
SQL> INSERT INTO geometry_examples (name, description, geom) VALUES
(
  '3-D Simple Solid as a Solid Box',
  '3-dimensional Solid with just the 2 corner vertices   ',
  SDO_GEOMETRY
  (
    3008,     -- SDO_GTYPE format: DOOT. Set to 3008 for a 3-dimensional Solid
    NULL,     -- No coordinate system
    NULL,  --- No data in SDO_POINT attribute
    SDO_ELEM_INFO_ARRAY(
       1,  -- Offset of a Simple solid element
       1007,  --- Etype for a Simple solid
       3  --  Solid Box type: only two corner vertices are specified
       ),
    SDO_ORDINATES_ARRAY
    (
      2,0,2,     4,2,4     -- min-corner and max-corner  for the solid
    )
  )
);
```

The solid object in Figure 4-27 (a) could represent a typical building in a city-modeling application. What if you want to model the open atrium inside the building? Let's say this open atrium is completely inside the building (does not touch any walls, ceiling, or ground) and by opening it, or *voiding* it, you do not want it to be modeled as part of the building geometry (you might model it as a separate structure). You can create the void in the building model by modeling this "open atrium" as an inner composite surface as shown in Figure 4-27 (b). Note that you have to represent the polygons of the inner composite surface such that their normals point outward from the entire solid.

(For determining the surface normal for a polygon, please refer to Figure 4-24 and to Table 4-5 if the polygon happens to be a rectangle.) The corresponding SQL is shown in Listing 4-40[11]; changes from Listing 4-38 are in bold.

Listing 4-40. *Simple Solid with an Inner Hole as in Figure 4-27 (b)*

```
SQL> INSERT INTO geometry_examples (name, description, geom) VALUES
(
  '3-D Simple Solid with inner hole',
  '3-dimensional Solid with 6 rectangle polygons as its boundary  ',
  SDO_GEOMETRY
  (
    3008,     -- SDO_GTYPE format: DOOT. Set to 3008 for a 3-dimensional Solid
    NULL,     -- No coordinate system
    NULL,  --- No data in SDO_POINT attribute
    SDO_ELEM_INFO_ARRAY(
      1,   -- Offset of a Simple solid element
      1007,  --- Etype for a Simple solid
      1,  -- Indicates all surfaces are specified explicitly
      1,   -- Offset of composite element
      1006,  --- Etype for composite surface element
       6,  -- # of composing elements; element triplets for each element follow
        1,1003,3, --Axis-aligned Rectangle element descriptor
         7,  1003,3,--Axis-aligned Rectangle element descriptor
         13,1003,3 , --Axis-aligned Rectangle element descriptor
         19, 1003,3, -- Axis-aligned Rectangle element descriptor
         25,  1003,3, --Axis-aligned Rectangle element descriptor
         31,1003,3,  --Axis-aligned Rectangle element descriptor
       37, 2006, 6,  -- Inner composite surface
          37, 2003,3, --  Axis-aligned Rectangle element ; note etype is 2003
          43,  2003,3, --Axis-aligned Rectangle element descriptor
          49,  2003,3 , --Axis-aligned Rectangle element descriptor
          55,  2003,3, -- Axis-aligned Rectangle element descriptor
          61,  2003,3, --Axis-aligned Rectangle element descriptor
          67,  2003,3  --Axis-aligned Rectangle element descriptor
                                                    ),
    SDO_ORDINATE_ARRAY
    (
     --- All polygons oriented such that normals point outward from solid
     ---
      ------- Ordinates for the rectangles of the outer composite surface
      4,2,2,   2,0,2, -- Back face
      2,0,4,   4,2,4, -- Front face
      4,0,2,   4,2,4, -- Right face
      2,2,4,   2,0,2, -- Left face
      4,0,4,   2,0,2, -- Bottom face
      2,2,2,   4,2,4, -- Top face
       ---
       ------- Ordinates for the rectangles of inner/hole composite surface
       --------      representing the atrium
        2.5, 0.5, 2.5,   3.5, 1.5, 2.5, -- Back face
        3.5, 1.5, 3.5,   2.5, 0.5, 3.5, -- Front face
```

11. If you validate this geometry using functions discussed in Chapter 5, Oracle incorrectly raises an error. This behavior is reported and resolved as bug 6357707.

```
          3.5, 1.5, 3.5,    3.5, 0.5, 2.5, -- Right face
          2.5, 0.5, 2.5,    2.5, 1.5, 3.5, -- Left face
          2.5, 0.5, 2.5,    3.5, 0.5, 3.5, -- Bottom face
          3.5, 1.5, 3.5,    2.5, 1.5, 2.5  -- Top face

    )
  )
);
```

■ **Note** An inner composite surface of a solid cannot *topologically overlap* with an outer composite surface of the same solid.

Note that the atrium, that is, the interior solid, is modeled as the inner surface of the outer solid. There is a notable exception to this modeling. If the inner solid touches the boundary of the outer solid as in Figure 4-28, then it can no longer be modeled as an inner surface (the `sdo_geom.validate_geometry` described in Chapter 5 will return an error on such a geometry). Instead, you can model it as a simple solid with just the exterior surfaces. Figure 4-28 shows the example. Observe that you can represent the side faces as a single polygon.

For the top face (likewise the bottom one too) that has a hole in it, Oracle does not allow you to represent them as a polygon with an inner ring. So, you need to break it into the two polygon rings ABCDEF and AGEDHB, as shown in Figure 4-28. Listing 4-41 shows the example SQL.

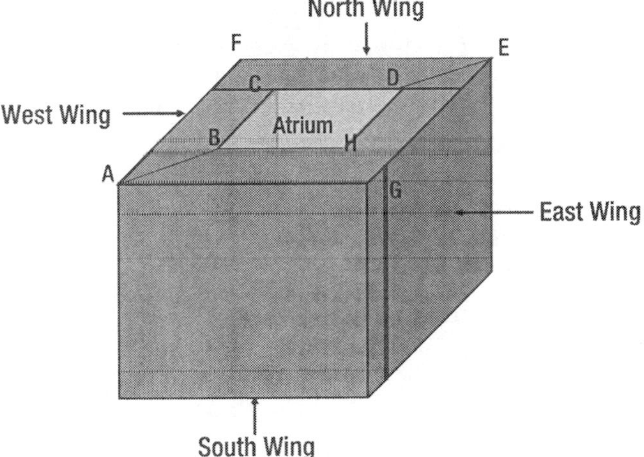

Figure 4-28. *Examples of a solid with the hole where the hole cannot be modeled as an inner surface (due to topological overlap of inner and outer composite surfaces)*

Listing 4-41. *Simple Solid with an Inner Hole That Touches Both Top and Bottom Faces*

```
SQL> INSERT INTO geometry_examples (name, description, geom) VALUES
(
  '3-D Simple Solid with inner hole touching top/bottom faces',
  '3-dimensional Solid with 8 rectangle polygons as its boundary  ',
  SDO_GEOMETRY
  (
```

```
    3008,    -- SDO_GTYPE format: DOOT. Set to 3008 for a 3-dimensional Solid
    NULL,    -- No coordinate system
    NULL,  --- No data in SDO_POINT attribute
    SDO_ELEM_INFO_ARRAY(
      1,   -- Offset of a Simple solid element
      1007,--- Etype for a Simple solid
      1,   -- Indicates all surfaces are specified explicitly
        1, -- Offset of composite element
        1006,  --- Etype for composite surface element
        8, -- # of composing elements; element triplets for each element follow
         1, 1003,3, --Axis-aligned Rectangle element descriptor  for left face
         7, 1003,3, --Axis-aligned Rectangle element descriptor for right face
         13,1003,3, --Axis-aligned Rectangle element descriptor  for back face
         19,1003,3, -- Axis-aligned Rectangle element descriptor for front face
         25,1003,1, -- Element descriptor for  ABCDEFA  on Top Face
         46,1003,1, -- Element descriptor for  AGEDHBA on Top Face
         67,1003,1, -- Element descriptor for equivalent ABCDEFA  on Bottom Face
         88,1003,1  -- Element descriptor for equivalent AGEDHBA on Bottom Face
          ),
    SDO_ORDINATE_ARRAY
    (
      -- Outer side walls
      4,2,2,   2,0,2,         -- Back face
      2,0,4,   4,2,4,         -- Front face
      4,0,2,   4,2,4,         -- Right side face
      2,2,4,   2,0,2,         -- Left side face
      --
      -- Inner side walls
      2.5,0,2.5,  3.5,2,2.5, -- Back Face
      3.5,2,3.5,  2.5,0,3.5, -- Front Face
      2.5,0,2.5,  2.5,2,3.5, -- Left Face
      3.5,2,3.5,  3.5,0,3.5, -- Right Face
      --
      -- Coordinates for  vertices A,B,C,D,E,F,A  on top face
      2,2,4, 2.5,2,3.5, 2.5,2,2.5, 3.5,2,2.5, 4,2,2, 2,2,2, 2,2,4,
      -- Coordinates for vertices A,G,E,D,H,B,A on top face
      2,2,4, 4,2,4, 4,2,2, 3.5,2,2.5, 3.5,2,3.5, 2.5,2,3.5, 2,2,4,
      -- Coordinates for polygon equivalent to ABCDEFA on bottom face
      2,0,4, 2,0,2, 4,0,2, 3.5,0,2.5, 2.5,0,2.5, 2.5,0,3.5, 2,0,4,
      -- Coordinates for polygon equivalent to AGEDHBA on bottom face
      2,0,4, 2.5,0,3.5, 3.5,0,3.5, 3.5,2,2.5, 4,0,2, 4,0,4, 2,0,4
    )
  )
);
```

Composite Solid

An alternate representation for the object in Figure 4-28 is a composite solid composed of four different simple solids, one each for the north wing, the south wing, the east wing, and the west wing, as shown in Figure 4-29. You can denote the solid element as a composite element by specifying the `ETYPE` as 1008. `SDO_ELEM_INFO` for this element will have a header triplet of the form `<offset, ETYPE=1008, N>` where `N` is the number of components. This triplet is followed by the triplets for the composing simple solid elements. Listing 4-42 shows the SQL for the solid object in Figure 4-29. Note that we use the solid box representation (just the two corner vertices) for each of the simple solids constituting the composite solid.

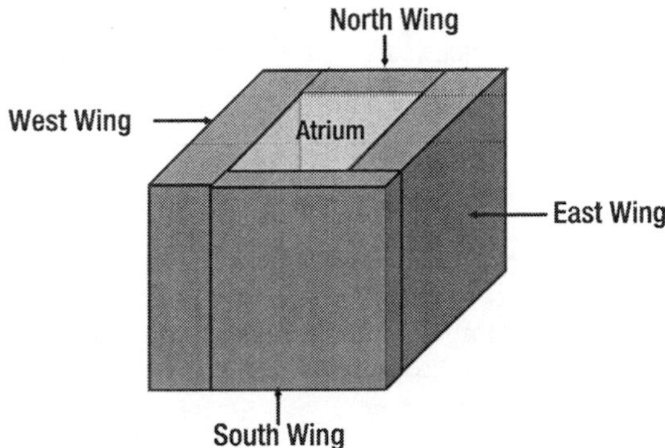

Figure 4-29. *Modeling the simple solid of Figure 4-28 as a composite solid*

Listing 4-42. *Example SQL for Composite Solid of Figure 4-29*

```
SQL> INSERT INTO geometry_examples (name, description, geom) VALUES
(
  '3-D Composite Solid of 4 simple solids',
  '3-dimensional composite solid  ',
  SDO_GEOMETRY
  (
    3008,     -- SDO_GTYPE format: DOOT. Set to 3008 for a 3-dimensional Solid
    NULL,     -- No coordinate system
    NULL,  --- No data in SDO_POINT attribute
    SDO_ELEM_INFO_ARRAY(
      1,   -- Offset of the composite solid element
      1008,  --- Etype for a composite solid
      4,  --Number of cimple solids making up the composite.
          --The simple solid descriptors next.
        1,   1007, 3,  -- Simple solid as a solid Box
        7,   1007, 3,  -- Simple solid as a solid box
        13, 1007, 3,  -- Simple solid as a solid box
        19, 1007, 3   -- Simple solid as a solid box
    ),
    SDO_ORDINATE_ARRAY
    (
      -- min-corner and max-corner  for the  West wing
      2,0,2,  2.5,2,4,
      -- min-corner and max-corner for the East wing,
      3.5, 0,2,  4,2,3.5,
      -- min-corner and max-corner for the North wing,
      2.5,0,2,  3.5,2,2.5,
      -- min-corner and max-corner for the South wing,
      2.5,0,3.5,  4,2,4
    )
  )
);
```

Note Every composite solid can also be represented as a simple solid. The composite solid type is provided only for natural and easier modeling of solids such as those in Figure 4-29.

Caution The composing elements of a composite solid element should be solid elements and should define a contiguous volume.

Collections

In the previous example, the south wing is attached to the west, the west wing to the north, the north to east, and so on. Because of the connected nature of these components, they are modeled as a composite solid. But what if the different parts of the building are not connected to each other as in Figure 4-30? You can model the components as a multisolid. Listing 4-43 shows the corresponding SQL for constructing this object.

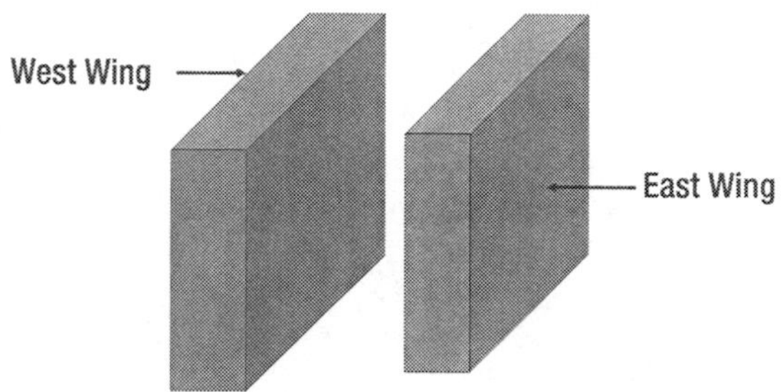

Figure 4-30. *Modeling different disjoint parts of a building as a multisolid*

Listing 4-43. *Example SQL for Multisolid of Figure 4-30*

```
SQL> INSERT INTO geometry_examples (name, description, geom) VALUES
(
  '3-D Multi Solid',
  '3-dimensional Multisolid with 2 solid boxes  ',
  SDO_GEOMETRY
  (
    3009,     -- SDO_GTYPE format: DOOT. Set to 3009 for a 3-dimensional MultiSolid
    NULL,     -- No coordinate system
    NULL,  --- No data in SDO_POINT attribute
    SDO_ELEM_INFO_ARRAY(
      1,   -- Offset of a simple solid element
      1007,  --- Etype for a simple solid
      3,  --  Solid box type: only two corner vertices are specified
      7, 1007, 3 - Solid Box for second solid),
    SDO_ORDINATES_ARRAY
    (
      -- min-corner and max-corner  for  first solid
      0,0,0,  4,4,4,
      --
      -- min-corner and max-corner for second solid.
       5,0,0,  9,4,4
    )
  )
);
```

Until now, we have described how to create buildings as solid and multisolid geometries. As shown in Figure 4-31, the windows and doors, however, are surface-type geometries that need to be associated with a building. How do you store the solid structure of the building along with the associated windows and doors as a single entity? The answer is to model it as a (heterogeneous) collection geometry. One element of this collection can be the composite solid representing the different wings of the building, and the other elements can be surfaces representing the windows.

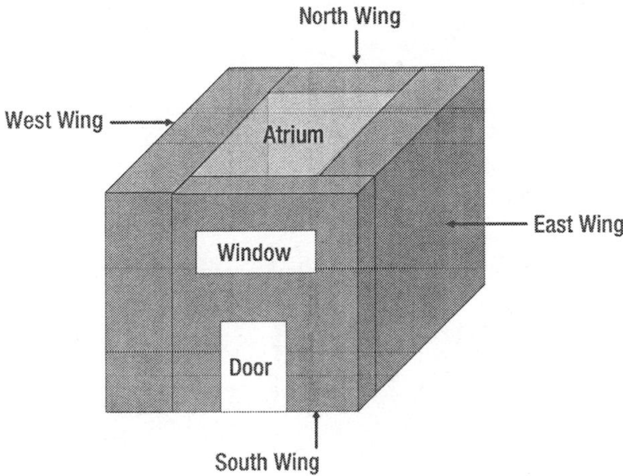

Figure 4-31. *Modeling the entire building (with windows, doors) as a (heterogeneous) collection*

Listing 4-44 shows the SQL for the building in Figure 4-31. You can observe that SDO_GTYPE is set to 3004 (heterogeneous collection). Elements of the collection are specified one after the other. First the composite solid element (along with its constituting solid elements) is specified. Then the window is specified as a polygon element, followed by the door as another polygon element.

Listing 4-44. *Example SQL for Buildings Modeled As a Collection*

```
SQL> INSERT INTO geometry_examples (name, description, geom) VALUES
(
  '3-D Building as a Collection',
  '3-dimensional collection as combination of a composite solid and 2 surfaces',
  SDO_GEOMETRY
  (
    3004,    -- SDO_GTYPE format: DOOT. Set to 3004 for a 3-dimensional Collection
    NULL,    -- No coordinate system
    NULL,  --- No data in SDO_POINT attribute
    SDO_ELEM_INFO_ARRAY(
      1, 1008,  4, --- Descriptor for a composite solid of 4 simple solids
         1, 1007, 3, --Simple solid as a solid Box
         7, 1007, 3,  -- Simple solid as a solid box
         13, 1007, 3,  -- Simple solid as a solid box
         19, 1007, 3,  -- Simple solid as a solid box,
         25, 1003, 3,  -- Descriptor for Door as a polygon
         31, 1003, 3 -- Descriptor for  Window as a polygon
    ),
```

```
    SDO_ORDINATE_ARRAY
    (
      -- min-corner and max-corner  for the  West wing
      2,0,2,  2.5,2,4,
      --
      -- min-corner and max-corner for the East wing,
      3.5, 0,2,  4,2,3.5,
      --
      -- min-corner and max-corner for the North wing,
      2.5,0,2,  3.5,2,2.5,
      --
      -- min-corner and max-corner for the South wing,
      2.5,0,3.5,  4,2,4,
      --
      -- min-corner and max-corner for the door,
      2.75, 0, 4,  3.25, 1, 4,
      --
      -- min-corner and max-corner for the window,
       2.5, 2, 4,   3.5, 3, 4
    )
  )
);
```

Summary

This chapter demonstrated that the SDO_GEOMETRY data type is a powerful structure in Oracle. You can use this data type to store point, line, polygon, surface, and solid geometries, as well as homogenous and heterogeneous collections of such geometries. The SDO_GTYPE attribute of SDO_GEOMETRY specifies the type (shape), and the SDO_ELEM_INFO and SDO_ORDINATES attributes together specify the ordinate information and connectivity for the shape object. The SDO_POINT attribute stores the location for two- or three-dimensional points. In short, you can store as an SDO_GEOMETRY any of the various two-dimensional types mentioned in OGC Simple Features Specification[12] or a major subset of the three-dimensional types (excluding parametric curves and surfaces) mentioned in the OGC GML 2.0 and 3.0 specifications.

In addition to the geometric structure, you can associate spatial referencing using appropriate coordinate systems with SDO_GEOMETRY objects. If the coordinate systems are based on the EPSG model, you can define your own transformation paths between different coordinate systems.

In your applications, you can utilize the SDO_GEOMETRY data type to model locations of customers, delivery sites, and competitors as two-dimensional points. You can model locations and the shapes of streets and highways as line strings, and you can model the shapes of city boundaries as polygons. For city-modeling or asset management applications, you can store not only the location but the exact structure of buildings as three-dimensional solids or collections using SDO_GEOMETRY type columns.

Having covered how to construct SDO_GEOMETRY objects for different types of spatial data, in the next chapter we will explain how to insert and load such objects into an Oracle table.

12. The native SDO_GEOMETRY type conforms to the OGC Simple Feature Specification. The ST_GEOMETRY type that is also supported in Oracle is compliant with the OGC Simple Feature Specification Object Model.

CHAPTER 5

Loading, Transporting, and Validating Spatial Data

To run the examples in this chapter, you need to import a dataset as shown in the following spatial schema. Please refer to the introduction for instructions on creating the spatial schema and other setup details.

```
imp spatial/spatial FILE=app_with_loc.dmp FULL=Y INDEXES=N
imp spatial/spatial FILE=city.dmp FULL=Y INDEXES=N
```

In the previous chapter, we introduced a new data type called SDO_GEOMETRY to store spatial data. This data type can store a variety of spatial objects: points (including those obtained by geocoding address strings), line strings, polygons, or more complex shapes. Points primarily represent the locations of application-specific entities such as businesses, customers, or suppliers. Line strings and polygons, on the other hand, represent the boundaries of geographical entities such as roads, cities, or states. In CAD/CAM-type applications, line strings and polygons can represent different entities such as the layouts of buildings, printed circuit boards, or shapes of different parts of an automobile.

In Chapter 3, we described how to add SDO_GEOMETRY columns to existing (application-specific) tables such as customers. We also described how to create tables with SDO_GEOMETRY columns to store geographic data such as states, counties, and interstates. These tables could be part of an e-business application or a variety of other spatial applications such as CAD/CAM, GIS, GPS, wireless, or telematics.

In this chapter, we work with our example business application, the tables for which we created in Chapter 3, and we move on to describe how to populate these tables with data and how to ensure that the data are valid and free of bugs. Specifically, we cover the following topics:

- *Inserting into a table with SDO_GEOMETRY columns.* We cover how to insert a single geometry into a table with SDO_GEOMETRY. This may not be the right approach to populate the application-specific and geographic tables because inserting geometries one by one may be time-consuming and error-prone. A better approach is to bulk load the data.
- *Loading and converting spatial data to and from Oracle databases.* We describe how to use Oracle utilities to bulk load spatial data into Oracle tables from operating system files or Oracle Import/Export (.dmp) files. We also describe a utility to convert third-party formats such as Environmental Systems Research Institute's (ESRI's) shapefiles to SQL*Loader files and load the resulting files into Oracle.

- *Validating spatial data.* We describe functions available to check whether the loaded spatial data are in a valid Oracle Spatial format.
- *Debugging spatial data.* We explain how to identify and correct any invalid spatial data in a table.

The functions that we describe in this chapter are part of two packages: SDO_GEOM and SDO_UTIL. The SDO_GEOM functions that we use in this chapter are part of the Locator product (shipped for free with Oracle Database Server). The SDO_UTIL package and the associated functions, however, are included only in the priced option of Spatial.

Inserting Data into an SDO_GEOMETRY Column

Let's create a table to model the sales regions of a business franchise. Listing 5-1 shows the SQL.

Listing 5-1. *Creating the* sales_regions *Table*

```
SQL> CREATE TABLE sales_regions
(
  id        NUMBER,
  geom      SDO_GEOMETRY
);
```

You can insert polygons representing sales regions into the geom column of this table. Listing 5-2 shows an example.

Listing 5-2. *Inserting a Polygon Geometry into the* sales_regions *Table*

```
SQL> INSERT INTO  sales_regions  VALUES
(
  10000,   -- SALES_REGIONS ID
  SDO_GEOMETRY  --  use  the SDO_GEOMETRY constructor
  (
    2003,  -- A two-dimensional Polygon
    8307,  -- SRID is GEODETIC
    NULL,  -- SDO_POINT_TYPE is null as it is not a point
    SDO_ELEM_INFO_ARRAY (1, 1003,  1),  -- A polygon with just one ring
    SDO_ORDINATE_ARRAY  -- SDO_ORDINATES field
    (
      -77.04487, 38.9043742,   -- coordinates of first vertex
      -77.046645, 38.9040983, -- other vertices
      -77.04815, 38.9033127, -77.049155, 38.9021368,
      -77.049508, 38.9007499, -77.049155, 38.899363, -77.048149, 38.8981873,
      -77.046645, 38.8974017, -77.04487, 38.8971258, -77.043095, 38.8974017,
      -77.041591, 38.8981873, -77.040585, 38.899363, -77.040232, 38.9007499,
      -77.040585, 38.9021368, -77.04159, 38.9033127, -77.043095, 38.9040983,
      -77.04487, 38.9043742    -- coordinates of last vertex same as first vertex
    )
  )
);
```

Note that the second argument is the SDO_GEOMETRY constructor presented in the previous chapter. You can insert any type of geometry into this column, be it a point, a line, a polygon, and so on. In this example, the geometry is a two-dimensional polygon geometry. The vertices of this polygon are stored in the SDO_ORDINATES attribute instantiated using the SDO_ORDINATE_ARRAY type. In Chapter 4, we noted that for a polygon the first and last vertex coordinates should be same. Accordingly, in Listing 5-2, the coordinates for the first and last vertices (shown in the first and the last lines of the SDO_ORDINATE_ARRAY object) are identical.

Caution INSERT statements with an SDO_GEOMETRY constructor cannot take more than 1,000 numbers in the SDO_ORDINATES array. One alternative is to create an SDO_GEOMETRY object in PL/SQL and bind this object in the INSERT statement (refer to Chapter 14 for details).

Populating tables by inserting the data rows one by one (as in Listing 5-2) is very time-consuming. In this chapter, we discuss how to load the data in bulk and how to check that the populated data are in the required Oracle Spatial format.

Loading and Converting Spatial Data

Spatial data can be loaded from different formats, including text files, Oracle export formats, or third-party proprietary formats. In the following sections, we describe each of these formats in sequence.

Loading from Text Files Using SQL*Loader

SQL*Loader is an Oracle utility to load data from files into Oracle tables. This utility performs *bulk loading*—that is, it can load more than one row into a table in one attempt.

Tip Always drop any associated spatial indexes before bulk loading into a table. Otherwise, spatial indexes may slow down the loading process.

SQL*Loader takes a control file that specifies how to break the file data into Oracle rows and how to separate these records into individual columns. We do not discuss all the details of SQL*Loader here. Instead, we highlight the object-specific issues that come into play when loading SDO_GEOMETRY columns.

Loading Point Data

First, let's look at how to insert data into the sales_regions table. Say the sales regions are point data. You can directly insert the regions into the x,y components of the geom column (SDO_GEOMETRY object) as described in the control file in Listing 5-3.

Listing 5-3. *Control File for Loading "Point"* sales_regions *Data*

```
LOAD DATA
INFILE *
INTO TABLE sales_regions
APPEND
FIELDS TERMINATED BY '|'
TRAILING NULLCOLS
(
  id NULLIF ID = BLANKS,
  geom COLUMN OBJECT
  (
```

```
    SDO_GTYPE       INTEGER EXTERNAL,
    SDO_POINT       COLUMN OBJECT
    (
      X             FLOAT EXTERNAL,
      Y             FLOAT EXTERNAL
    )
  )
)
BEGINDATA
1|2001|-76.99022|38.888654|
2|2001|-77.41575|38.924753|
```

Notice that there is no need to specify the SDO_SRID, the SDO_ELEM_INFO_ARRAY, and the SDO_ORDINATE_ARRAY components. These are automatically set to NULL. The control file in Listing 5-3 has two records, one with an ID of 1 and another with an ID of 2. Both records have the x,y components specified as the last two fields. Just as in other SQL*Loader control files, the fields in each record are terminated by the pipe symbol (because we specified fields terminated by |). We will use this "control" file to load the sales_regions data as shown in Listing 5-4. A log of the operation that records which rows are loaded and which are rejected is available in sales_regions.log.

Listing 5-4. *Using SQL*Loader to Load Data into the* sales_regions *Table*

```
SQLLDR spatial/spatial CONTROL=sales_regions.ctl
```

Note that the format for the data is specified in the initial part of the control file. The data are specified in the same control file right after the BEGINDATA keyword. Instead of specifying the data in the control file, you can store the data in a separate file, say sales_regions.dat. You can then specify the data file at the command line, as shown in Listing 5-5.

Listing 5-5. *Using SQL*Loader with a Data File*

```
SQLLDR spatial/spatial CONTROL=sales_regions.ctl DATA=sales_regions.dat
```

Alternatively, you can specify the data file name in the control file (and load the data, as in Listing 5-5). In the control file, you have to modify INFILE * to INFILE sales_regions.dat. The modified control file is shown in Listing 5-6, and the corresponding data file is shown in Listing 5-7. You can run the SQL*Loader command as in Listing 5-4 to load the data.

Listing 5-6. sales_regions.ctl *File*

```
LOAD DATA
INFILE  sales_regions.dat
INTO TABLE sales_regions
APPEND
FIELDS TERMINATED BY '|'
TRAILING NULLCOLS
(
  id NULLIF ID = BLANKS,
  geom COLUMN OBJECT
  (
    SDO_GTYPE       INTEGER EXTERNAL,
    SDO_POINT       COLUMN OBJECT
    (
      X             FLOAT EXTERNAL,
      Y             FLOAT EXTERNAL
```

```
      )
    )
)
```

Listing 5-7. `sales_regions.dat` *File*

```
1|2001|-76.99022|38.888654|
2|2001|-77.41575|38.924753|
```

Loading Nonpoint Data

What if the data you want to load contains nonpoint data? In that case, you need to populate the `SDO_ELEM_INFO` and `SDO_ORDINATES` fields of the `SDO_GEOMETRY` column. The control file in Listing 5-8 shows an example of how to do this for the `sales_regions` table, where most of the `sales_regions` are nonpoint geometries.

Listing 5-8. *Control File for Loading Nonpoint* `SDO_GEOMETRY` *Data*

```
LOAD DATA
INFILE *
CONTINUEIF NEXT(1:1)='#'
INTO TABLE sales_regions
APPEND
FIELDS TERMINATED BY '|'
TRAILING NULLCOLS
(
  id CHAR(6),
  geom COLUMN OBJECT
  (
    SDO_GTYPE INTEGER EXTERNAL,
    SDO_SRID INTEGER EXTERNAL,
    SDO_ELEM_INFO VARRAY terminated by '/'   (E FLOAT EXTERNAL),
    SDO_ORDINATES VARRAY terminated by '/' (O FLOAT EXTERNAL)
  )
)
BEGINDATA
 10000| 2003| 8307|
#1| 1003| 1|/
#-77.04487| 38.9043742| -77.046645| 38.9040983| -77.04815| 38.9033127|-77.049155|
#38.9021368| -77.049508| 38.9007499| -77.049155| 38.899363| -77.048149|
#38.8981873| -77.046645| 38.8974017| -77.04487| 38.8971258| -77.043095|
#38.8974017| -77.041591| 38.8981873| -77.040585| 38.899363| -77.040232|
#38.9007499| -77.040585| 38.9021368| -77.04159| 38.9033127| -77.043095|
#38.9040983| -77.04487| 38.9043742| -77.04487| 38.9043742|/
```

Note that SQL*Loader cannot process records that are more than 64KB in size if the data are included in the control file (as in Listing 5-3). (If the data are in a separate data file, the default limit for a record is 1MB, which can be increased up to 20MB by overriding the default using the `READSIZE` parameter.) To work around this restriction, the record is split into multiple lines. The line `CONTINUEIF NEXT(1:1)='#'` specifies that the record is continued if a hash mark (#) is the first character of each line. Note that the `SDO_ORDINATES` field could contain up to 1 million numbers. This means SQL*Loader will need to concatenate multiple records of a size less than 64KB to create one `SDO_ORDINATE_ARRAY` containing up to 1 million numbers.

■ **Caution** In direct path mode for SQL*Loader, spatial indexes that are associated with the tables being loaded are not maintained. You need to rebuild or drop and re-create such spatial indexes (see Chapter 8 for details on rebuilding/re-creating spatial indexes).

Transporting Spatial Data Between Oracle Databases

In the following sections, we discuss how to exchange spatial data between different Oracle databases. Oracle provides a variety of ways to perform such exchanges. These include the Import/Export utilities and the transportable tablespace mechanisms. In addition, Oracle Spatial provides a mechanism to migrate some of the pre-10*g* spatial formats to current formats using the `SDO_MIGRATE` function.

Import/Export Utilities

The easiest method to load data is through the use of Oracle's platform-independent `.dmp` files. These files are used by Oracle's Import/Export utilities. For instance, you can export the `customers` table from the `spatial` schema as shown in Listing 5-9.

Listing 5-9. *Exporting the* `customers` *Table into the* `customers.dmp` *File*

```
EXP spatial/spatial FILE=customers.dmp TABLES=customers
```

You can later import this data (that is, the `.dmp` file) into another schema, say the `scott` schema, using Oracle's Import utility. Listing 5-10 shows an example.

Listing 5-10. *Importing the* `customers` *Table into the* `scott` *Schema*

```
IMP scott/tiger  FILE=customers.dmp  IGNORE=Y INDEXES=N TABLES=CUSTOMERS
```

`ignore=y` ignores any warnings if objects already exist in the schema. If you do not specify any command-line arguments, the Import utility will prompt you to specify the import file name and the tables you want to import. You can then choose only a subset of the tables in `sample_data.dmp` to be imported.

Note that if the `location` column in the `customers` table had a spatial index before it was exported, then after the import, the spatial index will be automatically created on this table. The user `scott` in Listing 5-10 does not have to do anything specific in this instance to create the index. In addition, the spatial index will also populate the spatial metadata for the corresponding spatial layer (that is, the `location` column in the `customers` table) in the `USER_SDO_GEOM_METADATA` view. It uses the metadata from the exported database.

You can also import data into the `scott` schema using the `fromuser` and `touser` command-line arguments. The import command is run as a system account (`system/manager`). Listing 5-11 shows an example.

Listing 5-11. *Importing Using the* `fromuser` *and* `touser` *Arguments*

```
IMP SYSTEM/MANAGER FROMUSER=spatial TOUSER=scott FILE=customers.dmp
```

If the `customers` table has a spatial index, this will be re-created on import (as in Listing 5-10). Note that to re-create the index when you import with the `touser` argument, `scott` needs to have the `CREATE TABLE` and `CREATE SEQUENCE` privileges. You can use the following SQL to grant these privileges to `scott`:

```
SQL> CONNECT SYSTEM/MANAGER
SQL> GRANT create table to SCOTT;
SQL> GRANT create sequence to SCOTT;
```

You want to import just the table data without any indexes. You can then import the data by specifying indexes=n on the command line.

The Oracle Data Pump component provides alternate and more efficient mechanisms for transferring data between databases. It provides the EXPDP and IMPDP utilities, which are equivalent to the Export (EXP) and Import (IMP) utilities of Oracle.

Transportable Tablespaces

An alternate mechanism to transfer data between different Oracle databases is the use of transportable tablespaces. In this case, you can transport an entire tablespace (along with its contents) between two Oracle databases (10*g* or higher). For instance, if the customers table is part of a tablespace, TBS, then you can transport this tablespace. To ensure that any spatial indexes existing on the customers table are also transported, you need to perform the following steps:

1. Execute SDO_UTIL.PREPARE_FOR_TTS('TBS') before transporting the tablespace TBS.
2. Execute SDO_UTIL.INITIALIZE_INDEXES_FOR_TTS after transporting the tablespace TBS.

Listing 5-12 shows how to create the .dmp file for transporting the tablespace TBS from a source database.

Listing 5-12. *Transporting the Tablespace TBS from a Source Database*

```
SQLPLUS spatial/spatial
EXECUTE SDO_UTIL.PREPARE_FOR_TTS('TBS');
CONNECT SYSTEM/MANAGER AS SYSDBA
EXECUTE DBMS_TTS.TRANSPORT_SET_CHECK('TBS', TRUE);
ALTER TABLESPACE TBS READ ONLY;
EXIT;

EXP USERID = "'SYS/<password>'"  TRANSPORT_TABLESPACE=Y TABLESPACES=TBS
FILE=trans_ts.dmp
```

This will create the tablespace metadata in the file trans_ts.dmp. Copy this file and sdo_tts.dbf (the data file for the tablespace) to the target database system. You should create the spatial schema into which this data needs to be populated and then import the contents of trans_ts.dmp as shown in Listing 5-13.

Listing 5-13. *Creating the Transported Tablespace in the Target Database*

```
<copy the file to new system with user spatial created>
IMP USERID = "'SYS/<password>'"  TRANSPORT_TABLESPACE=Y FILE=trans_ts.dmp
DATAFILES='sdo_tts.dbf' TABLESPACES=tbs
```

This will create the tablespace and populate the contents in the target database. Note that the tablespace should not already exist in the target database. This restricts the import operation to being performed only once (as it creates the tablespace) in the target database.

After importing, you should alter the tablespace TBS to allow read/write operations and execute the SDO_UTIL.INITIALIZE_INDEXES_FOR_TTS procedure to enable spatial indexes. Listing 5-14 shows the corresponding SQL.

Listing 5-14. *Enabling Spatial Indexes for the Tables in the Transported Tablespace*

```
SQLPLUS SYS/<password>
ALTER TABLESPACE TBS READ WRITE;
CONNECT spatial/spatial;
EXEC SDO_UTIL.INITIALIZE_INDEXES_FOR_TTS;
```

The INITIALIZE_INDEXES_FOR_TTS function re-enables the spatial indexes that exist on the tables in the transported tablespace. *Spatial indexes, however, will work only if the endian format of the source and the target databases remains the same.* If the endian format is different, then the spatial indexes need to be rebuilt using the ALTER INDEX REBUILD command. Listing 5-15 shows an example for the customers_sidx index on the location column of the customers table. (Chapter 8 provides details on creating and rebuilding indexes.)

Listing 5-15. *Rebuilding a Spatial Index After Transporting Across Endian Platforms*

```
SQL> ALTER INDEX customers_sidx REBUILD;
```

Migrating from Prior Versions of Oracle Spatial

The SDO_GEOMETRY data type has evolved significantly over past releases of Oracle (see Chapter 2 for details), and it may continue to change in future releases. The SDO_MIGRATE package has functions, such as TO_CURRENT, to migrate spatial data from prior versions to the "current" version, whatever that is. Listing 5-16 shows an example to migrate the geometry data in the location column data of the customers table to Oracle10*g* (format). Note the third parameter specifies the commit interval as 100, which tells the database to commit after migration of every 100 rows of the customers table.

Listing 5-16. *Migrating* location *Column Data in the* customers *Table to the Current Format (10g)*

```
SQL> EXECUTE SDO_MIGRATE.TO_CURRENT('customers', 'location', 100);
```

This function has other signatures to accommodate migration of a single geometry instead of a set of geometries in a table. You can refer to the *Oracle Spatial User's Guide* for more details on this package. These migration functions work in only one direction—that is, they migrate data from older versions to the current version.

Loading from External Formats

Several GIS vendors have their own formats to store spatial data. The ESRI shapefile format is one such example. Oracle Spatial does not understand these formats. A variety of third-party converters are available to perform conversion between other formats and the Oracle Spatial format. A full discussion of these formats and the converters is beyond the scope of this book; however, to illustrate the concept, we will use the free but unsupported Oracle utility called SHP2SDO, which reads ESRI shapefiles and outputs SQL*Loader control and data files (see Listing 5-17). These files can then be used to populate the SDO_GEOMETRY column in an Oracle table.

Listing 5-17. *Using shp2sdo to Convert from ESRI Shapefiles*

```
SHP2SDO customers -g location  -x(-180,180) -y(-90,90) -s 8307 -t 0.5
```

Note that the command-line argument customers in Listing 5-17 indicates three different files as input: customers.shp, customers.shx, and customers.dbf. These three files contain different components of an ESRI shapefile named customers. The -x and -y arguments specify the extent of the data in x- and y-dimensions. The -t argument specifies the tolerance for the dimensions. The -s argument specifies the SRID (coordinate system) for the data.

The SHP2SDO utility outputs three files:

- `customers.sql`: This file creates the `customers` table and loads spatial metadata for the `customers` table (associated spatial layers). Listing 5-18 shows an example.
- `customers.ctl`: This file is the control file for SQL*Loader.
- `customers.dat`: This file contains the data for loading using SQL*Loader.

Listing 5-18. `customers.sql` *File*

```
DROPTABLE customers;
CREATE TABLE customers
(
  id                          NUMBER,
  datasrc_id                  NUMBER,
  name                        VARCHAR2(35),
  category                    VARCHAR2(30),
  street_number               VARCHAR2(5),
  street_name                 VARCHAR2(60),
  city                        VARCHAR2(32),
  postal_code                 VARCHAR2(16),
  state                       VARCHAR2(32),
  phone_number                VARCHAR2(15),
  customer_grade              VARCHAR2(15)
);
INSERT INTO USER_SDO_GEOM_METADATA VALUES
(
  'CUSTOMERS',                   -- Table_name
  'LOCATION',                    -- Column name
  MDSYS.SDO_DIM_INFO_ARRAY       -- Diminfo
  (
    MDSYS.SDO_DIM_ELEMENT('Longitude', -180, 180, 0.5), --Longitude dimension
    MDSYS.SDO_DIM_ELEMENT('Latitude', -90, 90, 0.5)     --Latitude dimension
  ),
  8307                           -- Geodetic SRID
);
```

■ **Note** See Chapter 3 for more information on different values in the SQL `INSERT` statement in Listing 5-18.

The `customers.ctl` and `customers.dat` files will be similar to those shown in Listings 5-6 and 5-7, respectively.

You can then load the data into the `customers` table in Oracle using SQL*Loader, as shown in Listing 5-19. This will create the table in Oracle and load the data into the table.

Listing 5-19. *Executing the Output Files from* SHP2SDO *to Load Data into Oracle*

```
SQLPLUS spatial/spatial @customers.sql
SQLLDR spatial/spatial CONTROL=customers.ctl
```

For more details on this utility, you can run `SHP2SDO -h`.

Converting Between SDO_GEOMETRY and WKT/WKB

SQL/MM is the ISO/IEC international standard for "Text, Spatial, Still Images, and Data Mining." SQL/MM specifies the well-known text (WKT) and the well-known binary (WKB) formats for specifying geometries (see Chapter 4 for details). You can convert these formats to an SDO_GEOMETRY (and store the data in Oracle Spatial), and vice versa. For instance, Listing 4-11 shows how to convert WKT to an SDO_GEOMETRY by taking the WKT and an SRID as parameters (you can also pass WKB and SRID as parameters in that example). Listing 5-20 shows how to do the reverse—that is, how to convert an SDO_GEOMETRY object to WKT format. This example uses the GET_WKT *method* of the SDO_GEOMETRY data type and returns the well-known text as a character large object (CLOB). Listing 5-21 shows an alternative to get the same result using the SDO_UTIL.TO_WKTGEOMETRY function.

Listing 5-20. *Converting from an* SDO_GEOMETRY *to* WKT *Format*

```
SQL> SELECT a.location.GET_WKT() wkt FROM customers a WHERE id=1;
WKT
---------------------------------
POINT (-76.9773898 38.8886508)
SQL> SELECT SDO_UTIL.TO_WKTGEOMETRY(a.location) wkt FROM customers a WHERE id=1;
WKT
---------------------------------
POINT (-76.9773898 38.8886508)
```

Listing 5-21. *Using* TO_WKTGEOMETRY *to Convert from an* SDO_GEOMETRY *to* WKT *Format*

```
SQL> SELECT SDO_UTIL.TO_WKTGEOMETRY(a.location)  wkt FROM customers a WHERE id=1;
WKT
---------------------------------
POINT (-76.9773898 38.8886508)
SQL> SELECT SDO_UTIL.TO_WKTGEOMETRY(a.location) wkt FROM customers a WHERE id=1;
WKT
---------------------------------
POINT (-76.9773898 38.8886508)
```

Analogously, the GET_WKB method of the SDO_GEOMETRY data type (or the equivalent SDO_UTIL.TO_WKBGEOMETRY function) converts an SDO_GEOMETRY object to WKB format. This method returns the result as a binary large object (BLOB).

Since WKT and WKB are standard formats for spatial data supported by many external spatial vendors, the preceding conversion methods enable the easy exchange of spatial data between Oracle Spatial (SDO_GEOMETRY) format and other external formats.

Converting SDO_GEOMETRY Data in GML

Geographic Markup Language (GML) is an XML-based encoding standard for spatial information. You can convert SDO_GEOMETRY data to/from GML format using various functions in the SDO_UTIL package. Note that the GML Specification (www.opengeospatial.org) has two major versions: GML 2.0 and GML 3.1.1. GML2.0 supports only two-dimensional data types. In contrast, GML 3.1.1 is quite rich and supports three-dimensional data types. Oracle Spatial has different functions to cater to each version of GML.

Converting to GML

To convert to GML 2.0, you can use the SDO_UTIL.TO_GMLGEOMETRY function. This function takes a single argument of type SDO_GEOMETRY and returns a GML-encoded document fragment in the form of a CLOB. This returned object contains information about the type of the geometry, the SRID, and the coordinates specified using appropriate GML tags.

Listing 5-22 shows an example of converting a customer location into a GML document fragment. The geometry information is specified between the <gml> and </gml> tags. The type is specified as a POINT, and coordinates are included between the <gml:coordinates> and </gml:coordinates> tags. Note that although we're using the point locations in the customers table for illustration, this function can work with arbitrary types of geometries (for example, polygons in the sales_regions or us_states table).

Listing 5-22. *Converting an* SDO_GEOMETRY *to a GML Document*

```
SQL> SELECT  TO_CHAR(SDO_UTIL.TO_GMLGEOMETRY(location)) gml_location
FROM customers
WHERE id=1;
GML_LOCATION
----------------
<gml:Point  srsName="SDO:8307"  xmlns:gml="http://www.opengis.net/gml">
     <gml:coordinates decimal="." cs="," ts=" ">
          -76.99022,38.888654
      </gml:coordinates>
</gml:Point>
```

To convert to GML 3.1.1, you can utilize the TO_GMLGEOMETRY311 function in the SDO_UTIL package. Note the suffix 311 to indicate the GML version. Listing 5-23 shows how to convert an axis-aligned solid box into GML311. Observe that the solid box is expanded, and all the six surfaces are represented as polygons of the exterior composite surface bounding the specified solid.

Listing 5-23. *Converting a Three-Dimensional Solid* SDO_GEOMETRY *to* GML311

```
SQL> SELECT TO_CHAR(SDO_UTIL.TO_GML311GEOMETRY(
  SDO_GEOMETRY
  (
    3008,     -- SDO_GTYPE format: DOOT. Set to 3008 for a 3-dimensional Solid
    NULL,     -- No coordinate system
    NULL,  --- No data in SDO_POINT attribute
    SDO_ELEM_INFO_ARRAY(
     1,   -- Offset of a Simple solid element
     1007,  --- Etype for a Simple solid
     3  -- Indicates an axis-aligned box
    ),
    SDO_ORDINATE_ARRAY
    (
      0,0,0,   --min-corners for box
      4,4,4    --min-corners for box
    )
  )
)) AS GML_GEOMETRY FROM DUAL;
GML_GEOMETRY
--------------------------------------------------------------------------------
<gml:Solid srsName="SDO:" xmlns:gml="http://www.opengis.net/gml">
   <gml:exterior>
      <gml:CompositeSurface>
         <gml:surfaceMember>
            <gml:Polygon><gml:exterior>
               <gml:LinearRing><gml:posList srsDimension="3">
                  0.0 0.0 0.0 0.0 4.0 0.0 4.0 4.0 0.0 4.0 0.0 0.0 0.0 0.0 0.0
```

```
            </gml:posList></gml:LinearRing></gml:exterior></gml:Polygon>
      </gml:surfaceMember>
      <gml:surfaceMember><gml:Polygon><gml:exterior><gml:LinearRing>
        <gml:posList srsDimension="3">
            4.0 4.0 4.0 0.0 4.0 4.0 0.0 0.0 4.0 4.0 0.0 4.0 4.0 4.0 4.0
        </gml:posList></gml:LinearRing></gml:exterior></gml:Polygon>
      </gml:surfaceMember>
      <gml:surfaceMember><gml:Polygon><gml:exterior><gml:LinearRing>
        <gml:posList srsDimension="3">
            0.0 0.0 0.0 4.0 0.0 0.0 4.0 0.0 4.0 0.0 0.0 4.0 0.0 0.0 0.0
          </gml:posList></gml:LinearRing></gml:exterior></gml:Polygon>
      </gml:surfaceMember>
        <gml:posList srsDimension="3">
            0.0 0.0 0.0 0.0 0.0 4.0 0.0 4.0 4.0 0.0 4.0 0.0 0.0 0.0 0.0
          </gml:posList></gml:LinearRing></gml:exterior></gml:Polygon>
      </gml:surfaceMember>
      </gml:surfaceMember>
        <gml:posList srsDimension="3">
            4.0 4.0 4.0 4.0 4.0 0.0 0.0 4.0 0.0 0.0 4.0 4.0 4.0 4.0 4.0
          </gml:posList></gml:LinearRing></gml:exterior></gml:Polygon>
      </gml:surfaceMember>
      </gml:surfaceMember>
        <gml:posList srsDimension="3">
            4.0 4.0 4.0 4.0 0.0 4.0 4.0 0.0 0.0 4.0 4.0 0.0 4.0 4.0 4.0
          </gml:posList></gml:LinearRing></gml:exterior></gml:Polygon>
      </gml:surfaceMember>
    </gml:CompositeSurface>
  </gml:exterior>
</gml:Solid>
```

Listings 5-21 and 5-22 convert each SDO_GEOMETRY to a GML geometry. You can encode multiple geometries in a GML document using the XMLFOREST function and other SQLX functions. Listing 5-24 shows an example using the XMLFOREST function. We refer interested readers to *Oracle XML Database Developer's Guide* or *Oracle XML API Reference Guide* for details on these functions.

Listing 5-24. *Converting Multiple Geometries to a GML Document Fragment*

```
SQL> SELECT xmlelement("State", xmlattributes(
    'http://www.opengis.net/gml' as "xmlns:gml"),
     xmlforest(state as "Name", totpop as "Population",
              xmltype(sdo_util.to_gmlgeometry(geom)) as
             "gml:geometryProperty"))
        AS theXMLElements
FROM spatial.us_states
WHERE state_abrv in ('DE', 'UT');
THEXMLELEMENTS
------------------------------------------
<State xmlns:gml="http://www.opengis.net/gml">
 <Name>Delaware</Name> <Population>666168</Population>
 <gml:geometryProperty><gml:Polygon srsName="SDO:8307"
 xmlns:gml="http://www.opengis.net/gml">
  <gml:outerBoundaryIs> <gml:LinearRing>
      <gml:coordinates decimal="." cs="," ts=" ">
        -75.788704,39.721699 ...
```

Converting GML to SDO_GEOMETRY

Listings 5-21 to 5-23 illustrated how to convert an SDO_GEOMETRY to GML. Now, we'll show how to perform the reverse operation: converting GML geometry fragments to SDO_GEOMETRY. You can find two functions in the SDO_UTIL package for this purpose: FROM_GMLGEOMETRY and FROM_GML311GEOMETRY. Listing 5-25 shows the SQL for converting the GML_GEOMETRY output of Listing 5-23 back to an SDO_GEOMETRY.

Listing 5-25. *Converting a GML Solid Geometry into an* SDO_GEOMETRY

```
SQL> SELECT SDO_UTIL.FROM_GML311GEOMETRY(
TO_CLOB(
'<gml:Solid srsName="SDO:" xmlns:gml="http://www.opengis.net/gml">
<gml:exterior>
  <gml:CompositeSurface>
   <gml:surfaceMember>
    <gml:Polygon>
     <gml:exterior>
      <gml:LinearRing>
       <gml:posList srsDimension="3">
        0.0 0.0 0.0 0.0 4.0 0.0 4.0 4.0 0.0 4.0 0.0 0.0 0.0 0.0 0.0
       </gml:posList>
      </gml:LinearRing>
     </gml:exterior>
    </gml:Polygon>
   </gml:surfaceMember>
   <gml:surfaceMember>
    <gml:Polygon>
     <gml:exterior>
      <gml:LinearRing>
       <gml:posList srsDimension="3">
         4.0 4.0 4.0 0.0 4.0 4.0 0.0 0.0 4.0 4.0 0.0 4.0 4.0 4.0 4.0
       </gml:posList>
      </gml:LinearRing>
     </gml:exterior>
    </gml:Polygon>
   </gml:surfaceMember>
   <gml:surfaceMember>
    <gml:Polygon>
     <gml:exterior>
      <gml:LinearRing>
       <gml:posList srsDimension="3">
        0.0 0.0 0.0 4.0 0.0 0.0 4.0 0.0 4.0 0.0 0.0 4.0 0.0 0.0 0.0
       </gml:posList>
      </gml:LinearRing>
     </gml:exterior>
    </gml:Polygon>
   </gml:surfaceMember>
   <gml:surfaceMember>
    <gml:Polygon>
     <gml:exterior>
      <gml:LinearRing>
       <gml:posList srsDimension="3">
        0.0 0.0 0.0 0.0 0.0 4.0 0.0 4.0 4.0 0.0 4.0 0.0 0.0 0.0 0.0
       </gml:posList>
       </gml:LinearRing>
      </gml:exterior>
```

```
      </gml:Polygon>
     </gml:surfaceMember>
    <gml:surfaceMember>
     <gml:Polygon>
      <gml:exterior>
       <gml:LinearRing>
        <gml:posList srsDimension="3">
         4.0 4.0 4.0 4.0 4.0 0.0 0.0 4.0 0.0 0.0 4.0 4.0 4.0 4.0 4.0
        </gml:posList>
       </gml:LinearRing>
      </gml:exterior>
     </gml:Polygon>
    </gml:surfaceMember>
    <gml:surfaceMember>
     <gml:Polygon>
      <gml:exterior>
       <gml:LinearRing>
        <gml:posList srsDimension="3">
         4.0 4.0 4.0 4.0 0.0 4.0 4.0 0.0 0.0 4.0 4.0 0.0 4.0 4.0 4.0
        </gml:posList>
       </gml:LinearRing>
      </gml:exterior>
     </gml:Polygon>
    </gml:surfaceMember>
   </gml:CompositeSurface>
  </gml:exterior>
  </gml:Solid>'
)) GEOM FROM DUAL;

GEOM(SDO_GTYPE, SDO_SRID, SDO_POINT(X, Y, Z), SDO_ELEM_INFO, SDO_ORDINATES)
--------------------------------------------------------------------------------
SDO_GEOMETRY(3008, NULL, NULL,
  SDO_ELEM_INFO_ARRAY(
       1, 1007, 1,    -- 1 Exterior Composite Surface (with explicit surfaces;
                                     not a box representation)
       1, 1006, 6,    -- Composite surface with 6 polygons
       1, 1003,1 16, 1003, 1, 31, 1003, 1, 46, 1003, 1, 61, 1003, 1, 76, 1003, 1
   ),
   SDO_ORDINATE_ARRAY(
     0, 0, 0, 0, 4, 0, 4, 4, 0, 4, 0, 0, 0, 0, 0,
     4, 4, 4, 0, 4, 4, 0, 0, 4, 4, 0, 4, 4, 4, 4,
     0, 0, 0, 4, 0, 0, 4, 0, 4, 0, 0, 4, 0, 0, 0,
     0, 0, 0, 0, 0, 4, 0, 4, 4, 0, 4, 0, 0, 0, 0,
     4, 4, 4, 4, 4, 0, 0, 4, 0, 0, 4, 4, 4, 4, 4,
     4, 4, 4, 4, 0, 4, 4, 0, 0, 4, 4, 0, 4, 4, 4
   )
 )
```

Note that although we started off in Listing 5-23 with a simple axis-aligned box solid format, what we got in Listing 5-25 from the GML fragment is the explicit representation of the solid by its six faces. This will be the behavior always: when a three-dimensional geometry is output as a result of a function in Oracle, it will be output in the full representation using all the components (no axis-aligned rectangles and no solid boxes will be used in the output).

For three-dimensional city models, the CityGML specification[1] describes an explicit set of entities to model the buildings, parks, vegetation, city furniture (lamp posts, and so on), and other architectural elements. Oracle provides a simple conversion tool for storing CityGML documents in the demo directory (`$ORACLE_HOME/md/demo/CityGML/examples`). You can compile and run the `CGMLToSDO` Java class to scan an input `CityGML.gml` file and store the geometry components as `SDO_GEOMETRY` columns in the database.

Extruding a Two-Dimensional Geometry to Three Dimensions

Many applications store the two-dimensional footprints of buildings and other three-dimensional objects. You can use the `EXTRUDE` function in the `SDO_UTIL` package to erect a building on the two-dimensional footprint. What you need to do is specify the ground height and the top height for each vertex of the two-dimensional geometry. Figure 5-1 shows an example of a two-dimensional geometry and how it looks when each vertex is extruded along the z-dimension by specifying a ground height of –1 and top height of 1.

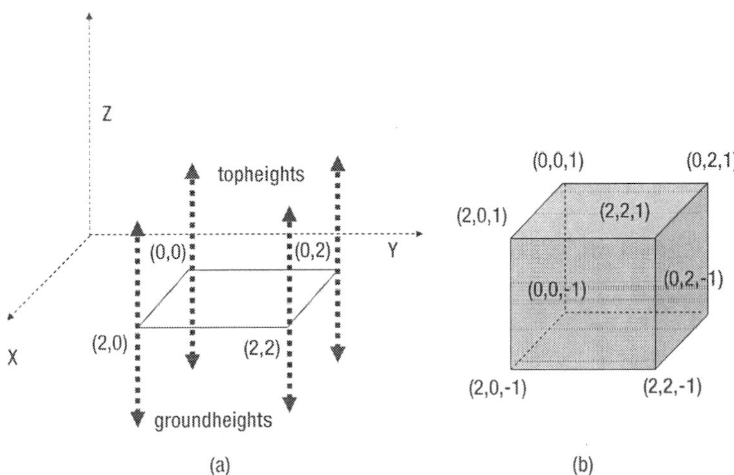

Figure 5-1. *(a) Example of a two-dimensional solid with the top heights and ground heights specified, and (b) the extruded solid*

The `EXTRUDE` function has the signature shown in Listing 5-26.

Listing 5-26. *Signature of the* `EXTRUDE` *Function*

```
SDO_UTIL.EXTRUDE
(
  geometry                          IN SDO_GEOMETRY,
  groundheights                     IN SDO_NUMBER_ARRAY,
  topheights                        IN SDO_NUMBER_ARRAY,
```

---

1. `www.citygml.org`. The specification is still under review by the Open Geospatial Consortium (OGC). It could be accepted as a standard for city models in the future.

```
  result_to_be_validated           IN VARCHAR2
  tolerance                        IN NUMBER
) RETURN SDO_GEOMETRY
```

The arguments are as follows:

- `geometry`: This specifies the input two-dimensional `SDO_GEOMETRY` object that needs to be extruded.
- `groundheights`: This is an array of numbers, one each for each vertex for use as the ground height (minimum z value). If only one number is specified, then all vertices get the same value (that is specified here).
- `topheights`: This is an array of numbers, one each for each vertex for use as the top height (minimum z value). If only one number is specified, then all vertices get the same value (that is specified here).
- `result_to_be_validated`: This is a character string that can be set to either `'TRUE'` or `'FALSE'`. This string informs Oracle whether to validate the resulting geometry.
- `tolerance`: This specifies the tolerance to use to validate the geometry (see Chapter 3 for details on tolerance).

A simple example is to specify a ground height and a top height for all the vertices. Listing 5-27 shows an example of how to extrude the two-dimensional polygon of Figure 5-1 (a) by specifying the ground height as –1 and top height as 1. You can observe that the solid returned corresponds to the one in Figure 5-1 (b).

Listing 5-27. *Extruding a Polygon to a Three-Dimensional Solid*

```
SELECT SDO_UTIL.EXTRUDE(
  SDO_GEOMETRY      -- first argument to validate is geometry
  (
    2003,           -- 2-D Polygon
    NULL,
    NULL,
    SDO_ELEM_INFO_ARRAY(1, 1003, 1   -- A polygon element
                       ),
    SDO_ORDINATE_ARRAY (0,0, 2,0, 2,2, 0,2, 0,0)  -- vertices of polygon
  ),
  SDO_NUMBER_ARRAY(-1),  -- Just 1 ground height value applied to all vertices
  SDO_NUMBER_ARRAY(1),   -- Just 1 top height value applied to all vertices
  'FALSE',               -- No need to validate
  0.5                    -- Tolerance value
) EXTRUDED_GEOM FROM DUAL;

EXTRUDED_GEOM(SDO_GTYPE, SDO_SRID, SDO_POINT(X, Y, Z), SDO_ELEM_INFO, SDO_ORDINA
--------------------------------------------------------------------------------
SDO_GEOMETRY(
  3008,    -- 3-Dimensional Solid  Type
  NULL, NULL,
 SDO_ELEM_INFO_ARRAY(
    1, 1007, 1,   -- Solid Element
    1, 1006, 6,   -- 1 Outer Composite Surface made up of 6 polygons
    1, 1003, 1,   -- First polygon element starts at offset 1 in SDO_ORDINATES array
    16, 1003, 1,  -- second polygon element starts at offset 16
    31, 1003, 1,  -- third polygon element starts at offset 31
    46, 1003, 1,  -- fourth polygon element starts at offset 46
```

```
    61, 1003, 1,  -- fifth polygon element starts at offset 61
    76, 1003, 1),  -- sixth polygon element starts at offset 76
  SDO_ORDINATE_ARRAY(  -- ordinates storing the vertices of the polygons
      0, 0, -1, 0, 2, -1, 2, 2, -1, 2, 0, -1, 0, 0, -1,
      0, 0, 1, 2, 0, 1, 2, 2, 1, 0, 2, 1, 0, 0, 1, 0, 0,
       -1, 2, 0, -1, 2, 0, 1, 0, 0, 1, 0, 0, -1, 2, 0,
      -1, 2, 2, -1, 2, 2, 1, 2, 0, 1, 2, 0, -1, 2, 2,
       -1, 0, 2, -1, 0, 2, 1, 2, 2, 1,2, 2, -1, 0, 2,
       -1, 0, 0, -1, 0, 0, 1, 0, 2, 1, 0, 2, -1))
```

The SQL script in Listing 5-28 uses the `SDO_UTIL.EXTRUDE` function to populate the `GEOM` column of the `buildings` table. As shown in the listing, you use the footprints in the `building_footprints` table and appropriate `groundheight` and `topheight` values for different groups of buildings. You can utilize this `city_buildings` data for indexing and analysis in Chapters 8 and 9.

Listing 5-28. *Script for Extruding Three-Dimensional Buildings from Their Footprints*

```
-- For buildings  4,5,9,13,16,17,  set topheight to 500
insert into city_buildings select id, type,
sdo_util.extrude(footprint,
                 SDO_NUMBER_ARRAY(0),
                 SDO_NUMBER_ARRAY(500),
                 'TRUE', 0.05) from building_footprints
where id in (4,5, 9, 13, 16, 17);

-- For buildings  3,10,15,  set topheight to 400


insert into city_buildings select id, type,
sdo_util.extrude(footprint,
                 SDO_NUMBER_ARRAY(0),
                 SDO_NUMBER_ARRAY(400),
                 'TRUE', 0.05) from building_footprints
where id in (3, 10, 15);

-- For buildings  14,  set topheight to 900

insert into city_buildings select id, type,
sdo_util.extrude(footprint,
                 SDO_NUMBER_ARRAY(0),
                 SDO_NUMBER_ARRAY(900),
                 'TRUE', 0.05) from building_footprints
where id=14  ;

-- For buildings  6,7,8,11,12,  set topheight to 650

insert into city_buildings select id, type,
sdo_util.extrude(footprint,
                 SDO_NUMBER_ARRAY(0),
                 SDO_NUMBER_ARRAY(650),
                 'TRUE', 0.05) from building_footprints
where id in (6, 7,  8, 11, 12)  ;

-- For rest of  buildings   set topheight to 600
```

```
insert into city_buildings select id, type,
sdo_util.extrude(footprint,
                 SDO_NUMBER_ARRAY(0),
                 SDO_NUMBER_ARRAY(600),
                 'TRUE', 0.05) from building_footprints
where id in (17, 18, 19) ;

-- Update the srid to 7407 and commit

update city_buildings a set a.geom.sdo_srid=7407;
commit;
```

Validating Spatial Data

Since the beginning of this chapter, you have seen numerous ways to populate the SDO_GEOMETRY columns in Oracle tables. Once the SDO_GEOMETRY data are in Oracle tables, you need to check whether they are in valid Spatial format. Otherwise, you may get wrong results, errors, or failures when performing spatial queries (discussed in Chapters 8 and 9).[2]

Validation Functions

Oracle Spatial provides two validation functions: VALIDATE_GEOMETRY_WITH_CONTEXT, which operates on a single geometry, and VALIDATE_LAYER_WITH_CONTEXT, which operates on a table of geometries. Both functions operate on two-dimensional as well as three-dimensional data and return an error string if the input geometry is invalid. These validation functions (and also the debugging functions described in next section) utilize a user-specified numeric value called tolerance to determine whether a geometry is valid. In Chapter 3, we described the significance of this parameter and how to set it. As explained there, this tolerance parameter is also stored in the DIMINFO column of the USER_SDO_GEOM_METADATA view. We'll cover the signature of these functions next.

VALIDATE_GEOMETRY_WITH_CONTEXT

This function is part of the SDO_GEOM package. It checks that a single specified geometry is in valid (Oracle Spatial) format. It has the two signatures, as shown in Listing 5-29, both of which return a VARCHAR2 string.

Listing 5-29. *Signatures of the* VALIDATE_GEOMETRY_WITH_CONTEXT *Function*

```
SDO_GEOM.VALIDATE_GEOMETRY_WITH_CONTEXT
(
  geometry          IN SDO_GEOMETRY,
  tolerance         IN NUMBER
) RETURN VARCHAR2;

SDO_GEOM.VALIDATE_GEOMETRY_WITH_CONTEXT
(
  geometry          IN SDO_GEOMETRY,
  diminfo           IN SDO_DIM_ARRAY
) RETURN VARCHAR2;
```

2. Oracle does not perform a full validation in spatial queries (Chapters 8 and 9) as such validation substantially increases the execution time for spatial queries.

The arguments are as follows:

- geometry: This specifies the input SDO_GEOMETRY object that needs to be validated.
- tolerance: This specifies the tolerance to use to validate the geometry (see Chapter 3 for details on tolerance).
- diminfo: This specifies dimension (bounds) information and tolerance information.

The function returns the string 'TRUE' if the geometry is valid. If it is invalid, it returns the Oracle error number if it is known; otherwise, it returns 'FALSE'.

VALIDATE_LAYER_WITH_CONTEXT

Instead of validating geometries one by one, you can validate the geometries in an entire table using the VALIDATE_LAYER_WITH_CONTEXT procedure. This procedure is also part of the SDO_GEOM package and has the signature in Listing 5-30.

Listing 5-30. *Signature of the* VALIDATE_LAYER_WITH_CONTEXT *Procedure*

```
SDO_GEOM.VALIDATE_LAYER_WITH_CONTEXT
(
  table_name       IN VARCHAR2,
  column_name      IN VARCHAR2,
  result_table     IN VARCHAR2
  [,
  commit_interval  IN NUMBER
  ]
)
```

The arguments are as follows:

- table_name and column_name: These specify the names of the table and column storing the SDO_GEOMETRY data.
- result_table: This specifies the table where the validation results, specifically the ROWIDs of invalid geometries, will be stored. This table should have been created with the following fields prior to the execution of this function. The SDO_ROWID field stores the ROWID, and STATUS stores either a specific validation error or the string 'FALSE' (to indicate that the row is invalid).

  ```
  SDO_ROWID     ROWID
  STATUS        VARCHAR2(2000)
  ```

- commit_interval: This optional argument specifies the frequency at which the updates to the results table are to be committed. If this argument is set to 100, then the validation results are committed to result_table after validating every 100 geometries.

Validation Criteria

How does Oracle determine whether a geometry is valid or invalid? First, Oracle looks at the SDO_GTYPE of the geometry for validation. For various elements in a geometry, the SDO_ETYPE is used as a guide. From the class diagram in Figure 4-2, recall that an SDO_GEOMETRY can store a wide variety of geometry types—points, line strings, rings, surfaces (polygons and composite surfaces), and solids (simple and composite). Next, we'll go over the different validation rules for each of these types based on the topology of the geometry with some specific examples.

Point

Note that the second signature to the VALIDATE_GEOMETRY_WITH_CONTEXT function specifies diminfo instead of tolerance as a second parameter. This signature/usage has an advantage: in addition to basic validation, the function checks whether all the coordinates are within the bounds specified in the diminfo attribute. This is the only validation rule for a point geometry. Consider the point geometry with longitude=-80 and latitude=20. If the diminfo is set to (0, 50) for both dimensions, then the point will be invalid, as shown in Listing 5-31. The SQL returns the ORA-13011 error. This error implies that the longitude value of –80 is out of range (0 to 50) for that dimension.

Listing 5-31. *Using the* diminfo *Parameter in the* VALIDATE_GEOMETRY_WITH_CONTEXT *Function*

```
SQL> SELECT SDO_GEOM.VALIDATE_GEOMETRY_WITH_CONTEXT
(
  SDO_GEOMETRY      -- first argument to validate is geometry
  (
    2001,           -- point type
    NULL,
    SDO_POINT_TYPE(-80,20,NULL), -- point is <-80,20> and is out of range.
    NULL,
    NULL
  ),
  SDO_DIM_ARRAY     -- second argument is diminfo (of type SDO_DIM_ARRAY)
  (

    SDO_DIM_ELEMENT('X', 0, 50, 0.5),  -- lower, upper bound range is 0 to 50
    SDO_DIM_ELEMENT('Y', 0, 50, 0.5)   -- lower, upper bound range is 0 to 50
  )
) is_valid FROM DUAL;
IS_VALID
--------------------------------------------------------------------------------
13011 -- Coordinate value out of dimension range
```

If you don't specify the SDO_DIM_ARRAY argument as second parameter and specify just the tolerance, the previous point will be returned as "valid." Listing 5-32 shows the corresponding SQL.

Listing 5-32. *Using the* tolerance *Parameter in the* VALIDATE_GEOMETRY_WITH_CONTEXT *Function*

```
SQL> SELECT SDO_GEOM.VALIDATE_GEOMETRY_WITH_CONTEXT
(
  SDO_GEOMETRY      -- first argument to validate is geometry
  (
    2001,           -- point type
    NULL,
    SDO_POINT_TYPE(-80,20,NULL), --point not out of range as no range specified
    NULL,
    NULL
  ),
  0.5
) is_valid FROM DUAL;

IS_VALID
--------------------------------------------------------------------------------
TRUE
```

Line String

A line string should satisfy the following validation rules. Listing 5-33 shows the result of validating a line string with duplicate points:

- All points in the line are distinct.
- A line should have two or more points.

Listing 5-33. *Validating a Line String with Duplicate Points*

```
SQL> SELECT SDO_GEOM.VALIDATE_GEOMETRY_WITH_CONTEXT
(
  SDO_GEOMETRY     -- first argument to validate is geometry
  (
    2002,          -- Line String type
    NULL,
    NULL,
    SDO_ELEM_INFO_ARRAY(1,2,1), -- Line String
    SDO_ORDINATE_ARRAY (
       1,1,     -- first vertex
       2,2,     -- second vertex
       2,2      -- third vertex: same as second
   )
  ),
  0.5              -- second argument: tolerance
) is_valid FROM DUAL;
  2   3   4   5   6   7   8   9  10  11  12
IS_VALID
--------------------------------------------------------------------------------
13356 [Element <1>] [Coordinate <2>]
```

The return string `'13356'` corresponds to ORA-13356 (adjacent points in a geometry are redundant). The return string also indicates which element has the error and the vertex (coordinate) that has this error. In this case, the error is on the second vertex (or coordinate).

Polygons

Polygons define a contiguous area bounded by one outer ring on the exterior and by zero or more inner rings on the interior. A ring is a planar closed line string. Polygons have the following characteristics:

- *Validity of rings:* The rings in a polygon are valid. This means each satisfies the following rules:
    - *Closedness:* The first and last vertices of the ring are identical.
    - *Planarity:* All vertices of the ring are on the same plane (within a *planarity-tolerance* error).
    - *Nonintersection of edges:* If edge e_i connects vertices $<V_i, V_{i+1}>$ and edge e_j connects $<V_j, V_{j+1}>$, then e_i and e_j have the following properties:
        - If (j=i+1 mod n), where n is the number of distinct vertices, then e_i and e_j touch only at vertex V_j.
        - Otherwise, e_i and e_j do not intersect.

- *Linestring:* The ring is a valid line string (that is, adjacent vertices V_i, V_{i+1} should not represent the same point in space. V_i, V_{i+1} are considered to duplicates of the same point if the distance between V_i, and V_{i+1} is less than a *tolerance* error).
- *Co-planarity of rings:* Since the polygon defines an area in a plane, all rings are on the same plane (within the specified tolerance).
- *Proper orientation:* The inner rings (if any) must have the opposite orientation compared to the outer ring.
- *Single contiguous area:* Together the outer ring and the interior rings define a single area. This means the inner rings cannot partition the polygon into disjoint areas.
- *Nonoverlapping rings:* No two rings can overlap (tolerance) with each other, but the rings can touch at a point (without violating the single contiguous area condition).
- *Inner-outer disjointedness:* Every inner ring must be inside the outer ring and can touch (tolerance) at only a single point (under the single contiguous area condition).
- For two-dimensional polygons, the outer ring should be specified in a counterclockwise manner, and inner rings should be specified in a clockwise manner. For three-dimensional polygons, there is no such restriction.

Figure 5-2 shows examples of invalid polygons. Listing 5-34 illustrates what happens when the geometry in Figure 5-2 (a) is validated.

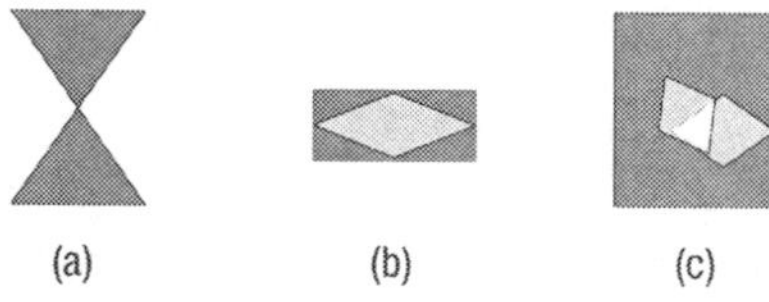

Figure 5-2. *Invalid polygons: invalid due to (a) edges of the ring of the polygon cross each other, (b) inner-outer ring intersect more than at one point, and (c) inner rings overlap*

Listing 5-34. *Validation on a Self-Crossing Geometry in Figure 5-2 (a)*

```
SQL> SELECT SDO_GEOM.VALIDATE_GEOMETRY_WITH_CONTEXT
(
  SDO_GEOMETRY
  (
    2003,         -- 2-D Polygon
    NULL,
    NULL,
    SDO_ELEM_INFO_ARRAY
    (
      1, 1003,1  -- Polygonal ring connected by lines
    ),
   SDO_ORDINATE_ARRAY
    (
      2,2,        -- first vertex
      3,3.5,      -- second vertex. Edge 1 is between previous and this vertex.
      2,5,
```

```
            5,5,
            3,3.5,      -- fifth vertex. Edge 4 is between previous and this vertex.
            5,2,
            2,2
        )
        ),
        0.000005
)
FROM dual;

SDO_GEOM.VALIDATE_GEOMETRY_WITH_CONTEXT(MDSYS.SDO_GEOMETRY(200
3,NULL,NULL,MDSYS.
--------------------------------------------------------------------------------
13349 [Element <1>] [Ring <1>][Edge <1>][Edge <4>]
```

The result indicates that element 1 is invalid. For this element, edge 1 connecting (2, 2) with (3, 3.5) and edge 4 connecting (5, 5) and (3, 3.5) are self-crossing (in other words, the polygon boundary crosses itself).

Composite Surfaces

A composite surface defines a single contiguous area formed by 1 or more adjacent planar polygons. The validation rules are defined as follows:

- *Validity of polygons*: Each of the polygons has to be a valid polygon.
- *Nonoverlapping but edge-sharing nature*: Any two polygons P_i and P_j should not overlap. In other words, if P_i and P_j are in the same plane, the area of intersection of the two polygons has to be zero. However, two polygons may touch (tolerance) in a (part of a) line/edge.
- *Contiguous area*: Every polygon in the composite should be reachable from any other polygon by appropriate tracing of the shared (parts of) edges.

Figure 5-3 shows examples of invalid composite surfaces. Listing 5-35 shows the result of validating the geometry in Figure 5-3 (a).

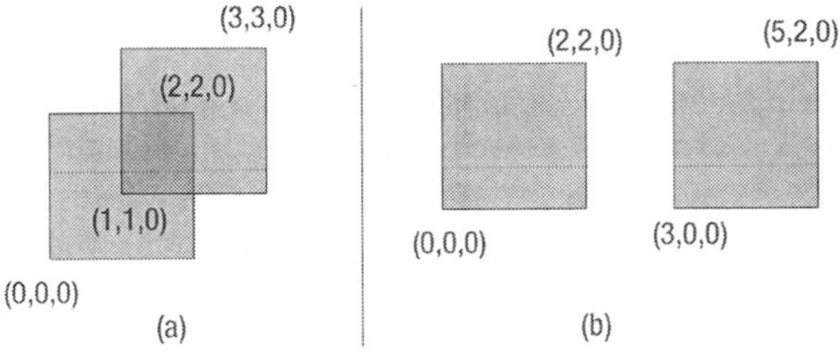

Figure 5-3. *Invalid composite surfaces: invalid due to violation of (a) nonoverlapping polygon rule and (b) single contiguous area rule*

Listing 5-35. *Validation on the Composite Surface in Figure 5-3 (a)*

```
SQL> SELECT SDO_GEOM.VALIDATE_GEOMETRY_WITH_CONTEXT
(
  SDO_GEOMETRY      -- first argument to validate is geometry
  (
    3003,           -- 3-D Polygon/Surface type
    NULL,
    NULL,
    SDO_ELEM_INFO_ARRAY(1, 1006, 2, -- Composite Surface with 2 Polygons
                        1, 1003, 1,   -- 1st polygon
                        16, 1003, 1   -- 2nd polygon
                       ),
    SDO_ORDINATE_ARRAY (
         0,0,0,  2,0,0, 2,2,0, 0,2,0,  0,0,0, -- vertices of first polygon
         1,1,0,  3,1,0, 3,3,0, 1,3,0,  1,1,0  -- vertices of second polygon
                       )
  ),
  0.5               -- second argument: tolerance
) is_valid FROM DUAL;
IS_VALID
--------------------------------------------------------------------------------
54515 Point:0,Edge:2,Ring:1,Polygon:1,
```

Observe that Oracle returns ORA-54515: "Outer rings in a composite surface intersect." It also indicates that the second edge from vertex (2,0,0) to vertex (2,2,0) from first polygon intersecting with another edge (you need to identify that edge manually).

Simple Solid

A solid in Oracle defines a single contiguous volume bounded by one composite surface on the exterior and zero or more inner composite surfaces on the interior. Based on this definition, the validation rules are as follows:

- *Single volume check*: The volume should be contiguous.
- *Closedness test*: The boundary has to be closed. This is verified by checking that every edge is traversed twice in the solid.
- *Connectedness test*: This means each component (surface, solid) of the solid should be reachable from any other component. Inner boundaries can never intersect but only touch under the condition that the solid remains connected (see the preceding bulleted item).
- *Inner-outer check*: Every surface marked as an inner boundary should be inside the solid defined by the exterior boundary.
- *Orientation check*: The polygons in the surfaces are always oriented such that the normals of the polygons point outward from the solid that they bound. The normal of a planar surface is defined by the "right thumb" rule (if the fingers of the right hand curl in the direction of the sequence of the vertices, the thumb points in the direction of the normal).
- *Validity of composite surfaces*: Every specified surface is a valid surface.
- *No inner ring in polygons*: In the composite surfaces of a solid, no inner rings are allowed.

Figure 5-4 shows a solid that is not closed (the top face on the y=4 plane is missing). Likewise, in Figure 5-5 (a), the solid has two exterior components (shown as dark boxes) and six inner components (shown in faded lines). The six inner components are attached to each of the smaller dark box and in that sense separate it from the outer solid. This solid is invalid because the volume is separated into two pieces (one each in the dark solids). By adding a small connecting solid between the two dark boxes as in Figure 5-5 (b), the solid becomes a valid solid because the two volumes are now connected.

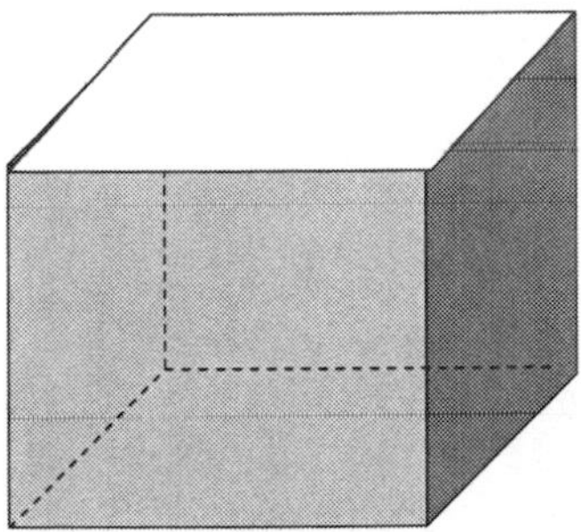

Figure 5-4. *The solid geometry is invalid because it is not closed on the top side.*

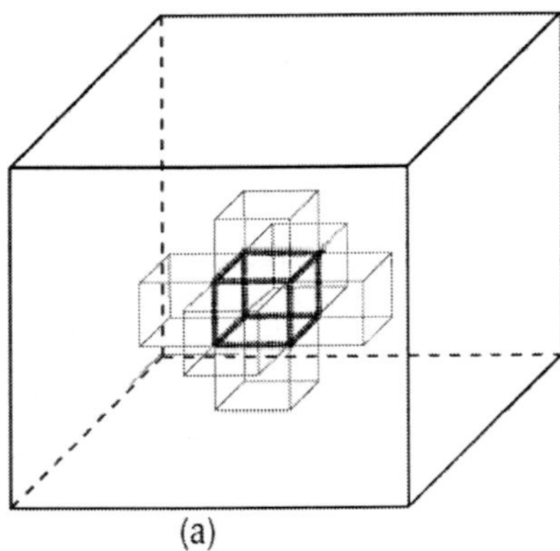

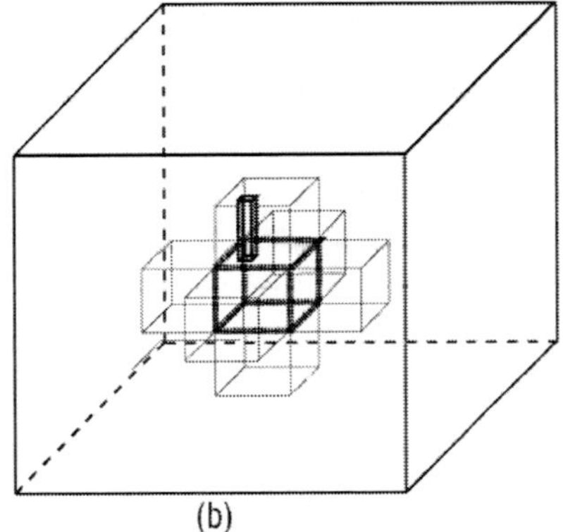

Figure 5-5. *(a) Invalid solid because the volume in the dark boxes (thick lines) is separated by the holes defined as boxes with thin lines. (b) The solid becomes valid because the volume is connected by adding a conduit between the two disjoint volumes.*

You can run validation on the solid in Figure 5-4 using the SQL in Listing 5-36. The SQL returns error ORA-542502: "Solid is not closed." It also indicates that the solid is open at the edge connecting (0,4,0) and (4,4,0). In other words, this edge is not traversed twice (once each in opposite directions in two polygons) in the solid specification.

Listing 5-36. *Validating the Simple Solid in Figure 5-4*

```
SQL> SELECT SDO_GEOM.VALIDATE_GEOMETRY_WITH_CONTEXT
(
  SDO_GEOMETRY(3008, NULL, NULL,
    SDO_ELEM_INFO_ARRAY(
       1, 1007, 1,    -- Solid element
       1, 1006, 5,    -- Composite surface with 5 polygons
       1, 1003,1, 16, 1003, 1, 31, 1003, 1, 46, 1003, 1, 61, 1003, 1
    ),
    SDO_ORDINATE_ARRAY(
      0, 0, 0, 0, 4, 0, 4, 4, 0, 4, 0, 0, 0, 0, 0,
      4, 4, 4, 0, 4, 4, 0, 0, 4, 4, 0, 4, 4, 4, 4,
      0, 0, 0, 4, 0, 0, 4, 0, 4, 0, 0, 4, 0, 0, 0,
      0, 0, 0, 0, 0, 4, 0, 4, 4, 0, 4, 0, 0, 0, 0,
      4, 4, 4, 4, 0, 4, 4, 0, 0, 4, 4, 0, 4, 4, 4
    )
  ),
  0.5
) is_valid FROM DUAL;

IS_VALID
--------------------------------------------------------------------------------
54502 Point:0,Edge:2,Ring:1,Polygon:1,Comp-Surf:1,
```

Composite Solids

A composite solid defines a single contiguous volume formed by a combination of one or more simple solids. Composite solids have the following characteristics:

- *Component validity*: Each component simple solid of a composite is valid.
- *Shared-face but no-volume intersection*: Intersection of two simple solid components of a composite solid has to be a zero volume (can be non-zero area).
- *Connectedness*: The volume of the composite is contiguous. In other words, you can go from any point in one component to any other component without going out of the composite solid.

Figure 5-6 shows examples of some invalid composite solids. Figure 5-6 (a) is invalid because the two simple solids that compose the composite solid are overlapping and their intersection has a non-zero volume. Figure 5-6 (b) is invalid because the two components are not connected (that is, the composite is not a single volume).

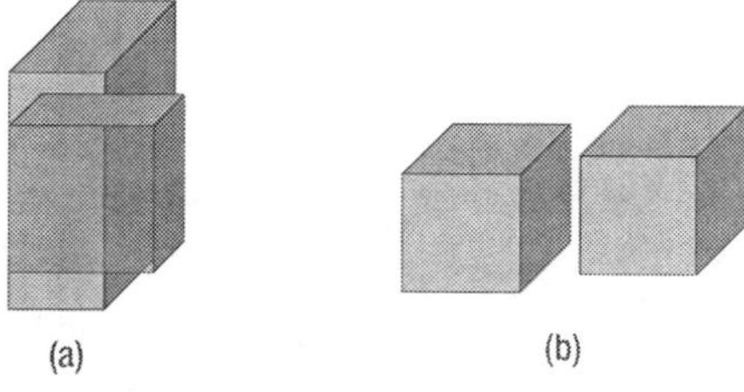

Figure 5-6. *Composite solids invalid due to (a) overlapping volume and (b) not being a single volume (violate connectedness)*

Note that composite solids are just for convenience: every composite solid can be represented by a single simple solid by removing the shared faces in the representation of the solids. Figure 5-7 shows an example.

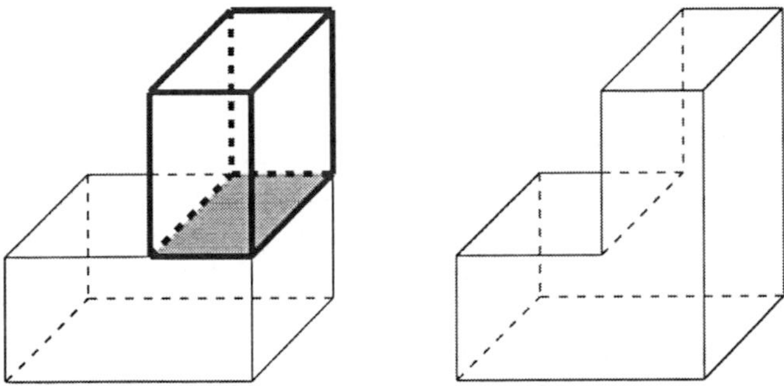

Figure 5-7. *Composite solid and an equivalent simple solid*

Collections

For collections of multiple elements, Oracle requires that all the individual elements are valid. In addition, if the collection is a homogenous collection such as multipoint, multiline string, multisurface (multipolygon), or multisolid, the elements of the collection have to be of the same conforming type.

Until now, all the examples are performing validation on a single geometry. What if you want to validate all the geometries in a table? You use the `VALIDATE_LAYER_WITH_CONTEXT` function. To illustrate the usage with an example, run this procedure on the `sales_regions` table. Listing 5-37 shows the corresponding SQL.

Listing 5-37. *Using the* `VALIDATE_LAYER_WITH_CONTEXT` *Procedure*

```
SQL> CREATE TABLE validate_results(sdo_rowid ROWID, status VARCHAR2(2000));

Table created.

SQL>
BEGIN
  SDO_GEOM.VALIDATE_LAYER_WITH_CONTEXT
  (
    'SALES_REGIONS',
    'GEOM',
    'VALIDATE_RESULTS'
  );
END;
/

SQL> SELECT * FROM validate_results;
SDO_ROWID                     STATUS
--------------------          --------------------------------------------
AAALctAADAAATRvAAA            13356 [Element <1>] [Coordinate <17>][Ring <1>]
```

Note that this returns the `ROWID` of the geometry with `ID=10000`, which is invalid. The reason is that the coordinates of vertex 17 and the subsequent one are duplicates.

Debugging Spatial Data

How do you remove the duplicate vertices? Oracle Spatial provides a number of functions to debug and clean data loaded into an SDO_GEOMETRY column. In the following sections, we describe these functions, because they will be useful in cleaning spatial data. These functions are part of the SDO_UTIL package.

REMOVE_DUPLICATE_VERTICES

This function removes duplicate vertices from an SDO_GEOMETRY object. It takes in an SDO_GEOMETRY and a tolerance value as input and returns a new SDO_GEOMETRY that does not have duplicate vertices. The SQL in Listing 5-38 shows its usage.

Listing 5-38. *Example of Removing Duplicate Vertices in a Geometry*

```
SQL> SELECT geom, SDO_UTIL.REMOVE_DUPLICATE_VERTICES(sr.geom,0.5) nodup_geom
FROM sales_regions sr
WHERE id=1000;

GEOM
------------
SDO_GEOMETRY
(
  2003, 8307, NULL, SDO_ELEM_INFO_ARRAY(1, 1003, 1),
  SDO_ORDINATE_ARRAY
  (
    -77.04487, 38.9043742, -77.046645, 38.9040983, -77.04815, 38.9033127,
    -77.049155, 38.9021368, -77.049508, 38.9007499, -77.049155, 38.899363,
    -77.048149, 38.8981873, -77.046645, 38.8974017, -77.04487, 38.8971258,
    -77.043095, 38.8974017, -77.041591, 38.8981873, -77.040585, 38.899363,
    -77.040232, 38.9007499, -77.040585, 38.9021368, -77.04159, 38.9033127,
    -77.043095, 38.9040983, -77.04487, 38.9043742, -77.04487, 38.9043742
  )
)
NODUP_GEOM
----------------------
SDO_GEOMETRY
(
  2003, 8307, NULL, SDO_ELEM_INFO_ARRAY(1, 1003, 1),
  SDO_ORDINATE_ARRAY
  (
    -77.04487, 38.9043742, -77.046645, 38.9040983, -77.04815, 38.9033127,
    -77.049155,38.9021368, -77.049508, 38.9007499, -77.049155, 38.899363,
    -77.048149, 38.8981873,-77.046645, 38.8974017, -77.04487, 38.8971258,
    -77.043095, 38.8974017, -77.041591,38.8981873, -77.040585, 38.899363,
    -77.040232, 38.9007499, -77.040585, 38.9021368, -77.04159, 38.9033127,
    -77.043095, 38.9040983, -77.04487, 38.9043742
  )
)
```

Notice that the last two vertices (look at the bold four numbers) of the original geometry are the same. After invoking the REMOVE_DUPLICATE_VERTICES function, the duplicate vertex (which is the 18th in this case) is removed (both ordinates of this vertex are removed) from the geometry. If you rerun the VALIDATE_GEOMETRY_WITH_CONTEXT function on this result geometry as shown in Listing 5-39, it returns the string 'TRUE'. Since the geometry is a polygon (sdo_gtype=2003), observe that the first point (at –77.04487, 38.9043742) and the last point (at –77.04487, 38.9043742) are the same.

Listing 5-39. *Validating After Removing the Duplicate Vertices*

```
SQL> SELECT  SDO_GEOM.VALIDATE_GEOMETRY_WITH_CONTEXT
(
  SDO_UTIL.REMOVE_DUPLICATE_VERTICES(a.geom, 0.5),
  0.5
) is_valid
FROM sales_regions a
WHERE id=10000;

IS_VALID
--------------------------------------------------------------------------------
TRUE
```

EXTRACT

This function extracts a specific element from an SDO_GEOMETRY object. It comes in handy while debugging multielement geometries such as multipolygons. This function takes as arguments an SDO_GEOMETRY, an element number, and, optionally, a ring number (within the element). It returns the extracted element as an SDO_GEOMETRY object.

Listing 5-40 shows an example of how to extract the second element of a multipolygon geometry. Note that the second argument, 2, in the EXTRACT function specifies that the second element is to be fetched. Looking at SDO_ELEM_INFO_ARRAY (1,1003,3, 5, 1003,1), you have two element descriptor triplets (1,1003,3) for the first element (specifying a rectangle polygon; see Figure 4-10 and the accompanying listing for examples) and (5, 1003,1) for the second element. This means the second element starts at ordinate 5 (that is, the third vertex). This is the element that will be extracted.

■ **Caution** The EXTRACT function described here is for use only with two-dimensional geometries. For three-dimensional geometries, there is a separate function called EXTRACT3D that we describe at the end of the section.

Listing 5-40. *Extracting the Second Element from a Geometry*

```
SQL> SELECT SDO_UTIL.EXTRACT
(
  SDO_GEOMETRY
  (
    2007,  -- multipolygon collection type geometry
    NULL,
    NULL,
    SDO_ELEM_INFO_ARRAY
    (
      1,1003,3,    -- first element descriptor triplet: for rectangle polygon
                   -- (see Figure 4-10 and the accompanying listing in Chapter 4)
      5, 1003, 1   -- second element descriptor triplet:
                   -- starting offset 5 means it starts at  the 5th ordinate
    ),
    SDO_ORDINATE_ARRAY
    (
      1,1,2,2,                        -- first element ordinates (four for mbr)
      3,3, 4, 3, 4,4, 3,4, 3,4,3,3 -- second element starting at 5th ordinate:
                                      -- this second element is returned
    )
  ),  -- End of the Geometry
```

```
  2   -- specifies the element number to extract
) second_elem
FROM dual;
SECOND_ELEM(SDO_GTYPE, SDO_SRID, SDO_POINT(X, Y, Z), SDO_ELEM_INFO,
SDO_ORDINATE
--------------------------------------------------------------------------------
SDO_GEOMETRY
(
  2003,
  NULL,
  NULL,
  SDO_ELEM_INFO_ARRAY(1, 1003, 1),
  SDO_ORDINATE_AR RAY
  (
    3, 3,     -- first vertex coordinates
    4, 3,     -- second vertex coordinates
    4, 4,     -- third vertex coordinates
    3, 4,     -- fourth vertex coordinates
    3, 4,     -- fifth vertex coordinates
    3, 3      -- sixth vertex coordinates (same as first for polygon)
  )
)
```

After extracting the appropriate element, you can perform validation on the specific element to identify what is wrong with it. Listing 5-41 shows an example.

Listing 5-41. *Validation of an Extracted Geometry*

```
SQL> SELECT  SDO_GEOM.VALIDATE_GEOMETRY_WITH_CONTEXT
(
  SDO_UTIL.EXTRACT
  (
    SDO_GEOMETRY
    (
      2007, null, null,
      SDO_ELEM_INFO_ARRAY(1,1003,3, 5, 1003, 1),
      SDO_ORDINATE_ARRAY
      (
        1,1,2,2,                        -- first element of  multipolygon geometry
        3,3, 4, 3, 4,4, 3,4, 3,4,3,3  -- second element of multipolygon geometry
      )
    ),
    2                                   -- element number to extract
  ),
  0.00005
)
FROM dual;
```

Note that the highlighted (bold) portion of the SQL in Listing 5-41 is the same as the SQL in Listing 5-40. That means Listing 5-41 is equivalent to performing the validation check on the result of Listing 5-40. Listing 5-42 shows the SQL rewritten using the result of Listing 5-40.

Listing 5-42. *Validation on the Result of* `SDO_UTIL.EXTRACT`

```
SQL> SELECT SDO_GEOM.VALIDATE_GEOMETRY_WITH_CONTEXT
(
  SDO_GEOMETRY
```

```
  (
    2003, NULL, NULL,
    SDO_ELEM_INFO_ARRAY(1, 1003, 1),
    SDO_ORDINATE_ARRAY
    (
      3, 3,      -- first vertex coordinates
      4, 3,      -- second vertex coordinates
      4, 4,      -- third vertex coordinates
      3, 4,      -- fourth vertex coordinates
      3, 4,      -- fifth vertex coordinates
      3, 3       -- sixth vertex coordinates (same as first for polygon)
    )
  ),
  0.00005        -- tolerance
) FROM dual;

SDO_GEOM.VALIDATE_GEOMETRY_WITH_CONTEXT(SDO_UTIL.EXTRACT(SDO_GE
OMETRY(2007,NULL,
--------------------------------------------------------------------------------
13356 [Element <1>] [Coordinate <4>][Ring <1>]
```

The result of 13356 <Coordinate 4> indicates a duplicate vertex at the fourth (and fifth) vertex *coordinates* of the SDO_ORDINATE_ARRAY5. The ordinate array is (3, 3, 4, 3, 4, 4, 3, 4, 3, 4, 3, 3), and the fourth and fifth vertexes (coordinates) are at (3, 4) and (3, 4), which are duplicates. You can remove this duplicate coordinate using the REMOVE_DUPLICATE_VERTICES function, as shown in Listing 5-43. This function removes the duplicate vertex from the geometry.

Listing 5-43. *Removing Duplicate Vertices*

```
SQL> SELECT SDO_UTIL.REMOVE_DUPLICATE_VERTICES
(
  SDO_UTIL.EXTRACT
  (
    SDO_GEOMETRY
    (
      2007, NULL, NULL,
      SDO_ELEM_INFO_ARRAY(1,1003,3, 5, 1003, 1),
      SDO_ORDINATE_ARRAY
      (
        1,1,2,2,
        3,3, 4, 3, 4,4, 3,4, 3,4,3,3
      )
    ),
    2
  ),
  0.00005
)
FROM  dual;

SDO_UTIL.REMOVE_DUPLICATE_VERTICES(SDO_UTIL.EXTRACT(SDO_GEOMETRY(
2007,NULL,NULL,
--------------------------------------------------------------------------------
  SDO_GEOMETRY
  (
    2003,
    NULL,
    NULL,
```

```
    SDO_ELEM_INFO_ARRAY(1, 1003, 1),
    SDO_ORDINATE_ARRAY
    (
      3, 3,     -- first vertex coordinates
      4, 3,     -- second vertex coordinates
      4, 4,     -- third vertex coordinates
      3, 4,     -- fourth vertex coordinates (duplicate (3,4) at fifth removed)
      3, 3      -- fifth vertex coordinates (same as first for polygon)
    )
  )
```

■ **Tip** You can directly run REMOVE_DUPLICATE_VERTICES on the collection geometry, and that will remove the duplicate vertex. Listing 5-41 uses SDO_UTIL.EXTRACT mainly for illustration.

APPEND

How do you recombine the new element after removing the duplicate with element 1? The SDO_UTIL.APPEND function combines multiple geometries as long as they do not intersect. This function takes two geometries and a tolerance and appends them into a single geometry. Listing 5-44 shows an example. This function first expands the first element, specified as a rectangle polygon (see Figure 4-10 in Chapter 4 for example) using the triplet <1,1003,3> in SDO_ELEM_INFO_ARRAY to five vertices for the polygon (four vertices for each corner and the first vertex repeated as the fifth vertex repeated for closure of the ring). The function then performs an append of the vertices of the first element and the second element, removing any duplicates automatically in that process.

Listing 5-44. *Example of* SDO_UTIL.APPEND

```
SQL> SELECT
SDO_UTIL.APPEND
(
  SDO_UTIL.EXTRACT
  (
    SDO_GEOMETRY
    (
      2007, NULL, NULL,
      SDO_ELEM_INFO_ARRAY(1,1003,3,    -- First element is as a rectangle polygon
                                                5, 1003, 1),
      SDO_ORDINATE_ARRAY(1,1,2,2,
      3,3, 4, 3, 4,4, 3,4, 3,4,3,3)
    ),
    1
  ),
  SDO_UTIL.REMOVE_DUPLICATE_VERTICES
  (
    SDO_GEOMETRY
    (
      2007, NULL, NULL,
      SDO_ELEM_INFO_ARRAY(1,1003,3, 5, 1003, 1),
      SDO_ORDINATE_ARRAY
      (
        1,1,2,2,
        3,3, 4, 3, 4,4, 3,4, 3,4,3,3
      )
```

```
      ),
    0.00005
    )
) combined_geom
FROM  dual;

COMBINED_GEOM(SDO_GTYPE, SDO_SRID, SDO_POINT(X, Y, Z), SDO_ELEM_INFO,
SDO_ORDINATES)
--------------------------------------------------------------------------------
SDO_GEOMETRY
(
  2007, NULL, NULL,
  SDO_ELEM_INFO_ARRAY(1, 1003, 1, 11, 1003, 1),
  SDO_ORDINATE_ARRAY
  (1, 1, 2, 1, 2, 2, 1, 2, 1, 1, 3, 3, 4, 3, 4, 4, 3, 4, 3, 3)
)
```

GETNUMELEM, GETNUMVERTICES, and GETVERTICES

These functions allow you to inspect the number of elements or vertices or get the set of vertices in an SDO_GEOMETRY object. These functions are also part of the SDO_UTIL package. The SQL in Listing 5-45 shows an example of the usage of the first two functions.

Listing 5-45. *Finding the Number of Elements in a Geometry*

```
SQL> SELECT SDO_UTIL.GETNUMELEM(geom) nelem
FROM  sales_regions
WHERE id=10000;
NELEM
----------
1
SQL> SELECT  SDO_UTIL.GETNUMVERTICES(geom) nverts
FROM sales_regions
WHERE id=10000;
NVERTS
----------
18
```

EXTRACT3D

The EXTRACT function described earlier takes an input geometry and at most two additional numeric parameters. This function works only with two-dimensional geometries. For three-dimensional geometries, you may need to specify more than two parameters to get a point or an edge, for example, of a solid geometry. For working with three-dimensional geometries, you can use the EXTRACT3D function. This function takes an input three-dimensional geometry and a LABEL string that uniquely identifies each element of the input geometry. The LABEL string is a comma-delimited string of ID numbers specifying the subset geometry to be returned, and they should be of the form PointID, EdgeId, RingID, PolygonID, CSurfId, SolidId, MultiID. You can specify values for these IDs as follows:

- PointID: ID of the point to be retrieved. Specify 0 if you do not want to retrieve a point but you want to retrieve a higher-level element such as an edge, ring, polygon, surface, solid, or multisolid.
- EdgeID: ID of the edge to be retrieved. Specify 0 if you do not want to retrieve an edge but you want to retrieve a higher-level element such as a ring, polygon, surface, solid, or multisolid.

- RingID: ID of the ring to be retrieved. Specify 0 if you do not want to retrieve a ring but you want to retrieve a higher-level element such as a polygon, surface, solid, or multisolid.
- PolygonID: ID of the polygon to be retrieved. Specify 0 if you do not want to retrieve a polygon but you want to retrieve a higher-level element such as a composite surface, solid, or multisolid.
- CSurfID: ID of the surface in a solid to be retrieved. Specify 0 otherwise. This ID is used to identify a specific surface in the set of outer and inner composite surfaces that make up a solid element. You specify a value of 1 for the outer surface and values greater than 1 for the inner surfaces of the solid element.
- SolidID: ID of the solid component of a composite solid element to be retrieved. Specify 0 otherwise.
- MultiID: ID of the component in a collection to be retrieved.

The MultiID will be useful only in the case of collections, and it can be omitted otherwise. Likewise, you can specify as many of the elements as apply for the specific geometry type (that is, you do not have to specify solidId if the geometry is a point, line polygon, or surface).

Using this function, let's identify the edge that caused the problem in Listing 5-36. The error string was "Point:0, Edge:2, Ring:1, Polygon:1, Csurf:1." You can plug in the same values of point_id=0 (this means you are not interested in this but instead a higher-level element such as a line or polygon), edgeID=2, RingID=1, PolygonID=1, and CsurfID=1 as the LABEL string for the EXTRACT3D function. Listing 5-46 shows the corresponding SQL. As mentioned in the discussion for Listing 5-36, the edge that is not closed is the edge from (0,4,0) to (4,4,0) (corresponding to one of the edges on the top face of the solid of Figure 5-4 mentioned in Listing 5-36).

Listing 5-46. *Extracting the Invalid Edge for Listing 5-36*

```
SQL> SELECT SDO_UTIL.EXTRACT3D
(
  SDO_GEOMETRY(3008, NULL, NULL,
    SDO_ELEM_INFO_ARRAY(
       1, 1007, 1,    -- Solid element
       1, 1006, 5,    -- Composite surface with 5 polygons
       1, 1003,1, 16, 1003, 1, 31, 1003, 1, 46, 1003, 1, 61, 1003, 1
    ),
    SDO_ORDINATE_ARRAY(
      0, 0, 0,   0, 4, 0,  4, 4, 0,  4, 0, 0, 0, 0, 0,  -- Vertices of 2nd edge bold
      4, 4, 4, 0, 4, 4, 0, 0, 4, 4, 0, 4, 4, 4, 4,
      0, 0, 0, 4, 0, 0, 4, 0, 4, 0, 0, 4, 0, 0, 0,
      0, 0, 0, 0, 0, 4, 0, 4, 4, 0, 4, 0, 0, 0, 0,
      4, 4, 4, 4, 0, 4, 4, 0, 0, 4, 4, 0, 4, 4, 4
    )
  ),
 '0,2,1,1,1'    -- LABEL String for extracting the
                -----2nd edge of Ring1, Polygon1,Comp Surface1
) edge FROM DUAL;

EDGE(SDO_GTYPE, SDO_SRID, SDO_POINT(X, Y, Z), SDO_ELEM_INFO, SDO_ORDINATES)
-------------------------------------------------------------------------------
SDO_GEOMETRY(3002, NULL, NULL, SDO_ELEM_INFO_ARRAY(1, 2, 1), SDO_ORDINATE_ARRAY(
0, 4, 0, 4, 4, 0))
```

Miscellaneous Functions

The SDO_UTIL package has a number of other functions to manipulate SDO_GEOMETRY objects. The following is a list of functions that may aid in debugging or cleaning up spatial data. We will discuss other functions at appropriate times throughout the book.

- SDO_CONCAT_LINES: This function concatenates two line string geometries. The line strings are expected to be nonintersecting. Because of this assumption, this function executes much faster than the SDO_UNION function, which we will discuss in Chapter 9.
- SDO_REVERSE_LINESTRING: This function reverses the order of vertices in a line string. Such functions may be useful in routing and other navigation applications.
- SDO_POLYGONTOLINE: This function converts a polygon to a line string geometry.

In short, the SDO_UTIL and SDO_GEOM packages provide a rich set of functions to validate and debug SDO_GEOMETRY data.

Summary

In this chapter, we described how to load data into and out of SDO_GEOMETRY columns. We discussed how to load from text files using SQL*Loader and how to load using the Oracle utilities such as Import/Export and transportable tablespaces. We also described how to convert SDO_GEOMETRY data to GML format.

Once data are loaded into SDO_GEOMETRY columns, the data need to be validated. We described how to perform validation to check for conformity with Oracle Spatial formats. In case of invalid data, we described a set of functions that are helpful in debugging such geometries and correcting the inaccuracies.

We also explained how to import data into the example application described in Chapter 3. In the next chapter, we will describe how to derive the SDO_GEOMETRY data from the address columns of an application's table. You can use this alternate method to populate the columns in application-specific tables such as branches and customers. Once the spatial data is populated in the tables, we will describe how to perform analysis and visualization in Chapters 8 to 11.

CHAPTER 6

Geocoding

To run the examples in this chapter, you need to import the following dataset. For complete details on creating this user and loading the data, refer to the introduction.

```
imp spatial/spatial file=gc.dmp ignore=y full=y
```

In preceding chapters, we discussed how to perform spatial searches and analysis. In each example, the entities manipulated (customers, ATMs, stores, and so on) were spatially located. They all included an SDO_GEOMETRY column containing their spatial location using geographical coordinates (longitude and latitude).

But how did this happen? Where did this information come from? Certainly, you cannot ask your customers to give their geographical coordinates when they register with you or when they place an order! We used a process called *geocoding*—we geocoded addresses and stored the resulting locations as SDO_GEOMETRY objects.

By *geocoding*, we mean a process that converts an address (for example, "3746 Connecticut Avenue NW, Washington, D.C. 20008, United States") to geographical coordinates (longitude = –77.060283, latitude = 38.9387083). In addition, geocoding may also *normalize* and *correct* the input address (HouseNumber=3746; StreetName=Connecticut Avenue NW; City=Washington; State=D.C.; Zip=20008; Country=US).

In this chapter, we describe the functionality of the geocoder in Oracle Spatial and how to use it to location-enable a business application. We start with a brief overview of the geocoding process. This will give you an understanding of how the conversion from addresses to SDO_GEOMETRY objects happens.

Next, we discuss how to set up the reference data used by the geocoder. This reference data is used to determine/extrapolate the location for a specified address. You can obtain this data from a data provider such as NAVTEQ.

Then we describe different geocoding functions that use the reference data. We provide generic examples to illustrate their functionality.

We go on to describe how to add SDO_GEOMETRY columns to application data and how to populate them using the Oracle geocoder. We illustrate this using different functions/APIs of the geocoder.

Finally, we show how to set up and use the Geocoding web service, provided with Oracle Spatial since 10*g* Release 2.

What Is Geocoding?

Geocoding serves two purposes. The main purpose is to associate geographical coordinates with an address. Listing 6-1 shows an example of how to get the coordinates from an address using the simple GEOCODE_AS_GEOMETRY function that returns a point SDO_GEOMETRY object. That object contains the geographical coordinates that the geocoder associated with this address.

Listing 6-1. *Geocoding an Address*

```
SQL> SELECT SDO_GCDR.GEOCODE_AS_GEOMETRY
(
  'SPATIAL',
  SDO_KEYWORDARRAY
  (
    '3746  CONNECTICUT AVE NW',
    'WASHINGTON, DC 20008'
  ),
  'US'
) geom
FROM DUAL;

GEOM(SDO_GTYPE, SDO_SRID, SDO_POINT(X, Y, Z), SDO_ELEM_INFO, SDO_ORDINATES)
----------------------------------------------------------------------------
SDO_GEOMETRY(2001, 8307, SDO_POINT_TYPE(-77.060283, 38.9387083, NULL), NULL, NULL)
```

What would happen if the address were misspelled? This brings us to the second purpose of geocoding, which is to correct various errors in addresses. This process is often called *address normalization*, and it involves structuring and cleaning the input address.

Address normalization is important: it corrects mistakes and ensures that all address information is complete, well structured, and clean. A set of clean and normalized addresses is necessary to derive meaningful location information and to remove duplicates.

It is common, for instance, to find variations of the same customer address in a customer database. The same customer might provide the information at different occasions in slightly different ways, and without normalization, this would lead to semantic duplicates that are treated as separate entries in the customer database.

Listing 6-2 shows how to obtain corrections for a misspelled address using the GEOCODE function. "Connecticut" is spelled as "Connectict" here, and the postal code is incorrect.

Listing 6-2. *Geocoding and Normalizing an Address*

```
SQL> SELECT SDO_GCDR.GEOCODE
(
    'SPATIAL',
    SDO_KEYWORDARRAY
    (
      '3746  CONNECTICT AVE NW',
      'WASHINGTON, DC 20023'
    ),
    'US',
    'DEFAULT'
  ) geom
FROM DUAL;

GEOM(ID, ADDRESSLINES, PLACENAME, STREETNAME, INTERSECTSTREET, SECUNIT,
SETTLEM
----------------------------------------------------------------------------
SDO_GEO_ADDR
(0, SDO_KEYWORDARRAY(NULL), NULL, 'CONNECTICUT AVE NW', NULL, NULL,
 'WASHINGTON', NULL, 'DC', 'US', '20008', NULL, '20008', NULL, '3746', 'CONNECT
ICUT', 'AVE', 'F', 'F', NULL, 'NW', 'L', .944444444, 18571166, '????#E?UT?B281C
??', 10, 'DEFAULT', -77.060283, 38.9387083)
```

The result of this function is a fairly complex structure of type SDO_GEO_ADDR. For now, we merely note that the structure contains the correct street name and the correct postal code. Later in this chapter, we cover the structure in more depth, and you will see how to format it in a readable way.

Architecture of the Oracle Geocoder

How is geocoding done? Figure 6-1 illustrates this process. First, the geocoder requires reference data—a list of addresses with known coordinates such as roads and streets but also towns, postal codes, and so on, with their geographical locations and shapes.

With this reference data, the geocoder performs the following three steps:

1. Parse the input address.
2. Search for an address with a matching name.
3. Compute a location (spatial coordinates) for the address that was found.

Let's examine these three steps in detail.

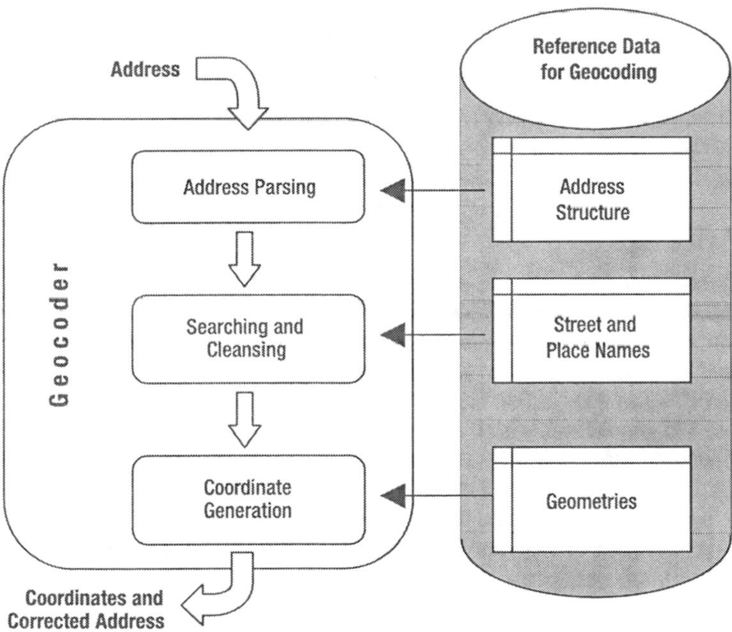

Figure 6-1. *Oracle geocoder architecture*

Parsing the Input Address

The geocoder first recognizes the parts of a street address and separates them into recognizable elements such as street name, street type (street, avenue, boulevard, and so on), house number, postal code, and city.

This process can be tricky—there are many ways to write the same address, especially in different countries, cultures, and languages. For example, the street type can precede (such as Rue de la Paix), follow (such as Elm Square), or be attached to the street name (such as Bahnhofstraße).

The Oracle geocoder recognizes a variety of address formats in various countries and languages. The formats are defined in one table, GC_PARSER_PROFILEAFS, in the reference data. Table 6-1 illustrates the effect of parsing some common international addresses.

Table 6-1. *Parsing International Addresses*

Address Element	United States	Germany	France
Full address	3746 Connecticut Avenue NW Washington, D.C. 20008	Arabellastraße 6 D-81925 München	12, Avenue Robert Soleau 06600 Antibes
House number	3746	6	12
Street base name	Connecticut	Arabella	Robert Soleau
Street type	Avenue	Strasse	Avenue
Street suffix	NW		
City	Washington	München	Antibes
Postal code	20008	81925	06600
Region	D.C		

■ **Note** Postal organizations have defined an official way to format addresses. The Universal Postal Union (www.upu.int) compiles and publishes this information.

Searching for the Address

Once the address has been parsed into recognizable elements, the geocoder can search the list of street names for the one that most closely matches the given address.

This search is *fuzzy*, meaning it finds a match even if the input address is misspelled (such as "avenue" spelled as "avnue" or "Van Ness" spelled as "Van Neus") or represented differently from the stored addresses (such as "street" entered as "st." or "strasse" entered as "straße").

The various keywords used in an address, with their multiple spellings (including common spelling errors), are stored in the GC_PARSER_PROFILES table in the reference data. For example, JUNCTION can be spelled JCT, JCTN, JUNCTN, or even JCTION or JUNCTON.

The search may also be "approximate"—that is, if the exact street cannot be found, then the geocoder will fall back to the postal code or city name. The user is able to specify whether this is acceptable by passing a *matching mode* parameter. We will cover the various possible modes later in the chapter.

In some cases, there may be multiple matches. For example, the chosen street name "Warren Street" may not exist, but "Warren Place" and "Warren Avenue" might. In such a case, both results will be returned. It is up to the calling application to decide which result to choose or, more likely, to let the user of the application choose.

One important result of the address search is a cleaned-up address, with the correct formatting and spelling of the street name, complete with elements that were missing from the input address, such as the postal code.

Computing the Spatial Coordinates

Once the proper street has been located, the geocoder needs to convert it into a geographical point. Let's examine this final step of the geocoding process.

The geocoding reference data used by the Oracle geocoder holds the house numbers at each end of a street segment, on each side of that street. When the input address contains a house number, the geocoder computes the geographical position of the house number by *interpolation*.

Figure 6-2 illustrates this process. The figure shows a section of Elm Street. Only the numbers of houses at each end are known: numbers 10 and 11 are at one end, and numbers 18 and 19 are at the other end. Where, then, is "13 Elm St"? The Oracle geocoder assumes that houses are regularly spaced along the linear geometry that represents the street segment, and positions (that is, interpolates) house number 13 accordingly.

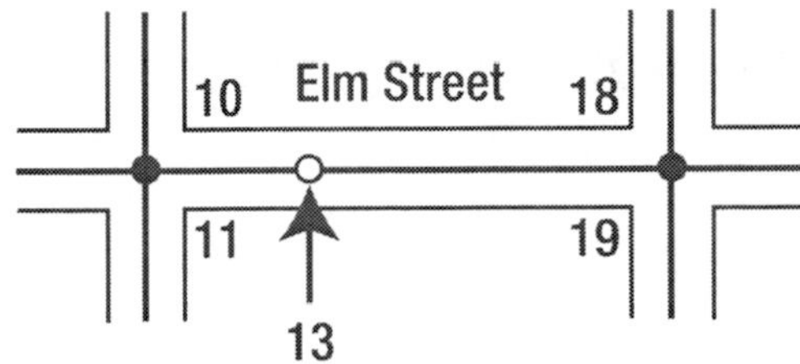

Figure 6-2. *Interpolation example*

When there is a good correlation between the house numbers and the distance along the road, the result will be quite precise. Otherwise, it will be approximate and may be erroneous. Even in the latter case, the margin of error is generally small.

■ **Note** Streets are modeled as line strings, the "centerline" of the actual street. The Oracle geocoder actually positions houses on the centerline—that is, the actual coordinates are in the middle of the street!

Note that the input address may be incomplete. This is what happens when the input address has missing components:

- When no house number is given in the address, the geocoder returns the midpoint of the street. The reference data of the Oracle geocoder stores the precomputed location of the house number at the midpoint.
- When no street is given in the input address or when the street is not found, the geocoder falls back to the postal code or city (built-up area, settlement, or municipality). In those cases, it returns a geographical point that corresponds to the "center" of the postal code or city.

Note that the required precision of a geographical location for a given address varies with the application:

- For an application that returns the current weather at a chosen location, geocoding at the postal code or city level is quite sufficient.
- For an application that compares customer locations with branch (business) locations or sales territories, geocoding at the street level is generally sufficient.
- For a pizza delivery or taxi pickup application, geocoding at the house level is nice, but just knowing the street segment (that is, the city block) and the side of the street is generally sufficient.

■ **Note** The coordinates returned by the geocoder are always in the coordinate system used in the reference data. For most data providers (as is the case for NAVTEQ) this will be longitude, latitude (WGS84) but the geocoder will work with any coordinate system.

In the next section, we discuss how to set up the reference data for the geocoder. We then illustrate the previously discussed geocoding process with appropriate examples.

Setting Up the Reference Data for the Geocoder

The reference data used by the Oracle geocoder is a set of tables with a specific structure. All the tables start with the `GC_` prefix. There are two kinds of tables:

- *Parameter tables* control the operation of the geocoder.
- *Data tables* contain the place names and their geographical coordinates.

The way you load those tables depends on the way your data supplier provides them. At the time of this writing, only NAVTEQ supplies the reference data for the geocoder, in Oracle export (`.dmp`) files or transportable tablespaces. Other suppliers may choose other mechanisms, such as SQL*Loader and SQL scripts, to provide their data.

For the examples in this book, we use the sample data that NAVTEQ provides, which covers San Francisco, California, and Washington, D.C. For ease of use, the data is provided to you as a single Oracle export file.

Loading this reference data for the Oracle geocoder is as easy as running the following import command. This will create all tables (parameter as well as data) and populate them.

```
imp spatial/spatial file=gc.dmp full=y ignore=y
```

For real geocoder reference data, you will most likely need to perform multiple such imports, because the data for each country is provided as one or more dump files. Note that you can load the data for different countries in the same Oracle schema or in different schemas. The data for each country uses different tables. See the "Data Tables" section of this chapter for details.

The rest of this section describes the overall structure and purpose of all tables in the reference data. You do *not* need to understand the details of the tables to use the geocoder.

Parameter Tables

Three tables contain information about the structuring of addresses in each country supported by the Oracle geocoder. You should not change the content of these tables.

GC_COUNTRY_PROFILE

This table contains general information about each country known to the Oracle geocoder, such as the definition of administrative levels for that country. One important piece of information is the suffix of the data tables for that country (more on this later).

GC_PARSER_PROFILEAFS

This table describes the structuring of the addresses for each country supported by the Oracle geocoder. There is one row per country, with the address structure defined in an XML notation.

GC_PARSER_PROFILES

The Oracle geocoder uses this table to recognize some address elements. It defines address elements with their synonyms, including possible misspellings. For example, it defines that AV, AVE, AVEN, AVENU, AVN, and AVNUE are all possible spellings for AVENUE. It also defines 1ST and FIRST as synonyms.

Data Tables

The data tables have names with a country-specific suffix (defined in the GC_COUNTRY_PROFILE table). For example, the reference data for France is in tables with the FR suffix, while the data for the United States is in tables with the US suffix. The xx in the following descriptions represents this suffix.

GC_AREA_xx

This table stores information on all administrative areas. The Oracle geocoder defines three levels of administrative areas: REGION, MUNICIPALITY, and SETTLEMENT. The way administrative areas are mapped to those levels varies from country to country.

For the United States, the administrative areas correspond to states, counties, and cities. For the United Kingdom, they correspond to counties, postal towns, and localities.

Note that the same area can appear multiple times—this is the case when an area has multiple names in different languages.

GC_POSTAL_CODE_xx

This table describes all postal codes, and it also contains the coordinates of the *center point* for each postal code. The center point is the point returned by the geocoder when the street name in the input address is invalid (or the input address contains no street name).

GC_POI_xx

This table contains a selection of points of interest (hospitals, airports, hotels, restaurants, parking garages, ATMs, and so on). The number of points of interest (POIs) and their classification varies among data suppliers.

GC_ROAD_xx

This is the main table used for address searches. It contains one row per road per settlement and postal code. If a road crosses multiple postal codes, then it will appear multiple times in this table.

GC_ROAD_SEGMENT_xx

This table provides the information needed to compute the coordinates of an address by interpolation. It contains one row for each segment of a road with the geometric shape of that road segment (an SDO_GEOMETRY type), as well as the house numbers on each side, at each end of the segment.

GC_INTERSECTION_xx

When multiple road segments meet, they form an intersection. This table defines one row for each couple of such road segments.

Using Geocoder Functions

The geocoding API is simple: it is composed of a PL/SQL package (SDO_GCDR) with only a few functions. All of them accept an address as input and return geographical coordinate information as the geocoded result. The difference between the functions is in the amount of information they return as well as the format of the input address. Table 6-2 summarizes the functions and their behaviors.

Table 6-2. *Comparing the Geocoding Functions*

Function	Address Conversion	Address Correction	Description
GEOCODE_AS_GEOMETRY	Yes	No	Returns a geometric point (with the geographical coordinates) for the address. It returns no indication as to the precision or quality of the result. This is best used when the addresses are known to be valid.
GEOCODE	Yes	Yes	Returns the geographical coordinates and a corrected address with detailed indications of the quality of the result. The input is an unstructured address, passed as a set of address lines.
GEOCODE_ADDR	Yes	Yes	Same as GEOCODE, but uses a structured address as input.
GEOCODE_ALL	Yes	Yes	Like GEOCODE, but can return multiple matches if the input address is ambiguous. This is best used for interactive applications, when the end user chooses which of the matches is correct.
GEOCODE_ADDR_ALL	Yes	Yes	Like GEOCODE_ALL, but uses a structured address as input.

In the rest of this section, we cover each function in detail with examples.

■ **Note** The first call to a geocoding function in a session requires more time (is longer) than the subsequent calls. This is because the function needs to load and parse the profile tables.

GEOCODE_AS_GEOMETRY

This is the simplest function to use. You just pass it the address to geocode, and it returns an SDO_GEOMETRY object with the corresponding geographical location for that address. Recall that we used this function to illustrate geocoding in Chapters 2 and 3.

Here is the syntax of the function:

```
SDO_GCDR.GEOCODE_AS_GEOMETRY (
       username          IN VARCHAR2,
       addr_lines        IN SDO_KEYWORDARRAY,
       country           IN VARCHAR2
) RETURN SDO_GEOMETRY;
```

Function Parameters

The following sections outline the parameters for the GEOCODE_AS_GEOMETRY function.

username

This is the name of the Oracle schema that contains the geocoding tables for the specified country. It is a required argument. If the data is in the same schema as the one that calls the function, then you can also use the SQL built-in USER.

■ **Note** If the geocoding tables are in a different schema than the one you are connected as, then you must have the SELECT access right on those tables.

---

addr_lines

The type SDO_KEYWORDARRAY is a simple array (VARRAY) of character strings that is used to pass address lines to the geocoding functions. Fill each array entry with one line of the street address to geocode as illustrated in the list that follows.

The lines of the address must be passed according to the structure described in GC_PARSER_PROFILEAFS. They should be in the order defined and formatted properly. This formatting varies from country to country. If an address is incorrectly formatted, then the geocoder will reject it (that is, it will return NULL).

There is, however, a certain degree of flexibility in the formatting. For example, all of the following are valid ways to format the U.S. address "1250 Clay Street, San Francisco, CA 94108":

- The state and postal code are on separate lines:

```
SDO_KEYWORDARRAY (
  '1250 Clay St',
  'San Francisco',
  'CA',
  '94108'
)
```

- The state and postal code are together on a separate line:

```
SDO_KEYWORDARRAY (
  '1250 Clay St',
  'San Francisco',
  'CA 94108'
)
```

- The city, state, and postal code are on the same line:

```
SDO_KEYWORDARRAY (
  '1250 Clay St',
  'San Francisco CA 94108'
)
```

The following, however, is incorrect:

- The address is on one line:

```
SDO_KEYWORDARRAY (
  '1250 Clay St, San Francisco CA 94108'
)
```

country

This is the two-letter ISO code for the country to which the address to be geocoded belongs.

Function Result: SDO_GEOMETRY

The result of the function is a simple `SDO_GEOMETRY` object that contains a point geometry.

If the function is unable to parse the input address (because it is incorrectly formatted) or if it is unable to geocode the address (because it could not find any place at all with the provided information), then it returns a `NULL` geometry.

Let's look at a few examples.

Examples

Listing 6-3 shows how to geocode a street address in San Francisco.

Listing 6-3. *Using the* `GEOCODE_AS_GEOMETRY` *Function*

```
SQL> SELECT SDO_GCDR.GEOCODE_AS_GEOMETRY
(
  'SPATIAL',
  SDO_KEYWORDARRAY('1250 Clay Street', 'San Francisco, CA'),
  'US'
  )
FROM DUAL;
SDO_GEOMETRY(2001, 8307, SDO_POINT_TYPE -122.41356, 37.7932878, NULL), NULL, NULL)
```

The result is a simple point geometry object that contains the geographical coordinates for that address. The coordinates may not point exactly to number 1250 on Clay Street; they are computed by interpolation between known house numbers.

If the house number does not exist, such as in the example in Listing 6-4 (the highest house number on Clay Street is 3999), you still get a valid geometry pointing to a house on the street, but you have no indication of the exact house on which the geocoder positioned the coordinates.

Listing 6-4. *Using the* `GEOCODE_AS_GEOMETRY` *Function with an Invalid House Number*

```
SQL> SELECT SDO_GCDR.GEOCODE_AS_GEOMETRY
(
  'SPATIAL',
  SDO_KEYWORDARRAY('4500 Clay Street', 'San Francisco, CA'),
  'US'
)
FROM DUAL;
SDO_GEOMETRY(2001, 8307, SDO_POINT_TYPE(-122.41437, 37.79318, NULL), NULL, NULL)
```

The geocoder tries its best to always return a geographic location. If the street does not exist at all, then you get a location in the middle of the town (or postal code if one was specified). If the town does not exist, then you will get a location in the middle of the state (for U.S. addresses). If nothing is found at all, then you will get a `NULL` geometry back. This is illustrated in Listing 6-5.

Listing 6-5. *Using the* `GEOCODE_AS_GEOMETRY` *Function with an Invalid Street Name*

```
SQL> SELECT SDO_GCDR.GEOCODE_AS_GEOMETRY
(
  'SPATIAL',
  SDO_KEYWORDARRAY('Cloy Street', 'San Francisco, CA'),
  'US'
)
FROM DUAL;

SDO_GEOMETRY(2001, 8307, SDO_POINT_TYPE(-122.49586, 37.77904, NULL), NULL, NULL)
```

The drawback of this function is that you have no indication of the quality of the result—the address you passed may contain a house number that does not exist. In this case, the address may have been matched to the house halfway down the street, but you have no way of knowing that. Or the street may not exist, and the address is then positioned in the middle of the postal code area or city. You also have no way to tell the geocoder what precision level (match mode) to use; it always uses the DEFAULT mode. The previous example is a good illustration of this problem: the location returned is actually a point in the middle of San Francisco (as stored in the GC_AREA_US table). This is probably not what you want.

Therefore, you will mostly use the GEOCODE_AS_GEOMETRY function on addresses that you know are valid, such as the existing shipping addresses of your customers.

On the other hand, sometimes you cannot be sure that the input address is valid, for example, when you register a new customer in your database in your order-entry system or when a user types an address to find the nearest store to that address. In those cases, you will use the GEOCODE or GEOCODE_ALL function, which we describe next.

GEOCODE

GEOCODE is the main geocoding function. Contrary to the GEOCODE_AS_GEOMETRY function, which returns only coordinates, the GEOCODE function also returns a fully formatted address and codes that tell you precisely how the address matched.

This is the syntax of the GEOCODE function:

```
SDO_GCDR.GEOCODE
(
  username       IN VARCHAR2,
  addr_lines     IN SDO_KEYWORDARRAY,
  country        IN VARCHAR2
  match_mode     IN VARCHAR2
) RETURN SDO_GEO_ADDR;
```

Function Parameters

The following sections outline the parameters for the GEOCODE function. They are the same as those of the GEOCODE_AS_GEOMETRY function, except for the additional MATCH_MODE parameter.

username

This is the name of the Oracle schema that contains the geocoding tables for the specified country. It is a required argument. If the data is in the same schema as the one that calls the function, then you can also use the SQL built-in USER.

addr_lines

This is a simple array (VARRAY) of character strings that is used to pass address lines. See the GEOCODE_AS_GEOMETRY function for a detailed explanation.

country

This is the two-letter ISO code for the country to which the address to be geocoded belongs.

match_mode

The match mode lets you decide how closely the elements of an input address must match the data in the geocoding catalog. Note that you do not specify this parameter for the GEOCODE_AS_GEOMETRY function—it always uses the DEFAULT mode.

The match mode can be specified as shown in Table 6-3.

Table 6-3. *Match Modes and Their Meanings*

Match Mode	Meaning
EXACT	All fields provided must match exactly.
RELAX_STREET_TYPE	The street type can be different from the official street type.
RELAX_POI_NAME	The POI name does not have to match exactly.
RELAX_HOUSE_NUMBER	The house number and street type do not have to match.
RELAX_BASE_NAME	The street (base) name, house number, and street type do not have to match.
RELAX_POSTAL_CODE	The postal code (if provided), street (base) name, house number, and street type do not have to match.
RELAX_BUILTUP_AREA	This mode searches the address outside the city specified, but within the same county, and includes RELAX_POSTAL_CODE.
RELAX_ALL	Same as RELAX_BUILTUP_AREA.
DEFAULT	Same as RELAX_POSTAL_CODE.

You will see the effect of the various modes in the upcoming examples.

Function Result: SDO_GEO_ADDR

This structure contains the detailed results of a geocoding operation. See Table 6-4 for the exact content of the structure.

As you can see, this structure is quite rich and contains many pieces of information. They can be summarized as follows:

- LONGITUDE and LATITUDE: The coordinates of the address.
- MATCHCODE and ERRORMESSAGE: Together, they indicate how close the match is. The possible values are detailed later.
- SIDE: The side of the street on which this address lies (L for left; R for right).
- PERCENT: The relative position of the address on the road segment when traveling from lower to higher numbered addresses. This is expressed as a percentage. A setting of 50 percent indicates that the address is halfway down the road segment.
- EDGE_ID: The ID of the road segment on which this address is located.

The other attributes hold the cleansed and completed address, broken down into individual components. This includes settlement, municipality, and region names; postal code; and street base name, suffix, prefix, and so on.

Table 6-4. SDO_GEO_ADDR *Object Structure*

Column Name	Data Type
ID	NUMBER
ADDRESSLINES	SDO_KEYWORDARRAY
PLACENAME	VARCHAR2(200)
STREETNAME	VARCHAR2(200)
INTERSECTSTREET	VARCHAR2(200)
SECUNIT	VARCHAR2(200)
SETTLEMENT	VARCHAR2(200)
MUNICIPALITY	VARCHAR2(200)
REGION	VARCHAR2(200)
COUNTRY	VARCHAR2(100)
POSTALCODE	VARCHAR2(20)
POSTALADDONCODE	VARCHAR2(20)
FULLPOSTALCODE	VARCHAR2(20)
POBOX	VARCHAR2(100)
HOUSENUMBER	VARCHAR2(100)
BASENAME	VARCHAR2(200)
STREETTYPE	VARCHAR2(20)
STREETTYPEBEFORE	VARCHAR2(1)
STREETTYPEATTACHED	VARCHAR2(1)
STREETPREFIX	VARCHAR2(20)
STREETSUFFIX	VARCHAR2(20)
SIDE	VARCHAR2(1)
PERCENT	NUMBER
EDGEID	NUMBER
ERRORMESSAGE	VARCHAR2(20)
MATCHCODE	NUMBER
MATCHMODE	VARCHAR2(30)
LONGITUDE	NUMBER
LATITUDE	NUMBER
MATCHVECTOR	VARCHAR2(20)

Interpreting the Results of a Geocode Operation

The results of the GEOCODE function indicate the way the input address was matched with the list of addresses from the reference data. All that was returned from the GEOCODE_AS_GEOMETRY function was a geographical point. The GEOCODE function allows you to find out whether there were any mistakes in the input address. Three attributes of the SDO_GEO_ADDR structure give you this information: MATCHCODE, ERRORMESSAGE, and MATCHVECTOR.

MATCHCODE

The MATCHCODE attribute indicates the general "quality" of the match and is described in Table 6-5.

Table 6-5. *Match Codes and Their Meanings*

Match Code	Meaning
1	Exact match. The city name, postal code, street base name, street type/suffix/prefix, and house number are all matched.
2	The city name, postal code, street base name, and house number are matched, but the street type and suffix or prefix is not matched.
3	The city name, postal code, and street base name are matched, but the house number is not matched.
4	The postal code and city name are matched, but the street address is not matched.
10	The city name is matched, but the postal code is not matched.
11	The postal code is matched, but the city name is not matched.

Note that the code specifies how close the match is with only those address elements that are specified in the input address. It does not consider the ones that are not passed. For example, an address such as "Clay St, San Francisco, CA" receives a match code of 1, even though no house number or postal code was specified. On the other hand, an address such as "9650 Clay St, San Francisco, CA 92306" receives a match code of 10, which indicates that neither the postal code nor the house number matched.

ERRORMESSAGE

The ERRORMESSAGE attribute further details the quality and precision of the match by telling you how each individual address element matched.

The error message is a character string in which each character specifies how each address element was matched. When the address element is not matched, then its corresponding character position contains a question mark (?). Table 6-6 shows the meaning of each position in the ERRORMESSAGE string.

Table 6-6. *Detailed* ERRORMESSAGE *Structure*

Position	Meaning	Value When Matched
5	House or building number	#
6	Street prefix	E
7	Street base name	N
8	Street suffix	U
9	Street type	T
10	Secondary unit	S
11	Built-up area or city	B
14	Region	1
15	Country	C
16	Postal code	P
17	Postal add-on code	A

Used together, the MATCHCODE and ERRORMESSAGE attributes let your application decide whether to accept the results of a geocode operation or reject the results and flag the containing record for later resolution by a human. Common reasons for rejecting a geocode are as follows:

- The geocoder was unable to correct errors in the address (such as an invalid house number).
- The application wants all addresses to be geocoded at the street level at a minimum, but the address was geocoded at the postal code or city level.

MATCHVECTOR

The ERRORMESSAGE attribute allows you to find out about any errors in the input address; for example, the postal code may be incorrect, or the street name may be misspelled. But it does not give any indication as to the accuracy of the result.

For example, an address may be supplied without any house number. In this case, we will match it to a random location on the specified street (actually, we will just use the coordinates for the center house number specified in the GC_ROAD_xx table). This will be diagnosed as an "exact match": the MATCHCODE attribute will be set to 1, and the ERRORMESSAGE vector will indicate that the house number was found.

However, this may not be satisfactory for your application. If you want to use the location and address for home deliveries, then an address without any house number is not useful. The MATCHVECTOR attribute will tell you not just whether an address element matched but also whether it was present.

Like ERRORMESSAGE, the MATCHVECTOR attribute contains a string. Each character of this string indicates the match status of an address attribute. Table 6-7 shows the meaning of each position in the MATCHVECTOR string.

Table 6-7. *Detailed* MATCHVECTOR *Structure*

Position	Meaning
5	House or building number
6	Street prefix
7	Street base name
8	Street suffix
9	Street type
10	Secondary unit
11	Built-up area or city
14	Region
15	Country
16	Postal code
17	Postal add-on code

Each character position in the MATCHVECTOR string can have one of the values detailed in Table 6-8.

Table 6-8. *Codes Used in the* `MATCHVECTOR` *Structure*

Value	Meaning	Example
0	`MATCHED` = The address element was specified and was successfully matched.	Your address contained the correct postal code.
1	`ABSENT` = The address element was not specified and not replaced.	Your address did not contain any postal code, and the geocoder did not supply one.
2	`CORRECTED` = The address element was specified but was not matched and was replaced by a different value from the database.	Your address contained an invalid postal code, which was replaced with the correct one.
3	`IGNORED` = The address element was specified but was not matched and not replaced.	Your address has a house number, but the street could not be found, so the house number was ignored.
4	`SUPPLIED` = The address element was not specified and was filled with a value from the database	Your address did not specify any postal code. The correct postal code was supplied from the database.

Examples

Let's look at a various examples. We start with valid addresses, and then we move on to show what happens when addresses contain various errors.

A Street Address Without a House Number

Listing 6-6 shows the geocoding of a street address in San Francisco. The address specifies the street name and town but no postal code.

Listing 6-6. *Example of Calling the* `GEOCODE` *Function*

```
SQL> SELECT SDO_GCDR.GEOCODE
(
  'SPATIAL',
  SDO_KEYWORDARRAY('Clay Street', 'San Francisco, CA'),
  'US',
  'DEFAULT'
)
FROM DUAL;
SDO_GEO_ADDR(0, SDO_KEYWORDARRAY(NULL), NULL, 'CLAY ST', NULL, NULL, 'SAN
FRANCISCO',
NULL, 'CA', 'US', '94108', NULL, '94108', NULL, '978', 'CLAY', 'ST', 'F',
 'F', NULL,
NULL, 'L', 0, 1, 23600689, 'nul?#ENUT?B281CP?', 1, 'DEFAULT', -122.40904, 37.79385)
```

The result is hard to read, so we will write a PL/SQL stored procedure that will format and display the result in a more readable way. Procedure `FORMAT_GEO_ADDR` takes an `SDO_GEO_ADDR` object as input and formats it using the `DBMS_OUTPUT` package. Listing 6-7 details the procedure.

Listing 6-7. `FORMAT_GEO_ADDR` *Procedure*

```
SQL>
CREATE OR REPLACE PROCEDURE format_geo_addr
(
  address SDO_GEO_ADDR
)
```

```
AS
BEGIN
  dbms_output.put_line ('- ID                   ' || address.ID);
  dbms_output.put_line ('- ADDRESSLINES');
  if address.addresslines.count() > 0 then
    for i in 1..address.addresslines.count() loop
      dbms_output.put_line ('- ADDRESSLINES['||i||']      ' ||
          address.ADDRESSLINES(i));
    end loop;
  end if;
  dbms_output.put_line ('- PLACENAME            ' || address.PLACENAME);
  dbms_output.put_line ('- STREETNAME           ' || address.STREETNAME);
  dbms_output.put_line ('- INTERSECTSTREET      ' || address.INTERSECTSTREET);
  dbms_output.put_line ('- SECUNIT              ' || address.SECUNIT);
  dbms_output.put_line ('- SETTLEMENT           ' || address.SETTLEMENT);
  dbms_output.put_line ('- MUNICIPALITY         ' || address.MUNICIPALITY);
  dbms_output.put_line ('- REGION               ' || address.REGION);
  dbms_output.put_line ('- COUNTRY              ' || address.COUNTRY);
  dbms_output.put_line ('- POSTALCODE           ' || address.POSTALCODE);
  dbms_output.put_line ('- POSTALADDONCODE      ' || address.POSTALADDONCODE);
  dbms_output.put_line ('- FULLPOSTALCODE       ' || address.FULLPOSTALCODE);
  dbms_output.put_line ('- POBOX                ' || address.POBOX);
  dbms_output.put_line ('- HOUSENUMBER          ' || address.HOUSENUMBER);
  dbms_output.put_line ('- BASENAME             ' || address.BASENAME);
  dbms_output.put_line ('- STREETTYPE           ' || address.STREETTYPE);
  dbms_output.put_line ('- STREETTYPEBEFORE     ' || address.STREETTYPEBEFORE);
  dbms_output.put_line ('- STREETTYPEATTACHED   ' || address.STREETTYPEATTACHED);
  dbms_output.put_line ('- STREETPREFIX         ' || address.STREETPREFIX);
  dbms_output.put_line ('- STREETSUFFIX         ' || address.STREETSUFFIX);
  dbms_output.put_line ('- SIDE                 ' || address.SIDE);
  dbms_output.put_line ('- PERCENT              ' || address.PERCENT);
  dbms_output.put_line ('- EDGEID               ' || address.EDGEID);
  dbms_output.put_line ('- ERRORMESSAGE         ' || address.ERRORMESSAGE);
  dbms_output.put_line ('- MATCHVECTOR              ' || address.MATCHVECTOR);
  dbms_output.put_line ('-    '||  substr (address.errormessage,5,1)  ||' '||
     substr (address.matchvector,5,1)  ||' House or building number');
  dbms_output.put_line ('-    '||  substr (address.errormessage,6,1)  ||' '||
     substr (address.matchvector,6,1)  ||' Street prefix');
  dbms_output.put_line ('-    '||  substr (address.errormessage,7,1)  ||' '||
    substr (address.matchvector,7,1)  ||' Street base name');
  dbms_output.put_line ('-    '||  substr (address.errormessage,8,1)  ||' '||
    substr (address.matchvector,8,1)  ||' Street suffix');
  dbms_output.put_line ('-    '||  substr (address.errormessage,9,1)  ||' '||
    substr (address.matchvector,9,1)  ||' Street type');
  dbms_output.put_line ('-    '||  substr (address.errormessage,10,1) ||' '||
    substr (address.matchvector,10,1) ||' Secondary unit');
  dbms_output.put_line ('-    '||  substr (address.errormessage,11,1) ||' '||
    substr (address.matchvector,11,1) ||' Built-up area or city');
  dbms_output.put_line ('-    '||  substr (address.errormessage,14,1) ||' '||
    substr (address.matchvector,14,1) ||' Region');
  dbms_output.put_line ('-    '||  substr (address.errormessage,15,1) ||' '||
    substr (address.matchvector,15,1) ||' Country');
  dbms_output.put_line ('-    '||  substr (address.errormessage,16,1) ||' '||
    substr (address.matchvector,16,1) ||' Postal code');
  dbms_output.put_line ('-    '||  substr (address.errormessage,17,1) ||' '||
    substr (address.matchvector,17,1) ||' Postal add-on code');
  dbms_output.put_line ('- MATCHCODE                ' ||
```

```
    address.MATCHCODE || ' = ' ||
    case address.MATCHCODE
      when  1 then 'Exact match'
      when  2 then 'Match on city, postal code, street base name and number'
      when  3 then 'Match on city, postal code and street base name'
      when  4 then 'Match on city and postal code'
      when 10 then 'Match on city but not postal code'
      when 11 then 'Match on postal but not on city'
    end
  );
  dbms_output.put_line ('- MATCHMODE          ' || address.MATCHMODE);
  dbms_output.put_line ('- LONGITUDE          ' || address.LONGITUDE);
  dbms_output.put_line ('- LATITUDE           ' || address.LATITUDE);
END;
/
show errors
```

Listing 6-8 shows how to use the procedure with the previous example.

Listing 6-8. *Example of Using the* FORMAT_GEO_ADDR *Procedure*

```
SQL> SET SERVEROUTPUT ON
SQL> BEGIN
       FORMAT_GEO_ADDR (
         SDO_GCDR.GEOCODE (
           'SPATIAL',
           SDO_KEYWORDARRAY('Clay Street', 'San Francisco, CA'),
           'US',
           'DEFAULT'
         )
       );
     END;
     /
- ID                 0
- ADDRESSLINES
- PLACENAME
- STREETNAME         CLAY ST
- INTERSECTSTREET
- SECUNIT
- SETTLEMENT         SAN FRANCISCO
- MUNICIPALITY
- REGION             CA
- COUNTRY            US
- POSTALCODE         94108
- POSTALADDONCODE
- FULLPOSTALCODE     94108
- POBOX
- HOUSENUMBER        978
- BASENAME           CLAY
- STREETTYPE         ST
- STREETTYPEBEFORE   F
- STREETTYPEATTACHED F
- STREETPREFIX
- STREETSUFFIX
- SIDE               L
- PERCENT            0
- EDGEID             23600689
```

```
- ERRORMESSAGE        ????#ENUT?B281CP?
- MATCHVECTOR         ????4101010??004?
-   # 4 House or building number
-   E 1 Street prefix
-   N 0 Street base name
-   U 1 Street suffix
-   T 0 Street type
-   ? 1 Secondary unit
-   B 0 Built-up area or city
-   1 0 Region
-   C 0 Country
-   P 4 Postal code
-   ? ? Postal add-on code
- MATCHCODE           1 = Exact match
- MATCHMODE           DEFAULT
- LONGITUDE           -122.40904
- LATITUDE            37.79385
```

We receive a geographical point that lies on Clay Street. We also receive a corrected address with the street name as CLAY ST, and a ZIP code, 94108. The house number returned (978) corresponds to the middle point of the part of Clay Street that lies in ZIP code 94108 (Clay Street actually spreads over five postal codes, as shown in Listing 6-9).

The MATCHCODE returned is 1, indicating that we had a full match, including street type. The ERRORMESSAGE is ????#ENUT?B281CP?, and the MATCHVECTOR is ????4101010??004?. Their combination indicates how address elements matched. Table 6-9 shows the details.

Table 6-9. *Matching Elements in the* ERRORMESSAGE *and* MATCHVECTOR

Code	Match	Address Element	Explanation
#	4	House or building number	No house number specified, filled by the geocoder
E	1	Street prefix	No street prefix, none in the database
N	0	Street base name	Street name found
U	1	Street suffix	No street suffix
T	0	Street type	Street type found
B	0	Built-up area or city	City name found
1	0	Region	State name found
C	0	Country	Country found
P	4	Postal code	No postal code specified, filled by the geocoder

Notice the letter T in the error message code. It indicates a match on the street type, even though the input address used "Street" and the actual type is "St."

However, the ERRORMESSAGE also contains the characters # and P, which indicate matches on the house number and postal code, despite that the input address contained no house number or postal code. The MATCHVECTOR correctly reflects this; the value 4 for house number and postal code indicates they were missing from the input address.

Caution The indication of a positive match for an address element in ERRORMESSAGE does not necessarily mean that the corresponding address element actually matched—the address element may simply be missing from the input address. Use MATCHVECTOR to determine this.

Dissecting Clay Street

For the following examples, it is useful to know more about the house numbers on Clay Street. This will help you understand the preceding example as well as those that follow. Listing 6-9 shows how to find out the house numbers for a street.

Listing 6-9. *Getting Street Details from the Geocode Reference Data*

```
SQL> SELECT road_id, name, postal_code, start_hn, center_hn, end_hn
FROM gc_road_us
WHERE name = 'CLAY ST' AND postal_code like '94%'
ORDER BY start_hn;

   ROAD_ID NAME                  POSTAL   START_HN  CENTER_HN     END_HN
---------- -------------------- ------ ---------- ---------- ----------
       767 CLAY ST              94111           1        398        699
       427 CLAY ST              94108         700        978       1299
       505 CLAY ST              94109        1300       1698       1999
      1213 CLAY ST              94115        2200       2798       3299
      1446 CLAY ST              94118        3300       3698       3999
```

The results show the house numbers on Clay Street for each postal code: the first house number, the last house number, and the number of the house halfway down the street.

Since our address did not include any explicit postal code, the geocoder picked the one with the smallest number (94108) and then the center house number (978).

A Street Address with a House Number

The example in Listing 6-10 includes a house number but does not specify the street type. Note that we use the FORMAT_GEO_ADDR procedure to make the results clearer.

Listing 6-10. *Using the* GEOCODE *Function with a Valid House Number*

```
SQL> SET SERVEROUTPUT ON
SQL> BEGIN
       FORMAT_GEO_ADDR (
         SDO_GCDR.GEOCODE (
           'SPATIAL',
           SDO_KEYWORDARRAY('1350 Clay', 'San Francisco, CA'),
           'US',
           'DEFAULT'
         )
       );
     END;
     /
- ID                    0
- ADDRESSLINES
- PLACENAME
- STREETNAME            CLAY ST
- INTERSECTSTREET
```

```
- SECUNIT
- SETTLEMENT          SAN FRANCISCO
- MUNICIPALITY
- REGION              CA
- COUNTRY             US
- POSTALCODE          94109
- POSTALADDONCODE
- FULLPOSTALCODE      94109
- POBOX
- HOUSENUMBER         1350
- BASENAME            CLAY
- STREETTYPE          ST
- STREETTYPEBEFORE    F
- STREETTYPEATTACHED F
- STREETPREFIX
- STREETSUFFIX
- SIDE                L
- PERCENT             .49
- EDGEID              23600696
- ERRORMESSAGE        ????#ENU??B281CP?
- MATCHVECTOR         ????0101410??004?
-   # 0 House or building number
-   E 1 Street prefix
-   N 0 Street base name
-   U 1 Street suffix
-   ? 4 Street type
-   ? 1 Secondary unit
-   B 0 Built-up area or city
-   1 0 Region
-   C 0 Country
-   P 4 Postal code
-   ? ? Postal add-on code-
- MATCHCODE           2 = Street type not matched
- MATCHMODE           DEFAULT
- LONGITUDE           -122.4152166
- LATITUDE            37.7930729
```

This time, the MATCHCODE returned is 2. This is because we did not match on the street type (we specified only the street base name). The letter T no longer appears in the error message code, and the match vector value of 4 for street type indicates it was not specified in the input address but was filled in the output address.

Notice also that we received the correct postal code (94109) that corresponds to the house number we specified. Number 1350 is in the range of houses from 1300 to 1999, in postal code 94109.

Correcting Invalid Addresses

If the house number does not exist on this street, you still get a successful match, as shown in Listing 6-11.

Listing 6-11. *Using the* GEOCODE *Function with an Invalid House Number*

```
SQL> SET SERVEROUTPUT ON
SQL> BEGIN
       FORMAT_GEO_ADDR (
         SDO_GCDR.GEOCODE (
           'SPATIAL',
```

```
        SDO_KEYWORDARRAY('4500 Clay Street', 'San Francisco, CA'),
        'US',
        'DEFAULT'
      )
    );
  END;
  /
- ID                  0
- ADDRESSLINES
- PLACENAME
- STREETNAME          CLAY ST
- INTERSECTSTREET
- SECUNIT
- SETTLEMENT          SAN FRANCISCO
- MUNICIPALITY
- REGION              CA
- COUNTRY             US
- POSTALCODE          94108
- POSTALADDONCODE
- FULLPOSTALCODE      94108
- POBOX
- HOUSENUMBER         1299
- BASENAME            CLAY
- STREETTYPE          ST
- STREETTYPEBEFORE    F
- STREETTYPEATTACHED F
- STREETPREFIX
- STREETSUFFIX
- SIDE                R
- PERCENT             0
- EDGEID              23600695
- ERRORMESSAGE        ?????ENUT?B281CP?
- MATCHVECTOR         ????2101010??004?
-   ? 2 House or building number
-   E 1 Street prefix
-   N 0 Street base name
-   U 1 Street suffix
-   T 0 Street type
-   ? 1 Secondary unit
-   B 0 Built-up area or city
-   1 0 Region
-   C 0 Country
-   P 4 Postal code
-   ? ? Postal add-on code
- MATCHCODE           3 = House number not matched
- MATCHMODE           DEFAULT
- LONGITUDE           -122.41437
- LATITUDE            37.79318
```

This time, the MATCHCODE returned is 3, confirming that the house number did not match. The coordinates returned are positioned on the highest house number in the first segment of the street (that is, the postal code with the smallest number): house 1299 in postal code 94108. The MATCHVECTOR value of 2 for the house number indicates that the original house number in the input address was replaced by one coming from the database.

Contrast this with the "naive" use of the GEOCODE_AS_GEOMETRY function in Listing 6-4, where we received coordinates but had no way of knowing that the house number was actually invalid and that the coordinates were pointing elsewhere. The GEOCODE function gives us this indication, allowing our application to reject the address or flag it as requiring human correction.

Let's see what happens if the postal code in the address is invalid. As illustrated in Listing 6-12, we still get the right answer, including a corrected postal code.

Listing 6-12. *Using the* GEOCODE *Function with an Invalid Postal Code*

```
SQL> SET SERVEROUTPUT ON
SQL> BEGIN
       FORMAT_GEO_ADDR (
         SDO_GCDR.GEOCODE (
           'SPATIAL',
           SDO_KEYWORDARRAY('1350 Clay St', 'San Francisco, CA 99130'),
           'US',
           'DEFAULT'
         )
       );
     END;
     /
- ID                 0
- ADDRESSLINES
- PLACENAME
- STREETNAME         CLAY ST
- INTERSECTSTREET
- SECUNIT
- SETTLEMENT         SAN FRANCISCO
- MUNICIPALITY
- REGION             CA
- COUNTRY            US
- POSTALCODE         94109
- POSTALADDONCODE
- FULLPOSTALCODE     94109
- POBOX
- HOUSENUMBER        1350
- BASENAME           CLAY
- STREETTYPE         ST
- STREETTYPEBEFORE   F
- STREETTYPEATTACHED F
- STREETPREFIX
- STREETSUFFIX
- SIDE               L
- PERCENT            .49
- EDGEID             23600696
- ERRORMESSAGE       ????#ENUT?B281C??
-   # House or building number
-   E Street prefix
-   N Street base name
-   U Street suffix
-   T Street type
-   B Built-up area or city
-   1 Region
-   C Country
- MATCHCODE          10 = Match on city but not postal code
- MATCHMODE          DEFAULT
- LONGITUDE          -122.4152166
- LATITUDE           37.7930729
```

The resulting MATCHCODE is 10, indicating that the postal code was not matched. However, the coordinates are correctly positioned on number 1350 Clay Street, and the correct postal code (94109) is given back to us.

Using the EXACT Match Mode

All the previous examples use the default match mode, RELAX_BASE_NAME. However, if we repeat the last geocode using a stricter match mode such as EXACT, then the operation fails, as shown in Listing 6-13.

Listing 6-13. *Using the* GEOCODE *Function with an Invalid Postal Code (in* EXACT *Mode)*

```
SQL> SET SERVEROUTPUT ON
SQL> BEGIN
       FORMAT_GEO_ADDR (
         SDO_GCDR.GEOCODE (
           'SPATIAL',
           SDO_KEYWORDARRAY('1350 Clay St', 'San Francisco, CA 99130'),
           'US',
           'EXACT'
         )
       );
     END;
     /
- ID                  0
- ADDRESSLINES
- PLACENAME
- STREETNAME
- INTERSECTSTREET
- SECUNIT
- SETTLEMENT
- MUNICIPALITY
- REGION
- COUNTRY
- POSTALCODE
- POSTALADDONCODE
- FULLPOSTALCODE
- POBOX
- HOUSENUMBER
- BASENAME
- STREETTYPE
- STREETTYPEBEFORE    F
- STREETTYPEATTACHED F
- STREETPREFIX
- STREETSUFFIX
- SIDE
- PERCENT             0
- EDGEID              0
- ERRORMESSAGE        Not found
- MATCHCODE           0 =
- MATCHMODE           DEFAULT
- LONGITUDE           0
- LATITUDE            0
```

Here the MATCHCODE is 0 and the ERRORMESSAGE is Not found.

Geocoding on Business Name

This final example demonstrates a powerful technique: instead of specifying an address, we specify the name of a POI. This allows us to find POIs by just specifying their name, for example, "City Hall," "Central Station," or "General Hospital." The result will be not only the coordinates of the POI, but also its full address.

Listing 6-14 shows how to find the location and address of the Transamerica Pyramid in San Francisco.

Listing 6-14. *Using the* `GEOCODE` *Function to Find a POI*

```
SQL> SET SERVEROUTPUT ON
SQL> BEGIN
       FORMAT_GEO_ADDR (
         SDO_GCDR.GEOCODE (
           'SPATIAL',
           SDO_KEYWORDARRAY('Transamerica Pyramid', 'San Francisco, CA'),
           'US',
           'DEFAULT'
         )
       );
     END;
     /
- ID                        0
- ADDRESSLINES
- PLACENAME                 TRANSAMERICA PYRAMID
- STREETNAME                MONTGOMERY ST
- INTERSECTSTREET
- SECUNIT
- SETTLEMENT                SAN FRANCISCO
- MUNICIPALITY
- REGION                    CA
- COUNTRY                   US
- POSTALCODE                94111
- POSTALADDONCODE
- FULLPOSTALCODE            94111
- POBOX
- HOUSENUMBER               600
- BASENAME
- STREETTYPE
- STREETTYPEBEFORE          F
- STREETTYPEATTACHED        F
- STREETPREFIX
- STREETSUFFIX
- SIDE                      R
- PERCENT                   0
- EDGEID                    23611721
- ERRORMESSAGE              ????#ENUT?B281CP?
- MATCHVECTOR               ????4101110??004?
-   # 4 House or building number
-   E 1 Street prefix
-   N 0 Street base name
-   U 1 Street suffix
-   T 1 Street type
-   ? 1 Secondary unit
-   B 0 Built-up area or city
-   1 0 Region
```

```
-    C 0 Country
-    P 4 Postal code
-    ? ? Postal add-on code
- MATCHCODE              1 = Exact match
- MATCHMODE              DEFAULT
- LONGITUDE              -122.40305
- LATITUDE               37.79509
```

The response contains the exact address of the Transamerica Pyramid: 600 Montgomery Street, San Francisco, CA 94111, as well as its geographical position (longitude and latitude).

The GEOCODE function is powerful, but it has a limitation: it returns only one match. When the input address results in multiple matches, the GEOCODE function returns only the first one. The GEOCODE_ALL function returns *all* matches.

GEOCODE_ALL

Some addresses may be ambiguous and result in multiple matches. For example, the address "12 Presidio, San Francisco, CA" is ambiguous—there are several matching streets. Is "12 Presidio Avenue" intended or "12 Presidio Boulevard"? Perhaps "12 Presidio Terrace"? The GEOCODE function returns only one of them. To see them all, use the GEOCODE_ALL function.

Another cause for ambiguity is when a street extends into multiple postal codes and no house number or postal code is passed to refine the match. Finally, when geocoding to a POI, the name of that POI may be that of the brand or a chain with multiple branches (such as "Bank of America" or "Hertz").

The GEOCODE_ALL function is similar to the GEOCODE function; it takes the same input arguments. However, instead of returning a single match in an SDO_GEO_ADDR object, it returns an array of SDO_GEO_ADDR objects as an object of type SDO_ADDR_ARRAY.

The syntax of the GEOCODE_ALL function is as follows:

```
SDO_GCDR.GEOCODE_ALL (
      username           IN VARCHAR2,
      addr_lines         IN SDO_KEYWORDARRAY,
      country            IN VARCHAR2
      match_mode         IN VARCHAR2
) RETURN SDO_ADDR_ARRAY;
```

Function Parameters

The following sections outline the parameters for the GEOCODE_ALL function. They are the same as those of the GEOCODE function.

username

This is the name of the Oracle schema that contains the geocoding tables for the specified country. It is a required argument. If the data is in the same schema as the one that calls the function, then you can also use the SQL built-in USER.

addr_lines

This is a simple array (VARRAY) of character strings that is used to pass address lines. See the GEOCODE_AS_GEOMETRY function for a detailed explanation.

country

This is the two-letter ISO code for the country to which the address to be geocoded belongs.

match_mode

The match mode lets you decide how closely the elements of an input address must match the data in the geocoding catalog. For a detailed explanation of possible values and their meanings, see the GEOCODE function.

Function Result: SDO_ADDR_ARRAY

This is a VARRAY of up to 1,000 SDO_GEO_ADDR objects. Each SDO_GEO_ADDR object contains the details about one matching address. The structure of each SDO_GEO_ADDR is the same as the one returned by the GEOCODE function.

Examples

Before running the actual examples, we create a stored procedure that will help in decoding the results of a call to the GEOCODE_ALL function. That procedure calls the procedure FORMAT_GEO_ADDR that we created previously, and it is shown in Listing 6-15.

Listing 6-15. FORMAT_ADDR_ARRAY *Procedure*

```
CREATE OR REPLACE PROCEDURE format_addr_array
(
  address_list SDO_ADDR_ARRAY
)
AS
BEGIN
  IF address_list.count() > 0 THEN
    FOR i in 1..address_list.count() LOOP
      dbms_output.put_line ('ADDRESS['||i||']');
      format_geo_addr (address_list(i));
    END LOOP;
  END IF;
END;
/
show errors
```

Our first example is to geocode the ambiguous address "12 Presidio." Listing 6-16 shows this operation.

Listing 6-16. *Using* GEOCODE_ALL *Over an Ambiguous Address*

```
SQL> SET SERVEROUTPUT ON SIZE UNLIMITED
SQL> BEGIN
       FORMAT_ADDR_ARRAY (
         SDO_GCDR.GEOCODE_ALL (
           'SPATIAL',
           SDO_KEYWORDARRAY('12 Presidio', 'San Francisco, CA'),
           'US',
           'DEFAULT'
         )
       );
     END;
     /
ADDRESS[1]
- ID                  1
- ADDRESSLINES
```

```
- PLACENAME
- STREETNAME          PRESIDIO AVE
- INTERSECTSTREET
- SECUNIT
- SETTLEMENT          SAN FRANCISCO
- MUNICIPALITY
- REGION              CA
- COUNTRY             US
- POSTALCODE          94115
- POSTALADDONCODE
- FULLPOSTALCODE      94115
- POBOX
- HOUSENUMBER         12
- BASENAME            PRESIDIO
- STREETTYPE          AVE
- STREETTYPEBEFORE    F
- STREETTYPEATTACHED F
- STREETPREFIX
- STREETSUFFIX
- SIDE                R
- PERCENT             .8877551020408163
- EDGEID              23614728
- ERRORMESSAGE        ????#ENU??B281CP?
- MATCHVECTOR         ????0101410??004?
-   # 0 House or building number
-   E 1 Street prefix
-   N 0 Street base name
-   U 1 Street suffix
-   ? 4 Street type
-   ? 1 Secondary unit
-   B 0 Built-up area or city
-   1 0 Region
-   C 0 Country
-   P 4 Postal code
-   ? ? Postal add-on code
- MATCHCODE               2 = Street type not matched
- MATCHMODE           DEFAULT
- LONGITUDE           -122.44757091836735
- LATITUDE            37.7915968367347

ADDRESS[2]
- ID                      1
- ADDRESSLINES
- PLACENAME
- STREETNAME              PRESIDIO BLVD
- INTERSECTSTREET
- SECUNIT
- SETTLEMENT              SAN FRANCISCO
- MUNICIPALITY
- REGION                  CA
- COUNTRY                 US
- POSTALCODE              94129
- POSTALADDONCODE
- FULLPOSTALCODE          94129
- POBOX
- HOUSENUMBER             12
- BASENAME                PRESIDIO
```

```
- STREETTYPE            BLVD
- STREETTYPEBEFORE      F
- STREETTYPEATTACHED    F
- STREETPREFIX
- STREETSUFFIX
- SIDE                  L
- PERCENT               .7931034482758621
- EDGEID                23622533
- ERRORMESSAGE          ????#ENU??B281CP?
- MATCHVECTOR           ????0101410??004?
-   # 0 House or building number
-   E 1 Street prefix
-   N 0 Street base name
-   U 1 Street suffix
-   ? 4 Street type
-   ? 1 Secondary unit
-   B 0 Built-up area or city
-   1 0 Region
-   C 0 Country
-   P 4 Postal code
-   ? ? Postal add-on code
- MATCHCODE             2 = Street type not matched
- MATCHMODE             DEFAULT
- LONGITUDE             -122.45612528011925
- LATITUDE              37.798262171909265

ADDRESS[3]
- ID                    1
- ADDRESSLINES
- PLACENAME
- STREETNAME            PRESIDIO TER
- INTERSECTSTREET
- SECUNIT
- SETTLEMENT            SAN FRANCISCO
- MUNICIPALITY
- REGION                CA
- COUNTRY               US
- POSTALCODE            94118
- POSTALADDONCODE
- FULLPOSTALCODE        94118
- POBOX
- HOUSENUMBER           12
- BASENAME              PRESIDIO
- STREETTYPE            TER
- STREETTYPEBEFORE      F
- STREETTYPEATTACHED    F
- STREETPREFIX
- STREETSUFFIX
- SIDE                  R
- PERCENT               .6428571428571429
- EDGEID                28488847
- ERRORMESSAGE          ????#ENU??B281CP?
- MATCHVECTOR           ????0101410??004?
-   # 0 House or building number
-   E 1 Street prefix
-   N 0 Street base name
-   U 1 Street suffix
```

```
-    ? 4 Street type
-    ? 1 Secondary unit
-    B 0 Built-up area or city
-    1 0 Region
-    C 0 Country
-    P 4 Postal code
-    ? ? Postal add-on code
- MATCHCODE               2 = Street type not matched
- MATCHMODE               DEFAULT
- LONGITUDE               -122.46105691438208
- LATITUDE                37.788768523050976
```

The result of the function is an array of three SDO_GEO_ADDR objects, each describing one match, complete with normalized address and geographical location.

So, what do we do with this result? Which of the matches is the right one for the address passed as input? There is no way for a program to decide that. The proper approach is to ask the end user. If the geocoding request is done in an interactive application (web or client/server), then the application can display the list of matches and allow the user to pick the right one. This would be the case for a call-center application where the operator asks the caller to clarify his or her address.

If the geocoding request is done in batch mode (that is, without direct user interaction), then the application program should just flag the record for later manual investigation or write it out to a "rejected addresses" table or report.

Our second example is to geocode a POI whose name appears multiple times in the geocoding reference data, such as a chain brand name (hotel, car rental company, and so on) or a common name. The geocoder then returns a list of those POIs that match the given name.

The example in Listing 6-17 (still using the FORMAT_ADDR_ARRAY function) shows how to get the full address and geographical location of the two YMCAs in San Francisco.

Listing 6-17. *Using* GEOCODE_ALL *Over an Ambiguous Address*

```
SQL> SET SERVEROUTPUT ON SIZE 10000
SQL> BEGIN
       FORMAT_ADDR_ARRAY (
         SDO_GCDR.GEOCODE_ALL (
           'SPATIAL',
           SDO_KEYWORDARRAY('YMCA', 'San Francisco, CA'),
           'US',
           'DEFAULT'
         )
       );
     END;
     /

ADDRESS[1]
- ID                     1
- ADDRESSLINES
- PLACENAME              YMCA
- STREETNAME             GOLDEN GATE AVE
- INTERSECTSTREET
- SECUNIT
- SETTLEMENT             SAN FRANCISCO
- MUNICIPALITY
- REGION                 CA
- COUNTRY                US
- POSTALCODE             94102
- POSTALADDONCODE
```

```
- FULLPOSTALCODE          94102
- POBOX
- HOUSENUMBER             220
- BASENAME
- STREETTYPE
- STREETTYPEBEFORE        F
- STREETTYPEATTACHED      F
- STREETPREFIX
- STREETSUFFIX
- SIDE                    L
- PERCENT                 0
- EDGEID                  23605184
- ERRORMESSAGE            ????#ENUT?B281CP?
- MATCHVECTOR             ????4101110??004?
-   # 4 House or building number
-   E 1 Street prefix
-   N 0 Street base name
-   U 1 Street suffix
-   T 1 Street type
-   ? 1 Secondary unit
-   B 0 Built-up area or city
-   1 0 Region
-   C 0 Country
-   P 4 Postal code
-   ? ? Postal add-on code
- MATCHCODE               1 = Exact match
- MATCHMODE               DEFAULT
- LONGITUDE               -122.41412
- LATITUDE                37.78184

ADDRESS[2]
- ID                      1
- ADDRESSLINES
- PLACENAME               YMCA
- STREETNAME              SACRAMENTO ST
- INTERSECTSTREET
- SECUNIT
- SETTLEMENT              SAN FRANCISCO
- MUNICIPALITY
- REGION                  CA
- COUNTRY                 US
- POSTALCODE              94108
- POSTALADDONCODE
- FULLPOSTALCODE          94108
- POBOX
- HOUSENUMBER             855
- BASENAME
- STREETTYPE
- STREETTYPEBEFORE        F
- STREETTYPEATTACHED      F
- STREETPREFIX
- STREETSUFFIX
- SIDE                    R
- PERCENT                 0
- EDGEID                  23615793
- ERRORMESSAGE            ????#ENUT?B281CP?
- MATCHVECTOR             ????4101110??004?
```

```
-    # 4 House or building number
-    E 1 Street prefix
-    N 0 Street base name
-    U 1 Street suffix
-    T 1 Street type
-    ? 1 Secondary unit
-    B 0 Built-up area or city
-    1 0 Region
-    C 0 Country
-    P 4 Postal code
-    ? ? Postal add-on code
- MATCHCODE                 1 = Exact match
- MATCHMODE                 DEFAULT
- LONGITUDE                 -122.40685
- LATITUDE                  37.7932
```

The response contains two matches (that is, two SDO_GEO_ADDR objects): one for the YMCA at 220 Golden Gate Avenue and the other for the YMCA at 855 Sacramento Street (with, of course, their geographical coordinates).

Caution Do not use the GEOCODE_ALL function as a way to search for businesses in a city. The proper way is to perform proximity searches ("within distance" or "nearest neighbor") on POI tables using the techniques described in Chapter 8.

Geocoding Using Structured Addresses

The GEOCODE and GEOCODE_ALL functions work on unformatted addresses: you pass the address as an array of strings, where each string represents one line of the address. The geocoder then needs to parse those lines into distinct address components.

Sometimes, however, your database already contains formatted addresses. For example, your customer table contains columns such as STREET_NAME, HOUSE_NUMBER, ZIP_CODE, CITY_NAME, ..., or your input form to your web application breaks down an address into the same elements.

In those cases, it will be simpler and more efficient to provide the address elements to the geocoding functions in a structured way: the geocoder will no longer need to parse the address, and your multinational application will no longer need to worry about formatting the address lines correctly for each country.

To use this technique, just call the GEOCODE_ADDR or GEOCODE_ADDR_ALL functions. They are identical to the GEOCODE and GEOCODE_ALL functions, respectively, except for their input arguments.

GEOCODE_ADDR

GEOCODE_ADDR is identical to the GEOCODE function, except it takes an SDO_GEO_ADDR object as input, instead of an SDO_KEYWORDARRAY. Note that the other parameters (country and match_mode) are now also passed inside the SDO_GEO_ADDR object.

This is the syntax of the GEOCODE_ADDR function:

```
SDO_GCDR.GEOCODE_ADDR
(
  username       IN VARCHAR2,
  address     IN SDO_GEO_ADDR
) RETURN SDO_GEO_ADDR;
```

Using the SDO_GEO_ADDR Object

Filling an SDO_GEO_ADDR object using its full constructor is difficult because of all its attributes. The attributes must all be filled explicitly, most of them with nulls. But you can use a simplified constructor, as illustrated in Listing 6-18.

Listing 6-18. *Example of Calling the* GEOCODE_ADDR *Function*

```
SQL> SELECT SDO_GCDR.GEOCODE_ADDR
(
  'SPATIAL',
  SDO_GEO_ADDR
  (
    'US',                 -- COUNTRY
    'DEFAULT',            -- MATCHMODE
    '1200 Clay Street',   -- STREET
    'San Francisco',      -- SETTLEMENT
    NULL,                 -- MUNICIPALITY
    'CA',                 -- REGION
    '94108'               -- POSTALCODE  )
)
FROM DUAL;
```

Note that you must specify a value for all arguments to the SDO_GEO_ADDR constructor. If you do not have a value for some argument, then specify the NULL value.

If you want to geocode a point of interest for which you do not have any address, then you can use your own stored function to populate the PLACENAME attribute of the SDO_GEO_ADDR object. Listing 6-19 shows an example of such a function.

Listing 6-19. *A Function Producing an* SDO_GEO_ADDR *Object*

```
SQL> CREATE OR REPLACE FUNCTION geo_addr_poi (
  country  VARCHAR2,
  poi_name VARCHAR2
)
RETURN SDO_GEO_ADDR
AS
  geo_addr SDO_GEO_ADDR := SDO_GEO_ADDR();
BEGIN
  geo_addr.country := country;
  geo_addr.placename := poi_name;
  geo_addr.matchmode := 'DEFAULT';
return geo_addr ;
end;
/
```

The example in Listing 6-20 illustrates how to use this function in order to find the location of the Moscone Center.

Listing 6-20. *Example of Calling the* GEOCODE_ADDR *Function*

```
SQL> SELECT SDO_GCDR.GEOCODE_ADDR
(
  'SPATIAL',
  GEO_ADDR_POI
  (
    'US',                 -- COUNTRY
```

```
    'Moscone Center'    -- POI_NAME
  )
)
FROM DUAL;
SDO_GEO_ADDR(0, SDO_KEYWORDARRAY(NULL), 'MOSCONE CENTER', 'HOWARD ST', NULL, NULL,
'SAN FRANCISCO', NULL, 'CA', 'US', '94103', NULL, '94103', NULL, '747', NULL, NULL,
'F', 'F', NULL, NULL, 'R', 0, 23607005, '????#ENUT?B281CP?', 1, 'DEFAULT',
-122.40137, 37.7841, '????4141114??404?')
```

GEOCODE_ADDR_ALL

GEOCODE_ADDR_ALL is identical to the GEOCODE_ALL function, except it takes an SDO_GEO_ADDR object as input, instead of an SDO_KEYWORDARRAY. Note that the other parameters (country and match_mode) are now also passed inside the SDO_GEO_ADDR object.

This is the syntax of the GEOCODE_ADDR_ALL function:

```
SDO_GCDR.GEOCODE_ADDR _ALL
(
  username        IN VARCHAR2,
  address      IN SDO_GEO_ADDR
) RETURN SDO_GEO_ADDR_ARRAY;
```

Reverse Geocoding

As the name implies, *reverse geocoding* performs the reverse operation of geocoding; given a spatial location (coordinates of a point), it returns the corresponding street address.

Reverse geocoding is useful for many applications. For example, GPS devices may be used to track buses or delivery vehicles. The reverse geocoding process will allow you to know approximately at what street address the bus or truck currently is.

Another common use is to identify locations from a click on a map. The click is first converted into geographical coordinates (MapViewer will do this automatically), then the reverse geocoding returns the corresponding street address.

The reverse geocoder performs four steps:

1. Locate the road segment. This is done using a nearest neighbor search, that is, using the SDO_NN spatial operator that you will see in Chapter 8.
2. Project the input location on the road segment, that is, find the point on the road segment that corresponds to the shortest distance between the input location and the road segment.
3. Compute the house number at that point by interpolation between the known house numbers at each end of the road segment. The house number returned will be on the same side of the road as the geographical point given as input.
4. Find all other address details (street name, postal code, city, and so on).

To perform reverse geocodings, use the REVERSE_GEOCODE function.

REVERSE_GEOCODE

Here is the syntax of the REVERSE_GEOCODE function:

```
SDO_GCDR.REVERSE_GEOCODE
(
  username        IN VARCHAR2,
  location        IN SDO_GEOMETRY,
```

```
  country         IN VARCHAR2
) RETURN SDO_GEO_ADDR;
```

Function Parameters

The following sections outline the parameters for the REVERSE_GEOCODE function.

username

This is the name of the Oracle schema that contains the geocoding tables for the specified country. It is a required argument. If the data is in the same schema as the one that calls the function, then you can also use the SQL built-in USER.

location

This is the geographic point to locate.

country

This is the two-letter ISO code for the country to which the address to be geocoded belongs.

Function Result: SDO_GEO_ADDR

This structure contains the detailed results of a geocoding operation. See Table 6-4 and the discussion of the GEOCODE function for the exact content of the structure and how to use it.

■Note The table GC_ROAD_SEGMENT_xx must have a spatial index in order to allow reverse geocoding.

Examples

The example in Listing 6-21 illustrates the REVERSE_GEOCODE function. To make the result more readable, we will format them using the FORMAT_GEO_ADDR procedure.

Listing 6-21. *Example of Calling the* REVERSE_GEOCODE *Function*

```
SQL> SET SERVEROUTPUT ON
SQL> BEGIN
       FORMAT_GEO_ADDR (
         SDO_GCDR.REVERSE_GEOCODE (
           'SPATIAL',
           SDO_GEOMETRY (
             2001,
             8307,
             SDO_POINT_TYPE (-122.4152166, 37.7930, NULL),
             NULL, NULL
           ),
           'US'
         )
       );
     END;
     /
```

```
- ID                      0
- ADDRESSLINES
- PLACENAME
- STREETNAME              CLAY ST
- INTERSECTSTREET
- SECUNIT
- SETTLEMENT              SAN FRANCISCO
- MUNICIPALITY
- REGION                  CA
- COUNTRY                 US
- POSTALCODE              94109
- POSTALADDONCODE
- FULLPOSTALCODE          94109
- POBOX
- HOUSENUMBER             1351
- BASENAME                CLAY
- STREETTYPE              ST
- STREETTYPEBEFORE        F
- STREETTYPEATTACHED      F
- STREETPREFIX
- STREETSUFFIX
- SIDE                    R
- PERCENT                 .484531914156248
- EDGEID                  23600696
- ERRORMESSAGE
- MATCHVECTOR             ????4141414??404?
-     4 House or building number
-     1 Street prefix
-     4 Street base name
-     1 Street suffix
-     4 Street type
-     1 Secondary unit
-     4 Built-up area or city
-     4 Region
-     0 Country
-     4 Postal code
-     ? Postal add-on code
- MATCHCODE               1 = Exact match
- MATCHMODE               DEFAULT
- LONGITUDE               -122.415225677046
- LATITUDE                37.7930717518897
```

Notice that the coordinates returned are different from the ones passed. This is because the input point is some distance away from the line that represents the centerline of the road.

Geocoding Business Data

Now that you know how to use the geocoder, how can you use it to location-enable business data—that is, the `customers`, `branches`, and `competitors` tables?

Adding the Spatial Column

The first step is to add a spatial column (type `SDO_GEOMETRY`) to the tables. You can easily do this using an `ALTER` statement, as shown in Listing 6-22. We previously explained the process in Chapter 3.

Listing 6-22. *Adding a Spatial Column*

```
SQL> ALTER TABLE customers ADD (location SDO_GEOMETRY);
SQL> ALTER TABLE branches ADD (location SDO_GEOMETRY);
SQL> ALTER TABLE competitors ADD (location SDO_GEOMETRY);
```

Geocoding the Addresses: The "Naive" Approach

As you have seen, geocoding an address is really quite simple when you are certain that the address is valid. Just use the result of the `GEOCODE_AS_GEOMETRY` function to update the `location` column you just added, as shown in Listing 6-23 for the `branches` table. The process is identical for the other tables (they all have the same structure).

Listing 6-23. *Populating the* `location` *Column of the* `branches` *Table*

```
SQL> UPDATE branches
SET location = SDO_GCDR.GEOCODE_AS_GEOMETRY
(
  'SPATIAL',
  SDO_KEYWORDARRAY
  ( street_number || ' ' || street_name, city  || ' ' || state || ' '
    || postal_code),
  'US'
  );
SQL> COMMIT;
```

The `GEOCODE_AS_GEOMETRY` function expects the input address to be passed as a series of formatted lines. However, the `branches` table already contains a structured address (that is, it has address elements in multiple columns):

```
STREET_NUMBER                                     VARCHAR2(5)
STREET_NAME                                       VARCHAR2(60)
CITY                                              VARCHAR2(32)
POSTAL_CODE                                       VARCHAR2(16)
STATE                                             VARCHAR2(32)
```

All you need is to construct a multiline address using this information. You can do this simply by concatenating the address elements:

- *First address line*: `street_number || ' ' || street_name`
- *Second address line*: `city  || ' ' || state || ' ' || postal_code`

Then, just pass each resulting string as one element to the `SDO_KEYWORDARRAY` object constructor.

We assume that all addresses are U.S. addresses, but this may not be the case. Addresses in different countries must be formatted according to the formatting rules of addresses in those countries before being passed to the geocoder.

For example, if you were geocoding German addresses, Listing 6-24 shows what the previous code becomes.

Listing 6-24. *Populating the* `location` *Column of the* `branches` *Table for German Addresses*

```
SQL> UPDATE branches
SET location = SDO_GCDR.GEOCODE_AS_GEOMETRY
(
  'SPATIAL',
  SDO_KEYWORDARRAY
  ( street_name || ' ' || street_number  || postal_code || ' ' || city),
```

```
  'DE'
);
SQL> COMMIT;
```

The address lines are now formatted according to the German rules: the house number follows the street name, and the postal code precedes the city. There is no state. The country code (DE) passed indicates that this is a German address. Note that we assume that the geocoding reference data tables (GC_ROAD_DE and so on) are in the database schema called SPATIAL.

However, the better way to handle multinational addresses is to use the structured addressing mechanism, that is, passing address elements in an SDO_GEO_ADDR structure.

■ **Note** For U.S. addresses, the state is optional if the address contains a postal code.

Address Verification and Correction

The preceding approach is simple to use, but it has limitations:

- You cannot be sure of the quality of the geocoding result (that is, there may be errors in the input addresses). Failed or ambiguous addresses should be flagged for later manual correction, but status information is not returned from the GEOCODE_AS_GEOMETRY function.
- If an address contains errors (such as an invalid postal code), you should be able to update it with the corrected information.
- For large data sets, it is not practical to do the update as a single transaction. You may need to perform intermediate commits.

To overcome these limitations, you need to use PL/SQL. The procedure in Listing 6-25 geocodes the addresses in the customers table.

Listing 6-25. *Address Geocoding and Correction*

```
SET SERVEROUTPUT ON SIZE 32000
DECLARE
  type match_counts_t is table of number;

  input_address      sdo_geo_addr;          -- Input address to geocode

  geo_addresses      sdo_addr_array;        -- Array of matching geocoded addresses
  geo_address        sdo_geo_addr;          -- Matching address
  geo_location       sdo_geometry;          -- Geographical location

  address_count      number;                -- Addresses processed
  geocoded_count     number;                -- Addresses successfully geocoded
  corrected_count    number;                -- Addresses geocoded and corrected
  ambiguous_count    number;                -- Ambiguous addresses (multiple matches)
  error_count        number;                -- Addresses rejected

  match_counts       match_counts_t         -- Counts per matchcode
    := match_counts_t();

  update_address     boolean;               -- Should update address ?
```

```
BEGIN

  -- Clear counters
  address_count := 0;
  geocoded_count := 0;
  error_count := 0;
  corrected_count := 0;
  ambiguous_count := 0;
  match_counts.extend(20);
  for i in 1..match_counts.count loop
    match_counts(i) := 0;
  end loop;

  -- Range over the customers
  for b in
    (select * from customers)
  loop

    -- Format the input address
    input_address := sdo_geo_addr();
    input_address.streetname  := b.street_name;
    input_address.housenumber := b.street_number;
    input_address.settlement  := b.city;
    input_address.postalcode  := b.postal_code;
    input_address.region      := b.state;
    input_address.country     := 'US';
    input_address.matchmode   := 'DEFAULT';

    -- Geocode the address
    geo_addresses := sdo_gcdr.geocode_addr_all (
      'SPATIAL',
      input_address
    );

    -- Check results
    update_address := false;
    address_count := address_count + 1;

    if geo_addresses.count() > 1 then

      -- Address is ambiguous: reject
      geo_location := NULL;
      ambiguous_count := ambiguous_count + 1;

    else
      -- Extract first or only match
      geo_address := geo_addresses(1);

      -- Keep counts of matchcodes seen
      match_counts(geo_address.matchcode) :=
        match_counts(geo_address.matchcode) + 1;

      -- The following matchcodes are accepted:
      --   1 = exact match
      --   2 = only street type or suffix/prefix is incorrect
      --  10 = only postal code is incorrect
```

```
      if geo_address.matchcode in (1,2,10) then
        -- Geocoding succeeded: construct geometric point
        geo_location := sdo_geometry (2001, 8307, sdo_point_type (
          geo_address.longitude, geo_address.latitude, null),
          null, null);
        geocoded_count := geocoded_count + 1;

        -- If wrong street type or postal code (matchcodes 2 or 10)
        -- accept the geocode and correct the address in the database
        if geo_address.matchcode <> 1 then
          update_address := true;
          corrected_count := corrected_count + 1;
        end if;

      else
        -- For all other matchcodes, reject the geocode
        error_count := error_count + 1;
        geo_location := NULL;
      end if;

    end if;

    -- Update location and corrected address in database
    if update_address then
      update customers
      set location = geo_location,
          street_name = geo_address.streetname,
          postal_code = geo_address.postalcode
      where id = b.id;
    else
      update customers
      set location = geo_location
      where id = b.id;
    end if;

  end loop;

  -- Display counts of records processed
  dbms_output.put_line ('Geocoding completed');
  dbms_output.put_line (address_count || ' Addresses processed');
  dbms_output.put_line (geocoded_count || ' Addresses successfully geocoded');
  dbms_output.put_line (corrected_count || ' Addresses corrected');
  dbms_output.put_line (ambiguous_count || ' ambiguous addresses rejected');
  dbms_output.put_line (error_count || ' addresses with errors');

  for i in 1..match_counts.count loop
    if match_counts(i) > 0 then
      dbms_output.put_line ('Match code '|| i || ': ' || match_counts(i));
    end if;
  end loop;

END;
/
```

Let's now look at some of the important parts of that procedure.

The following is where you do the actual geocoding of each address. The address elements are stored in a SDO_GEO_ADDR structure passed to the GEOCODE_ADDR_ALL function, which returns a list of matches.

```
-- Format the input address
input_address := sdo_geo_addr();
input_address.streetname  := b.street_name;
input_address.housenumber := b.street_number;
input_address.settlement  := b.city;
input_address.postalcode  := b.postal_code;
input_address.region      := b.state;
input_address.country     := 'US';
input_address.matchmode   := 'DEFAULT';

-- Geocode the address
geo_addresses := sdo_gcdr.geocode_addr_all (
  'SPATIAL',
  input_address
);
```

If the function returned multiple results in the SDO_ADDR_ARRAY, that means the address is *ambiguous* and we reject it.

```
if geo_addresses.count() > 1 then
  -- Address is ambiguous: reject
  geo_location := NULL;
  ambiguous_count := ambiguous_count + 1;
else
...
```

If the function returned one result, we can find out the quality of the result by looking at the MATCHCODE for that result. Match codes 1, 2, and 10 are accepted. Match code 1 indicates an exact match—the address was found and a geographical location was returned.

Match code 2 indicates that the street type, prefix, or suffix is in error. This is a common mistake. For example, the address is stored as "1250 Clay Avenue," when it should really be "1250 Clay *Street*."

Match code 10 indicates that the postal code is incorrect. This is also an easy mistake to make, especially for streets that span multiple postal codes. For example, for the address "1250 Clay Street, San Francisco, CA 94109" the correct postal code is 94108.

In both cases, we choose to accept the corrected information returned by the geocoder, and we use it to update the address in the table.

We also construct an SDO_GEOMETRY object using the coordinates returned. Notice that the coordinate system is set to 8307 (longitude/latitude, WGS84), which we know is the coordinate system used for the geocoding reference data.[1]

Finally, if the match code is anything else, we reject the result.

```
if geo_address.matchcode in (1,2,10) then
    -- Geocoding succeeded: construct geometric point
    geo_location := sdo_geometry (2001, 8307, sdo_point_type (
      geo_address.longitude, geo_address.latitude, null),
      null, null);
    geocoded_count := geocoded_count + 1;

    -- If wrong street type or postal code (matchcodes 2 or 10)
    -- accept the geocode and correct the address in the database
```

1. We know this because NAVTEQ, the supplier of the geocoder reference data, uses this coordinate system.

```
      if geo_address.matchcode <> 1 then
        update_address := true;
        corrected_count := corrected_count + 1;
      end if;
    else
      -- For all other matchcodes, reject the geocode
      error_count := error_count + 1;
      geo_location := NULL;
    end if;

  end if;
```

We can now update the table row inside the database. If the address error (if any) can be corrected, we do so. We replace the `street_name` and `postal_code` columns with the values returned by the geocoder.

In all cases, we update the `location` column with the geographical point object that contains the coordinates of the address. If the address was ambiguous or if the geocoder indicated a problem that we chose not to correct automatically, then the `location` column is set to `NULL` to indicate failure.

```
  -- Update location and corrected address in database
  if update_address then
    update customers
    set location = geo_location,
        street_name = geo_address.streetname,
        postal_code = geo_address.postalcode
    where id = b.id;
  else
    update customers
    set location = geo_location
    where id = b.id;
  end if;
```

When all addresses have been processed, we print out some statistics. Those numbers are useful to measure the quality of the input addresses. A *hit rate* can be computed as the ratio of successfully geocoded addresses to the total addresses to process.

```
  -- Display counts of records processed
  dbms_output.put_line ('Geocoding completed');
  dbms_output.put_line (address_count || ' Addresses processed');
  dbms_output.put_line (geocoded_count || ' Addresses successfully geocoded');
  dbms_output.put_line (corrected_count || ' Addresses corrected');
  dbms_output.put_line (ambiguous_count || ' ambiguous addresses rejected');
  dbms_output.put_line (error_count || ' addresses with errors');
```

Running the preceding code produces results like the following:

```
SQL> @geocode_customers.sql
Geocoding completed
3173 Addresses processed
3146 Addresses successfully geocoded
6 Addresses corrected
10 ambiguous addresses rejected
17 addresses with errors
Match code 1: 3140
Match code 2: 6
Match code 4: 9
Match code 11: 8
PL/SQL procedure successfully completed.
```

The hit rate for this run is 99.1 percent. Out of 3,173 addresses, 3,146 were successfully geocoded, among which 6 had minor errors that were corrected. Twenty-seven addresses were rejected; 10 addresses are ambiguous; and 17 addresses have various errors, for example, street name errors (match code 4) or city name errors (match code 11).

The next step is for someone to look at those failed addresses and correct them manually. Finding them is easy; we need look at only those rows where the `location` column is `NULL`. Once those addresses are corrected, we can rerun the process, possibly on only the new addresses.

Further Refinements

You can build upon and improve the preceding code in several ways:

- Turn it into a stored procedure that takes a `table_name` column as input. Use dynamic SQL to make the procedure work with any table.
- Perform periodic commits. This allows you to easily restart the process in case of failure by just skipping those addresses that you already processed.
- Only geocode those addresses that have the `location` column set to `NULL`. This allows you to use the same process after correcting the rejected addresses. It also enables you to restart the process should it fail for any reason. It will skip those addresses that were already geocoded.
- Add a `match_code` column to the data tables and populate it with the match codes returned by the geocoder. This can help the user who later corrects the addresses to better understand the nature of each error.

Automatic Geocoding

The geocoder is invoked using simple function calls. Those function calls can be used from anywhere, including from triggers. This is a powerful mechanism—it allows addresses to be geocoded automatically whenever an address is changed. Listing 6-26 shows a simple trigger that automatically geocodes addresses in the `branches` table.

Listing 6-26. *Automatic Geocoding of the* `branches` *Table Using a Simple Trigger*

```
CREATE OR REPLACE TRIGGER branches_geocode
  BEFORE INSERT OR UPDATE OF street_name, street_number, postal_code, city, state
  ON branches
  FOR EACH ROW
DECLARE
  geo_location SDO_GEOMETRY;
BEGIN
  geo_location := SDO_GCDR.GEOCODE_AS_GEOMETRY (
    'SPATIAL',
    SDO_KEYWORDARRAY (
      :new.street_number || ' ' || :new.street_name,
      :new.city || ' ' || :new.state || ' ' ||:new.postal_code),
    'US'
  );
  :new.location := geo_location;
END;
/
```

This trigger uses the "naive" approach: the new location is accepted no matter what errors exist in the new address. Consider the following example, in which the address of one of our branches is changed. The branch is currently at 1 Van Ness Avenue.

```
SQL> SELECT name, street_number, street_name, city, postal_code, location
     FROM branches
     WHERE id = 77;

NAME                 STREE STREET_NAME          CITY          POSTAL_CODE
-------------------- ----- -------------------- ------------- -------------------
LOCATION(SDO_GTYPE, SDO_SRID, SDO_POINT(X, Y, Z), SDO_ELEM_INFO, SDO_ORDINATES)
-------------------------------------------------------------------------------
BANK OF AMERICA      1     S VAN NESS AVE       SAN FRANCISCO 94103
SDO_GEOMETRY(2001, 8307, SDO_POINT_TYPE(-122.41915, 37.7751038, NULL), NULL, NULL)
```

The branch relocates to 1500 Clay Street:

```
SQL> UPDATE branches
     SET street_name = 'Clay Street', street_number = 1500
     WHERE id = 77;
1 row updated.
```

This is the result:

```
SQL> SELECT name, street_number, street_name, city, postal_code, location
     FROM branches
     WHERE id = 77;

NAME                 STREE STREET_NAME          CITY          POSTAL_CODE
-------------------- ----- -------------------- ------------- -------------------
LOCATION(SDO_GTYPE, SDO_SRID, SDO_POINT(X, Y, Z), SDO_ELEM_INFO,
SDO_ORDINATES)
-------------------- ----- -------------------- ------------- -------------------
BANK OF AMERICA      1500  Clay Street          SAN FRANCISCO 94103
SDO_GEOMETRY(2001, 8307, SDO_POINT_TYPE(-122.41768, 37.7927675, NULL), NULL, NULL)
```

The branch now has the new address, and the geographic coordinates point to the new address. However, the address has the wrong postal code—we forgot to change it!

A better approach is to proceed as in the previous example—that is, use the GEOCODE_ALL procedure and use the result to automatically correct the address in addition to simply geocoding it. The trigger in Listing 6-27 illustrates this technique.

Listing 6-27. *Automatic Geocoding with Address Correction*

```
CREATE OR REPLACE TRIGGER branches_geocode
  BEFORE INSERT OR UPDATE OF street_name, street_number, postal_code, city, state
  ON branches
  FOR EACH ROW
DECLARE
  input_address SDO_GEO_ADDR;
  geo_location SDO_GEOMETRY;
  geo_addresses SDO_ADDR_ARRAY;
  geo_address SDO_GEO_ADDR;
  update_address BOOLEAN;

BEGIN
  -- Format the input address
  input_address := sdo_geo_addr();
  input_address.streetname  := :new.street_name;
  input_address.housenumber := :new.street_number;
  input_address.settlement  := :new.city;
  input_address.postalcode  := :new.postal_code;
```

```
  input_address.region      := :new.state;
  input_address.country     := 'US';
  input_address.matchmode   := 'DEFAULT';

  -- Geocode the address
  geo_addresses := sdo_gcdr.geocode_addr_all (
    'SPATIAL',
    input_address
  );

  -- Check results
  if geo_addresses.count() > 1 then
    -- Address is ambiguous: reject
    geo_location := NULL;
  else
    -- Extract first or only match
    geo_address := geo_addresses(1);
    -- The following matchcodes are accepted:
    --   1 = exact match
    --   2 = only street type or suffix/prefix is incorrect
    --  10 = only postal code is incorrect
    if geo_address.matchcode in (1,2,10) then
      -- Geocoding succeeded: construct geometric point
      geo_location := sdo_geometry (2001, 8307, sdo_point_type (
        geo_address.longitude, geo_address.latitude, null),
        null, null);
      -- If wrong street type or postal code (matchcodes 2 or 10)
      -- accept the geocode and correct the address in the database
      if geo_address.matchcode <> 1 then
        update_address := true;
      end if;
    else
      -- For all other matchcoded, reject the geocode
      geo_location := NULL;
    end if;
  end if;

  -- Update location
  :new.location := geo_location;
  -- If needed, correct address
  :new.street_name := geo_address.streetname;
  :new.postal_code := geo_address.postalcode;

END;
/
```

Once this trigger is created, let's see what happens if we perform the same address change of branch 77 from 1 Van Ness Avenue to 1500 Clay Street:

```
SQL> UPDATE branches
     SET street_name = 'Clay Street', street_number = 1500
     WHERE id = 77;
1 row updated.
```

This is the result:

```
SQL> SELECT name, street_number, street_name, city, postal_code, location
FROM branches WHERE id = 77;

NAME                 STREE STREET_NAME          CITY          POSTAL_CODE
-------------------- ----- -------------------- ------------- -------------------
LOCATION(SDO_GTYPE, SDO_SRID, SDO_POINT(X, Y, Z), SDO_ELEM_INFO,
SDO_ORDINATES)
---------------------------------------------------------------------------------
BANK OF AMERICA      1500  CLAY ST              SAN FRANCISCO 94109
SDO_GEOMETRY(2001, 8307, SDO_POINT_TYPE(-122.41768, 37.7927675, NULL), NULL, NULL)
```

The geographical location is the same as computed previously, but notice that the street name was corrected to match the name in the reference data and, more important, the postal code is now the right one for that location.

Let's say the branch moves again, this time to 1200 Montgomery Street:

```
SQL> UPDATE branches SET street_name = 'Montgommery street', street_number = 1200
WHERE id = 77;
```

Notice that again we did not specify any postal code, but we also made a typing mistake: *Montgommery* instead of *Montgomery*. The result of the update is as follows:

```
SQL> SELECT name, street_number, street_name, city, postal_code, location
     FROM branches
     WHERE id = 77;

NAME                 STREE STREET_NAME          CITY          POSTAL_CODE
-------------------- ----- -------------------- ------------- -------------------
LOCATION(SDO_GTYPE, SDO_SRID, SDO_POINT(X, Y, Z), SDO_ELEM_INFO,
SDO_ORDINATES)
---------------------------------------------------------------------------------
BANK OF AMERICA      1200  MONTGOMERY ST        SAN FRANCISCO 94133
SDO_GEOMETRY(2001, 8307, SDO_POINT_TYPE(-122.40405, 37.8001438, NULL), NULL, NULL)
```

The street name was automatically corrected, and the postal code is also now correct for that section of Montgomery Street.

If the address given cannot be corrected or is ambiguous, then the `location` column is automatically set to `NULL`.

The major benefit of this approach is that it allows addresses to be automatically geocoded and corrected without needing any changes to the existing applications.

The Geocoding Server

Using SQL calls to geocode addresses is nice but requires a tight coupling between your application and the database via JDBC connections. Another possibility is to set up a web service that will perform the geocoding calls on your behalf. This is the role of the Geocoding Server web service: you send it geocoding requests, expressed in XML, and it returns the results also in XML.

Architecture

The architecture of the Geocoding Server is illustrated in Figure 6-3. The Geocoding Server is a pure Java server component (a Java servlet) that needs a Java application server environment. You can deploy it in the Oracle Application Server, as well as any J2EE-compliant application server.

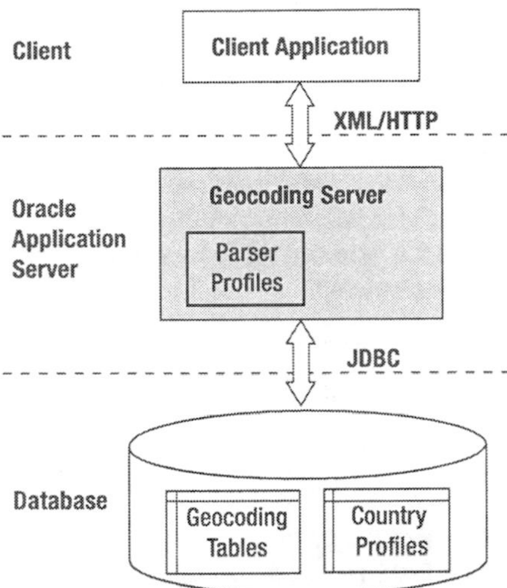

Figure 6-3. *Oracle Geocoding Server architecture*

The Geocoding Server does not use the geocoding procedures that you saw in previous sections. Rather, it runs the geocoding logic directly and uses JDBC only to read from the database geocoding data tables. It uses its own local copy of the parser profiles, instead of the `GC_PARSER_PROFILES` and `GC_PARSER_PROFILEAFS` tables. It does, however, load country profiles from the `GC_COUNTRY_PROFILE` table.

Figure 6-4 illustrates the way your application talks to the Geocoding Server. Your application must first format the geocoding request in XML and then send it to the server. Once the server has found a matching location, it will send another XML document back to your application, which you then need to parse and use.

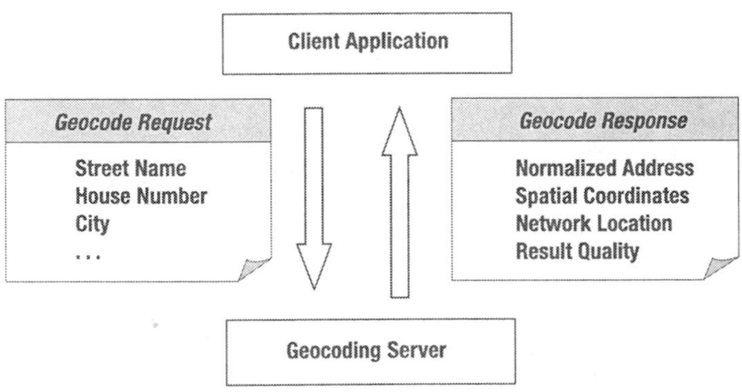

Figure 6-4. *Oracle Geocoding Server request/response flow*

The geocode request contains the address to process. You can pass it unstructured, as a set of address lines, or (for U.S. addresses) among a small number of semistructured encodings. The geocode response contains essentially the same information as the `SDO_GEO_ADDR` structure you learned about earlier.

Installation and Configuration

The Geocoding Engine is provided as a standard J2EE archive (EAR) format. See the introduction for details on how to install and configure OC4J and how to deploy applications using the OC4J console. The installation EAR file for the Geocoding Engine is provided in `$ORACLE_HOME/md/jlib/geocoder.ear`.

Once installed, you need to configure the geocoding server. Do this by manually editing the `geocodercfg.xml` file in `$OC4J_HOME/j2ee/home/applications/geocoder/web/WEB-INF/config`. To make the geocoder use your modified configuration, you need to restart it. You can do so by stopping and restarting the geocoder application using the OC4J administration console.

■ **Tip** You can also edit the configuration file and restart the geocoder using its own administration tool. You can access it from the Geocoder's home page, shown in Figure 6-5.

■ **Caution** The `geocodercfg.xml` file provided with the Geocoding Engine contains a database connection definition that points to a nonexistent database. This will make the engine fail the first time it starts, right after deployment.

The following is an example of a configuration file. All settings are the ones in the initial configuration. The only parameters you must change are those that define the database connection.

```
<GeocoderConfig >
  <logging log_level="finest" log_thread_name="false" log_time="true">
  </logging>
  <geocoder>
    <database name="local"
              host="localhost"
              port="1521"
              sid="orcl"
              mode="thin"
              user="gc"
              password="gc" />
    <data_source name="NAV" />
    <parameters cache_admin="false"
              cache_postcode="false"
              fuzzy_string_distance="70"
              fuzzy_leading_char_match="4"
              debug_level="0"/>
  </geocoder>
  <addressparser>
    <parameters debug_level="0" />
  </addressparser>
</GeocoderConfig>
```

Logging

The Geocoding Server can generate a log of its operation. The `<logging>` element enables you to control how detailed this logging should be. The following is an example setting:

```
<logging log_level="info" log_thread_name="true" log_time="true">
</logging>
```

The element contains the following attributes:

- log_level: This attribute defines the level of detail to log. It can range from less detailed (fatal) to very detailed (finest). The default (info) is a good compromise. The debug and finest settings are useful only to help in diagnosing problems or to better understand the operation of the geocoder. The finest level involves each request and response getting logged. Do not use it in production.
- log_thread_name: When this attribute is set to true, the name of each geocoder thread is logged with each message.
- log_time: When this attribute is set to true, a time stamp is logged with each message.

Note that you have no way to decide where the information is logged. It goes on the OC4J console, as well as to a file: $OC4J_HOME/j2ee/home/applications/geocoder/web/WEB-INF/log/geocoder.log.

■ **Caution** The log file gets reset every time the geocoding server starts or restarts.

Database Connection

The following lets you define the connection to your database:

```
<database name="local"
             host="localhost"
             port="1521"
             sid="orcl"
             mode="thin"
             user="gc"
             password="gc"
/>
```

where the following is true:

- name is a name for this database.
- host is the name or IP address of the system hosting the Oracle database.
- port is the port on which the database is listening. By default, databases listen on port 1521.
- sid is the name of the database.
- mode defines the kind of JDBC driver to use (specify as thin or oci).
- user is the user name to connect to the database.
- password is the password of the user connecting to the database.

Geocoding Parameters

The following lets you exercise some control on the behavior of the geocoder.

```
<parameters
      cache_admin="false"
      cache_postcode="false"
      fuzzy_string_distance="70"
      fuzzy_leading_char_match="4"
      load_db_parser_profiles="false"
/>
```

where the following is true:

- `cache_admin`: This specifies whether to cache the admin areas in memory.
- `cache_postcode`: This specifies whether to cache the postal codes in memory.
- `fuzzy_string_distance`: The geocoder assigns a score (0–100) to each candidate street name. The score 100 means an exact match. A lower score means the name is less like the input name. This parameter sets the minimum string match score for qualified candidate street names. Only names with score equal or greater than this value will be considered possible match candidates.
- `fuzzy_leading_char_match`: This is the number of leading characters in a street base name that are required to match.
- `load_db_parser_profiles`: Set this to `true` to load the parser profiles from the database instead of the local `ppr` files.

Using the Geocoder: XML Queries and Responses

You should now be able to start submitting geocoding requests.

Go to `http://oc4j_server:8888/geocoder` using your web browser, where `oc4j_server` is the name or IP address of the machine where you installed OC4J. For example, you would use `http://127.0.0.1:8888/ geocoder` if you installed OC4J on your desktop machine. You should see the page shown in Figure 6-5.

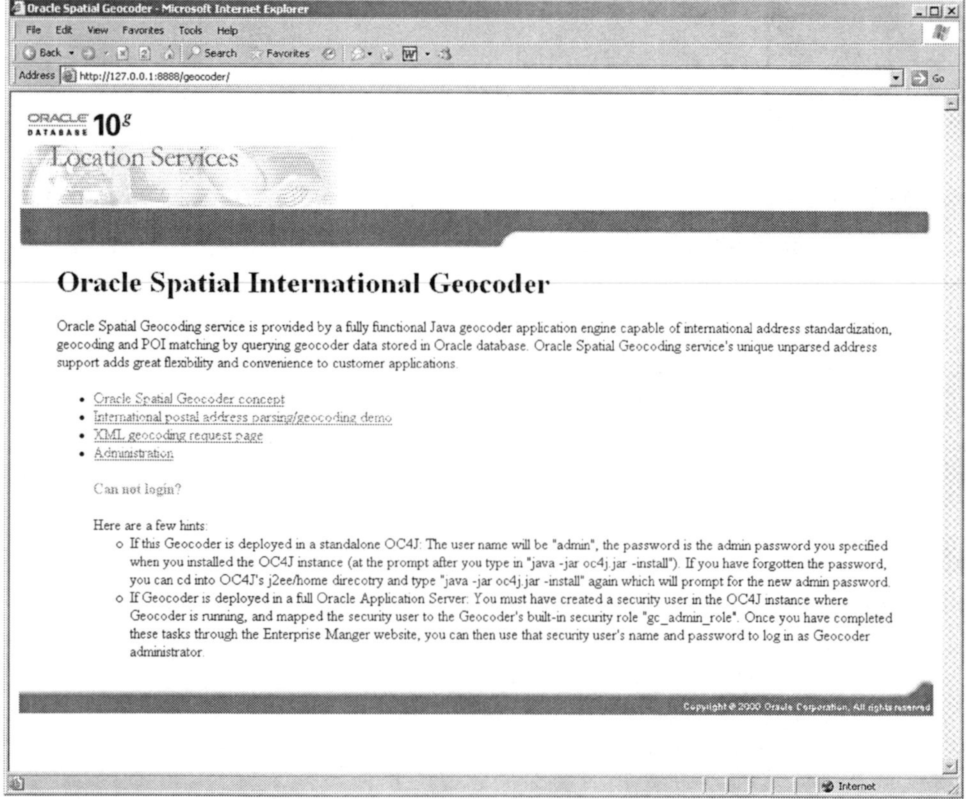

Figure 6-5. *The Geocoding Server home page*

From this page, you can choose links to various examples. If you click the link "XML geocoding request page," you will be taken to the page shown in Figure 6-6. This page allows you to enter any XML geocoding request and send it to the server.

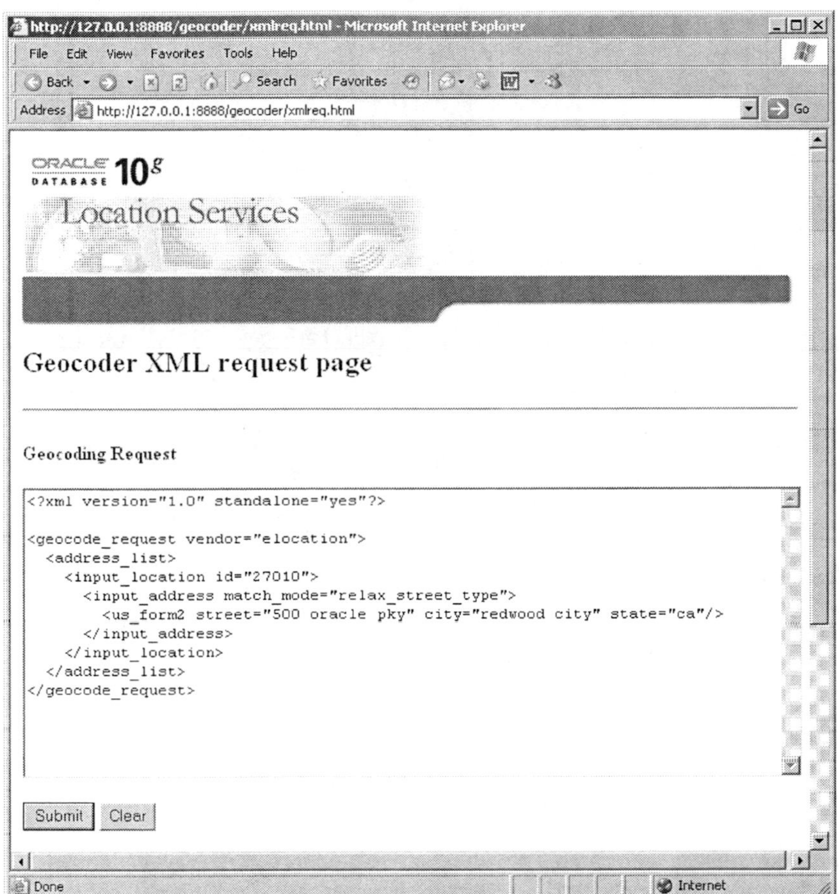

Figure 6-6. *Geocoding request page*

Just click the submit button for the first example. You should get a page back that looks like the one shown in Figure 6-7. Congratulations, you just completed your first geocoding request.

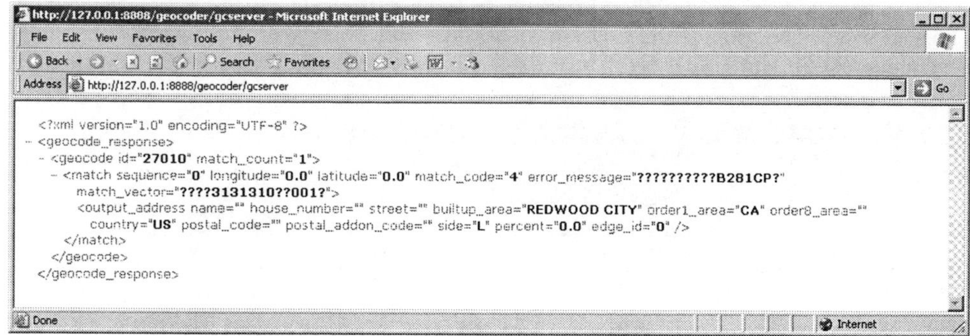

Figure 6-7. *Geocoding response*

Notice that the geocoder did not find the exact address (Oracle Parkway). This is because the dataset does not cover this area.

Geocoding Requests

The following is a simple geocoding request:

```
<geocode_request>
  <address_list>
    <input_location id="1" >
      <input_address>
        <unformatted country="US" >
          <address_line value="1250 Clay St" />
          <address_line value="San Francisco, CA 94108" />
        </unformatted >
      </input_address>
    </input_location>
  </address_list>
</geocode_request>
```

This request uses the generic, unformatted notation for street addresses. The geocoder supports a few alternate formats, specifically for U.S. addresses. For example, the request in Figure 6-7 uses one of those formats. The response is like this:

```
<geocode_response>
  <geocode id="1" match_count="1">
    <match sequence="0" longitude="-122.4135615" latitude="37.7932878"
      match_code="1"
      error_message="????#ENUT?B281CP?"
      match_vector="????0101010??000?">
      <output_address name="" house_number="1250" street="CLAY ST"
        builtup_area="SAN FRANCISCO"
        order1_area="CA" order8_area="" country="US" postal_code="94108"
        postal_addon_code=""
        side="L" percent="0.49" edge_id="23600695" />
    </match>
  </geocode>
</geocode_response>
```

You will notice that the response contains the same information as that returned by the `SDO_GCDR.GEOCODE()` function in the `SDO_GEO_ADDR` structure.

The following request is ambiguous; you do not specify the house number you want on Clay Street, and you do not specify any ZIP code:

```
<geocode_request>
  <address_list>
    <input_location id="1" >
      <input_address>
        <unformatted country="US" >
          <address_line value="Clay St" />
          <address_line value="San Francisco, CA" />
        </unformatted >
      </input_address>
    </input_location>
  </address_list>
</geocode_request>
```

Since Clay Street has several ZIP codes, you get a list of matches back:

```
<geocode_response>
  <geocode id="1" match_count="5">
    <match sequence="0" longitude="-122.42093" latitude="37.79236"
      match_code="1" error_message="????#ENUT?B281CP?"
      match_vector="????4101010??004?">
      <output_address name="" house_number="1698" street="CLAY ST"
        builtup_area="SAN FRANCISCO"
        order1_area="CA" order8_area="" country="US" postal_code="94109"
        postal_addon_code=""
        side="L" percent="0.0" edge_id="23600700" />
    </match>
    <match sequence="1" longitude="-122.40904" latitude="37.79385"
      match_code="1" error_message="????#ENUT?B281CP?"
      match_vector="????4101010??004?">
      <output_address name="" house_number="978" street="CLAY ST"
        builtup_area="SAN FRANCISCO"
        order1_area="CA" order8_area="" country="US" postal_code="94108"
        postal_addon_code=""
        side="L" percent="0.0" edge_id="23600689" />
    </match>
    <match sequence="2" longitude="-122.40027" latitude="37.79499"
      match_code="1" error_message="????#ENUT?B281CP?"
      match_vector="????4101010??004?">
      <output_address name="" house_number="398" street="CLAY ST"
        builtup_area="SAN FRANCISCO"
        order1_area="CA" order8_area="" country="US" postal_code="94111"
        postal_addon_code=""
        side="L" percent="0.0" edge_id="23600678" />
    </match>
    <match sequence="3" longitude="-122.43909" latitude="37.79007"
      match_code="1" error_message="????#ENUT?B281CP?"
      match_vector="????4101010??004?">
      <output_address name="" house_number="2798" street="CLAY ST"
        builtup_area="SAN FRANCISCO"
        order1_area="CA" order8_area="" country="US" postal_code="94115"
        postal_addon_code=""
        side="L" percent="0.0" edge_id="23600709" />
    </match>
    <match sequence="4" longitude="-122.45372" latitude="37.78822"
      match_code="1" error_message="????#ENUT?B281CP?"
```

```
      match_vector="????4101010??004?">
      <output_address name="" house_number="3698" street="CLAY ST"
        builtup_area="SAN FRANCISCO"
        order1_area="CA" order8_area="" country="US" postal_code="94118"
        postal_addon_code=""
        side="L" percent="0.0" edge_id="23600718" />
    </match>
  </geocode>
</geocode_response>
```

Batch Geocoding

You probably noticed the <address_list> tag in the geocoding request. As you may have guessed, this allows you to geocode multiple addresses in one single request, like this:

```
<geocode_request>
  <address_list>
    <input_location id="0" >
      <input_address>
        <unformatted country="US" >
          <address_line value="747 Howard Street" />
          <address_line value="San Francisco, CA" />
        </unformatted >
      </input_address>
    </input_location>
    <input_location id="1" >
      <input_address>
        <unformatted country="US" >
          <address_line value="1300 Columbus" />
          <address_line value="San Francisco, CA" />
        </unformatted >
      </input_address>
    </input_location>
    <input_location id="2" >
      <input_address>
        <unformatted country="US" >
          <address_line value="1450 California St" />
          <address_line value="San Francisco, CA" />
        </unformatted >
      </input_address>
    </input_location>
    <input_location id="3" >
      <input_address>
        <unformatted country="US" >
          <address_line value="800 Sutter Street" />
          <address_line value="San Francisco, CA" />
        </unformatted >
      </input_address>
    </input_location>
  </address_list>
</geocode_request>
```

The response, predictably, contains multiple <geocode> elements. Note that if an address is ambiguous, then its <geocode> element would include multiple <match> elements. Notice also that the id parameter lets you relate each result unambiguously with an input address.

```
<geocode_response>
  <geocode id="0" match_count="1">
    <match sequence="0" longitude="-122.4014128" latitude="37.7841193"
      match_code="1" error_message="????#ENUT?B281CP?"
      match_vector="????0101010??004?">
      <output_address name="" house_number="747" street="HOWARD ST"
        builtup_area="SAN FRANCISCO"
        order1_area="CA" order8_area="" country="US" postal_code="94103"
        postal_addon_code=""
        side="R" percent="0.53" edge_id="23607005" />
    </match>
  </geocode>
  <geocode id="1" match_count="1">
    <match sequence="0" longitude="-122.41833266666666" latitude="37.80600866666666"
      match_code="2" error_message="????#ENU??B281CP?"
      match_vector="????0101410??004?">
      <output_address name="" house_number="1300" street="COLUMBUS AVE"
        builtup_area="SAN FRANCISCO"
        order1_area="CA" order8_area="" country="US" postal_code="94133"
        postal_addon_code=""
        side="R" percent="0.03333333333333333" edge_id="23601015" />
    </match>
  </geocode>
  <geocode id="2" match_count="1">
    <match sequence="0" longitude="-122.4181062" latitude="37.790823100000004"
      match_code="1" error_message="????#ENUT?B281CP?"
      match_vector="????0101010??004?">
      <output_address name="" house_number="1450" street="CALIFORNIA ST"
        builtup_area="SAN FRANCISCO"
        order1_area="CA" order8_area="" country="US" postal_code="94109"
        postal_addon_code=""
        side="L" percent="0.49" edge_id="23599392" />
    </match>
  </geocode>
  <geocode id="3" match_count="1">
    <match sequence="0" longitude="-122.4134665" latitude="37.788557899999994"
      match_code="1" error_message="????#ENUT?B281CP?"
      match_vector="????0101010??004?">
      <output_address name="" house_number="800" street="SUTTER ST"
        builtup_area="SAN FRANCISCO"
        order1_area="CA" order8_area="" country="US" postal_code="94109"
        postal_addon_code=""
        side="L" percent="0.99" edge_id="23618424" />
    </match>
  </geocode>
</geocode_response>
```

Reverse Geocoding

To do a reverse geocoding, that is, to obtain the address that corresponds to a spatial location, use the following:

```
<geocode_request>
  <address_list>
    <input_location id="1" country="us"
```

```
      longitude="-122.4014128" latitude="37.7841193" />
  </address_list>
</geocode_request>
```

The result shows that we correctly matched back to the original address.

```
<geocode_response>
  <geocode id="1" match_count="1">
    <match sequence="0" longitude="-122.4014128" latitude="37.7841193"
      match_code="1" error_message="" match_vector="????4141414??404?">
      <output_address name="" house_number="747" street="HOWARD ST"
        builtup_area="SAN FRANCISCO"
        order1_area="CA" order8_area="" country="US" postal_code="94103"
        postal_addon_code=""
        side="R" percent="0.53" edge_id="23607005" />
    </match>
  </geocode>
</geocode_response>
```

Summary

In this chapter, you learned how to location-enable your data by converting street addresses into geographical locations that you can then use for spatial searches and various analyses. This is the first step in adding spatial intelligence to your applications.

You also learned that the geocoder can do much more than just generate geographical coordinates; it can also correct and clean errors in the input addresses.

The next step is to use the geocoded locations for spatial analysis. In the next few chapters, we describe spatial operators and functions to perform this spatial analysis.

CHAPTER 7

Manipulating SDO_GEOMETRY in Application Programs

So far, you have seen how to define and load spatial objects using the SDO_GEOMETRY type. You have also seen how to read spatial objects from SQL using SQL*Plus. In this chapter, we cover how to manipulate SDO_GEOMETRY types in the PL/SQL and Java programming languages.

Note that there are actually few occasions when you need to write explicit code to manipulate SDO_GEOMETRY types in your application. In most cases, you can directly examine the contents of an SDO_GEOMETRY in SQL. For instance, you can obtain the geographical coordinates from an SDO_GEOMETRY object as shown in Listing 7-1.

Listing 7-1. *Extracting Coordinates*

```
SQL> SELECT b.name,
b.location.sdo_point.x b_long,
b.location.sdo_point.y b_lat
FROM branches b
WHERE b.id=42 ;

NAME                                    B_LONG      B_LAT
----------------------------------- ---------- ----------
BANK OF AMERICA                      -122.4783 37.7803596
```

This example illustrates a simple yet powerful technique for extracting information from objects: *dot notation*. You can use this technique to extract any scalar value from geometry objects—in other words, the geometry type (SDO_GTYPE); spatial reference system ID (SDO_SRID); and the X, Y, and Z attributes of the point structure (SDO_POINT.X, .Y, and .Z).

This technique is generic; it applies to all object types, not just the SDO_GEOMETRY type. The advantage of this technique is that the result set produced does not include any object types—only native types—so it can be processed using any application tool, without the need to manipulate objects.

Caution To use this technique, you *must* use a table alias (b in Listing 7-1). If you forget, your query will fail with the "ORA-00904: invalid identifier" error.

In most application scenarios, you will be either extracting information from SDO_GEOMETRY as in Listing 7-1 or selecting data based on spatial relationships using spatial operators and functions (as discussed in Chapters 8 and 9). Listing 7-2 shows the selection of customers within a quarter-mile distance of a specific branch. All you need for such spatial selection is a spatial operator, called SDO_WITHIN_DISTANCE, in the WHERE clause of the SQL statement.

Listing 7-2. *Simple Spatial Query*

```
SELECT c.name, c.phone_number
  FROM branches b, customers c
 WHERE b.id=42
   AND SDO_WITHIN_DISTANCE (c.location,b.location,'distance=0.25 unit=mile')
       = 'TRUE';

NAME                               PHONE_NUMBER
---------------------------------- ---------------
GLOWA GARAGE                       415-7526677
PUERTOLAS PERFORMANCE              415-7511701
TOPAZ HOTEL SERVICE                415-9744400
CLEMENT STREET GARAGE              415-2218868
ST MONICA ELEMENTARY SCHOOL        NULL
```

Including SQL statements such as the ones in Listing 7-1 or Listing 7-2 in your application is no different from including any regular query. They may include spatial predicates (operators or functions, as discussed in Chapters 8 and 9) but return regular data types. They can be submitted and processed from any programming language.

Nonetheless, there are cases in which you need to deploy specific functionalities. In these cases, it may be necessary to develop specific code to read or write SDO_GEOMETRY types. This is typically an advanced use of Oracle Spatial but one that makes the difference in practice.

Typical cases in which you may need to manipulate SDO_GEOMETRY data are as follows:

- *Advanced location analysis*: You may want to create geometries for new branch locations, for appropriate sales regions, or for tracking the route of a delivery truck in a business application. In addition to creating geometries, you may need to know how to update existing geometries. You may want to create new functions for such creation/manipulation.
- *Data conversion*: You may need to load data that comes in a format for which no standard converter exists. Many commercial tools provide format-translation facilities, but there are still numerous cases in which legacy databases store spatial and/or attribute data in specific proprietary formats. This is also a relatively frequent issue when importing CAD/CAM diagrams in Oracle Spatial. In all these cases, you need to create interfaces between the external format and the Oracle Spatial objects.
- *Visualization analysis*: You may decide to write your own graphical map renderer and not use a standard component for this, such as Oracle MapViewer. This may not be a frequent need, but be aware that there are many specific viewing tools that fetch objects from Oracle Spatial for display on computer, handheld, and phone displays. The companies that create these tools need to develop software that has in-depth access to the spatial objects in the SDO_GEOMETRY column to perform efficient visualizations.

These tasks may require more than issuing SQL statements from application programs—you may need to know how to manipulate Oracle objects (because SDO_GEOMETRY is an object type) in the programming language in which the application is coded. In the rest of this chapter, we cover how to manipulate SDO_GEOMETRY data in detail in PL/SQL and then Java. The types of manipulations that we describe include the following:

- Mapping the object into corresponding data structures for that language
- Reading/writing SDO_GEOMETRY objects into an application program

- Extracting information from SDO_GEOMETRY objects
- Creating new SDO_GEOMETRY objects in the program
- Modifying existing SDO_GEOMETRY objects (PL/SQL)

Whenever possible, we illustrate these types of manipulations using typical tasks in a business application, such as creating a new branch location, creating a new sales region, updating delivery routes, and so on. However, such manipulation can be used for a variety of other different purposes in different applications, as described earlier.

Manipulating Geometries Using PL/SQL

Listing 7-3 shows a sample application using SDO_GEOMETRY objects in PL/SQL. This PL/SQL code creates a new branch location, computes a rectangular sales region, creates a delivery route for its business, and extends the delivery route as the delivery truck moves on.

Listing 7-3. *Sample Application in PL/SQL*

```
SQL>
DECLARE
  b_long            NUMBER;
  b_lat             NUMBER;
  new_long          NUMBER;
  new_lat           NUMBER;
  new_branch_loc    SDO_GEOMETRY;
  sales_region      SDO_GEOMETRY;
  route             SDO_GEOMETRY;
BEGIN
  -- Obtain old location for branch id=1
  SELECT br.location.sdo_point.x, br.location.sdo_point.y
  INTO b_long, b_lat
  FROM branches br
  WHERE id=1;

  -- Compute new coordinates: say the location is displaced by 0.0025 degrees
  new_long := b_long+ 0.0025;
  new_lat := b_lat + 0.0025;

  -- Create new branch location using old location
  new_branch_loc :=
    point
    (
      X=>    new_long,
      Y=>    new_lat,
      SRID=> 8307
     ) ;

  -- Compute sales region for this branch
  sales_region :=
    rectangle
    (
      CTR_X=> new_long,
      CTR_Y=> new_lat,
      EXP_X=> 0.005,
      EXP_Y=> 0.0025,
```

```
      SRID=>  8307
    ) ;

  -- Create Delivery Route
  route :=
    line
    (
      FIRST_X=> -122.4804,
      FIRST_Y=> 37.7805222,
      NEXT_X=> -123,
      NEXT_Y=> 38,
      SRID=>  8307
    ) ;

  -- Update Delivery Route by adding new point
  route :=
    add_to_line
    (
      GEOM=> route,
      POINT => POINT(-124, 39, 8307)
    ) ;

  -- Perform additional analysis such as length of route
  -- or # of customers in sales region (we give examples in Chapters 8 and 9)
  -- ...
  -- Update geometry in branches table
  UPDATE branches SET LOCATION = new_branch_loc WHERE id=1;

END;
/
```

First, note that all SQL types can be directly used in PL/SQL, so no explicit mapping needs to be done to use an SDO_GEOMETRY in PL/SQL. As you can observe in Listing 7-3, you use the SDO_GEOMETRY type in your code in the same way as you use native types (NUMBER, VARCHAR, and so on). In general, you can do the following:

- Declare variables of type SDO_GEOMETRY to hold geometry objects. For instance, we have declared three variables, new_branch_loc, sales_region, and route, in Listing 7-3, each of type SDO_GEOMETRY.
- Use regular PL/SQL operations to extract information from these geometry objects or to modify their structure. Listing 7-3 shows an example of how to extract the x and y coordinates of an SDO_GEOMETRY object.
- Use SDO_GEOMETRY objects as bind (or result) variables in static or dynamic SQL statements. This allows SDO_GEOMETRY objects to be read from and written to database tables. Listing 7-3 shows how to pass an SDO_GEOMETRY object to a SQL statement that updates the location of a branch.
- Create stored functions that may take SDO_GEOMETRY type arguments and/or return SDO_GEOMETRY objects. For instance, in Listing 7-3, the point function is a stored function that takes scalar (numeric) arguments and returns an SDO_GEOMETRY object. The add_to_line function has an SDO_GEOMETRY as the first argument and returns an SDO_GEOMETRY.

Next we will fill the gaps in Listing 7-3 and describe how to code some of the stored functions in Listing 7-3. The code for the point, rectangle, and line stored functions illustrates how to create new geometries in PL/SQL, and the code for the add_to_line function shows how to modify existing geometries.

Since an SDO_GEOMETRY object contains two VARRAY structures, SDO_ELEM_INFO and SDO_ORDINATES (as described in Chapter 4), it would be wise for us to take a detour here and present a primer on manipulating VARRAYs. These VARRAY structures are primarily used to store polygons and line strings, such as the sales region of a branch or the route of the delivery truck in our application. If you are already familiar with how to manipulate VARRAYs in PL/SQL, you can skip to the "Reading and Writing SDO_GEOMETRY Objects" section.

VARRAY Manipulation Primer

VARRAYs (short for *varying arrays*) behave pretty much like arrays in any programming language: they hold a *fixed* number of elements, but they can be extended and shrunk. They also have a *maximum capacity* beyond which you cannot extend them. They use sequential numbers as subscripts, starting from 1. They also have a number of methods that allow you to manipulate the entries in the array. Methods are called by appending them to the name of the VARRAY variable.

VARRAYs (as well as NESTED TABLES, another collections form) are not really new; they have been available in the Oracle database since version 8.0. They are a fundamental part of the object/relational aspects of Oracle. They make it possible to define multivalued attributes: and so to overcome a fundamental characteristic (some would say limitation) of the relational model, an attribute (for example, a column) can hold only one value per row.

What makes VARRAYs especially powerful is that their elements can themselves be object types. And those objects can themselves contain other VARRAYs. This makes it possible to construct complex structures such as collections or matrices and therefore represent complex objects. The SDO_GEOMETRY type, however, does not use such complex structures. It contains only two VARRAYs of NUMBERs.

Another important property of VARRAYs is that they are *ordered*. This is especially useful for geometric primitives, since the order in which points are defined is important—a shape defined by points A, B, C, and D is obviously not the same as one defined by A, C, B, and D.

The code in Listing 7-4 illustrates various array manipulations.

Listing 7-4. *Manipulating* VARRAYs

```
SET SERVEROUTPUT ON
DECLARE

  -- Declare a type for the VARRAY
  TYPE MY_ARRAY_TYPE IS VARRAY(10) OF NUMBER;

  -- Declare a VARRAY variable
  V               MY_ARRAY_TYPE;

  -- Other variables
  I               NUMBER;
  K               NUMBER;
  L               NUMBER;
  ARRAY_CAPACITY  NUMBER;
  N_ENTRIES       NUMBER;

BEGIN
  -- Initialize the array
  V := MY_ARRAY_TYPE (1,2,3,4);

  -- Get the value of a specific entry
  DBMS_OUTPUT.PUT_LINE('* Values for specific array entries');
  K := V(3);
  DBMS_OUTPUT.PUT_LINE('V(3)='|| V(3));
```

```
I := 2;
L := V(I+1);
DBMS_OUTPUT.PUT_LINE('I=' || I);
DBMS_OUTPUT.PUT_LINE('V(I+1)=' || V(I+1));

-- Find the capacity of a VARRAY:
DBMS_OUTPUT.PUT_LINE('* Array capacity');
ARRAY_CAPACITY := V.LIMIT();
DBMS_OUTPUT.PUT_LINE('Array Capacity: V.LIMIT()='||V.LIMIT());
N_ENTRIES := V.COUNT();
DBMS_OUTPUT.PUT_LINE('Current Array Size: V.COUNT()='||V.COUNT());

-- Range over all values in a VARRAY
DBMS_OUTPUT.PUT_LINE('* Array Content');
FOR I IN 1..V.COUNT() LOOP
  DBMS_OUTPUT.PUT_LINE('V('||I||')=' || V(I));
END LOOP;

FOR I IN V.FIRST()..V.LAST() LOOP
 DBMS_OUTPUT.PUT_LINE('V('||I||')=' || V(I));
END LOOP;

I := V.COUNT();
WHILE I IS NOT NULL LOOP
  DBMS_OUTPUT.PUT_LINE('V('||I||')=' || V(I));
  I := V.PRIOR(I);
END LOOP;

-- Extend the VARRAY
DBMS_OUTPUT.PUT_LINE('* Extend the array');
I := V.LAST();
V.EXTEND(2);
V(I+1) := 5;
V(I+2) := 6;

DBMS_OUTPUT.PUT_LINE('Array Capacity: V.LIMIT()='||V.LIMIT());
DBMS_OUTPUT.PUT_LINE('Current Array Size: V.COUNT()='||V.COUNT());
FOR I IN 1..V.COUNT() LOOP
  DBMS_OUTPUT.PUT_LINE('V('||I||')='|| V(I));
END LOOP;

-- Shrink the VARRAY
DBMS_OUTPUT.PUT_LINE('* Trim the array');
V.TRIM();

DBMS_OUTPUT.PUT_LINE('Array Capacity: V.LIMIT()='||V.LIMIT());
DBMS_OUTPUT.PUT_LINE('Current Array Size: V.COUNT()='||V.COUNT());
FOR I IN 1..V.COUNT() LOOP
  DBMS_OUTPUT.PUT_LINE('V('||I||')='|| V(I));
END LOOP;

-- Delete all entries from the VARRAY
DBMS_OUTPUT.PUT_LINE('* Empty the array');
V.DELETE();

DBMS_OUTPUT.PUT_LINE('Array Capacity: V.LIMIT()='||V.LIMIT());
DBMS_OUTPUT.PUT_LINE('Current Array Size: V.COUNT()='||V.COUNT());
```

```
  FOR I IN 1..V.COUNT() LOOP
    DBMS_OUTPUT.PUT_LINE('V('||I||')='|| V(I));
  END LOOP;
END;
/
```

Let's look at this code in detail next.

Declaring and Initializing VARRAY Variables

You cannot declare a VARRAY variable directly. You must first declare a type that includes the maximum capacity of the array:

```
TYPE MY_ARRAY_TYPE IS VARRAY(10) OF NUMBER;
```

You can then declare your VARRAY variable using this type:

```
V   MY_ARRAY_TYPE;
```

Before you can do anything with the array, it must be initialized. You can do this at the same time as you declare it, or you can initialize it later by assigning it a value. The following shows the simultaneous declaration and initialization of an array:

```
V   MY_ARRAY_TYPE := MY_ARRAY_TYPE ();
```

Getting the Value of a Specific Entry

Just use the number of the entry as a subscript. The subscript can be any expression that returns an integer equal to or less than the number of entries in the array, for example:

```
K := V(3);
I := 2;
L := V(I+1);
```

Finding the Capacity of a VARRAY

Use the COUNT() method on the VARRAY variable. Note that you do not have to specify the parentheses, since this method takes no arguments:

```
N_ENTRIES := V.COUNT();
```

This tells you the number of entries currently in use in the array. A VARRAY also has a maximum capacity that was specified when the type was declared. You can find out that capacity using the LIMIT() method:

```
ARRAY_CAPACITY := V.LIMIT();
```

Ranging Over All Values in a VARRAY

You can use several techniques. The simplest is to use a FOR loop:

```
FOR I IN 1..V.COUNT() LOOP
   DBMS_OUTPUT.PUT_LINE('V('||I||')='  || V(I));
END LOOP;
```

You can also use the FIRST() and LAST() methods. FIRST() returns the subscript of the first entry in the array (which is always 1), and LAST() returns the subscript of the last entry in the array (which is always the same as COUNT):

```
FOR I IN V.FIRST()..V.LAST() LOOP
   DBMS_OUTPUT.PUT_LINE('V('||I||')=' || V(I));
END LOOP;
```

You could also use the PRIOR(n) and NEXT(n) methods, which return the subscript of the entry that precedes or follows a given entry, respectively. For example, use this to range backward over the array:

```
I := V.COUNT();
WHILE I IS NOT NULL LOOP
  DBMS_OUTPUT.PUT_LINE('V('||I||')=' || V(I));
  I := V.PRIOR(I);
END LOOP;
```

PRIOR(n) is really the same as n-1, and NEXT(n) is the same as n+1, but PRIOR(1) and NEXT(V.COUNT()) return NULL.

Extending a VARRAY

Use the EXTEND(k) method. This method adds k new entries at the end of the VARRAY. When k is not specified, the array is extended by a single entry. The new entries have no value yet (they are set to NULL), but they can now be initialized. The COUNT() and LAST() methods now reflect the new capacity of the VARRAY. The following adds two entries to the array and initializes them:

```
I := V.LAST();
V.EXTEND(2);
V(I+1) := 5;
V(I+2) := 6;
```

Note that you cannot extend a VARRAY beyond its maximum capacity (returned by the LIMIT() method). Note also that the VARRAY must be instantiated before you can extend it. The following does *not* work:

```
VT MY_ARRAY_TYPE;
VT.EXTEND(5);
```

but the following does work:

```
VT MY_ARRAY_TYPE;
VT := MY_ARRAY_TYPE();
VT.EXTEND(5);
```

Shrinking a VARRAY

Use the TRIM(k) method. This method removes the last k entries from the end of the VARRAY. When k is not specified, the last entry of the array is removed. The values of the removed entries are lost. COUNT() and LAST() reflect the new capacity. The following removes the last entry from the VARRAY:

```
V.TRIM;
```

You can trim all entries from the array, like this:

```
V.TRIM(V.COUNT());
```

or you can use the DELETE() method, which has the same effect. It removes all entries from the array and sets its capacity to zero (that is, V.COUNT() now returns 0).

```
V.DELETE()
```

Now that you know how to manipulate VARRAYs, let's apply those techniques to the SDO_GEOMETRY type. We will start by covering the techniques to extract information from an SDO_GEOMETRY object, and then we will present an example of how to update an SDO_GEOMETRY object.

Next, we will revert to our original discussion on how to read/write SDO_GEOMETRY data, how to create new geometries, how to extract information from existing ones, and how to modify existing geometries. We cover each of these topics in a separate subsection.

Reading and Writing SDO_GEOMETRY Objects

Reading and writing SDO_GEOMETRY data in a PL/SQL program is easy. You define new variables of SDO_GEOMETRY and read from or write to these variables while executing a SQL statement. Listing 7-3 shows an example of both reading the x,y components of a branch location and updating the new location in the branches table.

Creating New Geometries

In this section, we illustrate how to create new geometries using stored functions, as described in Listing 7-3. These functions simplify the writing of some SQL statements and hide some of the complexities in dealing with geometries. You can use these constructors to populate new branch locations or to create new sales regions, for example.

Point Constructor

Inserting point geometries using the SDO_GEOMETRY constructor may seem unduly complicated. Listing 7-5 shows a simple stored function that makes this operation easier by hiding some of the complexity of spatial objects from developers and/or end users.

Listing 7-5. *Point Constructor Function*

```
CREATE OR REPLACE FUNCTION point (
  x NUMBER, y NUMBER, srid NUMBER DEFAULT 8307)
RETURN SDO_GEOMETRY
DETERMINISTIC
IS
BEGIN
  RETURN SDO_GEOMETRY (
          2001, srid, SDO_POINT_TYPE (x,y,NULL), NULL, NULL);
END;
/
```

As you can see, you just declare the function to return an SDO_GEOMETRY type. It is then a simple matter to use the standard constructor of SDO_GEOMETRY to generate a proper point object using the arguments provided (X, Y, and an optional spatial reference system).

You can then use this new constructor to simplify your SQL statements. For example, here is how to update the geographical location of a new branch using the constructor in Listing 7-5:

```
UPDATE branches
    SET location = point (-122.48049, 37.7805222, 8307)
WHERE id = 1;
```

■ **Tip** Always use the DETERMINISTIC keyword when the result of the function depends only on the input arguments (and not on the database state). This will help you reuse cached evaluations of the function when the same arguments are passed in, and it also results in better overall performance.

Rectangle Constructor

Listing 7-3 uses the rectangle function to create a new geometry to represent a sales region around a branch location. You can code this function to define a region around the branch location by expanding from the location by a specified amount in each of the two dimensions. Listing 7-6 shows the corresponding SQL. Note that rectangles are used extensively in visualization; many interactions that select objects to include on a map use rectangles to define the area of interest. As for the point constructor, the goal here is to simplify the writing of SQL statements that need to use rectangles.

Listing 7-6 shows how to define a rectangular shape. The function takes the coordinates of the center of the rectangle, the distances from the center to each side, and optionally a spatial reference system ID. As shown in Listing 7-6, the SDO_ORDINATES attribute in the SDO_GEOMETRY constructor stores the lower-left and upper-right points. Note that all you do here is create a new object using the SDO_GEOMETRY constructor, populate it with the appropriate information, and return the object as the function result.

Listing 7-6. *Rectangle Constructor*

```
CREATE OR REPLACE FUNCTION rectangle (
  ctr_x NUMBER, ctr_y NUMBER, exp_x NUMBER, exp_y NUMBER, srid NUMBER)
RETURN SDO_GEOMETRY
DETERMINISTIC
IS
  r SDO_GEOMETRY;
BEGIN
  r := SDO_GEOMETRY (
    2003, srid, NULL,
    SDO_ELEM_INFO_ARRAY (1, 1003, 3),
    SDO_ORDINATE_ARRAY (
      ctr_x - exp_x, ctr_y - exp_y,
      ctr_x + exp_x, ctr_y + exp_y));
  RETURN r;
END;
/
```

You can use this function anywhere in your SQL statements. For example, the following code counts the number of customers in a rectangular window, grouped by grade. Without the rectangle function, you would have to use the more complex generic SDO_GEOMETRY constructor.

```
SELECT count(*), customer_grade
  FROM customers WHERE SDO_INSIDE (location,
         rectangle (-122.47,37.79,  0.01, 0.01, 8307)) = 'TRUE'
GROUP BY customer_grade;

  COUNT(*) CUSTOMER_GRADE
---------- ---------------
       307 GOLD
         4 PLATINUM
       457 SILVER
```

Line Constructor

In Listing 7-3, we used the line function to create a new line geometry with a start point and an end point. Listing 7-7 shows how to write such a function.

Listing 7-7. *Line Constructor*

```
CREATE OR REPLACE FUNCTION line (
  first_x NUMBER, first_y NUMBER, next_x NUMBER, next_y NUMBER, srid NUMBER)
RETURN SDO_GEOMETRY
DETERMINISTIC
IS
  l SDO_GEOMETRY;
BEGIN
  l := SDO_GEOMETRY (
    2002, srid, NULL,
    SDO_ELEM_INFO_ARRAY (1, 2, 1),
    SDO_ORDINATE_ARRAY (
      first_x, first_y,
      next_x, next_y));
  RETURN l;
END;
/
```

Extracting Information from Geometries

In this section, we illustrate the manipulation of geometries with two examples. The first is simple and demonstrates how to find out the number of points in a geometry. The second is a slightly more complex example in which we show how to write a function to extract a specific point from a line geometry.

The functions we present here are intended primarily to illustrate the techniques you can use to manipulate geometry objects in PL/SQL.

Counting the Number of Points in a Geometry

The get_num_points function in Listing 7-8 computes the number of points in a geometry by dividing the count of elements in the SDO_ORDINATES array (that is, the total number of ordinates) by the dimensionality of the geometry (that is, the number of ordinates per point).

Listing 7-8. *Counting the Number of Points in a Geometry*

```
CREATE OR REPLACE FUNCTION get_num_points (
  g SDO_GEOMETRY)
RETURN NUMBER
IS
BEGIN
  RETURN g.SDO_ORDINATES.COUNT() / SUBSTR(g.SDO_GTYPE,1,1);
END;
/
```

You can use the function as follows to find out the number of points in a geometry:

```
SELECT get_num_points(geom) FROM us_states WHERE state = 'California';
GET_NUM_POINTS(GEOM)
--------------------
                1146
```

Extracting a Point from a Line

Let's assume you have an application that keeps track of the route followed by a delivery truck. When the truck is moving, it reports its position every minute. Those points are stringed together to form a line geometry that represents the route followed by the truck so far. (This operation is described later in this chapter.)

Listing 7-9 shows a function that extracts a selected point from a geometry. The function takes two input arguments: a geometry object and the number of the point in that geometry. The first point in the geometry is point number 1. It then returns a new geometry object that contains only the selected point.

Listing 7-9. *Function to Extract a Point from a Geometry*

```
CREATE OR REPLACE FUNCTION get_point (
  geom SDO_GEOMETRY, point_number NUMBER DEFAULT 1
) RETURN SDO_GEOMETRY
IS
  g MDSYS.SDO_GEOMETRY; -- Updated Geometry
  d NUMBER;             -- Number of dimensions in geometry
  p NUMBER;             -- Index into ordinates array
  px NUMBER;            -- X of extracted point
  py NUMBER;            -- Y of extracted point

BEGIN
  -- Get the number of dimensions from the gtype
  d := SUBSTR (geom.SDO_GTYPE, 1, 1);

  -- Verify that the point exists
  IF point_number < 1
  OR point_number > geom.SDO_ORDINATES.COUNT()/d THEN
    RETURN NULL;
  END IF;

  -- Get index in ordinates array
  p := (point_number-1) * d + 1;

  -- Extract the X and Y coordinates of the desired point
  px := geom.SDO_ORDINATES(p);
  py := geom.SDO_ORDINATES(p+1);

  -- Construct and return the point
  RETURN
    MDSYS.SDO_GEOMETRY (
      2001,
      geom.SDO_SRID,
      SDO_POINT_TYPE (px, py, NULL),
      NULL, NULL);
END;
/
```

In this function, you perform some error checking. If the number of the point is larger than the number of points in the object, then you return a NULL object. If the point number is not specified, then you just return the first point of the geometry. Notice that the extracted point is always returned as a two-dimensional point (even if the geometry is three- or four-dimensional). The returned point is always in the same coordinate system as the input geometry.

Further refinements to the function could be to make it throw an exception if the point number is incorrect or if the geometry is not a line.

Listing 7-10 shows some examples of how to use this function to get the first, middle, and last points of a line string (the line that represents Interstate 95).

Listing 7-10. *Getting the First, Middle, and Last Points of a Line String*

```
-- Getting the first point of a line string
SELECT get_point(geom) p
FROM us_interstates
WHERE interstate='I95';
P(SDO_GTYPE, SDO_SRID, SDO_POINT(X, Y, Z), SDO_ELEM_INFO, SDO_ORDINATES)
------------------------------------------------------------------------
SDO_GEOMETRY(2001, 8307, SDO_POINT_TYPE(-80.211761, 25.74876, NULL), NULL, NULL)

-- Getting the last point of a line string
SELECT get_point(geom, get_num_points(geom)) p
FROM us_interstates
WHERE interstate='I95';
P(SDO_GTYPE, SDO_SRID, SDO_POINT(X, Y, Z), SDO_ELEM_INFO, SDO_ORDINATES)
------------------------------------------------------------------------
SDO_GEOMETRY(2001, 8307, SDO_POINT_TYPE(-74.118584, 40.754608, NULL), NULL, NULL)

-- Getting the middle point of a line string
SELECT get_point(geom, ROUND(get_num_points(geom)/2)) p
FROM us_interstates
WHERE interstate='I95';
P(SDO_GTYPE, SDO_SRID, SDO_POINT(X, Y, Z), SDO_ELEM_INFO, SDO_ORDINATES)
------------------------------------------------------------------------
SDO_GEOMETRY(2001, 8307, SDO_POINT_TYPE(-68.118683, 46.120701, NULL), NULL, NULL)
```

Modifying Existing Geometries

Array manipulation techniques are most useful when updating geometries. In this section, we present a few examples. They are all stored functions that take an SDO_GEOMETRY object as input and return a new SDO_GEOMETRY object.

Removing a Point from a Line

A common editing operation on geometries is to add and remove points from a geometry, which is what this and the next stored function do. First you'll look at the removal of a point using the remove_point function in Listing 7-11.

Listing 7-11. remove_point *Function*

```
CREATE OR REPLACE FUNCTION remove_point (
  geom SDO_GEOMETRY, point_number NUMBER
) RETURN SDO_GEOMETRY
IS
  g MDSYS.SDO_GEOMETRY; -- Updated Geometry
  d NUMBER;             -- Number of dimensions in geometry
  p NUMBER;             -- Index into ordinates array
  i NUMBER;             -- Index into ordinates array
BEGIN
  -- Get the number of dimensions from the gtype
  d := SUBSTR (geom.SDO_GTYPE, 1, 1);
```

```
    -- Get index in ordinates array
    -- If 0 then we want the last point
    IF point_number = 0 THEN
      p :=  geom.SDO_ORDINATES.COUNT() - d + 1;
    ELSE
      p := (point_number-1) * d + 1;
    END IF;

    -- Verify that the point exists
    IF p > geom.SDO_ORDINATES.COUNT() THEN
      RETURN NULL;
    END IF;

    -- Initialize output line with input line
    g := geom;

    -- Step 1: Shift the ordinates "up"
    FOR i IN p..g.SDO_ORDINATES.COUNT()-d LOOP
      g.SDO_ORDINATES(i) := g.SDO_ORDINATES(i+d);
    END LOOP;

    -- Step 2: Trim the ordinates array
    g.SDO_ORDINATES.TRIM (d);

    -- Return the updated geometry
    RETURN g;
  END;
  /
```

Just like in the get_point() function, you begin by converting the number of the point to be removed into the index of the SDO_ORDINATE element where the ordinates of the point start (p).

Figure 7-1 illustrates the subsequent process. You first remove the point by shifting the ordinates "up." Assume you want to remove the third point (point C) from the line string. Its index in the ordinate array is 5. The ordinates for points D, E, and F are then shifted up from elements 7–12 into elements 5–10. This is step 1 in the figure.

	Original Ordinates		Step 1		Step 2
1	Xa	1	Xa	1	Xa
2	Ya	2	Ya	2	Ya
3	Xb	3	Xb	3	Xb
4	Yb	4	Yb	4	Yb
5	Xc	5	Xd	5	Xd
6	Yc	6	Yd	6	Yd
7	Xd	7	Xe	7	Xe
8	Yd	8	Ye	8	Ye
9	Xe	9	Xf	9	Xf
10	Ye	10	Yf	10	Yf
11	Xf	11	Xf		
12	Yf	12	Yf		

Figure 7-1. *Removing a point from a line*

Then, you trim the array by removing the last elements you no longer need. This is step 2 in the figure.

You can use this function, for example, to remove the last point from I-95:

```
UPDATE US_INTERSTATES
   SET GEOM = REMOVE_POINT (GEOM, 0)
 WHERE INTERSTATE = 'I95';
```

Adding a Point to a Line

This is the reverse of the previous operation: you now insert a new point into a line string. The function needs the geometry to update, the geometry of the point to insert, and an indication of where to insert the new point in the line. You do this by passing the number of the point *before* which the new point should be inserted.

To insert the point at the start of the line, pass the value 1. To append it at the end of the line, pass the value 0. Listing 7-12 shows the SQL.

Listing 7-12. *Adding a Point in a Line String (*add_to_line *in Listing 7-3)*

```
CREATE OR REPLACE FUNCTION add_to_line (
  geom         SDO_GEOMETRY,
  point        SDO_GEOMETRY,
  point_number NUMBER DEFAULT 0
) RETURN SDO_GEOMETRY
IS
  g   SDO_GEOMETRY;         -- Updated geometry
  d   NUMBER;               -- Number of dimensions in line geometry
  t   NUMBER;               -- Geometry type
  p   NUMBER;               -- Insertion point into ordinates array
  i   NUMBER;
BEGIN
  -- Get the number of dimensions from the gtype
  d := SUBSTR (geom.SDO_GTYPE, 1, 1);

  -- Get index in ordinates array
  -- If 0, then we want the last point
  IF point_number = 0 THEN
    p :=  geom.SDO_ORDINATES.COUNT() + 1;
  ELSE
    p := (point_number-1) * d + 1;
  END IF;

  -- Verify that the insertion point exists
  IF point_number <> 0 THEN
    IF p > geom.SDO_ORDINATES.LAST()
    OR p < geom.SDO_ORDINATES.FIRST() THEN
      RAISE_APPLICATION_ERROR (-20000, 'Invalid insertion point');
    END IF;
  END IF;

  -- Initialize output line with input line
  g := geom;

  -- Step 1: Extend the ordinates array
  g.SDO_ORDINATES.EXTEND(d);
```

```
  -- Step 2: Shift the ordinates "down".
  FOR i IN REVERSE p..g.SDO_ORDINATES.COUNT()-d LOOP
    g.SDO_ORDINATES(i+d) := g.SDO_ORDINATES(i);
  END LOOP;

  -- Step 3: Store the new point
  g.SDO_ORDINATES(p) := point.SDO_POINT.X;
  g.SDO_ORDINATES(p+1) := point.SDO_POINT.Y;
  IF d = 3 THEN
    g.SDO_ORDINATES(p+2) := point.SDO_POINT.Z;
  END IF;

  -- Return the new line string
  RETURN g;
END;
/
```

Again, you begin by converting the place to insert the new point into the index of the first SDO_ORDINATE element of the point before you want to insert the new point.

Figure 7-2 illustrates the process for inserting the point. You begin, in step 1, by extending the SDO_ORDINATE array by the number of elements needed to represent a point, according to the dimensionality (two-, three-, or four-dimensional) of the line string. Then in step 2, you make room for the new point by shifting the ordinates "down." Assume you want to insert a new point (point G) before point D (the fourth point). The index of point D in the ordinate array is 7. The ordinates for points D, E, and F are then shifted down from elements 7–12 into elements 9–14. Finally, in step 3 you fill elements 7 and 8 with the x and y of the new point G.

	Original Ordinates	Step 1	Step 2	Step 3
1	Xa	Xa	Xa	Xa
2	Ya	Ya	Ya	Ya
3	Xb	Xb	Xb	Xb
4	Yb	Yb	Yb	Yb
5	Xc	Xc	Xc	Xc
6	Yc	Yc	Yc	Yc
7	Xd	Xd	Xd	Xg
8	Yd	Yd	Yd	Yg
9	Xe	Xe	Xd	Xd
10	Ye	Ye	Yd	Yd
11	Xf	Xf	Xe	Xe
12	Yf	Yf	Ye	Ye
13			Xf	Xf
14			Yf	Yf

Figure 7-2. *Inserting a point into a line*

Note The previous example assumes you add a point to an already existing valid line. Constructing the line from scratch is left as an exercise to the reader.

Manipulating Geometries in Java

As you have seen, spatial objects are stored in database tables as SDO_GEOMETRY types. To process them in Java, you must first read them from the database using JDBC, and then you need to map them to Java classes.

Mapping an SDO_GEOMETRY type into a Java class is easy, thanks to the API provided with Oracle Spatial. The API itself is simple: it contains one main package (oracle.spatial.geometry) that contains two main classes (JGeometry and J3D_Geometry). The API has been significantly enhanced in Oracle Database 11*g*. It now comes with a number of geometry processing functions, as well as utility functions that allow you to convert geometries to/from some standard formats (GML, WKT, ESRI shapefiles). Those are in a package called oracle.spatial.util.

The Java API for Oracle Spatial is distributed in two JAR files (sdoapi.jar and sdoutl.jar) located in the Oracle installation (at $ORACLE_HOME/md/jlib[1]). To use the API in your applications, be sure to include them in your classpath. You will also need the JDBC driver, as well as the XML parser (this is only for processing GML). Here is how your classpath setting would look in a Windows environment:

```
C:\>set classpath=.;%ORACLE_HOME%\jdbc\lib\ojdbc14.jar;
%ORACLE_HOME%\md\jlib\sdoapi.jar;%ORACLE_HOME%\md\jlib\sdoutl.jar;
%ORACLE_HOME%\lib\xmlparserv2.jar;
```

The documentation (Javadoc) is available with the full Oracle documentation set, as well as in your Oracle installation, in the files $ORACLE_HOME/md/doc/sdoapi.zip and sdoutl.zip.

On the Apress website you will find a number of complete examples that illustrate how to read, write, and process geometries in Java. Table 7-1 lists the programs.

Table 7-1. *Example Programs*

Program	Information Returned
SdoPrint.java	Prints the structure of geometries in any table
SdoExport.java	Exports all or some geometries from a table into a flat file in a choice of formats (WKT, WKB, GML, etc.)
SdoImport.java	Imports previously exported geometries back into a table

Using the JGeometry Class

The main tool to manipulate geometries in Java is the JGeometry class. It allows you to read and write geometries from and to the database, but it also allows you to inspect the geometries, to create new geometries, and even to perform a number of transformations on those geometries.

Reading and Writing Geometries

When you read an object type (such as the SDO_GEOMETRY type) using a SQL SELECT statement, JDBC returns a Java structure—more precisely, an oracle.sql.STRUCT object. To write an object type

1. Note that in version 10*g* of the Oracle Database, the JAR files were in $ORACLE_HOME/md/lib.

(using an INSERT or UPDATE statement), you are also expected to pass an oracle.sql.STRUCT object. Decoding and constructing STRUCTs is rather complex, and the main goal of the Oracle Spatial Java API (the JGeometry class) is to make that task easy.

The JGeometry class provides two methods to convert a STRUCT into a JGeometry object:

- The load() method reads the STRUCT and returns a JGeometry object. Use it when you convert the geometries returned by a SELECT statement.
- The store() method performs the reverse conversion to the load() method. It converts a JGeometry object into a STRUCT that you can then write back to the database using an INSERT or UPDATE statement.

Figure 7-3 illustrates this conversion process.

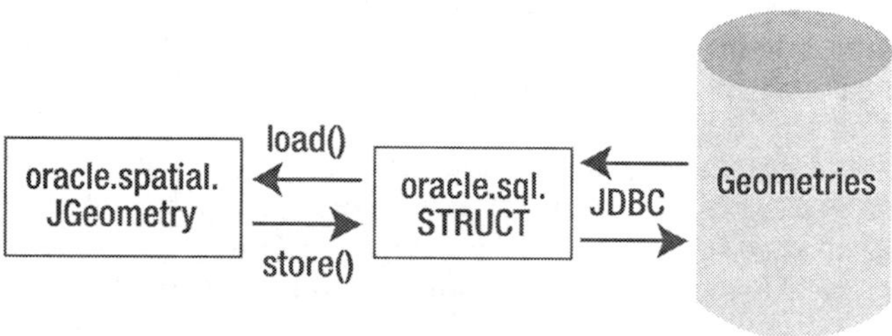

Figure 7-3. *Reading and writing geometries in Java*

In Oracle Database 11g, the load() and store() methods have been enhanced to provide their own "pickling"[2] and "unpickling" methods optimized for geometry objects and so should perform better. For reading a geometry, read the object into a byte array and pass that array to the load() method. Figure 7-4 illustrates the process.

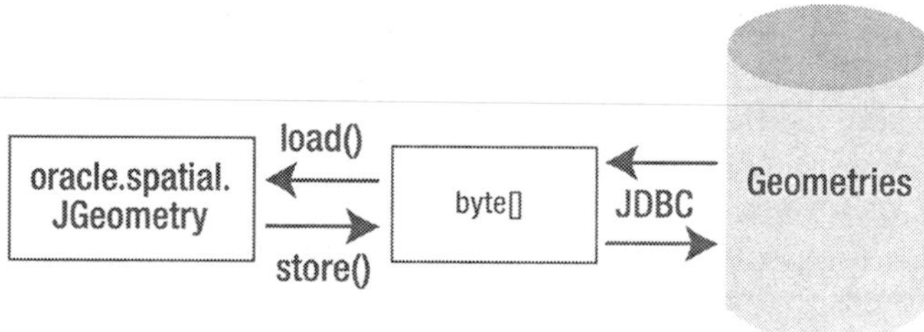

Figure 7-4. *Reading and writing geometries in Java using the optimized "pickler"*

The following is an example. First use the getObject() method of the result set to extract the geometry object for each row into a STRUCT and then use the static load() method of JGeometry to convert it into a JGeometry object.

2. *Pickling* is the process by which an object is serialized or converted into a byte stream. *Unpickling* is the reverse process.

```
STRUCT dbObject = (STRUCT) rs.getObject(1);
JGeometry geom = JGeometry.load(dbObject);
```

To use the optimized unpickler, first use the `getBytes()` method of the result set to extract the geometry into a `byte` array. Then again use the static `load()` method of `JGeometry` to convert it to a `JGeometry` object.

```
byte[] image = rs. getBytes (1);
JGeometry geom = JGeometry.load(image);
```

Inspecting Geometries

You can now use one of the many `get()` methods to extract information from the geometry object. Table 7-2 summarizes the main methods. The additional `is()` methods listed in Table 7-3 detail the nature of the geometry.

Table 7-2. *Main* `JGeometry get()` *Methods*

Method	Information Returned
`getType()`	Type of geometry (1 for a point, 2 for a line, and so on).
`getDimensions()`	Dimensionality.
`getSRID()`	Spatial reference system ID.
`getNumPoints()`	Number of points in the geometry.
`getPoint()`	Coordinates of the point object (if the geometry is a point).
`getFirstPoint()`	First point of the geometry.
`getLastPoint()`	Last point of the geometry.
`getMBR()`	MBR of the geometry.
`getElemInfo()`	Content of the `SDO_ELEM_INFO` array.
`getOrdinatesArray()`	Content of the `SDO_ORDINATES` array.
`getLabelPoint()`	Returns the coordinates of the `SDO_POINT` structure. When filled for a line or polygon geometry, this is often used as a labeling point.
`getJavaPoint()`	For a single-point object, returns the coordinates of the point as a `java.awt.geom.Point2D` object.
`getJavaPoints()`	For a multipoint object, returns an array of `java.awt.geom.Point2D` objects.
`getElements()`	Gets an array of `JGeometry` objects, each representing one element of the geometry.
`getElementAt()`	Extracts one element of the geometry as a `JGeometry`.
`createShape()`	Converts the geometry into a `java.awt.Shape` object, ready for use by the drawing and manipulation facilities of the `java.awt` package.

Table 7-3. *Main* `JGeometry is()` *Methods*

Method	Information Returned
`isPoint()`	Is this a point?
`isOrientedPoint()`	Is this an oriented point?
`isCircle()`	Is this a circle?
`isGeodeticMBR()`	Is this a geodetic MBR?
`isMultiPoint()`	Is this a multipoint?
`isRectangle()`	Is this a rectangle?
`hasCircularArcs()`	Does the geometry contain any arcs?
`isLRSGeometry()`	Is this a "linear referenced" geometry?

Two of the methods in Table 7-3 (`getElements()` and `getElementAt()`) allow you to inspect the structure of complex geometries: they allow you to extract individual elements as separate `JGeometry` objects. The first method returns all elements into an array of separate `JGeometry` objects. The second returns one specific element identified by its position in the geometry.

Caution The term *element* must be understood as defined in the OGC Simple Features for SQL specification. For example, a polygon with `voids` is considered as a single element, even though it is composed of multiple rings (each being an element in the Oracle sense). The validation functions discussed in Chapter 5 (`VALIDATE_GEOMETRY_WITH_CONTEXT()` and `EXTRACT()`) behave the same way. This means the `getElements()` method will not allow you to extract a void from a polygon with voids.

Caution The numbering of the elements starts at 1, not 0.

Creating Geometries

Writing a geometry to the database (in an `INSERT` or `UPDATE` statement) requires that you create a new `JGeometry` object, convert it into a `STRUCT` using the static `JGeometry.store()` method, and then pass the `STRUCT` to an `INSERT` or `UPDATE` statement. Just like for the `load()` method, you can also use the faster spatial pickler. Figures 7-3 and 7-4 illustrate both methods.

The following is an example of both approaches. First use the static `store()` method of `JGeometry` to convert it to a `STRUCT`, and then use the `setObject()` method to set it into the prepared SQL statement.

```
STRUCT dbObject = JGeometry.store (geom, dbConnection);
stmt.setObject (1,dbObject);
```

Using the optimized pickler is very much the same except that the order of the arguments to the `store()` method is reversed: first specify the database connection object and then the `JGeometry` object!

```
STRUCT dbObject = JGeometry.store (dbConnection, geom);
stmt.setObject (1,dbObject);
```

There are two ways you can construct new `JGeometry` objects. One way is to use one of the constructors listed in Table 7-4. The other way is to use one of the static methods that create various geometries. Table 7-5 lists those methods.

Table 7-4. `JGeometry` *Constructors*

Constructor	Purpose
`JGeometry (double x, double y, int srid)`	Constructs a point
`JGeometry (double x, double y, double z, int srid`	Constructs a three-dimensional point
`JGeometry (double minX, double minY, double maxX, double maxY, int srid)`	Creates a rectangle
`JGeometry (int gtype, int srid, int[] elemInfo, double[] ordinates)`	Constructs a generic geometry

Table 7-5. *Static* `JGeometry` *Creation Methods*

Creation Method	Purpose
`createPoint(double[] coord, int dim, int srid)`	Creates a point
`createLinearLineString (double[] coords, int dim, int srid)`	Creates a simple line string
`createLinearPolygon (double[] coords, int dim, int srid)`	Creates a simple polygon
`createMultiPoint (java.lang.Object[] coords, int dim, int srid)`	Creates a multipoint object
`createLinearMultiLineString (java.lang.Object[] coords, int dim, int srid)`	Creates a multiline string object
`createLinearPolygon (java.lang.Object[] coords, int dim, int srid)`	Creates a multipolygon
`createCircle(double x1, double y1, double x2, double y2, double x3, double y3, int srid)`	Creates a circle using three points on its circumference
`createCircle(double x, double y, double radius, int srid)`	Creates a circle using a center and radius

Modifying Existing Geometries

The `JGeometry` class does not provide any method that lets you modify a geometry. For example, there is no method to remove a point from a line or to add one more point to a line. To perform those updates, you need to extract the list of points using a method such as `getOrdinatesArray()`, then update the resulting Java arrays, and then create a new `JGeometry` object with the results.

To write the modified geometries to the database, proceed as discussed previously: convert the `JGeometry` object into a `STRUCT` using the `store()` method, and then pass the `STRUCT` to your SQL `INSERT` or `UPDATE` statement.

Processing Geometries

The Java API also provides you with a number of methods that perform various transformations on geometries. Table 7-6 lists the main ones. They take a `JGeometry` object as input and generate a new geometry as a result. Note that most of those functions are also provided via PL/SQL calls in the database that will be discussed in detail in Chapter 9.

Table 7-6. *Geometry-Processing Functions*

Method	Purpose
`buffer(double bufferWidth)`	Generates a buffer around a geometry
`simplify(double threshold)`	Simplifies a geometry
`densifyArcs(double arc_tolerance)`	Densifies all arcs in a geometry
`clone()`	Duplicates a geometry
`affineTransforms(...)`	Applies affine transformations on the input geometry based on the parameters supplied: translation, scaling, rotation, shear, reflection
`projectToLTP(double smax, double flat)`	Projects a geometry from longitude/latitude to a local tangent plane
`projectFromLTP()`	Projects a geometry from a local tangent plane to longitude/latitude

The API also provides some helper methods, summarized in Table 7-7. Those functions (except for `equals`) do not deal with `JGeometry` objects but are provided to help certain processing tasks.

The `equals()` method compares two `JGeometry` objects and determines whether they are the same. However, the comparison is based on the internal encoding of the geometry: two geometries will be considered as equal if the coordinates of all their points are the same and in the same sequence. The method does not perform a true geometric comparison involving tolerance.

Table 7-7. *Geometry Helper Functions*

Method	Purpose
`equals()`	Determines whether two geometries are identical
`computeArc(double x1, double y1, double x2, double y2, double x3, double y3)`	Computes the center, radius, and angles for this arc from the three coordinate points
`linearizeArc(double x1, double y1, double x2, double y2, double x3, double y3)`	Converts an arc into an array of 2D line segments
`reFormulateArc(double[] d)`	Reformulates an arc by recomputing the angles
`expandCircle(double x1, double y1, double x2, double y2, double x3, double y3)`	Linearizes the circle by converting it into an array of 2D segments
`monoMeasure(double[] coords, int dim ()`	Determines whether a line has increasing or decreasing measures

Using 3D Geometries: the J3D_Geometry Class

One of the major new capabilities in Oracle Database 11*g* is the ability to model complex 3D objects: surfaces and solids. The new `J3D_Geometry` class will help you manipulate those structures. Notice it is a subclass of `JGeometry`, so all the methods you have seen so far are applicable.

To read `J3D_Geometry` objects from the database, proceed the same way as with `JGeometry`, and then construct a `J3D_Geometry` from the `JGeometry` object. For example:

```
byte[] image = rs. getBytes (1);
JGeometry geom = JGeometry.load(image);
J3D_Geometry geom3D = new J3D_Geometry (
   geom.getType(), geom.getSRID(),
   geom.getElemInfo(), geom.getOrdinatesArray()
);
```

To write `J3D_Geometry` objects to the database, just use the regular `JGeometry.store()` method:

```
STRUCT dbObject = JGeometry.store (dbConnection, geom3d);
stmt.setObject (1,dbObject);
```

Just like `JGeometry`, it provides you with a number of methods that allow you to manipulate the geometry in various ways. Table 7-8 summarizes those methods.

Table 7-8. *3D Geometry Processing Functions*

Method	Purpose
`anyInteract(J3D_Geometry A, double tolerance)`	Determines whether two three-dimensional geometries interact in any way
`extrusion(JGeometry polygon, double grdHeight, double height, Connection conn, boolean cond, double tolerance)`	Returns a three-dimensional geometry extruded from a two-dimensional polygon
`closestPoints(J3D_Geometry A, double tolerance)`	Computes the closest points of approach between two three-dimensional geometries
`getMBH(J3D_Geometry geom)`	Returns the three-dimensional bounding box of a three-dimensional geometry[3]
`validate(double tolerance)`	Verifies the validity of a three-dimensional geometry.
`area(double tolerance)`	Computes the area of a surface or of the sides of a solid
`length(int count_shared_edges, double tolerance)`	Computes the length of a three-dimensional shape
`volume(double tolerance)`	Computes the volume of a three-dimensional solid
`distance(J3D_Geometry A, double tolerance)`	Computes the distance between two three-dimensional geometries

Extracting Elements from 3D Geometries: the ElementExtractor Class

3D objects can be complex. This is especially the case for solids. A complex solid is formed of multiple simple solids. The simple solids are formed from surfaces, some of them forming voids in the solid. Surfaces themselves are formed of elements, which are formed of rings.

3. This really returns a Minimum Bounding Hexahedron (MBH), that is, a solid with six faces, aligned with the axis of the coordinate system.

The ElementExtractor class makes it easy for you to inspect a complex object and extract individual components, such as one or more of the surfaces that form a solid. Note that you can also use the extractor on regular two-dimensional geometries. This can be useful to extract, for example, the linear contour of one of the rings in a complex polygon.

You can use the extractor in two ways: one is to extract one specific element. The other is to iterate over all available elements.

■ **Tip** The ElementExtractor class is not restricted to 3D geometries. It will also work on 2D geometries. However, since its input must be a J3D_Geometry object, you must first convert your JGeometry object into a J3D_Geometry.

Extracting a Single Element

All you need is to call the static getElementByLabel() method, passing it a "label" that uniquely identifies the geometry element to extract. The label is a comma-delimited string of ID numbers that specify the subset geometry to be returned. Specify as many of the following elements as apply. (For any null elements before the last specified element, enter a comma for the element.)

- Point ID
- Edge ID
- Ring ID
- Polygon ID
- Surface ID
- Solid ID
- Multisolid ID

Those ID numbers are really sequence numbers for each element at each level. The sequence numbers begin with 1: the first polygon in a multipolygon is polygon 1. Its rings are numbered from 1 to N. The second polygon is polygon 2, and its rings are again numbered from 1.

For example, the following will return polygon number 3 in surface 2 of a simple solid:

```
J3D_Geometry ring = ElementExtractor.getElementByLabel (solid,"0,0,0,3,2");
```

Note that the validate() method of J3D_Geometry will return such a label when it finds an error. You can then simply pass this label to ElementExtractor.getElementByLabel() to isolate the element on which the error was detected.

Iterating Over Elements

Create an ElementExtractor object, passing it the parameters for your query. This will essentially create an iterator that you initialize at a certain level of detail. You can then use its nextElement() method to extract the components of the object one by one. You can then use another ElementExtractor object to further inspect each of the elements you receive from the first loop.

The parameters to use when you create an ElementExtractor object are detailed in Table 7-9. Those parameters control the way the extractor behaves.

Table 7-9. *Parameters of the* `ElementExtractor`

Parameter	Purpose
`geometry`	The 3D geometry to analyze.
`firstElement`	The place to start the extraction, specified as an offset in the `SDO_ELEM_INFO` array of the geometry. By default, this will be 0.
`extractionLevel`	This is a code that indicates the way the iterator will process the elements in the geometry. See the "Extraction Levels" section for a detailed discussion.
`allow_comp_sub_elements`	Specify as `true` (the default) or `false`. In `MULTICOMP_TOSIMPLE` extraction level, users can also arrange to extract directly simple geometries from multi or composite geometries by setting this parameter to `FALSE`. The default value is `TRUE`, which means users will extract composite geometry first (if any) from a multigeometry.

Extraction Levels

The `extractionLevel` parameter allows you to control the way the extractor operates. Specify it as one of the following values. The names are those of the constants defined in the class.

- `Level 0 = MULTICOMP_TOSIMPLE`: This returns the successive elements in a multigeometry. For example, it will return each solid in a multisolid or each polygon in a multipolygon. Think of it as a "horizontal" scan through the elements.
- `Level 1 = INNER_OUTER`: This returns the inner/outer elements if any. For polygons, it returns the outer ring first, followed by inner rings.
- `Level 2 = LOWER_LEVEL`: This returns the subelements; that is, it returns the elements at the next level of hierarchy (for example, for a solid the next level will be surfaces, and for a polygon the next level will be edges, and so on).

Let's consider a simple example of a multipolygon where the polygons have multiple voids. To fully decompose the geometry, use the `MULTICOMP_TOSIMPLE` scan first. This will break the multipolygon into its constituent polygons.

The next step is to extract the rings of those polygons. For that, use the `INNER_OUTER` scan on each of the polygons returned from the first step. For a polygon without voids, the result stays the same. For those polygons that have voids, you will receive a polygon representing the outer ring first, then one or more polygons representing the inner rings.

Finally, to further decompose the geometry, use the `LOWER_LEVEL` scan on each of the rings. This scan will break each ring into a set of *edges*—a set of simple line strings with two vertices each.

Here is an example of using the extractor to break a multigeometry into its elements:

```
// Create new extractor
ElementExtractor e = new ElementExtractor (
  geom3d, 0, ElementExtractor.MULTICOMP_TOSIMPLE);
// Geometry to receive extracted element(s)
J3D_Geometry g;
// Used to receive the type of element (1=outer, 2=inner)
int is_a_hole[] = {0};
// Extract the elements
while ((g = e.nextElement(is_a_hole)) != null) {
  // Process extracted element
}
```

Notice that the nextElement() needs an output parameter that it will use to indicate whether the element it returned is an "outer" element or an "inner" element. The parameter must be defined as an int[] of one element, whose first element will be set to 1 (for an outer element) or 2 (for an inner element). This applies only to a LOWER_LEVEL scan, but the output parameter is required in all cases.

Recursive Decomposition

You do not have to specify the extractionLevel parameter. If you omit it, the extractor will automatically determine the most appropriate level to use for the geometry to analyze. This makes it easy to decompose a geometry recursively in its constituents, all the way to individual line segments. This is illustrated in the following example:

```
void decomposeGeometry (J3D_Geometry geom, int level, int seq)
  throws Exception
{
  System.out.println ("Level: "+ level+" Sequence: "+seq);
  if ((geom.getType() == geom.GTYPE_CURVE) ||
     (geom.getType() == geom.GTYPE_POINT))
    return;
  MyElementExtractor e = new MyElementExtractor (geom);
  int i = 0;
  J3D_Geometry g;
  int h[] = {0};
  while ((g = e.nextElement(h)) != null) {
    decomposeGeometry (g, level + 1, i+1);
    i++;
  }
}
```

Using Standard Notations: WKT, WKB, GML

In Chapter 5 we talked about PL/SQL functions and methods to convert between SDO_GEOMETRY types and the standard notations defined by the Open Geospatial Consortium (OGC): Well-Known Text (WKT), Well-Known Binary (WKB), and Geographic Markup Language (GML). We will now briefly explain how to perform those conversions in Java.

The classes we will use to manipulate those formats are all in package oracle.spatial.util. The SdoExport.java and SdoImport.java programs, available for download from the Apress website, provide fully functional examples of reading and writing the WKT, WKB, and GML formats.

Reading and Writing WKT

The WKT notation is a structured textual notation for encoding geometries. It was originally designed as a standard way for exchanging geometries between multiple environments. A point encoded in WKT would look like this:

```
POINT (-111.870478 33.685992)
```

A simple polygon would look like this:

```
POLYGON ((-119.308006 37.778061,  ... -119.308006 37.778061))
```

To convert a JGeometry object to the WKT notation, we will use method fromJGeometry() of class WKT in package oracle.spatial.util. Note that this method actually produces a byte array, which you may need to convert into a string before writing it out to a file. This is illustrated in the following example:

```
// Create a WKT processor
WKT  wkt  = new WKT();
...
// Convert the geometry to WKT
String s = new String(wkt.fromJGeometry(geom));
```

To convert WKT string back to a `JGeometry` object, just use method `toJGeometry()` of class `WKT`. This method also uses a byte array as input. The process is illustrated in the following example:

```
// Create a WKT processor
WKT  wkt  = new WKT();
...
// Convert the WKT  to geometry
JGeometry geom = wkt.toJGeometry(s.getBytes());
```

Caution The WKT and WKB notations do not provide any mechanism for indicating the projection of the geometry; this information is lost when converting a geometry to either of the formats. If you want to preserve it, you need to write it separately and add it back to the geometry using the `setSRID()` method.

Reading and Writing WKB

The WKB encoding, as the name implies, encodes geometries in binary, a more compact format than the WKT. Using it is similar to the way you proceeded previously. The `fromJGeometry()` method of class `WKB` also produces a byte array, which you can then write to a file. We will show how to write to a java `DataOutputStream` (called `ds` in the example) that allows you to write primitive Java data types in a portable way.

First you convert the `JGeometry` object into WKB. This results in the creation of a byte array. Then you write the size of this array to the output stream, followed by the SRID of the geometry. Finally you write the byte array proper.

```
// Create a WKB processor
WKB  wkb  = new WKB(ByteOrder.BIG_ENDIAN);
...
// Convert JGeometry to WKB
byte[] b = wkb.fromJGeometry(geom);
// First write the number of bytes in the array
ds.writeInt(b.length);
// Then write the SRID of the geometry
ds.writeInt(geom.getSRID());
// Then write the binary array
ds.write(b);
```

Notice the `ByteOrder.BIG_ENDIAN` parameter. It indicates the kind of binary encoding to use: *big endian* or *little endian*. The default is to produce a big endian encoding. You may need to adapt this to the encoding accepted by the tools that will process the WKB. Note that the chosen encoding method is itself flagged in the first byte of the binary result.

To convert a WKB back to a `JGeometry` object, just use method `toJGeometry()` of class `WKB`. This method also uses a byte array as input. The following example illustrates this process. You can assume that we're reading the data from the file written previously. You first read the size of the WKB and then the SRID of the geometry. Then you read exactly the number of bytes needed to rebuild the WKB. Finally you convert the WKB to a `JGeometry` object and set the SRID back using the `setSRID` method.

```
// Create a WKB processor
WKB  wkb  = new WKB();
...
// Read the size of the byte array
int n = ds.readInt();
// Read the SRID of the geometry
int srid = ds.readInt();
// Read the byte array that contains the WKB
byte[] b = new byte[n];
int l = ds.read (b, 0, n);
// Convert to JGeometry
geom = wkb.toJGeometry(b);
// Add the SRID
geom.setSRID(srid);
```

We did not need to specify the style of binary encoding (big or little endian) to use. This is because the toJGeometry() method recognizes the encoding automatically and handles both of them transparently.

Reading and Writing GML

The WKT and WKB have many limitations: they support only simple 2D shapes. They do not support any 3D shapes, and they do not support arcs or circles. In addition, they have no way to specify the projection of a geometry. For a more powerful solution, use Geographic Markup Language (GML), which is an XML encoding for geographical information.

To read and write GML, we will show how to use a set of four classes and methods, summarized in Table 7-10. The reason for having multiple classes is that the GML standard is evolving. There are currently two major versions of the standard: GML2 and GML3, with GML3 providing support for 3D shapes (surfaces and solids) and other advanced facilities.

Table 7-10. *Classes and Methods for GML Processing*

GML Version	Writing GML	Reading GML
GML2	GML2.to_GMLGeometry()	GML.fromNodeToGeometry()
GML3	GML3.to_GML3Geometry()	GML3g.fromNodeToGeometry()

Note that GML3 is a superset of GML2, so any GML2-encoded geometries will be readable by a GML3 reader. However, the reverse is not true.

Converting a JGeometry object to GML is easy, as shown in the following example:

```
// Create a GML2 Processor
GML2 gml  = new GML2();
...
String s = gml.to_GMLGeometry(geom);
```

As you can see, the to_GMLGeometry() method returns a string that you can now directly write out. You can also include the result (an XML string) in other XML documents. The previous example uses GML2. To use GML3, just use the proper class and method.

Converting a GML string back to a JGeometry object is more convoluted. The conversion methods (GML.fromNodeToGeometry() and GML3g.fromNodeToGeometry()) do not take a GML string as input but as a parsed document. So before using any of those methods, you must first parse the GML string yourself. The following example shows this process:

```
// Create a GML3 Processor
GML3 gml  = new GML3g();
...
// Read GML string from input stream
String s = ds.readLine();
// Setup an XML DOM parser
DOMParser parser = new DOMParser();
// Parse the XML string
parser.parse(new StringReader(s));
// Get the parsed document
Document document = parser.getDocument();
// Get the top level node of the document
Node node = document.getDocumentElement();
// Convert to geometry
geom = gml.fromNodeToGeometry(node);
```

Note that this uses the GML3 processor. To use the GML2 processor, just switch to class `GML` instead of `GML3g`.

Caution Make sure not to mix up the class names involved in GML processing.

Using ESRI Shapefiles

The ESRI shapefile format is a popular format for transferring geographical data. In Chapter 5 we used a simple command-line tool to convert shapefiles and load them into spatial tables. We will now show how to read and write shapefiles in Java. For that we will use a set of classes from the `oracle.spatial.util` package.

If all you need is to load an ESRI shapefile into a database table, then the `oracle.spatial.util` package has just what you need. Just invoke class `SampleShapefileToJGeomFeature` and pass it the appropriate parameters. If you don't know them, just invoke it without any parameters, and it will tell you. Here is an example that loads the content of shapefile `shp_cities` into table `us_cities`:

```
C:\>java oracle.spatial.util.SampleShapefileToJGeomFeature -h 127.0.0.1 -p 1521
-s orcl111 -u spatial -d spatial -t us_cities -f shp_cities -r 8307
host: 127.0.0.1
port: 1521
sid: orcl111
db_username: spatial
db_password: spatial
db_tablename: us_cities
shapefile_name: shp_cities
SRID: 8307
Connecting to Oracle10g using...
127.0.0.1, 1521, orcl111, spatial, spatial, us_cities, shp_cities, null, 8307
Dropping old table...
Creating new table...
Converting record #10 of 195
Converting record #20 of 195
Converting record #30 of 195
Converting record #40 of 195
Converting record #50 of 195
Converting record #60 of 195
Converting record #70 of 195
```

```
Converting record #80 of 195
Converting record #90 of 195
Converting record #100 of 195
Converting record #110 of 195
Converting record #120 of 195
Converting record #130 of 195
Converting record #140 of 195
Converting record #150 of 195
Converting record #160 of 195
Converting record #170 of 195
Converting record #180 of 195
Converting record #190 of 195
195 record(s) converted.
Done.
```

The class will create the table, load it, and insert the proper metadata in USER_SDO_GEOM_METADATA.

A Short Note on Shapefiles

The name *shapefile* is somewhat misleading. Each shapefile consists of a collection of at least three files, all sharing the same file name, and they're distinguished only by their file extensions. For example, in the previous example, the shape file shp_cities is really a collection of the following files:

- shp_cities.shp: The "shape" file proper. This is the file that contains the actual geometry definitions.
- shp_cities.shx: A spatial index on the shapes.
- shp_cities.dbf: A dBASE IV file containing the attributes for each geometry.

Some shapefiles can also come with other files, such as shp_cities.prj or shp_cities.sbn. Those are ignored by the Oracle Spatial Java classes.

When specifying the name of a shapefile, do not include the .shp extension. All files that form the shapefile must be stored together in the same directory.

Loading a Shapefile in Your Program

The oracle.spatial.util package contains three classes you can use from your own programs in order to read and load shapefiles. Table 7-11 summarizes them.

Table 7-11. *Classes for Shapefile Processing*

Class Name	Purpose
ShapefileReaderJGeom	Provides all the functions you need to read shapes (geometries) from the shapefile and convert them to JGeometry objects
DBFReaderJGeom	Provides functions for reading attributes from the DBF file, as well as to get the names and types of the attributes
ShapefileFeatureJGeom	Uses the two reader classes to provide you with high-end functions to create database tables and load them from a shapefile

The following example shows how to use the shapefile-processing classes to easily incorporate a shapefile loader in your application. Start by opening the input files and setting up the helper class. Remember that shapeFileName contains only the generic name of the shapefile, without any extension.

```
// Open SHP and DBF files
ShapefileReaderJGeom shpr = new ShapefileReaderJGeom(shapeFileName);
DBFReaderJGeom dbfr = new DBFReaderJGeom(shapeFileName);
ShapefileFeatureJGeom sf = new ShapefileFeatureJGeom();
```

Then extract the dimensions of the shapefile, that is, the minimum and maximum values of all coordinates of the geometries in the file in all dimensions:

```
// Get shapefile bounds and dimension
double minX = shpr.getMinX();
double maxX = shpr.getMaxX();
double minY = shpr.getMinY();
double maxY = shpr.getMaxY();
double minZ = shpr.getMinZ();
double maxZ = shpr.getMaxZ();
double minM = shpr.getMinMeasure();
double maxM = shpr.getMaxMeasure();
int shpDims = shpr.getShpDims(shpFileType, maxM);
```

You can now construct the spatial metadata. Method getDimArray() will generate the proper metadata definition based on the bounds and the dimensions of the data in the shapefile. Notice an oddity in the usage of this method: the minimum and maximum values for the X and Y dimensions must be passed as strings. The minimum and maximum for the Z and M dimensions are passed as numbers.

```
// Construct the spatial metadata
String dimArray = sf.getDimArray(
  shpDims, String.valueOf(tolerance),
  String.valueOf(minX), String.valueOf(maxX),
  String.valueOf(minY), String.valueOf(maxY),
  minZ, maxZ, minM, maxM
);
```

Then you can create the table in the database. The method will drop the existing table first and then create a new table using the proper Oracle data types that match the types of the attributes in the DBF file. It will also insert the spatial metadata in USER_SDO_GEOM_METADATA. Specify the name to be given to the SDO_GEOMETRY column (in geoColumn). You can also optionally specify the name of an identification column (idColumn). This column will be automatically filled with sequential numbers during the load.

```
// Create table before loading
sf.prepareTableForData(
  dbConnection, dbfr, tableName, geoColumn, idColumn,
  srid, dimArray
);
```

You can now load the data from the shapefile into the database table just created. The insertFeatures method takes a number of arguments: the name of the identification column (idColumn), the value to start numbering from (firstId), the commit frequency (commitFrequency), and the frequency of the progress messages (printFrequency) printed during the load.

```
// Load the features
sf.insertFeatures(dbConnection, dbfr, shpr, tableName,
  idColumn, firstId,
  commitFrequency, printFrequency, srid,
  dimArray
);
```

Finally, don't forget to close the input files:

```
// Close input file
shpr.closeShapefile();
dbfr.closeDBF();
```

Building Your Own Loader

If you want more flexibility, such as the ability to choose which attributes to load, to rename them, or to perform some processing on the geometries before loading, then you can use the low-level methods of the ShapefileReaderJGeom and DBFReaderJGeom classes. Table 7-12 and Table 7-13 summarize them.

Table 7-12. ShapefileReaderJGeom *Methods*

Method	Purpose
getMinX()	Returns the minimum value for the x-dimension
getMaxX()	Returns the maximum value for the x-dimension
getMinY()	Returns the minimum value for the y-dimension
getMaxY()	Returns the maximum value for the y-dimension
getMinZ()	Returns the minimum value for the z-dimension
getMaxZ()	Returns the maximum value for the z-dimension
getMinMeasure()	Returns the minimum value for the m-dimension
getMaxMeasure()	Returns the maximum value for the m-dimension
getShpFileType()	Returns the type of geometries contained in that shapefile: 1 for points, 3 for lines, 5 for polygons
getShpDims()	Returns the number of dimensions of the geometries
numRecords()	Returns the number of records in the shapefile
getGeometryBytes(int nth)	Extracts the *n*th geometry from the shape file as a byte array
getGeometry(byte[] recBuffer, int srid) ()	Converts a geometry from the shape binary encoding into a JGeometry object
closeShapefile()	Closes the shapefile

Table 7-13. DBFReaderJGeom *Methods*

Method	Purpose
numRecords()	Returns the number of records in the DBF file. This should match the number of records in the shapefile proper.
numFields()	Returns the number of attributes (= columns) in the DBF file.
getFieldName(int nth)	Returns the name of the *n*th field as a string.
getFieldType(int nth)	Returns the type of the *n*th field as a single-character code.
getFieldLength(int nth)	Returns the length of the *n*th field (number of bytes it occupies in the file).
getRecord(int nth)	Returns the *n*th record in the file as a byte array.
getFieldData(int nth, byte[] rec)	Extracts the value of the *n*th field from a binary record.
closeDBF()	Closes the DBF file.

Using those methods, you can now extract the names, types, and size of the attributes stored in the DBF file. Using that information, you have the complete flexibility to create a database table. The following shows how to map the DBF data types into their Oracle equivalents:

```
int numFields = dbfr.numFields();
String[] fieldName   = new String[numFields];
byte[]   fieldType   = new byte[numFields];
int[]    fieldLength = new int[numFields];
String[] oracleType  = new String[numFields];
for (int i=0; i<numFields; i++) {
  fieldName[i] = dbfr.getFieldName(i);
  fieldType[i] = dbfr.getFieldType(i);
  fieldLength[i] = dbfr.getFieldLength(i);
  switch (fieldType[i]) {
    case 'C':   // Character
      oracleType[i] = "VARCHAR2(" + fieldLength[i] + ")";
      break;
    case 'L':  // Logical
      oracleType[i] = "CHAR(1)";
      break;
    case 'D':  // Date
      oracleType[i] = "DATE";
      break;
    case 'I':  // Integer
    case 'F':  // Float
    case 'N':  // Numeric
      oracleType[i] = "NUMBER";
      break;
    default:
      throw new RuntimeException("Unsupported DBF field type " + fieldType[i]);
  }
}
```

Creating the corresponding table is easy. Just assemble the `CREATE TABLE` statement by appending the names of the attributes.

```
String createTableSql = "CREATE TABLE " + tableName + "(";
for (int i=0; i<numFields; i++)
  createTableSql = createTableSql + fieldName[i] + " " + oracleType[i] + ",";
createTableSql = createTableSql + geoColumn + " SDO_GEOMETRY)";
```

Finally, reading and inserting the data into the database needs a loop to fetch and process each SHP and DBF record one after the other. We assume that you built and prepared an `INSERT` statement that takes one bind variable for each column to fill.

```
for (int rowNumber = 0; rowNumber < numRows; rowNumber++)
{
  // Extract attributes values from  current DBF record
  byte[] a = dbfr.getRecord (rowNumber);
  for (int i = 0; i< dbfr.numFields(); i++) {
    stmt.setString (i+1,dbfr.getFieldData(i, a));
  }
  // Extract geometry from current SHP record
  byte[] s = shpr.getGeometryBytes (rowNumber);
  JGeometry geom = ShapefileReaderJGeom.getGeometry (s, srid);
```

```
    // Convert JGeometry object into database object
    Struct dbObject = JGeometry.store (dbConnection, geom);
    stmt.setObject (numFields+1, dbObject);

    // Insert row into the database table
    stmt.execute();
  }
```

Summary

In this chapter, you learned how to map geometry types into data structures that you can use in application programs for PL/SQL and Java to read, write, and manipulate them. Note that there are a few occasions when you will need to perform such manipulations, and Oracle Spatial provides a rich set of operators and functions that should cover the majority of cases. We will cover those operators and functions in the next two chapters.

PART 3

Spatial and Network Analysis

CHAPTER 8

Spatial Indexes and Operators

To run the examples in this chapter, you need to import the following datasets:

```
imp spatial/spatial file=app_with_loc.dmp full=y indexes=n
imp spatial/spatial file=map_large.dmp full=y
imp spatial/spatial file=citybldgs.dmp full=y
```

In previous chapters, we showed how to store location information in Oracle tables. We augmented existing tables, such as branches, customers, and competitors, with an SDO_GEOMETRY column to store locations of data objects. In this chapter, we describe how to use this spatial information to perform proximity analysis.

Proximity analysis refers to query/analysis using the locations of data objects. Specifically, in a business application, you might be interested in (but not limited to) the types of proximity analysis shown in Table 8-1.

Table 8-1. *Types of Proximity Analyses in a Business Application*

Analysis Type	Description
Customer analysis	Identify customers nearest to, or within a specified radius from, a branch or a competitor. For customers close to a competitor, you might provide certain promotions to retain them. You may specifically target this analysis on GOLD customers whom you want to retain at any cost.
Sales region analysis	Build sales regions (that is, quarter-mile buffers) around branch and competitor locations. Identify which of these overlap with one another or with state and county boundaries. If sales regions of branches overlap substantially, you could merge such branches.

We describe how to perform these (and additional) varieties of proximity analysis in detail in this chapter. To perform efficient proximity analysis, you will use three basic elements of Oracle's spatial technology:

- *Spatial operators*: Just as you can specify relational operators in a SQL statement, such as < (less than), > (greater than), or = (equal to), and so on, you can likewise use a spatial operator to search the location (SDO_GEOMETRY) columns of a table for proximity with respect to a query location.

  The following SQL shows how to search the customers table using a spatial operator:

  ```
  SELECT COUNT(*)
  FROM branches b, customers c
  WHERE b.id=1
  AND SDO_WITHIN_DISTANCE
     (c.location, b.location, 'DISTANCE=0.25 UNIT=MILE')='TRUE';
  ```

  This example counts the customers within a quarter mile of a specified store (id=1). The equality operator, b.id=1, selects only the row that has an ID of 1 from the branches table. You then specify a spatial predicate using the SDO_WITHIN_DISTANCE operator, with which you identify the customers that are within a quarter mile of the specified store.

- *Spatial indexes*: Analogous to B-tree indexes, spatial indexes facilitate fast execution of spatial operators on SDO_GEOMETRY columns of Oracle tables. A B-tree index on the id column of the branches table would facilitate searches based on branch ID. Similarly, a spatial index on the location column of the customers table would facilitate fast execution of the SDO_WITHIN_DISTANCE operator.

- *Geometry processing functions*: These functions perform a variety of operations, including computation of the spatial interaction of two or more SDO_GEOMETRY objects. Spatial functions do not use spatial indexes, and they enable a more rigorous analysis of spatial data than is possible with spatial operators.

In this chapter, we focus on only the first two topics listed previously: *spatial indexes* and *spatial operators*. We will describe the third topic, *geometry processing functions*, in Chapter 9. A majority of the functionality of spatial indexes and spatial operators is part of Oracle Locator (included in all editions of the Oracle Database). This means all Oracle applications can leverage the functionality described in this chapter.

The remainder of the chapter is structured as follows:

- First, we discuss how to create spatial indexes on SDO_GEOMETRY columns.

- Then, we describe spatial operators that perform different types of proximity analysis and how to use these operators in a SQL statement.

- Finally, we cover more advanced topics regarding spatial indexing and spatial queries. These include *function-based spatial indexing*, *parallel* and *partitioned* indexing, and *spatial joins*. Function-based spatial indexing allows spatial indexes to be created on functions that return SDO_GEOMETRY values. Partitioned indexing allows local indexes to be created for each partition of a partitioned table. Parallel indexing allows the creation of a spatial index in parallel. Spatial joins enable fast joining of multiple tables based on a spatial criterion. Some of these advanced topics, such as partitioned indexes, are included only in the Enterprise Edition of Oracle (as priced options).

Spatial Indexes

Spatial operators enable proximity analysis on SDO_GEOMETRY columns. Listing 8-1 shows how to search for customers within a half mile of a branch location.

Listing 8-1. SDO_WITHIN_DISTANCE *Spatial Operator in SQL*

```
SQL> SELECT COUNT(*)
FROM branches b , customers c
WHERE  b.id=1
  AND SDO_WITHIN_DISTANCE
  (c.location, b.location,  'DISTANCE=0.5 UNIT=MILE')='TRUE';
ERROR at line 1:
ORA-13226: interface not supported without a spatial index
ORA-06512: at "MDSYS.MD", line 1723
ORA-06512: at "MDSYS.MDERR", line 8
ORA-06512: at "MDSYS.SDO_3GL", line 387
```

The error in Listing 8-1 indicates that to use spatial operators, you first need to create a spatial index on the location column of the customers table. As an application developer, creating spatial indexes on the SDO_GEOMETRY columns is one of the first steps to undertake when enabling proximity analysis in your application.

As noted earlier, spatial indexes in Oracle are analogous to conventional indexes such as B-trees. Just as a B-tree index on a name column speeds up queries of the sort where name = 'Larry', so do spatial indexes enable fast searching on the indexed SDO_GEOMETRY columns. Spatial indexes are required to ensure effective response times for queries that use spatial operators, such as the one in Listing 8-1. You will learn of how they are structured and how they work in the "Spatial Index Concepts" section. But first we'll cover how to create the spatial index.

Just like B-tree indexes, spatial indexes are created using SQL. For instance, you can create a spatial index on the location column of the customers table, as shown in Listing 8-2.

Listing 8-2. *Creating an Index*

```
SQL> CREATE INDEX customers_sidx ON customers(location)
INDEXTYPE  IS MDSYS.SPATIAL_INDEX;
```

Note that the statement is similar to creating a B-tree index except that the INDEXTYPE IS MDSYS.SPATIAL_INDEX clause specifies that the index to be created is a spatial index instead of a regular B-tree index.

However, this statement may fail, as illustrated in the following code, if you have not already populated the appropriate metadata for the spatial layer (corresponding to <customers table, location column>):

```
ERROR at line 1:
ORA-29855: error occurred in the execution of ODCIINDEXCREATE routine
ORA-13203: failed to read USER_SDO_GEOM_METADATA view
ORA-13203: failed to read USER_SDO_GEOM_METADATA view
ORA-06512: at "MDSYS.SDO_INDEX_METHOD_10I", line 10
ORA-06512: at line 1
```

Caution Always insert metadata for a spatial layer (table_name, column_name) prior to creating a spatial index.

You may recall that we discussed how to add spatial metadata for a spatial layer in Chapter 3. We briefly recap that discussion in the next section.

Inserting Metadata for a Spatial Layer Prior to Indexing

Spatial metadata for a spatial layer (identified by `<table_name, column_name>`) is inserted in the `USER_SDO_GEOM_METADATA`[1] view. This view has the fields shown in Listing 8-3 that need to be populated appropriately.

Listing 8-3. `USER_SDO_GEOM_METADATA` *View*

```
SQL> DESCRIBE USER_SDO_GEOM_METADATA;
 Name                            Null?        Type
-----------------------         --------     -------------------
TABLE_NAME                      NOT NULL     VARCHAR2(32)
COLUMN_NAME                     NOT NULL     VARCHAR2(1024)
DIMINFO                                      MDSYS.SDO_DIM_ARRAY
SRID                                         NUMBER
```

You can populate these fields as shown in Listing 8-4.

Listing 8-4. *Inserting Metadata for the Spatial Layer Corresponding to the* `location` *Column of the* `customers` *Table*

```
SQL> INSERT INTO  user_sdo_geom_metadata
(table_name, column_name, srid, diminfo)
VALUES
(
  'CUSTOMERS',        -- TABLE_NAME
  'LOCATION',         -- COLUMN_NAME
  8307,               -- SRID specifying a geodetic coordinate system
  SDO_DIM_ARRAY       -- DIMINFO attribute for storing dimension bounds, tolerance
  (
    SDO_DIM_ELEMENT
    (
      'LONGITUDE',     -- DIMENSION NAME for first dimension
      -180,            -- SDO_LB for the dimension: -180 degrees
      180,             -- SDO_UB for the dimension: 180 degrees
      0.5              -- Tolerance of 0.5 meters (not 0.5 degrees: geodetic SRID)
    ),
     SDO_DIM_ELEMENT
     (
      'LATITUDE',      -- DIMENSION NAME for second dimension
      -90,             -- SDO_LB for the dimension: -90 degrees
      90,              -- SDO_UB for the dimension: 90 degrees
      0.5              -- Tolerance of 0.5 meters (not 0.5 degrees: geodetic SRID)
     )
  )
   );
```

The `table_name` and `column_name` fields, which identify the spatial layer, are set to `customers` and `location`, respectively. The `srid` field is set to `8307` to indicate a geodetic coordinate system. The `diminfo` field specifies the bounds and tolerance for each dimension. It is set using an `SDO_DIM_ARRAY` object containing two elements. The first element specifies the longitude dimension as `dimension_name`

---

1. Although we loosely refer to `USER_SDO_GEOM_METADATA` as a *view*, it is an *updatable* view based on an underlying table `SDO_INDEX_METADATA_TABLE` in the `MDSYS` schema. Inserts, deletes, and updates on the view are implemented as instead-of triggers on the underlying table.

and –180 (degrees) and 180 (degrees) as the lower and upper bounds for this dimension. The tolerance is set to 0.5 (meters). The second element specifies the latitude dimension as `dimension_name` and –90 (degrees) and 90 (degrees) as the lower and upper bounds for this dimension. The tolerance is set again to 0.5 (meters).

Creating a Spatial Index

Now that you have populated the metadata, you can create the spatial index. However, if the index creation failed earlier, you first need to drop the index that failed. Note that this behavior is different from that of a B-tree (when B-tree index creation fails, you don't need to explicitly drop the B-tree index). The command to drop a spatial index, shown in Listing 8-5, is the same as that for other indexes, such as B-trees.

Listing 8-5. *Dropping a Spatial Index*

```
SQL> DROP INDEX customers_sidx;
```

Now you are ready to re-create a spatial index on the `location` column of the `customers` table, as shown in Listing 8-6.

Listing 8-6. *Creating a Spatial Index on the* `location` *Column of the* `customers` *Table*

```
SQL> CREATE INDEX customers_sidx ON customers(location)
INDEXTYPE  IS MDSYS.SPATIAL_INDEX;
```

Note During index creation, Oracle checks whether the `SDO_SRID` in the column being indexed matches the SRID in the `USER_SDO_GEOM_METADATA` for the corresponding spatial layer. If these values do not match, Oracle raises the ORA-13365 error. Oracle, however, does not run any validation checks during index creation. You need to explicitly run validation (see Chapter 5 for details) if you are unsure of the validity of the spatial data.

Spatial Indexing Concepts

You have created a spatial index on the `location` column of the `customers` table, and you know that this will facilitate fast execution of spatial operator queries. However, before you move on to look at some more examples, it is important to understand how a spatial index works.

The `spatial_index` is internally implemented as an *R-tree* index,[2] a B-tree-like hierarchical structure that stores rectangle approximations of geometries as key values. Figure 8-1 shows an example of an R-tree `spatial_index` for customer locations represented by points.

---

2. Norbert Beckmann, Hans-Peter Kriegel, Ralf Schneider, and Bernhard Seeger. "The R*-tree: An Efficient and Robust Access Method for Points and Rectangles." Proceedings of the ACM SIGMOD International Conference on the Management of Data, 1990, p. 322–31.

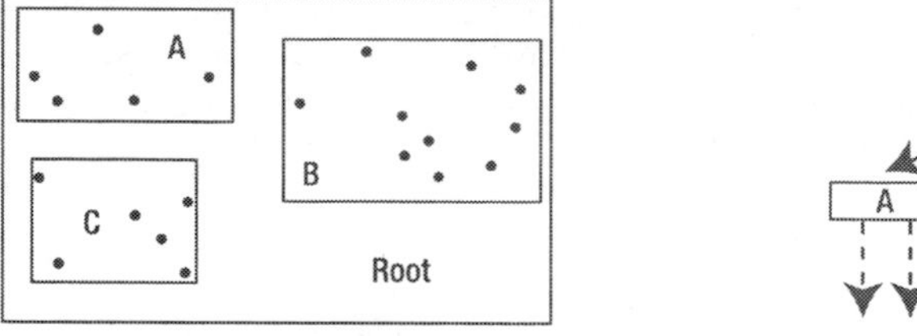

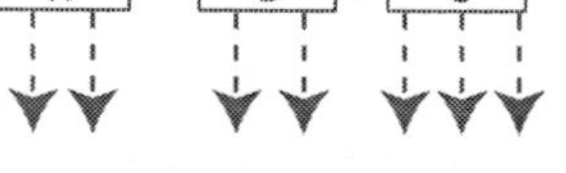

Rectangles: Index Approximations
• (dots): Point Geometries from Table

ROWIDs and MBRs from Data Table

Figure 8-1. *Example of an R-tree for a set of points*

Say that the black dots in Figure 8-1 represent the locations of customers stored as point geometries in the `location` (`SDO_GEOMETRY`) column of the `customers` table. For each `SDO_GEOMETRY` in the `location` column, the R-tree computes a *minimum bounding rectangle* (MBR) enclosing the `SDO_GEOMETRY`, and it creates a hierarchy of MBRs.

For instance, in Figure 8-1, the point locations are clustered into three nodes: A, B, and C. Each node is associated with an MBR that encloses the locations of the data in the subtree. The left side of Figure 8-1 shows the points and the MBRs for nodes A, B, and C. These nodes are further clustered into a single "root" node. In this manner, an R-tree constructs a hierarchical tree structure using the MBRs of the `SDO_GEOMETRY` data in a table. It then uses this hierarchy of MBRs to guide queries to appropriate branches of the tree and finally to the rows of the data table.

Figure 8-2 illustrates how the R-tree index is stored in Oracle. The logical tree structure is stored as an Oracle table that starts with the prefix `MDRT`. Each node of the tree structure is stored as a separate row in this table.

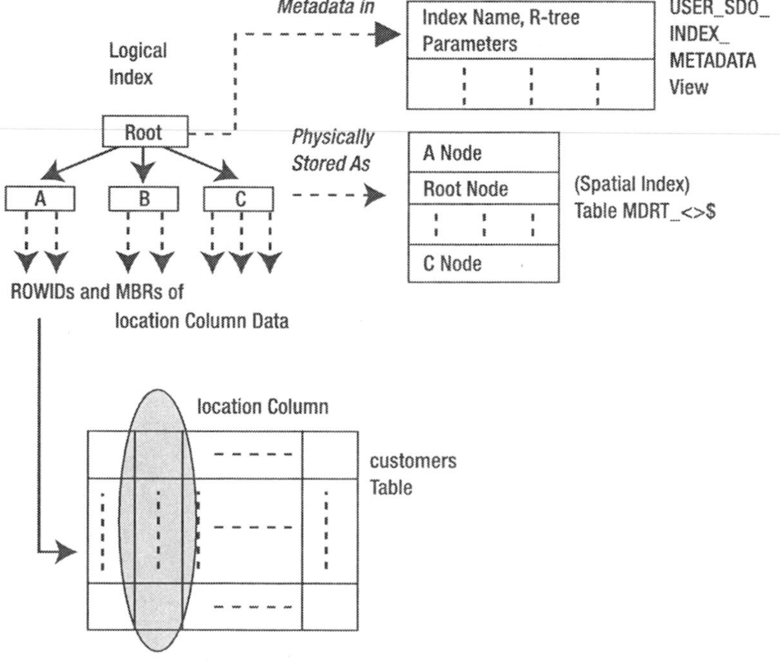

Figure 8-2. *Storage of a spatial (R-tree) index*

The metadata for the spatial index is stored in the view USER_SDO_INDEX_METADATA. (You should not confuse this view with the USER_SDO_GEOM_METADATA view that stores information about spatial layers.) This view stores the spatial index name (as SDO_INDEX_NAME), the table storing the index (as SDO_INDEX_TABLE), the root ROWID for the R-tree index, the branching factor or *fanout* (maximum number of children) of an R-tree node, and other relevant parameters. You can consult this view to identify the spatial index (MDRT) table (or SDO_INDEX_TABLE) corresponding to a specific spatial index. As an alternative, you can consult the simpler USER_SDO_INDEX_INFO view.

Note The USER_SDO_INDEX_INFO and USER_SDO_INDEX_METADATA views store all the VARCHAR2 fields in uppercase. You should compare these fields with uppercase literals (as in Listing 8-7).

As shown in Listing 8-7, the SDO_INDEX_TABLE (that is, the spatial index table) has the name MDRT_D81F$. Note that you may get a different name, but the name will always start with the prefix MDRT. You can identify all spatial index tables by querying the SDO_INDEX_TABLE column in the USER_SDO_INDEX_INFO view and take appropriate steps so that they are not moved around by an unwary DBA.

Listing 8-7. *Identifying the* SDO_INDEX_TABLE *That Stores the Spatial Index on the* customers *Table*

```
SQL> SELECT SDO_INDEX_TABLE FROM USER_SDO_INDEX_INFO
WHERE  TABLE_NAME = 'CUSTOMERS' AND COLUMN_NAME='LOCATION';
SDO_INDEX_TABLE
--------------------------------
MDRT_D81F$
```

Caution The SDO_INDEX_TABLE for a spatial index (for example, the one returned in the preceding SQL) should never be treated as a regular Oracle table—that is, it should not be moved from one tablespace to another, dropped, copied, and so on. Otherwise, this will render the spatial index invalid and could lead to the failure of subsequent spatial query operators[3] or spatial index rebuilding.

Spatial Index Parameters

In B-tree indexes, you can specify where to place the index data. Can you do that for the spatial index table associated with a spatial index? Yes. The CREATE INDEX statement in Listing 8-6 can take an additional PARAMETERS clause that can be used to specify a number of parameters, including where to store the index information. Listing 8-8 shows the syntax for creating a spatial index, including the PARAMETERS clause (in bold).

Listing 8-8. *Syntax for Creating a Spatial Index*

```
CREATE INDEX  <indexname> ON  <tablename>(<columnname>)
INDEXTYPE  IS MDSYS.SPATIAL_INDEX
PARAMETERS ('parameter_string');
```

The parameter_string is a list of parameter_name=value pairs. Let's examine some important parameters that you're likely to use in applications.

---

3. In this context, *operators* are binary predicates that operate on an SDO_GEOMETRY column that is indexed and a query SDO_GEOMETRY argument.

TABLESPACE Parameter

You can specify which tablespace to use for storing the spatial index table with this parameter. For instance, TABLESPACE=TBS_3 puts the spatial index table in the TBS_3 tablespace. Listing 8-9 shows an example.

Listing 8-9. *Creating a Spatial Index in Tablespace* TBS_3

```
SQL> CREATE INDEX customers_sidx ON customers(location)
INDEXTYPE IS MDSYS.SPATIAL_INDEX
PARAMETERS ('TABLESPACE=TBS_3');
```

You can specify the INITIAL and NEXT extents in addition to the TABLESPACE parameter, as shown in Listing 8-10.

Listing 8-10. *Creating an Index with the* INITIAL *and* NEXT *Extents for an Index Table*

```
SQL> CREATE INDEX customers_sidx ON customers(location)
INDEXTYPE IS MDSYS.SPATIAL_INDEX
PARAMETERS ('TABLESPACE=TBS_3 NEXT=5K INITIAL=10K');
```

If your tablespaces are *locally managed* (see the *Oracle Reference* for more details), you do not need these parameters, and Oracle will ignore them even if specified.

■ **Note** If the tablespace specified is an ASSM tablespace (you can verify this by checking that segment_space_management is AUTO in user_tablespaces for the specified tablespace), the LOBs created in the index are SECUREFILE LOBs. Otherwise, the LOBs created will be BASIC LOBs. Secure File LOBs are expected to be faster than BASIC LOBs.

WORK_TABLESPACE Parameter

During index creation, the R-tree index performs sorting operations on the entire dataset. As a result, it creates some working tables that are dropped at the end of index creation. Creating and dropping many tables with different sizes can fragment the space in a tablespace. To avoid this, you can specify a separate tablespace for these working tables using the WORK_TABLESPACE parameter, as shown in Listing 8-11.

Listing 8-11. *Creating an Index with* WORK_TABLESPACE *As* TBS_3

```
SQL> CREATE INDEX  customers_sidx ON  customers(location)
INDEXTYPE  IS MDSYS.SPATIAL_INDEX
PARAMETERS ('WORK_TABLESPACE=SYSAUX');
```

In this example, WORK_TABLESPACE=TBS_3 places all working tables in tablespace TBS_3. This ensures the existing tablespaces holding the index and/or data are not fragmented because of index creation work. The total size (in bytes) used in such a "work tablespace" will be approximately 200–300 times the number of rows in the customers table.

■ **Note** These working tables are regular tables and not "temporary" tables. You cannot use the temporary tablespace in Oracle for this purpose. Also note that if WORK_TABLESPACE is not specified, the working tables are created in the same tablespace as the index.

LAYER_GTYPE Parameter

You can use this parameter to specify that the geometry data in the location column of the customers table are *specific*-type geometries such as points (by default, all types are permitted). This will help in integrity checking and sometimes in speeding up the query operators.

For instance, as shown in Listing 8-12, you can set the parameter string to LAYER_GTYPE = POINT to indicate that the customers table has only point data. Trying to insert a line geometry into this column will raise an error. In general, you can set the value to the names of the SDO_GTYPEs (point, line, polygon, and so on), as discussed in Chapter 4.

Listing 8-12. *Creating an Index for Specific-Type (Point) Geometries*

```
SQL> CREATE INDEX  customers_sidx ON  customers(location)
INDEXTYPE  IS MDSYS.SPATIAL_INDEX
PARAMETERS ('LAYER_GTYPE=POINT');
```

SDO_INDX_DIMS Parameter

This parameter specifies that the dimensionality of the spatial_index. By default, this is set to 2. The R-tree can index three- and four-dimensional geometries. Listing 8-13 shows an example for setting the index dimensionality explicitly to 2. You can set this parameter to 3 or 4 to create a three- or four-dimensional R-tree index.

Listing 8-13. *Creating an R-tree Index with Dimensionality Specified*

```
SQL> CREATE INDEX  customers_sidx ON  customers(location)
INDEXTYPE  IS MDSYS.SPATIAL_INDEX
PARAMETERS ('SDO_INDX_DIMS=2');
```

SDO_DML_BATCH_SIZE Parameter

Inserts and deletes to a table containing a spatial index are not directly incorporated in the spatial index. Instead, they are incorporated in the index at commit time in batches. This parameter specifies the batch size for the batched insert/delete/update in a transaction. (For transactions with large number of inserts, set this parameter to 5000 or 10000.) Listing 8-14 shows an example.

Listing 8-14. *Creating an Index with the* SDO_DML_BATCH_SIZE *Parameter*

```
SQL> CREATE INDEX  customers_sidx ON  customers(location)
INDEXTYPE  IS MDSYS.SPATIAL_INDEX
PARAMETERS ('SDO_DML_BATCH_SIZE=5000');
```

This parameter, if not specified, is internally set to 1000. This means inserts in a transaction are incorporated in the index in batches of 1,000. This is a good value for most transactions that have a mix of queries and inserts, deletes, and updates. However, if your transactions have a large number of inserts, deletes, and updates (say, on the order of 5,000 or 10,000 or more), you may want to set the SDO_DML_BATCH_SIZE parameter to a higher value, for example, 5000 or 10000. This will substantially improve the performance of the commit operation (that is, the incorporation of the updates in the index at commit time). Note, however, that this might consume more memory and other system resources. In general, you should always set this parameter to be in the range of 1 to 10000.

■ **Tip** If you expect to perform a substantial number of insert (or delete or update) operations within a transaction on a table having a spatial index, set the SDO_DML_BATCH_SIZE parameter to 5000 or 10000 in the CREATE INDEX statement or in a subsequent ALTER_ INDEX REBUILD statement.

SDO_LEVEL Parameter

Instead of an R-tree index (which is the default), you can create a quadtree index by specifying the SDO_LEVEL parameter in the PARAMETERS clause (search the documentation for *Oracle Spatial Quadtree Indexing*). Quadtrees, unlike R-trees, need explicit tuning (the SDO_LEVEL parameter needs to be tuned for best performance) and are discouraged. Quadtrees can index only two-dimensional non-geodetic data. Listing 8-15 shows an example.

Listing 8-15. *Creating a Quadtree Type of Spatial Index*

```
SQL> CREATE INDEX customers_sidx ON customers(location)
INDEXTYPE  IS MDSYS.SPATIAL_INDEX
PARAMETERS ('SDO_LEVEL=8');
```

USER_SDO_INDEX_METADATA View

All the previously described parameters that can be used in the CREATE INDEX statement are stored in the USER_SDO_INDEX_METADATA view. For instance, after creating a spatial index, you can check the SDO_DML_BATCH_SIZE value for this index, as shown in Listing 8-16.

Listing 8-16. *Examining the* USER_SDO_INDEX_METADATA *View for Index Parameters*

```
SQL> SELECT SDO_DML_BATCH_SIZE  FROM USER_SDO_INDEX_METADATA
WHERE  SDO_INDEX_NAME = 'CUSTOMERS_SIDX';
SDO_DML_BATCH_SIZE
------------------
              1000
```

■ **Note** Again, observe that the USER_SDO_INDEX_METADATA view stores all its VARCHAR2 fields in uppercase. You should compare these fields with uppercase literals (as in Listings 8-7 and 8-16).

Listing 8-16 shows that the SDO_DML_BATCH_SIZE parameter is set to the default value of 1,000. Likewise, you can examine the SDO_TABLESPACE parameter (and other parameters) in the USER_SDO_INDEX_METADATA view to verify that the index is stored in the tablespace you specified.

Spatial Index Size Requirements

For a set of *N* rows in a table, the R-tree spatial index roughly requires 100*3**N* bytes of storage space for the spatial index table. Also, during index creation, it requires an additional 200 3 *N* to 300 3 *N* bytes for temporary worktables. You can use the utility function in Listing 8-17 to roughly estimate the size (in megabytes) of an R-tree spatial index table.

Listing 8-17. *Estimating the Size of a Spatial Index on the* `location` *Column of the* `customers` *Table*

```
SQL>  SELECT   sdo_tune.estimate_rtree_index_size
(
  'SPATIAL',       -- schema name
  'CUSTOMERS',     -- table name
  'LOCATION'       -- column name on which the spatial index is to be built
)  sz
FROM dual;

        SZ
----------
         1
```

The first parameter specifies the schema name, the second specifies the table name, and the third specifies the column name on which the spatial index is to be built. For building a spatial index on the `location` column of the `customers` table, this function indicates you need roughly 1MB of space. Note that this is the final index size. You may need two to three times this space during the index creation process

In addition, when you create a spatial index, the session parameter `SORT_AREA_SIZE` should be set to 1MB to optimize the index creation process.

Given this background on spatial indexes, let's move on to look at associated spatial operators and how to perform proximity analysis using such operators.

Spatial Operators

In this section, we describe the different spatial operators that Oracle Spatial supports for performing spatial analysis. We start with an overview of spatial operators, their general syntax, their semantics (along with any required privileges), and their evaluation using spatial indexes. Next, we take a closer look at different spatial operators and describe how to perform different kinds of proximity analyses (including those discussed in Table 8-1) using those operators. Then, we describe how specifying appropriate "hints" can ensure faster evaluation of spatial operators.

Oracle Spatial supports a variety of spatial operators for performing proximity analysis. Just like the relational operators <, >, and =, the spatial operators can be used in the `WHERE` clause of a regular SQL statement. Let's examine the syntax and the semantics of these operators.

Syntax of Spatial Operators

These operators have the generic syntax described in Listing 8-18.

Listing 8-18. *General Syntax of Spatial Operators*

```
<spatial_operator>
(
  table_geometry       IN SDO_GEOMETRY  (or ST_GEOMETRY),
  query_geometry       IN SDO_GEOMETRY  (or ST_GEOMETRY)
  [, parameter_string  IN VARCHAR2
   [, tag              IN NUMBER ]]
)
='TRUE'
```

In Listing 8-18, the following is true:

- table_geometry is the SDO_GEOMETRY (or ST_GEOMETRY) column of the table on which the operator is applied.
- query_geometry is the query location. This could be an SDO_GEOMETRY (or ST_GEOMETRY) column of another table, a bind variable, or a dynamically constructed object.
- parameter_string specifies the parameters specific to the spatial operator. As the opening square bracket indicates, this argument is optional in some operators.
- tag specifies a number used only in specific spatial operators. Again, the opening square bracket indicates that this argument is optional. This argument can be specified only in conjunction with the parameter_string argument.

You should note three things in the preceding syntax and explanation. First, the table_geometry column *must* be spatially indexed. Spatial operators raise an error otherwise. Second, the operator should always be equated to the string 'TRUE' in the preceding signature. This makes it a *predicate* to be evaluated with respect to every row of the indexed table. Finally, the columns can be either the native SDO_GEOMETRY type defined in Oracle or the ST_GEOMETRY type or the subtypes of ST_GEOMETRY such as ST_POINT, ST_LINESTRING, or ST_POLYGON that are mentioned in the "Spatial Data in SQL/MM and OGC" section of Chapter 4. The ST_GEOMETRY and its subtypes conform to the exact defined types in the SQL/MM standard. Although we describe all the operator examples with SDO_GEOMETRY type in the rest of the chapter, you can also use the ST_GEOMETRY and its subtypes in these examples.

Note When evaluating the spatial operators, Oracle Spatial sets the tolerance value to 0.005 if table_geometry is of type ST_GEOMETRY or one of its subtypes. Otherwise (that is, if table_geometry is of type SDO_GEOMETRY), Oracle obtains the tolerance value from the USER_SDO_GEOM_METADATA view for the specified table_geometry column.

Semantics of Spatial Operators

When you specify a spatial operator in a SQL statement, Oracle selects only those rows for which the operator evaluates to TRUE. This means the operator selects only those rows of the associated table where the corresponding table_geometry (SDO_GEOMETRY column) values satisfy a specified operator relationship with respect to the query_geometry (query location). This type of selection is analogous to selection with relational operators using a specific predicate such as id>=10.

Let's look at an example of spatial operator usage. Listing 8-19 shows our first spatial query using the SDO_WITHIN_DISTANCE operator in the WHERE clause.

Listing 8-19. *Spatial Operator Usage in a SQL Statement*

```
SQL> SELECT COUNT(*)
FROM branches b, customers c
WHERE  b.id=1
  AND SDO_WITHIN_DISTANCE
  (c.location, b.location, 'DISTANCE=0.5 UNIT=MILE') = 'TRUE';
  COUNT(*)
----------
       108
```

The first column of the SDO_WITHIN_DISTANCE operator specifies the column name (that is, the location column) that is indexed in the customers table. The second column specifies a query location. In this case, the query location is selected from the branches table. The third argument specifies the parameters for the operator. In the case of the SDO_WITHIN_DISTANCE operator, this parameter specifies the distance (and the units) to search. The operator returns all rows of the customers table where the location column satisfies the spatial-operator relationship with respect to the query location. In this example, it returns all customers within 0.5 miles of the query location.

All spatial operators, including the SDO_WITHIN_DISTANCE operator in the previous example, use the spatial index (associated with their first argument, the table_geometry) to prune irrelevant rows. Unlike the geometry processing functions described in Chapter 9, spatial operators are *tied* to the spatial index. In other words, they *require* that a spatial index exist on the table_geometry column specified as the first argument of an operator. For instance, if you executed the SQL in Listing 8-6 after dropping the customers_sidx index, you would get an ORA-13226 ("Interface not supported without a spatial index") error.

Evaluation of Spatial Operators

Next, we briefly discuss how spatial operators are evaluated. An understanding of this will help ensure the best execution strategies for a spatial operator.

Since spatial operators are tied to the spatial index, they are, in most cases, evaluated in a two-stage filtering mechanism involving the spatial index. As shown in Figure 8-3, a spatial operator is first evaluated using the spatial index. This evaluation using the index is referred to as the *primary filter*. Here, the approximations in the index (the MBRs stored in the spatial index table) are used to identify a candidate set of rows that satisfies the operator relationship with respect to the query location. The identified rows are then passed through the Geometry Engine, referred to as the *secondary filter*, to return the correct set of rows for the specified operator. Note that all of this processing is transparent to the user: just specifying the operator in the WHERE clause of a SQL statement will internally invoke the appropriate index (primary filter) and the Geometry Engine (secondary filter) functionality to identify the correct set of rows.

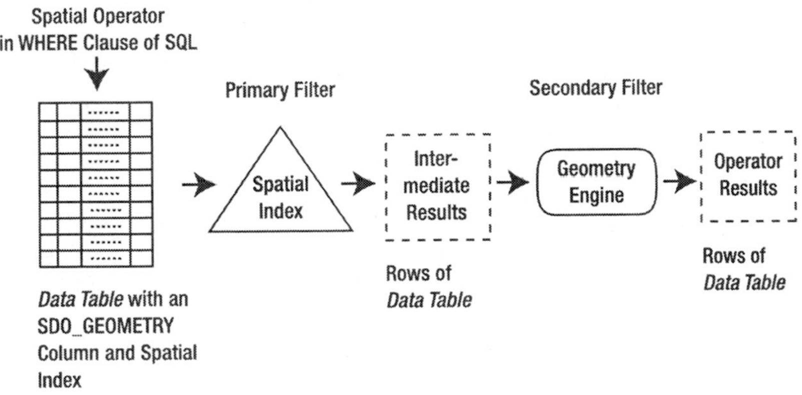

Figure 8-3. *Spatial operator evaluation using an associated spatial index*

In some cases, however, the optimizer may decide to bypass the spatial index. It then invokes the secondary filter (that is, the Geometry Engine functions) directly on appropriate rows of the table. (This might happen for a variety of reasons, including insufficient cost estimates for the spatial operator. Note that Oracle Spatial provides only rough estimates for the spatial operator evaluation with and without spatial indexes.) Not using the spatial index has the following implications:

- It might result in inefficient execution strategies whenever the SQL involves multiple tables or spatial and nonspatial predicates on the same table. Such cases might need tuning by providing explicit hints to use appropriate indexes.
- Oracle Spatial requires that the `SDO_NN` operator be evaluated using a spatial index. Sometimes you need explicit hints to ensure the use of a spatial index.

We discuss these cases and the remedies using explicit hints later in the "Hints for Spatial Operators" section.

A Closer Look at Spatial Operators

Now that you have some background on how spatial operators are evaluated in Oracle, we next describe the semantics of different spatial operators. Oracle Spatial provides different operators to perform the following types of proximity analyses. These operators can be used to enable the different analyses listed in Table 8-1 for a business application.

- *Find all data within a specified distance from a query location*: This operator is called `SDO_WITHIN_DISTANCE` or simply the *within distance* operator. This operator will enable customer analysis, as described in Table 8-1.
- *Find the nearest neighbors to a query location*: This operator is called `SDO_NN` or simply the *nearest-neighbor* operator. This operator can be useful in performing customer analysis, as described in Table 8-1.
- *Find neighbors that interact with or relate to a query location*: The primary operator to solve this purpose is called `SDO_RELATE`. There are other variants for determining specific types of relation. If only the index approximations are to be used, you can use a simpler variant (operator) called `SDO_FILTER`. These operators enable sales region analysis, as described in Table 8-1.

In this section of the chapter, we discuss each of these operators in sequence and how to use them for performing analysis in a business application.

■ **Caution** If the `sdo_indx_dims` is set to 3 as in Listing 8-13, only the following operators are supported: `SDO_FILTER`, `SDO_NN`, `SDO_WITHIN_DISTANCE`, and `SDO_RELATE` with `mask=ANYINTERACT` (or the equivalent `SDO_ANYINTERACT` operator) in Oracle 11 Release 1. The remaining operators such as `SDO_CONTAINS`, `SDO_INSIDE`, `SDO_TOUCH`, and `SDO_COVEREDBY` are not supported.

SDO_WITHIN_DISTANCE Operator

First, we will describe the `SDO_WITHIN_DISTANCE` operator. This operator is one of the simplest spatial operators, and you can start your proximity analysis with it. This operator facilitates analysis such as the identification of customers within a quarter-mile radius of a store site.

Given a set of locations, the `SDO_WITHIN_DISTANCE` operator returns all locations that are within a specified distance from a query location. Figure 8-4 shows an example. The `SDO_WITHIN_DISTANCE` operator specifies a distance *d* from the query location Q. The spatial index will retrieve the objects A, B, and C that are within this specified distance *d*. Objects D and E are eliminated, because they are farther than distance *d* from query location Q.

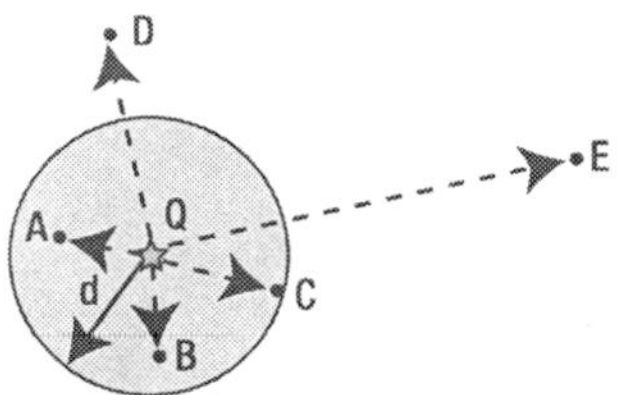

Figure 8-4. *The* SDO_WITHIN_DISTANCE *operator specifies a maximum distance d.*

The SDO_WITHIN_DISTANCE operator has the following syntax. You can observe that this operator conforms to the generic spatial_operator syntax in Listing 8-18. The cutoff distance *d* is specified in the third argument, parameter_string, using the parameter distance=d. Note that Oracle Spatial stipulates that the operator always be evaluated to the string 'TRUE'.

```
SDO_WITHIN_DISTANCE
(
  table_geom        IN SDO_GEOMETRY,
  query_geom        IN SDO_GEOMETRY,
  parameter_string  IN VARCHAR2
)
='TRUE'
```

where the following is true:

- table_geom is the SDO_GEOMETRY column of the table that is searched.
- query_geom is the SDO_GEOMETRY specifying the query location. This could be a column of another table, a bind variable, or a dynamically constructed object.
- parameter_string specifies the parameter *distance* and optionally the parameter *unit* (for the distance specified). The string will be of the form 'DISTANCE=<numeric value> [UNIT=<string>] [min_resolution=a] [max_resolution=b]'.

Note The default unit for geodetic data is meter.

Listing 8-20 shows the usage of the SDO_WITHIN_DISTANCE operator. Here, the customers within a quarter-mile distance of a specific competitor store (store id=1) are identified.

Listing 8-20. SDO_WITHIN_DISTANCE *Operator Retrieving All Customers Within a Quarter-Mile Radius of a Competitor Store*

```
SQL> SELECT ct.id, ct.name
FROM competitors comp, customers ct
WHERE comp.id=1
  AND SDO_WITHIN_DISTANCE
  (ct.location, comp.location, 'DISTANCE=0.25 UNIT=MILE ' )='TRUE'
```

```
ORDER BY ct.id;
        ID NAME
---------- -----------------------------------
        25 BLAKE CONSTRUCTION
        28 COLONIAL PARKING
        34 HEWLETT-PACKARD DC GOV AFFAIRS
        41 MCGREGOR PRINTING
        48 POTOMAC ELECTRIC POWER
        50 SMITH HINCHMAN AND GRYLLS
       270 METRO-FARRAGUT NORTH STATION
       271 METRO-FARRAGUT WEST STATION
       468 SAFEWAY
       809 LINCOLN SUITES
       810 HOTEL LOMBARDY
      1044 MUSEUM OF THE THIRD DIMENSION
      1526 INTERNATIONAL FINANCE
      1538 MCKENNA AND CUNEO
      2195 STEVENS ELEMENTARY SCHOOL
      6326 HOTEL LOMBARDY
      7754 EXECUTIVE INN
      7762 PHILLIPS 66
      7789 SEVEN BUILDINGS
      7821 RENAISSANCE MAYFLOWER HOTEL
      8138 ST GREGORY HOTEL
      8382 EXXON
      8792 DESTINATION HOTEL & RESORTS

23 rows selected.
```

Can you also report the distance of these returned customers from the corresponding store? Yes, but you have to use a spatial function called SDO_GEOM.SDO_DISTANCE for this purpose. Listing 8-21 shows the corresponding SQL.

Listing 8-21. SDO_WITHIN_DISTANCE *Operator Retrieving All Customers in a Quarter-Mile Radius of a Competitor Store and Also Reporting Their Distances*

```
SQL> col dist format 999
SELECT ct.id, ct.name,
SDO_GEOM.SDO_DISTANCE(ct.location, comp.location, 0.5, ' UNIT=YARD ') dist
FROM competitors comp, customers ct
WHERE comp.id=1
  AND SDO_WITHIN_DISTANCE
    (ct.location,  comp.location, 'DISTANCE=0.25 UNIT=MILE' )='TRUE'
ORDER BY  ct.id;
        ID NAME                                DIST
---------- ----------------------------------- ----
        25 BLAKE CONSTRUCTION                   319
        28 COLONIAL PARKING                     398
        34 HEWLETT-PACKARD DC GOV AFFAIRS       428
        41 MCGREGOR PRINTING                    350
        48 POTOMAC ELECTRIC POWER               355
        50 SMITH HINCHMAN AND GRYLLS            252
       270 METRO-FARRAGUT NORTH STATION         345
       271 METRO-FARRAGUT WEST STATION          272
       468 SAFEWAY                              252
       809 LINCOLN SUITES                       104
       810 HOTEL LOMBARDY                       313
```

```
1044 MUSEUM OF THE THIRD DIMENSION          153
1526 INTERNATIONAL FINANCE                  236
1538 MCKENNA AND CUNEO                       97
2195 STEVENS ELEMENTARY SCHOOL              305
6326 HOTEL LOMBARDY                         329
7754 EXECUTIVE INN                          375
7762 PHILLIPS 66                            303
7789 SEVEN BUILDINGS                        355
7821 RENAISSANCE MAYFLOWER HOTEL            322
8138 ST GREGORY HOTEL                       359
8382 EXXON                                  326
8792 DESTINATION HOTEL & RESORTS            159

23 rows selected.
```

Note that the SDO_GEOM.SDO_DISTANCE function takes as the first two arguments the locations of a customer and a store that satisfy the SDO_WITHIN_DISTANCE predicate. The third argument specifies the tolerance, and the fourth argument specifies the optional units parameter to retrieve the distances in appropriate units. In this case, the unit is set to yard. You will learn about this function in more detail in Chapter 9.

Note The SDO_GEOM.SDO_DISTANCE function is part of Locator.

Suppose you want to display the customers for the specified store on a map (the exact details of map creation will be discussed in Chapter 11). To construct the map, you need to retrieve additional background layers such as streets stored in the map_streets table. Listing 8-22 shows the SQL for getting the street names.

Listing 8-22. *Getting the Streets Around 0.25 Miles of the Competitor Store*

```
SQL> SELECT s.street_name
FROM competitors comp, map_streets s
WHERE comp.id=1
  AND SDO_WITHIN_DISTANCE
  (s.geometry, comp.location,
   'DISTANCE=0.25 UNIT=MILE ' )='TRUE'
ORDER BY s.street_name;

STREET_NAME
18TH ST NW
19TH ST NW
20TH ST NW
21ST ST NW
CONSTITUTION CT NW
DESALES ST NW
EYE ST NW
H ST NW
JEFFERSON PL NW
L ST NW

10 rows selected.
```

Now what if you wanted to restrict the previous search to only streets that are not too small or not too large? One way to do that is by obtaining the minimum bounding rectangle of the streets and checking for the area. Another alternative is to specify the restriction in the parameters clause of the SDO_WITHIN_DISTANCE query. Starting in Oracle 11, two additional parameters can be specified in parameter clause of the SDO_WITHIN_DISTANCE query:

- min_resolution = <a>. This criterion excludes too small data geometries from query result.
- max_resolution = <b>. This criterion excludes too large data geometries from query result.

If min_resolution is specified as a, then all data whose minimum bounding rectangles have both sides less than a units (for geodetic data, the units is meters) are not considered in the query. Likewise, if max_resolution is specified as b, then all data whose MBRs have both sides greater than b units are excluded. The query will be processed only on the data geometries that are not thus excluded. The units for min_resolution and max_resolution are always the default units for the coordinate system (for example, if the SRID attribute in street_name is 8307, it is meters) and are not affected by the UNITS specified in the query. Listing 8-23 shows the SQL (modified from that of Listing 8-22) to obtain only those streets that are at least 200 meters in length. Notice that distance units are specified in MILEs but the min_resolution units are in meters. The streets are at least 200m in length.

Listing 8-23. *Getting the Streets Around 0.25 Miles of the Competitor Store*

```
SQL> SELECT s.street_name
FROM competitors comp, map_streets s
WHERE comp.id=1
  AND SDO_WITHIN_DISTANCE
  (s.geometry, comp.location,
   'DISTANCE=0.25 UNIT=MILE  min_resolution=200 ' )='TRUE'
ORDER BY s.street_name;
STREET_NAME
----------------------------
18TH ST NW
19TH ST NW
20TH ST NW
21ST ST NW
EYE ST NW
H ST NW
L ST NW

7 rows selected.
```

Now how do you eliminate streets that are larger than 500 meters? You can use the max_resolution parameter for this purpose. Listing 8-24 shows the SQL (modified from Listing 8-23).

Listing 8-24. *Getting the Streets Around 0.25 Miles of the Competitor Store*

```
SQL> SELECT s.street_name
FROM competitors comp, map_streets s
WHERE comp.id=1
  AND SDO_WITHIN_DISTANCE
  (s.geometry, comp.location,
   'DISTANCE=0.25 UNIT=MILE  min_resolution=200 max_resolution=500 ' )='TRUE'
ORDER BY s.street_name;

STREET_NAME
-------------------------
21ST ST NW
H ST NW

2 rows selected.
```

The min_resolution and max_resolution parameters can be used only with SDO_FILTER, SDO_WITHIN_DISTANCE, and SDO_RELATE operators. These two parameters cannot be used with SDO_NN query.

SDO_NN Operator

The SDO_WITHIN_DISTANCE operator retrieves all objects within a specified distance *d* from a query location. What if there are no objects within distance *d*? What if the nearest object is at distance 2 * *d*? The SDO_WITHIN_DISTANCE operator is not appropriate when you need to obtain a specific number of neighbors, no matter how far they are from the query location. For these cases, the SDO_NN operator is appropriate.

Given a set of locations, the SDO_NN operator retrieves data in order of their distance to a query location. Figure 8-5 shows an example. A, B, C, D, and E are locations in a table that is spatially indexed. Q is a query location. The SDO_NN operator orders the items A, B, C, D, and E based on their distance to Q and returns them in the order of distance. If only one neighbor is requested, then A is returned. If two neighbors are requested, A and B are returned.

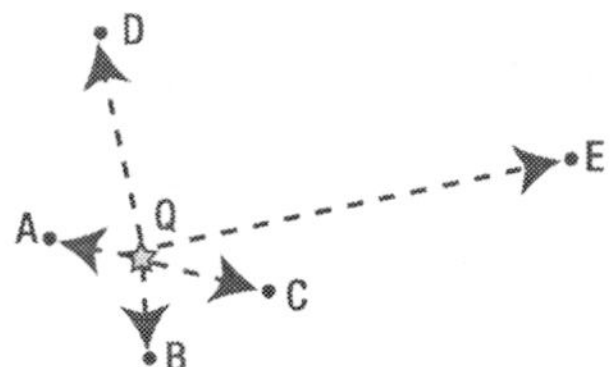

Figure 8-5. SDO_NN *on five locations: A, B, C, D, and E*

The SDO_NN operator has the following syntax. Observe that this syntax conforms to the generic signature (for any <spatial_operator>) in Listing 8-6, with some minor modifications. Note again that Oracle Spatial requires that the operator always evaluate to 'TRUE'.

```
SDO_NN
(
  table_geometry        IN SDO_GEOMETRY,
  query_geometry        IN SDO_GEOMETRY
  [, parameter_string   IN VARCHAR2
  [, tag                IN NUMBER ]]
)
='TRUE'
```

where the following is true:

- table_geom specifies the SDO_GEOMETRY column of the table whose spatial index is to be used.
- query_geom specifies the SDO_GEOMETRY for the query location. This could be a column of another table or a bind variable.
- parameter_string, an optional argument, specifies one of two tuning parameters, SDO_BATCH_SIZE or SDO_NUM_RES. We discuss these parameters in the next sections.
- tag, another optional argument, allows the SDO_NN operator to be bound to an ancillary distance operator. We discuss it in the later part of this section. Note that this tag can be specified only if parameter_string is specified.

The SDO_NN operator facilitates proximity analysis in the business application. For instance, you can use it to identify the nearest customers to a competitor store (whose ID is 1). Listing 8-25 shows a simple example.

Listing 8-25. *A Simple Example of the* SDO_NN *Operator*

```
SQL> SELECT ct.id, ct.name
FROM competitors comp, customers ct
WHERE comp.id=1
  AND SDO_NN(ct.location,  comp.location)='TRUE' ;
        ID NAME
---------- ----------------------------------
      1538 MCKENNA AND CUNEO
    .......
3173 rows selected.
```

The query in Listing 8-25 returns all 3,173 customer ids (from the customers table) in order of their distance from the location of the specified competitor store (id=1). But in general, we do not want to look at all the customers; rather, we want to select only the closest five or ten. To enforce this restriction, we specify ROWNUM<=N in the preceding SQL, where N is the number of neighbors that we are interested in. Listing 8-26 shows the SQL when N is 5 (that is, it retrieves the five nearest customers to the competitor id=1).

Listing 8-26. SDO_NN *Operator Retrieving the Five Nearest Customers to a Specific Competitor*

```
SQL> SELECT ct.id, ct.name, ct.customer_grade
FROM competitors comp, customers ct
WHERE comp.id=1
  AND SDO_NN(ct.location,  comp.location)='TRUE'
  AND ROWNUM<=5
ORDER BY ct.id;

        ID NAME                               CUSTOMER_GRADE
---------- ---------------------------------- ---------------
       809 LINCOLN SUITES                     GOLD
      1044 MUSEUM OF THE THIRD DIMENSION      SILVER
      1526 INTERNATIONAL FINANCE              SILVER
      1538 MCKENNA AND CUNEO                  SILVER
      8792 DESTINATION HOTEL & RESORTS        GOLD

5 rows selected.
```

Note that the customers have been graded into GOLD, SILVER, PLATINUM, and other categories. You want to retain the GOLD customers at any cost and should not let the competitors decrease your market share by poaching these important customers. So, how do you identify these customers? One mechanism is to focus on the nearest GOLD customers to each competitor. You can modify Listing 8-26 to return the five nearest GOLD customers instead of any nearest five customers.

Listing 8-27 shows the SQL for competitor id=1. Note that the customer_grade='GOLD' predicate is added to the WHERE clause.

Listing 8-27. SDO_NN *Operator Retrieving the Five* GOLD *Customers Nearest to a Specific Competitor*

```
SQL> SELECT ct.id, ct.name, ct.customer_grade
FROM competitors comp, customers ct
WHERE comp.id=1
  AND ct.customer_grade='GOLD'
  AND SDO_NN(ct.location,  comp.location)='TRUE'
  AND ROWNUM<=5
ORDER BY ct.id;
```

```
        ID NAME                                CUSTOMER_GRADE
---------- ----------------------------------- ---------------
       809 LINCOLN SUITES                      GOLD
       810 HOTEL LOMBARDY                      GOLD
      6326 HOTEL LOMBARDY                      GOLD
      7821 RENAISSANCE MAYFLOWER HOTEL         GOLD
      8792 DESTINATION HOTEL & RESORTS         GOLD

5 rows selected.
```

Note that all the customers returned are GOLD customers. The SILVER customers are filtered out.

In general, you can use the SDO_NN operator in different applications. For instance, Chapter 2 has some examples for obtaining the five nearest restaurants (or, more specifically, the five nearest Pizza Hut restaurants) to a certain highway.

The SDO_NN operator, as shown in Listing 8-27, can be used with other predicates in the same SQL statement. However, there are some restrictions:

- The SDO_NN operator *must always* be evaluated using the spatial index. Otherwise, an Oracle error is raised.
- If there is a nonspatial predicate on the same table (for example, customer_grade='GOLD') and this column (customer_grade) has an index, then that index should not be used in the execution.

Specifying appropriate hints such as ORDERED and INDEX will help ensure that the spatial index is used. We cover how to specify these hints in the "Hints for Spatial Operators" section later in this chapter.

SDO_BATCH_SIZE Tuning Parameter

Note that in the query in Listing 8-27, the five nearest GOLD customers are not the five nearest customers to the specified competitor (see Listing 8-26). As a result, the spatial index will iteratively return neighbors in *batches* until all the predicates in the WHERE clause are satisfied. For example, to find the five nearest GOLD customers, the index will first return the ten nearest customers. If there are fewer than five GOLD customers among these ten nearest customers, then the index will return the next batch of ten customers. It continues returning the customers in batches until all the predicates in the SQL are satisfied, including customer_grade='GOLD' and ROWNUM<=5.

The size of these batches is determined by the index. However, you can set this "batch" size using the SDO_BATCH_SIZE parameter. For instance, if you know that the five nearest GOLD customers are within the first 100 nearest customers, you can pass this information to the index by specifying 'SDO_BATCH_SIZE=100'. This may speed up the query processing.

Listing 8-28 shows the SQL of Listing 8-27 with the SDO_BATCH_SIZE parameter specified. Note that even if the estimate is incorrect (that is, the fifth GOLD customer is the 101st neighbor), the query returns correct results. SDO_BATCH_SIZE is set to 100.

Listing 8-28. SDO_NN *Operator Retrieving the Five* GOLD *Customers Nearest to a Competitor*

```
SQL> SELECT ct.id, ct.name, ct.customer_grade
FROM  competitors comp, customers ct
WHERE comp.id=1
  AND ct.customer_grade='GOLD'
  AND SDO_NN(ct.location,  comp.location, 'SDO_BATCH_SIZE=100' )='TRUE'
  AND ROWNUM<=5
ORDER BY ct.id;
```

```
        ID NAME                                 CUSTOMER_GRADE
---------- ----------------------------------- ---------------
       809 LINCOLN SUITES                       GOLD
       810 HOTEL LOMBARDY                       GOLD
      6326 HOTEL LOMBARDY                       GOLD
      7821 RENAISSANCE MAYFLOWER HOTEL          GOLD
      8792 DESTINATION HOTEL & RESORTS          GOLD

5 rows selected.
```

SDO_NUM_RES Tuning Parameter

In most cases, you do not have to qualify the neighbors being retrieved—that is, you may just be interested in five nearest customers instead of five nearest GOLD customers. You already saw in Listing 8-26 how to obtain the nearest neighbors in such cases. However, by specifying the SDO_NUM_RES=<N> parameter, the SDO_NN operator returns exactly N neighbors and may be evaluated faster than without the parameter (as in Listing 8-26).

Note Since the spatial index returns exactly N neighbors, you do not have to prune the search with the ROWNUM<=N predicate in the SQL.

Listing 8-29 shows the equivalent for Listing 8-26. Notice that there is no rownum<=5 predicate, because the spatial index retrieves exactly five neighbors because of the additional parameter SDO_NUM_RES=5 in the SDO_NN invocation. Also note that the order of the neighbors returned in Listing 8-29 is not the same as in Listing 8-26 (although the same neighbors are returned in both).

Listing 8-29. SDO_NN *Operator Retrieving the Five Customers Nearest to a Specific Competitor*

```
SQL> SELECT ct.id, ct.name, ct.customer_grade
FROM  competitors comp, customers ct
WHERE comp.id=1
  AND SDO_NN(ct.location,  comp.location, 'SDO_NUM_RES=5')='TRUE' ;

        ID NAME                                 CUSTOMER_GRADE
---------- ----------------------------------- ---------------
       809 LINCOLN SUITES                       GOLD
      1044 MUSEUM OF THE THIRD DIMENSION        SILVER
      1526 INTERNATIONAL FINANCE                SILVER
      1538 MCKENNA AND CUNEO                    SILVER
      8792 DESTINATION HOTEL & RESORTS          GOLD

5 rows selected.
```

Caution Using SDO_NUM_RES=<N> returns the N nearest neighbors to a specified query location, but the order of neighbors in the result set may not correspond to their distance to the query location.

SDO_NN with the Ancillary SDO_NN_DISTANCE Operator

In Listings 8-23 and 8-26, you saw how to obtain the five customers nearest to a competitor. In Listing 8-28, you saw how to obtain the five GOLD customers nearest to a competitor. In other words, you saw how to combine the SDO_NN operator with other predicates in the same SQL statement.

Instead of just identifying the nearest customers, why don't you find out how far away they are? In some cases, the first neighbor could be within 1 mile, but the next one could be 25 miles away. Knowing the distances will help you better understand the results. Fortunately, you can know the distances without paying any additional cost. The SDO_NN operator internally computes the distances to identify the customers. You can retrieve these distances by using the SDO_NN_DISTANCE ancillary operator.

To fully use the nearest-neighbor functionality, you augment the SDO_NN operator with an ancillary operator to provide the distance of each neighbor. This ancillary operator, called SDO_NN_DISTANCE, is specified as part of the SELECT list and is bound to an SDO_NN operator in the WHERE clause. Listing 8-30 shows how to augment the SQL of Listing 8-29 to retrieve the distances of the neighbors.

■ **Caution** To use the ancillary operator, you will have to specify one of the tuning parameters, either SDO_NUM_RES or SDO_BATCH_SIZE. In other words, you cannot use the SDO_NN_DISTANCE operator with the two-argument signature in Listing 8-26. If you do not know to what value to set SDO_BATCH_SIZE, then set it to 0, and the index will use the appropriate batch size internally.

Listing 8-30. SDO_NN *Operator Retrieving the Five Customers Nearest to a Specific Competitor Along with Their Distances*

```
SQL> col dist format 999
SELECT ct.id, ct.name, ct.customer_grade, SDO_NN_DISTANCE(1) dist
FROM competitors comp, customers ct
WHERE comp.id=1
  AND SDO_NN(ct.location,  comp.location, 'SDO_NUM_RES=5',1)='TRUE'
ORDER BY ct.id;
        ID NAME                                CUSTOMER_GRADE  DIST
---------- ----------------------------------- --------------- ----
       809 LINCOLN SUITES                      GOLD              95
      1044 MUSEUM OF THE THIRD DIMENSION       SILVER           140
      1526 INTERNATIONAL FINANCE               SILVER           216
      1538 MCKENNA AND CUNEO                   SILVER            89
      8792 DESTINATION HOTEL & RESORTS         GOLD             146

5 rows selected.
```

Note that SDO_NN_DISTANCE(1) specifies a *numeric tag*, 1, in braces. This numeric tag is also specified as the fourth argument to the SDO_NN operator. This tag serves the purpose of binding the SDO_NN_DISTANCE ancillary operator to an instance of the SDO_NN operator in the WHERE clause. As a result, the SQL in Listing 8-30 returns the distances (to competitor id=1) along with the customer ids. Likewise, you can augment Listing 8-28 to return the distances of the five nearest GOLD customers and their distances. The resulting SQL is shown in Listing 8-31.

Listing 8-31. SDO_NN *Operator Retrieving the Five GOLD Customers Nearest to a Specific Competitor Along with Their Distances*

```
SQL> SELECT ct.id, ct.name, ct.customer_grade, SDO_NN_DISTANCE(1) dist
FROM competitors comp, customers ct
WHERE comp.id=1
  AND ct.customer_grade='GOLD'
  AND SDO_NN(ct.location,  comp.location, 'SDO_BATCH_SIZE=100', 1  )='TRUE'
  AND ROWNUM<=5
ORDER BY ct.id;
```

```
        ID NAME                              CUSTOMER_GRADE  DIST
---------- --------------------------------- --------------- ----
       809 LINCOLN SUITES                    GOLD              95
       810 HOTEL LOMBARDY                    GOLD             286
      6326 HOTEL LOMBARDY                    GOLD             301
      7821 RENAISSANCE MAYFLOWER HOTEL       GOLD             295
      8792 DESTINATION HOTEL & RESORTS       GOLD             146

5 rows selected.
```

By the way, in which units are the distances? Meters, kilometers, or miles? In general, the distances returned will be in the units for the coordinate system (refer to the information on SRID of the geometries and the MDSYS.CS_SRS tables in Chapter 4). Since the SRID for this dataset is 8307, a geodetic coordinate system, the distances returned are in meters. However, you can specify the desired units, such as miles, in the third argument, the parameter_string part of the query. Listing 8-32 and Listing 8-33 correspondingly modify the SQL in Listings 8-30 and 8-31 to return the distances in miles. The 'UNIT=MILE' parameter is added to the parameter string of the SDO_NN operator in these examples.

Listing 8-32. *Rewriting Listing 8-30 with Mile As the Distance Unit*

```
SQL> col dist format 9.99
SELECT ct.id, ct.name, ct.customer_grade, SDO_NN_DISTANCE(1) dist
FROM competitors comp, customers ct
WHERE comp.id=1
  AND SDO_NN(ct.location,  comp.location, 'SDO_NUM_RES=5 UNIT=MILE',1)='TRUE'
ORDER BY ct.id;
        ID NAME                              CUSTOMER_GRADE  DIST
---------- --------------------------------- --------------- ----
       809 LINCOLN SUITES                    GOLD             .06
      1044 MUSEUM OF THE THIRD DIMENSION     SILVER           .09
      1526 INTERNATIONAL FINANCE             SILVER           .13
      1538 MCKENNA AND CUNEO                 SILVER           .06
      8792 DESTINATION HOTEL & RESORTS       GOLD             .09

5 rows selected.
```

Listing 8-33. *Rewriting Listing 8-31 with Mile As the Distance Unit*

```
SQL> col dist format 9.99
SELECT ct.id, ct.name, ct.customer_grade, SDO_NN_DISTANCE(1) dist
FROM competitors comp, customers ct
WHERE comp.id=1
  AND ct.customer_grade='GOLD'
  AND SDO_NN
    (ct.location,  comp.location, 'SDO_BATCH_SIZE=100 UNIT=MILE', 1 )='TRUE'
  AND ROWNUM<=5
ORDER BY ct.id;
        ID NAME                              CUSTOMER_GRADE  DIST
---------- --------------------------------- --------------- ----
       809 LINCOLN SUITES                    GOLD             .06
       810 HOTEL LOMBARDY                    GOLD             .18
      6326 HOTEL LOMBARDY                    GOLD             .19
      7821 RENAISSANCE MAYFLOWER HOTEL       GOLD             .18
      8792 DESTINATION HOTEL & RESORTS       GOLD             .09

5 rows selected.
```

Note that in the SDO_NN operator queries, the closest neighbors can be at 0.06 miles (as in Listing 8-33) or sometimes at 200 miles. In the latter case, the neighbor found even though the closest may not be worth targeting for a promotion. This means you need a mechanism to limit the search space in the nearest neighbor query. In Oracle 11, Spatial allows the specification of distance=<a> in an SDO_NN query in addition to the SDO_NUM_RES or SDO_BATCH_SIZE parameter. Using this parameter, you can limit the search to a distance of 0.1 miles in Listing 8-32. Listing 8-34 shows the corresponding SQL.

Listing 8-34. *Augmenting Listing 8-32 to Limit the Search Space to 0.1 Mile Distance*

```
SQL> col dist format 9.99
SELECT ct.id, ct.name, ct.customer_grade, SDO_NN_DISTANCE(1) dist
FROM competitors comp, customers ct
WHERE comp.id=1
  AND SDO_NN(ct.location,  comp.location, 'SDO_NUM_RES=5 DISTANCE=0.1 UNIT=MILE',
1)='TRUE' ORDER BY ct.id;
        ID NAME                                CUSTOMER_GRADE   DIST
---------- ----------------------------------- --------------- -----
       809 LINCOLN SUITES                      GOLD              .06
      1044 MUSEUM OF THE THIRD DIMENSION       SILVER            .09
      1538 MCKENNA AND CUNEO                   SILVER            .06
      8792 DESTINATION HOTEL & RESORTS         GOLD              .09

4 rows selected.
```

Note that only four rows are returned although sdo_num_res is set to 5. This is because of the five closest customers, only four of them are within the specified 0.1 mile distance. Listing 8-33 using the SDO_BATCH_SIZE parameter can likewise be modified to include a cutoff distance of 0.1 miles. Listing 8-35 shows the corresponding SQL.

Listing 8-35. *Augmenting Listing 8-33 with a Limit of 0.1 Mile Distance*

```
SQL> col dist format 9.99
SELECT ct.id, ct.name, ct.customer_grade, SDO_NN_DISTANCE(1) dist
FROM competitors comp, customers ct
WHERE comp.id=1
  AND ct.customer_grade='GOLD'
  AND SDO_NN
    (ct.location,  comp.location,
      'SDO_BATCH_SIZE=100 DISTANCE=0.1 UNIT=MILE', 1 )='TRUE'
  AND ROWNUM<=5
ORDER BY ct.id;

        ID NAME                                CUSTOMER_GRADE   DIST
---------- ----------------------------------- --------------- -----
       809 LINCOLN SUITES                      GOLD              .06
      8792 DESTINATION HOTEL & RESORTS         GOLD              .09

2 rows selected.
```

This refines the results of Listing 8-33 and returns only those rows that are within the 0.1 mile distance specified in the query. Together, these examples illustrate the power of the SDO_NN operator in performing various types of spatial analyses.

Operators for Spatial Interactions (Relationships)

Until now, we have discussed how to identify interesting locations based on their distance to a query location. Next let's look at operators to find locations/geometries that interact with a query geometry. Such operators are used frequently in applications for analysis using buffer zones.

For example, you could precompute quarter-mile to 2-mile buffer zones around existing branch or competitor locations. Say you have constructed quarter-mile buffer zones around competitor locations using the SDO_GEOM.SDO_BUFFER function, as shown in Listing 8-36.

Note We discuss the SDO_GEOM.SDO_BUFFER function in detail in Chapter 9.

This function takes the location of each competitor as the first argument and buffers it by 0.25 (the second argument) miles (specified in fourth argument). It takes the tolerance of 0.5 meters as the third argument. Let this buffer region denote the sales region (or *area of influence*) of each competitor. Likewise, you can compute the area of influence (or sale region) of each branch. Listing 8-36 shows the SQL for creating these tables.

Listing 8-36. *Creating the Sales Region (Area of Influence) for Each Competitor/Branch*

```
SQL> CREATE TABLE COMPETITORS_SALES_REGIONS AS
SELECT id, name, SDO_GEOM.SDO_BUFFER
(cmp.location, 0.25, 0.5, 'UNIT=MILE ARC_TOLERANCE=0.005') geom
FROM competitors cmp;

SQL> CREATE TABLE SALES_REGIONS AS
SELECT id, name, SDO_GEOM.SDO_BUFFER
(b.location, 0.25, 0.5, 'UNIT=MILE ARC_TOLERANCE=0.005') geom
FROM branches b;
```

Listing 8-37 shows the SQL to create spatial indexes on these tables.

Listing 8-37. *Creating Indexes on Sales Regions of Competitors/Branches*

```
Rem Metadata for Sales_regions table: copied from the metadata for Branches table
SQL> INSERT INTO USER_SDO_GEOM_METADATA
SELECT 'SALES_REGIONS','GEOM', DIMINFO, SRID
FROM USER_SDO_GEOM_METADATA
WHERE TABLE_NAME='BRANCHES';

Rem Metadata for Competitors_regions table:
Rem  -- copied from the metadata for Branches table

SQL> INSERT INTO USER_SDO_GEOM_METADATA
SELECT 'COMPETITORS_SALES_REGIONS','GEOM', DIMINFO, SRID
FROM USER_SDO_GEOM_METADATA
WHERE TABLE_NAME='COMPETITORS';

Rem Index-creation for Sales_regions table
SQL> CREATE INDEX sr_sidx ON sales_regions(geom)
INDEXTYPE IS MDSYS.SPATIAL_INDEX;

Rem Index-creation for Competitors_sales_regions table
SQL> CREATE INDEX cr_sidx ON competitors_sales_regions(geom)
INDEXTYPE IS MDSYS.SPATIAL_INDEX;
```

You can then identify how many customers are inside the buffer regions of each competitor (and target them for explicit promotions). Note that this functionality can also be accomplished by the SDO_WITHIN_DISTANCE operator you saw in Listing 8-20. However, this buffer region–based approach offers more rigorous analysis, such as how many customers are "inside"; how many, if any, customers are on the border (that is, exactly at a distance of a quarter mile); and so on. Note that this supplements all types of analyses in Table 8-1.

Additionally, you can perform analysis using demographic or transportation data such as city and state boundaries and highway and transportation networks. For instance, you can identify which sales regions intersect each another or city/county/state boundaries and possibly compute the area of intersection, the number of customers in each such intersection area, and so on (see Chapter 9 for details). This will help in detailed analysis, such as how many customers are from New Hampshire versus how many are from Massachusetts for a specific branch. From among several candidates, we can choose the region with best metrics. This enables the sales region analysis described in Table 8-1.

Figure 8-6 shows an example of a circular buffer zone query Q. A, B, C, D, and E are arbitrarily shaped data geometries. Using the interaction-based operators with Q as the query geometry, you can identify geometries that *intersect* Q (A, C, and D), that are *inside* Q (A), and that *touch* Q (C).

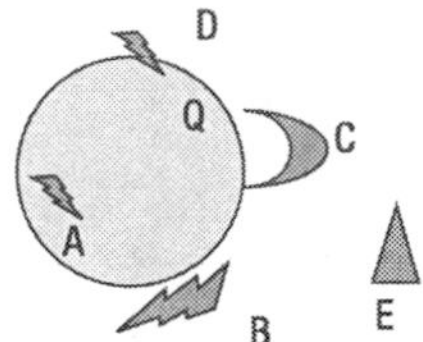

Figure 8-6. *Arbitrarily shaped data geometries (A, B, C, D, and E) are shown in black. A circular query geometry (Q) is shown in gray.*

There are two primary spatial operators for such interaction detection. Like the SDO_NN and SDO_WITHIN_DISTANCE operators, these operators are evaluated using the index-based model of Figure 8-3 and use the syntax of Listing 8-18.

- SDO_FILTER: This operator identifies all geometries whose MBRs intersect with the MBR of a query geometry. This operator primarily uses the spatial index without invoking a Geometry Engine function.
- SDO_RELATE: This operator identifies all geometries that interact in a specified manner with a query geometry. The specified type of interaction could involve intersection, touching the boundaries, being completely inside, and so on.
- SDO_ANYINTERACT, SDO_CONTAINS, SDO_COVERS, SDO_COVEREDBY, SDO_EQUAL, SDO_INSIDE, SDO_ON, SDO_OVERLAPS, and SDO_TOUCH: These operators are simplified variants of the SDO_RELATE operator for specific types of interactions. Instead of specifying the SDO_RELATE operator with an appropriate parameter to identify a specific relationship, you can directly use the corresponding simplified variant.

Next, we examine each of these operators in further detail.

SDO_FILTER Operator

The SDO_FILTER operator identifies all rows of a table where the MBRs of the column geometry intersect with the MBR of a specified query geometry. This operator always returns a superset of results for other interaction-based operators. In that sense, this operator is an approximation of other interaction-based operators.

Figure 8-7 shows how the SDO_FILTER operator evaluates for the data of Figure 8-6. It computes the MBRs around the data and the query geometries. It returns the data geometries A, B, C, and D as the result, because their MBRs intersect the MBR of the circular query Q.

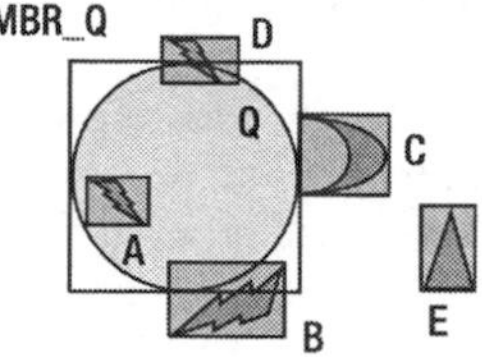

Figure 8-7. *In* SDO_FILTER, *the MBRs of data/query geometries are compared.*

The SDO_FILTER operator has the following syntax:

```
SDO_FILTER
(
  table_geometry       IN SDO_GEOMETRY,
  query_geometry       IN SDO_GEOMETRY
  [, parameter_string  IN VARCHAR2 ]
)
= 'TRUE'
```

where the following is true:

- table_geometry is the column name of the table whose spatial index is to be used.
- query_geometry is the query location. This could be a column of another table or a bind variable.
- parameter_string is always set to querytype=window. This parameter is optional (as indicated by the enclosing square brackets in the preceding syntax) and can be safely omitted in Oracle 10g and newer versions. However, in prior releases, this parameter is mandatory. Additional parameters that can be specified include min_resolution=<a> and max_resolution=<b> to eliminate too small or too large data geometries from the query result. You can find a detailed discussion on their usage in the section on SDO_WITHIN_DISTANCE operators (Listings 8-22, 8-23, and 8-24).

Listing 8-38 shows the use of the SDO_FILTER operator to identify all customers within a competitor's area of influence. Note that this query may return more customers than those that actually fall within a competitor's service area.

Listing 8-38. SDO_FILTER *Operator Retrieving All Customers Within a Competitor's Service Area*

```
SQL> SELECT  ct.id, ct.name
FROM competitors_regions comp, customers ct
WHERE comp.id=1
  AND SDO_FILTER(ct.location,  comp.geom)='TRUE'
ORDER BY ct.id;
        ID NAME
---------- -----------------------------------
        25 BLAKE CONSTRUCTION
        28 COLONIAL PARKING
        34 HEWLETT-PACKARD DC GOV AFFAIRS
        38 KIPLINGER WASHINGTON EDITORS
        41 MCGREGOR PRINTING
```

```
      42 MCI COMMUNICATIONS
      48 POTOMAC ELECTRIC POWER
      50 SMITH HINCHMAN AND GRYLLS
     270 METRO-FARRAGUT NORTH STATION
     271 METRO-FARRAGUT WEST STATION
     468 SAFEWAY
     809 LINCOLN SUITES
     810 HOTEL LOMBARDY
    1044 MUSEUM OF THE THIRD DIMENSION
    1081 GEORGE WASHINGTON UNIVERSITY
    1178 AVIS RENT-A-CAR
    1526 INTERNATIONAL FINANCE
    1538 MCKENNA AND CUNEO
    1901 CLUB QUARTERS WASHINGTON
    2195 STEVENS ELEMENTARY SCHOOL
    6326 HOTEL LOMBARDY
    7387 ELLIPSE
    7754 EXECUTIVE INN
    7762 PHILLIPS 66
    7789 SEVEN BUILDINGS
    7821 RENAISSANCE MAYFLOWER HOTEL
    8138 ST GREGORY HOTEL
    8382 EXXON
    8792 DESTINATION HOTEL & RESORTS
    8793 LOEWS HOTELS REGIONAL

30 rows selected.
```

In general, the SDO_FILTER operator returns more candidates—30 rows in Listing 8-38—than those that actually intersect a query geometry (23 rows, as you will see in Listing 8-40). Why would anyone use this operator? The reasons are it is fast (compared to other spatial operators) and it does prune a majority of the geometries (except the 30 returned out of 3,100+ rows) in the customers table that do not fall in the neighborhood of the query geometry. In that sense, the SDO_FILTER operator works as a fast approximation of other interaction-detecting operators such as SDO_RELATE.

Applications such as map visualizers, which can tolerate such approximations in the result set, use the SDO_FILTER operator to render maps. A typical query from Oracle MapViewer would look like Listing 8-39.

Listing 8-39. *Typical Query from MapViewer Using the* SDO_FILTER *Operator*

```
SELECT location
FROM customers
WHERE SDO_FILTER
  (
  location,
  SDO_GEOMETRY
  (
    2003, 8307, null,
    SDO_ELEM_INFO_ARRAY(1, 1003, 3),  -- Rectangle query window
    SDO_ORDINATE_ARRAY(-122.43886,37.78284,-122.427195,37.79284)
  )
) = 'TRUE';
```

Typically, the query window in such map-rendering applications would be a rectangle corresponding to the window displayed on the screen. This window will be modified as the user navigates (for example, zooms in and out, and pans) on the map.

■ **Tip** Unlike all other operators, which work only for two-dimensional geometries, SDO_FILTER can work with two-, three-, and four-dimensional geometries. The index can be three- or four-dimensional by setting the SDO_INDX_DIMS parameter in the CREATE INDEX statement (see Listing 8-14).

SDO_RELATE Operator

As shown earlier in Figure 8-7, not all objects returned by the SDO_FILTER operator intersect with the query geometry Q (for example, object B). The SDO_FILTER operator always returns the exact result set and possibly more geometries (a superset). How do you find geometries that interact with the query in a specified manner? The SDO_RELATE operator provides this functionality.

For example, as shown in Figure 8-6, you can specify the interaction to be ANYINTERACT (intersection), and the SDO_RELATE operator will return A, C, and D. If you specify the interaction to be INSIDE, it returns A. If you specify the interaction to be TOUCH, it returns C. In general, the SDO_RELATE operator has the following syntax. Note that the SDO_RELATE operator, as with other spatial operators, should be compared to the string 'TRUE'.

```
SDO_RELATE
(
  table_geometry        IN SDO_GEOMETRY,
  query_geometry        IN SDO_GEOMETRY,
  parameter_string      IN VARCHAR2
)
= 'TRUE'
```

where the following is true:

- table_geometry is the column name of the table whose spatial index is to be used.
- query_geometry is the query location. This could be a column of another table or a bind variable.
- parameter_string is set to 'querytype=window MASK=<interaction-type> [min_resolution=<a>] [max_resolution=<b>]'. The SDO_RELATE operator is true if table_geometry has an <interaction-type> relation with query_geometry (the query). The interaction-type or mask-type could be one of several types, which we discuss next. Note that the parameters min_resolution=<a> and max_resolution=<b> can be specified to eliminate too small or too large data geometries from the query result. You can find a detailed discussion on their usage in the section on SDO_WITHIN_DISTANCE operators (Listings 8-22, 8-23, and 8-24).

Before we describe the different interactions for an SDO_RELATE operator, you should understand what constitutes a geometry. Every geometry is composed of three parts:

- *Boundary*: This is the outer border for the geometry. Figure 8-8 shows the boundary in solid black for different types of geometries. For a point geometry, there is only a boundary point. For a line-string geometry, the two endpoints are the boundary. For a polygon (with or without voids), the rings forming the polygon are the boundary.
- *Interior*: Everything in the geometry inside the boundaries is considered interior. This is shown in gray in Figure 8-8.
- *Exterior*: This is everything outside the geometry. This is implicitly white in Figure 8-8.

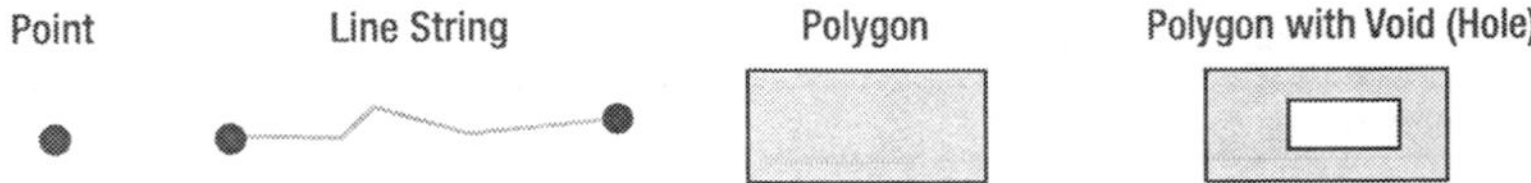

Figure 8-8. *The boundary is solid black, and the interior is gray for different types of geometries.*

Interactions in SDO_RELATE

Now that you understand the interior and boundary parts of geometries, we'll resume our discussion on the different interaction types for the `SDO_RELATE` operator. Figure 8-9 illustrates these interactions. The two geometries Q and A in Figure 8-9 correspond to `query_geometry` and `table_geometry`, respectively, in the preceding signature for `SDO_RELATE`.

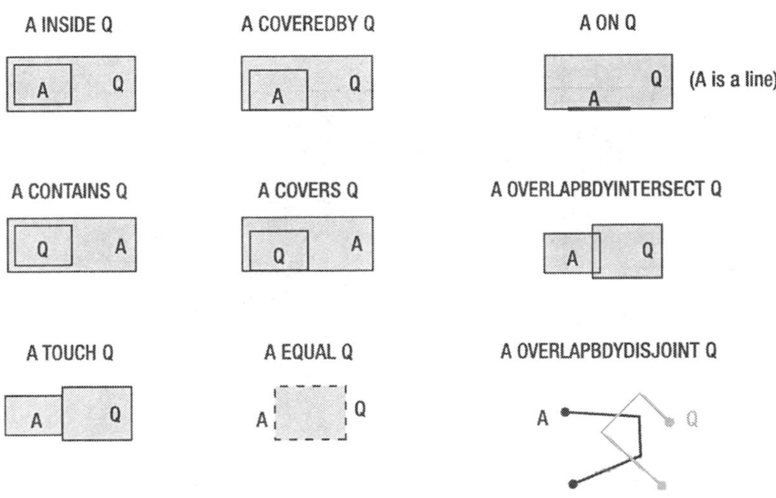

ANYINTERACT: *True* if any of the above interactions is *true*

DISJOINT: *True* if ANYINTERACT is *false*

Figure 8-9. *Interactions between a data geometry A and a query geometry Q for the* `SDO_RELATE` *operator*

The different relationships/interactions between Q and A are due to different interactions between the interior and boundary of one geometry with those of the other. Note that each of these interactions has an equivalent simplified operator. You can use either the `SDO_RELATE` operator with the appropriate mask specification or the corresponding simplified operator in your queries, as shown in Table 8-2. Like all other operators, the `SDO_RELATE` and equivalent simplified operators need to be evaluated to the string `'TRUE'`.

Table 8-2. *Names, Semantics, and Operators of the Interactions in Figure 8-9*

Interaction	Description	Simplified Operator
INSIDE	This interaction holds if the boundary and interior of geometry A (data geometries) are inside the interior of the query Q. In Figure 8-5, geometry A is *inside* query Q.	SDO_INSIDE (A, Q)
CONTAINS	This holds if the boundary and interior of Q are inside the interior of A (data geometry). This relationship is the reverse of INSIDE (that is, if A is inside Q, then Q contains A).	SDO_CONTAINS (Q, A)
COVEREDBY	A is COVEREDBY Q if the interior and boundary of A (data geometries) are inside the interior of Q (query), except that the boundaries overlap.	SDO_COVEREDBY (A, Q)
ON	The interior and boundaries of A interact exclusively with the boundary of Q (line string completely on the boundary of a polygon). Note that A is a line string here.	SDO_ON (A, Q)
COVERS	This interaction is true if the interior and boundary of query Q is inside the interior of A and the boundaries overlap. This is the reverse of COVEREDBY (i.e., if Q is covered by A, then A covers Q). Alternatively, you can use the following operator for the same semantics.	SDO_COVERS (A, Q)
TOUCH	This holds if the boundaries of two geometries touch, but the interiors do not intersect. In Figure 8-5, geometry C *touches* query Q.	SDO_TOUCH (C, Q)
OVERLAPBDYINTERSECT	This holds if the boundaries and interiors of A and query Q intersect.	SDO_OVERLAPBDYINTERSECT (A, Q)
OVERLAPBDYDISJOINT	This holds if the interior of one intersects the interior and boundary of the other, but the two boundaries do not intersect.	SDO_OVERLAPBDYDISJOINT (A, Q)
EQUAL	This holds if the interior and boundary of A exactly match those of Q.	SDO_EQUAL (A, Q)
ANYINTERACT	This interaction is true if either the boundary or interior of A intersects with the boundary or interior of Q. In other words, if there is any intersection between the two geometries (i.e., any of the previous interactions are true). In Figure 8-5, geometries A, C, and D have an ANYINTERACT relation with query Q.	SDO_ANYINTERACT (A, Q)

SQL/MM (where MM stands for multimedia) is the *extended* standard for specifying spatial and multimedia operators in SQL statements. This standard specifies a standard set of query relationships that start with the prefix ST. You can use these SQL/MM functions with the same name in Oracle: ST_Contains, ST_Within, ST_Overlaps, ST_Crosses, ST_Intersects, ST_Touches, ST_Equals, and ST_Disjoint. Each of these functions operates on a pair of ST_Geometry objects: a data geometry and a query geometry. In Oracle, you can also use these relationships as *operators*, that is, operate on a table of data geometries and a query geometry. Table 8-3 shows the SQL/MM relationships (ISO IEC 13249) and the corresponding operators in Oracle Spatial.

Table 8-3. *SQL/MM Spatial Relationships and the Equivalent Oracle Spatial Operators*

SQL/MM Relationship	Oracle Spatial Operator
ST_Contains	SDO_RELATE operator with mask=CONTAINS+COVERS
ST_Within	SDO_RELATE operator with mask=INSIDE+COVEREDBY
ST_Overlaps	SDO_OVERLAPS operator
ST_Crosses	(Only supported as ST_CROSSES function)
ST_Intersects	SDO_RELATE operator with mask=ANYINTERACT (or SDO_ANYINTERACT operator)
ST_Touches	SDO_RELATE operator with mask=TOUCH (or SDO_TOUCH operator)
ST_Equals	SDO_RELATE operator with mask=EQUAL (or SDO_EQUAL operator)
ST_Disjoint	Negation of SDO_ANYINTERACT (use MINUS to subtract SDO_ANYINTERACT results from the entire set)

Now that we've covered the different spatial relationships determined by the SDO_RELATE operator (or the equivalent simplified operators), we'll describe how to use this operator to perform customer analysis and sales region analysis, as described in Table 8-1.

First, we'll use the SDO_RELATE operator for customer analysis. We'll identify all customers *inside* or *on the boundary of* the buffer zones of each competitor store using the ANYINTERACT interaction mask. Listing 8-40 shows the SQL for a specific competitor (id=1).

Listing 8-40. SDO_RELATE *Operator Retrieving All Customers in a Quarter-Mile Buffer Zone of a Competitor Store*

```
SQL> SELECT  ct.id, ct.name
FROM competitors_sales_regions comp, customers ct
WHERE comp.id=1
  AND SDO_RELATE(ct.location,  comp.geom, 'MASK=ANYINTERACT ' )='TRUE'
ORDER BY ct.id;

        ID NAME
---------- -----------------------------------
        25 BLAKE CONSTRUCTION
        28 COLONIAL PARKING
        34 HEWLETT-PACKARD DC GOV AFFAIRS
        41 MCGREGOR PRINTING
        48 POTOMAC ELECTRIC POWER
        50 SMITH HINCHMAN AND GRYLLS
       270 METRO-FARRAGUT NORTH STATION
       271 METRO-FARRAGUT WEST STATION
       468 SAFEWAY
       809 LINCOLN SUITES
       810 HOTEL LOMBARDY
```

```
      1044 MUSEUM OF THE THIRD DIMENSION
      1526 INTERNATIONAL FINANCE
      1538 MCKENNA AND CUNEO
      2195 STEVENS ELEMENTARY SCHOOL
      6326 HOTEL LOMBARDY
      7754 EXECUTIVE INN
      7762 PHILLIPS 66
      7789 SEVEN BUILDINGS
      7821 RENAISSANCE MAYFLOWER HOTEL
      8138 ST GREGORY HOTEL
      8382 EXXON
      8792 DESTINATION HOTEL & RESORTS

23 rows selected.
```

To identify the `DISJOINT` relationship, use *negation* of `ANYINTERACT` (that is, subtract the results of `ANYINTERACT` from the entire set). Listing 8-41 shows the SQL to identify all customers that are disjoint from competitor region (`id=1`):

Listing 8-41. *Identifying a* `DISJOINT` *Relationship*

```
SELECT  ct1.id, ct1.name
FROM  customers ct1
WHERE NOT EXISTS
(
  SELECT 'X'
  FROM competitors_sales_regions comp, customers ct2
  WHERE comp.id=1
  AND ct2.id = ct2.id
    AND SDO_RELATE(ct2.location, comp.geom, 'MASK=ANYINTERACT')='TRUE'
);
```

Note that Listing 8-40 is the exact equivalent of Listing 8-20, except it executes a little slower than Listing 8-20. In general, the following tip should be useful.

Tip Specifying the `ANYINTERACT` mask in an `SDO_RELATE` query (with buffered regions) as in Listing 8-40 is equivalent to Listing 8-20 with the `SDO_WITHIN_DISTANCE` operator. The question that arises is, which usage is better and when? The solution is to use `SDO_WITHIN_DISTANCE` wherever possible. The `SDO_WITHIN_DISTANCE` operator, in most cases, will be faster since it prunes based on distance rather than trying to check whether a customer is inside, as in `SDO_RELATE`.

The next question to ask is, when is the `SDO_RELATE` operator useful? The `SDO_RELATE` operator offers much more power than the `SDO_WITHIN_DISTANCE` operator. Instead of specifying the `ANYINTERACT` relationship, you can specify a variety of other relationships such as `INSIDE`, `TOUCH`, `OVERLAPBDYDISJOINT`, and so on. These relationships are especially useful while performing analysis with nonpoint data that occur in geographic datasets such as the `us_states` or `us_counties` table. We referred to such analysis as "sales region analysis" in Table 8-1.

For instance, you can analyze the influence of the competitors inside and outside the District of Columbia (D.C.) region. Some competitor branches extend their area of influence to neighboring states. First, look at how many competitor regions intersect the D.C. region. Listing 8-42 shows an example.

Listing 8-42. SDO_RELATE *Operator Identifying All Competitors in the D.C. Region*

```
SQL> SELECT COUNT(*)
FROM us_states st, competitors_sales_regions comp
WHERE st.state_abrv='DC'
  AND SDO_RELATE(comp.geom,  st.geom, 'MASK=ANYINTERACT ' )='TRUE';
  COUNT(*)
----------
       286

1 row selected.
```

Not all these competitors sales regions are inside D.C. To get the competitors whose influence is completely inside the D.C. area, you should use the SDO_RELATE operator with the INSIDE relationship. Listing 8-43 shows the SQL.

Listing 8-43. SDO_RELATE *Operator Identifying All Competitors in the D.C. Region*

```
SQL> SELECT COUNT(*)
FROM us_states st, competitors_sales_regions comp
WHERE st.state_abrv='DC'
  AND SDO_RELATE(comp.geom,  st.geom, 'MASK=INSIDE ' )='TRUE';

  COUNT(*)
----------
       268

1 row selected.
```

For those competitors whose influence extends beyond but also overlaps the D.C. area, you should use the SDO_RELATE operator with the OVERLAPBDYINTERSECT relationship. Listing 8-44 shows the corresponding SQL.

Listing 8-44. SDO_RELATE *Operator Identifying All Competitors That Overlap the D.C. Region*

```
SQL> SELECT COUNT(*)
FROM us_states st, competitors_sales_regions comp
WHERE st.state_abrv='DC'
  AND SDO_RELATE(comp.geom,  st.geom, 'MASK=OVERLAPBDYINTERSECT ' )='TRUE'  ;
  COUNT(*)
----------
        18

1 row selected.
```

From the examples in Listings 8-42 to 8-44, you can note that there are 286 competitor regions in the D.C. area, of which 268 are completely inside and 18 overlap. You could use this analysis to target the 18 competitors and the customers in their area of influence as you pursue business expansion outside the D.C. area. Within D.C., you can target the 268 competitor regions.

Caution In general, if the underlying tolerance associated with a table in the USER_SDO_GEOM_METADATA view is modified, some of the relationships may change. For instance, a TOUCH relationship may become DISJOINT. Always set the tolerance value to suit your application (see the related discussion in Chapter 3).

Next, we will show how to analyze which sales regions overlap. After identifying such sales regions, you can possibly merge the corresponding branches if the overlap is significant. To this end, we will identify all sales regions that overlap or touch the sales region of a specific branch (id=51). You can perform similar analysis for other branches. Instead of specifying multiple masks, you can perform this analysis using the ANYINTERACT mask in SDO_RELATE. Listing 8-45 shows the SQL to identify all sales regions that intersect a specified sales region.

Listing 8-45. *Identifying Sales Regions That Intersect a Specific Sales Region (*id=51*)*

```
SQL> SELECT sr1.id
FROM sales_regions sr2, sales_regions sr1
WHERE sr2.id=51
  AND sr1.id <> 51
  AND SDO_RELATE(sr1.geom,  sr2.geom, 'MASK=ANYINTERACT' )='TRUE';

     A.ID
----------
        63
        54
        72
        69
        43
        66
        50
        75
        76

9 rows selected.
```

Tip In Oracle, specifying ANYINTERACT in SDO_RELATE (or using SDO_ANYINTERACT) is recommended over specifying SDO_RELATE with the equivalent combination of multiple masks. Oracle optimizes the processing for the ANYINTERACT mask.

Multiple Masks in SDO_RELATE

Before considering merging the sales regions returned in Listing 8-45 with the query sales region (id=51), you should do further analysis to determine how many of these sales regions are "touching" and how many are "overlapping" the query sales region (id=51). (Note that they won't be inside or contain the query region, because all sales regions are of the same size—that is, they're constructed using quarter-mile radius buffers.) You can determine the exact relationship by using the SDO_GEOM.RELATE function discussed in Chapter 9. Here, we describe an alternate approach using just the SDO_RELATE operator and appropriate masks to determine the type of intersection.

First you will see how many sales regions *overlap* the query sales region (id=51). This involves specifying two masks, OVERLAPBDYDISJOINT and OVERLAPBDYINTERSECT, in the parameter_string of the SDO_RELATE operator. You can combine multiple such masks using a plus sign (+) in the mask specification. Listing 8-46 shows an example.

Listing 8-46. *Identifying All Sales Regions That Overlap a Specific Sales Region (*id=51*)*

```
SQL> SELECT sr1.id
FROM sales_regions sr2, sales_regions sr1
WHERE sr2.id=51
  AND sr1.id <> 51
```

```
  AND SDO_RELATE
  (sr1.geom,  sr2.geom, 'MASK=OVERLAPBDYDISJOINT+OVERLAPBDYINTERSECT')='TRUE' ;
        ID
----------
        63
        54
        72
        69
        43
        66
        50
        75

8 rows selected.
```

Note that only eight out of the nine returned in Listing 8-45 are overlapping. This means the other region, which intersected the query sales region (id=51), was actually "touching" it. You can verify this using the query in Listing 8-47.

Listing 8-47. *Verifying That a Sales Region Touches Another Sales Region (*id=51*)*

```
SQL> SELECT a.id
FROM sales_regions b, sales_regions a
WHERE b.id=51
  AND a.id <> 51
  AND SDO_RELATE(a.geom, b.geom, 'MASK=TOUCH' )='TRUE' ;
        ID
----------
        76
```

Another useful combination is that of the INSIDE and COVEREDBY masks. For instance, you can use the INSIDE+COVEREDBY mask in Listing 8-43 instead of just the INSIDE mask. This will retrieve all sales regions of competitors that are inside and may also touch the border of the D.C. boundary.

■ **Tip** In Oracle, the combination of INSIDE and COVEREDBY is optimized. The combination of CONTAINS and COVERS is also optimized.

Together with the SDO_FILTER operator, the SDO_RELATE operator provides a rich set of functionality for use in a wide variety of applications. Whereas the SDO_NN and SDO_WITHIN_DISTANCE operators provide simple and easy-to-use distance-based analysis, the SDO_RELATE operator provides a detailed analysis of query geometry-data geometry relationships.

Tuning Parameter for SDO_RELATE on Nongeodetic Data Tables

During the evaluation of an SDO_RELATE query on nongeodetic data, an R-tree index in Oracle Spatial uses the MBR of the query to internally compute tiles (by recursively subdividing the MBR) that cover the query geometry (in that sense, the R-tree of Oracle Spatial is much different from the ones published in research literature[4]). It then uses the tiles to eliminate candidate data geometries without performing the expensive secondary filter (Geometry Engine) operations (see Figure 8-3). The

4. For an overview of the Oracle R-tree, see Ravikanth V. Kothuri and Siva Ravada. "Efficient Processing of Large Spatial Queries using Interior Approximations." Proceedings of the 7th International Symposium on Spatial and Temporal Databases (SSTD), 2001.

user does not have to do anything to invoke this optimization. The R-tree automatically invokes this optimization. However, for some query geometries, there may be a need for fine-tuning. Figure 8-10 shows an example.

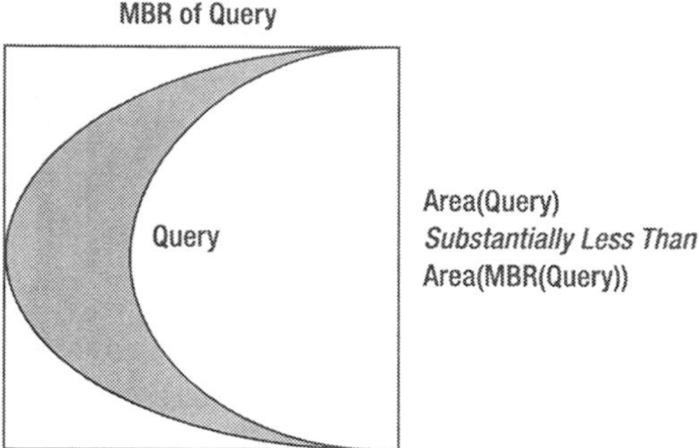

Figure 8-10. *Example of a query geometry*

Consider the query geometry in Figure 8-10. The area of the query geometry is substantially (say 75 percent) less than the area of the MBR for the query geometry. In this case, specifying `SDO_LEVEL=6` in the `parameter_string` of the `SDO_RELATE` operator may improve the response time for this operator. This is because of the elimination of more data prior to the expensive secondary filter. Note that Oracle does not allow you to specify the `SDO_LEVEL` as 7 or higher, because this is likely to degrade the performance because of an increase in the cost of tile generation. The queries implicitly use a value of 4 for `SDO_LEVEL`. Listing 8-48 shows an example that adds the tuning parameter to Listing 8-43.

Listing 8-48. *Adding the* `SDO_LEVEL=6` *Parameter to an* `SDO_RELATE` *Query*

```
SQL> SELECT COUNT(*)
FROM  us_states st, competitors_sales_regions comp
WHERE st.state_abrv='DC'
  AND SDO_RELATE(comp.geom,  st.geom, 'MASK=INSIDE SDO_LEVEL=6' )='TRUE'  ;
```

Hints for Spatial Operators

Recall that during our discussion on operator evaluation, we noted that the optimizer cannot choose the spatial index. This might happen when the spatial operator is used in conjunction with other nonspatial operators (on the same table) or in a multitable join. Oracle Spatial does not provide cost and selectivity estimates for spatial operators that are comparable to other operators in SQL. As a result, the choice made by the optimizer to use or not to use the spatial index may be incorrect. Specifying explicit hints will ensure an appropriate execution plan. In this section, we cover specific cases where you may need appropriate hints and how to specify these hints.

To determine whether a spatial operator is evaluated using the spatial index, you can trace the execution plan for the SQL statement involving the operator. Before tracing, you first have to load the `utlxplan` script (once). You can then use `SET AUTOTRACE ON` to view the execution plan output (see the *Oracle Reference* for more information). Alternatively, you can use the `EXPLAIN PLAN` statement. Listing 8-49 illustrates this with an example.

Listing 8-49. *Explaining the Execution Plan for a SQL Statement*

```
SQL> @$ORACLE_HOME/rdbms/admin/utlxplan  -- Load only once
SQL> SET AUTOTRACE ON
SQL> SELECT ct.id
FROM  customers ct
WHERE SDO_WITHIN_DISTANCE
(
  ct.location,
  ( SELECT location FROM competitors WHERE id=1),
  'DISTANCE=0.25 UNIT=MILE '
)='TRUE' ;
```

The plan looks like the following:

```
Execution Plan
----------------------------------------------------------
Plan hash value: 2227105339

--------------------------------------------------------------------------------
----------------

| Id  | Operation                      | Name            | Rows  | Bytes | Cost (%
CPU)| Time     |

--------------------------------------------------------------------------------
----------------

|   0 | SELECT STATEMENT               |                 |    32 |  4864 |      5
 (0)| 00:00:01 |

|   1 |  TABLE ACCESS BY INDEX ROWID   | CUSTOMERS       |    32 |  4864 |      3
 (0)| 00:00:01 |

|*  2 |   DOMAIN INDEX                 | CUSTOMERS_SIDX  |       |       |
    |          |

|   3 |    TABLE ACCESS BY INDEX ROWID| COMPETITORS     |     1 |   137 |      2
 (0)| 00:00:01 |

|*  4 |     INDEX UNIQUE SCAN          | COMPETITORS_PK  |     1 |       |      1
 (0)| 00:00:01 |
--------------------------------------------------------------------------------
----------------
```

If you see a statement like `DOMAIN INDEX of <index_name>`, it means the optimizer is using the spatial index referred to by `<index_name>`. The spatial index and other non-native indexes such as the context index are referred to as *domain indexes* in Oracle. In most cases, you do not have to specify any hints—the optimizer automatically picks the spatial domain index whenever it sees a spatial operator. However, there are exceptions:

- When the SQL has multiple predicates on the same table
- When the SQL has multiple tables being joined

Let's look at each of these cases and how the `NO_INDEX`, `ORDERED`, and `INDEX` hints can help.

Spatial Operator with Other Predicates on the Same Table

Say the spatial operator is not an SDO_NN operator—that is, the operator is, for instance, an SDO_WITHIN_DISTANCE operator. You do not have to do anything here. Otherwise, if the SQL has an SDO_NN operator and one or more additional nonspatial predicates such as customer_grade='GOLD' on the same table, you may need to specify explicit hints. Let's look at this in detail in the following section.

Spatial Operator Is an SDO_NN Operator

Consider the examples in Listings 8-27, 8-28, and 8-31. Here you want to identify the five nearest customers whose grade is GOLD. (Note that you cannot use the SDO_NUM_RES=5 parameter, as in Listing 8-29 or 8-30, to answer this query correctly because that query will return the five nearest customers, of which two are not GOLD customers. In effect, it returns only three GOLD customers instead of the required five.) Listings 8-27, 8-28, and 8-31 answer the query correctly and return the customers in order of their distance to the query. Listing 8-50 repeats the SQL in Listing 8-31 for ease of reference.

Listing 8-50. SDO_NN *Operator Retrieving the Five* GOLD *Customers Nearest to a Specific Competitor Along with Their Distances*

```
SQL> col dist format 999
SELECT ct.id, ct.customer_grade, SDO_NN_DISTANCE(1) dist
FROM competitors comp, customers ct
WHERE comp.id=1
  AND ct.customer_grade='GOLD'
  AND SDO_NN(ct.location,  comp.location, 'SDO_BATCH_SIZE=100', 1  )='TRUE'
  AND ROWNUM<=5
ORDER BY ct.id;

        ID     CUSTOMER_GRADE              DIST
----------     ---------------             ----
       809     GOLD                        95
       810     GOLD                        286
      6326     GOLD                        301
      7821     GOLD                        295
      8792     GOLD                        146

5 rows selected.
```

The query works fine because there is no index on the customer_grade column (that is, on the column involved in the *equality* predicate). Now, say you have created an index on the customer_grade column of the customers table. Then you re-execute the example in Listing 8-50, as shown in Listing 8-51.

Listing 8-51. *Creating an Index on* customer_grade *and Rerunning Listing 8-50*

```
SQL> CREATE INDEX cust_grade ON customers(customer_grade);
SQL> col dist format 9999
SELECT ct.id, ct.customer_grade, SDO_NN_DISTANCE(1) dist
FROM competitors comp, customers ct
WHERE comp.id=1
  AND ct.customer_grade='GOLD'
  AND SDO_NN(ct.location,  comp.location, 'SDO_BATCH_SIZE=100', 1  )='TRUE'
  AND ROWNUM<=5
ORDER BY ct.id;
```

```
        ID CUSTOMER_GRADE   DIST
---------- ---------------             -----
       777 GOLD                        2487
       778 GOLD                        3953
       780 GOLD                          552
       781 GOLD                        3950
       796 GOLD                        1466


Execution Plan
----------------------------------------------------------
Plan hash value: 4235074169

--------------------------------------------------------------------------------
----------------------

| Id  | Operation                         | Name            | Rows  | Bytes | C
ost (%CPU)| Time     |

--------------------------------------------------------------------------------
----------------------

|   0 | SELECT STATEMENT                  |                 |     5 |  1445 |
  14  (15)| 00:00:01 |

|   1 |  SORT ORDER BY                    |                 |     5 |  1445 |
  14  (15)| 00:00:01 |

|*  2 |   COUNT STOPKEY                   |                 |       |       |
          |          |

|   3 |    NESTED LOOPS                   |                 |    11 |  3179 |
  13   (8)| 00:00:01 |

|   4 |     TABLE ACCESS BY INDEX ROWID   | COMPETITORS     |     1 |   137 |
   2   (0)| 00:00:01 |

|*  5 |      INDEX UNIQUE SCAN            | COMPETITORS_PK  |     1 |       |
   1   (0)| 00:00:01 |

|   6 |     TABLE ACCESS BY INDEX ROWID   | CUSTOMERS       |    11 |  1672 |
  13   (8)| 00:00:01 |

|   7 |      BITMAP CONVERSION TO ROWIDS  |                 |       |       |
          |          |

|   8 |       BITMAP AND                  |                 |       |       |
          |          |

|   9 |        BITMAP CONVERSION FROM ROWIDS|               |       |       |
          |          |

|  10 |         SORT ORDER BY             |                 |       |       |
          |          |
```

```
|* 11 |          DOMAIN INDEX                  | CUSTOMERS_SIDX |        |        |
       |         |

|  12 |        BITMAP CONVERSION FROM ROWIDS|                  |        |        |
       |         |

|* 13 |         INDEX RANGE SCAN               | CUST_GRADE     |        |        |
   3   (0)| 00:00:01 |
```

Listing 8-51 gives incorrect results (in fact, it may give different results at different times too). This erroneous behavior happens for the following reason: the SDO_NN returns, say, the 100 nearest neighbors in order of their distance to query geometry. The order, however, is lost when they are bitmap-merged with the results of the B-tree index on customer_grade. This behavior is documented in the *Oracle Spatial User's Guide.*

You can avoid the preceding erroneous behavior by ensuring the following hints in the "Hints for the SDO_NN Operator" sidebar.

HINTS FOR THE SDO_NN OPERATOR

Here are some hints for the optimizer to ensure correct execution of SDO_NN:

- Force the optimizer to use the associated spatial index for the SDO_NN operator. This is required because the SDO_NN operator is actually a distance-ordering operator and cannot be evaluated (in current releases) without the spatial index (an Oracle error ORA-13249 will be raised if index is not chosen).
- Force the optimizer to `not use` indexes on other predicates on the same table as the SDO_NN operator operates on. (Otherwise, it may return incorrect results, as shown in Listing 8-51.)

You can rewrite Listing 8-51 as shown in Listing 8-52 to ensure the preceding two criteria are satisfied. Specify the `INDEX/NO_INDEX` hints with the table alias (or table name) as the first argument and the index name as the second. Listing 8-52 executes correctly and returns the customers in distance order. Note that these results are identical to those of Listing 8-50 (or Listing 8-31).

Listing 8-52. *Usage of Hints with* SDO_NN *and Other Operators on the Same Table*

```
SQL> SELECT /*+ NO_INDEX(ct cust_grade) INDEX(ct customers_sidx) */
ct.id, ct.customer_grade, SDO_NN_DISTANCE(1) dist  FROM
competitors comp, customers ct
WHERE comp.id=1
  AND ct.customer_grade='GOLD'
  AND SDO_NN(ct.location,  comp.location, 'SDO_BATCH_SIZE=100', 1  )='TRUE'
  AND ROWNUM<=5
ORDER BY ct.id;

        ID CUSTOMER_GRADE   DIST
---------- --------------- -----
       809 GOLD               95
       810 GOLD              286
      6326 GOLD              301
      7821 GOLD              295
      8792 GOLD              146
```

```
Execution Plan
----------------------------------------------------------
Plan hash value: 2605535536

----------------------------------------------------------------------------
----------------

| Id  | Operation                     | Name            | Rows  | Bytes | Cost (
%CPU)| Time     |

----------------------------------------------------------------------------
----------------

|   0 | SELECT STATEMENT              |                 |     5 |  1445 |    12
  (9)| 00:00:01 |

|   1 |  SORT ORDER BY                |                 |     5 |  1445 |    12
  (9)| 00:00:01 |

|*  2 |   COUNT STOPKEY               |                 |       |       |
     |          |

|   3 |    NESTED LOOPS               |                 |    11 |  3179 |    11
  (0)| 00:00:01 |

|   4 |     TABLE ACCESS BY INDEX ROWID| COMPETITORS    |     1 |   137 |     2
  (0)| 00:00:01 |

|*  5 |      INDEX UNIQUE SCAN        | COMPETITORS_PK  |     1 |       |     1
  (0)| 00:00:01 |

|*  6 |     TABLE ACCESS BY INDEX ROWID| CUSTOMERS      |    11 |  1672 |    11
  (0)| 00:00:01 |

|*  7 |      DOMAIN INDEX             | CUSTOMERS_SIDX  |       |       |
     |          |

----------------------------------------------------------------------------
```

Spatial Operator with Multiple Tables in a SQL Statement

If the operator is an SDO_NN operator, you should apply the criteria and hints in the "Hints for the SDO_NN Operator" sidebar. In addition, the following general guidelines apply for all spatial operators.

When a SQL statement has more than one table, the optimizer may or may not choose the spatial index. If you want the spatial index to be used (for performance reasons), you should specify the table whose spatial index is to be used as the *inner* table. You can enforce this by specifying this table to be the last in the FROM clause of the SELECT statement and specifying the ORDERED hint. Listing 8-53 shows the usage with the customers and competitors tables. Note that you want to use the spatial index on the customers table, so you specify it as the inner table (that is, the last table in the FROM clause).

Listing 8-53. *Spatial Operator with Multiple Hints in a SQL Statement with Two Tables*

```
SQL>  SELECT /*+ ORDERED */ ct.id, ct.name
FROM competitors comp, customers ct
WHERE comp.id=1
  AND SDO_WITHIN_DISTANCE
  (ct.location, comp.location, 'DISTANCE=0.25 UNIT=MILE ' )='TRUE'
ORDER BY ct.id ;

        ID NAME
---------- -----------------------------------
        25 BLAKE CONSTRUCTION
        28 COLONIAL PARKING
        34 HEWLETT-PACKARD DC GOV AFFAIRS
        41 MCGREGOR PRINTING
        48 POTOMAC ELECTRIC POWER
        50 SMITH HINCHMAN AND GRYLLS
       270 METRO-FARRAGUT NORTH STATION
       271 METRO-FARRAGUT WEST STATION
       468 SAFEWAY
       809 LINCOLN SUITES
       810 HOTEL LOMBARDY
      1044 MUSEUM OF THE THIRD DIMENSION
      1526 INTERNATIONAL FINANCE
      1538 MCKENNA AND CUNEO
      2195 STEVENS ELEMENTARY SCHOOL
      6326 HOTEL LOMBARDY
      7754 EXECUTIVE INN
      7762 PHILLIPS 66
      7789 SEVEN BUILDINGS
      7821 RENAISSANCE MAYFLOWER HOTEL
      8138 ST GREGORY HOTEL
      8382 EXXON
      8792 DESTINATION HOTEL & RESORTS

23 rows selected.


Execution Plan
----------------------------------------------------------
Plan hash value: 4243869098

--------------------------------------------------------------------------------
----------------

| Id  | Operation                    | Name             | Rows  | Bytes | Cost (%
CPU)| Time     |

--------------------------------------------------------------------------------
----------------

|   0 | SELECT STATEMENT             |                  |    32 |  9248 |     5
(20)| 00:00:01 |

|   1 |  SORT ORDER BY               |                  |    32 |  9248 |     5
(20)| 00:00:01 |
```

```
|  2 |   NESTED LOOPS                 |                 |   32 |  9248 |    4
 (0)| 00:00:01 |

|  3 |    TABLE ACCESS BY INDEX ROWID| COMPETITORS     |    1 |   137 |    2
 (0)| 00:00:01 |

|* 4 |     INDEX UNIQUE SCAN          | COMPETITORS_PK |    1 |       |    1
 (0)| 00:00:01 |

|  5 |    TABLE ACCESS BY INDEX ROWID| CUSTOMERS       |   32 |  4864 |    4
 (0)| 00:00:01 |

|* 6 |     DOMAIN INDEX               | CUSTOMERS_SIDX |      |       |
    |          |

---------------------------------------------------------------------------
```

Note the order of the tables in Listing 8-53. The `customers` table, whose index needs to be used, is specified last (that is, as the *inner* table). In general, if the first argument of the `spatial_operator` is from table A and the second is from table B, always ensure that table B precedes table A in the `FROM` clause of the SQL statement. The `ORDERED` hint, in such a SQL, informs the optimizer to use table B as the *outer* table and table A as the *inner* table.

You can generalize the preceding guidelines and specify the `ORDERED`, `INDEX`, and/or `NO_INDEX` hints in a SQL with multiple tables or multiple *indexed* operators (domain index, B-tree, bitmap, IOT operators) to ensure an appropriate execution.

Advanced Spatial Index Features

In the following sections, we cover some advanced spatial indexing features that are useful for large spatial repositories. These include function-based indexing, online index rebuilds, three-dimensional indexing, parallel indexing, and local partitioned indexing. For each of these features, we describe how to create the associated spatial index and how to use spatial operators.

Function-Based Spatial Indexes

Oracle allows you to create a B-tree index on a function operating on one or more columns of a table. You can do the same with a spatial index. Instead of creating indexes on a column of `SDO_GEOMETRY`, you can create indexes on *any deterministic function* that returns an `SDO_GEOMETRY` using existing columns of a table. For instance, you can indirectly use the `SDO_GCDR.GEOCODE_AS_GEOMETRY` function that returns an `SDO_GEOMETRY` from the address fields of the `customers` table as described in Chapters 3 and 6. (Note that the `SDO_GCDR` package is available only in the priced option of Spatial—it is not available in Locator.) This means you do not have to explicitly materialize the location from the address fields of the `customers` table to create spatial indexes. Instead, you can create functions that return `SDO_GEOMETRY` from existing columns of a table.

Note that the `SDO_GCDR.GEOCODE_AS_GEOMETRY` function is not defined as a deterministic function. So, you create a `deterministic` function, called `gcdr_geometry`, around the `SDO_GCDR.GEOCODE_AS_GEOMETRY`, as shown in Listing 8-54. You can then use `gcdr_geometry` as the function in the function-based spatial index.

Listing 8-54. *Creating a Deterministic Function to Return an* `SDO_GEOMETRY` *Using Address Attributes of the* `customers` *Table*

```
CREATE or REPLACE FUNCTION gcdr_geometry(street_number varchar2,
street_name varchar2, city varchar2, state varchar2, postal_code varchar2)
RETURN MDSYS.SDO_GEOMETRY DETERMINISTIC is
BEGIN
   RETURN (sdo_gcdr.geocode_as_geometry('SPATIAL',
                   sdo_keywordarray(street_number || ' ' ||street_name ,
                   city || ' ' || state || ' ' || postal_code), 'US'));
END;
/
```

As a side note, declaring a function to be deterministic helps with performance if the function is called multiple times in the same SQL statement. Listing 8-55 shows a SQL statement with two invocations of the `gcdr_geometry` function. The optimizer will evaluate this function just once if it is declared as `DETERMINISTIC`.

Listing 8-55. *SQL Example Where a Deterministic Function Is Evaluated Only Once Even When Called Twice*

```
SQL> SELECT
gcdr_geometry(street_number,street_name,city,state,postal_code).sdo_point.x,
gcdr_geometry(street_number,street_name,city,state,postal_code).sdo_point.y
FROM customers WHERE id=1;
```

You also need to populate the `USER_SDO_GEOM_METADATA` view that has the `TABLE_NAME`, `COLUMN_NAME`, `DIMINFO`, and `SRID` columns. All columns except the `column_name` field can be populated as described in Listing 8-4. The `column_name` to be inserted is not a regular column of the table. Instead, it is a pseudo-column, obtained using the `GCDR_GEOMETRY` function. So, you set the `column_name` to be an invocation of the function with associated arguments. The SQL for inserting this information into the metadata is shown in Listing 8-56.

Listing 8-56. *Inserting the Metadata for a* `<table, function-based pseudo-column>`

```
SQL> INSERT INTO user_sdo_geom_metadata VALUES
(
  'CUSTOMERS',
  'SPATIAL.GCDR_GEOMETRY(street_number,street_name,city,state,postal_code)',
  MDSYS.SDO_DIM_ARRAY
  (
    MDSYS.SDO_DIM_ELEMENT('X', -180, 180, 0.5),
    MDSYS.SDO_DIM_ELEMENT('Y', -90, 90, 0.5)
  ),
  8307
);
```

■ **Caution** While inserting into the metadata view, do not include any spaces between the arguments of the `GCDR_GEOMETRY` function—that is, do not have the arguments as `street_number, <space> street_name`. This will cause errors during index creation. Also, make sure to put the schema owner of the function in the column name, that is, set the column name to `'spatial.gcdr_geometry...'` and not as `'gcdr_geometry...'`. (To make your code more portable, you can dynamically obtain the schema owner instead of hard-coding it as `SPATIAL` using the following: `sys_context('userenv', 'CURRENT_SCHEMA')|| '.GCDR_GEOMETRY (street_number,street_name,city,state,postal_code)' ),`.

Now you can create an index on the customers table using the function-based virtual column. This virtual column is a function, GCDR_GEOMETRY, that returns an SDO_GEOMETRY using the street_number, street_name, city, state, and postal_code columns of the table. Listing 8-57 shows the corresponding SQL.

Listing 8-57. *Creating a Spatial Index on a Function Returning an* SDO_GEOMETRY

```
SQL> CREATE INDEX customers_spatial_fun_idx ON  customers
(
  gcdr_geometry(street_number, street_name, city,  state, postal_code)
)
INDEXTYPE  IS MDSYS.SPATIAL_INDEX
PARAMETERS ('LAYER_GTYPE=POINT');
```

Note that you can augment the preceding CREATE INDEX with a parameter string to specify appropriate parameters as in Listings 8-8 through 8-15. Specifically, 'LAYER_GTYPE=POINT' should be used since the geocoded addresses will always be points.

As in the case of function-based indexes on B-trees, to create and use function-based spatial indexes, the user needs to have the QUERY REWRITE privilege (GLOBAL QUERY REWRITE if creating index in another schema). Besides, the QUERY_REWRITE_ENABLED parameter must be set to TRUE, and the QUERY_REWRITE_INTEGRITY parameter must be set to TRUSTED. You can set them either in the parameter file used at database start-up or in a particular session as shown in Listing 8-58.

Listing 8-58. *Setting Session Parameters to Enable Query Rewrite on Function-Based Indexes (Not Necessary in Oracle 10g (and Newer)*

```
SQL> ALTER SESSION SET QUERY_REWRITE_INTEGRITY = TRUSTED;
SQL> ALTER SESSION SET QUERY_REWRITE_ENABLED = TRUE;
```

Once an index is created using a function-based index, the function will serve as the virtual column for the table. You can use this column in spatial operators just like a regular SDO_GEOMETRY column in a table. The SQL in Listing 8-59 shows an example using the SDO_NN operator. This example is the equivalent of Listing 8-29, except it uses the function-based virtual column. The function is specified as the first argument (that is, as the indexed column) to the spatial operator.

Listing 8-59. SDO_NN *Operator Retrieving the Five Customers Nearest to Each Competitor Using the Function-Based Index*

```
SQL>  SELECT /*+ ORDERED */ ct.id, ct.name, ct.customer_grade
FROM  competitors comp, customers ct
WHERE comp.id=1
  AND SDO_NN
  (
    gcdr_geometry
      (ct.street_number,ct.street_name, ct.city, ct.state, ct.postal_code),
    comp.location,
    'SDO_NUM_RES=5'
  )='TRUE'
ORDER BY ct.id;
```

```
        ID NAME                                CUSTOMER_GRADE
---------- ----------------------------------- ---------------
       809 LINCOLN SUITES                      GOLD
      1044 MUSEUM OF THE THIRD DIMENSION       SILVER
      1526 INTERNATIONAL FINANCE               SILVER
      1538 MCKENNA AND CUNEO                   SILVER
      8792 DESTINATION HOTEL & RESORTS         GOLD

5 rows selected.
```

■ **Tip** Always specify 'LAYER_GTYPE=POINT' in the CREATE INDEX statement if you are creating a spatial index on a function that geocodes addresses to SDO_GEOMETRY objects. If you do not specify this parameter, queries will be slow. A better alternative, then, would be to explicitly store the geocoded addresses as SDO_GEOMETRY columns and index them.

To summarize, functional-based indexing could be used whenever the location data cannot be explicitly materialized for various reasons (for example, if existing table definitions cannot be changed), but the power and functionality of Oracle Spatial is desired.

Local Partitioned Spatial Indexes

Table partitioning, a priced option of Oracle, is an important Oracle feature to achieve scalability and manageability in large databases. For instance, you can have the customers table partitioned on the customer_grade attribute as illustrated in Listing 8-60.

Listing 8-60. *Creating a Partitioned Table*

```
SQL>
DROP INDEX customers_sidx;  -- Drop the spatial index
RENAME customers TO customers_old;  -- Store old data
CREATE TABLE customers
(
  NAME                    VARCHAR2(64),
  ID                      NUMBER,
  STREET_NUMBER           VARCHAR2(14),
  STREET_NAME             VARCHAR2(80),
  CITY                    VARCHAR2(64),
  STATE                   VARCHAR2(64),
  POSTAL_CODE             VARCHAR2(16),
  CUSTOMER_GRADE          VARCHAR2(15),
  LOCATION                SDO_GEOMETRY
)
PARTITION by RANGE(CUSTOMER_GRADE)
(
  PARTITION GOLD        VALUES LESS THAN ('GOLDZZZZZZ'),
  PARTITION PLATINUM    VALUES LESS THAN ('PLATINUMZZZZZZ'),
  PARTITION SILVER      VALUES LESS THAN ('SILVERZZZZZZ')
);

INSERT INTO customers
SELECT name, id, street_number, street_name, city, state,
               postal_code, customer_grade, location  FROM customers_old;
COMMIT;
```

In Listing 8-60 partitions are created based on *ranges*. For instance, the first partition GOLD will have all customers whose grade will be less than 'GOLDZZZZZZ'. This means the customer grade GOLD (less than 'GOLDZZZZZZ') will be in this partition. You define other partitions analogously.

Creating Local Indexes on Partitioned Tables

If you create an index using the SQL in Listing 8-6, this will create a single global spatial index on all the partitions. Alternatively, you can create a local index, one for each partition, by specifying the keyword LOCAL at the end of the CREATE INDEX statement in Listing 8-6 and specifying some optional partition-specific parameters. Listing 8-61 shows the SQL syntax for a local partitioned index.

Listing 8-61. *Creating a Local Partitioned Spatial Index*

```
CREATE INDEX customers_sidx ON customers(location)
INDEXTYPE  IS MDSYS.SPATIAL_INDEX
[PARAMETERS ('parameter_string')]
LOCAL  [PARAMETERS(sequence of 'partition-specific parameters')] ;
```

Caution You can create local spatial indexes only on range-partitioned tables (created as in Listing 8-60). You cannot create local spatial indexes on list- or hash-partitioned tables.

What is the advantage of creating *local* indexes as opposed to creating one *global* index for all the partitions? Manageability and scalability are two primary advantages of local partitioned indexing:

- *Manageability*: You can rebuild the local index associated with a specific partition without affecting other partitions. As with B-tree indexes, you can take advantage of all the partitioning features, such as exchange partitions and split partitions, while maintaining the associated spatial indexes.
- *Scalability*: Queries can be targeted to specific partitions, improving performance. This means you will be searching only a subset of the data as opposed to the entire set.
  - By specifying different tablespaces for each partition and mapping each tablespace to a different I/O device, you can obtain I/O parallelism in queries.
  - Likewise, spatial indexes can be created on each partition in parallel.

In addition to the LOCAL keyword, you can specify partition-specific parameters. These parameters will override the default parameters specified before the LOCAL keyword. Listing 8-62 shows an example.

Listing 8-62. *Creating a Local Partitioned Spatial Index with Partition-Specific Parameters*

```
SQL> CREATE INDEX customers_sidx ON customers(location)
INDEXTYPE  IS MDSYS.SPATIAL_INDEX
PARAMETERS ('TABLESPACE=USERS')
LOCAL
(
  PARTITION IP1 PARAMETERS('TABLESPACE=TBS_3'),
  PARTITION IP2,
  PARTITION IP3
);
```

Note that in the preceding CREATE INDEX statement, index partition names IP1, IP2, and IP3 correspond to the table partitions GOLD, SILVER, and PLATINUM, respectively (matched based on the order/sequence of specification). The index for partition IP1 is placed in tablespace TBS_3, whereas the indexes for all other partitions are placed in the default tablespace USERS specified before the LOCAL keyword.

Caution Parameters specified per partition must be compatible (the same type of index: R-tree or quadtree), with the default parameters and the parameters for other partitions.

Querying Using Local Partitioned Indexes

If a table is partitioned and you have created a local partitioned index on it, there is nothing specific to be done at the time of queries. There's little overhead if the SQL contains only the spatial operator without any partition key. If a partitioned key is specified in the WHERE clause of the SQL statement along with a spatial operator, Oracle automatically prunes irrelevant partitions using the partition key and applies the spatial operator only on relevant partitions. Listing 8-63 includes the partition key in the query of Listing 8-20.

Listing 8-63. SDO_WITHIN_DISTANCE *Operator on a Partitioned Table*

```
SQL> SELECT /*+ ORDERED */ ct.id, ct.name
FROM competitors comp, customers ct
WHERE comp.id=1
  AND customer_grade='GOLD'
  AND SDO_WITHIN_DISTANCE
    (ct.location,  comp.location, 'DISTANCE=0.25 UNIT=MILE ' )='TRUE'
  ORDER BY ct.id;
        ID NAME
---------- -----------------------------------
       809 LINCOLN SUITES
       810 HOTEL LOMBARDY
      6326 HOTEL LOMBARDY
      7821 RENAISSANCE MAYFLOWER HOTEL
      8138 ST GREGORY HOTEL
      8792 DESTINATION HOTEL & RESORTS
6 rows selected.
```

This query, instead of returning 23 rows as in Listing 8-20, returns only 6 rows. Since the majority of the rows are eliminated in the search, the query may also execute faster. This example demonstrates how local spatial indexes extend the performance advantages of table partitioning to spatial analysis.

For all partitions that satisfy the partitioning key (or all the partitions if there is no partition pruning), the spatial operators execute using the local indexes on each partition, aggregate the results, and return them to the user. As a consequence, the results for the SDO_WITHIN_DISTANCE, SDO_FILTER, and SDO_RELATE operators would be the same as the results if the table *were* not partitioned.

The results for the SDO_NN operator differ, however. The SDO_NN operator will return the specified number of neighbors for each partition (instead of for all the partitions satisfying the query). For example, if the query specifies SDO_NUM_RES=5 in the parameter string of the SDO_NN operator, then each partition that satisfies the SQL returns the five nearest neighbors from its associated local index. This means if there are three partitions, SDO_NN will return a total of 3 ⊇ 3 5 = 15 results when SDO_NUM_RES=5 is specified. To get the five nearest neighbors, the SQL has to be modified as shown in Listing 8-64. Note that the results match those in Listing 8-27.

Listing 8-64. *Obtaining the Five Customers Nearest to Each Competitor When the* customers *Table Has a Local Partitioned Index*

```
SQL> SELECT id, name FROM
(
  SELECT /*+ ORDERED */ a.id , a.name, SDO_NN_DISTANCE(1) dist
  FROM  competitors b, customers a
  WHERE b.id=1
  AND SDO_NN(a.location,  b.location, 'SDO_NUM_RES=5' , 1)='TRUE' ORDER BY dist
)
WHERE ROWNUM<=5
ORDER BY id;
        ID NAME
---------- -----------------------------------
       809 LINCOLN SUITES
      1044 MUSEUM OF THE THIRD DIMENSION
      1526 INTERNATIONAL FINANCE
      1538 MCKENNA AND CUNEO
      8792 DESTINATION HOTEL & RESORTS

5 rows selected.
```

Parallel Indexing

Just as in the case of B-trees, you can create spatial indexes in parallel. For this, you can specify the PARALLEL clause with an optional parallel_degree parameter at the end of the CREATE INDEX statement, as shown in Listing 8-65.

Listing 8-65. *Creating a Spatial Index with the* PARALLEL *Keyword*

```
CREATE INDEX customers_sidx ON customers(location)
INDEXTYPE IS MDSYS.SPATIAL_INDEX
[PARAMETERS ('parameter_string')]  [LOCAL [Partition-specific parameters]]
PARALLEL [parallel_degree];
```

All optional parameters are specified in square brackets. The parallel_degree parameter, which is also optional, specifies the degree of parallelism. This degree specifies the number of slaves to work in parallel to create the index. If parallel_degree is omitted, Oracle uses the degree associated with the table (this is stored in the USER_TABLES dictionary view). You can alter the degree to 2 (or more) for a table using the SQL in Listing 8-66. You can do the same for a specific index too.

Listing 8-66. *Setting the Degree of Parallelism to 2 for a Table and Creating the Index*

```
SQL> ALTER TABLE customers PARALLEL 2 ; -- set degree

DROP INDEX customers_sidx;  -- drop existing index

CREATE INDEX customers_sidx ON customers(location)
INDEXTYPE IS MDSYS.SPATIAL_INDEX  PARALLEL;  -- no need to specify degree
```

Whether the index being created is a local partitioned index or a global index, index creation is performed in parallel if the *parallel degree* is more than 1. However, that is not the case with queries.

Spatial indexes do not perform any explicit parallel processing at query time (except for the parallelism for the underlying table scans). However, if the spatial index is a local partitioned index, then the query processing on multiple partitions is performed in parallel. This means partitioning and parallelism go hand in hand. Using partitioning and setting the table degree to more than 1 (as in Listing 8-66) implicitly improves the performance of proximity analysis operations using spatial indexes.

You will learn about some of the best practices relating to partitioning in Chapter 14.

Online Index Rebuilds

When there are too many deletes, typically 30 percent, from a spatially indexed table such as customers, a rebuild of the associated spatial index may make the index quite compact and efficient for subsequent queries. You can rebuild an index on a table, say `customers`, using the `ALTER INDEX` statement, as shown in Listing 8-67.

Listing 8-67. *Using* `ALTER INDEX ... REBUILD` *Statement to Rebuild the Entire Index*

```
SQL> ALTER  INDEX customers_sidx  REBUILD ;
```

Just as in the case of a `CREATE-INDEX` statement, you can specify parameters such as `layer_gtype`, `tablespace`, and `sdo_indx_dims` using a `PARAMETERS` clause, as shown in Listing 8-68. The effect of the `ALTER INDEX` SQL is the same as a `DROP INDEX` followed by a `CREATE INDEX` with the specified parameters.

Listing 8-68. `ALTER INDEX ... REBUILD` *with* `PARAMETERS` *Clause*

```
SQL> ALTER  INDEX customers_sidx REBUILD
PARAMETERS ('layer_gtype=POINT');
```

Note that the `ALTER INDEX` statement is a DDL statement and hence will commit any active transaction in the current session. Besides, `ALTER INDEX ... REBUILD` is also a blocking statement. This means if there are any concurrent DML (possibly in a separate session) executing on the index, this command will block till it gets exclusive lock on the index (that is, the associated `MDRT_<>$` table), and if there are any concurrent DML statements that are issued against the table/index after the rebuild starts, the DML will likewise be blocked. So, if a user issues a spatial operator query against the table/index, that query could be blocked because of an `ALTER INDEX ... REBUILD` that is executing in a separate session.

One way to not block queries when the index is being rebuilt is to specify the keyword `ONLINE` in the `ALTER INDEX ... REBUILD` statement.

Recollect from Figure 8-2 that the spatial index is stored as an Oracle table that starts with prefix `MDRT` (the exact name is stored in the `USER_SDO_INDEX_METADATA` view). For the SQL in Listing 8-69, the index is built using the existing data into a new table prefixed with `MDOT` while any concurrent queries are still evaluated using the index information in the table with the `MDRT` prefix. This is shown in Figure 8-11.

Listing 8-69. `ALTER INDEX ... REBUILD` *Without Blocking Any Concurrent Queries*

```
SQL> ALTER  INDEX customers_sidx REBUILD  ONLINE
PARAMETERS ('layer_gtype=POINT');
```

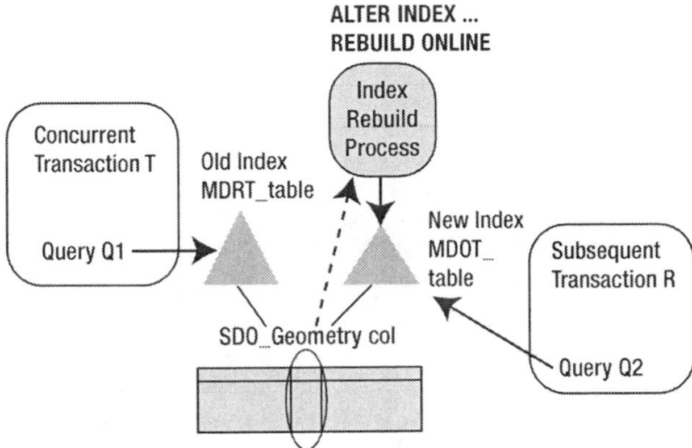

Figure 8-11. *Online index rebuilding and concurrent query processing*

At the end of the rebuild, the metadata is updated so that subsequent queries can use the latest index information in the index table with `MDOT` prefix. Subsequent rebuilds can switch the index table from `MDOT` prefix to `MDRT` prefix. This latest feature ensures queries are never blocked when the index on a spatial column is being rebuilt with the `ONLINE` keyword specified.

Spatial Joins

Listing 8-20 identified all customers inside a quarter mile of a specific competitor (`id=1`). Say you now want to look at all customers within 200 meters of all competitors. What if you wanted to perform this operation for all competitors instead of just the one with `id=1`? You could remove the `comp.id=1` predicate in Listing 8-20 (and set the distance to 200 meters). This would result in the SQL shown in Listing 8-70.

Listing 8-70. `SDO_RELATE` *Operator Retrieving All Customers Inside (and Touching the Border of) Each Competitor Region*

```
SQL> SELECT COUNT(DISTINCT ct.id)
FROM competitors comp, customers ct
WHERE SDO_WITHIN_DISTANCE
    (ct.location,  comp.location, 'DISTANCE=200 UNIT=METER ' )='TRUE';

COUNT(DISTINCTCT.ID)
--------------------
                1145
```

This query executes in a *nested loop*, performing the `SDO_WITHIN_DISTANCE` operation for each row in the `competitors` table. What if there is a spatial index on the `competitors` table? You can use this index in addition to the index on the customers in the preceding operation. This will speed up the query significantly for large datasets.

To use both indexes, you need to use the `SDO_JOIN` table function. This function has the following syntax:

```
SDO_JOIN
(
  table1                  IN VARCHAR2,
  col1                    IN VARCHAR2,
  table2                  IN VARCHAR2,
  col2                    IN VARCHAR2
  [, parameter_string     IN VARCHAR2     DEFAULT NULL
  [, preserve_join_order  IN NUMBER       DEFAULT 0
  [, table1_partition     IN VARCHAR2     DEFAULT NULL,
  [ , table2_partition    IN VARCHAR2     DEFAULT NULL]]]]
)
RETURNS SDO_ROWIDSET
```

where the following is true:

- `table1` and `col1` refer to the first table name and the corresponding geometry column name.
- `table2` and `col2` refer to the second table name and the corresponding geometry column name.
- `parameter_string` is optional. Just as in the `SDO_RELATE` and `SDO_WITHIN_DISTANCE` operators, this parameter can specify either `MASK=<mask-type>` or `DISTANCE=<val> [UNIT=<unit-spec>]`. If the `parameter_string` is not specified, then `SDO_JOIN` will operate only as the primary filter (that is, it will be equivalent to `SDO_FILTER`).
- `preserve_join_order` can be either 0 or 1. If the tables are of different sizes, then `SDO_JOIN` may internally reorder the tables for join processing. You may set this to 1 only if you prefer to override this reordering. For all practical purposes, just leave it as the default value of 0 (or do not specify this parameter).
- `table1_partition` is optional. If not `NULL`, this parameter restricts the scope of the join to a specified partition of table `table1`.
- `table2_partition` is optional. If not `NULL`, this parameter restricts the scope of the join to a specified partition of table `table2`.
- The `SDO_JOIN` returns an `SDO_ROWIDSET`. This is the *table* of `rowid` pairs of the form `<rowid1, rowid2>`. The first `rowid`, `rowid1`, corresponds to the rows of `table1`, and the second `rowid`, `rowid2`, corresponds to the rows of the second table, `table2`.

Using this syntax for the `SDO_JOIN`, you can rewrite Listing 8-70 to use the indexes of both tables. This query, shown in Listing 8-71, is likely to be faster than the query in Listing 8-70.

Listing 8-71. `SDO_JOIN` *Operator Analyzing the Number of Customers Inside All the Competitor Regions*

```
SQL> SELECT COUNT(DISTINCT ct.id)
FROM competitors comp, customers ct,
  TABLE
  (
    SDO_JOIN
      (
      'competitors', 'location',  -- first table and the SDO_GEOMETRY column
      'customers', 'location',    -- second table and the SDO_GEOMETRY column
      'DISTANCE=200 UNIT=METER'   -- specify mask relationship
    )
  ) jn
WHERE  ct.rowid=jn.rowid2 and  comp.rowid = jn.rowid1;
COUNT(DISTINCTCT.ID)
--------------------
                1145
```

Note that SDO_JOIN is a table function and is included in the FROM clause of the SQL. In contrast, the SDO_WITHIN_DISTANCE operator in Listing 8-70 is included in the WHERE clause of a SQL statement. In general, the SDO_JOIN function will execute faster than the equivalent SDO_RELATE or the SDO_WITHIN_DISTANCE operators, as SDO_JOIN uses both the spatial indexes.

Note that if the parameter_string is omitted, SDO_JOIN operates just like an SDO_FILTER operation. Listing 8-72 is therefore equivalent to Listing 8-73. However, since SDO_JOIN uses two spatial indexes instead of one in SDO_FILTER, the SQL in Listing 8-73 (using SDO_JOIN) may run significantly faster than that in Listing 8-72.

Listing 8-72. SDO_FILTER *Operator Retrieving All Customers Whose MBRs Intersect Those of Competitor Regions*

```
SQL> SELECT COUNT(DISTINCT ct.id)
FROM competitors_sales_regions comp, customers ct
WHERE SDO_FILTER(ct.location,  comp.geom)='TRUE';
  COUNT(*)
----------
      2171
```

Listing 8-73. SDO_JOIN *Operator Retrieving All Customers Whose MBRs Intersect the MBRs of Competitor Regions (Filter Operation Is Used)*

```
SQL> SELECT COUNT(DISTINCT ct.id)
FROM competitors_sales_regions comp, customers ct,
  TABLE
  (
    SDO_JOIN
    (
      'competitors_sales_regions', 'geom',   -- first table and column
      'customers', 'location'                -- second table and column
    )
  ) jn
WHERE  ct.rowid=jn.rowid2 AND comp.rowid = jn.rowid1;
  COUNT(*)
----------
      2171
```

What if you wanted to restrict the scope to only GOLD customers rather than all customers? Since the customers table is already partitioned on the customer_grade column, you can restrict the join to just the GOLD partition of the customers table. To use the local index on the GOLD partition, you will have to re-create the index as a local partitioned index for this purpose. Listing 8-74 rewrites the SDO_JOIN query of Listing 8-73 to restrict the scope to just the GOLD customers. You can observe that the query retrieves fewer results (and is also expected to execute faster).

Listing 8-74. *Rewriting Listing 8-73 to Restrict the Scope of* SDO_JOIN *to Just the Customers in the* GOLD *Partition*

```
SQL>
-- First, drop and re-create the index as a local partitioned index
DROP INDEX customers_sidx;
CREATE INDEX customers_sidx on customers(location)
INDEXTYPE IS mdsys.spatial_index LOCAL;

-- Now perform the query on a specific partition
SELECT COUNT(DISTINCT ct.id)
FROM competitors_sales_regions comp, customers PARTITION(GOLD) ct,
  TABLE
  (
    SDO_JOIN
    (
      'competitors_sales_regions', 'geom',  -- first table and column
      'customers', 'location',               -- second table and column
       NULL,   -- parameters list is set to NULL
       0,         -- preserve_join_order  set to default value
       NULL,   -- competitors_sales_region is the entire table
       'GOLD' --  GOLD partition of customers table
    )
  ) jn
WHERE  ct.rowid=jn.rowid2 AND comp.rowid = jn.rowid1;
  COUNT(*)
----------
       498
```

■ **Note** If a partitioned table has a local partitioned spatial index, you have to specify a valid partition in the SDO_JOIN for that table (if a NULL is specified for the partition parameter in SDO_JOIN, Oracle raises an error).

Three-Dimensional Analysis

The preceding discussion mainly focused on analysis using two-dimensional data such as customer locations or street networks. In certain applications such as city modeling, the data is not two-dimensional but three-dimensional in nature. In Chapter 4, we examined how to build city buildings and other architectural elements as three-dimensional solids, and three-dimensional surfaces. With the onset of impressive visualization tools such as Google Earth, streaming and visualizing the data in three dimensions has become a differentiating aspect of many successful analyses. In this section, we cover how to index and query three-dimensional data that was discussed in Chapter 4.

Consider the three-dimensional buildings that you created in Chapter 5 and stored as the shape column in the city_buildings table. Figure 8-12 shows a bird's-eye view (two-dimensional top view) of this data. The trajectory of a helicopter is also shown as a *line geometry*. To create a three-dimensional spatial index on this column, first you need to insert extent information in the USER_SDO_GEOM_METADATA view. Listing 8-75 shows the SQL.

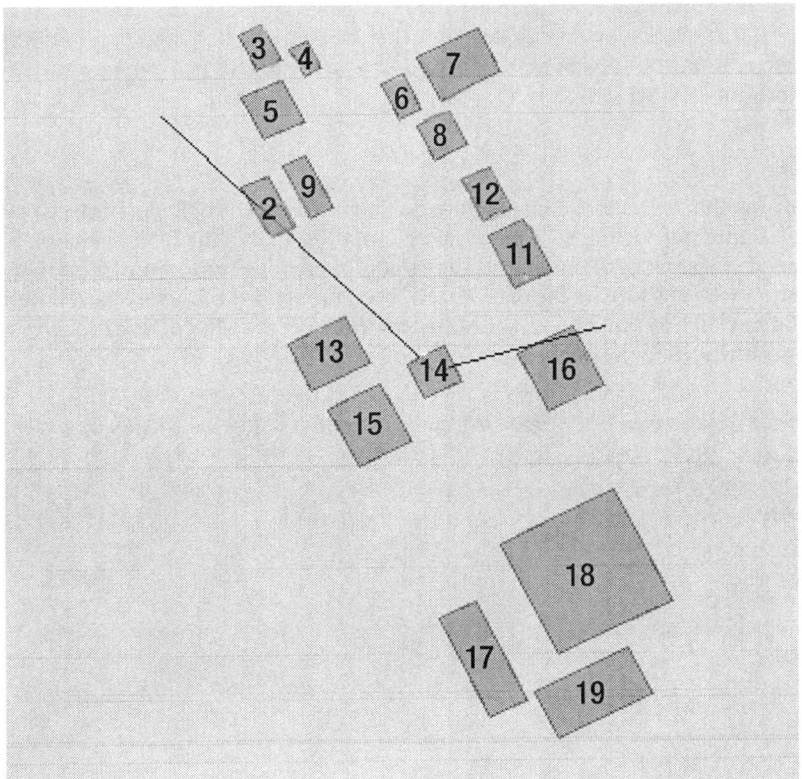

Figure 8-12. *Three-dimensional city buildings: a bird's eye view. The black line shows the trajectory a helicopter.*

Listing 8-75. *Inserting Metadata for the* `city_buildings` *Table (Extents in all Three Dimensions Are Entered)*

```
SQL> insert into user_sdo_geom_metadata values
('CITY_BUILDINGS', 'GEOM',
  SDO_DIM_ARRAY(
   SDO_DIM_ELEMENT('X', 29214140, 29219040, 0.05),
   SDO_DIM_ELEMENT('Y',  43364000, 43372640, 0.05),
   SDO_DIM_ELEMENT('Z', 0, 2000, 0.05)),
  7407);
```

You can now create the three-dimensional spatial index as shown in Listing 8-76. Observe that you need to specify 3 for parameter `sdo_indx_dims` to explicitly set the index dimensionality to three dimensions in this `CREATE INDEX` statement.

Listing 8-76. *Creating an R-tree Index on Three-Dimensional City Data*

```
SQL> CREATE INDEX  city_bldg_sidx  ON  city_buildings(geom)
INDEXTYPE  IS MDSYS.SPATIAL_INDEX
PARAMETERS ('SDO_INDX_DIMS=3');
```

Once the index is built, you can perform a variety of proximity analyses using the three-dimensional spatial index. These analyses come in handy in various situations.

For instance, the CEO of a company has a meeting at Building 14 (in the `city_buildings` table). His helicopter has a specific trajectory in or out of the city, which is stored in the `trajectory` column of the `trip_route` table. You can identify buildings that need additional security by performing a variety of proximity analyses using the spatial operators.

Relationship Analysis

One approach to identifying the approximate set of buildings that intersect the helicopter trajectory is by using the SDO_FILTER operator. Listing 8-77 shows an example. Recall that the filter operation is an approximate intersection operation. It compares the three-dimensional minimum bounding volume (MBV) of the query with the MBV of the data. That is, even though the trajectory itself does not intersect some buildings such as Building 12, the MBV does intersect the MBV of that building and hence the building is included in the query result.

Listing 8-77. *Identifying the Buildings Intersecting a Helicopter Trajectory Using* SDO_FILTER *Operator*

```
SQL> SELECT id FROM trip_route t, city_buildings c
           WHERE SDO_FILTER(c.geom,  t.trajectory)='TRUE'
           ORDER BY id;

    ID
------
     6
     8
    11
    12
    14

5 rows selected.
```

To perform an exact intersection operation using the three-dimensional geometries, you can use the SDO_ANYINTERACT (or the equivalent SDO_RELATE with mask=ANYINTERACT) operator to get the exact set of buildings that intersect the query window. Note that this returns only Building 14 as the result. The reason is that the helicopter lands only on Building 14 and flies over all the other buildings (that is, the helicopter trajectory does not intersect all the "additional rows" that are in Listing 8-77 but not in Listing 8-78).

Listing 8-78. *Identifying the Exact Set of Buildings Intersecting a Helicopter Trajectory Using* SDO_ANYINTERACT *Operator*

```
SQL> SELECT id FROM trip_route t, city_buildings c
           WHERE SDO_ANYINTERACT(c.geom,  t.trajectory)='TRUE';

        ID
----------
        14

1 row selected.
```

■ **Note** You can always substitute the SDO_ANYINTERACT operator with the equivalent 'mask=ANYINTERACT' type SDO_RELATE operator (that is, specify mask=ANYINTERACT in the third parameter of the SDO_RELATE operator).

Caution Relationship masks—CONTAINS, INSIDE, TOUCH, OVERLAPBDYDISJOINT, OVERLAPBDYINTERSECT, and COVEREDBY—that are used in an SDO_RELATE operator (or the respective equivalent operators SDO_CONTAINS, SDO_INSIDE, SDO_TOUCH, and so on) are not supported for three-dimensional spatial indexes.

Distance-Based Analysis

The problem with Listing 8-78 is that only Building 14 that intersects the trajectory is identified. Buildings close to the trajectory are not included. For this type of analysis, you can use the SDO_NN operator. Listing 8-79 identifies the three buildings that are close to the helicopter trajectory. The distance to the trajectory is reported using the SDO_NN_DISTANCE ancillary operator. Note that you can utilize the different variants of the SDO_NN operator (using the SDO_NUM_RES parameter or the SDO_BATCH_SIZE parameter) for three-dimensional data too. Listing 8-79 shows the SQL using the SDO_NUM_RES parameter. The SDO_BATCH_SIZE parameter can come in handy when screening for buildings of a certain type.

Listing 8-79. *Identifying the Five Closest Buildings to a Helicopter Trajectory*

```
SQL> SET numformat 99999
SELECT id, SDO_NN_DISTANCE(1) dist FROM trip_route t, city_buildings c
           WHERE SDO_NN(c.geom, t.trajectory,  'sdo_num_res=3', 1)='TRUE'
           ORDER BY dist;

    ID   DIST
------ ------
    14      0
    16    187
    10    321

3 rows selected.
```

Since we didn't specify the UNITS parameter in the previous query, the distances reported in the query result are in the default distance FEET. You can determine the units using the coordinate System Reference ID (SRID) for the data. In this case, the data has an SRID of 7407, a compound coordinate system. As determined by Listing 8-80 (also check Listing 4-10), this compound system combines a horizontal coordinate system (for first two dimensions) identified by CMPD_HORIZ_SRID and a vertical coordinate system (for the third dimension) identified by CMPD_VERT_SRID.

Listing 8-80. *Identifying the Component SRIDs for Compound Coordinate System 7407*

```
SQL> SELECT srid, cmpd_horiz_srid, cmpd_vert_srid
FROM sdo_coord_ref_sys WHERE srid=7407;
  SRID       CMPD_HORIZ_SRID     CMPD_VERT_SRID
  ------     ---------------     --------------
  7407       32037               5702
```

The horizontal coordinate system SRID is 32037, and the vertical coordinate system SRID is 5702.

You can then examine the wktext for the horizontal SRID in the cs_srs table and search for the UNIT string as shown in Listing 8-81.

Listing 8-81. *Identifying the Units for Horizontal Coordinate System SRID 32037*

```
SQL> SELECT wktext FROM cs_srs WHERE srid=32037;
WKTEXT
--------------------------------------------------------------------------------
PROJCS ["NAD27 / Texas North",
 GEOGCS[ "NAD27",
   DATUM ["North American Datum 1927 (EPSG ID 6267)",
      SPHEROID
        ["Clarke 1866 (EPSG ID 7008)", 6378206.4,
         294.978698213905820761610537123195175418],
         -3, 142, 183, 0, 0, 0, 0],
   PRIMEM [ "Greenwich", 0.000000 ],
   UNIT ["Decimal Degree", 0.01745329251994328]
 ],
 PROJECTION ["Lambert Conformal Conic"], PARAMETER ["Latitude_Of_Origin", 34],
 PARAMETER ["Central_Meridian", -101.5], PARAMETER ["Standard_Parallel_1", 34.65],
 PARAMETER ["Standard_Parallel_2", 36.183333333333333333333333333333333333],
 PARAMETER ["False_Easting", 2000000],
 PARAMETER ["False_Northing", 0],
 UNIT ["U.S. Foot", .3048006096012192024384048768097536195072]
]
```

You can see in the last line that UNIT is U.S. Foot for the horizontal SRID 32037. You can then identify the units for the vertical coordinate system by looking up the value after UoM in the result of Listing 8-82. You can note that the unit is ftUS, which is the equivalent of USFoot for horizontal component.

Listing 8-82. *Identifying the Units for Vertical Coordinate System SRID 5702*

```
SQL> SELECT coord_sys_name FROM sdo_coord_sys a, sdo_crs_vertical b
    WHERE b.srid=5702 and a.coord_sys_id = b.coord_sys_id;
COORD_SYS_NAME
----------------------------------------------------------------------
Gravity-related CS. Axis: height (H). Orientation: up.  UoM: ftUS.
```

Although convoluted, the SQL examples in Listings 8-80 to 8-82 illustrate how to ascertain that the default units in the horizontal and vertical coordinate systems of a compound coordinate system are equivalent.

Caution If the units of horizontal and vertical components of a compound coordinate system are different, Oracle does not normalize the distances (in the first release of Oracle 11*g*[6]), and the resulting distance computations using all three dimensions (two dimensions from the horizontal and one dimension from the vertical coordinate system) may be incorrect.

What if you want to identify buildings within a specified distance from the trajectory? You can utilize the SDO_WITHIN_DISTANCE operator for this purpose. Listing 8-83 shows the SQL for identifying buildings that are within 200 units of distance from the trajectory.

5. This may change in subsequent releases and patches of Oracle 11*g*.

Listing 8-83. *Identifying the Closest Buildings to a Helicopter Trajectory Within 200 Feet*

```
SQL> SELECT id FROM trip_route t, city_buildings c
            WHERE SDO_WITHIN_DISTANCE(c.geom, t.trajectory,
                 'distance = 200 unit=FOOT ')='TRUE'
            ORDER BY id;

        ID
----------
        14
        16

2 rows selected.
```

■ **Caution** If the data is in Geographic3D coordinate systems, the distance computation is on the geodetic surface (that is, height is ignored). Only compound coordinate systems, such as SRID 7407, that use the projected 2D component should be used for explicit consideration of the height as the third dimension. Please refer to Chapter 4 to understand how to identify compound coordinate systems. You can refer to the Oracle Spatial User's Guide for details on how to create a new compound coordinate system that combines a specific projected coordinate system with a vertical coordinate system.

Besides being useful in city modeling, medical, virtual reality, and gaming applications, three-dimensional querying will come in handy when creating impressive three-dimensional visualization scenarios using tools such as Google Earth, LandXplorer, 3D StudioMax, Maya, and Aristoteles.

Summary

In this chapter, we discussed how to perform proximity analysis using spatial indexes and associated operators. We explained how to create spatial indexes on SDO_GEOMETRY columns of Oracle tables. Once these indexes are created, they help in the fast processing of several spatial operators that are useful in proximity analysis. These operators include SDO_NN and SDO_WITHIN_DISTANCE, which provide distance-based analysis, and SDO_RELATE and SDO_FILTER, which provide interaction-based analysis.

The majority of the functionality described in this chapter (except that in the "Advanced Spatial Index Features" section) is part of Locator, which is included with the Oracle Database Server. As a result, most applications running on Oracle can readily leverage this functionality for supporting proximity analysis. In the next chapter, we will complement this analysis with additional functions on SDO_GEOMETRY objects.

CHAPTER 9

Geometry Processing Functions

To run the examples in this chapter, you need to import the following datasets:

```
imp spatial/spatial file=app_data_with_loc.dmp ignore=y full=y
imp spatial/spatial file=citybldgs.dmp full=y ignore=y
imp spatial/spatial file=map_large.dmp full=y ignore=y
```

In Chapter 8, we discussed how to perform proximity analysis using a spatial index and associated spatial operators. In this chapter, we describe *geometry processing* functions, which are also referred to as *spatial functions* (whenever there is no ambiguity), which complement this functionality. In contrast to the spatial operators, these geometry processing functions

- do not require a spatial index,
- provide more detailed analyses than the spatial operators associated with a spatial index, and
- can appear in the SELECT list (as well as the WHERE clause) of a SQL statement.

We supplement the customer analysis and sales region analysis of Chapter 8 with the additional types of analyses presented in Table 9-1, which use the spatial functions described in this chapter. The new analyses are shown in bold in the table.

The analyses in Table 9-1 are much more detailed than was possible in Table 8-1 using spatial indexes and associated operators. In this chapter, you will learn about spatial functions that enable such complex analysis on SDO_GEOMETRY objects. These spatial functions can be classified into the following broad categories:

- *Buffering functions*: The SDO_BUFFER function creates a buffer around an existing SDO_GEOMETRY object. The object can be of any type—point, line, polygon, or collection. For instance, you can create buffers around the point locations in the branches table. The buffers created around such business/branch locations may represent the *sales regions* for those businesses/branches.
- *Relationship analysis functions*: These functions determine the relationship between two SDO_GEOMETRY objects. For example, using these functions, you can compute the distance between a potential customer and a branch (business) location (then you can know whether the customer is within a quarter-mile from the branch location). Alternatively, you can determine whether a customer or a supplier is *inside* a specified buffer zone around a branch location.

- *Geometry combination functions*: These functions perform intersection, union, and other geometry combination functions on pairs of geometries. You can use these functions to identify pairs of sales regions that intersect (or overlap) and find the intersection areas. You can target customers in these intersection areas for specific promotions.
- *Geometric analysis functions*: These functions perform analysis such as area calculations on individual geometric objects. For instance, for the overlap region of two sales regions, you can compute the area and check whether this area (of the overlap region) is significantly large. If it is, then the corresponding branch locations can be marked as potential candidates for *merging*.
- *Aggregate functions*: The preceding analysis functions analyze individual or pairs of geometries. Spatial also has *aggregate* functions that perform *aggregation* analyses on an arbitrary set of geometries instead of individual or pairs of geometries. These sets of geometries can result from any arbitrary selection criterion in the `WHERE` clause of a SQL statement.

Table 9-1. *Augmenting Proximity Analyses from Table 8-1 Using Geometry Processing Functions*

Analysis Type	Description
Customer analysis	Identify customers nearest to, or within a specified radius from, a branch or a competitor. For customers close to a competitor, you might provide certain promotions to retain them. You may specifically target this analysis on `GOLD` customers whom you want to retain at any cost. **Identify appropriate regions to start a new branch (in other words, a new business unit) to cater to a group of customers.**
Sales region analysis	Build sales regions (in other words, quarter-mile buffers) around branch and competitor locations. Identify which of these overlap one another or overlap state and county boundaries. If sales regions of branches overlap substantially, you could merge such branches. **Create buffers around branches and competitors to indicate sales regions or coverage. Identify the overlapping portion of two sales regions, determine the area of the overlapping portion, examine the customer population in this portion, and so on. If the area exceeds a threshold and the number of customers is significant, you may consider merging the sales regions (in other words, merging the corresponding branches). Determine the total coverage of all the branches (or store locations). This indicates in which parts of the city/country the business has a presence and in which parts the business is not represented. Identify the coverage of competitors (or a specific competitor), and target customers who are in exclusive regions of the coverage.**

With the exception of the spatial aggregate functions, all other spatial functions discussed in this chapter are part of the SDO_GEOM package. This means you can use them as SDO_GEOM.<function_name> in SQL statements. These functions can appear wherever a user-defined function can occur in a SQL statement. The spatial aggregate functions, on the other hand, can appear only in the SELECT list of a SQL statement.

For three-dimensional objects, only the following relationship functions are supported in Oracle 11*g* Release 1: distance (for computing the distance between two three-dimensional geometries), closestpoints (for finding the closest pair of points on two geometries), and anyinteract (for determining whether two three-dimensional geometries intersect). For three-dimensional objects, only the following geometric analysis functions are supported: length, area, and volume. You can use these functions via the SDO_GEOM PL/SQL package or via the J3D_Geometry class in the Java API. The J3D_Geometry class (first discussed in Chapter 7) extends the JGeometry class for three-dimensional objects and defines specific methods to implement this functionality.

Most of the spatial functions described previously take one or two SDO_GEOMETRY arguments, a tolerance argument, and other optional arguments. The tolerance argument has the same meaning as described in Chapter 8. To recap, tolerance in a geometry reflects the distance that two points must be apart to be considered different (for example, to accommodate rounding errors). The tolerance for *geodetic*[1] geometries (where interpolation between points is the shortest distance on the surface of the earth) is specified in meters and is usually set to 0.1 or 0.5. For nongeodetic geometries, this tolerance will be set based on the application.

In this chapter, we discuss each of the spatial functions in turn. We use these functions to perform analyses on two sets of data:

- The branches and customers tables of the business application
- The us_states, us_counties, and us_parks tables that constitute the geographic data in the business application

Buffering Functions

The first function we discuss is SDO_BUFFER. This function constructs a buffer around a specified geometric object or a set of geometric objects. For instance, you can use this function to create a quarter-mile buffer around a delivery site location. This buffer geometry will be a circle around the delivery site with a radius of a quarter mile. Likewise, a buffer around an L-shaped road will be the merged area of two sausage shapes (flattened ovals), one for each segment of the road.

Figure 9-1 shows examples of the constructed buffers for different types of geometries, with the pre-buffered geometries shown. Note that only simple geometries are shown here. The SDO_BUFFER function can work with complex SDO_GEOMETRY objects, such as compound polygons and collections. Note that if the input geometric object has a large enough interior hole, the resultant buffer zone may also have an interior hole (but one that is shrunk in size, as shown in the polygon with a hole in Figure 9-1).

1. To determine whether a geometry is *geodetic*, look at the SRID value, and compare it to those in the MDSYS.GEODETIC_SRIDS table.

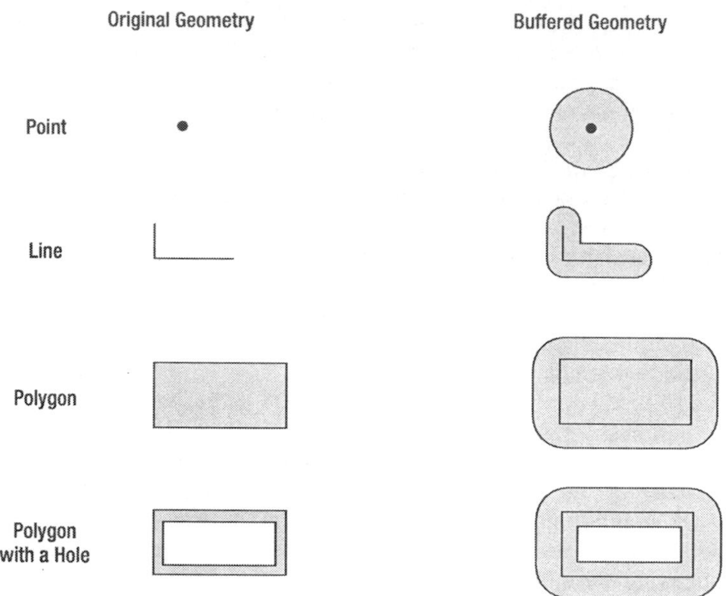

Figure 9-1. *Geometric objects and buffered geometries for some simple types*

Next, let's examine how to construct these buffers using the SDO_BUFFER function. This function has the following syntax:

```
SDO_BUFFER
(
  geometry      IN SDO_GEOMETRY,
  distance      IN NUMBER,
  tolerance     IN NUMBER
  [, params     IN VARCHAR2]
)
RETURNS an SDO_GEOMETRY
```

where the following is true:

- geometry is a parameter that specifies an SDO_GEOMETRY object to be buffered.
- distance is a parameter that specifies a numerical distance to buffer the input geometry.
- tolerance is a parameter that specifies the tolerance.
- params is the optional fourth argument that specifies two parameters, unit=<value_string> and arc_tolerance=<value_number>.

The unit=<value_string> parameter specifies the unit in which the distance is specified. You can obtain possible values for the units by consulting the MDSYS.SDO_DIST_UNITS table.

The arc_tolerance=<value_number> parameter is required if the geometry is geodetic (in other words, if SDO_SRID in the geometry is set to a geodetic SRID such as 8307 or 8265). In geodetic space, arcs are not permitted. Instead, they are represented using straight-line approximations. The arc tolerance parameter specifies the maximum distance between an arc and its straight-line approximation. Figure 9-2 shows this arc tolerance.

Figure 9-2. *The arc tolerance is the maximum distance between the arc and the lines approximating the arc.*

You should note the following:

- `arc_tolerance` always has to be greater than the tolerance for the geometry.
- The tolerance is specified in units of meters for geodetic data. `arc_tolerance`, however, is always in the units specified in `parameter_string`.
- The `units` parameter, if specified, applies to both `arc_tolerance` and the buffer distance.

Using this signature, you can construct a quarter-mile buffer around each branch location in the `branches` table, as shown in Listing 9-1. We're storing these buffers in a `sales_regions` table for use in subsequent analysis.

Listing 9-1. *Creating Buffers Around Branches*

```
SQL> CREATE TABLE sales_regions AS
SELECT id,
SDO_GEOM.SDO_BUFFER(b.location, 0.25, 0.5, 'arc_tolerance=0.005 unit=mile') geom
FROM branches b
```

Note that the first parameter is the geometry to be buffered. The second parameter specifies the buffer distance as 0.25. The third parameter specifies the tolerance to be 0.5 meters, which is the tolerance unit for geodetic geometries. The `parameter_string` parameter in the fourth argument specifies the units for the buffer distance (of 0.25). In this case, the units are miles. The buffer distance, then, is 0.25 miles. Additionally, the `parameter_string` parameter also specifies an arc tolerance of 0.005. Since the units are miles, the arc tolerance will be interpreted as 0.005 miles (equivalent to 26.4 feet or 8.1 meters).

Likewise, you can create buffers around competitor stores, as shown in Listing 9-2.

Listing 9-2. *Creating Buffers Around Competitor Locations*

```
SQL>  CREATE TABLE COMPETITORS_SALES_REGIONS AS
SELECT id,
SDO_GEOM.SDO_BUFFER(cmp.location, 0.25, 0.5, 'unit=mile arc_tolerance=0.005') geom
FROM competitors cmp
```

Note that you need to create spatial indexes for both tables. You can refer to Chapter 8 for details on how to create the metadata and the spatial index. Here, we provide the script to do just that:

```
Rem Metadata for Sales_regions table
SQL> INSERT INTO user_sdo_geom_metadata
SELECT 'SALES_REGIONS',
'GEOM', diminfo, srid FROM user_sdo_geom_metadata
WHERE table_name='BRANCHES';

Rem Metadata for Competitors_sales_regions table
SQL> INSERT INTO user_sdo_geom_metadata
SELECT 'COMPETITORS_SALES_REGIONS',
'GEOM', diminfo, srid FROM user_sdo_geom_metadata
WHERE table_name='COMPETITORS';
```

```
Rem Index-creation for Sales_regions table
SQL> CREATE INDEX sr_sidx ON sales_regions(geom)
INDEXTYPE IS mdsys.spatial_index;

Rem Index-creation for Competitors_sales_regions table
SQL> CREATE INDEX cr_sidx ON competitors_sales_regions(geom)
INDEXTYPE IS mdsys.spatial_index;
```

Relationship Analysis Functions

In the following sections, we cover two functions to analyze the relationship between two SDO_GEOMETRY objects. The first function is SDO_DISTANCE. This function determines how far apart two geometries are. The second function is RELATE. This function determines whether two geometries interact in any specified manner. For instance, you can use this function to identify whether there are any customers *inside* the buffers created in Listing 9-2.

SDO_DISTANCE

The SDO_DISTANCE function computes the *minimum* distance between any two points on the two geometries. Figure 9-3 shows some examples. This distance computation takes into account both vertices and the interpolated curves of each geometry. In the line geometry example, one of the vertices of the line is closest to the second (point) geometry. In the polygon example, one of the curves is closest to the second (point) geometry.

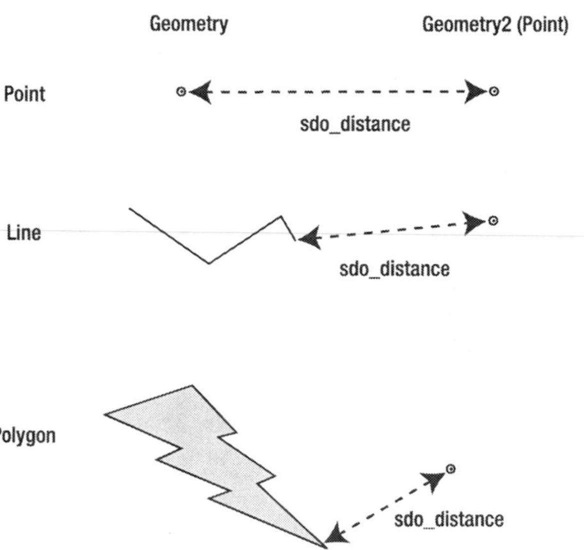

Figure 9-3. *The* SDO_DISTANCE *function for different pairs of geometric objects*

The SDO_DISTANCE function has the following syntax:

```
SDO_DISTANCE
(
  geometry1        IN SDO_GEOMETRY,
  geometry2        IN SDO_GEOMETRY,
```

```
  tolerance         IN NUMBER
  [, params         IN VARCHAR2]
)
  RETURNS a NUMBER
```

where the following is true:

- geometry1 and geometry2 are the first two arguments, and they specify SDO_GEOMETRY objects.
- tolerance specifies the tolerance for the dataset. For geodetic data, this is usually 0.5 or 0.1 (0.5 meters or 0.1 meters). For nongeodetic data, this is set appropriately to avoid rounding errors (see Chapter 8 for details).
- params is the optional fourth parameter in a string of the form 'unit=<value_string>'. This specifies the units in which the distance should be returned. You can obtain possible values for the units by consulting the MDSYS.SDO_DIST_UNITS table.

This function returns the minimum distance between geometry1 and geometry2 in the units specified. If no unit is specified, the default unit for the coordinate system is used (this can be determined by inspecting the SDO_SRID attribute in the SDO_GEOMETRY objects and looking at the WKTEXT attribute in the MDSYS.CS_SRS table for that SRID).

Using this function, you can identify the customers within a quarter-mile radius of a competitor location, as shown in Listing 9-3.

Listing 9-3. *Identifying Customers Within a Quarter-Mile of a Competitor Location*

```
SQL> SELECT ct.id, ct.name
FROM competitors comp, customers ct
WHERE comp.id=1
AND SDO_GEOM.SDO_DISTANCE(ct.location, comp.location, 0.5, 'unit=mile') < 0.25
ORDER BY ct.id;
        ID NAME
---------- -----------------------------------
        25 BLAKE CONSTRUCTION
        28 COLONIAL PARKING
        34 HEWLETT-PACKARD DC GOV AFFAIRS
        41 MCGREGOR PRINTING
        48 POTOMAC ELECTRIC POWER
        50 SMITH HINCHMAN AND GRYLLS
       270 METRO-FARRAGUT NORTH STATION
       271 METRO-FARRAGUT WEST STATION
       468 SAFEWAY
       809 LINCOLN SUITES
       810 HOTEL LOMBARDY
      1044 MUSEUM OF THE THIRD DIMENSION
      1526 INTERNATIONAL FINANCE
      1538 MCKENNA AND CUNEO
      2195 STEVENS ELEMENTARY SCHOOL
      6326 HOTEL LOMBARDY
      7754 EXECUTIVE INN
      7762 PHILLIPS 66
      7789 SEVEN BUILDINGS
      7821 RENAISSANCE MAYFLOWER HOTEL
      8138 ST GREGORY HOTEL
      8382 EXXON
      8792 DESTINATION HOTEL & RESORTS

23 rows selected.
```

Note that the preceding query will have the same semantics as Listing 8-20, which uses the SDO_WITHIN_DISTANCE operator. The SDO_WITHIN_DISTANCE operator in Listing 8-20 uses the spatial index, but the SDO_GEOM.SDO_DISTANCE function does not. As a result, Listing 9-3 will be much slower in comparison. You should use the SDO_WITHIN_DISTANCE operator wherever possible. You should use the SDO_DISTANCE function to do only the following:

- To operate on nonindexed tables
- To augment the SDO_WITHIN_DISTANCE operator

Here is an example of where the SDO_DISTANCE function will come in handy. In Listing 9-4, the SDO_WITHIN_DISTANCE operator identifies the rows that are within a specified distance. The SDO_DISTANCE function in the SELECT list of the SQL identifies the exact distance of each of these rows to the query geometry. Note that the unit is specified as yard in the SDO_DISTANCE function. As a result, the distances are returned in yards.

Listing 9-4. *Using the* SDO_DISTANCE *Function with the* SDO_WITHIN_DISTANCE *Spatial Operator in SQL*

```
SQL> SELECT ct.id, ct.name,
SDO_GEOM.SDO_DISTANCE(ct.location, comp.location, 0.5, 'unit=yard')  distance
FROM competitors comp, customers ct
WHERE comp.id=1
  AND SDO_WITHIN_DISTANCE
  (ct.location, comp.location, 'distance=0.25 unit=mile')='TRUE'
ORDER BY ct.id;
        ID NAME                                 DISTANCE
---------- ---------------------------------- ----------
        25 BLAKE CONSTRUCTION                 319.038526
        28 COLONIAL PARKING                   398.262506
        34 HEWLETT-PACKARD DC GOV AFFAIRS     427.660664
        41 MCGREGOR PRINTING                  350.463038
        48 POTOMAC ELECTRIC POWER             354.721567
        50 SMITH HINCHMAN AND GRYLLS          252.366911
       270 METRO-FARRAGUT NORTH STATION       344.955038
       271 METRO-FARRAGUT WEST STATION        271.905717
       468 SAFEWAY                            252.001358
       809 LINCOLN SUITES                     103.915921
       810 HOTEL LOMBARDY                     313.088568
      1044 MUSEUM OF THE THIRD DIMENSION      152.658273
      1526 INTERNATIONAL FINANCE              235.987835
      1538 MCKENNA AND CUNEO                  96.9728115
      2195 STEVENS ELEMENTARY SCHOOL          304.662483
      6326 HOTEL LOMBARDY                     329.301433
      7754 EXECUTIVE INN                      374.571287
      7762 PHILLIPS 66                        302.628637
      7789 SEVEN BUILDINGS                    354.721567
      7821 RENAISSANCE MAYFLOWER HOTEL        322.143941
      8138 ST GREGORY HOTEL                   359.219279
      8382 EXXON                              326.165809
      8792 DESTINATION HOTEL & RESORTS        159.234843

23 rows selected.
```

You can also use the SDO_DISTANCE function on three-dimensional objects. Listing 9-5 shows the SQL for determining the distance between a helicopter trajectory and, say, one of the closest buildings, building 16 (from Figure 8-12). Since the buildings are modeled as three-dimensional solids and the helicopter trip route is modeled as a three-dimensional line string, the distance will be the three-dimensional distance. From Listing 9-5, you can understand that building 16 is 150.0003 feet away from the helicopter trajectory.

Listing 9-5. *Using the* `SDO_DISTANCE` *Function to Determine the Distance Between Building 16 and the Helicopter Trajectory*

```
SQL> SELECT cbldg.id,
  SDO_GEOM.SDO_DISTANCE(cbldg.geom, tr.trajectory, 0.05, 'UNIT=foot') dist
FROM trip_route tr, city_buildings cbldg
WHERE cbldg.id=16;

        ID           DIST
----------      ----------
        16      187.258607
```

In Java, you can perform the same distance operation using the distance method in the `J3D_Geometry` class. As described in Chapter 7, to read `J3D_Geometry` objects from the database, proceed the same way as with `JGeometry`, and then construct a `J3D_Geometry` object from the `JGeometry` object. You can then compute the distance between the `J3D_Geometry` objects, `traj` and `bldg16`, corresponding to the helicopter trajectory and building 16. Listing 9-6 shows the code snippet that is equivalent to Listing 9-5. Note the second argument to the `distance` function is the value for the tolerance (see Chapter 3 for appropriate values).

Listing 9-6. *Using the* `J3D_Geometry.DISTANCE` *Method to Determine the Distance Between Building 16 and the Helicopter Trajectory*

```
// Assume traj and bldg16 represent the J3D_Geometry objects
// for trajectory and building 16
double dist = traj.distance(bldg16, tol);
```

Note For three-dimensional *geodetic* geometries, the distance computed is always the two-dimensional (ground) distance.

SDO_CLOSEST_POINTS

In the previous examples, you computed the distance between two geometries. In Listings 9-5 and 9-6, the geometries are three-dimensional city buildings and a helicopter trajectory. (Likewise, in Listing 9-4, the geometries are two-dimensional locations of competitor businesses and customers.) What if you want not just the distance but also the closest point of approach? In other words, what if you want to find the specific points on the building and the trajectory that are the closest? You can obtain such closest points using the `SDO_CLOSEST_POINTS` procedure (notice that it is not a function) in the `SDO_GEOM` package in PL/SQL. The syntax for this procedure is as follows:

```
SDO_CLOSEST_POINTS
(
  geometry1        IN SDO_GEOMETRY,
  geometry2        IN SDO_GEOMETRY,
  tolerance        IN NUMBER,
  params           IN VARCHAR2,
  dist             OUT NUMBER,
  pt1              OUT SDO_GEOMETRY,
  pt2              OUT SDO_GEOMETRY
)
```

where the following is true:

- `geometry1` and `geometry2` are the `SDO_GEOMETRY` objects for which you want the distance and the closest points computed.
- `tolerance` specifies the tolerance for the dataset. For geodetic data, this is usually 0.5 or 0.1 (0.5 meters or 0.1 meters). For nongeodetic data, this is set appropriately to avoid rounding errors (see Chapter 8 for details).
- `params` is a string of the form `'unit=<value_string>'`. This specifies the units in which the distance should be returned. You can obtain possible values for the units by consulting the `MDSYS.SDO_DIST_UNITS` table.

The procedure returns the following values:

- `dist` is the distance between `geometry1` and `geometry2`.
- `pt1` is the point on `geometry1` that contributes to this distance.
- `pt2` is the point on `geometry2` that contributes to this distance.

You can use this function to compute the closest points on building 16 and the helicopter trajectory as in Listing 9-7. (Note that the SRIDs were set to `NULL` because this procedure is returning an error with the default SRID of 7407 (bug 6201938). Observe that the procedure returns a distance of 150 feet and the closest points on building 16 and the helicopter trajectory that have this distance.

■Note If there are multiple pairs satisfying the same closest distance, *any one* of those pairs is returned.

Listing 9-7. *Obtaining the Closest Points on Building 16 and Helicopter Trajectory*

```
set serverout on
declare
  traj sdo_geometry;
  bldg16 sdo_geometry;
  dist number;
  trajpt sdo_geometry;
  bldg16pt sdo_geometry;
begin
  select geom INTO bldg16 from city_buildings where id=16;
  select trajectory into traj from trip_route where rownum<=1;
  bldg16.sdo_srid:=null;   -- Workaround for Bug 6201938
  traj.sdo_srid:=null;         -- Workaround for Bug 6201938

  sdo_geom.sdo_closest_points(traj, bldg16, 0.05, 'UNIT=FOOT',
                             dist, trajpt, bldg16pt);
  dbms_output.put_line('Distance= '  || TO_CHAR(dist));
  dbms_output.put_line('Pt on Trajectory:' ||
    TO_CHAR(trajpt.sdo_point.x) || ',  ' ||
    TO_CHAR(trajpt.sdo_point.y) || ',  ' ||
    TO_CHAR(trajpt.sdo_point.z));
  dbms_output.put_line('Pt on Bldg16:' ||
    TO_CHAR(bldg16pt.sdo_point.x) || ',  ' ||
    TO_CHAR(bldg16pt.sdo_point.y) || ',  ' ||
    TO_CHAR(bldg16pt.sdo_point.z));

end;
/
```

```
Distance= 187.258232
Pt on Trajectory:29217975.2129243, 43368860.78637, 685.800311
Pt on Bldg16:29217954.2883524, 43368850.4882017, 500

PL/SQL procedure successfully completed.
```

The corresponding method in the J3D_Geometry class is called closestPoints. Given an input geometry and tolerance value as arguments, this method computes the closest points on the reference geometry and the input geometry and returns them as an ArrayList. In contrast to the PL/SQL procedure, the equivalent closestPoints in the Java API does not return the distance. You have to call distance separately to get the distance. Listing 9-8 shows the Java code snippet for Listing 9-7.

Listing 9-8. *Finding the Closest Points Using the* J3D_Geometry *Java API*

```
// Assume traj and bldg16 represent the J3D_Geometry objects
// for trajectory and building 16

  ArrayList closest_pts = traj.closestPoints(bldg16, tol);  // tol is the tolerance
  J3D_Geometry pt1 = (J3D_Geometry) closest_pts.get(0);
  J3D_Geometry pt2 = (J3D_Geometry) closest_pts.get(1);
  Double dist = pt1.distance(pt2, tol);
```

RELATE

In Listing 9-2, you created buffers around competitor locations. What do you do with these buffers around the branch locations and competitor locations? You can perform relationship analysis to identify customers inside these sales regions and competitor regions. You can do this using either the SDO_RELATE operator (as in described in Chapter 8) or the RELATE function in the SDO_GEOM package. The RELATE function has the following syntax:

```
RELATE
(
  Geometry_A      IN SDO_GEOMETRY,
  mask,           IN VARCHAR2,
  Geometry_Q,     IN SDO_GEOMETRY,
  Tolerance       IN NUMBER
)
RETURNS a relationship of type VARCHAR2
```

where the following is true:

- Geometry_A and Geometry_Q are arguments that specify geometric objects.
- The mask argument can take one of the following values:
    - DETERMINE, which determines the relationship or interaction Geometry_A has with Geometry_Q
    - Any relationship specified in Figure 8-8, including the following: INSIDE, COVEREDBY, COVERS, CONTAINS, EQUAL, OVERLAPBDYDISJOINT, OVERLAPBDYINTERSECT, ON, and TOUCH
    - ANYINTERACT if any of the preceding relationships holds
    - DISJOINT if none of the preceding relationships holds

This RELATE function returns the following:

- 'TRUE' if the geometries intersect and the ANYINTERACT mask is specified
- The value of mask if Geometry_A satisfies the specified mask-type relationship with Geometry_Q
- 'FALSE' if the relationship between the geometries does not match the relationship specified in the second argument, mask
- The type of relationship, if the mask is set to 'DETERMINE'

Using this signature for the RELATE function, you can perform proximity analyses using your buffer zones around branches and competitors. You can identify all customers who are in competitors_sales_regions (in other words, the buffer zones around competitors), as shown in Listing 9-9.

Listing 9-9. *Identifying Customers in a Competitor's Sales Region*

```
SQL> SELECT ct.id, ct.name
FROM customers ct, competitors_sales_regions comp
WHERE SDO_GEOM.RELATE (ct.location, 'INSIDE',  comp.geom, 0.5) = 'INSIDE'
  AND comp.id=1
ORDER BY ct.id;
        ID NAME
---------- -----------------------------------
        25 BLAKE CONSTRUCTION
        28 COLONIAL PARKING
        34 HEWLETT-PACKARD DC GOV AFFAIRS
        41 MCGREGOR PRINTING
        48 POTOMAC ELECTRIC POWER
        50 SMITH HINCHMAN AND GRYLLS
       270 METRO-FARRAGUT NORTH STATION
       271 METRO-FARRAGUT WEST STATION
       468 SAFEWAY
       809 LINCOLN SUITES
       810 HOTEL LOMBARDY
      1044 MUSEUM OF THE THIRD DIMENSION
      1526 INTERNATIONAL FINANCE
      1538 MCKENNA AND CUNEO
      2195 STEVENS ELEMENTARY SCHOOL
      6326 HOTEL LOMBARDY
      7754 EXECUTIVE INN
      7762 PHILLIPS 66
      7789 SEVEN BUILDINGS
      7821 RENAISSANCE MAYFLOWER HOTEL
      8138 ST GREGORY HOTEL
      8382 EXXON
      8792 DESTINATION HOTEL & RESORTS

23 rows selected.
```

Note that this query returns only those customers at a distance of less than 0.25 miles from (in other words, that are inside the sales region of) the specified competitor (id=1). This does not, however, return the customers who are exactly 0.25 miles from the competitor (in other words, those that touch or are on the boundary of the competitor buffer zone). To include those, you can simply specify the ANYINTERACT mask, as shown in Listing 9-10. Note that the function is compared with

'TRUE' instead of 'ANYINTERACT'.[2] Note that the result of Listing 9-10 is the same as that of Listing 9-9 because there are no customers on the boundary (but there may be a difference for other datasets or query windows).

Listing 9-10. *Identifying Customers Who Interact with a Competitor's Sales Region*

```
SQL> SELECT ct.id, ct.name
FROM customers ct, competitors_sales_regions comp
WHERE SDO_GEOM.RELATE (ct.location, 'ANYINTERACT',  comp.geom, 0.5) = 'TRUE'
  AND comp.id=1
ORDER BY ct.id;

        ID NAME
---------- -----------------------------------
        25 BLAKE CONSTRUCTION
        28 COLONIAL PARKING
        34 HEWLETT-PACKARD DC GOV AFFAIRS
        41 MCGREGOR PRINTING
        48 POTOMAC ELECTRIC POWER
        50 SMITH HINCHMAN AND GRYLLS
       270 METRO-FARRAGUT NORTH STATION
       271 METRO-FARRAGUT WEST STATION
       468 SAFEWAY
       809 LINCOLN SUITES
       810 HOTEL LOMBARDY
      1044 MUSEUM OF THE THIRD DIMENSION
      1526 INTERNATIONAL FINANCE
      1538 MCKENNA AND CUNEO
      2195 STEVENS ELEMENTARY SCHOOL
      6326 HOTEL LOMBARDY
      7754 EXECUTIVE INN
      7762 PHILLIPS 66
      7789 SEVEN BUILDINGS
      7821 RENAISSANCE MAYFLOWER HOTEL
      8138 ST GREGORY HOTEL
      8382 EXXON
      8792 DESTINATION HOTEL & RESORTS

23 rows selected.
```

For three-dimensional geometries, you can specify the ANYINTERACT mask only as the second argument to the RELATE function. Using the SQL in Listing 9-11, you can determine which buildings intersect the helicopter trajectory using the SDO_GEOM.RELATE function.

Listing 9-11. *Identifying Buildings That Intersect the Helicopter Trajectory*

```
SQL> SELECT cbldg.id
FROM city_buildings cbldg, trip_route tr
WHERE SDO_GEOM.RELATE (cbldg.geom, 'ANYINTERACT',  tr.trajectory, 0.5) = 'TRUE';
        ID
----------
        14
```

2. You have to specify the masks in single quotes as is the case with all Oracle strings.

Note For three-dimensional geometries, you can specify the ANYINTERACT mask only in the RELATE function. If you specify any other mask, it will return "no rows selected" (the behavior may change in future releases).

The equivalent method in J3D_Geometry for determining ANYINTERACT type of relationship between two geometries is the anyInteract method in the J3D_Geometry class. Listing 9-12 shows the Java code snippet for Listing 9-11. The anyInteract method takes a building geometry bldg and a tolerance value tol and returns true if the bldg intersects with the reference geometry, in this case, the trajectory.

Listing 9-12. *Using the* J3D_Geometry.anyinteract *Method to Determine the Buildings That Intersect the Helicopter Trajectory*

```
// Assume ids of the buildings from city_buildings table
// are fetched into the ArrayList idarr;
// and corresponding geom column is fetched into the ArrayList bldgarr
for (int i=0; i<bldg_geom.length; i++) {
   J3D_Geometry bldg = (J3D_Geometry) bldgarr.get(i);
   int id = idarr.get(i);
   if (traj.anyInteract(bldg, tol) = true) // tol is the tolerance value
     System.out.println(id);
}
```

When to Use the RELATE Function

Observe that the result in Listing 9-11 is the same as that in Listing 8-69 from Chapter 8 where you used the SDO_RELATE operator to perform the same analysis but using a spatial index. The SDO_GEOM.RELATE function, as mentioned earlier, does not utilize the spatial index and evaluates for all rows (in other words, all possible pairs in the tables city_buildings and trip_route). Likewise, for the two-dimensional data/query in Listing 9-10, notice that the result is identical to that of Listing 8-35. Again, this query uses the SDO_GEOM.RELATE spatial function, whereas the query in Listing 8-35 uses the SDO_RELATE operator. Because operators are evaluated using the spatial index, Listing 8-35 will execute faster. In contrast, the SDO_GEOM.RELATE function in Listing 9-10 does not use any index and is evaluated for every row of the customers table. This might result in a much slower evaluation. Why and when should the SDO_GEOM.RELATE function be used? The RELATE function is never to be used if the SDO_RELATE operator can serve the same purpose.

However, the SDO_GEOM.RELATE function can be useful in certain scenarios—for example, to operate on nonindexed tables or subsets of geometries such as the suppliers table in Listing 9-13. Note that the suppliers table does not have a spatial index.

Listing 9-13. *Identifying Suppliers in a Quarter-Mile Buffer Around a Competitor*

```
SQL> SELECT  s.id
FROM suppliers s, competitors_sales_regions cs
WHERE SDO_GEOM.RELATE (s.location, 'ANYINTERACT',  cs.geom, 0.5) = 'TRUE'
AND cs.id=1;
```

You can also use the SDO_GEOM.RELATE function to complement the SDO_RELATE operator. For instance, you can use the SDO_RELATE operator with the ANYINTERACT mask (or a combination of masks) to identify a candidate set of rows. You can then use the SDO_GEOM.RELATE function to determine the relationship for each row that is returned. Listing 9-14 shows how to complement the functionality of Listing 8-35 using the SDO_GEOM.RELATE function.

Listing 9-14. *Identifying Customers in a Quarter-Mile Buffer Around a Competitor*

```
SQL> SELECT  ct.id, ct.name,
SDO_GEOM.RELATE (ct.location, 'DETERMINE',  comp.geom, 0.5)  relationship
FROM customers ct, competitors_sales_regions comp
WHERE comp.id=1
  AND SDO_RELATE(ct.location, comp.geom, 'mask=anyinteract')='TRUE';

    ID NAME                                   RELATIONSHIP
------ -----------------------------------    -------------------------------------
    25 BLAKE CONSTRUCTION                     INSIDE
  7821 RENAISSANCE MAYFLOWER HOTEL            INSIDE
  8138 ST GREGORY HOTEL                       INSIDE
  8382 EXXON                                  INSIDE
  6326 HOTEL LOMBARDY                         INSIDE
  1526 INTERNATIONAL FINANCE                  INSIDE
   810 HOTEL LOMBARDY                         INSIDE
    50 SMITH HINCHMAN AND GRYLLS              INSIDE
   271 METRO-FARRAGUT WEST STATION            INSIDE
  7762 PHILLIPS 66                            INSIDE
    34 HEWLETT-PACKARD DC GOV AFFAIRS         INSIDE
  1538 MCKENNA AND CUNEO                      INSIDE
  1044 MUSEUM OF THE THIRD DIMENSION          INSIDE
    28 COLONIAL PARKING                       INSIDE
    41 MCGREGOR PRINTING                      INSIDE
  7754 EXECUTIVE INN                          INSIDE
   270 METRO-FARRAGUT NORTH STATION           INSIDE
  2195 STEVENS ELEMENTARY SCHOOL              INSIDE
   809 LINCOLN SUITES                         INSIDE
  8792 DESTINATION HOTEL & RESORTS            INSIDE
   468 SAFEWAY                                INSIDE
    48 POTOMAC ELECTRIC POWER                 INSIDE
  7789 SEVEN BUILDINGS                        INSIDE

23 rows selected.
```

Another interesting analysis that you can perform in the example business application is the identification of sales regions that intersect each other. You can use the combination of the SDO_RELATE operator to identify pairs of sales regions that intersect each other and then perform the SDO_GEOM.RELATE to determine whether they just *touch* or *overlap* with each other. Listing 9-15 shows the SQL to retrieve all sales regions that intersect a sales region with id=51.

Listing 9-15. RELATE *Function Complementing the* SDO_RELATE *Operator*

```
SQL> SELECT sra.id,
SDO_GEOM.RELATE(sra.geom, 'DETERMINE', srb.geom, 0.5) relationship
FROM sales_regions srb, sales_regions sra
WHERE srb.id=51 AND sra.id<>51 AND
  SDO_RELATE
  (sra.geom, srb.geom,
  'mask=TOUCH+OVERLAPBDYDISJOINT+OVERLAPBDYINTERSECT'
  )='TRUE'
ORDER BY sra.id;
```

```
        ID      RELATIONSHIP
----------      --------------------------------
        43      OVERLAPBDYINTERSECT
        50      OVERLAPBDYINTERSECT
        54      OVERLAPBDYINTERSECT
        63      OVERLAPBDYINTERSECT
        66      OVERLAPBDYINTERSECT
        69      OVERLAPBDYINTERSECT
        72      OVERLAPBDYINTERSECT
        75      OVERLAPBDYINTERSECT
        76      TOUCH

9 rows selected.
```

Instead of doing two queries as in Listing 8-46 and Listing 8-47, Listing 9-15 will tell you, in a single SQL query, which sales regions overlap and which touch.

■ **Tip** Use SDO_GEOM.RELATE and SDO_RELATE in combination to identify specific types of interactions.

Listing 9-15 shows the sales regions that overlap with a specific sales region (with id=51). But can you extract just the overlap (or intersection) region—that is, the area that is common to both sales regions? Based on the size of these intersection regions and the number of customers in these intersection regions, you can designate the corresponding pair of branch locations as potential candidates for merging. In the next section, we discuss functions to extract the intersection regions of overlapping geometric objects.

Geometry Combination Functions

In mathematics, two *sets of items*, A and B, can be combined using different *set-theory* operations such as A minus B, A union B, and A intersection B. Here, we cover similar functions that act on a pair of geometries instead of a pair of sets. If A and B are two geometries, the semantics of each of the geometry combination functions are illustrated in Figure 9-4.

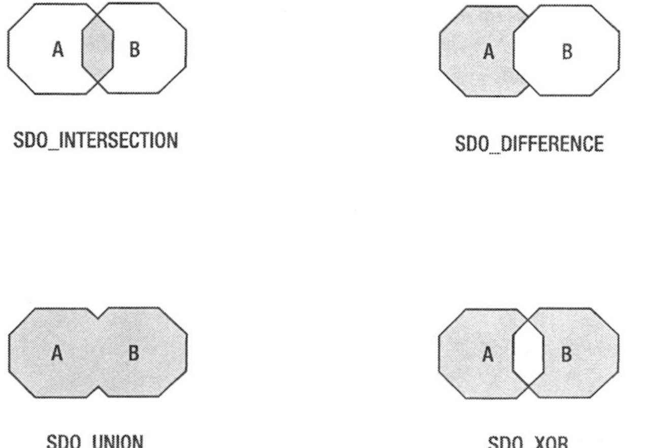

Figure 9-4. *Semantics of geometry combination functions for octagon-shaped polygon geometries A and B. The shaded region shows the result of each specific function.*

The values returned by each function described in Figure 9-4 are as follows:

- A SDO_INTERSECTION B: Returns the region of A that is also shared by B.
- A SDO_UNION B: Returns the region covered by A or B.
- A SDO_DIFFERENCE B: Returns the region covered by A that is not also covered by B.
- A SDO_XOR B: Returns the region of A and B that is not shared by both. This function is equivalent to (A SDO_UNION B) SDO_DIFFERENCE (A SDO_INTERSECTION B).

Each of these functions has the following signature:

```
SDO_<set_theory_fn>
(
  Geometry_A       IN SDO_GEOMETRY,
  Geometry_B       IN SDO_GEOMETRY,
  Tolerance        IN NUMBER
)
  RETURNS SDO_GEOMETRY
```

where the following is true:

- Geometry_A and Geometry_B are SDO_GEOMETRY objects (with the same SRIDs).
- Tolerance is the tolerance value for the geometric objects.

The function returns an SDO_GEOMETRY that computes the appropriate geometry combination function for Geometry_A with respect to Geometry_B.

Caution In Oracle 11, the geometry combination functions operate only on two-dimensional geometries. You cannot perform the union of two solids.

Now that you understand the semantics and syntax, let's look at examples of how to use these functions to perform proximity analysis.

SDO_INTERSECTION

In Listing 9-15, you identified all sales regions that overlapped (or touched) a specific sales region (with id=51). Here, you can perform more rigorous analysis with each such pair of overlapping sales regions and determine whether they are good candidates for merging.

Consider sales regions with ids 51 and 63. Listing 9-16 shows the SQL for identifying the intersection geometry for each pair of overlapping sales regions. The sales_intersection_zones table stores these intersection regions. Listing 9-17 shows the ids of sales regions that overlap with sales region 51 (the ids are the same as in Listing 9-15).

Listing 9-16. SDO_INTERSECTION *of Two Geometries*

```
SQL> CREATE TABLE sales_intersection_zones AS
SELECT sra.id id1, srb.id id2,
SDO_GEOM.SDO_INTERSECTION(a.geom, b.geom, 0.5) intsxn_geom
FROM sales_regions srb, sales_regions sra
WHERE sra.id<> srb.id
AND SDO_RELATE(sra.geom,  srb.geom, 'mask=anyinteract' )='TRUE' ;
```

Listing 9-17. *Sales Regions Intersecting the Sales Region with* `id=51`

```
SQL> SELECT id2 FROM sales_intersection_zones WHERE id1=51;
   ID2
------
    43
    50
    54
    63
    66
    69
    72
    75
    76

9 rows selected.
```

You can use the *intersection geometry* (the `intsxn_geom` column) stored in the `sales_intersection_zones` table for subsequent analysis on sales regions. Listing 9-18 shows how to use this geometry to identify customers in the intersection area of two specific sales regions with `ids` 51 and 43. The result of this SQL indicates that there are only two customers common to both sales regions.

Listing 9-18. *Identifying Customers in* `sales_ intersection_zones`

```
SQL> SELECT count(*)
FROM sales_intersection_zones siz, customers ct
WHERE siz.id1=51 AND  siz.id2=43
AND SDO_RELATE(ct.location, siz.intsxn_geom, 'mask=anyinteract')='TRUE';
  COUNT(*)
----------
         2
```

You can perform the preceding intersection analysis without materializing the intersection regions in a separate table. Listing 9-19 shows the corresponding SQL to identify customers in the intersection of sales regions 51 and 43. Note that the result is the same as that of Listing 9-18.

Listing 9-19. *Identifying Customers in the Intersection of Sales Regions 51 and 43*

```
SQL> SELECT COUNT(*)
FROM customers ct
WHERE SDO_RELATE
(
  ct.location,
  (
    SELECT SDO_GEOM.SDO_INTERSECTION(sra.geom, srb.geom, 0.5)
    FROM sales_regions sra, sales_regions srb
    WHERE sra.id = 51 and srb.id = 43
  ),
  'mask=anyinteract'
)='TRUE';
  COUNT(*)
----------
         2
```

SDO_UNION

You can use the SDO_UNION function to compute the geometry covered by two sales regions. You can then use the resulting union geometry to identify the total number of customers. Listing 9-20 shows the SQL for sales regions 43 and 51.

Listing 9-20. SDO_UNION *of Two Geometries*

```
SQL> SELECT  count(*)
FROM
(
  SELECT SDO_GEOM.SDO_UNION (sra.geom, srb.geom, 0.5) geom
  FROM sales_regions srb, sales_regions sra
  WHERE sra.id=51 and srb.id=43
) srb, customers sra
WHERE SDO_RELATE(sra.location, srb.geom, 'mask=anyinteract')='TRUE';
  COUNT(*)
----------
       124

1 row selected.
```

The number of customers returned is 124. Compare this with the two customers returned in Listing 9-19 using the intersection region. This means there are 122 customers who are not common to both sales regions. Since less than 2 percent of the customers are common to both sales regions, you may decide not to combine the two sales regions with ids 51 and 43.

What if you want to know the coverage of all your businesses in the Washington, D.C., area? This will involve not just two sales region geometries, but all geometries in the sales_regions table. You can repeatedly perform the union in an iterative fashion, as the PL/SQL procedure in Listing 9-21 demonstrates.

Listing 9-21. *Coverage of the Sales Regions: Performing a Union of All the Sales Regions*

```
CREATE TABLE sales_region_coverage (coverage SDO_GEOMETRY);
DECLARE
  coverage  SDO_GEOMETRY := NULL;
BEGIN
  FOR g IN (SELECT geom FROM sales_regions) LOOP
    coverage := SDO_GEOM.SDO_UNION(coverage, g.geom, 0.5);
  END LOOP;
  INSERT INTO sales_region_coverage values (coverage);
  COMMIT;
END;
/
```

Note that the procedure in Listing 9-21 computes the coverage by performing a union of all the sales regions and inserts the coverage geometry into the sales_region_coverage table. It assumes the table exists and contains only one column of type SDO_GEOMETRY. Later in the chapter, you will look at alternate methods using spatial aggregate functions to perform the same task.

SDO_DIFFERENCE

The SDO_DIFFERENCE function subtracts the second geometry from the first geometry. In effect, it returns the region that is exclusive to the first geometry. Note that this is meaningful only in the following situations:

- Both the first and second geometries have area (in other words, polygons or multipolygons, and so on).
- The second geometry is a polygon or a line and the first geometry is a line.
- The first geometry is a point.

If the preceding conditions are not met, the SDO_DIFFERENCE operation returns the first geometry as the result.

Using the SDO_DIFFERENCE function, you can compare the sales regions with the competitor regions, as shown in Listing 9-22. For instance, you want to target customers exclusively served by a specific competitor (with id=2). First, you identify all sales regions that intersect this competitor region using a simple SDO_RELATE query (left as an exercise to the reader). Only one sales region (id=6) intersects competitor region 2. To find customers exclusive to competitor region 2, you first compute the difference of the competitor region with respect to sales region 6. The resulting region is exclusive to competitor region 2.

Listing 9-22. SDO_DIFFERENCE *of Competitor Region 2 with Sales Region 6*

```
SQL> CREATE TABLE exclusive_region_for_comp_2 AS
SELECT SDO_GEOM.SDO_DIFFERENCE(b.geom, a.geom, 0.5) geom
FROM sales_regions sr, competitors_sales_regions csr
WHERE csr.id=2 and sr.id=6  ;
```

Once you construct the region that is exclusive to competitor region 2, you can identify customers in this exclusive zone, as shown in Listing 9-23. You probably can target such customers with special promotions to wean them from the specific competitor (id=2).

Listing 9-23. *Identifying Customers in an Exclusive Zone of a Competitor*

```
SQL> SELECT ct.id, ct.name
FROM exclusive_region_for_comp_2 excl, customers ct
WHERE SDO_RELATE(ct.location, excl.geom, 'mask=anyinteract')='TRUE'
ORDER BY ct.id;

    ID NAME
------ -----------------------------------
    51 STUDENT LOAN MARKETING
   487 GETTY
   795 FOUR SEASONS HOTEL WASHINGTON DC
   796 HOTEL MONTICELLO-GEORGETOWN
   798 GEORGETOWN SUITES
   821 LATHAM HOTEL
  1022 C AND O CANAL BOAT TRIPS
  1161 GEORGETOWN SUITES HARBOR BLDG
  1370 BIOGRAPH THEATRE
  1377 FOUNDRY
  1558 US OFFICE PRODUCTS
  2067 WASHINGTON INTERNATIONAL SCHOOL
  6685 SONESTA INTERNATIONAL HOTELS
  6953 FOUNDRY MALL
  6956 WASHINGTON HARBOUR
  6957 WASHINGTON HARBOUR
  7163 GEORGETOWN VISITOR CENTER
  7164 GEORGETOWN VISITOR CENTER
  7176 CHESAPEAKE & OHIO CANAL
  7601 MASONIC LODGE

20 rows selected.
```

Note that you can combine Listings 9-22 and 9-23 into a single SQL statement as shown in Listing 9-24. You obtain the same 20 customers as in Listing 9-23.

Listing 9-24. *Combining Listings 9-22 and 9-23*

```
SQL> SELECT  ct.id, ct.name
FROM sales_regions sr, competitors_sales_regions csr, customers ct
WHERE csr.id=2 AND sr.id=6
  AND SDO_RELATE
  (
    ct.location,
    SDO_GEOM.SDO_DIFFERENCE(csr.geom, sr.geom, 0.5),
    'mask=anyinteract'
  )='TRUE'
ORDER BY ct.id;
    ID NAME
------ -----------------------------------
    51 STUDENT LOAN MARKETING
   487 GETTY
   795 FOUR SEASONS HOTEL WASHINGTON DC
   796 HOTEL MONTICELLO-GEORGETOWN
   798 GEORGETOWN SUITES
   821 LATHAM HOTEL
  1022 C AND O CANAL BOAT TRIPS
  1161 GEORGETOWN SUITES HARBOR BLDG
  1370 BIOGRAPH THEATRE
  1377 FOUNDRY
  1558 US OFFICE PRODUCTS
  2067 WASHINGTON INTERNATIONAL SCHOOL
  6685 SONESTA INTERNATIONAL HOTELS
  6953 FOUNDRY MALL
  6956 WASHINGTON HARBOUR
  6957 WASHINGTON HARBOUR
  7163 GEORGETOWN VISITOR CENTER
  7164 GEORGETOWN VISITOR CENTER
  7176 CHESAPEAKE & OHIO CANAL
  7601 MASONIC LODGE

20 rows selected.
```

SDO_XOR

You can rewrite this function as the SDO_DIFFERENCE of the SDO_UNION and the SDO_INTERSECTION of the two geometries. You can use this function as an alternate mechanism to identify whether two overlapping sales regions need to be merged. For instance, if sales regions 1 and 2 overlap, you can compare the number of customers in the SDO_XOR of these regions to those in the SDO_UNION of these regions. If the number in the SDO_XOR is close to that in the SDO_UNION, then these two sales regions, although overlapping, have few common customers. This is the case in Listing 9-25. The result of 122 customers is close to that from the SDO_UNION (as in Listing 9-20). As a result, these sales regions don't need to be merged.

Listing 9-25. `SDO_XOR` *of Sales Regions 43 and 51 to Identify Customers Who Are Not Shared Between Them*

```
SQL> SELECT count(*)
FROM
(
  SELECT SDO_GEOM.SDO_XOR (a.geom, b.geom, 0.5) geom
  FROM sales_regions srb, sales_regions sra
  WHERE sra.id=51 and srb.id=43
) srb, customers sra
WHERE SDO_RELATE(sra.location, srb.geom, 'mask=anyinteract')='TRUE';
    COUNT(*)
----------
       122

1 row selected.
```

Geometric Analysis Functions

In the previous section, we examined how to construct geometries that represent the intersection, union, or difference of a pair of geometries. In the following sections, we describe how to perform further analysis on individual geometries. These individual geometries can be columns of existing tables, or they can be the result of other operations such as unions and intersections. For instance, you can compute the area of the intersection region for each pair of overlapping sales regions. Next, you can identify the pair (of sales regions) that has the maximum area for the overlap. The pair can then be marked as a potential candidate for merging associated business units.

Area, Length, and Volume Functions

We will start with functions for calculating the area, length, or volume of an input `SDO_GEOMETRY` object. You can use these functions on a two-dimensional geometry or a three-dimensional geometry. These functions have the following generic syntax in PL/SQL. For three-dimensional geometries, you can also use the equivalent `area`, `length`, and `volume` methods defined in the `J3D_Geometry` class.

```
Function_name
(
  Geometry          IN SDO_GEOMETRY,
  tolerance         IN NUMBER
  [, units_params   IN VARCHAR2]
)
RETURN NUMBER
```

where the following is true:

- `Geometry` specifies the geometry object to be analyzed.
- `tolerance` specifies the tolerance to be used in this analysis.
- `units_params` is an optional third argument that specifies the units in which the area/length is to be returned. This argument is of the form `'unit=<value_string>'`. You can obtain possible values for the units by consulting the `MDSYS.SDO_DIST_UNITS` table for length functions and the `MDSYS.SDO_AREA_UNITS` table for area functions. There is no such table defined for volume functions (in other words, no unit conversion is performed).

■ Note Only the PL/SQL functions support the conversion between different units or different coordinate systems, whereas the Java methods do not.

Accuracy of Area and Length Computations for Geodetic Data

The area and length functions take the curvature of the earth into account during calculations. For a geodetic geometry, the accuracy of the area function varies based on geometry size and how much it varies in latitude:

- For small geometries such as New Hampshire, the area function is accurate to within 0.0001 percent.
- For larger geometries of the size of India, the accuracy is within 0.001 percent.
- For much larger geometries, the accuracy is within 0.1 percent.

The length function, on the other hand, is accurate to within 0.00000001 percent. This also holds true for distance calculations between point geometries using the SDO_DISTANCE function.

Next, let's look at examples of the area and length functions.

SDO_AREA

This function computes the area of an SDO_GEOMETRY object. For instance, if a rectangle object has a length of 10 units and a width of 20 units, the area would be 10 * 20 = 200 square units. Likewise, for arbitrary geometric objects, this function returns the area covered by them.

Listing 9-26 shows how to compute the area of the intersection of sales region 51 with sales region 43 in the sales_regions table (this could be used in addition to the analysis in Listing 9-18 to determine whether to merge these sales regions). Note that the unit is specified as 'sq_yard' to indicate square yards.

Listing 9-26. *Area of the Intersection Region of Sales Region 43 and Sales Region 51*

```
SQL> SELECT SDO_GEOM.SDO_AREA
(SDO_GEOM.SDO_INTERSECTION(sra.geom, srb.geom, 0.5), 0.5, ' unit=sq_yard ' ) area
FROM sales_regions srb, sales_regions sra
WHERE sra.id=51 and srb.id=43;
      AREA
-----------
 26243.3702
```

The area function makes sense only for a polygon, surface, or solid (or collection) geometry. For a point or a line string, the area will always be 0. For solids, you can use the area function to calculate the surface area of the solid. For ease of illustration, we'll insert a new building with dimensions 200 feet by 200 feet by 400 feet into the city_buildings table. It will be easier to understand the area, length, and volume computations on this building. Listing 9-27 shows the insertion of this building into the city_buildings table.

Listing 9-27. *Inserting a New Building of Dimensions 200 Feet by 200 Feet by 400 Feet into* city_buildings

```
SQL> insert into city_buildings (id, geom) values (1,    -- ID of the building
  sdo_geometry(3008, 7407, null,
      sdo_elem_info_array(1,1007,3),     -- 3 represents a Solid Box representation
                                         -- using just the corner points
      sdo_ordinate_array(
          27731202, 42239124, 0,     -- Min values for  x, y, z
          27731402, 42239324, 400  -- Max values for x, y, z
                                       )
                            )
);

commit;
```

Listing 9-28 illustrates the computation of surface area for building 1 of the city_buildings table. The area function sums the area of each of the six faces of the solid.

Listing 9-28. *Surface Area of Building 1 (in Default Units of Square Feet)*

```
SQL> SELECT id, SDO_GEOM.SDO_AREA(geom, 0.05) SURFACE_AREA
FROM city_buildings
WHERE id=1;

           ID  SURFACE_AREA
------------- -------------
            1         400000
```

For computing the area of a three-dimensional object in Java, you can utilize the area method in the J3D_GEOMETRY class. This method takes an input tolerance value and computes the area for the reference geometry. (Note the absence of a units parameter: the Java interfaces do not support conversions between different units.) Listing 9-29 shows equivalent Java code for Listing 9-28.

Listing 9-29. *Surface Area of Building 1 (in Default Units of Square Feet) in Java*

```
// Assume bldg1 is loaded into the J3D_Geometry object as described in Chapter 7.
double area = bldg1.area(tol);  // tol is the tolerance value
```

SDO_LENGTH

This function returns the *length* for a line string and the *perimeter* for a polygon, surface, or solid. For points, this function returns 0.

You can use this function to identify connectors between multiple interstates. Usually, these connectors are short in length, on the order of 1 or 2 miles. Opening a new store close to these connectors is ideal, because the location would be close to multiple main interstates. Listing 9-30 shows the interstates (connectors) that are not more than 1 mile in length. These interstates usually connect multiple major interstates and are ideal sites for new businesses.

Listing 9-30. *Identifying Interstates Shorter Than 1 Mile*

```
SQL> SELECT interstate
FROM us_interstates
WHERE SDO_GEOM.SDO_LENGTH(geom, 0.5, 'unit=mile') < 1;
```

```
INTERSTATE
-----------------------------------
I10/I45
I40/I65
I30/I35E
I564
I71/I670
I55B
I90/I87
I94S
I94/I35E
I94/I35W
I670/315
I96S

12 rows selected.
```

For three-dimensional surfaces and solids, you can use the sdo_length function to determine the total length of the connecting edges that make up the geometry. Such analysis may be useful in identifying the amount of trim material needed for the building. Since there are some edges that may be shared, the function takes an additional numeric parameter, called count_shared_edges (with possible values 1 or 2), to denote whether the shared edges are counted once (if the parameter value is 1) or as many times as they occur (if parameter value is 2). Listing 9-31 and Listing 9-32 determine the length of the edges in building 1 for both values of count_shared_edges. Recall from Chapter 5 that every edge in a valid solid has to be traversed twice. So, the length with a value of 2 for count_shared_edges will be roughly double that of the length with a value of 2 for count_shared_edges, as verified by Listings 9-31 and 9-32.

Listing 9-31. *Length of the Building 1 (in Units of Feet) with* count_shared_edges *Set to 1*

```
SQL> SELECT SDO_GEOM.SDO_LENGTH(
        geom,  -- input geometry
        0.05,  -- tolerance value
        'UNIT=FOOT',  -- units parameter
        1      -- count_shared_edges only once
       ) LENGTH
FROM city_buildings
WHERE id=1;

    LENGTH
----------
3200.0064000126
```

Listing 9-32. *Length of the Building 1 (in Units of Feet) with* count_shared_edges *Set to 2*

```
SQL> SELECT SDO_GEOM.SDO_LENGTH(
        geom,  -- input geometry
        0.05,  -- tolerance value
        'UNIT=FOOT',  -- units parameter
        2      -- count_shared_edges only once
       ) LENGTH
FROM city_buildings
WHERE id=1;

    LENGTH
----------
6400.0128000252
```

For computing the length of a three-dimensional object in Java, you can utilize the `length` method in the `J3D_GEOMETRY` class. This method takes the `count_shared_edges` parameter as the first argument and a tolerance value as the second argument and computes the length for the reference geometry. (Note the absence of a `units` parameter: the Java interfaces do not support conversions between different units.) Listing 9-33 shows equivalent Java code for Listing 9-31.

Listing 9-33. *Length of Building 1 (in Default Units of Feet) in Java*

```
// Assume bldg1 is loaded into the J3D_Geometry object as described in Chapter 7.
int count_shared_edges = 1;  // count shared edges only once
double area = bldg1.length(count_shared_edges, tol);  // tol is the tolerance value
```

SDO_VOLUME

This function takes a geometry and a tolerance value and returns the *volume* if the input geometry is a three-dimensional solid or a multisolid geometry. For all other types of geometries, this function returns 0. Listing 9-34 computes the volume (in default units of cubic feet) for building 1 in the `city_buildings` table. As mentioned earlier, this building has dimensions of 200 feet by 200 feet by 400 feet, and hence the volume is 200 * 200 * 400 =16000000 cubic feet.

Listing 9-34. *Volume of Building 1 (in Default Units of Cubic Feet)*

```
SQL> set numwidth 15
SQL> SELECT SDO_GEOM.SDO_VOLUME(
        GEOM,  -- INPUT GEOMETRY
        0.05  -- TOLERANCE VALUE
       ) VOLUME
FROM city_buildings
WHERE id=1;

         VOLUME
---------------
       16000000
```

For computing the volume of a three-dimensional object in Java, you can utilize the `volume` method in the `J3D_GEOMETRY` class. This method takes the tolerance value as a parameter and computes the volume for the reference geometry. (Note the absence of a `units` parameter: the Java interfaces do not support conversions between different units.) Listing 9-35 shows equivalent Java code for Listing 9-34.

Listing 9-35. *Volume of Building 1 (in Default Units of Cubic Feet) in Java*

```
// Assume bldg1 is loaded into the J3D_Geometry object as described in Chapter 7.
double vol = bldg1.volume(tol);  // tol is the tolerance value
```

MBR Functions

If you want to show geometry on a map, you usually need to specify the *extent*—that is, the lower bound and upper bound in each dimension. You can use the *minimum bounding rectangle* (MBR) for this purpose. This rectangle is usually specified by the lower-left (all the minimum values) and upper-right (all the maximum values) corner vertices. Figure 9-5 shows an example of the MBR for different geometries.

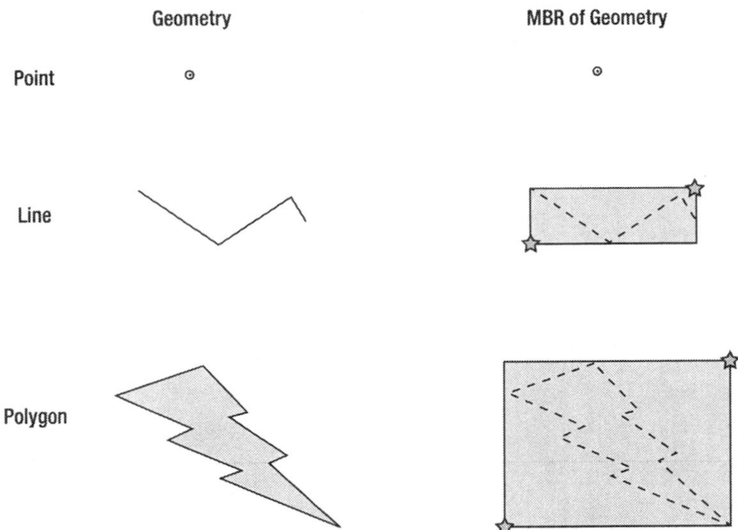

Figure 9-5. *SDO_MBR for different geometries. The stars mark the lower-left and upper-right corners of the MBRs.*

Note that the MBR of a geometry will usually cover more area than the original geometry. For a point geometry, the MBR is also a point (in other words, a degenerate MBR where the lower-left and upper-right corners are the same).

Spatial provides several functions to compute the MBR and associated components.

SDO_MBR

The SDO_MBR function takes an SDO_GEOMETRY as an argument and computes the MBR for the geometry. It returns an SDO_GEOMETRY object.

- If the input is a *point*, then the SDO_MBR function returns the point geometry.
- If input is a *line string* parallel to the x- or y-axis, then the function returns a linear geometry.
- Otherwise, the function returns the MBR of the input geometry as an SDO_GEOMETRY object.

Listing 9-36 shows how to get the extent or the MBR for a specific sales region in the sales_regions table.

Listing 9-36. *Computing the MBR of a Geometry*

```
SQL> SELECT SDO_GEOM.SDO_MBR(sr.geom) mbr FROM sales_regions sr
WHERE sr.id=1;

MBR(SDO_GTYPE, SDO_SRID, SDO_POINT(X, Y, Z), SDO_ELEM_INFO,
SDO_ORDINATES)
------------------------------------------------------------------------------
SDO_GEOMETRY(2003, 8307, NULL, SDO_ELEM_INFO_ARRAY(1, 1003, 3),
SDO_ORDINATE_ARR
AY(-77.049535, 38.8970816, -77.040259, 38.90433))

1 row selected.
```

For an input three-dimensional object, the SDO_MBR function returns the extent, in other words, the minimum and maximum values in all three dimensions as a three-dimensional geometry.[3] Listing 9-37 shows an example for building 1 of the city_buildings table. You can utilize this function in setting the window extent in three-dimensional visualization client tools such as Google Earth or LandXplorer.

Listing 9-37. *Computing the Extent of a Three-Dimensional Object*

```
SQL> SELECT SDO_GEOM.SDO_MBR(geom) extent
FROM city_buildings cbldg
WHERE id=1;

EXTENT(SDO_GTYPE, SDO_SRID, SDO_POINT(X, Y, Z), SDO_ELEM_INFO, SDO_ORDINATES)
-----------------------------------------------------------------------------

SDO_GEOMETRY(3008, 7407, NULL,
    SDO_ELEM_INFO_ARRAY(1, 1007, 3),
     SDO_ORDINATE_ARRAY(27731202, 42239124, 0, 27731402, 42239324, 400))
```

You can compute the extent in Java by using the getMBR function in the JGeometry class (the superclass of the J3D_Geometry class). Note that this function returns a double array where the first three numbers represent the minimum values in x,y,z and the last three numbers represent the maximum values in x,y,z dimensions. Listing 9-38 shows equivalent Java code for Listing 9-37.

Listing 9-38. *Computing the Extent of Building 1 in Java*

```
// Assume bldg1 is loaded into the JGeometry object as described in Chapter 7.
double [] mbr = bldg1.getMBR();  // tol is the tolerance value
```

Caution The functions SDO_AGGR_UNION, SDO_AGGR_CENTROID, and SDO_CONVEXHULL work only on two-dimensional geometries.

SDO_MIN_MBR_ORDINATE and SDO_MAX_MBR_ORDINATE

Instead of getting the extent in both dimensions, sometimes you may be interested in the extent in a specific dimension. You can obtain this using the SDO_MIN_MBR_ORDINATE and SDO_MAX_MBR_ORDINATE functions, which return the minimum and maximum ordinates of a geometry in a specified dimension, respectively. Listing 9-39 shows how to get the extent in the first dimension.

3. Note that the returned object can no longer be a rectangle (polygon) but a solid, although the R in SDO_MBR indicates a rectangle. Oracle retained the name SDO_MBR instead of changing it to something more appropriate such as SDO_EXTENT so as not to break existing two-dimensional applications.

Listing 9-39. *Obtaining the* MIN_ORDINATE*s and* MAX_ORDINATE*s in a Specific Dimension*

```
SQL> SELECT SDO_GEOM.SDO_MIN_MBR_ORDINATE(sr.geom, 1) min_extent,
SDO_GEOM.SDO_MAX_MBR_ORDINATE(sr.geom, 1) max_extent
FROM sales_regions sr WHERE sr.id=1;
MIN_EXTENT      MAX_EXTENT
----------      ----------
-77.049535      -77.040259

1 row selected.
```

You can use these functions on three-dimensional objects too. Listing 9-40 shows an example for building 1 in the city_buildings table.

Listing 9-40. *Obtaining* MIN_ORDINATE *and* MAX_ORDINATE *in the Third Dimension*

```
SQL> SELECT SDO_GEOM.SDO_MIN_MBR_ORDINATE(geom, 3) min_extent,
SDO_GEOM.SDO_MAX_MBR_ORDINATE(geom, 3) max_extent
FROM city_buildings cbldg
WHERE id=1;

MIN_EXTENT MAX_EXTENT
---------- ----------
         0        400
```

Miscellaneous Geometric Analysis Functions

In addition to the MBR functions are several other functions to perform simple *geometric* analyses such as computing the centroid or computing the convex hull (in Oracle 11g Release 1, neither of these functions is supported for three-dimensional geometries). Each of these functions has the following generic signature:

```
<Function_name>
(
  Geometry          IN SDO_GEOMETRY,
  Tolerance         IN NUMBER
)
RETURNS SDO_GEOMETRY
```

where the first argument is an SDO_GEOMETRY object and the second specifies the tolerance for the geometry.

Let's look at each of these functions in turn.

SDO_CONVEXHULL

The MBR is a very coarse approximation of a geometric object. A finer approximation is the convex hull of that object. A geometric set is *convex* if for every pair of points in the set, the line joining those two points is contained completely within the geometry. The convex hull of a geometry is the smallest convex set that contains all of that geometry. Thus, a convex hull of a polygon simplifies by eliminating the concave vertices (where the boundary bends inward) in its boundary. Figure 9-6 shows the convex hull for different types of geometries.

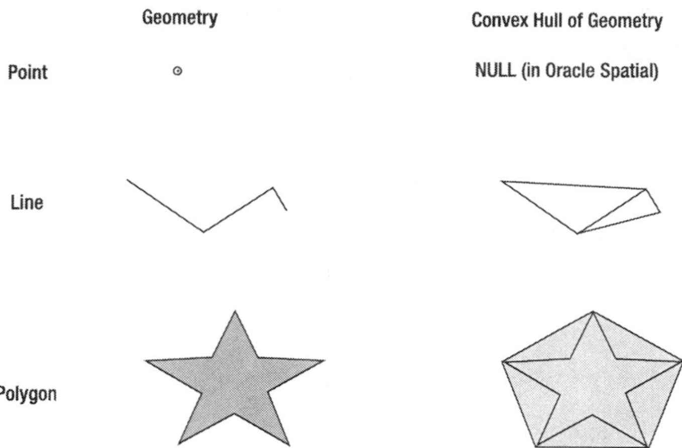

Figure 9-6. *Example of* SDO_CONVEXHULL *for different geometry objects*

The SDO_CONVEXHULL function computes the convex hull of an SDO_GEOMETRY. Listing 9-41 illustrates this for the state of New Hampshire. Note that the geometry for the state of New Hampshire has 709 vertices. In contrast, the convex hull shown in Listing 9-41 reduces it to 30 (in other words, a total of 60 numbers in the SDO_ORDINATE_ARRAY attribute of the resulting SDO_GEOMETRY). In this case, the convex hull simplifies the geometry without compromising too much on its shape. It can be used as a finer approximation of the geometry than the MBR in applications involving computational geometry algorithms.

Listing 9-41. *Computing the Convex Hull for the State of New Hampshire*

```
SQL> SELECT SDO_GEOM.SDO_CONVEXHULL(st.geom, 0.5) cvxhl
FROM us_states st
WHERE st.state_abrv='NH';

CVXHL(SDO_GTYPE, SDO_SRID, SDO_POINT(X, Y, Z), SDO_ELEM_INFO,
SDO_ORDINATES)
--------------------------------------------------------------------------------
SDO_GEOMETRY
(
  2003, 8307, NULL,
  SDO_ELEM_INFO_ARRAY(1, 1003, 1),    -- A Polygon
  SDO_ORDINATE_ARRAY                  -- Vertices of polygon
  (
   -71.294701, 42.6968992, -71.182304, 42.7374992, -70.817787, 42.8719901,
   -70.712257, 43.042324, -70.703026, 43.057457, -70.7052, 43.0709,
   -71.084816, 45.3052478, -71.285332, 45.3018647, -71.301582, 45.2965197,
   -71.443062, 45.2383418, -72.068199, 44.273666, -72.379906, 43.5740009,
   -72.394676, 43.5273279, -72.396866, 43.5190849, -72.553307, 42.8848878,
   -72.556679, 42.8668668, -72.557594, 42.8524128, -72.542564, 42.8075558,
   -72.516022, 42.7652279, -72.458984, 42.7267719, -72.412491, 42.7253529,
   -72.326614, 42.722729, -72.283455, 42.721462, -71.98188, 42.7132071,
   -71.773003, 42.7079012, -71.652107, 42.7051012, -71.630905, 42.7046012,
   -71.458282, 42.7004362, -71.369682, 42.6982082, -71.294701, 42.6968992
  )
)

1 row selected.
```

Caution The SDO_CONVEXHULL function is not defined—that is, it returns NULL for any geometry with less than three noncolinear points or if all the points are collinear.

The convex hull function is traditionally used to calculate the smallest convex geometry covering a set of points or a set of polygons. However, the function in Listing 9-41 generates the hull for a single geometry. How do you operate on sets of geometries? One option is to perform a union of geometries as in Listing 9-21 and then compute the convex hull for the resulting union. An alternative and easier approach is to use the equivalent spatial aggregate function that operates on sets of geometries. We discuss this aggregate function later in the chapter.

Note In Oracle 11*g*, the SDO_CONVEXHULL function works only on a two-dimensional geometry.

SDO_CENTROID

Suppose you want to label each intersection region with a name on a map. Where do you put the label? One place to put the label is at the *centroid* (in other words, the center of mass or gravity) for the geometry. Mathematically speaking, the centroid of a geometric object is defined by an average position of all points within the object. If the number of points is finite, such as a set of points, the centroid's x-value is the average of all the point's x-values, and the centroid's y-value is the average of all the point's y-values. For an infinite number of points (such as a curve or polygon), you use this equivalent integral from calculus:

$$\int_g p\,d\mu \Big/ \int_g d\mu$$

where g is the geometry, p is the point value, and μ is any uniform integral measure.

The SDO_CENTROID function computes the geometric centroid of an SDO_GEOMETRY object. Figure 9-7 shows examples of centroids for different geometries. Note that the centroid is not defined for lines in Oracle Spatial. The centroid for inverted C-shaped polygons can be outside the polygon.

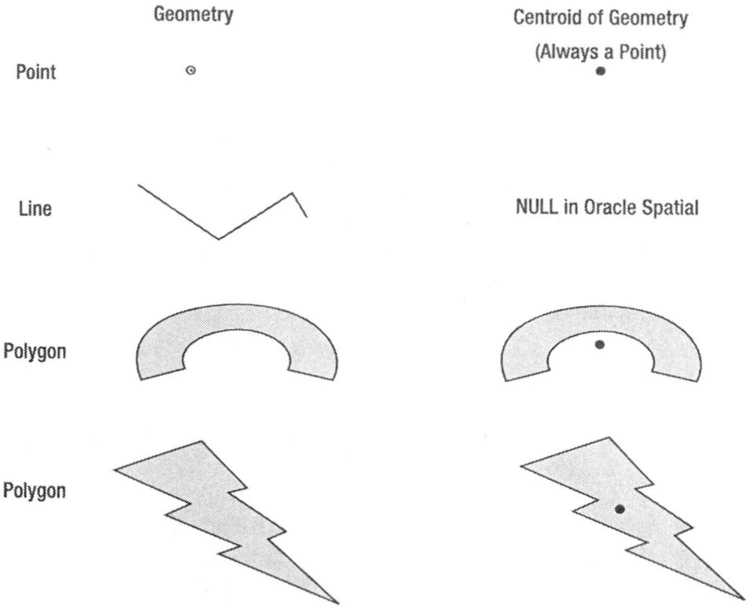

Figure 9-7. SDO_CENTROID *for different geometries*

The centroid of any geometry is always a point. This centroid may or may not lie on the geometry itself. The inverted C-shaped polygon in Figure 9-7 is one such example. The SDO_CENTROID function also returns NULL for linear geometries.

Listing 9-42 shows how to compute the centroid for the state of New Hampshire using the SDO_CENTROID function. You can use the location of the centroid to place a label for the state while displaying it on a map.

Listing 9-42. *Computing the Centroid for the State of New Hampshire*

```
SQL> SELECT SDO_GEOM.SDO_CENTROID(st.geom, 0.5) ctrd
FROM us_states st WHERE st.state_abrv='NH';
CTRD(SDO_GTYPE, SDO_SRID, SDO_POINT(X, Y, Z), SDO_ELEM_INFO,
SDO_ORDINATES)
--------------------------------------------------------------------------------
SDO_GEOMETRY
(2001, 8307, SDO_POINT_TYPE(-71.580917, 43.6792049, NULL), NULL, NULL)

1 row selected.
```

■ **Note** In Oracle 11*g*, the SDO_CENTROID function works only on two-dimensional geometries.

SDO_POINTONSURFACE

Since the centroid of a polygon may or may not lie within that polygon, it might be useful to put a label on some other point on the surface of the geometry. This is also necessary when creating some types of polygonal maps. You can get one such point using the SDO_POINTONSURFACE function as shown in Listing 9-43.

Listing 9-43. *Obtaining a Point on the Surface of the Geometry of the State of Massachusetts*

```
SQL> SELECT SDO_GEOM.SDO_POINTONSURFACE(st.geom, 0.5) pt
FROM us_states st
WHERE state_abrv='MA';

PT(SDO_GTYPE, SDO_SRID, SDO_POINT(X, Y, Z), SDO_ELEM_INFO,
SDO_ORDINATES)
--------------------------------------------------------------------------------
SDO_GEOMETRY(2001, 8307, SDO_POINT_TYPE(-73.265411, 42.745861, NULL),
NULL, NULL)

1 row selected.
```

You can use this function on three-dimensional geometries too. Listing 9-44 shows an example.

Listing 9-44. *Obtaining a Point on Building 1*

```
SQL> SELECT SDO_GEOM.SDO_POINTONSURFACE(geom, 0.05) pt
FROM city_buildings cbldg
WHERE id=1;

PT(SDO_GTYPE, SDO_SRID, SDO_POINT(X, Y, Z), SDO_ELEM_INFO, SDO_ORDINATES)
--------------------------------------------------------------------------
SDO_GEOMETRY(3001, 7407, SDO_POINT_TYPE(27731202, 42239124, 0), NULL, NULL)
```

■ **Caution** The only assurance for the SDO_POINTONSURFACE function is that the returned point will be in the boundary/interior of the polygon passed in. (In the current implementation, it actually returns the first point in the SDO_ORDINATE_ARRAY of the polygon geometry.) No other assumptions can be made.

Aggregate Functions

Until now, you have seen spatial functions that operate either on a single geometric object or on a pair of geometric objects. Next, we describe *spatial aggregate* functions that operate on a set of SDO_GEOMETRY objects. Like other aggregate functions in Oracle, these spatial aggregates are specified in the SELECT list of a SQL statement.

Aggregate MBR Function

Suppose you want to find out the extent covered by a set of SDO_GEOMETRY objects. (Usually, you will need this information to populate the USER_SDO_GEOM_METADATA view before creating an index.) Figure 9-8 shows the aggregate MBR for a set of point geometries.

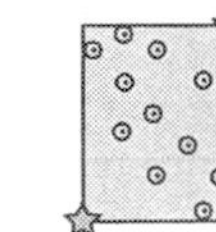

Figure 9-8. SDO_AGGR_MBR *for a set of points. The stars mark the lower-left and upper-right vertices of the computed MBR.*

You can compute the MBR of a collection using the SDO_AGGR_MBR function. Listing 9-45 illustrates its usage by computing the aggregate MBR for all the locations in the branches table.

Listing 9-45. *Finding the Extent of a Set of Geometries Using* SDO_AGGR_MBR

```
SQL> SELECT  SDO_AGGR_MBR(location) extent FROM branches;

EXTENT(SDO_GTYPE, SDO_SRID, SDO_POINT(X, Y, Z), SDO_ELEM_INFO,
SDO_ORDINATES)
--------------------------------------------------------------------------------
SDO_GEOMETRY
(
  2003, 8307, NULL,
  SDO_ELEM_INFO_ARRAY(1, 1003, 3),  -- A Rectangle-type polygon
  SDO_ORDINATE_ARRAY(-122.49836, 37.7112075, -76.950947, 38.9611552)
)
```

Note that this returns the coordinate extent or the MBR of the set of geometries as an SDO_GEOMETRY object. You may need to use the SDO_MIN_MBR_ORDINATE and SDO_MAX_MBR_ORDINATE functions on the resulting MBR to appropriately set the SDO_DIM_ARRAY elements in the USER_SDO_GEOM_METADATA view.

The SDO_AGGR_MBR works even on three-dimensional geometries. Listing 9-46 shows how to compute the extent of all the geometries in the city_buildings table.

Listing 9-46. *Computing the Three-Dimensional Extent of the Buildings in the* city_buildings *Table*

```
SQL> SELECT SDO_AGGR_MBR(geom) extent FROM city_buildings;

EXTENT(SDO_GTYPE, SDO_SRID, SDO_POINT(X, Y, Z), SDO_ELEM_INFO, SDO_ORDINATES)
--------------------------------------------------------------------------------
SDO_GEOMETRY(3008, 7407, NULL,
   SDO_ELEM_INFO_ARRAY(1, 1003, 3),
   SDO_ORDINATE_ARRAY(27731202, 42239124, 0, 29882178.9, 45466602.5, 900))
```

Other Aggregate Functions

In addition to the MBR, you may want to compute the union or the convex hull of a set of geometries. You can use the SDO_AGGR_UNION or SDO_AGGR_CONVEXHULL function for this purpose. Unlike the SDO_AGGR_MBR function, which takes an SDO_GEOMETRY as the argument, these functions take an SDOAGGRTYPE as the argument. The SDOAGGRTYPE has the following structure:

```
SQL> DESCRIBE SDOAGGRTYPE;
Name                     Null?     Type

GEOMETRY                           MDSYS.SDO_GEOMETRY
TOLERANCE                          NUMBER
```

Note The functions SDO_AGGR_UNION, SDO_AGGR_CENTROID, and SDO_CONVEXHULL work only on two-dimensional geometries.

SDO_AGGR_UNION

The aggregate function SDO_AGGR_UNION computes the union of a set of geometries. The union is returned as an SDO_GEOMETRY object. Figure 9-9 shows the union for a set of points.

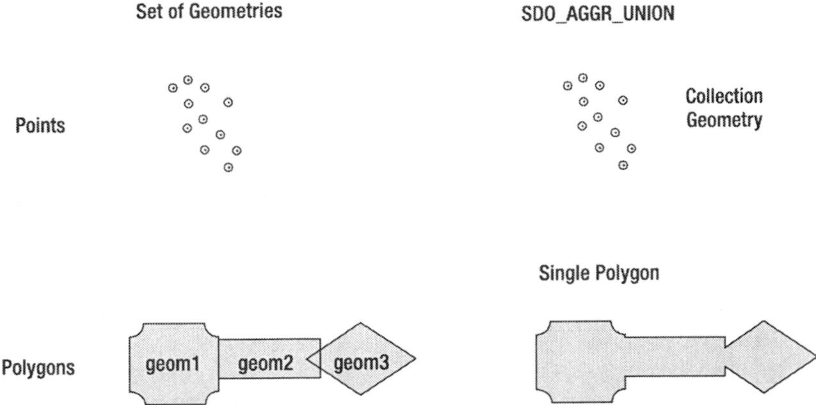

Figure 9-9. *Two examples of* SDO_AGGR_UNION

For a set of point geometries, the union is a geometry *collection*. For a set of three overlapping polygon geometries, the union is a single polygon. Note that the interior edges vanish on the union polygon shown at the right of Figure 9-9.

You can create a union of all the locations in the branches table to identify the coverage of stores, as shown in Listing 9-47. This creates a collection of all 77 point locations for the branches.

Listing 9-47. *Finding the Coverage of Branch Locations Using* SDO_AGGR_UNION

```
SQL>SELECT SDO_AGGR_UNION(SDOAGGRTYPE(location, 0.5)) coverage
FROM branches;

COVERAGE(SDO_GTYPE, SDO_SRID, SDO_POINT(X, Y, Z), SDO_ELEM_INFO,
SDO_ORDINATES)
--------------------------------------------------------------------------------
SDO_GEOMETRY
(
  2005, 8307, NULL,
  SDO_ELEM_INFO_ARRAY(1, 1, 77),    -- collection of 77 points
  SDO_ORDINATE_ARRAY
  (
    -122.41915, 37.7751038, -122.39489, 37.793174, -122.39686, 37.793595,
    -77.02601, 38.8945028, -77.033619, 38.8991971, -122.40839, 37.788633,
    -122.49045, 37.7339297, -122.43403, 37.7511713, -122.40361, 37.7839342,
    -122.40007, 37.7998365, -122.40415, 37.7702542, -122.4025, 37.791987,
    -122.46898, 37.7380652, -122.40473, 37.730593, -122.4076, 37.7845683,
    -122.39796, 37.7438371, -122.40876, 37.7991795, -122.43855, 37.7440736,
    -122.47552, 37.726909, -122.42232, 37.7906913, -122.4308, 37.7974994,
    -122.47685, 37.7429851, -122.40781, 37.794415, -122.40864, 37.788168,
    -122.4359, 37.7238284, -122.4886, 37.75362, -122.40145, 37.7881653,
    -122.40255, 37.792281, -122.44138, 37.7160032, -122.42035, 37.744667,
    -122.41864, 37.753694, -122.40391, 37.7112075, -122.4787, 37.763452,
    -122.46635, 37.7640397, -122.40599, 37.7933898, -122.4783, 37.7803596,
    -122.44957, 37.7821163, -122.43418,37.7907946, -122.43879, 37.7738425,
    -122.41713, 37.7392079, -122.46537, 37.7828694, -122.4395, 37.800408,
    -122.43495, 37.7607737, -122.45275, 37.78649, -122.41914, 37.7751346,
    -122.39652, 37.7782523, -122.40047, 37.7958989, -122.49836, 37.7756795,
    -122.40905, 37.7527288, -122.39119, 37.7330824, -77.032016, 38.8993045,
```

```
    -77.033679, 38.8987586, -76.950947, 38.8925976, -77.006755, 38.93653,
    -77.042079, 38.9026399, -77.037653, 38.9295113, -76.989522, 38.8655141,
    -76.993059, 38.9001983, -77.033158, 38.9035919, -77.023716, 38.9331479,
    -77.062822, 38.9431214, -77.09677, 38.9442554, -77.083759, 38.9570281,
    -77.009721, 38.9611552, -76.995893, 38.90018, -77.001773, 38.8215786,
    -77.017477, 38.8765101, -77.003477, 38.887564, -77.02956, 38.8982647,
    -77.039476, 38.9012157, -77.046673, 38.9037307, -77.06342, 38.9075175,
    -77.044112, 38.9092715, -77.043592, 38.9214703, -77.051909, 38.9242888,
    -77.057711, 38.9344998, -77.044897, 38.9007058
  )
)
```

Note that the union returns a geometry *collection* where each element is a point in the input set. This is because the individual points do not intersect. Let's look at another example where there is a union of two overlapping polygons, sales regions 51 and 43, and a third disjoint, region 2. This will return a collection of two polygon elements: one element after merging overlapping regions 1 and 7 and another element for disjoint region 2. This is illustrated in Listing 9-48. Compare this with Listing 9-20, where you could perform only a union of two regions (1 and 7) at a time using the SDO_UNION function.

Listing 9-48. *Union of Three Sales Regions (ids 43, 51, and 2)*

```
SQL> SELECT SDO_AGGR_UNION(SDOAGGRTYPE(geom, 0.5)) union_geom
FROM sales_regions
WHERE id=51 or id=43 or id=2 ;
UNION_GEOM(SDO_GTYPE, SDO_SRID, SDO_POINT(X, Y, Z), SDO_ELEM_INFO,
SDO_ORDINATES
-------------------------------------------------------------------------------
SDO_GEOMETRY
(
  2007, 8307, NULL,                              -- Collection Geometry
  SDO_ELEM_INFO_ARRAY(1, 1003, 1, 35, 1003, 1), -- Two polygonal rings
  SDO_ORDINATE_ARRAY                             -- Vertices of the polygons
  (
    -77.061998, 38.9358866, -77.062351, 38.9344997, -77.061997,
    38.9331128, -77.060992, 38.9319371, -77.059486, 38.9311515, -77.057711,
    38.9308756,-77.055935, 38.9311515, -77.05443, 38.9319371, -77.053424,
    38.9331128, -77.05307, 38.9344997, -77.053423, 38.9358866, -77.054429,
    38.9370624, -77.055935, 38.9378481, -77.057711, 38.938124, -77.059486,
    38.9378481, -77.060992, 38.9370624, -77.061998, 38.9358866, -122.41056,
    37.7933897, -122.41021, 37.7920025, -122.40922,37.7908265, -122.40774,
    37.7900408, -122.40599, 37.7897649, -122.40541, 37.7898563, -122.40567,
    37.7895524, -122.40602, 37.7881652, -122.40567, 37.7867781, -122.40468,
    37.7856021, -122.4032, 37.7848164, -122.40145, 37.7845404, -122.3997,
    37.7848164, -122.39822, 37.7856021, -122.39723, 37.7867781, -122.39688,
    37.7881652, -122.39723, 37.7895524, -122.39822, 37.7907285, -122.3997,
    37.7915143, -122.40145, 37.7917902, -122.40203, 37.7916988, -122.40177,
    37.7920025, -122.40142, 37.7933897, -122.40177, 37.7947769, -122.40276,
    37.7959529, -122.40424, 37.7967387, -122.40599, 37.7970147, -122.40774,
    37.7967387, -122.40922, 37.7959529, -122.41021, 37.7947769, -122.41056,
    37.7933897
  )
)

1 row selected.
```

Likewise, you can compute the coverage (in other words, the union of all the sales_regions) as in Listing 9-49. Note that this will be the equivalent of the coverage obtained in Listing 9-21. Unlike Listing 9-21, the following usage is much simplified without the need for PL/SQL code. Listing 9-49 illustrates the power of spatial aggregate functions.

Listing 9-49. *Union of All Sales Regions to Obtain Business Coverage*

```
SQL> SELECT  SDO_AGGR_UNION(SDOAGGRTYPE(geom, 0.5)) coverage
FROM sales_regions;
-- output too big to be shown: result geometry more than 100 vertices
```

SDO_AGGR_CONVEXHULL

The resulting unions in Listings 9-48 and 9-49 are complex geometries with some concave vertices. As an alternative, you can compute the SDO_AGGR_CONVEXHULL to compute the convex hull from the set of sales_regions. Figure 9-10 shows the aggregate convex hull for the point set in Figure 9-8. Listing 9-50 shows the code for computing the coverage of sales regions using the SDO_AGGR_CONVEXHULL function.

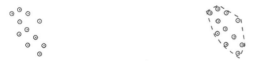

Figure 9-10. SDO_AGGR_CONVEXHULL *for a set of points*

Listing 9-50. *Finding the Coverage of* sales_regions *Using* SDO_AGGR_CONVEXHULL

```
SQL> SELECT SDO_AGGR_CONVEXHULL(SDOAGGRTYPE(geom, 0.5)) coverage
FROM sales_regions;
COVERAGE(SDO_GTYPE, SDO_SRID, SDO_POINT(X, Y, Z), SDO_ELEM_INFO,
SDO_ORDINATES)
-------------------------------------------------------------------------------
SDO_GEOMETRY
(
  2003, 8307, NULL,                        -- Polygon type geometry
  SDO_ELEM_INFO_ARRAY(1, 1003, 1),
  SDO_ORDINATE_ARRAY                       -- Vertices of the polygon
  (
    -122.48595, 37.6881575, -76.865425, 38.7930326, -76.86362, 38.7927488,
    -76.861815, 38.7930202, -76.860283, 38.7938054, -76.85926, 38.7949851,
    -76.80744, 38.8662751, -76.807079, 38.8676696, -76.807438, 38.8690665,
    -76.808461, 38.8702533, -76.868265, 38.9394471, -76.869798, 38.9402428,
    -122.55129, 37.7783805, -122.62661, 37.7497019, -122.62812, 37.7489059,
    -122.62913, 37.7477192, -122.62948, 37.7463226, -122.62912, 37.7449286,
    -122.62811, 37.7437496, -122.62661, 37.742965, -122.51969, 37.6946774,
    -122.48949, 37.6881485, -122.48772, 37.687876, -122.48595, 37.6881575
  )
)

1 row selected.
```

Note that as opposed to the union geometry in Listing 9-49 (or the union of the branches in 9-42), the aggregate convex hull computed has fewer vertices. This might result in significantly faster computation if the convex hull approximation of the coverage is used (instead of the actual union) in further proximity analyses.

■ **Caution** SDO_AGGR_CONVEXHULL returns NULL if all the vertices of all the input geometries are collinear or if there is only one vertex (one point).

SDO_AGGR_CENTROID

Assume you have identified that a group of customers in the customers table is too far from existing branch locations. You may want to start a new store to cater to this group of customers. What might be the best location for this new store? The *centroid* of the group is a reasonable choice. The centroid of the customer locations minimizes the average distance from the customers to the new store location. Figure 9-11 illustrates the centroid for a set of points.

Figure 9-11. SDO_AGGR_CENTROID *for a set of points*

The SDO_AGGR_CENTROID function allows you to compute this centroid for an arbitrary group of customers as shown in Listing 9-51.

Listing 9-51. *Finding the Centroid of Customer Locations Using* SDO_AGGR_CENTROID

```
SQL> SELECT SDO_AGGR_CENTROID(SDOAGGRTYPE(location, 0.5)) ctrd
FROM customers;
WHERE  id>100;
CTRD(SDO_GTYPE, SDO_SRID, SDO_POINT(X, Y, Z), SDO_ELEM_INFO,
SDO_ORDINATES)
-----------------------------------------------------------------------------
SDO_GEOMETRY
(2001, 8307, SDO_POINT_TYPE(-103.19018, 38.0963807, NULL), NULL, NULL)
```

As shown in Listing 9-51, you can have any arbitrary spatial or attribute filtering in the WHERE clause of the SQL statement. The aggregate function, CENTROID in this case, operates only on the subset of the geometries that satisfy the WHERE clause as collected by the GROUP BY clause, if any.

Summary

In this chapter, we described how to perform proximity analysis using spatial functions to solve real application problems. We described functions to perform relationship analysis, unions, intersections, and other geometry combination functions on pairs of geometric objects. We covered how to create buffers around geometric objects and use them in relationship analysis with other geometries. We also examined how to identify the extents, centroids, and convex hulls of individual geometric objects or groups of geometric objects.

Together, these functions aid in the analysis of business demographics, such as number of customers in appropriate buffers and intersecting regions. Such analysis is vital to making strategic decisions, such as starting new businesses at appropriate locations, merging existing businesses, or targeting specific customers with additional promotions.

CHAPTER 10

Network Modeling

In the previous chapters, we described geographical objects as points, lines, and polygons. In Chapters 8 and 9, you saw how to search geographical objects based on the way they are positioned with respect to other objects. In particular, you learned how to find objects that are within some distance from another object (with the SDO_WITHIN_DISTANCE operator) or simply to find the object nearest to another one (with the SDO_NN operator).

Those operations are useful, no doubt. However, they find and select objects based solely on the shortest absolute distance ("as the crow flies") between them. This may be very different from the actual distance you would need to travel to reach your destination. Unless you are a bird, you are obliged by nature (if not by law!) to travel along only well-defined paths—that is, you follow streets and roads, and you obey traffic regulations such as one-way streets and speed limits.

Consider the set of points illustrated in Figure 10-1. The point nearest to point D is point B. However, if the points are placed on a network, as illustrated in Figure 10-2, then the point nearest to point D is now point E.

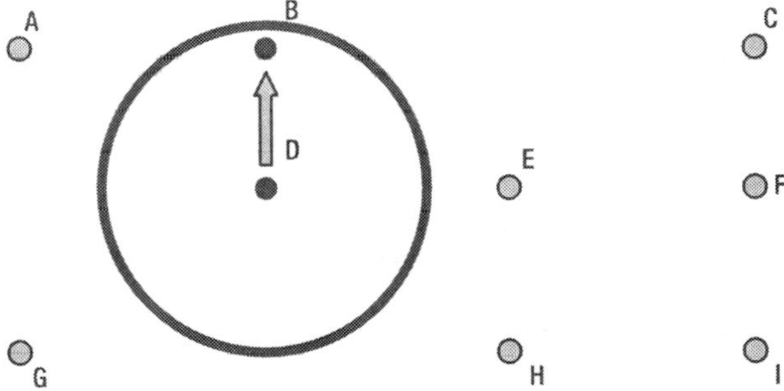

Figure 10-1. *Nearest point "as the crow flies"*

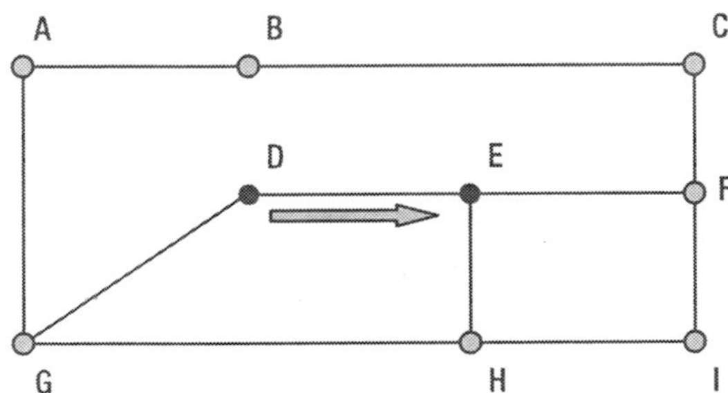

Figure 10-2. *Nearest point along a network*

Things get complicated if you introduce one-way streets, as illustrated in Figure 10-3. Then the nearest point to D is G.

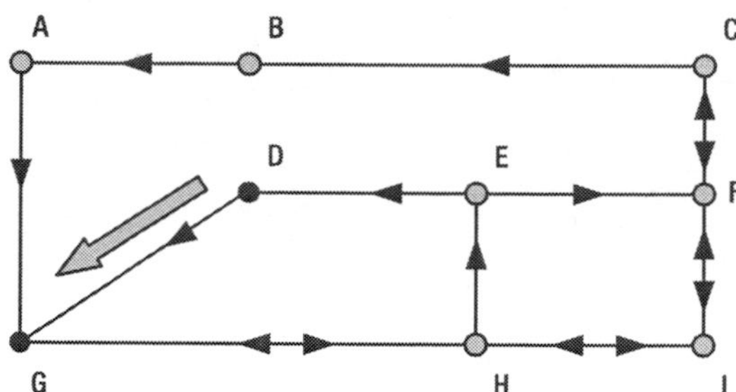

Figure 10-3. *Nearest point along a directed network*

By representing the links between objects, you can answer the following questions:

- What is the shortest or fastest route between two cities?
- What is the closest hotel to an airport?
- How many customers live less than 30 minutes driving time from a particular store?
- How can you reroute traffic if a road is closed for repairs?

More specifically, you can now revisit the types of analyses you studied in previous chapters. Table 10-1 shows some examples of analyses you can perform on your business data (customers, stores, and branches) once you have positioned them on a road network.

Table 10-1. *Examples of Network-Based Proximity Analyses*

Type of Network Analysis	Usage
Nearest neighbor	Identify the branch nearest to a specific customer.
Route computation	Determine the optimal route from a branch to a customer location. Determine the optimal route for a salesperson to visit a series of customers.
Within distance	Identify customers who live within 30 minutes driving distance of a specific branch.

These analyses are similar to those in Tables 8-1 and 9-1, except they use *network* distances instead of *spatial* distances. In this chapter, we describe how to perform these types of network analyses.

In this chapter, we first cover the general concepts and terminology of network modeling, and then we describe how they are used in the Oracle Network Data Model. We also explain the data structures. Next, we describe how to define and load networks in the Oracle database. We then show how to use the Java API to perform network analyses and apply all the concepts we describe to your business data.

General Network Modeling Concepts

We all have an intuitive understanding of what constitutes a network. Nevertheless, we think it is useful to start with some generic formal definitions of networking concepts, as illustrated in Figure 10-4. The figure shows a set of city streets, with a network representation of those streets.

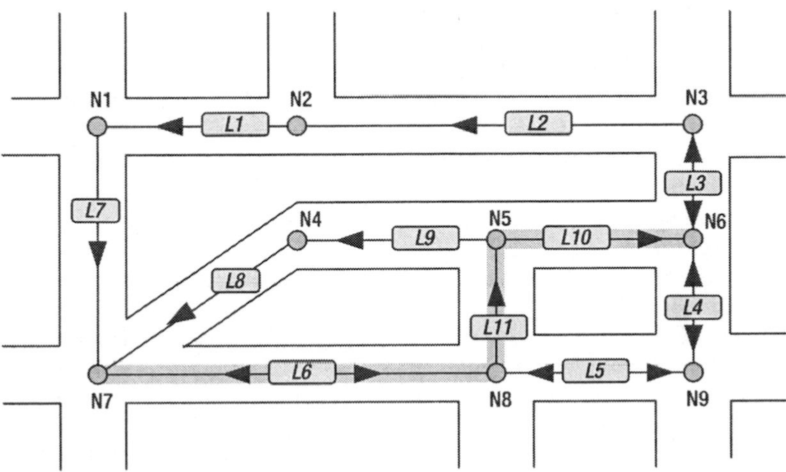

Figure 10-4. *Network concepts: nodes and link*

A *network* is a type of mathematical graph that captures relationships between objects using connectivity. A network consists of nodes and links.

A *node* represents an object of interest on the network. For a road network, nodes are the intersections, as illustrated in Figure 10-4.

A *link* represents a relationship between two nodes. Each link connects two and only two nodes. Multiple links can leave from and meet at the same node. Two nodes can be connected by multiple links. Links can be *directed* or *undirected*. An undirected link can be traversed in either direction, whereas a directed link allows traffic in only one direction. Nodes define the direction of a link: a directed link is considered to "flow" from its *start node* to its *end node*. The *colink* of a directed link is the link that "flows" between the same nodes, in the opposite direction.

On a road network, links represent road and street segments between intersections. A directed link represents a one-way street. In Figure 10-4, links L1 and L2 represent one-way streets. Links L3 and L4 represent two-way streets.

Network elements (links and nodes) may have geometric information associated with them. A *logical network* contains connectivity information but no geometric information. A *spatial network* contains both connectivity information and geometric information.

In Oracle Spatial, in a spatial network, the nodes and links are `SDO_GEOMETRY` objects representing points and lines, respectively.

Note A spatial network can also use other kinds of geometry representations. One variant lets you use linear-referenced geometries. Another lets you use topology objects. We do not cover these possibilities in this chapter. We cover linear referencing in Appendix B, and we discuss topology in Appendix C.

A *path* represents a route through the network. It is formed by a sequence of nodes and links between two nodes. There can be multiple paths between two nodes. A path can be *simple* or *complex*. In a simple path, the links form an ordered list that can be traversed from the start node to the end node, with each link visited once. A complex path represents a subnetwork between a start node and a destination node. Figure 10-4 shows a path from node N7 to node N6, going through links L6, L11, and L10.

Cost is a numeric attribute that can be associated with links or nodes. Costs are used for computing paths between two nodes: the cost of a path is the sum of the costs of all nodes and links on that path. The *minimum cost path* is the path that has the smallest total cost from a start node to an end node—for example, the shortest distance or time. Links and nodes can have multiple costs, but only one is used at a time.

On a road network, the cost of a link is typically the *length* of the street or road segment represented by that link. This is good for computing the *shortest* route between two places. Most road networks also include the typical driving *time* along the road segment. This is used to compute the *fastest* route between two places.

Reachable nodes are all nodes that can be reached from a given node. *Reaching* nodes are all nodes that can reach a given node.

The *spanning tree* of a network is a tree (in other words, a graph with no cycles) that connects all nodes of the network. (The directions of links are ignored in a spanning tree.) The *minimum cost spanning tree* (MCST) is a tree that connects all nodes and has the minimum total cost. Spanning trees are commonly used to find the optimal way to build transportation networks (road, rail, and air) to connect a number of places. See Figure 10-20 later in this chapter for an example of an MCST.

Finally, network *constraints* are restrictions defined on network searches. On a road network, for example, driving routes may be required to include only those roads that are accessible to trucks or to avoid toll roads. Other constraints can be time based, such as mountain-pass closures during the winter, ferry operation hours, or turns prohibited during peak traffic hours.

Examples of Networks

Networks are used to solve many different problems. In this book, we concentrate on networks that represent spatial objects (roads, rivers, and so on). The following sections present a sampling of network applications.

Road Networks

In a typical road network, the intersections of roads are nodes, and the road segments between two intersections are links. The spatial representation of a road is not inherently related to the nodes and links in the network. For example, a shape point in the spatial representation of a road (reflecting a sharp turn in the road) is not a node in the network if that shape point is not associated with an intersection, and a single spatial object may make up several links in a network (such as a straight segment intersected by three crossing roads).

An important operation with a road network is to find the path from a start point to an end point, minimizing either the travel time or the distance. There may be additional constraints on the path computation, such as having the path go through a particular landmark or avoiding a particular intersection.

Train Networks

The subway network of any major city is probably best modeled as a logical network, assuming that the precise spatial representation of the stops and tracks is unimportant. In such a network, all stops on the system constitute the nodes of the network, and a link is the connection between two stops if a train travels directly between these two stops. Important operations with a train network include finding all stations that can be reached from a specified station, finding the number of stops between two specified stations, and finding the travel time between two stations.

Utility Networks

Utility networks, such as power lines or cable networks, must often be configured to minimize cost. An important operation with a utility network is to determine the connections among nodes by using MCST algorithms to provide the required quality of service at the minimum cost. Another important operation is reachability analysis so that, for example, if a station in a water network is shut down, you know which areas will be affected and how the affected areas can be supplied with water from other stations.

Biochemical Networks

Biochemical processes can be modeled as biochemical networks to represent reactions and regulations in living organisms. For example, metabolic pathways are networks involved in enzymatic reactions, while regulatory pathways represent protein-protein interactions. In this example, a pathway is a network; genes, proteins, and chemical compounds are nodes; and reactions among nodes are links. Important operations for a biochemical network include computing paths and the degrees of nodes. Specialized tools such as Cytoscape are able to use and update networks in the Oracle database using the appropriate plug-in.

Finance Networks

Many multinational companies with subsidiaries in multiple countries are linked together in a financial network, which is used to transport funds (dividends, royalties, and interests) between them. Tax rates in the various countries and tax treaties between countries are modeled as "costs" on the network links. Various network operations can help find the best way to transfer capital and optimize tax costs.

Project Networks

Our final network example relates to project plans. A *project* is really a network with activities and dependencies represented as links and nodes. Activities have costs (for example, the time to complete an activity or the resources needed).

Oracle Network Data Model

The network support in Oracle Database 10*g* is composed of the following elements:

- A data model to store networks inside the database as a set of network tables. This is the *persistent* copy of a network.
- SQL functions to define and maintain networks (the `SDO_NET` package).
- Network analysis functions in Java. The Java API works on a copy of the network loaded from the database. This is the *volatile* copy of the network. Results of analyses (in other words, computed network paths) and network changes can be written back to the database.
- Network analysis functions in PL/SQL (the `SDO_NET_MEM` package). Note, however, that this API is really a "wrapper" over the Java API, which then executes inside the database. This technique still uses a volatile copy of the network, which is now loaded in Java-managed memory, inside the database.

Figure 10-5 and Figure 10-6 illustrate the relationship between these elements. Figure 10-6 shows how the PL/SQL and Java APIs relate to each other.

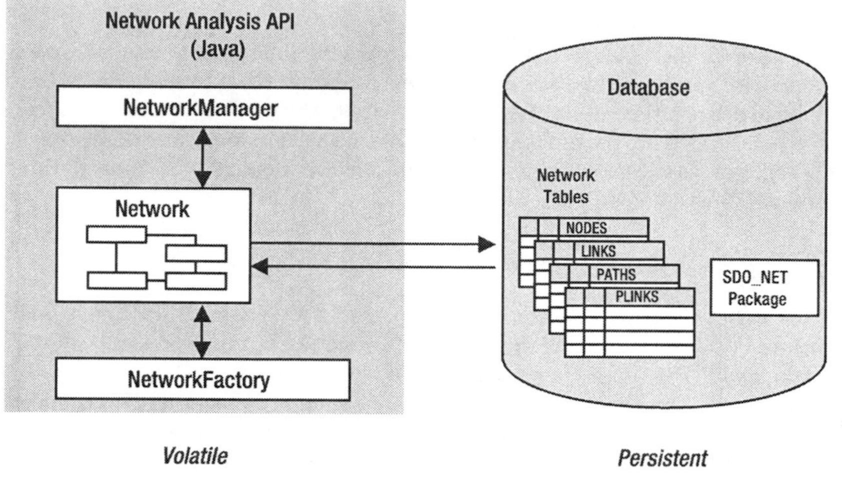

Figure 10-5. *Oracle Network Data Model*

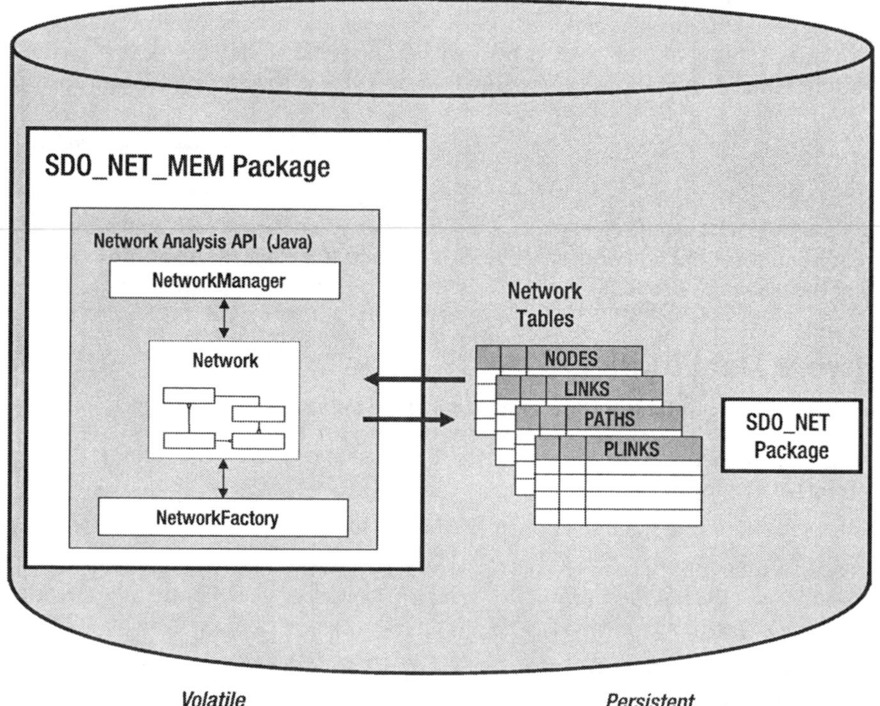

Figure 10-6. *The PL/SQL and Java APIs*

Data Structures: The Network Tables

We will first explain how you define your network elements as tables. A network is defined using two tables: a *node* table and a *link* table. You must provide those tables with the proper structure and content to model your network.

A network can also have a *path* table and a *path link* table. These tables are optional and are filled with the results of analyzes performed in the Java API, such as the shortest path between two nodes. They are needed only if applications want to make analysis results available to other applications by storing them in the database.

Other optional tables are the *partition* tables. Those will be discussed separately in the section that covers network partitioning.

Figure 10-7 shows the relationships between the tables that describe a network.

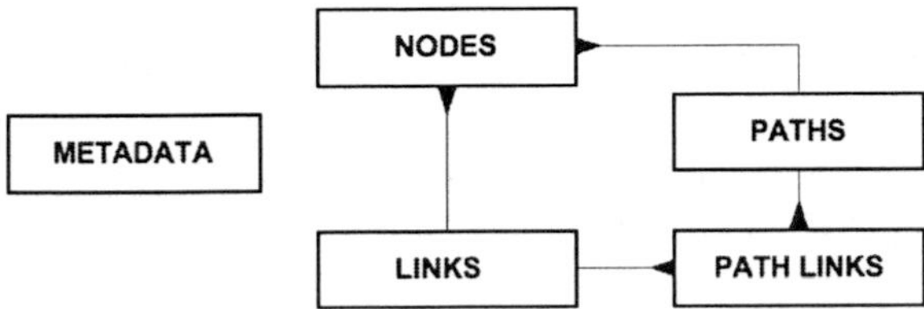

Figure 10-7. *Main network tables*

The tables can be named in any way you like, but they must follow a well-defined structure. Or, to be more precise, they must contain a certain minimum number of columns, some with predefined names.

You have a large degree of flexibility in structuring the tables—some columns can be named in any way you like (the *geometry* and *cost* columns, in particular), and their order is unimportant. You can also include any other columns to hold additional information. And finally, the tables could actually be views over existing tables.

The actual naming of the tables that constitute a network and their structure is defined in a separate metadata table called `USER_SDO_NETWORK_METADATA`, which you update the same way as the basic spatial metadata (`USER_SDO_METADATA`). In particular, this is where you specify the name of the column in the *node* and *link* tables that defines the *cost* value, or the name of the *geometry* column. This also allows you to define multiple networks on the same set of tables, using different cost columns—for example, one network based on distances and another based on travel times.

There are several techniques for defining the data structures for a network. At one extreme, a simple procedure call does everything; it creates all tables with default names and populates the metadata. At the other extreme, you create all the tables manually (or create views on existing tables) and fill the metadata manually. Functions are provided to verify that the data structures are valid and coherent.

In the following sections, we present an overview of the structure of each of the network tables. For each table, we indicate those columns that are required and those that are optional. Columns with names in lowercase can have any name. Their actual name is defined in the metadata.

Node Table

The *node* table, as shown in Table 10-2, describes all nodes in the network. Each node has a unique numeric identifier (the NODE_ID column). This is the only required column—all others are actually optional.

Table 10-2. *The* Node *Table*

Column	Data Type	Meaning
NODE_ID[a]	NUMBER	Unique identification for that node in the network. This is also the primary key of the table.
geometry_column	SDO_GEOMETRY	A point geometry object that contains the coordinates of the node. This is present only for spatial networks. Logical networks contain no geometries.
cost_column	NUMBER	A numeric value representing the cost for traversing that node. There could be multiple costs associated with a node. The actual cost column used for network analysis is defined in the network metadata. When no cost column is defined, then all nodes are assumed to have a cost of 0.
HIERARCHY_LEVEL	NUMBER	For hierarchical networks only. This is the level of the node.
PARENT_NODE_ID	NUMBER	For hierarchical networks only. This is the identifier of the parent node for this node.
ACTIVE	CHAR(1)	Defines whether the node is active (visible in the network)—'Y' or 'N'. An inactive node will not be used by the network analysis functions. When the column is not defined, then all nodes are considered to be active.
NODE_NAME	VARCHAR2(32)	Name of the node. Fill this with any descriptive name (not used by the network analysis functions).
NODE_TYPE	VARCHAR2(24)	Type of node. Fill this with any descriptive code or text.

[a] *This column is required. The remaining columns in the table are optional.*

Link Table

The *link* table, as shown in Table 10-3, describes all links in the network. Each link has a unique numeric identifier (the LINK_ID column) and contains the identifiers of the two nodes it connects. All other columns are optional.

Table 10-3. *The* Link *Table*

Column	Data Type	Meaning
LINK_ID[a]	NUMBER	Unique identification for that link in the network. This is also the primary key of the table.
START_NODE_ID[a]	NUMBER	Unique identifier of the node from which the link originates.
END_NODE_ID[a]	NUMBER	Unique identifier of the node at which the link terminates.
geometry_column	SDO_GEOMETRY	A line geometry object that describes the shape of the link. This is present only for spatial networks. Logical networks contain no geometries.

Column	Data Type	Meaning
cost_column	NUMBER	A numeric value representing the cost for traversing that link. There could be multiple costs associated with a link. The actual cost column used for network analysis is defined in the network metadata. When no cost column is defined, then all links are assumed to have a cost of 1.
BIDIRECTED	CHAR(1)	Defines whether the link is directed. A directed link (BIDIRECTED='N') can be traversed only from the start node to the end node. An undirected link (BIDIRECTED='Y') can be traversed either way. This column is applicable only if the network is defined as directed. If this column is absent and the network is defined as directed, then the link is assumed to be directed.
PARENT_LINK_ID	NUMBER	For hierarchical networks only. This is the identifier of the parent link for this node.
ACTIVE	CHAR(1)	Defines whether the link is active (visible in the network)—'Y' or 'N'. An invisible link will not be used by the network analysis functions. When the column is not defined, then all nodes are considered to be active.
LINK_LEVEL	NUMBER	Priority of the link.
LINK_NAME	VARCHAR2	Name of the link. Fill this with any descriptive name (not used by the network analysis functions).
LINK_TYPE	VARCHAR2	Type of link. Fill this with any descriptive code or text.

[a] *These columns are required. All others are optional.*

Path Table

The *path* table, as shown in Table 10-4, stores the start and end node of a path and its total cost. Note that the *cost* column is always present and is named COST. The list of the links that describe a path is in the *path link* table (described in the next section). Remember that the *path* and *path link* tables are optional—you need to create them only if you want to retain paths computed by the network analysis Java API.

Table 10-4. *The Path Table*

Column	Data Type	Meaning
PATH_ID[a]	NUMBER	Unique identification for that path in the network. This is also the primary key of the table.
START_NODE_ID[a]	NUMBER	Unique identifier of the node from which the path originates.
END_NODE_ID[a]	NUMBER	Unique identifier of the node at which the path terminates.
COST[a]	NUMBER	A numeric value representing the total cost for the path.
SIMPLE[a]	CHAR(1)	Contains Y if the path is simple path or N if it is complex. If the column does not exist, then all paths are considered simple. Note that all paths produced by the Java API are simple.
geometry_column	SDO_GEOMETRY	A line geometry object that describes the shape of the path, formed by linking together the geometries of all links in the path. This is present only when the network is spatial.
PATH_NAME	VARCHAR2	Name of the path. Fill this with any descriptive name.
PATH_TYPE	VARCHAR2	Type of path. Fill this with any descriptive code or text.

[a] *These columns are required. All others are optional.*

Path Link Table

The *path link* table, as shown in Table 10-5, stores the list of all links that define a path. The PATH_ID and LINK_ID form the primary key of the table. All columns are required.

Table 10-5. *The Path Link Table*

Column	Data Type	Meaning
PATH_ID	NUMBER	Path identification
LINK_ID	NUMBER	Link identification
SEQ_NO	NUMBER	Sequence of that link in the path

Network Metadata

The view USER_SDO_NETWORK_METADATA, as shown in Table 10-6, describes the elements that compose a network: the names of the tables and the names of optional columns such as costs and geometries.

Table 10-6. *The* USER_SDO_NETWORK_METADATA *View*

Name	Data Type	Meaning
NETWORK	VARCHAR2(24)	Unique name of the network. Note that this is limited to 24 characters.
NETWORK_ID	NUMBER	Unique network number (optional).
NETWORK_CATEGORY	VARCHAR2(12)	The network category is SPATIAL if the network nodes and links are associated with spatial geometries and LOGICAL if the network nodes and links are not associated with spatial geometries.
GEOMETRY_TYPE	VARCHAR2(24)	Type of spatial geometry if the network category is SPATIAL. This is typically set to SDO_GEOMETRY, but it could also be set to LRS_GEOMETRY or TOPO_GEOMETRY (not covered in this book).
NETWORK_TYPE	VARCHAR2(24)	User-defined string to describe the type of network.
NO_OF_HIERARCHY_LEVELS	NUMBER	Number of levels in the network hierarchy. It contains 1 if there is no hierarchy.
NO_OF_PARTITIONS	NUMBER	Number of partitions in the network.
LINK_DIRECTION	VARCHAR2(12)	Specifies whether the links of the network are directed (DIRECTED or UNDIRECTED).
NODE_TABLE_NAME	VARCHAR2(32)	Name of the node table.
NODE_GEOM_COLUMN	VARCHAR2(32)	Name of the geometry column in the node table (if the network category is SPATIAL).
NODE_COST_COLUMN	VARCHAR2(1024)	Name of the cost column in the node table. If this is not specified, then network analysis does not use any node costing (in other words, all nodes have a cost of 0).
LINK_TABLE_NAME	VARCHAR2(32)	Name of the link table.
LINK_GEOM_COLUMN	VARCHAR2(32)	Name of the geometry column in the link table (if the network category is SPATIAL).
LINK_COST_COLUMN	VARCHAR2(1024)	Name of the cost column in the link table. If this is not specified, then network analysis does not use any link costing (in other words, all links have a cost of 1).

Name	Data Type	Meaning
PATH_TABLE_NAME	VARCHAR2(32)	Name of the path table. This is optional. If it is not specified, then the network does not use any path table.
PATH_LINK_TABLE_NAME	VARCHAR2(32)	Name of the path link table. This is optional. Specify it only if the network uses a path table.
PATH_GEOM_COLUMN	VARCHAR2(32)	Name of the geometry column in the path table.
LRS_TABLE_NAME	VARCHAR2(32)	Name of the table that contains the LRS geometries (only when GEOMETRY_TYPE is LRS_GEOMETRY).
LRS_GEOM_COLUMN	VARCHAR2(32)	Name of the geometry column in the LRS table.
PARTITION_TABLE_NAME	VARCHAR2(32)	Name of the table that contains the network partitions.

The simplest possible network is one that contains a *node* table with only a NODE_ID column and a *link* table that contains LINK_ID, START_NODE_ID, and END_NODE_ID columns. This is a logical network without costs.

Defining Networks

As mentioned earlier, you have several ways to define the data structures for a network. At one extreme, a simple procedure call will do everything. At the other extreme, you create all the tables manually.

All operations are provided by procedures and functions of the SDO_NET package.

"Automatic" Network Definition

You can use the CREATE_SDO_NETWORK or CREATE_LOGICAL_NETWORK procedure to create all the structures of a network.

The example in Listing 10-1 creates a spatial network called US_ROADS. The links are directed, and the nodes have no cost. No names are provided for the various tables; they will receive default generated names. In this and the following example, we use the *named* notation for parameters. This notation is more verbose, but it makes your code easier to read and maintain. It is especially useful for calling procedures or functions that have a long list of parameters.

Listing 10-1. *Creating a Spatial Network Using Default Table Names*

```
SQL> BEGIN
       SDO_NET.CREATE_SDO_NETWORK (
         NETWORK => 'US_ROADS',
         NO_OF_HIERARCHY_LEVELS => 1,
         IS_DIRECTED => TRUE,
         NODE_WITH_COST => FALSE
     );
     END;
     /
```

The call can be shortened to the following (using the positional parameter notation):

```
SQL> EXEC SDO_NET.CREATE_SDO_NETWORK ('US_ROADS',1,TRUE,FALSE)
```

The procedure creates four network tables called US_ROADS_NODE$, US_ROADS_LINK$, US_ROADS_PATH$, and US_ROADS_PLINK$, and it adds information to the network metadata. The geometry columns in the *node, link,* and *path link* tables are called GEOMETRY. The *link* table has a cost column called COST. The *path* and *path link* tables are created, even if you do not want any. Listing 10-2 shows the structure of the resulting tables.

Listing 10-2. *Structure of Default Network Tables*

```
SQL> describe US_ROADS_NODE$
 Name                                      Null?    Type
 ----------------------------------------- -------- --------------------
 NODE_ID                                   NOT NULL NUMBER
 NODE_NAME                                          VARCHAR2(32)
 NODE_TYPE                                          VARCHAR2(24)
 ACTIVE                                             VARCHAR2(1)
 PARTITION_ID                                       NUMBER
 GEOMETRY                                           MDSYS.SDO_GEOMETRY

SQL> describe US_ROADS_LINK$
 Name                                      Null?    Type
 ----------------------------------------- -------- --------------------
 LINK_ID                                   NOT NULL NUMBER
 LINK_NAME                                          VARCHAR2(32 CHAR)
 START_NODE_ID                             NOT NULL NUMBER
 END_NODE_ID                               NOT NULL NUMBER
 LINK_TYPE                                          VARCHAR2(24 CHAR)
 ACTIVE                                             VARCHAR2(1 CHAR)
 LINK_LEVEL                                         NUMBER
 GEOMETRY                                           MDSYS.SDO_GEOMETRY
 COST                                               NUMBER
 BIDIRECTED                                         VARCHAR2(1)

SQL> describe US_ROADS_PATH$
 Name                                      Null?    Type
 ----------------------------------------- -------- --------------------
 PATH_ID                                   NOT NULL NUMBER
 PATH_NAME                                          VARCHAR2(32 CHAR)
 PATH_TYPE                                          VARCHAR2(24 CHAR)
 START_NODE_ID                             NOT NULL NUMBER
 END_NODE_ID                               NOT NULL NUMBER
 COST                                               NUMBER
 SIMPLE                                             VARCHAR2(1 CHAR)
 GEOMETRY                                           MDSYS.SDO_GEOMETRY

SQL> describe US_ROADS_PLINK$
 Name                                      Null?    Type
 ----------------------------------------- -------- --------------------
 PATH_ID                                   NOT NULL NUMBER
 LINK_ID                                   NOT NULL NUMBER
 SEQ_NO                                             NUMBER
```

Note that the tables have primary keys defined (using default constraint names). No foreign key constraints are defined, however.

■ **Note** The network creation function is not atomic. If it fails to complete, then you may be left with a half-created network (in other words, some tables are created). Before you try to create the network again, you must first manually drop the existing network using the DROP_NETWORK procedure.

The second example (see Listing 10-3) illustrates the creation of the same US_ROADS network with explicit table and column names. The example also shows the complete list of parameters you can pass to the procedure.

Listing 10-3. *Network Creation with Explicit Table and Column Names*

```
SQL> BEGIN
  SDO_NET.CREATE_SDO_NETWORK (
    NETWORK => 'US_ROADS',
    NO_OF_HIERARCHY_LEVELS => 1,
    IS_DIRECTED => TRUE,
    NODE_TABLE_NAME  => 'US_INTERSECTIONS',
    NODE_GEOM_COLUMN => 'LOCATION',
    NODE_COST_COLUMN => NULL,
    LINK_TABLE_NAME  => 'US_STREETS',
    LINK_GEOM_COLUMN => 'STREET_GEOM',
    LINK_COST_COLUMN => 'STREET_LENGTH',
    PATH_TABLE_NAME  => 'US_PATHS',
    PATH_GEOM_COLUMN => 'PATH_GEOM',
    PATH_LINK_TABLE_NAME => 'US_PATH_LINKS'
  );
END;
/
```

When no name is given for a *geometry* column, it is named GEOMETRY. When no name is given for a *cost* column, then no cost column is created.

"Manual" Network Definition

The "automatic" creation method you just saw is not flexible. It gives you very little control over the actual structuring of the tables, and it gives you no control at all over their physical storage (tablespaces, space management, partitioning, and so on). But it is easy to use. In particular, it automatically populates the network metadata and makes sure the table structures are consistent.

The alternative is to create the network tables manually. This gives you total flexibility over the table structures, but you must manually update the network metadata and ensure that the table structures are consistent with the metadata.

Listing 10-4 illustrates the process for manually creating the US_ROADS spatial network with only the columns we need. Note that for simplicity, we do not include any storage parameters for the tables, and we define the primary key constraints inline. A better practice is to create explicit indexes and use them to define the constraints.

Note that the us_streets table contains two columns that can be used as cost: street_length represents the length of the street segment, whereas travel_time contains the time needed to drive along that street segment.

■ **Note** Travel times are usually derived from the type of street segment (interstate or motorway, local road, and so on). This is often referred to in road-navigation databases as the functional class of the street segment. Travel times may also include local specific speed limits.

Listing 10-4. *Manual Network Creation*

```
SQL> -- Create the node table
SQL> CREATE TABLE us_intersections (
 node_id         NUMBER,
 location        SDO_GEOMETRY,
 CONSTRAINT us_intersections_pk PRIMARY KEY (node_id)
     );
SQL> -- Create the link table
     CREATE TABLE us_streets (
       link_id          NUMBER,
       start_node_id    NUMBER NOT NULL,
       end_node_id      NUMBER NOT NULL,
       active           CHAR(1),
       street_geom      SDO_GEOMETRY,
       street_length    NUMBER,
       travel_time      NUMBER,
       bidirected       CHAR(1),
       CONSTRAINT us_streets_pk PRIMARY KEY (link_id)
     );
SQL> -- Create path table
SQL> CREATE TABLE us_paths (
       path_id          NUMBER,
       start_node_id    NUMBER NOT NULL,
       end_node_id      NUMBER NOT NULL,
       cost             NUMBER,
       simple           VARCHAR2(1),
       path_geom        SDO_GEOMETRY,
       CONSTRAINT us_paths_pk PRIMARY KEY (path_id)
     );
SQL> -- Create path link table
SQL> CREATE TABLE us_path_links (
       path_id          number,
       link_id          number,
       seq_no           number,
       CONSTRAINT us_path_links_pk PRIMARY KEY (path_id, link_id)
    );
```

This code only creates the tables that define the network. You still need to "glue" them together as an actual network, which you can do manually by inserting the proper information into the network metadata (USER_SDO_NETWORK_METADATA), as illustrated in Listing 10-5.

Listing 10-5. *Setting Up Network Metadata*

```
SQL> INSERT INTO USER_SDO_NETWORK_METADATA (
       NETWORK,
       NETWORK_CATEGORY,
       GEOMETRY_TYPE,
       NO_OF_HIERARCHY_LEVELS,
       NO_OF_PARTITIONS,
       LINK_DIRECTION,
       NODE_TABLE_NAME,
       NODE_GEOM_COLUMN,
       NODE_COST_COLUMN,
       LINK_TABLE_NAME,
       LINK_GEOM_COLUMN,
       LINK_COST_COLUMN,
```

```
    PATH_TABLE_NAME,
    PATH_GEOM_COLUMN,
    PATH_LINK_TABLE_NAME
  )
  VALUES (
    'US_ROADS',           -- network (primary key)
    'SPATIAL',            -- network_category
    'SDO_GEOMETRY',       -- geometry_type
    1,                    -- no_of_hierarchy_levels
    1,                    -- no_of_partitions
    'DIRECTED',           -- link_direction
    'US_INTERSECTIONS',   -- node_table_name
    'LOCATION',           -- node_geom_column
    NULL,                 -- node_cost_column (no cost at node level)
    'US_STREETS',         -- link_table_name
    'STREET_GEOM',        -- link_geom_column
    'STREET_LENGTH',      -- link_cost_column
    'US_PATHS',           -- path_table_name
    'PATH_GEOM',          -- path_geom_column
    'US_PATH_LINKS'       -- path_link_table_name
  );
SQL> COMMIT;
```

This insert can be tricky. Because of the large number of columns to fill, it is easy to make mistakes. So, it is important to verify that your definitions are consistent using the validation functions provided by Oracle. We will discuss those functions shortly.

Note You can also create the network tables individually, using the `SDO_CREATE_xxx_TABLE` procedures (where `xxx` stands for `NODE`, `LINK`, and so on). Those procedures are of little interest, because they give no option to control the storage parameters for the tables, and you must still manually update the network metadata and make sure it is consistent with the tables you created. We do not discuss those procedures here.

Defining Multiple Networks on the Same Tables

In the preceding example, the `us_streets` table contains two cost columns: `street_length` and `travel_time`. We defined the `US_ROADS` network as using `street_length` for the cost column. This means you can use this network for computing the *shortest* routes between nodes.

But you may also want to compute the *fastest* routes between nodes. For this, all you need to do is define a second network on the same tables, this time using `travel_time` as the cost column for the links. This is illustrated in Listing 10-6, which defines a new network called `US_ROADS_TIME`.

Listing 10-6. *Setting Up Metadata for a Time-Based Road Network*

```
SQL> INSERT INTO USER_SDO_NETWORK_METADATA (
    NETWORK,
    NETWORK_CATEGORY,
    GEOMETRY_TYPE,
    NO_OF_HIERARCHY_LEVELS,
    NO_OF_PARTITIONS,
    LINK_DIRECTION,
    NODE_TABLE_NAME,
    NODE_GEOM_COLUMN,
```

```
      NODE_COST_COLUMN,
      LINK_TABLE_NAME,
      LINK_GEOM_COLUMN,
      LINK_COST_COLUMN,
      PATH_TABLE_NAME,
      PATH_GEOM_COLUMN,
      PATH_LINK_TABLE_NAME
    )
    VALUES (
      'US_ROADS_TIME',       -- network (primary key)
      'SPATIAL',             -- network_category
      'SDO_GEOMETRY',        -- geometry_type
      1,                     -- no_of_hierarchy_levels
      1,                     -- no_of_partitions
      'DIRECTED',            -- link_direction
      'US_INTERSECTIONS',    -- node_table_name
      'LOCATION',            -- node_geom_column
      NULL,                  -- node_cost_column (no cost at node level)
      'US_STREETS',          -- link_table_name
      'STREET_GEOM',         -- link_geom_column
      'TRAVEL_TIME',         -- link_cost_column
      'US_PATHS',            -- path_table_name
      'PATH_GEOM',           -- path_geom_column
      'US_PATH_LINKS'        -- path_link_table_name
    );
SQL> COMMIT;
```

Notice that the US_ROADS_TIME network uses the same *path* and *path link* tables as the US_ROADS network. If you want, you can create and use different tables. That way, you can keep separate the results of distance-based searches and time-based searches.

Defining a Network Over Existing Structures

In the previous example, you were able to define the network structures entirely from scratch. What if you already have a network defined (as *node* and *link* tables) and used in existing applications?

One way is to create a copy of the existing network into tables suitable for the Oracle Network Data Model. This approach has drawbacks: it doubles the storage costs and adds complexities to maintaining the two copies of the network in sync.

A simpler approach is to define a network directly on the existing tables by just setting up the network metadata to point to the existing tables. That may, however, not be directly possible. Even though the structure of network tables is flexible, there are still some constraints—for example, the primary key of the node table must be called NODE_ID.

The solution is to create views over the existing tables and rename columns in the views so that they match the naming conventions of the network tables. This approach is illustrated in the following simple example. Consider that an existing application already uses a water distribution network, defined as a set of pipes and valves. Those tables were created by the application shown in Listing 10-7.

Listing 10-7. *Existing Water Network Tables*

```
SQL> CREATE TABLE valves (
       valve_id      NUMBER PRIMARY KEY,
       valve_type    VARCHAR2(20),
       location      SDO_GEOMETRY
       -- ... other columns ...
     );
```

```
SQL> CREATE TABLE pipes (
      pipe_id       NUMBER PRIMARY KEY,
      diameter      NUMBER,
      length        NUMBER,
      start_valve   NUMBER NOT NULL REFERENCES valves,
      end_valve     NUMBER NOT NULL REFERENCES valves,
      pipe_geom     SDO_GEOMETRY
      -- ... other columns ...
    );
```

The first step is to define views over the existing tables, as illustrated in Listing 10-8. Notice that column valve_id in the original valves table is renamed to node_id in the net_pipes view. Similar renaming takes place in the net_pipes view.

Listing 10-8. *Views Over Existing Tables*

```
SQL> CREATE VIEW net_valves (node_id, valve_type, location) AS
      SELECT valve_id,
             valve_type,
             location
             -- ...other columns ...
      FROM   valves;
SQL> CREATE VIEW net_pipes
      (link_id, start_node_id, end_node_id, length, pipe_geom)
    AS
      SELECT pipe_id,
             start_valve,
             end_valve,
             length,
             pipe_geom
             -- ... other columns ...
      FROM pipes;
```

The second step is optional. If you want to keep the results of any network traces or analyses, then you need to also create *path* and *path link* tables (see Listing 10-9). There is little flexibility in creating those tables—all you can do is choose the name of the tables and choose a name for the SDO_GEOMETRY column in the *path* table.

Listing 10-9. *Creating the* Path *and* Path Link *Tables*

```
SQL> CREATE TABLE net_paths (
      path_id          NUMBER,
      start_node_id    NUMBER NOT NULL,
      end_node_id      NUMBER NOT NULL,
      cost             NUMBER,
      simple           VARCHAR2(1),
      path_geom        SDO_GEOMETRY,
      CONSTRAINT net_paths_pk PRIMARY KEY (path_id)
    );
SQL> CREATE TABLE net_path_links (
      path_id          NUMBER,
      link_id          NUMBER,
      seq_no           NUMBER,
      CONSTRAINT net_path_links_pk PRIMARY KEY (path_id, link_id)
    );
```

The final step is to set up the network metadata for the water network, as shown in Listing 10-10. Notice that this is an *undirected* network—in a pipe, water can flow in any direction.

Listing 10-10. *Metadata for a Network on Existing Structures*

```
SQL> INSERT INTO USER_SDO_NETWORK_METADATA (
       NETWORK,
       NETWORK_CATEGORY,
       GEOMETRY_TYPE,
       NO_OF_HIERARCHY_LEVELS,
       NO_OF_PARTITIONS,
       LINK_DIRECTION,
       NODE_TABLE_NAME,
       NODE_GEOM_COLUMN,
       NODE_COST_COLUMN,
       LINK_TABLE_NAME,
       LINK_GEOM_COLUMN,
       LINK_COST_COLUMN,
       PATH_TABLE_NAME,
       PATH_GEOM_COLUMN,
       PATH_LINK_TABLE_NAME
     )
     VALUES (
       'WATER_NET',          -- network (primary key)
       'SPATIAL',            -- network_category
       'SDO_GEOMETRY',       -- geometry_type
       1,                    -- no_of_hierarchy_levels
       1,                    -- no_of_partitions
       'UNDIRECTED',         -- link_direction
       'NET_VALVES',         -- node_table_name
       'LOCATION',           -- node_geom_column
       NULL,                 -- node_cost_column (no cost at node level)
       'NET_PIPES',          -- link_table_name
       'PIPE_GEOM',          -- link_geom_column
       'LENGTH',             -- link_cost_column
       'NET_PATHS',          -- path_table_name
       'PATH_GEOM',          -- path_geom_column
       'NET_PATH_LINKS'      -- path_link_table_name
     );
SQL> COMMIT;
```

Validating Network Structures

You may make mistakes when defining all network structures and metadata manually. We recommend you verify the correctness of your definitions using one of the functions provided.

The main function is `VALIDATE_NETWORK`. It verifies the consistency between the metadata and the network tables, and it verifies that the tables are correctly defined (in other words, that they contain the right columns with the right data types). The function takes only one argument: the name of the network to validate.

The result of the function is a string that can take the following values:

- `NULL` if the network does not exist
- `TRUE` if the network is correctly defined
- A string with diagnostics if the network is not correctly defined

For example, if the us_streets table in the previous example were created without the street_length column, the validation of network US_ROADS would fail, as illustrated in Listing 10-11.

Listing 10-11. *Validating a Network Definition*

```
SQL> select sdo_net.validate_network('us_roads') from dual;
SDO_NET.VALIDATE_NETWORK('US_ROADS')
------------------------------------------------------------------------------
  Link Schema Error:  [COST]
```

You can also use individual VALIDATE_xxxx_SCHEMA functions (where xxxx stands for NODE, LINK, or PATH) to verify the correctness of each table in a network.

Populating Network Tables

You can populate network tables (*link* and *node* tables) using any tool: inserts from an application program, SQL*Loader, and so on.

Dropping a Network

To drop a network, use the DROP_NETWORK procedure. It will drop all tables related to a network and remove the definition of the network from the metadata. The example in Listing 10-12 removes the US_ROADS network.

Listing 10-12. *Dropping a Network*

```
SQL> EXEC SDO_NET.DROP_NETWORK ('US_ROADS');
PL/SQL procedure successfully completed.
```

The procedure locates the tables that compose a network as indicated in the network metadata. If the metadata is incorrect—for example, if it contains the wrong name for a node table—then the procedure will attempt to drop the table whose name is in the metadata. Note that it also automatically removes any spatial metadata from USER_SDO_GEOM_METADATA.

■ Caution If you want only to modify the network definition, do not use the DROP_NETWORK procedure, since it will also drop the complete network data. Instead, simply delete the definition from USER_SDO_NETWORK_METADATA and reinsert the new one. If the network is defined using views (such as WATER_NET), then the procedure only removes the views without touching the tables on which the views are based.

Creating Spatial Indexes on Network Tables

For spatial networks in which tables contain SDO_GEOMETRY columns, it may be necessary to set up spatial indexes. This is not a requirement; network analysis functions do not need spatial indexes.

Spatial indexes need spatial metadata in the USER_SDO_GEOM_METADATA table. You can insert the metadata manually, or you can use the INSERT_GEOM_METADATA procedure to set the metadata for all tables that are part of the network and that contain an SDO_GEOMETRY column, as illustrated in Listing 10-13. The function takes the name of the network as an input parameter, followed by the bounds definitions and the SRID.

Listing 10-13. *Adding Spatial Metadata to Network Tables*

```
SQL> BEGIN
       SDO_NET.INSERT_GEOM_METADATA (
         'US_ROADS',
         SDO_DIM_ARRAY (
           SDO_DIM_ELEMENT ('Long', -180, +180, 1),
           SDO_DIM_ELEMENT ('Lat',   -90,  +90, 1)
         ),
         8307
       );
     END;
     /
SQL> COMMIT;
```

Getting Information About a Network

To find out the details about the structure of a network (the name of the *link* table, the name of the *cost* column in the *node* table, and so on), just query the USER_SDO_NETWORK_METADATA view. Be aware that the output may be hard to read.

You can alternatively use one of the many functions in the SDO_NET package that return an individual piece of information. The functions' names are self-descriptive. They all take one argument: the name of the network to examine. We do not list them all here.

Listing 10-14 shows a convenient procedure that uses all those functions in order to display information about a network in a readable way. Listing 10-15 shows the results of executing the procedure on the US_ROADS network.

Listing 10-14. *Convenient Procedure for Getting Network Details*

```
CREATE OR REPLACE PROCEDURE SHOW_NET_DETAILS (NETWORK_NAME VARCHAR2) AS
BEGIN
  DBMS_OUTPUT.PUT_LINE ('NETWORK_EXISTS() =                ' ||
    SDO_NET.NETWORK_EXISTS(NETWORK_NAME));
  DBMS_OUTPUT.PUT_LINE ('IS_HIERARCHICAL() =               ' ||
    SDO_NET.IS_HIERARCHICAL(NETWORK_NAME));
  DBMS_OUTPUT.PUT_LINE ('IS_LOGICAL() =                    ' ||
    SDO_NET.IS_LOGICAL(NETWORK_NAME));
  DBMS_OUTPUT.PUT_LINE ('IS_SPATIAL() =                    ' ||
    SDO_NET.IS_SPATIAL(NETWORK_NAME));
  DBMS_OUTPUT.PUT_LINE ('GET_NETWORK_CATEGORY() =          ' ||
    SDO_NET.GET_NETWORK_CATEGORY(NETWORK_NAME));
  DBMS_OUTPUT.PUT_LINE ('SDO_GEOMETRY_NETWORK() =          ' ||
    SDO_NET.SDO_GEOMETRY_NETWORK(NETWORK_NAME));
  DBMS_OUTPUT.PUT_LINE ('GET_NETWORK_TYPE() =              ' ||
    SDO_NET.GET_NETWORK_TYPE(NETWORK_NAME));
  DBMS_OUTPUT.PUT_LINE ('GET_GEOMETRY_TYPE() =             ' ||
    SDO_NET.GET_GEOMETRY_TYPE(NETWORK_NAME));
  DBMS_OUTPUT.PUT_LINE ('GET_NO_OF_HIERARCHY_LEVELS() =    ' ||
    SDO_NET.GET_NO_OF_HIERARCHY_LEVELS(NETWORK_NAME));
  DBMS_OUTPUT.PUT_LINE ('GET_LINK_DIRECTION() =            ' ||
    SDO_NET.GET_LINK_DIRECTION(NETWORK_NAME));
  DBMS_OUTPUT.PUT_LINE ('GET_NODE_TABLE_NAME() =           ' ||
    SDO_NET.GET_NODE_TABLE_NAME(NETWORK_NAME));
```

```
  DBMS_OUTPUT.PUT_LINE ('GET_NODE_COST_COLUMN() =         ' ||
    SDO_NET.GET_NODE_COST_COLUMN(NETWORK_NAME));
  DBMS_OUTPUT.PUT_LINE ('GET_NODE_GEOM_COLUMN() =         ' ||
    SDO_NET.GET_NODE_GEOM_COLUMN(NETWORK_NAME));
  DBMS_OUTPUT.PUT_LINE ('GET_LINK_TABLE_NAME() =          ' ||
    SDO_NET.GET_LINK_TABLE_NAME(NETWORK_NAME));
  DBMS_OUTPUT.PUT_LINE ('GET_LINK_COST_COLUMN() =         ' ||
    SDO_NET.GET_LINK_COST_COLUMN(NETWORK_NAME));
  DBMS_OUTPUT.PUT_LINE ('GET_LINK_GEOM_COLUMN() =         ' ||
    SDO_NET.GET_LINK_GEOM_COLUMN(NETWORK_NAME));
  DBMS_OUTPUT.PUT_LINE ('GET_PATH_TABLE_NAME() =          ' ||
    SDO_NET.GET_PATH_TABLE_NAME(NETWORK_NAME));
  DBMS_OUTPUT.PUT_LINE ('GET_PATH_GEOM_COLUMN() =         ' ||
    SDO_NET.GET_PATH_GEOM_COLUMN(NETWORK_NAME));
  DBMS_OUTPUT.PUT_LINE ('GET_PATH_LINK_TABLE_NAME() =     ' ||
    SDO_NET.GET_PATH_LINK_TABLE_NAME(NETWORK_NAME));
END;
```

Listing 10-15. *Getting Network Details*

```
SET SERVEROUTPUT ON
SQL> EXEC show_net_details ('US_ROADS');
NETWORK_EXISTS() =             TRUE
IS_HIERARCHICAL() =            FALSE
IS_LOGICAL() =                 FALSE
IS_SPATIAL() =                 TRUE
GET_NETWORK_CATEGORY() =       SPATIAL
SDO_GEOMETRY_NETWORK() =       TRUE
GET_NETWORK_TYPE() =
GET_GEOMETRY_TYPE() =          SDO_GEOMETRY
GET_NO_OF_HIERARCHY_LEVELS() = 1
GET_LINK_DIRECTION() =         DIRECTED
GET_NODE_TABLE_NAME() =        US_INTERSECTIONS
GET_NODE_COST_COLUMN() =
GET_NODE_GEOM_COLUMN() =       LOCATION
GET_LINK_TABLE_NAME() =        US_STREETS
GET_LINK_COST_COLUMN() =       STREET_LENGTH
GET_LINK_GEOM_COLUMN() =       STREET_GEOM
GET_PATH_TABLE_NAME() =        US_PATHS
GET_PATH_GEOM_COLUMN() =       PATH_GEOM
GET_PATH_LINK_TABLE_NAME() =   US_PATH_LINKS
PL/SQL procedure successfully completed.
```

Verifying Network Connectivity

The SDO_NET package provides some other functions, summarized in Table 10-7, to help you locate any errors inside the network data such as isolated nodes or dangling links. All the functions take a network name as parameter.

Table 10-7. *Network Verification Functions*

Function	Usage
`SDO_NET.GET_NO_OF_NODES()`	Returns the number of nodes in the network
`SDO_NET.GET_NO_OF_LINKS()`	Returns the number of links in the network
`SDO_NET.GET_ISOLATED_NODES()`	Returns the nodes that are not related to any link
`SDO_NET.GET_INVALID_LINKS()`	Returns the links with nonexistent start or end nodes
`SDO_NET.GET_INVALID_PATHS()`	Returns the paths with nonexistent start or end nodes, or with nonexistent links

■ **Note** You can prevent errors such as isolated nodes or dangling links using referential integrity constraints in the link table, as illustrated in the definition of the `pipes` table in Listing 10-7.

Some other functions, listed in Table 10-8, allow you to find out details about individual nodes in the network. They all take two parameters: the name of the network and the identifier of the node to examine.

Table 10-8. *Node Detail Functions*

Function	Usage
`SDO_NET.GET_NODE_DEGREE()`	Returns the number of links that originate and terminate at that node
`SDO_NET.GET_NODE_IN_DEGREE()`	Returns the number of links that terminate at that node (in other words, those links that have this node's ID as `END_NODE_ID`)
`SDO_NET.GET_NODE_OUT_DEGREE()`	Returns the number of links that originate at that node (in other words, those links that have this node's ID as `START_NODE_ID`)
`SDO_NET.GET_IN_LINKS()`	Returns a list containing the IDs of all links that terminate at that node (as an `SDO_NUMBER_ARRAY` type)
`SDO_NET.GET_OUT_LINKS()`	Returns a list containing the IDs of all links that originate at that node (as an `SDO_NUMBER_ARRAY` type)

Example Network

We will now create and load two simple networks called UNET and DNET. We will use those networks extensively later to illustrate network analysis functions.

UNET: A Simple Undirected Network

Figure 10-8 shows a simple network (UNET) with undirected links. Links have a cost proportional to their length; the cost of each link is shown in parentheses. Listing 10-16 shows the creation of the network, and Listing 10-17 shows the loading of the network. Note that the ordering of the nodes in the `start_node_id` and `end_node_id` columns in the `unet_links` table is unimportant.

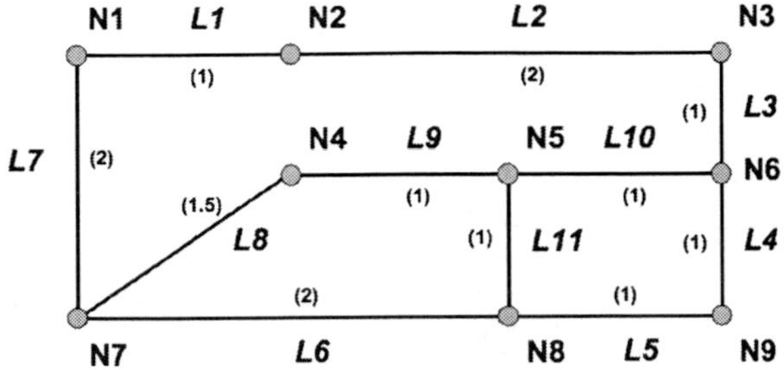

Figure 10-8. *A simple undirected network*

Listing 10-16. *Defining the UNET Network*

```
SQL> BEGIN
       SDO_NET.CREATE_SDO_NETWORK (
         NETWORK => 'UNET',
         NO_OF_HIERARCHY_LEVELS => 1,
         IS_DIRECTED => FALSE,
         NODE_TABLE_NAME => 'UNET_NODES',
         NODE_GEOM_COLUMN => 'GEOM',
         NODE_COST_COLUMN => NULL,
         LINK_TABLE_NAME => 'UNET_LINKS',
         LINK_COST_COLUMN => 'COST',
         LINK_GEOM_COLUMN => 'GEOM',
         PATH_TABLE_NAME => 'UNET_PATHS',
         PATH_GEOM_COLUMN => 'GEOM',
         PATH_LINK_TABLE_NAME => 'UNET_PLINKS'
       );
     END;
     /
```

Listing 10-17. *Loading the UNET Network*

```
SQL> -- Populate the node table
SQL> INSERT INTO unet_nodes (node_id, node_name, geom)
       VALUES (1, 'N1',
         SDO_GEOMETRY (2001, NULL, SDO_POINT_TYPE (1,3,NULL), NULL, NULL));
  ...
SQL> COMMIT;
SQL> -- Populate the link table
SQL> INSERT INTO unet_links
       (link_id, link_name, start_node_id, end_node_id, cost, geom)
       VALUES ( 1, 'L1',  1,  2,  1,
          SDO_GEOMETRY (2002, NULL, NULL,
            SDO_ELEM_INFO_ARRAY (1,2,1),
            SDO_ORDINATE_ARRAY (1,3, 2,3))
       );
...
SQL> COMMIT;
```

DNET: A Simple Directed Network

In Oracle Database 10*g* Release 1, the directed/undirected nature of the network was global—that is, all links were directed. Bidirectional links had to be represented as two links, one in each direction: a link and a colink, as illustrated in Figure 10-9.

The usual convention in network modeling is to identify a link and its colink using the same number with opposite signs. For example, link L6 goes from node N8 to node N7, whereas link –L6 goes from node N7 to node N8.

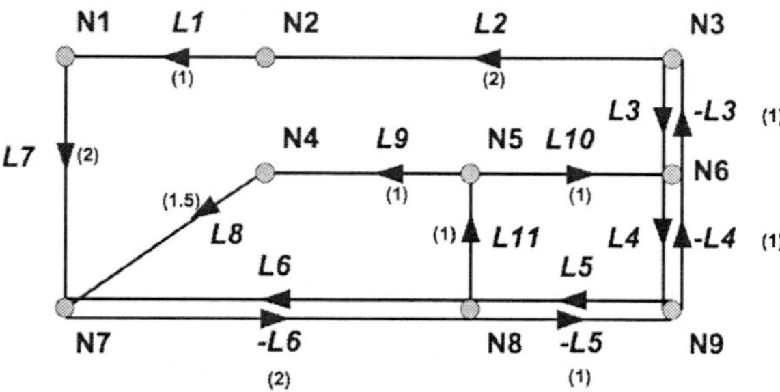

Figure 10-9. *Directed network with dual links*

Since Oracle Database 10*g* Release 2, you no longer need two links to represent a bidirectional link. Now, each link in a directed network can be classified as bidirected or not. You indicate this in the `bidirected` column of the `link` table. This greatly reduces the storage space for a road network; in a typical road network, the vast majority of the road segments allow two-way traffic. In Oracle Database 10*g* Release 1, each of those segments had to be modeled using two links. Since Oracle Database 10*g* Release 2, you can model all those road segments using just one link per segment.

Figure 10-10 shows the same network as earlier but this time using bidirectional links. Note, however, that link L6 is still represented as two links, a link and a colink. This is useful if you want different attributes in each direction; after all, they could have different costs or types. An example would be a one-way street with a bus lane going in the opposite direction. In this example, link L6 has a cost of 3, whereas link –L6 has a cost of 2.

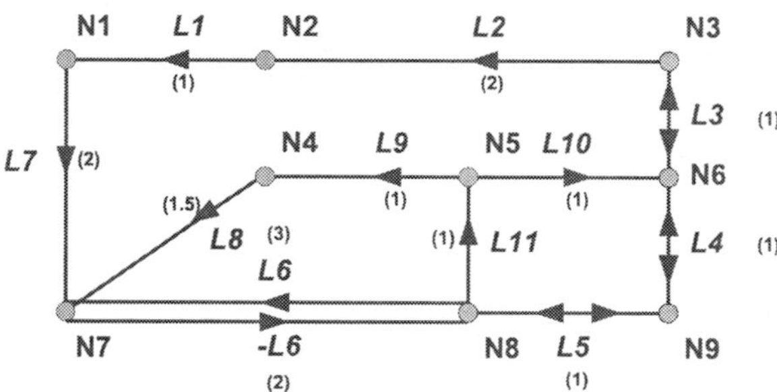

Figure 10-10. *Directed network using bidirected links*

Listing 10-18 shows the creation of the network, and Listing 10-19 shows the loading of the network. Note that the ordering of the nodes in the `start_node_id` and `end_node_id` columns in the `dnet_links` table is important—it determines the direction of the directed links.

■ **Note** When a link is flagged as "directed" (that is, column `bidirected` is set to `'N'`), its orientation is always from the start node to the end node. If you want to orient the link in the opposite direction, then you need to swap its start and end node (that is, swap the contents of the `start_node_id` and `end_node_id` columns).

Listing 10-18. *Defining the DNET Network*

```
SQL> BEGIN
       SDO_NET.CREATE_SDO_NETWORK (
         NETWORK => 'DNET',
         NO_OF_HIERARCHY_LEVELS => 1,
         IS_DIRECTED => TRUE,
         NODE_TABLE_NAME => 'DNET_NODES',
         NODE_GEOM_COLUMN => 'GEOM',
         NODE_COST_COLUMN => NULL,
         LINK_TABLE_NAME => 'DNET_LINKS',
         LINK_COST_COLUMN => 'COST',
         LINK_GEOM_COLUMN => 'GEOM',
         PATH_TABLE_NAME => 'DNET_PATHS',
         PATH_GEOM_COLUMN => 'GEOM',
         PATH_LINK_TABLE_NAME => 'DNET_PLINKS'
       );
     END;
     /
```

Listing 10-19. *Loading the DNET Network*

```
SQL> -- Populate The Node Table
SQL> INSERT INTO dnet_nodes (node_id, node_name, geom)
       VALUES (1, 'N1',
         SDO_GEOMETRY (2001, NULL, SDO_POINT_TYPE (1,3,NULL), NULL, NULL));
...
SQL> COMMIT;
SQL> -- Populate The Link Table
SQL> INSERT INTO dnet_links
       (link_id, link_name, start_node_id, end_node_id, cost, geom, bidirected)
       VALUES ( 1, 'L1',  2,  1,  1,
         SDO_GEOMETRY (2002, NULL, NULL,
           SDO_ELEM_INFO_ARRAY (1,2,1),
           SDO_ORDINATE_ARRAY (2,3, 1,3)),
         'N'
       );
...
SQL> COMMIT;
```

■ **Note** The geometric representation does not have to match the logical representation exactly. In particular, the orientation of the line geometry for a link does not have to match the direction of the link. In this section's example, link L1 goes from node N2 to node N1, whereas the line string goes in the opposite direction. It is, however, a good idea to make the physical orientation of a link (its digitizing order) match its logical direction.

Analyzing and Managing Networks Using the Java API

Network analysis uses a Java API that provides a range of analysis functions. This is actually where the value of the network data model truly lies. You use that API to find the cheapest path between nodes, the nearest nodes to a node, and so on.

The Java API is very rich. We will list only the most important methods here. For a complete reference, see the Javadoc documentation for the API, provided with the standard set of manuals. The Javadoc pages are next to the other manuals for Oracle Spatial, in the "Unstructured Data" category. You will also find a copy in your Oracle installation at `$ORACLE_HOME/md/doc/sdonm.zip`. Note that there is no other documentation of the Java API.

The Java API is provided as a package called `oracle.spatial.network` in a Java archive (JAR) file called `sdonm.jar`. You will find it in your Oracle installation at `$ORACLE_HOME/md/jlib`. To use it in your Java applications, just include it in your classpath. Note that you also need other packages to use the Java API. All necessary packages are summarized in Table 10-9.

Table 10-9. *Packages Needed to Use the Network Java API*

Package	JAR File	Usage	Location
`oracle.spatial.network`	`sdonm.jar`	Network analysis	`$ORACLE_HOME/md/jlib`
`oracle.spatial.geometry`	`sdoapi.jar`	`JGeometry` object	`$ORACLE_HOME/md/jlib`
`oracle.spatial.util`	`sdoutl.jar`	Various utilities	`$ORACLE_HOME/md/jlib`
(multiple)	`ojdbc14.jar`	JDBC driver	`$ORACLE_HOME/jdbc/lib`

The API is composed of three main sets of classes:

- `Network`, `Node`, `Link`, and `Path`: These classes store and maintain networks and network elements.
- `NetworkManager`: This class performs network analysis, and it also reads networks from the database and writes them back.
- `NetworkFactory`: This class creates networks and network elements.

■ **Caution** In versions of Oracle Database prior to 11*g*, the directory holding the JAR files was called `lib`. It is now called `jlib`.

We will now cover each of the classes in turn. We will start with `NetworkManager`, because this is the class that is at the heart of network analysis.

■ **Note** You must use a Java 1.5 JDK in order to use the Java API. Your Oracle 11*g* installation comes with a complete Java 1.5 SE JDK in `$ORACLE_HOME/jdk`

Analyzing Networks: The NetworkManager Class

The fundamental use of the Network Data Model is to find paths between nodes. There can be many paths between any two nodes, and the model can help find them all or choose the "best" one (in other words, the one with the lowest cost).

The analysis functions are all provided by methods of the NetworkManager class. The methods operate on a memory-resident copy of the network. Therefore, the first step in a program is to load the network from the database.

Loading a Network

The readNetwork() method loads a network from the database into a Network object. The method needs a connection to a database and the name of the network to load. By default, it loads the entire network, but you can also specify a subset of the network: either a certain level or all elements in a chosen rectangular window.

The following loads the complete network called UNET from the database:

```
Network UNet =
  NetworkManager.readNetwork(dbConnection, "UNET");
```

This example loads the network in "read-only" mode. If you intend to update it in your application, then you must say so when you first load it from the database. For example:

```
Network UNet =
    NetworkManager.readNetwork(dbConnection, "UNET", true);
```

Only one user at a time is allowed to load a network (or a subset of the network) in updatable mode at a time. If another user tries loading the same network (or the same subset) in updatable mode, that user will receive an error. Note that this "single updater" restriction is implemented using SELECT ... FOR UPDATE statements on all loaded network elements. This means the network elements loaded by a user are also locked for updates from any other application.

■ **Note** Loading a network in "read-only" mode still allows you to perform network updates in memory. However, you will not be able to apply the changes to the database.

Updating a Network

The writeNetwork() method writes a network back to the database. The method's name is a misnomer; it actually takes only the changes you made to the memory-resident network and applies them to the persistent copy stored in the database.

The main use of the writeNetwork() method is to store the paths calculated by the analysis functions into the *path* and *path link* tables in the database. To use that method, you must first have loaded the network in "update" mode.

Finding the Shortest Path Between Two Nodes

A common operation on a network is to find the shortest path between two nodes. The shortestPath() method does just this; it returns the "best" path between two nodes in a network. The inputs to the method are the network on which to perform the analysis and the start and end nodes. This is probably the *most useful analysis function,* and it is the building block for all routing engines and others that provide driving directions.

The best path between two nodes is the one with the smallest cost. Remember that the cost of a node or link is a numeric value defined in the network tables. That cost can represent anything, such as the length of a road segment or the time needed to travel along that road segment. When no cost column is present, then all links are considered to have a cost of 1, and nodes have a cost of 0. Only active nodes and links are considered—in other words, those that have an ACTIVE column set to 'Y'.

The code in Listing 10-20 returns the shortest path from node N4 to node N3 on the UNET undirected network shown in Figure 10-8. Figure 10-11 shows the resulting path. The shortestPath()

method returns a Path object. We use a number of methods of the Path object to extract various pieces of information, such as the cost of the path and the number of links. We also extract the detailed structure of the path as an array of Link objects. We then proceed to extract details from each of the Link objects.

Note We detail how to use the Path, Link, and Node objects later in this chapter.

Listing 10-20. *Using the* shortestPath() *Method*

```
// Get shortest path from node N4 to N3
Network testNet = uNet;
startNodeId = 4;
endNodeId = 3;
Path path = NetworkManager.shortestPath (testNet, startNodeID ,endNodeId);

// Show path cost and number of links
System.out.println ("Path cost: " + path.getCost() );
System.out.println ("Number of links: "+ path.getNoOfLinks());
System.out.println ("Simple path? "+ path.isSimple());

// Show the links traversed
System.out.println ("Links traversed:");
Link[] linkArray = path.getLinkArray();
for (int i = 0; i < linkArray.length; i++)
  System.out.println ("  Link " + linkArray[i].getID() + "\t"
    + linkArray[i].getName() +"\t" + linkArray[i].getCost());

// Show the nodes traversed
System.out.println ("  Nodes traversed:");
Node [] nodeArray = path.getNodeArray();
for (int i = 0; i < nodeArray.length; i++)
  System.out.println ("    Node " + nodeArray[i].getID() + "\t"
    + nodeArray[i].getName() +"\t" + nodeArray[i].getCost());
```

Here are the results of executing the code in Listing 10-20:

```
Path cost: 3.0
Number of links: 3
Simple path? true
Links traversed:
  Link 9      L9      1.0
  Link 10     L10     1.0
  Link 3      L3      1.0
Nodes traversed:
  Node 4      N4      0.0
  Node 5      N5      0.0
  Node 6      N6      0.0
  Node 3      N3      0.0
```

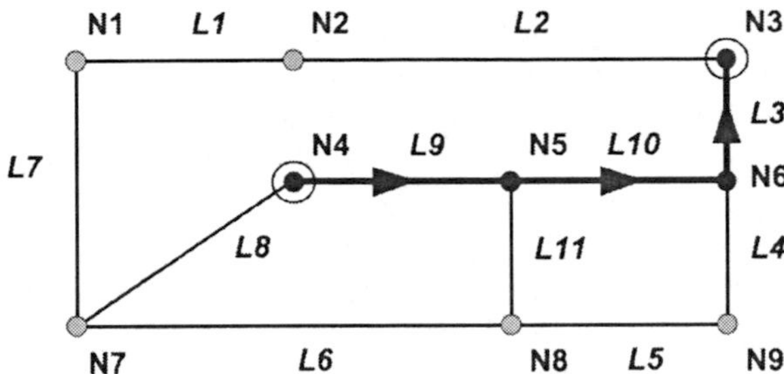

Figure 10-11. *The path from node N4 to node N3 (undirected network)*

Performing the same operation on the directed network DNET (from Figure 10-10) gives the following results, as shown in Figure 10-12:

```
Path cost: 6.5
Number of links: 5
Simple path? true
Links traversed:
  Link 8      L8     1.5
  Link -6     L6     2.0
  Link 11     L11    1.0
  Link 10     L10    1.0
  Link -3     L3     1.0
Nodes traversed:
  Node 4      N4     0.0
  Node 7      N7     0.0
  Node 8      N8     0.0
  Node 5      N5     0.0
  Node 6      N6     0.0
  Node 3      N3     0.0
```

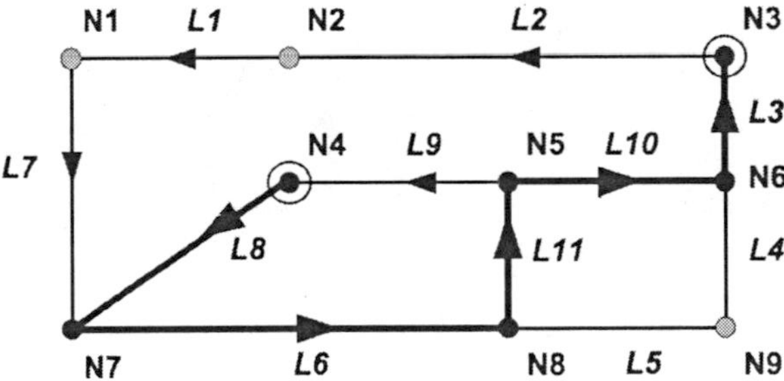

Figure 10-12. *The path from node N4 to node N3 (directed network)*

You can see that the shortest path is no longer as straightforward as in the previous example. It now has to follow the one-way links in the right direction!

The `shortestPath()` method uses the A* algorithm to find the shortest path between the nodes. You can also use the `shortestPathDijkstra()` method, which uses the algorithm developed by Professor E. W. Dijkstra. Discussing the relative merits of the two algorithms is beyond the scope of this book.

Saving the Computed Path

The Path object obtained by running one of the preceding functions is a stand-alone object; it is not related to any network. To store that path into the database, you need to complete it with some information before adding it to the network and writing it to the database, as illustrated in the following code example:

```
// Give a name to the path - construct it using the path id.
path.setName ("P" + path.getID() + " Friday excursion");

// Compute the geometry of the path
path.computeGeometry(0.05);

// add the path to the network
network.addPath(path);
```

Notice that the path has automatically received a unique ID (a sequential number), which you can override if you want. Note also the computeGeometry() method generates a geometry object that will make it easy to display the resulting path graphically on a map.

The addPath() method adds the path only into the memory-resident copy of the network. To store the path in the database tables, you still need to use the NetworkManager.writeNetwork() method.

The path returned by the shortestPath() method is sufficient to find a route through a water or electricity network. The list of the pipes traversed is sufficient to locate the network elements (the pipes and valves). For a road network, it will list the street segments traversed, in the right order.

Finding the Nearest Neighbors

Another common network analysis operation is to find the nearest node(s) to a starting node. This is similar to the SDO_NN spatial operator, with the major difference being that the SDO_NN operator locates the nearest neighbors based on straight-line distances (in other words, ignoring any road travel constraints), whereas the nearestNeighbors() method follows the network links.

An example of the use of the nearestNeighbors() method is to find the gas station nearest to your current location. The SDO_NN operator will happily point you to a station that is right across a canal, with no bridge in sight.

The code in Listing 10-21 finds the two nearest nodes from node N4 on the undirected network UNET. The nearestNeighbors() method returns an array of Path objects. Not only does it tell you who the nearest nodes are, but it also tells you how to reach them.

Listing 10-21. *Using the* nearestNeighbors() *Method*

```
// Find the two nearest neighbors of node N4
Network testNet = uNet;
startNodeId = 4;
numNeighbors = 2;
Path[] pathArray =
  NetworkManager.nearestNeighbors (testNet, startNodeId, numNeighbors);

// Display the resulting paths
System.out.println ("  " + pathArray.length + " nearest neighbors of node "
  + startNodeId + " in network " + testNet.getName());
for (int i = 0; i < pathArray.length; i++)
{
  Path path = pathArray[i];
  System.out.println("    node " + path.getEndNode().getID() +
    ", path cost " + path.getCost());
}
```

Running the code in Listing 10-21 gives the following results, which are illustrated in Figure 10-13:

```
2 nearest neighbors of node 4 in network UNET
  node 5, path cost 1.0
  node 7, path cost 1.5
```

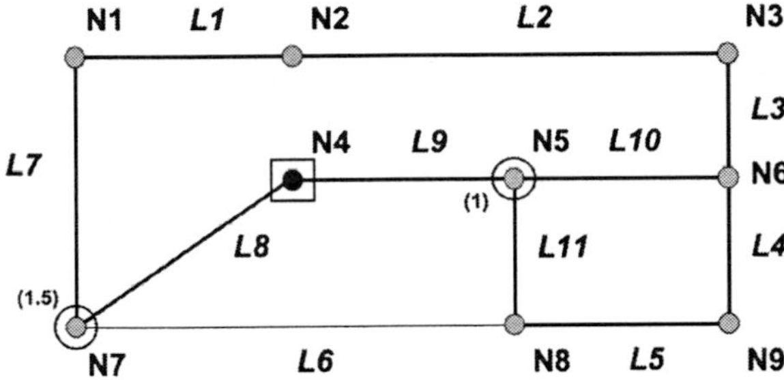

Figure 10-13. *The two nearest nodes to node N4 (undirected network)*

Performing the same operation on the directed network DNET (from Figure 10-10) gives the following results, which are illustrated in Figure 10-14:

```
2 nearest neighbors of node 4 in network DNET
  node 7, path cost 1.5
  node 8, path cost 3.5
```

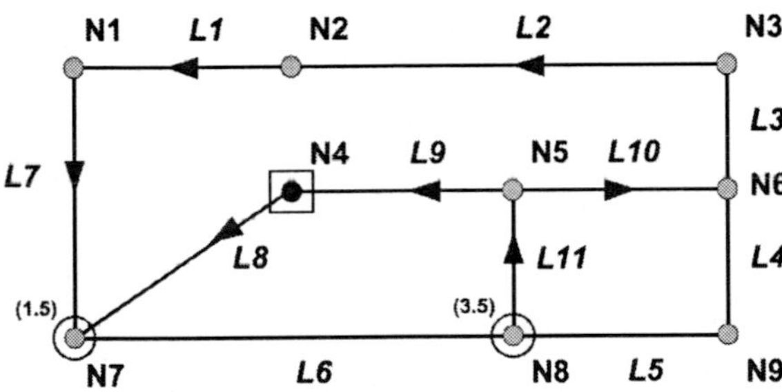

Figure 10-14. *The two nearest nodes to node N4 (directed network)*

The directions on the network links change the results; node N5 is no longer the nearest.

Finding All Nodes Within Some Distance

Another common network analysis operation selects nodes based on the distance that separates them from a starting node. This is comparable to the `SDO_WITHIN_DISTANCE` spatial operator, with the difference being that `SDO_WITHIN_DISTANCE` uses straight-line distances, whereas the `withinCost()` method uses distances along the network.

A typical example of using the `withinCost()` method is to find the network nodes (road intersections) that are within a certain driving distance or driving time from a given store. The polygon that includes all those points represents the *traction zone* of the store. It would not include customers who are directly across a river from the store but have no means to cross the river because the nearest bridges are far away. Multiple analyses using different driving times produce polygons that represent *isochrones* (in other words, zones that are at the same distance [in time] from a location).

The code in Listing 10-22 finds the nodes that are at a distance of less than three "cost units" from node N4 on the UNET network. Just like `nearestNeighbors()`, the `withinCost()` method returns an array of `Path` objects.

Listing 10-22. *Using the* `withinCost()` *Method*

```
// Find nodes that are less than or equal to 3 'cost units' from node N2
Network testNet = uNet;
startNodeId = 2;
maxCost = 3;
Path[] pathArray =
  NetworkManager.withinCost (testNet, startNodeId, maxCost);

// Display the resulting paths
System.out.println ("   " + pathArray.length + " nodes from node "
  + startNodeId + " in network " + testNet.getName() +
  " within a cost of " + maxCost + ": ");
for (int i = 0; i < pathArray.length; i++)
{
  Path path = pathArray[i];
  System.out.println("     node " + path.getEndNode().getID() +
    ", path cost " + path.getCost());
}
```

The output from running the code in Listing 10-22 is as follows:

```
4 nodes from node 2 in network UNET within a cost of 3.0:
  node 1, path cost 1.0
  node 3, path cost 2.0
  node 6, path cost 3.0
  node 7, path cost 3.0
```

Figure 10-15 shows the results graphically.

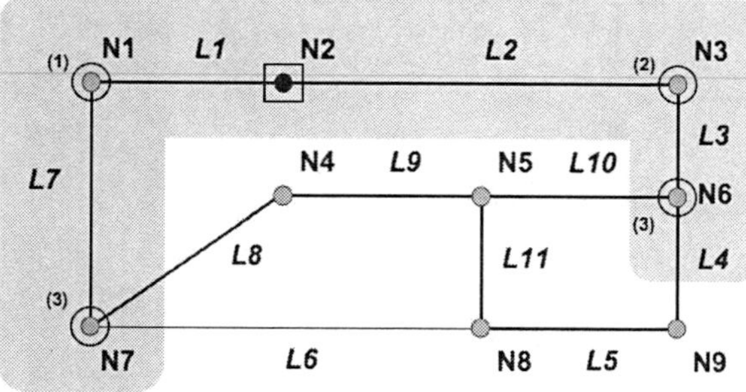

Figure 10-15. *Nodes less than three "cost units" from node N2 (undirected network)*

Performing the same operation on the directed network DNET gives the following results, as shown in Figure 10-16:

```
2 nodes from node 2 in network DNET within a cost of 3.0:
  node 1, path cost 1.0
  node 7, path cost 3.0
```

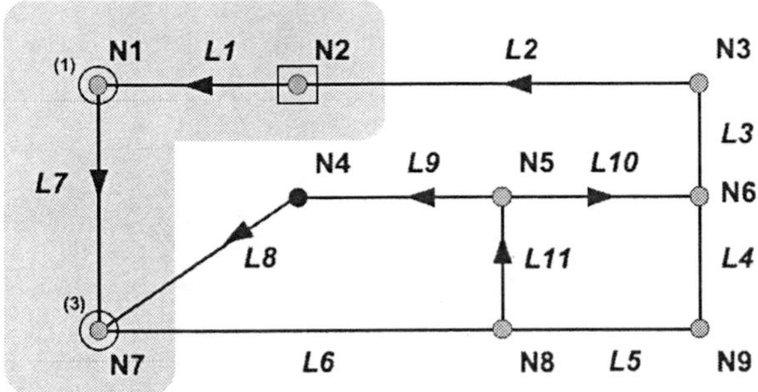

Figure 10-16. *Nodes less than three "cost units" from node N2 (directed network)*

Traveling Salesperson Problem

A traveling salesperson visits many customers in a day. The customers are spread out geographically. The salesperson really does not want to go crisscrossing the country from one visit to the other. The salesperson does not want to waste unnecessary time driving up and down roads. The salesperson wants to visit customers in the most optimal order so as to minimize travel time.

The `tspPath()` method is available to solve the *traveling salesperson problem* (TSP). You pass it the list of the nodes to visit, and the method returns the shortest path that passes through all the nodes you specified. You can optionally specify that you want to return to your starting point.

You also need a way to get the list of nodes to visit in the order proposed. Of course, they are all in the returned `Path` object, but they are mixed with all the nodes that you traverse on the way. The `getTspNodeOrder ()` method will return the nodes on the TSP in the right order.

The following code obtains the optimal route for an example trip on network UNET. We start at node N7 and need to visit nodes N2, N3, and N5. Then we come back to N7. Listing 10-23 shows how to use the `tspPath()` method.

Listing 10-23. *Using the* `tspPath()` *Method*

```
// Traveling Salesperson Problem: nodes N7, N2, N3, N5, then back to N7
Network testNet = uNet;
int[] nodeIds = {7,2,3,5};
boolean isClosed = true;
boolean useExactCost = true;
Path tspPath = NetworkManager.tspPath (testNet, nodeIds, isClosed,
  useExactCost, null);

// Display the resulting path
Link[] linkArray = tspPath.getLinkArray();
System.out.println ("  Path cost: " + tspPath.getCost() );
System.out.println ("  Number of links: "+ tspPath.getNoOfLinks());
System.out.println ("  Simple path? "+ tspPath.isSimple());
for (int i = 0; i < linkArray.length; i++)
  System.out.println ("    Link " + linkArray[i].getID() + "\t"
    + linkArray[i].getName()
    + "\t(cost: " + linkArray[i].getCost() + ")" );

// Display the visitation order
Node[]visitedNodes =  tspPath.getTspNodeOrder();
System.out.println ("  Actual node visitation order : " );
for (int i = 0; i < visitedNodes.length; i++)
  System.out.println ("    Node " + visitedNodes [i].getID() + "\t" +
     visitedNodes [i].getName());
```

The result of executing the code in Listing 10-23 is as follows:

```
Path cost: 9.5
  Number of links: 7
  Simple path? true
    Link 8      L8      (cost: 1.5)
    Link 9      L9      (cost: 1.0)
    Link 10     L10     (cost: 1.0)
    Link 3      L3      (cost: 1.0)
    Link 2      L2      (cost: 2.0)
    Link 1      L1      (cost: 1.0)
    Link 7      L7      (cost: 2.0)
  Actual node visitation order :
    Node 7      N7
    Node 5      N5
    Node 3      N3
    Node 2      N2
    Node 7      N7
```

Figure 10-17 shows the path chosen. The large circles are the nodes to visit. The square (N7) is our starting and ending point.

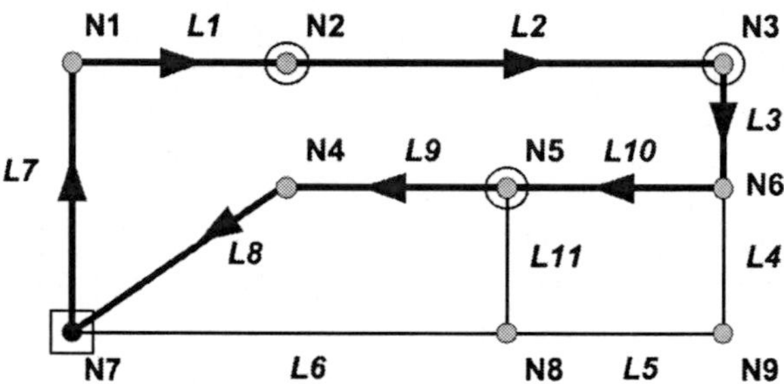

Figure 10-17. *Solution for the TSP*

Let's try the same operation on the directed network DNET. We get a different path, which is expected since we now have to consider the one-way links. Here are the results, with the path shown in Figure 10-18:

```
Path cost: 10.0
Number of links: 7
Simple path? true
  Link -6     L6      (cost: 2.0)
  Link 11     L11     (cost: 1.0)
  Link 10     L10     (cost: 1.0)
  Link -3     L3      (cost: 1.0)
  Link 2      L2      (cost: 2.0)
  Link 1      L1      (cost: 1.0)
  Link 7      L7      (cost: 2.0)
Actual node visitation order :
  Node 7      N7
  Node 5      N5
  Node 3      N3
  Node 2      N2
  Node 7      N7
```

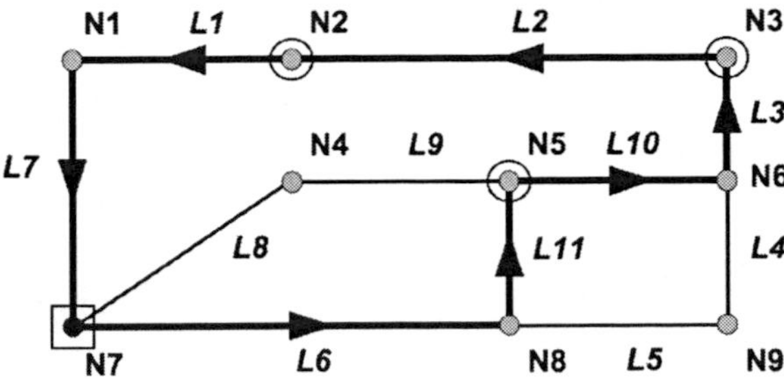

Figure 10-18. *TSP and one-way streets*

Notice that there's one important difference between the two examples: the nodes are not visited in the same order. In the first case, we actually visit the nodes in the order in which they are listed in the `nodeIds` parameter, but that is just because this happens to match the optimal path. In the second case, however, the visitation order is different. We start at node N7 and then visit nodes N5, N3, and N2 before coming back to node N7.

Discovering Reachability

A different kind of problem is not to find the best path between two nodes but simply to determine whether there indeed exists a path between the nodes. This operation is most useful in utility networks and "what if?" analyses. For example, what happens if you close this valve or if this circuit breaker trips? Will some customers no longer be serviced?

There are three methods available to determine reachability:

- `findReachableNodes()` returns all nodes that can be reached from the source node.
- `findReachingNodes()` returns all nodes that can reach the target node.
- `isReachable()` checks whether the source node can reach the target node.

Consider the network shown in Figure 10-19. It is the same network you have been playing with (UNET), except that two links are no longer accessible.

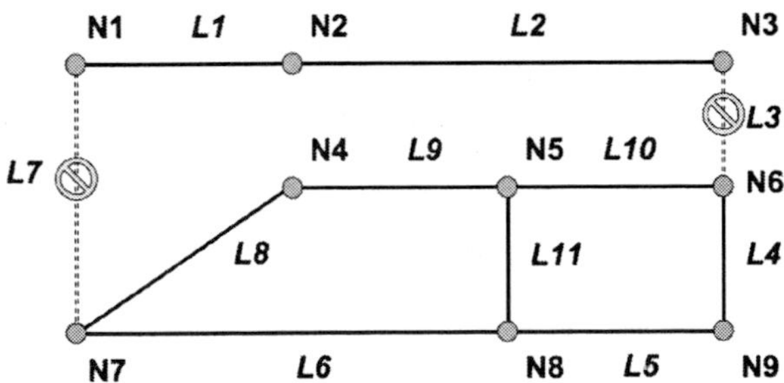

Figure 10-19. *UNET network with two links disabled*

The two links may have been removed from the network entirely, but a more likely scenario is that they still exist but are no longer active (in other words, the `ACTIVE` attribute has been set to `'N'`). For example, they could represent roads that are closed for repairs.

You can change the status of a link or node by updating the network tables in the database:

```
update unet_links set active = 'N' where link_id in (7,3);
commit;
```

You can also change the state directly on the memory-resident copy:

```
testNet.getLink(7).setState(false);
testNet.getLink(3).setState(false);
```

The code in Listing 10-24 illustrates the use of the `findReachableNodes()` method. The method returns an array of `Node` objects.

Listing 10-24. *Using the* `findReachableNodes()` *Method*

```
// Find nodes that can be reached from node N4
Network testNet = uNet;
nodeId = 4;
Node[] nodeArray = NetworkManager.findReachableNodes (testNet, nodeId);

// Display the results
System.out.println ("  " + nodeArray.length + " nodes in network "
  + testNet.getName() + " are reachable from node " + nodeId);
for (int i = 0; i < nodeArray.length; i++)
  System.out.println("    node " + nodeArray[i].getID());
```

The code in Listing 10-24 produces the following results. Note that nodes N1, N2, and N3 are not reachable because of the inactive links L3 and L7.

```
5 nodes in network UNET are reachable from node 4
  node 9      N9
  node 8      N8
  node 7      N7
  node 6      N6
  node 5      N5
```

The `findReachingNodes()` method works the same way.

In a large, fully connected network, those methods can return many nodes. As a matter of fact, they would return `all` nodes in the network, since they are all ultimately connected to one another. Such a result would not be very useful.

So, both methods let you limit the scope of the search by including either (or both) of the following parameters:

- *A rectangular geographical area*: Only those nodes inside the rectangle will be searched for reachability.
- *A maximum search depth, as a number of links to traverse*: Only those nodes less than the specified number of links away from the search node are considered.

Minimum Cost Spanning Tree

A *spanning tree* is a tree that connects all nodes in a graph. A *minimum cost spanning tree* (MCST) is the spanning tree with the minimum cost. Practically speaking, it tells you how you should wire together all nodes in your network at the lowest cost.

Typical applications are in the design of actual networks (utilities, telecommunications, transportation, and so on). For example, designing a gas pipeline in such a way that it follows an MCST approach can save a great deal money in equipment, construction, and operation costs.

There are two methods for obtaining the MCST of a network: `mcstLinkArray()` and `mcst()`. The `mcstLinkArray()` method returns an array containing all the `Link` objects in the tree. The `mcst()` method returns a new `Network` object that contains only those links and nodes that form the spanning tree. This is helpful because you can now use this new network for performing direct searches, such as shortest paths or nearest neighbors. You can write this new network to the database and use it for further analyses.

The code in Listing 10-25 gets the MCST for the undirected test network (UNET).

Listing 10-25. *Using the* `mcst()` *Method*

```
// Compute the Minimum Spanning Cost Tree
Network mcstNet = NetworkManager.mcst(uNet);

// Inspect the resulting network
System.out.println ("  Nodes: " + mcstNet.getNoOfNodes());
System.out.println ("  Links: " + mcstNet.getNoOfLinks());

// Display MCST network links
Link[] linkArray = mcstNet.getLinkArray();
double treeCost = 0;
for (int i = 0; i < linkArray.length; i++) {
  System.out.println ("    Link " + linkArray[i].getID() + "\t"
    + linkArray[i].getName()+ "\t"
    + linkArray[i].getCost());
  treeCost = treeCost + linkArray[i].getCost();
}
System.out.println ("  Total cost: \t\t" + treeCost);
```

The results of the code in Listing 10-25 are as follows. Figure 10-20 shows the resulting tree.

```
Nodes: 9
Links: 8
  Link 2     L2     2.0
  Link 4     L4     1.0
  Link 8     L8     1.5
  Link 9     L9     1.0
  Link 1     L1     1.0
  Link 3     L3     1.0
  Link 10    L10    1.0
  Link 5     L5     1.0
Total cost:         9.5
```

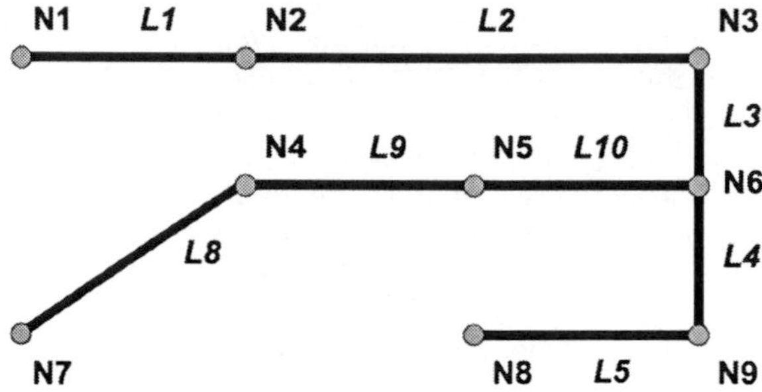

Figure 10-20. *MCST on network UNET*

Multiple Path Searches

You have two more methods to examine: `allPaths()` and `shortestPaths()`. The `allPaths()` method returns *all* possible paths between two nodes, and the `shortestPaths()` method (notice the plural) returns the shortest paths from one node to *all* the other nodes. Both methods return an array of `Path` objects.

Finding All Paths Between Two Nodes

Obviously, on a large, fully connected network, the `allPaths()` method could return a very large number of responses, and the computation could take a long time. So, this method lets you limit the search space by specifying one or more of the following bounds:

- *Depth*: Return only the solutions that have less than the specified number of links.
- *Cost*: Return only the solutions whose cost is less than the specified value.
- *Solutions*: Return only the *N* best solutions.

The example in Listing 10-26 illustrates the search for all paths between nodes N3 and N4 on the undirected network (UNET). The bounds are set to a high value to get all possible solutions.

Listing 10-26. *Using the* `allPaths()` *Method*

```
// Get all paths between nodes 3 and 4
maxDepth = 1000;
maxCost = 1000;
maxSolutions = 1000;
Path[] pathArray =
   NetworkManager.allPaths(uNet, 3, 4, maxDepth, maxCost, maxSolutions);;

// Display the solutions found
for (int i = 0; i < pathArray.length; i++)
{
  Path p = pathArray[i];
  int numLinks = p.getNoOfLinks();
  double cost = p.getCost();
  System.out.println ("    path["+i+"] links:" + numLinks + ", path cost "+ cost);
}
```

The results of the code in Listing 10-26 are as follows:

```
path[0] links:3, path cost 3.0
path[1] links:5, path cost 5.0
path[2] links:4, path cost 6.5
path[3] links:5, path cost 6.5
path[4] links:5, path cost 6.5
path[5] links:6, path cost 9.0
path[6] links:8, path cost 11.0
```

To limit the results to only those solutions with four or fewer links, set the `maxDepth` parameter in the code to `4`. The results then become as follows:

```
path[0] links:3, path cost 3.0
path[1] links:4, path cost 6.5
```

Finding All Shortest Paths from a Node

The `shortestPaths()` method returns the shortest path between a chosen node and each of the reachable nodes in the network. It takes no search restrictions, so it will return one solution for each reachable node. The results are ordered by cost, with the "nearest" nodes returned first.

Listing 10-27 shows how to use this method on node N4 in network UNET.

Listing 10-27. *Using the* `shortestPaths()` *Method*

```
// Get the shortest paths between node 4 and all other nodes
Path[] pathArray = NetworkManager.shortestPaths(uNet, 4);
for (int i = 0; i < pathArray.length; i++)
{
  Path p = pathArray[i];
  int endNodeId = p.getEndNode().getID();
  int numLinks = p.getNoOfLinks();
  double cost = p.getCost();
  System.out.println ("    path["+i+"] to node " + endNodeId + ", links:"
    + numLinks + ", path cost "+ cost);
}
```

The results of Listing 10-27 are as follows:

```
path[0] to node 5, links:1, path cost 1.0
path[1] to node 7, links:1, path cost 1.5
path[2] to node 6, links:2, path cost 2.0
path[3] to node 8, links:2, path cost 2.0
path[4] to node 3, links:3, path cost 3.0
path[5] to node 9, links:3, path cost 3.0
path[6] to node 1, links:2, path cost 3.5
path[7] to node 2, links:3, path cost 4.5
```

On a complex, fully connected network, this method will return a large number of results. You need a way to limit the number of results. You can do this using *network constraints*.

Limiting the Search Space: The SystemConstraint Class

The `SystemConstraint` class is a specific example of a network constraint. It lets you define a set of constraints to limit the search space for *any* of the methods you have seen so far.

Specifically, the `SystemConstraint` class lets you define the following constraints:

- `MaxCost`: The maximum cost.
- `MaxDepth`: The maximum search depth (the number of links in the paths).
- `MaxDistance`: The maximum geographical distance from the start node and any candidate node (in other words, consider only those nodes within that distance from that start node).
- `MaxMBR`: Consider only those nodes that are inside the MBR.
- `MustAvoidLinks`: A list of links to avoid.
- `MustAvoidNodes`: A list of nodes to avoid.

To use the class, just create a `SystemConstraint` object, and configure it with one or more of the preceding constraints using specific methods such as `setMaxDepth()`. You can then pass it as the last parameter to any of the analysis methods you have seen so far, with the exception of the `mcst()` method.

Listing 10-28 shows how to set up a constraint that avoids node N5 and limits the cost of any solution to ten "cost units." Then use the `shortestPath()` method to find the optimal path between nodes N3 and N4, and pass it the `SystemConstraint` just defined.

■ **Note** When you set up a list of nodes to avoid, the links associated to those nodes are automatically put on the list of links to avoid.

Listing 10-28. *Using the* `SystemConstraint` *Class*

```
// Set up a system constraint with a list of nodes to avoid and a cost limit
int[] avoidNodes = {5};        // Nodes to avoid
SystemConstraint myConstraint = new SystemConstraint (uNet, avoidNodes);
myConstraint.setMaxCost(10);

// Get shortest path from node N4 to N3 considering the constraint
Path path = NetworkManager.shortestPath (uNet, 3, 4, myConstraint);

// Show path cost and number of links
System.out.println ("Path cost: " + path.getCost() );
System.out.println ("Number of links: "+ path.getNoOfLinks());
System.out.println ("Simple path? "+ path.isSimple());

// Show the links traversed
System.out.println ("Links traversed:");
Link[] linkArray = path.getLinkArray();
for (int i = 0; i < linkArray.length; i++)
  System.out.println ("  Link " + linkArray[i].getID() + "\t"
    + linkArray[i].getName() +"\t" + linkArray[i].getCost());

// Show the nodes traversed
System.out.println ("  Nodes traversed:");
Node [] nodeArray = path.getNodeArray();
for (int i = 0; i < nodeArray.length; i++)
  System.out.println ("    Node " + nodeArray[i].getID() + "\t"
```

```
+ nodeArray[i].getName() +"\t" + nodeArray[i].getCost());
```

Because node N5 is now prohibited, you get a different answer from the one in Listing 10-20. Figure 10-21 shows the new path.

```
Path cost: 6.5
Number of links: 4
Simple path? true
Links traversed:
  Link 8     L8     1.5
  Link 7     L7     2.0
  Link 1     L1     1.0
  Link 2     L2     2.0
Nodes traversed:
  Node 4     N4     0.0
  Node 7     N7     0.0
  Node 1     N1     0.0
  Node 2     N2     0.0
  Node 3     N3     0.0
```

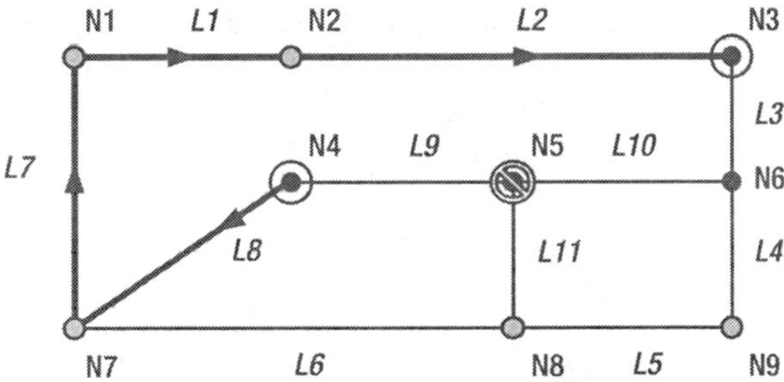

Figure 10-21. *The path from node N4 to node N3, avoiding node N5*

Advanced Analysis: Network Constraints

The analyses you have performed so far consider only relatively simple variables: network connectivity, link directions, node and link state, and costs. However, many real-life scenarios require more sophisticated choices.

Route calculations on a road network need to consider restricted maneuvers. One-way streets can easily be modeled using directed links. The dynamic aspect of the road network (such as streets closed because of repairs) can be modeled using the active/inactive states.

But some restrictions may be seasonal or time dependent—for instance, a mountain pass is open only during the summer months, and a ferry operates only at certain times of year. Other restrictions may be legal, such as a left turn on a busy boulevard or a U-turn. Those restrictions may apply only at certain times (for example, the left turn is prohibited during peak traffic hours but allowed otherwise).

Finally, the restrictions may apply differently to different classes of vehicles. For example, a private access road cannot be used to carry public traffic, but it is always open to emergency vehicles. Or a low tunnel or weak bridge prevents trucks but not cars from using a road. Or on a canal network, barges can travel only on those sections that are wide and deep enough, whereas small boats can go anywhere.

Similar issues exist for other kinds of networks. In an electrical or telecommunications network, nodes may represent complex equipment whose behavior is more sophisticated than a simple On/Off status.

You can implement those kinds of constraints using the NetworkConstraint interface, specifically with the isSatisfied() method. This method is passed an AnalysisInfo object that provides sufficient context information for you to decide whether to accept or reject the proposed link. Use one of the methods shown in Table 10-10 to find out the current state of the solution being computed.

Table 10-10. AnalysisInfo *Methods*

Method	Meaning
getCurrentCost()	Returns the current path cost
getCurrentDepth()	Returns the current path depth
getCurrentNode()	Returns the current node
getCurrentLink()	Returns the current link, that is, the link leading to the current node
getNextLink()	Returns the next link, that is, the link being considered
getNextNode()	Returns the next node, that is, the node at the end of the link being considered
getNextCost()	Returns the path cost including the proposed link
getNextDepth()	Returns the path depth including the proposed link (same as getCurrentDepth()+1)
getPathLinkVec()	Returns the current path links as a Vector
getPathNodeVec()	Returns the current path nodes as a Vector
getStartNode()	Returns the start node

Caution The meaning of methods getCurrentCost() and getCurrentDepth() has changed in Oracle Database 11*g*. In Oracle Database 10*g*, both methods included the next link (the link being considered). Now they include only the links in the path determined when your constraint method is called. To get the cost and depth including the link being considered, use getNextCost() and getNextDepth().

If you accept to use the proposed link, then return true. Return false to indicate that the next link should be skipped.

We will now illustrate how to use network constraints with a simple example. Suppose that the UNET network represents a canal network. Each link in our network has a link_level column, which you can use to define the class of each canal as a number from 1 to 3. A class 1 canal is wide and deep; any boat can travel through such a canal. Class 2 canals are narrower and not as deep as class 1 canals. Class 3 canals are still smaller and can accept only small boats.

Boats also have a size. Size 1 boats are large and heavy, and they can travel only through class 1 canals. Size 2 boats are smaller than size 1 boats, and they can travel through class 1 or class 2 canals. Size 3 boats are smaller still and can travel on any class of canal (1, 2, or 3).

The code in Listing 10-29 sets the link_level column in the unet_links table. Figure 10-22 shows the resulting UNET network.

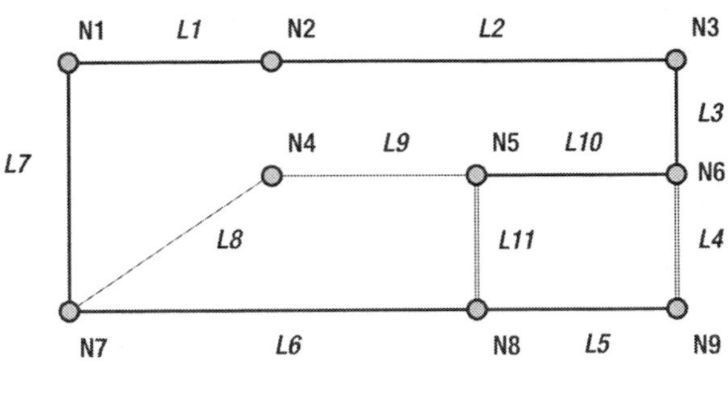

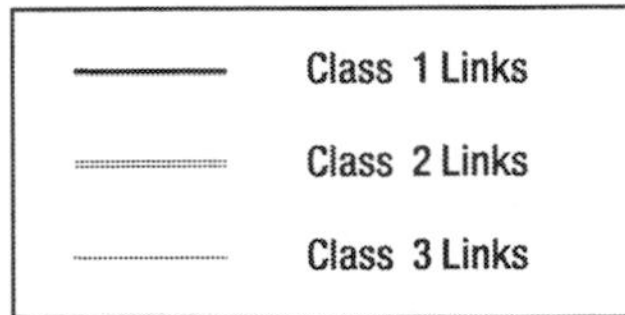

Figure 10-22. *Network with multiple link levels*

Listing 10-29. *Setting Link Levels for the UNET Network*

```
SQL> UPDATE unet_links SET link_level = 1 WHERE link_id IN (1, 2, 3, 5, 6, 7, 10);
SQL> UPDATE unet_links SET link_level = 2 WHERE link_id IN (4, 11);
SQL> UPDATE unet_links SET link_level = 3 WHERE link_id IN (8, 9);
SQL> COMMIT;
```

You can now write a network constraint that will make sure that boats travel only through the canals that can accommodate them. Listing 10-30 shows the code for the `LinkLevelConstraint` class.

Listing 10-30. *Network Constraint*

```
import java.util.*;
import oracle.spatial.network.*;
/**
 * The following network constraint assumes that
 * 1. each link has a link level (stored as LINK_LEVEL in { 1,2,3 })
 * 2. for a given target level (in { 1,2,3 } ), the following must hold:
 *    target Level 1 can only travel on link Level 1
 *    target Level 2 can travel on link Level 1 and 2
 *    target Level 3 can travel on link Level 1, 2, and 3
 */
public class LinkLevelConstraint implements NetworkConstraint {
  int targetLevel = 0; // Default; no restriction

  public LinkLevelConstraint (int newTargetLevel) {
    targetLevel = newTargetLevel;
  }

  public boolean requiresPathLinks() {
    return false ;
  }
```

```
  public boolean isSatisfied (AnalysisInfo info) {
    if ( targetLevel == 0 ) // no restriction
      return true ;
    Link link = info.getNextLink() ; // potential link candidate
    int linkLevel = link.getLinkLevel(); // get link Level
    if ( link != null && targetLevel >= linkLevel )
      return true;
    else
      return false;
  }
}
```

You can now use the network constraint just created to find the shortest path from node N7 to node N5 on the modified UNET network, as shown in Listing 10-31.

Listing 10-31. *Using the Network Constraint*

```
// Set up network constraint
int targetLevel = 1;
LinkLevelConstraint netConstraint = new LinkLevelConstraint (targetLevel);

// Get shortest path from node N7 to N5
Network testNet = uNet;
startNodeId = 7;
endNodeId = 5;
Path path = NetworkManager.shortestPath (testNet, startNodeID ,endNodeId);

// Show path cost and number of links
System.out.println ("Path cost: " + path.getCost() );
System.out.println ("Number of links: "+ path.getNoOfLinks());
System.out.println ("Simple path? "+ path.isSimple());

// Show the links traversed
System.out.println ("Links traversed:");
Link[] linkArray = path.getLinkArray();
for (int i = 0; i < linkArray.length; i++)
  System.out.println ("    Link " + linkArray[i].getID() + "\t"
   + linkArray[i].getName() +"\t"
   + linkArray[i].getLinkLevel() + "\t"
   + linkArray[i].getCost() );
// Show the nodes traversed
System.out.println ("  Nodes traversed:");
Node [] nodeArray = path.getNodeArray();
for (int i = 0; i < nodeArray.length; i++)
  System.out.println ("    Node " + nodeArray[i].getID() + "\t"
    + nodeArray[i].getName() +"\t"
    + nodeArray[i].getCost());
```

You can now try to find the shortest path between nodes N7 and N5 with various settings of the `targetLevel` parameter. You should see the following results. Remember that the `targetLevel` value passed to the constraint represents the size of the boat; the smaller the value, the larger the boat. With `targetLevel` set to 1 (in other words, for a *large* boat), the result of running the code in Listing 10-31 is as follows. The path is long because the boat can travel only through the largest (class 1) canals.

```
Path cost: 7.0
Number of links: 5
Simple path? true
Links traversed:
  Link 7      L7      1       2.0
  Link 1      L1      1       1.0
  Link 2      L2      1       2.0
  Link 3      L3      1       1.0
  Link 10     L10     1       1.0
Nodes traversed:
  Node 7      N7      0.0
  Node 1      N1      0.0
  Node 2      N2      0.0
  Node 3      N3      0.0
  Node 6      N6      0.0
  Node 5      N5      0.0
```

Running the same code with the targetLevel set to 2, which indicates a *medium* boat, you should get the following results. The path is shorter, indicating the boat can travel through class 1 and class 2 canals.

```
Path cost: 3.0
Number of links: 2
Simple path? true
Links traversed:
  Link 6      L6      1       2.0
  Link 11     L11     2       1.0
Nodes traversed:
  Node 7      N7      0.0
  Node 8      N8      0.0
  Node 5      N5      0.0
```

With targetLevel set to 3 (for a *small* boat), you can travel on any link:

```
Path cost: 2.5
Number of links: 2
Simple path? true
Links traversed:
  Link 8      L8      3       1.5
  Link 9      L9      3       1.0
Nodes traversed:
  Node 7      N7      0.0
  Node 4      N4      0.0
  Node 5      N5      0.0
```

The same constraint could be used for a road network, where the link_level could be used to indicate the type of vehicles that can pass a link. Level 3 links could be used to indicate bridges or tunnels that heavy trucks cannot use.

More sophisticated constraints, such as time-based turn restrictions, need additional information. That information can be fetched from the database when the network constraint object is instantiated.

If you are curious about the way the network search algorithms operate, you can write a network constraint that does nothing but print the information provided in its input AnalysisInfo object. This will show you the "reasoning" of the search process: the links it tries and the order it tries them.

Listing 10-32 shows the code of such a constraint, aptly called NetworkTraceConstraint.

Listing 10-32. *Network Constraint for Tracing and Debugging*

```
/*
  This shows how to use the NetworkConstraint mechanism to trace and
  observe the search process used by the network API.
  It does not alter the search process: all it does is to dump out
  context information whenever it is called.
 */

import java.util.*;
import oracle.spatial.network.*;

public class NetworkTraceConstraint implements NetworkConstraint {

  private boolean firstCall = true;

  public boolean requiresPathLinks() {
    return false ;
  }

  public boolean isSatisfied (AnalysisInfo info) {
    this.dumpContext(info);
    return true;
  }

  private void dumpContext(AnalysisInfo info) {
    Link    cl  = info.getCurrentLink();
    Node    cn  = info.getCurrentNode();
    Link    nl  = info.getNextLink();
    Node    nn  = info.getNextNode();
    String  dbg = "";
    if (cn != null)
      dbg += "# " + cn.getID();
    else
      dbg += "# NULL";
    dbg += "\t" + info.getCurrentCost();
    dbg += "\t" + info.getCurrentDepth();
    dbg += "\t" + info.getCurrentDuration();
    if (nl != null)
      dbg += "\t" + nl.getID();
    else
      dbg += "\tNULL";
    if (nn != null)
      dbg += "\t" + nn.getID();
    else
      dbg += "\tNULL";
    dbg += "\t" + info.getNextCost();
    dbg += "\t" + info.getNextDepth();
    dbg += "\t" + info.getNextDuration();
    if (firstCall) {
      System.out.println ("# Trace level "+traceLevel);
      System.out.println ("# ➥
          CNode\tCCost\tCDepth\tCDur\tNLink\tNnode\tNCost\tNDepth\tNDur");
      firstCall = false;
    }
    System.out.println (dbg);
  }
}
```

To illustrate how this constraint works, we will use it to get the shortest path between nodes 7 and 5 on the UNET network, like we did in the code in Listing 10-31. The result of running this code will be as follows:

```
# CNode CCost   CDepth  CDur    NLink   Nnode   NCost   NDepth  NDur
# 7     0.0     0       0.0     7       1       2.0     1       0.0
# 7     0.0     0       0.0     6       8       2.0     1       0.0
# 7     0.0     0       0.0     8       4       1.5     1       0.0
# 4     1.5     1       0.0     9       5       2.5     2       0.0
  Path cost: 2.5
  Number of links: 2
  Simple path? true
  Links traversed:
    Link 8      L8      1       1.5
    Link 9      L9      1       1.0
  Nodes traversed:
    Node 7      N7      0.0
    Node 4      N4      0.0
    Node 5      N5      0.0
```

The trace shows that we started from node 7 (our start node) and then checked the links leading out from node 7: links 7, 6 and 8. We pick the latter, leading to node 4, from which we pick link 9, which takes us to node 5, our goal.

If you want, you can now try this technique with other network searches. For example, try it with the `shortestPathDijkstra()` method, which uses Dijkstra's algorithm instead of the A* algorithm.

Network Structures: The Network, Node, Link, and Path Classes

The `Network` class stores and maintains networks. The classes `Node`, `Link`, and `Path` define individual network elements.

Network Class

The methods of the `Network` class let you select, add, modify, and delete network elements, as well as find out general information about the network.

A `Network` object is either created from scratch using the `NetworkFactory` class or instantiated from the database using the `readNetwork()` method of the `NetworkManager` class.

Note that you cannot instantiate the `Node`, `Link`, and `Path` classes (they are actually interfaces). To create any of them, use the proper methods of the `NetworkFactory` class.

Maintaining the Network

The `addNode()`, `addLink()`, and `addPath()` methods add node, link, and path elements, respectively, to a network. Their inputs are `Node` and `Link` objects produced by the `NetworkFactory` class. The `Path` objects are typically produced by analysis functions of the `NetworkManager` class.

For example, the following adds node `n1` to network `graph`:

```
graph.addNode(n1);
```

The `deleteNode()`, `deleteLink()`, and `deletePath()` methods remove elements from a network. You can pass them either a `Node`, `Link`, or `Path` object or their numeric identifier.

The `setState()` method allows you to turn network elements "on" and "off." The method alters the `ACTIVE` state of the link of node. An inactive link or node is not considered by any network analysis operation.

The Network class remembers the changes you make. When you write it back to the database (using the writeNetwork() method of the NetworkManager class), only the changes are applied to the database. The method performs an automatic commit.

Extracting Network Elements

A large number of methods extract elements from a network. Examples of these elements are single nodes, links, paths (based on their identifier), or collections of nodes or links based on various criteria: all active nodes or links; all elements at a certain hierarchy level; all elements of a certain type; or simply all of the nodes, links, and paths in the network.

You can also extract the entire network at a given hierarchy level or the network contained in a given rectangular window.

Finding Information About the Network

Methods are available to extract metadata information: name, type, and name of the network structures in the database (table and column names).

Other methods return element counts: the number of nodes, links, or paths in the network; a count of those elements at a certain hierarchy level; or only the active elements.

Yet more methods return the current maximum identifier for nodes, links, and paths. Since identifiers must be unique, this is useful to generate new identifiers for new elements.

Node and Link Classes

These classes are used to describe elements in the network. A number of *get* and *set* methods enable you to obtain details on each element and modify it. The major get methods on the Node and Link classes are shown in Table 10-11 and Table 10-12. *Set* methods (not listed here) allow you to modify nodes and links.

Table 10-11. *Main* get *Methods on the* Node *Object*

Method	Meaning
getCost()	Returns the stored cost for the node
getID()	Returns the unique numeric identifier of the node (from the column NODE_ID in the NODE table)
getName()	Returns the name of the node (from the column NODE_NAME in the NODE table)
isActive()	Returns true if the node is active (derived from the column ACTIVE in the NODE table)
getGeometry()	Returns the geometric point for the node
getInLinks()	Returns an array of the links that terminate at this node
getOutLinks()	Returns an array of the links that originate from this node

Table 10-12. *Main* get *Methods on the* Link *Object*

Method	Meaning
getCost()	Returns the stored cost for the link
getID()	Returns the unique numeric identifier of the link (from the column LINK_ID in the LINK table)
getName()	Returns the name of the link (from the column LINK_NAME in the LINK table)
isActive()	Returns true if the link is active (derived from the column ACTIVE in the LINK table)
getLinkLevel()	Returns the level of this link (derived from the column LINK_LEVEL in the LINK table)
getGeometry()	Returns the geometric line for the link
getStartNode()	Returns the start node for that link
getEndNode()	Returns the end node for the link
getCoLink()	Returns the colink of the link (in other words, the link that goes in the opposite direction)

Path Class

Path objects are primarily used to store the results of analysis functions—for example, the result of the shortestPath() method of the NetworkManager class.

The main method of the Path class is getLinkArray(), which returns a list of all links that compose the path, as an array. Alternate notations return the list of links as an *iterator* or a *vector*.

The Path class has many other useful methods:

- The getXxxx() and isXxxx() methods return various information about the path: whether it is closed, whether it is simple or complex, its total cost and the number of links that compose it, the start and end nodes, and so on. The list goes on and on. Table 10-13 lists the main methods.
- The path search method contains() finds out whether a path contains a specific Node or Link, and the getLinkAt() and getNodeAt() methods extract specific path elements.
- The path editing methods are clip(), split(), insertLink(), removeLink(), and concatenate() (to join two paths).
- The computeGeometry() method computes the geometry of the complete path from the geometries of all the links that form the path.

Table 10-13. *Main* get *Methods on the* Path *Object*

Method	Meaning
getCost()	Returns the total computed cost for the path
getNoOfLinks()	Returns the total number of links in the path
getLinkArray()	Returns an array of the links in the path
getGeometry()	Returns the geometric shape of the path

Creating Networks: The NetworkFactory Class

Use the `NetworkFactory` class to create new networks and network elements (nodes, links, and paths). Those elements are transient; the `NetworkManager` class lets you write them to the database.

Creating Networks

The `createLogicalNetwork()` and `createSDONetwork()` methods create an empty network (logical or spatial). You can optionally specify the names of the tables for storing the network in the database.

For example, the following code creates a new spatial network called `NH_ROADS`, which is single level, is directed, and uses an `SRID` of 8307 and two-dimensional geometries:

```
Network nhRoads = NetworkFactory.createSDONetwork("NH_ROADS", 1, true, 8307, 2);
```

The tables for this network will use default names (in other words, `NH_ROADS_NODE$`).

Creating Network Elements

The `createNode()`, `createLink()`, and `createPath()` methods create nodes, links, and paths. Those are stand-alone elements. Methods of the `Network` class enable you to add them to a network.

For example, the following code creates node `n1` with the identifier `1`. No other information is given—the node has no cost and no geometry.

```
Node n1 = NetworkFactory.createNode(1);
```

The `Node` and `Link` classes also provide many methods to connect link and node objects.

Creating Network Tables

Other methods let you create the physical table structures in the database. `createNetworkTables()` will create all the tables for a network (using the names you specified when creating the network or using default names if you did not specify any). Methods such as `createNodeTable()` let you create individual tables.

The preceding methods create empty tables. To actually populate the tables with the network data, use the `writeNetwork()` method of the `NetworkManager` class.

Network Creation Example

The code in Listing 10-33 illustrates how to create and populate a network using the Java interface. It produces the same network as the simple undirected logical network (UNET) illustrated in Figure 10-8 that was defined and created in the database using SQL statements in Listings 10-16 and 10-17.

Listing 10-33. *Creating a Network Using the Java API*

```
// Create the network object
String networkName = "MY_NET";
Network myNet = NetworkFactory.createLogicalNetwork(
  networkName,                  // networkName
  1,                            // noOfHierarchyLevels
  true,                         // isDirected
  networkName+"_NODE",          // nodeTableName
  "COST",                       // nodeCostColumn
  networkName+"_LINK",          // linkTableName
  "COST",                       // linkCostColumn
```

```
  networkName+"_PATH",          // pathTableName
  networkName+"_PLINK"          // pathLinkTableName
);

// Create the nodes
Node n1 = NetworkFactory.createNode (1, "N1");
Node n2 = NetworkFactory.createNode (2, "N2");
Node n3 = NetworkFactory.createNode (3, "N3");
Node n4 = NetworkFactory.createNode (4, "N4");
Node n5 = NetworkFactory.createNode (5, "N5");
Node n6 = NetworkFactory.createNode (6, "N6");
Node n7 = NetworkFactory.createNode (7, "N7");
Node n8 = NetworkFactory.createNode (8, "N8");
Node n9 = NetworkFactory.createNode (9, "N9");

// Create the links
Link l1  = NetworkFactory.createLink ( 1, "L1",  n1, n2, 1);
Link l2  = NetworkFactory.createLink ( 2, "L2",  n2, n3, 2);
Link l3  = NetworkFactory.createLink ( 3, "L3",  n3, n6, 1);
Link l4  = NetworkFactory.createLink ( 4, "L4",  n6, n9, 1);
Link l5  = NetworkFactory.createLink ( 5, "L5",  n9, n8, 1);
Link l6  = NetworkFactory.createLink ( 6, "L6",  n8, n7, 2);
Link l7  = NetworkFactory.createLink ( 7, "L7",  n7, n1, 2);
Link l8  = NetworkFactory.createLink ( 8, "L8",  n7, n4, 1.5);
Link l9  = NetworkFactory.createLink ( 9, "L9",  n4, n5, 1);
Link l10 = NetworkFactory.createLink (10, "L10", n5, n6, 1);
Link l11 = NetworkFactory.createLink (11, "L11", n5, n8, 1);

// Add the nodes to the network
myNet.addNode (n1);
myNet.addNode (n2);
myNet.addNode (n3);
myNet.addNode (n4);
myNet.addNode (n5);
myNet.addNode (n6);
myNet.addNode (n7);
myNet.addNode (n8);
myNet.addNode (n9);

// Add the links to the network
myNet.addLink (l1);
myNet.addLink (l2);
myNet.addLink (l3);
myNet.addLink (l4);
myNet.addLink (l5);
myNet.addLink (l6);
myNet.addLink (l7);
myNet.addLink (l8);
myNet.addLink (l9);
myNet.addLink (l10);
myNet.addLink (l11);

// Create the network tables in the database
NetworkFactory.createNetworkTables (dbConnection, myNet);

// Write the network (this also writes the metadata)
NetworkManager.writeNetwork (dbConnection, myNet);
```

Debugging Network Structures

All classes have a `toString()` method that formats their content in a readable way. For example, the following dumps the `myNet` network just created:

```
System.out.println (myNet);
```

and produces the following output:

```
User    Name:   [null]
Network Name:   [MY_NET]
Network Category:   [LOGICAL]
Geometry Type:  []
No. Of Hierarchy Levels: [1]
Link    Dir.  :   [DIRECTED]
Node    Table :  MY_NET_NODE[null ]:(DIM:0,SRID:0)
Link    Table :  MY_NET_LINK[null ]:(DIM:0,SRID:0)
LRS     Table :  null
Path    Table :  MY_NET_PATH[null ]:(DIM:0,SRID:0)
Path-Link Table: MY_NET_PLINK
Link Cost Column: [COST]
Node Cost Column: [COST]

Network Node Table:
NodeID: 2[H:1] , Name: N2, Type: null, Cost: 0.0 InLinks: 1  OutLinks: 2
NodeID: 4[H:1] , Name: N4, Type: null, Cost: 0.0 InLinks: 8  OutLinks: 9
NodeID: 9[H:1] , Name: N9, Type: null, Cost: 0.0 InLinks: 4  OutLinks: 5
NodeID: 8[H:1] , Name: N8, Type: null, Cost: 0.0 InLinks: 5 11  OutLinks: 6
NodeID: 6[H:1] , Name: N6, Type: null, Cost: 0.0 InLinks: 3 10  OutLinks: 4
NodeID: 1[H:1] , Name: N1, Type: null, Cost: 0.0 InLinks: 7  OutLinks: 1
NodeID: 3[H:1] , Name: N3, Type: null, Cost: 0.0 InLinks: 2  OutLinks: 3
NodeID: 7[H:1] , Name: N7, Type: null, Cost: 0.0 InLinks: 6  OutLinks: 7 8
NodeID: 5[H:1] , Name: N5, Type: null, Cost: 0.0 InLinks: 9  OutLinks: 10 11

Network Link Table:
LinkID: 2[H:1] , Name: L2, Type: null, State: true, Cost: 2.0, Level: 1,
StartNode: 2, EndNode: 3,
CoLink ID:none
LinkID: 4[H:1] , Name: L4, Type: null, State: true, Cost: 1.0, Level: 1,
StartNode: 6, EndNode: 9,
CoLink ID:none
LinkID: 9[H:1] , Name: L9, Type: null, State: true, Cost: 1.0, Level: 1,
StartNode: 4, EndNode: 5,
CoLink ID:none
LinkID: 8[H:1] , Name: L8, Type: null, State: true, Cost: 1.5, Level: 1,
StartNode: 7, EndNode: 4,
CoLink ID:none
LinkID: 11[H:1] , Name: L11, Type: null, State: true, Cost: 1.0, Level: 1,
StartNode: 5, EndNode: 8,
CoLink ID:none
LinkID: 6[H:1] , Name: L6, Type: null, State: true, Cost: 2.0, Level: 1,
StartNode: 8, EndNode: 7,
CoLink ID:none
LinkID: 1[H:1] , Name: L1, Type: null, State: true, Cost: 1.0, Level: 1,
StartNode: 1, EndNode: 2,
CoLink ID:none
LinkID: 3[H:1] , Name: L3, Type: null, State: true, Cost: 1.0, Level: 1,
```

```
StartNode: 3, EndNode: 6,
CoLink ID:none
LinkID: 10[H:1] , Name: L10, Type: null, State: true, Cost: 1.0, Level: 1,
StartNode: 5, EndNode: 6,
CoLink ID:none
LinkID: 7[H:1] , Name: L7, Type: null, State: true, Cost: 2.0, Level: 1,
StartNode: 7, EndNode: 1,
CoLink ID:none
LinkID: 5[H:1] , Name: L5, Type: null, State: true, Cost: 1.0, Level: 1,
StartNode: 9, EndNode: 8,
CoLink ID:none
```

Analyzing Networks Using the PL/SQL API

Instead of the Java API, you can also use a PL/SQL API. In other words, you can perform almost all the network searches we discussed in previous sections by calling various PL/SQL functions and procedures. Those functions and procedures are in the SDO_NET_MEM package.

The SDO_NET_MEM package is really a wrapper over the Java API; each function and procedure in the package invokes a method on a Java object, which runs in the Java virtual machine embedded in the Oracle 11g database. The procedures and functions are grouped and named in such a way that you can easily relate them with their Java equivalents. For example, here is how you can get the shortest path between two nodes in Java:

```
Path path = NetworkManager.shortestPath (testNet, startNodeID ,endNodeId);
```

The equivalent in PL/SQL will look like this:

```
path_id := sdo_net_mem.network_manager.shortest_path
  (network_name, start_node_id, end_node_id);
```

Table 10-14 summarizes the main Java classes and their PL/SQL equivalents.

Table 10-14. *Network Java API Classes and Their PL/SQL Equivalents*

Class	PL/SQL	Purpose
NetworkManager	SDO_NET_MEM.NETWORK_MANAGER	Performs all network analyses
Network	SDO_NET_MEM.NETWORK	Network maintenance (add and remove nodes, links, or paths)
Node	SDO_NET_MEM.NODE	Get and set node attributes
Link	SDO_NET_MEM.LINK	Get and set link attributes
Path	SDO_NET_MEM.PATH	Get and set path attributes

The association between individual methods in the Java API and the PL/SQL procedures and functions is not exact; some methods have no equivalent, and some PL/SQL functions may combine multiple Java methods. For example, there is no equivalent to the NetworkFactory class. The methods of NetworkFactory are provided by SDO_NET_MEM.NETWORK_MANAGER.

The names of the Java methods are slightly different in the PL/SQL API. Since PL/SQL is fundamentally case-insensitive, the capitalizations in the names are removed and replaced by underscores. For example, path.getNoOfLink() becomes SDO_NET_MEM.PATH.GET_NO_OF_LINKS(). However, that does not work for all methods. For example, path.getLinkArray() becomes SDO_NET_MEM.PATH.GET_LINK_IDS().

Another difference between the Java and PL/SQL APIs is that the PL/SQL API is not object-oriented. All function and procedure calls must be passed the name of the network against which they are used. Also, individual network entities (nodes, links, paths) are identified using their unique numeric identifiers. Where a Java method returns an object (for example a `Path`), the equivalent PL/SQL function will return the identifier of that path. Passing, for example, a `Node` object to a method in Java becomes the passing of the unique numeric identifier of that node. For example, the following Java code:

```
Path path = NetworkManager.shortestPath (testNet, startNodeId, endNodeId);
int cost = path.getCost();
```

becomes the following in PL/SQL:

```
PATH NUMBER;
COST NUMBER;
...
PATH := SDO_NET_MEM.NETWORK_MANAGER.SHORTEST_PATH (
  NETWORK_NAME, START_NODE_ID,  END_NODE_ID);
COST := SDO_NET_MEM.PATH.GET_COST(NETWORK_NAME, PATH);
```

At this point you may wonder about the implementation of the `SDO_NET_MEM` package and how the functions and procedures got grouped. You may have tried to get details on all the functions and procedures using a `DESCRIBE` command. You did not get anything interesting back:

```
SQL> DESCRIBE SDO_NET_MEM
PROCEDURE SET_MAX_MEMORY_SIZE
 Argument Name                  Type                    In/Out Default?
 ------------------------------ ----------------------- ------ --------
 BYTES                          NUMBER                  IN
```

This is because the functions and procedures are really implemented as methods on object types, and the package is really only a container for those objects. To actually find out the signatures of the functions and procedures, you just need to describe those objects. Table 10-15 lists the describe commands to use.

Table 10-15. *Describing the Functions and Procedures in* `SDO_NET_MEM`

Main Groups	`DESCRIBE` **Commands**
SDO_NET_MEM.NETWORK_MANAGER	DESCRIBE SDO_NETWORK_MANAGER_T
SDO_NET_MEM.NETWORK	DESCRIBE SDO_NETWORK_T
SDO_NET_MEM.NODE	DESCRIBE SDO_NODE_T
SDO_NET_MEM.LINK	DESCRIBE SDO_LINK_T
SDO_NET_MEM.PATH	DESCRIBE SDO_PATH_T

■ **Note** You cannot call the API functions in SQL. This is because of the multilevel names, which are not recognized by SQL. For example, `SELECT SDO_NET_MEM.NETWORK_MANAGER.LIST_NETWORKS FROM DUAL` will fail with the error `ORA-00904: invalid identifier`. You can call them only from within PL/SQL (functions, procedures, or anonymous blocks).

Using a Memory Object

Just like in the Java environment, you must first load the network in memory. The network will be loaded as a collection of Java objects into your private session memory. This is the first step you must perform before doing any kind of analysis on the network.

The following loads the complete network called UNET from the database:

```
SQL> EXECUTE SDO_NET_MEM.NETWORK_MANAGER.READ_NETWORK('UNET','FALSE');
```

The second argument indicates that the network is read-only. This does not prevent you from updating the network in memory (adding the results of analyzes, and so on). It prevents you only from making those changes permanent, that is, from writing the changes to the network tables.

Caution Just like when using the Java API, only one session at a time can load a network in updatable mode. Any number of sessions can load the same network in read-only mode (together with at most one updatable session). While a network is loaded by an updatable session, all network objects (nodes, links, paths) will be locked, preventing anyone from updating or deleting any of them.

You can load multiple networks. To find out what networks you have loaded in your session memory, do this:

```
DECLARE
  NETWORKS_LIST VARCHAR2(128);
BEGIN
  NETWORKS_LIST := SDO_NET_MEM.NETWORK_MANAGER.LIST_NETWORKS();
  DBMS_OUTPUT.PUT_LINE(networks_list);
END;
/
```

If you performed updates to the network—for example, you added a path resulting from a search—you can now make those changes permanent by writing the network back to the database, provided that you specified the updatable option when you loaded the network. Only the changes will be applied to the network tables.

```
SQL> EXECUTE SDO_NET_MEM.NETWORK_MANAGER.WRITE_NETWORK('UNET');
```

Once you are done with your network, you can remove it from memory by doing this:

```
SQL> EXECUTE SDO_NET_MEM.NETWORK_MANAGER.DROP_NETWORK('UNET');
```

Caution The procedure `SDO_NET_MEM.NETWORK_MANAGER.DROP_NETWORK('UNET')` removes the network only from your session memory. Do not confuse it with `SDO_NET.DROP_NETWORK('UNET')`, which removes the network from the database by dropping all tables for that network.

The network will be loaded into your session private memory in a section managed by the Java virtual machine. You may need to adjust your session in order to make that region large enough to accommodate the entire network. To do this, use the only function directly provided by the `SDO_NET_MEM` package: `SET_MAX_MEMORY_SIZE`. Use this function to set the maximum size (in bytes) of the Java heap in your current session. This is equivalent to setting the `-Xmx` option with the `java` command. Here is how you can use this function:

```
SQL> EXECUTE SDO_NET_MEM.SET_MAX_MEMORY_SIZE(512*1024*1024);
```

You may also want to find out what the current setting is for your session. Oracle does not provide a built-in function to do so, but you can easily build one yourself. All you need is to write a simple PL/SQL function wrapper on a Java function. Listing 10-34 shows how to do this. It also shows the function to set the maximum size.

Listing 10-34. *Functions to Get and Set the Maximum Java Heap Size*

```
CREATE OR REPLACE PROCEDURE set_max_memory_size(bytes NUMBER) AS
 LANGUAGE JAVA
 NAME 'oracle.aurora.vm.OracleRuntime.setMaxMemorySize(long)';
/

CREATE OR REPLACE FUNCTION get_max_memory_size RETURN NUMBER AS
 LANGUAGE JAVA
 NAME 'oracle.aurora.vm.OracleRuntime.getMaxMemorySize() returns long';
/
```

You can now us those functions to get and set memory size:

```
SQL> select get_max_memory_size() from dual;

GET_MAX_MEMORY_SIZE()
---------------------
           268435456

SQL> exec set_max_memory_size (get_max_memory_size()*2);
PL/SQL procedure successfully completed.

SQL> select get_max_memory_size() from dual;

GET_MAX_MEMORY_SIZE()
---------------------
           536870912
```

■ **Caution** Remember that your network will be loaded into your private local session memory. You will not be able to share this loaded network with any other session. Anyone else wanting to also work on the same network will have to load it again in their own session. All networks you loaded will be automatically removed from memory when you disconnect your session.

Analyzing Networks

We will illustrate only a few of the searches we already covered while reviewing the Java API. Essentially they are transpositions of the Java examples in PL/SQL. Our goal is to point out the differences in approaches.

In all examples, we assume that the network was previously loaded as explained earlier.

Finding the Shortest Path Between Two Nodes

The code in Listing 10-35 uses the PL/SQL API to get the shortest path from node N4 to node N3 on the UNET undirected network shown in Figure 10-8. The `SDO_NET_MEM.NETWORK.SHORTEST_PATH()` call returns the unique numeric identifier of the path object it produced. You can then use a number of methods of the `SDO_NET_MEM.PATH` object to extract various pieces of information, such as the cost of the path and the number of links. You then proceed to show details from each of the links and nodes in the path.

Notice that when the search finds no result, it returns NULL. This is true for all network searches.

Listing 10-35. *Using the* SHORTEST_PATH() *Function*

```
DECLARE
  test_net      VARCHAR2(30) := 'UNET';
  start_node_id NUMBER   := 4;
  end_node_id   NUMBER   := 3;
  constraint    VARCHAR2(30) := 'LinkLevelConstraint';
  path          NUMBER;
  link_array    SDO_NUMBER_ARRAY;
  node_array    SDO_NUMBER_ARRAY;
BEGIN
  -- Get shortest path between two nodes
  path := SDO_NET_MEM.NETWORK_MANAGER.SHORTEST_PATH
  (test_net, start_node_id, end_node_id, constraint);
  -- Make sure we have a result
  IF path IS NULL THEN
    DBMS_OUTPUT.PUT_LINE('No path found');
    RETURN;
  END IF;

  -- Show path cost and number of links
  DBMS_OUTPUT.PUT_LINE('Path cost: ' || SDO_NET_MEM.PATH.GET_COST(test_net, path));
  DBMS_OUTPUT.PUT_LINE('Number of links: ' ||
    SDO_NET_MEM.PATH.GET_NO_OF_LINKS(test_net, path));
  DBMS_OUTPUT.PUT_LINE('Simple path? ' ||
    SDO_NET_MEM.PATH.IS_SIMPLE(test_net, path));

  -- Show the links traversed
  DBMS_OUTPUT.PUT_LINE('Links traversed:');
  link_array := SDO_NET_MEM.PATH.GET_LINK_IDS(test_net, path);
  FOR i IN link_array.first..link_array.last LOOP
    DBMS_OUTPUT.PUT_LINE('* Link ' || link_array(i) || ' ' ||
      SDO_NET_MEM.LINK.GET_NAME (test_net, link_array(i)) || ' ' ||
      SDO_NET_MEM.LINK.GET_COST (test_net, link_array(i))
    );
  END LOOP;

  -- Show the nodes traversed
  DBMS_OUTPUT.PUT_LINE('Nodes traversed:');
  node_array := SDO_NET_MEM.PATH.GET_NODE_IDS(test_net, path);
  FOR i IN node_array.first..node_array.last LOOP
    DBMS_OUTPUT.PUT_LINE('* Node ' || node_array(i) || ' ' ||
       SDO_NET_MEM.NODE.GET_NAME (test_net, node_array(i)) || ' ' ||
       SDO_NET_MEM.LINK.GET_LEVEL (test_net, link_array(i)) || ' ' ||
       SDO_NET_MEM.NODE.GET_COST (test_net, node_array(i))
    );
  END LOOP;
END;
/
```

Here are the results of executing the code in Listing 10-35. As you can see, and as you would expect, they are identical to the results you got by doing the same operation using the Java API.

```
Path cost: 3
Number of links: 3
```

```
Simple path? TRUE
Links traversed:
* Link 9  L9  3 1
* Link 10 L10 1 1
* Link 3  L3  1 1
Nodes traversed:
* Node 4 N4 0
* Node 5 N5 0
* Node 6 N6 0
* Node 3 N3 0
```

Function SDO_NET_MEM.PATH.GET_LINK_IDS() returns an array of link identifiers. Note that we used the SDO_NUMBER_ARRAY type to hold this list. As the name implies, it is just a simple array of numbers. We will use it whenever we need to extract a list of elements, such as the links in a path. Getting details on each link is then a simple matter of walking down that array and using other functions to extract the details, passing it the ID of each link.

Saving the Computed Path

The path obtained is a stand-alone object; it is not related to the network. To store that path into the database, you need to complete it with additional information, such as giving it a name and then adding it to the network. To actually store the path into the network tables (path and path link), you just need to write the network to the database, as you've already seen.

The following example illustrates the process:

```
-- Give a name to the path - construct it using the path id.
SDO_NET_MEM.PATH.SET_NAME (test_net, path, 'P' || path);

-- Compute the geometry of the path
SDO_NET_MEM.PATH.COMPUTE_GEOMETRY(test_net, path, 0.05);

-- Add the path to the network
SDO_NET_MEM.NETWORK.ADD_PATH(test_net, path);
```

Traveling Salesperson Problem

Listing 10-36 shows how to use the PL/SQL API to obtain the optimal route that passes through a list of nodes on network UNET. You start at node N7 and need to visit nodes N2, N3, and N5, and then you come back to N7.

Listing 10-36. *Using the* TSP_PATH() *Function*

```
DECLARE
  test_net        VARCHAR2(30) := 'UNET';
  node_ids        SDO_NUMBER_ARRAY := SDO_NUMBER_ARRAY(7,2,3,5);
  is_closed       CHAR(5) := 'TRUE';
  use_exact_cost  CHAR(5) := 'TRUE';
  path            NUMBER;
  link_array      SDO_NUMBER_ARRAY;
  node_array      SDO_NUMBER_ARRAY;
BEGIN
  -- Traveling Salesperson Problem: nodes N7, N2, N3, N5, then back to N7
  path := SDO_NET_MEM.NETWORK_MANAGER.TSP_PATH (
    test_net, node_ids, is_closed, use_exact_cost);
```

```
  -- Make sure we have a result
  IF path IS NULL THEN
    DBMS_OUTPUT.PUT_LINE('No path found');
    RETURN;
  END IF;

  -- Show path cost and number of links
  DBMS_OUTPUT.PUT_LINE('Path cost: ' || SDO_NET_MEM.PATH.GET_COST(test_net, path));
  DBMS_OUTPUT.PUT_LINE('Number of links: ' ||
    SDO_NET_MEM.PATH.GET_NO_OF_LINKS(test_net, path));
  DBMS_OUTPUT.PUT_LINE('Simple path? ' ||
    SDO_NET_MEM.PATH.IS_SIMPLE(test_net, path));

  -- Show the links traversed
  DBMS_OUTPUT.PUT_LINE('Links traversed:');
  link_array := SDO_NET_MEM.PATH.GET_LINK_IDS(test_net, path);
  FOR i IN link_array.first..link_array.last LOOP
    DBMS_OUTPUT.PUT_LINE('* Link ' || link_array(i) || ' ' ||
      SDO_NET_MEM.LINK.GET_NAME (test_net, link_array(i)) || ' ' ||
      SDO_NET_MEM.LINK.GET_LEVEL (test_net, link_array(i)) || ' ' ||
      SDO_NET_MEM.LINK.GET_COST (test_net, link_array(i))
    );
  END LOOP;
END;
/
```

The result of executing the code in Listing 10-36 is as follows:

```
Path cost: 9.5
Number of links: 7
Simple path? TRUE
Links traversed:
* Link 8  L8  3 1.5
* Link 9  L9  3 1
* Link 10 L10 1 1
* Link 3  L3  1 1
* Link 2  L2  1 2
* Link 1  L1  1 1
* Link 7  L7  1 2
```

Unfortunately, the PL/SQL API does not offer any equivalent to the `tspPath.getTspNodeOrder()` method in Java, so we are unable to present the actual visitation order of the TSP nodes.

Creating and Updating Networks

The PL/SQL API does not provide access to the `NetworkFactory` class in the Java API, but the equivalent methods are available in `SDO_NET_MEM.NETWORK_MANAGER` and `SDO_NET_MEM.NETWORK`.

Creating Networks

The `SDO_NET_MEM.NETWORK_MANAGER.CREATE_LOGICAL_NETWORK()` and `CREATE_SDO_NETWORK()` methods create an empty network (logical or spatial). You can optionally specify the names of the tables for storing the network in the database.

For example, the following code creates a new spatial network called NH_ROADS, which is single level and directed, using an SRID of 8307 and two-dimensional geometries:

```
EXECUTE SDO_NET_MEM.NETWORK_MANAGER.CREATE_SDO_NETWORK( -
  'NH_ROADS', -
  1, 'TRUE', 8307, 2, -
  'NH_ROADS_NODE', 'GEOM', 'COST', -
  'NH_ROADS_LINK', 'GEOM', 'COST', -
  'NH_ROADS_PATH', 'GEOM', -
  'NH_ROADS_PLINK', -
  'FALSE');
```

Note that the network is created only in memory. Use SDO_NET_MEM.NETWORK_MANAGER.WRITE_NETWORK() to create and populate the network tables and metadata.

Creating Network Elements

Use the procedures SDO_NET_MEM.NETWORK.ADD_NODE, SDO_NET_MEM.NETWORK.ADD_LINK, and SDO_NET_MEM.NETWORK.ADD_PATH to create new nodes, links, and paths and add them to a network.

For example, the following code creates node with the identifier 7325 and adds it to network 'NH_ROADS':

```
EXECUTE SDO_NET_MEM.NETWORK.ADD_NODE ('NH_ROADS', 7325, 'N-7325', 0, 0);
```

The SDO_NET_MEM.NODE and SDO_NET_MEM.LINK objects provide many methods to set details on nodes and links. For example, the following sets the proper geometry for the node you just created:

```
EXECUTE SDO_NET_MEM.NODE.SET_GEOMETRY ('NH_ROADS', 7325, -
  SDO_GEOMETRY(2001, 8307, SDO_POINT_TYPE(-71.48891, 42.75104, NULL), NULL, NULL) -
);
```

■ **Caution** Do not use the SDO_NET_MEM.NETWORK.ADD_SDO_NODE() function. It allows you to directly specify the geographical coordinates of the node, but it does not allow you to specify the coordinate system of the geographic point. The resulting point in the database will be created with an SRID set to NULL. Use SDO_NET_MEM.NETWORK.ADD_NODE() and then SDO_NET_MEM.NODE.SET_GEOMETRY() to set the geometric point.

Updating and Deleting Network Elements

Procedures such as SDO_NET_MEM.NETWORK.DELETE_NODE allow you to delete nodes, links, and paths from a network.

To update network elements, use the setters specific for each type of element, for example, SDO_NET_MEM.NODE.SET_NAME(), SDO_NET_MEM.LINK.SET_COST(), and so on.

Network Creation Example

The code in Listing 10-37 illustrates how to create and populate a network using the PL/SQL interface. It produces the same network as the simple undirected logical network (UNET) illustrated in Figure 10-8 that was defined and created in the database using SQL statements in Listings 10-16 and 10-17 and using the Java API in Listing 10-32.

Listing 10-37. *Creating a Network Using the PL/SQL API*

```
DECLARE
  network_name VARCHAR2(20) := 'MY_NET';
BEGIN
  -- Create the network object in memory
  SDO_NET_MEM.NETWORK_MANAGER.CREATE_LOGICAL_NETWORK(
    network_name,            -- network_name
    1,                       -- no_of_hierarchy_levels
    'TRUE',                  -- is_directed
    network_name||'_NODE', -- node_table_name
    'COST',                  -- node_cost_column
    network_name||'_LINK', -- link_table_name
    'COST',                  -- link_cost_column
    network_name||'_PATH', -- path_table_name
    network_name||'_PLINK',-- path_link_table_name
    'FALSE'                  -- is_complex
  );

  -- Create and add the nodes
  SDO_NET_MEM.NETWORK.ADD_NODE(network_name, 1, 'N1', 0, 0);
  SDO_NET_MEM.NETWORK.ADD_NODE(network_name, 2, 'N2', 0, 0);
  SDO_NET_MEM.NETWORK.ADD_NODE(network_name, 3, 'N3', 0, 0);
  SDO_NET_MEM.NETWORK.ADD_NODE(network_name, 4, 'N4', 0, 0);
  SDO_NET_MEM.NETWORK.ADD_NODE(network_name, 5, 'N5', 0, 0);
  SDO_NET_MEM.NETWORK.ADD_NODE(network_name, 6, 'N6', 0, 0);
  SDO_NET_MEM.NETWORK.ADD_NODE(network_name, 7, 'N7', 0, 0);
  SDO_NET_MEM.NETWORK.ADD_NODE(network_name, 8, 'N8', 0, 0);
  SDO_NET_MEM.NETWORK.ADD_NODE(network_name, 9, 'N9', 0, 0);

  -- Create and add the links
  SDO_NET_MEM.NETWORK.ADD_LINK(network_name,  1, 'L1',  1, 2, 1);
  SDO_NET_MEM.NETWORK.ADD_LINK(network_name,  2, 'L2',  2, 3, 2);
  SDO_NET_MEM.NETWORK.ADD_LINK(network_name,  3, 'L3',  3, 6, 1);
  SDO_NET_MEM.NETWORK.ADD_LINK(network_name,  4, 'L4',  6, 9, 1);
  SDO_NET_MEM.NETWORK.ADD_LINK(network_name,  5, 'L5',  9, 8, 1);
  SDO_NET_MEM.NETWORK.ADD_LINK(network_name,  6, 'L6',  8, 7, 2);
  SDO_NET_MEM.NETWORK.ADD_LINK(network_name,  7, 'L7',  7, 1, 2);
  SDO_NET_MEM.NETWORK.ADD_LINK(network_name,  8, 'L8',  7, 4, 1.5);
  SDO_NET_MEM.NETWORK.ADD_LINK(network_name,  9, 'L9',  4, 5, 1);
  SDO_NET_MEM.NETWORK.ADD_LINK(network_name, 10, 'L10', 5, 6, 1);
  SDO_NET_MEM.NETWORK.ADD_LINK(network_name, 11, 'L11', 5, 8, 1);

  -- Write the network (this also creates the tables and writes the metadata)
  SDO_NET_MEM.NETWORK_MANAGER.WRITE_NETWORK(network_name);
END;
/
```

Using Network Constraints

The PL/SQL API also allows you to use network constraints. You still need to write the constraint in Java, as discussed previously, but how can you then pass a constraint (that is, a Java class) to the PL/SQL functions so they can use it?

Simple. You will load the Java class that implements the constraint into the database and pass its name to the network PL/SQL search functions. There are, however, some specifics and gotchas with this process. We will now review them.

We will start first with the simple `NetworkTraceConstraint` we wrote earlier and show the steps for using it in the PL/SQL API.

Having compiled the Java class, you must load it into the database. The easiest is to use the `loadjava` tool, like this:

```
loadjava -user spatial/spatial -verbose NetworkTraceConstraint.class
```

Then you must tell the PL/SQL network API about it. This you do by inserting a row in a new metadata view, `USER_SDO_NETWORK_CONSTRAINTS`, whose structure is shown in Table 10-16.

Table 10-16. *The* `USER_SDO_NETWORK_CONSTRAINTS` *View*

Name	Data Type	Meaning
CONSTRAINT	VARCHAR2(32)	Unique name given to the constraint. This name will be used to identify the constraint in applications.
DESCRIPTION	VARCHAR2(200)	Descriptive text (optional).
CLASS_NAME	VARCHAR2(4000)	The fully qualified name of the Java class that implements the constraint.
CLASS	BLOB	Used to hold the binary code of the class (contents of the class file).

Listing 10-38 shows how to insert a constraint definition in view `USER_SDO_NETWORK_CONSTRAINTS`.

Listing 10-38. *Defining a Network Constraint for Use by the PL/SQL API*

```
INSERT INTO user_sdo_network_constraints (constraint, description, class_name)
VALUES (
  'MyConstraint',
  'Tracing network algorithms',
  'NetworkTraceConstraint'
);
COMMIT;
```

Remember to specify the fully qualified name of your class, that is, to prefix the name of the class with the hierarchical name of the Java package it is part of, if any.

For example, if `NetworkTraceConstraint` is defined in package `com.Acme.net.constraints`, then the class name to specify in the previous statement will be `com/Acme/net/constraints/NetworkTraceConstraint`. This will also be the name of the class stored in the database by the `loadjava` tool.

To replace the constraint with a new version, simply compile it, and reload the new version using `loadjava`. The new version will automatically replace the existing one.

To remove the constraint, just delete the row from `USER_SDO_NETWORK_CONSTRAINTS`, and delete the class from the database using the `DROP JAVA` statement:

```
SQL> DROP JAVA CLASS "NetworkTraceConstraint";
Java dropped.
```

Again, do not forget to specify the fully qualified name if applicable.

The REGISTER_CONSTRAINT Mechanism

There is another way to load and define a constraint: using the REGISTER_CONSTRAINT() procedure, as shown in Listing 10-39.

Listing 10-39. *Defining a Network Constraint Using* REGISTER_CONSTRAINT()

```
EXECUTE SDO_NET_MEM.NETWORK_MANAGER.REGISTER_CONSTRAINT ( -
    'MyConstraint', -
    'NetworkTraceConstraint', -
    'CONSTRAINTS_CLASSES_DIR', -
    'Tracing network algorithms' -
);
```

This technique has the advantage of performing both of the steps needed: loading the Java class and populating USER_SDO_NETWORK_CONSTRAINTS. Its major drawback is that the database administrator must first define a directory object in the database and grant access to this directory, as illustrated in Listing 10-40.

Listing 10-40. *Defining a Directory Object*

```
CREATE DIRECTORY constraints_classes_dir AS 'D:\Files\Code\Constraints';
GRANT READ ON DIRECTORY constraints_classes_dir TO spatial;
```

To remove a constraint, use the DEREGISTER_CONSTRAINT() procedure, as shown in Listing 10-41.

Listing 10-41. *Removing a Network Constraint Using* DEREGISTER_CONSTRAINT()

```
EXECUTE SDO_NET_MEM.NETWORK_MANAGER.DEREGISTER_CONSTRAINT ( -
    'MyConstraint' -
);
```

This will delete the reference to the constraint from USER_SDO_NETWORK_CONSTRAINTS and also drop the class from the database.

To install a new version of the constraint, you can deregister and reregister it or, more simply, reload it using loadjava.

■ **Note** The DEREGISTER_CONSTRAINT() procedure will first load the contents of the class file in the BLOB column of USER_SDO_NETWORK_CONSTRAINTS. This is just an intermediate storage place from which the procedure then loads the class into the database by calling the CREATE JAVA statement.

Using a Constraint

To use a constraint in your network searches, you just need to pass its name to the function you call. For example:

```
path := SDO_NET_MEM.NETWORK_MANAGER.SHORTEST_PATH ('UNET', 4, 3, 'MyConstraint');
```

However, if you run this search, you will see no difference in output from that of the original code that does not use the constraint. Whatever happened to the trace that the constraint is suppose to print? That output is produced on Java's System.out, and to see it, you need to tell your JVM that you want it redirected to the standard server output mechanism. This you do by calling DBMS_JAVA.SET_OUTPUT() and using the SET SERVEROUTPUT command in SQL*Plus:

```
SQL> set serveroutput on size unlimited
SQL> exec dbms_java.set_output(32000);
PL/SQL procedure successfully completed.
```

From now on, you will see the output produced by your constraint on your SQL*Plus console.

A Parameterized Constraint

`NetworkTraceConstraint` was simple to load and use; it does not require any parameter. What about the other constraint you used, `LinkLevelConstraint`? That one needs a parameter; in the Java examples, you passed when instantiating the constraint object.

This approach is no longer possible with the PL/SQL API. You give only the name of the constraint to apply, and the instantiation of the corresponding class happens deep inside the API routines. You have no way to pass any start-up parameter to the class.

Actually, if you try to use the `LinkLevelConstraint` like you did for `NetworkTraceConstraint`, your network search call will fail with a `java.lang.InstantiationException` error. This is because your class contains an explicit constructor (needed to pass the target link-level parameter) and therefore does not provide the default constructor, which is the one used by the PL/SQL API to instantiate the class.

So, the first change to the `LinkLevelConstraint` class is to add an explicit default constructor:

```
public LinkLevelConstraint () {
}
```

Now the class will be correctly instantiated and used in your network searches. However, that does not do much good, since you are unable to control the constraint, that is, pass it a target link level. To achieve this, you will first add a "setter" method to the class, which will enable you to control the value of the target link level:

```
public static void setTargetLevel (int newTargetLevel) {
  targetLevel = newTargetLevel;
}
```

And while we are at it, let's also create a "getter" function:

```
public static int getTargetLevel () {
  return targetLevel;
}
```

Notice those are `static` methods. This is because you will call them using PL/SQL wrappers, and this is possible only for `static` methods. As a result, `targetLevel` must also now be made `static`:

```
private static int targetLevel = 0;
```

Listing 10-42 gives the new and improved `LinkLevelConstraint`.

Listing 10-42. *Network Constraint for the PL/SQL API*

```
import java.util.*;
import oracle.spatial.network.*;

/**
 * The following network constraint assumes that
 * 1. each link has a link level (stored as LINK_LEVEL in { 1,2,3 })
 * 2. for a given target level (in { 1,2,3 } ), the following must hold:
 *    target Level 1 can only travel on link Level 1
 *    target Level 2 can travel on link Level 1 and 2
 *    target Level 3 can travel on link Level 1, 2, and 3
 */
```

```
public class LinkLevelConstraint implements NetworkConstraint {
  static int targetLevel = 0; // Default; no restriction

  public LinkLevelConstraint () {
  }

  public LinkLevelConstraint (int newTargetLevel) {
    targetLevel = newTargetLevel;
  }

  public static void setTargetLevel (int newTargetLevel) {
    targetLevel = newTargetLevel;
  }

  public static int getTargetLevel () {
    return targetLevel;
  }

  public boolean requiresPathLinks() {
    return false ;
  }

  public boolean isSatisfied (AnalysisInfo info) {
    if ( targetLevel == 0 ) // no restriction
      return true ;
    Link link = info.getNextLink() ; // potential link candidate
    int linkLevel = link.getLinkLevel(); // get link Level
    if ( link != null && targetLevel >= linkLevel )
      return true;
    else
      return false;
  }
}
```

The last step is to define PL/SQL wrappers over `setTargetLevel()` and `getTargetLevel()` so that you can call them from SQL and PL/SQL. Listing 10-43 shows those wrappers.

Listing 10-43. *Defining PL/SQL Wrappers*

```
CREATE OR REPLACE PACKAGE link_level_constraint AS
  PROCEDURE set_target_level (new_target_level NUMBER);
  FUNCTION get_target_level RETURN NUMBER;
END;
/
CREATE OR REPLACE PACKAGE BODY link_level_constraint AS
  PROCEDURE set_target_level (new_target_level NUMBER)
    AS LANGUAGE JAVA
    NAME 'LinkLevelConstraint.setTargetLevel(int)';

  FUNCTION get_target_level RETURN NUMBER
    AS LANGUAGE JAVA
    NAME 'LinkLevelConstraint.getTargetLevel() return int';
END;
/
```

You can now use those wrappers to get and set the target link level. Let's put everything together. First, compile the new NetworkConstraint class, and then load it into the database:

```
loadjava -user spatial/spatial -verbose NetworkTraceConstraint.class
```

Then define the constraint in the USER_SDO_NETWORK_CONSTRAINTS view:

```
INSERT INTO user_sdo_network_constraints (constraint, description, class_name)
VALUES (
  'LinkLevelConstraint',
  'Filters links based on level',
  'LinkLevelConstraint'
);
COMMIT;
```

Now load the network UNET:

```
SQL> EXECUTE SDO_NET_MEM.NETWORK_MANAGER.READ_NETWORK('UNET','FALSE');
```

Check the current target link level used by the constraint:

```
SQL> SELECT link_level_constraint.get_target_level() FROM DUAL;

LINK_LEVEL_CONSTRAINT.GET_TARGET_LEVEL()
----------------------------------------
                                       0
```

The target level is 0. This is the default value you specified. Then set it to the value 1. This means that the constraint will accept links only at level 1.

```
SQL> EXECUTE link_level_constraint.set_target_level(1)
```

Get the shortest path from node 7 to node 5, using the constraint. See the full code in Listing 10-44.

Listing 10-44. *Using the* SHORTEST_PATH() *Function with a Network Constraint*

```
DECLARE
  test_net       VARCHAR2(30) := 'UNET';
  start_node_id NUMBER   := 7;
  end_node_id    NUMBER   := 5;
  constraint     VARCHAR2(30) := 'LinkLevelConstraint';
  path           NUMBER;
  link_array     SDO_NUMBER_ARRAY;
  node_array     SDO_NUMBER_ARRAY;
BEGIN
  -- Get shortest path between two nodes
  path := SDO_NET_MEM.NETWORK_MANAGER.SHORTEST_PATH (
    test_net, start_node_id, end_node_id, constraint);

  -- Make sure we have a result
  IF path IS NULL THEN
    DBMS_OUTPUT.PUT_LINE('No path found');
    RETURN;
  END IF;

  -- Show path cost and number of links
  DBMS_OUTPUT.PUT_LINE('Target link level: ' ||
    link_level_constraint.get_target_level());
  DBMS_OUTPUT.PUT_LINE('Path cost: ' || SDO_NET_MEM.PATH.GET_COST(test_net, path));
```

```
  DBMS_OUTPUT.PUT_LINE('Number of links: ' ||
    SDO_NET_MEM.PATH.GET_NO_OF_LINKS(test_net, path));
  DBMS_OUTPUT.PUT_LINE('Simple path? ' ||
    SDO_NET_MEM.PATH.IS_SIMPLE(test_net, path));

  -- Show the links traversed
  DBMS_OUTPUT.PUT_LINE('Links traversed:');
  link_array := SDO_NET_MEM.PATH.GET_LINK_IDS(test_net, path);
  FOR i IN link_array.first..link_array.last LOOP
    DBMS_OUTPUT.PUT_LINE('* Link ' || link_array(i) || ' ' ||
      SDO_NET_MEM.LINK.GET_NAME (test_net, link_array(i)) || ' ' ||
      SDO_NET_MEM.LINK.GET_LEVEL (test_net, link_array(i)) || ' ' ||
      SDO_NET_MEM.LINK.GET_COST (test_net, link_array(i))
    );
  END LOOP;

  -- Show the nodes traversed
  DBMS_OUTPUT.PUT_LINE('Nodes traversed:');
  node_array := SDO_NET_MEM.PATH.GET_NODE_IDS(test_net, path);
  FOR i IN node_array.first..node_array.last LOOP
    DBMS_OUTPUT.PUT_LINE('* Node ' || node_array(i) || ' ' ||
       SDO_NET_MEM.NODE.GET_NAME (test_net, node_array(i)) || ' ' ||
       SDO_NET_MEM.NODE.GET_COST (test_net, node_array(i))
    );
  END LOOP;
END;
/
```

The result shows that you had to take a long way, using only level-1 links:

```
Target link level: 1
Path cost: 7
Number of links: 5
Simple path? TRUE
Links traversed:
* Link 7  L7  1 2
* Link 1  L1  1 1
* Link 2  L2  1 2
* Link 3  L3  1 1
* Link 10 L10 1 1
Nodes traversed:
* Node 7 N7 0
* Node 1 N1 0
* Node 2 N2 0
* Node 3 N3 0
* Node 6 N6 0
* Node 5 N5 0
```

Change the target link level to 2, which means you can use links at level 1 or 2:

```
SQL> EXECUTE link_level_constraint.set_target_level(2)
```

Repeat the search shown in Listing 10-44. The result is now as follows:

```
Target link level: 1
Target link level: 2
Path cost: 3
Number of links: 2
Simple path? TRUE
```

```
Links traversed:
* Link 6  L6  1 2
* Link 11 L11 2 1
Nodes traversed:
* Node 7 N7 0
* Node 8 N8 0
* Node 5 N5 0
```

The Network Editor

All the examples you have seen so far have used either SQL or Java but with no actual graphical results and little interaction. Oracle provides a nice graphical editor that lets you experiment visually with actual data and try all the network analysis functions.

Starting the Editor

The editor is a Java program supplied as a JAR file, `sdondme.jar`. Make sure to include all the required JAR files in the Java classpath (see Table 10-17).

Table 10-17. *JAR Files Used by the Network Editor*

JAR File	Usage	Location
sdondme.jar	Network Editor	$ORACLE_HOME/md/jlib
sdoapi.jar	Spatial SDO API	$ORACLE_HOME/md/jlib
sdonm.jar	Network Java API	$ORACLE_HOME/md/jlib
sdoutl.jar	Spatial utilities	$ORACLE_HOME/md/jlib
ojdbc14.jar	JDBC driver	$ORACLE_HOME/jdbc/lib
xmlparserv2.jar	XML parser	$ORACLE_HOME/lib

Since the network API loads networks in memory, you may want to provide sufficient memory to Java using the `-Xms` and `-Xmx` options.

The main class of the editor is `oracle.spatial.network.editor.NetworkEditor`. Listing 10-45 shows how you can start the editor in a Windows environment. Make sure to change `ORACLE_HOME` to point to the home of your own Oracle Database 11*g* installation.

Listing 10-45. *Starting the Network Editor*

```
set ORACLE_HOME=D:\Oracle\Ora111
set JAR_LIBS=%ORACLE_HOME%/md/jlib/sdondme.jar;
%ORACLE_HOME%/lib/xmlparserv2.jar; %ORACLE_HOME%/jdbc/lib/classes12.jar;
%ORACLE_HOME%\md/jlib/sdonm.jar; %ORACLE_HOME%/md/jlib/sdoapi.jar;
%ORACLE_HOME%/md/jlib/sdoutl.jar
java -Xms512M -Xmx512M -cp %JAR_LIBS% oracle.spatial.network.editor.NetworkEditor
```

You should now see the window shown in Figure 10-23.

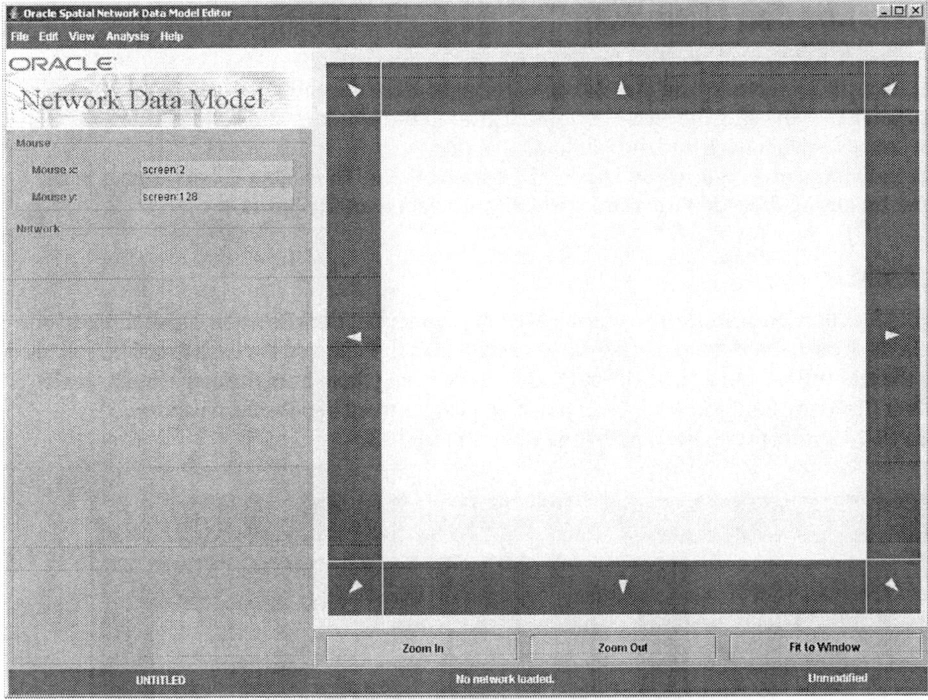

Figure 10-23. *Main window of the Network Editor*

Connecting to the Database

Select the Connect to Database option from the File menu, and then fill the next dialog box with the usual JDBC connection information: host name, port, database name, user name, and password.

■ **Tip** You can specify the connection parameters on the command line that starts the Network Editor.

Loading a Network from the Database

Select the Read Network from Database option from the File menu. This opens a dialog box much like the connection box, where you can select the network to load from the Network Name drop-down list.

Depending on the size of the network you load, this may take some time. For the networks we used in the preceding examples, this will be fast, of course.

■ **Note** The Network Editor can manipulate spatial networks only.

Using the Loaded Network

Once the network has loaded, you will see it entirely in the main map window. Use the Zoom In and Zoom Out buttons to zoom in and out. You can also right-click the mouse to drag a rectangle to zoom into. You can pan using the arrow buttons all around the window. The Fit to Window button brings the entire network back into the window.

Select individual objects (links and nodes) by clicking them. The object details appear in the left window, including drop-down lists from which you select related objects.

Network Analysis

The `Analysis` function lets you select an individual analysis function. Each function corresponds to one of the methods of the `NetworkManager` class you have studied in this chapter. For each function, you need to provide the relevant parameters. You identify nodes by selecting them from the map window (or by entering their IDs in the form window). Other parameters are entered into the form window.

Figure 10-24 shows the shortest path from node 7 to node 3.

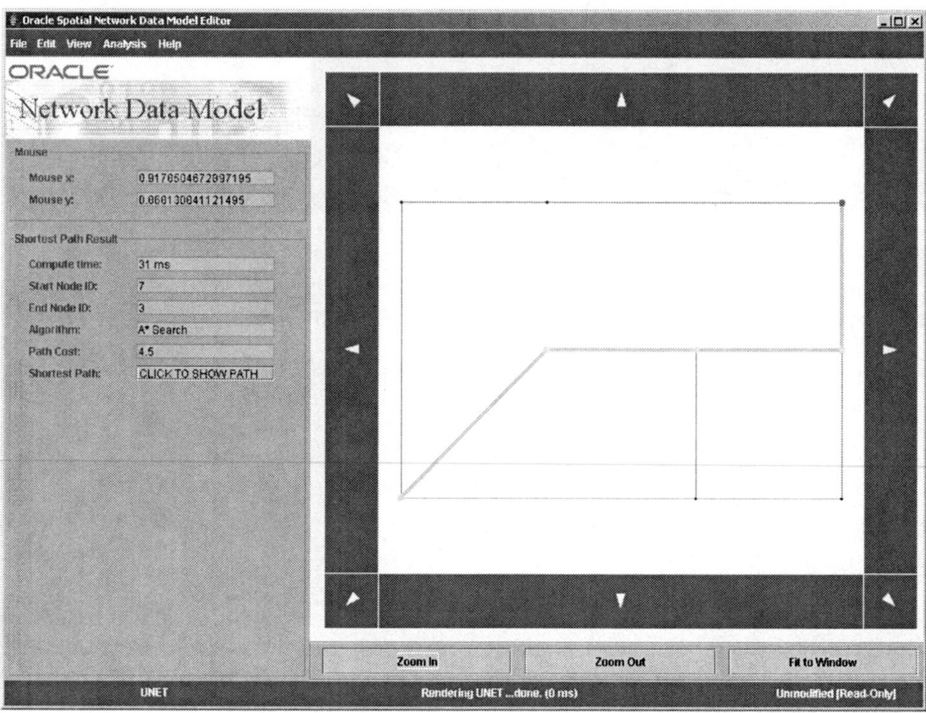

Figure 10-24. *Shortest path from node 7 to node 3 on network UNET*

Network Editing

From the Edit menu, you can modify the network by adding and removing nodes and links.

To add a node, click the spot on the screen where you want the new node to be placed. The left window is then filled with the x and y coordinates of the node, as well as with a new ID for the node. You just need to fill in the other information, such as node cost and status, before clicking the Create button.

You can add links only between existing nodes. Click the start node and then the end node. The IDs of the two nodes appear in the left window (but you can also enter them manually). Fill in the rest of the form, and click the Create button.

You can delete links or nodes by selecting them and then using the Delete Selected option of the Edit menu.

Once you have finished changing the network, you can write it back to the database using the Write Network to Database option from the File menu. If you forget to do this before exiting the editor or loading another network, you will be reminded.

Example Data: The Streets of San Francisco

The network analysis on the simple networks (UNET and DNET) you have been working with is interesting but not very spectacular.

In the Downloads area of the Apress website (`www.apress.com`), you will find a dataset that contains a street network for San Francisco, California. See the introduction for instructions on how to get the files. This network contains some 17,000 links and 11,000 nodes. Use the Oracle Import tool to load it, as shown in Listing 10-46. Notice the additional step to insert the network metadata in `USER_SDO_NETWORK_METADATA`.

Listing 10-46. *Loading the Network Data*

```
imp spatial/spatial file=net.dmp full=y
SQL> INSERT INTO USER_SDO_NETWORK_METADATA
       SELECT * FROM my_network_metadata;
SQL> commit;
```

The network is called `NET_SF`. Once you have loaded it in the Network Editor, you will see a window like the one shown in Figure 10-25.

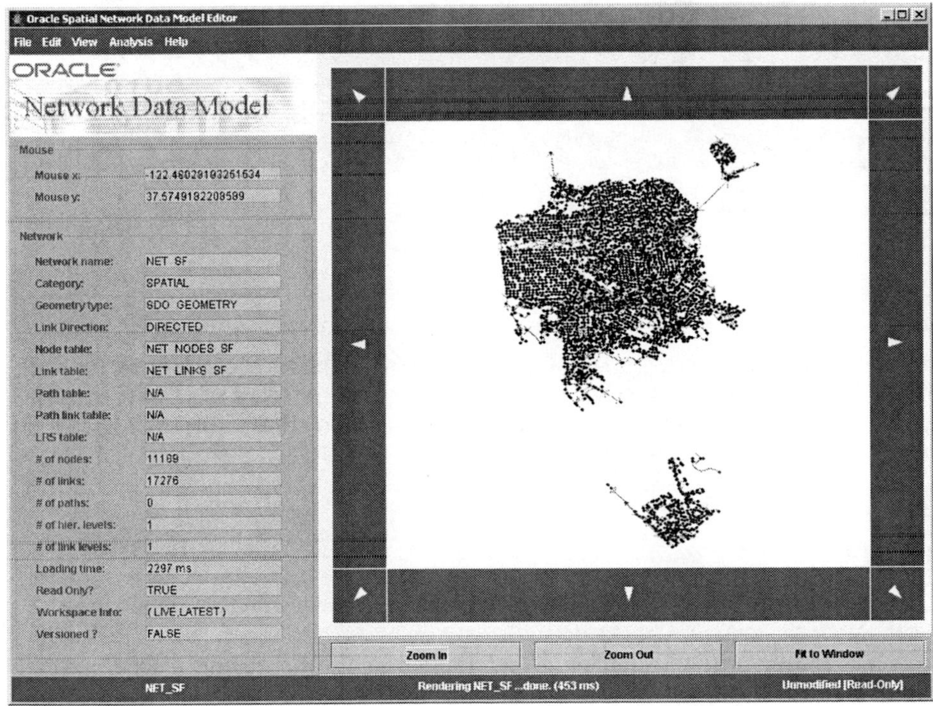

Figure 10-25. *The streets of San Francisco*

Zoom in until you see the links and nodes in sufficient detail. Each link represents a street segment between two intersections. Nodes are intersections. This is a directed network, and arrows indicate the direction of each link.

Try performing some analysis functions. For example, select the Nearest N Nodes from a Given Node Choice from the Analysis menu, select a node by clicking it, enter the number of neighbors to search, and click the Compute button. A typical result should look like Figure 10-26.

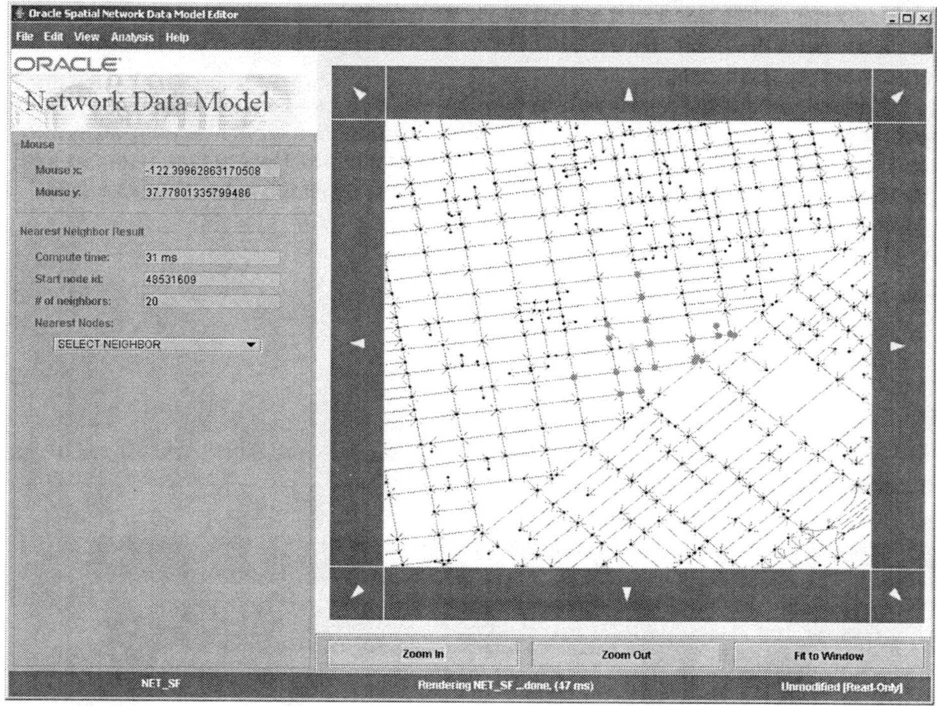

Figure 10-26. *A nearest-neighbors search in San Francisco*

■ **Caution** Some analysis functions may need to process a great deal of information—this is the case for the functions that return all paths between two nodes or those that find all nodes that are reachable or that can reach a given node. By default, those functions perform unbounded searches that can take a long time to complete. Make sure to limit the results by providing a maximum depth, cost, or number of solutions. The MCST function has no limit; it always runs on the complete network.

Summary

In this chapter, you learned how to define and load networks. You also learned how to use the APIs provided with the Oracle Network Data Model to perform such network-based analyses as finding the shortest path between two nodes, finding all nodes within some distance from a node, and discovering the nearest neighbors to a node.

CHAPTER 11

The Routing Engine

In order to run the examples in this chapter, you need to import the following dataset:

```
imp spatial/spatial file=routing.dmp full=y
```

Using the techniques described in Chapter 10, you know how to obtain the shortest path between two network nodes. The result of the search was a *logical path*, or a list of links traversed. You could also get the *geographical path*, or the geometry of the path.

Let's assume you want to tell a customer how to get to your nearest store. Using the Network Data Model shortest-path search, you received the geometry of the path. You can use it to show the shortest route to your store on a map.

But this can be hard to read and hard to use. It would be better if you could also tell your customer how to reach your store: the streets to follow, when to turn left or right, how long to drive, and so on. The list of links received from the shortest-path search is insufficient: it just lists all street segments traversed but does not give instructions. Giving instruction is the role of the Oracle Spatial Routing Engine.

Contrary to the Network Data Model that provides an API to be used only in your own application, the Routing Engine is a *web service*: you send it routing requests expressed in XML, and it returns the best computed route, also in XML.

Note You may think that the Routing Engine uses the Network Data Model APIs and data structures. This is unfortunately not the case. The two features are completely separate, although they can be made to work against the same data structures. We hope future versions of Oracle Spatial will unite the two features.

Table 11-1 compares the Network Data Model to the Routing Engine.

Table 11-1. *The Network Data Model vs. the Routing Engine*

Network Data Model	Routing Engine
Java and PL/SQL APIs.	XML API.
Returns lists of links.	Returns driving directions.
Can do any kind of network searches.	Can compute the shortest path only.
Network tables can have any names.	Network tables have fixed names.
Can use bidirected links.	Can use directed links only.
Uses one cost per network only.	Can use either time or distance (for fastest or shortest calculations).

Architecture

Figure 11-1 illustrates the architecture of the Routing Engine. The Routing Engine is a pure Java server component (a Java servlet) that needs a Java application server environment. You can deploy it in the Oracle Application Server, as well as in any J2EE-compliant application server.

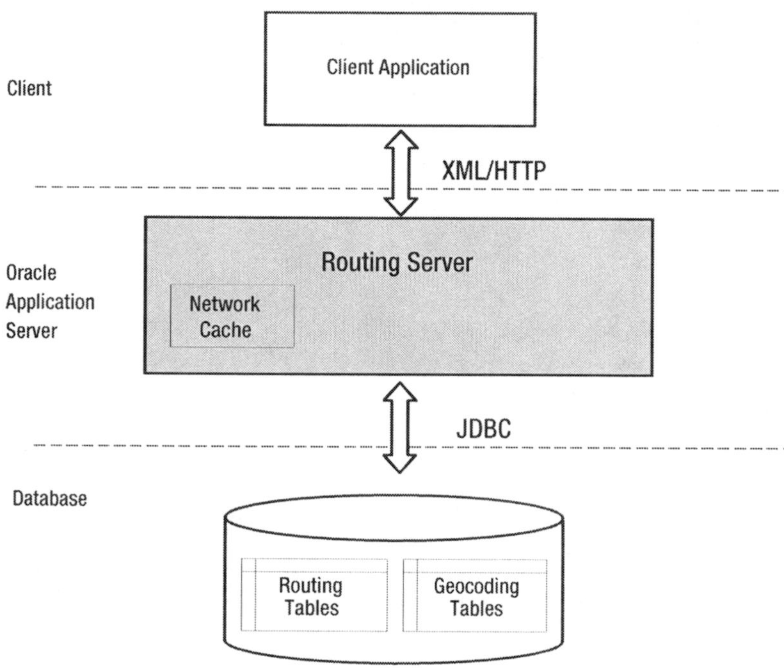

Figure 11-1. *Oracle Routing Engine architecture*

The road network used for routing is stored in the database in a set of tables. We will discuss the exact organization of those tables later in this chapter. Notice also the presence of geocoding tables. This is because your application will typically pass the street address of the start and end locations. The Routing Engine will automatically call the proper geocoding functions in order to convert those addresses to network locations.

The Routing Engine will not load the entire network in memory. Rather, it will load only the necessary subsets of the network (called *partitions*) in memory. You can control the size of the partition cache. You will also need to partition the network using functions supplied with the Routing Engine. You'll learn more about this in the "Partitioning" section later in this chapter.

Note that the Routing Engine can also be configured to use a Geocoding Server web service instead, as illustrated in Figure 11-2. The Geocoding Server web service is the one you saw in Chapter 6.

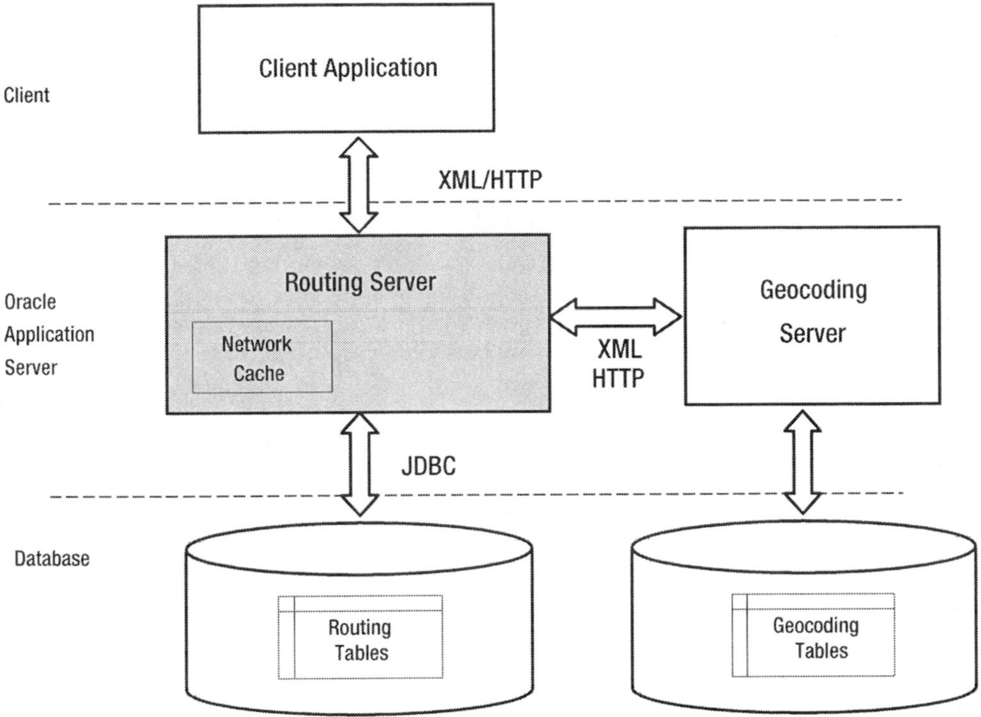

Figure 11-2. *Oracle Routing Engine architecture using the Geocoding Server web service*

Figure 11-3 illustrates the way your application talks to the Routing Engine. Your application must first format the routing request in XML and then send it to the server. Once the server has computed the correct route and driving directions, it will send another XML document to your application, which you then need to parse and use.

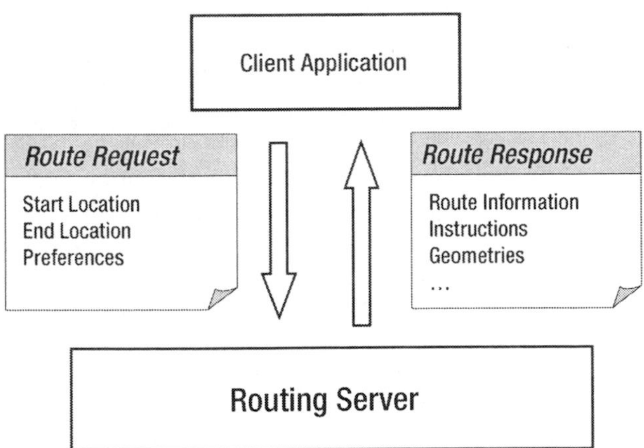

Figure 11-3. *Oracle Routing Engine request/response flow*

Routing requests are flexible. You can pass the start and end locations as full addresses, but you can also pass them just as spatial coordinates. This is helpful when you get the start and/or end locations from a mouse click. You can also specify preferences: whether to get the shortest or the fastest path, what units should be used in the resulting directions (minutes, kilometers, miles, and so on), what language to use, and many more. We will review the API later in this chapter.

Installation and Configuration

The Routing Engine is provided as a standard J2EE archive (EAR) format. See the introduction for details on how to install and configure OC4J and how to deploy applications using the OC4J console. The installation EAR file for the Routing Engine is provided in `$ORACLE_HOME/md/jlib/routeserver.ear`.

To configure the routing server, you need to manually edit the `web.xml` file in `$OC4J_HOME/j2ee/home/applications/routeserver/web/WEB-INF`.

■ **Caution** The `web.xml` file provided with the Routing Engine contains a number of parameter settings that will make the engine fail on start-up: connections to nonexistent databases, and so on.

The parameters in the `web.xml` file are encoded using a name/value pair approach. For example, here is how you specify the default language for the driving directions returned by the router:

```
<init-param>
  <param-name>language</param-name>
  <param-value>English</param-value>
      <description>
        Language to use to give driving directions.
      </description>
</init-param>
```

Table 11-2 lists the parameters you can specify. They are pretty much self-descriptive.

Table 11-2. *Routing Engine Parameters*

Parameter	Meaning
Connection to Routing Tables	
`routeserver_schema_jdbc_connect_string`	Connection string to the database that contains the routing tables. Specify as `jdbc:oracle:thin@<server>:<port>:<sid>`.
`routeserver_schema_username`	Database user who owns the routing tables.
`routeserver_schema_password`	Password of that user. Specify it with a leading exclamation point (!). The routing server will replace it with an encrypted version.
`routeserver_schema_connection_cache_min_limit`	Minimum number of database connections established by the server.
`routeserver_schema_connection_cache_max_limit`	Maximum number of database connections.
Type of Geocoder to Use	
`geocoder_type`	Type of geocoder to use: `thinclient` or `httpclient`.
`geocoder_match_mode`	The match mode for geocoder calls. See Chapter 6 for possible values and their effects.

Parameter	Meaning
Connection to Geocoding Tables (`geocoder_type = "thinclient"`)	
`geocoder_schema_host`	Host name of database server containing the geocoding tables.
`geocoder_schema_port`	Port number.
`geocoder_schema_sid`	Database SID.
`geocoder_schema_username`	Database user who owns the geocoding tables.
`geocoder_schema_password`	Password for that user.
`geocoder_schema_mode`	Type of JDBC driver to use (`thin` or `oci8`).
Connection to Geocoding Server (`geocoder_type="httpclient"`)	
`geocoder_http_url`	URL to the geocoding service.
`geocoder_http_proxy_host`	Name or IP address of the proxy server, if any.
`geocoder_http_proxy_port`	Port of the proxy server.
Logging	
`log_filename`	Name of a log file. If you specify a relative path (for example, `log/routeserver.log`), it will be interpreted as based on `$OC4J_HOME/j2ee/home`.
`log_level`	Level of detail of the information logged. Specify as `FATAL`, `ERROR`, `WARN`, `INFO`, `DEBUG`, or `FINEST`.
`log_thread_name`	Specify whether to log thread names (as `true` or `false`).
`log_time`	Specify whether to log timestamps.
Routing Parameters	
`max_speed_limit`	Maximum speed limit in meters per second. Set by default to 34 meters per second, which corresponds approximately to 122 kilometers per hour or 75 miles per hour.
`highway_cost_multiplier`	Factor by which to make highways less attractive when computing a route with a preference for local roads.
`driving_side`	Side of the road on which you drive, as `R` or `L`.
`language`	Default language used to give driving directions. This can be overridden in the routing requests. The supported languages are English (the default), French, German, Italian, and Spanish.
`distance_function_type`	Which method to use for computing distance. Specify as `geodetic` or `euclidean`.
`long_ids`	Set this to `true` to force the router to use Java `long` types to store edge and node IDs.
`partition_cache_size_limit`	Maximum number of network partitions to keep in memory at any point.
`partition_table_name`	Name of the partition table. Set to `PARTITION` by default.

To change parameters, just edit the `web.xml` file using your favorite editor. You probably want to use an editor that is able to color-code the XML elements.

Tip You have to stop and restart the complete OC4J server for the routing server to pick up your changes. Just stopping and starting the `routeserver` application using the OC4J console is not enough.

Data Structures

Just like the Network Data Model, the Routing Engine needs a network graph, that is, a set of connected links and nodes. Links and nodes are also stored in tables, whose structure is similar—but not identical—to that used by the Network Data Model. One important difference is that the names of the tables are fixed, as is their structure (column names and types).

The routing network is composed of two main tables: the `NODE` table, which describes all network nodes, and the `EDGE` table, which describes all network links. There is no equivalent to the path and path link tables: the Routing Engine does not store the computed routes in the database, so they are not needed. There is, however, a new table, `SIGN_POST`, which describes the indications on signposts at highway exits.

The node table is similar to that used for the Network Data Model. The main difference is that the routing node table must be called `NODE` and have exactly the structure shown in Table 11-3. Notice the `PARTITION_ID` column: it is originally empty and will be filled when the network is partitioned before use.

Table 11-3. *The* `NODE` *Table*

Column	Data Type	Meaning
NODE_ID	NUMBER	Unique identification for that node in the network. This is also the primary key of the table.
GEOMETRY	SDO_GEOMETRY	A point geometry object that represents the node.
PARTITION_ID	NUMBER	Numeric identifier of the partition that contains this node. This is originally empty and will be filled when partitioning the network.

The `EDGE` table is also similar to a link table used for the Network Data Model. It has the structure shown in Table 11-4. One important difference, however, is that the routing edges are all directed. This means a two-way road segment must be modeled using two edges, one in each direction.

Table 11-4. *The* `EDGE` *Table*

Column	Data Type	Meaning
EDGE_ID	NUMBER	Unique identification for that edge in the network. This is also the primary key of the table.
START_NODE_ID	NUMBER	Unique identifier of the node from which the edge originates.
END_NODE_ID	NUMBER	Unique identifier of the node at which the edge terminates.
PARTITION_ID	NUMBER	Numeric identifier of the partition that contains this node. This is originally empty and will be filled when partitioning the network.
FUNC_CLASS	NUMBER	Functional class of that edge. This is a number from 1 to 5.
LENGTH	NUMBER	Length of the edge in meters.

Column	Data Type	Meaning
SPEED_LIMIT	NUMBER	Speed limit on that edge, in meters per second.
GEOMETRY	SDO_GEOMETRY	A line geometry object that describes the shape of the edge.
NAME	VARCHAR(128)	Name of this edge. This will be the name used in driving directions.
DIVIDER	CHAR(1)	Defines whether the edge is divided. Specify as N to indicate the edge is not divided. Any other value indicates the edge is divided.

The FUNC_CLASS column is important for routing. It represents the functional class of the edge as a number from 1 to 5, with 1 indicating a large, high-speed, high-volume road, and each successive class is generally smaller in size, speed, and volume. Table 11-5 explains the values and their meanings.

Table 11-5. *Functional Classes*

Functional Class	Meaning
1	Large high-speed, high-volume roads such as U.S. interstates or U.K. motorways
2	Roads with consistent speed, used to get traffic to and from functional class 1 roads
3	High-volume roads, used to connect functional class 2 roads
4	Used to move traffic between neighborhoods
5	All other roads and streets

The Routing Engine uses the value in the DIVIDER column to determine whether the vehicle can make a U-turn at the start or end of a route. When set to N, it indicates that the edge allows U-turns without restriction. Any other value indicates the presence of some restriction.

■ **Caution** The DIVIDER column must always contain a value (in other words, NULLs are not allowed and will cause failures if present).

The SIGN_POST table stores information about road signs. The information it contains will be used in the driving directions generated by the router, such as "Take exit xxx toward xxx." It is not used to compute routes. Table 11-6 describes its structure.

Table 11-6. *The* SIGN_POST *Table*

Column	Data Type	Meaning
FROM_EDGE_ID	NUMBER	Number of the edge to which this sign applies.
TO_EDGE_ID	NUMBER	Number of the edge to which the sign points.
RAMP	VARCHAR(64)	Ramp text. Typically this will be the major road ID, such as I-280 S or US-101.
EXIT	VARCHAR(8)	For exit ramps: the name or number of the exit.
TOWARD	VARCHAR(64)	Indicates where the exit is heading to, such as DOWNTOWN or SIXTH STREET.

Example Data: The Streets of San Francisco

In the example data you can download from Apress's catalog page for this book, you will find a routing dataset that contains a street network for San Francisco, California. (See the introduction for instructions on how to get the files.) This network is identical to the network you loaded in Chapter 10 for use in the Network Editor. It has the same number of nodes but almost twice the number of edges (links). This is because, as already noted, each two-way street segment needs two edges in the routing tables, whereas one link is sufficient in the Network Data Model.

Use the Oracle Import tool to load the street network, as shown in Listing 11-1. Notice the additional step to rename the tables to match the names expected by the Routing Engine.

Listing 11-1. *Loading the Routing Data*

```
imp spatial/spatial file=routing.dmp full=y
SQL>
DROP TABLE EDGE;
DROP  NODE;
DROP TABLE SIGN_POST;
RENAME ROUTE_EDGES_SF TO EDGE;
RENAME ROUTE_NODES_SF TO NODE;
RENAME ROUTE_SIGN_POSTS_SF TO SIGN_POST;
```

You can use the San Francisco street network with the network APIs as well as the Network Editor. All you need is to create views on the NODE and EDGE tables, renaming columns on the way, and insert an entry in the USER_SDO_NETWORK_METADATA view, as shown in Listing 11-2. You can then load network NET_ROUTE_SF in the Network Editor. Once loaded, you should see a window identical to the one shown in Figure 11-4.

Listing 11-2. *Defining a Network Over the Routing Data*

```
SQL> CREATE OR REPLACE VIEW route_node_sf_v AS
  SELECT  node_id,
          geometry,
          partition_id
  FROM    node;

SQL> CREATE OR REPLACE VIEW route_edge_sf_v AS
  SELECT  edge_id AS link_id,
          start_node_id,
          end_node_id,
          partition_id,
          func_class,
          length,
          speed_limit,
          geometry,
          name AS link_name,
          divider
  FROM    edge;

SQL> DELETE FROM user_sdo_network_metadata
WHERE network = 'NET_ROUTE_SF';

SQL> INSERT INTO user_sdo_network_metadata (
  NETWORK,
  NETWORK_CATEGORY,
  GEOMETRY_TYPE,
```

```
  NODE_TABLE_NAME,
  NODE_GEOM_COLUMN,
  LINK_TABLE_NAME,
  LINK_GEOM_COLUMN,
  LINK_DIRECTION,
  LINK_COST_COLUMN
)
VALUES (
  'NET_ROUTE_SF',
  'SPATIAL',
  'SDO_GEOMETRY',
  'ROUTE_NODE_SF_V',
  'GEOMETRY',
  'ROUTE_EDGE_SF_V',
  'GEOMETRY',
  'DIRECTED',
  'LENGTH'
);
SQL> COMMIT;
```

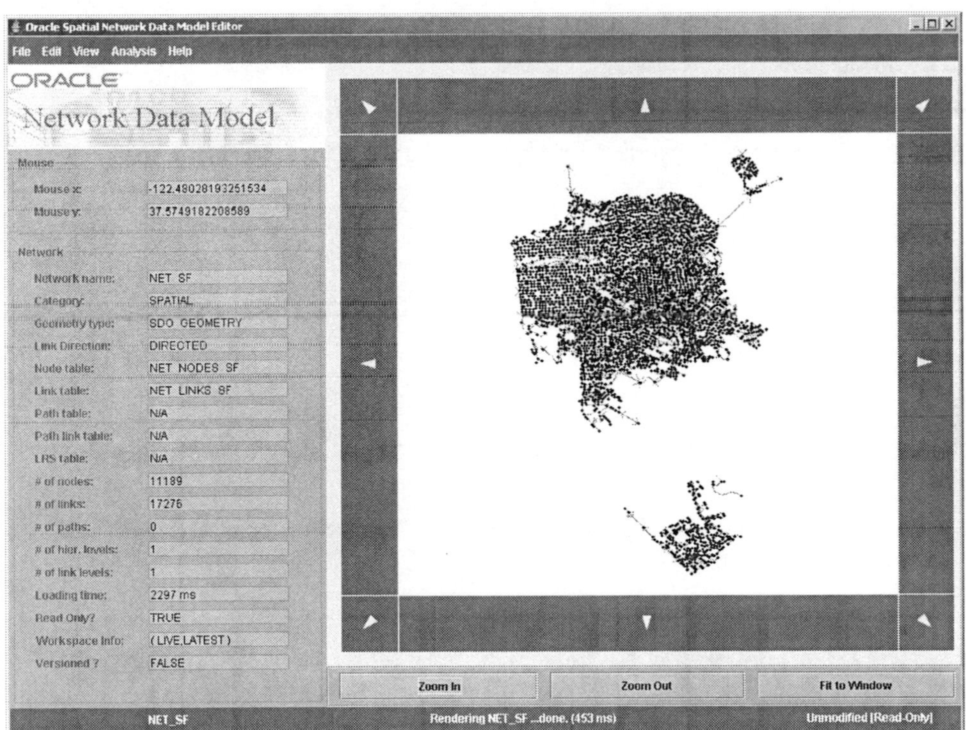

Figure 11-4. *The routing network shown in the Network Editor*

Partitioning

As already noted, the Routing Engine loads parts of the network as necessary. Those parts are called *partitions*. The original network graph (in other words, the NODE and EDGE tables) are not partitioned. You must perform the partitioning before the router can use the network.

Partitioning a network is easy; you just need to call the SDO_ROUTER_PARTITION.PARTITION_ROUTER() procedure, passing it the name of a "node partition" table, as well as the number of network nodes to be used for each partition.

However, before you can invoke the partitioning procedure, you must set up your environment so that the procedure can write its progress to a log file. This must be done by a privileged user (such as SYSTEM), as illustrated in Listing 11-3. Notice that you need to grant access to the log directory and file using Java-specific grants. This is because the partitioning procedure invokes a Java function to do the actual partitioning.

Listing 11-3. *Setting Up the Rights for Partitioning*

```
SQL>
-- Create the directory
CREATE DIRECTORY sdo_router_log_dir AS 'D:\Work';
-- Grant access to the user that will perform the partitioning
GRANT READ, WRITE ON DIRECTORY sdo_router_log_dir TO spatial;
-- Grant java write access on the file
exec dbms_java.grant_permission( 'SPATIAL', 'SYS:java.io.FilePermission',
    'D:\Work\sdo_router_partition.log', 'write' )
-- Also to MDSYS
exec dbms_java.grant_permission( 'MDSYS', 'SYS:java.io.FilePermission',
    'D:\Work\sdo_router_partition.log', 'write' )
```

■ **Caution** You can store the log file anywhere, but it must be called SDO_ROUTER_PARTITION.LOG.

Let's first examine the full syntax of the procedure:

```
SDO_ROUTER_PARTITION.PARTITION_ROUTER (
  p_tab_name     IN VARCHAR2 DEFAULT 'NODE_PART',
  max_v_no       IN NUMBER   DEFAULT 10000,
  driving_side   IN VARCHAR2 DEFAULT 'R',
  make_equal     IN BOOLEAN  DEFAULT TRUE
);
```

The following are the parameters for the PARTITION_ROUTER procedure. Note that they are all optional.

- p_tab_name: This is the name of an intermediate table that the procedure creates to hold a copy of all nodes in the network.

■ **Caution** Do not specify anything other than 'node_part'. This is because the procedure uses this name hard-coded in several places. Specifying any other name will make the procedure fail.

- max_v_no: This is the maximum number of nodes to store in each partition.
- driving_side: Specify this as L or R (the default).
- make_equal: Specify as TRUE (the default) or FALSE. If TRUE, the partitioning logic will attempt to distribute the nodes as evenly as possible between the partitions.

To invoke the partitioning procedure, do as shown in Listing 11-4. Notice that this script calls the procedure and then cleans up all the intermediate tables it leaves around.

Listing 11-4. *Performing the Partitioning*

```
SQL>
exec sdo_router_partition.partition_router('NODE_PART', 1000);
-- Now delete temporary tables left over by the partitioning
drop table EDGE_PART purge;
drop table FINAL_PARTITION purge;
drop table NODE_PART purge;
drop table PARTITION_TMP_2 purge;
drop table PARTITION_TMP_3 purge;
drop table SUPER_EDGE_IDS purge;
drop table SUPER_NODE_IDS purge;
purge recyclebin;
```

You can monitor the progress of the partitioning process by watching the log file (SDO_ROUTER_PARTITION.LOG), which is updated on the fly. The log provides useful timing information about the job's progress. After the call completes, you will have a new table in your schema, called PARTITION, whose structure is detailed in Table 11-7. The table contains one row for each partition produced, identified by a unique sequential number. Note that the PARTITION_ID column in the NODE and EDGE tables also contains the ID of the partition to which each network element was assigned.

Table 11-7. *The Partition Table*

Column	Data Type	Meaning
PARTITION_ID	NUMBER	Unique identification for that partition
SUBNETWORK	BLOB	The binary representation of the subnetwork for that partition
NUM_NODES	NUMBER	Number of nodes in the partition
NUM_NON_BOUNDARY_EDGES	NUMBER	Number of edges fully contained in the partition
NUM_OUTGOING_BOUNDARY_EDGES	NUMBER	Number of edges that originate in that partition and terminate in another partition
NUM_INCOMING_BOUNDARY_EDGES	NUMBER	Number of edges that originate in another partition and terminate in this partition

Note that the table contains one more partition than the number you may expect. This is partition 0 and represents the "supernetwork," that is, the network that links all the partitions (subnetworks) together.

Using the Router: XML Queries and Responses

You now have a fully functional router network, and you can start using it from the router web service. Assuming you have updated your router configuration as outlined in Table 11-2, you should now be able to start your OC4J or application server, and you should be able to start submitting routing requests.

Go to http://oc4j_server:8888/routeserver using your web browser, where oc4j_server is the name or IP address of the machine where you just installed OC4J. For example, you would use http://127.0.0.1:8888/routeserver if you installed OC4J on your desktop machine. You should see the page shown in Figure 11-5.

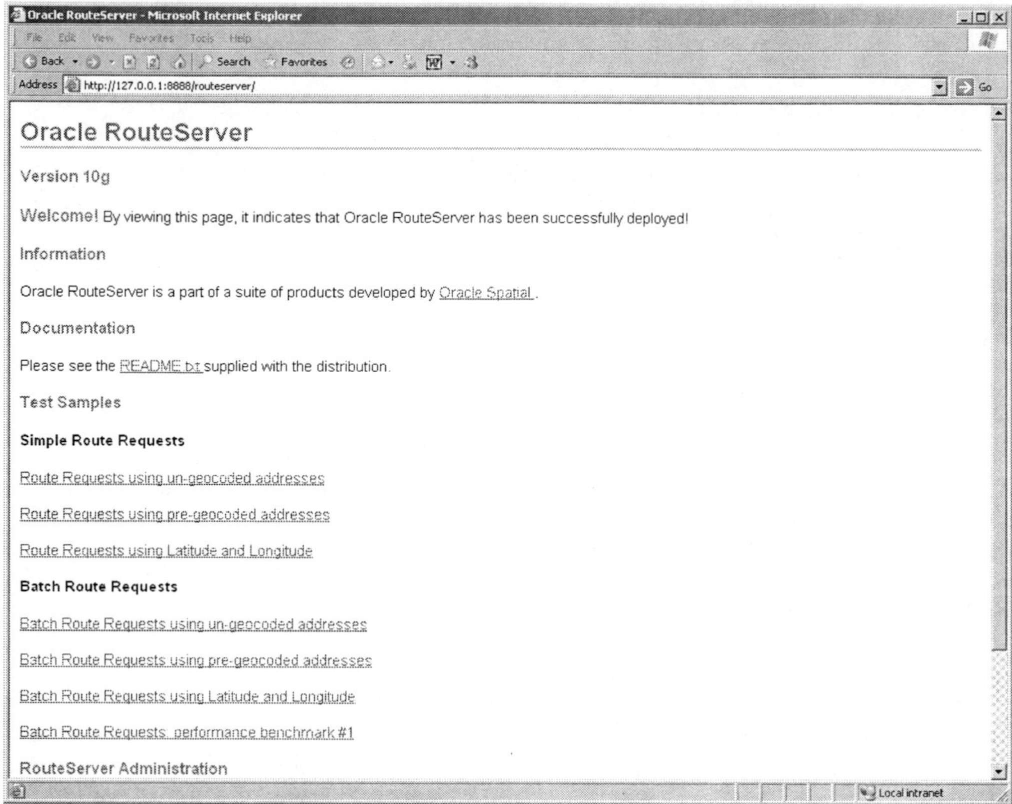

Figure 11-5. *The routing server home page*

From this page, you can choose links to various examples. If you click the first link ("Route Requests using un-geocoded addresses"), you will be taken to the page shown in Figure 11-6.

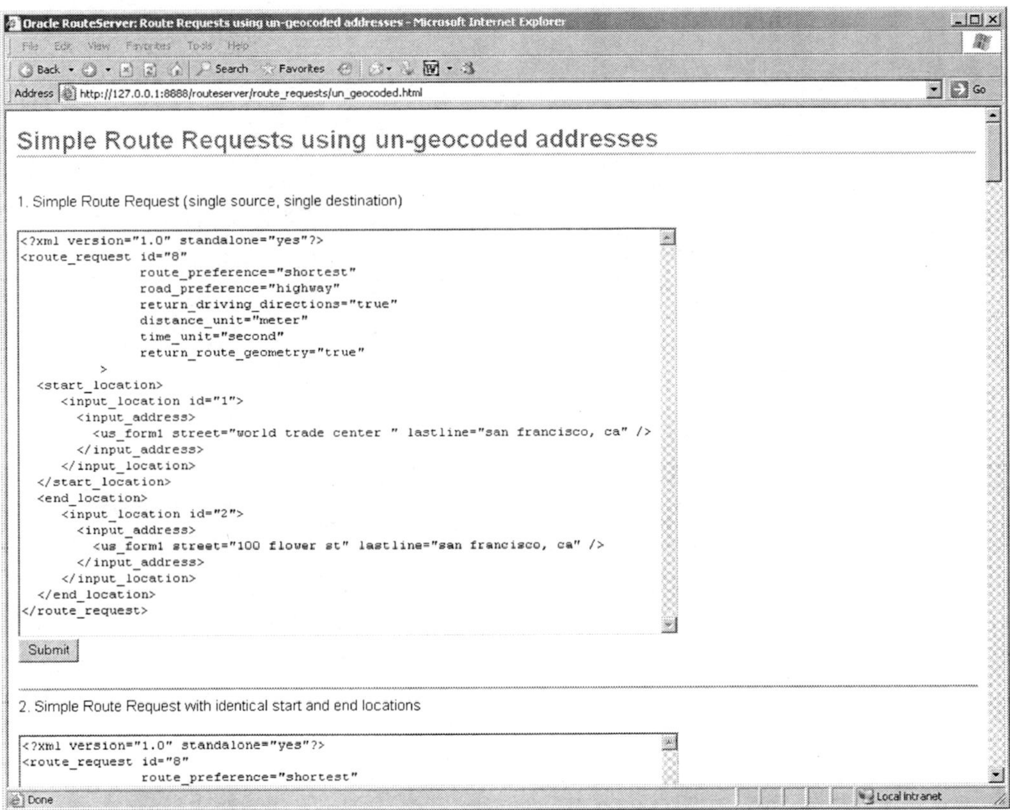

Figure 11-6. *Routing request example page*

Just click the Submit button for the first example. You should see a page that looks like the one shown in Figure 11-7. Congratulations, you just completed your first routing request.

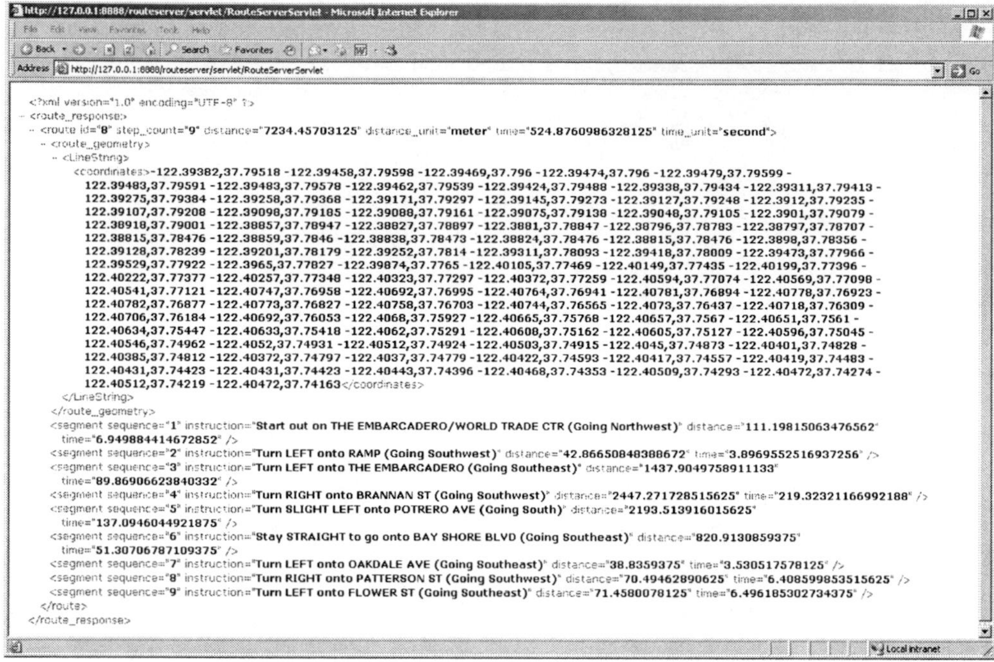

Figure 11-7. *Routing response*

The routing response contains overall information about the route: number of steps, total distance, and total duration. Then you get the geometry of the route and finally the step-by-step directions with their distance and duration. You can get different results by altering the input request, such as getting the response in a different language, using different time and distance units, and so on.

Routing Requests

Let's first examine a simple routing request:

```
<route_request id="1"
  route_preference="shortest"
  return_driving_directions="true"
  distance_unit="mile" time_unit="minute"
  return_route_geometry="true">
  <start_location>
    <input_location id="1" >
      <input_address>
        <unformatted country="US" >
          <address_line value="747 Howard Street" />
          <address_line value="San Francisco, CA" />
        </unformatted >
      </input_address>
    </input_location>
  </start_location>
  <end_location>
    <input_location id="2" >
      <input_address>
        <unformatted country="US" >
```

```
        <address_line value="1300 Columbus" />
        <address_line value="San Francisco, CA" />
      </unformatted >
    </input_address>
   </input_location>
  </end_location>
</route_request>
```

This request uses the generic, unformatted notation for street addresses. The router supports a few alternate formats, specifically for U.S. addresses. For example, the request in Figure 11-6 uses one of those formats. For more details on how to format addresses, see Chapter 6.

Apart from the start and end locations, the request specifies a number of preferences and options you can use to control the way the router determines the route, as well as the level of detail it returns.

Routing Options

The routing options are passed as attributes on the `<routing_request>` element. Some parameters influence the route computed by the router:

- `route_preference` allows you to choose between the `fastest` or `shortest` route (the default).
- `road_preference` allows you to decide whether to use `highways` or only `local` roads.

Other parameters control the level of details of the result. Specify them as `true` or `false` (the default):

- `return_driving_directions` returns the detailed step-by-step directions.
- `return_route_geometry` returns the line string that represents the geometry of the route. This is useful if you want to show the route on a map.
- `return_segment_geometry` returns a line string for the geometry of each step in the route. Use this if you want to show a small map for each step.
- `return_detailed_geometry` returns fully detailed geometries or returns simplified (generalized) geometries.
- `return_route_edge_ids` returns the list of all edges traversed by the route.
- `return_segment_edge_ids` returns the list of edges traversed by each step in the route.

Finally, the following parameters control the way the route instructions are returned to the user:

- `language` allows you to specify the language to be used for the instructions. If not specified, then the instructions will be returned in the default language specified in the router configuration file. Possible values are `ENGLISH`, `FRENCH`, `GERMAN`, `ITALIAN`, or `SPANISH`. If no language is specified at all, then the directions are returned in English.
- `distance_unit`: Specify as `kilometer`, `mile`, or `meter`. If not specified, the distances will be returned in miles.
- `time_unit`: Specify as `hour`, `minute`, or `second`. If not specified, the times will be returned in minutes.

Pregeocoded Start and End Locations

The default mechanism is to specify the locations as full street addresses, as shown earlier. However, your application may already have verified and geocoded the addresses in a previous step. It would be a waste of resources to have the router geocode them again. By specifying the attribute pre_geocoded_locations = "true" in the routing request, you can specify the locations using the information returned by the geocoder. This is illustrated in the following example, which specifies the same location as the preceding example but this time as network references:

```
<route_request id="1"
  return_driving_directions="true"
  distance_unit="mile" time_unit="minute"
  pre_geocoded_locations="true">
  <start_location>
    <pre_geocoded_location id="1">
      <edge_id>23607005</edge_id>
      <percent>0.53</percent>
      <side>R</side>
    </pre_geocoded_location>
  </start_location>
  <end_location>
    <pre_geocoded_location id="2">
      <edge_id>23601015</edge_id>
      <percent>0.33</percent>
      <side>R</side>
    </pre_geocoded_location>
  </end_location>
</route_request>
```

For each of the locations, specify the edge ID, percentage, and side returned by the geocoder. See Chapter 6 for details.

Geographic Start and End Locations

Finally, you may not have any start or end location. Rather, the locations are provided by a geographic point obtained, for example, from a click on a map or possibly collected from a GPS receiver. The following is an example that again uses the same locations as in the previous examples but this time as longitude/latitude coordinates:

```
<route_request id="1"
  return_driving_directions="true"
  distance_unit="mile" time_unit="minute">
  <start_location>
    <input_location id="1"
      longitude="-122.4014128" latitude="37.7841193" />
  </start_location>
  <end_location>
    <input_location id="2"
      longitude="-122.4183326" latitude="37.805999" />
  </end_location>
</route_request>
```

The router will call the reverse geocoding function of the geocoder to convert the geographical coordinates to an address and network location.

Batch Routing

The batch routing mechanism allows you to specify multiple end locations. Its purpose is to compute the best route (shortest or fastest depending on your preferences) from your start location to each of the end locations.

The batch routing request will not return the full driving directions for each route; it returns only the distance and duration for each route, but it can order the routes by either distance or duration and can also limit the result to only those routes that are less than some maximum distance. This makes the batch routing mechanism a powerful way to sort locations (for example, stores) by their travel time or distance from another location (for example a customer).

Just like for regular routing requests, locations can be passed as street addresses, network connections (that is, pregeocoded locations), or longitude/latitude points.

Here is an example of a batch route request with three destinations:

```
<batch_route_request id="1" route_preference="fastest"
  distance_unit="km" time_unit="minute">
  <start_location>
    <input_location id="0" >
      <input_address>
        <unformatted country="US" >
          <address_line value="747 Howard Street" />
          <address_line value="San Francisco, CA" />
        </unformatted >
      </input_address>
    </input_location>
  </start_location>
  <end_location>
    <input_location id="1" >
      <input_address>
        <unformatted country="US" >
          <address_line value="1300 Columbus" />
          <address_line value="San Francisco, CA" />
        </unformatted >
      </input_address>
    </input_location>
  </end_location>
  <end_location>
    <input_location id="2" >
      <input_address>
        <unformatted country="US" >
          <address_line value="1450 California St" />
          <address_line value="San Francisco, CA" />
        </unformatted >
      </input_address>
    </input_location>
  </end_location>
  <end_location>
    <input_location id="3" >
      <input_address>
        <unformatted country="US" >
          <address_line value="800 Sutter Street" />
          <address_line value="San Francisco, CA" />
        </unformatted >
      </input_address>
    </input_location>
  </end_location>
</batch_route_request>
```

And here is the response returned from the router. Notice the routes are returned in the order in which you specified the destinations.

```
<batch_route_response id="1">
  <route id="1" step_count="0" distance="3.731" distance_unit="km"
    time="4.12" time_unit="minute" />
  <route id="2" step_count="0" distance="2.725" distance_unit="km"
```

```
    time="3.04" time_unit="minute" />
  <route id="3" step_count="0" distance="2.045" distance_unit="km"
    time="2.50" time_unit="minute" />
</batch_route_response>
```

The routing options are passed as attributes on the `<batch_route_request>` element. The following parameters are identical to those of the regular routing request:

- `route_preference`: This allows you to choose between the `fastest` or `shortest` route (the default).
- `road_preference`: This allows you to decide whether to use `highways` or only `local` roads.
- `distance_unit`: Specify as `kilometer`, `mile`, or `meter`. If not specified, the distances will be returned in miles.
- `time_unit`: Specify as `hour`, `minute`, or `second`. If not specified, the times will be returned in minutes.

The following parameters are specific to batch routing:

- `sort_by_distance`: Specify as `true` if you want the results to be ordered by distance; that is, the shortest routes appear first in the result set. If not specified, then results will be returned in random sequence.
- `cutoff_distance`: Use this to limit the results; that is, any result longer than the value you specify will not be returned. The distance you specify is expressed in the unit you indicate using the `distance_unit` parameter.

If you add the parameter `sort_by_distance="true"` to the previous batch routing request, the routes are now returned ordered by distance:

```
<batch_route_response id="1">
  <route id="3" step_count="0" distance="2.045" distance_unit="km" time="2.50"
    time_unit="minute" />
  <route id="2" step_count="0" distance="2.725" distance_unit="km" time="3.04"
    time_unit="minute" />
  <route id="1" step_count="0" distance="3.731" distance_unit="km" time="4.12"
    time_unit="minute" />
</batch_route_response>
```

And it you add `cutoff_distance="3"`, then the response is limited to only those locations that are less than 3 kilometers from the start location:

```
<batch_route_response id="1">
  <route id="2" step_count="0" distance="2.725" distance_unit="km"
    time="3.04" time_unit="minute" />
  <route id="3" step_count="0" distance="2.049" distance_unit="km"
    time="2.50" time_unit="minute" />
</batch_route_response>
```

Summary

In this chapter, you learned how to use the Oracle Routing Engine to obtain driving directions.

In Chapter 12, you will use some of the techniques you learned in this chapter in a complete application.

PART 4

Visualization

CHAPTER 12

Defining Maps Using MapViewer

So far, you have seen how to use spatial-based queries and how to manipulate spatial objects. However, one important aspect is still missing: the visualization of spatial objects using maps. After all, location information is all about maps, and to paraphrase a common saying, a map is certainly worth 1,000 words. In this chapter and the next, you will see how to enable a map-based visualization of spatial data in your applications using Oracle MapViewer.

MapViewer is a server-side component that constructs maps by reading appropriate database views and tables and returns the maps to the client applications in the appropriate formats. Each map constructed is specified using one or more layers, or *themes*. Each theme represents a logical grouping of geographic spatial features, such as roads, customer locations, rivers, and so on. These features are rendered with specific *styles*. In this chapter, we will describe in detail how to create these maps using Oracle MapViewer by covering the following topics:

- The need for maps in Spatial applications and an overview of Oracle MapViewer
- How to install, deploy, and configure MapViewer
- How to define maps with themes and styles and how to store their definitions in the database using the map definition tool Map Builder
- How to use MapViewer and the maps you have defined in your applications using one of the many available APIs: JavaScript (Ajax), Java, XML, or PL/SQL
- How to manage and administer the MapViewer server (that is, how to manage data sources, caches, map definitions, and so on)

Note Oracle MapViewer is a feature of the Oracle Application Server and as such follows a release cycle that is largely independent from that of the Oracle Database. In this chapter, we base our discussion on the version of MapViewer included with Oracle Fusion Middleware 11*g*, version 11.1.

Why Use Maps in Location-Enabled Applications?

We are all familiar with maps. We used maps in geography classes. We currently use maps to decide where to go for our vacations or to find our way when we are lost on the road. In this section, you will see how maps enable the visualization of location data in your applications.

To start, consider the query in Listing 12-1, which selects all the branches in San Francisco.

Listing 12-1. *Branches in San Francisco*

```
SQL> SELECT street_number num,
            street_name,
            city,
            postal_code
       FROM branches
      WHERE city = 'SAN FRANCISCO';

NUM   STREET_NAME               CITY          POSTAL_CODE
----- ------------------------- ------------- -----------
420   POST ST                   SAN FRANCISCO 94102
944   STOCKTON ST               SAN FRANCISCO 94108
1007  TARAVAL ST                SAN FRANCISCO 94116
1995  UNION ST                  SAN FRANCISCO 94123
1640  VAN NESS AVE              SAN FRANCISCO 94109
245   WINSTON DR                SAN FRANCISCO 94132
5268  DIAMOND HEIGHTS BLVD      SAN FRANCISCO 94131
1455  STOCKTON ST               SAN FRANCISCO 94133
2090  JERROLD AVE               SAN FRANCISCO 94124
1     POWELL ST                 SAN FRANCISCO 94102
2485  SAN BRUNO AVE             SAN FRANCISCO 94134
288   W PORTAL AVE              SAN FRANCISCO 94127
315   MONTGOMERY ST             SAN FRANCISCO 94104
680   8TH ST                    SAN FRANCISCO 94103
915   FRONT ST                  SAN FRANCISCO 94111
150   4TH ST                    SAN FRANCISCO 94103
4098  24TH ST                   SAN FRANCISCO 94114
1515  SLOAT BLVD                SAN FRANCISCO 94132
445   POWELL ST                 SAN FRANCISCO 94102
50    CALIFORNIA ST             SAN FRANCISCO 94111
45    SPEAR ST                  SAN FRANCISCO 94105
1200  MONTGOMERY ST             SAN FRANCISCO 94133
5000  3RD ST                    SAN FRANCISCO 94124
2850  24TH ST                   SAN FRANCISCO 94110
3701  BALBOA ST                 SAN FRANCISCO 94121
500   BATTERY ST                SAN FRANCISCO 94111
501   BRANNAN ST                SAN FRANCISCO 94107
1525  MARKET ST                 SAN FRANCISCO 94102
3565  CALIFORNIA ST             SAN FRANCISCO 94118
501   CASTRO ST                 SAN FRANCISCO 94114
2200  CHESTNUT ST               SAN FRANCISCO 94123
600   CLEMENT ST                SAN FRANCISCO 94118
433   CORTLAND AVE              SAN FRANCISCO 94110
1275  FELL ST                   SAN FRANCISCO 94117
2310  FILLMORE ST               SAN FRANCISCO 94115
2835  GEARY BLVD                SAN FRANCISCO 94118
5500  GEARY BLVD                SAN FRANCISCO 94121
701   GRANT AVE                 SAN FRANCISCO 94108
800   IRVING ST                 SAN FRANCISCO 94122
1945  IRVING ST                 SAN FRANCISCO 94122
6     LELAND AVE                SAN FRANCISCO 94134
2701  MISSION ST                SAN FRANCISCO 94110
3250  MISSION ST                SAN FRANCISCO 94110
5150  MISSION ST                SAN FRANCISCO 94112
345   MONTGOMERY ST             SAN FRANCISCO 94104
33    NEW MONTGOMERY ST         SAN FRANCISCO 94105
```

```
2325  NORIEGA ST                    SAN FRANCISCO  94122
15    OCEAN AVE                     SAN FRANCISCO  94112

48 rows selected.
```

Compare this textual response to Figure 12-1, which positions those branches on a map of San Francisco, and Figure 12-2, which compares those branch positions with positions of competitors. Notice how the map clearly points out the placement of the branches and those of the competitors.

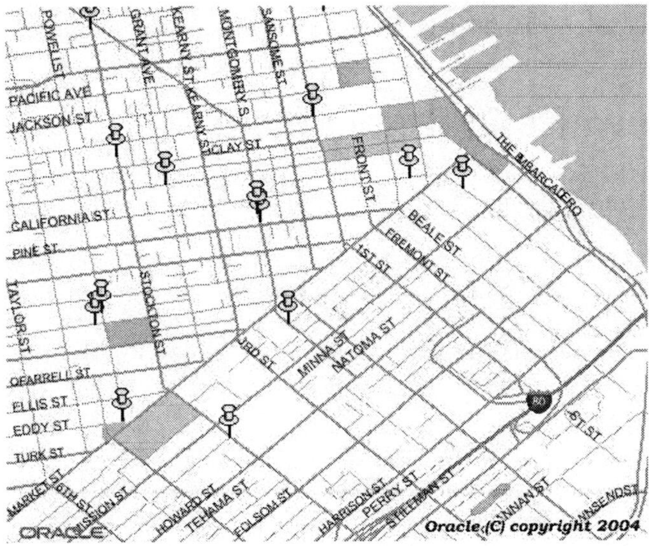

Figure 12-1. *A map showing the position of the branches*

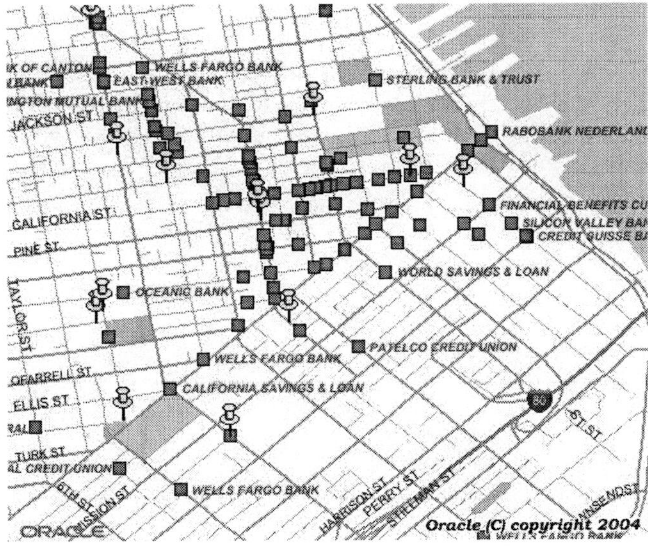

Figure 12-2. *A map showing the position of the branches and those of the competitors*

As you can see from these images, maps are meaningful geometric representations of the world rendered in a human-readable size and format. Maps are so fundamental to the way in which we perceive the world that they predate everything but the cave paintings humans created in an attempt to understand the world and to find ways to communicate that understanding. Whether scratched in the sand with a stick, printed on papyrus or paper, or displayed on a screen, a map can convey an understanding of the shape of the environment and the relationships among things within it in a manner more efficient and understandable than any number of spoken or written words.

Computer-generated maps are much like paper maps, except they are dynamically generated from information stored in databases. They give you a certain level of control and interaction; you can choose to see more or less information, to see different regions, to zoom in and out, and so on.

Overview of MapViewer and Oracle Maps

In this chapter, you'll learn to use two Oracle features—MapViewer and Maps—to add mapping functionality to your applications. Before getting into how to use the features, we'll give you some background on each.

Oracle MapViewer

MapViewer is a pure Java server-side component included with Oracle Application Server. The main components, illustrated in Figure 12-3, are as follows:

- *A map-rendering engine running in Oracle Application Server*: The rendering engine is exposed as a servlet that processes *requests* sent by client applications, fetches the proper information from spatial tables, and constructs maps in a variety of graphical formats (GIF, PNG, JPEG, or SVG), which it then returns to the requesting client. In addition to the core mapping servlet, the MapViewer server also provides a map cache server and a feature of interest (FOI) server.
- *Map definitions*: The map definitions are stored in the database. This is where you describe your maps: which tables to use, how the maps should be rendered (colors, line thickness, and fonts), and so on.
- *A series of application programming interfaces (APIs)*: Those APIs allow you to access MapViewer features from a variety of application development environments. These APIs include XML, Java, PL/SQL, and JavaScript (Ajax) interfaces. The Java API also includes JavaServer Pages (JSP) tags to ease the inclusion of maps in JSPs.
- *A graphical Map Builder tool*: This is a stand-alone program that helps you manage the map definitions stored in the database.

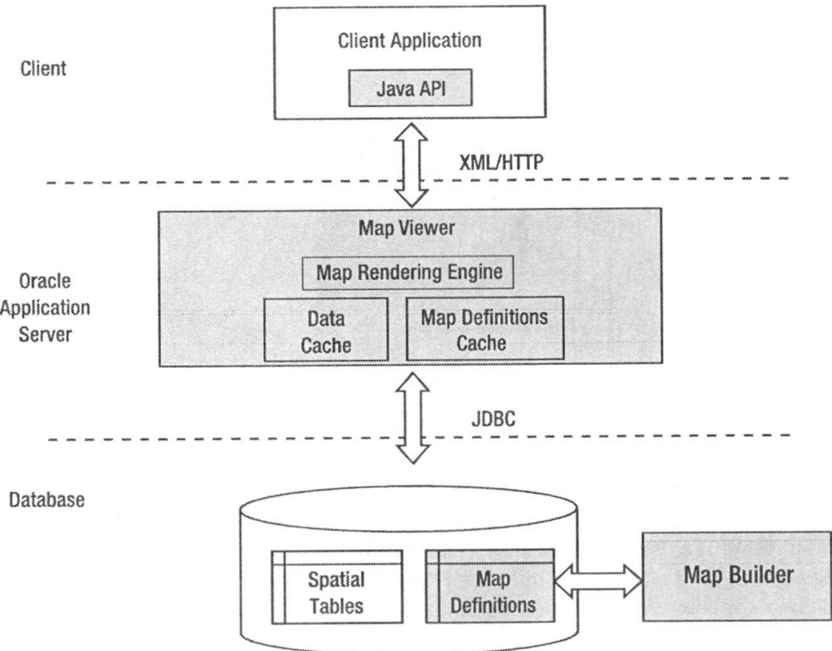

Figure 12-3. *Oracle MapViewer core architecture*

The client applications talk to the MapViewer servlet over HTTP in a request/response model, as illustrated in Figure 12-4. Requests and responses are encoded in XML. Java clients can use the Java API, which takes care of constructing and sending the XML requests, as well as reading and parsing the XML responses.

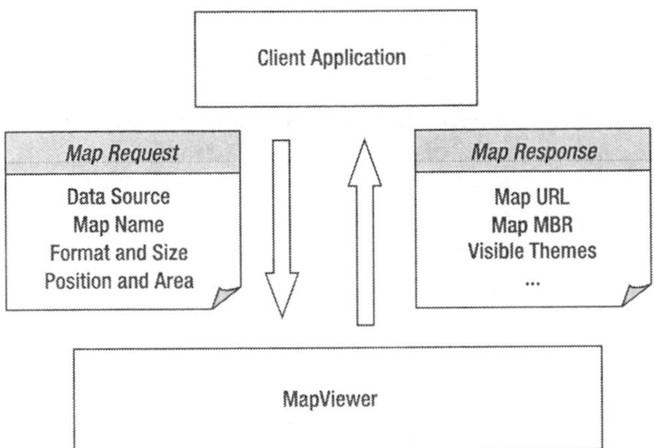

Figure 12-4. *MapViewer request/response flow*

An alternative to the flow in Figure 12-4 is for MapViewer to stream the map image directly to the client application instead of returning a URL to the generated map, as illustrated in Figure 12-5.

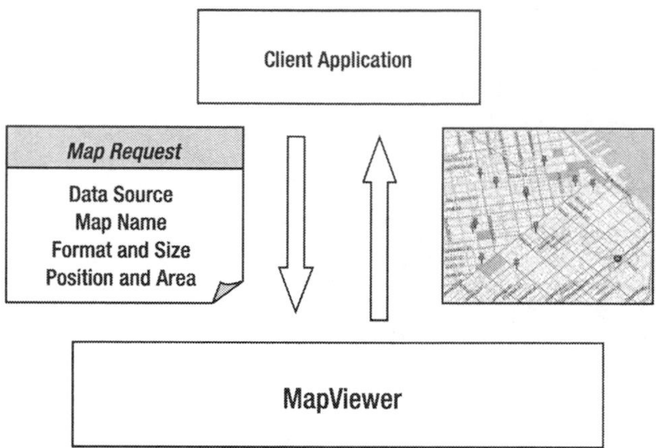

Figure 12-5. *MapViewer request/response flow with image streaming*

Since MapViewer is a pure Java tool, it can run on any platform where Java is available. However, that does not mean it can be used only from Java applications. Its lowest-level API (XML over HTTP) allows any application to use its services.

Oracle Maps

Oracle Maps is the name of a suite of technologies provided by MapViewer that allows you to build highly dynamic and highly performant mapping applications. The MapViewer architecture with Oracle Maps is illustrated in Figure 12-6 and uses the following main components:

- *A map cache server*: This server automatically caches tiles of the maps generated by the map-rendering engine to satisfy application requests and serves those tiles to any application that requests the same maps. The goal of the map cache server is to process the static background maps (vector or raster). Because map tiles are pregenerated and cached, application users experience fast map-viewing performance. Note that the map cache is persistent (map tiles are stored using files) and is shared by all users.
- *A feature of interest (FOI) server*: The FOI server reads and renders dynamic features from spatial tables. Those represent the dynamic entities managed by your application: customers, pipes, trucks, and so on.
- *An Ajax-based JavaScript mapping client API*: The JavaScript library provides all functions needed by applications to browse and interact with maps in a highly dynamic way: smooth dragging and zooming, info tips, information windows, queries, and selections.

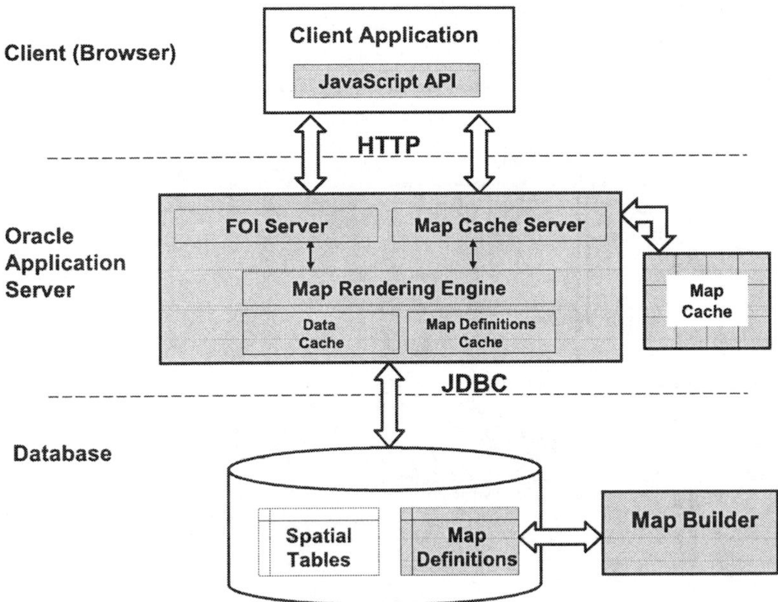

Figure 12-6. *Oracle Maps architecture*

MapViewer is not an end-user tool; rather, it is a component developers use to add maps to their applications. With that in mind, we'll now show how to use MapViewer to create maps such as these and then how to use them in an application. The first step is to install and configure MapViewer for use.

Getting Started

MapViewer is provided as a standard J2EE archive (EAR) format. See the introduction for details on how to install and configure OC4J and how to deploy applications using the OC4J console. The EAR file for MapViewer is available for download from the Oracle Technology Network website at `http://otn.oracle.com/software/products/mapviewer`. The result is a file called `mapviewer.ear` (approximately 9MB in size).

As discussed, MapViewer is a pure Java component, as is OC4J, so you can install MapViewer and OC4J on any platform that has a suitable Java environment. MapViewer needs a Java 2 Platform Standard Edition Software Development Kit from Sun Microsystems (J2SE SDK) 1.5 or newer. Your Oracle Database 11*g* installation includes such a JDK in `$ORACLE_HOME/jdk`.

Tip MapViewer needs a graphical environment in order to generate maps. The "headless" mechanism in J2SE SDK enables MapViewer to run on Linux or Unix systems without setting any X11 DISPLAY variable. To enable AWT headless mode on Linux or Unix systems, specify the following on the command line to start the OC4J server: `-Djava.awt.headless=true`.

You can confirm that MapViewer was successfully installed by going to `http://oc4j_server:8888/mapviewer` in your web browser (for example, `http://127.0.0.1:8888/mapviewer` if you installed OC4J on your own desktop system). You should see the home page of MapViewer, as shown in Figure 12-7.

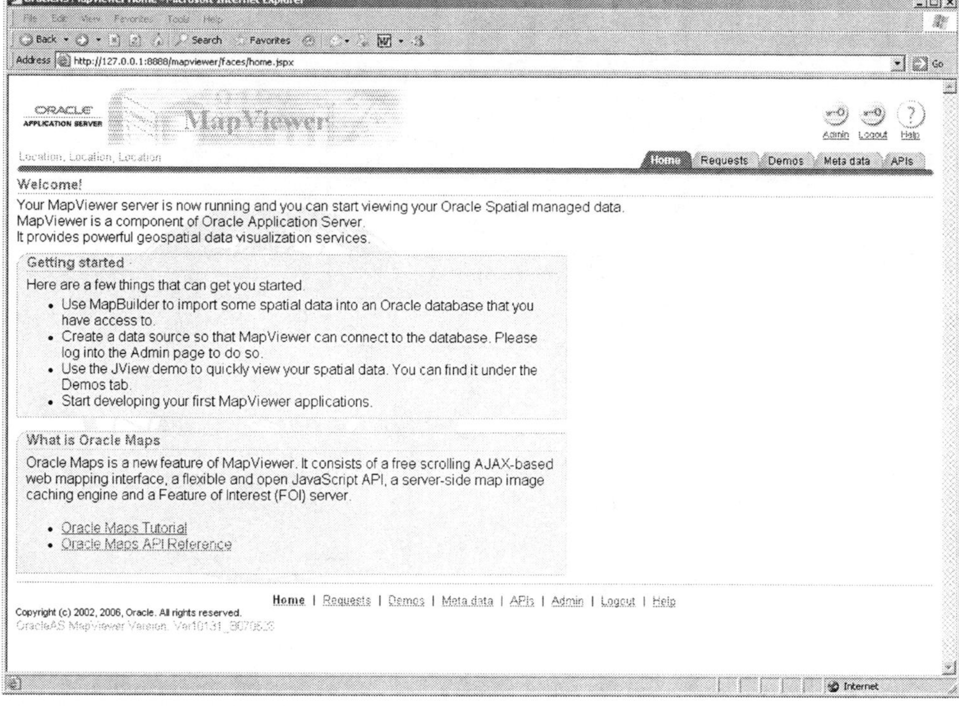

Figure 12-7. *MapViewer home page*

At this point, MapViewer is ready for use. The default settings are adequate for you to start using it, although a little later in the chapter we will cover some of the configuration settings. We have yet to discuss how to define new maps, but you are already in a position to display a first predefined map. To do this, perform these steps:

1. Load the sample data into your database, together with predefined map definitions.
2. Define a MapViewer data source.
3. Install the example applications so they can be retrieved using your OC4J server.

Load the Sample Data

To work through all the examples shown in this chapter, you need to populate your database with the sample data provided on the Apress website (`www.apress.com`). So far, we have been using only the application data (`customers`, `branches`, and `competitors` tables) without any references to other spatial data. If you want to see application data on maps, you also need the geographical data that will appear on the maps: streets, administrative boundaries, natural features, and so on.

Location-Enable the Application Data

If you have performed the steps detailed in Chapter 6 and you have run the examples in the following chapters, you should now have your `customers`, `branches`, and `competitors` tables spatially enabled and ready for use.

In case you did not complete those steps, you can now load them in the "spatially enabled" format by importing the file `app_data_with_loc.dmp` as follows:

```
imp spatial/spatial file=app_data_with_loc.dmp full=y
```

Load the Geographical Data

For clarity and ease of use, we provide the data as several Oracle dump files (you can find details on the tables and their structure in Appendix E):

- Large-scale data (countries, states, counties, and so on) are provided in the file `map_large.dmp`.
- Detailed data (city streets, and so on) are provided in the file `map_detailed.dmp`.

Load the data using the Oracle Import tool as illustrated in the following code. Note that this will create the tables, load the tables with data, load the spatial metadata, and create the spatial indexes. Once the import is complete, the tables are ready for use.

```
imp spatial/spatial file=map_large.dmp full=y
imp spatial/spatial file=map_detailed.dmp full=y
```

Load Maps, Themes, Style, and Map Cache Definitions for MapViewer

Maps, themes, and style definitions, as well as map caches, are provided ready for use. To use them, you simply need to perform these steps:

1. Import them into the database. This creates and populates three tables: `my_maps`, `my_themes`, `my_styles`, and `my_cached_maps`.
2. Load the definitions into the dictionary tables used by MapViewer.

Listing 12-2 illustrates the full process.

Listing 12-2. *Loading Maps, Themes, Style, and Cache Definitions*

```
imp spatial/spatial file=styles.dmp full=y

SQL> INSERT into user_sdo_styles
       select * from my_styles;
SQL> insert into user_sdo_themes
       select * from my_themes;
SQL> insert into user_sdo_maps
       select * from my_maps;
SQL> insert into user_sdo_cached_maps
       select * from my_cached_maps;
SQL> commit;
```

Define a Data Source

The next step is to define a permanent data source in MapViewer's configuration file. This is not strictly necessary, since you could also add a data source via MapViewer's administration page, but having a permanent data source makes it easier for you when you stop and start OC4J and MapViewer.

To add the data source, you edit the configuration file, as explained in the previous section. The file is located at `$OC4J_HOME/j2ee/home//applications/mapviewer/web/WEB-INF/conf/MapViewerConfig.xml`. Add the following definition in the main `<MapperConfig>` element:

```
<map_data_source name="spatial"
                 jdbc_host="127.0.0.1"
                 jdbc_port="1521"
                 jdbc_sid="orcl111"
                 jdbc_user="spatial"
                 jdbc_password="!spatial"
                 jdbc_mode="thin"
                 max_connections="5"
                 number_of_mappers="3"
/>
```

Replace the JDBC connection details (`host`, `port`, `sid`, `user`, and `password`) with your own information. The user name should be the one into which you loaded the example data.

If your OC4J server is not up and running, then start it now by going to `$OC4J_HOME/j2ee/home` and entering the command `java -jar oc4j.jar`.

Caution When you edit the XML configuration file, make sure to insert the new definitions in the proper places. In particular, make sure you do not put them in existing comments. We recommend you use a text editor that is able to recognize and color-code XML syntax elements or an XML-aware editor such as XMLSpy. We also recommend you make backup copies of any configuration file you modify, just in case.

Install Example Applications

The MapViewer examples provided with this book are available in a file called `web-examples.zip`. Expand it into `$OC4J_HOME/j2ee/home/applications/mapviewer/web/spatial-book`.

Note In all the examples, it is assumed that you installed OC4J on your desktop machine, so you will access it using the `localhost` address (`127.0.0.1`).

In your browser, go to the home page for the book examples at `http://127.0.0.1:8888/mapviewer/spatial-book`. You should see the page shown in Figure 12-8.

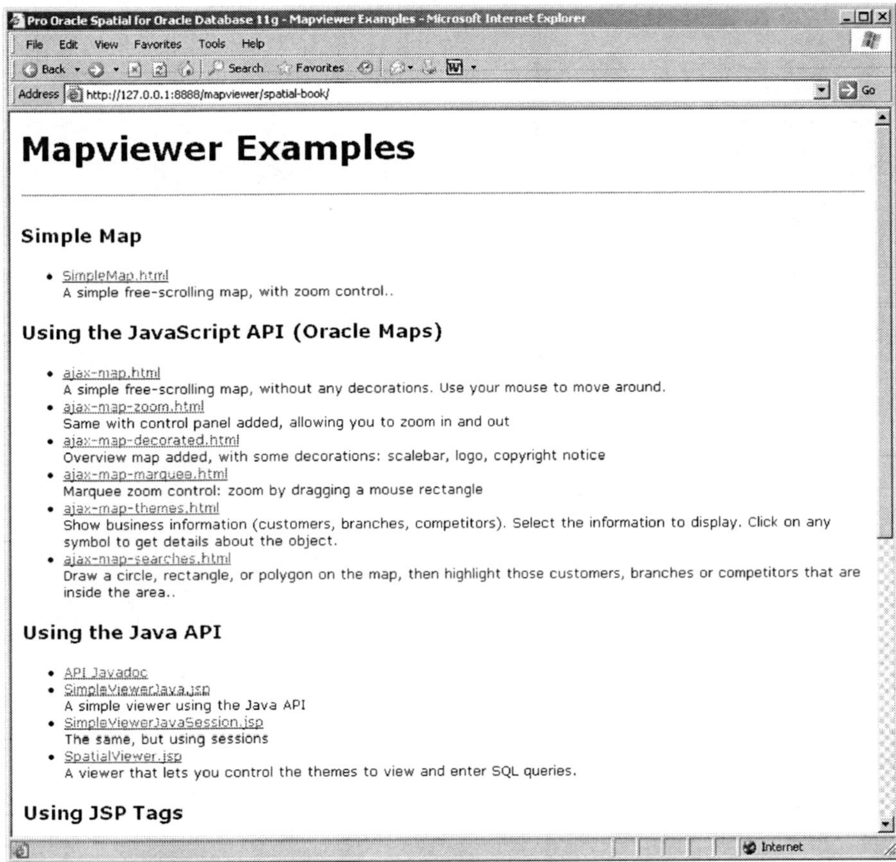

Figure 12-8. *Home page for the MapViewer examples*

The links on the page in Figure 12-8 take you to various examples that illustrate how to use MapViewer's API. You may want to take some time to explore those examples as you read this chapter. If you click the first link (`SimpleMap.html`), you should see the page shown in Figure 12-9. Use your mouse and the Control Panel to explore the map.

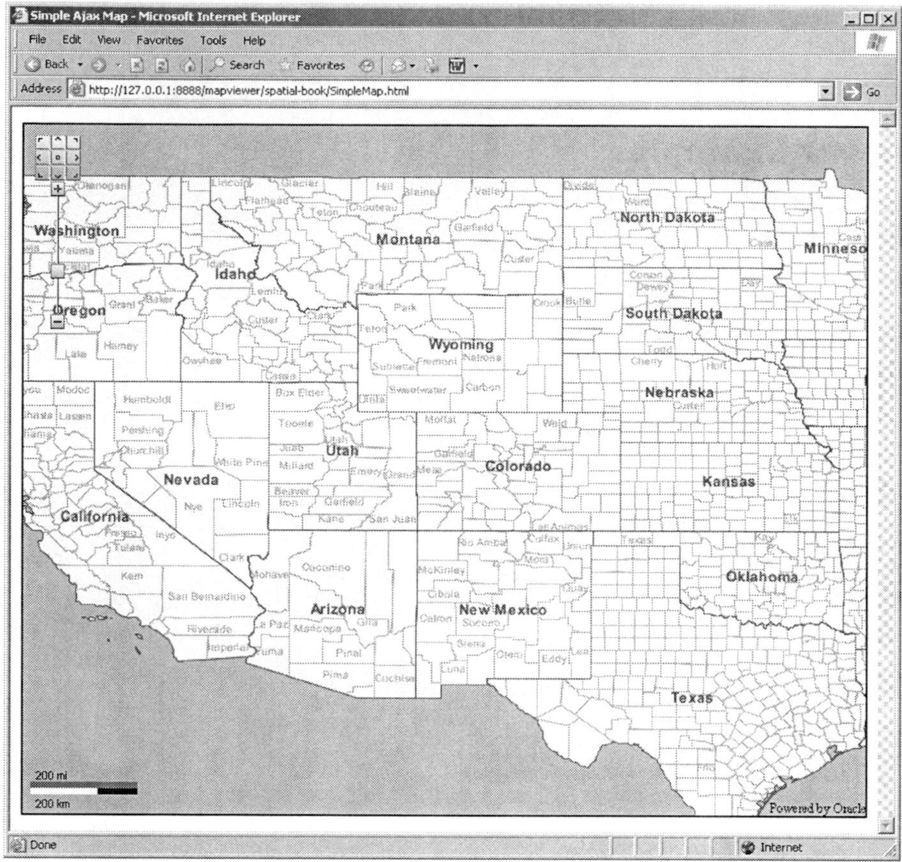

Figure 12-9. *Your first map*

In the rest of this chapter, you will learn how this map was defined and how to define your own maps. Then you will learn how to embed maps in your applications and allow users to interact with the maps. Before we move on to that, however, it is worth taking a quick look at some of the MapViewer configuration options.

Configuring MapViewer

Although the MapViewer default settings are adequate for you to start using MapViewer, at some point you will probably want to change some configuration parameters. Those parameters are coded in XML. You can find the configuration file at `$OC4J_HOME/lbsj2ee/home/mapviewer/web/WEB-INF/conf/mapViewerConfig.xml`. You can change parameters by editing this file, preferably using an XML-aware editor, but Notepad or vi will do as well. You can also modify the file using MapViewer's own administration console. The file contains many comments, which makes it easier for you to apply changes.

Note that MapViewer will apply the changes only when you restart it, either by stopping and starting the entire OC4J component or by restarting only the MapViewer application via the administrative API or the administration console of the application server.

Using the Administration Console

To invoke the administration console, start from MapViewer's home page, shown in Figure 12-7. Click the Admin link at the top right of the page. You will then be asked to provide the name and password of the administrative account for your application server installation. For a stand-alone OC4J installation, the username is `oc4jadmin`, and the password is the one you specified when you installed OC4J. Figure 12-10 shows the main page of the administration console.

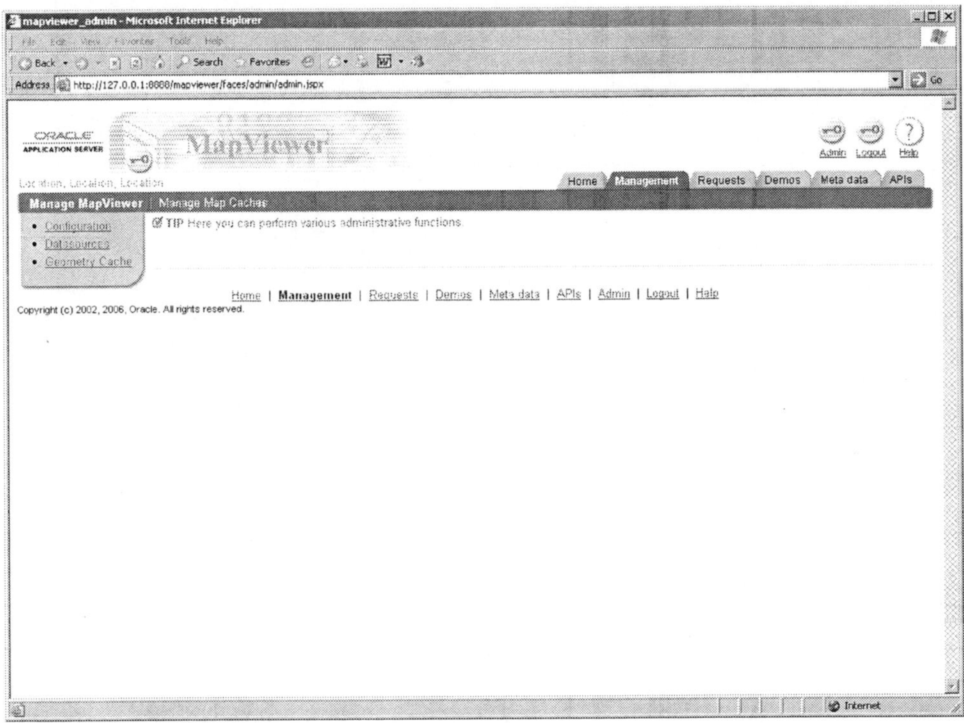

Figure 12-10. *MapViewer administration console*

Editing the Configuration File

Clicking the first link on the left (Configuration) opens a form, shown in Figure 12-11, where you can edit the content of the configuration file. Once you are done, click the Save button at the bottom of the page. If you want your changes to take effect immediately, click the Save and Restart button, which will instruct MapViewer to reload the configuration file.

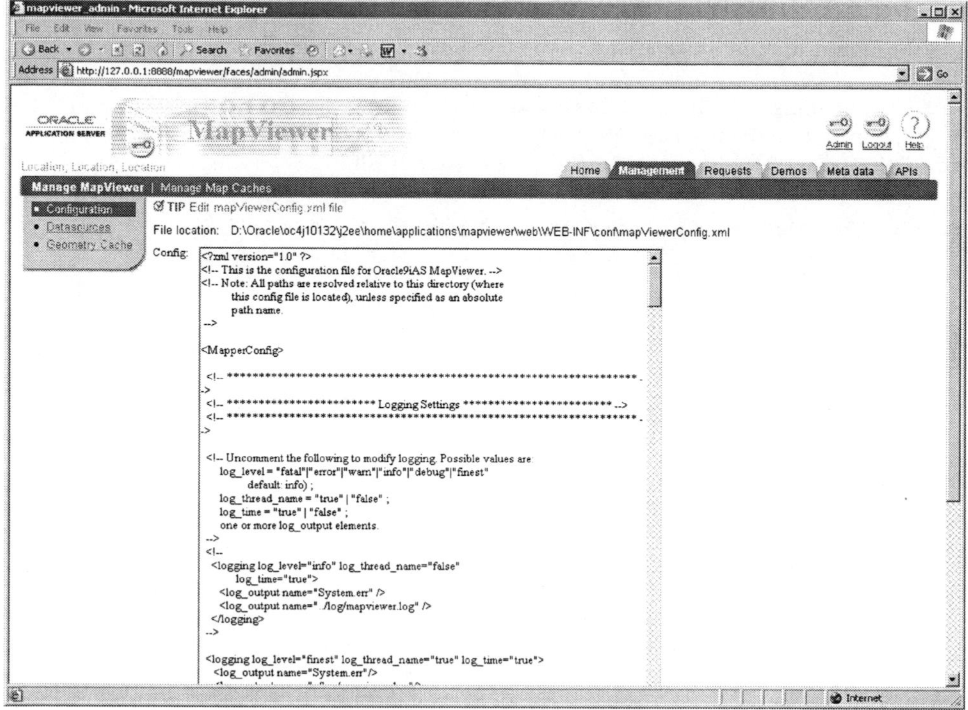

Figure 12-11. *Editing the configuration file*

Maintaining Data Sources

Clicking the second link on the left (Datasources) opens a form like the one shown in Figure 12-12. This form allows you to define a new data source. Note that this data source is dynamic; that is, it will disappear the next time you stop or restart MapViewer. To define a permanent data source, you must include it in the configuration file, as explained later in this chapter.

The form also allows you to delete a data source: this removes only the definition from MapViewer's memory (it has no effect on the definitions in the configuration file). You can also purge all map, theme, and style definitions for that data source (using the Purge Cached Metadata button). Use this to force MapViewer to use the changes you made to map definitions in the database (using Map Builder).

■ Note The Edit button has no effect. To modify a permanent data source, edit the configuration file. For a dynamic data source, delete it, and then redefine it.

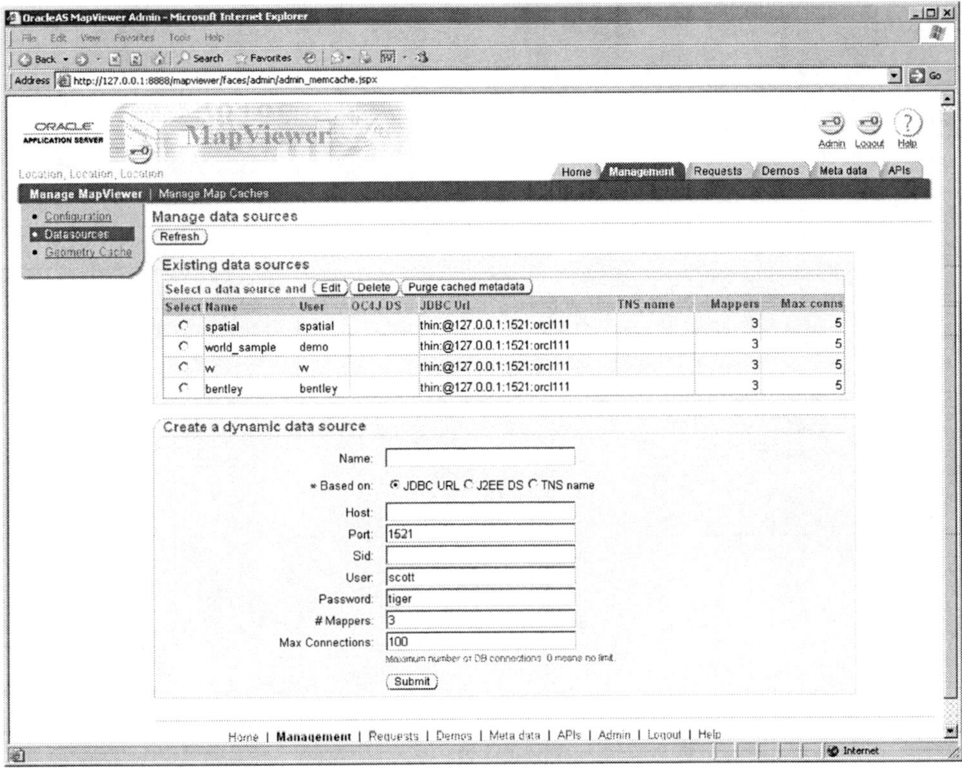

Figure 12-12. *Maintaining data sources*

Maintaining Geometry Caches

Clicking the third link on the left (Geometry Caches) opens a form like the one shown in Figure 12-13. Use it to clear geometries retained in memory for a data source. You have the option to clear the geometries cached for all themes or just for one specific theme.

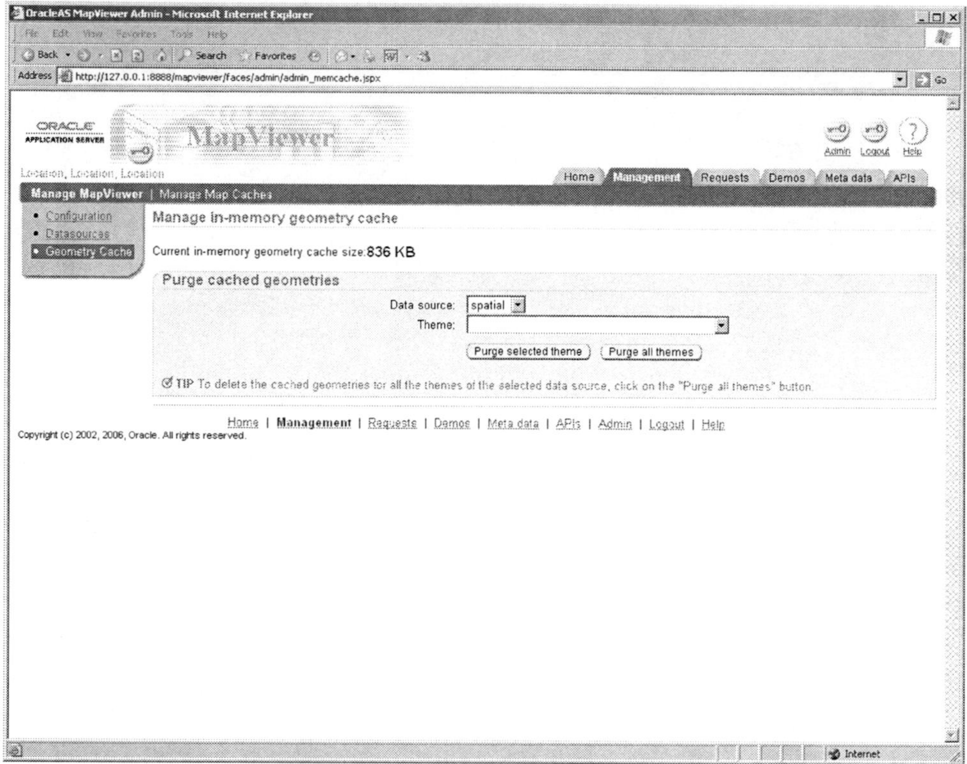

Figure 12-13. *Maintaining geometry caches*

The form shows the current size of the geometry cache. Set the maximum size of the cache by editing the configuration file.

Configuration Parameters

The configuration parameters are specified as a set of XML elements, with each element covering one aspect of MapViewer's operation.

Logging

MapViewer can generate a log of its operation. The `<logging>` element enables you to control how detailed this logging should be and where it should go. The following is an example setting:

```
<logging log_level="info" log_thread_name="true" log_time="true">
  <log_output name="System.err"/>
  <log_output name="../log/mapviewer.log"/>
</logging>
```

The element contains the following attributes:

- `log_level`: This attribute defines the level of detail to log. It can range from less detailed (`fatal`) to very detailed (`finest`). The default (`info`) is a good compromise. The `debug` and `finest` settings are useful only to help in diagnosing problems or to better understand the operation of MapViewer. The `finest` level involves each request getting logged, together with each and every database SQL query. Do not use it in production.
- `log_thread_name`: When this attribute is set to `true`, the name of each MapViewer thread is logged with each message.
- `log_time`: When this attribute is set to `true`, a time stamp is logged with each message.

The `<logging>` element contains one or more `<log_output>` elements. Each `<log_output>` element defines one log destination. The destination `System.err` corresponds to the console of the OC4J container.

Note All file specifications are relative to the location of the configuration file. For example, `../log/mapviewer.log` is equivalent to `$OC4J_HOME/j2ee/home/mapviewer/web/WEB-INF/log/mapviewer.log`. This makes your configuration files portable between different installations. Notice that you can write the file specifications in the configuration file using forward slashes (/), even if you use a Windows platform.

Caution MapViewer starts a new log file each time the application server (or OC4J container) starts. Files are named by appending a number at the end (for example, `mapviewer_35.log`). The log files are not automatically removed.

Map Image Lifetime

The map images generated by MapViewer are stored in the file system on the application server. The `<save_images_at>` element enables you to control the lifetime of those files. The following is a typical setting:

```
<save_images_at file_prefix="omsmap"
                url="/mapviewer/images/"
                path="../../../web/images"
                life= "5"
                recycle_interval="10" />
```

The element uses XML attributes to define the following parameters:

- `file_prefix` is the prefix of the generated map files. Maps are numbered sequentially, and this number is appended to the prefix you choose. The default is `omsmap`, and we see no reason to change this.
- `url` is used to produce the URL that points to the generated maps, which is relative to the URL used to reach the MapViewer servlet. The default is `/mapviewer/images`, which corresponds to `$OC4J_HOME/j2ee/home/applications/mapviewer/web/images`. Again, we see no reason to change this.
- `path` is the folder in which images are stored. By default, the images go to `../../../web/images`, which is the same as `$OC4J_HOME/j2ee/home/applicationslbs/mapviewer/web/images`. There is no reason to change this.

- `life` specifies how long (in minutes) a generated map should remain on the server. By default, it is set to 0, which means that images are *never* deleted. This is probably not a good idea, since images will accumulate quickly.
- `recycle_interval` specifies how the interval (in minutes) between successive executions of the recycling thread, whose purpose is to remove old maps. By default, this happens every eight hours. In production systems, this process will probably need to happen more often.

Geometry Caching

When MapViewer reads data from spatial tables, it automatically retains a copy of the geometries in a JDBC object cache, thereby avoiding the need to read them again for subsequent map requests on the same geographical area. The cache is memory resident.

The `<spatial_data_cache>` element enables you to control the size of the cache. The following is an example setting:

```
<spatial_data_cache
  max_cache_size="32"
report_stats="false"
/>
```

where the following is true:

- `max_cache_size` is a parameter that specifies the size (in megabytes) of the memory cache. The default is 64MB.
- `report_stats` provides cache statistics. When this parameter is set to `true`, MapViewer will periodically (approximately every five minutes) report the current cache size and the number of cached objects as a log message.

Note Previous versions of MapViewer also included a disk-based cache for geometries. This is no longer the case. The old parameters `max_disk_cache_size` and `disk_cache_path` that used to control the size and location of the disk cache are now ignored.

Permanent Data Sources

MapViewer accesses databases via JDBC. A data source defines the parameters for a JDBC connection: host name, port, database name, user name, and password. Each data source has a unique name.

Data sources can be defined dynamically, using the administrative API, or they can be defined statically in the configuration file. A data source is defined in a `<map_data_source>` element. Here is an example that defines a data source over a database that runs on the same system as MapViewer:

```
<map_data_source name="spatial"
  jdbc_host="127.0.0.1"
  jdbc_port="1521"
  jdbc_sid="orcl1101"
  jdbc_user="spatial"
  jdbc_password="!spatial"
  jdbc_mode="thin"
  max_connections="10"
  number_of_mappers="3"
/>
```

where the following is true:

- name is the name of the data source. It must be unique.
- jdbc_host is the name or IP address of the system hosting the Oracle database.
- jdbc_port is the port on which the database is listening. By default, databases listen on port 1521.
- jdbc_sid is the name of the database.
- jdbc_user is the user name to connect to the database.
- jdbc_password is the password of the user connecting to the database. The password must be written with a leading ! symbol. MapViewer will automatically encrypt this password and replace it in the configuration file with the encrypted result.
- number_of_mappers defines the maximum number of concurrent map requests that this data source can handle.
- max_connections limits the number of connections used for the data source. MapViewer will use as many concurrent connections as needed for a request, and then it will close them up to the maximum number specified.

You can also tell MapViewer to use one of the data sources defined for OC4J. Those data sources are defined in the configuration file $OC4J_HOME/j2ee/home/config/data-sources.xml. For example, here is an OC4J data source definition:

```
<managed-data-source name="spatial"
  connection-pool-name="spatial-demos"
  jndi-name="jdbc/spatial"/>

<connection-pool name="spatial-demos">
  <connection-factory factory-class="oracle.jdbc.pool.OracleDataSource"
    user="spatial"
    password="spatial"
    url="jdbc:oracle:thin:@//localhost:1521/ORCL111">
  </connection-factory>
</connection-pool><data-source
```

You can use that data source for MapViewer by defining it as follows in the MapViewer configuration file:

```
<map_data_source name="spatial"
                 container_ds="jdbc/spatial"
                 max_connections="5"
                 number_of_mappers="3"
/>
```

Global Map Options

The <global_map_config> element enables you to define some settings that control the general look and feel of the produced maps. In particular, you can use it to set a copyright notice and logo on all the maps produced by your server. Here is a typical setting:

```
<global_map_config>
    <title text="MapViewer Demo" font="Courier" position="NORTH"/>
  <note text="Oracle (C) copyright 2004"
     font="Bookman Old Style Bold Italic"
     position="SOUTH_EAST"/>
  <logo image_path="../../../web/myicons/orcl_logo_test.gif"
     position="SOUTH_WEST"/>
```

```
  <rendering
     allow_local_adjustment="false"
     use_globular_projection="false" />
</global_map_config>
```

where the following is true:

- title defines the position of map titles on the generated maps. You can also specify a default title that will appear when a map is requested without any explicit title.
- note defines a text string that will appear on all maps—typically a copyright notice. The text and font parameters are self-explanatory. The position parameter lets you specify where the text should appear on the map using a keyword such as NORTH, SOUTH, EAST, WEST, NORTH_WEST, SOUTH_EAST, and so on. In the preceding example, the copyright notice appears at the lower right of the image.
- logo is a GIF logo that will appear on all maps. The position of the logo is specified the same way it is for the note. The image_path parameter specifies the file specification of the logo. Like all other file specifications, it is relative to the location of the configuration file.
- rendering represents advanced settings for controlling the appearance of maps on geodetic data.

Security

Several of the requests that applications can send to MapViewer are potentially dangerous. This is true for the administrative requests that allow applications to discover and define data sources (database connections). Those, however, can be sent only from properly authenticated clients. You can, however, also restrict the clients that are allowed to issue administration requests by using the <ip_monitor> element and specifying the lists of IP addresses or a range of addresses to allow or disallow.

Another potential security risk is the ability for applications to issue just any SQL SELECT statement against a data source. Those are typically issued by applications that need to find out details about spatial objects returned on a map. You can disable those requests by adding the following in your configuration:

```
<security_config>
  <disable_direct_info_request> true </disable_direct_info_request>
</security_config>
```

Be aware, however, that this will prevent applications from using any of the identification techniques (identify(), queryWithinRadius(), doQuery(), and so on) used in Java applications. Those techniques are discussed in Chapter 13.

One more security concern is the ability to send dynamic SELECT statements to the database straight from the browser. This capability is known as JDBC theme-based FOIs, and it allows JavaScript applications to build powerful dynamic queries to be performed by MapViewer's FOI server. However, this is also a security concern. By default, such queries are *not* allowed. To allow them against a specific data source, add the parameter allow_jdbc_theme_based_foi="true" to the definition of that data source. JDBC theme-based FOIs will be discussed in detail with the Oracle Maps JavaScript API.

Map Cache Server

Use the <map_cache_server> element to define some generic settings for the map cache server. Here is an example:

```
<map_cache_server>
  <cache_storage default_root_path="/scratch/mapcachetest/"/>
  <logging log_level="info" log_thread_name="true" log_time="true">
     <log_output name="System.err"/>
     <log_output name="../log/mapcacheserver.log"/>
   </logging>
</map_cache_server>
```

where the following is true:

- The `<cache_storage>` element defines the default location used by MapViewer to store the caches on the file system. If the location you specify does not exist, then the caches will all be stored in `$OC4J_HOME/j2ee/home/applications/mapviewer/web/mapcache`. Note that you can specify a specific location for each cache when you define it.
- The `<logging>` element lets you control the level of logging detail produced by the map cache server. Its syntax is identical to that of the general MapViewer logging.

Defining Maps

A map is constructed from one or more *themes*, which refer to styles. A theme is based on a table. Figure 12-14 illustrates these relationships.

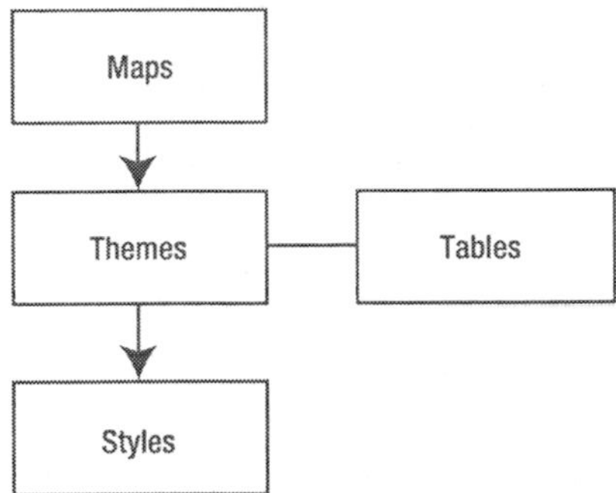

Figure 12-14. *Elements of map definitions*

Styles describe *how* the information shown on a map should look: color, symbols, and so on. Themes define *what* information should appear on a map and the style to use.

Figure 12-14 is a simplification; multiple maps can use the same theme, and multiple themes can use the same style. A theme can use many different styles. Also, multiple themes can be based on the same table. A table could also be a view or a dynamically defined SQL query.

The definitions are stored in the database in a set of three dictionary views: USER_SDO_MAPS, USER_SDO_THEMES, and USER_SDO_STYLES. Like all Oracle dictionary views, they come in three variants: USER, ALL, and DBA. Only the USER views are updatable—you define new styles (or themes or maps) by inserting them into the corresponding USER view. You can also remove styles (or themes, or maps) or update them by deleting or updating the USER views. The ALL views include all objects (styles, themes, or maps) that you are allowed to access. The DBA views include all objects in the database, but only DBAs are allowed to access them.

The relationships between the various elements are not implemented via referential integrity constraints; rather, a MAP definition contains a list of themes, and a THEME refers to a list of styles. Those lists are coded in the definition elements using an XML notation.

You can directly update the tables where map, theme, and style definitions are stored, but this requires that you understand precisely the structure of the tables, as well as the XML syntax. A better way is to use the map definition tool called Map Builder that is provided with MapViewer. Next, we'll give you a general overview of how to install and use Map Builder, and then we'll cover in greater detail how to define and modify the main mapping elements: styles, then themes, and finally base maps.

Using Map Builder

Download Map Builder from the Oracle Technology Network website at the same location from which you downloaded the MapViewer kit. Save it anywhere you like on your disk.

Map Builder is a stand-alone Java tool, provided as a single JAR file. You can run it on any platform, provided you have a Java 1.5 JDK. The JAR file is entirely self-contained: it contains not only Map Builder's own code but also the core MapViewer rendering classes, JDBC driver, and imagery and XML support libraries. To start Map Builder, just do this:

```
java -jar mapbuilder.jar
```

You will see the window in Figure 12-15 appear.

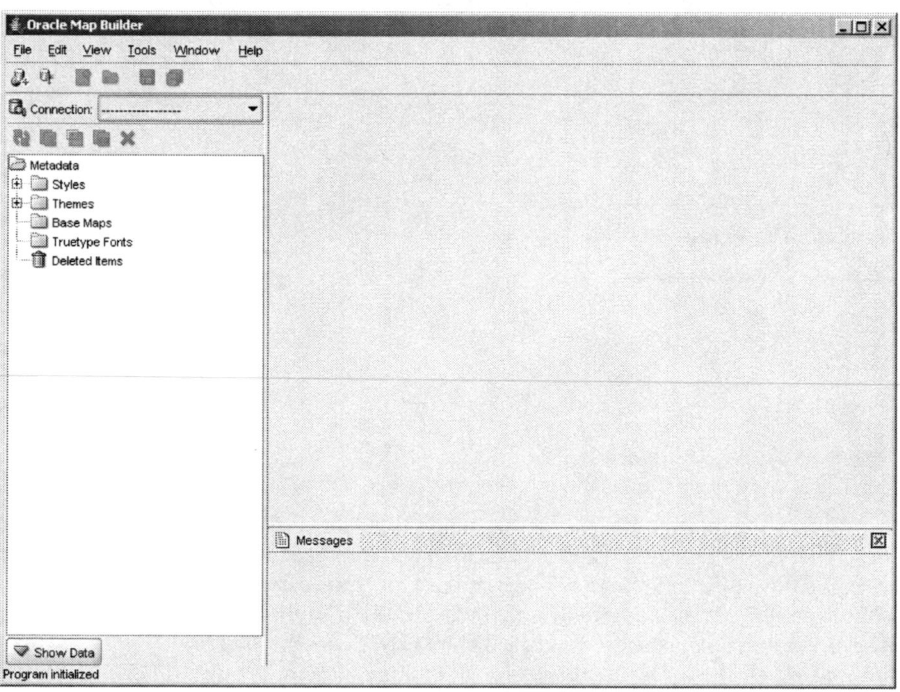

Figure 12-15. *Starting Map Builder*

To use the tool, you must first connect to the database where you will keep your styles and other definitions. Click the Add Connection icon on the top toolbar. You can also press Ctrl+N on your keyboard or select File ➤ New Connection. Another possibility is to click the drop-down list of connections and select Load/Add/Remove. All bring you to the box shown in Figure 12-16. Fill it with the usual JDBC connection information: host, port, database name (SID), user name, and password. The Test Connection button will verify that the information you entered is correct and that the database is up and running and accessible.

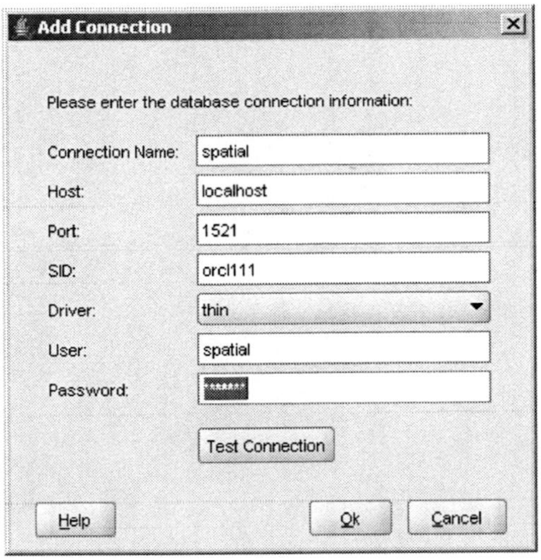

Figure 12-16. *Connecting to the database*

After clicking the Ok button, Map Builder will load all map definitions defined for the user you connected as. You can define any number of connections that way, including to different databases or different accounts in the same database. The connections will appear in the Connections drop-down list. Switch from one connection to another by just selecting the proper connection from the list. Map Builder remembers the connections and will provide them when you start it again.

■ **Note** On start-up, Map Builder automatically attempts to reconnect to all connections defined in your list. It will skip any invalid connection (for example, if the database is not available). It will also automatically load all map definitions from the first valid connection it finds. If you do not want this behavior, then specify the `-noconnect` option when starting Map Builder. The drop-down list of connections will be empty, but your connections will still be available via the Load/Add/Remove option of the Connections drop-down list.

Once you are successfully connected, you will see Map Builder's main window, as shown in Figure 12-17. The explorer window on the left lets you navigate through your styles, theme, and maps and then select the definition to modify.

- To create a new element (style, theme, map), click the Create Metadata icon on the top toolbar, or right-click the kind of element you want to create. You can also press Shift+Ctrl+N on your keyboard or select File ➤ New Metadata. All open a new form in a tab on the right area of the screen for you to fill.
- To update an existing element, double-click it from the list on the left side. Then modify the settings in the form that appears.
- To delete an element, select it, and click the red cross button at the top. You can also right-click it and select the Delete option or select the Edit ➤ Delete menu.

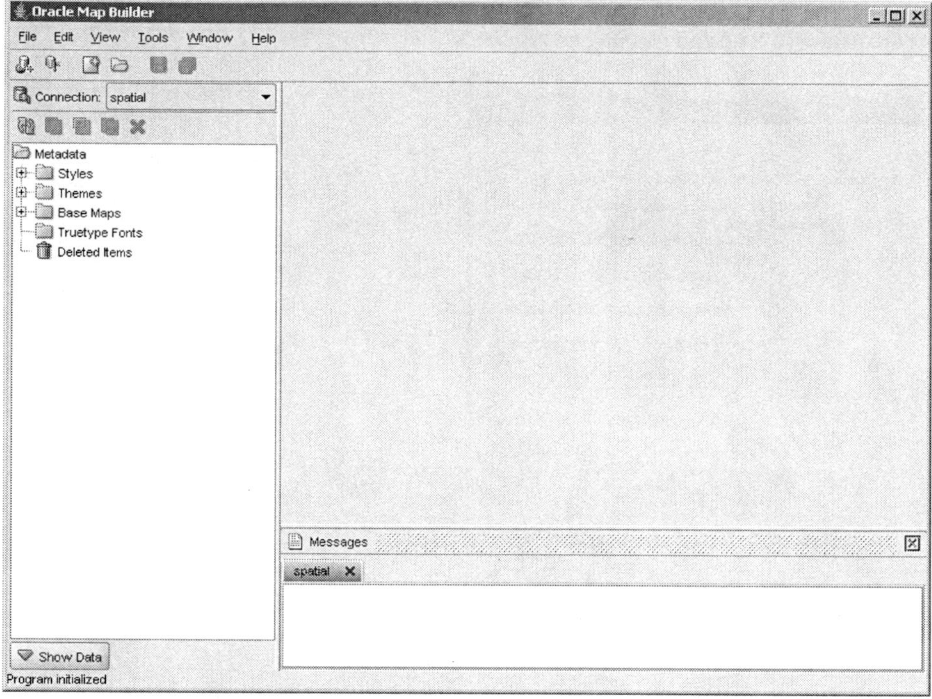

Figure 12-17. *Main Map Builder window*

When you create a new element or when you select an existing element to modify, the information on that element will appear in a tab in the right area of the screen. You can have any number of tabs open at any point in time. You can switch between those tabs, which means you can at the same time create a new style and modify the theme that uses that style. All elements have a preview mechanism that allows you so see how your choices will look in your applications.

When you make changes to an element (or create a new one), those changes are not final. They exist only in Map Builder's memory. You can always discard changes by closing the corresponding tab. You will be asked first whether to keep or discard the changes.

To save changes you made to an element to the database, click the Save icon in the top toolbar. If you want to save all your changes, click the Save All icon (or use the corresponding options from the File menu).

Note, however, that deletions are final. You will be asked to confirm the deletion, and if you do, the element will be permanently removed from the database.

One interesting possibility is to duplicate an existing element. Use this if you want a new element (for example, a complex line style) to be slightly different from an existing style. Right-click the element to duplicate, and provide a name for the new element.

■ **Tip** Map Builder provides no mechanism to rename an element. To rename an element, just duplicate it with the right name, and then delete the old one.

Figure 12-18 shows a typical Map Builder editing session. You can see three elements being edited: a color style, a theme, and a map. Notice that all element-editing tabs contain three subtabs accessible from the bottom of the screen: the Editor subtab proper, the XML subtab that shows the definition as it will appear in the database tables, and the Preview subtab where you can judge the result of your design efforts.

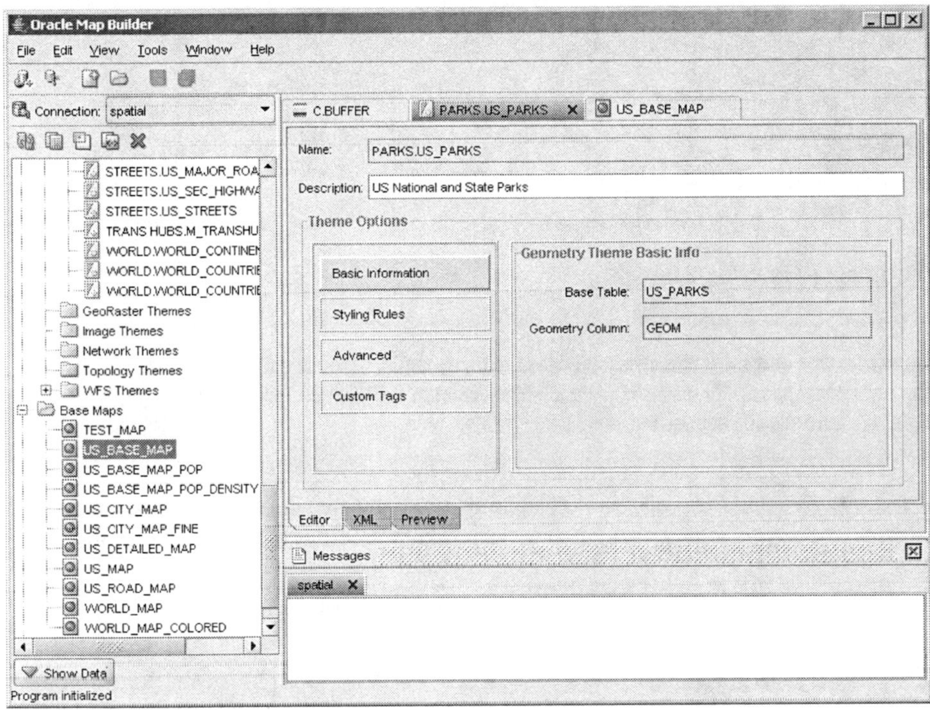

Figure 12-18. *Example of a Map Builder editing session*

Using Styles

Spatial information is stored in the database as geometric shapes: points, lines, and polygons. To draw those shapes on a map, you need to tell MapViewer how to do this (that is, what style to use). To do this, you associate each theme with a style.

A *style* is a visual attribute that represents a spatial feature. Basic map symbols and labels for representing point, line, and area features are defined and stored as individual styles. Symbology on a map can be simple and informal, or it can follow guidelines based on standard usages. Those graphical charts are typically defined by national mapping agencies, such the U.S. Federal Geographic Data Committee or the Ordnance Survey of Great Britain. Symbols should be chosen to reflect the culture, common understanding, and sensitivities of map viewers.

Proper use of styles can have a large impact on map readability and usability. For example, compare the two maps shown in Figure 12-19. Both maps show the same content; however, the left map uses no styling rules to speak of, whereas the right map uses a rich set of styles that allows you to clearly identify the features shown on the map.

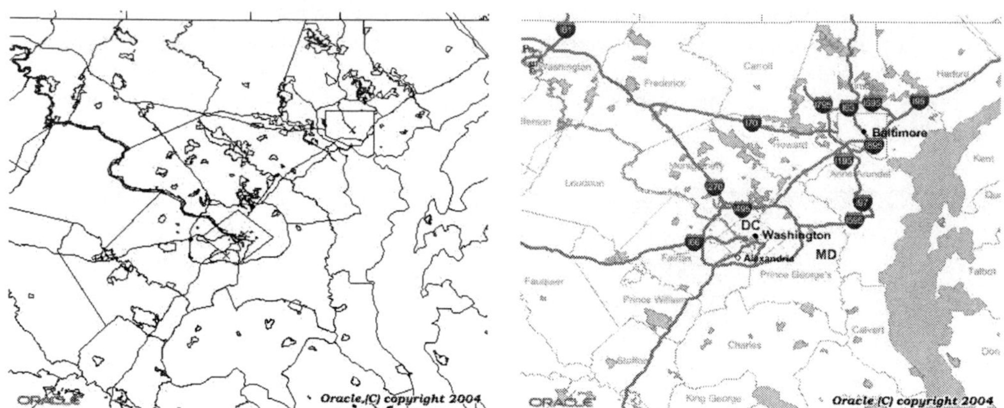

Figure 12-19. *Comparing styling rules*

■ **Note** The association of themes and styles may need to be dynamic, because different cultures are used to different map style conventions. For example, a French Michelin map, a British Ordnance Survey map, and an American Rand McNally atlas do not use the same conventions.

In the following sections, we will cover the various style types that are used for different geographic features that comprise maps, and then we will discuss how they are stored in the Oracle database.

Point Styles

Points are represented as graphic shapes: a cross, a star, a square, or a pictogram (for example, a small house or a church). These pictograms are often represented as small bitmap images, for example, with a plane representing an airport, a skier representing a ski resort, an ambulance representing a hospital, and so on.

Line Styles

Lines can be very complex to define. They are used to represent a variety of linear objects: highways, railroads, canals, rivers, electricity lines, sewers, and so on. A line typically needs many parameters: thickness, color, center and side lines, and hash marks, among others.

Area Styles

Areas are represented using a *fill* color (for example, the color of the interior of a polygon) and a *stroke* color (for example, the color of the boundary of the polygon).

Text Styles and Labeling

Objects shown on maps correspond to real-world features. Many of those features are named: cities, parks, streets, customers, stores, and so on. Labels containing those names can be used to identify the features.

Efficient labeling of map features is an art in itself. Labels must be placed so they can be clearly and unambiguously associated with the features they describe and in a manner that doesn't obscure symbols or other labels. If labels overlap, some may need to be moved or even omitted.

MapViewer automatically places labels on maps, but you still need to define the font and color to use for those labels.

Defining Styles: The USER_SDO_STYLES View

Styles are stored in the `USER_SDO_STYLES` view. This is the view you will update to define and maintain your *private* styles. The `ALL_SDO_STYLES` view lists all styles defined by all users in the database. In other words, this makes it easy for multiple users to share styles. Note that there are no privileges on styles—once you define a style in your `USER_SDO_STYLES` view, anyone can use that style in a map or application.

Each style has a unique name and defines one or more graphical elements using XML syntax. There are six types of styles:

- *Color*: Coloring for the fill (inside) and stroke (contour) of area features.
- *Marker*: A geometric shape (with a fill and stroke color) or an image for point features.
- *Line*: Used to represent linear features, defining width, color, center and edge lines, and hash marks. It also defines how lines end and how they join.
- *Area*: Fill patterns for areas.
- *Text*: Font, color, and highlighting for text labels.
- *Advanced*: A composite style used for thematic mapping.

Table 12-1 lists the columns of the `USER_SDO_STYLES` view. The `ALL` and `DBA` variants contain an additional `OWNER` column.

Table 12-1. *Structure of the* `USER_SDO_STYLES` *View*

Column Name	Data Type	Description
`NAME`	`VARCHAR2`	Name of the style
`TYPE`	`VARCHAR2`	Type of style (`COLOR`, `MARKER`, `LINE`, `AREA`, `TEXT`, or `ADVANCED`)
`DESCRIPTION`	`VARCHAR2`	Description of the style
`DEFINITION`	`CLOB`	XML definition of the style
`IMAGE`	`BLOB`	Image for marker styles

Managing Styles Using Map Builder

All screens for managing styles use a similar logic:

- To create a new style, right-click the kind of style you want to create (color, marker, and so on). You can also press Shift+Ctrl+N on your keyboard, or select File ➤ New Metadata. This opens a new form in a tab on the right area of the screen for you to fill.
- To update a style, double-click it from the list on the left side. Then modify the settings in the form that appears.
- To delete a style, select it, and click the red cross button at the top. Right-click it, and choose the Delete option.

Your styles must have unique names. However, different users can define their own styles using the same names.

Note The styles provided with MapViewer as well as those provided with the book examples have names that begin with *C.* for colors, *M.* for markers, and so on, but this is just a convention. You can name your styles in any way you like.

Color Styles

Color styles are primarily used to render area features. A color is defined by the following primitive constructs:

- A *fill* color (that is, the coloring of the inside of the feature)
- A *stroke* color (that is, the coloring and thickness of the contour of the feature)

Both settings are optional. If no fill is set, then the interior of the area features will be empty. If no stroke is set, then adjacent areas will merge without any visible separation.

In addition, you can set the *opacity* of the fill and stroke. This lets you control how much of the underlying features shows through this area. When the opacity is set to 100 percent (the default), the area is totally opaque. If you set the opacity to 0, the area is totally transparent.

You have several techniques for choosing colors: a picker, a hue-saturation-brightness model, and a red-green-blue model. You can also enter colors manually using the hexadecimal encoding.

Notice the small preview window: this allows you to see how your style will really look like.

Figure 12-20 shows the definition of a new color.

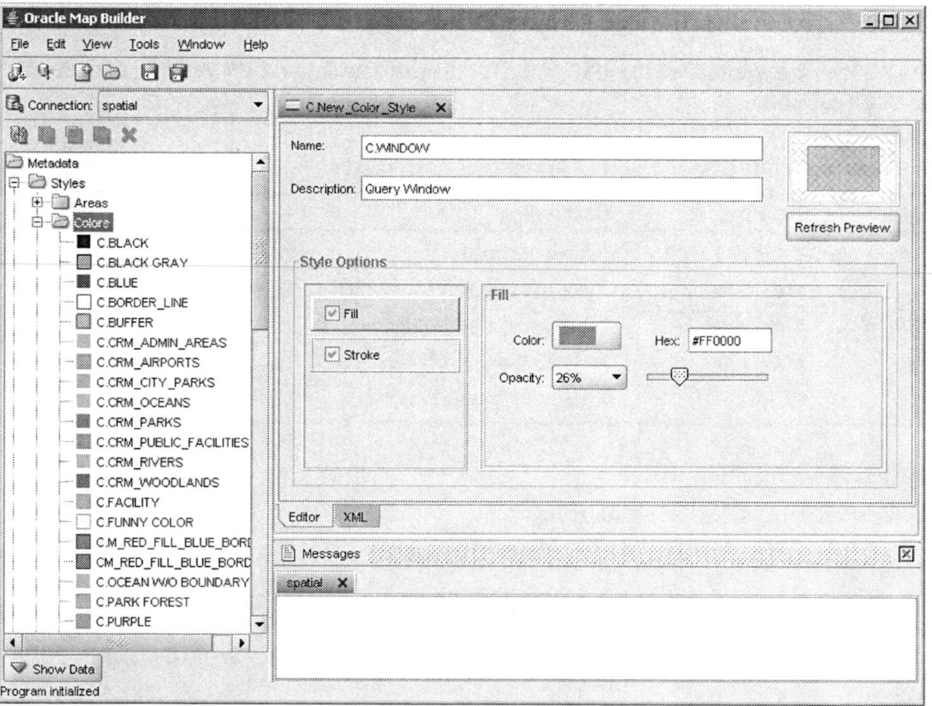

Figure 12-20. *Defining a color*

Marker Styles

Markers define symbols for point features. You can define them in two ways:

- *As vector drawings (circles, polygons, and so on)*: See Figure 12-21 for an example of a circle marker. The actual shape is described by a set of coordinates (for a generic polygon) or by a radius (for a circle). You can specify a fill and stroke color with opacity and thickness.

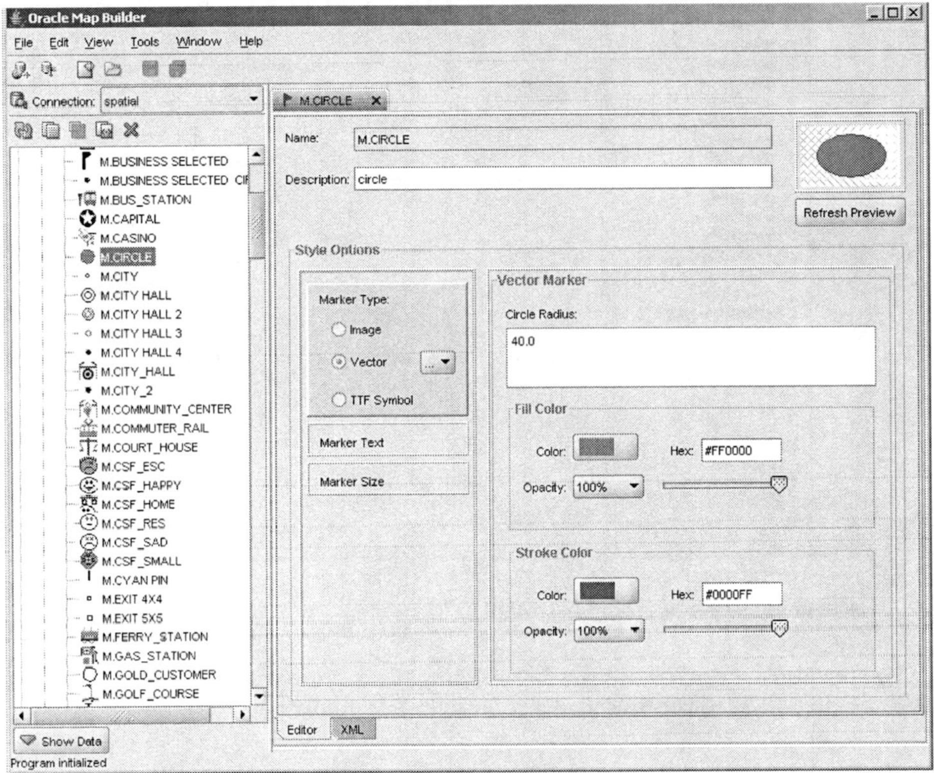

Figure 12-21. *Defining a circle marker*

- *As bitmap images*: See Figure 12-22 for an example of a bitmap symbol.

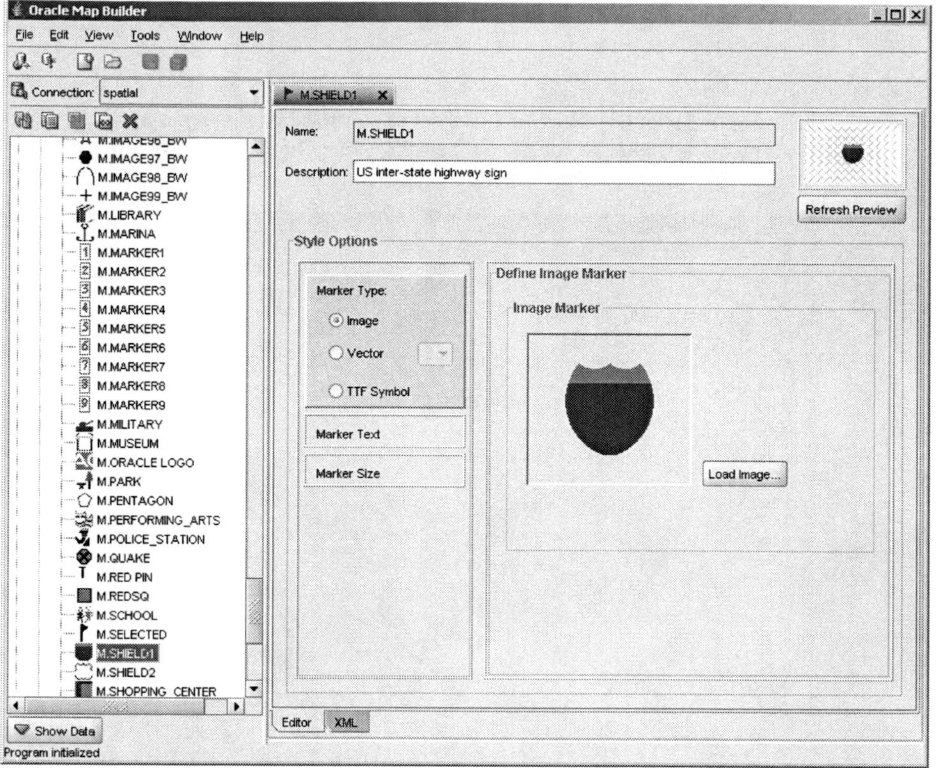

Figure 12-22. *Defining a bitmap symbol*

You can also use markers as styles for rendering labels. For example, the bitmap symbol illustrated in Figure 12-22 will be used to render the interstate numbers.

Line Styles

Lines are rather complex graphic objects. They are defined by the combination of several characteristics (all optional):

- A general color, thickness, and opacity
- A center line, with color, thickness, and dash styling
- Side lines, with color, thickness, and dash styling
- Hash marks on the center line, with color, length, and frequency

You can also define the way lines terminate and the way multiple lines connect. Figure 12-23 shows the definition of a line style for divided highways.

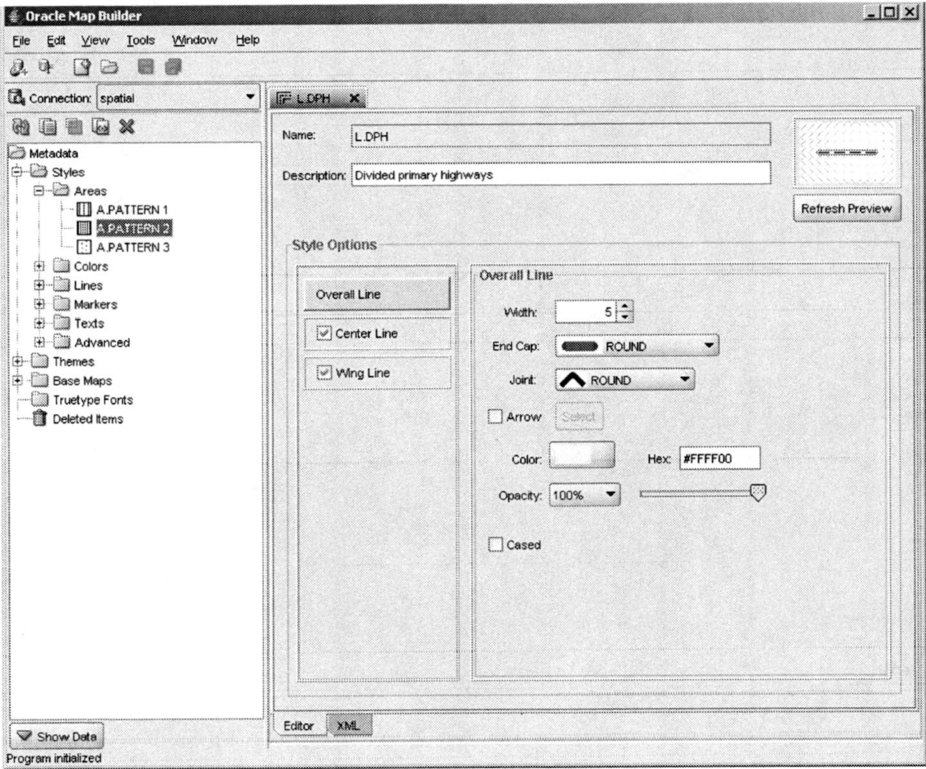

Figure 12-23. *Defining a line style*

Area Styles

Area styles are bitmaps used for filling an area with some patterns instead of a color style. They are loaded from bitmaps. Figure 12-24 shows the definition of a pattern.

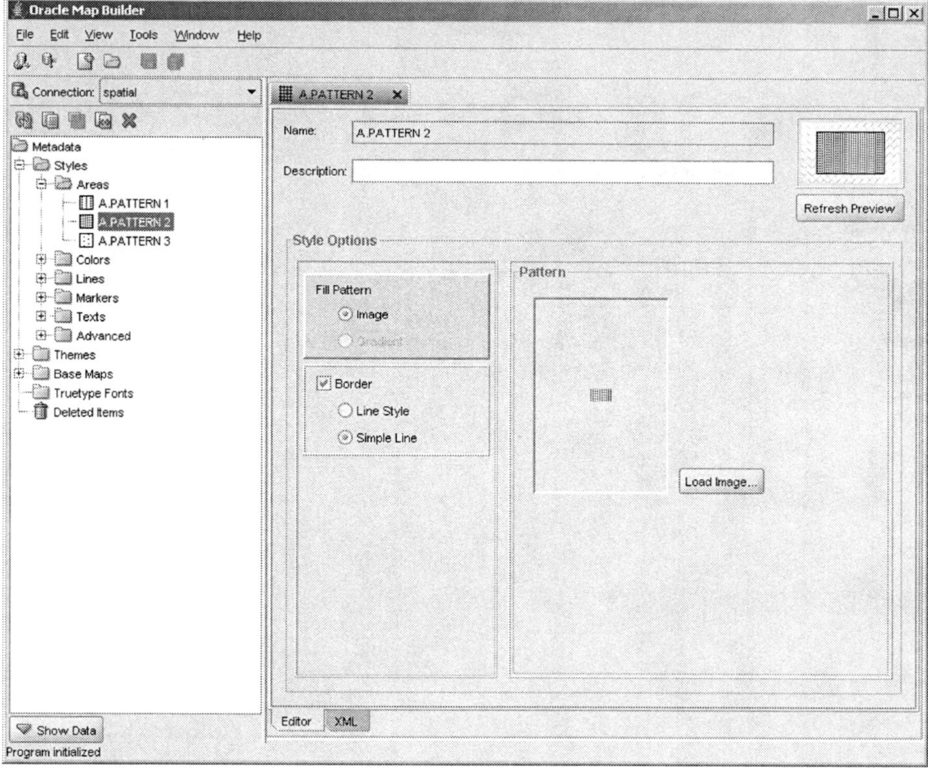

Figure 12-24. *Defining an area pattern style*

Text Styles

Text styles define the way labels should be rendered. A text style combines a font with a color, size, halo, and bolding, and/or italicizing. You can also control the spacing between letters and specify how a label should be placed on lines. See Figure 12-25 for an example.

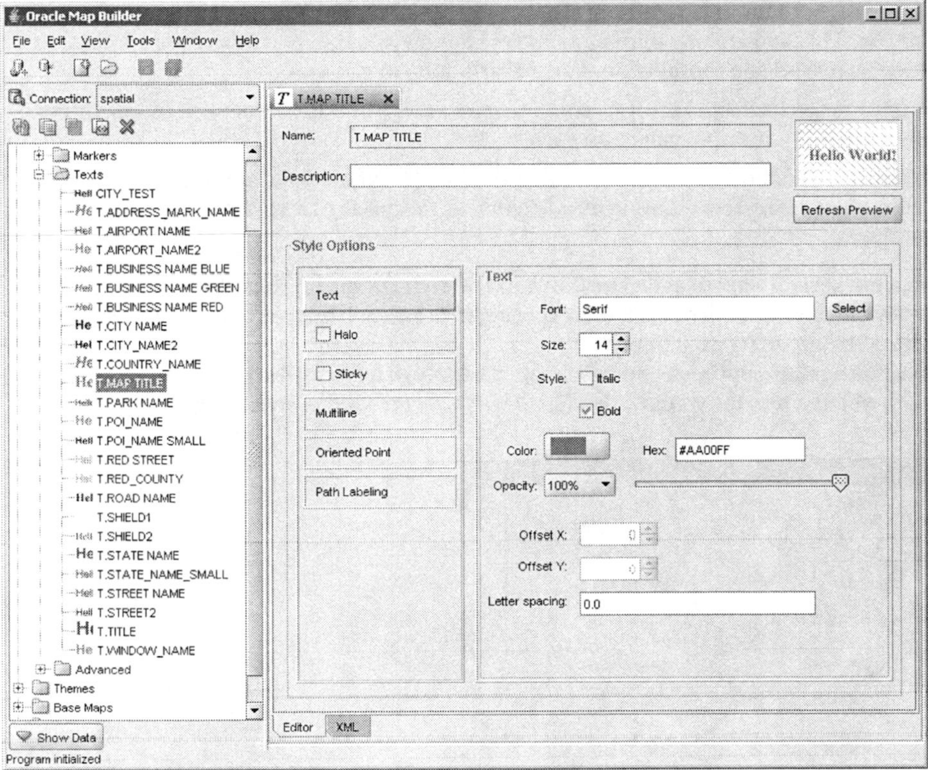

Figure 12-25. *Defining a text style*

Advanced Styles

Advanced styles are the most complex, but also the most powerful, of all styles. You can use them to define thematic maps by providing the ability to render features differently based on the value of one or more columns of a table, called the *control variables* in the following discussion. Note that you do not specify those variables when creating the advanced style; you will specify them when creating a theme that uses this advanced style.

Thematic maps are often used in conjunction with statistical analysis of geographical information. An example of a thematic map is one that shows the type of underlying geology or one that presents counties in different colors depending in the population density (an example of this is shown later in Figure 12-40). Other thematic maps could be used to represent stores with different-sized symbols based on the revenue of each store.

MapViewer provides two major categories of advanced styles: those that render complete features in a different way depending on some value, such as using different colors for counties depending on population density, and those that produce pie charts or bar charts. We will now cover each category of advanced styles in turn.

Advanced Styles for Thematic Mapping

The principle of thematic mapping is to distribute the values of a control column (for example, population density or sales volume) into a set of *buckets* and to associate a *primitive style* (color, marker, line) to each bucket. The buckets can be defined in three ways:

- *Equal range*: All buckets represent the same range of values. You need to specify only the number of buckets and the minimum and maximum values. Equal ranges are appropriate if your control variable contains a uniform distribution of values.
- *Variable range*: Each bucket represents a separate range of values. You need to specify the minimum and maximum values for each bucket.
- *Collection*: Each bucket represents a single value. The value does not have to be numeric. It could be a string representing a code (such as the grade of a customer as Silver, Gold, or Platinum).

You can use several ways to associate the primitive styles to the buckets. You can use a color that gradually darkens for each bucket, use a specific style for each bucket, or even use a marker symbol whose size grows for each bucket.

By combining those options, you can create a variety of advanced styles, summarized in Figure 12-26, which is also the window that lets you choose the kind of style to create.

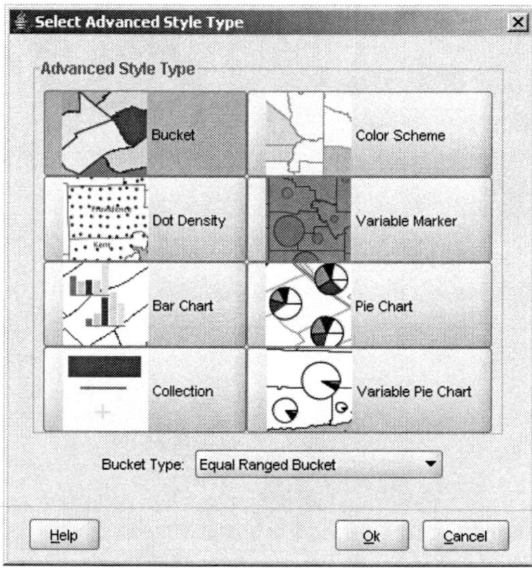

Figure 12-26. *Types of advanced styles*

Here are the main advanced styles for building thematic maps:

- *Color Scheme*: This style associates a gradually darkening color to a set of buckets. The buckets can be of any kind (equal range, variable range, or collection). All you need is to specify the base color.
- *Bucket*: This style gives you finer control over the way you associate styles to buckets. Like for the Color Scheme style, you can choose between equal range, variable range, or collections bucket distributions. Then you associate one specific style for each bucket (or value in a collection).
- *Variable Marker*: Somewhat similar to the Color Scheme style, this style associates gradually larger marker symbols to the buckets. Specify the base marker symbol (which can be any existing marker style, vector, or raster image) and the bucket ranges.

Another advanced style for thematic mapping is Dot Density. This style does not use any bucket mechanism. Rather, it fills a region with dots (of your chosen marker style and size) proportionally to the value of a control column, such as population density.

Figure 12-27 shows one example of a *variable color scheme* style that associates a range of colors to a range of values. Specify a base color and the ranges of values. Each range will be associated to a gradually darker variant of the base color. We will use this style for producing a thematic map highlighting population density in U.S. counties.

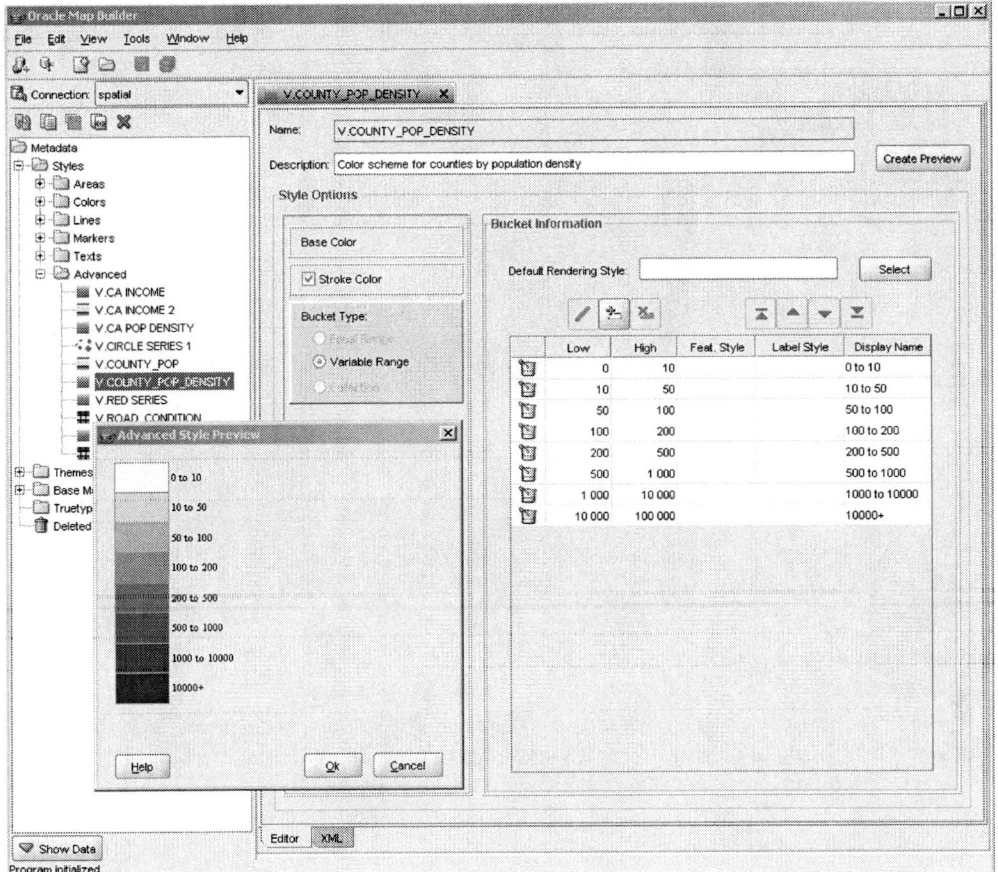

Figure 12-27. *Variable color scheme style*

Figure 12-28 illustrates a *variable marker* style, where the value of an attribute is represented using circles of varying sizes. The base marker can be any existing marker style, including bitmap markers.

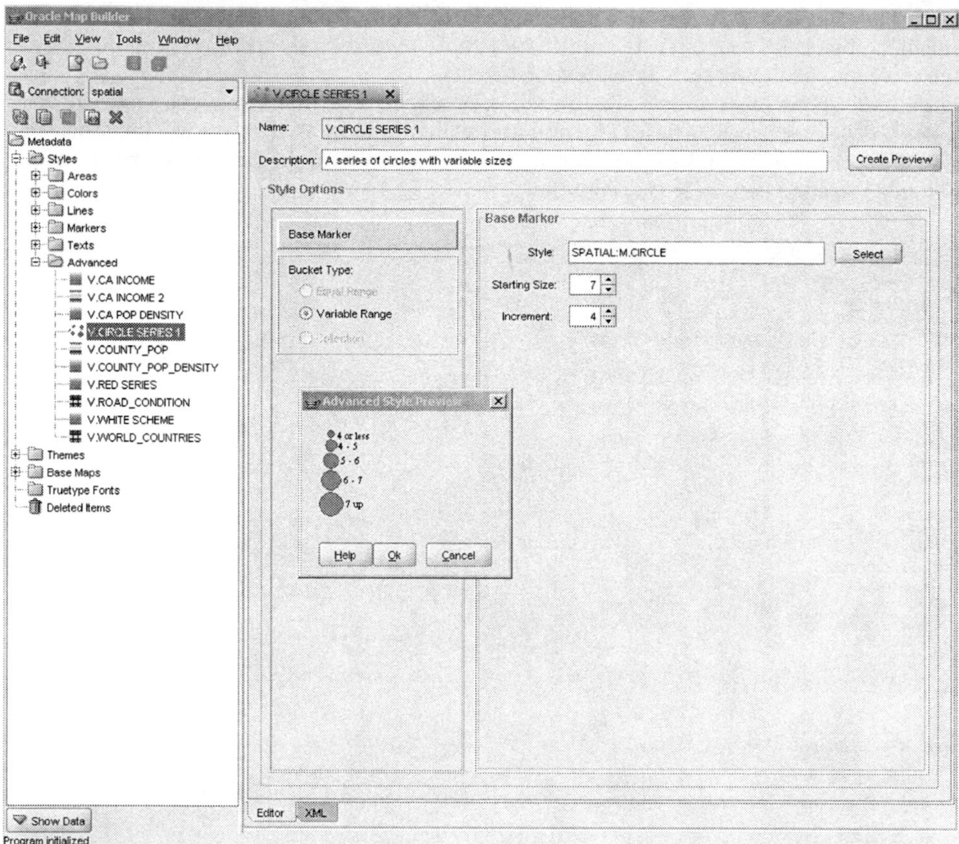

Figure 12-28. *Variable size marker style*

Figure 12-29 illustrates a *collection bucket* style, where the value of an attribute, here the condition of a road, is represented using different semitransparent-colored lines. A theme built using this style can be overlaid on a road network to highlight roads in poor condition.

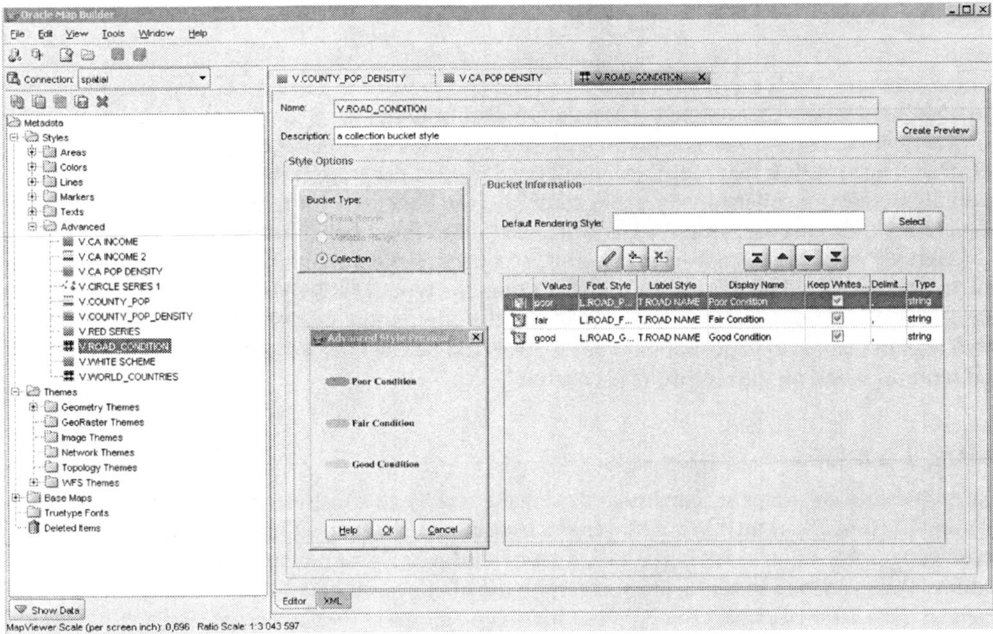

Figure 12-29. *Collection bucket style*

Advanced Styles for Statistical Graphs

The thematic mapping allows you to observe only one variable. Other advanced styles allow you to observe multiple variables by adding bar or pie charts to your maps. Those need multiple control variables (one for each slice or bar of the chart).

- *Pie chart*: Specify the color for each slice of the pie, as well as the size of the pie chart.
- *Bar chart*: Specify the color for each bar. You can also specify the width of the bars as well as the minimum and maximum values of the values used to build the bars.
- *Variable pie chart*: This makes the size of the pie chart vary with some other control variable. Use this for example to build pie charts where each slice represents the relative sales volume for each product group and the size of the pie represents the total volume of sales for a sales territory.

Combining Styles

The Collection style allows you to group multiple styles and use the resulting combination when defining a theme. This is especially useful when you always want to show, for example, state boundaries together with pie charts showing population distribution.

One approach is to define two themes: one for the states and one for the pie charts. The drawback of that approach is that MapViewer will need to read the states table twice, once for each theme. By building a collection style that combines the base style for rendering states with the advanced style for pie charts, MapViewer will need to read the state table only once.

Thematic maps are often used in conjunction with statistical analysis of geographical information. An example of a thematic map is one that shows the type of underlying geology or one that presents counties in different colors depending on the population density (an example of this is shown later in Figure 12-40). Other thematic maps could be used to represent stores with different-sized symbols based on the revenue of each store.

Using Themes

As already discussed, maps are constructed using themes. Themes are also often called *layers* in GIS and mapping tools. You can think of a layer as a transparent sheet on which you have drawn a set of related geographic objects, such as roads, a set of land parcels, or points representing customer locations. You get a map by laying those sheets on top of one another (and, of course, aligning them correctly). This is exactly what cartographers have done for more than a century, and light tables with transparent media with registration marks have been the tools of geographic analysis since the late 1800s.

Themes are a powerful concept. You use them to group spatial objects in logical subsets. Typical examples of themes that you will see in mapping applications are as follows:

- Political boundaries (countries, country subdivisions, states, provinces, counties, city limits, and so on)
- Natural features (rivers, forests, lakes, and so on)
- Transportation networks (roads, streets, railways, and so on)
- Customer or store locations, truck positions, and so on

Figure 12-30 shows a map composed of five themes: cities, interstates, national parks, counties, and states.

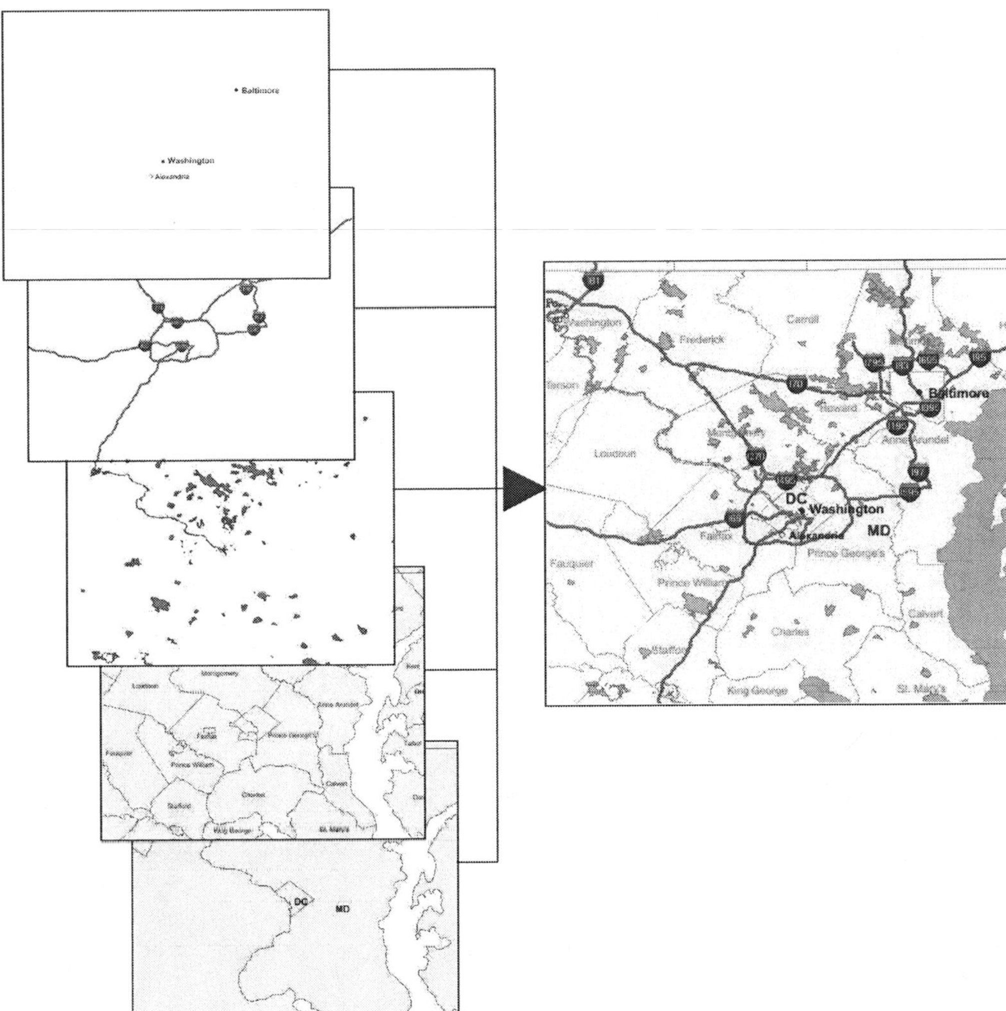

Figure 12-30. *A map with multiple themes*

The way you group your spatial objects in themes is important. This grouping will determine the way users interact with your maps. Users can decide which data they want to see on a map by selecting complete themes (turning them "on" or "off"). You could, for example, mix rivers and railroads in the same layer, but that would mean users would never be able to see rivers without also seeing railroads.

Themes do not have to be homogeneous. In other words, a theme can contain different types of spatial objects—for example, lines and polygons. A typical example is a "hydro" theme that combines lakes (which are polygons) and rivers (which are lines).

You can define multiple themes on the same table essentially by defining a sequence of SQL queries, one for each theme. For example, assume that all roads are defined in a single spatial table. You can define multiple themes on that table, where each theme selects a subset of the table: motorways, national roads, country roads, and so on.

As another example, if you are especially interested in roads that cross bridges of a certain character, you can separate them as a theme and define a symbology for them. This is a handy visual tool for the spatial analysis needed to plan the routes of oversize or very heavy trucks.

Defining Themes: The USER_SDO_THEMES View

Themes are defined in the USER_SDO_THEMES view. This is the view you update to define and maintain your private themes. The ALL_SDO_THEMES view lists the themes defined by users on tables that you can access. You will see a theme in your ALL_SDO_THEMES view only if you have been granted access on the underlying table (in other words, if that table also appears in your ALL_TABLES view).

Table 12-2 lists the columns of the USER_SDO_THEMES view. The ALL and DBA variants contain an additional OWNER column.

Table 12-2. *Structure of the* USER_SDO_THEMES *View*

Column Name	Data Type	Description
NAME	VARCHAR2	Name of the theme
DESCRIPTION	VARCHAR2	Description of the theme
BASE_TABLE	VARCHAR2	Name of the table used by this theme
GEOMETRY_COLUMN	VARCHAR2	Name of the geometry column
STYLING_RULES	CLOB	XML definition of the theme

Managing Themes Using Map Builder

To define a new theme, right-click the Theme category, and select the Create Geometry Theme option. This launches a wizard that will take you through the steps for creating your theme.

Using the first step of the wizard, shown in Figure 12-31, choose a unique name for your theme (other users could, however, define their own themes with the same name). Next, choose the base table (or view) this theme should use by selecting it from the Base Table drop-down list. After that, you can choose the name of the geometry column from the Spatial Column drop-down list.

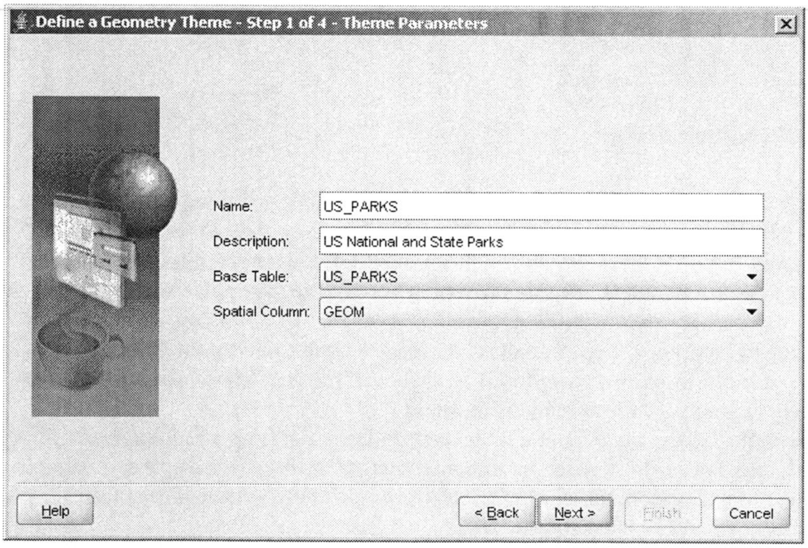

Figure 12-31. *Theme-building wizard: table and column name*

Choosing a Feature Style

The second step of the wizard, shown in Figure 12-32, is where you specify the style to use for rendering the features. Select the kind of style to apply (color, marker, line, advanced), and then choose the style using the style picker, as shown in Figure 12-33. Notice that the style picker allows you to use styles defined by other users, not just your own styles. When building the styling rules, Map Builder will automatically prefix each style name with the name of its owner.

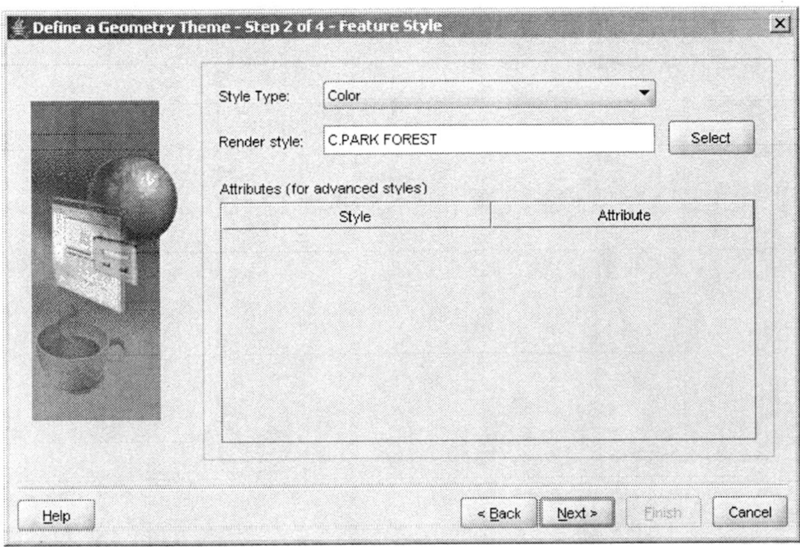

Figure 12-32. *Theme-building wizard: feature style*

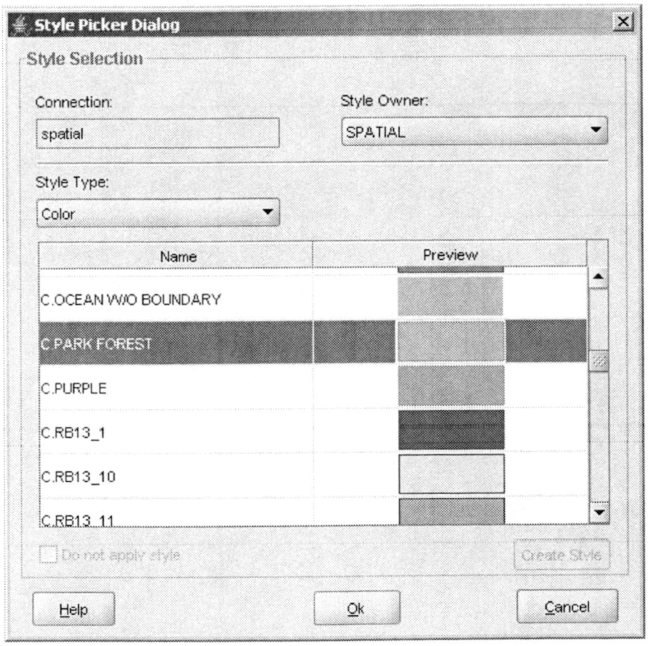

Figure 12-33. *The style picker*

Labeling

The third step of the wizard, shown in Figure 12-34, lets you choose a column whose content will be used for labeling the features, as well as the style to use for the labels. Note that labeling is optional.

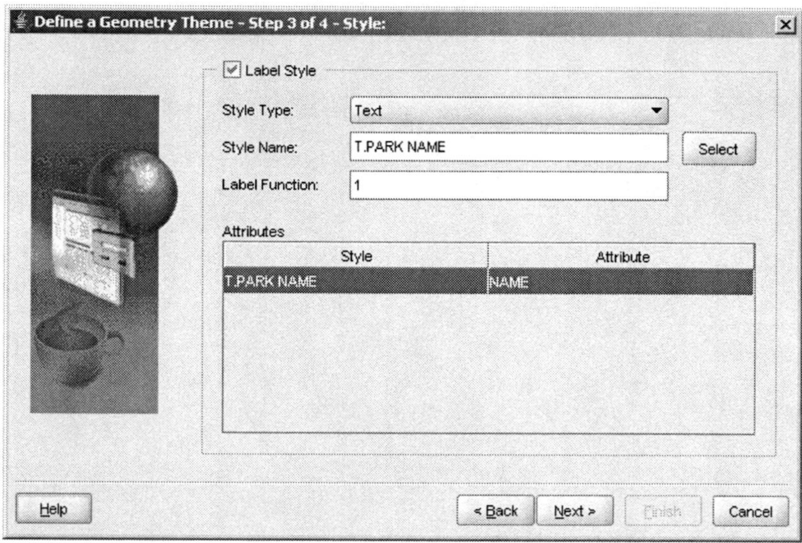

Figure 12-34. *Theme-building wizard: labeling*

Query Condition

The fourth and final step of the wizard, shown in Figure 12-35, allows you to enter a query condition to select only those features from the table you want to include on the theme. Leave it empty if you want to include the entire table.

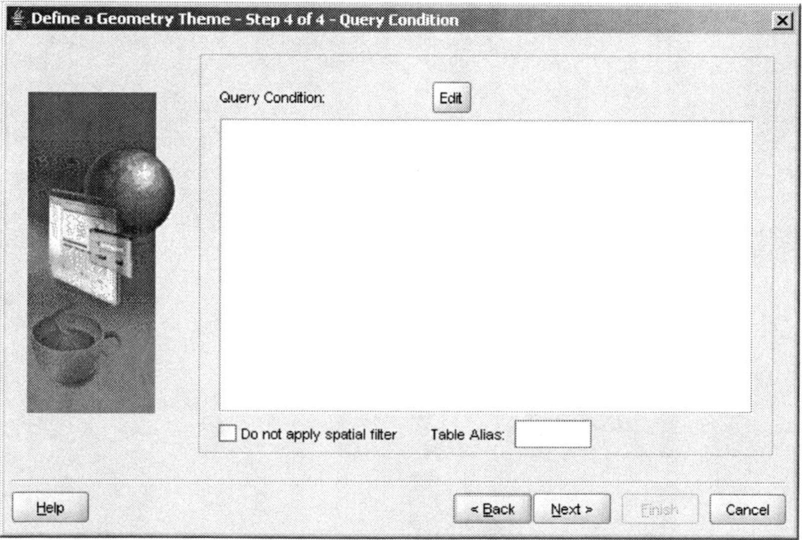

Figure 12-35. *Theme-building wizard: query condition*

Fine-Tuning Your Theme

When the wizard has completed, it shows the details about your theme, as illustrated in Figure 12-36. This is also the window you will be taken to when you modify your theme. The information about a theme is grouped in several topics: Basic Information, Styling Rules, Advanced, and Custom Tags.

Basic Information is the name of the table and geometry column; you cannot change that. If you want to use the theme against a different table, you need to duplicate it and specify a different table and column for the copy.

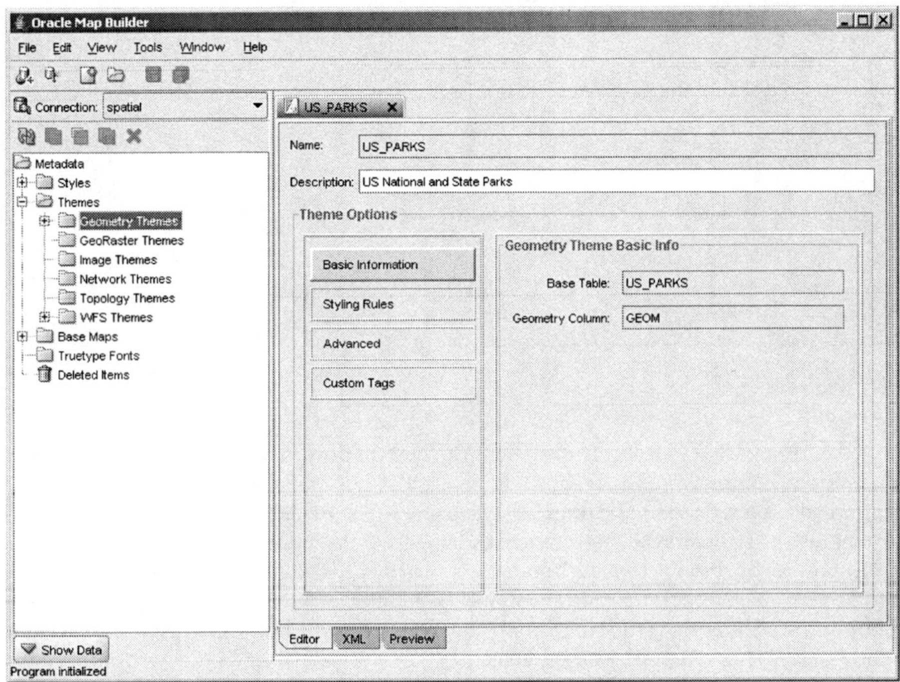

Figure 12-36. *Editing a theme definition*

The main part of a theme definition is in the Styling Rules section, illustrated in Figure 12-37.

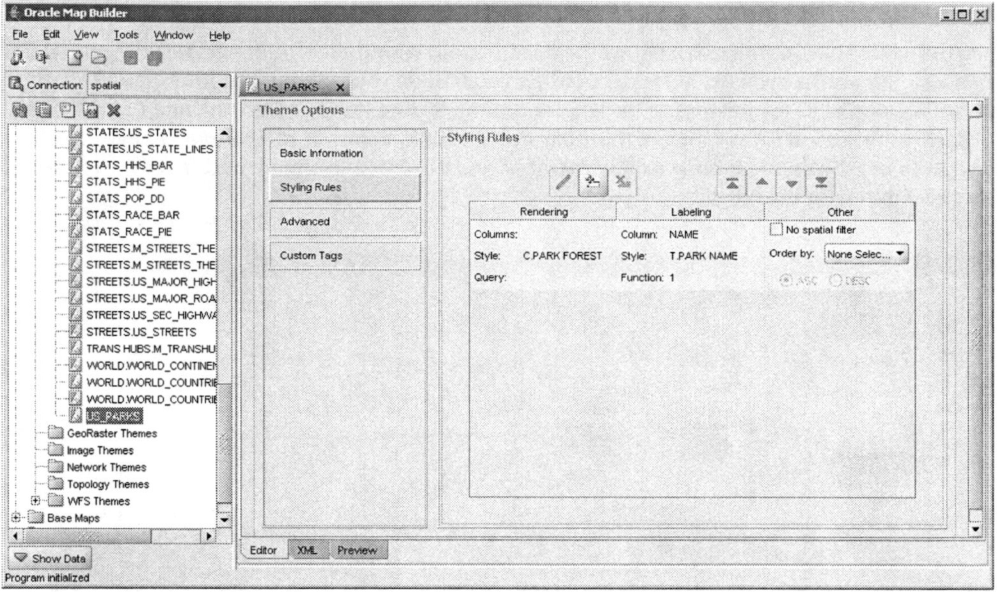

Figure 12-37. *Styling rules*

To edit a styling rule, click it to select it, and then use the Edit button on the toolbar just above the rules. This opens an editing window, as shown in Figure 12-38. In this window you can change all the information you entered when creating the style using the wizard. Notice, however, the Layer Function entry set to 1. This means the features will be labeled. If the value were 0, then no feature would be labeled. You could actually replace this value by a call to a SQL function returning 0 or 1, allowing you to decide which individual features should be labeled.

Another important parameter is the No Spatial Filter check box. If checked, then MapViewer will *not* apply any spatial filter when that theme is read.

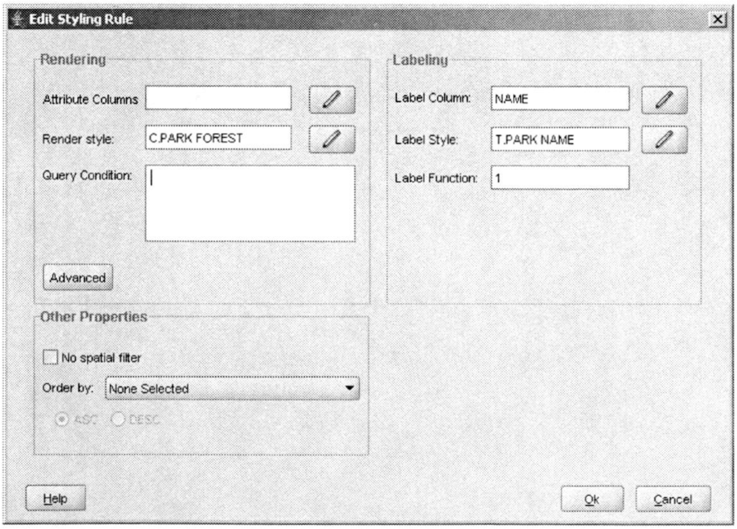

Figure 12-38. *Edit Styling Rule dialog box*

Multiple Styling Rules

When you define multiple styling rules, MapViewer will apply different styles to different rows in the table. See Figure 12-39 for an example.

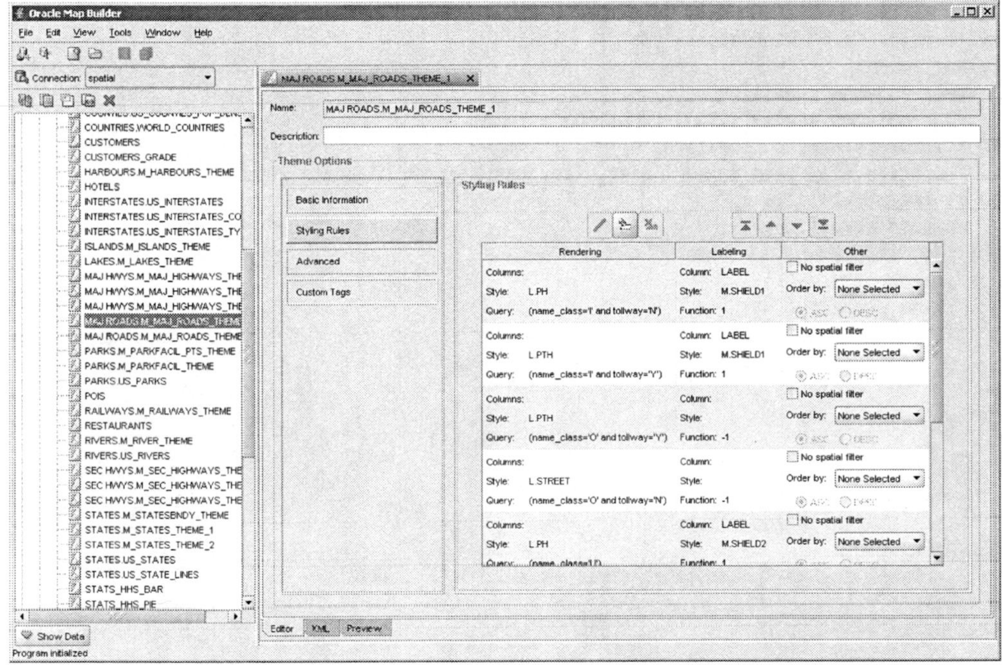

Figure 12-39. *Theme with multiple styling rules*

This theme describes the rendering for the `MAP_MAJOR_ROADS` table. That table contains road segments of different kinds that need to be displayed using different colors and thicknesses and different labeling styles. One styling rule is defined for each kind of road, and each rule uses a different feature and label style. Some rules do not have any labeling at all.

To identify which rule should be applied to which rows, you just need to provide a SQL expression in the Query Condition box to select the relevant rows. MapViewer will include this expression in the `WHERE` clause of the `SELECT` statement it generates to read the table for this theme.

Buttons at the top of the window let you insert a new rule, remove a rule, or move rules in the list. Note that the order of the rules is unimportant.

Templated Themes

A templated theme is one where the SQL expression used in the Query Condition box contains references to bind variables, with the actual values being provided at runtime. For example, a theme on the `CUSTOMERS` table could have the SQL expression `CUSTOMER_GRADE = :1`, allowing the application to choose the kind of customers to show at runtime.

Using Complex SQL

The SQL queries generated by MapViewer for a theme are simple queries that may contain at most one `WHERE` clause to restrict the rows to be returned. But you may want to define a theme that would be the result of a complex join between multiple tables. One way would be to define a view for that query. Another is just to include the complete query straight in the query condition for the theme.

For example, the following query joins a table called US_INTERSTATES_LRS with another one called US_ROAD_CONDITIONS and uses a linear referencing function to clip the sections of interstates based on their condition (Appendix B discusses linear referencing):

```
<?xml version="1.0" standalone="yes"?>
<styling_rules>
    <rule column="condition">
        <features style="V.ROAD_CONDITION">
select i.interstate, c.condition,
       sdo_lrs.clip_geom_segment(geom, from_measure, to_measure) geom
from us_interstates_lrs i,
     us_road_conditions c
where sdo_filter(
        geom,
        sdo_geometry(
          2003, 8307, null,
          sdo_elem_info_array(1, 1003, 3),
          sdo_ordinate_array (
            ?, ?, ?, ?)
        ),
        'querytype=window'
      ) ='TRUE'
and i.interstate = c.interstate
</features>
        <label column="interstate" style="M.SHIELD1"> 1 </label>
  </rule>
</styling_rules>
```

Notice that you must provide a complete query, including the spatial filter, usually added automatically by MapViewer. Notice also that you must include the four question marks; MapViewer will replace them at runtime with the actual bounds of the current map window.

Advanced Parameters

Now that you have defined the styling rules for your theme, you can progress to the Advanced Parameters option. Use this to specify the following:

- *The key column for this theme*: MapViewer must be able to uniquely identify the rows returned for that theme. By default, it will use the ROWID of the objects fetched. However, if the theme is based on a view or a complex query, then this is not possible, and you need to specify the name of a unique identifying column. Notice that you must enter the name manually; there is no drop-down list of column names from which to choose.
- *The level of caching for the theme*: Fetching geometries from the database is fairly expensive, so MapViewer will try to avoid repeatedly fetching the same geometries—a common case when zooming in or out—by retaining them in a memory cache. The size of that cache is specified in MapViewer's configuration file, as you have seen. However, caching may not be appropriate for all themes. Specify the level of caching as follows:
  - NORMAL: Geometries will be cached and retained on an LRU basis.
  - ALL: The theme will be fully loaded in memory on first access. You can use this for small spatial tables that are used for the majority of maps.
  - NONE: The theme will not be cached at all. This is the setting to use for anything that changes dynamically. Note that themes for which you provide the full SELECT statement to run (like the earlier example) are never cached.

- *Information columns*: Here you specify the names of columns from the base table used by the theme and associate a label to each name. The columns could actually be SQL expressions. Those columns will be available in Oracle Maps (that is, the JavaScript API) and will be shown in the information window displayed when the user clicks a dynamic feature. We will discuss this in detail in Chapter 13 when we cover Oracle Maps.

Thematic Mapping: Using Advanced Styles

Another way to get MapViewer to render features depending on some attribute value is to use an advanced style. This technique is called *thematic mapping*. See Figure 12-40 for an example of a theme that uses an advanced style.

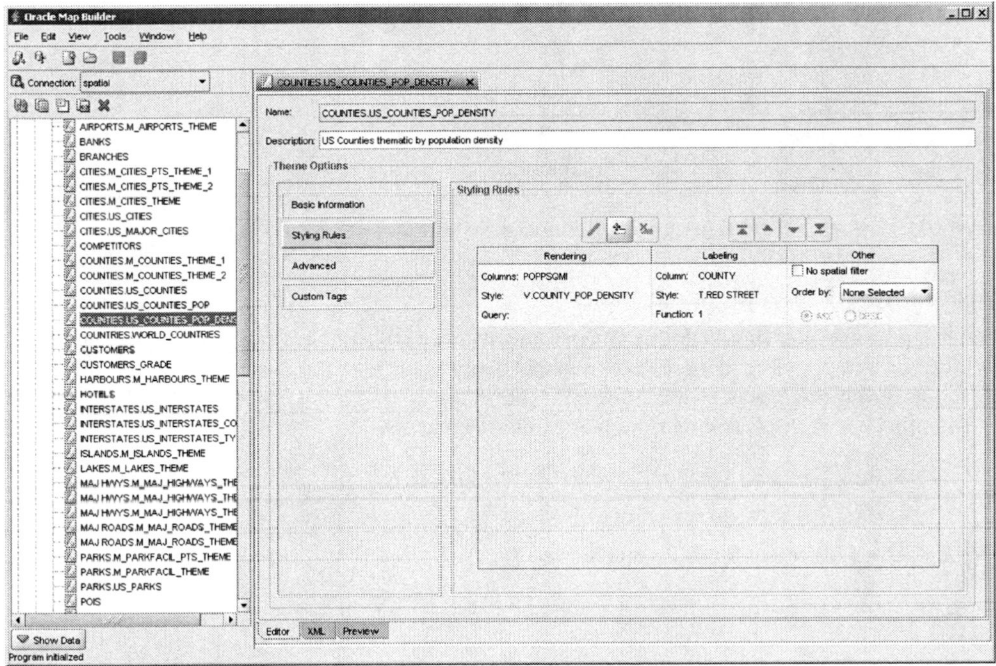

Figure 12-40. *A theme that uses an advanced style*

For this theme, U.S. counties should be rendered in such a way that the color of each county varies with the population density in that county.

To achieve this, we will use the advanced style we defined previously (see Figure 12-27). In addition, we need to specify the name of the attribute whose value will control the rendering. Here we use the column POPPSQMI, which contains the average population per square mile in each county. We choose this column from the Attribute Column drop-down list. Figure 12-41 shows a map that uses this style.

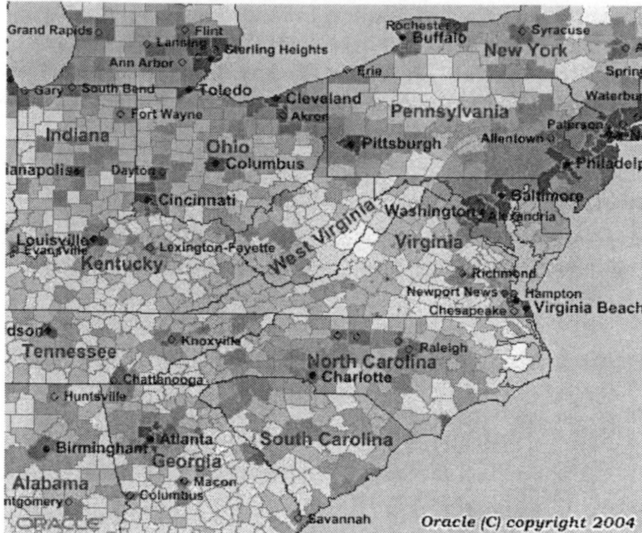

Figure 12-41. *A thematic map showing population density in U.S. counties*

Advanced Style vs. Multiple Styling Rules

Whenever possible, you should define and use an advanced style rather than multiple styling rules. This is because each styling rule generates a spatial query against the database, whereas an advanced style requires only one query, so it is more efficient.

You must use multiple styling rules in the following cases:

- The styling is based on a combination of attributes.
- The styling is not based on a range of values.
- Labeling is different for different features.

Using Maps

As you have seen, a map is a collection of themes. However, constructing a map is more than just listing the themes that should appear on that map. The order in which the themes are listed is important. In addition, the map definition enables you to control the amount of information to include, depending on the scale of the map. Both concepts are very important, and we will examine them in the sections that follow.

Theme Ordering

The themes in a map must be assembled in the correct order depending on the type of symbology for each layer and its relative importance. To return to the transparent sheets metaphor, if the counties are drawn as colored polygons, then the "counties" sheet should be placed at the bottom of the stack so that the "roads" sheet and the "customers" sheet can be seen. If the "counties" sheet is placed on the top, then it will obscure (hide) the other sheets.

For computer-generated maps, the order in which the themes are defined controls the `rendering` or `display` order of those themes. The first theme to appear is rendered, and then the others are rendered successively on top of one another until you have the complete map, as illustrated in Figure 12-23.

For MapViewer, the themes are listed in the order of rendering—that is, the first theme in the list is rendered first, then the second, and so on. The theme at the end of the list is rendered last.

Note Most mapping tools list the themes in the opposite order; in other words, the theme that appears at the bottom of the list is the one rendered first, and the others are layered on top of one another. The topmost theme is rendered last. MapViewer uses the opposite convention.

Note that you can define one or more themes to use transparent styles. Such a theme can be defined as the last theme to be rendered (that is, at the end of the theme list) and can allow other themes to be partially seen.

Map Scale and Zoom Level

One important advantage of generating maps on the fly is to show more or less information depending on the current scale of the map. Let's examine what this means.

The scale of a map determines the size of the geographical area shown on that map. The scale represents the ratio of a distance on the map to the actual distance on the ground. For example, if 2 cm on the map represents 1 km on the ground, then the scale would be 2 cm/1 km, which is the same as 2 cm/100,000 cm, or 1/50,000. The scale is then 1:50,000. At that scale, each centimeter on the map represents 0.5 kilometer on the ground.

Geographers talk commonly about large- and small-scale maps. A large-scale map—for example, 1:1,000 (remember, this is the fraction 1/1,000)—shows a small area with great detail and is useful for analysis that deals with small areas, such as site planning for construction or a walk in the park. At that scale, 1 centimeter on the map corresponds to 10 meters on the ground. A small-scale map, such as 1:1,000,000 (1/1,000,000), shows a large area with little detail and is useful for large-area applications such as routing a truck or flying an airplane. At that scale, 1 centimeter on the map corresponds to 10 kilometers on the ground. The *larger* the denominator in the scale expression, the *smaller* the scale of the map and the *larger* the area of coverage for a particular display size, and vice versa.

Zooming in or out is nothing but changing the scale of a map—that is, asking for a new map to be produced at a different scale.

The amount of information shown on a map depends on the scale of that map. Maps at a small scale (that is, showing the entire United States) will show less detail than maps at a large scale (that is, showing the southern tip of Manhattan). It would be meaningless for a map of the continental United States to show the details on each street in every city and town, as well as each and every gas station and ATM. Not only would the map be hard to read, but it would also take a long time to produce because of the amount of data to read and render. A map at that scale would reasonably include only the boundaries of the U.S. states, some major cities, and the major interstate highways.

Then as you zoom in, you should see gradually more details: counties start to appear, then secondary highways, then major roads, then streets, then building outlines, and so on. This is a fundamental concept in cartography often referred to as *scale-dependent content* or *scale-dependent symbology*. On the other hand, when you zoom in very closely, it probably makes no sense to show country or state boundaries anymore.

To make this possible, you associate a *scale range* to individual themes. A theme will appear on a map only when the scale of the map is inside that range. Setting scale ranges correctly is important—it determines how readable and useful your maps will be. It can also determine the performance of your application.

USER_SDO_MAPS View

Maps are defined in the USER_SDO_MAPS view. This is the view you will update to define and maintain your maps. The ALL_SDO_MAPS view lists all maps in the database.

Table 12-3 lists the columns of the USER_SDO_MAPS view. The ALL and DBA variants contain an additional OWNER column.

Table 12-3. *Structure of the* USER_SDO_MAPS *View*

Column Name	Data Type	Description
NAME	VARCHAR2	Name of the map
DESCRIPTION	VARCHAR2	Optional description of the map
DEFINITION	CLOB	XML definition of the map

Managing Maps Using Map Builder

To define a map, right-click the Base Maps category, and select the Create Base Map option. This launches a wizard that will take you through the steps for creating a new map.

The first step in the wizard lets you specify the name of your map. This name must be unique. However, other users could define their own maps with the same name.

The second step, illustrated in Figure 12-42, is where you specify the themes to appear on your map. Select a theme from the list of themes at the top, and then click the Add Theme button on the bottom toolbar to add it to the map. If you make a mistake, click the Delete Theme button. Change the ordering of the themes using the arrow buttons on the toolbar.

To enter scale limits, double-click the Min Scale and Max Scale data items in the list.

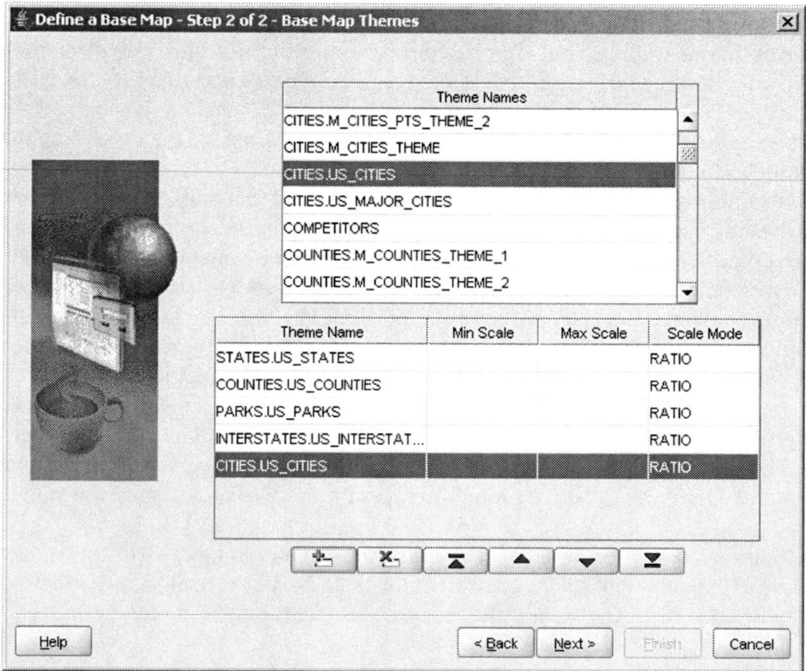

Figure 12-42. *The map-building wizard*

When you are done defining the map using the wizard, you will be taken to the screen shown in Figure 12-43, which is also the screen you get to update an existing map.

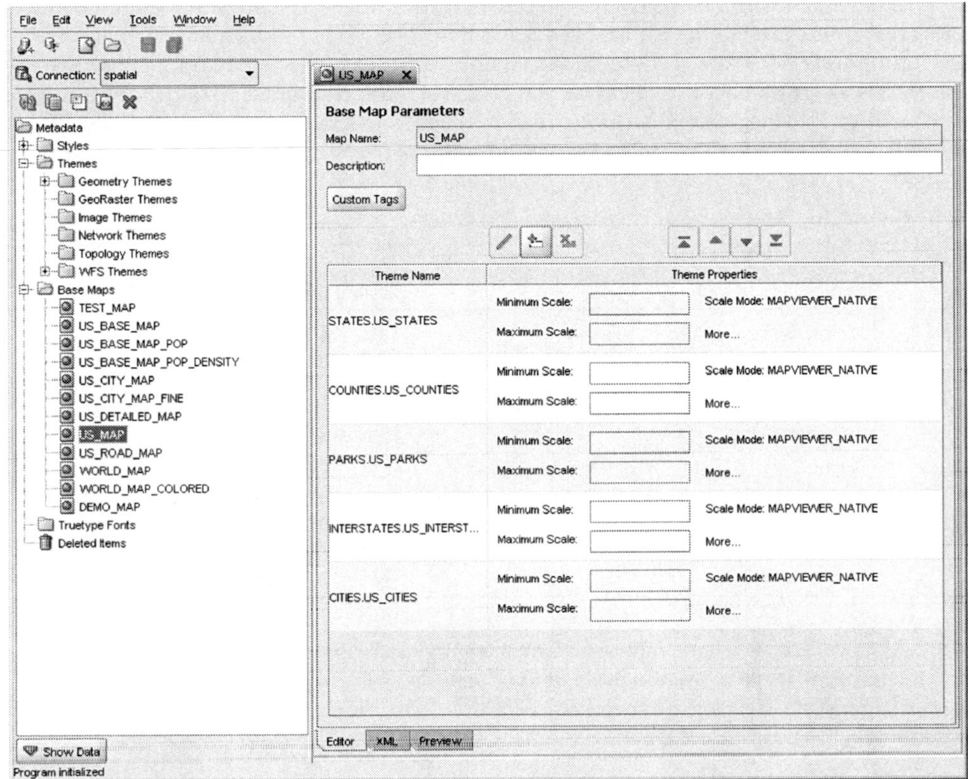

Figure 12-43. *Editing a map definition*

Themes are listed in the order of rendering; the first theme in the list is rendered first, then the second, and so on. The theme at the end of the list is rendered last. You can control and change the ordering of the themes using the buttons at the bottom of the form. For the map shown in the example, MapViewer will first render the `US_STATES` theme and then the `US_COUNTIES`, `US_PARKS`, and `US_INTERSTATES` themes. The `US_CITIES` theme is rendered last.

Scale Dependency

The Min Scale and Max Scale parameters define the visible scale range of each theme. They control whether the theme is displayed, depending on the current map scale. When no values are specified, then the theme is always visible.

MapViewer allows you to define the scale of a map in two modes, called `RATIO` and `MAPVIEWER_NATIVE`. The first mode (`RATIO`) corresponds to the description given earlier. Specify scale values as the denominator of the scale expression. A scale value of 1000 corresponds to a scale of 1:1000.

You can also use the other way (called MAPVIEWER_NATIVE), which was the only one available up to version 10 of MapViewer. In this mode, the scale value represents the distance on the ground that corresponds to 1 inch on the map. That distance is expressed in the units of the coordinate system of the spatial tables. With data in a geodetic coordinate system (that is, in latitude, longitude), the scale value represents the number of decimal degrees that correspond to 1 inch on the map.

Converting scale values between the two notations is fairly easy. See Table 12-4. In this table we use value 0.0254 as the number of inches per meter and 111195 as an approximation of the number of meters per degree in longitude (this value can differ slightly depending in the actual coordinate system used). In this table, we assume that projected coordinate systems use the meter as base unit.

Table 12-4. *Converting Between Ratio and Screen Inch Scales*

Coordinate System	Ratio to Screen Inch	Screen Inch to Ratio
Projected	`screen_inch = ratio * 0.0254` Example: A ratio scale of 1:50000 is equivalent to 50000 * 0.0254 = 1270 meters per screen inch.	`ratio = screen_inch / 0.0254` Example: A screen inch scale of 1,000 meters per inch is equivalent to 1000 / 0.0254 = 39370, that is, a ratio scale of 1:39370.
Geodetic	`screen_inch = ratio * 0.0254 / 111195` Example: A ratio scale of 1:50000 is equivalent to 50000 * 0.0254/111195 = 0.0009982 degrees per screen inch.	`ratio = screen_inch * 111195 / 0.0254` Example: A screen inch scale of 0.5 degrees per inch is equivalent to 0.5 / 0.0254 * 111195 = 2188877, that is, a ratio scale of 1:2188877.

A high Min Scale or Max Scale value is associated with less map detail and a smaller scale in cartographic terms, whereas a low Min Scale or Max Scale value is associated with greater map detail and a larger scale in cartographic terms. The Min Scale value is always larger than the Max Scale value.

- *Min Scale* is the value to which the display must be zoomed in for the theme to be displayed.
- *Max Scale* is the value beyond which the display must be zoomed in for the theme to not be displayed.

For example, if a theme called Parks has a Min Scale value of 50000 and a Max Scale value of 20000, it means it will appear on maps at scales only from 1:50000 up to (but not including) 1:20000. If the initial map is at scale 1:80000 and you start zooming in, parks will appear as soon as you reach a scale of 1:50000. They remain visible as you keep on zooming in, until you go beyond the scale of 1:20000, at which point they no longer appear on the map.

Figure 12-44 illustrates the use of scale dependency. Map US_BASE_MAP contains two themes based on the US_STATES table: US_STATES and US_STATE_LINES. The US_STATE_LINES theme uses a style without any fill color (that is, it shows only the border of the states). This means states can be rendered on top of the counties, without hiding them. Notice also the two themes for cities: US_CITIES and US_MAJOR_CITIES. Both are defined on the US_CITIES table, but US_MAJOR_CITIES includes only those cities with a population of more than 250,000.

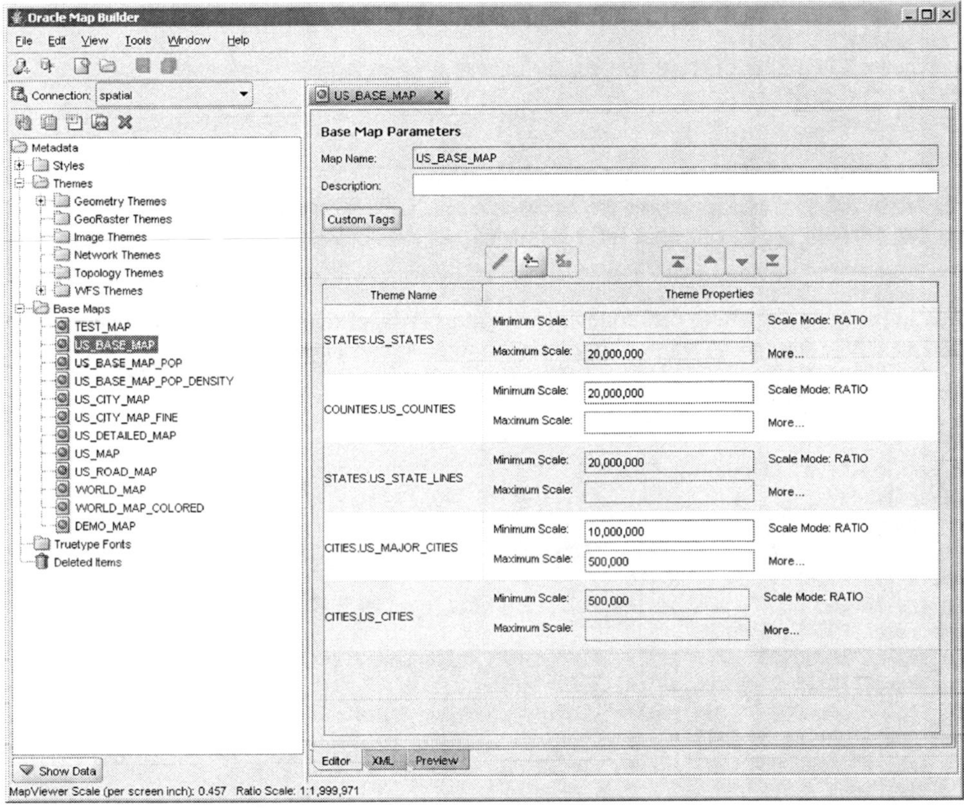

Figure 12-44. *Defining a map with scale-dependent content*

On the initial small-scale map, you see only the states (theme US_STATES). Then as you zoom in, you stop seeing the states and see only the counties (theme US_COUNTIES) with the state boundaries (theme US_STATE_LINES). As you zoom in further, you begin to see the major cities (theme US_MAJOR_CITIES), which are finally replaced by all cities (theme US_CITIES).

Viewing and Updating Map Definitions in SQL

In addition to using Map Builder, you can also update the map, theme, and style definitions by directly updating the USER_SDO_MAPS, USER_SDO_THEMES, and USER_SDO_STYLES views using standard SQL statements.

Viewing the definitions is simple; just use a SELECT statement. For example, here is how to view the XML definition of map US_BASE_MAP:

```
SQL> select definition from user_sdo_maps where name = 'US_BASE_MAP';

<?xml version="1.0" standalone="yes"?>
<map_definition>
  <theme name="STATES.US_STATES" min_scale="Infinity" max_scale="2.0E7"
    scale_mode="RATIO"/>
  <theme name="COUNTIES.US_COUNTIES" min_scale="2.0E7" max_scale="-Infinity"
    scale_mode="RATIO"/>
  <theme name="STATES.US_STATE_LINES" min_scale="2.0E7" max_scale="-Infinity"
    scale_mode="RATIO"/>
```

```
  <theme name="CITIES.US_MAJOR_CITIES" min_scale="1.0E7" max_scale="500000.0"
    scale_mode="RATIO"/>
  <theme name="CITIES.US_CITIES" min_scale="500000.0" max_scale="-Infinity"
    scale_mode="RATIO"/>
</map_definition>
```

Tip By default, SQL*Plus displays only the first 80 characters of CLOB columns. To make sure it displays the complete XML definition, use the command `set long 32000` prior to executing the `SELECT` statement.

Creating or updating a map definition element (map, style, or theme) is just as easy. Simply use an `INSERT` or `UPDATE` statement. For example, here is how to define a new map called `US_MAP`:

```
insert into user_sdo_maps (name, description, definition)
values (
'US_MAP','',
'<?xml version="1.0" standalone="yes"?>
<map_definition>
  <theme name="STATES.US_STATES"
    min_scale="Infinity"  max_scale="20000000"  scale_mode="RATIO"/>
  <theme name="COUNTIES.US_COUNTIES"
    min_scale="20000000"  max_scale="-Infinity" scale_mode="RATIO"/>
  <theme name="PARKS.US_PARKS"
    min_scale="8000000"   max_scale="-Infinity" scale_mode="RATIO"/>
  <theme name="INTERSTATES.US_INTERSTATES"
    min_scale="8000000"   max_scale="-Infinity" scale_mode="RATIO"/>
  <theme name="CITIES.US_CITIES"
    min_scale="10000000"  max_scale="-Infinity" scale_mode="RATIO"/>
</map_definition>
');
```

Exporting and Importing Map Definitions

Map definitions are stored in dictionary tables, so they will not be included when you export data from one database to another. To transfer map definitions successfully using the Oracle export/import tools, use the following technique:

1. In the source database, before running the export, save a copy of the map definitions in regular tables:

   ```
   create table my_styles as select * from user_sdo_styles;
   create table my_themes as select * from user_sdo_themes;
   create table my_maps as select * from user_sdo_maps;
   ```

2. In the target database, load the definitions back in the dictionary:

   ```
   insert into user_sdo_styles select * from my_styles;
   insert into user_sdo_themes select * from my_themes;
   insert into user_sdo_maps select * from my_maps;
   ```

3. If definitions already exist in the target database, you may need to remove the old definitions first:

   ```
   delete from user_sdo_maps where name in (select name from my_maps);
   delete from user_sdo_themes where name in (select name from my_themes);
   delete from user_sdo_styles where name in (select name from my_styles);
   ```

Defining Map Caches

To use a base map in the JavaScript API (Oracle Maps), you must first define a cache on that map. The simplest way to define a map cache is to use the MapViewer console. But you can also define caches by manually editing the contents of the USER_SDO_CACHED_MAPS view, an approach that allows greater flexibility.

Map caches can be of two kinds: internal and external caches. Internal caches are those defined on base maps defined in the database (using Map Builder). External caches are defined on external web map providers, such as other MapViewer servers. External web map providers are accessed using specific adapters.

The USER_SDO_CACHED_MAPS View

The definitions of map caches are stored in the USER_SDO_CACHED_MAPS view. This is the view you update to define and maintain map cache definitions. The ALL_SDO_CACHED_MAPS view lists the caches defined by all.

Table 12-5 lists the columns of the USER_SDO_CACHED_MAPS view. The ALL and DBA variants contain an additional OWNER column.

Table 12-5. *Structure of the* USER_SDO_CACHED_MAPS *View*

Column Name	Data Type	Description
NAME	VARCHAR2	Name of the cache.
DESCRIPTION	VARCHAR2	Description of the cache (optional).
BASE_MAP	VARCHAR2	Name of the base map.
DEFINITION	CLOB	XML definition of the map cache.
TILES_TABLE	VARCHAR2	(Currently not used.)
IS_ONLINE	VARCHAR2	Specifies whether the cache is online (YES). When a cache is offline, then the map cache server returns a blank image for all tiles not found in the cache.
IS_INTERNAL	VARCHAR2	YES if the map source is an internal base map.
MAP_ADAPTER	BLOB	Stores the binary class that implements the adapter for an external source.

Managing Caches Using the MapViewer Console

To manage existing map caches, use the MapViewer administration console, shown in Figure 12-10, and click the Manage Map Caches link, which brings you to a page like the one in Figure 12-45.

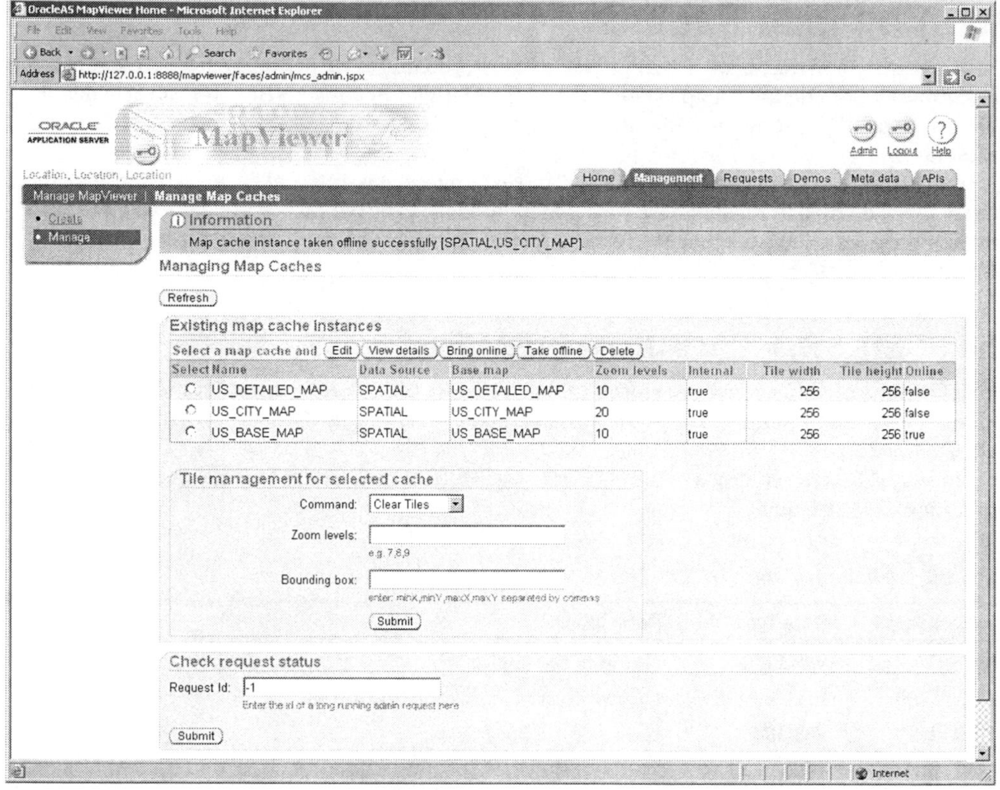

Figure 12-45. *Managing map caches*

The form allows you to view the XML definition of a cache (View Details button). Use it also to take a cache offline or bring it back online. Finally, you can also delete a cache, which will delete the definition of the cache from the database (the USER_SDO_CACHED_MAPS view) and will also remove all files for that cache from the file system.

The form also allows you to clear, populate, or refresh selected tiles of a map cache. Specify the zoom levels to process as well as the bounding box representing the area to process. Those operations could take a long time to complete, so the map cache server will process them in an asynchronous way. Use the Check Request Status form to monitor the progress of a request. Figure 12-46 illustrates the refreshing of all tiles at zoom level 1 for the cache US_BASE_MAP.

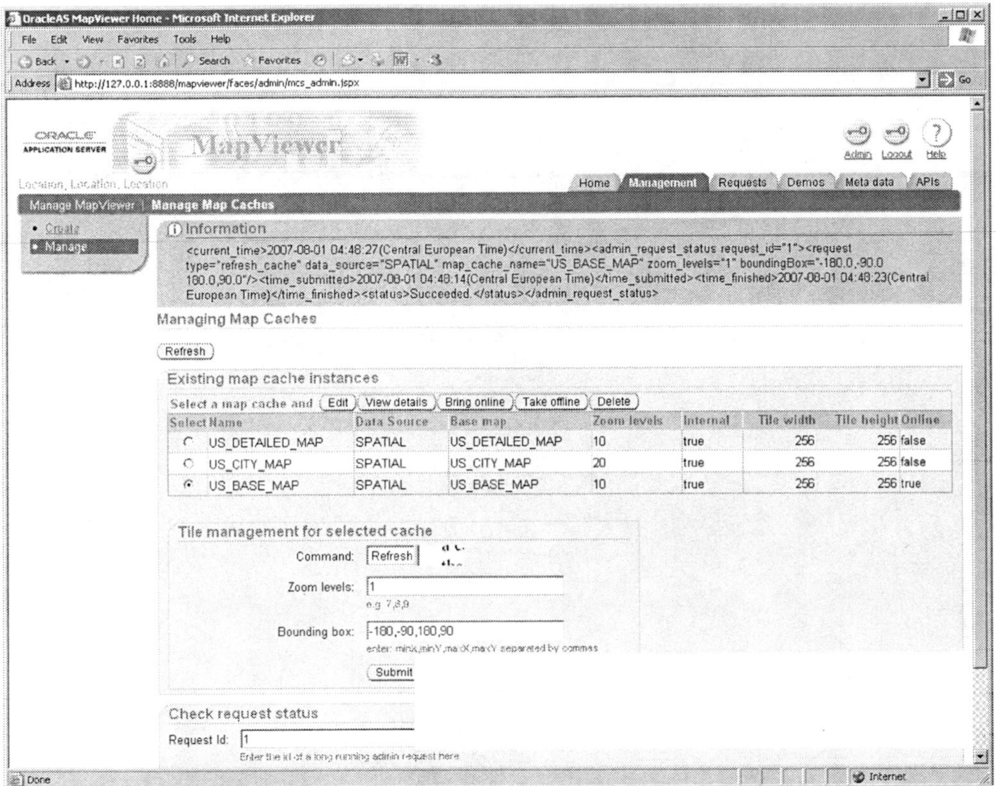

Figure 12-46. *Refreshing map tiles*

Note The Edit button is inoperative. To change the definition of a map cache, delete it first, and then redefine it.

Creating a New Map Cache

Click the Create link at the top left of the map cache administration page shown in Figure 12-44, and then select the type of map cache to create. Choose Internal to define a cache based on a base map defined in your database. This will open a form such as the one in Figure 12-47, which you will now fill with the parameters that define the cache. Choosing External will direct you to a different form to define a cache based on an external data source. We discuss external caches later in this chapter.

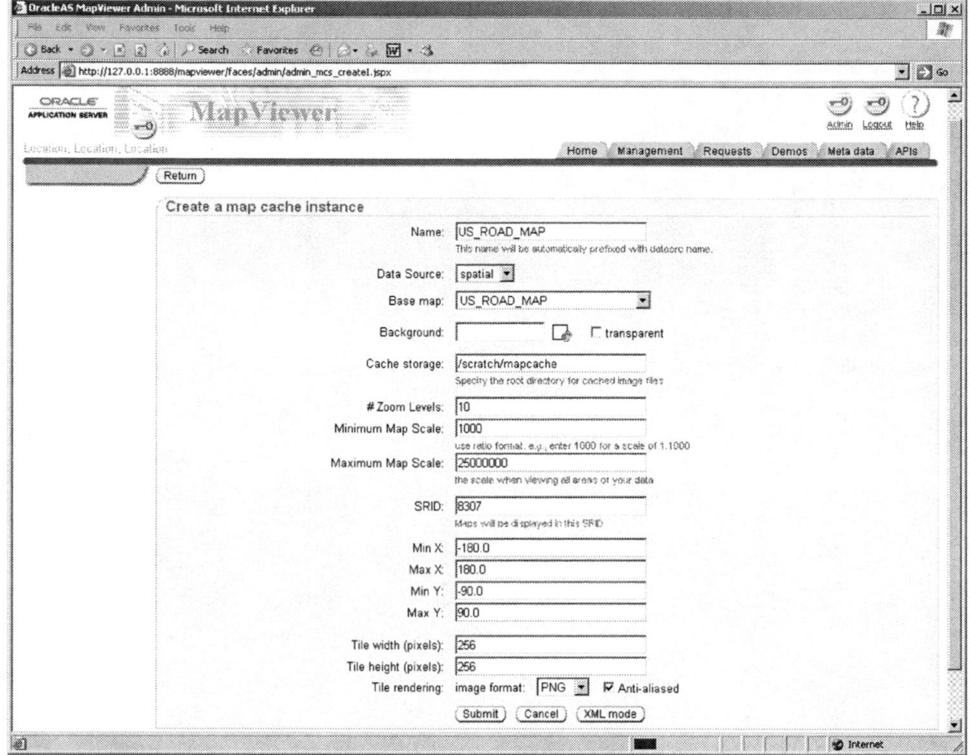

Figure 12-47. *Defining a new map cache*

To define a new map cache, specify the following information:

- The name of the cache. You can use any name, but it is a good practice to give the same name as that of the base map the case uses. In the example, the cache is called `US_ROAD_MAP` to match the name of the base map.
- The name of the data source and the name of the base map for the cache.
- Optionally, a background color and whether that background should be transparent.
- Optionally, the location in the file system of the application server, where the files for that cache will be stored. If this setting is omitted or invalid, then the files go in `$OC4J_HOME/j2ee/home/applications/mapviewer/web/mapcache`.
- The number of zoom levels in the cache, as well as the minimum and maximum scales, specified in ratio notation; a minimum scale of 1000 means a ratio scale of 1:1000. The maximum scale setting will be used for zoom level 0, and the maximum scale setting will be associated with zoom level `N-1` (where `N` is the number of zoom levels). The scales associated with the intermediate zoom levels are automatically computed by MapViewer. In the example, the cache goes from zoom level 0 (at scale 1:25,000,000) to zoom level 9 (at scale 1:1000).

- The coordinate system (SRID) in which to produce the tiles for the cache and the minimum and maximum values of the x,y coordinates for that coordinate system. Note that the tables used to build the base map could be in a different coordinate system. If this is the case, then MapViewer will automatically transform the source data into the coordinate system you specified.
- The size (in pixels) of the map tiles and the format of the tiles. In the example, the tiles are 256 × 256 pixels, in PNG.

When you are satisfied with your parameters, click the Submit button. This has the effect of defining the cache in USER_SDO_CACHED_MAPS and of creating the file system structures to hold the tiles for the cache.

Creating Map Caches Using SQL

The previous approach generates a set of uniform zoom levels; the scales for the intermediate zoom levels are automatically computed so that the zoom levels are uniformly distributed in the interval. You can see the zoom levels that have been generated by querying the details of the cache definition, using the Show Details button on the cache management page illustrated in Figure 12-44. You can also see them by just querying the view USER_SDO_CACHED_MAPS, as illustrated in Listing 12-3.

Listing 12-3. *Details of a Cache Definition*

```
SQL> SELECT DEFINITION FROM user_sdo_cached_maps WHERE name = 'US_ROAD_MAP';

<cache_instance name="US_ROAD_MAP" image_format="PNG" antialias="true">
  <internal_map_source base_map="US_ROAD_MAP" data_source="SPATIAL"/>
  <cache_storage root_path=""/>
  <coordinate_system srid="8307" minX="-180.0" maxX="180.0" minY="-90.0"
    maxY="90.0"/>
    <tile_image width="256" height="256"/>
    <zoom_levels levels="10" min_scale="1000" max_scale="25000000">
      <zoom_level tile_width="15.286028158107968"
        tile_height="15.286028158107968" level_name="level0" scale="2.5E7"/>
      <zoom_level tile_width="4.961746909541633"
        tile_height="4.961746909541633" level_name="level1" scale="8114840.0"/>
      <zoom_level tile_width="1.6105512127664132"
        tile_height="1.6105512127664132" level_name="level2" scale="2634025.0"/>
      <zoom_level tile_width="0.5227742142726501"
        tile_height="0.5227742142726501" level_name="level3" scale="854987.0"/>
      <zoom_level tile_width="0.16968897570090388"
        tile_height="0.16968897570090388" level_name="level4" scale="277523.0"/>
      <zoom_level tile_width="0.05507983954154727"
        tile_height="0.05507983954154727" level_name="level5" scale="90082.0"/>
      <zoom_level tile_width="0.017878538533723076"
        tile_height="0.017878538533723076" level_name="level6" scale="29240.0"/>
      <zoom_level tile_width="0.005803187729944108"
        tile_height="0.005803187729944108" level_name="level7" scale="9491.0"/>
      <zoom_level tile_width="0.0018832386690789012"
        tile_height="0.0018832386690789012" level_name="level8" scale="3080.0"/>
      <zoom_level tile_width="6.114411263243185E-4"
        tile_height="6.114411263243185E-4" level_name="level9" scale="1000.0"/>
   </zoom_levels>
</cache_instance>
```

You can control the exact configuration of the cache by directly editing the XML definition. Do this either by using the XML interface via the XML Mode button on the map cache creation form (Figure 12-46) or by simply updating the map cache definition in SQL. You can also use SQL to create a new map cache. The code in Listing 12-4 creates the same map cache as the one you created using the administration console.

Listing 12-4. *Creating a Cache in SQL*

```
SQL> INSERT INTO user_sdo_cached_maps (name, description, tiles_table,
  is_online,  is_internal, definition, base_map)
VALUES (
'US_ROAD_MAP',
'Map Cache for overview US Road Map',
'TILES_US_ROAD_MAP',
'YES',
'YES',
'<cache_instance name="US_ROAD_MAP" image_format="PNG" antialias="true">
   <internal_map_source base_map="US_ROAD_MAP" data_source="SPATIAL"/>
   <cache_storage root_path=""/>
   <coordinate_system srid="8307" minX="-180" maxX="180"
     minY="-90" maxY="90"/>
   <tile_image width="256" height="256"/>
   <zoom_levels levels="10" min_scale="1000" max_scale="25000000">
   </zoom_levels>
</cache_instance>',
'US_ROAD_MAP'
);
```

Notice that you specify only the minimum and maximum scales and the number of zoom levels. MapViewer will update the definition with the actual breakdown in zoom levels the first time you use the map cache in an application. MapViewer will also create the directory structure that will hold the map tiles.

■ **Caution** When you create a new cache using direct SQL statements, it will not appear immediately in the administration console. It will appear only after an application has used the map cache.

By manually editing the XML definition, you can fine-tune your cache and specify exactly the scale for each zoom level. This allows you to adjust the zoom levels to better feed your needs. For example, if your original map (at zoom level 0) covers the entire globe, then you could set up the first zoom level to zoom in by large steps and the later zoom level to zoom by finer steps. This is illustrated in Listing 12-5.

Listing 12-5. *Creating a Cache in SQL with Detailed Zoom Levels*

```
SQL> INSERT INTO user_sdo_cached_maps (name, description, tiles_table,
  is_online, is_internal, definition, base_map)
VALUES (
'US_ROAD_MAP',
'Map Cache for detailed US Road Map covering the lower 48 states only',
'TILES_US_ROAD_MAP',
'YES',
'YES',
'<cache_instance name="US_ROAD_MAP" image_format="PNG" antialias="true">
```

```
    <internal_map_source base_map="US_ROAD_MAP" data_source="SPATIAL"/>
    <cache_storage root_path=""/>
    <coordinate_system srid="8307" minX="-180" maxX="180"
      minY="-90" maxY="90"/>
    <tile_image width="256" height="256"/>
    <zoom_levels levels="20" min_scale="1000" max_scale="25000000">
      <zoom_level level_name="level0"  scale="25000000"/>
      <zoom_level level_name="level1"  scale="22000000"/>
      <zoom_level level_name="level2"  scale="20000000"/>
      <zoom_level level_name="level3"  scale="15000000"/>
      <zoom_level level_name="level4"  scale="10000000"/>
      <zoom_level level_name="level5"  scale=" 7500000"/>
      <zoom_level level_name="level6"  scale=" 5000000"/>
      <zoom_level level_name="level7"  scale=" 2000000"/>
      <zoom_level level_name="level8"  scale=" 1500000"/>
      <zoom_level level_name="level9"  scale=" 1000000"/>
      <zoom_level level_name="level10" scale="  500000"/>
      <zoom_level level_name="level11" scale="  200000"/>
      <zoom_level level_name="level12" scale="  100000"/>
      <zoom_level level_name="level13" scale="   80000"/>
      <zoom_level level_name="level14" scale="   50000"/>
      <zoom_level level_name="level15" scale="   20000"/>
      <zoom_level level_name="level16" scale="   10000"/>
      <zoom_level level_name="level17" scale="    5000"/>
      <zoom_level level_name="level18" scale="    2000"/>
      <zoom_level level_name="level19" scale="    1000"/>
    </zoom_levels>
</cache_instance>',
'US_ROAD_MAP'
);
```

In this example, we use 20 zoom levels and specify explicit scale values for each level. Notice that we do not specify the size of the tiles at each zoom level. This information will be automatically computed and added when the map cache is accessed the first time by an application. The zoom levels are defined by the order they appear in the list. The first one is zoom level 0, the second one is zoom level 1, and so on. Each zoom level can also receive a `description` attribute. Use it to explain the usage of each level, such as `city block level`, `city level`, `district level`, and so on.

Another way to define the zoom levels is to specify tile sizes instead of scales, as illustrated in Listing 12-6. Note that the minimum and maximum tile width are expressed in the units of the coordinate system for the map—here they are in decimal degrees. MapViewer will automatically compute the tile sizes for each intermediate zoom level. You can of course also explicitly specify the tile size at each zoom level, like you specified detailed scale levels.

Listing 12-6. *Creating a Cache in SQL Using Tile Sizes*

```
SQL> INSERT INTO user_sdo_cached_maps (name, description, tiles_table,
  is_online,  is_internal, definition, base_map)
VALUES (
'US_ROAD_MAP',
'Map Cache for overview US Road Map',
'TILES_US_ROAD_MAP',
'YES',
'YES',
'<cache_instance name="US_ROAD_MAP" image_format="PNG" antialias="true">
    <internal_map_source base_map="US_ROAD_MAP" data_source="SPATIAL"/>
    <cache_storage root_path=""/>
```

```
    <coordinate_system srid="8307" minX="-180" maxX="180"
      minY="-90" maxY="90"/>
    <tile_image width="256" height="256"/>
    <zoom_levels levels="10" min_tile_width="0.0005" max_tile_width="15">
    </zoom_levels>
</cache_instance>',
'US_ROAD_MAP'
);
```

Cache Data Structures

The map cache server keeps the tiles it generates as files on the file system used by the host application server. The top-level directory for a map cache has the same name as the cache, prefixed by the name of the data source for the cache. For example, the cache shown on Listing 12-5 is in directory `SPATIAL.US_ROAD_MAP`. In that directory you will find one directory for each zoom level, named `0` to `19`. Each directory either contains tile files or is further subdivided into directories, possibly in multiple levels at the higher zoom levels.

Exporting Cache Definitions

Since the definitions of your map caches are stored in the database (in view `USER_SDO_CACHED_MAPS`), you can transfer those definitions to other databases (for example, from a development to a production environment) by exporting the contents of that view.

Since Oracle's export/import tools do not allow you to export views, you must first extract the definitions into a table:

```
create table my_cached_maps as select * from user_sdo_cached_maps;
```

Export this table and import it into your target database, and then load the map definitions:

```
insert into user_sdo_cached_maps select * from my_cached_maps;
```

If the map cache already exists in the target system, you must first remove it. You can do this using the administration console (which will remove the definition and any existing tiles)—or you can do it by manually by deleting the existing definition from `USER_SDO_CACHED_MAPS` and then removing the cache from the file system by deleting its top-level directory. MapViewer will automatically re-create the proper directory structure when the next time it starts up and opens the cache.

Purging and Refreshing Cache Contents

Once MapViewer has generated a tile for a map cache, the corresponding file will remain on the file system forever. If you update your database with a new version of the data used to build the tiles in a map cache, then the stored tiles are now obsolete and must be regenerated.

The simplest way to achieve this is simply to manually delete all directories contained in the top-level directory for the cache. The map cache server will then automatically and gradually rebuild the cache as applications request map tiles. Obviously, this will add overhead to map requests as the map tiles get regenerated.

Another approach is to use the administration interface of the map cache server, which allows you to clear selected portions of a cache but also to refresh or populate selected portions. See Figure 12-46 for an example.

■ **Tip** MapViewer never removes any tiles from a map cache, so it could possibly grow too large. You can always recover disk space by deleting part or all of the files and folders in the cache. A possible tactic, for example, is to schedule automatic cleanups of the lower levels of the cache (highest zoom levels) while retaining the higher levels, without stopping MapViewer. The map cache server will automatically rebuild any sections of the cache you removed.

Using External Data Sources

External data sources are mapping servers accessible via HTTP. Examples of such servers are Web Map Services (WMS)—web services that implement the ISO/DIS 19128 specification. Other examples are MapViewer servers.

Accessing those external servers through map caches is a powerful capability; it will reduce the number of times those external services are queried, since the map tiles returned by the external servers will be retained in the cache and reused.

MapViewer accesses external data sources via an adapter mechanism. It comes with two such adapters: one to access other MapViewer servers and one to access Web Map Services. MapViewer also provides you with a mechanism to implement your own adapter to other data sources.

Using the Standard Adapters

The two adapters provided with MapViewer are in the directory `$OC4J_HOME/j2ee/home/applications/mapviewer/web/WEB-INF/mapcache/mvadapter`. This directory contains the file `mvadapter.jar`, which is the JAR file that contains the classes for both adapters. The subdirectory `mcsadapter` contains the source code of the two adapters.

To use the adapters, the simplest is to copy the JAR file `mvadapter.jar` to MapViewer's main JAR library directory: `$OC4J_HOME/j2ee/home/applications/mapviewer/web/WEB-INF/lib`.

Creating a Map Cache on a Web Map Service

Click the Create link at the top left of the map cache administration page, as illustrated in Figure 12-45, and then select External as the type of map source to use. This will direct you to a form like that in Figure 12-48.

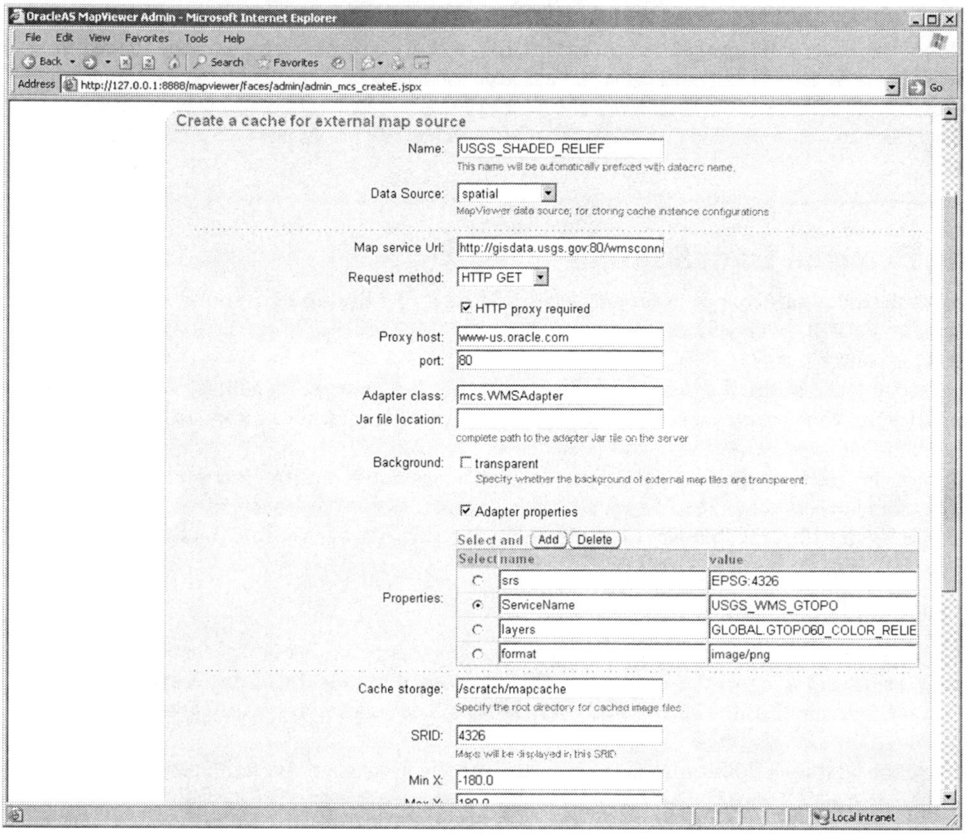

Figure 12-48. *Defining a new external map cache*

The following illustrates how to define a map cache on a public WMS server run by the U.S. Geological Survey. Here are the parameters you need to specify. For details on the WMS protocol and how to formulate WMS requests, see the next chapter where we discuss MapViewer's own WMS server.

- A name for the cache.
- The name of the data source in which the definition will be stored.
- The service URL for the Web Map Service. Use `http://gisdata.usgs.gov:80/wmsconnector/com.esri.wms.Esrimap/USGS_EDC_Elev_GTOPO`.
- The request method; use the GET method.
- If you access the Internet via a proxy server, enter its name and port.
- The adapter class to use; specify `mcsadapter.WMSAdapter`.
- The location of the JAR file. If you copied the JAR file provided with MapViewer as instructed, then you can leave this empty.
- Adapter properties. This is a list of name and value pairs that get passed as request parameters to the WMS service. Some of them are part of the standard WMS protocol. Some are specific to the service being called. For the USGS WMS server, specify them as shown in Table 12-6.
- The remaining parameters deal with the way you organize your cache in terms of storage and zoom levels. They are identical to those for an internal cache.

Table 12-6. *Parameters to Access the USGS Web Map Service*

Parameter	Value	Usage
srs	EPSG:4326	The coordinate system in which the service will return the map tiles.
layers	GLOBAL.GTOPO60_COLOR_RELIEF	The layer to query. This layer returns a colored relief map of the world. Another layer is GLOBAL.GTOPO60_BW_RELIEF, which returns a relief map in grayscale.
format	image/png	The format of the map tiles. This should match the format you specify for the tiles in your map cache. The service can also return the tiles in GIF or JPEG format.
ServiceName	USGS_WMS_GTOPO	(Specific to the USGS server.) The name of the service that provides the relief maps.

When you are satisfied with your parameters, click the Submit button. This has the effect of defining the cache in USER_SDO_CACHED_MAPS and of creating the file system structures to hold the tiles for the cache.

Listing 12-7 illustrates how to define the same map cache using SQL.

Listing 12-7. *Creating a Cache on an External WMS*

```
SQL> INSERT INTO user_sdo_cached_maps (name, description, tiles_table,
  is_online,  is_internal, definition, base_map)
VALUES (
'USGS_SHADED_RELIEF',
'Map Cache external Mapviewer data source',
'TILES_USGS_SHADED_RELIEF',
'YES',
'YES',
'<cache_instance name="USGS_SHADED_RELIEF" image_format="PNG" antialias="true">
  <external_map_source
    url="http://gisdata.usgs.gov:80/wmsconnector/com.esri.wms.Esrimap
/USGS_EDC_Elev_GTOPO"
    adapter_class="mcsadapter.WMSAdapter"
    proxy_host="www-us.oracle.com"
    proxy_port="80"
    timeout="5000"
  >
    <properties>
      <property name="srs" value="EPSG:4326"/>
      <property name="serviceName" value="USGS_WMS_GTOPO"/>
      <property name="layers" value="GLOBAL.GTOPO60_COLOR_RELIEF"/>
      <property name="format" value="image/png"/>
      <property name="transparent" value="false"/>
    </properties>  />
  </external_map_source>
  <cache_storage root_path=""/>
    <coordinate_system srid="4326" minX="-180" maxX="180"
      minY="-90" maxY="90"/>
    <tile_image width="512" height="512"/>
    <zoom_levels levels="10" min_scale="1000" max_scale="25000000">
    </zoom_levels>
 </cache_instance>',
'USGS_SHADED_RELIEF'
);
```

Notice that the SQL approach allows you to also specify a timeout value—this is not possible using the administration console. The timeout value (expressed in milliseconds) specifies how long MapViewer will wait for the web map server to reply. If you do not specify any timeout value, MapViewer will use a default of 15 seconds.

Creating a Map Cache on a MapViewer Service

Listing 12-8 illustrates how to define a map cache on another MapViewer server using SQL.

Listing 12-8. *Creating a Cache on an External MapViewer Server*

```
SQL> INSERT INTO user_sdo_cached_maps (name, description, tiles_table,
  is_online,  is_internal, definition, base_map)
VALUES (
'ELOCATION_MAP',
'Map Cache external Mapviewer data source',
'TILES_ELOCATION_MAP',
'YES',
'YES',
'<cache_instance name="ELOCATION_MAP" image_format="PNG" antialias="true">
  <external_map_source
    url="http://elocation.oracle.com/elocation/lbs"
    adapter_class="mcsadapter.MVAdapter"
    proxy_host="www-proxy.us.oracle.com"
    proxy_port="80"
    timeour="5000"
  >
    <properties>
      <property name="data_source" value="elocation"/>
      <property name="base_map" value="us_base_map"/>
    </properties>  />
  </external_map_source>
  <cache_storage root_path=""/>
    <coordinate_system srid="8307" minX="-180" maxX="180"
      minY="-90" maxY="90"/>
    <tile_image width="512" height="512"/>
    <zoom_levels levels="10" min_scale="1000" max_scale="25000000">
    </zoom_levels>
 </cache_instance>',
'ELOCATION_MAP'
);
```

The parameters describing the MapViewer server are in the `<external_map_source>` element. Here are the parameters you need to provide:

- The URL of the MapViewer mapping servlet.
- If necessary, the URL and port of your web proxy server, as well as a timeout value.
- The name of the adapter class. `mcsadapter.MVAdapter` is the class that implements the MapViewer adapter.
- The name of the base map to use and the data source where this base map is defined. Note that those names belong to the remote MapViewer service.

Summary

In this chapter, you learned how to define maps, themes, and styles, as well as map caches. In the next chapter, you will learn how to build applications using those maps.

CHAPTER 13

Using Maps in Your Applications

In the preceding chapter, you saw the overall architecture of MapViewer and how to install and configure it. You also learned how to define the various elements that make up a map: styles, themes, and maps, as well as map caches. In this chapter, you will learn how to use maps in your applications using the many application programming interfaces available with MapViewer.

We begin with an overview of the available APIs and a comparison of their capabilities. We continue with a study of fundamental principles and mechanisms to interact with maps. We then proceed to the bulk of this chapter. We offer detailed descriptions of the available APIs—first the new Oracle Maps (Ajax-based interface), then the more classic Java interfaces, and finally the lowest-level interface such as direct XML exchanges and the administrative API (XML only) that allows your application to manage the MapViewer server.

We finally conclude the chapter with a brief overview of the Web Map Service (WMS) API, an international standard defined by the Open Geospatial Consortium (OGC) that allows you to publish maps for access by any WMS-capable tool.

Overview of MapViewer's APIs

As you saw in the preceding chapter, MapViewer is a server-side component—actually a series of servlets. Your application interacts with the server using a request/response mechanism. MapViewer provides you with a variety of methods (APIs) to perform those exchanges. The method you choose will have a major impact on the way you develop your application but also on the way your application will interact with its users. The available methods fall into two main categories, each offering a different approach than the way you interact with MapViewer.

The first approach is to use one of the "classic" APIs that MapViewer has offered since its first version. These APIs allow you to use MapViewer from almost any development environment and use any programming language using direct XML exchanges or via one of the client libraries for Java, Java Server Pages, or PL/SQL.

The second approach is to use the new JavaScript/Ajax interface called Oracle Maps. This allows you to build highly dynamic interfaces using the JavaScript language from your favorite browser. We will now cover both approaches in further detail.

XML, Java, JSPs, and PL/SQL

The lowest level of interaction is direct XML. Your application needs to be capable only of constructing XML requests, sending them to the server via HTTP, and then parsing MapViewer's response. Because it is so generic, this technique is available from any programming environment capable of sending HTTP requests and manipulating XML: Java, .NET, and C#, but also Perl, PHP, and Python.

If you develop in Java, then you can use MapViewer's Java API that isolates your program from the intricacies of XML generation and parsing or from handling HTTP. One additional variant allows you to use Java Server Pages with MapViewer's specific tags. Then you may want to use MapViewer from database-centric environments, in other words, from PL/SQL code executing in your database. This is possible with the PL/SQL API.

Regardless of the API you choose, the flow of operation for requesting a map using any of the "classic" interfaces is the same. Refer to Figure 13-1 for the components of MapViewer involved in processing a request:

1. The client application constructs a web service request to obtain a map. The request contains the name of the data source (database) to read, the information to include on the map, its format (GIF, PNG, or JPEG), its size in pixels, and the area covered by the map. The application can construct the XML request manually, or it can use a client API to generate it: Java, JSPs, or PL/SQL.
2. The client calls the MapViewer map-rendering servlet over HTTP, passing the XML request as a parameter. Again, this can be done manually or via a client API.
3. The MapViewer map-rendering servlet parses the request, reads the necessary map definitions from the database, selects from the spatial tables, and generates a map in GIF, PNG, or JPEG format. The map is written out as a file. Note that the server caches map definitions. The server can also optionally cache part or all of the spatial data it reads.
4. The server constructs an XML response that includes the URL to the generated image file and returns it to the client.
5. The client then parses the XML and extracts the map image URL, which it then forwards to the client browser. If the client uses the client Java API, it needs only to invoke the proper method to extract the URL. An alternative is for MapViewer to return the resulting map directly by streaming it to the client instead of returning an XML document. This is possible only when using the XML API directly. In this case, no image file is generated on the server.

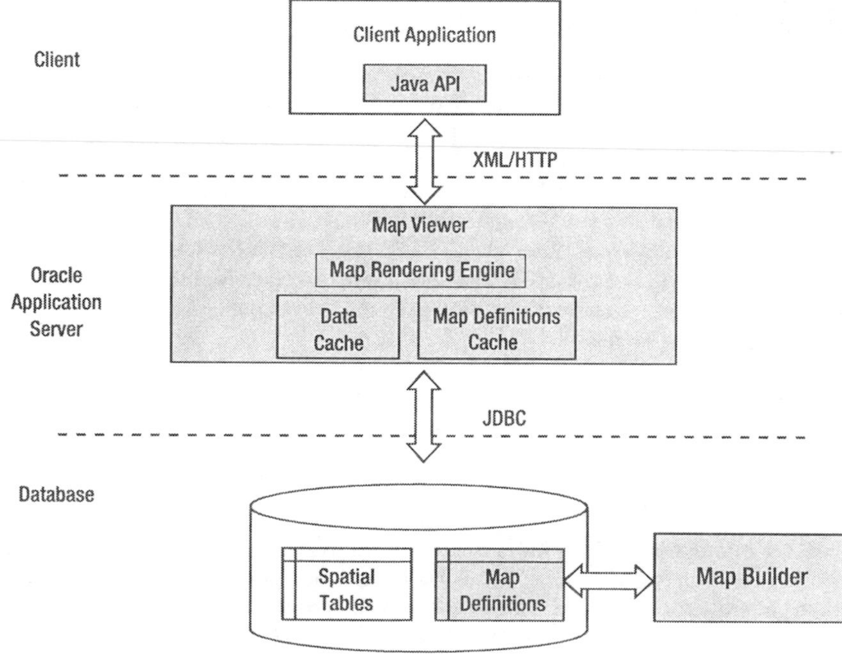

Figure 13-1. *Oracle MapViewer architecture*

Regardless of the API you use (XML, Java, JSPs, or PL/SQL), the MapViewer server will perform a complete map generation cycle. It will read all the data needed, read all map definitions, apply your styles, and generate a complete new map from scratch, even if no data changed and all you did was ask for a refresh of the map.

JavaScript and Ajax: Oracle Maps

The Oracle Maps technology offers a different approach and a different flow. Using Oracle Maps, the application no longer addresses the main MapViewer server (the *map-rendering engine*). Rather, it interacts with two servers: map cache and FOI that themselves invoke the map-rendering engine. Figure 13-2 illustrates the flow between the application and the servers.

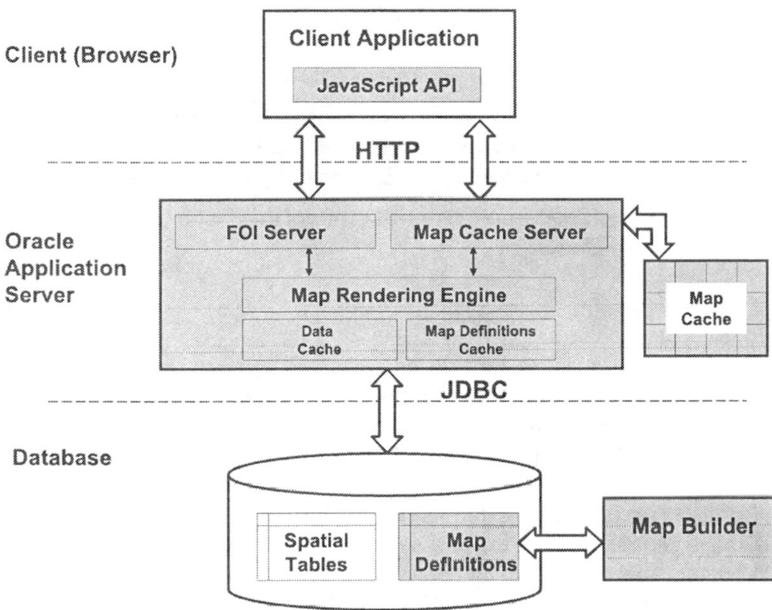

Figure 13-2. *Oracle Maps architecture*

The interactions between the client (your web browser) and MapViewer occur using the Ajax paradigm—Asynchronous JavaScript and XML—which exploits the ability for the web browser to send HTTP requests to a web server (and receive responses) in a fully asynchronous manner, transparently to the user. This simple yet powerful technique allows the development of highly dynamic applications that no longer rely on the classic browser cycle, which calls for a complete page refresh even if only some minor icon or value has changed. Using the Ajax paradigm, applications can now choose to update only those sections of the page that actually changed or to call a server as a result of some user interaction, such as mouse movements.[1] Contrary to the "classic" interfaces, you have no way to directly interact with the map cache server or the FOI server. Rather, the interaction between your application and MapViewer is via MapViewer's Ajax-based JavaScript mapping library from your browser. Many of those interactions happen automatically as a result of actions by the end user: panning, zooming, clicking dynamic features, and so on.

1. For more details about AJAX and browser-dependencies, refer to *Foundations of Ajax* by Ryan Asleson and Nathaniel T. Schutta (Apress, 2005).

The client application interacts with MapViewer as follows:

- With the map cache server:
    - The JavaScript client library determines the map tiles it needs to satisfy the current map requests at the required scale. It sends multiple requests to the map cache servlet, instructing it to return the desired tiles.
    - The map cache servlet then checks its cache. If it finds the tiles, it streams them back to the client. If one or more of the tiles are absent from the cache, it invokes the map-rendering servlet and instructs it to generate the map tiles, which it then saves in the cache before returning them to the requesting client.
- With the FOI server:
    - The JavaScript client sends a request to the FOI servlet, asking it to fetch the dynamic features (*features of interest*) to be displayed on the current map. The client can either specify the name of a predefined theme or provide an SQL `select` statement.
    - The FOI servlet then performs a spatial query to retrieve the features from the database tables. It also generates the graphical rendering of each spatial object it finds and returns the graphics together with any attributes to the requesting client.
- Finally, the JavaScript client assembles the map tiles and overlays them with the FOI objects before showing the result to the end user.

Choosing an API

The Ajax JavaScript mapping library handles automatically all exchanges between your application and the MapViewer servers (map cache and FOI). It also handles automatically all user interactions, such as zooming and panning, identifying and selecting features, and so on. This makes your application code lighter and easier to write. Your application, written in JavaScript, will run inside the user browser.

The other APIs (Java and XML) are typically used in server-side development environments, such as servlets or JSPs, although you can also use the Java API in a browser applet. The XML API can be used from any environment able to produce and parse XML and issue HTTP requests, such as .NET. The PL/SQL API can be used only from inside an Oracle database. In all those environments, your application will be responsible for handling all user interactions (zooming and panning) via your own custom code.

Another important difference between the Java/XML/PLSQL APIs and the JavaScript API lies with the presence of the map cache server. Since the server generates map tiles only at the zoom levels that you specified when defining the cache, your JavaScript application is therefore restricted to showing the maps only at those exact predefined zoom levels. Also, you can no longer change the rendering of base maps, since their constituent tiles are retained in the map cache.

On the contrary, the other APIs offer you the full flexibility to generate any map with any content at any scale. But that of course comes at the extra cost that MapViewer must always regenerate a full map for each request.

Table 13-1 summarizes some key differences between the various APIs.

Table 13-1. *Comparing the MapViewer APIs*

API	Application Environment	Scales	Maps Reused?	User Interactions
Java	Any Java environment: Servlets, JSPs, applets, thick clients	Any	Never	User-developed
XML	Any environment: Java, .NET, and so on	Any	Never	User-developed
PL/SQL	Database	Any	Never	User-developed
JavaScript	Any browser	Fixed	Always	Automatic

In the rest of this chapter, we will cover the various APIs in greater detail. We will start with the JavaScript API, then cover the Java and JSP APIs, and finally conclude with the lowest-level technique, which is XML. But before that, we will study the general principles for generating maps and interacting with them. You will find those principles in all interfaces: JavaScript as well as Java, XML, and PL/SQL APIs.

Anatomy of a Map Request

The exchanges between the client application and the MapViewer server are simple. The application sends mapping requests to MapViewer, and MapViewer sends back responses that include the resulting map, possibly with additional details, such as, for example, the actual geographical area covered by the map.

Whatever API you use to interact with MapViewer, a map request always contains three pieces of information: *what, where*, and *how*.

What: The Information That Should Appear on the Map

First, you must specify the spatial features you want to include on the map. You can specify them as one or more of the following elements. All are optional.

- *A predefined base map*: A base map is composed of a number of themes. Those themes will be visible depending on the scale at which the map is generated. Your application has no possibility to decide that certain themes, part of the base map, should be shown or not. It also has no control over the order in which the themes are displayed.
- *One or more predefined themes*: Using this approach, your application has more flexibility to build maps that exactly match your needs. In other words, it can list those exact themes to be used for each individual map. Your application can also change in which the themes are displayed.
- *One or more dynamic themes*: These are built using SQL statements generated by your application, possibly constructed from user input or selections. This is what gives your application the greatest degree of flexibility. It can decide not only what spatial tables to include on a map but also exactly what rows from those tables to display. For example, using this technique you can choose to show only those customers that have ordered more than a certain value over the last year and whose birthday is in the next week.
- *One or more dynamic features*: These are geometric shapes produced by your application. Those could be generated by your application. For example, a user may click a map and ask for all features within some distance of that point. Your application can then ask MapViewer to highlight the corresponding circle on the map.

Note that all those elements are actually optional! This means you are not required to define maps or themes in the database. You can actually build fully dynamic applications using only dynamic themes, where the content and structure of each map is fully controlled by your application and/or the users of your application.

Where: The Geographical Area to Be Covered by the Map

Then you need to specify the area covered by the map in a variety of ways:

- *As a rectangular box*: Specify the coordinates of the lower-left and upper-right corners of the box.
- *As a center and size*: Specify the coordinates of the center of the map, together with the size (height) of the map in ground units. For example, you can specify that the map should cover an area of 100 kilometers from top to bottom.
- *As a center and scale*: Specify the coordinates of the center of the map, together with the ratio scale at which the map should be built. For example, you can request a map at 1:50000 centered on a given location.
- *Using a bounding theme*: Specify that one of the themes (predefined or dynamic) should be used as a bounding theme, in other words, that the map should be centered on all the objects returned for that theme. For example, one of your themes may return the geometry corresponding to one of your sales regions. If you indicate that this should be your bounding theme, then the resulting map will be automatically centered and sized so that it shows the complete sales region.
- *Specifying no area at all*: If you do not specify any bounds, then MapViewer will automatically generate your map in such a way as to contain all the information you asked for. For example, if all the spatial objects on your map concern the state of California only, then the map will automatically be generated to show all of California only. The map will also be scaled to match the size of the spatial objects on your map. For example, a map that shows everything about Rhode Island will show more detail (be at a smaller scale) than a map that shows all of California.

■ Caution If you specify the map area using a box geometry, you must make sure to set the map size (width and height in pixels) to the same aspect ratio as this box. Failure to do so will result in distorted output, because MapViewer will "squeeze" or "expand" the map so that if fits fully in the size you asked.

How: The Format and Size of the Resulting Map

Finally, you need to specify the size of the map (in pixels) as well as its format (JPEG, PNG, and so on). You can also specify the styles to be used for rendering the various elements you want to appear on the map. For base maps, you have no choice: the rendering always happens based on the styles associated with the predefined themes on that map. For predefined themes, MapViewer will apply the style defined in the database, but you can override it with another (database-defined or dynamic) style. For dynamic themes or dynamic features, you must specify a style.

However, in all cases, you can specify your own dynamically constructed style. This gives you yet a larger degree of flexibility. Your application could even allow end users to dynamically choose styles to apply or even to build them (for example from a color palette).

Interacting with Maps

Some applications may be content with just producing static maps. This could be the case, for example, if all you want is to display a map on your home page showing the location of your stores. This may be sufficient for many applications, but your customers may want to see more details. For example, some of your stores may be close to each other, making them hard to distinguish on the map. Or some of your new stores may actually be outside the area covered by your map.

To answer those needs, you must provide your users with the ability to interact with your maps: zoom in and out, pan, select objects, and so on. Let's now review the techniques you can use to enable users to interact with maps. The JavaScript API provides all the facilities to interact with maps, without any specific programming from your part. The other APIs, however, require that you implement the controls yourself in your application.

Controlling the Level of Detail: Zoom In and Zoom Out

The most frequently used movement controls are zooming in and zooming out. *Zooming in* means you focus in on a smaller area in greater detail. When you *zoom out*, you see a larger area and less detail. From a mapping point of view, zooming in and out is easily performed by changing the scale of the current map.

The MapViewer server does not provide any specific method for zooming in or zooming out—this is all under the control of the client application. To zoom in by a chosen factor, the application just resubmits the same map request but specifies a size reduced (or enlarged) by the desired factor. MapViewer then generates a new map. Note that MapViewer will automatically adjust the amount of information that appears on the map; it includes only those themes that should be visible at the current scale, based on the `min_scale` and `max_scale` parameters of the theme definition.

A simple approach to implement zoom controls in applications is to use two buttons: one for zooming in (by a fixed factor) and one for zooming out (by the same factor). Whenever one of the buttons is clicked, the application simply computes a new map (by multiplying or dividing the current size or scale by the chosen factor) and requests a new map at that size or scale. More sophisticated techniques use a range of buttons, each associated with a fixed scale factor, a slider bar, or an edit box where you type in the desired factor or scale.

The Oracle Maps JavaScript API provides the end user with built-in zooming controls, and it also automatically handles all zoom requests, greatly simplifying your application code.

A common technique, called *marquee zoom*, is to let the user select a rectangular window on the map using a mouse *drag*. This approach requires some additional logic in the browser, typically via JavaScript. The Oracle Maps JavaScript library provides this facility.

Controlling the Area Shown on the Map: Pan and Recenter

The next most frequently used movement is a lateral pan. *Panning* is the action of shifting the map window so that another part of the map is shown.

As with zoom in and zoom out, the MapViewer server does not provide any specific method for panning—again, this is all under the control of the client application. The application simply needs to decide on a new center and resubmit the same map request with that new center position. The map content and size remain the same. MapViewer then generates a new map covering the new location.

A common approach to implement panning is to use a set of four (up, down, left, and right) or eight buttons (at the corners). Whenever one of the buttons is clicked, the application computes a new center by offsetting one or both coordinates (x and y) by a fixed factor (for example, half the current width or height of the map). It then submits a request for a new map, centered on the computed point.

Another common approach is to *recenter* the map on the spot where a user clicked. This technique requires that the application capture the coordinates of the click and use those coordinates to compute a new center. Note that this requires a conversion from image coordinates to the equivalent ground coordinates. *Image* coordinates are in pixels, with an origin at the upper-left corner of the image, whereas *ground* coordinates are in the units of the coordinate system of the map. MapViewer's Java API provides methods to perform this transformation.

A powerful and user-friendly technique is to use a mouse drag to move the map: click the map, hold, and move the map around. This approach requires some intelligence in the browser, typically via some custom JavaScript code. The Oracle Maps JavaScript API provides this naturally via its built-in controls, again greatly simplifying your applications code.

Note that scrollbars are rarely seen in mapping applications since they usually imply by their size the maximum area available. The earth is pretty big, so this can be confusing.

Selecting Features: Identify

The `identify` operation lets the user select a spatial object graphically, via a mouse click, and obtain additional information about that object, such as coordinates or attribute information not displayed on the map.

The common approach is for the application to capture the coordinates of the mouse click, convert them from image coordinates to ground coordinates, and then use this information to perform a spatial search.

Once again, the Oracle Maps JavaScript API provides all the facilities for selecting and identifying features without your application having to do anything special.

The other APIs (Java and XML) require that you write specific code to capture the coordinates of the mouse click and perform a spatial search. Note that selecting point or line objects poses additional challenges; clicking exactly on a point or on a line is almost impossible, so the application needs to convert the clicked point into a square region of a few pixels around the clicked point and use this region to perform the spatial search. MapViewer's Java API provides a number of methods to easily perform those spatial searches. The JavaScript API handles this automatically.

More sophisticated techniques let the user select multiple objects from a rectangular or circular window drawn on the map, or even from any arbitrary user-drawn polygon. Again, the JavaScript API provides facilities for doing this.

Choosing the Information to Appear on the Map: Layer Control

The application may let the user choose the amount of information that should appear on the maps by allowing the user to select the themes to include.

The common simple approach is to use a check box–like select list constructed from a list of available themes. The user picks from the list those themes that should appear on the map, and the application includes those themes on the subsequent map requests.

Applications may provide more sophisticated user interfaces and let the user also select the order in which the themes appear on the map or let the user dynamically associate a style to the themes.

Finally, the application may let the user construct new dynamic themes on the fly. The application can, for example, construct SQL statements based on user input and add them to the map as dynamic themes.

Oracle Maps: The JavaScript API

The main component of Oracle Maps is the Ajax-based JavaScript mapping client. This library provides all the functions for browsing and interacting with maps, zooming, panning, identifying, selecting, and so on, via a flexible JavaScript API. It allows you to develop applications that will run in your web browser and interact with a MapViewer server.

The JavaScript API is distributed as a JS (JavaScript source) file located in your MapViewer installation at `$OC4J_HOME/j2ee/home/applications/mapviewer/web/fsmc/jslib/oraclemaps.js`. All you need is to incorporate it into your web page via a `<script>` tag.

■ **Note** The `oraclemaps.js` JavaScript library is distributed in a compressed format. This makes the code of the library hard to read, but it reduces significantly the size of the library so that browsers will load it quickly.

We will cover the main features of the JavaScript API. For the fine details on the API, refer to the Javadoc documentation of the API. This documentation is available online in your MapViewer installation at `$OC4J_HOME/j2ee/home/applications/mapviewer/web/fsmc/apidoc`, and you can access it directly at `http://127.0.0.1:8888/mapviewer/fsmc/apidoc` as well as from a direct link from your MapViewer home page.

■ **Tip** MapViewer comes with a well-written tutorial for Oracle Maps. You will find a link to the tutorial from your MapViewer home page, or you can access it directly from `http://127.0.0.1:8888/mapviewer/fsmc/tutorial/index.html`. The tutorial takes you to a progressive set of examples; each example illustrates one aspect of the API. To run those examples, you must first have uploaded the example data downloadable from Oracle's OTN site.

The other major components of Oracle Maps run in the MapViewer server: the map cache and the FOI servers. We will discuss them later in this chapter—mostly you will learn how to create, monitor, and manage your map caches.

Displaying a Map

Incorporating a map in your application is simple and is illustrated in Listing 13-1.

Listing 13-1. *Displaying a Map Using the JavaScript API*

```
<!DOCTYPE html PUBLIC "-//W3C//DTD HTML 4.01 Transitional//EN">
<html>
<head>
<meta http-equiv="Content-Type" content="text/html; charset=UTF-8">
<title> Simple Free-Scrolling Map</title>
<script language="JavaScript" src="/mapviewer/fsmc/jslib/oraclemaps.js"></script>
<script language="JavaScript">
  function loadMainMap()
  {
    // Set up the connection to MapViewer
    var baseURL = "http://"+document.location.host+"/mapviewer";
    var mapview = new MVMapView(document.getElementById("map_div"), baseURL);

    // Add a base map
    mapview.addBaseMapLayer(new MVBaseMap("SPATIAL.US_DETAILED_MAP"));

    // Set up initial map center and zoom level
    var center  = MVSdoGeometry.createPoint(-122.5, 37.7, 8307);
    mapview.setCenter(center);
    mapview.setZoomLevel(9);
```

```
    // Display the map
    mapview.display();
  }
</script>

</head>
<body onload="loadMainMap()">
<div id="map_div"
   style="left:0px; top:0px; width:100%; height:100%; border:2px solid">
</div>
</body>
</html>
```

Calling this page in your browser should give you a map that looks like Figure 13-3.

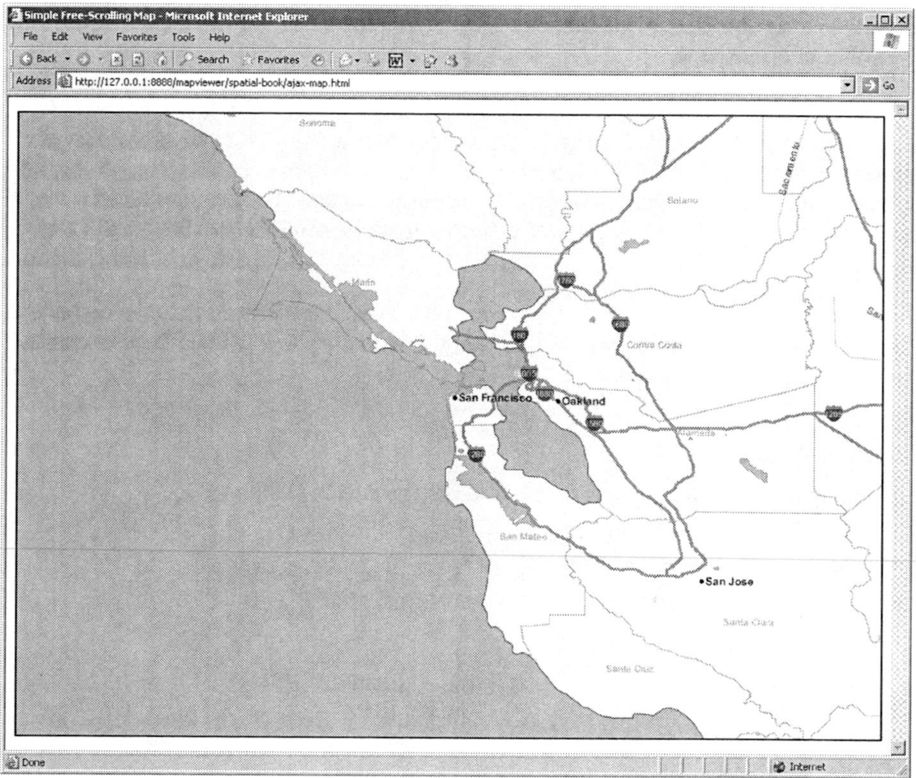

Figure 13-3. *A simple free-scrolling map*

Let's now dissect the code you had to write to get this map. The first step is to tell the browser to load the Oracle Maps JavaScript library:

```
<script language="Javascript" src="/mapviewer/fsmc/jslib/oraclemaps.js"></script>
```

The second step is to define a section in your HTML page that will be used to hold the map:

```
<div id="map_div"
   style="left:0px; top:0px; width:100%; height:100%; border:2px solid">
</div>
```

Then you can write the actual JavaScript code to produce the map. You initialize the connection to the MapViewer server by creating a `MVMapView` object. You need to specify the URL to be used for reaching the MapViewer server—which we assume here to be on the same server because that is where we loaded the HTML page from. We also link our `MVMapView` object to the HTML section (`map_div`) it will use for displaying the map.

```
var baseURL = "http://"+document.location.host+"/mapviewer";
var mapview = new MVMapView(document.getElementById("map_div"), baseURL);
```

You can now set up the `MVMapView` object. First, add a base map layer. Note that the name you specify is really that of a map cache built on a base map. Most of the time, you will have only one map cache for a given base map, so it is good practice to give the cache the same name as the base map it serves. We discuss map caches later in this chapter. The name of the map cache is prefixed with the name of the owner of the cache.

```
mapview.addBaseMapLayer(new MVBaseMap("SPATIAL.US_DETAILED_MAP"));
```

■ **Note** The map cache you specify must exist, but it can be empty, that is, contain no map tiles yet. It will be filled automatically.

Then set up the geographical point on which the initial map will be centered, as well as the zoom level at which the initial map will be displayed. The zoom level corresponds to one of the levels you defined for the map cache. Zoom levels start at 0 and can go to any depth you specified when you created the cache, for example, 9 for a 10-level cache. If you do not specify any zoom level, then the initial map will be at level 0, that is, the highest level, corresponding to the level with the least detail (= at the smallest scale). Zoom levels are discussed in detail with map caches.

```
var center  = MVSdoGeometry.createPoint(-122.5, 37.7, 8307);
mapview.setCenter(center);
mapview.setZoomLevel(9);
```

The final step in the JavaScript code is to tell the Oracle Maps client to display the map. The Oracle Maps client now contacts the map cache server, and it instructs it to build the necessary map and return it to the browser for displaying in the HTML section you told it to use. At that point, the control of your HTML page passes to the Oracle Maps client, which will handle all user interactions: zooming, panning, and so on.

```
mapview.display();
```

■ **Caution** The `mapview.display()` call never returns. Any code that follows it will never be executed.

There is, however, one more thing to do: make sure the JavaScript code you just wrote gets executed. It could be triggered via a URL link or by the user clicking a button. But most of the time, it will be automatically executed when the page gets loaded. This is done via the `onload` action on your HTML body:

```
<body onload="loadMainMap()">
```

Our HTML page now shows the map. You can interact with this map in only one way: you can click the map, hold the mouse button, and move the map around by dragging it.

Interacting with Maps: Zooming and Panning

Only allowing a user to move around a map (that is, panning) may be sufficient for your application but is probably not sufficient for the majority of applications. We are now going to look at how to provide more interactions. The main interaction users will want is the ability to zoom in and out of the map. For that we will add a navigation panel to our map view by simply adding the following line to the previous code:

```
mapview.addNavigationPanel();
```

The new map will look like Figure 13-4, with a navigation panel placed on the top-left side of the map.

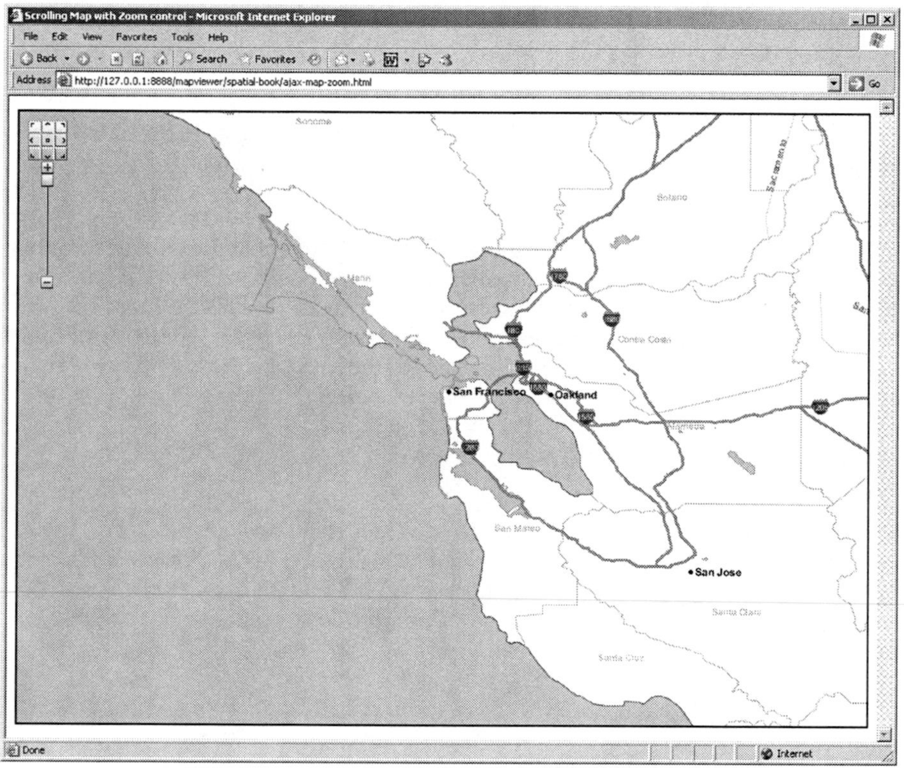

Figure 13-4. *A simple map with navigation panel*

Using the navigation panel, you can now zoom in and out by clicking the + and – buttons or by dragging the scroll bar up and down. The arrow buttons at the top will pan the map in the desired direction. Notice that zooming happens in steps: the + and – buttons increase or decrease the zoom level by one step. This is also the case when you zoom in and out using the scrollbar.

You can customize your navigation panel by passing parameters to the function call. The first parameter lets you choose where to place the panel on the map (`EAST` or `WEST`). The other three parameters let you decide which of the individual components of the panel you want: panning buttons, zooming bar, or zooming buttons (specify as `true` or `false`).

The button at the center of the panning arrow buttons is the "home" button. Clicking it will reset the map to a home position that you have previously defined by

```
mapview.setHomeMap(center, mapZoom);
```

■ **Caution** You must set the home position before adding the navigation panel; otherwise, the navigation will have no home button.

Another way of panning the map is via the arrow keys on your keyboard. This capability is enabled by default, but you can disable it by doing this:

```
mapview.enableKeyboardPanning(false);
```

Note that you could also disable map dragging entirely:

```
mapview.enableDragging(false);
```

Finally, double-clicking anywhere on the map will recenter the map at that point. You can change this to zoom in one step with the following:

```
mapview.setDoubleClickAction("zoomin");
```

Adding Map Decorations

You can place additional elements on the map, called *decorations*. Decorations are stationary: they do not move when a map is dragged, zoomed, or recentered. We start by looking at standard decorations: scale bar and copyright note.

A scale bar is handy to help users better understand the size of the map and of objects on the map. Add one like this:

```
mapview.addScaleBar();
```

Just like the navigation panel, you can control the location of your scale bar. By default, it will be located at the lower-left corner of the map, but you can choose to position it in any corner of the map by passing a number to the previous function: 1 for upper-right, 2 for lower-left, 3 for lower-right, and 4 for upper-left. You can also specify horizontal and vertical offsets from the sides of the corner you positioned the scale bar.

The scale bar shows distances in both metric (meters, kilometers) and imperial (feet, miles) units. It is dynamic: it always reflects the scale of the map at the current zoom level. The bar expands and contracts automatically so that the measures shown are always integers (such as 500 m).

Another element you may want to add on a map is a copyright note. This is often required by the provider of the spatial information you use for your base maps. Add such a note by doing this:

```
mapview.addCopyRightNote("Powered by Oracle Maps");
```

The copyright note is always placed in the lower-right corner of your map.

Adding Generic Decorations

Oracle Maps also provides a mechanism that allows you to add just about any custom decoration to your map. First you need to define your decoration. The following builds a clickable logo at the upper-left corner of your map:

```
homeURL = '<a href="http://www.oracle.com"><img src="/mapviewer/myicons/oracle_logo.gif">
</a>';
homeURLcontainer= new MVMapDecoration(homeURL, 0, 0);
```

Then add the decoration to your map:

```
mapview.addMapDecoration(homeURLcontainer);
```

You can further customize your decoration. For example, your application can generate its content dynamically, hide the decoration, and make it visible again. It can also handle mouse events against the decoration. Events are described later in this chapter.

To remove a decoration from the map, do the following:

```
mapview.removeMapDecoration(homeURLcontainer);
```

Creating an Overview Map

Sometimes you need to move rapidly to an area that is far away from the area currently shown on your map. Dragging the map to the new location can be cumbersome—and slow—if you are zoomed to a deep level of detail. For example, imagine you are looking at a street-level map of San Francisco and then want to move to Washington, D.C. Dragging your map all the way is too hard. The usual solution is either to zoom out far enough so that you can see both San Francisco and Washington on your map or to at least zoom out to a level where you can easily drag the map from one place to the other.

A better way is to use an "overview" map, that is, a small map showing less detail (is at lower zoom level) that you can drag directly. The main map will be dragged accordingly. For example, the overview map could show a small map of the entire United States, making panning very fast.

The overview map can be displayed anywhere in your web page. You just need to set up an HTML section (`<div>`) to host it. But you will use a smarter technique. You will add the overview map inside the main map as a decoration and make it collapsible—that is, the user will be able to hide it at will when he/she does not need it.

The first step in the process is to define the new map decoration, make it collapsible, and add it to the map:

```
ovcontainer = new MVMapDecoration(null,null,null,200,150) ;
ovcontainer.setCollapsible(true);
mapview.addMapDecoration(ovcontainer);
```

Notice that you do not specify any content for the decoration (the first argument is `null`). The following two arguments are `null` too. They are used to position the decoration on the map. The last two arguments define the size of the decoration in pixels.

Now you can define the overview map:

```
var over=new MVOverviewMap(ovcontainer.getContainerDiv(), 7);
```

The first argument—`ovcontainer.getContainerDiv()`—extracts the `<div>` section that holds the content of the decoration you just added to the map. This tells the overview map where it should build itself. The second argument—7—is the zoom difference between the main map and the overview map. Here it means that when you are zoomed all the way down, say at zoom level 9, the overview map will be at zoom level 2. Obviously, the overview map will stay at zoom level 0 when you zoom the main map out to level 6 or less.

All that is left now is to link the overview map to the main map view:

```
mapview.addOverviewMap(over)
```

Figure 13-5 shows the resulting map with all decorations and a collapsible overview map. Note that you also changed the code so that the navigation panel is now on the right side of the map.

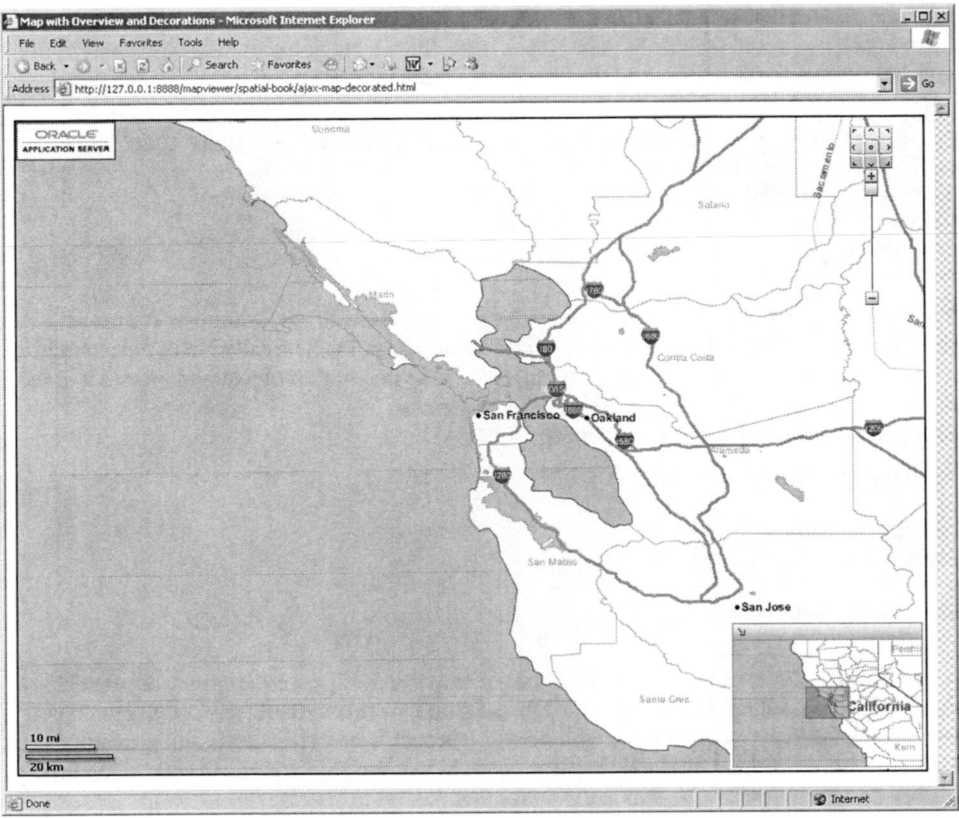

Figure 13-5. *A map with overview map and scale bar*

Notice that the area covered by the main map is shown as a rectangle in the overview map (you can also customize the look of this rectangle if you want). You can now drag this rectangle around or just drag the overview map proper. The main map and overview map will now move in concert as you move either of them.

Clicking the little arrow on the overview map will hide it completely.

Caution At the time of writing, you cannot control the positioning of collapsible decorations. They always go in the lower-right corner. This means they will hide the copyright notice. It also means you can have only one collapsible decoration on a map.

Rectangular (Marquee) Zooming

A common way to zoom on a map is to use the mouse to draw a rectangle that represents the area to zoom into. This technique is called *marquee zoom* and is not enabled by default. You can enable and disable it via simple method calls, but you must first add a mechanism to your map to let users switch between "normal" mode (where dragging the mouse drags the map) and "marquee" mode (where dragging the mouse draws a rectangle on the map).

Let's first construct a tool to control the marquee zoom. What you essentially need is a simple check box, which you could include in your HTML page. But we are going to take advantage of the map decorations mechanism to embed the check box on the map.

```
var toolBar =
  '<div style="width:50;height:40;background-color:white;border:2px solid black;">'+
  ' <b>Marquee Zoom: </b>'+
  '<input type="checkbox" onclick="toggleMarqueeZoom(this)" unchecked/>'
  '</div>';
md = new MVMapDecoration(toolBar, 0, 0) ;
mapview.addMapDecoration(md);
```

The first statement builds the HTML that produces a simple check box. Whenever the user checks or unchecks that box, the JavaScript function `toggleMarqueeZoom()` will be called with the check box passed as a parameter. The second statement builds the map decoration object and locates it at the top-left corner of the map. The last statement adds it to the map.

Here is the `toggleMarqueeZoom()` function:

```
function toggleMarqueeZoom(checkBox)
{
  if(checkBox.checked)
    mapview.startMarqueeZoom("continuous");
  else
    mapview.stopMarqueeZoom() ;
}
```

As you can see, all the function does is to start or stop the marquee zoom mode depending on the setting of the controlling check box. Note, however, that for this to work, the `MVMapView` object (`mapview`) must be defined as a global variable so that it is visible in all functions and procedures.

To use marquee zooming, the user now just needs to tick the zoom box, and then using the mouse, click and drag a rectangle. Notice the parameter passed to `startMarqueeZoom()`. This can take one of the following values:

- `continuous`: In this mode, the user can use the marquee zoom tool to zoom the map by rectangle drawing repeatedly. After each rectangle drawing and zooming, the user can immediately start drawing another rectangle and zooming the map by clicking and dragging the mouse. The marquee zoom tool stays active until `stopMarqueeZoom()` is invoked.
- `one_time`: In this mode, the user can use the marquee zoom tool only once. After zooming the map by rectangle drawing for the first time, the marquee zoom tool becomes inactive, and the user is no longer able to draw rectangle and zoom the map unless this method is invoked once again.
- `prompt`: In this mode, the user can use the marquee zoom tool to zoom the map by rectangle drawing repeatedly. After each rectangle drawing, the user needs to click the rectangle to zoom the map. If the user clicks the other part of the map, the rectangle disappears, and the map will not be zoomed. The marquee zoom tool stays active until `stopMarqueeZoom()` is invoked.

Figure 13-6 shows a map with the marquee zoom control and a zoom window.

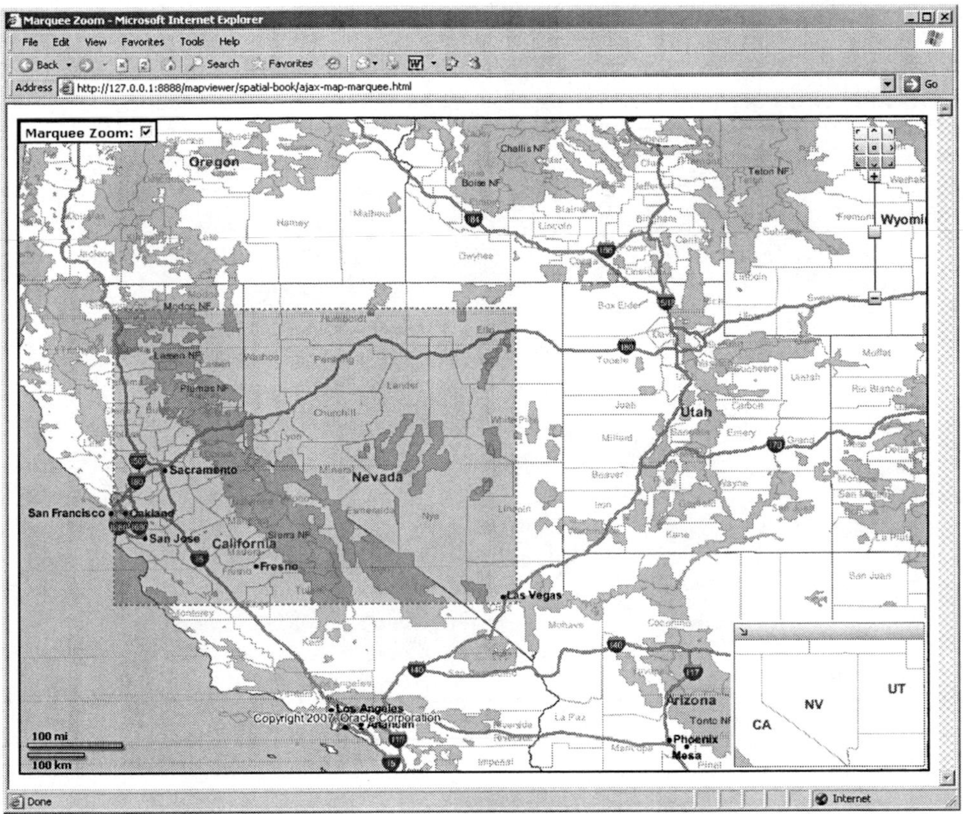

Figure 13-6. *A map with marquee zoom*

Adding Dynamic Information: Theme-Based FOIs

The maps we have defined so far are all static. To build actual applications, you need to add the business information to those maps: customers, pipes, sales regions, trucks, and so on. In Oracle Maps parlance, those are called *features of interest* (FOIs), and they originate from database tables. They are served by MapViewer using its FOI server.

Adding our customers to the map view is simply done like this:

```
customers = new MVThemeBasedFOI('customers','SPATIAL.CUSTOMERS');
mapview.addThemeBasedFOI(customers);
```

The first parameter passed to the `MVThemeBasedFOI` constructor is the name you choose to give to the theme in your map view. The second parameter (`'SPATIAL.CUSTOMERS'`) is the name of a theme defined in the database, prefixed with the owner of the theme.

FOI themes are always produced from information stored in the database. They are also automatically refreshed as you zoom or pan the map. When the mouse moves over one of the FOI objects, the label of the objects is displayed. When you click one, you see an information window. Figure 13-7 shows a map that includes multiple themes: customers, branches, and competitors, as well as an information window.

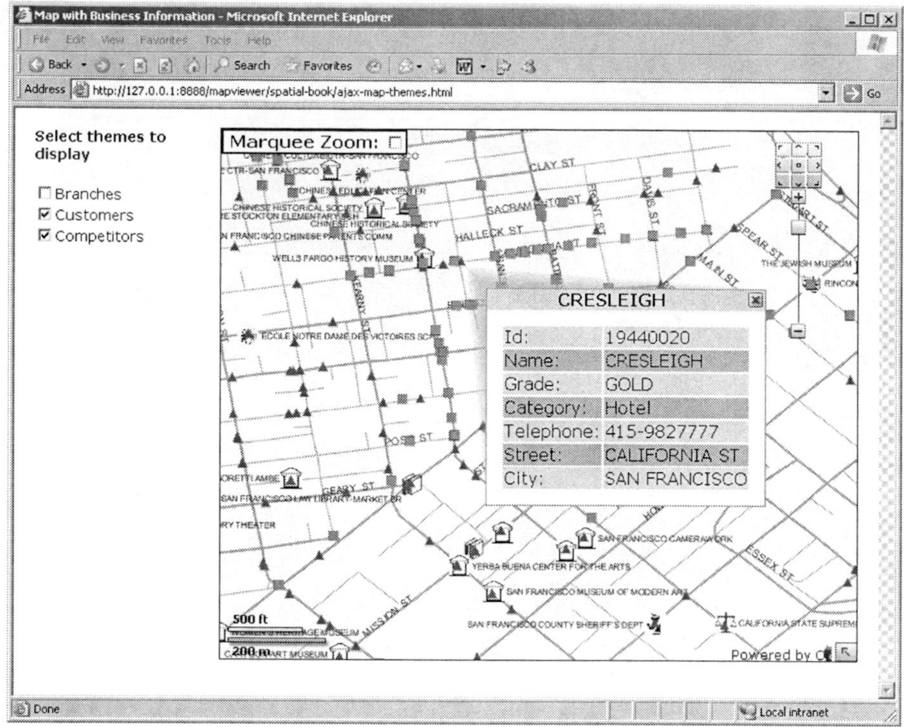

Figure 13-7. *A map with FOI themes*

The application in Figure 13-7 also includes check boxes that enable the user to choose whether the themes should be included on the map. The check boxes are defined like this:

```
<dl>
  <dt><input type="checkbox" value="branches"
    onclick="toggleTheme(this)" unchecked/>Branches
  <dt><input type="checkbox" value="customers"
    onclick="toggleTheme(this)" unchecked/>Customers
  <dt><input type="checkbox" value="competitors"
    onclick="toggleTheme(this)" unchecked/>Competitors
</dl>
```

Here is the `toggleTheme()` function that will turn a theme on or off to make it visible or hide it:

```
function toggleTheme(checkBox)
{
  theme = mapview.getThemeBasedFOI (checkBox.value);
  if(checkBox.checked)
    theme.setVisible(true);
  else
    theme.setVisible(false);
}
```

You have a number of options to control the way an FOI theme is displayed. Those options are controlled using methods of the `MVThemeBasedFOI` object for a theme. Here are the main ones:

- `enableInfoTip()` enables the display of the FOI label (that is, the content of the column you specified as the label column when defining the theme. By default info tips are always enabled.
- `enableInfoWindow()` enables the display of an information window when you click an FOI object. The information window will list the name and values of all the "information columns" specified when defining the theme). By default info windows are always enabled. The method `enableInfoWindowForMouseOver()` allows you to have the information windows pop up automatically on mouseover. Other methods allow you to customize the information windows.
- `setAutoRefresh()` indicates that the FOIs on a map should be refreshed automatically as you refresh the map by panning and zooming. This is also the default.
- `refresh()` allows you to manually control when to refresh FOIs, such as when using a Refresh button.
- `setVisible()` allows you to make FOIs objects in a theme visible or not. This switching happens in the browser; it does not trigger any refresh from the database.
- `setBoundingTheme()` instructs MapViewer to use this theme as a bounding theme, in other words, center and zoom the map so that it shows all the objects in this theme.

FOIs are represented in the browser as JavaScript objects. Having a large number of FOIs in your browser can slow it down significantly in addition to making maps very cluttered. The `MVThemeBasedFOI()` object allows you to control the zoom levels at which FOIs are shown:

- `setMinVisibleZoomLevel()`: Starting from this zoom level, FOIs are shown on the map.
- `setMaxWholeImageLevel()`: Up to (and including) this zoom level, FOIs are shown, but only as images.
- `setMinClickableZoomLevel()`: Starting from this zoom level, FOIs are active; you get an info window when you click them and an info tip when you mouse over them.
- `setMaxVisibleZoomLevel()`: Above this level, FOI are no longer shown.

Figure 13-8 illustrates the relationships between those various levels.

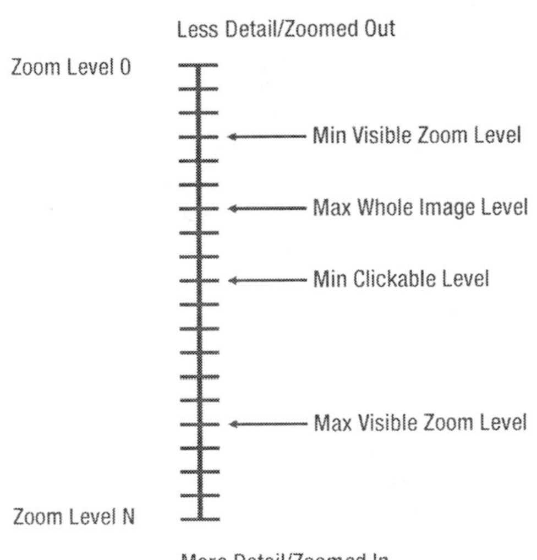

Figure 13-8. *Zoom levels and FOI visibility*

You should set those levels in such a way that your FOIs are displayed only at the zoom level that fits the density of your data and meets the needs of your application. A good rule is to set the zoom levels so that a map will show at most 200 FOIs.

When MapViewer fetches FOIs from the database, it actually prefetches more than the number shown on the map. This is to limit the number of database fetches when panning or zooming to adjust the map window. The following method allows you to control how many more FOIs MapViewer will fetch from the database:

- `setQueryWindowMultiplier(multiplier)`

This method sets the size multiplier of the query window used to query the FOI layer. This multiplier is applied to both the x- and y-dimensions of the map window. The default multiplier is 2, which means MapViewer will query a window that is four times larger than the actual map window. To disable this prefetching of additional FOIs, just set the multiplier to 1.

Templated Themes

A templated theme is one whose SQL expression contains references to bind variables, with the actual values being provided at run time. For example, a theme on the `CUSTOMERS` table could have an SQL expression `CUSTOMER_GRADE = :1`, allowing the application to choose the kind of customers to show at runtime. The following will select only the `GOLD` customers for inclusion on our map:

```
customers = new MVThemeBasedFOI('customers','SPATIAL.CUSTOMERS_GRADE');
customers.setQueryParameters ("GOLD");
mapview.addThemeBasedFOI(customers);
```

Highlighted Themes

A common need in mapping applications is to highlight features that are located in a specific area. To do this, apply a geometry to the theme using the `setFilteringGeom()` method, and then instruct the theme to show only those features that are inside the geometry you passed, using the `setHighlightOnly()` method. You can optionally change the rendering style of the selected features.

The following shows how to display only those customers whose location is in a region whose geometry is contained in `regionGeom`, which is an `MVSdoGeometry` object:

```
customers.setHighlightOnly(true);
customers.setFilteringGeom(regionGeom);
customers.setRenderingStyle("M.CYAN PIN");
```

The geometry used for highlighting could come from any source. Later in this section, you will learn how to use manually drawn shapes (circles, rectangles, or any polygon) to generate geometries. Still later, you will learn how to select individual features and use their geometries.

Dynamic JDBC Themes

The ultimate degree of flexibility is for your application to generate a theme based on a `SELECT` statement generated fully dynamically. The following example adds all `GOLD` customers that are located less than 100 meters from any of the branches:

```
SqlSelect =
  "select c.id, c.name, c.phone_number, c.location, b.id nearest_branch " +
  "from customers c, branches b "+
  "where c.customer_grade='GOLD' "+
  "and sdo_within_distance(c.location, b.location, 'distance=100 unit=m')='TRUE' ";
jdbcTheme =
```

```
  "<themes>"+
  " <theme name='selected_customers' >" +
  "   <jdbc_query asis='true' spatial_column='location' jdbc_srid='8307' " +
  "     render_style='M.GOLD_CUSTOMER' datasource='spatial'>" +
  SqlSelect +
  "   </jdbc_query>"+
  "  </theme>"+
  "</themes>";
selectedCustomers = new MVThemeBasedFOI('SELECTED_CUSTOMERS',jdbcTheme);
mapview.removeThemeBasedFOI(selectedCustomers);
mapview.addThemeBasedFOI(selectedCustomers);
```

The first statement builds the `SELECT` statement, possibly using input supplied by the application user. The second statement defines a theme over that statement (using the XML syntax for theme definitions that you will see later when studying the XML API). Finally, you create the `MVThemeBasedFOI` object and add it to the map view. Notice that before adding the new theme to the map view, you remove any previous version of that theme.

■ **Caution** Allowing JavaScript applications to dynamically generate `SELECT` statements is a potential security risk. Therefore, you must explicitly allow them by specifying the parameter `allow_jdbc_theme_based_foi="true"` in the data source definitions that should support this technique. By default, dynamic JDBC themes are not allowed.

Accessing FOI Data

When MapViewer reads FOIs from the database, it does not just read their geometries; it also reads a selected set of attributes—the "information columns" specified when defining the theme. Those are the attributes shown on the information window.

Your application can get access to the attributes of all the FOIs in a chosen theme that are displayed on the current map using the `getFOIData()` method. The FOI data entries are returned as an array, with each element specifying one FOI data entry. Each entry has the following attributes:

- `id`: A string that uniquely identifies the FOI data entry. By default, this will be the ROWID of the table row (but you can specify another column when defining the theme using MapBuilder).
- `name`: The name of the FOI data entry. This is the value of the label column for the theme, also used for the info tips.
- `gtype`: The geometry type of the FOI.
- `X`: The x coordinate of the FOI location.
- `Y`: The y coordinate of the FOI location.
- `width`: The width (in screen pixels) of the FOI image.
- `height`: The height (in screen pixels) of the FOI image.
- `attrs`: An array that specifies the FOI attributes (one value for each information column).
- `attrnames`: An array that specifies the names of the FOI attributes.

Adding Individual FOIs

Sometimes the features you want to add to your map do not come from any database table but are created by your application—possibly based on user input or based on some processing in your application. For this, you will use the `MVFOI` object.

FOI objects that you create this way have the same capabilities as the theme-based FOIs you have just seen; you will get an info tip on mouseover, you can click them and get an information window, you can turn them on and off, and you can use them for providing some animations—by changing their location. Use FOI objects, for example, to indicate the start and end points of a route calculation.

Here is how you could add a marker at the center of the map:

```
mapCenter = MVSdoGeometry.createPoint(mapCenterX, mapCenterY, mapSRID);
centerFOI = new MVFOI("MAP CENTER", mapCenter, "SPATIAL.M.CYAN PIN");
centerFOI.setWidth(40);
centerFOI.setHeight(60);
mapview.addFOI(centerFOI);
```

You're assuming that `mapCenterX` and `mapCenterY` contain the coordinates of the center of the map (and `mapSRID` is the coordinate system). You begin by creating an `MVSdoGeometry` object for this point.

Then you create the MVFOI object. You give it a unique identifier (here `MAP CENTER`) and then specify its geometry and the name of the style to be used.

The next two statements customize the FOI. Since the FOI is a point object, you need to specify the size (in pixels) of the marker for that point. Finally, you add the FOI to the map.

Here are the main methods you can use to customize your FOI:

- `setWidth()` and `setHeight()` let you specify the size of the marker for point objects.
- `setInfoTip()` lets you specify the text to be displayed as an info tip when you mouse over the FOI.
- `setInfoWindow()` allows you to specify the content of the information window (displayed when you click the FOI). Specify this as an HTML string, which means you can have any content in your information window, such as URLs, images, forms, and so on.
- `setHTMLElement()` allows you to associate some HTML content to the FOI. That content will be displayed on the map at the location of the FOI or at some optional offset.
- `updateGeometry()` use this to alter the geometry of the FOI. For points, this means moving the FOI to a new location.
- `reDraw()` forces the FOI to be redrawn on the map.
- `setVisible()` allows you to make the FOI object visible.
- `setTopFlag()` instructs MapViewer to always display this FOI at the "top" of the map, that is, over any other object. This applies only to line and polygon FOIs (point FOIs are always displayed last).

In addition, two convenient static methods allow you to build FOIs:

- `createHTMLFOI()` constructs an FOI built with an HTML string.
- `createMarkerFOI()` constructs an FOI whose marker image comes from a URL.

Controlling Styles

In all the previous examples, we used predefined rendering styles, that is, styles stored in the `USER_SDO_STYLES` table. Another possibility is for your application to define the styles it needs dynamically. First you need to create an appropriate style using one of the following JavaScript objects:

- MVStyleColor: Builds a color style.
- MVStyleMarker: Builds a marker style for point objects.
- MVXMLStyle: Allows you to build any style by specifying its encoding in the SVG notation used in the USER_SDO_STYLES table.

Other objects allow you to do build advanced styles for thematic mapping:

- MVBarChartStyle: Builds a bar chart style.
- MVBucketStyle: Builds a generic thematic style.
- MVPieChartStyle: Builds a pie chart style.

Once the style is defined, you can use it for rendering any of your themes. The following illustrates how to define a new marker style and apply it to one of your themes.

```
goldCustomerStyle = new MVStyleMarker ("M.GOLD_CUSTOMER", "vector");
goldCustomerStyle.setVectorShape("c:50");
goldCustomerStyle.setSize(10, 10);
goldCustomerStyle.setFillColor("ff0000");
goldCustomerStyle.setStrokeColor("000000");
goldCustomerStyle.setStrokeWidth("1.5");
```

The first argument to all style objects is the name for that style. Each kind of style objects has specific methods that allow you to define various aspects. In the previous example, we specify the shape of the marker (here a circle), the size of the marker (10 by 10 pixels), the color of the inside of the marker, and the contour (the stroke) of the marker.

To use the style for a theme, first add it to the theme, and then indicate that it should be used for rendering the features in this theme. The following shows how to use the new style for rendering the dynamic JDBC theme selected_customers:

```
selectedCustomers.addStyle(goldCustomerStyle);
selectedCustomers.setRenderingStyle("M.GOLD_CUSTOMER");
```

Capturing User Input: Tools and Selectors

Three tools allow you to capture geometric shapes; use them to draw shapes on the map and capture those shapes in your application. You can draw a circle, a rectangle, or any polygon shape using one of the available classes:

- MVCircleTool allows you to draw a circle of any size by clicking a point and dragging the mouse.
- MVRectangleTool allows you to draw a rectangle by clicking and dragging.
- MVRedlineTool allows you to build any polygon shape by clicking a series of points.

Figure 13-9 shows an application that allows you to select objects (customers, branches, or competitors) that are in an area you draw on the map.

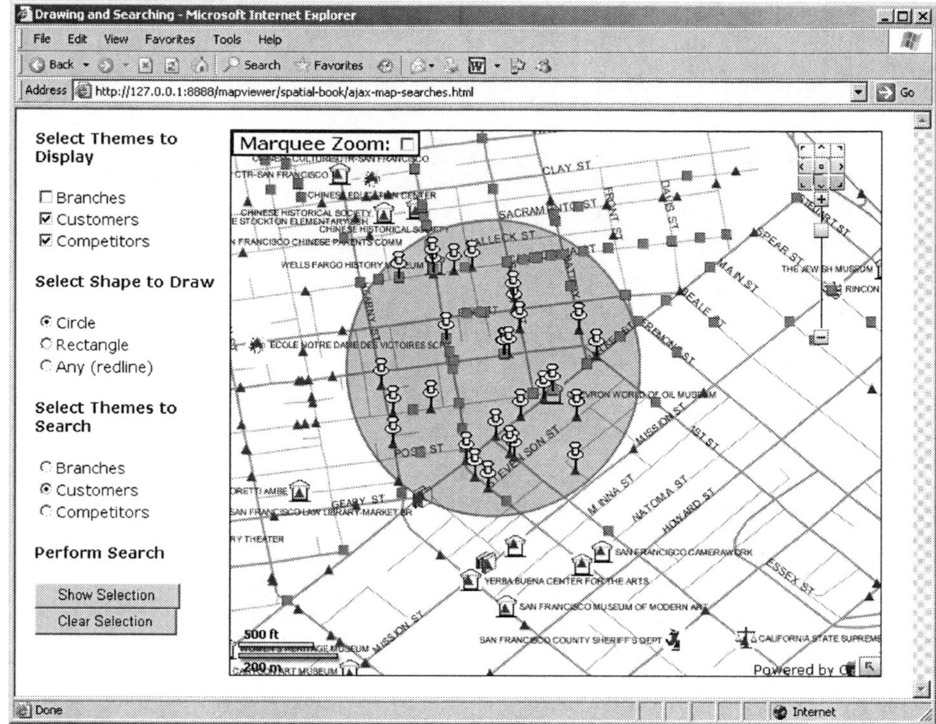

Figure 13-9. *Drawing a shape and selecting objects*

The following sections cover the steps you need to follow in order to use any of those tools.

Create the Tool

First, you need to create the tool. Specifically, create a new `MVCircleTool`, `MVRectangleTool`, or `MVRedlineTool` object, and add the tool to the map view using the appropriate method, which is `addCircleTool()`, `addRectangleTool()`, or `addRedlineTool()`. Here is an example of creating a new redlining tool:

```
redlineTool = new MVRedlineTool("SPATIAL.DRAWING_LINE","SPATIAL.DRAWING_FILL" );
```

The constructor of the tool takes two arguments. They are both names of styles, prefixed with the name of the data source where they are defined. The first style is a *line* style. It will be used to render the shape of the polygon as you draw it. The second style is a *color* style. The inside of the final polygon will be rendered using this style. Here is how to create a circle and a rectangle tool. Note that those tools do not allow you to specify a color style for filling the resulting shape:

```
circleTool = new MVCircleTool("SPATIAL.DRAWING_LINE")
rectangleTool = new MVRectangleTool("SPATIAL.DRAWING_FILL");
```

Then you can add the tools to the map view. Here is how to add the redline tool just created:

```
mapview.addRedLineTool(redlineTool);
```

Activate the Tool

You can now activate the tool by calling its `init()` method:

```
redlineTool.init();
```

The application user can now draw the desired shape by clicking a series of points.

For a circle, the user clicks the map to place the center of the circle and then drags the mouse to the desired size. For a rectangle, the user will click the upper-left corner and then drag the mouse to the lower-right corner.

If necessary, your application can determine the state of the drawing (not started, in progress, completed) by calling the `getStatus()` method of the drawing tool.

■ Note For drawing a polygon (using the redline tool), the user does not need to close the polygon, that is, does not need to click the starting point. The polygon will be closed automatically using the `generateArea()` method.

Extract the Captured Shape

Once the user has finished drawing the shape, you can capture that shape in your application. For a redline tool, you need to first generate the polygon from the points clicked:

```
redlineTool.generateArea();
```

This has the effect of transforming the suite of points clicked into a polygon. Then you can extract the geometry of that polygon (as an `MVSdoGeometry` object):

```
redlineGeom = redlineTool.getPolygon();
```

For a circle or polygon tool, there is no need to generate the area first. Call directly the appropriate method:

```
circleGeom = circleTool.getCircle();
rectangleGeom = rectangleTool.getRectangle();
```

The resulting shape is actually processed by MapViewer as an individual FOI. You can extract that FOI and customize it just like any other FOI. For example, here is how you can fill the interior of a circle to your liking:

```
circleFOI = circleTool.getCircleFOI();
circleFOI.setRenderingStyle("SPATIAL.DRAWING_AREA");
circleFOI.reDraw();
```

You can also extract various pieces of information from the shape just drawn. Table 13-2 summarizes the information you can extract.

Table 13-2. *Extracting Information About the Drawn Shape*

Shape Type	Method	Information Returned
Circle	`getRadius()`	The radius of the circle. You can specify the unit in which the radius should be expressed.
Circle	`getCircle()`	A geometric point (`MVSdoGeometry`) representing the center point of the circle.
Rectangle	`getHeight()`	The height of the rectangle in your chosen unit.
Rectangle	`getWidth()`	The width of the rectangle in your chosen unit.

Use the Shape

The most common use of the returned shape is to highlight spatial features related to that shape, such as all customers inside the redline polygon just drawn. Just use a highlighted theme. The following example adds a new theme, `selected_customers`, that highlights those customers who are in the area built using the drawing tool—here the polygon selected by redlining.

```
selectedCustomers = new MVThemeBasedFOI('selected_customers', 'SPATIAL.CUSTOMERS');
selectedCustomers.setHighlightOnly(true);
selectedCustomers.setFilteringGeom(redlineGeom);
selectedCustomers.setRenderingStyle("M.CYAN PIN");
mapview.addThemeBasedFOI(selectedCustomers);
```

Clear the Shape

Finally, once you are done using the shape, remove it from the map by calling its `clear()` method:

```
redlineTool.clear();
```

Responding to Events

The JavaScript environment is fundamentally event-driven; it allows you to react on a variety of user actions, typically mouse clicks and moves, which enable you to build dynamic and responsive applications.

Most of the objects available in the MapViewer JavaScript library allow you to define events using the `addEventListener()` method. The method takes two arguments:

- The name of the event on which you want to act
- The name of the JavaScript function that will be called to handle the event

In the following sections, we will cover the major events available with each MapViewer object and show how you can use them. Note that some of your event handling functions will receive parameters specific to the event. You can handle events on various categories of mapping elements: the map view itself but also individual FOIs and even drawing tools.

Events on the Map View

Use events on the map view to be notified when the map is refocused, that is, zoomed or panned. You can also use mouse-click events to provide custom actions. For example, you could use a right mouse click to display some contextual menu.

- `mouse_click`, `mouse_right_click`, and `mouse_double_click`: The user clicked the map. Note that the default action of a double click is to recenter the map to the point clicked. No parameter is passed to your handling function; it should call the `getMouseLocation()` method of the map view to get the coordinates of the point the user clicked.
- `recenter`: The user recentered the map (via mouse dragging or via the navigation panel). Use this, for example, if you want your application to always show the coordinates of the current center point of the map. Use the `getCenter()` method to get the new center.
- `zoom_level_change` and `before_zoom_level_change`: Called after (or before) the map zoom level is changed. Two parameters are passed to the listener function when it is invoked. The first parameter specifies the map zoom level before the zoom level change, and the second parameter specifies the map zoom level after the zoom level change. Use this if you want to show the current zoom level of the map. You can also use this to switch to a different base map depending on the zoom level.

Events on Theme-Based FOI

Those events apply to individual features. Use the mouse click event to display your own customized information window. The mouseover events allow you to display customized pop-up windows. The refresh events allow you to be notified when the features currently shown on a map for a theme have changed, for example, as a result of a pan or zoom action. Use this event to automatically update other sections of your web page—such as, for example, a counter of features on the map or a list of those features.

- `mouse_click` and `mouse_right_click`: The user clicked any of the FOIs in that theme. Your handling function will receive the location of the mouse click (as an `MVSdoGeometry` object) and an FOI data object that contains all attributes of the FOI object (just like `MVThemeBasedFOI.getFOIData()` returns).
- `mouse_over` and `mouse_out`: The user moved the mouse on, or out of, one of the FOIs. Your handling function receives the same arguments as earlier.
- `before_refresh` and `after_refresh`: Called before or after the theme is refreshed, either as a result of a map move (drag, pan, zoom) if the theme is in "autorefresh" mode or after calling the `refresh()` method. Use this event if you want to show a list of currently displayed FOIs in a table of your HTML page, and have this list automatically update as you drag or zoom the map.

Events on Individual FOIs

Those events are identical to the events on theme-based FOIs, except they apply to one individual FOI only:

- `mouse_click` and `mouse_right_click`: The user clicked this FOI. Your handling function will receive the location of the mouse click (as an `MVSdoGeometry` object) and the FOI object.
- `mouse_over` and `mouse_out`: The user moved the mouse on, or out of, the FOI. Your handling function receives the same arguments as earlier.

Events on Drawing Tools

Events allow you to monitor the progress of the drawing in progress. The following events apply to the circle (`MVCircleTool`) and rectangle (`MVRectangleTool`) tools:

- `on_start` is called when the user starts drawing, that is, when the user clicks the screen before dragging the mouse.
- `on_drag` is called when the user drags the mouse to draw the circle or rectangle.
- `on_finish` is called when the user completes the drawing, that is, releases the mouse button. This event allows you to automatically use the resulting circle or rectangle, such as applying it as filtering geometry on a theme.

The redline tool (`MVRedlineTool`) has only one event:

- `new_shape_point` is called each time the user clicks a point.

Events on Map Decorations

You can also handle some mouse events on your map decorations:

- `mouse_click`: The user clicked the decoration.
- `mouse_over` and `mouse_out`: The user moved the mouse on, or out of, the decoration.

Using the Java API

The Java API to MapViewer is distributed as a JAR file located in your MapViewer installation (at `$OC4J_HOME/j2ee/home/applications/mapviewer/web/WEB-INF/lib/mvclient.jar`). It consists of a single class: `oracle.lbs.mapclient.MapViewer`. To use the API in your applications, make sure to include `mvclient.jar` in your classpath. This will already be the case when you use the API from Java applications (servlets or JSPs) that execute in the same OC4J instance that is running MapViewer.

The documentation (Javadoc) is available in your MapViewer installation as well, at `$OC4J_HOME/j2ee/home/applications/mapviewer/web/mapclient`, and you can access it directly at `http://127.0.0.1:8888/mapviewer/mapclient`. Please refer to the Javadoc for the precise syntax of the various methods.

We will cover only the main features of the API. We begin by covering simple map requests, and then we will examine various interactions: zooming and panning, theme and style control, and adding dynamic features and legends. We do not detail the full syntax and parameter lists of the methods. To get the details, refer to MapViewer's Javadoc or user guide.

Although you can use the Java API from any Java-capable development environments (such as stand-alone programs or applets), our discussion mostly focuses on Java Server Pages and servlets.

Map Requests

Let's first consider the construction and execution of a simple map request. The basic flow of operation when using the MapViewer bean is as follows:

1. Create a MapViewer object.
2. Set up request parameters in the MapViewer object (using various `set()` methods).
3. Send the request to the server (invoking the `run()` method).
4. Extract the results from the object (using `get()` methods).

Create a MapViewer Object

Your application needs to import the `oracle.lbs.mapclient.MapViewer` package and create a MapViewer object. Before you can use the object, you must pass it the URL of the MapViewer servlet, which establishes the connection with the MapViewer server. You can do this at the time you create the object, like this:

```
MapViewer mv = new MapViewer(MapViewerURL);
```

Alternatively, you can pass it later using the `setServiceURL` method, like this:

```
MapViewer mv = new MapViewer();
...
mv.setServiceURL(MapViewerURL);
```

The service URL has the form `http://<host>:<port>/mapviewer/omserver`. When you use the API from a JSP page or servlet and your JSP page or servlet runs in the same container as the MapViewer servlet, then you can construct the URL from the request parameters:

```
mapViewerURL = "http://"
  + request.getServerName()+":"
  + request.getServerPort()
  + request.getContextPath()
  + "/omserver";
```

Set Up the Map Request

The MapViewer class provides a number of "set" methods that let you control the parameters for a map request: data source, base map, and so on.

First, you define the general parameters for the map:

- `setDataSourceName()` sets the name of the data source to use.
- `setBaseMapName()` sets the name of the base map to display. This is optional.
- `setImageFormat()` selects the format of the image to produce. For servlets or JSP pages, this must be `FORMAT_GIF_URL`, `FORMAT_PNG_URL`, or `FORMAT_JPEG_URL`. For "thick" clients, you can also set this to `FORMAT_RAW_COMPRESSED`, which instructs MapViewer to return the image in `java.awt.Image` format.
- `setDeviceSize()` defines the size of the requested map in pixels (horizontal and vertical).
- `setMapRequestSRID()` sets the coordinate system in which the map will be produced.

Then you define the area to be covered by the map. You can do this in multiple ways. The first approach is to specify the exact rectangular area for the map.

- `setBox()` sets the box to query as the coordinates of the lower-left and upper-right corners.

The second approach is to define the center point of the map, together with the height of the map:

- `setCenter()` sets the center (x and y coordinates).
- `setSize()` sets the size of the map (height from top to bottom in ground units). The width of the map will be automatically computed to match the size you specified for the resulting map in pixels (`setDeviceSize()` method).
- `setCenterAndSize()` sets both center and size in one operation.

The third approach is to define the center point of the map, together with the desired scale for the map:

- `setCenter()` sets the center (x and y coordinates).
- `setScale()` sets the scale at which the map should be produced. The scale is a ratio scale. For example, specify 25000 to get a map at scale 1:25000.
- `setCenterAndScale()` sets both center and scale in one operation.

Finally, the last approach is to not specify any size at all:

- `setFullExtent()` requests a map to cover the full extent of all features to display. Note that the map could then also be limited in size by that of the bounding theme (if any).
- `setBoundingThemes()` specifies the names of the themes whose data will be used to determine the area covered by the map. The themes can be part of the base map, or they can be any static or dynamic theme added to the map (see later).

You can also specify some processing options:

- `setAntiAliasing()` is either `true` or `false` (the default).
- `setBackgroundColor()` should be used only if you want a background different from the default "ocean blue" color.

There are many other methods you can use to set or add legends, select the themes to display, add dynamic themes, add features, and so on, which we will examine in the following sections.

Note that the API does not verify the parameters when you set them. For example, if you specify an invalid data source, you will get an error only when you attempt to send the request to the MapViewer service. Also note that most "set" methods have a corresponding "get" method.

The following shows the basic steps of setting up a map request:

```
// Set up map request
mv.setDataSourceName(dataSource);                    // Data source
mv.setBaseMapName(baseMap);                          // Base map
mv.setMapTitle(" ");                                 // No title
mv.setImageFormat(MapViewer.FORMAT_PNG_URL);         // Map format
mv.setDeviceSize(
  new Dimension(mapWidth, mapHeight));               // Map size
mv.setCenterAndSize(cx, cy, mapSize);
```

Send the Request to the MapViewer Server

The main method for sending a request is `run()`. This method constructs the XML request from the properties currently set in the MapViewer object, sends it to the MapViewer service, reads the XML response, and parses the response. All failures are signaled via Java exceptions.

```
// Send map request
mv.run();
```

■ **Caution** The parameters you specified for a request are checked only when you send the map request. Only an invalid data source will cause an error to be returned to your application code as a Java exception. Other errors will not get reported. For example, if you specify an invalid base map, then the resulting map will not include that map and so may be returned as an empty blue image.

Extract Information from the Map Response

Once a request has completed, you can extract its results from the MapViewer object using "get" methods. Mostly, you will extract the URL of the generated image.

- `getGeneratedMapImageURL()` extracts the URL of the image generated by MapViewer on the server, provided you asked for an image in `FORMAT_PNG_URL`, `FORMAT_GIF_URL`, or `FORMAT_JPEG_URL`. This is the normal case for all servlets and JSP pages.
- `getGeneratedMapImage()` extracts the image in `java.awt.Image` format, provided you asked for an image in `FORMAT_RAW_COMPRESSED` format.
- `getMapMBR()` extracts the minimum bounding rectangle (MBR) of the generated map. The result is an array of `doubles` that contains the `xmin`, `ymin`, `xmax`, and `ymax` of the current map's MBR.
- `getMapResponseThemeNames()` extracts the names of those themes that actually appear on the resulting map. For example, if the area you zoomed on does not contain any of your customers, then the `CUSTOMER` theme will not be listed in the map response. This is useful for dynamically adjusting the legend so it shows only those themes that are visible at any point in time. Note that the list of themes also contains those themes that are defined in the base map.
- `getMapRequestString()` and `getMapResponseString()` return the XML string sent to the MapViewer and the XML response. This is mostly useful for debugging purposes.

Listing 13-2 shows how to extract information returned by the MapViewer server.

Listing 13-2. *Processing the Map Response*

```
// Get URL to generated Map
imgURL = mv.getGeneratedMapImageURL();

// Get the XML request sent to the server
String mapRequest = mv.getMapRequestString();

// Get the XML response received from the server
String mapResponse = mv.getMapResponseString();

// Get the names of rendered themes
String[] names = mv. GetMapResponseThemeNames();

// Get size and center of new map
double mapSize = mv.getRequestSize();
Point2D center = mv.getRequestCenter();
double cx = center.getX();
double cy = center.getY();

// Get the MBR of the map
double box[] = mv.getMapMBR();
double boxLLX = box[0];
double boxLLY = box[1];
double boxURX = box[2];
double boxURY = box[3];
```

Zooming and Panning

There are two techniques you can use for controlling the zooming and panning. The first approach is to compute a new map center and size based on user actions and request a new map using the `run()` method. This technique is good for "stateless" applications. The MapViewer object is rebuilt from scratch for each map request, and there is no need to save it in servlet session. This is illustrated in the Listing 13-3.

Listing 13-3. *Zooming and Panning*

```
if (userAction.equals("Get Map")) {
  // User clicked the 'Get Map' button and
  // chose a new datasource or map name,
  // or manually entered a new map center and size
  // Nothing to do: new settings already
  // extracted from request parameters
}

// User clicked one of the 'Zoom' buttons:
// Zoom in or out by a fixed factor (2x)
else if (userAction.equals("Zm In"))
  mapSize = mapSize/2;
else if (userAction.equals("Zm Out"))
  mapSize = mapSize*2;

// User clicked one of the 'Pan' buttons:
// shift map 50% in the desired direction.
else if (userAction.equals("Pan W."))
  cx = cx - mapSize/2;
```

```
else if (userAction.equals("Pan N."))
  cy = cy + mapSize/2;
else if (userAction.equals("Pan S."))
  cy = cy - mapSize/2;
else if (userAction.equals("Pan E."))
  cx = cx + mapSize/2;

// User clicked on the map. Get the coordinates of the clicked point
// convert to map coordinates, and use it as new map center
else if (userAction.equals("reCenter")) {
  imgCX = Integer.valueOf(request.getParameter("mapImage.x")).intValue();
  imgCY = Integer.valueOf(request.getParameter("mapImage.y")).intValue();
  cx = boxLLX+imgCX/mapWidth*(boxURX-boxLLX);
  cy = boxURY-imgCY/mapHeight*(boxURY-boxLLY);
}
```

The second technique is to use the run() method only when requesting a new map and then use the zoomIn(), zoomOut(), or pan() method for zooming or panning. This technique requires that the MapViewer object be retained between successive invocations of the JSP page or servlet. In other words, it must be saved in session context and restored on each execution.

Note that the parameters of those methods are always expressed in *device coordinates*—that is, they are in pixels on the map image (their origin is at the upper-left corner of the image). This means you can use the coordinates you receive from a click directly on the image.

You can use the zoomIn() method in several ways:

- zoomIn(double factor) zooms in by the chosen factor.
- zoomIn(int x, int y, double factor) recenters the map on the chosen point (in device coordinates) and zooms by the chosen factor. This combines a zoom and pan.
- zoomIn(int x1, int y1, int x2, int y2) zooms in on the specified device rectangle.

Here is how you can use the zoomOut() method:

- zoomOut(double factor) zooms out by the chosen factor.
- zoomOut(int x, int y, double factor) recenters the map on the chosen point (in device coordinates) and zooms out by the chosen factor.

Here is how you can use the pan() method:

- pan(int x, int y) recenters the map on the chosen point (in device coordinates).

Listing 13-4 illustrates the use of the zoomIn(), zoomOut(), and pan() methods.

Listing 13-4. *Using the* zoom() *and* pan() *Methods*

```
// Fetch saved MapViewer object from session (if any)
MapViewer mv = (MapViewer) session.getAttribute("mvhandle");
if (mv==null) {
  // No MapViewer object found - must create and initialize it
  mv = new MapViewer(MapViewerURL);
  session.setAttribute("mvhandle", mv);       // keep client handle in the session
}
```

```
if (userAction.equals("Get Map")) {
  // User clicked the 'Get Map' button and
  // choose a new datasource or map name,
  // or manually entered a new map center and size
  // Initialize the MapViewer object with the entered
  // information
  mv.setDataSourceName(dataSource);                    // Data source
  mv.setBaseMapName(baseMap);                          // Base map
  mv.setMapTitle("  ");                                // No title
  mv.setImageFormat(MapViewer.FORMAT_PNG_URL);         // Map format
  mv.setDeviceSize(new Dimension(mapWidth, mapHeight)); // Map size
  mv.setCenterAndSize(cx, cy, mapSize);
  // Send map request
  mv.run();
}

// User clicked one of the 'Zoom' buttons:
// Zoom in or out by a fixed factor (2x)
else if (userAction.equals("Zm In"))
  mv.zoomIn(2);
else if (userAction.equals("Zm Out"))
  mv.zoomOut(2);

// User clicked one of the 'Pan' buttons:
// shift map 50% in the desired direction.
else if (userAction.equals("Pan W."))
  mv.pan (0, mapHeight/2);
else if (userAction.equals("Pan N."))
  mv.pan (mapWidth/2, 0);
else if (userAction.equals("Pan S."))
  mv.pan (mapWidth/2, mapHeight);
else if (userAction.equals("Pan E."))
  mv.pan (mapWidth, mapHeight/2);

// User clicked on the map. Get the coordinates of the clicked point
// convert to map coordinates, and use it as new map center
else if (userAction.equals("reCenter")) {
  imgCX = Integer.valueOf(request.getParameter("mapImage.x")).intValue();
  imgCY = Integer.valueOf(request.getParameter("mapImage.y")).intValue();
  mv.pan (imgCX, imgCY);
}
```

Theme Control

The MapViewer bean gives you extensive control over the themes in a map. Themes are kept in an ordered list inside the map request. This ordering of themes is very important, because it determines the order in which the themes are rendered on the map; the first theme in the list gets rendered first, and then the others are rendered one after the other. The last theme listed gets rendered last.

The following methods add and delete themes:

- addPredefinedTheme() adds a predefined theme to the current map request. You can optionally specify the position at which the theme should be added in the list of existing themes. If you do not specify a position, then the theme is added at the end of the list of themes. The first theme in the list is number 0.
- addThemesFromBaseMap() lets you compose a map with only themes (in other words, without any base map). It adds to the current map request all themes defined for the specified base map. This is equivalent to finding out all the themes listed in the base map and then calling addPredefinedTheme() and setThemeScale() for each theme in the list. Note that this actually sends an "administrative" request to the MapViewer server to get the theme list. The themes are loaded in the order in which they appear in the base map, but you are able to change that order if you desire.
- addJDBCTheme() adds a JDBC theme for which you must supply a SQL query. There are two main variants of that method: one that uses a data source name to identify the database to connect to and one that needs explicit JDBC connection parameters (host, port, database, user name, and password). You can optionally specify the position at which the theme should be added in the list of existing themes. If you do not specify a position, then the theme is added at the end of the list of themes.
- deleteTheme() removes a theme from the current map request.

If the theme is parameterized, that is, if its definition includes references to bind variables, use the following method to supply values for those bind variables:

- setThemeBindingParameters() passes the values for bind parameters as an array of strings.

The following methods are for enabling and disabling themes (note that all themes are originally enabled):

- setThemeEnabled() enables or disables one specific theme.
- enableThemes() enables a list of themes.
- setAllThemesEnabled() enables or disables all themes in the map request.

These methods are for controlling the order of the themes:

- moveThemeDown() moves a specific theme down one position in the list of themes. The theme to move is identified by its sequence in the list of themes.
- moveThemeUp() moves a theme up one position in the list.

These methods are for controlling theme and label visibility:

- setThemeScale() sets the minimum and maximum scale values for displaying a theme. Note that this is not needed for themes added from a base map using the addThemesFromBaseMap() method; those themes have the scale values defined in the base map definition. Use setThemeScaleMode() to specify the mode in which you indicate the scale, as in MAPVIEWER_NATIVE (the default) or RATIO.
- setThemeRenderLabels() controls whether MapViewer labels the features in a theme.
- setLabelAlwaysOn() controls whether MapViewer labels all features in a theme even if two or more labels will overlap.
- setThemeTransparency () allows you to control the transparency of a theme. Specify as an *alpha* value between 0 and 1, where 0 means that the theme will be invisible (fully transparent) and 1 means that it will be fully opaque.

Use these methods to find information about themes:

- `hasThemes()` checks to see whether the current map request has any explicitly added themes. If the map request contains only a base map, then this method returns `FALSE`.
- `getThemeNames()` returns the list of all themes in the map request.
- `getEnabledThemes()` returns the list of all themes that are currently enabled in the map request.
- `getThemePosition()` gets the position of a theme in the list of themes in the map request.
- `getActiveTheme()` gets the name of the topmost theme (that is, the one at the end of the theme list).

See Figure 13-10 for an example of the output of the `SpatialViewer.jsp` page that lets you select the themes to display. The selection is done via a series of check boxes that is dynamically constructed from the list returned by the `getThemeNames()` method.

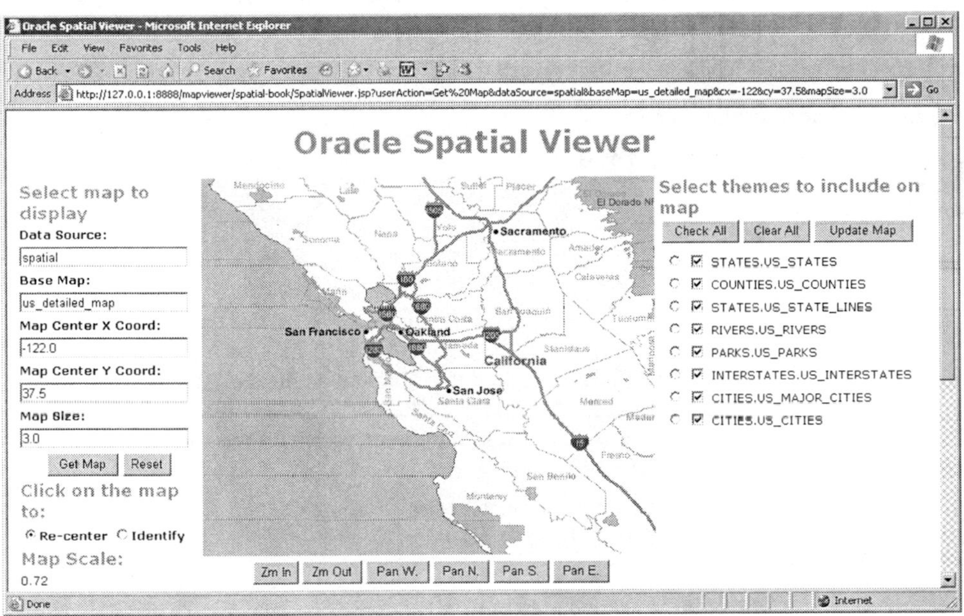

Figure 13-10. *Selecting the themes to display*

The initial list of themes is set when the MapViewer object is constructed:

```
mv.addThemesFromBaseMap(baseMap); // Themes from base map
mv.setAllThemesEnabled(true); // Enable all themes
```

Here is how the check-box list is constructed in the HTML code:

```
<table>
    <% String[] ts = mv.getThemeNames(); %>
    <% for(int i=0; i<ts.length; i++) {%>
    <tr><td>
      <input type="checkbox"
        name="checkedThemes"
        value="<%=ts[i]%>"
        <%=mv.getThemeEnabled(ts[i])?"checked":""%>
      >
      <%= ts[i] %>
    </td></tr>
  <%}%>
</table>
```

The result of selecting check boxes is then passed back to the JSP page. The following statement extracts the checked themes in an array of strings:

```
String[] checkedThemes = request.getParameterValues("checkedThemes");
```

Finally, enabling the themes on the map is done like this:

```
// Enable the themes selected by the user
if (checkedThemes != null)
  mv.enableThemes(checkedThemes);
else
  mv.setAllThemesEnabled(false);
```

Dynamic Themes

As just explained, you use the `addJDBCTheme()` method to add dynamic themes (that is, themes based on the results of JDBC queries).

The `SpatialViewer.jsp` page lets you enter a SQL statement, which it then adds as a theme called `SQL_QUERY`. Here is the code that achieves this:

```
// If necessary, run the SQL query entered by the user
if (sqlQuery != null && sqlQuery.length() > 0) {
  // Add a JDBC theme for the query
  mv.addJDBCTheme (
      dataSource,                   // dataSource
      "[SQL_QUERY]",                // Theme name
      sqlQuery.replace(';',' '),    // SQL Query (remove trailing semicolon if any)
      null,                         // Name of spatial column
      null,                         // srid
      "SQL_QUERY",                  // renderStyle
      null,                         // labelColumn
      null,                         // labelStyle
      true);                        // passThrough
}
```

Figure 13-11 shows this technique used to highlight Yosemite National Park on the map. Note that the JDBC theme appears as a regular theme in the map. You can therefore turn it "on" or "off" just like any other theme.

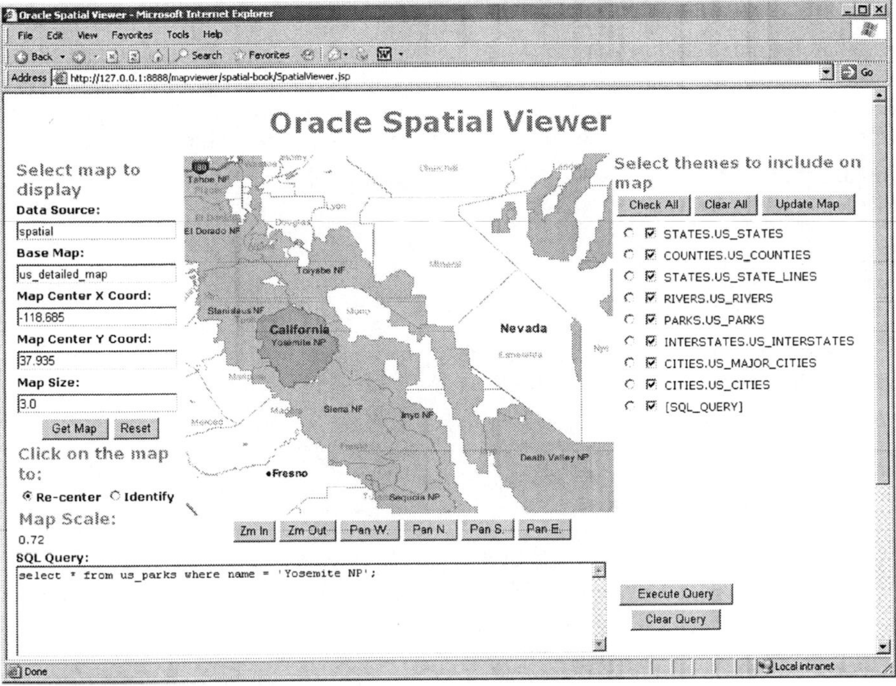

Figure 13-11. *Displaying the result of an SQL query*

WMS and WFS Themes

Two methods allow you to include information coming from an external web map server or web feature server:

- `addWMSMapTheme()` adds a WMS theme to the map. At the minimum, specify the URL of the web map server, together with the list of layers to include on the map and their styles. Additional parameters let you specify the projection you want the WMS to return the map in, the format of the image (PNG, JPEG, and so on), whether the background of the map should be transparent, and so on.
- `addWFSTheme()` adds a WFS theme to the map. Specify the URL of the WFS, the name of the feature class to query, the names of the feature attributes to fetch, and a query condition to apply. Specify also the name of the feature attributes to be used as geometry and label columns and the names of the MapViewer styles to use.

A WFS server returns geographic features, and MapViewer will do the rendering according to the styles you indicate. On the other hand, a WMS server returns map images. The rendering is done by the WMS, and the names of the styles requested by your application are known by the WMS, not by MapViewer.

Style Control

Styles are defined in the database, but you can also dynamically define new styles and add them to the map request.

To add a style to your request, first construct it using one of the StyleModel interfaces, and then add it to the request using the addStyle() method. This approach is illustrated here:

```
// Setup a color style model. Fill color is red, transparent, stroke is blue:
ColorStyleModel csm = new ColorStyleModel();
csm.setFillColor(new Color(255, 0, 0, 40));
csm.setStrokeColor(new Color(0, 0, 255, 100));
// Add the color to your map request
mv.addStyle ("SQL_QUERY", csm);
```

The other possible approach is to use one of the many specialized methods (add<Xxx>Style()) for defining and adding styles. The following adds the same color style as earlier:

```
// Add a color style. Fill color is red, transparent, stroke is blue:
mv.addColorStyle (
  "SQL_QUERY",                // Style name
  "blue",                     // Stroke color
  "red",                      // Fill color
  255,                        // Stroke opacity
  40);                        // Fill opacity
```

The following methods let you manage the dynamically created styles:

- listAllDynamicStyles() returns the names of all the dynamic styles you added to the current map request.
- deleteStyle() deletes the named style from the map request.
- removeAllDynamicStyles() deletes all dynamically added styles from the map request.

■ **Note** When you define a style with the same name as a permanent style, your definition overrides the permanent style for the execution of the current map request. This allows you to build applications that can adapt the styles based on user preferences. When you delete a dynamic style, MapViewer reverts to the permanent style definition.

Identification and Queries

Identification is the ability to select a spatial object graphically, via a mouse click, and obtain additional information about that object. The JSP file SpatialViewer.jsp illustrates how to do this. Figure 13-12 shows the result of selecting one county. Notice that the radio button for the US_COUNTIES theme is selected. Also, the radio button on the left ("Click on the map to:") is set to Identify. A blue pin is set on the map to indicate the point clicked, and information about the county is displayed under the map.

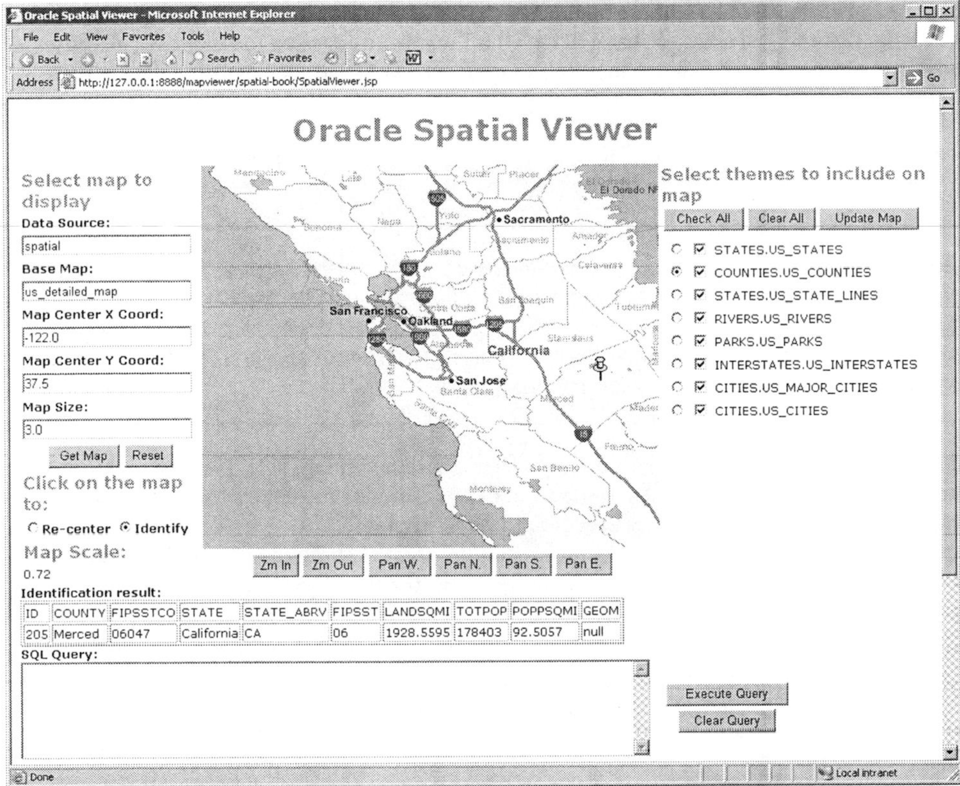

Figure 13-12. *Identifying spatial objects*

The main method to use is `identify()`. You just need to pass it the name of the table to query and the name of the spatial column, as well as the coordinates of the mouse click. Note that you can pass directly the image (pixel) coordinates—MapViewer will automatically convert them to ground coordinates.

The function also allows you to pass a rectangle as search criteria, instead of a point. This will be useful when you want to identify a point object; it allows you to enlarge the clicked area so that your query can return the proper point.

Other methods are available to select objects within various spatial shapes. They all select from a chosen *theme* (not a table) and can use indifferently image (pixel) or ground coordinates.

- `queryAtPoint()` selects features at a chosen point. Note that this works fine for polygons (areas) but not for points or lines, since it is impossible to guarantee that the mouse click falls exactly on the point or line.
- `queryWithinRadius()` selects all features that are completely inside a chosen radius from a point.
- `queryWithinRectangle()` selects all features that are completely inside a chosen rectangle (defined using the lower-left and upper-right corners).
- `queryWithinArea()` selects features that are inside a chosen polygon area.
- `queryNN()` selects the nearest features to a point.

A parameter common to all of these methods is the list of columns to select. This is passed as an array of strings (`String[]`). Passing a single string (*) is the same as passing the names of all columns.

Finally, you can use the following methods to perform any SQL query against a data source.

- `doQuery()` performs the SQL query you passed, as is.
- `doQueryInMapWindow()` performs the SQL query you passed but appends a spatial filter that limits the results to only those objects that are within the bounds of the current map window.

Caution The `doQuery()` method allows you to perform any `SELECT` statement against the data source—within the limits of the rights granted to the user defined for that data source in MapViewer's configuration. Nevertheless, this capability is a potential security risk. You can disable this risk by removing the possibility of performing nonmap requests from applications. See the "Configuring MapViewer" section in Chapter 12 for details. Disabling nonmap requests will disable all of the previous queries.

All methods return their results as an array of string arrays (`String[][]`). The first row of strings contains the names of the columns. Each subsequent row contains the values for each column in each matching row. This format is easy to output in an HTML table.

Let's examine how the example in Figure 13-12 is programmed. You construct the radio button for choosing the themes to select in much the same way as the theme selector you saw in an earlier example:

```
<table>
    <% String[] ts = mv.getThemeNames(); %>
    <% for(int i=0; i<ts.length; i++) {%>
    <tr><td>
    <input type="radio"
       name="identifyTheme"
       value="<%=ts[i]%>"
       <%=ts[i].equals(identifyTheme)?"checked":""%>
    >
    <%= ts[i] %>
    </td></tr>
  <%}%>
</table>
```

The result of checking the radio box is passed back to the JSP page. Here is how the name of the selected theme is extracted:

```
String identifyTheme = request.getParameter("identifyTheme");
```

The actual identification is performed as follows. You need to extract the coordinates of the mouse click:

```
imgCX = Integer.parseInt(request.getParameter("mapImage.x"));
imgCY = Integer.parseInt(request.getParameter("mapImage.y"));
```

Then you query the feature at that point:

```
String[] colsToSelect = new String[]{"*"};
String[][] featureInfo = mv.queryAtPoint (
    dataSource,             // Datasource
    identifyTheme,          // Theme name
    colsToSelect,           // Names of columns to select
    imgCX, imgCY,           // Mouse click
    null,                   // No extra conditions
    true);                  // Coords are in pixels
```

and you add a point at the place you clicked:

```
Point2D p = mv.getUserPoint(imgCX,imgCY);
mv.addPointFeature (p.getX(), p.getY(), 8307,"M.CYAN PIN", null, null, null);
```

Finally, you format the results as an HTML <table>:

```
<table border="1">
  <% for (int i=0; i<featureInfo.length; i++) {%>
    <tr>
    <% String[] row = featureInfo[i];
       for (int k=0; k<row.length; k++) {%>
        <td><%= row[k] %></td>
      <% } %>
    </tr>
  <% } %>
</table>
```

Dynamic Features

Some methods enable you to draw features on top of the map:

- addPointFeature() adds a point feature to the current map request.
- addLinearFeature() adds a line feature to the current map request.
- addPolygonFeature() adds a polygon feature to the current map request.
- getNumGeoFeatures() returns the number of dynamic features added to the current map request. You can also use more specific methods, such as getNumPointFeatures(), getNumLinearFeatures(), or getNumPolygonFeatures().
- removeAllPointFeatures() removes all the point features from the map request.
- removeAllLinearFeatures() removes all the line features from the map request.
- removeAllPolygonFeatures() removes all the polygon features from the map request.

The features are defined by a list of coordinates, a rendering style, and a label style. The style names refer to styles that must exist on the MapViewer server, either as permanent styles or as dynamic styles that you created previously. For point features, you can optionally specify the radius for a number of circles to be drawn around the point, as well as variable values, that can be used to build complex markers, based on an advanced style.

Legends

Once your map becomes complex and includes many different features, your users will need assistance in understanding the meaning of your many different symbols. For that, you will add a legend to your map. A legend essentially lists the styles used on your map, together with a short explanatory text. Figure 13-13 illustrates a map with a legend that explains the meaning of the various symbols used.

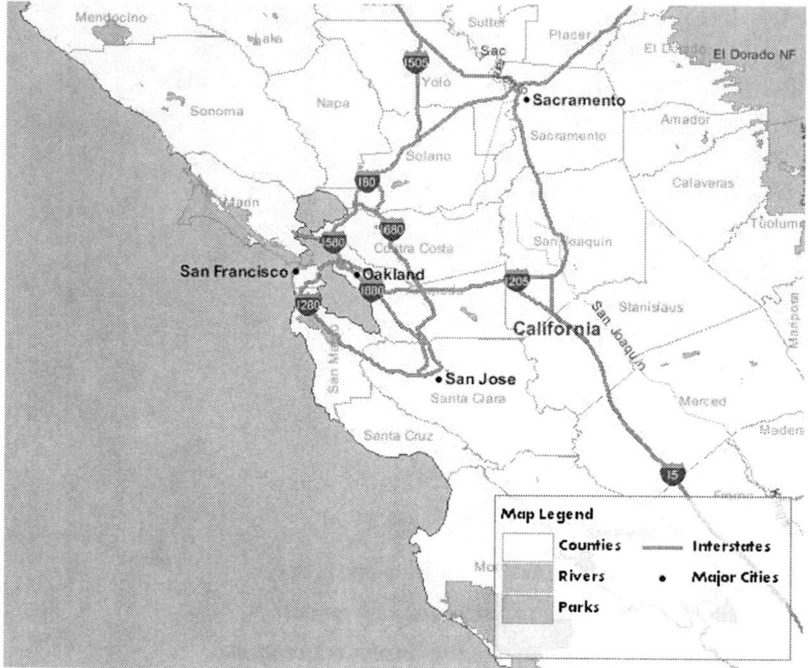

Figure 13-13. *Example of a legend*

The following methods let you define a legend:

- `setMapLegend()` sets the map legend. You need to define the elements that make up the legend as a Java `String` array.
- `getMapLegend()` gets the map legend.
- `deleteMapLegend()` deletes the legend.

Listing 13-5 explains how to generate the legend shown in Figure 13-13.

Listing 13-5. *Building a Legend*

```
String[][][] legend = new String[][][]
{
  {
    {"Map Legend",  null,                "true",  null, "false"},
    {"Counties",    "C.US MAP YELLOW",   "false", null, "false"},
    {"Rivers",      "C.RIVER",           "false", null, "false"},
    {"Parks",       "C.PARK FOREST",     "false", null, "false"}
  },
  {
    {"",            null,                "false", null, "true" },
    {"Interstates", "L.PH",              "false", null, "false"},
    {"Major Cities","M.CITY HALL 4",     "false", null, "false"}
  }
};

mv.setMapLegend(
```

```
  "white",        // Fill color
  "128",          // Fill opacity
  "red",          // Stroke color
  "medium",       // Legend size
  "SOUTH_EAST",   // Legend position
  legend          // Legend array
);
```

To define the legend, you need to fill a three-dimensional array of strings. The first dimension represents the columns in your legend; in our example, we place the legend on two columns. The second dimension represents the entries in each column. In our case, the first column has four entries, while the second one has only three entries.

Finally, the third dimension describes the content of each entry. Here you need to specify five items:

- The descriptive text to include for that entry
- The name of the style
- Whether this entry is a title (specify as `"true"` or `"false"`)
- Whether this entry is a tabulation (specify as `"true"` or `"false"`)
- Whether this entry is a separator (specify as `"true"` or `"false"`)

You can now call the `setMapLegend()` method and pass it the array you just built, together with additional parameters to set the color and transparency of the backdrop of the legend, the color of the line around the legend, the size (as `SMALL`, `MEDIUM`, or `LARGE`), and the location of the legend on the map (for example, `SOUTH_EAST` to position it in the lower-right corner).

■ **Note** You can also construct the legend definition in XML and pass that directly to the `setMapLegend()` method. We will cover the syntax of this XML later in the chapter when covering the XML API. Note that the `getMapLegend()` method actually returns the definition of your legend in this XML notation.

Map Decorations

The Java API provides you with a number of methods to control map decorations: title, footnote, logo, and scale bar. Adding a title or footnote is easy.

- `setMapTitle()` sets the map title. Set it to a blank string (not an empty string) if you want no title at all. If you do not specify any title (or specify a `null` title), then MapViewer will automatically include the title you specified in the global configuration file. The title will go in the position you specified for the default title in the configuration—you have no way to override this position.
- `setMapTitleStyleName()` sets the style for the map title.
- `setMapFootNote()` sets a footnote on the map. Set it to a blank string if you want no footnote. If you do not specify any footnote, then MapViewer automatically displays the note specified in the configuration file.
- `setMapFootNoteStyleName()` sets the style for the footnote.

Adding a scale bar is a little more involved. You must first create a separate ScaleBarDef object and then add it to the map. The following example creates a scale bar that shows both a metric and an imperial scale, located in the bottom-right corner of the map. Other methods give you finer control over the colors, label styles, and size of the scale bar.

```
// Define and setup a new scale bar
ScaleBarDef myScaleBar = new ScaleBarDef();
myScaleBar.setPosition("SOUTH_EAST");
myScaleBar.setMode("DUAL_MODES");

// Add the scale bar to your request
mv.setScaleBar(myScaleBar);
```

Finally, you can choose to not show the decorations on a map request. Just disable and reenable them using the following method:

- setMapPiecesRendered() enables or disables the rendering of map decorations.

Using the Map Cache

A powerful possibility is the ability to combine map caches with the Java API. You can use a map cache in two ways: at the map level and at the theme level.

At the map level, you must first decide whether you want to use the cache for a map:

- setUseCachedBaseMap() sets whether to use the cached base map. If true, MapViewer will use the base map image cached by the map cache server. This setting takes effect only if a cache exists for the base map. If no cache exists for the base map, then a custom map is built.

Then you need to specify the way the map cache should be used:

- setSnapToCachedZoomLevel() sets whether to snap the map scale to match the cached zoom levels.

If you specify false (the default setting), then the cached base map will be used only when the map scale specified by the map request matches exactly that of one of the predefined cached zoom levels. For requests at other scales, MapViewer will generate a custom map the usual way.

If you specify true, the cached base map will be used even when the map scale specified by the map request does not match any of the predefined cached zoom levels. In this case, MapViewer will automatically adjust your query window so that the scale matches a predefined cached zoom level.

This technique means you could program your application so that the zoom levels available to the end user match those of the map cache, thus providing high performance to common zoom operations while still giving the user the ability to use custom zoom controls in exceptional cases (or giving this ability only to selected users).

Another powerful possibility is to define a theme on a cached base map:

- addMapCacheTheme() adds a cached base map as a new theme in the current map request.

Just like when using a full base map from the cache, you can specify the snapping behavior for that theme. This possibility is especially interesting to include WMS-based themes in your map. By accessing the WMS via a map cache, you can avoid having to get map tiles from the WMS on every zoom or pan and instead let the map cache server get the map tiles from its cache.

Discovering Data Sources, Maps, Themes

In all of the previous discussions, we assumed that you know which data sources are available, which maps are defined, which themes exist, and so on. However, sometimes you may need to discover dynamically what information exists. This is what the following methods let you do:

- `getDataSources()` gets the names of the data sources defined on the server. Those can be permanent data sources (defined in MapViewer's configuration file) or data sources dynamically added using the administrative API.
- `dataSourceExists()` determines whether a data source exists on the server.
- `getBaseMapNames()` gets the names of all base maps defined in a data source.
- `getPredefinedThemes()` gets the name of all themes defined in a data source. A variant lets you find the themes used by a specific base map.
- `getPermanentStyles()` gets the list of styles defined in a data source.
- `styleExists()` determines whether a style exists on the server.

You can also dynamically define a new data source using the `addDataSource()` method. You need to pass the usual information needed for setting up a JDBC connection to an Oracle database (that is, host name, port number, database name, user name, and password).

Using JSP Tags

Some applications may not need the full flexibility of the MapViewer Java API. For such applications, you can use a set of JSP tags that let you embed maps in JSP with minimal programming. Note that tags use the MapViewer Java API internally, which enables you to combine the use of the tags and the Java API in the same application.

The definition of the JSP tags is in your MapViewer installation (at `$OC4J_HOME/j2ee/home/applications/mapviewer/web/WEB-INF/mvtaglib.tld`). You need to include a pointer to this file in your JSP pages.

Figure 13-14 shows the output of the `SimpleViewerTags.jsp` page. The center of the page shows the map produced by MapViewer. Interacting with the map uses a different technique from the previous examples; all interactions take place via mouse clicks on the map. A radio button underneath the map defines what happens when you click the map:

- *Recenter*: A new map is produced, centered on the point clicked.
- *Zoom In*: The new map is centered on the point clicked, zoomed in by a factor of two.
- *Zoom Out*: The new map is centered on the point clicked, zoomed out by a factor of two.
- *Identify*: The application fetches the details about the county in which the mouse click is located and displays those details at the bottom of the page.

Under the radio buttons are the coordinates of the current center of the map, as well as the scale of the current map.

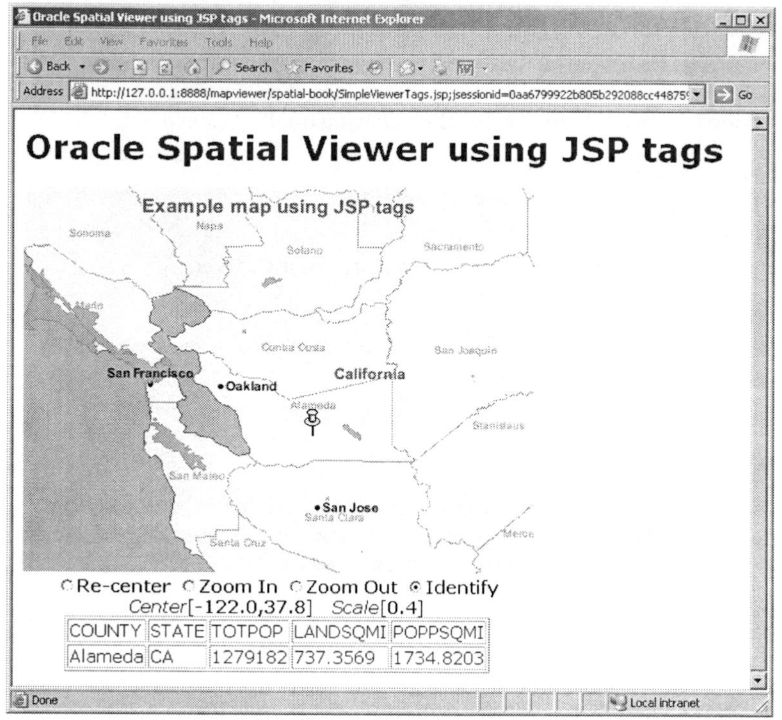

Figure 13-14. *JSP page that uses the MapViewer JSP tags*

Table 13-3 lists the JSP tags available.

Table 13-3. *JSP Tags for MapViewer*

Tag Name	Usage
`init`	Creates the MapViewer bean and places it in the current session. This tag must appear before any other MapViewer JSP tags.
`setParam`	Specifies one or more parameters for the current map request.
`importBaseMap`	Adds the predefined themes that are in the specified base map to the current map request.
`addPredefinedTheme`	Adds a predefined theme to the current map request.
`addJDBCTheme`	Adds a dynamically defined theme to the map request.
`makeLegend`	Creates a legend (map inset illustration) drawn on top of the generated map.
`run`	Submits the current map request to the MapViewer service for processing. The processing can be to zoom in or out, to recenter the map, or to perform a combination of these operations.
`getParam`	Gets the value associated with a specified parameter for the current map request.
`getMapURL`	Gets the HTTP URL for the currently available map image, as generated by the MapViewer service.
`identify`	Gets nonspatial attribute (column) values associated with spatial features that interact with a specified point or rectangle on the map display and optionally uses a marker style to identify the point or rectangle.

We will now cover the main JSP tags and the way they are used in the example application.

Initialization and Setup: The init Tag

Your JSP application must include a pointer to the JSP tags library. It also must indicate that the JSP uses sessions to keep context. Finally, you can import the definitions of the MapViewer Java API if you want to use some of its features in conjunction with the JSP tags, as is the case in the example:

```
<%@ taglib uri="/WEB-INF/mvtaglib.tld" prefix="mv" %>
<%@ page session="true" %>
<%@ page import="oracle.lbs.mapclient.MapViewer" %>
```

Use the `init` tag to initialize the connection with the MapViewer servlet; it creates a `MapViewer` object and saves it in the session for the JSP page:

```
<!-- Initialize MapViewer handle and save it in the session -->
<mv:init
  url="<%=mapViewerURL%>"
  datasource="spatial"
  id="mvHandleSimpleViewerTags" />
```

- The `url` argument specifies the URL to the MapViewer server. Note that it is provided by a JSP substitution from variable `mapViewerURL`. This allows you to construct it dynamically from the request parameters, as shown in the discussion of the Java API.
- The `datasource` argument defines the name of the data source. This could also come from a substituted variable.
- The `id` argument is the name used to save the MapViewer object into the session for the JSP page. It must be constant (no substituted variable).

Setting Up the Map

Several tags are available to specify the format and content of the map. Here is how they are used in the example page.

First, we define the general size of the map in pixels, as well as the title to show on the map:

```
<!-- Set map format and size -->
<mv:setParam
  title="Example map using JSP tags"
  width="480"
  height="360"/>
```

Then we define the name of the base map to display together with any additional predefined themes:

```
<!-- Add themes from the base map -->
<mv:importBaseMap name="us_base_map"/>
<!-- Additional themes -->
<mv:addPredefinedTheme name="parks.us_parks"/>
```

Finally, we set the center and size of the map:

```
<!--  Set initial map center and size -->
<mv:setParam
  centerX="-122.0"
  centerY="37.8"
  size="1.5" />
```

In addition, you can use the `addJDBCTheme` tag to add themes based on SQL queries. This technique is not used in the example.

Interacting with the Map: The run Tag

The previously discussed tags define only the parameters for the map. To actually generate the map, use the run tag. The run tag does more than just generate a new map—it also allows you to dynamically interact with the map.

```
<mv:run
  action="<%=userAction%>"
  x="<%= imgCX %>"
  y="<%= imgCY %>" />
```

- The action argument defines the action to take against the current map. It can be specified as recenter, zoomin, or zoomout.
- The x and y arguments define the coordinates of the center of the new map. They are passed as image coordinates (that is, they represent the coordinates of the mouse click in the map image).

In the preceding example, the action argument is provided by the userAction variable, which contains the current setting of the radio button displayed underneath the map image on the HTML page:

```
String userAction = request.getParameter("userAction");
```

The userAction request parameter contains the current setting of the radio button. Here is the HTML definition of the button:

```
<!-- Map click action  -->
<tr>
  <td align="center">
    <input type="radio" name="userAction" value="recenter"
      <%= "recenter".equals(userAction)?"checked":""%> ><B>Re-center</B>
    <input type="radio" name="userAction" value="zoomin"
      <%= "zoomin".equals(userAction)?"checked":""%> ><B>Zoom In</B>
    <input type="radio" name="userAction" value="zoomout"
      <%= "zoomout".equals(userAction)?"checked":""%> ><B>Zoom Out</B>
    <input type="radio" name="userAction" value="identify"
      <%= "identify".equals(userAction)?"checked":""%> ><B>Identify</B>
  </td>
</tr>
```

The x and y arguments are set from variables (imgCX and imgCY) that contain the coordinates of the mouse click:

```
String imgCX = request.getParameter("userClick.x");
String imgCY = request.getParameter("userClick.y");
```

Displaying the Map: The getMapURL Tag

This tag returns the URL of the map image produced by the run tag. Use it in your HTML code to display the map in an <img> tag or in an <input type="image"> tag, as follows:

```
<!-- Map display  -->
<tr>
  <td valign="top" align="center" >
  <input type="image"
     border="1"
     src="<mv:getMapURL />"
     name="userClick"
```

```
    alt="Click on the map for selected action"
  >
  </td>
</tr>
```

Getting Feature Details: The identify Tag

The identify tag lets you extract details about a selected feature and flag it on the map:

```
<mv:identify
  id="identifyResults"
  table="us_counties"
  spatial_column="geom"
  srid="8307"
  x="<%= imgCX %>" y="<%= imgCY %>"
  style="M.CYAN PIN">
  county, state_abrv state, totpop, landsqmi, poppsqmi
</mv:identify>
```

Here's what the attributes mean:

- id is the name of the variable (of type String[][]) that receives the results of the identification query. The first row of strings contains the names of the columns. Each subsequent row contains the values for each column in each matching row. This format is easy to output in an HTML table.
- table is the name of the table to query.
- spatial_column is the name of the spatial column to query in that table (of type SDO_GEOMETRY).
- srid is the coordinate system for that spatial column.
- x and y are the coordinates of the mouse click (in image coordinates).
- style is optional. If specified, it indicates the style to use for the symbol that marks the spot clicked on the resulting map. If omitted, then no mark is set on the map.

The content of the tag (county, and so on) represents the names of the columns to read from the specified table. Notice that the state_abrv column is renamed to state.

The results of the query are formatted as an HTML <table> as follows:

```
<!-- Identification result -->
<% if (featureInfo !=null && featureInfo.length>0) {%>
  <tr><td align="center">
  <table border="1">
    <% for (int i=0; i<featureInfo.length; i++) {%>
      <tr>
      <% String[] row = featureInfo[i];
         for (int k=0; k<row.length; k++) {%>
          <td><%= row[k] %></td>
         <% } %>
      </tr>
    <% } %>
  </table>
  </td></tr>
<% } %>
```

Combining MapViewer JSP Tags and the Java API

Since the JSP tags use a `MapViewer` object, you can combine the tags with MapViewer's Java API. This is particularly useful for extracting various pieces of information from the `MapViewer` object not accessible through the JSP tags.

Before using MapViewer's Java API, you need to extract the `MapViewer` object saved in the page session:

```
MapViewer mvHandle = (MapViewer) session.getAttribute("mvHandleSimpleViewerTags");
```

The following HTML code displays the coordinates of the center of the current map, as well as the scale of that map, using the `getRequestCenter()` and `getMapScale()` methods of the `MapViewer` object:

```
<!-- Current position -->
<tr>
  <td align="center">
    <i>Center</i>[<b>
      <%=mvHandle.getRequestCenter().getX()+ ","+
        mvHandle.getRequestCenter().getY()%></b>]
    <i>Scale</i>[<b><%=mvHandle.getMapScale()%></b>]
  </td>
</tr>
```

Using the XML API

Let's now examine how to use the XML API. This is the most basic technique to use MapViewer, and you can use it from any application development environment: Java servlets, Java Server Pages (JSP), Java applets, C or C++, .NET, PHP, Perl, and so on. All you need is the ability to send XML to an HTTP URL and parse an XML response.

We will not go through the details of submitting the requests to MapViewer, since this is very dependent on the development environment you use. We will cover only a number of typical map requests.

If you installed the examples provided with the book, you will be able to access those requests at `http://127.0.0.1:8888/mapviewer/spatial-book/map-requests.html`. The XML requests are shown in a set of forms. Clicking the Submit button on each form sends the request for execution by your MapViewer installation.

You can interact with the MapViewer server using the XML API in two ways, depending on the format you specify for the resulting map:

- If the format is `GIF_URL` (the default), `PNG_URL`, or `JPEG_URL`, then you are returned an XML form that contains a URL to the generated map.
- If the format is `GIF_STREAM`, `PNG_STREAM`, or `JPEG_STREAM`, then the image is returned directly. No XML parsing is needed. The examples in the `map-requests.html` page use the "stream" technique so that you can easily see the results.

■ **Note** Map requests return XML. To view this XML correctly, you should use a browser that is able to show an XML document in a tree structure, such as Microsoft Internet Explorer 6 or Firefox 2.

Simple Map Requests

Let's first examine a simple map request. It looks like this:

```
<map_request
  title="Simple Map"
  basemap="US_BASE_MAP"
  datasource="spatial"
  width="480"
  height="400"
  format="PNG_STREAM">
  <center size="12">
    <geoFeature>
      <geometricProperty>
        <Point>
          <coordinates>-120.0, 39.0</coordinates>
        </Point>
      </geometricProperty>
    </geoFeature>
  </center>
</map_request>
```

As its name implies, the `<map_request>` element describes a request to MapViewer. Its parameters define the generic format and aspect of the map:

- `datasource` is the name of the JDBC data source from which to get the map. That data source can be a permanent one (defined in the configuration file) or one that was dynamically added via the administrative API. This is a required parameter.
- `basemap` is the name of the base map to display. This corresponds to a map defined in the `USER_SDO_MAPS` table in the database. This is actually an optional parameter, since a map can also be constructed from a list of themes (as we will show in the next example).
- `width` and `height` represent the size (in pixels) of the resulting image.
- `format` is the format of the image to produce. MapViewer is able to produce maps in the GIF, PNG, or JPEG graphic format. In addition, it can return the image in one of the following two ways:
  - As a URL in an XML response: Specify `GIF_URL`, `PNG_URL`, or `JPEG_URL`.
  - As a directly streamed image: Specify `GIF_STREAM`, `PNG_STREAM`, or `JPEG_STREAM`.

  The default is `GIF_URL`.
- `title` is an optional string that will appear on the map as a title. The title is positioned as specified in the configuration file. By default, it goes at the top of the map. If no title is specified, then the default title from the configuration file is used. If you do not want the default title to appear, then pass an empty string.

Some other parameters not mentioned in the preceding example are as follows:

- `bgcolor` is the color to use for the background. The default is to use an "ocean blue" backdrop. To get a white background instead, set it to `#FFFFFF`.
- `antialiasing` can be `true` or `false` (the default). When this parameter is set to `true`, MapViewer renders the map image in an antialiased manner. This usually provides the map with better graphic quality, but it may take longer for the map to be generated.

You still need to specify the area to be included in the map. You do this by specifying the center point of the map and its size using the `<center>` element. The `<center>` element contains a `<geoFeature>` element, which contains a `<geometricProperty>` element, which itself contains a `<Point>` element, which finally contains a `<coordinates>` element that defines the x,y coordinates of the map center point.

Note The `<geometricProperty>` element is coded using the OGC GML v1.0 specification.

The `size` parameter of the `<center>` element sets the size of the map (actually, the height of the map). It is expressed in the units of the spatial tables used for the map. In the preceding example, we use geodetic data, so the size is expressed in decimal degrees. The value 180 means that you want a map that goes from the South Pole to the North Pole.

When you run the preceding example, you should get the map shown in Figure 13-15 as a result.

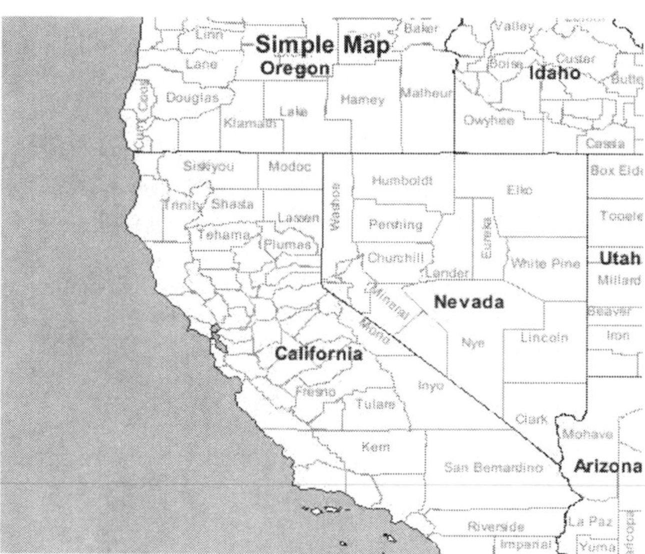

Figure 13-15. *A simple map*

If you modify the `format` parameter to be `PNG_URL`, then the map image is generated as a file on the OC4J server, and you are returned an XML form that contains the URL to the generated image, as shown in Figure 13-16.

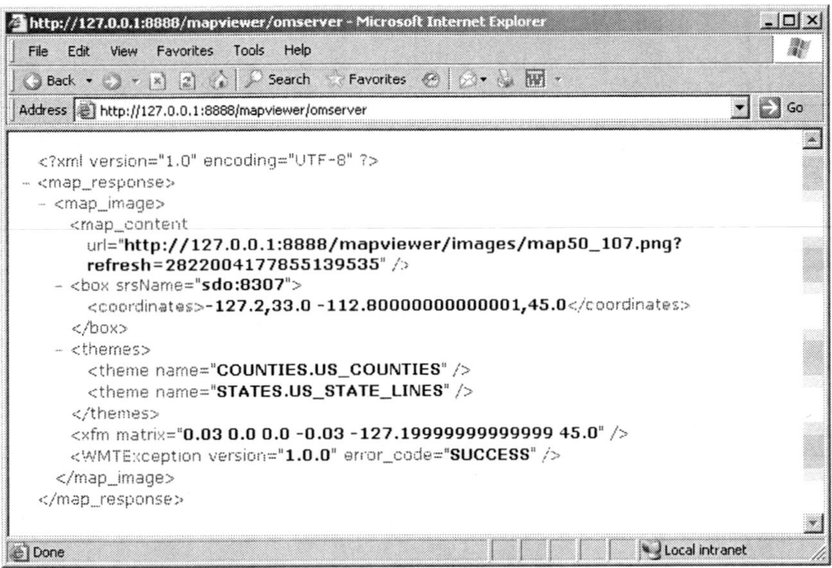
http://127.0.0.1:8888/mapviewer/omserver - Microsoft Internet Explorer
File Edit View Favorites Tools Help
Back Search Favorites
Address http://127.0.0.1:8888/mapviewer/omserver
Go
<?xml version="1.0" encoding="UTF-8" ?>
- <map_response>
- <map_image>
<map_content url="http://127.0.0.1:8888/mapviewer/images/map50_107.png?refresh=2822004177855139535" />
- <box srsName="sdo:8307">
<coordinates>-127.2,33.0 -112.80000000000001,45.0</coordinates>
</box>
- <themes>
<theme name="COUNTIES.US_COUNTIES" />
<theme name="STATES.US_STATE_LINES" />
</themes>
<xfm matrix="0.03 0.0 0.0 -0.03 -127.19999999999999 45.0" />
<WMTException version="1.0.0" error_code="SUCCESS" />
</map_image>
</map_response>
Done
Local intranet

Figure 13-16. *XML response*

Another possibility is to use a <box> element instead of a <center> element. In this case, you specify the exact geographical area to display by specifying the coordinates of the lower-left and upper-right corners of that area. The XML request becomes the following:

```
<?xml version="1.0" standalone="yes"?>
<map_request
  title="Box query"
  basemap="US_BASE_MAP"
  datasource="spatial"
  width="400"
  height="400"
  format="PNG_STREAM">
  <box>
    <coordinates>-126,33 -114,45</coordinates>
  </box>
</map_request>
```

Adding Themes to a Base Map

You can complement your map with additional themes that are not defined in the base map. This lets you control which themes appear on the map. Consider the following example. It is identical to our first simple map request, but we now ask for interstates and parks to appear on top of the base information.

```
<?xml version="1.0" standalone="yes"?>
<map_request
  title="Base Map with Additional Themes"
  basemap="US_BASE_MAP"
  datasource="spatial"
  width="480"
  height="400"
  format="PNG_STREAM">
  <center size="12">
```

```
    <geoFeature>
      <geometricProperty>
        <Point>
          <coordinates>-120.0,39.0</coordinates>
        </Point>
      </geometricProperty>
    </geoFeature>
  </center>
  <themes>
    <theme name="PARKS.US_PARKS"  />
    <theme name="INTERSTATES.US_INTERSTATES"  />
  </themes>
</map_request>
```

When you run the preceding example, you should get the map shown in Figure 13-17 as a result.

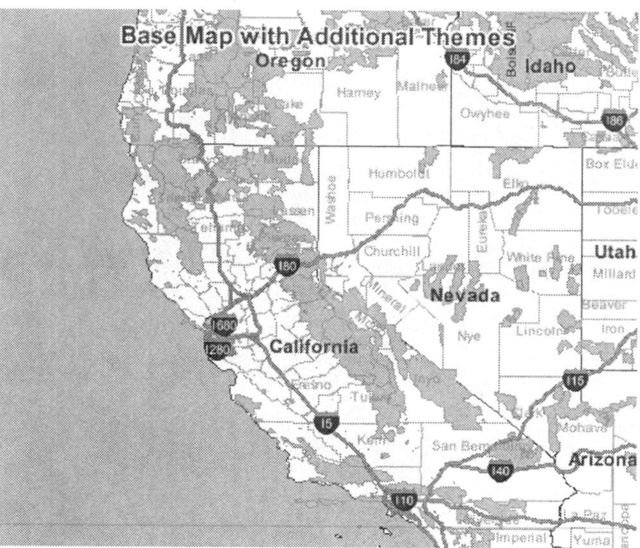

Figure 13-17. *A simple map with additional themes*

Note that the order in which you specify the additional themes is important. The themes in the base map are rendered first (in the order they are defined in the map definition), and then the additional layers are rendered in the order they appear. In the preceding example, parks are rendered first, and then interstates are rendered on top of the parks.

Using Multiple Data Sources

The preceding example assumes that all the data needed to produce a map exist in a single data source. In real applications, it is common to separate application data (for example, the `branches` and `competitors` tables) from the base geographical data tables (for example, `US_STATES`). Use the `datasource` parameter in the `<theme>` element to indicate where each theme comes from. If no data source is specified, then the theme is assumed to come from the main data source (defined by the `datasource` parameter in the top-level `<map_request>` element).

This technique is illustrated in the following example. The data source for each additional theme is explicitly specified. The resulting map is identical to that from the previous example.

```
<?xml version="1.0" standalone="yes"?>
<map_request
  title="Base Map with Additional Themes"
  basemap="US_BASE_MAP"
  datasource="spatial"
  width="480"
  height="400"
  format="PNG_STREAM">
  <center size="12">
    <geoFeature>
      <geometricProperty>
        <Point>
          <coordinates>-120.0,39.0</coordinates>
        </Point>
      </geometricProperty>
    </geoFeature>
  </center>
  <themes>
    <theme name="PARKS.US_PARKS" datasource="spatial" />
    <theme name="INTERSTATES.US_INTERSTATES" datasource="spatial" />
  </themes>
</map_request>
```

Constructing a Map from Themes

You can construct a map entirely from individual themes. In this case, there is no basemap parameter in the map request; instead, you list the themes to appear on the map. The themes must be listed in the order in which they should be rendered—that is, the first theme listed gets rendered first, and then the others are rendered one after the other. The last theme listed is rendered last.

As you just saw, each theme could come from a different data source:

```
<?xml version="1.0" standalone="yes"?>
<map_request
  title=""
  datasource="spatial"
  width="480"
  height="400"
  format="PNG_STREAM">
  <center size="1.5">
    <geoFeature>
      <geometricProperty>
        <Point>
          <coordinates>-77.0,39.0</coordinates>
        </Point>
      </geometricProperty>
    </geoFeature>
  </center>
  <themes>
    <theme name="STATES.US_STATES"  />
    <theme name="COUNTIES.US_COUNTIES" />
    <theme name="RIVERS.US_RIVERS" />
    <theme name="PARKS.US_PARKS" />
    <theme name="INTERSTATES.US_INTERSTATES" />
    <theme name="CITIES.US_CITIES" />
  </themes>
</map_request>
```

This technique is useful to let the application (or the user of the application) control which themes should be displayed. The Java examples will show an application that lets the end user select the themes to display.

Note that in the preceding example, all themes are always rendered, irrespective of the zoom level. This may not be what you want. If you want the themes to be rendered only at the appropriate zoom level, you then need to include scale limits in the theme definitions, like this:

```
<theme name="STATES.US_STATES"
  min_scale="100000000" max_scale="20000000" scale_mode="RATIO" />
<theme name="COUNTIES.US_COUNTIES"
  min_scale="20000000" max_scale="0.0" scale_mode="RATIO" />
<theme name="STATES.US_STATE_LINES"
  min_scale="20000000" max_scale="0.0" scale_mode="RATIO" />
<theme name="CITIES.US_MAJOR_CITIES"
  min_scale="10000000" max_scale="0.0" scale_mode="RATIO" />
<theme name="CITIES.US_CITIES"
  min_scale="500000.0" max_scale="0.0" scale_mode="RATIO" />
```

Dynamic Themes

The examples you have seen so far construct maps from predefined theme definitions. We will now add information from themes that we will dynamically define for a specific map request. We do this using a <jdbc_query> element inside a <theme> element. The <jdbc_query> element includes a SQL query that selects the additional information to display on the map.

Consider the following example:

```
<?xml version="1.0" standalone="yes"?>
<map_request
  title=" "
  basemap="US_CITY_MAP_FINE"
  datasource="SPATIAL"
  width="480"
  height="400"
  format="PNG_STREAM">
  <center size="0.02">
    <geoFeature>
      <geometricProperty>
        <Point>
          <coordinates>-122.40, 37.79</coordinates>
        </Point>
      </geometricProperty>
    </geoFeature>
  </center>
  <themes>
    <theme name="Branches">
       <jdbc_query
         datasource="SPATIAL"
         spatial_column="LOCATION"
         jdbc_srid="8307"
         render_style="M.CYAN PIN">
           select * from branches
       </jdbc_query>
    </theme>
  </themes>
</map_request>
```

The `<jdbc_query>` element contains the SQL query to execute and has the following parameters:

- `datasource` is the name of a JDBC data source to use for executing the query. This is a required setting.
- `spatial_column` is the name of the spatial column (of type `SDO_GEOMETRY`) returned by the SQL query.
- `jdbc_srid` is the coordinate system of the geometries returned by the SQL query.
- `render_style` is the name of the style to apply.
- `label_column` is the name of the column used for labeling the features in this theme.
- `label_style` is the name of the style to use for labeling.

This assumes that the table processed by the SQL statement is in a data source known to MapViewer. You can also get data from any other database by specifying the JDBC connection details:

- `jdbc_host`: Server name
- `jdbc_port`: Database port (1521 is the default)
- `jdbc_sid`: Database name
- `jdbc_user`: User name for the connection
- `jdbc_password`: Password for the user name
- `jdbc_mode`: Driver type (OCI8 or thin)

See Figure 13-18 for the map produced by running the preceding request. It overlays the branches on top of a map of San Francisco. This is the same as the map in Figure 12-1 in Chapter 12.

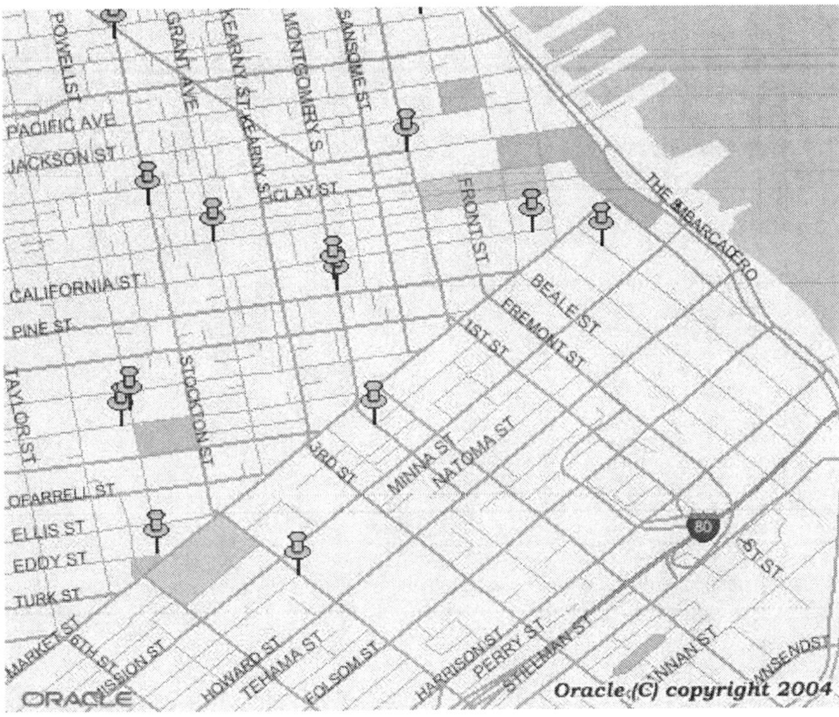

Figure 13-18. *A map with a dynamically constructed theme*

You can include any number of dynamic and static themes in a map request. You must, however, make sure that all dynamic themes have names and that those names are unique (that is, no two themes should have the same name).

There is no limit to the number of dynamic themes you can include in a map. The following example shows the same map as the preceding example, but this time we include the location of the branches as well as the competitors. This results in the map shown in Figure 12-2 in the previous chapter.

```
<?xml version="1.0" standalone="yes"?>
<map_request
  title=" "
  basemap="US_CITY_MAP_FINE"
  datasource="SPATIAL"
  width="480"
  height="400"
  format="PNG_STREAM">
  <center size="0.02">
    <geoFeature>
      <geometricProperty>
        <Point>
          <coordinates>-122.40, 37.79</coordinates>
        </Point>
      </geometricProperty>
    </geoFeature>
  </center>
  <themes>
    <theme name="Competitors">
       <jdbc_query
         datasource="SPATIAL"
         spatial_column="LOCATION"
         render_style="M.BUSINESS RED SQUARE"
         label_column="NAME"
         label_style="T.BUSINESS NAME RED"
         jdbc_srid="8307">
           select * from competitors
       </jdbc_query>
    </theme>
    <theme name="Branches">
       <jdbc_query
         datasource="SPATIAL"
         spatial_column="LOCATION"
         render_style="M.CYAN PIN"
         jdbc_srid="8307">
           select * from branches
       </jdbc_query>
    </theme>
  </themes>
</map_request>
```

■ **Note** Contrary to static (predefined) themes, the information fetched by dynamic themes is never cached.

Dynamic Features

In addition to having a map display features extracted from a database, you can also add manually defined features onto the map. These are generally constructed by the client application, for example, to visualize the place where a user clicked the map.

You do this with the <geoFeature> element. This element includes a <geometricProperty> element that describes the geometric shape (using GML v1.0 notation), as well as parameters for rendering and labeling styles.

The first example is to visualize the center of the current map. All you need to do is add some rendering information to the existing <geoFeature> element that defines the map center, like this:

```
<?xml version="1.0" standalone="yes"?>
<map_request
  title=" "
  basemap="US_BASE_MAP"
  datasource="SPATIAL"
  width="480"
  height="400"
  format="PNG_STREAM">
  <center size="4">
    <geoFeature
      render_style="M.CYAN PIN"
      label="Map center" label_always_on="true"
      text_style="T.TITLE"
      radius="100000,150000,200000">
      <geometricProperty>
        <Point srsName="SDO:8307">
          <coordinates> -82.0,35.0 </coordinates>
        </Point>
      </geometricProperty>
    </geoFeature>
  </center>
</map_request>
```

Here are the parameters you supply to the <geoFeature> element:

- render_style is the style to use for rendering the map's center point.
- label is the hard-coded text to use as a label for the center point.
- text_style is the style to use for rendering the label.
- label_always_on is optional. It tells MapViewer to always show the center label, even if it collides with other labels.
- radius is a comma-separated list of radius values. MapViewer will draw a circle around the center point at each of the radii you specify.

See Figure 13-19 for the map produced by running the preceding request.

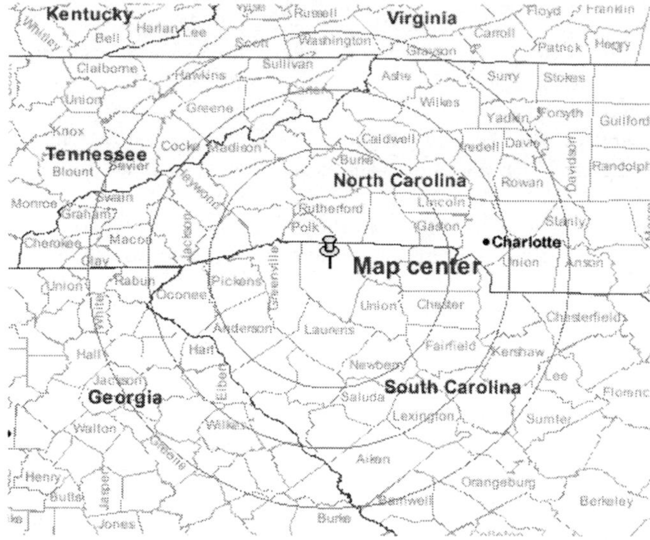

Figure 13-19. *Circles around the map center*

■ Note Make sure to specify the coordinate system used to specify the map center. In this section's first example, it is passed to the `<Point>` element as the parameter `srsName`. That way, you can specify the radius values in meters.

The second example draws a polygon on top of a map:

```
<?xml version="1.0" standalone="yes"?>
<map_request
  title=" "
  basemap="US_BASE_MAP"
  datasource="SPATIAL"
  width="480"
  height="400"
  format="PNG_STREAM">
  <center size="6">
    <geoFeature>
      <geometricProperty>
        <Point>
          <coordinates> -82.0,35.0 </coordinates>
        </Point>
      </geometricProperty>
    </geoFeature>
  </center>
  <geoFeature
    label="Query Window"
    text_style="T.WINDOW_NAME"
    render_style="C.WINDOW">
    <geometricProperty>
      <Polygon>
        <outerBoundaryIs>
```

```
          <LinearRing>
            <coordinates>
            -84.0,35.0 -83.0,34.0 -81.0,34.0 -80.0,35.0 -80.0,36.0
            -82.0,37.0 -84.0,35.0
            </coordinates>
          </LinearRing>
        </outerBoundaryIs>
      </Polygon>
    </geometricProperty>
  </geoFeature>
</map_request>
```

We described the label, text_style, and render_style parameters of the <geoFeature> element earlier. The <geometricProperty> element is used to describe the geometric shape in GML v1.0 notation. In the preceding example, we draw a polygon shape. A MapViewer request can include any number of <geoFeature> elements. See Figure 13-20 for the map produced by running the preceding request.

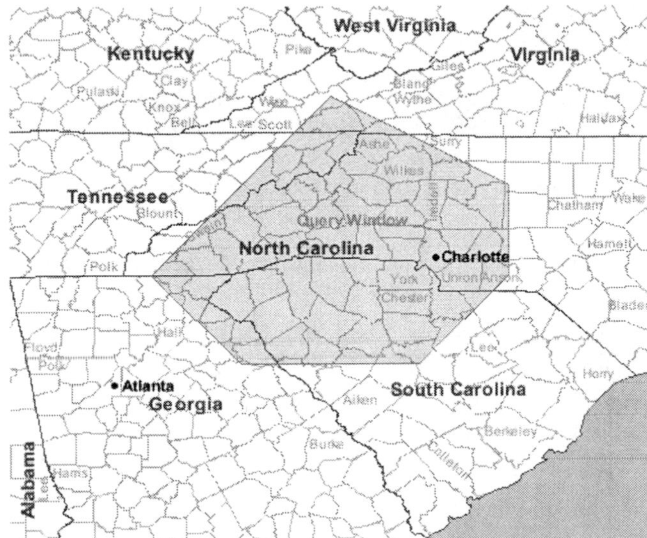

Figure 13-20. *A map with a polygon overlay*

Legends

Legends are an important aid to make maps readable. Here is an example of a map request that includes a legend:

```
<?xml version="1.0" standalone="yes"?>
<map_request
  title=" "
  basemap="US_BASE_MAP"
  datasource="spatial"
  width="480"
  height="400"
  format="GIF_STREAM">
  <center size="8.0">
    <geoFeature>
```

```
      <geometricProperty>
        <Point>
          <coordinates>-94.0,37.0</coordinates>
        </Point>
      </geometricProperty>
    </geoFeature>
  </center>
  <legend profile="MEDIUM" position="SOUTH_EAST">
    <column>
      <entry text="Map Legend" is_title="true" />
      <entry text="Counties"     style="C.US MAP YELLOW" />
      <entry text="Rivers"       style="C.RIVER" />
      <entry text="Parks"        style="C.PARK FOREST" />
    </column>
    <column>
      <entry text=" " is_title="true" />
      <entry text="Interstates"  style="L.PH" />
      <entry text="Major Cities" style="M.CITY HALL 4" />
    </column>
  </legend>
</map_request>
```

The legend is defined in a <legend> element and by groups of <entry> elements. Each <entry> element corresponds to a theme shown on the map. There are special kinds of entries to represent titles or separators. Entries are further grouped into columns.

The <legend> element has a number of optional parameters that let you control the size, position, and background of the legend:

- size can be specified as SMALL, MEDIUM, or LARGE. The default is MEDIUM, which should be adequate for most cases.
- position is one of NORTH, SOUTH, EAST, or WEST, or a corner such as NORTH_EAST or SOUTH_WEST. The default is SOUTH_EAST (that is, the lower-right corner of the map).
- bgstyle lets you specify the background of the legend. You code this using an SVG notation. For example, "fill:#ffffff;stroke:#ff0000" sets the legend to a white background with a red boundary.

Each <entry> element should correspond to a layer on the map. For each entry, you specify two parameters:

- text: A text string to appear on the legend (it should be the name of a theme)
- style: A style name (it should be the style for that theme)

Figure 13-21 shows the map produced by running the preceding request.

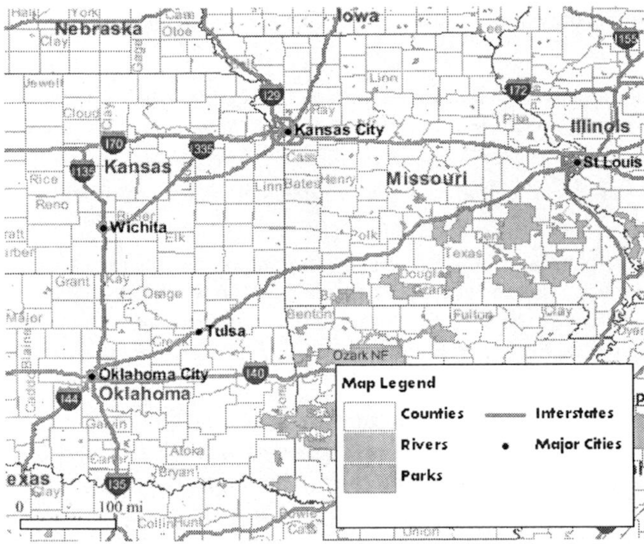

Figure 13-21. *A map with a legend*

The XML Map Response

Unless you asked for MapViewer to return a map image directly to you (in the format `GIF_STREAM`, `PNG_STREAM`, or `JPEG_STREAM`), you need to parse the XML map response to extract the URL to the map that MapViewer generated on the server.

A typical map response looks like this:

```
<?xml version="1.0" encoding="UTF-8"?>
<map_response>
 <map_image>
  <map_content url="/mapviewer/images/omsmap63.tif?refresh=-3991419801814O4304" />
  <box srsName="default">
     <coordinates> -18.0,-15.0  18.0,15.0 </coordinates>
  </box>
  <themes>
    <theme name="COUNTIES.US_COUNTIES"/>
    <theme name="STATES.US_STATE_LINES"/>
    <theme name="CITIES.US_MAJOR_CITIES"/>
  </themes>
  <xfm matrix="0.075 0.0 0.0 -0.075 -18.0 15.0" />
  <WMTException version="1.0.0" error_code="SUCCESS">
  </WMTException>
 </map_image>
</map_response>
```

The `<map_response>` element contains only one element, `<map_image>`, which itself contains the following main elements:

- `<map_image>` contains the `url` parameter, which in turn contains the relative URL to the generated map image (constructed using the `url` parameter of the `<save_images_at>` element in the MapViewer configuration file).
- `<box>` defines the actual area covered by the map as the coordinates of the lower-left and upper-right corners of the map.
- `<themes>` lists only those themes that are actually visible on the map at the current scale. Note that the list includes not only the themes you explicitly specified in your map request but also the themes implicitly defined in the base map you specified. You can use this information in your application to dynamically adjust the map legend to reflect the exact content of the map at all times.
- `<xfm>` represents the matrix values that are the parameters for an `AffineTransform`, which you can use to convert a screen coordinate (such as a user's mouse click position on the returned map image) to the coordinate in the user's data space. This happens automatically in the Java API.

In case the request failed, you will receive an error response similar to this:

```
<?xml version="1.0" encoding="UTF-8"?>
<oms_error>
  Message:[oms] : data source not found.
  Sat Jan 24 00:41:35 CET 2004
  Severity: 0
  Description:
     at oracle.lbs.mapserver.oms.doPost(oms.java:273)
     ...
     at java.lang.Thread.run(Thread.java:536)
</oms_error>
```

Using the PL/SQL API

You always had the possibility of using MapViewer from PL/SQL. All you needed was to build suitably formatted XML requests and then send them to the MapViewer server using functions from the `UTL_HTTP` package. However, that approach was rather cumbersome and involved the parsing of XML responses. MapViewer now provides a dedicated API.

The PL/SQL API is provided as a set of functions and procedures in a package called `SDO_MVCLIENT`. This package is not present in the database. To use it, you must first install it.

Installing the API

The package is provided in your MapViewer installation at `$OC4J_HOME/j2ee/home/applications/mapviewer/sql`. To install the package, connect to the database as system, and then run both SQL scripts provided in the folder indicated.

```
SQL> connect system/********
SQL> @sdomvclh.sql
SQL> @sdomvclb.sql
```

Installing the package is not all you have to do. The functions and procedures actually call the equivalent methods of the Java API. Therefore, you must also install the Java API in your database. Do this using the `loadjava` tool as shown next. The `mvclient.jar` file is in `$OC4J_HOME/j2ee/home/applications/mapviewer/web/WEB-INF/lib`.

```
loadjava -force -schema mdsys -grant PUBLIC -user system/******* mvclient.jar
```

You still need to go through one more step before you are able to use the API. You need to grant yourself the proper rights that will allow the Java API library to perform HTTP network calls. Do this by executing the following (again, connected as SYSTEM). Note that you must also grant the same rights to user MDSYS.

```
SQL> connect system/********
SQL> call dbms_java.grant_permission('SPATIAL', 'SYS:java.net.SocketPermission',
     '127.0.0.1:8888', 'connect, resolve');
SQL> call dbms_java.grant_permission('MDSYS', 'SYS:java.net.SocketPermission',
     '127.0.0.1:8888', 'connect, resolve');
```

A Simple Example

The functions and procedures correspond almost exactly to the methods of the `Mapviewer` class in the Java API.

Your first step is to connect to the MapViewer server, like this:

```
SQL> call sdo_mvclient.createmapviewerclient( 'http://127.0.0.1:8888/mapviewer/omserver');
```

Note that this call does not actually set up the connection to the MapViewer server. The connection will take place only on the first call that needs information from the server. To confirm that you can actually use the server, get the list of available data sources, like this:

```
SQL> select sdo_mvclient.getdatasources() datasources from dual;

DATASOURCES
--------------------------------------------------------------------------------
SDO_1D_STRING_ARRAY('spatial', 'world_sample')
```

You can now set up a map request by calling the appropriate functions, much like you would do in Java:

```
SQL> call sdo_mvclient.setDataSourceName('SPATIAL');
SQL> call sdo_mvclient.setImageFormat('PNG_URL');
SQL> call sdo_mvclient.setMapTitle('Simple Map');
SQL> call sdo_mvclient.setBaseMapName('US_BASE_MAP') ;
SQL> call sdo_mvclient.setCenter(-120, 39);
SQL> call sdo_mvclient.setSize(12);
SQL> call sdo_mvclient.setDevicesize(480,400);
```

You can also add dynamic styles:

```
SQL> call sdo_mvclient.addColorStyle('C.FUNNY COLOR', 'blue', 'yellow', 100,100);
```

or add a dynamic (JDBC) theme to your request:

```
SQL> select sdo_mvclient.addJDBCTheme(
       'SPATIAL',
       'SELECTED-STATES',
       'select * from us_states where state_abrv = ''CA''',
       'geom',
       '8307', 'C.RED', null, null, 'FALSE')
     from dual ;
```

and then send the map request:

```
SQL> select sdo_mvclient.run() from dual;

SDO_MVCLIENT.RUN()
--------------------------------------------
TRUE
```

Note that this is actually a function call that returns a string always set to 'TRUE'. You can also use such methods as `sdo_mvclient.zoomIn()` and `sdo_mvclient.zoomOut()` to get zoomed maps.

Finally, you can now extract results from the request. The most common result will be the URL of the map produced.

```
SQL> select sdo_mvclient.getgeneratedMapImageURL() from dual;

SDO_MVCLIENT.GETGENERATEDMAPIMAGEURL()
-------------------------------------------------------------------------
http://127.0.0.1:8888/mapviewer/images/map15_29.tif?refresh=-725304371952178
```

Using the Administrative API

In addition to the map request APIs (XML and Java) described previously, MapViewer also provides an administrative API, which lets applications perform such actions as discovering data sources, maps, themes, and styles or managing data sources and caches.

Browsing Map Definitions

The functions in the administrative API are useful for building generic applications that enable users to discover what map definitions exist. They let you find out the data sources defined on the MapViewer server, as well as browse the maps, themes, and styles defined in a data source. You can access those functions via the MapViewer home page (`http://host:port/mapviewer`).

Listing Data Sources

The following XML request returns a list of the data sources known by the server:

```
<?xml version="1.0" standalone="yes"?>
<non_map_request>
  <list_data_sources />
</non_map_request>
```

The response is an XML form that looks like this:

```
<?xml version="1.0" ?>
<non_map_response>
  <map_data_source_list succeed="true">
    <map_data_source name="spatial />
    <map_data_source name="mvdemo" />
  </map_data_source_list>
</non_map_response>
```

Note that this gives you only the names of the data sources. To obtain further details, such as JDBC connection details, you need to use a secure variant, which we discuss shortly.

You can also verify the existence of a data source:

```
<?xml version="1.0" standalone="yes"?>
<non_map_request>
```

```
  <data_source_exists data_source="mvdemo"/>
</non_map_request>
```

Listing Maps

The following XML request returns a list of the base maps defined for a data source:

```
<?xml version="1.0" standalone="yes"?>
<non_map_request>
  <list_maps data_source="spatial" />
</non_map_request>
```

The response is an XML form like this:

```
<?xml version="1.0" ?>
<non_map_response>
  <map_list succeed="true">
    <map name="CITY_MAP" />
    <map name="US_BASE_MAP" />
    <map name="US_CITY_MAP" />
    <map name="US_DETAILED_MAP" />
    <map name="WORLD_MAP" />
    <map name="WORLD_MAP_COLORED" />
  </map_list>
</non_map_response>
```

Listing Themes

Use the following request to get the list of all themes defined in a data source:

```
<?xml version="1.0" standalone="yes"?>
<non_map_request>
  <list_predefined_themes data_source="spatial" />
</non_map_request>
```

The response is an XML form that contains the names of the themes:

```
<?xml version="1.0" ?>
<non_map_response>
  <predefined_theme_list succeed="true">
    <predefined_theme name="COUNTRIES.WORLD_COUNTRIES" />
    <predefined_theme name="COUNTIES.US_COUNTIES" />
    <predefined_theme name="RIVERS.US_RIVERS" />
    <predefined_theme name="STATES.US_STATES" />
    <predefined_theme name="WORLD.WORLD_CONTINENTS" />
    <predefined_theme name="WORLD.WORLD_COUNTRIES" />
    <predefined_theme name="WORLD.WORLD_COUNTRIES_COLORED" />
  </predefined_theme_list>
</non_map_response>
```

You can also get the themes used in a specific base map:

```
<?xml version="1.0" standalone="yes"?>
<non_map_request>
  <list_predefined_themes data_source="spatial" map="US_BASE_MAP"/>
</non_map_request>
```

The response lists the themes with their scale limits:

```
<?xml version="1.0" ?>
<non_map_response>
```

```
  <predefined_theme_list succeed="true">
    <predefined_theme name="STATES.US_STATES"
      min_scale="1.0E8" max_scale="2.0E7" scale_mode="RATIO" />
    <predefined_theme name="COUNTIES.US_COUNTIES"
      min_scale="2.0E7" max_scale="0.0" scale_mode="RATIO" />
    <predefined_theme name="STATES.US_STATE_LINES"
      min_scale="2.0E7" max_scale="0.0" scale_mode="RATIO" />
    <predefined_theme name="CITIES.US_MAJOR_CITIES"
      min_scale="1.0E7" max_scale="0.0" scale_mode="RATIO" />
    <predefined_theme name="CITIES.US_CITIES"
      min_scale="500000.0" max_scale="0.0" scale_mode="RATIO" />
  </predefined_theme_list>
</non_map_response>
```

Listing Styles

Use the following request to get the names of all styles defined in a data source. This list contains only the permanent styles (those stored in the database). Dynamically created styles do not appear.

```
<?xml version="1.0" standalone="yes"?>
<non_map_request>
  <list_styles data_source="spatial" />
</non_map_request>
```

The response is an XML form that looks like this:

```
<?xml version="1.0" ?>
<non_map_response>
  <style_list succeed="true">
    <style name="A.PATTERN 1" />
    ...
    <style name="V.WORLD_COUNTRIES" />
  </style_list>
</non_map_response>
```

You can restrict the list to specific style types by adding a `style_type` parameter.

Managing the MapViewer Server

The normal way to manage the MapViewer server is via its administration console, which you have seen in the previous chapter (see Figure 12-10). But you can also control MapViewer directly via XML requests that allow you to do the following:

- Manage data sources (JDBC connections) by adding, removing, and listing data sources.
- Manage caches by clearing data and metadata caches.
- Restart MapViewer after you change its configuration settings.

Security and Access Control

The management functions are protected. When you attempt to call one, you will be asked to specify a user name and password.

If MapViewer is deployed in a stand-alone OC4J, then the user name will be `oc4jadmin`. The password is the administrative password you specified when you started the OC4J server for the first time.

When MapViewer is deployed in the Oracle Internet Application Server, you need to create an administration user in the OC4J instance where MapViewer is running and map this administration user to MapViewer's built-in security role, `map_admin_role`.

Managing Data Sources

One of the major functions of the administrative API is that it lets you dynamically manage the data sources. You can define new data sources, redefine existing data sources, and remove data sources. Those changes are temporary; they take place only in the running MapViewer server. Any new data source you define disappears if the MapViewer server is restarted.

Adding a Data Source

Here is the XML request you submit to define a new data source:

```
<?xml version="1.0" standalone="yes"?>
<non_map_request>
  <add_data_source
        name="spatial"
        jdbc_host="127.0.0.1"
        jdbc_port="1521"
        jdbc_sid="orcl111"
        jdbc_user="spatial"
        jdbc_password="spatial"
        jdbc_mode="thin"
        number_of_mappers="3" />
</non_map_request>
```

The data source will be available to all users of the MapViewer server. However, its definition is not persistent; the data source definition will disappear at the next shutdown of the server.

Listing Data Sources

The following XML request returns a list of the data sources known by the server:

```
<?xml version="1.0" standalone="yes"?>
<non_map_request>
  <list_data_sources />
</non_map_request>
```

The response is an XML form that looks like this:

```
 <?xml version="1.0" ?>
  <non_map_response>
    <map_data_source_list succeed="true">
      <map_data_source name="spatial" host="127.0.0.1" sid="orcl111"
        port="1521" user="spatial" mode="thin" numMappers="3" />
      <map_data_source name="mvdemo" host="127.0.0.1" sid="orcl111"
        port="1521" user="mvdemo" mode="thin" numMappers="3" />
    </map_data_source_list>
  </non_map_response>
```

Note that this request can also be sent in a "nonprivileged" mode—that is, without being logged in as the MapViewer administrator. In that case, the XML response lists only the data source names.

Modifying a Data Source

The following XML request changes `number of mappers` (the maximum number of concurrent threads) and the maximum number of connections for a data source:

```
<?xml version="1.0" standalone="yes"?>
<non_map_request>
  <redefine_data_source
        name="spatial"
        jdbc_host="127.0.0.1"
        jdbc_port="1521"
        jdbc_sid="orcl111"
        jdbc_user="spatial"
        jdbc_password="spatial"
        jdbc_mode="thin"
        number_of_mappers="4"
        max_connections="40" />
</non_map_request>
```

Note that you cannot change the host, port, user name, or password. Those must match exactly the values specified when the data source was defined. If they do not, then you will receive an error indicating that the data source cannot be found.

To modify any of those parameters, you need to remove the data source and re-create it with the new parameters. You can modify the parameters for a permanent data source (one defined in MapViewer's configuration file), but those changes will disappear when MapViewer is restarted.

Removing a Data Source

To remove a data source, you must provide the JDBC password for that data source:

```
<?xml version="1.0" standalone="yes"?>
<non_map_request>
  <remove_data_source data_source="spatial" jdbc_password="spatial" />
non_map_request>
```

You can remove a permanent data source (one defined in MapViewer's configuration file), but it will come back when MapViewer is restarted.

Managing Caches

The MapViewer server maintains a cache for the data it reads from the database, as well as a cache for the map definitions, called the *metadata cache*. The following commands enable you to clear those caches.

Clearing the Data Cache

Use this request to clear the data cache for a named theme in a named data source:

```
<?xml version="1.0" standalone="yes"?>
<non_map_request>
  <clear_theme_cache data_source="spatial" theme="us_states" />
</non_map_request>
```

Clearing the Metadata Cache

The following request clears the styles, maps, and themes from the cache of the MapViewer server for a given data source:

```
<?xml version="1.0" standalone="yes"?>
<non_map_request>
  <clear_cache data_source="spatial" />
</non_map_request>
```

This operation is necessary if you change any style, theme, or map definition in the database. It forces MapViewer to reload the definitions from the database the next time they are needed.

Restarting MapViewer

The following restarts the MapViewer server. All data and metadata caches are cleared, all data sources are closed, and all dynamically added data sources are removed. MapViewer then rereads the configuration file and starts up again.

```
<?xml version="1.0" standalone="yes"?>
<non_map_request>
  <restart/>
</non_map_request>
```

This operation is necessary if you change settings in MapViewer's configuration file, such as if you add a new permanent data source or if you modify the logging parameters.

Web Map Service (OGC WMS) Interface

The WMS protocol is an international standard (ISO/DIS 19128:2005) originally defined by the OGC. The standard describes the behavior of a service that produces spatially referenced maps dynamically from geographic information. It specifies operations to retrieve a description of the maps offered by a server, to retrieve a map, and to query a server about features displayed on a map.

MapViewer implements the WMS protocol, specifically the WMS 1.1.1 implementation specification. MapViewer supports the `GetMap`, `GetFeatureInfo`, and `GetCapabilities` requests as defined in the WMS standard. The URL to invoke the Web Map Service is `http://server:port/mapviewer/wms`, where `server` and `port` are the name and port of your MapViewer server.

The GetCapabilities Request

WMS requests are passed as annotated URLs. For example, the following URL will return the capabilities of your local Web Map Service, that is, the list of data sources, base maps, and themes known to the MapViewer server:

```
http://127.0.0.1:8888/mapviewer/wms
?REQUEST=GetCapabilities
&SERVICE=WMS
&VERSION=1.1.1
```

■ **Note** The URLs shown in this section are broken down so that each request parameter occupies one line. This is only for making the examples more readable. In reality, all parameters must be attached to form a single line.

The response will be an XML document. For the exact structure of this document, please refer to the official WMS standard definition.[2] Listing 13-6 shows an excerpt of a typical response.

2. The specification is available from the Open Geospatial Consortium at `http://www.opengeospatial.org/standards/wms`.

Listing 13-6. *Example* GetCapabilities *Response*

```
<?xml version="1.0" encoding="UTF-8" ?>
<WMT_MS_Capabilities version="1.1.1">
  <Service>
    <Name>OGC:WMS</Name>
    <Title>WMS 1.1 interface for Oracle Application Server MapViewer</Title>
    <Fees>none</Fees>
    <AccessConstraints>none</AccessConstraints>
  </Service>
  <Capability>
    <Request>
      <GetCapabilities>
        <Format>application/vnd.ogc.wms_xml</Format>
      </GetCapabilities>
      <GetMap>
        <Format>image/png</Format>
        <Format>image/gif</Format>
        <Format>image/jpeg</Format>
        <Format>image/svg+xml</Format>
        <Format>image/png8</Format>
      </GetMap>
      <GetFeatureInfo>
        <Format>text/xml</Format>
      </GetFeatureInfo>
    </Request>
    <Exception>
      <Format>text/xml</Format>
    </Exception>
    <Layer>
      <Name>WMS</Name>
      <Title>Oracle WebMapServer Layers by data source.</Title>
      <SRS>EPSG:4326</SRS>
      <LatLonBoundingBox
        minx="-180.0" miny="-90.0" maxx="180.0" maxy="90.0"/>
      <Layer>
        <Name>spatial</Name>
        <Title>Datasource spatial</Title>
        <Layer>
          <Name>US_BASE_MAP</Name>
          <Title>Basemap US_BASE_MAP</Title>
          <SRS>EPSG:4326</SRS>
          <LatLonBoundingBox minx="-180.0" miny="-90.0" maxx="180.0" maxy="90.0"/>
          <Layer queryable="1">
            <Name>US_STATES</Name>
            <Title>US_STATES</Title>
            <SRS>EPSG:4326</SRS>
            <BoundingBox SRS="EPSG:4326"
              minx="-180.0" miny="-90.0"
              maxx="180.0" maxy="90.0"
              resx="1.0" resy="1.0"/>
             <ScaleHint min="1000000" max="5.0"/>
          </Layer>
          <Layer queryable="1">
            <Name>US_COUNTIES</Name>
            <Title>US_COUNTIES</Title>
            <SRS>EPSG:4326</SRS>
```

```
          <BoundingBox SRS="EPSG:4326"
            minx="-180.0" miny="-90.0"
            maxx="180.0" maxy="90.0"
            resx="1.0" resy="1.0"/>
          <ScaleHint min="5.0" max="0.0"/>
        </Layer>
        <Layer queryable="1">
          <Name>US_CITIES</Name>
          <Title>US_CITIES</Title>
          <SRS>EPSG:4326</SRS>
          <BoundingBox SRS="EPSG:4326"
            minx="-180.0" miny="-90.0"
            maxx="180.0" maxy="90.0"
            resx="1.0" resy="1.0"/>
          <ScaleHint min="0.15" max="0.0"/>
        </Layer>
      </Layer>
    </Layer>
  </Layer>
 </Capability>
</WMT_MS_Capabilities>
```

Notice that the response contains a series of nested `<layer>` elements. The top `<layer>` element is always called `WMS`. It contains one `<layer>` element for each data source. Each data source further contains one `<layer>` element per base map, which in turns contains one `<layer>` element for each theme it uses.

The GetMap Request

The `GetMap` request is the main mapping request; use it to tell the Web Map Service what data to use and how to format the resulting map. The response of the `GetMap` request is a streamed image. Here is an example of a `GetMap` request:

```
http://127.0.0.1:8888/mapviewer/wms
?VERSION=1.1.1
&REQUEST=GetMap
&FORMAT=image/gif
&WIDTH=480
&HEIGHT=400
&SRS=EPSG:4326
&BBOX=-126,33,-114,45
&LAYERS=US_STATES,US_COUNTIES,US_PARKS,US_INTERSTATES,US_CITIES
&BASEMAP=US_BASE_MAP
&DATASOURCE=spatial
```

Table 13-4 lists the main parameters you can pass with a `GetMap` request. Again, you should refer to the official WMS standard definition for the full details. Note that the WMS standard allows implementers to add their own specific parameters to the requests. This is the case for the `BASEMAP` and `DATASOURCE` parameters, which are specific to MapViewer. Some parameters are not supported by MapViewer and will be ignored if used.

Table 13-4. *Main WMS* GetMap *Request Parameters*

Parameter	Usage
FORMAT	Specifies the format of the resulting map image. The formats supported by the server are listed in the response to the GetCapabilities request. They correspond to the formats supported by MapViewer: image/png, image/gif, and image/jpeg, as well as image/jpeg+svg and image/png8.
WIDTH	The width in pixels of the resulting map image.
HEIGHT	The width in pixels of the resulting map image.
BGCOLOR	Color to be used for the background of the map. Specify using the hexadecimal RGB notation. The default is 0xFFFFFF, or white. To get an "ocean-blue" background (the default for regular MapViewer requests) use 0xA6CAE0.
TRANSPARENT	A string (TRUE or FALSE, the default) indicating whether the background of the map should be transparent. This parameter applies only if the output format is PNG.
SRS	The spatial reference system of the resulting map. This is specified as a namespace (here EPSG) followed by the number of the spatial reference system (here 4326). See the "Spatial Reference Systems (SRS) Mapping" section for a discussion on the mapping of EPSG codes to Oracle Spatial codes.
BBOX	The spatial coordinates of the area covered by the map. The coordinates are in the coordinate system specified by the SRS parameter.
LAYERS	A comma-separated list of layers to include on the map. Note that the server will render the layers in the opposite order from that of MapViewer, in other words, by drawing the leftmost in the list bottommost, the next one over that, and the first in the list at the top.
MapViewer-Specific Extensions	
BASEMAP	The name of a base map.
DATASOURCE	The name of a data source. If not specified, then the server will use a default data source called WMS.
DYNAMIC_STYLES	A list of style descriptors, encoded in XML.
MVTHEMES	A list of themes, encoded in XML.
LEGEND_REQUEST	A legend descriptor, encoded in XML.
Parameters Not Supported by MapViewer	
TIME	The time dimension.
ELEVATION	The elevation dimension.
STYLES	Styled layer descriptors.

Caution The LAYERS parameter is required, even if all you want is to display a base map. If this is the case, specify LAYERS=NULL.

The GetFeatureInfo Request

Use the GetFeatureInfo request to get attribute information about features located at a specific location on the map produced by a GetMap request. The goal of the GetFeatureInfo request is to allow an application to capture the point a user clicked on and query the server for features located on the map at that point. The point is passed in image coordinates, that is, in pixels from an origin (0,0) at the upper-left corner of the map.

Here is an example of a GetFeatureInfo request that queries three layers for features at a given point location:

```
http://127.0.0.1:8888/mapviewer/wms
?VERSION=1.1.1
&REQUEST=GetFeatureInfo
&FORMAT=image/gif
&WIDTH=480
&HEIGHT=400
&SRS=EPSG:4326
&BBOX=-126,33,-114,45
&LAYERS=US_STATES,US_COUNTIES,US_RIVERS,US_PARKS,US_INTERSTATES,US_CITIES
&DATASOURCE=spatial
&INFO_FORMAT=text/xml
&QUERY_LAYERS=US_STATES,US_COUNTIES,US_PARKS
&X=240&Y=200
```

When calling the GetFeatureInfo request, you must include the same parameters as those you passed to the GetMap request, followed by the additional query parameters, listed in Table 13-5.

Table 13-5. *Main WMS* GetFeatureInfo *Request Parameters*

Parameter	Usage
INFO_FORMAT	Specifies the format of the resulting output. The only format supported by MapViewer is text/xml.
QUERY_LAYERS	A comma-separated list of layers to query. The list must be a subset of the layers shown on the map (listed in the LAYERS parameter).
X	The X location of the query point (in image coordinates, in other words, in pixels counted down from the top of the map).
Y	The Y location of the query point (in image coordinates, in other words, in pixels counted from the left of the map).
FEATURE_COUNT	The number of features to return (1 by default). If more features than the specified number exist at the query point, then MapViewer will return a random subset of those features.
MapViewer-Specific Parameters	
QUERY_TYPE	The standard spatial selection mechanism proposed by the WMS protocol is to select features that interact with a given point. The QUERY_TYPE parameter allows you to use other kinds of spatial queries: AT_POINT (the default) is identical to the WMS default; NN returns the nearest neighbors with the number of results specified in FEATURE_COUNT; and WITHIN_RADIUS (or WITHIN_DISTANCE) returns the features that are within the distance specified by the RADIUS parameter.
RADIUS	The radius value for the QUERY_TYPE=WITHIN_RADIUS search.
UNIT	The unit in which the RADIUS value is specified. Use one of the units known to MapViewer, defined in the SDO_DIST_UNITS view.

The result of the previous query is an XML document:

```
<?xml version="1.0" encoding="UTF-8"?>
<GetFeatureInfo_Result>
  <ROWSET name="STATES.US_STATES" >
    <ROW num="1">
      <ROWID>AAAQykAAEAAACFUAAE</ROWID>
    </ROW>
  </ROWSET>
```

```
  <ROWSET name="COUNTIES.US_COUNTIES" >
    <ROW num="1">
      <COUNTY>Tuolumne</COUNTY>
      <LAND>2235.2656</LAND>
      <POPULATION>48456</POPULATION>
    </ROW>
  </ROWSET>
  <ROWSET name="PARKS.US_PARKS" >
  </ROWSET>
</GetFeatureInfo_Result>
```

The query found one state and one county at the designated location, but no park. For the state, the query returned only the ROWID of the feature. For the county, the query returned a number of attributes; those are the attributes defined as "information columns" in the theme definition.

Spatial Reference Systems (SRS) Mapping

MapViewer's WMS server supports two namespaces for encoding spatial reference systems: EPSG and SDO. The EPSG namespace uses the numbers defined by the European Petroleum Support Group (EPSG). SDO uses Oracle's native numbers.

The WMS specification recommends using EPSG codes for identifying coordinate systems. To ease the transition between Oracle's numbering and the EPSG numbering, MapViewer provides a built-in mapping list for some common coordinate systems. For example, EPSG:4326 is the same as SDO:8307. Both represent the WGS84 coordinate system.

You can use either notation interchangeably in your Getmap and GetFeatureInfo requests. The GetCapabilities response always attempts to return EPSG codes, provided it has a mapping in its internal table. For example, see the response in Listing 13-5. The layers are really stored using SRID 8307, but the response returns the corresponding EPSG code. If it cannot find a mapping, then it just returns SDO: followed by the Oracle SRID.

You can also use your own set of mappings by writing them into a text file. Use one line per mapping, where each line is in the format sdo_srid=epsg_srid. Specify the name of the file in the <srs_mapping> element in MapViewer's configuration file. For example:

```
<srs_mapping>
  <sdo_epsg_mapfile>
    ../conf/epsg_srids.properties
  </sdo_epsg_mapfile>
</srs_mapping>
```

Summary

In this chapter, you learned how to add maps to your applications and how to let your users interact with your maps. MapViewer is a very powerful product, and we touched on only the most important aspects of it. In the next chapter, we will use many of the techniques we presented here to build two complete applications, one using the Oracle Maps (Ajax/JavaScript) approach and one using a Java Server Page approach.

PART 5

Spatial in Applications

CHAPTER 14

Sample Applications

To create the sample application in this chapter, you need to load the following datasets and run the following scripts:

```
imp spatial/spatial file=app_data.dmp full=y
imp spatial/spatial file=gc.dmp full=y
imp spatial/spatial file=map_large.dmp full=y
imp spatial/spatial file=map_detailed.dmp full=y
imp spatial/spatial file=styles.dmp full=y
```

Throughout this book, you have learned many techniques relating to spatial technology: how to location-enable an application, how to perform spatial analysis, and how to view the results using dynamically generated maps.

The time has come to use all of these techniques in a single application that integrates spatial analysis and visualization. This chapter presents and dissects two such applications. Both are web-based applications. The first one uses Ajax and MapViewer's JavaScript API (Oracle Maps). The second one uses MapViewer's Java API in a JSP page. Table 14-1 lists the main requirements for the applications, along with the features of Oracle Spatial exercised and the chapters that discuss those features.

Table 14-1. *Application Requirements*

Application Requirement	Features Used
Display a map showing the locations of customers, competitors, and branches, along with additional geographical information such as streets, public buildings, administrative boundaries, and so on.	Map generation (Chapters 12 and 13)
Select the information to appear on the map, and allow the usual map navigation, such as zoom in and out, pan, and recenter.	Map generation (Chapters 12 and 13)
Enter a street address, and center the map on that address.	Geocoding (Chapter 6)
Find all customers, competitors, or branches within a specified distance from a location on the map. This location could be the location of a branch, a customer, a competitor, or a street address. The results are highlighted on the map.	Proximity analysis and geometry processing (Chapters 8 and 9)
Find a specified number of neighboring customers, competitors, or branches closest to a specified location on this map. This location could be the location of a customer, a competitor, a branch, or a street address. The results are highlighted on the map.	Proximity analysis and geometry processing (Chapters 8 and 9)

We begin this chapter with a study of the data needed by the applications. Much of that data should have been loaded and prepared as you proceeded through the examples in the preceding chapters.

We then walk you through the applications, showing you how to install and run them, how to use them, and how the various functions of the applications were implemented.

You will find the complete source code for both applications on the Apress website (`www.apress.com`).

Data Preparation and Setup

The sample applications require several types of data before you can actually run them:

- *Geographical data*: This is the data that will appear as a "backdrop" on your map. Without it, you would see only colored dots, without anything to relate them to. This data includes the data used by the geocoder.
- *Location-enabled application tables*: The `branches`, `customers`, and `competitors` tables contain only street addresses. To use them in the application, they must first be extended with a spatial column (`SDO_GEOMETRY`), and this column must be populated.
- *Map definitions and styles*: The applications use a predefined map, themes, and styles.

Loading the Geographical Data

If you have not done so yet, now is the time to load your database with the base geographical data. For clarity and ease of use, we provide the data as several Oracle dump files.

You need to import those files using the Oracle Import tool. The code shown in Listing 14-1 performs the following actions:

- Loads the large-scale data (countries, states, counties, and so on)
- Loads the detailed data (city streets, and so on)
- Loads the geocoding data

Listing 14-1. *Loading the Geographical Data*

```
imp spatial/spatial file=map_large.dmp full=y
imp spatial/spatial file=map_detailed.dmp full=y
imp spatial/spatial file=gc.dmp full=y
```

Location-Enabling the Application Data

If you have performed the steps detailed in Chapter 6 and you have run the examples in the following chapters, you should now have your `customers`, `branches`, and `competitors` tables spatially enabled and ready for use.

In case you did not complete those steps, you can now load them in the "spatially enabled" format by importing the file `app_data_with_loc.dmp` as follows:

```
imp spatial/spatial file=app_data_with_loc.dmp full=y
```

Loading Map, Theme, Style, and Map Cache Definitions for MapViewer

Maps, themes, and style definitions are provided ready for use. All you need to do is import them into the database. Importing the style dump file creates and populates three tables: `my_maps`, `my_themes`, and `my_styles`. The definitions must still be loaded into the dictionary tables used by MapViewer. Listing 14-2 illustrates this process. Note that you also load the definitions of map caches needed by the Oracle Maps application.

Listing 14-2. *Loading Map Definitions*

```
imp spatial/spatial file=styles.dmp full=y

SQL> INSERT into user_sdo_styles
       select * from my_styles;
SQL> insert into user_sdo_themes
       select * from my_themes;
SQL> insert into user_sdo_maps
       select * from my_maps;
SQL> insert into user_sdo_cached_maps
       select * from my_cached_maps;
SQL> commit;
```

Applications Setup

To run the sample applications, you must have a running Oracle Application Server or, at a minimum, the stand-alone Oracle Containers for Java (OC4J) software. You also need to have the MapViewer component up and running. If you ran any of the examples presented in Chapters 12 and 13, then you should be all set. If not, just refer to Chapter 12; specifically, review the section "Getting Started with MapViewer." That section includes instructions on how to install and set up the OC4J software.

The sample applications, together with all the MapViewer examples used in this book, are in a file called `web-examples.zip`. Expand it into `$OC4J_HOME/j2ee/home/applications/mapviewer/web/spatial-book`, where `$OC4J_HOME` is the root folder where you installed OC4J.

The next step is to define a permanent data source in MapViewer's configuration file. This is not strictly necessary, since you could also add a data source via MapViewer's administration page, but having a permanent data source makes it easier for you when you stop and start OC4J and MapViewer.

To add the data source, you edit the configuration file, as explained in Chapter 12. The file is located at `$OC4J_HOME/j2ee/home/applications/mapviewer/web/WEB-INF/conf/MapViewerConfig.xml`. Add the following definition in the main `<MapperConfig>` element:

```
<map_data_source name="spatial"
                 jdbc_host="127.0.0.1"
                 jdbc_port="1521"
                 jdbc_sid="orcl111"
                 jdbc_user="spatial"
                 jdbc_password="!spatial"
                 jdbc_mode="thin"
                 max_connections="5"
                 number_of_mappers="3"
/>
```

Replace the JDBC connection details (`host`, `port`, `sid`, `user`, and `password`) with your own information. The user name should be the one into which you loaded the example data.

If your OC4J server is not up and running, then start it now by going to `$OC4J_HOME/j2ee/home` and entering the command `java -jar oc4j.jar`.

The JavaScript Application

The first application is written in JavaScript and uses MapViewer's JavaScript mapping library. It allows your users to view the location of your branches, your customers, and the branches of your competitors on a street-level map, as well as to find details about them and search them. It also lets your users position the map on a street address and perform searches around that address.

Application Walk-Through

Let's first walk through the application from a user's perspective and see what it can do. Then we will look under the hood to see how the various features and functions are implemented.

Starting the Application

Enter the following URL in your browser:

```
http://127.0.0.1:8888/mapviewer/spatial-book/sample-app/SampleApplication.html
```

Note that this URL assumes you installed OC4J on your local machine. If you installed it on some other machine, then just replace the IP address 127.0.0.1 with that of your server.

If your setup is correct, you should now see a page like the one shown in Figure 14-1.

Figure 14-1. *Home page of the sample JavaScript application*

The map is centered to downtown San Francisco. You can also center it to Washington, D.C., by clicking the link in the "Direct Links" section.

The home page of the application consists of three main areas:

- The center area contains the map proper with its controls and decorations: scale bar, navigation panel, overview map, and marquee zoom control.
- The left area lets you control what application data should appear on the map—that is, which application themes (branches, customers, or competitors) should be enabled—and whether the application data should refresh automatically as you pan and zoom. It also lets you enter an address on which to position the map.
- The area on the right (not shown on the figure) will list the details about the application objects shown on the current map. This is also where the results of searches and queries will appear.

You can move around the map by dragging it, using the navigation panel, or using the overview map. To zoom, use the navigation panel, or use marquee zoom.

Adding Application Data to the Map

You can add application features to the map by selecting one or more of the check boxes on the left. As you click a box, the corresponding features will be read from the database and shown on the map. Details about each feature also appear in a list in the area at the right of the map area, as shown in Figure 14-2, which shows the map with the branches and competitors themes enabled.

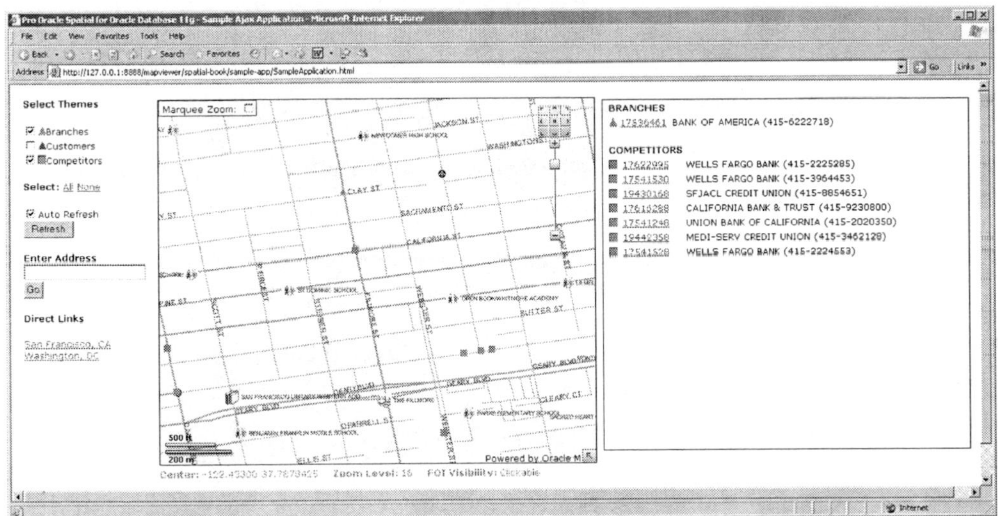

Figure 14-2. *Map with branches and competitors shown*

As you move around the map, the application features will be automatically refreshed, together with the list in the right window. To disable this automatic updating, just uncheck the Auto Refresh box. You can always ask for a manual refresh by clicking the Refresh button.

Identifying an Application Feature

Clicking an application feature on the map opens an information window, as shown in Figure 14-3. You can also get that window by clicking a details line.

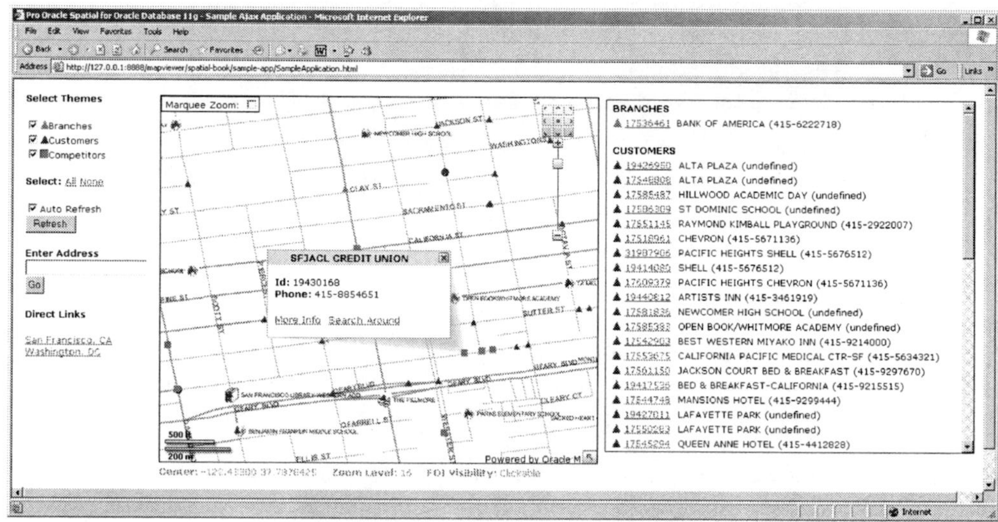

Figure 14-3. *An information window*

Clicking the More Info link will replace the right window with full details on the feature you selected. See Figure 14-4 for an example.

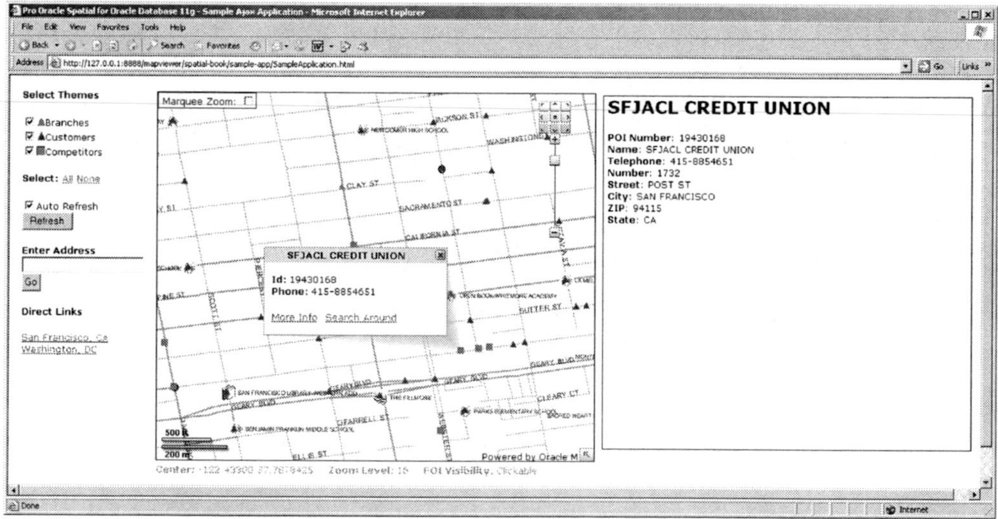

Figure 14-4. *Full details about an application feature*

Searching "Within Radius"

Clicking the Search Around link in the information window expands it, as shown in Figure 14-5. Choose the kind of features to search and a radius in meters. Then click the Search button.

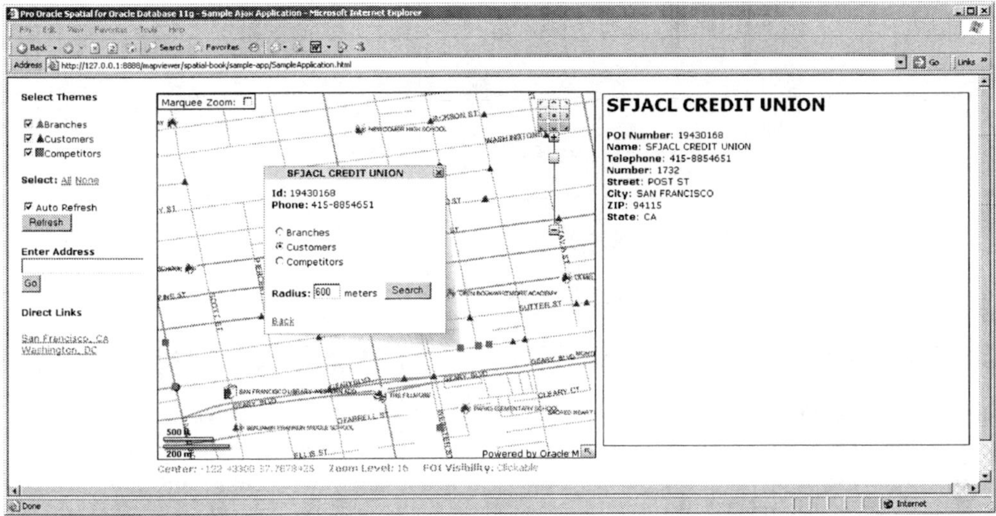

Figure 14-5. *Searching around a feature*

MapViewer will then issue a spatial search to retrieve those features of your chosen type that are within the chosen distance from the originally selected feature. Figure 14-6 shows the results of such a search. The map shows the area searched, and the features found are highlighted with small pins. You will notice that the map was automatically recentered and expanded in such a way that it shows the full search area.

■ **Note** The search area is a circle, but the map shows an ellipse. This is just a side effect of the projection currently used by MapViewer to produce its maps.

The area on the right contains a list of the features found. Clicking any of the features (or a feature in the list) will open a new information window, allowing you to repeat the process if you want.

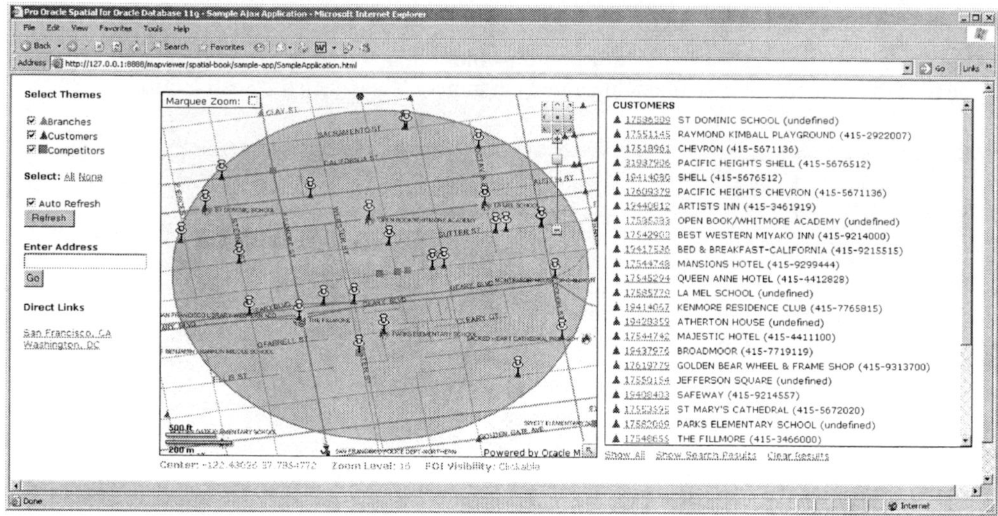

Figure 14-6. *Map with highlighted search results*

To dismiss the results of the search, click the Clear Results link. The Show All and Show Search Results links allow you to toggle between showing all the features on the current map or only the results of your search.

Positioning on a Street Address

Just enter an address in free form into the input box on the left, and click the Go button. The map then centers on the location of that address, highlighted using a yellow pin marker, with an information window pointing to it, as shown in Figure 14-7.

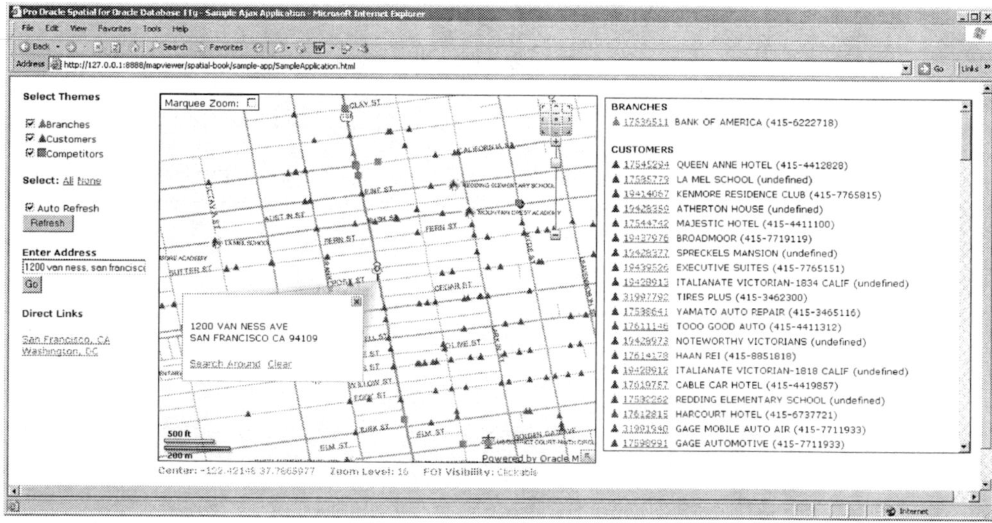

Figure 14-7. *Map positioned on a street address*

Notice that MapViewer automatically refreshed the features shown on the map (and their details in the right window).

To remove the address marker and the information window, just click the Clear link in that window. The Search Around link allows you to search for features around the address, just like you have seen before.

Under the Hood

We'll now explain in detail how to implement the various functions we have just walked you through. All the logic of the application is written in JavaScript, contained in a file called `SampleApplication.js`. The overall structure and appearance of the HTML page is in two separate files, `SampleApplication.html` and `SampleApplication.css`.

Creating the HTML Page

The HTML page is essentially a collection of empty <DIV> sections organized in a table structure to help place them precisely on the page. Those sections will be filled dynamically by the application. The size of the <DIV> sections is specified in the style sheet. Listing 14-3 shows the content of the page.

Listing 14-3. *The Application HTML Page*

```
<!DOCTYPE html PUBLIC "-//W3C//DTD HTML 4.01//EN">
<html>
<head>
  <META http-equiv="Content-Type" content="text/html;">
  <title> Pro Oracle Spatial for Oracle Database 11g  - Sample Ajax
     Application</title>
  <link rel="stylesheet" href="SampleApplication.css" type="text/css">
  <script language="Javascript"
    src="/mapviewer/fsmc/jslib/oraclemaps.js"></script>
  <script language="JavaScript"
    src="SampleApplication.js"> </script>
</head>
<body onLoad="loadMainMap(0);" style="width:100%;">
  <table>
    <tr>
      <td valign="top">
        <div id="PANEL_CONTROL">
        <form name="controlPanel">
          <b>Select Themes</b>
          <div id="THEMES_LIST"></div>
          <b>Select:</b>
          <a href="javascript:toggleAllThemes(true)" >All</a>
          <a href="javascript:toggleAllThemes(false)" >None</A>
          <p><input type="checkbox" name="autoRefresh"
            onclick="toggleAutoRefresh(this);">Auto Refresh
          <br><input type=button onclick="refreshAllThemes();" value="Refresh">
          <p><b>Enter Address</b>
          <br><input type="text" id="address" size="24"/>
          <br><input type=button onclick="geocodeAddress();" value="Go">
          <p><b>Direct Links</b>
          <div id="DIRECT_LINKS"></div>
        </form>
        </div>
      </td>
      <td valign="top">
```

```
        <table>
          <tr><td valign="top"> <div id="PANEL_MAP"> </div> </td></tr>
          <tr><td valign="top"> <div id="PANEL_STATUS" > </div> </td> </tr>
        </table>
      </td>
      <td valign="top">
        <table>
          <tr>
          <tr><td valign="top"> <div id="PANEL_INFO" > </div> </td> </tr>
            <td valign="top">
              <div id="PANEL_SEARCH_CONTROL">
                <a href="javascript:showSearch(false)">Show All</a>
                <a href="javascript:showSearch(true)">Show Search Results</a>
                <a href="javascript:clearSearch()">Clear Results</a>
              </div>
            </td>
          </tr>
        </table>
      </td>
    </tr>
  </table>
</body>
</html>
```

You load two JavaScript libraries in the header of the page: `oraclemaps.js`, which is the main MapViewer (Oracle Maps) library providing all mapping functions, and the application code, which is `SampleApplication.js`.

The <body> specification contains the `onLoad="loadMainMap(0);"` specification, which instructs your browser to automatically invoke the application's main entry point when the page is loaded.

The page contains a number of links (`href`) and buttons. All invoke JavaScript functions contained in the application code.

Creating the JavaScript Code

The JavaScript code of the application begins with some global variables, visible to all functions. The majority are actually constants used to configure the application, such as the name of the base map and data source, the projection (SRID) of the map, and the list of the application data themes and various zoom levels.

There are also true global variables, used to share information between the various functions that make up the application. The main one is the variable used to hold the `MVMapView` object:

```
var mapview = null;
```

It will be set during initialization and then used in many of the functions.

Initializing the Application

The application begins its execution with the `loadMainMap()` function, automatically invoked when the HTML page gets loaded. The function receives one input parameter (`location`), which is the number of the location to start from. Locations are defined in an array:

```
var locations = new Array (
  new Array ("San Francisco, CA", -122.433028333333328, 37.7878425, 16),
  new Array ("Washington, DC",    -77.016167,           38.90505,   16)
)
```

Each location is defined by a name, the longitude and latitude, and the zoom level to use when showing this location.

You first create and initialize the MVMapView object:

```
// Define initial map center and scale based on chosen location
mapCenterX = locations[location][1];
mapCenterY = locations[location][2];
mapZoom =    locations[location][3];

// Create an MVMapView instance to display the map
mapview = new MVMapView(document.getElementById("PANEL_MAP"), baseURL);

// Add a base map layer as background.
var basemap = new MVBaseMap(datasourceName+"."+baseMapName);
mapview.addBaseMapLayer(basemap);

// Set the initial map center and zoom level
var center=MVSdoGeometry.createPoint(mapCenterX, mapCenterY, mapSRID);
mapview.setCenter(center);
mapview.setZoomLevel(mapZoom);
```

Then you add some decorations and tools, such as a navigation panel, scale bar, overview map, and so on:

```
// Add a navigation panel on the right side of the map
mapview.setHomeMap(center, mapZoom);
mapview.addNavigationPanel("EAST");

// Add a scale bar
 mapview.addScaleBar();

// Add a copyright notice
mapview.addCopyRightNote("Powered by Oracle Maps");
```

You also build and add a marquee-zoom control:

```
// Add a marquee zoom control
var toolBar =
'<div style="background-color:white; border:1px solid black;">'+
' Marquee Zoom: '+
'<input id="marqueezoom" type="checkbox" value="marqueezoom" ' +
  'onclick="toggleMarqueeZoom(this)" unchecked/>'+
'</div>'
md = new MVMapDecoration(toolBar, 0, 0) ;
mapview.addMapDecoration(md);
```

The next step is to set up and add the application data layers as FOI themes to the map view. Just like the locations, they are defined in a constant table:

```
var foiThemes = new Array(
  "BRANCHES",
  "CUSTOMERS",
  "COMPETITORS"
);
```

Here is how the FOI themes are defined:

```
for (i in foiThemes) {
  theme = new MVThemeBasedFOI(foiThemes[i],datasourceName+"."+foiThemes[i]);
  theme.setMinVisibleZoomLevel(minVisibleZoomLevel);
```

```
  theme.setMaxWholeImageLevel(maxWholeImageLevel);
  theme.setMinClickableZoomLevel(minClickableZoomLevel);
  theme.setAutoRefresh(autoRefresh);
  theme.enableInfoWindow(false);
  theme.addEventListener('mouse_click', foiMouseClickEvent) ;
  theme.addEventListener('after_refresh',foiAfterRefreshEvent);
  theme.setVisible(false);
  mapview.addThemeBasedFOI(theme);
}
```

You begin by setting the zoom levels that control the visibility of the themes. See Chapter 13 for explanations of the meaning of the various levels:

```
theme.setMinVisibleZoomLevel(minVisibleZoomLevel);
theme.setMaxWholeImageLevel(maxWholeImageLevel);
theme.setMinClickableZoomLevel(minClickableZoomLevel);
```

Set the theme to refresh automatically (or not) based on setting one of the configuration constants:

```
theme.setAutoRefresh(autoRefresh);
```

Disable the display of the standard information window; you will use a custom-built window instead:

```
theme.enableInfoWindow(false);
```

Add event listeners; one will be called each time you click one of the features in this theme. This is how you will trigger your own information window. The second event will be called each time the theme is refreshed by dragging the map or zooming. This will be used to maintain the side list of features.

```
theme.addEventListener('mouse_click', foiMouseClickEvent) ;
theme.addEventListener('after_refresh',foiAfterRefreshEvent);
```

Finally, add the theme to the map. But before that, set it to be invisible. Nothing will happen with this theme (no data read, no display) until it is set to be visible again.

```
theme.setVisible(false);
mapview.addThemeBasedFOI(theme);
```

The final step in the initialization sequence is to display the map:

```
mapview.display();
```

This effectively passes the control to MapViewer. All the other functions in our application will be called as a consequence of some explicit or implicit user action, including mouse clicks, button presses, URLs, and so on. This also means that control never returns from this call. Any code that follows will never be executed.

Displaying the List of Features Currently on the Map

Whenever you move the map around by panning or zooming, whether directly or using the overview map of the navigation panel, details about the features currently visible on the map will be shown in a list format in the window at the right side of the map (the information panel). This works thanks to the `after_refresh` event you declared for each FOI theme. The function `foiAfterRefreshEvent()` handles the event and simply calls `refreshInfoPanel()`.

```
function foiAfterRefreshEvent()
{
  refreshInfoPanel()
}
```

The function refreshInfoPanel() shown in Listing 14-4 is actually called from multiple places: when enabling or disabling a theme or when clicking the Refresh button. The information panel can contain either the full list of visible features or the list of features returned by a radius query. The function calls a separate function to handle each case.

Listing 14-4. *Function* refreshInfoPanel()

```
// ---------------------------------------------------------------------------
// refreshInfoPanel()
// Updates the list of FOIs currently displayed in the info panel
// ---------------------------------------------------------------------------
function refreshInfoPanel()
{
  if (showSearchResults)
    showSelectedFOIs();
  else
    showAllVisibleFOIs();
}
```

Function showAllVisibleFOIs() shown in Listing 14-5 processes the case where you are showing all visible features. It runs through the list of themes, retaining only those that are currently visible and, if they are, calls displayFOIList() to format the list of features currently on the map for that theme. The function showSelectedFOIs() processes only the list of features selected in the current radius search and also calls displayFOIList() to format them.

Listing 14-5. *Function* showAllVisibleFOIs()

```
// ---------------------------------------------------------------------------
// showAllVisibleFOIs()
// List all currently visible FOIs in the right panel (PANEL_INFO)
// Do this only if FOIs are clickable, i.e. if the current zoom level
// is >= minClickableZoomLevel
// ---------------------------------------------------------------------------
function showAllVisibleFOIs()
{
  if (mapview.getZoomLevel() < minClickableZoomLevel)
    return;
  var html = '';
  for (var i in foiThemes) {
    theme = mapview.getThemeBasedFOI(foiThemes[i]);
    if (theme.isVisible())
      html += displayFOIList(theme, foiThemes[i]);
  }
  document.getElementById("PANEL_INFO").innerHTML=html;
}
```

The function displayFOIList() formats the list of features to be shown in the information panel. It does so by dynamically generating an HTML table. See Listing 14-6.

Listing 14-6. *Function* displayFOIList()

```
// ---------------------------------------------------------------------------
// displayFOIList()
// Display a list of FOIs
// ---------------------------------------------------------------------------
function displayFOIList (theme, themeName)
{
```

```
  // Extract the FOIs in this theme
  var fois = theme.getFOIData();
  // Nothing to display if list is empty
  if (!fois)
    return '';
  var html = '<table>';
  html += '<tr><td colspan="3"><b>'+themeName+'</b></td></tr>';
  for (var i in fois) {
    // Build URL to display function
    var href = 'javascript:locateFOI("' + themeName + '","' + fois[i].id + '")';
    html += '<tr>';
    // Marker symbol
    html += '<td>' +
      '<a href=' + href + '>' +
      '<img src=' + baseURL + '/omserver?sty=m.' + themeName + '&ds=' +
         datasourceName +'&f=png&w=12&h=12&aa=true" border="0">' +
      '</a></td>';
    // FOI ID
    html += '<td>' +
       '<a href=' + href + '>' + fois[i].attrs[0] + '</a></td>';
    // FOI Name and telephone
    html += '<td>' +
      '<td>'+ fois[i].attrs[1] + ' ('+fois[i].attrs[2] +')</td>'
    html += '</tr>';
  }
  html += '</table><br>';
  return html;
}
```

Notice that you add a link in each entry of the list that, when clicked, will display an information window for this feature. The link calls the JavaScript function locateFOI(), which gets passed two arguments: the name of the theme this feature belongs to (as in CUSTOMERS, BRANCHES, or COMPETITORS) and the unique identifier of the feature.

Creating the Information Window

Just like the feature list is refreshed, an information window is displayed when triggered by an event. This is the mouse_click event, handled by function foiMouseClickEvent(). The event handler receives two input parameters: the location of the click and an object containing the data of the feature. You ignore the location of the click, since the actual location of the feature is contained in the data object. Note that you save the data object in the global variable currentFOI. This is because you need to pass the data object around between multiple functions invoked via dynamically generated links.

```
function foiMouseClickEvent (loc, foi)
{
  currentFOI = foi;
  displayInfoWindow()
}
```

The function displayInfoWindow() shown in Listing 14-7 formats the information window using input from the data object saved in the global variable and then adds it to the map view. It adds two links on the window, both calling JavaScript functions. One of the links calls showFOIDetails() to display the complete content of the data object in the information panel at the right side of the map. The other calls displaySearchWindow() to handle the search function.

Listing 14-7. *Function* `displayInfoWindow()`

```
// -----------------------------------------------------------------------------
// displayInfoWindow()
// Displays the information window when a FOI object is clicked.
// -----------------------------------------------------------------------------
function displayInfoWindow()
{
  foi = currentFOI
  var html = '';
  html += '<b>Id: </b>'+foi.attrs[0]+'<br>';
  html += '<b>Phone: </b>'+foi.attrs[2]+'<br>';
  html += '<p><a href="javascript:showFOIDetails()">More Info<a>  ';
  html += '<a href="javascript:displaySearchWindow()">Search Around<a>';
  width = 250;
  height = 120;
  loc = MVSdoGeometry.createPoint(foi.x,foi.y);
  mapview.displayInfoWindow(loc, html, width, height,
    "MVInfoWindowStyle1", "  "+foi.name+"  ");
}
```

Listing 14-8 shows the function `showFOIDetails()`. All it does is format the content of variable `currentFOI` into the information panel.

Listing 14-8. *Function* `showFOIDetails()`

```
// -----------------------------------------------------------------------------
// showFOIDetails()
// Shows details about one selected FOI in the INFO panel
// -----------------------------------------------------------------------------
function showFOIDetails()
{
  foi = currentFOI;
  var html = '<h2>'+foi.name+'</h2>';
  for (var i=0; i<foi.attrs.length; i++)
    html += '<b>'+foi.attrnames[i]+'</b>: '+foi.attrs[i]+'<br>';
  document.getElementById("PANEL_INFO").innerHTML=html;
}
```

Searching "Within Radius"

Searching begins with the function `displaySearchWindow()` detailed in Listing 14-9 whose goal it is to redraw the information window, allowing the user to select the parameters to be used for the search. The parameters are a set of radio buttons allowing the user to choose the theme to search, then a text input to enter the radius to search (in meters), and finally a button that, when clicked, calls the function `searchAround()` to perform the actual search.

Listing 14-9. *Function* `displaySearchWindow()`

```
// -----------------------------------------------------------------------------
// displaySearchWindow()
// Redisplays the information window with search selection information
// -----------------------------------------------------------------------------
function displaySearchWindow()
{
  foi = currentFOI;
  var html = '';
```

```
  html += '<b>Id: </b>'+foi.attrs[0]+'<br>';
  html += '<b>Phone: </b>'+foi.attrs[2]+'<br>';
  html += '<dl>';
  for (i in foiThemes) {
    html += '<dt>' +
      '<input type="radio" name="searchThemes" value="' + foiThemes[i] + '"/>' +
      foiThemeLabels[i];
  }
  html += '</dl>';
  html += '<b>Radius: </b><input id="searchRadiusInput" size=2 value=500> meters';
  html += '  <input type=button onclick="searchAround();" '+
    'value="Search">'
  html += '<p><a href="javascript:displayInfoWindow()">Back<a>';
  width = 250;
  height = 120;
  loc = MVSdoGeometry.createPoint(foi.x,foi.y);
  mapview.displayInfoWindow(loc, html, width, height,
    "MVInfoWindowStyle1", "  "+foi.name+"  ");
}
```

The function searchAround() extracts the name of the theme to search as well as the radius from named HTML elements in the information window. Before going any further, it makes sure the radio button selects a theme. It then proceeds to construct two more themes and adds them to the map view. See Listing 14-10 for the source code.

Listing 14-10. *Function* searchAround()

```
// -----------------------------------------------------------------------------
// searchAround()
// Selects all features around the currently selected FOI
// -----------------------------------------------------------------------------
function searchAround()
{
  // Get the currently selected FOI
  var foi = currentFOI;

  // Get the value of the chosen radius
  var searchRadius = document.getElementById('searchRadiusInput').value;

  // Get the name of the theme to search
  var searchThemes = document.getElementsByName('searchThemes');
  var searchThemeName = null;
  for (var i=0; i<searchThemes.length; i++) {
    if (searchThemes[i].checked)
      searchThemeName = searchThemes[i].value;
  }
  if (!searchThemeName) {
    alert ("Please select the theme to search");
    return;
  }

  // Build the parameters for the search
  var loc = MVSdoGeometry.createPoint(foi.x,foi.y,mapSRID);
  var distanceString = 'distance='+searchRadius+' unit=m';

  // Add the search window theme to the map view
  if (searchBufferTheme)
```

```
    mapview.removeThemeBasedFOI(searchBufferTheme);
  searchBufferTheme = new MVThemeBasedFOI('buffer', 'DYNAMIC_CIRCULAR_BUFFER');
  searchBufferTheme.setQueryParameters(loc, searchRadius) ;
  searchBufferTheme.setBoundingTheme(true);
  searchBufferTheme.setClickable(false);
  searchBufferTheme.enableImageCaching(true);
  searchBufferTheme.setAutoRefresh(false);
  mapview.addThemeBasedFOI(searchBufferTheme);

  // Add the search theme to the map view. Remove it first if already shown
  if (searchTheme)
    mapview.removeThemeBasedFOI(searchTheme);
  searchTheme = new MVThemeBasedFOI('search', searchThemeName+'_WD');
  searchTheme.setQueryParameters(loc, distanceString) ;
  searchTheme.setRenderingStyle("M.CYAN PIN");
  searchTheme.enableImageCaching(true);
  searchTheme.setAutoRefresh(false);
  searchTheme.addEventListener('mouse_click', foiMouseClickEvent);
  searchTheme.addEventListener('after_refresh', foiAfterRefreshEvent);
  mapview.addThemeBasedFOI(searchTheme);

  // Make controls appear
  document.getElementById("PANEL_SEARCH_CONTROL").style.visibility="visible";
  showSearchResults = true;
}
```

The first theme it adds (searchBufferTheme) is the one that renders a circular buffer representing the area searched (in other words, a circle of the chosen radius), centered on the point location we search from. The buffer is generated using a predefined parameterized theme. Here is the definition of the theme:

```
insert into user_sdo_themes
  (name, description, base_table, geometry_column, styling_rules)
values ('DYNAMIC_CIRCULAR_BUFFER','Dynamic circular buffers','DUAL','BUFFER_GEOM',
'<?xml version="1.0" standalone="yes"?>
<styling_rules>
  <rule>
    <features asis="true" style="C.BUFFER">
      select sdo_geom.sdo_buffer (:1, :2, 0.05) buffer_geom from dual
    </features>
  </rule>
</styling_rules>'
);
```

The buffer is produced using the function SDO_GEOM.SDO_BUFFER(). The parameters to the function are set into the theme definition in JavaScript using this statement:

```
searchBufferTheme.setQueryParameters(loc, searchRadius) ;
```

The second theme added to the map view (searchTheme) is the one that actually selects the features within the chosen radius from the origin point location. It is also built on a predefined parameterized theme that corresponds to the theme being searched. Here is the definition of the theme for searching customers:

```
insert into user_sdo_themes
  (name, description, base_table, geometry_column, styling_rules)
values ('CUSTOMERS_WD','Searching customers','CUSTOMERS','LOCATION',
'<?xml version="1.0" standalone="yes"?>
```

```
<styling_rules>
  <hidden_info>
    <field column="DATASRC_ID" name="POI Number"/>
    <field column="NAME" name="Name"/>
    <field column="PHONE_NUMBER" name="Telephone"/>
    <field column="STREET_NUMBER" name="Number"/>
    <field column="STREET_NAME" name="Street"/>
    <field column="CITY" name="City"/>
    <field column="POSTAL_CODE" name="ZIP"/>
    <field column="STATE_ABRV" name="State"/>
    <field column="CUSTOMER_GRADE" name="Grade"/>
    <field column="CATEGORY" name="Category"/>
  </hidden_info>
  <rule >
    <features asis="true" style="M.CUSTOMERS">
    (sdo_within_distance (location, :1, :2) = &apos;TRUE&apos;)
    </features>
    <label column="NAME" style="T.BUSINESS NAME BLUE"> 1 </label>
  </rule>
</styling_rules>
');
```

Here the parameters get inserted into an SDO_WITHIN_DISTANCE() operator. The first parameter is the point location you search from, and the second is a distance expression. The following statement sets the parameter values in the theme definition:

```
var distanceString = 'distance='+searchRadius+' unit=m';
searchTheme.setQueryParameters(loc, distanceString) ;
```

Notice that you also add two event listeners to the theme:

```
searchTheme.addEventListener('mouse_click', foiMouseClickEvent);
searchTheme.addEventListener('after_refresh', foiAfterRefreshEvent);
```

Both events are handled by the same listeners you defined earlier on the regular application data themes. The mouse_click event allows the user to select individual features returned by the search, therefore also enabling the user to get the full details about a feature and perform more searches around a selected feature.

The after_refresh event makes sure the details of the features returned by the search appear in the information panel.

Positioning on a Street Address

The start point for positioning on an address is the function geocodeAddress(), detailed in Listing 14-11.That function is invoked when the user enters an address in the address input field and clicks the Go button next to it. You first extract the address from the input field and then split it up into an array of address lines, based on the commas present in the input. For example: 1250 Clay Street, San Francisco, CA will be split into three lines:

```
1250 Clay Street
San Francisco
CA
```

Then you build the XML request for the geocoding service. For details on the syntax of the XML requests and responses, see Chapter 6.

Listing 14-11. *Function* geocodeAddress()

```
// ---------------------------------------------------------------------------
// geocodeAddress()
// ---------------------------------------------------------------------------
function geocodeAddress()
{
  // Get input address and split it into lines
  var address = document.getElementById("address").value;
  if (!address)
    return;
  var addressLines = address.split(',');

  // Construct the XML request to the Geocoder
  gcXML = '<geocode_request>'
  gcXML += ' <address_list>'
  gcXML += '  <input_location id="1" >'
  gcXML += '   <input_address>'
  gcXML += '    <unformatted country="US" >'
  for (var i in addressLines)
    gcXML += '     <address_line value="'+addressLines[i]+'" />';
  gcXML += '    </unformatted >'
  gcXML += '   </input_address>'
  gcXML += '  </input_location>'
  gcXML += ' </address_list>'
  gcXML += '</geocode_request>'

  var serverURL = "http://"+document.location.host+"/"+"geocoder/gcserver";
  var queryString = encodeURI("xml_request="+gcXML);

  // Call the geocoder via an asynchronous XMLHTTPRequest call
  var response = callServer(serverURL, queryString, geocodeAddressComplete);
}
```

The last statement of the function calls the geocoding server. This is an asynchronous call. You call the function `callServer()`, which uses the `XMLHttpRequest` mechanism to send the query to the server. The `callServer()` function is detailed later in Listing 14-14. It needs three arguments:

- The first argument is the URL of the service to call.
- The second argument is the query string passed to the service.
- The third argument is the function to call when the response from the service is received.

In this case, when the call to the geocoding service completes, the function `geocodeAddressComplete()` will be called. This function will receive one argument: the response object returned by the `XMLHttpRequest` mechanism. See Listing 14-12 for the code of the function `geocodeAddressComplete()`.

Listing 14-12. *Function* geocodeAddressComplete()

```
// ---------------------------------------------------------------------------
// geocodeAddressComplete()
// This function gets called when the asynchronous XMLHTTPRequest call completes
// ---------------------------------------------------------------------------
function geocodeAddressComplete(response)
{
```

```
// The Geocode XML response looks like this:
/*
<geocode_response>
  <geocode id="1" match_count="1">
    <match sequence="0" longitude="-122.4135615" latitude="37.7932878"
      match_code="1"
      error_message="????#ENUT?B281CP?"
      match_vector="????0101010??000?">
      <output_address name="" house_number="1250" street="CLAY ST"
        builtup_area="SAN FRANCISCO"
        order1_area="CA" order8_area="" country="US" postal_code="94108"
        postal_addon_code=""
        side="L" percent="0.49" edge_id="23600695" />
    </match>
  </geocode>
</geocode_response>
*/

// Extract the results from the XML response returned by the server
var geocode = response.getElementsByTagName('geocode');
var match = geocode[0].getElementsByTagName('match');
var output_address = match[0].getElementsByTagName('output_address');

gc_longitude    = match[0].getAttribute('longitude');
gc_latitude     = match[0].getAttribute('latitude');
gc_house_number = output_address[0].getAttribute('house_number');
gc_street       = output_address[0].getAttribute('street');
gc_builtup_area = output_address[0].getAttribute('builtup_area');
gc_state        = output_address[0].getAttribute('order1_area');
gc_postal_code  = output_address[0].getAttribute('postal_code');

if (gc_longitude == 0) {
  alert ("Address not found");
  return;
}

// Delete existing marker, if any
if (gcMarker)
  mapview.removeFOI (gcMarker);
// Add a marker on the map
var gc_loc = MVSdoGeometry.createPoint(gc_longitude, gc_latitude, mapSRID);
gcMarker = new MVFOI("ADDRESS LOCATION", gc_loc, "SPATIAL.M.YELLOW PIN");
gcMarker.setWidth(30);
gcMarker.setHeight(50);
mapview.addFOI(gcMarker);

// Build  an info window and add it to the marker
var html = '';
html += gc_house_number + " " + gc_street + "<br>";
html += gc_builtup_area + " " + gc_state + " " + gc_postal_code +"<br>";
html += '<p><a href="javascript:displayMarkerSearchWindow()">Search Around<a>';
html += '  <a href="javascript:removeMarker()">Clear<a>';
width = 250;
height = 120;
gcMarker.setInfoWindow (html, width, height);
```

```
  // Show the info window
  mapview.displayInfoWindow(gc_loc, html, width, height, "MVInfoWindowStyle1");

  // Center the map on the marker
  mapview.setCenter(gc_loc) ;

  // Save the marker
  currentFOI = gcMarker;
}
```

The function first extracts the relevant information from the XML response, which includes the longitude and latitude but also the corrected and completed address elements. The values are saved in global variables so that they can easily be used by other functions.

Note The parsing as done is not very sophisticated. All you do is extract the information from the first match in the result, and you really do not check the various response codes (`match_code`, `error_message`, and `match_vector`).

The following step is to add a stand-alone FOI on the map at the point indicated by the coordinates returned from the geocoder and to build an information window on the marker.

Finally, you display that information window and center the map on the location of the marker.

Searching Around the Street Address

Just like for regular information windows, the one built on the address marker contains a Search Around link, pointing to the function `displayMarkerSearchWindow()`, shown in Listing 14-13.

Listing 14-13. *Function* `displayMarkerSearchWindow()`

```
// -----------------------------------------------------------------------------
// displayMarkerSearchWindow()
// Redisplays the information window with search selection information
// -----------------------------------------------------------------------------
function displayMarkerSearchWindow()
{
  var foi = currentFOI;
  var html = '';
  html += gc_house_number + " " + gc_street + "<br>";
  html += gc_builtup_area + " " + gc_state + " " + gc_postal_code +"<br>";
  html += '<dl>';
  for (i in foiThemes) {
    html += '<dt>' +
      '<input type="radio" name="searchThemes" value="' + foiThemes[i] + '"/>' +
      foiThemeLabels[i];
  }
  html += '</dl>';
  html += '<b>Radius: </b><input id="searchRadiusInput" size=2 value=500> meters';
  html +=
    '  <input type=button onclick="searchAround();" value="Search">'
  html += '<p><a href="javascript:displayInfoWindow()">Back<a>';
  width = 250;
  height = 120;
  loc = MVSdoGeometry.createPoint(foi.x,foi.y);
  mapview.displayInfoWindow(loc, html, width, height, "MVInfoWindowStyle1");
}
```

The information window is very much like the one you built before for other searches. It allows the user to choose the theme to query and the radius to use. The Search button links to the same `searchAround()` function we have already discussed.

Using the XMLHTTPRequest Mechanism

Listing 14-14 shows the functions used for the asynchronous server call. They are pretty much standard Ajax calls. The first function, `callServer()`, sends the request to the server, checks the result, and invokes the response handler function.

The second function, `getXMLHttpRequest()`, contains the browser-dependent way to get the `XMLHttpRequest` object.[1]

Listing 14-14. *The* `XMLHTTPRequest` *Mechanism*

```
// -------------------------------------------------------------------------------
// callServer()
// -------------------------------------------------------------------------------
function callServer(url, query, handler)
{
  var req = getXMLHttpRequest();
  req.open("POST", url, true);
  req.setRequestHeader("Content-Type","application/x-www-form-urlencoded");
  req.onreadystatechange = function() {
    try {
      if (req.readyState == 4)
        if (req.status==200)
          handler(req.responseXML);
        else
          alert ('Server call failed - '+req.status+' '+req.statusText);
    }
    catch (e) {
      alert(e);
    }
  }
  req.send(query);
}

// -------------------------------------------------------------------------------
// getXMLHttpRequest()
// Get the XMLHttpRequest object (browser-dependent)
// -------------------------------------------------------------------------------
function getXMLHttpRequest ()
{
  if(window.ActiveXObject)
  {
    var req = null ;
```

1. For more details about Ajax and browser-dependencies, refer to *Foundations of Ajax* by Ryan Asleson and Nathaniel T. Schutta (Apress, 2005).

```
    try
    {
      req=new ActiveXObject("Microsoft.XMLHTTP");
    }
    catch(e)
    {
      req=new ActiveXObject("Msxml2.XMLHTTP");
    }
    return req;
  }
  else
    return new XMLHttpRequest();
}
```

The Java (JSP) Application

The second example application is written in Java, embedded in JavaServer Page (JSP), which includes both the logic and the HTML code. To interact with MapViewer, you'll use MapViewer's Java API.

The features of the application are fairly similar to those of the JavaScript variant. The users will be able to view the location of your branches, your customers, and the branches of your competitors on a street-level map. They can find details about them and search them. They can enter a street address, position the map on that address, and perform searches around that address.

Application Walk-Through

Just like for the JavaScript application, we will first walk you through the application and see what it can do. Then we will explain how to implement the various features.

Starting the Application

Enter the following URL in your browser:

```
http://127.0.0.1:8888/mapviewer/spatial-book/sample-app/SampleApplication.jsp
```

If your setup is correct, you should now see a page like the one shown in Figure 14-8.

Just like for the JavaScript application, the map is centered on downtown San Francisco. The initial center and size of the map is actually controlled by parameters you can pass to the application. For example, the following URL positions the initial map on downtown Washington, D.C.:

```
http://127.0.0.1:8888/mapviewer/spatial-book/sample-app/SampleApplication.jsp➥
?initialCx=-77.03497825&initialCy=38.90819015
```

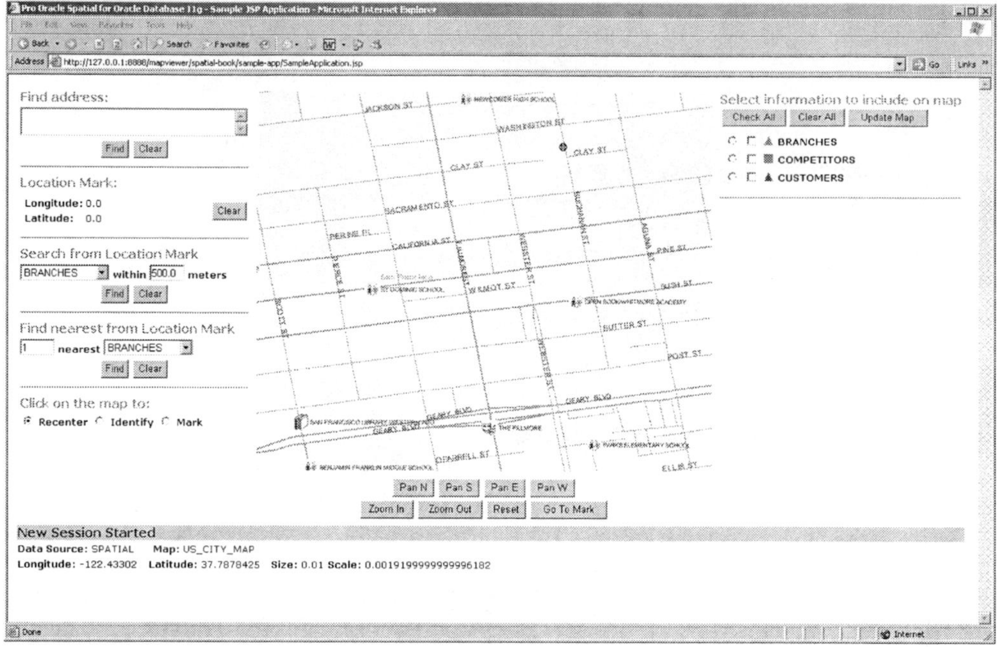

Figure 14-8. *Home page of the sample JSP application*

Creating Application Home Page

The home page of the application consists of three main areas:

- The center area contains the map proper, with navigation buttons and controls.
- The left area lets you enter an address on which to position the map. It shows the current position of the location mark (see the next section for details) and lets you perform searches around it. This is also where you indicate what should happen when you click the map.
- The right area lets you control what application data should appear on the map—that is, which application themes (branches, customers, or competitors) should be enabled. Once a theme is displayed on a map, the application will allow you to click that theme (such as, a particular branch) and display details specific to that theme. This information will also appear in the right window (though none appears in Figure 14-8).

The bottom of the page contains a status area (the gray area where "New Session Started" appears). This is where the application displays the SQL statements it sends to the database. It also uses the status window to report any errors.

Underneath you can see various pieces of information, such as the name of the data source used to connect to the database and the name of the base map used. The second row shows the current center and size of the map, as well as the current scale.

Setting the Location Mark

The left area shows the current position (longitude and latitude) of a *location mark*. Initially, there is no mark set, and the coordinates are shown as zero.

The location mark is the pivotal concept of the application. You use functions provided by the application to set the location mark and other functions to perform searches and analyses from that mark.

You can set the location mark by entering a street address; by selecting a branch, customer, or competitor; or simply by clicking the map, as illustrated in Figure 14-9.

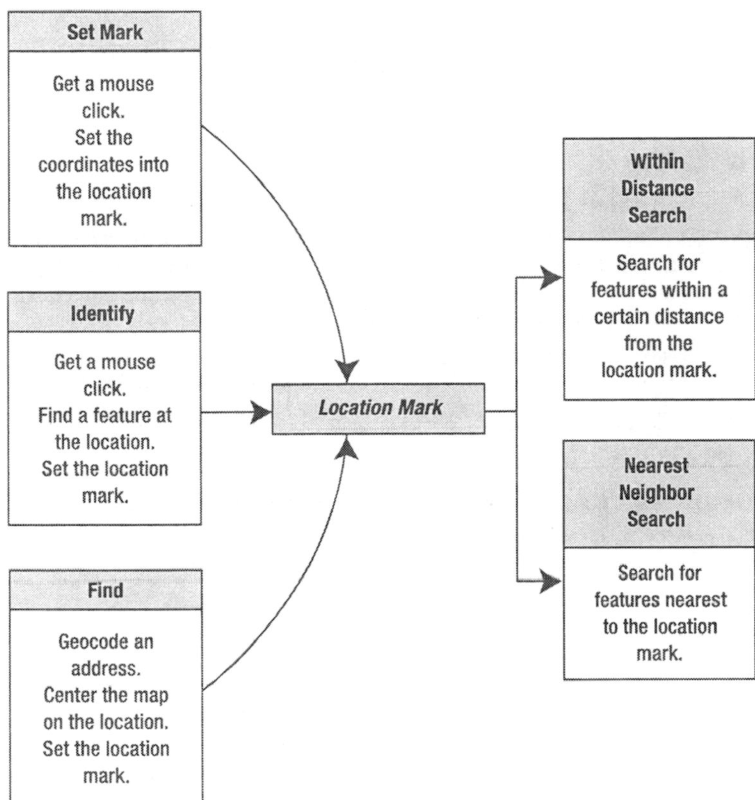

Figure 14-9. *Using the location mark*

The current position of the location mark is shown on the map using a yellow pin. The Clear button next to the Location Mark setting resets it to zero. It also removes the yellow pin marker from the map.

Zooming, Panning, and Recentering

The application provides buttons for navigating around the map and adjusting the zoom level:

- The Pan buttons are used to shift the map in the indicated direction.
- The Zoom In and Zoom Out buttons do exactly what you would expect them to do.
- The Reset button essentially restarts the application. It resets the map to the origin settings and clears all query and search results as well as the location mark.
- The Go to Mark button is an easy way to recenter the map on the current coordinates of the location mark.

You can also reposition the map by simply clicking it. Make sure the radio button on the left is set to Recenter.

Adding Application Data to the Map

The area on the right side of the page shows a list of business tables, from which you can select data to incorporate into the map. Next to each table name is a radio button and a check box. Select the check box for each of the tables you want to use to populate the map, and click the Update Map button. The radio button lets you choose which of the application theme to query when you click the map to identify objects. You'll learn more about that later in this chapter.

The map in the center window is then refreshed with the tables you have chosen. Branches appear as green triangles, customers appear as blue lozenges, and competitors appear as red squares. Notice that not all these elements are labeled. This is because MapViewer tries its best to not overlay labels, as shown in Figure 14-10.

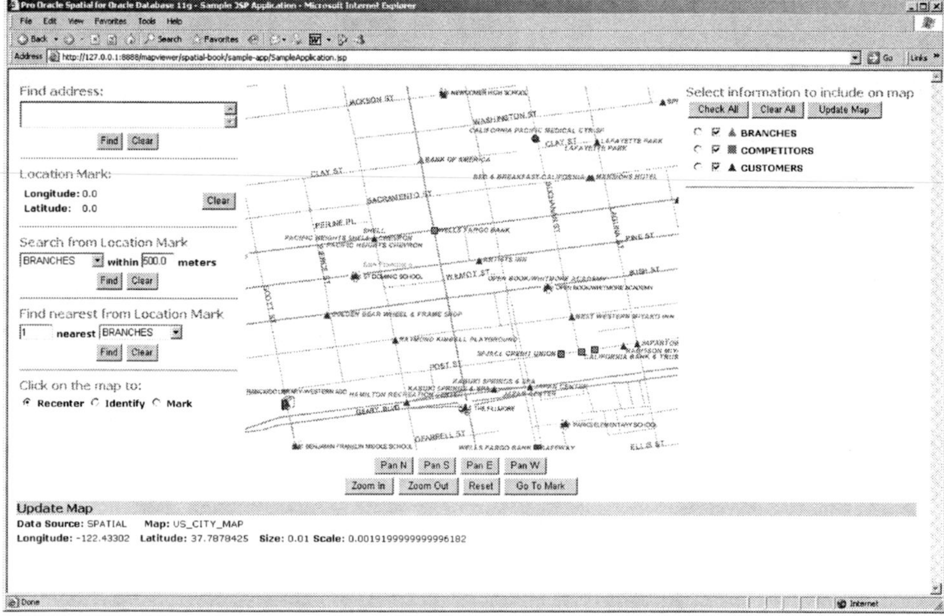

Figure 14-10. *Map showing the business information*

The Clear All and Check All buttons clear and set all application themes, respectively. Note that you still need to click the Update Map button to refresh the map.

Positioning on a Street Address

You can reposition the map at any time by simply entering a valid street address in the window at the top left and clicking the Find button. Be sure to format the address on two lines. For example, you can enter the following address:

```
600 Stockton Street
San Francisco, CA
```

The address is marked with a yellow pin. The right-side window shows the normalized and corrected address.

■ Note `The first time you position the map to a street address after starting up the application server, you will notice a delay. This is because the Oracle geocoder initializes itself by reading and parsing the address-description parameters in the database.

If the address you entered is incorrect or could not be found, the status window at the bottom of the page will indicate this. Otherwise, you will see the SQL statement sent to the database to call the geocoding function.

Note that the yellow pin indicates the current position of your location mark. The coordinates (longitude and latitude) of that location mark are shown in the left area. This mark is important, because you will use it as a starting point for searches. The status area shows the SQL statement issued to perform the geocoding.

Figure 14-11 shows the result of positioning the map on the preceding address and showing the branches.

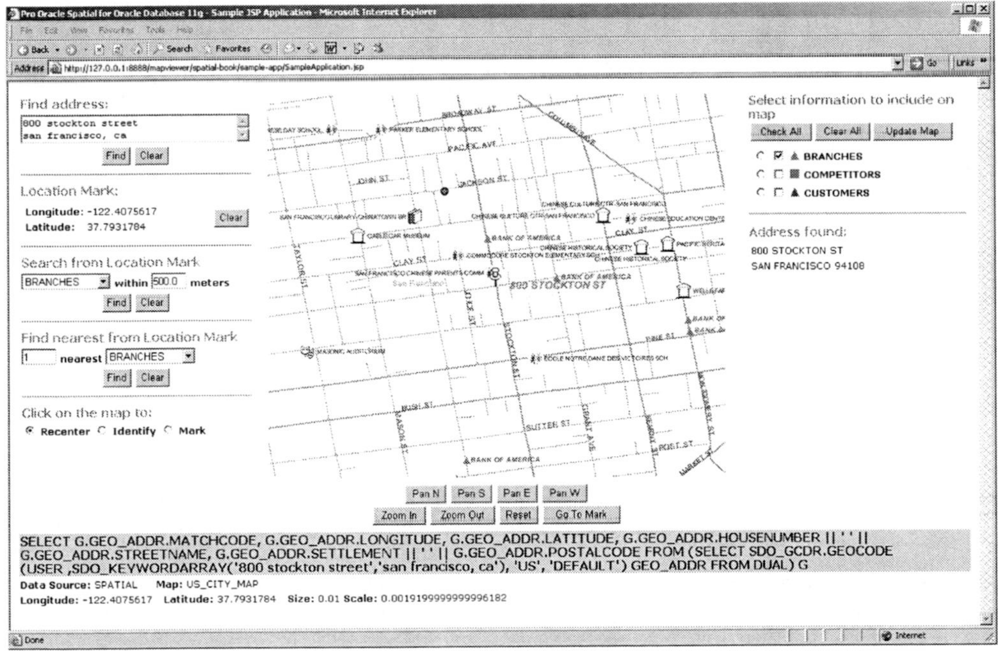

Figure 14-11. *Map positioned on an address*

Selecting and Identifying a Branch, Customer, or Competitor

Now that you can see all the application data (branches and so forth), you can find out more about them by selecting one of them using the mouse.

First, you need to tell the application what it should do when you click the map. For example, you should indicate that when you next click the map, you do not want to reposition it on the point you clicked; rather, you want to get information on the application theme object (the branch) that is on the map on that point. For that, make sure to select the Identify option.

Then you need to tell the application which of the application themes you will be selecting from by using the radio button in front of the theme names. For example, if you want to find out details of a branch by clicking the map, first select the radio button in front of the `branches` table in the selection area.

Now to select a branch, simply move the mouse on the symbol for that branch (the green triangle), and click. The branch will be flagged using a yellow pin, and details on the branch will be shown inside the right window.

Figure 14-12 shows the results of identifying a branch.

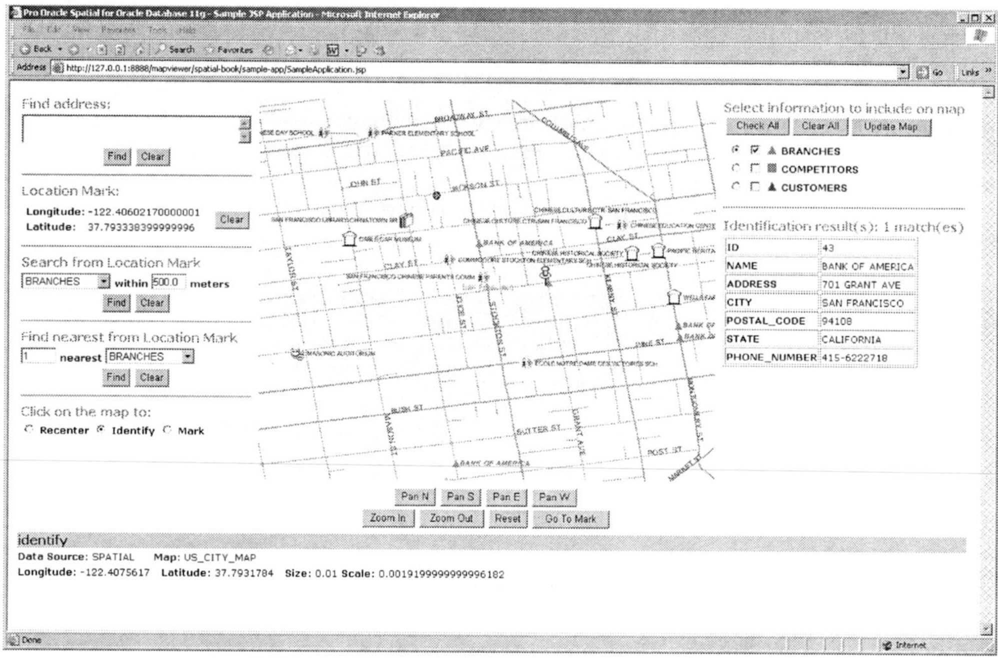

Figure 14-12. *Identifying a branch*

The location mark is now set to the location of the branch you just selected. You can use this mark to search from the selected branch. The process is identical to selecting a customer or a competitor.

Note The selection could actually return multiple matches (multiple customers or competitors) if they are at the same address or are close together.

Searching "Within Distance"

The application lets you search only for visible information. In other words, the theme you want to search (*branches*, *customers*, or *competitors*) must be shown on the map.

Remember that to make a theme visible, you need to select the check box directly in front of the theme's name in the right window and then click the Update Map button.

Next, go to the "Search from Location Mark" area. Select the competitors theme from the drop-down list and enter a distance (for example, 150 meters). Then click the Find button.

The new map marks all competitors within the specified distance with a blue pin. The competitors' details are shown in the right window, as illustrated in Figure 14-13, which shows the results of a search for all competitiors within 150 meters from the branch selected in the previous example. Notice the new SEARCH RESULTS theme that appears in the right window to represent the dynamic results of the search. You can uncheck it to remove the results from the map.

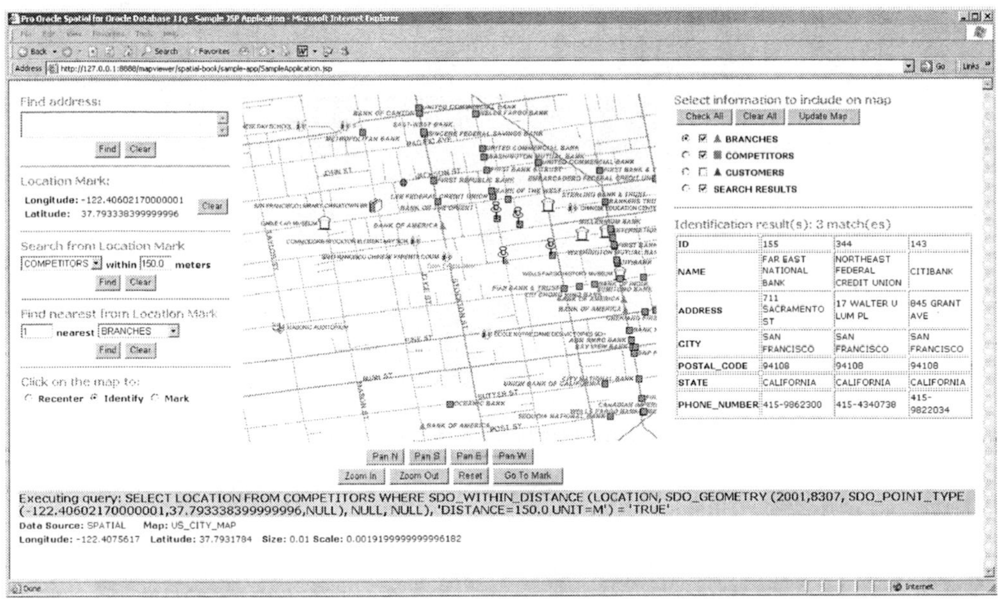

Figure 14-13. *Results of a "within distance" search*

Note that the search radius could be larger than the area currently shown on the map. All matches will be returned, even those that are outside the current map window. However, you will have to zoom out manually to make those matches appear on the map.

The SQL query used to find those competitors is shown in the status window. Clicking the Clear button in the search area removes the query results from the map.

You can repeat this operation for customers. First add the customers to the map, then select the `customers` table from the drop-down list, and finally click the Find button.

Setting a Mark on the Map

You can also set the location mark directly on the map. This lets you perform searches from anywhere. All you need to do is select the Mark option under the map window and then click anywhere on the map.

The location mark, identified by the yellow pin, is now set to the place you clicked.

Searching for Nearest Neighbors

Navigate to the "Find nearest from Location Mark" area of the left window. Select the branches table from the drop-down list, and enter the number of branches to show. Then click the Find button.

The result is much like the one from the previous search; the nearest branches to the location mark you set are marked with blue pins, and their details are shown in the window on the right. See Figure 14-14 for an illustration.

Note that the nearest branch may actually be far away and outside the area currently shown on the map. You will see it by zooming out.

The status window shows the SQL query used to find the nearest branch.

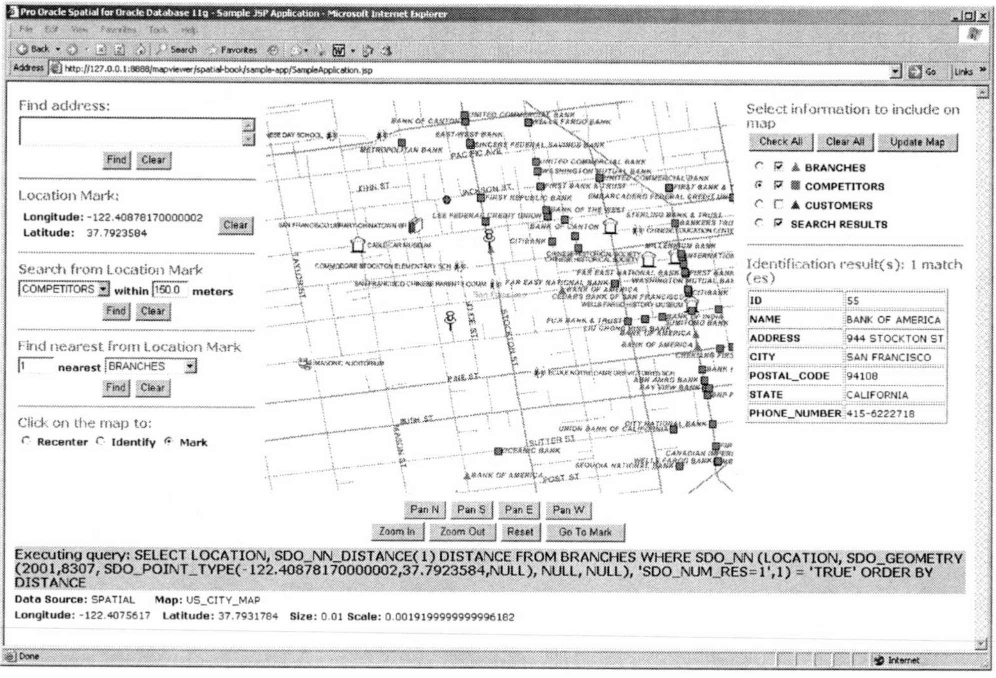

Figure 14-14. *Results of a "nearest neighbor" search*

Under the Hood

The general logic of the application is fairly simple, as shown in Figure 14-15. The application is written as a single JSP page, which contains the application logic proper (in Java) as well as the HTML output.

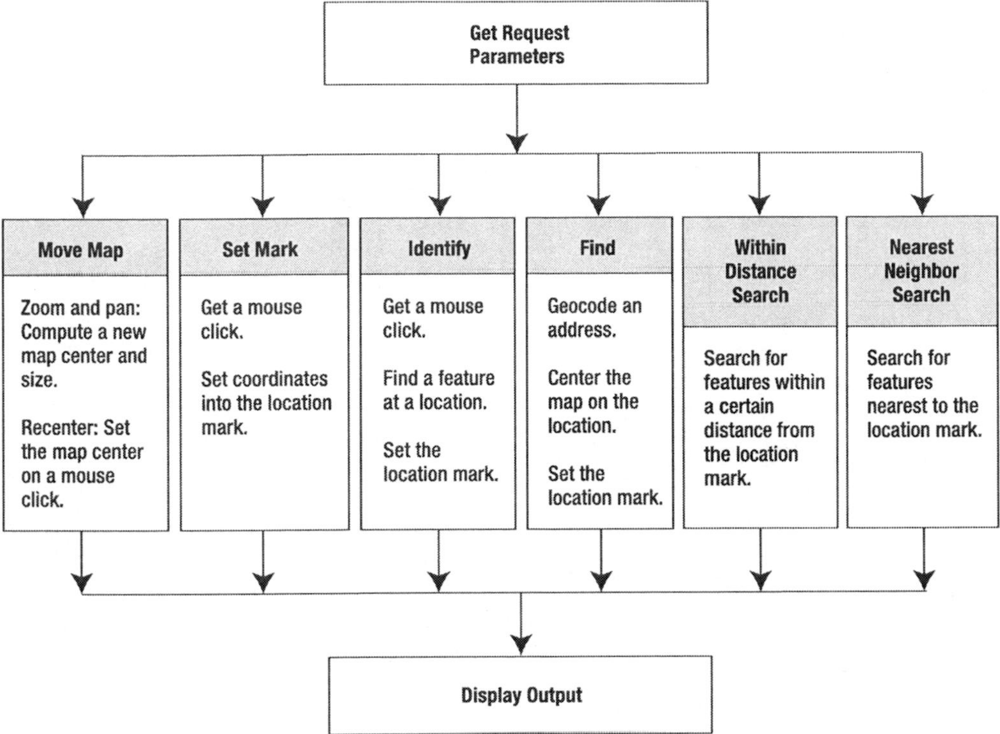

Figure 14-15. *Flow of the sample application*

The HTML page contains a single form. All user actions (for example, button presses and mouse clicks on the map) are posted back to the JSP as request parameters.

The main logic of the application is therefore as follows:

1. Parse the request parameters.
2. Process the user request.
3. Display the HTML output.

We will now look at the major functions implemented by the application.

Initializing the Application: The "Reset" Action

This is where you initialize the `MapViewer` object and save it in your session. Here, you also set up and request the initial map. See Listing 14-15 for the source code.

Note that this action is called under three circumstances:

- When the application is launched the first time
- When the user clicks the Reset button
- If the `MapViewer` object is no longer in the session, which means the session expired

The name of the base map, the data source, the initial center and size of the map, and the size of the map in pixels are all defined in variables. The defaults are such that the initial map is positioned on downtown San Francisco.

Listing 14-15. *Reset Action*

```
// -----------------------------------------------------------------------
// [Reset] button clicked
// Initialize the MapViewer object with the original center and size
// -----------------------------------------------------------------------
if (userAction.equals("Reset")) {

  // Create and initialize new MapViewer object)
  mv = new MapViewer(mapViewerURL);
  mv.setDataSourceName(dataSource);                    // Data source
  mv.setBaseMapName(baseMap);                          // Base map
  for(int i=0; i<appThemes.length; i++) {              // Additional themes
    mv.addPredefinedTheme(appThemes[i]);               // Theme name
    mv.setThemeScale(appThemes[i],
      appThemeMinScale, 0.0);                          // Scale limits
  }
  mv.setAllThemesEnabled(false);                       // Themes disabled
  mv.setMapTitle(" ");                                 // No title
  mv.setImageFormat(MapViewer.FORMAT_PNG_URL);         // Map format
  mv.setDeviceSize(new Dimension(mapWidth, mapHeight)); // Map size

  // Save MapViewer object in session
  session.setAttribute("MapviewerHandle", mv);

  // Set initial map position and display it
  mv.setCenterAndSize(initialCx, initialCy, initialSize);
  mv.run();

  // Set default options
  clickAction = "recenter";
  markX = 0;
  markY = 0;
}
```

Zooming, Panning, and Recentering

Zooming is straightforward. You just use the `zoomIn()` or `zoomOut()` method of the `MapViewer` object. Those methods take a zoom factor value as argument. To make the application more flexible, this factor is defined in a variable:

```
double zoomFactor = 1.5;              // Zoom factor
```

The `zoomIn()` and `zoomOut()` methods behave like the `run()` method. They submit a map request to the MapViewer server and process the response. Listing 14-16 shows the source code for using these methods.

Listing 14-16. *Zoom Actions*

```
// ------------------------------------------------------------------------
// [Zoom XXX] button clicked
// Zoom in or out by a fixed factor
// ------------------------------------------------------------------------
else if (userAction.equals("Zoom In"))
  mv.zoomIn(zoomFactor);
else if (userAction.equals("Zoom Out"))
  mv.zoomOut(zoomFactor);
```

Panning is just as straightforward as zooming. The `pan()` method of the `MapViewer` object recenters the map to a new location. Note that the coordinates that `pan()` expects should be in image coordinates (not in geographical coordinates).

Like the `zoomIn()` and `zoomOut()` methods, `pan()` submits a new map request to the MapViewer server and processes the response. Listing 14-17 shows the source code.

Listing 14-17. *Pan Actions*

```
// ------------------------------------------------------------------------
// [Pan XXX] button clicked
// Shift map 50% in the desired direction.
// ------------------------------------------------------------------------
else if (userAction.equals("Pan W"))
  mv.pan (0, mapHeight/2);
else if (userAction.equals("Pan N"))
  mv.pan (mapWidth/2, 0);
else if (userAction.equals("Pan S"))
  mv.pan (mapWidth/2, mapHeight);
else if (userAction.equals("Pan E"))
  mv.pan (mapWidth, mapHeight/2);
```

Recentering the map to the point identified by a mouse click is easy as well. All you need to do is extract the coordinates of the mouse click. They are passed as subattributes `.x` and `.y` of the attribute that corresponds to the map image on the HTML page (defined as an input element of type image).

Again, the fact that the `pan()` method uses image coordinates makes the repositioning easy to write—just pass it the coordinates of the mouse click directly. It will convert the coordinates to geographical coordinates and submit a new map request. Listing 14-18 shows the source code.

Listing 14-18. `reCenter` *Action*

```
// ------------------------------------------------------------------------
// Map clicked to recenter
// Use the coordinates of the clicked point as new map center
// ------------------------------------------------------------------------
else if (userAction.equals("reCenter")) {
  // Extract coordinates of mouse click
  int imgCX = Integer.parseInt(request.getParameter("mapImage.x"));
  int imgCY = Integer.parseInt(request.getParameter("mapImage.y"));
  // Pan to that position
  mv.pan (imgCX, imgCY);
}
```

Adding Application Data to the Map

The application themes (whose names are defined in the variable appThemes) are initially not visible. Their visibility is controlled using the enableThemes() method of the MapViewer object, as shown in Listing 14-19.

The list of themes to be enabled is in the variable checkedThemes[]. This is a string array that is populated from the request parameter of the same name, which itself gets set via a <checkbox> element in the HTML page. If that list is empty, then you use the setAllThemesEnabled(false) method to disable all the application themes. Finally, the run() method requests a refresh of the map.

Listing 14-19. updateMap *Action*

```
// ------------------------------------------------------------------------
// [Update Map] button clicked
// Enable the themes selected by the user and refresh the map
// ------------------------------------------------------------------------
else if (userAction.equals("Update Map")) {
  if (checkedThemes == null)
    mv.setAllThemesEnabled(false);
  else
    mv.enableThemes(checkedThemes);
  mv.run();
}
```

Positioning on a Street Address

Let's now examine how to position the map on a street address. For that, you call the geocoder and use the resulting coordinates. The format of the address must be acceptable to the geocoder. The application passes it to the geocoder exactly as you type it. For U.S. addresses, you can write the address on two, three, or more lines. See Chapter 6 for details.

After splitting the input address, you construct the SQL statement to call the geocoder. Here you will submit the query using the doQuery() method of the MapViewer object. However, just like identify(), the doQuery() method returns the result as arrays of strings—it cannot return objects. You therefore need to write the query in a slightly convoluted way to extract individual results from the SDO_GEO_ADDR object returned by the call to the geocoder.

A typical query sent to the database looks like this:

```
SELECT G.GEO_ADDR.MATCHCODE,
       G.GEO_ADDR.LONGITUDE,
       G.GEO_ADDR.LATITUDE,
       G.GEO_ADDR.HOUSENUMBER || ' ' || G.GEO_ADDR.STREETNAME,
       G.GEO_ADDR.SETTLEMENT || ' ' || G.GEO_ADDR.POSTALCODE
FROM (
  SELECT SDO_GCDR.GEOCODE(
           USER,
           SDO_KEYWORDARRAY(
              '600 Stockton Street','San Francisco, CA'),
           'US', 'DEFAULT')
           GEO_ADDR
  FROM DUAL) G
```

Once the query is completed, you extract the results: the match code, the longitude and latitude, and the first address line.

You then add a point feature (a yellow pin) at the location returned and save the coordinates as the new value for the location mark. Note that the point feature is also labeled with the corrected address returned by the geocoder.

Listing 14-20 shows the source code.

Listing 14-20. *Find Action*

```
// -------------------------------------------------------------------------
// [Find] button clicked:
// Geocode the entered address.
// Center map on the resulting coordinates.
// Set mark on that point.
// -------------------------------------------------------------------------
else if (userAction.equals("Find")) {

  // Extract address details
  String[] addressLines = findAddress.split("\r\n");

  // Construct query to geocoder
  String gcQuery =
    "SELECT "+
    "G.GEO_ADDR.MATCHCODE, G.GEO_ADDR.LONGITUDE, "+
    "G.GEO_ADDR.LATITUDE, " +
    "G.GEO_ADDR.HOUSENUMBER || ' ' || G.GEO_ADDR.STREETNAME, " +
    "G.GEO_ADDR.SETTLEMENT || ' ' || G.GEO_ADDR.POSTALCODE " +
    "FROM (SELECT SDO_GCDR.GEOCODE(USER ,SDO_KEYWORDARRAY(";
  for (int i=0; i<addressLines.length; i++) {
    gcQuery = gcQuery + "'" + addressLines[i] + "'";
    if (i < addressLines.length-1)
      gcQuery = gcQuery + ",";
  }
  gcQuery = gcQuery + "), 'US', 'DEFAULT') " +
  "GEO_ADDR FROM DUAL) G";

  // Send query
  String[][] f = mv.doQuery(dataSource, gcQuery);

  // Extract match code. Proceed only if > 0
  int matchCode = Integer.parseInt(f[1][0]);
  if (matchCode > 0) {

    // Extract X and Y coordinates from geocode result
    double destX = Double.valueOf(f[1][1]).doubleValue();
    double destY = Double.valueOf(f[1][2]).doubleValue();

    // Extract full street address from result
    String streetAddress = f[1][3];

    // Transform result from row-major to column-major
    geocodeInfo = new String[f[0].length-3];
    for (int i=0; i<f[0].length-3; i++)
      geocodeInfo[i] = f [1][i+3];

    // Center map on the new address and zoom in
    mv.setCenterAndSize(destX, destY, markerMapSize);

    // Remove any existing marker
    mv.removeAllPointFeatures();
```

```
        // Add a marker at the point clicked and label it
        // with the first address line
        mv.addPointFeature (
          destX, destY,
          mapSrid,
          markerStyle,
          streetAddress,
          markerLabelStyle,
          null,
          true);

        // Save new mark
        markX = destX;
        markY = destY;

        // Show SQL statement
        mapError = gcQuery;

        // Refresh map
        mv.run();
      }
      else
        mapError = "Address not found";
  }
```

Identifying a Branch, Customer, or Competitor

Here is how you get details about business data shown on the map, including branches, customers, and competitors.

The first step is, as for other map click actions, to get the coordinates of the point clicked on the map. You also verify that a theme (branches, customers, or competitors) is selected for identification and that the theme is also shown on the map.

You then use the `identify()` method of the `MapViewer` object. This method is passed the name of the theme to select from as well as the list of columns to return. It also needs the coordinates of the mouse click.

Since you are selecting points, it is impossible to click exactly on the point to identify. You therefore enlarge the area of the click by passing a small rectangular region to the method. This rectangle is constructed by specifying the coordinates of the lower-left and upper-right corners as 4 pixels away from the user click.

The `colsToSelect` argument defines the name of the columns to return:

```
String[] colsToSelect                // Columns to select for application themes
  = new String[]{
    "ID",
    "NAME",
    "STREET_NUMBER||' '||STREET_NAME ADDRESS",
    "CITY",
    "POSTAL_CODE",
    "STATE",
    "PHONE_NUMBER"
  };
```

Note that you ask for the street_number and street_name columns to be concatenated. The result of the identify() method is an array of string arrays (String[][]). The first row of strings contains the names of the columns, and the following row contains the value returned for each column. You transpose this result into another array so that the first column contains the column names and the subsequent columns contain the corresponding values.

Finally, proceed the same way as for the manual setting of the mark; add a point feature on the object found, and save the coordinates as the new value for the location mark.

Listing 14-21 shows the source code.

Listing 14-21. identify *Action*

```
// -----------------------------------------------------------------------
// Map clicked to identify a feature.
// Get the coordinates of the clicked point
// use them to query the feature from the selected theme
// -----------------------------------------------------------------------
else if (userAction.equals("identify")) {

  // Extract coordinates of mouse click
  int imgCX = Integer.parseInt(request.getParameter("mapImage.x"));
  int imgCY = Integer.parseInt(request.getParameter("mapImage.y"));

  if (identifyTheme == null)
    mapError = "No theme selected to identify";
  else if (!mv.getThemeEnabled(identifyTheme))
    mapError = "Theme "+identifyTheme+" is not visible";
  else {

    // Locate the feature and get details
    // Notes:
    //   1. The identify() method needs a TABLE NAME, not a theme name.
    //      We just assume that the theme and table name are the same.
    //   2. We query a rectangle of 4 pixels around the user click. Notice,
    //      however, that pixels have their origin at the UPPER-LEFT corner
    //      of the image, whereas ground coordinates use the LOWER-LEFT
    //      corner.
    String[][] f = mv.identify(dataSource, identifyTheme, colsToSelect,
      geoColumn, mapSrid,
      imgCX-4, imgCY+4,
      imgCX+4, imgCY-4,
      false);

    // The result is one row per matching record, but we want to display
    // results as one column per record.
    if (f!= null && f.length > 0) {
      featureInfo = new String[f[0].length][f.length];
      for (int i=0; i<f.length; i++)
        for (int j=0; j<f[i].length; j++)
          featureInfo[j][i] = f [i][j];
      featuresFound = f.length-1;
    } else
      mapError = "No matching " + identifyTheme + " found";
```

```
          if (featuresFound > 0) {

            // Remove any existing marker
            mv.removeAllPointFeatures();

            // Add a marker at the point clicked
            Point2D p = mv.getUserPoint(imgCX,imgCY);
            mv.addPointFeature (p.getX(), p.getY(),
              mapSrid, markerStyle, null, null, null);

            // Save new mark
            markX = p.getX();
            markY = p.getY();

            // Refresh map
            mv.run();
          }
        }
      }
```

■ **Note** The `identify()` method needs a table name as input, not a theme name. MapViewer does not provide a method to retrieve the name of the table associated with a theme. For this application, you assume the themes to identify have the same names as the tables they use. For example, the competitors theme is defined on the `competitors` table.

Setting a Mark on the Map

As for the `reCenter` action, you first must get the coordinates of the point just clicked for this action. You then use the `addPointFeature()` method to define a new point feature to the map.

However, the `addPointFeature()` method wants geographical coordinates, so you must first convert the mouse click from image to geographical coordinates by using the `getUserPoint()` method:

```
Point2D p = mv.getUserPoint(imgCX,imgCY);
```

This method returns a `java.awt.geom.Point2D` object from which you extract the x,y coordinates and pass them to `addPointFeature()`. You also save those coordinates as the location mark (that is, in the `markX` and `markY` variables).

The `markerStyle` argument defines the style to be used for rendering the location mark on the map. It is defined as follows:

```
String markerStyle ="M.YELLOW PIN"; // Style for location mark
```

Listing 14-22 shows the source code.

Listing 14-22. `setMark` *Action*

```
// ------------------------------------------------------------------
// Map clicked to set a mark
// Get the coordinates of the clicked point and use them to set a mark
// at that point
// ------------------------------------------------------------------
else if (userAction.equals("setMark")) {
```

```
    // Extract coordinates of mouse click
    int imgCX = Integer.parseInt(request.getParameter("mapImage.x"));
    int imgCY = Integer.parseInt(request.getParameter("mapImage.y"));

    // Remove any existing marker
    mv.removeAllPointFeatures();

    // Add a marker at the point clicked
    Point2D p = mv.getUserPoint(imgCX,imgCY);
    mv.addPointFeature (p.getX(), p.getY(),
      mapSrid, markerStyle, null, null, null);

    // Save new mark
    markX = p.getX();
    markY = p.getY();

    // Refresh map
    mv.run();
  }
```

Searching "Within Distance"

All the code you have seen so far deals with displaying the map and locating places, filling the location mark. The rest of the code will use the location mark as a starting point for performing searches.

The first search operation is to find all the customers, branches, or competitors that are within a chosen distance from the current location mark. Listing 14-23 shows the source code for this.

First check whether all the information is available to do the search; the location mark must have been set (either manually; by going to a street address; or by selecting a branch, customer, or competitor). The theme to search must be visible. You can search for customers, for example, only if they are shown on the map.

You want the results of the search in two formats:

- Highlight the matching objects on the screen (mark them with blue pins).
- Show information about each object (name, address, telephone number, and so on).

Unfortunately, MapViewer provides no method that can combine both effects. You therefore have to perform the two operations separately.

You will start by constructing a SQL query that uses the `SDO_WITHIN_DISTANCE` operator. You will then add this query to the map as a dynamic JDBC theme using the `addJdbcTheme()` method. The `queryStyle` argument defines the style to be used for rendering the results on the map. It is defined as follows:

```
String queryStyle = "M.CYAN PIN";   // Style for query result markers
```

Continue by using the `queryWithinRadius()` method. This method returns all objects in a theme that are within a chosen radius from a starting point. Just like the `identify()` and `doQuery()` methods, the results are returned as a string array that you have to reformat.

■ **Note** The distance is entered in meters. This is because `queryWithinRadius()` has no mechanism to let the user specify a unit for the radius to search. The radius is always assumed to be in the units used for the theme being queried or meters if the theme is in a geodetic coordinate system, which is the case in this example. Allowing the user to choose a different unit is left as an exercise for the reader.

Listing 14-23. distSearch *Action*

```
// -------------------------------------------------------------------------
// [distSearch] button clicked
// Search for all neighbors within distance D from the current set mark.
// -------------------------------------------------------------------------
else if (userAction.equals("distSearch")) {
  if (markX == 0 && markY == 0)
    mapError = "No address or mark set";
  else if (!mv.getThemeEnabled(distSearchTheme))
    mapError = "Theme "+distSearchTheme+" is not visible";
  else if (distSearchParam <= 0)
    mapError = "Enter search distance";
  else {

    // Construct spatial query
    String sqlQuery = "SELECT "+geoColumn+" FROM " + distSearchTheme
      + " WHERE SDO_WITHIN_DISTANCE ("+ geoColumn + ","
      + " SDO_GEOMETRY (2001," + mapSrid + ", SDO_POINT_TYPE("
      + markX + "," + markY + ",NULL), NULL, NULL), "
      + "'DISTANCE="+distSearchParam+" UNIT=M') = 'TRUE'";
    mapError = "Executing query: "+ sqlQuery;

    // Add a JDBC theme to highlight the results of the query
    mv.addJDBCTheme (
      dataSource,                 // Data source
      "SEARCH RESULTS",           // Theme to search
      sqlQuery,                   // SQL Query
      geoColumn,                  // Name of spatial column
      null,                       // srid
      queryStyle,                 // renderStyle
      null,                       // labelColumn
      null,                       // labelStyle
      true                        // passThrough
    );

    // Perform the query
    String[][] f = mv.queryWithinRadius(
      dataSource,                 // Data source
      distSearchTheme,            // Theme to search
      colsToSelect,               // Names of columns to select
      null,                       // Extra condition
      markX, markY,               // Center point (current mark)
      distSearchParam,            // Distance to search
      false                       // Center point is in ground coordinates
    );

    if (f!= null && f.length > 0) {

      // The result is one row per matching record, but we want to display
      // results as one column per record.
      featureInfo = new String[f[0].length][f.length];
      for (int i=0; i<f.length; i++)
        for (int j=0; j<f[i].length; j++)
          featureInfo[j][i] = f [i][j];
      featuresFound = f.length-1;
```

```
        // Refresh map
        mv.run();

      } else
        mapError = "No matching " + distSearchTheme + " found";

    }
  }
```

Searching for Nearest Neighbors

The "nearest neighbor" search is similar to the previous case. The only differences are that you generate a query that uses the `SDO_NN` operator and that you use the `queryNN()` method of the `MapViewer` object instead of the `queryWithinRadius()` method. Listing 14-24 shows the source code.

Listing 14-24. `nnSearch` *Action*

```
// ------------------------------------------------------------------
// [nnSearch] button clicked
// Search the N nearest neighbors from the current set mark.
// ------------------------------------------------------------------
else if (userAction.equals("nnSearch")) {
  if (markX == 0 && markY == 0)
    mapError = "No address or mark set";
  else if (!mv.getThemeEnabled(nnSearchTheme))
    mapError = "Theme "+nnSearchTheme+" is not visible";
  else if (nnSearchParam <= 0)
    mapError = "Enter number of matches to search";
  else {

    // Construct spatial query
    String sqlQuery = "SELECT "+geoColumn+", SDO_NN_DISTANCE(1) DISTANCE"
      + " FROM " + nnSearchTheme
      + " WHERE SDO_NN ("+ geoColumn + ","
      + " SDO_GEOMETRY (2001," + mapSrid + ", SDO_POINT_TYPE("
      + markX + "," + markY + ",NULL), NULL, NULL), "
      + "'SDO_NUM_RES="+nnSearchParam+"',1) = 'TRUE'"
      + " ORDER BY DISTANCE";
    mapError = "Executing query: "+ sqlQuery;

    // Add a JDBC theme to highlight the results of the query
    mv.addJDBCTheme (
      dataSource,                 // Data source
      "SEARCH RESULTS",           // Theme to search
      sqlQuery,                   // SQL Query
      geoColumn,                  // Name of spatial column
      null,                       // srid
      queryStyle,                 // renderStyle
      null,                       // labelColumn
      null,                       // labelStyle
      true                        // passThrough
    );

    // Perform the query
    String[][] f = mv.queryNN(
      dataSource,                 // Data source
```

```
          nnSearchTheme,            // Theme to search
          colsToSelect,             // Names of columns to select
          nnSearchParam,            // Number of neighbors
          markX, markY,             // Center point (current mark)
          null,                     // Extra condition
          false,                    // Center point is in ground coordinates
          null
        );

        if (f== null || f.length == 0)
          mapError = "No matching " + nnSearchTheme + " found";
        else {

          // The result is one row per matching record, but we want to display
          // results as one column per record.
          featureInfo = new String[f[0].length][f.length];
          for (int i=0; i<f.length; i++)
            for (int j=0; j<f[i].length; j++)
              featureInfo[j][i] = f [i][j];
          featuresFound = f.length-1;

          // Refresh map
          mv.run();
        }
      }
    }
```

Summary

In this chapter, we described how to create sample applications to perform a variety of spatial analyses and integrate the results with visualization using MapViewer.

We explained how to set up each component, such as the geocoder and MapViewer, and how to integrate these components in a simple application. This application can be easily integrated into the business logic of most Oracle applications.

In the next chapter, we describe several case studies using Oracle Spatial technology in different applications. These case studies will give you an idea of how businesses are using and integrating different components of spatial functionality.

CHAPTER 15

Case Studies

This chapter describes five case studies that illustrate how to use Oracle Spatial for storing, analyzing, visualizing, and integrating spatial data in business and government applications. These are large, complex applications that include several components and software tools besides Oracle Spatial, but they rely on Oracle Spatial for handling all spatial data.

The emphasis in this chapter is on the requirements and the implementation context for these applications, as well as on the way Oracle Spatial was introduced to satisfy these requirements. In each case study, we identify the main uses of Oracle Spatial and, where appropriate, provide some detailed examples. It is outside the scope of this chapter to provide a comprehensive and detailed description of the technical implementation of Oracle Spatial in these cases. However, most of the steps illustrated in detail in Chapter 14 have been used in these applications.

All solutions described here are in use, and a number have been in use for some time already. For each case study, we introduce the context in which the application was conceived and designed so that you can understand the needs and constraints of each implementation. We then focus on the part of the solution/system that uses Oracle Spatial and describe how, why, and with what benefits it was deployed.

Overview of the Case Studies

The first case study we examine in this chapter, *BusNet*, illustrates how to use Oracle Spatial for managing the bus network of London. It serves to improve the planning and management of the bus schedules and routes, to share information with users of this information, and to integrate the system with the de facto national standard for spatial data. The case study illustrates data loading and validation (see Chapter 5), spatial analysis (see Chapter 8), and network analysis (see Chapter 10). The system extensively uses the linear referencing model of Oracle Spatial (see Appendix B).

The *P-Info* case study describes a system to provide mobile, location-enabled access to mission-critical information for police officers operating in the field. P-Info provides secure access to all databases of the Dutch police from a handheld device that exchanges data with the servers using the GSM or UMTS telephone network. Spatial information is used for spatial selections and overlays (see Chapters 8 and 9), to visualize locations and maps (see Chapter 12), and to geocode and reverse geocode addresses (see Chapter 6).

The *Risk Repository for Hazardous Substances* is a national system in the Netherlands that gives access to information on risk and possible effects for all locations involved in storing, processing, and transporting hazardous substances. This information is available to citizens from the Web and to professional users involved in the prevention, response, and mitigation of incidents related to hazardous substances. This case study discusses spatial analysis (see Chapters 8 and 9) and data loading and validation (see Chapter 5).

The *USGS National Land Cover Visualization and Analysis Tool* case study provides a single access point to land-cover data for the United States. The tool provides to both expert and nonexpert users access to the USGS Land Cover data, which incorporates the entire 30m×30m-resolution National Land Cover Data repository for 1992 and 2001, as well as the changes occurred in the meantime. This case study discusses storing raster data in Oracle (see Appendix D) and the Oracle Java API (see Chapter 7).

The *MilitaryHOMEFRONT LBS* case study illustrates how to use Oracle Spatial for storing and accessing point-of-interest information, as well as for geocoding and routing. The MilitaryINSTALLATIONS web portal is intended as a source of information for troops and their families who relocate to a different site as part of their careers in the U.S. military. The site provides information on services, base layout, proximity to schools, clinics, and other points of interest to allow families to become accustomed with their new home. The case study illustrates the use of Oracle Spatial for storing and geocoding spatial data (see Chapter 6) and for routing (see Chapter 11).

Notice that these applications are fully deployed and operational and therefore utilize earlier versions of Oracle Spatial, usually 9*i* or 10*g*. This means all features and capabilities discussed in the case studies are part of Oracle Spatial 11g, but some features of Oracle Spatial 11*g* are not visible in these case studies.

Notice also that in these case studies, Oracle Spatial is used to store and retrieve all spatial data used in the applications. The applications also use the loading mechanisms discussed in Chapter 5, and they extensively use the spatial analysis discussed in Chapters 8 and 9; however, they also exploit the possibility of accessing the `SDO_GEOMETRY` objects in Java to implement specific functionalities required by the applications, as discussed in Chapter 7.

Spatial Information for Managing the London Bus Network

■ **Note** This section is based on the work of Olliver Robinson (business analyst at Transport for London, London Buses), Prashan Rampersad, and Terry Allen. The authors want also to thank Transport for London for making the background material available for this section of the chapter. You can find additional information on Transport for London at `www.tfl.gov.uk`.

London's transport system is one of the most comprehensive, complex, and articulate urban transport systems in the world. It covers a vast area with 13,600 km of roads, 3,730 km of bus routes, 205 km of dedicated bus lanes, 329 km of subway lines, 26 km of Docklands Light Railway (DLR) lines, 28 km of new tramways, and 788 km of national rail lines in Greater London. Every day, more than 27 million journeys are made in Greater London, 8.5 million of which take place on public transport (4.5 million by bus, 3 million by subway, and 1 million by rail). The London bus system plays a crucial role in getting and keeping London moving. About 6,500 buses are scheduled every day on more than 700 different routes, amounting to about 1.5 billion passengers per year.

Transport for London (TfL) is the body responsible for managing the London transport system. TfL is accountable for the planning and delivery of transport facilities, including London Buses, London Underground, DLR, and London Trams. London Buses manages the bus services in London and, along with London Underground, is the primary provider of urban public transport for the city. The extent of the bus network and the number of passengers carried makes London Buses one of the largest public transport providers in the world. The tasks of London Buses include bus route planning, service-level definition, and quality of service monitoring. London Buses does not include the bus services that are operated by private operators working under contract to London Buses. Each route is competitively tendered every five years.

London Buses is a success story of public transport that has been reshaped to meet the needs of 21st-century urban life. Thanks to a more modern, punctual, and customer-focused network, the buses of London are now carrying the highest number of passengers in more than 40 years. These results can be achieved only with the sophisticated management of the bus network and an appropriate information system. London Buses needs to manage and maintain a complex bus network that adapts continuously in response to changes in London's growth, spatial pattern, and economic and social developments. On average, half of the network is subject to some level of review each year. Oracle Spatial has been introduced by London Buses as the core spatial component of BusNet, the information system that supports the route network management.

BusNet

A variety of information systems are used to support London Buses' responsibilities, including systems to record passenger information and surveys, to manage contracts with operators, to support service controls, and to manage stops and shelters.

BusNet is the back-office application dedicated to bus-route network management. The system is networked to about 400 staff and enables TfL to maintain and share reference information supporting the following:

- *Route definition*: This includes the sequence of streets for each bus run on each route (containing a list of the road names composing the run) and the sequence of transit nodes (containing the list of service access points for the runs).
- *Version control for bus-route records for past, present, and future routes*: The bus routes change for several reasons, such as because of changes in the route segments, start and end points, or stops. For a given route, BusNet usually contains several past expired records, the current route, and one or more proposed versions for the future.
- *Service change records that aid task workflow and enforce business rules*: Examples are the issue of a briefing and an amended route description.
- *Detailed service definition*: This includes, for instance, the operator name, the vehicles used, the day type of service (for example, Monday–Friday nights), the time periods, the number of buses per hour, and so on.

The introduction of Oracle Spatial as a basis for BusNet came at a time when London Buses realized the need to improve the quality control of the route information, integrate the system with the de facto national reference set for road data (the Ordnance Survey's Integrated Transport Network [ITN], and its predecessor called OSCAR[1]), and share route geometry definitions among internal and external stakeholders such as local authorities. The existing systems were unable to achieve these goals, and a new integrated system, BusNet, was developed to replace them. Spatial information management is at the core of BusNet, which makes it possible to do the following:

- Store route diagrams as persistent data, based accurately on London's road network. This accommodates changes not only to bus routes over time but also to the road network itself. (A *route* is the composition of route runs, the sequence of streets composing the run, and turning points required at each extremity of the route or at intermediate points to allow buses running late to turn around and get back on schedule.)
- Establish directionality to diagrams so that sequential street names could be derived with no need for text data entry, in particular to support the route description document included in the contract with each operator to run a route.

---

1. www.ordnancesurvey.co.uk/oswebsite/products/osmastermap/itn/

- Support complex diagram patterns such as loops and figure eights.
- Support the recording of passenger drop-off and pick-up points at terminal and intermediate turning points on routes.
- Import and display related datasets such as bus stops owned by other systems so that they can be displayed in conjunction with the routes they serve.

Spatial Data and Oracle Spatial in BusNet

The data model implemented in BusNet reflects the information needs illustrated in Figure 15-1. This figure identifies an operator's view and a technical planner's view. The operator's view focuses on the detailed routing of a bus route and contains information such as the sequence of streets traversed for each route run, the turning points, and the stands. This information allows operators to implement the bus service on the route and is part of the contract with the operator. The technical planner's view includes details of how each route is physically operated in terms of legs of service, days of the week, frequency per hour, vehicle types, and so on.

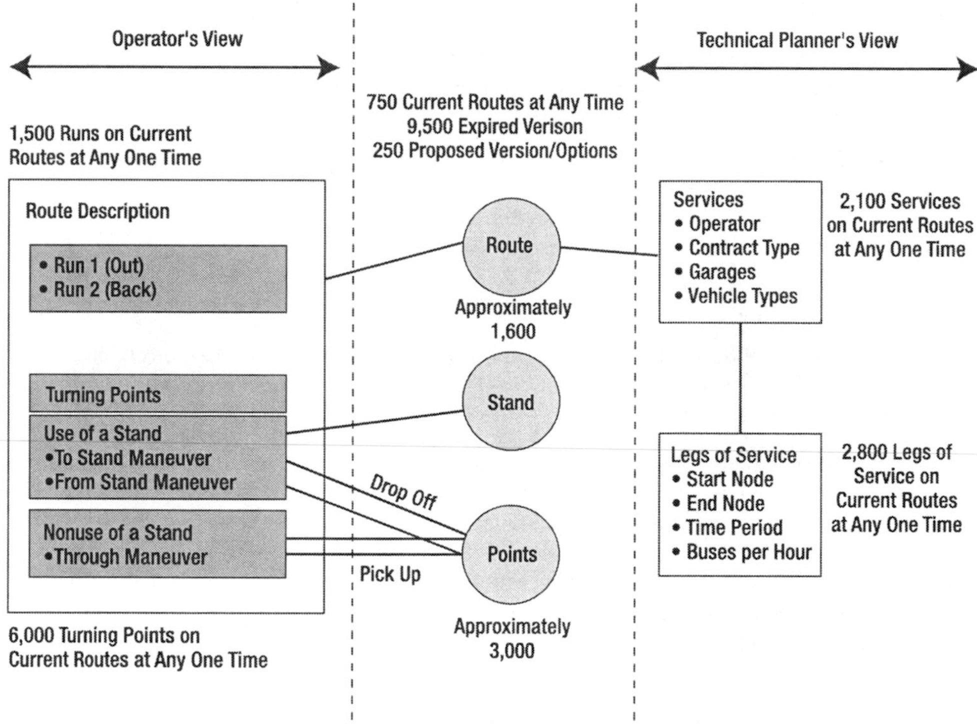

Figure 15-1. *The operator's and technical planner's views*

Figure 15-2 shows the data model used by BusNet to support just the operator's view. The road links are contained in a roads table (`oscar_road`) populated with the OSCAR road segments ("links" consisting of lines and nodes, with attributes including the road number; the road name; the form of the way, such as a divided highway or rotary; the road length; and so on). The passenger set-down and pick-up locations associated with turning points are contained in a points table (`point`), which also provides a warehouse for different types of spatial points, such as bus-stop locations, owned by and imported from other systems. These two tables contain an SDO_GEOMETRY column named geoloc in Figure 15-2 and are the source of most spatial data used by BusNet.

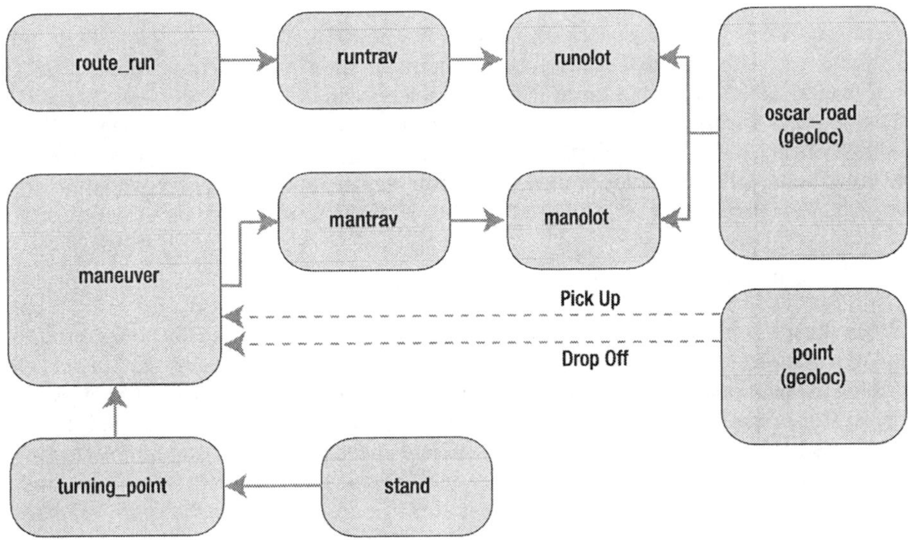

Figure 15-2. *The* oscar_road *and* point *tables contain an* SDO_GEOMETRY.

The road links are sequences in the runolot table. The runtrav table derives sequenced street names from the sequenced links and optionally chooses different street names where convenient (for example, on a rotary). The route_run table combines all the links into a single route geometry. The same data structure is used for maneuvers, which are micro-runs associated with the turning points at each extremity of the route.[2] Maneuvers also include set-down and pick-up point information from the point table.

The oscar_road table is populated from ITN files supplied by Ordnance Survey. The custom-built data-loading process is based on SQL*Loader, a bulk-loading utility used for moving data from external files into the Oracle database. The loading steps are as follows:

1. Create a SQL*Loader control file.
2. Load the ITN table in BusNet from SQL*Loader.
3. Update SDO_GEOM_METADATA to introduce x,y and m parameters, where *m* (measure) supports the Linear Referencing System (LRS).
4. Run SDO_LRS.REDEFINE_GEOM_SEGMENT to calculate the measure values (that is, the *m*s).
5. Run SDO_GEOM.VALIDATE_LAYER.
6. Create an R-tree index.

For each update of ITN, the new and live road datasets are compared with SDO_GEOM.RELATE, which returns "equals" if geometries match. If a segment exists in the live database but not in the new data, the status of the record is updated to Withdrawn. This prevents it from being used in new route diagrams but allows the system to retain it as part of historic, or Expired, status routes. If a record exists in the new dataset but not in the live one, the new record is inserted.

2. Note that to allow buses running late to turn around and get back on schedule, a number of turning points are also defined along the route.

BusNet is available to end users through a client interface developed in Visual Basic. The spatial functions provide the GIS interface to the system. This is particularly useful, for instance, in facilitating the route definition (a record in the `route_run` table) based on selection of road links. Links can be manually selected from the screen, or they can be identified automatically with an auto trace function. The auto trace selects the minimum distance path between two points on the route network graph and applies Dijkstra's shortest path algorithm. The algorithm is implemented in the client BusNet application, but it uses the `SDO_WITHIN_DISTANCE` function to select the links to evaluate for the shortest path algorithm. It also exploits the linear referencing model to weight the links based on their lengths. On completion of sequencing, the `runolot` and `runtrav` records are automatically saved to the database, and the `oscar` links thus used are combined into a single geometry to populate the `geoloc` column in the `route_run` table. The function `SDO_LRS.CONCATENATE_GEOM_SEGMENTS` is again used for this purpose.

User Interface for Spatial Data in BusNet

Figure 15-3 shows the result of a polygon spatial query (highlighted in the center of the image) around a small section of road outside the TfL London Buses office. The query is created using the BusNet GIS application, which makes it possible for users to define query areas of any shape. In the User Selection pane on the right side of the screen, all spatial business objects found by Oracle Spatial within the polygon are delivered as parent "labels," including the whole of each route run that intersects the polygon. This gives the user the choice of which of these he wants to view, because it is unlikely—and unwise—to want to see everything all at once. Note the dotted line around the coach station indicating a terminus turning point maneuver for route C10 around the block. Note also the passenger pick-up and set-down point, each near to its related bus stops icons (the small house images indicate each stop has a bus shelter with it).

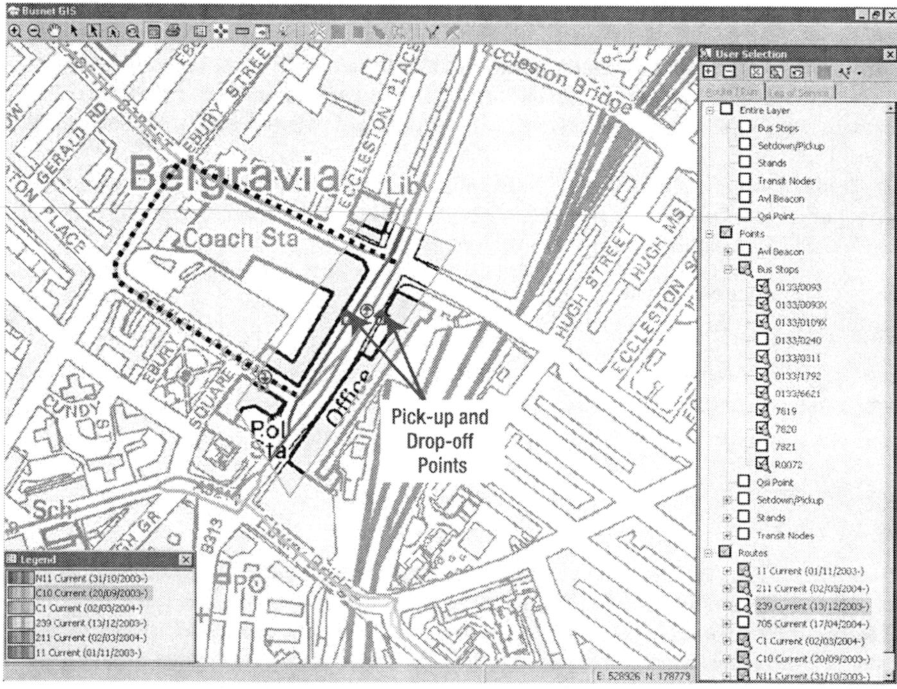

Figure 15-3. *Spatial query and visualization of route information*

Figure 15-4 shows a zoomed-out view from the same query in Figure 15-3, this time displaying bus stops in both directions (Runs 1 and 2) on Route 11. Note there is a *C* around two of the bus stop icons—one on the far left and one in the middle. This indicates a "Countdown" sign, which is the brand name of a dot-matrix indicator system showing passengers waiting at the stop when the next few buses on each route are predicted to arrive.

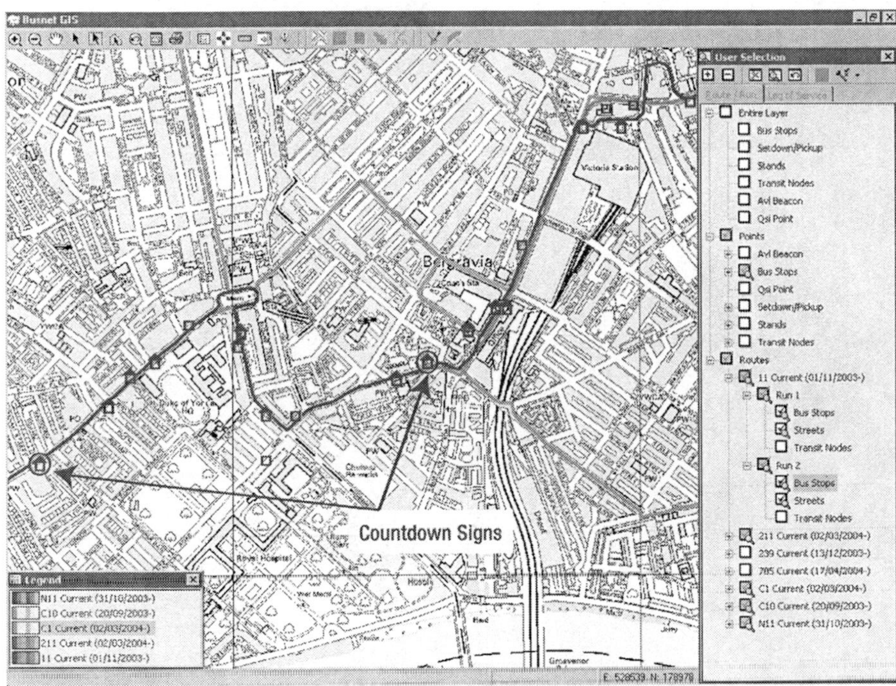

Figure 15-4. *Spatial query and visualization of route information: zoomed-out view*

Figure 15-5 shows the result of a query based on the planner's view of the BusNet object model, which enables calculation of combined buses-per-hour frequencies on a given day type and time period (in this case, Monday–Friday p.m. peak) at each service access point representing a bus stop or bus-stop pair. To get this result, the user must first run a polygon query, then run the function that runs a PL/SQL procedure to get all frequencies for each leg of service, and finally add them up to produce a total for each service access point. Note the different raster map background from the Ordnance Survey 1:10,000, in which the user interface has been designed to allow switching between easily during a session. All this is available to the user from a total of about five mouse clicks, whereas before this implementation all the information presented in this way would have taken at least a day to compile. It is all immediately available from the single BusNet Oracle database and requires no more daily data maintenance by users than the predecessor systems, from which no spatial data or GIS leverage was possible.

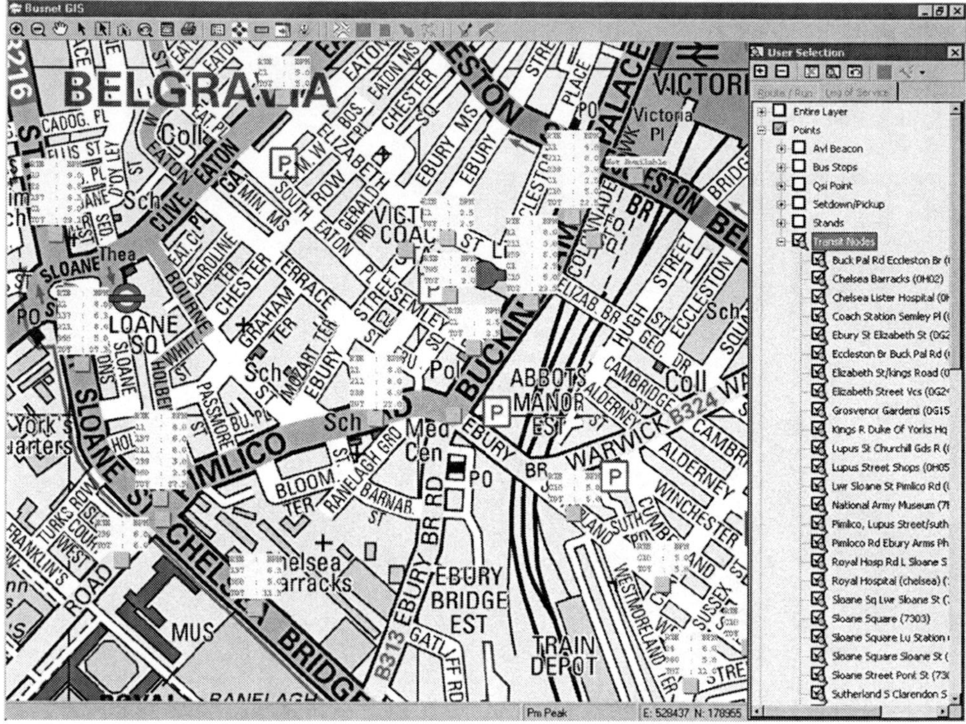

Figure 15-5. *The "planner's view"*

BusNet Conclusions

The introduction of BusNet makes it possible to simplify, standardize, and automate the distribution of reliable bus route information at London Buses. A key feature of the system is its data structure. It is both simple and flexible, and above all, it is strictly derived from the business logic applied by London Buses for its operations.

The spatial functionality of BusNet extensively uses the operators and functions of Spatial and the features of `SDO_GEOMETRY`, such as the linear referencing model. The availability of this model simplifies several operations in BusNet, such as data loading, data deduplication, and short-path searches. This was one of the reasons for choosing Oracle Spatial as a basis for BusNet. In general, BusNet benefits from the possibility of using one database for spatial and nonspatial data types and from the use of one language (SQL) for all data operations. The availability of a vast range of spatial PL/SQL options has made it possible to implement the needs of BusNet in a neat and straightforward manner. Oracle Spatial has also allowed BusNet to implement a clear separation between data and application layer, data model and functional logic, and application and storage layer. The structural features of Oracle Spatial, such as scalability, security, reliability, and support for Open Geospatial standards, are also important factors for BusNet.

P-Info: A Mobile Application for Police Forces

■ **Note** P-Info was developed by the IT Service Cooperative Association for the Dutch police, Judicial Authorities, and Public Safety Services (ISC) and by Geodan Mobile Solutions under the coordination of the Dutch Ministry of the Interior and Kingdom Relations and with the cooperation of regional police organizations.

The law enforcement sector faces an increasing demand for effective and efficient performance. Recent increases in urban criminality, the growing concern about youth crime, and the sense of insecurity generated by the threat of terrorism have led to a growing demand for security. The police and other law enforcement agencies are expected to ensure more timely responses and improve preventive measures. These demands, however, stress the capacity of these organizations and impose on them more serious requirements than ever before.

Police work has always relied heavily on information management. Proper and timely information makes it possible for law enforcement agencies to achieve expected goals, and it dictates the level of effectiveness and efficiency of their operations. The growing demands on this sector have rendered many of the current information systems inadequate. Simultaneously providing timely and accurate information to the field, locating the resources deployed (vehicles and personnel), allowing data communication during operations, and integrating multiple sources of information is often beyond the capacity of current police IT systems.

This gap needs to be filled if the increasing requirements of law enforcement are to be met. At the same time, there is a growing awareness that simply deploying more modern IT systems does not automatically ensure benefits to the organization. IT managers are facing increasing pressure to justify the large costs of IT investments. This can result in failed implementations, huge integration costs, and never-ending upgrades. There is a growing skepticism of the maxim "IT investment equals productivity gains."

In the year 2000, the Dutch police started investigating the use of wireless technology and location services to address the needs of officers in the field and of those in the control rooms. The result of this process is the P-Info system, currently implemented by several Dutch police regions and adopted by the national police organization in support of mobile police workers.

The application focuses on mobile officers, those who operate in the field to provide citizen security, response services, and investigative capabilities. In the Netherlands, about 20,000 police personnel operate in the field either full-time or part-time. A special group of these officers operates almost exclusively in the field and performs systematic patrol and policing in urban and rural areas. By focusing on crime prevention and mobilizing citizens' support locally, their work reduces the distance between citizens and the police while increasing mutual trust and cooperation. They are assigned to, and operate in, a small area with the support and coordination of regional police offices. They operate mostly outside of the office, and the goal of the police organization is to maximize their presence in the field. Hence, these officers suffer particularly from the lack of proper information availability. In several cases, they are forced to interrupt their fieldwork and return to the office simply to gather information that is useful to the field operations.

Figure 15-6 illustrates the P-Info system at work and shows the main features of the mobile interface, in this case displayed on a PDA device, which is one of the many devices supported by P-Info. The figure shows a police officer (left) using P-Info during a routine check, the main interface (center) of P-Info with access to all services, and an English version of the same interface (right) together with a sample illustration of a spatial search for incidents.

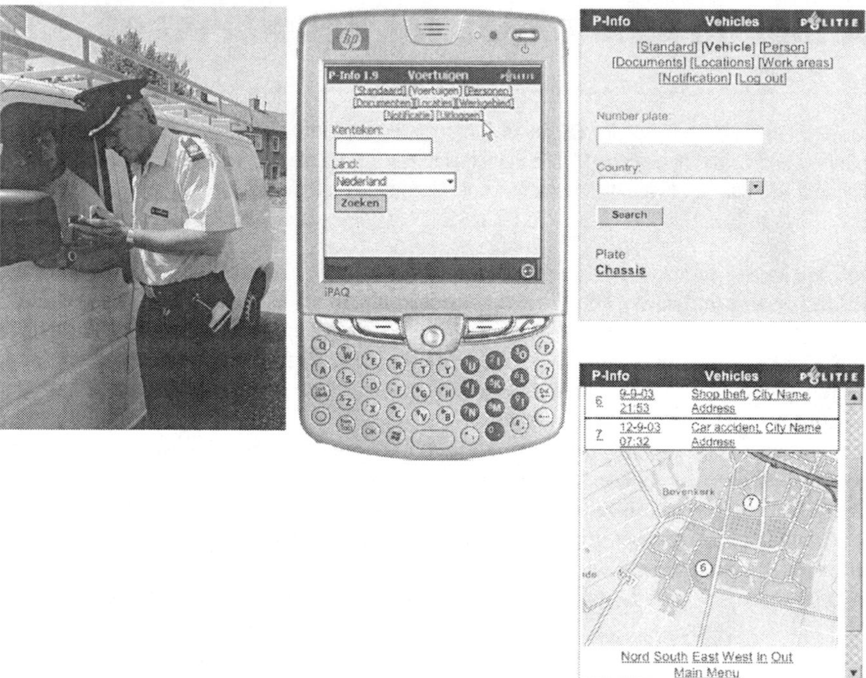

Figure 15-6. *The P-Info system at work*

P-Info Functionality

The P-Info system contains three functionality groups:

- Database and data services
- Location services
- Office automation

The central component of P-Info is the *database and data services* module. It provides integrated access to the whole range of regional, national, and international police databases. The information sources are the same as those available at the office, while information search and information provision is optimized for mobile users. Queries are predefined and the most used query forms (for example, query by entry code, person, license plate, date, address, area, time, and so on) are predefined for easy use. With this service, simultaneous searches in multiple databases are performed in the background, and the full search results are provided in a single form. The results are an overview of a given situation—for example, information about a suspect car collected from all databases containing the search items (car data are extracted from the national car registration system, any fines on the car are extracted from the regional databases where fines are registered, the charges to the car owner are extracted from the national databases, and so on). The databases connected to P-info include the following:

- Regional databases that contain all reports and their mutations, such as an incident report, a theft report, and so on. They are logged and edited by the control room or collected and edited by police staff on the basis of individual reports.
- A regional database of outstanding search warrants, fines, or parking tickets.
- National databases related to vehicles and driving licenses. They include vehicle registration systems, such as license plate numbers, ownership, annual maintenance checks, and so on, and driver's licenses with their status.
- A national criminal records database that includes information on search warrants, missing people, and stolen vehicles.
- NSIS, the national node of the European Schengen Information System (SIS), which coordinates public safety matter under the European Schengen Convention. It contains personal data supplied by member states relating to missing persons, people wanted as witnesses in criminal proceedings, people wanted for arrest for extradition, aliens who have been refused entry, and so on.

The main purpose of the *location services* is to provide location-enabled searches, such as proximity or area searches, to provide the visualization of results on a map, and in general to location-enable the P-Info content.

Spatial searches serve to locate incidents, or any other type of record that has location information, and to rank them based on how close or far they are from the user position or any other location.

Location services include a street guide that can be consulted directly to locate an address and display it on a map or that can be consulted directly by the P-Info server to associate coordinates to an address string or a certain database entry.

The ability to locate any database entry in space is at the basis of location notification services. Users who register for notification receive an automatic voice message briefly describing an event (for example, an incident) that occurred in the vicinity of the current position of the police officer.

Location functionality can also be used to locate the position of an officer on a map by applying telecom location capability (Cell ID or GPS). This can be used to optimize information and proximity searches, as well as to locate colleagues and other resources when needed. This functionality also allows the optimization of resource allocation in the field.

Office functionality includes e-mail, a calendar, contacts, and tasks. It is based on wireless access to the regular office facilities of the police. It is used to maintain communication between officers in the field, to check appointments made by the office assistants, and to receive documents and notifications while working in the field.

P-Info Architecture

Figure 15-7 illustrates the P-Info architecture. Mobile users access the system through a variety of handsets, such as PDAs, portable computers, or tablets. Data communication is currently based on GSM-GPRS, a standard that ensures data transfer rates of about 40Kbps. The system is designed to be bearer independent (thus it can work on, for example, GPRS, UMTS, or dedicated Tetra networks) and to be device independent. The interface is adapted to each device with style sheets, and it uses pure browser-based access to prevent any content from being stored on the handset. For security reasons, information is never stored or cached in the mobile device; it is always accessed online.

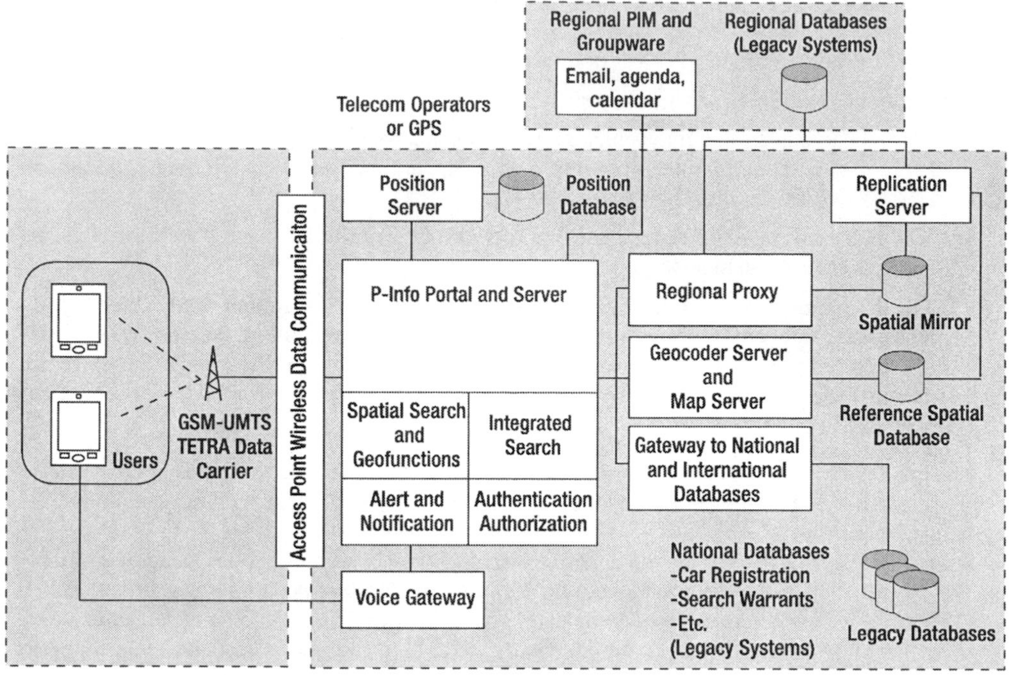

Figure 15-7. *Simplified architecture of the P-Info system*

The access point ensures that only authorized devices can access the P-Info portal and server, which in turn performs user authentication and authorization. The P-Info server and portal provides access to the underlying P-Info components. It routes the requests from the mobile users and dispatches them to the national gateway or to the regional proxy.

The national gateway includes a series of XML wrappers serving as an interface between XML (used within P-Info) and the legacy data models of some national databases.

The regional proxy plays a similar role as the national gateway, but in this case it decides whether a query can be dispatched directly to the regional databases (for example, for details of an incident) or whether it needs to access the P-Info spatial mirror. The term *spatial mirror* derives from the function of this database, which mirrors a small portion of the content of the regional databases while adding a spatial component to each record. In this way, each record in the regional database corresponds to a record in the mirror database. They share code and the name of the record, but the mirror version includes location information (the address in a standardized form and the x,y coordinates). This is necessary because the regional databases contain spatial information in the form of an address, but they do not account for x,y coordinates. Also, every address entry is a text string formatted in slightly different ways (abbreviations, spelling mistakes, truncations, and so on). The mirror database, which is an Oracle Spatial database, makes it possible to perform spatial search and proximity analysis without accessing the regional databases, thus ensuring coherent location information.

The mirror database and the regional database are coordinated by a replication server, which monitors entries in the regional databases and intercepts differences to the mirror database. When an addition is intercepted, the replication server invokes the geocoder to interpret and normalize the address string and to associate it with x,y coordinates. It then copies the essential information from the regional database and creates a new entry in the mirror table, from now on synchronized with the regional repository. Notice that the geocoder needs to perform the regular normalization and geocoding activities (such as normalize "Bond Street, 5" and associate it to x,y coordinates), but it also needs to interpret entries such as crossroads (such as an incident at the crossing between "Bond Street" and "Large Street") or building locations (such as a railway station).

Maps are created by an Open Geospatial–compliant web map server[3] that extracts information and spatial features from reference spatial databases (in Oracle Spatial) containing the full road network, geocoding information, and other essential spatial display and analysis features.

The alert and notification service provides voice messages to officers operating in a given area who have subscribed to the alert service. Based on the profile selected by the officer (such as "only thefts and burglaries"), P-Info performs a match between notification profiles and entries in the regional databases. When a match occurs—for instance, because a burglary has been notified to the emergency 112 number—the system creates a VoiceXML message that stores the basic information about the event (code, time, and location). The voice gateway makes a short call to the officer's mobile phone describing the essential information of the event. The full details can be checked in a dedicated notification area of P-Info reserved for each registered officer.

Finally, the integrated search provides a sophisticated mechanism to dispatch a search—for instance, for a certain name—to all connected databases simultaneously. Figure 15-8 shows a typical result. P-Info has found several entries in various databases for "GROE." The results are organized in a table with links to the entry list in each database. P-Info creates a series of nested hit lists, which contain all information available to the police regarding the search item. This mechanism saves officers a great deal of time and presents a coherent information picture to the users, independent of the database structures that contain the information.

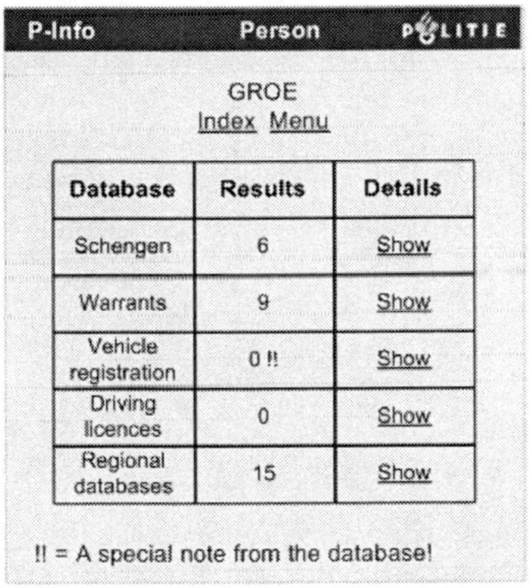

P-Info Person POLITIE

GROE
Index Menu

Database	Results	Details
Schengen	6	Show
Warrants	9	Show
Vehicle registration	0 !!	Show
Driving licences	0	Show
Regional databases	15	Show

!! = A special note from the database!

Figure 15-8. *Summary results of an integrated search*

All components of P-Info are developed in Java (J2EE and Java servlets) and run in any Java environment. Oracle Application Server is used in this case.

Use of Oracle Spatial in P-Info

Oracle Spatial is used by P-Info to store and retrieve spatial information, perform proximity analysis, and support overlay and spatial selections. The spatial mirror (see Figure 15-7) provides the basis for these operations. The main methods for selecting data from regional databases (those containing police reports) through the spatial mirror are as follows:

3. www.opengeospatial.org

- Select based on proximity to a current position.
- Select based on proximity to a certain address location.
- Select based on inclusion in a certain work area.

The spatial mirror contains only point objects. The table size grows continuously, with a rate of increase of several hundreds of thousands of records per year, for each of the 25 police regions. The table size at the national level grows at a rate of several million records per year.

Listing 15-1 shows the procedure to insert the spatial object for a new record into the table place_table of the spatial mirror. This procedure is used by the replication server (see Figure 15-7). The question marks are filled in by the application and represent the incident ID and the x and y coordinates, respectively.

Listing 15-1. *Inserting Records in the Spatial Mirror*

```
INSERT INTO place_table (point_id, geo, creation_date)
VALUES(?, MDSYS.SDO_GEOMETRY(2001, 90112, MDSYS.SDO_POINT_TYPE(?, ?, NULL),
NULL, NULL), sysdate)
```

The geocoding of the incident information is complicated by the fact that officers report the location of an event in three ways: address, crossing, and road section. Crossing and road section are often used to specify the location of a road accident. Although geocoding on an address is well supported (see Chapter 6), crossing and road-section geocoding required the development of specific procedures.

Reverse geocoding is used in P-Info to associate with an x,y coordinate to a specific address. The most common use is to find the closest address to the current location of the user (for example, based on GPS location or telecom location). Listing 15-2 shows an example. The query selects one road segment (sdo_num_res=1) from the table tblstreet (which contains the streets database) that is the closest to the current location. The location is represented by two question marks that are filled in by the application that calls the query and passes on the x,y coordinates of the current location.

Listing 15-2. *Reverse Geocoding in P-Info*

```
SELECT  d.street_id id, SDO_NN_DISTANCE(1) distance
FROM tblstreet d
WHERE SDO_NN(d.geo, MDSYS.SDO_GEOMETRY(2001,90112,
    sdo_point_type(?, ?,null),null,null), 'sdo_num_res=1', 1) = 'TRUE'
```

Officers in the field select items based on their location using either a selection of the *n* closest items (implemented using SDO_NN) or the items within a certain radius from the user (implemented using SDO_WITHIN_DISTANCE). Listing 15-3 shows an example of the first that relates to the selection of a certain number of incident locations (place codes and place names) that fall within the area of responsibility of an officer. The place_table table contains the objects to be selected, and the user_location table contains the officer's location, which can be the current position or a default position such as the center of the area of responsibility. The parameter $$nr_of_nearest_places specifies how many places are selected.

The query uses SDO_NN to rank places based on distance from the user location. The first and second AND conditions ensure that the location is that of the user, who logs in specifying a user name ($$user_name) and the code of the area of responsibility ($$regio_code). The third AND condition includes an SDO_RELATE statement that selects only places that fall within the area of responsibility (the geoloc of the table work_areas). This query discards places that are closer but not in the area for which the officer is responsible.

Listing 15-3. *Selecting Incidents Within a Certain Work Area*

```
SELECT place_code, place_name
FROM
(
   SELECT place_code, place_name
   FROM   place_table, user_location
   WHERE
       SDO_NN(place_table.geo, user_location.geo, sdo_num_res=500', 1) = 'TRUE'
       AND upper(user_location.fldid) = upper('$$user_name')
       AND upper(user_location.regio_id) = upper('$$regio_code')
       AND SDO_RELATE
                 (
                       place_table.geo,
                       (select geoloc from work_areas
                        where upper(areas_id) = upper('$$regio_code')
                        ),
                          'mask=INSIDE querytype=WINDOW'
                 ) = 'TRUE'
        ORDER BY SDO_NN_DISTANCE(1)
)
WHERE rownum <= $$nr_of_nearest_places
```

Bounding boxes are used in P-Info to display certain areas on a map. For orientation purposes, an officer can request a map of a street, postal code area, administrative area, and so on. Listing 15-4 shows an example of selecting the display area for a certain postal code area, here replaced by a question mark (as earlier, this is a parameter that is passed on by the Java code that calls the query). The table tblpostcode contains the list of postal codes and their spatial boundaries (polygons). The query results are passed on to the web-mapping application to display the full postal code area on the handheld screen.

Listing 15-4. *Selecting a Bounding Box for Display*

```
SELECT t.postcode,
    sdo_geom.sdo_min_mbr_ordinate(t.geo, m.diminfo, 1) left,
    sdo_geom.sdo_min_mbr_ordinate(t.geo, m.diminfo, 2) bottom,
    sdo_geom.sdo_max_mbr_ordinate(t.geo, m.diminfo, 1) right,
    sdo_geom.sdo_max_mbr_ordinate(t.geo, m.diminfo, 2) top,
    d.x_coordinaat_gem x,
    d.y_coordinaat_gem y
FROM   tblpostcode t, user_sdo_geom_metadata m
    WHERE  t.postcode = ?
```

Measurable Added Value of P-Info

The Dutch police corps have carried out various efficiency and effectiveness tests of P-Info. Their main goal was to measure whether P-Info was able to provide a tangible benefit to the police operations. The metrics used for the tests reflected two of the original goals of the system: to increase the visibility and presence of officers in the field and to be able to carry out the same work in less time. Among the various measurements suitable for this purpose, tests were carried out to measure the increase in time that agents would spend in the field and the amount of time required to carry out the same operation with and without P-Info.

In the first test, a group of five policemen were monitored over a period of about four weeks. Their field presence was compared to that of other colleagues who had the same tasks but operated without P-Info (the control group). The results showed that P-Info increased the time spent by officers in the field by about 20 percent. This means the same amount of fieldwork could be carried out by four rather than five agents or, alternatively, that a 20 percent larger area could be patrolled at the same quality level. Considering the personnel costs and the costs of P-Info, the balance was dramatically in favor of P-Info in terms of operation costs.

The second test regarded a comparison of work efficiency during roadblocks. Two roadblocks were set up with the same number of personnel, with one group operating with P-Info and the other group operating in the regular way (without P-Info). At the end of the operations, the number of cars checked and fines issued were compared. The test demonstrated that about 50 percent more cars could be screened using P-Info, with a proportional increase of the number of fines.

In spite of the limitations of the tests and the necessary caution in generalizing results, there is clear evidence that P-Info improves the effectiveness and efficiency of police forces. Considering the costs of P-Info and its benefits, a clear case can be made in favor of investing in P-Info.

It is worth stressing the role of location information in P-Info. Although there are some pure uses of location information in P-Info—for instance, to locate an address or a user location on a map—in the vast majority of cases, location information enables information search, provision, and visualization. P-Info is essentially a portal to multiple legacy information sources, organized to serve the specific needs of mobile officers. The combination of mobility requirements with legacy information systems put some hard requirements on the design and management of spatial data in P-Info. The result is a system that uses various forms of spatial data (reference road networks, geocoding databases, real-time user positions, and backdrop maps) and various types of services that exploit this data (such as spatial replication, visualization, and notification) within the general purpose of P-Info: providing extensive and meaningful information to officers in the field.

Risk Repository for Hazardous Substances

Note This system was developed by Getronics PinkRoccade BV and Geodan IT BV for the National Institute for Public Health and the Environment (RIVM) under supervision of the Netherlands Ministry of Housing, Spatial Planning, and the Environment (VROM).

On May 13, 2000, two explosions in a fireworks warehouse located in the urban center of the city of Enschede in the Netherlands detonated an estimated 100 tons of explosives. The blast was felt up to 40 km away, and within minutes the surrounding residential quarter was devastated. Twenty-two people died in the accident, and more than 1,000 people were injured. More than 400 houses were reduced to ashes, and another 1,000 were damaged. The material costs of the incident were estimated in the range between 500 million and 1 billion U.S. dollars.

In the aftermath of disasters such as this one, and also of Chernobyl (1986), Bhopal (1984), and Seveso (1976), governments in industrialized and developing countries have introduced or toughened legislation and controls over the transportation, storage, processing, and use of dangerous substances.

In the Netherlands, the Enschede disaster has triggered a number of important risk management initiatives that are meant to improve the prevention, preparedness, and repression of industrial incidents. One of those is the obligation to report to the authorities any situation that may involve a risk related to hazardous substances. Generally speaking, these risks are the result of storing, transporting, or processing a (bio)chemical substance.

The RRGS (the Dutch acronym for Register Risk Situations Hazardous Substances) is the central repository for this information. It provides a single source for all information regarding high-risk sources countrywide. The RRGS is accessible to professional users only, but the risk information is also accessible to the public through the provincial risk maps. For the public, the RRGS provides information to understand and assess possible risk situations in a certain neighborhood. National and local government organizations use the RRGS for spatial planning, risk management, and disaster prevention.

Emergency services agencies use the information in the repository to plan and organize rescue operations and emergency response. Figure 15-9 shows an example of the RRGS information, including the location of a gas station and its related risk contours.

The RRGS system is accessible through a web interface. It provides a set of forms, available to registered users, to manage the information concerning an industrial site or a transportation infrastructure and the nature and extent of the risks associated with these objects. The map interface serves to visualize the location of risk sources, the risk contours, and the areas surrounding a facility or a transport infrastructure affected by various risk levels. The RRGS include risk sources such as the following:

- Major industrial plants
- LPG filling stations
- Storage facilities for hazardous chemical and biochemical substances
- Storage facilities for explosives and ammunitions
- Nuclear reactors or nuclear waste storage facilities
- Railway yards for shunting trains with hazardous substances
- Containers of hazardous substances (for example, container shipments)

The RRGS addresses risks related to transportation by road, rail, water, or pipeline.

Figure 15-9. *Example of risk map for a gas station. Image © Provincie Utrecht* (`www.provincie-utrecht.nl`).

Table 15-1 shows the typical information included in the system. It is worth noting that risk contours and risk profiles usually require detailed studies, which are site and incident specific. In the case of RRGS, the risks are simplified representations of the actual risks and are based on generic risk models.[4] This allows a rapid risk assessment based on relatively limited information.

Table 15-1. *Example of Data Included in the RRGS*

General Data	Data on Hazardous Substances	Risk Data
Name of the installation	Name and identification numbers (for example, CAS, UN) of the substances	Risk contours for predefined risk thresholds, such as 10^{-5}/year, 10^{-6}/year, and 10^{-8}/year, and specific consequences
Address or coordinates of a location	Nature of the hazard (in other words, toxicity, explosion, flammable)	Average population density in the area around the establishment (or transport route) Effect distances

The information in the RRGS is also available to other systems. Other systems can use the RRGS as part of planning, logistics, or emergency management and to overlay risk maps on other type of maps. This is one of the main requirements of the RRGS that implies an extensive adoption of open standards and web services at all levels of the system.

RRGS Technology

The RRGS is based on a web services framework. Thanks to this architecture, the system can be used stand-alone, or it can be integrated in regional and local risk-information systems, such as desktop applications for the assessment or formulation of regional plans and development plans.

The RRGS implements the OpenGIS standard interfaces and services. The open standards permit a seamless integration of external systems with the objects in the RRGS. Compliance with these standards allows a faster, more consistent, and more economical structuring of the system. Figure 15-10 provides a simplified architecture overview, completely implemented in Java (J2EE).

4. According to the U.S. Department of Transportation, Office of Hazardous Material Safety, *hazard* is the characteristic of a substance that has the potential to cause harm to people, material goods, or the environment. *Consequence* is the direct effect of an event or incident. It can be a health effect (for example, death, injury, or exposure), property loss, environmental effect, and so on. *Risk* is the combination of the likelihood and the consequence of a specified hazard being realized. *Likelihood* is expressed as a probability, such as one in a million.

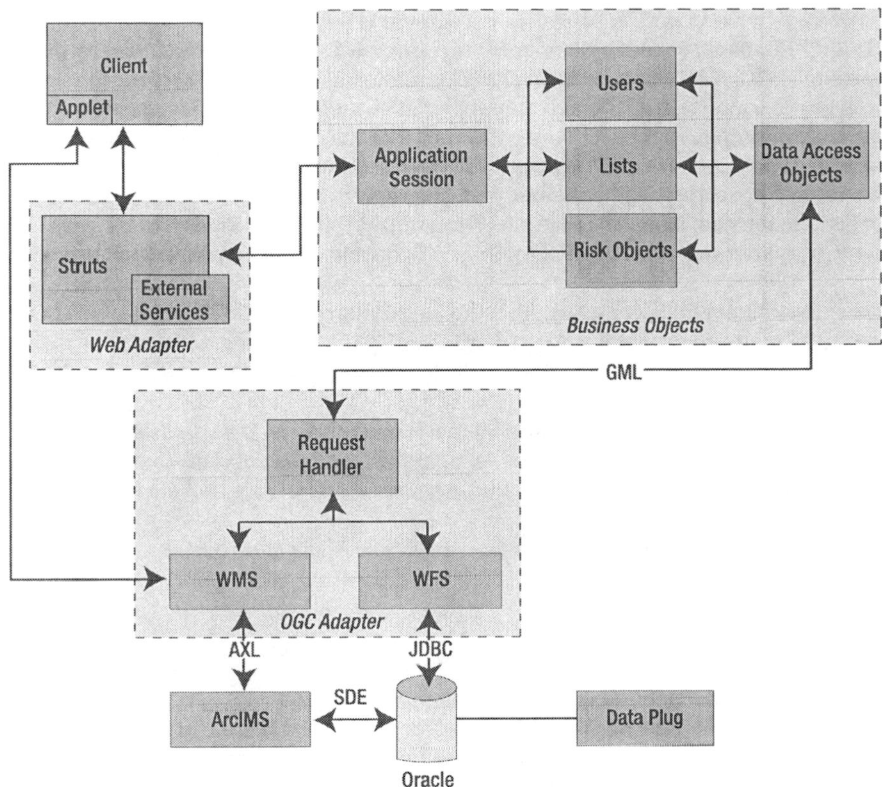

Figure 15-10. *Overview of the RRGS architecture*

The RRGS is accessible through a web interface and requires an applet for the map component of the application. The web adapter controls the main interfaces. The core of the web adapter is a Struts framework that manages the system interface and delegates tasks to the business objects.[5] Struts implements the Model View Controller (MVC) pattern. MVC organizes an interactive application into three modules. The first includes the application model, with its data representation and business logic. The second concerns the views that provide data presentation and user input. The third includes the controller that manages flows and dispatches requests. The web adapter also offers access to data services to external applications.

The business objects provide data handling, including data storage and access. The RRGS uses a Data Access Object (DAO) to communicate with the data services. A DAO abstracts and encapsulates all access to the data source and implements the access mechanism required to work with the data source (such as an RDBMS or LDAP). The business component that relies on the DAO uses the simpler interface exposed by the DAO, which hides the data source implementation details from its clients. Because the interface exposed by the DAO to clients does not change when the underlying data source implementation changes, this pattern allows the DAO to adapt to different storage schemes without affecting its business components. The DAO therefore acts as an adapter between the business object and the data source.

5. For more information on Struts, please visit `http://struts.apache.org`.

All communication between the DAO and the data sources is based on Geography Markup Language (GML), an XML-based encoding standard for geographic information developed by the OpenGIS Consortium (OGC). The data used by the RRGS is mediated by two OGC servers: the web feature server and the web map server. The web map server allows a client to overlay maps for display served from multiple web map services on the Internet. The web feature server allows a client to retrieve geospatial data encoded in GML from multiple web feature services.

The web feature server accesses alphanumeric and geographic objects from the database. The web map server generates a map in a certain format (for example, JPEG) and sends it to the map applet in the client. Maps are generated by ESRI ArcIMS, which connects to Oracle Spatial through ArcSDE.

The Oracle database, including Oracle Spatial, is the foundation of the RRGS, and it stores both spatial and nonspatial information, such as the risk information. A data plug is also added to the system to synchronize the content of the database with that of other databases, such as regional ones.

The reference geographic data stored in Oracle Spatial is essentially topographic data, at scales ranging from 1:10,000 to 1:250,000. This data can be very detailed, and the data can be used to identify single geographic objects such as parts of a building, a road infrastructure, or a bridge. The system manages more than 100 data layers.

The system runs on a cluster of Linux servers and uses Oracle Application Server as a Java container for the Java implementation.

Use of Oracle Spatial in the RRGS

Oracle Spatial is used to store background information, such as maps and road networks, and spatial information related to risk objects. All manipulation of spatial objects is done in Oracle Spatial, as well as many simple risk-modeling operations that correspond to spatial operators, such as a buffer.

The main tables with `SDO_GEOMETRY` columns are the tables containing the risk locations and the risk installations (a risk location can be a chemical plant that contains many installations, such as reactors, tanks, and so on). The geometry of risk locations is almost always a polygon, corresponding to the physical boundary of the plant or industrial premise. Risk installations, on the other hand, are always points. Each location and each installation is associated with several other `SDO_GEOMETRY` columns, which contain the risk and effect contours.

Risk contours for risk locations usually have specific shapes. The shape is computed by an external module (for example, an explosion model), and it is loaded in Oracle through the web feature server. The web feature server receives a GML containing the risk contour and parses it to create the structure of `INSERT` statements for loading the spatial object (the risk contour) in the appropriate `SDO_GEOMETRY` column. For linear transportation infrastructures, the risk contour is calculated by a buffer function. Java code creates a SQL statement for Oracle that creates a buffer polygon in an `SDO_GEOMETRY` column. Remaining risk installations are associated to circular risk contours.

Listing 15-5 shows the buffer generation using `SDO_BUFFER`, in this case applied to an object (`l_route`) for a buffer of `l_dist` meters around the object. Notice that `SDO_BUFFER` returns an `SDO_GEOMETRY` object, which in this case is the object of a densify function. With geometries in a projected coordinate system, such as in this case, circular arcs can be *densified* into polygons. The result is straight-line polygon geometry. The `arc_tolerance` parameter specifies the maximum distance between the original geometry and its approximated straight-line representation, in this case 1 meter. The RRGS uses this solution to increase rendering speed.

Listing 15-5. *Example of Generating a Buffer and Densifying Its Geometry*

```
l_buffer := sdo_geom.sdo_arc_densify
(sdo_geom.sdo_buffer(l_route, l_dim, l_dist), l_dim, 'arc_tolerance = 1');
```

Once the buffer is created, the geometry can be stored in the SDO_GEOMETRY containing the risk contour. Listing 15-6 shows an example for updating the table rgs_transportroutes (major roads and highways), inserting a risk contour polygon for the p_tre_id object through the function illustrated in Listing 15-5 for geometry column risk_contour_1 of table rgs_transportroutes.

Listing 15-6. *Example of Inserting a Geometry*

```
update rgs_transportroutes tre
set tre.risk_contour_1 = l_buffer
where tre.id = p_tre_id;
```

Notice that the tables containing risk location and risk installations have multiple SDO_GEOMETRY columns to accommodate for risk contours and effect contours, as well as various risk and effect levels. For instance, the risk location table contains seven different SDO_GEOMETRY columns. All spatial columns are indexed.

To display spatial objects with ArcSDE, the system defines a series of views. This is necessary to separate object types in tables (points, lines, polygons, and so on) into separate views that are rendered separately. The same applies to multiple SDO_GEOMETRY columns. Different views are created for each separate column and are rendered separately.

One of the main features of the RRGS is to identify all locations and installations that contribute to the total risk of any given location. When you click a point on the map, the system detects all sources of a certain risk or effect level, based on the risk and effect contours of locations and installations. This is based on the SDO_RELATE operator. Listing 15-7 shows an example of this selection (in this case, a cursor example). The query selects the IDs of installations (irg.id) from the table of risk installations (rgs_installations), for which the risk contour (irg.risk_contour_1) contains the object b_geom.

Listing 15-7. *Example of Selecting Risk Objects Causing a Certain Risk for a Point*

```
cursor c_irg_rcr5(b_geom in mdsys.sdo_geometry) is
  select irg.id id
  from   rgs_installations irg
  where  sdo_relate(irg.risk_countour_1, b_geom, 'mask=contains querytype=WINDOW')
= 'TRUE';
```

From Hazardous Substances to Risk Management

The RRGS system, which has been in operation since 2003, focuses on a specific type of risks related to hazardous substances. However, public risk managers need to address a much larger portfolio of situations that can cause serious consequences for people, material resources, and the environment. These situations include, for instance, transportation incidents (air, land, and water), earthquakes, epidemics, large fires in buildings or tunnels, floods, forest fires, and blackouts, among others. The RRGS represents only one of the sources of information needed to identify, prevent, and manage these risks.

The evolution of the RRGS is in the direction of supporting the definition of comprehensive risk maps based on multiple risk sources that interoperate and provide information to assess all types of risks. Figure 15-11 shows an example of a risk map that includes risks associated to hazardous substances together with flooding risks (dashed area) and water freight routes (blue lines). The combination of these sources of information provides risk managers with a comprehensive view of the risks to which a certain area is exposed.

These maps shown in this case study are publicly available from the website of the Dutch risk map (www.risikokaart.nl). Regional maps from most Dutch regions are now available online with the same look and feel and information format.

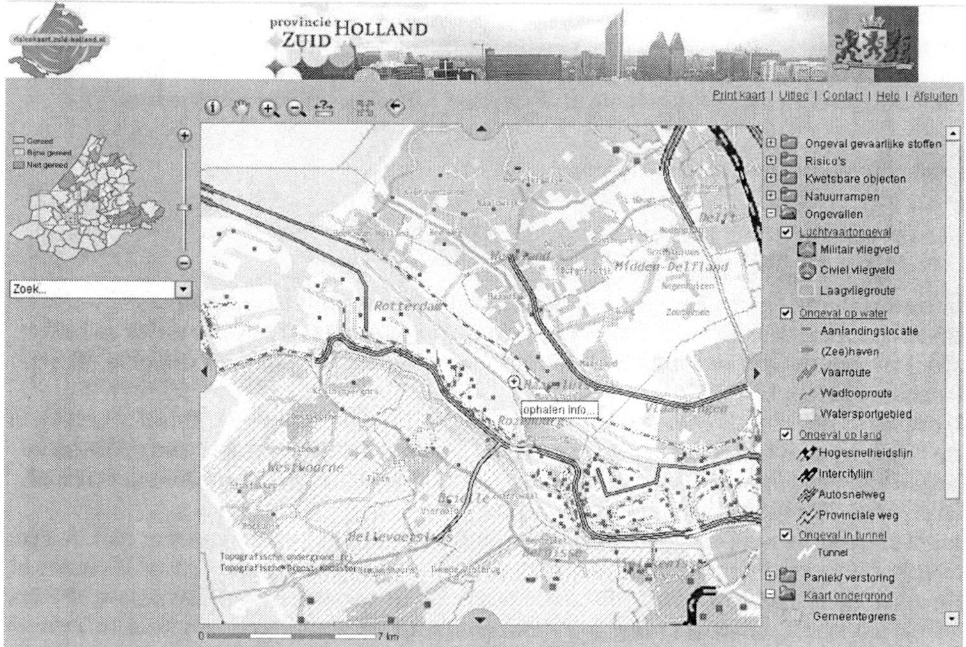

Figure 15-11. *Risk map for the province of Zuid Holland. Image © Provincie Zuid Holland (*`www.zuid-holland.nl`*).*

USGS National Land Cover Visualization and Analysis Tool

■ **Note** The USGS National Land Cover Visualization and Analysis tool was developed by eSpatial.[6] The authors would like to thank eSpatial for granting permission to publish the material in this section.[7]

Land-cover data is a largely untapped information resource. With increasing population and the challenging prospect of climate change, comprehensive information about the condition of our land and how it is changing becomes more and more vital. Land cover, the pattern of natural vegetation, agriculture, and urban areas, is shaped by both natural processes and human influences. Information about land cover is needed by managers of public and private lands, urban planners, agricultural experts, and scientists for studying such issues as climate change or invasive species.

The U.S. National Land Cover Dataset 1992 (NLCD 1992) was derived from the early to mid-1990s using LANDSAT[8] Thematic Mapper satellite data. The National Land Cover Dataset 2001 (NLCD 2001)

---

6. See `www.espatial.com/`.

7. At the time of writing, the system is not yet available to the public. The launch is scheduled for the second part of 2007.

8. Satellites managed by NASA that acquire imagery of the earth from space. The images are used in the areas of agriculture, geology, forestry, regional planning, global change, and national security.

is a second-generation land-cover database and maps land cover for 50 states with data captured about 10 years after the first campaign.

Land-cover data is useful in many operational settings and for strategic decisions:

- *Fire danger monitoring and forecasting*: Based on land-cover data as well as other data sources, the effects of fire can be consistently measured in terms of burn severity. This measures the magnitude of ecological change caused by fire and provides a reliable way to measure the effects and damage of a fire. The same land-cover data, combined with fire risk factors, can be used to predict the spatial likelihood and effect of fires and thus facilitate preparedness as well as emergency operations.
- *Biodiversity conservation*: Land cover is an essential indicator of the ability of a land to sustain ecosystems. Combined with ecological information and ecosystem maps, land cover provides the basic information for effective conservation measures, as well for optimal allocation of land to potentially conflicting activities, such as nature conservation and urban development.
- *Land-use planning*: In densely populated areas, land use is often the result of conflicting claims, with land contended between transportation, urban areas, agriculture, nature, or industrial areas. For policy makers, understanding the current situation as well as the changes that occurred in the recent past is essential to designing meaningful land-use policies that balance regional with local needs as well as the needs of conflicting land claims.
- *Climate change*: Land-cover data is used to understand and analyze the stocks and fluxes of carbon on the landscape (soils and biomass) to predict the impacts of future land management decisions on the global carbon cycle. This is the basis for understanding the effectiveness of mitigation measures to limit the impact of human activities on climate change, as well as to predict the effectiveness of adaptation measures to climate change and extreme events.
- *Flood and natural risk prevention*: Land-cover data, combined with simulation tools, serves to predict the risk and impact of events such as floods, hurricanes, or landslides. Information derived from these simulations can improve preparedness as well as emergency management.

The USGS National Land Cover Visualization and Analysis Tool provides to both expert and nonexpert users access to the USGS Land Cover data. The application incorporates the entire USGS 30m×30m-resolution National Land Cover Data repository, which includes nationwide data coverage for 1992 and 2001. A third dataset, the NLCD Change Product, shows how land cover has changed during this time.

The interface of the tool allows users to easily navigate to areas of interest through the map or by searching a gazetteer of areas of interest. Figure 15-12 shows the home page of the system, the map navigation pane, and the main selections available to the user. Figure 15-13 shows the 2001 land-cover data for a small area around Richmond, Virginia.

Simple analysis functionality allows reports to be generated showing the aggregate areas of each land cover type within the current map bounds or within a user-defined area. Figure 15-14 shows two sample reports for the data displayed in Figure 15-13. You can download the report results in multiple formats: CSV, XLS, or PDF.

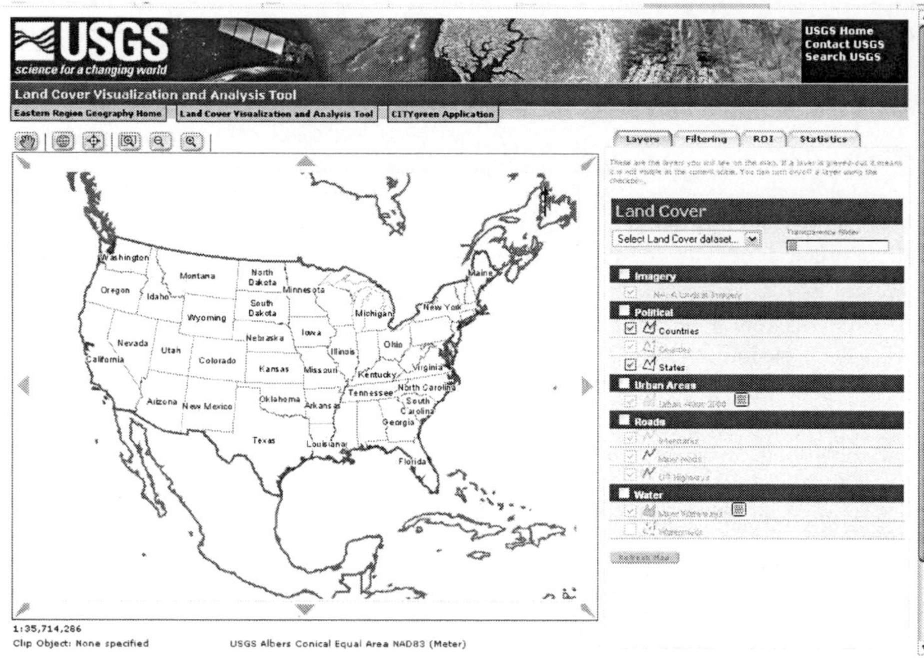

Figure 15-12. *The USGS visualization and analysis tool: home page*

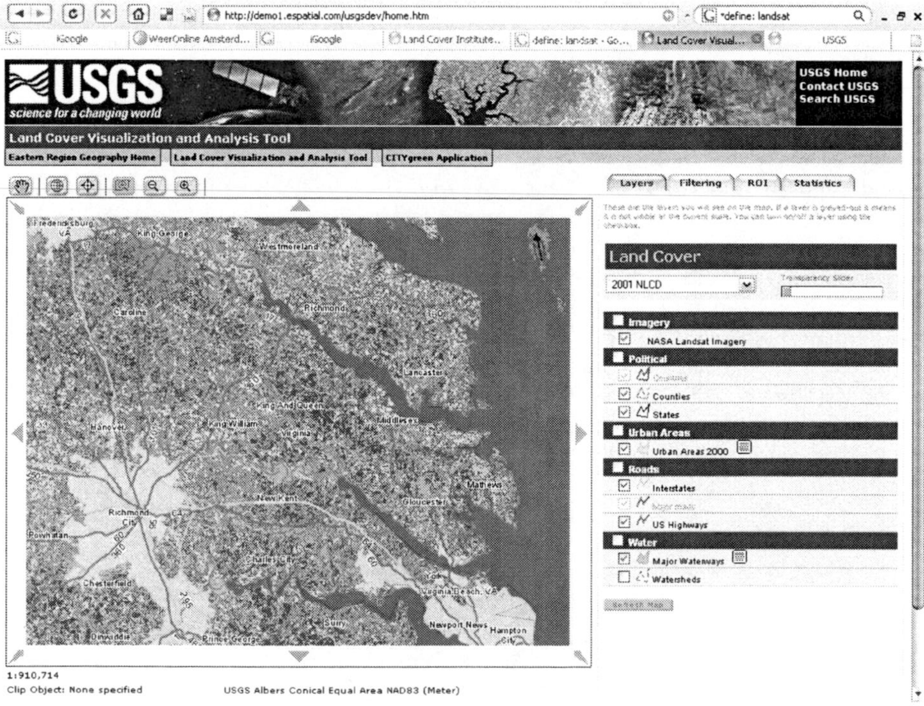

Figure 15-13. *The USGS visualization and analysis tool: details for an area around Richmond, Virginia, for the 2001 land-cover data*

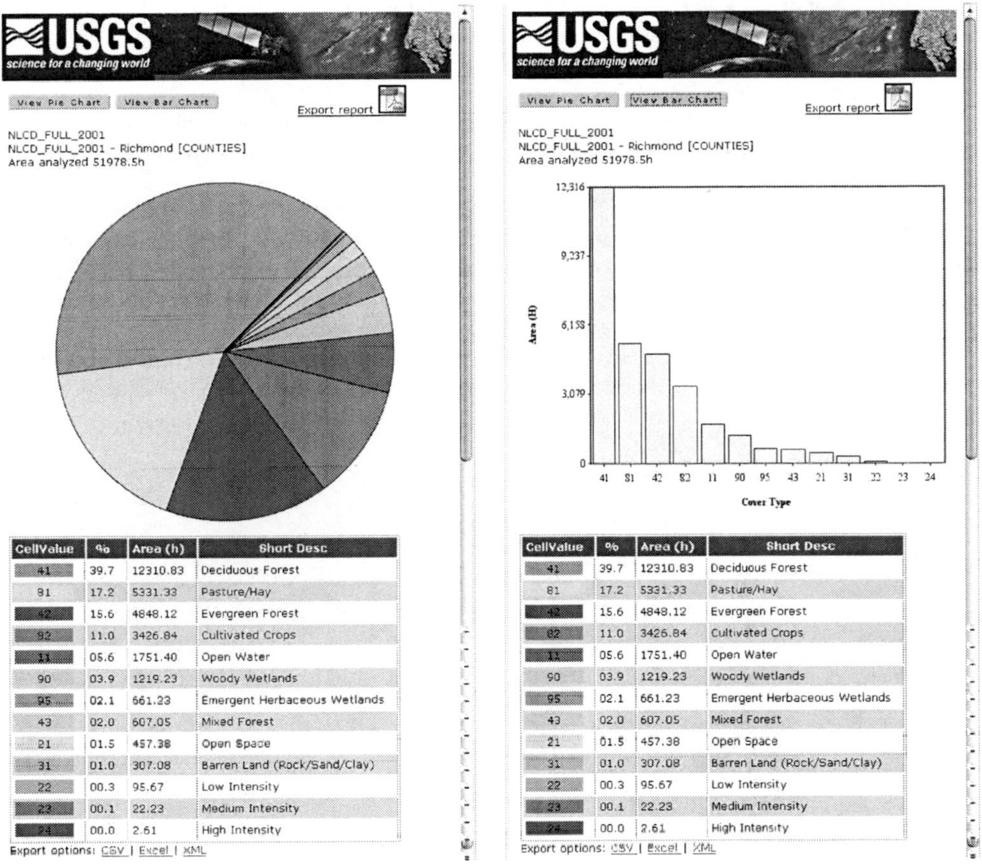

Figure 15-14. *The USGS visualization and analysis tool: land-cover statistics for Richmond, Virginia—pie chart (left) and histogram (right)*

The Architecture of USGS Visualization and Analysis Tool

The functionality of the USGS Land Cover Visualization and Analysis Tool includes the following:

- *Land-cover selection tool*: This serves to select the 1992, 2001, or 1992–2001 change data (raster format) and the overlay data, such as political boundaries, roads, and waterways (vector format).
- *Filtering and legend tool*: Land cover data consists of small colored cells (of 30×30 meters). This pane displays the color code of each land-cover type and its definition, as well the possibility of hiding any land-cover type.
- *Region of interest selector*: This tool serves to select a region of interest for further analysis. The selection can be based on a spatial feature (a state or county), on an area drawn on the screen by the user, or on an external boundary uploaded from a file.
- *A statistics tool*: This tool computes the frequency of occurrences of land-cover cell values for the region of interest selected and produces a pie chart or histogram of the data, which can be exported in a file.

Figure 15-15 shows the architecture of the system. The application runs on Oracle Application Server. It is written in Java and uses eSpatial's API in addition to the Oracle Spatial API to convert and reproject uploaded ESRI shapefiles[9] and the Oracle Spatial Georaster API to allow statistics to be gathered from a Java Georaster object.

Oracle Spatial stores about 70GB of georaster data in seamless coverage of the Unites States for 1992 and 2001. The system also includes the original LANDSAT images as georasters. All data is loaded into Oracle and mosaiced into seamless coverage using SQL scripts.

The Spring Framework[10] is used as the overall design model for the USGS Land Cover Visualization and Analysis Tool. Spring implements the Model View Controller (MVC) architectural pattern in which distinction is made between the client objects, such as browser pages, called *views*, server-side servlets that supply these pages and are called *controllers*, and the back-end data model and business logic that supports the views and controllers called the *model*.

The purpose of the MVC pattern is to allow developers to focus on a particular aspect of the application's function and to keep other nonrelated aspects out of the code. Views, for instance, should not access a database; controllers should not contain model objects.[11]

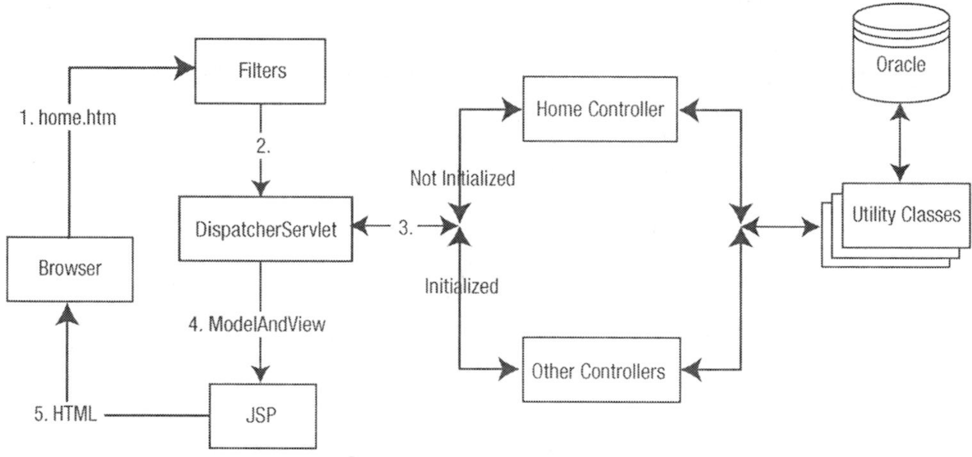

Figure 15-15. *USGS visualization and analysis tool: architecture*

Oracle Spatial in USGS Visualization and Analysis Tool

Three primary map overlays are used in the application:

- Imagery map sheet
  - Contains a map image derived from orthophoto (LANDSAT) or other imagery loaded into Oracle as georaster data
  - Is at the bottom of the map sheet stack

9. www.esri.com/library/whitepapers/pdfs/shapefile.pdf
10. www.springframework.org/
11. You can find a brief discussion of the MVC pattern at http://java.sun.com/blueprints/patterns/MVC-detailed.html.

- Grid map sheet
    - Contains a map image derived from Land Cover grid data in Oracle as georasters
    - Overlays the imagery map grid
    - Supports variable transparency
- Vector map sheet
    - Contains a map image derived from Oracle Spatial data as polygons, lines, and points
    - Overlays the two sheets below it
    - Has background transparency set by default

The geographic data are stored in Oracle as SDO_GEOMETRY and SDO_GEORASTER data types. Original ESRI shapefiles are loaded into Oracle Spatial using shp2sdo.

USGS uses a custom projection that was added to Oracle's Spatial Reference Identifiers to support the project. The following SQL (Listing 15-8) is used to create the necessary SRID within Oracle (see also Chapter 3). This projection is similar to the regular Albers Conical Equal Area projection but based on a different datum (NAD83 rather than NAD27).

Listing 15-8. *Creating the SRID in Oracle*

```
delete from sdo_coord_ref_system where srid = 1000000;
INSERT INTO SDO_COORD_REF_SYSTEM
(
SRID, COORD_REF_SYS_NAME, COORD_REF_SYS_KIND,
COORD_SYS_ID, DATUM_ID, GEOG_CRS_DATUM_ID,
SOURCE_GEOG_SRID, PROJECTION_CONV_ID, CMPD_HORIZ_SRID,
CMPD_VERT_SRID, INFORMATION_SOURCE,
DATA_SOURCE, IS_LEGACY,
LEGACY_CODE,
LEGACY_WKTEXT,
LEGACY_CS_BOUNDS,
IS_VALID,
SUPPORTS_SDO_GEOMETRY
)
VALUES
(
1000000, 'USGS Albers Conical Equal Area NAD83', 'PROJECTED',
4400, NULL, 10076,
2000006 , NULL, NULL,
NULL, 'USGS',
NULL, 'TRUE',
NULL,
'PROJCS["Equal-Area Projection (United States)",
   GEOGCS[ "NAD 83", DATUM ["NAD 83",
   SPHEROID ["GRS 80",6378137,298.2572221010002]],
   PRIMEM ["Greenwich",0], UNIT["Decimal degree",0.0174532925199433]],
   PROJECTION ["Albers Conical Equal Area"],
   PARAMETER ["Standard_Parallel_1",29.5],
   PARAMETER ["Standard_Parallel_2",45.5], PARAMETER ["Latitude_of_Origin",23],
   PARAMETER ["Central_Meridian",-96], UNIT ["Meter",1]]',
NULL,
'TRUE',
'TRUE'
);
```

The Oracle Spatial Java API is used to reproject uploaded ESRI shapefiles, which originally store the LANDSAT images and the derived land use data. The following code reprojects uploaded shapefiles to the custom USGS projection. The file upload uses Apache's commons file upload library. Once the shapefile is obtained, the procedure iterates through them, calling a method to project them.

Listing 15-9 and Listing 15-10 show two parts of the reprojection procedure. Listing 15-9 shows a call to the translate function, described in Listing 15-10. In the first listing we use the translate function and store the result into `newgeom`. This, together with the geometry key, is then stored in `customsGeomsMap` for later use.

Listing 15-9. *Call to the Translate Function*

```
//get a geometry from a Map of geometries
// this is within a loop - geom is of type JGeometry

            geom = (JGeometry)m.get("GEOM");
            JGeometry newgeom = null;
            if (geom != null) {
                try {
                    //call the method to reproject
                    newgeom = tr.translate(toSRID, geom);
                    // this key is composed of a String and concatenated
                    // unique ID of the shape
                    key = "CUSTOM-" + fIndex;
                    //the key and transformed geometry are added to a
                    // java.util.Map for storage in the session
                    customGeomsMap.put(key, newgeom);
                } catch (Exception e) {
                    logger.error("Here Controller Name: failed to translate geom");
                }
```

Listing 15-10 shows the actual reprojection function. The first part of the listing is the connection to the database. Once connected, we use the `SDO_CS.TRANSFORM`, which transforms a geometry representation using the coordinate system USGS SRID 1000000. This call is used inside a Java statement. The `while` loop at the end of the listing executes the transformation of the geometries.

Listing 15-10. *Reprojection Function*

```
private STRUCT s = null;
private JGeometry g = null;

private OracleConnection oraCon = null;
private PreparedStatement ps = null;
private ResultSet rs = null;

//accept an incoming SRID and a JGeometry
public JGeometry translate (int toSRID, JGeometry geom) throws Exception  {

if (oraCon == null) {
            //open a DB connection first time through
            InitialContext initial = new InitialContext();
            Object o = initial.lookup(dataSourceName);
            if (o==null) {
                log.error( "No datasource called "+dataSourceName+" found" );
            }
            oraCon = (OracleConnection) ((DataSource) o).getConnection();
        }
```

```
        try {
            //call the transform to custom USGS SRID 1000000
            ps = oraCon.prepareStatement(
                    "select SDO_CS.TRANSFORM(?,0.0005,1000000)
                    from DUAL");

            //put the JGeometry into a STRUCT
            s = JGeometry.store(geom, oraCon);
            ps.setObject(1,s);

            rs = ps.executeQuery();

            while (rs.next()) {
                //set the returned STRUCT back into a JGeometry
                g = JGeometry.load( (STRUCT)rs.getObject(1));
                if (g != null) log.debug(
                        "TranslateGeom: translate : got transformed");
            }

        } catch (SQLException e) { log.debug("TranslateGeom: translate " + e); }
        return g;
    }
```

A cleanup of objects and connections happens last at the end of the code.

Listing 15-9 and Listing 15-10 show two of the steps of the actual procedure used to translate the ESRI shape geometries. From the shapefile, a loop (not shown in the listing) gets a geometry from the map of geometries. The translate function utilizes an `SDO_CS.TRANSFORM` function that performs the actual translation. The result—the reprojected object—is stored in `customGeomsMap` for later use.

Benefits of USGS Visualization and Analysis Tool

Several benefits are associated with the USGS Land Cover Visualization and Analysis Tool:

- It is a single nationwide seamless dataset containing land-cover and other mapping data, something that until recently was available only to a restricted group of scientists and specialists.
- Data is available for any geographic area of the United States from any web browser without the need for specialized GIS software. This dramatically increases accessibility.
- It makes it possible to analyze land cover in an historical perspective, looking not only at the current situation but also at the past and the changes that occurred in between.
- It allows the analysis of selected areas by political, natural, or user-defined boundaries (hand-drawn area or specific region, such as state or county).
- It calculates land-cover statistics within selected areas for further analysis and prints simple reports.

The National Land Cover Dataset has to date been a largely untapped resource. It contains a host of information useful to managers of public and private lands, urban planners, agricultural experts, and scientists alike. Making it easily accessible over the Web and showing changes over time opens the potential of this rich dataset to a wide audience.

U.S. Department of Defense MilitaryHOMEFRONT LBS

■ Note The MilitaryHOMEFRONT LBS was developed by eSpatial.[12] The authors would like to thank eSpatial for granting permission to publish the material in this section. You can find additional information on eSpatial at `www.espatial.com/`.

Organizations are increasingly providing customized, web-based applications to allow their personnel access to location information relevant to their roles. The Office of the Under Secretary of Defense, Personal & Readiness, Military Community & Family Policy, Program Support Group (MC&FP PSG) is no exception. Troops are often required to relocate during their careers in the U.S. military. When considering relocation, they will want to know the answer to a variety of practical questions regarding the area where they relocate to, such as the following:

- Where is the installation located, and how do I get there?
- Where can I find a specific service such as a childcare center, barber, relocation office, and so on?
- Where can my kids go to school?
- How far away is the nearest hospital?
- What is today's weather like?
- What will the weather be like in winter?
- Are there nearby hotels for my family and friends to stay at if they come visit?

The MilitaryINSTALLATIONS web portal[13] site is intended as a source of information that can benefit the troops and their families. Information on services, base layout, access to services and their locations, and proximity to schools, clinics, and other points of interest allow families to become accustomed with their new home.

The location-based service (LBS) assists users to make more informed decisions regarding services available on and near military facilities installations worldwide. The user interface, modeled on the latest web mapping technologies, provides an intuitive interface for non-GIS users. Service personnel and their families are able to locate military installations by means of menus or interactively using a map to find details about the installation and the community surrounding it. The application simplifies planning moves and trips to a new installation. For example, a family relocating from Germany to a base in Oklahoma can search a specific installation to find on-base and off-base services, including schools, ATMs, pharmacies, parks, and other municipal services. Links are provided to additional information where available and directions to and from locations can be provided. The LBS can also be used to assist service personnel when traveling or planning travel to a military installation.

MilitaryINSTALLATIONS is part of the MilitaryHOMEFRONT[14] web portal. They are the central, trusted, and up-to-date sources for service members and their families to obtain information about Department of Defense Quality of Life programs and services. The site is a service of the MC&FP PSG and was first launched in August 2006.

12. See `www.espatial.com`.

13. `www.militaryinstallations.dod.mil`

14. `www.militaryhomefront.dod.mil`

Figure 15-16 shows the home page of MilitaryINSTALLATIONS. Users can select a program or service (such as schools or legal services), a branch or service agency (such as Navy or Air Force), and a specific installation. You can also choose the installation by clicking in the map, which will show the facilities in the state selected.

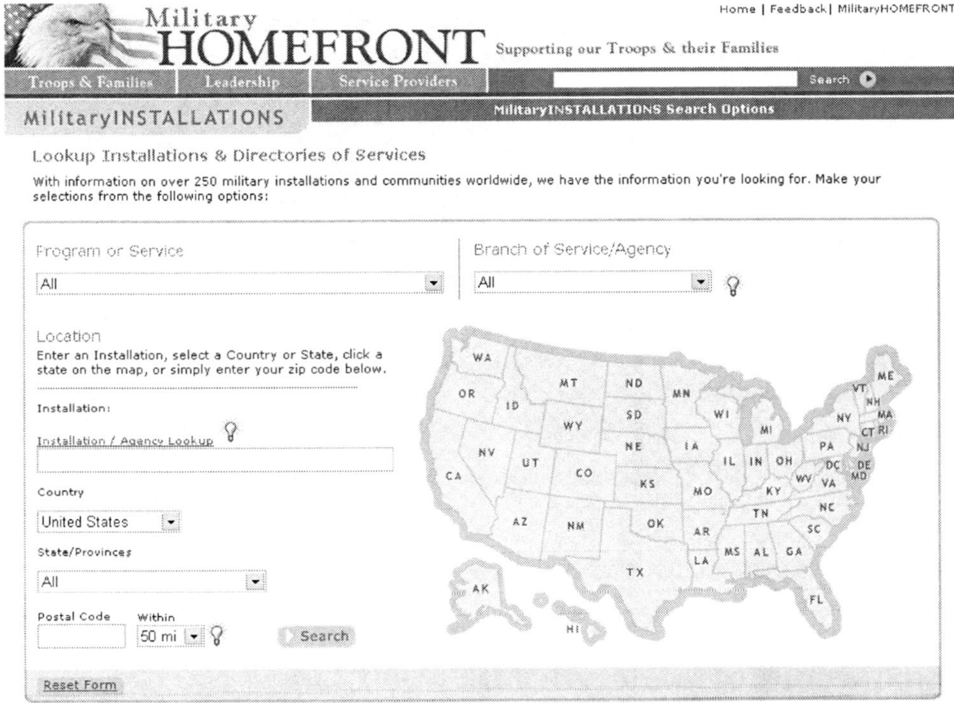

Figure 15-16. *The MilitaryINSTALLATIONS home page (*`www.militaryinstallations.MC&FP PSG.mil`*)*

The MilitaryINSTALLATIONS application is based on Oracle Spatial 10*g* and uses eSpatial's iSMART platform. Worldwide data for the system is provided using NAVTEQ's Premium Streets and Points of Interest (POI) datasets. This dataset has been augmented with additional application-specific data concerning military installations, services, and military-specific points of interest.

The application utilizes iSMART's web mapping software to provide a seamless user interface for navigating the spatial and business data. Navigation is enhanced with significant use of Ajax for a dynamic experience, including rich map navigation, mouseover pop-ups of information, and quick loading of data. Oracle Spatial is used to provide geocoding and routing services based on the NAVTEQ data. External data feeds are also incorporated, providing useful information such as local weather conditions.

The system integrates the existing geo-spatial data of the MC&FP PSG infrastructure, which stores address and service information for all of the U.S. military bases worldwide, with NAVTEQ worldwide premium map and POI data. The data is stored in Oracle 10*g*, and all spatial query functionality, routing, and geocoding is performed through the Oracle Spatial platform.

Figure 15-17 illustrates the results of a search for car services within a certain radius from an installation. The resulting map shows the installation and the closest services found in its surrounding. The results page allows for an extension of the search to a larger area or to a different set of POIs.

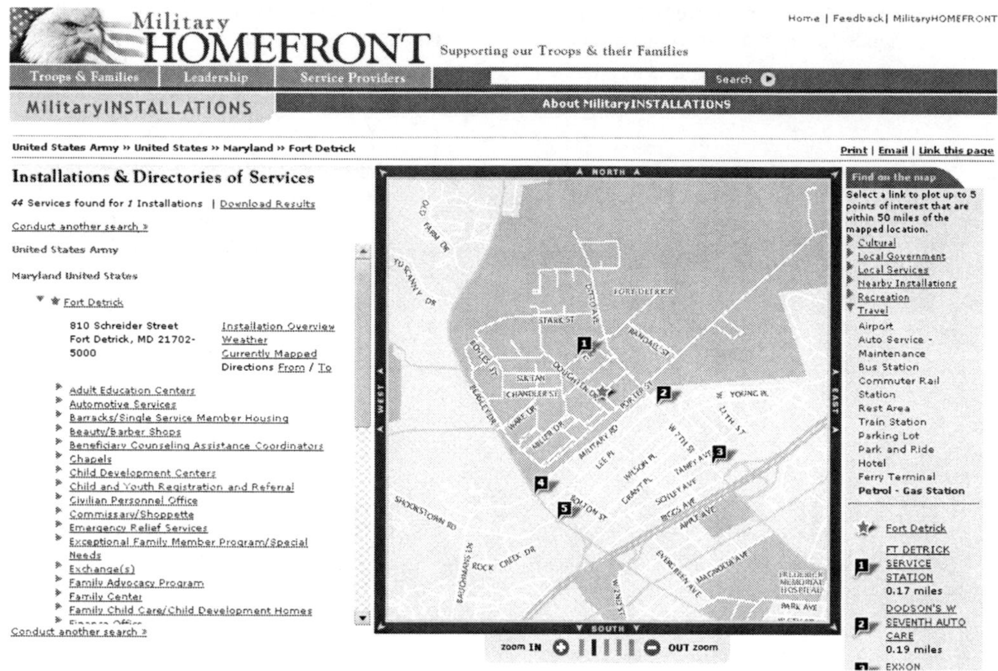

Figure 15-17. *The MilitaryINSTALLATIONS results page showing search results and nearby points of interest.*

The Architecture of MilitaryHOMEFRONT LBS

The MilitaryINSTALLATIONS system functionality includes the following:

- Installation and directory of services search. The search is based on location (such as country, state, or province), program or service (such as family or education centers), and branch of service (such as Navy or National Guard).
- Detailed information on each search result, such as location overview (such as mission, history, relocation assistance), weather conditions (from an external XML web services feed), contact information (phone numbers and facilities list for the installation), and other information.
- Proximity searches for locating other facilities and POI in the proximity of an installation (ATMs, cultural venues, schools or police stations, recreation, and so on).
- Point-to-point driving directions to determine the driving route between two locations (installations, POIs, or address) using custom route preferences such as type of road (highways or local roads) or fastest/shortest route.

MilitaryHOMEFRONT provides a diverse set of spatial and nonspatial datasets stored in an Oracle 10*g* database. Oracle Spatial stores the maps, addresses, POIs, and POI attributes. In particular, the repository contains the following:

- *Map data at various scales*: The base data of the MilitaryINSTALLATIONS application is provided by NAVTEQ. After loading, the data is processed for symbolization and performance. Data is split into separate layers to minimize query time and processing and to facilitate symbolizing. The data provided by NAVTEQ is of much higher precision than can be easily displayed at the application's viewing levels, so filtering and simplification is performed. Very large datasets (streams, lakes, roads, and so on) are simplified into multiple layers that are then displayed at separate scale levels for maximum performance and clarity. Data selection and filtering is applied for optimal display at all map scales. For example, only interstates and major highways are displayed at high levels, while minor roads are rendered when zoomed in further.
- *POI data*: The primary POI database is the existing MC&FP PSG database of installations and facilities that is integrated into the application. This provides the services and installation information searched through the main interface. The remainder of the POI data (gas stations, ATMs, restaurants, and so on) is a combination of the MC&FP PSG data and the NAVTEQ POI dataset. Additional information (phone numbers, websites, pictures) stored in these datasets is either displayed in-line with the results or as a secondary page linked in the results.
- *Address data*: These include the full address of a POI or of a certain location and their x,y coordinates. Address data is stored primarily for routing and display purposes, with geocoding both being preprocessed for the majority of the data. In cases where address data is not available or was not previously geocoded, the user is given the option to modify the address, which is then geocoded in real time using Oracle Spatial.
- *Road network data*: Road network data is supplied by NAVTEQ and includes all of the necessary tables and data structures for use with the Oracle Spatial Route Server.

The cartographic representation of the data is provided in an intuitive and easy-to-use form. Rendering performance is improved through the use of iSMART's transactional spatial data cache. Because of both the large amounts of spatial data being queried from the Oracle database and the large number of users accessing the site, this caching of data allows for significantly improved render times and query speeds.

The application uses "smart style" style sheets, which vary styles, symbols, or icons and sizes depending upon the preset zoom levels. The color selections try to convey the element type easily to the user (for example, park polygons in green, military base polygons in gray, and so on). POIs are displayed in their actual location on the map based on coordinates rather than showing the POI locations along the street centre line. This provides the user the ability to discern which side of the street the POI resides.

Figure 15-18 shows the architecture of the system. The application resides in the Oracle Application Server and uses three main components: the spatial query and display, the geocoding, and the routing. Oracle database is implemented in a cluster for maximum performance, scalability and reliability.

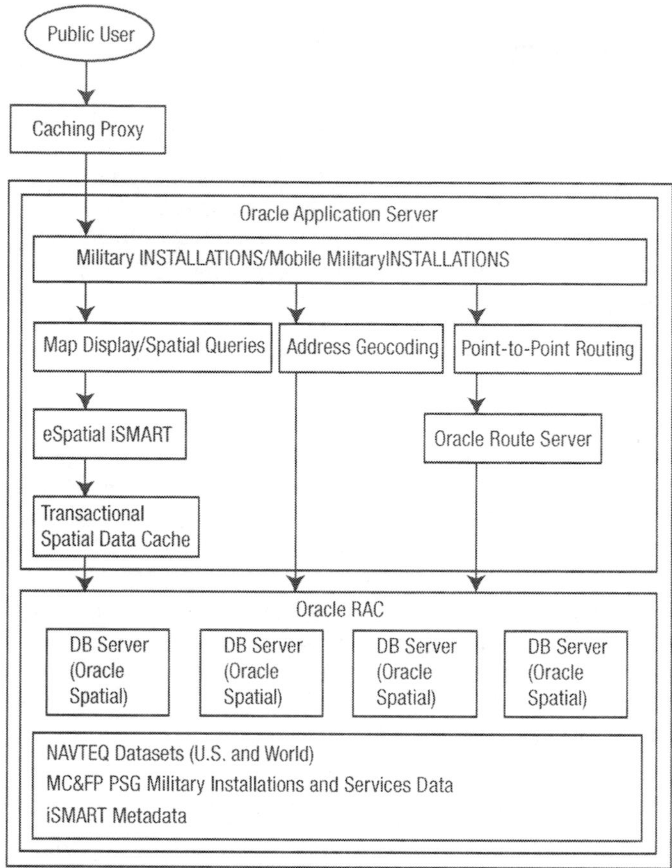

Figure 15-18. *The MilitaryINSTALLATIONS architecture*[15]

The use of an external OGC WMS[16] Image service is currently being evaluated to provide additional map data to the user. In the current implementation, this functionality is used to display raster imagery behind the vector dataset. WMS consumption was also tested to overlay weather information on top of the vector data, although this was abandoned in favor of the current separate page of weather information for simplicity of display.

The architecture, combined with iSMART's capabilities, allows for the MilitaryINSTALLATIONS map data to also be served internally through both web map server and web feature server[17] (read-only) services allowing other internal users the ability to consume the data in their own GIS applications.

15. RAC stands for Real Application Cluster.

16. Web Map Service (WMS) is a standard defined by the Open Geospatial Consortium (`www.opengeospatial.org`) that provides a standard interface for querying and accessing map layers from a mapping server. Clients and servers that adhere to the standard can share data independent of their implementation.

17. A web feature server is a standard interface specified by the Open Geospatial Consortium (`www.opengeospatial.org`) that allows interoperability of for geographical features across the Web. It uses the XML-based GML for data exchange.

Oracle Spatial in MilitaryHOMEFRONT

Oracle Spatial is used by MilitaryINSTALLATIONS to store and retrieve spatial information, to perform proximity analysis, to geocode locations, and to provide routing to and from military installations, services, and POIs.

The search for POIs in the proximity of an installation is based on an SDO_INSIDE query. In this case, it is preferred to use the SDO_INSIDE query instead of the SDO_NN query because the query may be applied for searches in fairly remote areas of the country/world, where the density of POI data can be very small and the search may extend for a very large area. Using SDO_INSIDE instead of SDO_NN improves performance in this case, because distances are calculated only for a subset of POIs.

Listing 15-11 shows the search of POIs close to a reference point with coordinates p_x and p_y. The query returns POIs within p_distance from the reference point.

The query joins two tables: the POI table (poi) and the geocoding table (gc). The POI table contains the information about a POI, such as name (poi_name), street name (street_name), or phone number (phone_number). The geocoding table adds information such as region name (region_name), postal code (postal_code), and municipality name (municipality_name).

The query creates a list of poi and gc records and includes a new column called distance_in_miles from the reference point (p_x, p_y). This column contains the distance from each POI to the reference point calculated with SDO_DISTANCE.

The first part of the where clause limits the selection to POI geometries (m.geometry) that fall inside a buffer of p_distance miles from the reference point. The buffer is computed on the fly by sdo_geom.sdo.buffer. The results are limited to POI of type p_poi_type.

Listing 15-11. *Selecting POIs Close to a Facility*

```
select
  m.poi_id,
  m.poi_name,
  m.poi_st_number,
  m.street_name,
  g.municipality_name,
  g.region_name,
  g.postal_code,
  m.phone_number,
  m.link_id,
  m.geometry.sdo_point.x,
  m.geometry.sdo_point.y,
  sdo_geom.sdo_distance(
       m.geometry, sdo_geometry(2001, 8307,
       sdo_point_type(<p_x>, <p_y>, NULL),
       NULL, NULL), 0.5, 'unit = mile')
       distance_in_miles
from
  us.poi m,
  us.gc g
where
  sdo_inside(m.geometry, sdo_geom.sdo_buffer(
       sdo_geometry(2001, 8307, sdo_point_type(<p_x>, <p_y>, NULL),
       NULL, NULL), <p_distance>, 0.5, 'unit=mile')) = 'TRUE'
and
  m.poi_type = <p_poi_type>
and
  m.poi_id = g.poi_id
order by distance_in_miles
```

The search of POIs can also be based on ZIP code instead of installation. The two following listings illustrate the POI searches (from the MC&FP PSG data) based the ZIP code. The key parts of the query are to obtain the ZIP code geometry used multiple times in the query and the search of the full dataset using the ZIP code geometry. The examples in Listing 15-12 and Listing 15-13 are part of a procedure that takes parameters such as the following:

- `p_postal_code`: A certain postal code
- `p_stat_id`: The ID of a certain state
- `p_within`: The distance from a postal code

Listing 15-12 serves to obtain the ZIP code geometry. The query scans the table `zip_usa` and selects the `shp_geometry` objects for which the field `shp_zip` equals the parameter `p_postal_code` and for which `shp_state` equals `p_stat_id`. The NLV statement allows also matches when `p_stat_id` is null. The query selects only one element that is stored in `zip_geometry` for use in the next listing.

Listing 15-12. *Obtaining Geometry of ZIP Code*

```
select shp_geometry into zip_geom from zip_usa
where shp_zip = p_postal_code
and shp_state = NVL(p_stat_id, shp_state)
and rownum <= 1;
```

Once the geometry of the ZIP code is obtained, the contact table is searched using this geometry below a section of the full query, which is also part of a procedure.

The first part of the query creates a set containing four fields: x, y, location geometry (from the table contact), and distance. Distance, set at -999 if `sdo_point x` is null, is the distance between `zip_geom` (extracted by Listing 15-12) and the points in the location column in the contact table, calculated with `SDO_DISTANCE`. The `where` clause, here a section of the full `where` clause, limits the selection to records that are within `p_within` miles. If `p_within` is not given, the query defaults to 25 miles.

Listing 15-13. *Selecting Geometries Close to the ZIP Geometry*

```
Select
...
c.location.sdo_point.x x,
c.location.sdo_point.y y,
c.location,
decode(c.location.sdo_point.x,
null, -999,
sdo_geom.sdo_distance(zip_geom, c.location, 0.5,
'unit=mile')
) distance
                              from
contact c
where
<...>
and sdo_within_distance(c.location, zip_geom,
   'distance=' || NVL(p_within, 25) || ' unit=mile') = 'TRUE') fcl2,
```

Geocoding is performed by querying the Oracle stored procedures through Java code. A set of classes encapsulate this functionality. Listing 15-14 illustrates the use of `SDO_GCDR.GEOCODE_ALL` (see Chapter 6). The prepared statement calls the `SDO_GCDR.GEOCODE_ALL` that uses four parameters, one of them being an array of two parameters in `SDO_KEYWORDARRAY`. The parameters are shown next to the

<prepare address for geocode> section. They are name (IDX_IN_SCHEMA), address lines (in this case IDX_IN_ADDR1 and IDX_IN_ADDR2), country (IDX_IN_COUNTRY), and the match mode (IDX_IN_MODE).

Listing 15-14. *Geocoding*

```
private static final String QUERY_GEOCODE  =
   "SELECT SDO_GCDR.GEOCODE_ALL(?, SDO_keywordArray(?, ?), ?, ?)
   FROM DUAL";private static final String MATCH_MODE = "RELAX_ALL";
private PreparedStatement buildGeocodeQuery(
   USForm2Address address, String geocodeCountry)
       throws SQLException {
           StringBuffer addressLine1 = new StringBuffer(100);
           StringBuffer addressLine2 = new StringBuffer(100);

<prepare address for geocoding>

            PreparedStatement ps = connection.prepareStatement(QUERY_GEOCODE);
            ps.setString(IDX_IN_SCHEMA,  schemaName);
            ps.setString(IDX_IN_ADDR1,   addressLine1.toString());
            ps.setString(IDX_IN_ADDR2,   addressLine2.toString());
            ps.setString(IDX_IN_COUNTRY, geocodeCountry);
            ps.setString(IDX_IN_MODE,    MATCH_MODE);

            return ps;
}
```

The actual call is shown in Listing 15-15, which contains the loop that executes the query and geocodes all the addresses. The variables address and geocodeCountry are the parameters to the query.

Listing 15-15. *Call to Geocoding*

```
ps = buildGeocodeQuery(address, geocodeCountry);
rs = ps.executeQuery();
Object[] addressess = (Object[])array.getArray();
for ( int i = 0; i < addressess.length; i++ ) {
          STRUCT st = (STRUCT) addressess[i];
          GeocoderAddress ga = GeocoderAddress.load(st);

<process the address>

          }
```

Routing is performed using the Oracle Spatial Route Server (see Chapter 11). Requests are composed into XML, sent using HttpClient, and then parsed out using SAX.[18] As with geocoding, a set of classes encapsulates this functionality.

Listing 15-16 illustrates the routing call. The first part of the code shows the preparation of the XML for the routing, including the parameters necessary to compute a route and the preferences for the routing. The second part of the code illustrates the HTTP request and the request sent to Oracle Route Server. The result is parsed into RouteResponse, which is the usable route information.

---

18. http://sax.sourceforge.net/

Listing 15-16. *Routing Call to Oracle Spatial Route Server*

```
public RouteResponse routeFromTo(StartLocation sl, EndLocation el) {
    RouteRequest rr = new RouteRequest();
    rr.setId("1");
    rr.setDistanceUnit(distanceUnits);
    rr.setTimeUnit(timeUnits);
    rr.setReturnDrivingDirections(true);
    rr.setReturnRouteGeometry(true);
    rr.setRoutePreference(routePreference);
    rr.setRoadPreference(roadPreference);
    rr.setDetailedGeometry(detailedGeometry);
    rr.setStartLocation(sl);
    rr.setEndLocation  (el);
   return route(rr);
}

public RouteResponse route(RouteRequest routeRequest) {
    String requestXML = routeRequest.buildXMLRequest();
    HttpClient client = new HttpClient();
    HttpMethod method = new PostMethod(routeserverUrl);
    method.setQueryString(new NameValuePair[] {
         new NameValuePair("xml_request", requestXML) });

   <send html request>

    InputSource is = new InputSource(method.getResponseBodyAsStream());
    RouteResponse routeResponse = rrp.parseInputSource(this, is);
    return routeResponse;
}
```

Mobile MilitaryINSTALLATIONS

MilitaryINSTALLATIONS offers also mobile access, enabling anyone with one of the supported mobile devices (Windows Mobile, Blackberry, Treo) to use the mobile version of the website.[19] Users with a mobile device can access any of the standard functionality of the application. For example, a user could route from an airport to their destination on a military base using only their mobile handset. They can locate POIs, such as banks, ATMs, restaurants, or museums, and obtain vital information such as a phone number or the current weather conditions. This mobile application serves as a "one-stop" service for all military personnel that are traveling and need information about programs and services at the base level.

MilitaryINSTALLATIONS is designed to recognize the device being used to access the application and provide the appropriate interface automatically. The majority of the functionality is available on both the mobile and desktop versions, although there are some differences:

- The mobile application is simplified to reduce bandwidth and screen size requirements.
- Most of the interactive elements of the application (pop-ups, dynamic page refreshes, and JavaScript form validation) are not possible on the mobile application because of the lack of consistent JavaScript support on mobile devices.
- Some of the information displayed is filtered to focus on important information and avoid displaying too much data on the smaller screens.
- Map navigation is simplified significantly because of the lack of JavaScript support.

---

19. http://militaryinstallations.MC&FPPSG.mil/mobile

Figure 15-19 shows four sample screens of the mobile application. The top-left image shows the home page and the service selection drop-down list. The top-right image shows the input screen for a search, in this case a search by country, state/province, or ZIP code, which is also part of the home page. The bottom-left image illustrates the results of the search, in this case the overview map. By scrolling down it is possible to see the list POIs meeting the search criteria. The bottom-right image shows a typical routing result, in this case the first five steps of the turn-by-turn directions.

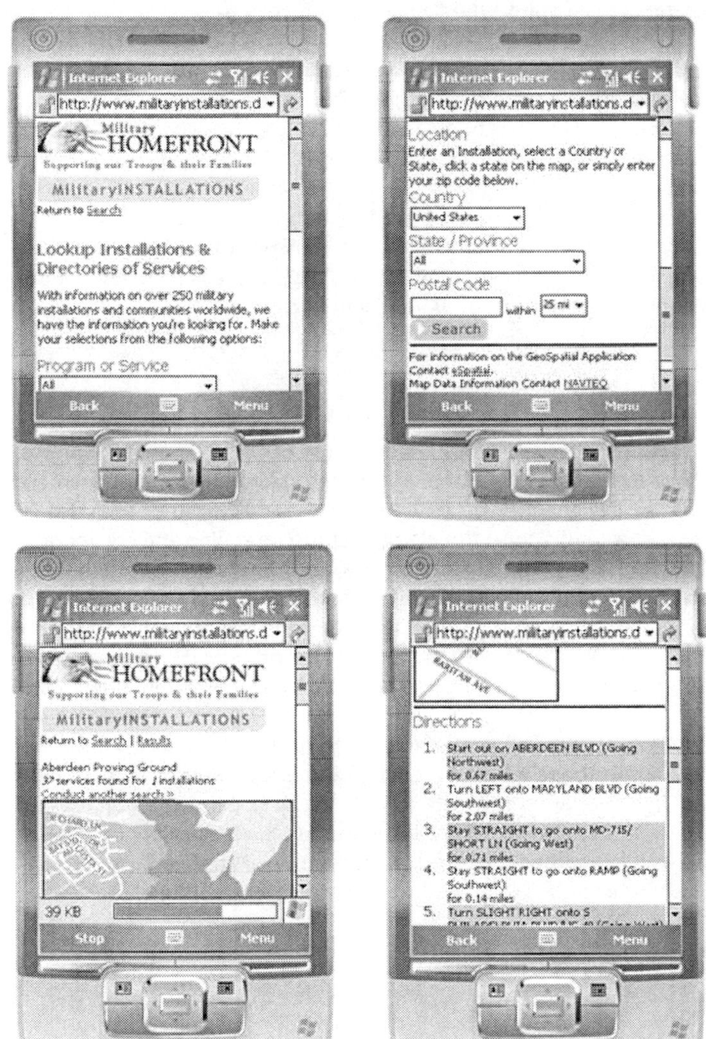

Figure 15-19. *Mobile home page for MilitaryHOMEFRONT (top left); location search (top right); results of location search (bottom left); turn-by-turn instructions (bottom right)*

Benefits of MilitaryHOMEFRONT LBS

Thanks to the technology selected, MC&FP PSG was able to produce an intuitive and easy-to-use website. The implementation of industry standards for data management and display made it possible to rapidly merge business and complex geospatial sets of information into a very user-friendly application.

The MC&FP PSG now has a comprehensive geospatial database platform that can be used to build multiple map-based applications that support the "supporting the troops and their families" mission.

The framework was designed to allow other applications to easily integrate into the MilitaryINSTALLATIONS architecture, providing the user a seamless transition from one application to another. As an example of this, the MilitaryHOMEFRONT has many instances where the driving directions, routing, or map display provided by the MilitaryINSTALLATIONS application are integrated into other MilitaryHOMEFRONT offerings.

By having the capability to add geospatial components to various operation applications, MC&FP PSG has moved to the realm of a truly spatially enabled enterprise that will benefit the entire community. By establishing this infrastructure now, MC&FP PSG can easily develop additional services and applications at no additional cost for data or software.

Summary

In this chapter, we described five case studies that demonstrate the use of Oracle Spatial in applications. The BusNet case illustrated how to use Oracle Spatial to improve the planning and management of the bus schedules and routes for the city of London. The P-Info case study described a system to provide mobile, location-enabled access to mission-critical information for police officers operating in the field. The Risk Repository for Hazardous Substances case study illustrated a system that gives access to information on risk and possible effects of storing, processing, and transporting hazardous substances. The USGS spatial data warehouse case described the use of Oracle Spatial to search, visualize, and analyze land-cover data for the United States. The MilitaryHOMEFRONT LBS case study illustrated how Oracle Spatial is used to locate and geocode information and how to provide street navigation to users.

Oracle Spatial is used to store and retrieve all spatial data used in the applications, and the spatial analysis performed in these applications is based on the methods and tools described in this book. The applications described in this chapter rely extensively on the scalability, security, and reliability of the Oracle database—another reason for the selection of Oracle Spatial in all these applications. Together, these case studies are meant to illustrate through real applications the variety of cases in which Oracle Spatial is used and to demonstrate the wide applicability of the Oracle Spatial technology.

CHAPTER 16

Tips, Common Mistakes, and Common Errors

Now that you have studied many techniques for how to location-enable your application and how to incorporate spatial analysis and visualization tools in your application, we think it is time for a little advice.

First, we present some advice on best practices—in other words, we give some tips for location-enabling your application. Next, we cover some of the common pitfalls that can trap unwary users as they set out to location-enable their business application. Finally, we enumerate common errors that you may encounter in location-enabling your application and the corrective actions to sort out these errors.

Tips

In this section, we provide several tips (best practices) for data modeling, improving spatial query performance, and managing large historical/temporal spatial databases. Note that we discuss only those tips not covered in prior chapters in detail. For tips covered in earlier chapters, we refer you directly to those chapters.

Data Modeling and Loading

We'll first examine some things you should keep in mind while modeling and loading spatial data.

Always Validate Your Data

You should always validate your data before proceeding with further analysis. You can use the SDO_GEOM.VALIDATE_* routines to perform this validation, as discussed in Chapter 5. Chapter 5 has routines to debug/correct invalid geometries as well. You can also use the SDO_MIGRATE.TO_CURRENT function to correct the orientation in any invalid *polygon* geometries. The SDO_MIGRATE.TO_CURRENT function works only for two-dimensional geometries in Oracle Database 11*g* Release 1 but is expected to work for three-dimensional geometries too in subsequent releases.

If your application involves network modeling, as described in Chapter 10, you should validate the network using the SDO_NET.VALIDATE_NETWORK function. See Chapter 10 for examples.

Always Store Two- and Three-Dimensional Points in SDO_POINT

To store a two- or three-dimensional point, you should always use the SDO_POINT attribute of the SDO_GEOMETRY data type. You should set the SDO_ELEM_INFO and SDO_ORDINATES attributes to NULL. This ensures less storage and faster access for such point data. Refer to Chapter 4 for more details and examples.

Use TO_CURRENT to Correct Orientation in a Polygon

As described in Chapter 5, you can correct the orientation of a polygon using the SDO_MIGRATE.TO_CURRENT function. For instance, you can run SDO_MIGRATE.TO_CURRENT on the polygon geometry in Listing 16-1 that is oriented clockwise. (Oracle Spatial expects the ring of the polygon boundary to be oriented counterclockwise.)

Listing 16-1. *Correcting the Orientation of a Polygon Geometry Using* TO_CURRENT

```
SQL> SELECT SDO_MIGRATE.TO_CURRENT
(
  SDO_GEOMETRY
  (
    2003, NULL, NULL,
    SDO_ELEM_INFO_ARRAY(1,1003,1 ),
    SDO_ORDINATE_ARRAY
    (
      2,2,         -- Vertices specified in clockwise order
      3,3.5,
      5,2,
      2,2
    )
  ),
  SDO_DIM_ARRAY
  (
    SDO_DIM_ELEMENT('1', -180, 180, 0.0000005),
    SDO_DIM_ELEMENT('2', -90, 90, 0.0000005)
  )
) FROM DUAL;

SDO_MIGRATE.TO_CURRENT(MDSYS.SDO_GEOMETRY(2003,NULL,NULL,MDSYS.SD
O_ELEM_INFO_ARRAY
--------------------------------------------------------------------------------
SDO_GEOMETRY
(
  2003, NULL, NULL,
  SDO_ELEM_INFO_ARRAY(1, 1003, 1),
  SDO_ORDINATE_ARRAY
  (
    2, 2,          -- Vertices specified in counterclockwise order
    5, 2,
    3, 3.5,
    2, 2
  )
)
```

Use the SDO_UNION Function to Correct a Self-Crossing Polygon

In Figure 5-2(a) (in Chapter 5), we show a self-crossing polygon geometry. If you model this geometry as a single polygon and try to validate it as shown in Listing 5-34 in that chapter, Oracle throws the ORA-13349 ("Polygon boundary crosses itself") error. One simple mechanism to correct this polygon geometry is to union (that is, run SDO_GEOM.SDO_UNION on) the geometry with itself. Listing 16-2 shows the code to correct the invalid geometry of Listing 5-34.

Listing 16-2. *Correcting a Self-Crossing Polygon Geometry Using* SDO_UNION

```
SQL> SELECT SDO_GEOM.SDO_UNION
(
  SDO_GEOMETRY    -- self-crossing 'polygon' geometry
  (
    2003,         -- A polygon type geometry: invalid because edges cross
    NULL, NULL,
    SDO_ELEM_INFO_ARRAY(1,1003,1 ),
    SDO_ORDINATE_ARRAY
    (
      2,2,
      3,3.5,
      2,5,
      5,5,
      3,3.5,
      5,2,
      2,2
    )
  ),
  SDO_GEOMETRY     -- self-crossing 'polygon' geometry (repeated)
  (
    2003,
    NULL, NULL,
    SDO_ELEM_INFO_ARRAY(1,1003,1 ),
    SDO_ORDINATE_ARRAY
    (
      2,2,
      3,3.5,
      2,5,
      5,5,
      3,3.5,
      5,2,
      2,2
    )
  ),
  0.0000005
) valid_gm FROM  DUAL;

VALID_GM(SDO_GTYPE, SDO_SRID, SDO_POINT(X, Y, Z), SDO_ELEM_INFO,
SDO_ORDINATES)
--------------------------------------------------------------------------------
SDO_GEOMETRY
(
  2007,            -- Corrected to a multipolygon rather than a single polygon
  NULL, NULL,
  SDO_ELEM_INFO_ARRAY  -- Two elements, each specifying a separate polygon
  (
    1, 1003, 1,    -- First Polygon Element starting at offset 1 in SDO_ORDINATES
```

```
    9, 1003, 1    -- Second Polygon Element starting at offset 9 in SDO_ORDINATES
  ),
  SDO_ORDINATE_ARRAY
  (
    3, 3.5,       -- First vertex of first polygon element
    2, 2,         -- Second vertex
    5, 2,         -- Third vertex
    3, 3.5,       -- Final vertex of first polygon element (same as 1st vertex)
    2, 5,         -- First vertex of second polygon element
    3, 3.5,       -- Second vertex
    5, 5,         -- Third vertex
    2, 5          -- Final vertex of second polygon element (same as 1st vertex)
  )
)
```

Note that the preceding listing corrects the geometry to be a multipolygon with two polygon elements. The polygon elements are disjoint (that is, the boundary does not cross). The resulting multipolygon geometry is in valid Oracle Spatial format.

Always Store Only As Many Dimensions/Digits As Needed

Some third-party tools export spatial data as three-dimensional data. The first two dimensions contain the longitude and latitude information, and the third dimension is always set to 0. This means the SDO_ORDINATES attribute will contain *three* ordinates for each point or vertex instead of *two*. For large geometries, this will translate into some wasted storage in the SDO_ORDINATES attribute of an SDO_GEOMETRY, which could have potential implications for storage and subsequent query performance (because of a greater number of I/Os). You should clean up such data by removing every third ordinate in the SDO_ORDINATES attribute (see Chapter 7 for details).

Likewise, third-party tools may also waste space by exporting too many digits for ordinate values in an SDO_GEOMETRY. For instance, if the data is in a projected coordinate system, an ordinate value with six or more decimal digits may specify a very high precision. Applications seldom require such high precision of data. By reducing the number of decimal digits (you can use the ROUND function in Oracle for this purpose), you can reduce the storage for an SDO_GEOMETRY with potential implications on the fetch performance (I/Os) of the geometry.

Performance of Spatial Operator Query

In most applications, selection based on spatial operators is much more expensive than selection using relational operators such as ' > and '. The cost of spatial operators increases with the complexity of spatial data.

Use Real Data for Performance Analysis

Given the complexity of spatial data, you should always run performance tests with realistic amounts of data instead of synthetic/artificial data, which may not model the complexity of spatial data well. Next, we focus on how to improve the performance of spatial operator queries.

A major portion of the time to answer a spatial operator query such as SDO_RELATE or SDO_NN goes into fetching the data rows from the data table. Consider the query in Listing 16-3 for identifying the nearest customers to a branch with id=1.

Listing 16-3. *Nearest-Neighbor Query on the* customers *Table*

```
SQL> SELECT COUNT(*)
FROM branches b, customers c
WHERE b.id=1 AND SDO_NN(c.location, b.location, 'SDO_NUM_RES=100')='TRUE';
```

This query is processed by Oracle Spatial in the following sequence (see Figure 16-1).

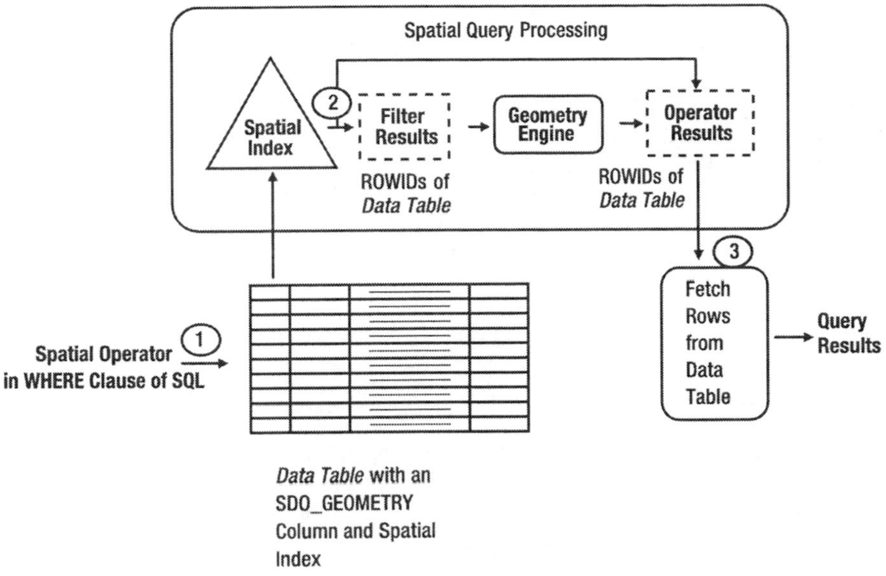

Figure 16-1. *Operator processing sequence in Oracle Spatial*

1. The query (store) location is passed to the spatial index.
2. The spatial index returns ROWIDs of the `customers` table that are closest to the query (store) location.
3. Oracle then fetches the rows corresponding to the ROWIDs returned by the spatial index.

The query returns the 100 nearest customers to the specified branch location. Steps 2 and 3 may access the row data (such as ID and location columns) corresponding to these 100 customers in the `customers` table. These 100 rows may result in random disk I/Os, because there is no clustering of the `customers` table rows based on the "location" columns. The performance of the query may suffer because of a high I/O cost. This might result in a high response time for queries. In the following sections, we suggest two important tips for improving the performance.

Specify the LAYER_GTYPE Parameter

The first tip for improving query performance is to specify the `LAYER_GTYPE=POINT` parameter at the time of index creation if the table contains just point data. This will completely avoid step 3 in query processing in Figure 16-1. Instead, it will use the information in the spatial index to evaluate the query. This will substantially speed up query performance. Listing 16-4 shows how you can specify the `LAYER_GTYPE` parameter in the `CREATE INDEX` statement. Refer to Chapter 8 for more details on the `CREATE INDEX` statement.

Listing 16-4. *Specifying* `LAYER_GTYPE` *During Spatial Index Creation*

```
SQL> CREATE INDEX customers_sidx ON customers(location)
INDEXTYPE IS MDSYS.SPATIAL_INDEX PARAMETERS('LAYER_GTYPE=POINT');
```

Reorganize the Table Data to Minimize I/O

In the previous example, the spatial data in the `location` column of the `customers` table has only *point* geometries. In other tables, this may not be the case; the corresponding spatial column may contain both *point* and *nonpoint* geometries. For such tables, you cannot employ the trick shown in Listing 16-4 of specifying `LAYER_GTYPE=POINT` to improve spatial query performance. However, you can still reduce I/O in step 3 of Figure 16-1 by an alternate mechanism: cluster the rows and avoid/minimize random I/O. What you specifically need is a reclustering of the table rows based on proximity of the geometry data in the `location` column. This means customer rows in the same city or state, or any other geometric region, should be stored in the same physical block or adjacent blocks if possible. This will ensure the rows that satisfy a spatial query (which is usually expensive compared to nonspatial predicates) are retrieved with very few block accesses (random I/Os).

■ **Caution** This tip is recommended only if spatial queries are the dominant part of the application workload and are the main bottlenecks in performance and wait-time analysis shows this is because of high I/O cost.

Two features can achieve such clustering of rows in Oracle: *table clusters* and *index-organized tables* (IOTs). Both features are not supported by Oracle Spatial. Clusters do not support the storage of objects (such as `SDO_GEOMETRY` columns), and Oracle Spatial does not support spatial indexes on IOTs.

In this section, we describe how to achieve similar performance gains as in Oracle IOTs and Oracle table clusters for mostly *static* spatial data. Some experiments using similar techniques indicate record performance gains.[1] The method involves a function called `linear_key` that takes as input an `SDO_GEOMETRY` and an `SDO_DIM_ARRAY` as parameters and returns a `RAW` string. You will work with the `us_streets` table in the following example.

First drop the index on the `us_streets` table, and then rename the `us_streets` to a new table called `us_streets_dup`. You can then re-create the `us_streets` table as an empty table with the same attributes as the `us_streets_dup` table, as shown in Listing 16-5. (Note that when you re-create the `us_streets` table, you may have to do additional management such as issuing grants on the table, and so on.) After you execute the SQL in Listing 16-5, you can observe that the `us_streets` table becomes empty (because of the `ROWNUM<=0` in the `WHERE` clause), and the data is transferred to the `us_streets_dup` table.

Listing 16-5. *Renaming and Re-creating the* `us_streets` *Table*

```
SQL> DROP INDEX us_streets_sidx;
RENAME  us_streets TO us_streets_dup;
-- Re-create the us_streets with the same fields as in us_streets_dup;
CREATE TABLE us_streets AS SELECT * FROM us_streets_dup  WHERE ROWNUM<=0;
```

For each row in the `us_streets_dup` table, compute the value of the function `linear_key` (described later in this section) using the `location` column for the row. Reinsert data from the `us_streets_dup` table into the `us_streets` table by ordering the rows using the value of the `linear_key` function. This approach is likely to store the rows in the `us_streets` table in the specified order. Listing 16-6 shows the SQL. Note that we assume the metadata for the spatial layer `<us_streets, location>` is populated.

---

1. T.P.M. Tijssen, C.W. Quak, and P.J.M. van Oosterom. "Spatial DBMS testing with data from Cadastre and TNO-NITG," `www.gdmc.nl/oosterom/kad6.pdf`, GISt Report No. 7 Delft, ISSN 1569-0245, ISBN 90-77029-02-8, March 2001.

Listing 16-6. *Reinserting into the* `us_streets` *Table Based on the* `linear_key` *Order*

```
SQL> INSERT INTO us_streets
SELECT * FROM us_streets_dup st
ORDER BY
  linear_key
  (
    st.location,
    (
      SELECT diminfo FROM USER_SDO_GEOM_METADATA
      WHERE table_name = 'US_STREETS' AND column_name='LOCATION'
    )
  );
```

You should be all set now. The preceding reorganization will ensure that the data in the repopulated `us_streets` table is more or less *spatially* clustered. You can now re-create the spatial index on the `location` column of the `us_streets` table. This reordering may improve the performance of subsequent queries on the table, because they might minimize random block accesses.

An alternative approach is to materialize the `linear_key` function value for each row as an additional column in the table and then *partition* the table using the values for this materialized column. Note that to use partitioning, you will need to license the Partitioning option of Oracle.

You can code the `linear_key` function in a number of ways. Listing 16-7 is a simple implementation in PL/SQL. Note that this example uses the `MD.HHENCODE` function, which encodes a two-dimensional point (such as the `CENTROID` or `POINTONSURFACE` of a geometry) into a `RAW` string. This function is provided by Oracle Spatial (in both Locator and Spatial options), and it uses the lower/upper bounds in each dimension and an encoding level as additional parameters.

Listing 16-7. *Using the* `linear_key` *Function to Order Geometry Rows Based on a "Spatial" Ordering*

```
CREATE OR REPLACE FUNCTION linear_key
(
  location    SDO_GEOMETRY,
  diminfo     SDO_DIM_ARRAY
)
RETURN RAW DETERMINISTIC
IS
  ctr          SDO_GEOMETRY;
  rval         RAW(48);
  lvl          INTEGER;
BEGIN

  -- Compute the centroid of the geometry
  -- Alternately, you can use the 'faster' sdo_pointonsurface function
  ctr := SDO_GEOM.SDO_CENTROID(location, diminfo);

  lvl := 8;  -- Specifies the encoding level for hhcode function
  rval :=
    MD.HHENCODE
    ( -- Specify value, lower and upper bounds, encoding level for each dimension
      location.sdo_point.x, diminfo(1).sdo_lb, diminfo(1).sdo_ub, lvl,
      location.sdo_point.y, diminfo(2).sdo_lb, diminfo(2).sdo_ub, lvl
    );
  RETURN  rval;
END;
/
```

Specify Appropriate Hints in a Query

In the case of a query specifying multiple tables, you should specify appropriate hints to ensure the desired evaluation plan. Refer to Chapter 8 for details on how to use the ORDERED, INDEX, and NO_INDEX hints to suggest an appropriate plan to the optimizer.

Performance of Other Spatial Processing Functions

Next, we discuss how to improve the performance of stored functions and geometry processing functions such as SDO_AGGR_UNION (see Chapter 9 for details). Unlike the spatial operators, the geometry processing functions do not use the spatial index.

Specify DETERMINISTIC for Stored Functions

Most queries on spatial data may involve a combination of spatial operators, geometry processing functions, and user-defined stored PL/SQL functions. Here is a tip you should bear in mind when coding such stored PL/SQL functions: if the return value of a PL/SQL function depends solely on the input parameter values (that is, it returns the same value for the same set of parameter values and the function does not depend on the state of the session variables and schema objects), then you should declare the function as DETERMINISTIC. This will allow the optimizer to avoid redundant function calls, and it may translate to a faster response time for queries. For example, in Listing 16-4 the linear_key function is declared as DETERMINISTIC.

If a DETERMINISTIC function is invoked multiple times with the same parameter values in a SQL statement, Oracle evaluates the function only once (and reuses the result in other invocations).

If your stored function returns an object such as an SDO_GEOMETRY, Oracle may evaluate this function multiple times. However, defining such a function as DETERMINISTIC will avoid such multiple evaluations and will improve the performance of any SQL query that uses such stored functions.

Use a Divide-and-Conquer Approach for SDO_AGGR_UNION

In some applications, you may have to compute the aggregate union of several SDO_GEOMETRY objects. For instance, you might want to compute the union of all the geometries in the us_counties table. Listing 16-8 shows the SQL to compute the union using the SDO_AGGR_UNION function (see Chapter 9 for details).

Listing 16-8. *Aggregate Union of All Geometries in the* us_counties *Table*

```
SQL> SELECT SDO_AGGR_UNION(SDOAGGRTYPE(geom, 0.5)) union_geom
FROM us_counties ;
```

The SDO_AGGR_UNION function is evaluated as follows. It first starts with a null value for the result (that is, union_geom). It then unions (uses the SDO_GEOM.SDO_UNION function) every geometry in the us_counties table with union_geom in an iterative fashion.

The problem with this approach is that union_geom becomes larger and more complex with every union operation. Computing the union operation (using the SDO_GEOM. SDO_UNION function) with a complex geometry such as union_geom as one of the operands will be increasingly slow after each iteration.

An alternate mechanism is to divide the set of geometries to be "unioned" into disjoint groups or subsets, S1, . . ., Sn. You can group them in any manner you like. First compute the SDO_AGGR_UNION for the geometries in each subset/group, and then compute the union of the results of all the groups.

The SQL in Listing 16-9 shows how to compute the union of all the counties in Massachusetts by grouping them using the first letter of the county name. The county names in each group start with the same letter.

Listing 16-9. *Computing the Aggregate Unions for Multiple Groups*

```
SQL> SELECT SDO_AGGR_UNION(SDOAGGRTYPE(geom, 0.5)),  SUBSTR(county,1,1)
FROM us_counties
WHERE state_abrv='MA'
GROUP BY  (SUBSTR(county,1,1));
```

The SQL in Listing 16-9 groups all counties with the same starting letter using the SUBSTR function. For each such group, the union of the county geometries is returned. An alternate grouping could be based on the ROWNUM pseudo-column. For instance, if you want ten groups each, with approximately the same number of counties, you can use the SQL in Listing 16-10.

Listing 16-10. *Computing the Aggregate Unions Grouped by the* ROWNUM *Pseudo-Column*

```
SQL> SELECT SDO_AGGR_UNION(sdoaggrtype(geom, 0.5)) union_geom
FROM us_counties
WHERE state_abrv='MA'
GROUP BY MOD(ROWNUM,10);
```

This returns the union geometries for each group. You can aggregate these geometries to obtain the aggregate union of all the counties. Listing 16-11 shows the corresponding SQL.

Listing 16-11. *Computing the Aggregate Union of Aggregate Unions Grouped by the* ROWNUM *Pseudo-Column*

```
SQL> SELECT SDO_AGGR_UNION(SDOAGGRTYPE(union_geom, 0.5))
FROM
(
  SELECT SDO_AGGR_UNION(SDOAGGRTYPE(geom, 0.5)) union_geom
  FROM us_counties
  WHERE state_abrv='MA'
  GROUP BY MOD(ROWNUM,10)
);
```

Note that Listing 16-11 uses Listing 16-10 in the FROM clause. This means the results of the SDO_AGGR_UNION in Listing 16-10 are *pipelined* to the outer-level SDO_AGGR_UNION in Listing 16-11. You can repeat this pipelining any number of times. Listing 16-12 shows a pipelining of results between three SDO_AGGR_UNION functions.

Listing 16-12. *Computing the Aggregate Union in a Pipelined Fashion*

```
SQL> SELECT SDO_AGGR_UNION(SDOAGGRTYPE(ugeom,0.5)) ugeom
FROM
(
  SELECT SDO_AGGR_UNION(SDOAGGRTYPE(ugeom,0.5)) ugeom
  FROM
  (
    SELECT SDO_AGGR_UNION(SDOAGGRTYPE(ugeom,0.5)) ugeom
    FROM
    (
      SELECT SDO_AGGR_UNION(SDOAGGRTYPE(geom,0.5)) ugeom
      FROM us_counties
      GROUP BY MOD (ROWNUM, 1000)
    )
    GROUP BY MOD (ROWNUM, 100)
  )
  GROUP BY MOD (ROWNUM, 10)
);
```

How many such SDO_AGGR_UNION functions should you use in this pipelined execution? We recommend you use as many as necessary to ensure that the innermost SDO_AGGR_UNION function does not have more than ten rows. (You can easily write a stored function to apply this guideline and perform SDO_AGGR_UNION as in Listing 16-12.) With this approach, the response time is likely to be minimized.

An analogous "divide-and-conquer" approach may help in improving the performance of the SDO_AGGR_CONVEXHULL and SDO_AGGR_MBR aggregate functions.

Performance of Inserts, Deletes, and Updates

If a table has a spatial index on one or more of its columns, then inserts, deletes, and updates on this table will take longer. This is because the associated spatial index(es) need to be kept up to date. Here are two alternatives to improve performance.

Drop the Index Before Modifying a Large Number of Rows

If you are modifying (inserting, deleting, or updating the geometry columns of) more than 30 percent of the total rows in a table, then it may be faster to drop the spatial indexes on columns of the table, perform the modification (either insert, delete, or update), and then re-create the spatial index.[2]

Perform Inserts, Deletes, and Updates in Bulk

You can minimize the performance overheads of spatial indexes if you batch multiple inserts, deletes, and/or update operations in the same transaction. If you expect to perform more than 1,000 such operations in a typical transaction,[3] you can fine-tune the performance by specifying the parameter SDO_DML_BATCH_SIZE=<numeric_value> in the CREATE INDEX parameters. By default, this value is set to 1000 (optimal if the transaction has 1,000 inserts/deletes/updates). The SQL in Listing 16-13 shows an example of setting SDO_DML_BATCH_SIZE to 5000.

Listing 16-13. *Setting the* SDO_DML_BATCH_SIZE *Parameter*

```
SQL> CREATE INDEX customers_sidx ON customers(location)
INDEXTYPE IS MDSYS.SPATIAL_INDEX
PARAMETERS('SDO_ML_BATCH_SIZE=5000');
```

The SDO_DML_BATCH_SIZE parameter should be in the range of 1 and 10,000. (You can inspect this value for your index in the USER_SDO_INDEX_METADATA view.) It is advisable not to increase this parameter to a value of more than 10,000, because this leads to a lot of memory consumption with no discernible performance improvements.

If you have already created the spatial index, you can alter this parameter by manually changing it in the SDO_INDEX_METADATA_TABLE[4] table in the MDSYS schema for a specific spatial index. Note that you should not modify other parameters in this table. If you do, operations that use the spatial index such as spatial operators may fail (see Chapter 8 for more information).

Next, you'll learn about the best practices for scalability and manageability of spatial data in tables with a large number of rows.

---

2. In the meantime (between dropping the index and re-creating it), be aware that you will not be able to use spatial operators, which require a spatial index.

3. Note that this recommendation applies whenever "each" transaction has more than 1,000 insert, delete, or update operations.

4. The USER_SDO_INDEX_METADATA and USER_SDO_INDEX_INFO dictionary views are based on this table.

Best Practices for Scalability and Manageability of Spatial Indexes

Oracle recommends table partitioning, a licensed option, to scale with and easily manage large tables (in other words, with tens of millions of rows or larger). In fact, table partitioning is the suggested mechanism to scale to even ultra-large databases (on the order of Exa- [10^{18}] bytes).[5] You can extend the benefits of such partitioning to tables with SDO_GEOMETRY columns, too. As you saw in Chapter 8, partitioning can help in spatial query performance by pruning irrelevant partitions when the partition key is specified. Oracle combines parallelism with partitioning to efficiently process queries that access multiple partitions.

Creating a spatial index is much slower than creating a B-tree index—in some cases, by several orders of magnitude. Table partitioning will help in faster creation and easy management of spatial indexes. Specifically, we suggest using partitioning and local spatial indexes for managing large tables with tens of millions of rows, and/or managing historical, temporal, or mobile data. In the following sections, we illustrate the best practices for scalability and easy manageability of spatial indexes using a specific application in which new data is added continuously.

Consider an application that collects and stores weather-pattern images for different regions of the world. In such an application, you need to add data continuously on a per-day (or per-month, or per-year) basis. And, after analyzing the access patterns, you may decide to store the data on a daily basis for the current month, on a monthly basis for the prior months of the current year, and on a yearly basis for prior years. Since the current month changes with time, the challenge is to effectively maintain this data organization and to ensure all associated spatial indexes are up to date.

Use Table Partitioning (and Local Spatial Indexes)

The solution for this problem is to use the Oracle table partitioning feature and create local spatial indexes for each partition. Listing 16-14 shows an example.

Listing 16-14. *Creating a Partitioned Table for Storing Temporal Weather-Pattern Data*

```
SQL> CREATE TABLE weather_patterns
(
    gid NUMBER,
    geom SDO_GEOMETRY,
    creation_date VARCHAR2(32)
)
PARTITION BY RANGE(CREATION_DATE)
(
    PARTITION p1 VALUES LESS THAN ('2000-01-01')  TABLESPACE tbs_3,
    PARTITION p2 VALUES LESS THAN ('2001-01-01')  TABLESPACE tbs_3,
    PARTITION p3 VALUES LESS THAN ('2002-01-01')  TABLESPACE tbs_3,
    PARTITION p4 VALUES LESS THAN ('2003-01-01')  TABLESPACE tbs_3,
    PARTITION p5 VALUES LESS THAN ('2004-01-01')  TABLESPACE tbs_3,
    PARTITION jan VALUES LESS THAN ('2004-02-01'),  -- Month of January, 2004
    PARTITION feb VALUES LESS THAN ('2004-03-01'),  -- Month of February, 2004
    PARTITION current_month VALUES LESS THAN (MAXVALUE)
);
```

5. See the following presentations for more information: "Oracle Database 10g: A VLDB Case Study" by Berik Davies and Xavier Lopez (www.oracle.com/openworld/archive/sf2003/solutions_bi.html) and the keynote speech titled "Journey to the Center of the Grid" given by Charles Rozwat at Oracle OpenWorld, San Francisco, September 10, 2003 (www.oracle.com/oracleworld/online/sanfrancisco/2003/keynotes.html).

■ **Note** Oracle 11*g* provides a new type of table partitioning called *interval partitioning* to simplify partition management for partitioning on a date or a numeric attribute. You cannot yet create spatial indexes (or any domain indexes for that matter) on such interval-partitioned tables.

The SQL in Listing 16-14 creates a partitioned table based on the `creation_date` column. The first five partitions, `p1` to `p5`, store the data for years before 2004. You specify that these partitions go into the tablespace `TBS_3`. The next three partitions store the data for the first three months of 2004. There is no tablespace specified. Hence, these partitions are stored in the default tablespace, `USERS`. The last partition, `current_month`, stores the data for the `current_month` month, which, let's say, is March. You could go further and organize the data for March into days and associate partitions with these, too. But this current organization is sufficient to illustrate the concepts.

You can create a local partitioned spatial index for this table. Listing 16-15 illustrates this. Note the `LOCAL` keyword at the end of the statement. This tells Oracle to create "local" indexes—that is, a separate index for each partition (but all managed by the same name, `weather_patterns_sidx`).

```
INSERT INTO USER_SDO_GEOM_METADATA VALUES
('WEATHER_PATTERNS', 'GEOM',
 SDO_DIM_ARRAY(
   SDO_DIM_ELEMENT('LONG', -180, 180, 0.5),
   SDO_DIM_ELEMENT('LAT', -90, 90, 0.5)
 ),
 8307
);
```

Listing 16-15. *Creating a Local Partitioned Spatial Index*

```
SQL> CREATE INDEX  weather_patterns_sidx ON weather_patterns(geom)
INDEXTYPE IS MDSYS.SPATIAL_INDEX LOCAL;
```

This will create a separate spatial index for each partition of the table. The index information is stored in the corresponding tablespace associated with the partition. For example, for the first five partitions, the index is stored in tablespace `TBS_3`. You can also specify the `parallel 4` clause after the `LOCAL` keyword to indicate that the index creation should be run in parallel using four slave processes.

Let's say that, after creating the local indexes for partitions `p1` to `p3`, the system runs out of space in the `TBS_3` tablespace. At that point, you need to add more space, drop the index, and re-create the index using the SQL in Listing 16-15.

Create the Local Index As UNUSABLE for Better Manageability

An alternative option for creating local spatial indexes avoids such pitfalls and offers more flexibility. Listing 16-16 shows the alternative mechanism for creating partitioned indexes. First you create the index as `UNUSABLE`. This will initialize the indexes for all partitions.

Listing 16-16. *Creating a Local Partitioned Spatial Index As "Unusable"*

```
SQL> CREATE INDEX  weather_patterns_sidx ON weather_patterns(geom)
INDEXTYPE IS MDSYS.SPATIAL_INDEX LOCAL UNUSABLE;
```

Note that the SQL in Listing 16-16 creates only a "dummy" index in each partition (more or less an instantaneous operation). After executing the SQL in Listing 16-16, Oracle marks all the partitions as `UNUSABLE`. Any spatial operator query, an insert/delete/update on the table, or a specific partition will raise an error that indicates the partition is `UNUSABLE`. You will need to rebuild the index on the partitions before proceeding.

Rebuild the Spatial Index for Each Partition Separately

You can rebuild the index for each table partition separately (that is, independent of one another). Listing 16-17 shows how to rebuild the local index for partition `p1`. Note that although we did not specify any tablespace parameter here, the index will be built in the "tablespace" used with the table partition in the prior `CREATE INDEX` statement. For partition `p1`, this tablespace is `TBS_3`. So, the index is built and stored in tablespace `TBS_3`.

Listing 16-17. *Rebuilding a Local Spatial Index*

```
SQL> ALTER INDEX weather_patterns_sidx REBUILD PARTITION P1;
```

Likewise, you can rebuild the local indexes for each partition separately. By rebuilding these indexes in multiple SQL*Plus sessions, you can achieve parallelism.

Rebuilding the local indexes separately gives you more control over partition index creation. If one partition fails, the whole index is not marked as failed. This means you do not have to rebuild the indexes for all partitions. Instead, you can rebuild the index only for the failed partition.

You can rebuild all `UNUSABLE` indexes (including the spatial index) for a partition in one attempt using the `ALTER TABLE ... REBUILD UNUSBALE INDEXES` command. Listing 16-18 shows the corresponding SQL. Note that this is an `ALTER TABLE` command instead of an `ALTER INDEX` command.

Listing 16-18. *Rebuilding All* `UNUSABLE` *Indexes for a Table Partition*

```
SQL> ALTER TABLE weather_patterns REBUIlD PARTITION P1 UNUSABLE LOCAL INDEXES;
```

Use EXCHANGE PARTITION to Work on FAILED Partitions

The rebuild of the spatial index as in Listing 16-18 may fail for a variety of reasons, including lack of space in the specified tablespace for the partition or invalid geometries in the indexed column of the table partition. In the former case, if you increase the size of the tablespace and reexecute (that is, rebuild the index as in Listing 16-18), the index will rebuild. However, if the partition has invalid geometries, then reexecuting Listing 16-18 will not help. Moreover, you may not be able to delete or update the rows corresponding to the invalid geometries. Oracle may raise the "Partition marked as `FAILED/UNUSABLE`" error for such operations.

To avoid such failures, you should always validate the spatial data before creating spatial indexes. See Chapter 5 for details on how to validate spatial data.

If you end up with an "index failed" situation, how do you recover from it? One solution is to use the `EXCHANGE PARTITION` clause of `ALTER TABLE`. You should first create a table, say `tmp`, with the same structure as the `weather_patterns` table. Then create a spatial index on this empty table `tmp` (after inserting the appropriate metadata in the `USER_SDO_GEOM_METADATA` view). Now you can execute the SQL in Listing 16-19 to exchange data between table `tmp` and partition `p1` of the `weather_patterns` table. Note that the `EXCLUDING INDEXES` clause at the end ensures that the indexes are not exchanged (only the data is exchanged).

Listing 16-19. *Exchanging* `tmp` *Data with Partition* `p1` *of* `weather_patterns` *Without Indexes*

```
SQL> ALTER TABLE weather_patterns EXCHANGE PARTITION current_month WITH
TABLE tmp EXCLUDING INDEXES;
```

If you examine the contents of the table `tmp`, you will see the rows that were earlier part of partition `p1` in `weather_patterns` table, and vice versa. Since `tmp` is not a partitioned table, you can perform regular DML (delete, update, and insert) operations on this table and correct the rows with invalid geometries. (You may want to drop the spatial index if there are too many such rows.) After correcting the rows, you can reexecute Listing 16-19 to put the corrected data in partition `p1`. You can then rebuild the index on this partition as in Listing 16-17.

Use EXCHANGE PARTITION with INDEXES for New Data

You may want to use the ALTER TABLE ... EXCHANGE PARTITION command for another purpose: keeping spatial indexes up to date with new data.

For instance, say you add new data to the current_month partition every day. How do you keep the data in the current_month partition up to date? One method is to add all new data to this partition directly. Inserting into partitions that have spatial indexes could be slow. Here are some tips to improve performance:

- *Add new data in large batches*: This means each insert transaction should have more than 1,000 inserts. Spatial indexes incorporate efficient algorithms to bulk load a substantial number of inserts (or deletes) within a single transaction.
- *Create a temporary table (say* tmp*) that has the new data along with the data in the* current_month *partition*: Create a spatial index on this tmp table. You can exchange the contents of the tmp table with the contents of the current_month partition in a split second. This will also exchange the associated spatial indexes.

Listing 16-20 shows an example of the second tip in practice.

Listing 16-20. *Adding New Data Using the* EXCHANGE PARTITION *Clause*

```
SQL> CREATE TABLE tmp (gid number, geom sdo_geometry, date varcahr2(32));
SQL> INSERT INTO TABLE tmp  VALUES (...);  --- new data

--  Also include data from current_month partition
SQL> INSERT INTO TABLE tmp
SELECT * FROM weather_partitions PARTITION(current_month);

-- Exchange table tmp with "current_month" partition of weather_patterns.
SQL> ALTER TABLE weather_patterns
EXCHANGE PARTITION current_month WITH TABLE tmp INCLUDING INDEXES;
```

Note that Listing 16-20 uses the INCLUDING INDEXES clause. This will exchange the (already created) indexes of partition p1 and table tmp almost instantaneously. The preceding tips can help ensure that the current_month partition is always up to date.

Other Tips for Partition Maintenance

Next, we'll show how to split a current_month partition as you enter a new month. At the end of the year, you may also want to consolidate/merge all monthly partitions into a single yearly partition.

Splitting the current_month Partition

As you enter into the month of April, you will need to split the current_month partition into two partitions: march and current_month (which holds the current month data). You can accomplish this using the SPLIT PARTITION clause of ALTER TABLE, as shown in Listing 16-21.

Listing 16-21. *Splitting the* current_month *Partition into* march *and* current_month *Partitions*

```
SQL> ALTER TABLE weather_patterns
SPLIT PARTITION current_month AT ('2004-04-1')  INTO
(
  PARTITION march,
  PARTITION current_month
);
```

The SQL in Listing 16-21 splits the `current_month` partition at April 1, 2004 (the key is `'2004-04-01'`), into the `march` and `current_month` partitions. You will need to rebuild the indexes, as shown in Listing 16-22, for each of these partitions to allow queries to succeed.

Listing 16-22. *Rebuilding the Indexes for the "Split" Partitions*

```
SQL> ALTER INDEX weather_patterns_sidx REBUILD PARTITION march;
SQL> ALTER INDEX weather_patterns_sidx REBUILD PARTITION current_month;
```

Merging Partitions

At the end of the year, you want to merge all the partitions into a single year partition. First, Listing 16-23 shows how to merge the partitions `jan` and `feb` into a single partition.

Listing 16-23. *Merging the Partitions for* `jan` *and* `feb` *into a Single Partition*

```
SQL> ALTER TABLE weather_patterns
MERGE PARTITIONS jan, feb INTO PARTITION  janfeb;
```

Note that the resulting partition is named `janfeb`. If you try to name it to `jan` in Listing 16-23, Oracle throws an error. Instead, you should first name the merged partition as `janfeb` as in Listing 16-23 and then later rename the `janfeb` partition to `jan` again as shown in Listing 16-24.

Listing 16-24. *Renaming a Partition*

```
SQL> ALTER INDEX weather_patterns_sidx RENAME PARTITION janfeb TO jan;
```

Likewise, using the SQL in Listings 16-23 and 16-24, you can merge partitions for other months into the `jan` partition. You can then rename the `jan` partition to an appropriate name such as `p2004` using the `ALTER INDEX ... RENAME PARTITION` command, as shown in Listing 16-25.

Listing 16-25. *Renaming the Merged Monthly Partition As a Year Partition*

```
SQL> ALTER INDEX weather_patterns_sidx RENAME PARTITION jan TO p2004;
```

Specify the Partition Key in the WHERE Clause

Specifying the partition key in the `WHERE` clause of a `SELECT` statement aids in pruning the number of partitions searched. If the `WHERE` clause does not have a predicate on the partition key, all partitions (and associated spatial indexes) are evaluated.

Specify the PARALLEL Clause to Ensure a Parallel Query on a Partitioned Index

To ensure queries on multiple partitions of a table are evaluated in parallel, you should do one of the following: specify the `PARALLEL` clause in `CREATE INDEX` (see Listing 8-65 for the syntax), alter the table by specifying a parallel degree (see Listing 8-66 for an example), or alter the index by specifying a parallel degree.

To summarize, table partitioning can be an effective mechanism to ensure scalability and manageability of spatial indexes on large tables of spatial data. The partitioning features come in handy when you are managing temporal and historical spatial data.

Common Mistakes

In the following sections, we look at some of the common pitfalls associated with location-enabling an application. You should consult this list before you design your application.

Bounds, Longitude and Latitude, and Tolerance for Geodetic Data

If the data in a layer is geodetic (that is, the SRID matches one of the values in the MDSYS.GEODETIC_SRIDS table), then the corresponding DIMINFO attribute (of type SDO_DIM_ARRAY) should be set as follows:

- The first dimension in the SDO_DIM_ARRAY should correspond to the longitude dimension. The lower and upper bounds (for this dimension) should always be set to values of –180 and 180. If other values are specified for the bounds, Oracle Spatial ignores them.
- The second dimension in SDO_DIM_ARRAY should correspond to the latitude dimension. The lower and upper bounds should always be set to values of –90 and 90. If other values are specified for the bounds, Oracle Spatial ignores them.
- The tolerance for the dimensions should always be specified in meters. The meter is the unit of distance in all geodetic coordinate systems in Oracle.

If the tolerance is set incorrectly, Oracle Spatial may return unexpected results. A value of 0.5 (0.5 meters) is suitable for most applications.

NULL Values for SDO_GEOMETRY

Setting the individual fields of SDO_GEOMETRY to NULL does not constitute a NULL SDO_GEOMETRY object. Instead, you should set the entire object to NULL. For example, you can set the location (SDO_GEOMETRY) column to NULL as in Listing 16-26.

Listing 16-26. *Setting the* location *Column in the* customers *Table to a* NULL *Value*

```
SQL> UPDATE customers SET location = NULL;
```

Use GEOCODE or GEOCODE_ALL

You should not use the naive GEOCODE_AS_GEOMETRY function to convert addresses to SDO_GEOMETRY data, if you suspect that the input address may be incorrect or misspelled. The GEOCODE_AS_GEOMETRY may return incorrect SDO_GEOMETRY objects if the input address has errors. In such cases, you should use the GEOCODE or GEOCODE_ALL functions to obtain corrected address(es) along with the quality of the match(es). See Chapter 6 for more details.

Specify "INDEXTYPE is mdsys.spatial_index" in CREATE INDEX

To create a spatial index on the column of a table, you should always specify INDEXTYPE is mdsys.spatial_index. See Listing 16-13 or 16-15, or see Chapter 8 for examples. If you do not specify this clause in the CREATE INDEX statement, Oracle will raise the ORA-02327 ("Cannot create index on expression with datatype ADT") error.

Always Use Spatial Operators in the WHERE Clause

Never use spatial operators such as SDO_RELATE, SDO_FILTER, SDO_ANYINTERACT, SDO_WITHIN_DISTANCE, and SDO_NN (see Chapter 8 for a full list) in the SELECT list of a SQL statement (in other words, do not use them as in SELECT SDO_RELATE() FROM us_states). Instead, you should always specify the spatial operators in the WHERE clause and evaluate them to TRUE (see examples in Chapter 8).

Use Spatial Functions When No Spatial Index Is Available

When you do not have a spatial index available, use spatial functions rather than spatial operators (if you use spatial operators when there is no spatial index, Oracle raises an error, as mentioned in Chapter 8). Listing 8-40 showed how to find the customers that are within competitors' sales regions using the SDO_RELATE operator. Instead of performing this analysis on all the customers, what if you want to do it only for the customer names that are schools (that is, have %SCHOOL% in the name)? You can add modify Listing 8-40 as in Listing 16-27.

Listing 16-27. *Performing* SDO_RELATE *on a Subset of Customers*

```
SQL> SELECT  ct.id, ct.name
FROM competitors_sales_regions comp, customers ct
WHERE comp.id=1
  AND SDO_RELATE(ct.location,  comp.geom, 'MASK=ANYINTERACT ' )='TRUE'
  AND ct.name LIKE '%SCHOOL%'
ORDER BY ct.id;
```

However, if you know that the ct.name LIKE '%SCHOOL%' is more selective, you can push it to the FROM clause in Listing 16-28.

Listing 16-28. *Performing* SDO_RELATE *on a Subquery Returning a Subset of Customers*

```
SQL> SELECT  ct.id, ct.name
FROM competitors_sales_regions comp,
   (SELECT c.name FROM customers c WHERE c.name LIKE '%SCHOOL') ct
WHERE comp.id=1
  AND SDO_RELATE(ct.location,  comp.geom, 'MASK=ANYINTERACT ' )='TRUE'
ORDER BY ct.id;
```

Since ct.location in the result of the subquery no longer has a spatial index, the query returns the ORA-13226 ("Interface not supported without spatial index") error. In these cases, you can utilize the SDO_GEOM.RELATE function as shown in Listing 16-29.

Listing 16-29. *Performing* SDO_GEOM.RELATE *on a Subquery Returning a Subset of Customers*

```
SQL> SELECT  ct.id, ct.name
FROM competitors_sales_regions comp,
   (SELECT c.name FROM customers c WHERE c.name LIKE '%SCHOOL') ct
WHERE comp.id=1
  AND SDO_GEOM.RELATE(ct.location, 'ANYINTERACT', comp.geom, 0.5 )='TRUE'
ORDER BY ct.id;
```

In this manner, all the relationship spatial operators can be easily replaced by the equivalent spatial functions. What about an SDO_NN operator? The SDO_NN operator internally utilizes the SDO_GEOM.SDO_DISTANCE function to order the neighbors. You can do the same: order the results of a subquery based on distance to a query geometry and get only the nearest ones. Listing 16-30 shows an example of how to return the closest customer to a specific competitor region (comp.id=1) that is also a school (note you can use the sdo_batch_size formulation, but this is another alternative).

Listing 16-30. *Computing the Nearest Neighbor on a Subquery Returning a Subset of Customers*

```
SQL> SELECT  ct.id, ct.name FROM (
  SELECT ct.id, ct.name, SDO_GEOM.DISTANCE(comp.geom, ct.location, 0.5) dist
  FROM competitors_sales_regions comp,
     (SELECT c.name FROM customers c WHERE c.name LIKE '%SCHOOL') ct
  WHERE comp.id=1
  ORDER BY dist
  )
  WHERE rownum <= 1; - substitute 1 by k for k-nearest neighbors
```

You would use the spatial functions (as in Listings 16-29 and 16-30) instead of the spatial operators when operating on small subsets of geometries. Otherwise, you can specify the predicates as part of a single query (as in Listing 16-26) and let the optimizer decide how to evaluate the various predicates.

Do Not Move, Import, or Replicate MDRT Tables

The MDRT_<>$ tables (and the associated MDRS_<>$ sequences) are used in storing information for spatial indexes. You should never operate on these tables as regular Oracle tables. This means the following:

- *You should not move the MDRT tables from one tablespace to another*: If you do, the corresponding spatial index becomes unusable, and all *spatial operators on the indexed table fail.* The only way to recover from this situation is to drop and re-create the spatial index. To avoid all these problems, make sure your DBA understands this restriction and does not move the MDRT tables around to perform some optimizations. You can specify the tablespace in which the MDRT table needs to be stored using the tablespace parameter during spatial index creation. Refer to Chapter 8 for more details.
- *You should not drop or alter the MDRT tables or the MDRS sequences*: You can drop them, however, if they are not associated with any spatial index (this should not happen under normal circumstances). You can identify all MDRT tables that are associated with the user's spatial indexes by inspecting the USER_SDO_INDEX_METADATA view:

  ```
  SQL> SELECT sdo_index_name, sdo_index_table, sdo_rtree_seq_name
  FROM USER_SDO_GEOM_METADATA;
  ```

- *You should not export the MDRT tables explicitly*: When you import a table, say customers, that has a spatial index, the appropriate spatial index information is also exported. During import, the spatial index (and the associated MDRT tables) will be re-created. You do not have to export or import any of the MDRT tables (or the MDRS sequences).
- *You should not replicate the MDRT tables to a replicated database*: If you want to replicate a user table, say customers, all you will have to replicate is that customers table. You will need to explicitly create the spatial index on the replicated instance.

Network Metadata

If you intend to define a network over existing structures or manually create the network, you should explicitly populate the USER_SDO_NETWORK_METADATA view. Refer to Chapter 10 for an example. If, however, you use the CREATE_SDO_NETWORK function as described in Chapter 10 to create the network, you do not need to populate the metadata.

Map Metadata

To create maps, you need to populate the USER_SDO_MAPS, USER_SDO_THEMES, and USER_SDO_STYLES dictionary views. Note that some of the columns (for example, DEFINITION) in these views store information using XML. You need to be careful in populating/updating these columns. See Chapter 12 for details.

Common Errors

In the following sections, we list some common errors that you may encounter while location-enabling your application (starting with some of the frequently encountered errors). We also suggest the corrective actions for each error. Note that this list is not exhaustive. For other errors not listed here, you should refer to *Oracle Spatial User's Guide* and Oracle Technical Support for assistance.

ORA-13226: Interface Not Supported Without a Spatial Index

This error happens when you are using a spatial operator that cannot be evaluated without the use of the spatial index. This could happen if either there is no index on the column that you are using or the optimizer does not choose the index-based evaluation. Listing 8-1 shows an example of this error.

Action: If there is no spatial index on the columns in the spatial operator, create an index. Otherwise, if the optimizer is not choosing the spatial index, then you should specify explicit hints such as INDEX or ORDERED to ensure that the spatial index is used. Refer to Chapter 8 for more details.

ORA-13203: Failed to Read USER_SDO_GEOM_METADATA View

This error occurs if the table you are trying to index does not have any metadata in the USER_SDO_GEOM_METADATA view. See Listing 8-2 for an example.

Action: Insert a row corresponding to the spatial layer (table_name, column_name) in this view. Listing 8-4 shows an example.

ORA-13365: Layer SRID Does Not Match Geometry SRID

This error implies that the SRID in a geometry column in a table does not match the SRID value in the corresponding layer in the USER_SDO_GEOM_METADATA view. For instance, if the layer corresponds to the location column in the customers table, you can inspect these values using the SQL in Listing 16-31. Note that the SRID must be set to the same value in the location columns of all rows in the customers table.

Listing 16-31. *Determining the* SRID *Value in the Location (Geometry) Columns of a Table*

```
SQL> SELECT ct.location.sdo_srid FROM customers ct WHERE ROWNUM=1;
```

This gives the SRID stored in the location column of the customers table. You should compare it to the SRID for the layer (in the USER_SDO_GEOM_METADATA view), as shown in Listing 16-32.

Listing 16-32. *Determining the* SRID *Value for a Spatial Layer (Specified by* table_name, column_name*)*

```
SQL> SELECT srid FROM USER_SDO_GEOM_METADATA
WHERE  table_name='CUSTOMERS' AND column_name='LOCATION';
```

Action: Modify the SRIDs (in the geometries and the USER_SDO_GEOM_METADATA view) to be the same value. This error occurs mostly during the creation or rebuilding of an index. You might have to drop the index before retrying the create-index/rebuild-index operation (after changing the SRID values).

ORA-13223: Duplicate Entry for <table_name, column_name> in SDO_GEOM_METADATA

This error indicates that the insertion of a new row for a specified <table_name, column_name> pair into the USER_SDO_GEOM_METADATA view failed. There is already a row that exists for the <table_name, column_name> pair in this view.

Action: Delete the rows in USER_SDO_GEOM_METADATA for <table_name, column_name> before inserting new values.

ORA-13249, ORA-02289: Cannot Drop Sequence/Table

This error occurs when you are trying to drop a spatial index. If the associated tables/sequences do not exist, the DROP INDEX statement raises these errors (ORA-13249 and ORA-02289).

Action: Append FORCE to the DROP INDEX statement, as in the following example in which the customers_sidx is dropped:

```
SQL> DROP INDEX customers_sidx  FORCE;
```

ORA-13249: Multiple Entries in sdo_index_metadata Table

This error occurs when you are trying to create a spatial index and there is leftover metadata from a failed DROP INDEX statement.

Action: You will have to explicitly clean up the metadata entries for the specified index in the SDO_INDEX_METADATA_TABLE table in the MDSYS schema, as shown in the following example:

```
SQL> connect mdsys/<mdsys-password>
SQL> DELETE FROM SDO_INDEX_METADATA_TABLE
WHERE sdo_index_owner = 'SPATIAL' AND sdo_index_name='CUSTOMERS_SIDX';
```

ORA-13207: Incorrect Use of the <operator-name> Operator

This error operator > occurs when the specified operator is used incorrectly. In most cases, this will happen when the SDO_RELATE, SDO_NN, or SDO_WITHIN_DISTANCE operator is used on a three- or four-dimensional index (created by specifying SDO_INDX_DIMS in the parameter clause of the CREATE INDEX statement; see Chapter 8 for details).

Action: You can use only the SDO_FILTER operator (and not others, such as SDO_RELATE) if the SDO_INDX_DIMS parameter is set to a value greater than 2 (the default operator > value) during index creation.

ORA-13000: Dimension Number Is Out of Range

This error occurs when you are operating with geometries that have the SDO_GTYPE value (in an SDO_GEOMETRY object) to be less than 10. This might be from prior versions of Oracle Spatial where the SDO_GTYPE contained only the type (T) information. Starting with Oracle 9*i*, the SDO_GTYPE in an SDO_GEOMETRY is of the D00T, where D indicates the dimensionality and T is the type. Refer to Chapter 4 for more details.

Action: Modify your data to reflect this change. Alternatively, use the SDO_MIGRATE.TO_CURRENT function to let Oracle Spatial make the change. This function also corrects the orientation of polygon geometries.

ORA-00904: . . . Invalid Identifier

You may get this error when executing SQL of the following form:

```
SQL> SELECT geom..sdo_srid FROM competitors WHERE id=1;
ORA-00904: "GEOM"."SDO_SRID": invalid identifier
```

This is because of not specifying an alias for the table when referring to attributes of an object. You can correct the SQL with a table alias as follows:

```
SQL> SELECT cmp.geom..sdo_srid FROM competitors cmp WHERE id=1;
```

ORA-00939: Too Many Arguments for Function

This error may occur while inserting an SDO_GEOMETRY with more than 1,000 ordinates in the SDO_ORDINATES array. For instance, it is likely to be raised by the following SQL statement:

```
SQL> INSERT INTO sales_regions VALUES
(
  1000,
  SDO_GEOMETRY
  (
    2004, - A multipoint geometry
    8307,
    NULL,
    SDO_ELEM_INFO_ARRAY(1, 1, 1100),  -- this geometry has 1100 points
    SDO_ORDINATE_ARRAY  -- store the ordinates
    (
      1,1, 1,1, 1,1, 1,1, 1,1 , -- repeat this line 99  times
      ......
      1,1, 1,1, 1,1, 1,1, 1,1
    )
  )
);
ERROR at line 5:
ORA-00939: too many arguments for function
```

Action: This is a SQL-level restriction. You can avoid this error by creating a PL/SQL variable (called geom in the following code) that holds this geometry and then binding this variable to the INSERT SQL statement:

```
SQL>
DECLARE
  geom SDO_GEOMETRY; -- PL/SQL variable to store the geometry with >999 ordinates
BEGIN
  -- construct the geometry here
  geom :=
    SDO_GEOMETRY
    (
      2004, 8307, NULL,
      SDO_ELEM_INFO_ARRAY(1, 1, 1100),
      SDO_ORDINATE_ARRAY
      (
        1,1, 1,1, 1,1, 1,1, 1,1 , -- repeat this line 99  times
```

```
        --
        1,1, 1,1, 1,1, 1,1, 1,1
      )
    );

    -- store the geometry in the sales_regions table using dynamic SQL
    EXECUTE IMMEDIATE
       'INSERT INTO sales_regions VALUES (1000, :gm )' USING geom;
END;
/
PL/SQL procedure successfully completed.
```

ORA-13030: Invalid Dimensionality for the SDO_GEOMETRY, or ORA-13364: Layer Dimensionality Does Not Match Geometry Dimensions

One of these errors may occur in a query if the dimensionality of the spatial index (layer) is greater than the dimensionality of the query window specified in a spatial operator. For instance, if you have a two-dimensional query that is coded on the threed table, which has three-dimensional geometries (and is indexed as three-dimensional), then these errors could occur.

```
SQL>
-- Create the threed table and a 3D index
CREATE TABLE threed (id  NUMBER, geom SDO_GEOMETRY);
INSERT INTO threed VALUES (1,
 SDO_GEOMETRY (3001, NULL, SDO_POINT_TYPE (1,1,1), NULL, NULL));
insert into user_sdo_geom_metadata values ('THREED', 'GEOM',
  mdsys.sdo_dim_array (
    mdsys.sdo_dim_element ('x', 1, 100, .0000005),
    mdsys.sdo_dim_element ('y', 1, 100, .0000005),
    mdsys.sdo_dim_element ('z', 1, 200, .0000005)), null);
CREATE INDEX threed_sidx ON threed(geom) INDEXTYPE IS MDSYS.SPATIAL_INDEX
PARAMETERS ('sdo_indx_dims=3');

-- Perform the query with 2D query window
SELECT b.id FROM threed b
  WHERE SDO_FILTER
  (
    b.geom,         -- 3-dimensional data (indexed as 3D, i.e., sdo_indx_dims=3)
    SDO_GEOMETRY    -- 2-dimensional query window
    (
      2003, NULL, NULL,
      SDO_ELEM_INFO_ARRAY(1, 1003, 3),
      SDO_ORDINATE_ARRAY(1,1, 3,3)
     )
   )='TRUE';
ERROR at line 1:
ORA-13030: Invalid dimension for the SDO_GEOMETRY object
```

You can verify the dimensionality of the index by examining the attribute sdo_indx_dims in the USER_SDO_INDEX_METADATA view. You can also determine the dimensionality of the query geometry by inspecting the SDO_GTYPE attribute of the geometry.

Even if the spatial index dimensionality is not greater than the query dimensionality, the ORA-13364 error may occur if all of the following are true:

- The table data has more than two dimensions.
- The spatial index on this table is two-dimensional.
- The query dimensionality is not the same as the data dimensionality.

Action: These errors can be resolved by changing the query geometry to match the dimensionality of the data. For instance, you can change the query window as follows:

```
SQL> SELECT b.id FROM threed
  WHERE SDO_FILTER
  (
    geom,         -- 3-dimensional data (indexed as 3-d, i.e., sdo_indx_dims=3)
    SDO_GEOMETRY   -- 2-dimensional query window
    (
      3003, NULL, NULL,
      SDO_ELEM_INFO_ARRAY(1, 1003, 3),
      SDO_ORDINATE_ARRAY(1,1,1,  3,3, 3)
     )
   )='TRUE';
```

Summary

In this chapter, we provided several tips to model spatial data; to tune the performance of spatial operators, functions, and updates; and to manage temporal or historical spatial data using table partitioning. We also covered several common pitfalls and errors and described corrective actions for these errors. This information should come in handy when you incorporate spatial analysis and visualization into your business application.

With this chapter, we come to the end of the book. We hope the information in these chapters helped you in location-enabling your application. In the following appendixes, we give a brief overview of additional functionality components of Oracle Spatial such as GeoRaster and Linear Referencing, which cater to specialized applications in GIS and CAD/CAM.

PART 6

Appendixes

APPENDIX A

Additional Spatial Analysis Functions

In Chapters 8 and 9 we described how to perform proximity analysis using the SDO_GEOMETRY data in Oracle tables. We described a variety of functions and index-based operators to perform proximity-based spatial analysis.

In this appendix, we describe more advanced functions to cater to specific business analysis. We consider the business application that is discussed throughout this book. Say, for example, that you want to start three new stores. Where are the best locations to start them? The advanced functions we discuss in this appendix enable the following types of analyses to aid in site selection:

- *Tiling-based analysis*: One approach is to examine population. Population statistics can be obtained using demographic datasets such as ZIP codes, census block groups, and so on. You can tile the possible set of locations and identify the tiles that have the greatest populations. In general, tiling-based analysis groups data into areas called *tiles* and computes aggregates for specified attributes (for example, income, age, spending patterns, and so on) inside the tiles.
- *Neighborhood analysis*: Another approach is to identify a candidate set of locations (by some other criterion, such as proximity to a highway). Then, you can choose among these candidate sets by estimating the population in the neighborhood of each location.
- *Clustering analysis*: Yet another approach to identify the best places to start new businesses is to analyze the customer locations that are not covered by existing stores. You can arrange the set of customer locations into groups, or clusters. The centers of these clusters may be good choices for locating new businesses.

The SDO_SAM package in Oracle Spatial includes functions to facilitate the kinds of spatial analyses just described. In this appendix, we give an overview of how to use these functions. You can find a detailed discussion in *Oracle Spatial User's Guide*.

Tiling-Based Analysis

First we cover how to identify regions/tiles that satisfy a business criterion. For the business application discussed in this book, we describe how to divide the two-dimensional coordinate space in which all locations are partitioned into small regions called *tiles*. We then describe functions to estimate population statistics for each tile using demographic data stored in other tables.

TILED_BINS

Tiling is the process of dividing a two-dimensional space into smaller regions. Figure A-1 shows an example. If the tiling level is specified as 1, then the range in each dimension is bisected once. In Figure A-1, the x-dimension is bisected once and the y-dimension is bisected once. This produces tiles at tiling level 1. The boundaries of these tiles are shown by a thick border. At level 2, each level-1 tile is bisected once along the x- and y-dimensions, again providing a total of 16 equal-sized tiles. This process is repeated until you obtain tiles of appropriate sizes (or at a specified tiling level).

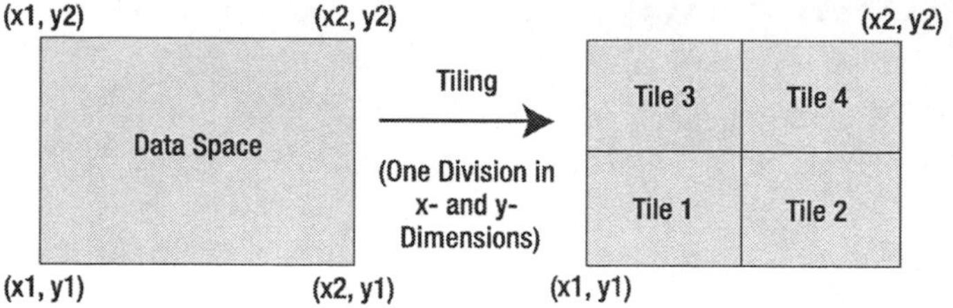

Figure A-1. *Tiling a two-dimensional space at level 1 by bisecting the range in x- and y-dimensions to yield four tiles*

How is tiling useful in business analysis? Tiling helps in dividing the entire two-dimensional space (over which the businesses and potential sites are located) into smaller regions. You can then analyze these regions and identify whether they are appropriate for the business task at hand.

The TILED_BINS function has the following syntax:

```
TILED_BINS
(
  lower_bound_in_dimension_1    NUMBER,
  upper_bound_in_dimension_1    NUMBER,
  lower_bound_in_dimension_2    NUMBER,
  upper_bound_in_dimension_2    NUMBER,
  tiling_level                  NUMBER,
  srid                          NUMBER DEFAULT NULL,
  xdivs                         NUMBER DEFAULT NULL,
  ydivs                         NUMBER DEFAULT NULL
)
RETURNS Table of SDO_REGION
```

where the SDO_REGION type has the following structure:

```
SQL> DESCRIBE SDO_REGION;
ID                                NUMBER
GEOMETRY                          SDO_GEOMETRY
```

If the tiling_level is set to 1, the function returns four tiles (one bisection of x- and y-dimensions, causing four disjoint regions). As you increase the tiling level by 1, each tile is further subdivided into four tiles. In general, for tiling level *k*, the function returns 4^k tiles. Each tile is returned as an SDO_REGION data type. This type includes the ID and the Geometry corresponding to the tile. The srid argument, if specified, indicates the spatial reference (coordinate) system for the returned geometries. Listing A-1 shows an example of this function. Note that the return type is a table, which means you should use the "table" casting operation as shown.

Listing A-1. *Tiling a Two-Dimensional Space*

```
SQL> SELECT * FROM TABLE
(SDO_SAM.TILED_BINS(-77.1027, -76.943996, 38.820813, 38.95911,1, 8307));
```

Note that the number of tiles is always a power of 4 if you specify the tiling_level parameter. For the tiling_level parameter of k, the number of tiles is 4^k. You can better control the number of tiles if you specify a grid of n by m, where n and m specify the number of divisions in the x-axis and the y-axis, respectively. This is possible by simply setting the tiling_level parameter to NULL, the xdivs parameter to n, and the ydivs parameter to m. This will divide the (range in the) x-axis n times and the (range in the) y-dimension m times, respectively. For example, if n=1, the range of values in x-dimension is divided once, that is, into two halves. In general, for a division on n times of the x-axis and m times of the y-axis, the total number of tiles returned will be (n+1)*(m+1). Listing A-2 shows an example with two divisions along the x-axis and three divisions along the y-axis, returning a total of 3*4=12 tiles.

Listing A-2. *Tiling a Two-Dimensional Space by Specifying the Number of Divisions Along x- and y-axes*

```
SQL> SELECT * FROM TABLE
(SDO_SAM.TILED_BINS(-77.1027, -76.943996, 38.820813, 38.95911, NULL, 8307, 2, 3 ));
```

TILED_AGGREGATES

The next function that we will cover is TILED_AGGREGATES. This function implicitly computes the tiles using the dimension bounds for a specified table in USER_SDO_GEOM_METADATA. For each computed tile, the function returns the aggregated estimate for a user-specified column such as population. This estimate is derived from a specified *demographic* or *theme* table, and it uses a proportion of overlap to calculate the aggregate value.

For instance, the table zip5_dc in Listing A-3 stores the ZIP code name, the ZIP code boundary (as an SDO_GEOMETRY object), and the population for each ZIP code in the District of Columbia in the United States. (Note that the population values in this table are for illustrative purposes only and may not match current real-world values.)

Listing A-3. *ZIP Code Table Used to Get Demographic Information*

```
SQL> desc zip5_dc;
 Name                                      Null?    Type
 ----------------------------------------- -------- ----------------------------
 STATE_ABRV                                         VARCHAR2(2)
 FILE_NAME                                          VARCHAR2(8)
 AREA                                               NUMBER
 PERIMETER                                          NUMBER
 ZCTA                                               VARCHAR2(5)
 NAME                                               VARCHAR2(90)
 LSAD                                               VARCHAR2(2)
 LSAD_TRANS                                         VARCHAR2(50)
 GEOM                                               SDO_GEOMETRY
 POPULATION                                         NUMBER
```

A variety of such theme tables store demographic information at different levels. The U.S. Census blocks, block groups, tracts, counties, and states are some examples. Such demographic data can be easily combined with application data to perform spatial analysis for business applications. For instance, you can use the ZIP code regions in the zip5_dc table to derive population estimates for an arbitrary tile or region (ref_geometry).

Only 20 percent of the ZIP code region from zip5_dc (demographic) table intersects, as shown in Figure A-2. The aggregate for ref_geometry is 20 percent of the aggregate associated with the ZIP code.

Figure A-2. *Estimating the aggregate for* `ref_geometry` *(tile or region)*

What if you have multiple ZIP codes intersecting the tile (or region)? You can specify how to combine the aggregate contributions from each of the intersecting ZIP codes. For instance, if 20 percent of ZIP code A intersects with the tile, 30 percent of ZIP code B intersects with the tile, and these need to be *summed* up, then the resulting population estimate (aggregate) for the tile is as follows:

```
sum(0.2*(population of zip code A), 0.3*(population of zip code B))
```

The `TILED_AGGREGATES` function computes these estimates using a specified theme (demographic) table. It has the following signature:

```
Tiled_Aggregates
(
  theme_table                 VARCHAR2,
  theme_geom_column           VARCHAR2,
  aggregate_type              VARCHAR2,
  aggregate_column            VARCHAR2,
  tiling_level                NUMBER,
  tiling_domain               SDO_DIM_ARRAY DEFAULT NULL
)
RETURNS Table of MDSYS.SDO_REGAGGR
```

where the `SDO_REGAGGR` type has the following structure:

```
SQL> DESCRIBE SDO_REGAGGR;
Name                          Type
----------------------------  ----------------------------
REGION_ID                     VARCHAR2(24)
GEOMETRY                      SDO_GEOMETRY
AGGREGATE_VALUE               NUMBER
```

This function returns a table of `SDO_REGAGGR` objects. `REGION_ID` corresponds to `tile_id`. `GEOMETRY` corresponds to the geometry of the corresponding tile. `AGGREGATE_VALUE` contains the aggregate value for the tile—for instance, the sum of the population or the number of customers.

The function takes the following arguments:

- `theme_table` and `theme_geom_column` specify the name of the theme table and the geometry column. For instance, these arguments could be `zip5_dc` and `geom` (the geometric boundary of the ZIP code).
- `aggregate_type` specifies how to combine multiple contributions from intersecting ZIP codes. This could be one of the SQL aggregates `SUM`, `COUNT`, `MIN`, and `MAX`.
- `aggregate_column` specifies which demographic attribute needs to be estimated. In the example application, this can be `POPULATION`.
- `tiling_level` specifies the tiling level to construct the tiles.
- `bounds` specifies the tiling domain for the tiles. If this argument is not specified, then the tiling domain is set to the bounds for the spatial layer corresponding to `<theme_table, theme_geom_column>` in the `USER_SDO_GEOM_METADATA` view.

■ **Caution** AVG and other aggregates are not supported. These aggregates need to be computed using the SUM and COUNT aggregates. For instance, if the AVG income needs to be computed, then it can be computed as `sum(total_income_per_tile)/sum(total_population_per_tile)`. `total_income_per_tile` and `total_population_per_tile` can be estimated with the TILED_AGGREGATES function using the `total_income` and `total_population` columns of the ZIP code tables (these two columns need to be explicitly materialized).

Listing A-4 shows an example of the TILED_AGGREGATES function. Note that by selecting only those tiles that have `aggregate_value` (population) greater than 30,000, you are identifying the most populated tiles from the set of tiles.

Listing A-4. *Searching for Regions (Tiles) That Have a Population Greater Than 30,000*

```
SQL> SELECT REGION_ID, AGGREGATE_VALUE, GEOMETRY FROM TABLE
(
  SDO_SAM.TILED_AGGREGATES
  ('ZIP5_DC', 'GEOM','SUM', 'POPULATION', 2)
  ) a
WHERE a.aggregate_value > 30000;
```

Note that the query returns tiles (regions) along with the population. In your site selection analysis, you can make these tiles (regions) the starting points for further analysis. In general, you can use the TILED_AGGREGATES function to determine candidate regions based on a selection criterion (for example, a high population).

You can visualize these tiles using Oracle MapViewer. For instance, you can use the `jview.jsp` file in the `mapviewr/demo` directory for this purpose. Specify `select geom from ZIP5_DC` as query1 and the SQL in Listing A-4 as query2.

Figure A-3 shows the ZIP codes in dark gray, and tile regions that have a population of more than 30,000 are shown in lighter gray boxes. You can further refine this analysis by identifying smaller tiles (that is, tiles at level 3 or 4). Additionally, you can superimpose locations of roads and other businesses to aid in the site selection process.

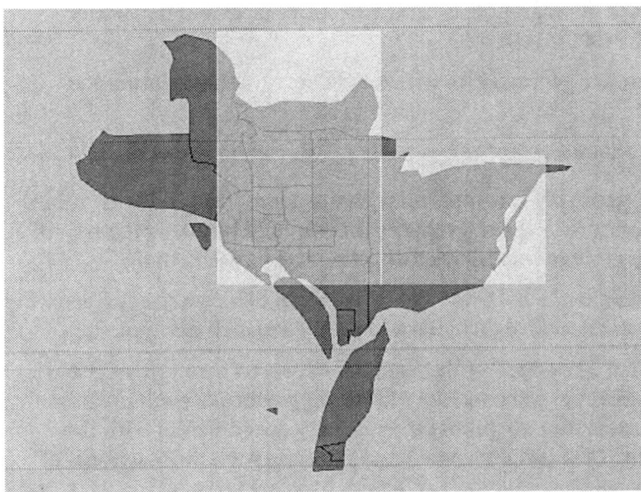

Figure A-3. *Displaying ZIP code boundaries and tiles that have population of more than 30,000*

Neighborhood Analysis

Instead of using tiles to compute estimates, can you compute the population for arbitrary sales regions? This might be useful if you already chose a set of candidate sites through other selection criteria. You can examine the population in the neighborhood of each such site (or location) by constructing a (quarter-mile) buffer around the location. The AGGREGATES_FOR_GEOMETRY function allows you to compute the estimates for an arbitrary geometry.

AGGREGATES_FOR_GEOMETRY

This function computes the estimated aggregate value from a theme table for a specified region: ref_geometry (as opposed to precomputed tiles in TILED_AGGREGATES). It uses the information in theme_table to compute this estimate. This function has the following signature:

```
AGGREGATES_FOR_GEOMETRY
(
  theme_table                VARCHAR2,
  theme_geom_column          VARCHAR2,
  aggregate_type             VARCHAR2,
  aggregate_column           VARCHAR2,
  ref_geometry               SDO_GEOMETRY,
  dist_spec                  VARCHAR2 DEFAULT NULL
)
RETURNS NUMBER
```

The function's arguments are as follows:

- theme_table and theme_geom_column specify the name of the theme table and the geometry column. For instance, these arguments could be zip5_dc and geom (the geometric boundary of the ZIP code). The demographic information at a fine or coarse level is stored in these tables.
- aggregate_type specifies how to combine multiple contributions from intersecting ZIP codes. This could be one of the SQL aggregates SUM, COUNT, MIN, and MAX.
- aggregate_column specifies which demographic attribute needs to be estimated. In the example application, this can be POPULATION.
- ref_geometry specifies the reference geometry for which the demographic information needs to be computed.
- dist_spec specifies additional parameters for ref_geometry. This can be one of the following:
  - NULL: In this case, the ref_geometry is compared with the geometries in theme_table. As in Figure A-1, the aggregate for the ref_geometry is computed by taking the area of intersection (of the theme geometries with the ref_geometry) into account.
  - *A string of the form* distance= <val> unit=<distance_unit>: In this case, the ref_geometry is expanded (buffered) by the specified distance and the aggregate is computed.
  - *A string of the form* sdo_num_res=<N>: In this case, the nearest N geometries (from theme_table) to the ref_geometry are considered. The aggregates of each neighbor are equally weighted, because the neighbors may or may not intersect with the ref_geometry. For instance, if N=2 and ZIP code A and ZIP code B are the neighbors of the ref_geometry, then the aggregate for the ref_geometry is sum(population of A and population B). The aggregate_type is sum and the aggregate_column is population in this example.

Caution AVG and other aggregates are not supported. These aggregates need to be computed using SUM and COUNT aggregates. For instance, if the AVG income needs to be computed, then it can be computed as sum(total_income_per_ref_geometry)/sum(total_population_per_ref_geometry). total_income_per_ref_geometry and total_population_per_ref_geometry can be estimated with the AGGREGATES_FOR_GEOMETRY function using the total_income and total_population columns of the ZIP code tables (these two columns need to be explicitly materialized: total_income=income*population.

Listing A-5 shows an example of the AGGREGATES_FOR_GEOMETRY function. In this example, you are computing the population for sales region 1 (id=1) in the sales_regions table. Note that the sales_regions table is a quarter-mile buffered region on an existing store location. Likewise, you can perform the same population analysis on other regions that correspond to potential new store locations.

Listing A-5. *Estimating the Population in Sales Region 1 Using the Demographic Information in the* zip5_dc *Table*

```
SQL> SELECT SDO_SAM.AGGREGATES_FOR_GEOMETRY
('ZIP5_DC', 'GEOM', 'SUM', 'POPULATION', a.geom) population
FROM sales_regions a WHERE a.id=1;
```

AGGREGATES_FOR_LAYER

Instead of analyzing sales regions one by one, you may want to compute the population for all sales regions in the sales_regions table. The AGGREGATES_FOR_LAYER function performs this operation.

This function computes the aggregates for a set of geometries in a specified ref_table (instead of a specific geometry). This function has the following signature:

```
AGGREGATES_FOR_LAYER
(
  theme_table                 VARCHAR2,
  theme_geom_column           VARCHAR2,
  aggregate_type              VARCHAR2,
  aggregate_column            VARCHAR2,
  ref_table                   VARCHAR2,
  ref_geom_col                SDO_GEOMETRY,
  dist_spec                   VARCHAR2
)
RETURNS Table of SDO_REGAGGR
```

where the SDO_REGAGGR type has the following structure:

```
SQL> DESCRIBE SDO_REGAGGR;
Name                          Type
----------------------------- ----------------------------
 REGION_ID                    VARCHAR2(24)
 GEOMETRY                     SDO_GEOMETRY
 AGGREGATE_VALUE              NUMBER
```

Note that the function arguments are mostly the same as in AGGREGATES_FOR_GEOMETRY. The only difference is that instead of taking in a single ref_geometry as in AGGREGATES_FOR_GEOMETRY, the AGGREGATES_FOR_LAYER function takes a table of such geometries. These are specified using the ref_table and ref_geom_col arguments. This function returns a table of SDO_REGAGGR objects, where each object contains the aggregate computed using the ref_geometry in a row of the ref_table. The SDO_REGAGGR object stores the ROWID in the region_id attribute, the ref_geometry in the geometry attribute, and the computed aggregate in the aggregate_value attribute.

Listing A-6 shows how to obtain the population for all sales regions in the sales_regions table.

Listing A-6. *Estimating the Population for All Rows in the* sales_regions *Table Using Demographic Information in the* zip5_dc *Table*

```
SQL> SELECT s.id, aggregate_value population FROM TABLE
(
  SDO_SAM.AGGREGATES_FOR_LAYER
  ('ZIP5_DC', 'GEOM','SUM', 'POPULATION', 'SALES_REGIONS', 'GEOM')
  ) a, sales_regions s
WHERE s.rowid = a.region_id;
```

Note that the population attribute is not part of the sales_regions table. It is derived from the demographic table. These functions allow you to easily incorporate external demographic information into business analysis.

Clustering Analysis

Another approach for site selection is to examine where the potential customers are. If you want to start three new stores to cater to these new customers, then you can group or cluster the customers into three groups. In the following sections, you will look at how to perform clustering of customer locations.

SPATIAL_CLUSTERS

This function computes the clusters for a set of geometries in a specified table. You can perform additional analysis to identify the cluster center or for visualization using Oracle MapViewer. This function has the following signature:

```
SPATIAL_CLUSTERS
(
  geometry_table              VARCHAR2,
  geometry_column             VARCHAR2,
  max_clusters                NUMBER
)
RETURNS Table of MDSYS.SDO_REGION
```

where the SDO_REGION type has the following structure:

```
SQL> DESCRIBE SDO_REGION;
Name                 Type
--------             ---------
ID                   NUMBER
GEOMETRY             SDO_GEOMETRY
```

The arguments to this function are as follows:

- geom_table specifies the name of the table storing the geometries.
- geom_column specifies the name of the SDO_GEOMETRY column. This column needs to have a spatial index. The geometries in this column are clustered and returned.
- max_clusters specifies the maximum number of clusters to be returned.

This function computes the clusters based on the geometry columns of the specified geometry table. It returns each cluster as a geometry in the SDO_REGION type. The ID value is set to a number from 0 to max_clusters – 1. The function returns a table of such SDO_REGION objects. Listing A-7 shows how to cluster the customer locations in the customers table.

Listing A-7. *Finding Three Clusters for Customer Locations*

```
SQL> SELECT ID, GEOMETRY FROM TABLE
(SDO_SAM.SPATIAL_CLUSTERS('CUSTOMERS', 'LOCATION', 3));
```

You can visualize the customer locations and the three clusters using Oracle MapViewer. Use jview.jsp in the demo directory of MapViewer, and specify select location from customers in query1 and the SQL in Listing A-6 for query2. Figure A-4 shows the customer locations (points with an *x*) in dark gray and the clusters (rectangular regions) in lighter gray.

Once the clusters are identified, you can determine their centers using the SDO_GEOM.SDO_CENTROID function. This will give candidate locations for starting new stores to cater to the three groups of customers.

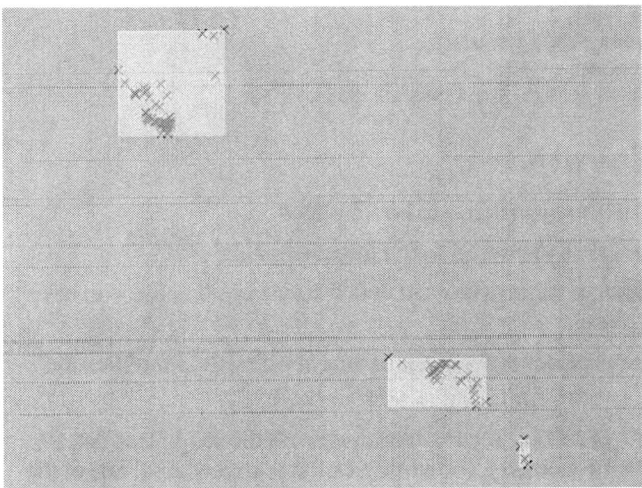

Figure A-4. *Displaying the customer regions and three clusters for Listing A-6*

Refining the Candidates for Site Selection

The spatial analyses functions (discussed in previous sections) enable users to identify regions (tiles or clusters) that satisfy a specific business criterion. For instance, the business criterion could be population>30000 in the tiling analysis. Once the candidate set of regions is identified, you can refine the set further using visual or other analysis techniques. For instance, you can refine the candidate set by visualizing these regions using Oracle MapViewer. As part of this visualization, you can overlay other appropriate data, such as roads and other business locations. Such combination of spatial analysis functions with other techniques, including visual refinement, can serve as an efficient and effective mechanism for site selection in business applications.

Geometry Simplification for Speeding Up Analysis

Most site-location analysis involves analyzing demographic data associated with county, ZIP code, tract, or block group regions. The boundaries of these entities are stored as complex shapes involving thousands of vertices. Spatial analysis using geometries with a large number of vertices tends to be slow and may not be acceptable in an interactive system that requires fast responses. To alleviate these performance issues, we can offer a simple solution: simplify each geometric shape in your demographic dataset (also known as *generalization* in GIS parlance). Oracle Spatial provides two functions for this purpose: the SIMPLIFY function in the SDO_UTIL package and the SIMPLIFY_GEOMETRY function in the SDO_SAM package (the latter is a wrapper around the former and hides complex usage). The SIMPLIFY_GEOMETRY function has two signatures: one with tolerance value (described in Chapter 3) as a parameter and another with diminfo (from the USER_SDO_GEOM_METADATA) as a parameter. Both signatures are described here:

```
FUNCTION simplify_geometry(geom mdsys.sdo_geometry,
                           dim mdsys.sdo_dim_array,
                           pct_area_change_limit number default 2)
RETURN mdsys.sdo_geometry;

FUNCTION simplify_geometry(geom mdsys.sdo_geometry,
                           tol number,
                           pct_area_change_limit number default 2)
RETURN mdsys.sdo_geometry;
```

The arguments to these functions are as follows:

- Geom.: This is the input SDO_GEOMETRY object that is to be simplified.
- Dim: This is the input SDO_DIM_ARRAY to use to obtain the tolerance value.
- Tolerance: This is the input tolerance value to be used to determine whether two vertices and edges can be collapsed into one.
- Pct_area_change_limit: This is the percentage change in area at which the simplification can stop.

As mentioned earlier, the SIMPLIFY_GEOMETRY function iteratively calls the SDO_UTIL.SIMPLIFY function for the simplification of the input geometry. The simplification is applied until one of the following criteria is met: the change in the area between the input geometry and the result geometry exceeds 2 percent, the number of iterations exceeds 20, or the number of vertices in the input geometry falls to less than 20. Note that the last two criteria are not exposed as tunable parameters, but only the pct_area_chng_limit is specified. In most cases, you can also skip this parameter and allow the default value of 2 (2 percent area change). Listing A-8 counts the number of vertices in the original geometry and the simplified geometry for the boundary of New Hampshire state. You can observe that the default value of 2 percent area change reduces the number of vertices from 709 to just 10 vertices. Such simplification to reduce the number of vertices comes in handy in many analysis and visualization applications.

Caution The generalization process in the simplify_geometry function simplifies line strings to have fewer vertices whenever possible. The simplified geometry may not cover the entire area as the original geometry. This is unlike the SDO_MBR and SDO_CONVEXHULL functions that guarantee that the area covered by the original geometry is always covered in their result.

Listing A-8. *Simplifying the Geometry for New Hampshire*

```
SQL> SELECT sdo_util.getnumvertices(geom) orig_num_vertices,
     sdo_util.getnumvertices(sdo_sam.simplify_geometry(geom, 0.5)) new_num_vertices
     FROM states
     WHERE state_abrv='NH';

ORIG_NUM_VERTICES    NEW_NUM_VERTICES
-----------------    ----------------
              709                  10
```

It is recommended that you simplify your demographic datasets using these functions before proceeding with analysis functions described in this appendix. Doing so may speed up spatial analysis functions such as `SDO_RELATE` and `TILED_AGGREGATES`. Note that the simplification may lead to changes in results and can be applied only if the application can tolerate small deviations in analysis results.

Summary

Spatial analysis functions in Oracle estimate attribute values for a region or a neighborhood. In addition, the functionality can cluster geometry objects into a specified number of clusters. These analysis functions can be combined with the visualization capability in Oracle MapViewer to aid in site selection applications. In warehouse applications, spatial analysis functions can be used to materialize the influence of neighborhoods in warehouse data and to mine for spatial patterns in the data.

APPENDIX B

Linear Referencing

In all the chapters of this book, we use coordinates to locate spatial objects on the surface of the earth. Coordinates locate objects in a two-dimensional space, such as longitude and latitude. As you saw in Chapter 4, a large number of different coordinate systems can be used in this way. They are all defined as *spatial reference systems*.

Spatial coordinates are not the only way to locate objects. Some objects are better identified by their position along a linear feature: their location can be described by a *measure* value (such as travel distance) with respect to some known point on the feature (such as its start point). This type of location referencing using a measure value (instead of the latitude/longitude values) is called a *Linear Referencing System* (*LRS*).

Let's say that the delivery truck for your business breaks down on a particular segment of a highway. How do you report its location to other agencies? One method is to mention the actual geographic coordinates, say –76.40804 degrees longitude and 45.79385 degrees latitude, obtained from a GPS receiver. An alternate method that is more frequently used in transportation applications is by specifying that the truck is "12 meters (measure) from Exit 5 (a reference point on the highway) going north on the highway." In short, this method specifies a reference point on a linear feature and the measure of the location from the reference point. This approach of specifying linear measures is widely used in transportation and utility (electric cables, gas pipelines, and so on) industries.

In this appendix, we will describe the functionality of the *Linear Referencing* component of Oracle Spatial. This functionality, available in the `SDO_LRS` package, allows you to associate *measures* with a linear feature stored in an `SDO_GEOMETRY` object. We will refer to such geometries as *linear referenced* or *LRS* geometries. In addition, Oracle allows you to perform the following operations on LRS geometries:

- *Project* a two-dimensional point onto a linear feature, and identify the corresponding measure along the linear feature. This functionality is useful to determine the closest milepost on a highway when a car breaks down. For example, the popular OnStar positioning system uses such an approach to convert the geographical coordinates of the car into the nearest milepost on the highway and inform the appropriate road service.[1]
- *Locate* a point using the measure value, and identify the corresponding two-dimensional coordinates. You can use this functionality to identify the coordinates of stop signs and other objects that are specified using measures along a linear feature.
- *Clip* a linear feature by specified start and end measure values. This function allows you, for example, to obtain specific sections of a road that will be closed to traffic.

---

1. The OnStar system, developed by General Motors Corporation, combines an onboard GPS and cellular phone and allows a driver to be located and get assistance at the press of a button.

In the next section, we will describe concepts of linear referencing and how it is used in applications. Then, we will show you how to create LRS geometries and perform *projection, location,* or *clipping* types of operations.

Concepts and Definitions

First we'll describe some basic concepts using the geometry in Figure B-1. The figure shows a line string from "Start" to "End." Such line strings could typically represent highways, flight paths, gas pipelines, electric cables, and so on.

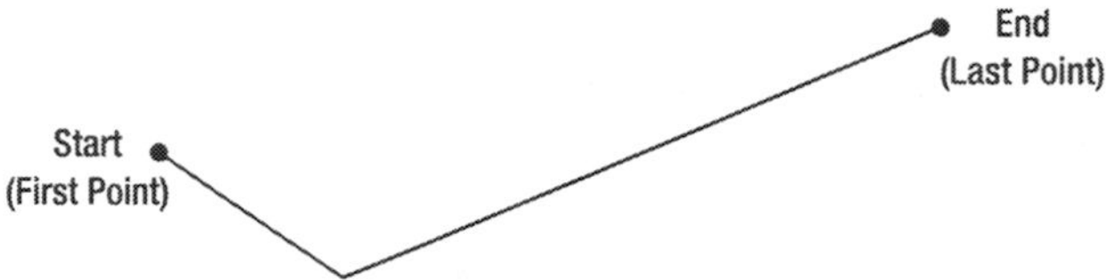

Figure B-1. *Linear feature with start (first) and end (last) points*

Measure

The *measure* of a point along a geometric segment is the linear distance to the point measured from the start point (for increasing values) or end point (for decreasing values) of the geometric segment. In Figure B-1, the start point may be associated with a measure value of 0 (or any other value). Likewise, other points of the line string may be associated with measure values.

Linear Referenced Segments

A *linear referenced segment* is a linear geometry with measures. It is usually a line string but could also be a multiline string or even the boundary of a polygon. For all the following examples, we consider only the most common case of simple line strings. In Figure B-1, if you associate measure information with the end points, the line string is a linear referenced, or LRS, geometry.

The measures may be increasing or decreasing along a linear feature, and they can start at any value.

Direction

The *direction* of a geometric segment is indicated from the start point of the geometric segment to the end point. The direction is determined by *the order of the vertices (from start point to end point) in the geometry definition*.

Shape Points

Shape points are those points of the line string that are assigned measure information. The start and end points of a line string must always have measure information. Intermediate points may or may not have measures.

Points that do not have any set measure will be populated by linear interpolation between the points with measures. Figure B-2 illustrates how missing measures are populated. We specified measures of 0 and 100 only for the start and end points, respectively, and the measure for an intermediate point is internally assigned as 25.

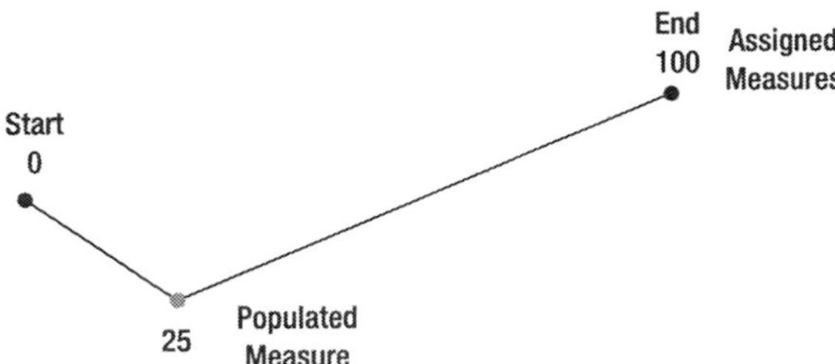

Figure B-2. *Populating measures for intermediate points*

Offset

The *offset* of a point along a geometric segment is the perpendicular distance between the point and the geometric segment. Figure B-3 shows an example. Offsets are positive if the points are on the left side along the segment direction and negative if they are on the right side. Points are on a geometric segment if their offsets to the segment are zero.

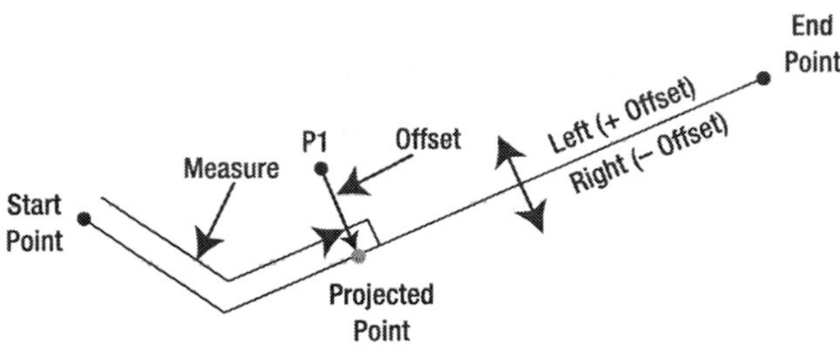

Figure B-3. *Offset of a point*

Typical Application

Linear referencing is widely used in transportation networks (flight paths, highways, and so on) and utility networks (gas pipelines, and so on). Linear referencing is most useful to *position* objects or information such as accidents, traffic conditions, road conditions, and road equipment (traffic lights, road signs, and so on) with reference to a linear feature. Figure B-4 illustrates this.

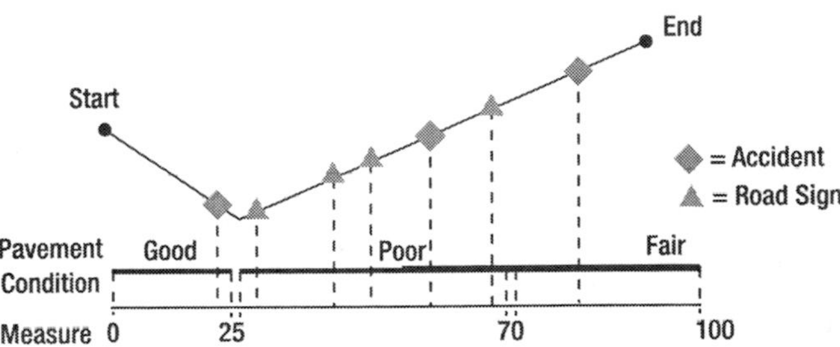

Figure B-4. *Accidents, road signs, and road conditions modeled using a linear feature*

An LRS application uses tables like the ones shown in Figure B-5: one table (`roads`) contains the actual LRS geometries. The other tables (`accidents`, `road signs`, and `pavement condition`) contain only references to the `roads` table together with their measure information.

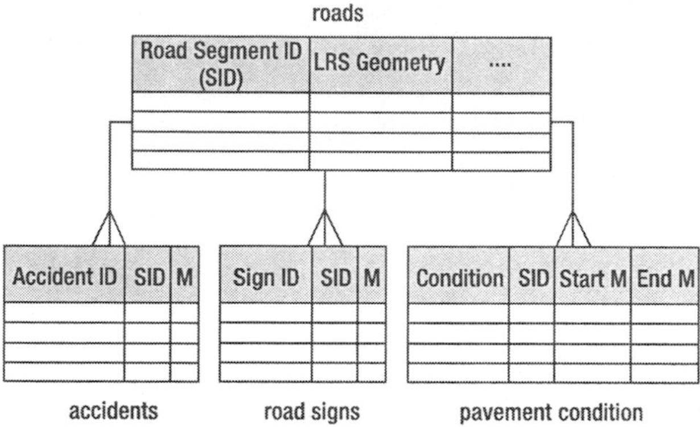

Figure B-5. *Tables in an LRS application*

To reference locations along a line, the line must first be registered with measure information: each point that describes the line has the usual *x* and *y* coordinates but also a *measure* that represents the distance from the start of the line.

For example, the linear referenced geometry in Figure B-6 is registered with measure information (start measure = 0 and end measure = 100).

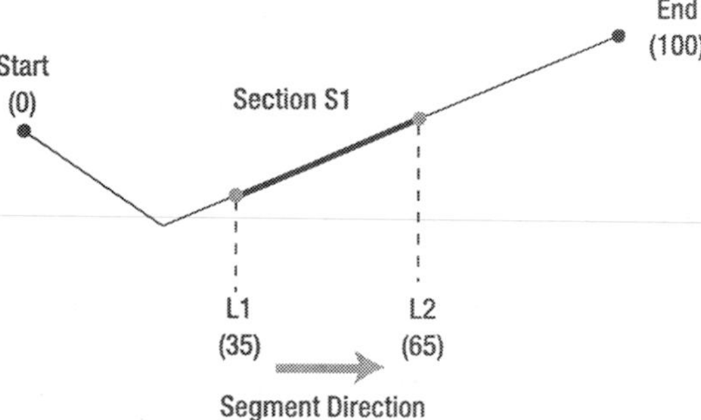

Figure B-6. *A linear referenced segment with dynamic segmentation*

Locations on this geometry can be described in terms of their measures on the geometry; for example, location L1 is at measure 35, and location L2 is at measure 65. Use this technique to represent *point events* such as accidents or road signs.

Sections are represented by specifying a start and end measure. In Figure B-6, section S1 is represented as having a start measure of 35 and end measure of 65 on the geometry. Use this technique to represent *line events* such as road works or road conditions.

You can now materialize locations and sections as new geometries using specific functions. The ability to generate points or line segments dynamically from measure information is called *dynamic segmentation*.

Note The measures on a line segment do not have to start at zero. For example, roads are typically modeled as multiple road segments, whereby each segment is a stretch of road between intersections. The end measure of one road segment is then usually carried on as the first measure of the next segment in sequence.

Measures do not have to represent distances: they can represent anything as long as all measures on a line segment are all increasing or decreasing. For example, they could represent the elapsed time on the route of a boat. This then allows you to find out where the boat was at a certain date and time.

Creating Linear Referenced Geometries

The easiest way to populate measures in a linear feature is by using the CONVERT_TO_LRS_GEOM function. This function takes as arguments an SDO_GEOMETRY object representing a linear feature and two numbers representing the measure values to be associated with the first and last vertices of the linear feature. The measure values for all intermediate vertices are linearly interpolated.

```
SQL> UPDATE road_segments SET geom =
SDO_LRS.CONVERT_TO_LRS_GEOM
(
  geom,
  0,   -- start measure value
  100  -- end measure value
);
```

You can also use the CONVERT_TO_LRS_LAYER function to convert a complete table. For example, here is how to LRS-enable the us_interstates table. You first take a copy of the table as us_interstates_lrs, together with its spatial metadata. Then you call the CONVERT_TO_LRS_LAYER function.

```
CREATE TABLE us_interstates_lrs AS
  SELECT * FROM us_interstates;
INSERT INTO user_sdo_geom_metadata
  SELECT 'US_INTERSTATES_LRS', column_name, diminfo, srid
  FROM  user_sdo_geom_metadata
  WHERE table_name = 'US_INTERSTATES';
DECLARE
  STATUS VARCHAR2(20);
BEGIN
  STATUS := SDO_LRS.CONVERT_TO_LRS_LAYER ('US_INTERSTATES_LRS', 'GEOM');
END;
/
```

Alternately, you can explicitly construct LRS geometries as follows: linear referenced geometries are stored in the SDO_GEOMETRY object just like regular lines. However, there are two exceptions: first, the SDO_GTYPE of an LRS geometry has additional information to indicate the measure dimension, and second, each point in the LRS geometry uses three ordinates (instead of two in the regular one): an x value, a y value, and an m value—the measure. First let's look at the changes for SDO_GTYPE in LRS geometries.

SDO_GTYPE in LRS Geometries

The geometry type attribute (SDO_GTYPE) described in Chapter 4 changes from D00T to DM0T. The second digit, M, specifies the position of the measure dimension. For instance, if this attribute is set to 3302, it means the following:

3 = Each point in the geometry uses three ordinates (x, y, m).

3 = The measure is in the third ordinate.

0 = Not used.

2 = This is a simple line string.

The presence of the digit 3 in the second position is what tells Oracle Spatial that this is an LRS-enabled line. A geometry with an SDO_GTYPE of 3002 is not an LRS-enabled line; it does contain three coordinates for each point (x, y, and something else), but the "something else" has no specific meaning to Oracle.

Constructing LRS Geometries

For example, the following SQL shows how to insert a (non-LRS) line segment into a database table:

```
INSERT INTO road_segments (id, geom) VALUES
(
  65328,
  SDO_GEOMETRY
  (
    2002,      -- SDO_GTYPE for regular geometries is of type DOOT (see chapter 4)
    8307, null,
    SDO_ELEM_INFO (1,2,1),
    SDO_ORDINATES
    (
      x1,y1,
      x2,y2,
      x3,y3,
      x4,y4,
      x5,y5,
      x6,y6,
      x7,y7,
      x8,y8,
      x9,y9
    )
  )
);
```

The same line segment with measures on shape points is inserted as follows:

```
INSERT INTO road_segments (id, geom) VALUES
(
  65328,
  SDO_GEOMETRY
  (
    3302,  -- SDO_GTYPE for LRS geometries is DMOT where M is the measure position
    8307, null,
    SDO_ELEM_INFO (1,2,1),
    SDO_ORDINATES
    (
      x1,y1, 20,  --  third number (in all following rows) is measure value
      x2,y2, null,
      x3,y3, null,
      x4,y4, 50,
      x5,y5, null,
      x6,y6, null,
      x7,y7,  100,
```

```
      x8,y8, null,
      x9,y9, 160
    )
  );
```

Note that some shape points have no explicit measure set; the measures are passed as NULL.

Metadata

The spatial metadata for a linear referenced layer must describe three dimensions: the x, the y, and the measure. For example, the SQL would look like the following:

```
INSERT INTO user_sdo_geom_metadata
  (table_name, column_name, diminfo, srid)
VALUES
(
  'ROAD_SEGMENTS',
  'GEOM',
  SDO_DIM_ARRAY
  (
    SDO_DIM_ELEMENT ('X', -180, 180, 1),
    SDO_DIM_ELEMENT ('Y', -90, 90, 1),
    SDO_DIM_ELEMENT ('M', 0, 1000, 1)
  ),
  8307
);
```

Spatial Indexes and Spatial Operators on LRS Geometries

Note that in the preceding example, the USER_SDO_GEOM_METADATA view specified three dimensions (in other words, three SDO_DIM_ELEMENTs in the DIMINFO attribute), one for the x, y, and m (measure) dimensions for the spatial layer corresponding to <road_segments, geom.>. To create a spatial index on the preceding spatial layer, use the same CREATE INDEX statement that you saw in Chapter 8. The following code shows the SQL:

```
SQL> CREATE INDEX roads_seg_sidx ON road_segments(geom)
INDEXTYPE IS MDSYS.SPATIAL_INDEX;
```

You can then use the spatial operators such as SDO_NN, SDO_WITHIN_DISTANCE, or SDO_RELATE on the geom column of the road_segments table. This column contains LRS geometries (that is, geometries populated with measure values), but the operators use only the x and y dimensions of the LRS geometries.

Dynamic Segmentation Operations

At the beginning of the appendix, you saw the principles of linear referencing, and we described the main dynamic segmentation operations: *clip*, *locate*, and *project*. Let's now examine how Oracle performs those operations.

Clip a Segment

This is the main dynamic segmentation function. Given a start and end measure, it extracts the section of a line between those two measures. Figure B-7 illustrates this process of extracting that part of the line between measures M1 and M2.

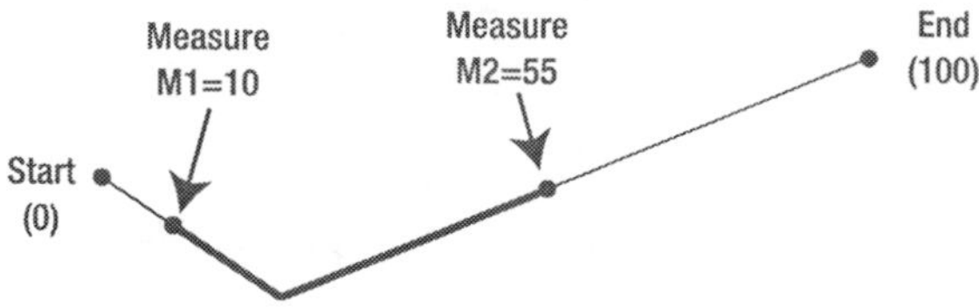

Figure B-7. *Clipping a line segment*

The following code shows how to use the `CLIP_GEOM_SEGMENT` function to perform this operation. This function takes an LRS geometry as the first argument and takes start and end measures (to use in clipping) as the second and third arguments.

```
SQL> SELECT SDO_LRS.CLIP_GEOM_SEGMENT
(
  geom,
  10,  -- measure value for the start of dynamic segment
  55   -- measure value for the end of dynamic segment
) new_lrs_geom
FROM road_segments;
```

Examples of Uses

Here are some examples of use:

- Extract the section of a street that will be closed to traffic because of road repairs.
- Extract the route that a boat followed on a certain day. The line is the route followed by the boat and measures represent time fixes. The start and end measures are the time stamp at the start and end of the day.

Locate a Point

Locating a point is similar to clipping, except it extracts a single point from the line. Given a measure, it returns the point located on a line at that measure. It can also position the point away from the line at a chosen offset. A positive offset locates the point on the left side of the line. A negative offset is on the right side of the line. Notion of left (right) implies left (right) of the geometry as you traverse from the start to the end of the geometry.

Figure B-8 shows how point P1 is located along a linear referenced segment from a measure and offset.

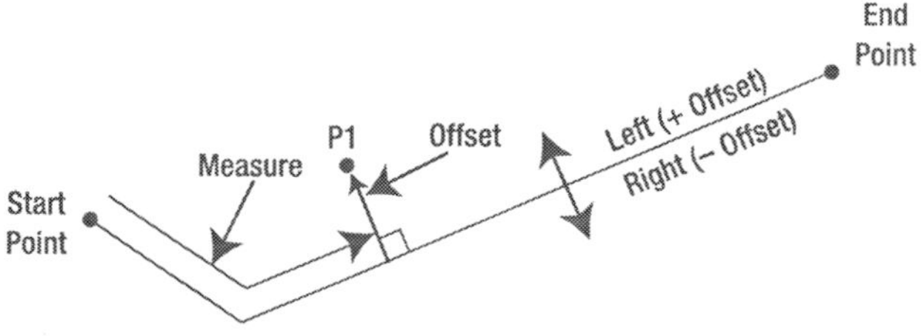

Figure B-8. *Locating a point on an LRS geometry*

The following code shows how to use the LOCATE_PT function to perform this operation. This function takes an LRS geometry as the first argument and a measure value as the second argument.

```
SQL> SELECT SDO_LRS.LOCATE_PT
(
  geom,
  55   -- measure value for the point to be located
) point_2d
  FROM road_segments;
```

Examples of Uses

Here are some examples of use:

- Locate a stop sign along a street. The measure indicates how far down the street the sign is located. The offset indicates how far on the left or right the sign is located.
- Find where a boat was on a certain date and time. The line is the route followed by the boat, with measures that represent time fixes. The measure of the point to locate is the time stamp to find.

Project a Point

This is the reverse of the locate operation: given a point and a line, it returns the measure of that point on the line. The point does not have to be on the line: the projection of a point on a line segment is the point on the segment that is on the perpendicular from the point and the geometric segment. Figure B-9 illustrates this.

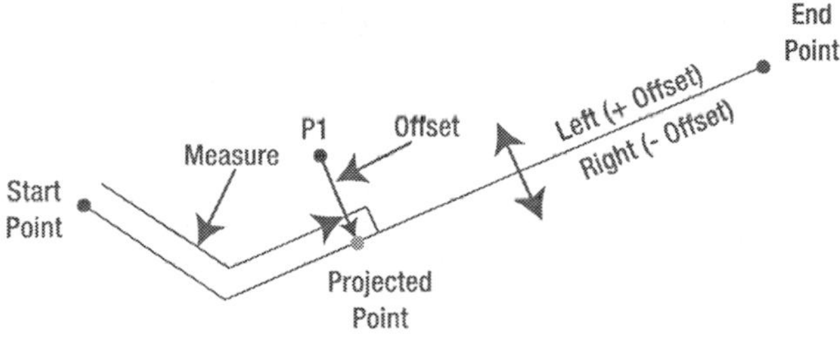

Figure B-9. *Projecting a point onto an LRS geometry*

The following code shows how to use the PROJECT_PT function to perform this operation. This function takes an LRS geometry as the first argument and a *reference point* (that is, the point to be projected) as the third argument.

```
SQL> SELECT SDO_LRS.PROJECT_PT
(
  geom,
  SDO_GEOMETRY(2003, 8307, SDO_POINT(-76, 45, NULL), NULL, NULL)   -- ref. point
) projected_pt
FROM road_segments;
```

The preceding SQL statement returns the point on the LRS geometry where the reference point is projected. You can combine the preceding code with the GET_MEASURE function to obtain the measure value for the projected point as follows:

```
SQL> SELECT SDO_LRS.GET_MEASURE
(
  SDO_LRS.PROJECT_PT
  (
    geom,
    SDO_GEOMETRY(2003, 8307, SDO_POINT(-76, 45, NULL), NULL, NULL)   -- ref point
  )  -- projected_pt
)
FROM road_segments;
```

Examples of Uses

Here are some examples of use:

- A car breaks down while traveling on a highway. The current location of the car (collected by the onboard GPS) is sent to a service center. A "projection" query returns the position of the car as a distance along the highway. The offset indicates the side of the road.

Intersecting LRS Segments with Standard Geometries

The SDO_GEOM.SDO_INTERSECTION() function you saw in Chapter 9 can be used to clip a line at the boundaries of a polygon. You can use that function, for example, to clip the section of an interstate at the border of a county.

The SDO_LRS.LRS_INTERSECTION() function behaves the same way, except it returns an LRS geometry; in other words, it also returns the measures of the points at which the interstate crosses the county boundary. You can then use other LRS functions to extract the exact location and measures of the points where the road intersects the county boundary.

The following example illustrates the process. It first computes the LRS intersection of I-25 and county El Paso in Colorado. Then it returns the measures of the I-25 as it crosses the boundary of the county.

```
SQL>
SELECT SDO_LRS.GEOM_SEGMENT_START_MEASURE (clip_geom),
SDO_LRS.GEOM_SEGMENT_END_MEASURE (clip_geom)
FROM (
  SELECT SDO_LRS.LRS_INTERSECTION (i.geom, c.geom, 0.5) clip_geom
  FROM us_interstates_lrs i, us_counties c
  WHERE i.interstate ='I25'
  AND   c.county = 'El Paso'
  AND   c.state_abrv = 'CO'
);
```

Validation of LRS Segments

Oracle provides several functions to determine whether an LRS geometry or measure value for a given segment is valid and whether the measure value is valid for a given segment using the functions VALID_GEOM_SEGMENT, VALID_MEASURE, and VALID_LRS_PT. Alternately, you can directly invoke VALIDATE_GEOMETRY_WITH_CONTEXT, described in Chapter 5, to validate an LRS geometry. The latter function invokes the corresponding LRS-specific validation functions internally.

Dynamic Segmentation on 3D Geometries

The dynamic segmentation operations can also operate on three-dimensional lines, that is, on lines with points defined by *x*, *y*, and *z* coordinates. They use the *z* values to compute measures, or in other words, they consider the slope of the lines.

These operations are particularly useful for working with lines where slope is important, such as water or gas pipes.

The 3D LRS operations are implemented using the same functions and procedures as listed previously, except that the function names end with the `_3D` suffix. For example, function `CLIP_GEOM_SEGMENT_3D` clips a line in 3D.

The lines must be defined as 3D geometries with measures: each point contains *x*, *y*, and *z* coordinates followed by a *measure*. The `SDO_GTYPE` for such a geometry will be 4402, where the second 4 indicates that the measure is in the last position.

Other Operations

There are a number of other operations on LRS geometries. These include concatenation, splitting, and offsetting.

Concatenate

Given two lines with measures, this returns a single line with measures. The second line may be in a different direction, and measures do not have to be continuous with those of the first line. The resulting line has measures adjusted from the two input lines. Figure B-10 illustrates this process.

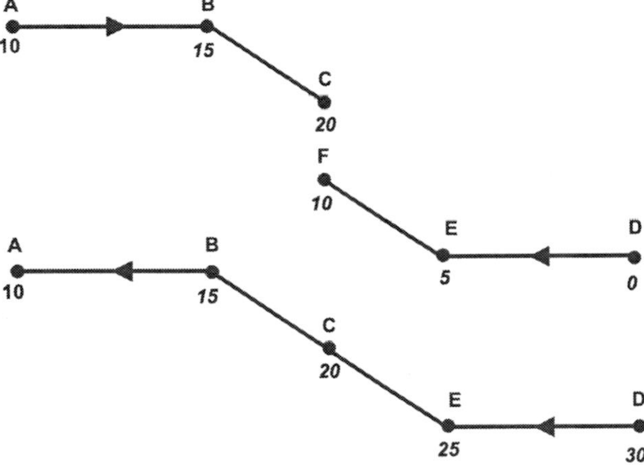

Figure B-10. *Concatenating two LRS segments*

The top of Figure B-10 shows two segments: `ABC` and `DEF`. The two segments are geometrically connected; this is, point `C` and point `F` have the same coordinates. Both segments have ascending measures, but the orientation of segment `DEF` is the opposite of that of segment `ABC`.

The bottom of the figure shows the result of concatenating the two segments. You now have a single line. The measures have been harmonized; they are ascending according to the orientation of the first segment (`ABC`). In addition, the orientation of the second segment (`DEF`) has been reversed to match that of the first segment.

Split

This splits a line into two lines at a chosen measure.

Offset

This is the same as the clip operation, but the resulting clipped line is shifted at a chosen offset (left or right from the input line).

Summary

In this appendix, we described how to associate measures with a linear feature stored in an SDO_GEOMETRY object. You can refer to locations on a linear feature using these measure values. This type of referencing, called *linear referencing*, is popular in the transportation and utility industries.

The Linear Referencing component in Oracle provides a powerful set of functionality to store, manage, and operate on linear referenced geometries. In this appendix, we presented a brief overview of this functionality, including how to convert from standard two-dimensional coordinates/geometries to linear referenced geometries, and vice versa.

APPENDIX C

Topology Data Model in Oracle

In the preceding chapters, we described how to store and perform analysis on SDO_GEOMETRY data in an Oracle database. In most cases, these geometries represent different *spatial features* such as roads, rivers, land parcels, city boundaries, property boundaries, and business locations. These features can be stored as columns in one or more tables in Oracle. For instance, an application may store land parcels and rivers that share edges as different features in different tables. Figure C-1 shows an example of this. Figure C-2 shows an example of what happens if a shared edge e is updated.

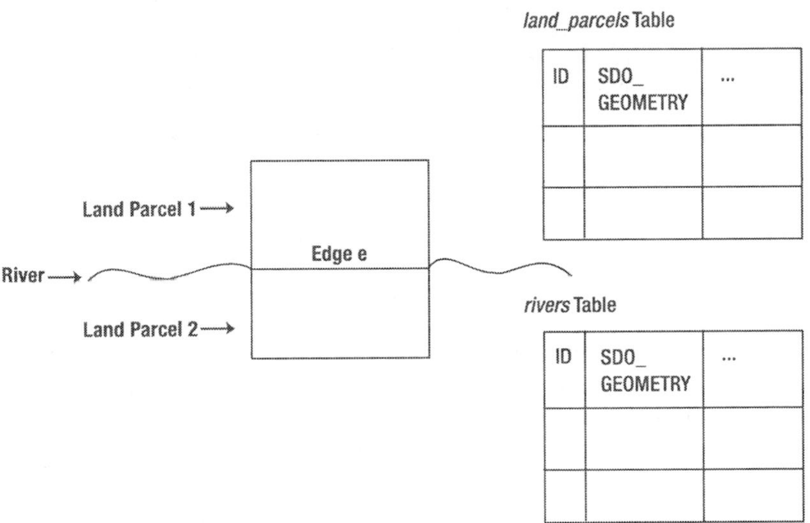

Figure C-1. *Spatial features of different types are stored in one or more tables as* SDO_GEOMETRY *objects. Features can share boundaries.*

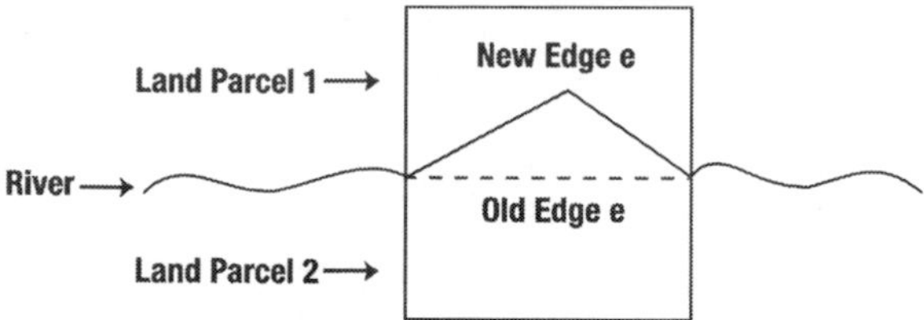

Figure C-2. *Updating edge e as the river changes course. Geometries for Land Parcel 1, Land Parcel 2, and River need to be updated in the* `land_parcels` *and* `rivers` *tables.*

In this appendix, we describe an alternate model, the Topology Data Model, for effective management of shared geometry features.

Sharing Boundaries

How can you effectively share and manage boundaries between multiple features? You can accomplish this using Oracle's Topology Data Model. The Topology Data Model stores the individual features using three topological primitive elements: nodes, edges, and faces. These elements, described next, are internally stored as `SDO_GEOMETRY` objects. Figure C-3 shows the topological elements that constitute the features of Figure C-1.

- *Node*: This is a point geometry that is shared by one or more features. A node can be an island (that is, not connected to any other node), or it can be connected to one or more edges (nodes). In Figure C-3, the topology has four nodes: n1, n2, n3, and n4.
- *Edge*: This is a line-string geometry that connects two nodes in a topology. Note that this line string may contain multiple vertices that are not considered as individual nodes in the topology. That means it may contain multiple line segments (connecting those vertices). For instance, edge e3 in Figure C-3 is a line string consisting of two vertical lines and a horizontal line. Likewise, edge e4 consists of two vertical lines and a horizontal line.
- *Face*: This is the polygonal area surrounded by a closed set (ring) of edges. The face is always a single polygon containing just one outer ring and any number of inner rings. The topology of Figure C-3 shows two faces: f1 and f2. Face f1 is the area bounded by edge e and e4 (connecting nodes n2 and n3). Face f2 is the area bounded by edges e and e3.

Note that the features in the corresponding feature tables are not stored as `SDO_GEOMETRY` objects. Instead, they are stored as `SDO_TOPO_GEOMETRY` objects, which we will describe later in this appendix. These objects specify a list of underlying topological elements to construct the feature. For instance, the River feature in Figure C-3 is specified as a list of edges: e1, e, and e2 (note that in this high-level model, the River feature is modeled as a line string, that is, a set of edges; a more detailed model can store the River feature as a set of polygonal faces). The Land Parcel 1 feature is represented using the face f1, and the Land Parcel 2 feature is represented using the face f2.

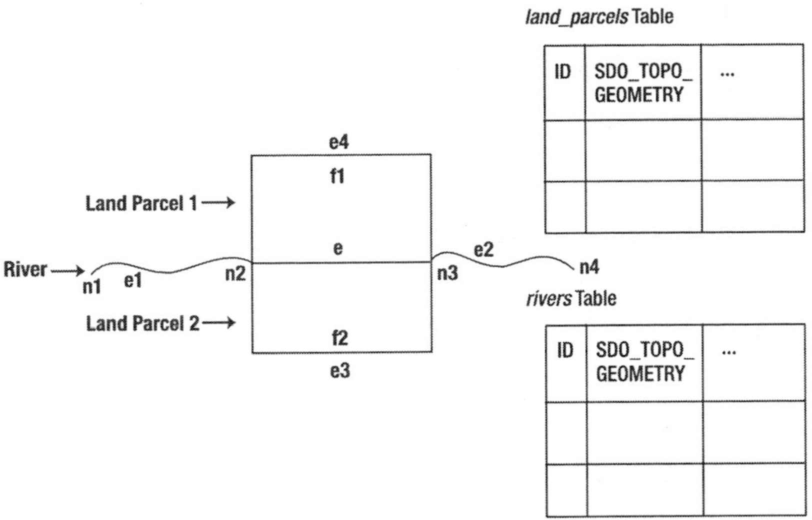

Figure C-3. *Representing features using the Topology Data Model. Each feature is represented using an* SDO_TOPO_GEOMETRY *object consisting of underlying topological elements such as nodes, edges, and faces.*

Benefits of the Topology Data Model

What are the advantages of representing spatial features using the Topology Data Model as opposed to storing them using simple SDO_GEOMETRY data? The benefits include the following:

- *No redundant storage of data*: For instance, edge e in Figure C-3, which is shared among multiple features, is stored just once. All features that include edge e just store (direct or indirect) references to the edge via the SDO_TOPO_GEOMETRY.
- *Data consistency*: Updating a topological element *implicitly defines* updates to all features that share the element. For instance, if edge e is modified (the associated geometry is updated), the Land Parcel and River features that share edge e are implicitly updated. This avoids possible data inconsistencies due to multiple updates at feature layers.
- *Fast topological relationships*: Since the topology is precomputed, the identification of all features that satisfy a specified *topological relationship* with a query feature is easy and efficient. The types of topological relationships that can be specified include TOUCH, ANYINTERACT, OVERLAPBDYDISJOINT, OVERLAPBDYINTERSECT, CONTAINS, INSIDE, COVERS, COVEREDBY, and EQUALS. We discussed these relationships in detail in Chapter 8. Note that topological relationships are preserved even if the coordinate space is stretched or twisted. Distance relationships are not topological relationships.

Because of these benefits, the Topology Data Model is widely used in GIS applications for land management, where the primary focus is on data consistency, nonredundant storage, and topological queries.

Storing a Topology Data Model in Oracle

Oracle Spatial allows users to share, update, and manage information between multiple feature layers using an associated topology. Figure C-4 shows the schematic for storing a topology constructed from two feature layers, land_parcels and rivers. As shown in Figure C-3, the features are decomposed into the constituent topological primitive elements, such as nodes, edges, and faces. The node elements are stored in the <topology-name>_NODE$ table, simply referred to as the NODE$ table. Likewise, the edge elements are stored in the corresponding EDGE$ table, and the face elements are stored in the corresponding FACE$ table. The RELATION$ table stores as individual rows all the constituent primitive elements for an SDO_TOPO_GEOMETRY in a feature layer. Oracle also refers to the SDO_TOPO_GEOMETRY as a *topology geometry*. As shown in Figure C-4, each element of the topology geometry is identified in the RELATION$ table by the ID of the feature layer (TG_LAYER_ID), the ID of that feature (TG_ID), the type of the element (TOPO_TYPE), and the ID of the element (TOPO_ID).

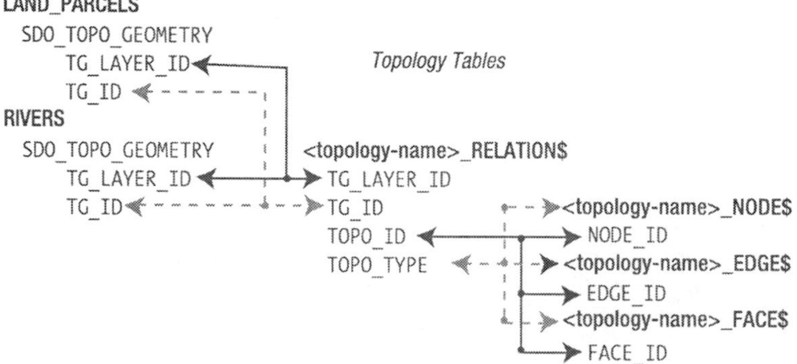

Figure C-4. *Associating a topology with two feature layers,* land_parcels *and* rivers

The topology model consists of the following tables:

- NODE$ table: This table stores all the node elements in the topology. This table has the following fields:
    - NODE_ID: This is a unique ID for the node.
    - EDGE_ID: This is the ID for the edge (if any) that has this node as a start_node or as an end_node.
    - FACE_ID: This is the ID for the face containing this node if the node is an island node.
    - GEOMETRY: This is a point-type SDO_GEOMETRY to represent the location of the node.
- EDGE$ table: This table stores all the edge elements in the topology. Edges have a direction. As a result, they have a start_node and an end_node. This table has the following fields:
    - EDGE_ID: This is a unique ID for the edge.
    - START_NODE_ID and END_NODE_ID: These are the IDs of the starting and ending nodes of the edge.
    - LEFT_FACE_ID and RIGHT_FACE_ID: These are the IDs of the left and right faces.
    - NEXT_LEFT_EDGE_ID, PREV_LEFT_EDGE_ID: These are the IDs of the *next* and the *previous* edges in the *left* face (face to the left side identified by LEFT_FACE_ID) of the current edge.
    - NEXT_RIGHT_EDGE_ID, and PREV_RIGHT_EDGE_ID: These are the IDs of the next and the previous edges in the *right* face (face to right side identified by RIGHT_FACE_ID) of the current edge.
    - GEOMETRY: This is a line string–type SDO_GEOMETRY that represents the shape and location of the edge. Note that for the edge, only the first and last vertices correspond to nodes in the topology. All other vertices do not have a corresponding node.

- FACE$ table: This table stores all the face elements in the topology. Faces can also store one or more *island* nodes and *island* edges. These island nodes and *island* edges are not on the boundary of the face but are inside the face. This table has the following fields:
  - FACE_ID: This is a unique ID for the face.
  - BOUNDARY_EDGE_ID: This is the ID of an edge on the boundary of the face. All other edges can be traced from this edge (by following the next and previous edge pointers for this edge).
  - ISLAND_EDGE_LIST and ISLAND_NODE_LIST: These are lists of IDs for the island edges and the island nodes.
  - MBR_GEOMETRY: This is a minimum bounding rectangle that encloses the face. Note that the geometry of the face is not explicitly stored here. The geometry is traced by constructing the boundary using the BOUNDARY_EDGE_ID.
- RELATION$ table: This table stores the topological primitive elements for each feature in an associated feature table. Note that the feature objects are stored using the SDO_TOPO_GEOMETRY object, which is also referred to as the *topology geometry* (TG) object. Spatial automatically generates an ID for each such TG object, called TG_ID. Each feature layer is referenced using a number called TG_LAYER_ID. This table has the following fields:
  - TG_LAYER_ID: This is the ID of the feature layer.
  - TG_ID: This is the ID of the feature object in the preceding feature layer.
  - TOPO_ID: This is the ID of the topological element associated with the feature object.
  - TOPO_TYPE: This is the type of the topological element: 1 for NODE, 2 for EDGE, and 3 for FACE.

The following are other attributes of the topology:

- For each feature object in a feature table that is associated with the topology, the RELATION$ table stores *N* rows if there are *N* associated topological elements. For instance, the Rivers feature in Figure C-3 has four nodes and three edges, so it will have seven rows in the RELATION$ table.
- The feature tables store the feature using the SDO_TOPO_GEOMETRY data type. Like the SDO_GEOMETRY data type, SDO_TOPO_GEOMETRY also captures the shape and location of a feature. But unlike SDO_GEOMETRY, SDO_TOPO_GEOMETRY does not store the coordinates explicitly. Instead, it stores only references to topological elements from which the shape can be derived. This data type has the following structure:
  - TG_TYPE: The type of topology (that is, feature) geometry; 1 indicates a point or multipoint, 2 indicates a line or multiline, 3 indicates a polygon or multipolygon, and 4 indicates a heterogeneous collection.
  - TG_ID: A unique ID generated by Spatial for this feature.
  - TG_LAYER_ID: A unique ID assigned by Spatial for this feature layer (which is stored as an SDO_TOPO_GEOMETRY column in a database table). This ID is assigned when the layer is associated with the topology.
  - TOPOLOGY_ID: A unique ID of the current topology. This ID is assigned by Spatial when the topology is created.

Figure C-5 shows the association between feature tables and topology tables. Given a feature ID (TG_ID) along with the feature table (TG_LAYER_ID), you can identify the topological elements that constitute this feature. The shape of this feature can be derived from these elements. The SDO_TOPO_GEOMETRY has a method to return the shape as an SDO_GEOMETRY object.

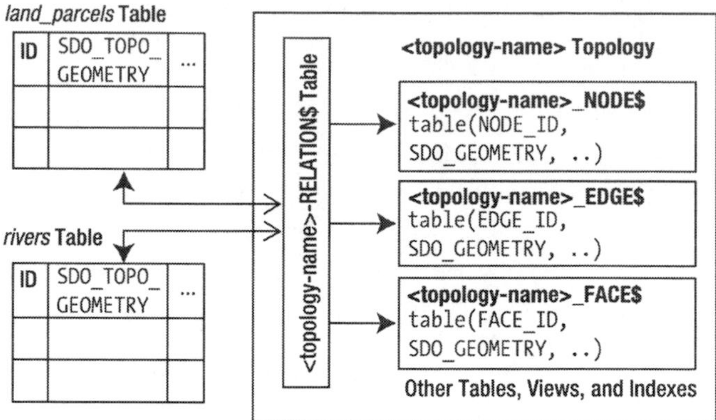

Figure C-5. *Association between feature tables and topology tables*

Given this background on how topology is stored in Oracle, next we will cover how to create a topology, associate feature tables with the topology, populate the tables, and query the topology.

Operating on a Topology in Oracle

Oracle Spatial provides the following functionality to operate on the Topology Data Model:

- Creating a new topology in the database. This includes creating new tables for storing topological primitive elements (nodes, edges, and faces) associated with a topology.
- Associating feature layers (tables) with a topology.
- Inserting new features into feature tables using the topological elements already in the topology.
- Updating the underlying topological elements.
- Querying features for topological relationships.
- Other functions to drop a topology, drop the association of a feature table with a topology, and so on.

Oracle Spatial provides both PL/SQL and Java APIs for the preceding operations. In this appendix, we will discuss only the PL/SQL functions. The `SDO_TOPO` package includes these functions, each of which we will describe in brief. For a detailed discussion, please consult *Oracle Spatial User's Guide*.

Creating a Topology

The `CREATE_TOPOLOGY` procedure creates a new topology in the database. This function takes a name for the topology, the tolerance to be used (see Chapter 3 for a discussion of tolerance), and the Spatial Reference ID (SRID) for the topology data. Currently, all data in a topology have to be in the same spatial reference (coordinate) system. The following SQL shows an example:

```
SQL> EXECUTE SDO_TOPO.CREATE_TOPOLOGY('CITY_DATA', 0.00000005, NULL);
```

This function creates the associated topology tables such as `CITY_DATA_NODE$`, `CITY_DATA_EDGE$`, and `CITY_DATA_FACE$`. We will refer to these tables as `NODE$`, `EDGE$`, and `FACE$` when there is no ambiguity. Since the SRID (the third parameter) is `NULL`, the spatial reference system will be the default (Euclidean coordinate system in two-dimensional space).

Populating a Topology

Note that the user has to populate the topology—that is, the related tables such as NODE$, EDGE$, and FACE$. You can bulk load the data into these tables using Oracle utilities such as SQL*Loader, Import/Export, and Data Pump. You can easily construct the topological element data for the example in Figure C-1 and load the data into these tables. We leave this as an exercise for the reader.

Associating a Feature Layer with a Topology

Once the topology is populated (that is, the topological element information is filled in), you can create a feature layer as follows:

```
SQL> CREATE TABLE land_parcels
(
  parcel_name     VARCHAR2(30) PRIMARY KEY,
  feature         SDO_TOPO_GEOMETRY
);
```

Another feature layer, streets, can store each street as a topology geometry.

```
SQL> CREATE TABLE streets
(
  street_name         VARCHAR2(30) PRIMARY KEY,
  feature             SDO_TOPO_GEOMETRY
);
```

You can then associate these feature layers with a topology using the ADD_TOPO_GEOMETRY_LAYER function in the SDO_TOPO package. This function takes the topology name as the first argument, the feature table name and the column name as the second and third arguments, and the type of the features (whether they are points, lines, or polygons) as the fourth argument. The following SQL shows how to add the land_parcels feature layer, which has just polygon data, to the city_data topology:

```
SQL>
BEGIN
-- Add the feature layer for land parcels
SDO_TOPO.ADD_TOPO_GEOMETRY_LAYER
('CITY_DATA',  -- name of the topology
 'LAND_PARCELS', 'FEATURE', 'POLYGON' - names of the feature table, column, & type
);

);

-- Add the feature layer for the street network
SDO_TOPO.ADD_TOPO_GEOMETRY_LAYER
('CITY_DATA', -- name of the topology
 'STREETS', 'FEATURE', 'POLYGON'  -- names of the feature table, column, and type
);

END;
/
```

After adding all feature layers to a topology, you want set up indexes on the NODE$, FACE$, and EDGE$ tables. Oracle will automatically do this when you execute the INITIALIZE_METADATA procedure, as shown in the following SQL:

```
SQL>  EXECUTE SDO_TOPO.INITIALIZE_METADATA('CITY_DATA');
```

Inserting, Updating, and Populating Feature Layers

Now, we'll show how to insert features into the feature layers. The features are of type SDO_TOPO_GEOMETRY, which has the following structure:

```
SQL> DESCRIBE sdo_topo_geometry;
 Name                                      Null?    Type
 ----------------------------------------- -------- ----------------------------
 TG_TYPE                                            NUMBER
 TG_ID                                              NUMBER
 TG_LAYER_ID                                        NUMBER
 TOPOLOGY_ID                                        NUMBER
...method descriptions omitted
```

Among the attributes listed are the ID of the topology (TOPOLOGY_ID) and the ID of the feature layer (TG_LAYER_ID). You can identify the TOPOLOGY_ID and the TG_LAYER_ID for a feature layer in a specific topology by consulting the USER_SDO_TOPO_METADATA view. The following SQL returns the TG_LAYER_ID for the LAND_PARCELS FEATURE layer in the CITY_DATA topology:

```
SQL>  SELECT topology_id, tg_layer_id FROM USER_SDO_TOPO_METADATA
          WHERE topology = 'CITY_DATA' and table_name='LAND_PARCELS'
            and column_name='FEATURE';
```

But what value should you give to the TG_ID in the SDO_TOPO_GEOMETRY object? Instead of creating the SDO_TOPO_GEOMETRY by yourself, you should use one of several predefined constructor functions that will then populate the TG_ID and other attributes for a new feature geometry. The following SQL shows an example using one such constructor function for SDO_TOPO_GEOMETRY. This function uses the IDs and types of topological primitive elements such as nodes, edges, and faces stored in the NODE$, EDGE$, and FACE$ tables, respectively.

```
SQL> INSERT INTO land_parcels (parcel_name, feature) VALUES
(
  'P1',
  SDO_TOPO_GEOMETRY -- construct using topology elements(no explicit geometry)
  (
    'CITY_DATA',  -- topology_name
    3,            -- topo_geometry_type for polygon (or multipolygon)
    1,            -- feature layer (TG_LAYER) ID representing 'Land Parcels',
    SDO_TOPO_OBJECT_ARRAY -- Array of 2 topo objects (two faces)
    (
      SDO_TOPO_OBJECT  -- Constructor for the object
      (
        3,        -- element ID (i.e., FACE_ID) from the associated topology
        3         -- element TYPE is 3 (i.e., a FACE)
      ),
      SDO_TOPO_OBJECT -- Constructor for topo object
      (
        6,        -- element ID (i.e., FACE_ID) from the associated topology
        3         -- element type is 3 (i.e., a FACE)
      )
    )
  )
);
```

The feature is a multipolygon composed of two faces, one with ID 3 and another with ID 6. These two face elements that constitute the feature are specified using the SDO_TOPO_OBJECT_ARRAY in the preceding SDO_TOPO_GEOMETRY constructor. This method will populate the RELATION$ table appropriately and insert a row in the land_parcels table with the TG_ID and TG_LAYER_ID filled appropriately (Spatial generated) in the SDO_TOPO_GEOMETRY column.

Updating features in a feature table can be processed by invoking the constructor method to generate the SDO_TOPO_GEOMETRY object.

Updating Topological Elements

As we mentioned earlier, the Topology Data Model is ideal for propagating updates on the underlying topology elements to the feature layers. For instance, if you update the geometry of edge e (with an EDGE_ID of 10, for instance) from g to g1, then this will be reflected in all features that contain edge e.

Oracle Spatial provides a variety of functions such as ADD_NODE, ADD_EDGE, and SPLIT_EDGE in the SDO_TOPO package to add, update, or delete topological primitive elements. Since topological primitive elements (such as nodes, edges, and faces) are shared across multiple features, updates from multiple applications are likely to conflict. Although Oracle implicitly obtains appropriate locks for such concurrent updates, because of efficiency reasons, typical topology applications would like to *lock* at a coarse granularity of a region of interest. To facilitate such coarse-grained updates, you can use the TopoMap object. A TopoMap object is a subset of a specified topology defined by a region of interest. The TopoMap object can be created and manipulated in PL/SQL using the SDO_TOPO_MAP package (in Java, the equivalent API is the TopoMap class). To perform updates using the TopoMap object, you need to perform following *sequence* of operations:

1. Initialize a TopoMap object.
2. Perform edits on the TopoMap object.
3. Finish the processing with the TopoMap object.

We'll illustrate this operation sequence with a typical topology update operation; say you want to add (and/or edit) a street called "Fifth Street" in Manhattan, New York, part of the CITY_DATA topology. You can do this by initializing a TopoMap object, performing edits, and committing the changes.

Initialization of TopoMap Object

Now say you want to call the TopoMap object "Manhattan Topology." To create the TopoMap object based on the CITY_DATA topology, you can use the following SQL:

```
SQL> EXEC SDO_TOPO_MAP.CREATE_TOPO_MAP('CITY_DATA', 'Manhattan Topology');
```

Next, you specify the extent of the TopoMap object and load it into the TopoMap cache by specifying the minimum and maximum longitude/latitude values for New York City. Let's say min_lat and max_lat are the minimum and maximum latitude values and min_long and max_long are the minimum and the maximum longitude values for the Manhattan region.

```
SQL>  EXEC SDO_TOPO_MAP.LOAD_TOPO_MAP(
                 'Manhattan Topology',
                 min_long, min_lat, max_long, max_lat);
```

The LOAD_TOPO_MAP procedure not only loads the subset of the topology for the Manhattan region into the TopoMap cache object; it also locks this region (and the associated edges, nodes, and faces that intersect with the extent of the specified region) and reserves the region for updates *exclusively* by the current application. This means any other application that needs to update topological elements in the same (Manhattan) region will be blocked until your application releases the locks (by committing or rolling back the TopoMap changes).

Editing the TopoMap Object

Now that you have exclusive access to the topological elements in the Manhattan region, you want to perform your edits on the topological elements in the loaded TopoMap object.

So, start by inserting the new segment for the Fifth Street in the Manhattan TopoMap object. Since this is a street feature, you can add the feature to the streets table using the CREATE_FEATURE function, as illustrated in the following SQL:

```
SQL> INSERT INTO STREETS  (street_name, feature)
          SELECT 'Fifth Street, Segment11',
               SDO_TOPO_MAP.CREATE_FEATURE(
                   'Manhattan Topology',
                   'ROAD_NETWORK',  -- Table where the feature is stored,
                   'FEATURE',  -- Column in the table storing the feature
                   -- Next,  specify the geometry for the Fifth street, segment 11
                   -- as line from x1,y1 to x2,y2
                   SDO_GEOMETRY(
                       2002, 8307, NULL,
                       SDO_ELEMENT_INFO_ARRAY(1,2,1),
                       SDO_ORDINATE_ARRAY(x1,y,1, x2,y,2)
                   )
               ) ;
```

Instead of updating the feature layers, you can directly manipulate the primitive topological elements such as nodes, edges, and faces. The editing functions you can use have self-explanatory names such as ADD_NODE, ADD_EDGE, REMOVE_NODE, and REMOVE_EDGE. (You can look up the full list of such editing functions in the “Oracle Topology Data Model” manual.) The following code adds the edge geometry gm between nodes 1 and 2:

```
SQL> EXEC SDO_TOPO_MAP.ADD_EDGE('Manhattan Topology',  1, 2, gm);
```

After performing your edits on the topological elements, you can validate the topology to make sure your edits did not violate any topological constraints:

```
SQL> EXEC SDO_TOPO_MAP.VALIDATE('Manhattan Topology');
```

Finishing Up with the TopoMap Object

After performing your edits on the TopoMap object, you can commit the changes to the underlying topology in the database, as shown in the following SQL:

```
SQL> EXEC SDO_TOPO_MAP.COMMIT_TOPO_MAP('Manhattan Topology');
```

This function will commit the changes and release all locks on the topological elements in the underlying topology. Other applications can now load them into their TopoMap objects and update them.

In some cases, you just want to discard your changes in the TopoMap object. The right way to do this is to use the ROLLBACK_TOPO_MAP function, as shown in the following SQL. This will release associated locks on the topological elements.

```
SQL> EXEC SDO_TOPO_MAP.ROLLBACK_TOPO_MAP('Manhattan Topology');
```

Finally, don't forget to drop the TopoMap object using the drop_topo_map procedure. This will release the memory associated with this “cache” object.

```
SQL> EXEC SDO_TOPO_MAP.DROP_TOPO_MAP('Manhattan Topology');
```

You can find more details on the SDO_TOPO_MAP PL/SQL API or the equivalent TopoMap Java API in the Oracle documentation titled “Spatial Topology and Network Data Models.”

Querying for Topological Relationships

Oracle Spatial provides a number of operators to query the features tables. These include the SDO_FILTER and SDO_RELATE operators discussed in Chapter 8. The SDO_RELATE operator specifies the desired topological relationship as a third parameter. If the desired relationship is ANYINTERACT (that is, any type of interaction other than being disjoint; see Chapter 8 for more details), then the SDO_ANYINTERACT operator can also be used. The following SQL shows an example of how to retrieve all Land Parcel features (features from the land_parcels table) that interact with River features:

```
SQL> SELECT a.parcel_name FROM land_parcels a, rivers b
WHERE SDO_ANYINTERACT (a.feature, b.feature) = 'TRUE';
```

Note that both the first and second arguments are SDO_TOPO_GEOMETRY objects. In some cases, the query window (the second argument to the SDO_ANYINTERACT operator in the preceding SQL) need not be a feature geometry that is part of the topology. Instead, it can be a query window represented using an SDO_GEOMETRY object. To support such queries, all the operators also allow the second (that is, the query) argument to be an SDO_GEOMETRY object. The following SQL shows an example of how to retrieve all Land Parcel features (features from the land_parcels table) that interact with a specified SDO_GEOMETRY query window:

```
SQL> SELECT a.parcel_name FROM land_parcels a
WHERE SDO_ANYINTERACT
(
  a.feature,
  SDO_GEOMETRY
  (
    2003,NULL, NULL,
    SDO_ELEM_INFO_ARRAY(1,1003,3)
    SDO_ORDINATE_ARRAY(14,20,15,22)
  )
) = 'TRUE';
```

Both queries use the topological information to identify the features that satisfy the query criterion. Since the topological information is precomputed and already stored persistently in the database, such queries will be answered efficiently.

Hierarchical Feature Model

The Oracle Topology Data Model supports a hierarchical feature model constructed in a bottom-up manner from the layers built on the topological primitive elements (nodes, edges, and faces). This means if you consider the Land Parcel and River features as Level-0 features that are derived/ constructed from the topological primitive elements (nodes, edges, and faces), you can construct Level-1 features using these Level-0 features. You can accomplish this by specifying Level-0 feature IDs (TGIDs) in the SDO_TOPO_GEOMETRY constructors (for the Level-1 features). In general, Level-*N* features can be derived from Level-(*N* – 1) features.

This hierarchical modeling of data is very useful in several applications. For instance, you can model the U.S. Census Bureau data hierarchically as follows:

- The Census *blocks* are Level-0 features constructed using the faces in a topological representation.
- The Census *blockgroups* are Level-1 features derived from the Census *blocks*.
- The Census *tracts* are Level-2 features derived from the *blockgroups*.
- The Census *counties* are Level-3 features derived from the *tracts*.

This hierarchy can be extended to multiple levels until we have the United States as a Level-7 feature derived from a list of regions.

You can construct similar examples for other countries. For instance, you could use data from the Ordnance Survey to construct such a hierarchy for Great Britain.

Summary

Oracle Spatial provides the Topology Data Model to store feature layers that share boundaries. This topology model is very effective in maintaining data consistency, in reducing or eliminating storage redundancy, and in identifying topological relationships. Updates to an underlying topology model can be reflected in the feature layers without any explicit updates to the feature tables. Since topological relationships are precomputed, features interacting with a query feature can be answered very efficiently. Distance queries such as nearest-neighbor queries, though, cannot be answered efficiently using this model. Spatial also provides validation routines to detect inconsistencies in the data. This functionality is widely used in land management and other GIS applications.

APPENDIX D

Storing Raster Data in Oracle

Real-world spatial features can be represented in either a *vector* or *raster* model. In a vector model, each spatial feature (a river, a road, a shop location, and so on) is represented as an object with geometric features (the shape and location) and a set of attributes. In Chapter 4, we discussed the SDO_GEOMETRY data type to store such vector spatial data. To represent the complexity of a city, for instance, you may need myriad points, lines, and polygons. A raster model, on the other hand, associates collections of *pixels* or *cells* to spatial entities by making a discrete approximation of spatial features into grid cells. Each cell takes on a single value. You can consider a raster object as a two-dimensional array or grid of regularly spaced cells. Some common examples of raster objects include satellite images, aerial photos, and digital elevation models.

A road in a vector model corresponds to a line object described by road attributes (for example, the road type, the road size, the pavement type, the last maintenance date, and so on). The same road in a raster model would be a collection of grid cells sharing the same value specific to that road. Vector and raster models are, in theory, equivalent: it is always possible to extract a vector model from a raster one, and vice versa. In practice, they have different uses and varying abilities to represent real-world spatial objects. Vector models are the most commonly used and are appropriate whenever you want to identify and describe spatial objects with their relationships. With vectors, it is easy to find overlaps between objects, create buffers around objects, calculate the distance between objects, and so on. Although the same operations can also be performed on the basis of a raster model, the raster model (and raster analysis) has the following differences:

- *Raster data* is typically used to model *spatially continuous* data such as elevations or environmental data, for instance, to display a digital elevation of land or to model the diffusion of a pollutant from a chemical spill. Currently, the bulk of raster data corresponds to satellite images, aerial pictures, digital terrain/elevation models, grid data, and medical images. Most of the rest is vector data.
- *Raster analysis* consists of spatial processing on a grid or a two-dimensional array/grid of cells. Typically the analysis includes map/matrix algebra operations such as overlay, addition and subtraction of multiple rasters, or neighborhood/clustering analysis functions on individual rasters.

To illustrate the difference between the raster and vector models, let's consider an example. In Figure D-1, (a) shows a small section of an urban area as seen from an aircraft, whereas (b) and (c) show the corresponding vector and raster representations (simplified here for convenience). As you can see, both models are capable of representing the same picture. In a vector model, objects are easy to identify and are modeled using points, lines, and other geometric shapes. In a raster model, the spatial patterns are more visible, and the objects are models using different-colored cells or pixels.

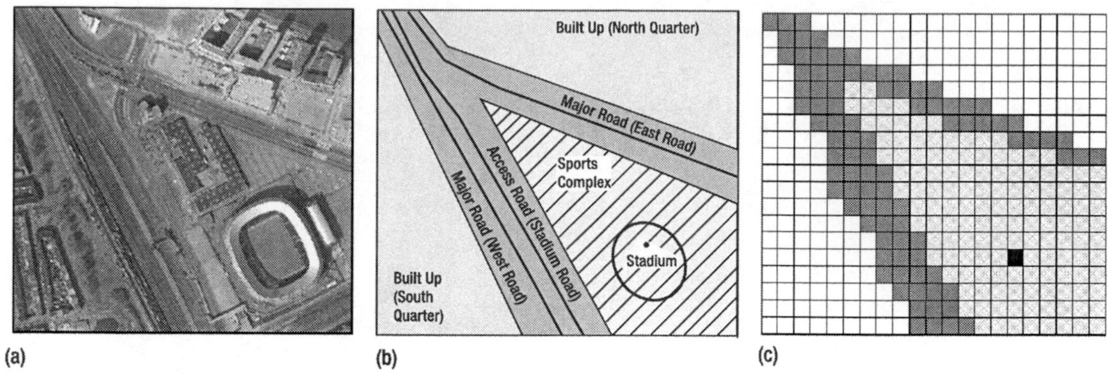

Figure D-1. *(a) An aerial photograph of a small section of an urban area, (b) a vector representation, and (c) a raster representation of the spatial objects in the picture shown in Figure D-1 (b)*

In this book, we primarily focus on how to store, analyze, and visualize spatial data in the vector model. The SDO_GEOMETRY (see Chapter 4 for more information) provides an easy mechanism to store spatial data in the vector format. The spatial indexes and geometry functions (see Chapters 8 and 9 for more information) provide an appropriate mechanism to search/analyze these vector data, and Oracle MapViewer (see Chapter 11 for more information) enables visualization of vector data. Typically in a business application, you will store the locations of businesses and customers as vector data. However, as shown in Figure D-1, you may also want to store and visualize aerial photographs of your businesses and other entities in addition to the vector data.

In this appendix, we describe how to work with "raster" spatial data in Oracle. Specifically, we examine the GeoRaster component in Oracle, which stores raster data using the SDO_GEORASTER data type and provides preliminary analysis functions (such as generating pyramids and subsetting). We then describe how to visualize the stored raster data using Oracle MapViewer. Note that GeoRaster enables only the storage and visualization of raster data (and very basic analysis). Once you store the raster data in Oracle, you can use a variety of third-party tools to perform more comprehensive analysis operations, such as map algebra, that are typical on raster data.

The SDO_GEORASTER Data Type

Oracle Spatial provides the SDO_GEORASTER data type to store spatial data in raster format. Conceptually, an SDO_GEORASTER object is an *N*-dimensional matrix of *cells*. The dimensions include a row dimension, a column dimension, and other optional dimensions. These optional dimensions can contain a *band* dimension to represent multiband or hyperspectral images, and/or a temporal dimension.

For most raster data, such as an RGB image, there will be a row, a column, and a band (or color) dimension. Each cell in an RGB image is addressed by (row, column, band) and specifies an intensity value for the corresponding pixel (row, column) in the specified color/band, as shown in Figure D-2.

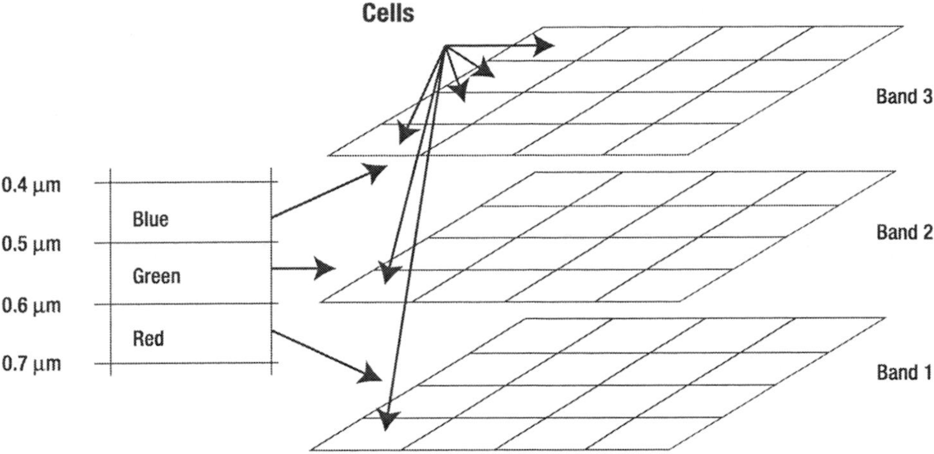

Figure D-2. *Bands in an RGB image*

The cell values in a GeoRaster object are stored in a *raster data table*, which we will explain later in this appendix. In addition to the raster information, SDO_GEORASTER could also capture information about which region on the earth's surface is represented by this raster object. This makes the raster object georeferenced.

The SQL in Listing D-1 shows how to add an SDO_GEORASTER column to the branches table. The idea is to store the aerial photograph for each branch (along with its location).

Listing D-1. *Altering the* branches *Table to Add the* georaster *Column*

```
ALTER TABLE branches ADD ( georaster    SDO_GEORASTER);
```

Next, we will explain the structure of the SDO_GEORASTER type, as shown in Listing D-2. Typically, a GeoRaster object can be very large. In the following sections, we will describe how to specify different storage options. If you just want a general idea of how to store raster objects, you can skip to the section "Populating SDO_GEORASTER Columns."

Listing D-2. *Structure of* SDO_GEORASTER

```
SQL> DESC SDO_GEORASTER;
 Name                                      Null?     Type
 ----------------------------------------- -------- ----------------------
 RASTERTYPE                                          NUMBER
 SPATIALEXTENT                                       MDSYS.SDO_GEOMETRY
 RASTERDATATABLE                                     VARCHAR2(32)
 RASTERID                                            NUMBER
 METADATA                                            SYS.XMLTYPE
```

The following list describes each attribute's purpose:

- `RASTERTYPE`: This specifies the type of the raster object. It is a number of the form `[d][b][t]01`.
    - `[d]` is the number of spatial dimensions. If the spatial dimensions include x,y,z in the model space that correspond to row, column, depth in the cell-coordinate space, then this number is set to 3. Currently only two spatial dimensions (x and y) are supported (that is, `d` should be set to 2).
    - `[b]` is either 0 or 1. It is 0 if the raster object has a single band, and it is 1 if the raster object has more than one band.
    - `[t]` specifies whether there is a temporal dimension. Currently it is set to 0 (not used).
- `SPATIALEXTENT`: This is an `SDO_GEOMETRY` object storing the minimum bounding rectangle (MBR) of the raster object on the earth's surface. This spatial extent is represented in a *model coordinate system* to model the earth's surface.
- `RASTERDATATABLE`: This is the name of the table that stores the cell information for the raster object. The two-dimensional row-column matrix of cells is referred to as the *cell coordinate system.*
- `RASTERID`: Combined with the `RASTERDATATABLE`, this is a unique identifier for the raster object.
- `METADATA`: This is an XML object that stores information regarding the raster object. For instance, it stores information on how to convert from the model coordinate system (for example, the spatial extent) to the cell coordinate system.

Storage for SDO_GEORASTER Data

Each `SDO_GEORASTER` object may be subdivided into multiple blocks, and the cell values in each block are stored as a binary large object (BLOB) in the raster data table. Figure D-3 shows how `SDO_GEORASTER` objects are internally stored using the raster data table. You could also have additional tables such as the Value-Attribute Table (VAT) to store a meaning/interpretation for each cell value. For instance, the value of 1 for a cell value in the red band indicates a light red color, and value of 3 indicates a dark red color.

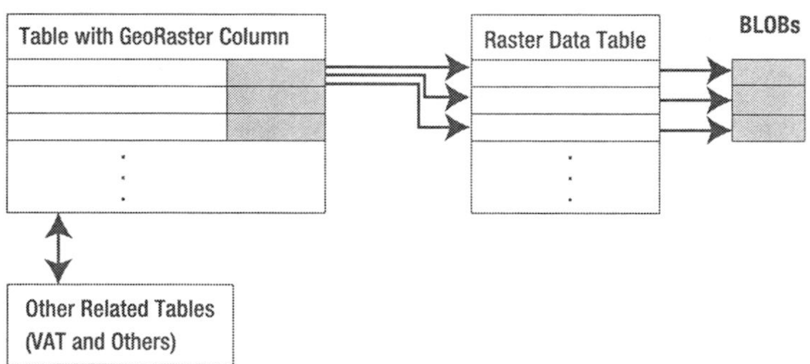

Figure D-3. *Storing* `SDO_GEORASTER` *objects in an Oracle table. Each* `SDO_GEORASTER` *object is internally stored using the BLOBs in the raster data table.*

Creating the Raster Data Table

The cell information for a raster object is stored in a raster data table associated with the GeoRaster object. Next, we will cover the raster data table. The raster data table is a table of the SDO_RASTER data type. This table splits a raster object into blocks and stores the two-dimensional matrix of cell values (indexed by rows and columns) for each block as a RASTERBLOCK object. This table needs to be created explicitly by the user. The table will be associated with a GeoRaster object using the SDO_GEOR.INIT procedure, which we describe later in this appendix. Listing D-3 shows how to create the raster data table.

Listing D-3. *Creating the Raster Data Table*

```
CREATE TABLE branches_rdt OF SDO_RASTER
(
  PRIMARY KEY
  (
    RASTERID, PYRAMIDLEVEL, BANDBLOCKNUMBER,
    ROWBLOCKNUMBER, COLUMNBLOCKNUMBER
  )
)
LOB(RASTERBLOCK) STORE AS (NOCACHE NOLOGGING);
```

The RASTERID attribute corresponds to the unique identifier for the raster object. We will explain other fields of the SDO_RASTER data type as we proceed in this section. The raster object is divided into smaller pieces called *blocks*. The cell values in each block are stored in the RASTERBLOCK.

Blocking a Large Raster Object

A raster object could consist of a large number of cells. In such cases, a more scalable approach is to divide the object into smaller pieces, called *blocks*, so that queries and updates can operate on blocks instead of the entire object. The cell values in each block are stored together as a single RASTERBLOCK (BLOB) object. Figure D-4 shows an example for a single-band raster object.

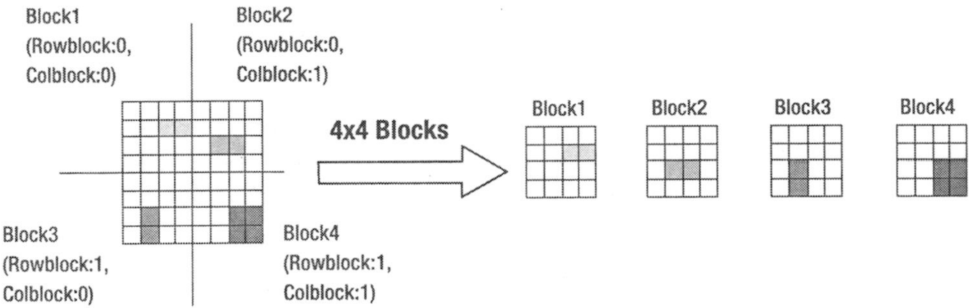

Figure D-4. *Blocking to store a 16-by-16 raster object using 4-by-4 blocks*

Note that each block is uniquely addressed by rowblocknumber and columnblocknumber (and bandblocknumber, if it exists) fields.

Interleaving of Bands in a Raster Object

What if you have multiple bands, as in Figure D-2? Let's name the cell values (by the band number for simplicity), as shown in Figure D-5. In what order do you store the cell values for each band? This is specified by the *interleaving* of bands.

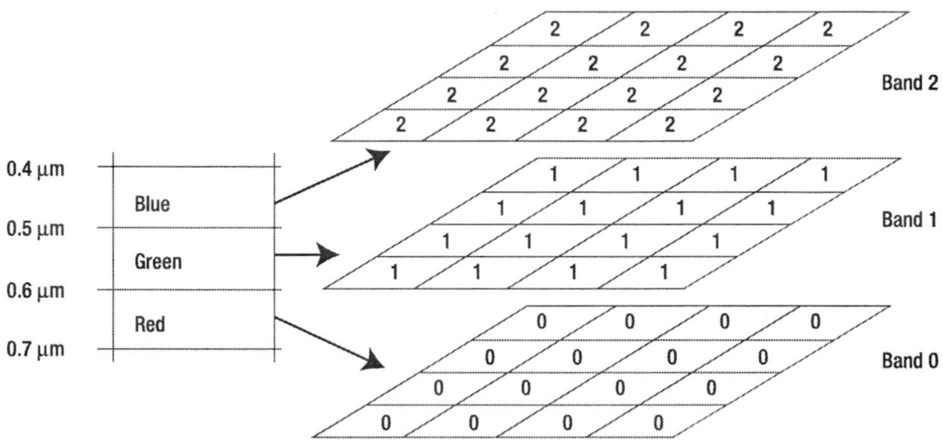

Figure D-5. *An RGB image (three-band raster object)*

You can store (cell values for) each band in sequence (that is, one after another). This interleaving is referred to as *Band Sequential* (BSQ). Figure D-6 shows the storage of cell values for this interleaving.

0	0	0	0	0	0	0	0	0	0	0	0	0	0	0	0	1	1	1	1	1	1	1	1	1	1	1	1	1	1
1	1	2	2	2	2	2	2	2	2	2	2	2	2	2	2	2	2												

Figure D-6. *BSQ interleaving for the RGB image in Figure D-5*

Alternatively, you can alternate the rows (lines) of each band. This means you store the row (that is, all four cells of the row) of band 0, then the row of band 1, and then the row of band 2. This interleaving is called *Band Interleaved by Line* (BIL). Figure D-7 shows the BIL interleaved storage of cell values for Figure D-5.

0	0	0	0	1	1	1	1	2	2	2	2	0	0	0	0	1	1	1	1	2	2	2	2	0	0	0	0	1	1
1	1	2	2	2	2	0	0	0	0	1	1	1	1	2	2	2	2												

Figure D-7. *BIL interleaving for the RGB image in Figure D-5*

A third alternative is to store each cell of each band one after another. This interleaving is called *Band Interleaved by Pixel* (BIP). Figure D-8 shows the BIP interleaved storage of cell values for Figure D-5.

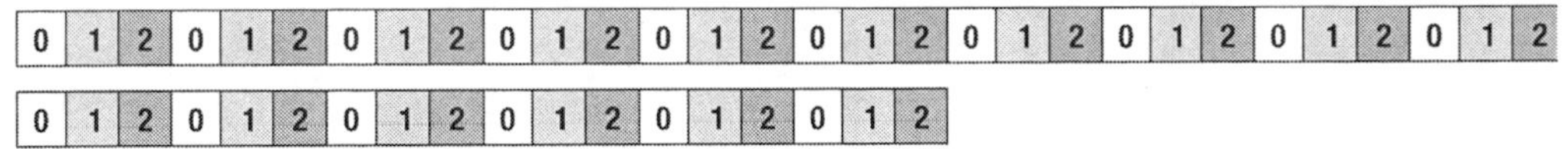

Figure D-8. *Band Interleaved by Pixel interleaving for the RGB image in Figure D-5*

Which of these interleaving options should you use? It depends on the application. For instance, if the application expects to retrieve one band at a time, you would achieve optimal performance with BSQ interleaving.

Metadata in SDO_GEORASTER Data

The last attribute of SDO_GEORASTER is an XMLType to store the metadata associated with a GeoRaster object. This metadata can include information regarding the blocking, interleaving, and so on. The metadata may also include parameters to convert from the model coordinate system to the cell coordinate system of the GeoRaster object. We refer you to Oracle Spatial GeoRaster documentation for a list of attributes that you can specify in the metadata field of SDO_GEORASTER.

Populating SDO_GEORASTER Columns

How do you populate the SDO_GEORASTER columns? As we described earlier, you create a column of the SDO_GEORASTER type and a raster data table to contain the cell data for the raster objects. You may also need to create a trigger on the table containing the SDO_GEORASTER column so that any updates, inserts, or deletes to this column are internally propagated to the raster data table. Listing D-4 shows how to create this trigger.

Listing D-4. *Creating a Trigger to Populate the Raster Data Table*

```
SQL> call SDO_GEOR_UTL.createDMLTrigger('BRANCHES','GEORASTER');
```

Starting in Oracle Database 10*g* Release 2 (that is, version 10.2), you no longer need to create this trigger. Instead, the trigger is implicitly created when you initialize a GeoRaster object. We'll illustrate how to initialize a GeoRaster object in the branches table. Listing D-5 shows the SQL involved. Note that the SDO_GEOR.INIT function takes the raster data table name, branches_rdt, and returns a SDO_GEORASTER object with the raster data table information populated.

Listing D-5. *Initializing the* georaster *Column in the* branches *Table*

```
SQL> UPDATE branches SET georaster = SDO_GEOR.INIT('BRANCHES_RDT') WHERE id=1;
```

Once you initialize the GeoRaster object, you can upload images from TIFF or other standard image formats into (or out of) the GeoRaster object using the SDO_GEOR.IMPORTFROM (or the SDO_GEOR.EXPORTTO) procedure. This procedure invokes internal adaptors to read from/write to different image formats such as TIFF, GeoTIFF, JPEG, GIF, PNG, BMP, or an ESRI world file.

The SDO_GEOR.IMPORTFROM procedure takes a GeoRaster object, the blocksize parameters, the type, and the location of the image file being uploaded into the GeoRaster object (along with some additional parameters). The PL/SQL block in Listing D-6 shows an example of loading the r1.tif image into the branches table for georaster id=1.

Listing D-6. *Populating the Georaster Column with a TIFF Image*

```
DECLARE
  g SDO_GEORASTER;
BEGIN

  -- Select the georaster column
  SELECT georaster INTO g FROM branches WHERE id = 1 FOR UPDATE;

  -- Import into the georaster object
  SDO_GEOR.IMPORTFROM
  (
    g,  'blocksize=(512,512)', 'TIFF', 'file',
    '/usr/rasters/r1.tif'  -- specify the name and location of the image file
  );

  -- update the column
  UPDATE branches SET georaster = g WHERE id = 1;
  COMMIT;
END;
/
```

Note You can export/import only GeoTIFF, JPEG, GIF, BMP, and PNG files. For other formats, you should use third-party GeoRaster ETL tools.

Before performing the preceding import procedure, you may want to ensure that the “spatial” schema and the MDSYS schema both have “read” permission to read the specified file into the database. You can grant this permission using the DBMS_JAVA.GRANT_PERMISSION procedure, as shown in Listing D-7. The first parameter specifies the schema name, the second parameter specifies the permission type, the third parameter specifies the file name, and the fourth parameter specifies the permission action.

Listing D-7. *Granting Permissions to Import Data into a GeoRaster Column*

```
SQL> CONNECT system/manager  -- Replace with password for system
-- Grant permission to user 'spatial'
SQL> CALL DBMS_JAVA.GRANT_PERMISSION( 'SPATIAL', 'SYS:java.io.FilePermission',
'/usr/rasters/r1.tif', 'read');
-- Grant permission to the MDSYS schema
SQL> CALL DBMS_JAVA.GRANT_PERMISSION( 'MDSYS', 'SYS:java.io.FilePermission',
'/usr/rasters/r1.tif', 'read');
SQL> connect spatial/spatial; -- connect back as spatial
```

Manipulating Raster Objects

Once raster objects are stored in the SDO_GEORASTER columns of a table, Oracle Spatial allows you to perform a number of operations on each of these objects. These operations include the following:

- Generating pyramids, an operation that allows you to generate raster objects of different resolutions
- Subsetting, which involves clipping the GeoRaster by band or specified region

- Georeferencing, which involves identifying a portion of an image by specifying the coordinates in the model coordinate system
- Changing the interleaving or blocking for a raster object
- Copying a raster object to another
- Generating the spatial extent of an image or a subset returned
- Creating a mosaic of all the GeoRaster data in a column of type `SDO_GEORASTER`

Oracle Spatial also provides additional functionality for advanced processing and viewing and loading GeoRaster objects. You can find a full reference for all the operations in the *Oracle Spatial GeoRaster Developer's Guide*. In the rest of this appendix, we present a synopsis for a subset of the operations on GeoRaster objects.

Generating Pyramids

In some cases, the raster objects are too large and have a high resolution. How do you reduce the size? You reduce the resolution by specifying a pyramid level. Figure D-9 shows an example of low-resolution objects created at different pyramid levels from the original raw object.

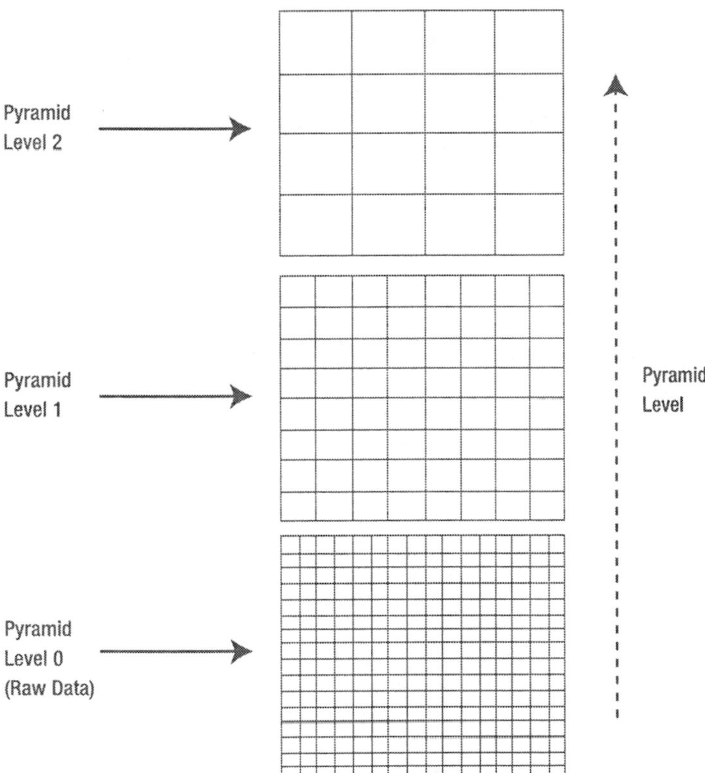

Figure D-9. *Generating raster objects at different resolutions. The higher the pyramid level, the lower the resolution (and the smaller the storage requirement of the object).*

You can generate pyramids for a raster object using the SDO_GEOR.GENERATEPYRAMID procedure. The SQL in Listing D-8 shows an example for generating pyramids for four levels. Note that the second parameter, 'rlevel=4', specifies the number of pyramid levels to generate. You can specify other parameters such as 'resampling=NN' to use a specific algorithm such as nearest-neighbor to create the pyramids.

Listing D-8. *Generating Pyramids for a GeoRaster Object in the* branches *Table*

```
DECLARE
  geor sdo_georaster;
BEGIN
  SELECT georaster INTO geor FROM branches WHERE id = 1 FOR UPDATE;

  -- Generate four levels of pyramids
  SDO_GEOR.GENERATEPYRAMID(geor, 'rlevel=4');

  UPDATE branches SET georaster = geor WHERE id = 1;
  COMMIT; -- commit and release the lock on the row
END;
/
```

Subsetting

Another important operation is subsetting. Here, you can clip the GeoRaster data by band and/or regions. For instance, you can select only the raw data (pyramid level 0) corresponding to band 0 for the specified window (in cell space), as shown in Listing D-9.

Listing D-9. *Subsetting a GeoRaster Object*

```
DECLARE
  g SDO_GEORASTER;
  b BLOB;
BEGIN
  SELECT georaster INTO g FROM branches WHERE id = 1;
  DBMS_LOB.CREATETEMPORARY(b, true);
  SDO_GEOR.GETRASTERSUBSET
  (
    georaster => g,
    pyramidlevel => 0,
    window => sdo_number_array(0,0,699,899),
    bandnumbers => '0',
    rasterBlob => b
  );
 END;
 /
```

The subset of blocks is returned as BLOB.

Georeferencing

Georeferencing associates real-world (referred to as *model space*) coordinates with a GeoRaster object. For georeferenced raster objects, Oracle Spatial enables you to specify real-world coordinates and convert them into cell coordinates in a GeoRaster object. Figure D-10 shows an example of a GeoRaster object covering a region that contains a national park and a restaurant. The national park will be represented by a subset of pixels in the cell coordinate system of the GeoRaster object. The restaurant will be represented by a single pixel in the GeoRaster object.

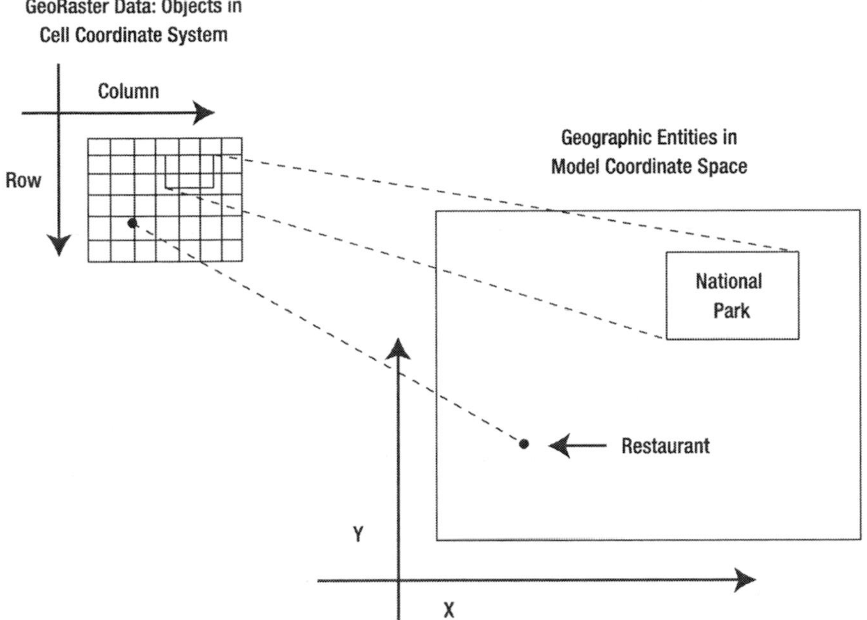

Figure D-10. *Georeferencing is the process of relating objects in model coordinate system (*`x,y` *space) to the objects in cell coordinate system. Oracle supports such model-to-cell space transformations for georeferenced raster objects.*

So, if `x,y` are the real-world (model space) coordinates, then you can identify the `row, col` of the GeoRaster object that corresponds to these coordinates using the following transformation, called the *affine transformation*:

```
row = a + b * x + c * y
col = d + e * x + f * y
```

The parameters *a, b, c, d, e,* and *f* are transformation coefficients and are stored in the metadata associated with the GeoRaster object. Note that determining the right values for these parameters is part of georeferencing. Such georeferencing is not supported by Oracle. Instead, Oracle supports the transformations between model space and cell space for georeferenced GeoRaster objects. Oracle provides the `SDO_GEOR.GEOREFERENCE` function to associate this transformation (generating coefficients *a, b, c, d, e,* and *f* from input ESRI WorldFile coefficients A, B, C, D, E, and F) with a GeoRaster object. Listing D-10 shows the example SQL.

Listing D-10. *Georeferencing a GeoRaster Object*

```
DECLARE
  g SDO_GEORASTER;
  b BLOB;
BEGIN
  SELECT georaster INTO g FROM branches WHERE id = 1  FOR UPDATE;
  SDO_GEOR.GEOREFERENCE
  (
    georaster => g,
    srid => 8307,
    modelcoordinatelocation => 0,   -- 0 for center of the cell
```

```
    xCoefficients => sdo_number_array(
        30, 0, 410000.0),    -- values for ESRI World File Coefficients ➥
        A, B, and C
    yCoefficients => sdo_number_array(
        0, -30, 3759000.0) -- values for ESRI World File Coefficients ➥
        D, E, and F
  );
  UPDATE branches SET georaster = g WHERE id = 1;
  COMMIT; -- commit and release lock on the row
END;
/
```

In Oracle 10*g*, affine transformations as described previously were the only supported transformations supported for georeferencing. In Oracle 11*g*, a much more powerful, complex, and generic functional-fitting transformation model is incorporated. You can use this model to specify transformations to a cell coordinate space (with `row, col` dimensions) from a two-dimensional (`x,y`) or a three-dimensional (`x,y,z`) ground coordinate system. This model allows you to define the following relationships to derive the `row, col` coordinates in cell coordinate space from the `x,y,z` ground coordinates.

```
row =  p(x,y,z) / q(x,y,z)
col = r(x,y,z) / s(x,y,z)
```

where `p,q,r` are polynomials on `x,y,z` of the form

$$\sum_{i=0}^{m1}\sum_{j=0}^{m2}\sum_{k=0}^{m3} a_{ijk} x^i y^j z^k$$

This functional-fitting transformation model is quite generic: by setting the various parameters (coefficients, powers) appropriately, it can support popular georeferencing transformations such as affine transformations, direct linear transformations (DLT), and rational polynomial coefficients (RPC). You can consult the *Oracle Spatial GeoRaster Developer's Guide* for full details on this model.

Attaching Bitmap Masks

What if you want to *mask* a sensitive portion of an image from being displayed in visualization applications? In GeoRaster, you can attach/detach such masks to the GeoRaster object: attaching a mask will physically store the bitmap as part of the GeoRaster itself (as opposed to manipulating the display in the renderer/visualizer application such as MapViewer). Given a GeoRaster object G of M by N cells, you associate to it a *bitmap* GeoRaster object B of exactly M by N cells. The bitmap object will be of just one band and will attach with each cell a value of 1 if you want to display the corresponding cell from GeoRaster G or a value of 0 if the corresponding cell value from GeoRaster G is not to be displayed. Once you define the bitmap GeoRaster B, you can attach it with GeoRaster G using the PL/SQL procedure shown in Listing D-11.

Listing D-11. *Attaching Bitmap GeoRaster B with GeoRaster G*

```
BEGIN
  SDO_GEOR.SETBITMAPMASK(
     geoRaster => G,          -- IN/OUT parameter: Input  for which mask B is applied
     layerNumber => 0,        -- IN parameter:  0 means all layers,
                              -- >0 implies a specific layer
     mask => B );             -- IN parameter: bitmap GeoRaster
END;
/
```

Note that the example in Listing D-11 attaches the bitmap mask with all layers (bands) of the GeoRaster by specifying the value of 0 for `layerNumber` in the `SETBITMAPMASK` procedure. However, if you want to attach the bitmap GeoRaster with only a specific layer, say layer 2, then you specify that value, 2, in the second, that is, the `layerNumber` parameter. In general, a bitmap mask is a special 1-bit-deep rectangular raster grid with each pixel having the value of 0 or 1. It is used to define an irregularly shaped region inside another image.

After you create a GeoRaster object, you may want to inspect the bitmap masks attached to it. You can use the `GETBITMAPMASK` function for this purpose. You can look up the details on this and other bitmap-related procedures in the *Oracle Spatial GeoRaster Developer's Guide.*

Registering NODATA Values

Let's say you are modeling the vegetation for a region using appropriate values for the cells of a GeoRaster object O. Let the number 1 to 100 denote different types of vegetation. What if you do not have any data for certain cells? You can give those cells a special value, say 1000, and designate this value as a `NODATA` value using the `SDO_GEOR.ADDNODATA` procedure. Note that the semantics of this `NODATA` value are similar to that of the `NULL` in SQL (but the `NODATA` value can be application-defined, and your applications can define multiple `NODATA` values). Listing D-12 shows the code to designate a value of 1000 as a `NODATA` value in a GeoRaster object.

Listing D-12. *Associating a* `NODATA` *Value of 1000 with GeoRaster G*

```
BEGIN
  SDO_GEOR.ADDNODATA(
      geoRaster => G,              -- IN/OUT parameter: Input  GeoRaster
      layerNumber => 0,            -- IN parameter:  0 means all layers,
                   >0,             -- implies a specific layer
      nodata => 1000 );            -- IN parameter: value that is treated as a NODATA
END;
/
```

Note that the Listing D-12 associates the `nodata` value with all layers (bands) of the GeoRaster by specifying the value of 0 for `layerNumber` in the previous procedure. However, if you want to associate the `nodata` value with only a specific layer, say layer 2, then you specify that value, 2, in the second, that is, the `layerNumber` parameter.

Instead of specifying a single value as a `NODATA` value, you can designate multiple *ranges* of values, say, 101–200, 301–330, as `NODATA` values. You can do this by specifying the third parameter in the `ADDNODATA` procedure as a `VARRAY` of `SDO_RANGE` type (specifying a lower bound and an upper bound for range; only lower bound is inclusive). Listing D-13 shows the corresponding PL/SQL code.

Listing D-13. *Associating a Set of* `NODATA` *Value Ranges with GeoRaster G*

```
BEGIN
  SDO_GEOR.ADDNODATA(
     geoRaster => G,            -- IN/OUT parameter: Input GeoRaster
     layerNumber => 0,          -- IN parameter:  0 means all layers,
                                -- >0 implies a specific layer
     nodata => SDO_RANGE_ARRAY(SDO_RANGE(101,200), SDO_RANGE(301,330)); END;
/
```

You can use the related `getnodata` and `deletenodata` procedures to retrieve and delete values associated with a GeoRaster object.

Using Compression in GeoRaster

As the number of GeoRaster objects and their sizes keep increasing, a useful feature that you want to exploit is compression of the stored rasters. Oracle provides two types of native compression to reduce storage space requirements for GeoRaster objects: JPEG (JPEG-B or JPEG-F) and DEFLATE. With both types, each block is compressed individually as a distinct raster representation; when a compressed GeoRaster object is decompressed, each block is decompressed individually.

There are no separate procedures for compressing and decompressing a GeoRaster object. Instead, compression is implicitly performed when you specify the `compression=<type>` keyword in the `storage` parameter of any of the following GeoRaster procedures: `SDO_GEOR.changeFormatCopy`, `SDO_GEOR.getRasterData`, `SDO_GEOR.getRasterSubset`, `SDO_GEOR.importFrom`, `SDO_GEOR.mosaic`, `SDO_GEOR.scaleCopy`, and `SDO_GEOR.subset`. Figure D-11 illustrates how these procedures use the `compression` keyword. Regardless of whether the input is compressed, the procedures always return the output in the user-specified compression format. Oracle allows you to specify one of the following keywords for the `compression` parameter.

- `JPEG-B`: Applies JPEG-B compression
- `JPEG-F`: Applies JPEG-F compression
- `DEFLATE`: Uses DEFLATE compression
- `NULL`: Uses decompression

Notice that the `NULL` value is used to return decompressed object in the output (if the input object is in a compressed format). If the compression parameter is not specified, then the output is returned in the same format as the input.

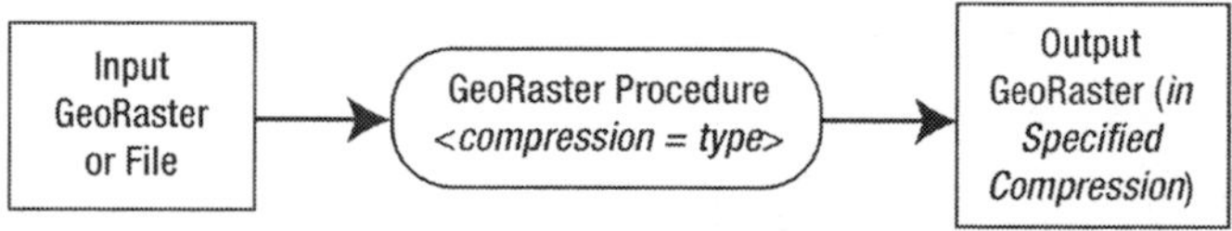

Figure D-11. *Using the* `compression` *parameter in a GeoRaster procedure*

For instance, let's say you want to store the imported image in Listing D-6 as a compressed JPEG-B GeoRaster object. To accomplish this, you modify the code of Listing D-6 by specifying `compression=JPEG-B` in the "storage" parameter of the `importFrom` procedure. Listing D-14 shows the modified code. Oracle will then load the image into the GeoRaster format and compress each block of the GeoRaster using JPEG-B compression. Later, when you retrieve a subset of the image using `getRasterSubset`, you can specify the `compression` parameter to perform a different compression or decompression (if `compression=null`).

Listing D-14. *Specifying JPEG-B Compression When Populating the Georaster Column with a TIFF Image*

```
DECLARE
  g SDO_GEORASTER;
BEGIN

  -- Select the georaster column
  SELECT georaster INTO g FROM branches WHERE id = 1 FOR UPDATE;

  -- Import into the georaster object
  SDO_GEOR.IMPORTFROM
```

```
  (
    g,
    'blocksize=(512,512), compression=JPEG-B',
     -- Specify compression type of JPEG-B
    'TIFF', 'file',
    '/usr/rasters/r1.tif'  -- specify the name and location of the image file
  );

  -- update the column
  UPDATE branches SET georaster = g WHERE id = 1;
  COMMIT; -- commit and release locks
END;
/
```

Visualizing Raster Data in Oracle MapViewer

Once you store raster data in Oracle, you can visualize the data using Oracle MapViewer version 10.1.2[1] (or the client-side GeoRasterViewer tool, which is not discussed in this appendix). To visualize GeoRaster data, MapViewer uses the GeoRaster themes. Before you can use MapViewer with the GeoRaster themes, you must perform the following actions with the GeoRaster data:

1. Georeference the GeoRaster data to establish a relationship between cell coordinates of the GeoRaster data and the real-world ground coordinates (or some other local coordinates). See Listing D-10 for an example.
2. Generate or define the spatial extent (footprint) associated with the raster data. You can do this by using the `GENERATESPATIALEXTENT` function as shown in the SQL in Listing D-15. (Observe that to refer to the `spatialextent` attribute of the `georaster` column of the `branches` table, you need to specify an alias `'b'` for the table.)

   Listing D-15. *Generating and Populating the Spatial Extent of the* `georaster` *Column*

   ```
   DECLARE
     extent SDO_GEOMETRY;
   BEGIN
     SELECT SDO_GEOR.GENERATESPATIALEXTENT(a.georaster) INTO extent
            FROM branches b WHERE b.id=1 FOR UPDATE;
     UPDATE branches b SET b.georaster.spatialextent = extent WHERE b.id=1;
     COMMIT;
   END;
   /
   ```

3. Insert a row into the `USER_SDO_GEOM_METADATA` view that specifies the name of the GeoRaster table and the `SPATIALEXTENT` attribute of the GeoRaster column (that is, the column of type `SDO_GEORASTER`). The SQL in Listing D-16 shows an example.

   Listing D-16. *Populating the Metadata for the Spatial Extent of the* `georaster` *Column*

   ```
   INSERT INTO USER_SDO_GEOM_METADATA VALUES
   ( 'branches',
     'georaster.spatialextent',
     SDO_DIM_ARRAY
   ```

1. This is not possible in MapViewer version 9.0.4.

```
    (
      SDO_DIM_ELEMENT('X', -180, 180, 0.5),
      SDO_DIM_ELEMENT('Y', -90, 90, 5)
    ),
    8307   -- SRID
  );
```

4. Create a spatial index on the spatial extent of the GeoRaster table. The SQL in Listing D-17 shows an example.

   Listing D-17. *Creating an Index on the Spatial Extent of the* georaster *Column*

   ```
   CREATE INDEX geor_idx ON branches(georaster.spatialextent)
   INDEXTYPE IS MDSYS.SPATIAL_INDEX;
   ```

5. Optionally, generate pyramid levels that represent the raster image or data at different sizes and degrees of resolution. See Listing D-8 for an example.

To support the visualization of GeoRaster data, MapViewer defines a new type of theme called the GEORASTER theme (see Listing D-18). This theme can have elements to specify the name of the raster data table.

Listing D-18. *Creating a Predefined Theme for the* georaster *Column in the* branches *Table*

```
INSERT INTO user_sdo_themes  VALUES
(
   'BRANCHES_Images',  -- Theme name
   'Tiff Image',       -- Description
   'BRANCHES',         -- Base table name
   'GEORASTER',        -- Column name storing georaster object in table
   '<?xml version="1.0" standalone="yes"?>
    <styling_rules theme_type="georaster" raster_table="BRANCHES_RDT"
                   raster_id="1" >
    </styling_rules>'  --  Theme style definition
);
```

You can use this predefined theme in the definition of a map. Alternatively, you can create a *dynamic* theme using the JDBC_GEORASTER_QUERY element, as shown in Listing D-19.

Listing D-19. *Creating a Dynamic Theme for GeoRaster Objects*

```
<theme name="georaster_theme" >
  <jdbc_georaster_query
    georaster_table="branches"
    georaster_column="georaster"
    jdbc_srid="8307"
    datasource="mvdemo"
    asis="false"> SELECT georaster FROM branches WHERE id =1
  </jdbc_georaster_query>
</theme>
COMMIT;
```

Once you incorporate either the predefined themes or the dynamic themes in a client request for a map, you can view the raster data at different pyramid levels as you zoom in and out using MapViewer. MapViewer automatically determines which pyramid level to use; you don't have to do anything special.

Summary

Oracle Spatial provides a data type and storage mechanism called `SDO_GEORASTER` for storing spatial objects in a raster (image/grid) format. Oracle Spatial provides a number of adapters to import and export data into this `SDO_GEORASTER` format from external image and raster formats. You can also utilize third-party tools from companies such as PCI Geomatics and Safe Software for importing from or exporting to tens of external raster formats. Once the object is in an `SDO_GEORASTER` column, you can perform a variety of query and manipulation procedures such as subsetting, pyramid generation, and bitmap masking. You can specify compression parameters to return the output of various GeoRaster procedures in JPEG-B, JPEG-F, or DEFLATE compression formats. You can visualize the raster data using Oracle MapViewer. In short, the Oracle GeoRaster component provides the efficient storage, retrieval, query, and manipulation of a variety of raster data, including aerial photos, satellite images, digital terrain/elevation models, and gridded data inside the Oracle database server.

APPENDIX E

Three-Dimensional Modeling Using Point Clouds and TINs in Oracle

Due to the recent advances in laser-scanning technologies, the acquisition of location and height information using laser scanners and other such equipment has become quite popular. Many companies utilize such laser-scanning techniques to create three-dimensional point datasets (the first two dimensions, x,y, for location, and the third dimension, z, for height) in a variety of applications including city modeling, bathymetry (ocean floor modeling), and three-dimensional object modeling. Since such point datasets are usually dense, they are referred to as *point clouds*. Figure E-1 shows the typical workflow for creating three-dimensional representations of objects using point clouds in one such application:

1. The objects are first scanned using laser scanners, and a point cloud representation of the object is created. This point cloud representation is a set of three-dimensional point values with depth/height values for different x,y scan locations.
2. Using the points in the point cloud, a surface representation using triangles is generated. Typically a specific type of triangulation, called *Delaunay triangulation*, is used. (You will learn about it later in the chapter.)
3. The triangulated surface is further refined in successive steps to create a smooth three-dimensional object representation in the appropriate format.

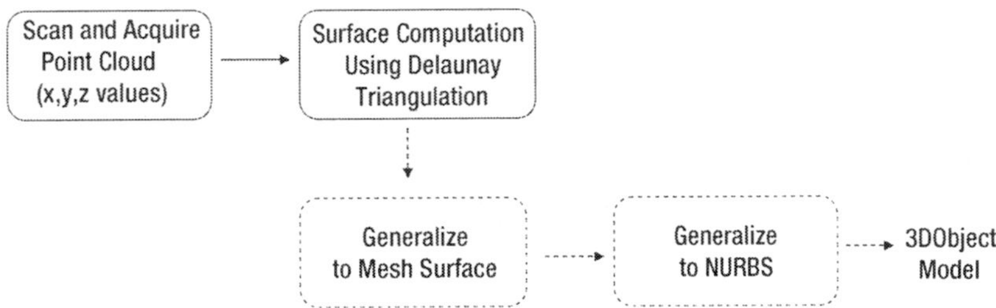

Figure E-1. *Typical workflow in a three-dimensional modeling framework*

The first two steps of the workflow are employed not only in three-dimensional object modeling but also for obtaining representations of city landscapes. Oracle Spatial provides tools to aid in the first two steps of such a modeling workflow. You can create, store, and query a large set of points, or point clouds, using a new data type called SDO_PC (PC is short for *point cloud*). You can also create a triangulated irregular network (TIN) for a given set of points and store the TIN persistently (perform queries) in the database using the SDO_TIN data type. In this appendix, you will learn about each of these data types in turn.

Storing Large Point Sets

In a three-dimensional modeling framework, the acquired three-dimensional datasets tend to be relatively large, typically of the order of hundreds of thousands (or more) of points for each scan. Storing such three-dimensional point data as a multipoint collection using the SDO_GEOMETRY type may not be an ideal solution for two reasons: the number of ordinates in the SDO_GEOMETRY cannot exceed the 1 million limit, and the entire set of points is stored as a single array, which means you cannot search and access the point set piecemeal by area of interest. For such large point sets, you can use a new data type in Oracle called SDO_PC.

The SDO_PC Data Type

Starting in Oracle Database 11g, you can use the SDO_PC type to model a point cloud object in Oracle (we will use the terms *point cloud* and SDO_PC interchangeably from now on). Figure E-2 shows the storage architecture for a point cloud using the SDO_PC type in Oracle. As shown in the figure, you can have a table, say pc_tab, with a column of type SDO_PC. This column stores the metadata associated with the point cloud. The points of the point cloud are, however, divided into subsets and stored as multiple rows (in the points BLOB column) of a separate table, say pc_blktab. We refer to the table that stores the SDO_PC column as the *base table* and the table that stores the point cloud blocks as the *block table*. Listing E-1 and Listing E-2 show the SQL for creating the base table named pc_tab and a block table named pc_blktab. The block table is created using the columns in the table MDSYS.SDO_PC_BLK_TABLE.

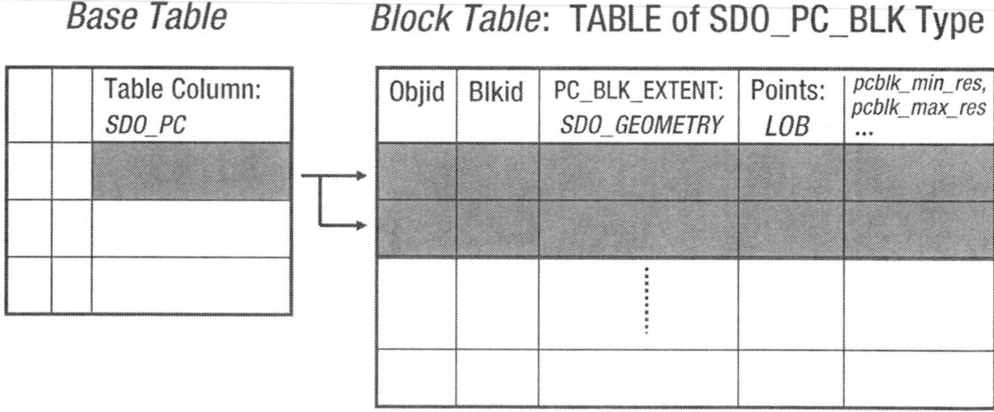

Figure E-2. *Scalable storage framework for a point cloud in Oracle*

Listing E-1. *Adding an* SDO_PC *Column to Store Point Cloud Data*

```
SQL> CREATE TABLE pc_tab  (pc SDO_PC);
```

Listing E-2. *Creating* pc_blktab *As the Block Table for the Point Cloud Data*

```
SQL> CREATE TABLE pc_blktab AS SELECT * FROM MDSYS.SDO_PC_BLK_TABLE;
```

Observe that you have to create the block table yourself as shown in Listing E-2. You can see that we created a table pc_blktab to have the same fields as the table MDSYS.SDO_PC_BLK_TABLE. By always creating the block table in this manner, you will not have to change your code even if Oracle changes the attributes for the block table.

Note You can create the block table directly by naming the columns and their types. But the block table should at least have the same columns as the table MDSYS.SDO_PC_BLK_TABLE and can contain additional columns.

The advantages of this storage model for a point cloud (which includes storing the metadata of the point cloud in the base table and storing the points as multiple blocks/rows in the block table) include the following:

- No upper bound on the number of points in a point cloud object (because there is no limit on the number of rows in a table).
- Efficient selection of a subset of the point cloud by specifying a query window or a block (blk_id); the query accesses only relevant blocks for the specified query window or block.
- Efficient update of specific blocks of a point cloud (not in Oracle 11.1.0.6 but will be available in subsequent releases of Oracle).
- Use of Oracle table partitioning features for the block table. You can create the block table as an Oracle-partitioned table based on blk_id ranges. This will extend all the features of partitioning such as manageability and parallel scans of partitions for point clouds.
- Use of secure LOB structure for the points column in the block tables. Since the creation and management of the block table is in your hands, you can alter the points column to use SecureFiles[1] for LOB storage. This will extend the performance features of Oracle SecureFiles to point clouds.
- Automatic cleanup of the block table when a point cloud object is deleted from the base table.
- Automatic cleanup of the block table when a base table is truncated.

Given this understanding of how a point cloud can be stored in an Oracle database using the SDO_PC data type, you can now proceed to populate the base tables with point cloud objects. You can look up all manipulation functions for a point cloud in the package SDO_PC_PKG.

Populating a Point Cloud

We'll now illustrate how to populate an input set of points stored in a table or view, called INPTAB, into a point cloud (SDO_PC column) in Oracle. First, Oracle stipulates INPTAB has the structure shown in Listing E-3 (if it does not, you can create a view with those columns).

---

1. Please refer to the *Oracle Database SecureFiles and Large Objects Developer's Guide* to learn about this feature.

Listing E-3. *Structure of the Table Storing Input Set of Points*

```
SQL> DESC INPTAB;
 Name                                      Null?    Type
 ----------------------------------------- -------- ----------------------------
 RID                                                VARCHAR2(40)
 VAL_D1                                             NUMBER
 VAL_D2                                             NUMBER
 VAL_D3                                             NUMBER
```

The RID column in Listing E-3 is a unique identifier for a point. The VAL_D1, VAL_D2, and VAL_D3 represent the ordinates for a three-dimensional point. If the total number of dimensions is N, INPTAB has to have columns of the form RID, VAL_D1, VAL_D2, . . . VAL_DN.

■ **Tip** INPTAB does not have to be a physical table. It can be an external table interface where the data is stored in a file. See the Oracle documentation for information about how to use external tables.

To populate a point cloud object in the pc_tab table, you need to perform the following operations. Listing E-5 later in the chapter shows the PL/SQL block for these operations.

1. Initialize a point cloud object using the SDO_PC_PKG.INIT function. Here you specify a variety of parameters for the point cloud including the following:
    - The name of the base table
    - The column in which this SDO_PC object is being inserted
    - The block table that stores the blocks of the SDO_PC object
    - The maximum block capacity of each point cloud block
    - The extent of the SDO_PC object specified as an SDO_GEOMETRY
    - The tolerance associated with the SDO_PC object
    - The total number of dimensions that are stored in the SDO_PC object

    Note that the dimensionality of the extent specifies how many dimensions are to be used for partitions (for example, if it is 2, that is, if the SDO_GTYPE in extent is 2003, then the first two dimensions are used for partitioning the input point set). The total number of dimensions, on the other hand, specifies the total number that is stored with each point. In other words, this includes additional dimensions such as z values (or intensity values, and so on).
2. Insert the SDO_PC object in the pc_tab table.
3. Insert an input set of points from the INPTAB table into the initialized point cloud object using the SDO_PC_PKG.CREATE_PC procedure. This procedure reads the points from the INPTAB table, partitions them into subsets, and inserts each subset of points into a separate row in the block table associated with the point cloud. You can *optionally* specify a third parameter for a result table, RESTAB. If the result table is specified, Oracle populates it with the input set of points, after augmenting each point with two additional attributes: ptn_id and point_id. ptn_id refers to the block (blk_id) in whose points BLOB the point is stored. point_id is the offset for the point in the points LOB. This means for INPTAB listed in Listing E-3, the result table has to be created as shown in Listing E-4.

Listing E-4. *Result Table for Three-Dimensional Point Data*

```
SQL> CREATE TABLE restab (ptn_id NUMBER, point_id NUMBER,
rid VARCHAR2(24), val_d1 NUMBER, val_d2 NUMBER, val_d3 NUMBER);
```

Listing E-5 shows the PL/SQL block for populating a point cloud using an input set of points. This code performs all the operations mentioned earlier: initializing a point cloud object pc, inserting into a table called pc_tab, and inserting an input point set from table inptab into the point cloud object.

Listing E-5. *Initializing, Inserting, and Populating a Point Cloud with an Input Set of Points*

```
SQL> -- Initialize a PointCloud object and populate it using the points in INPTAB.
DECLARE
  pc sdo_pc;
BEGIN
  -- Initialize the point cloud object.
  pc := SDO_PC_PKG.INIT(
          'PC_TAB', -- Table that has the SDO_POINT_CLOUD column defined
          'PC',   -- Column name of the SDO_POINT_CLOUD object
          'PC_BLKTAB', -- Table to store blocks of the point cloud
           'blk_capacity=50', -- max # of points per block
           SDO_GEOMETRY(2003, 8307, NULL,
          -- Extent: 2 in 2003 in preceding line indicates that
          -- ptn_dimensionality is 2. This means only the first 2 dimensions are
          -- used in partitioning the input point set. The index on the block table
          -- will also have a dimensionality of 2 in this case.
          --
             SDO_ELEM_INFO_ARRAY(1,1003,3),
             SDO_ORDINATE_ARRAY(-180, -90, 180, 90)
            ),
           0.5, -- Tolerance for point cloud
           3, -- Total number of dimensions is 3; the third dimension is stored
               -- but not used for partitioning
           NULL  -- This parameter is for enabling compression but  always set to
                       -- NULL in  Oracle 11gR1;
   );

  -- Insert the point cloud object  into the "base" table.
  INSERT INTO pctab (pc) VALUES (pc);

  -- Create the blocks for the point cloud.
  SDO_PC_PKG.CREATE_PC(
    pc,       -- Initialized PointCloud object
    'INPTAB' -- Name of input table to ingest into the point cloud
    'RESTAB'     -- Name of output table that stores the points
                        -- (with addl. Columns ptn_id,pt_id)  );
END;
/
```

The code in Listing E-5 populates the blocks in the block table. You can verify that the number of points in INPTAB matches the sum of the number of points in each block of the pc_blktab using the SQL in Listings E-6 and E-7.

Listing E-6. *Number of Points in* INPTAB

```
SQL>  SELECT count(*) FROM INPTAB;
```

Listing E-7. *Verifying Number of Points in the Point Cloud (Associated Block Table)*

```
SQL> SELECT sum(num_points) FROM pc_blktab;
```

■ **Caution** The `sdo_pc_pkg.create_pc` procedure is a DDL[2] operation. If you want to roll back the operation of inserting points into a point cloud object, you need to explicitly delete the point cloud object from the base table (which will implicitly clean up the corresponding entries in the block table). When applicable, use `truncate` instead of `delete`, because `truncate` will be faster.

Querying a Point Cloud

Once you have populated a point cloud, you can query it by specifying a query window using the `SDO_PC_PKG.CLIP_PC` function. This function takes as input an `SDO_PC` object, an `SDO_GEOMETRY` as the query window, and additional `NULL` parameters (see the documentation for details) to return a table of `MDSYS.SDO_PC_BLK_TABLE` (that is, essentially a new block table), where the points completely intersect the query window. You can store the returned rows as a table `QRYRES`, as shown in Listing E-8.

Listing E-8. *Querying a Point Cloud Object*

```
SQL> CREATE TABLE qryres AS SELECT * FROM MDSYS.SDO_PC_BLK_TABLE;

-- Query
DECLARE
  inp  sdo_pc;
BEGIN
  SELECT pc INTO inp  FROM pc_tab WHERE rownum=1;
  INSERT INTO qryres
  SELECT * FROM
    TABLE(SDO_PC_PKG.CLIP_PC
          (
            inp,  -- Input point cloud object
            SDO_GEOMETRY(2003, 8307, NULL,
              SDO_ELEM_INFO_ARRAY(1, 1003, 3),
              SDO_ORDINATE_ARRAY(-74.1, -73.9, 39.99999,40.00001)
             ), -- QUERY
            NULL, NULL, NULL, NULL));
END;
/
```

Observe that the table `QRYRES` has the same columns as the table `MDSYS.SDO_PC_BLK_TABLE`. This means the intersecting points are returned in the `points` BLOB column of the table. You have to read the points into your application and unmarshal the BLOB to extract the point information (the LOB format is published by Oracle). Alternately, you can convert the points in the BLOB to an `SDO_GEOMETRY` object using the `SDO_PC_PKG.TO_GEOMETRY` function. This function takes as input the input BLOB of points, the exact number of points in the BLOB, the total dimensionality of each point, and an optional `SRID` to set in the result geometry. Listing E-9 shows an example.

Listing E-9. *Get the Points in Each Block As a Multipoint Collection* `SDO_GEOMETRY`

```
SQL> SELECT blk_id, SDO_PC_PKG.TO_GEOMETRY(
                    r.points,    -- LOB containing the points
                    r.num_points, -- # of points in the LOB
```

---

2. DDL is short for Data Definition Language in database parlance. A DDL statement ends (commits) current transaction (if any) in the session.

```
                3, -- Total dimensionality of the points in the LOB
                8307 -- SRID
              ) FROM  qryres r;
```

What if you just wanted the IDs of the points returned in a query and stored in the RESQRY table? You can simply use the SDO_PC_PKG.GET_PT_IDS function for this purpose. This function takes an input points BLOB, the exact number of points in the LOB, and their total dimensionality. The function returns an array of numbers where each pair of numbers indicates the <ptn_id, pt_id> values for a point. Listing E-10 shows the SQL. You can take this information and join with the RESTAB table to obtain all the attributes of all intersecting points for a given query window.

Listing E-10. *Selecting the Point IDs in Each Block As an Array of* <ptn_id, point_id> *Pairs*

```
SQL> SELECT SDO_PC_PKG.GET_PT_IDS(
                r.points,     -- LOB containing the points
                r.num_points, -- # of points in the LOB
                3 -- Total dimensionality of the points in the LOB
              ) FROM resqry r WHERE num_points >0;
```

Other Manipulation Functions for Point Clouds

If you intend to have your own way of dividing a point cloud into smaller pieces and storing those pieces, you can still utilize the SDO_PC storage framework in Oracle. All you need to do is populate the relevant columns such as blk_id, num_points, and blk_extent, as well as the points BLOB in the block table. For this, you will have to contact Oracle for the published structure of the points BLOB.

Another common type of functionality associated with point clouds is the ability *to generate and query using coarser resolution of point clouds.* Oracle does not provide any functionality for generating a coarser resolution point cloud from a given point cloud. However, there are well-known algorithms to do that. If you generate coarser resolution point clouds, you can store them in the same block table as for the original point cloud. The pcblk_min_res and pcblk_max_res values for the coarser-resolution point cloud have to be set to nonzero (0 is the default resolution for the original point cloud blocks). Once you compute the coarser resolutions, you can still utilize Oracle's CLIP_PC procedure to perform a query not just on a query window but also a range on the resolution. The CLIP_PC takes as its fourth and fifth arguments, qry_min_res (minimum resolution level) and qry_max_res (maximum resolution level), to include in the query. Blocks that do not satisfy this resolution range are excluded from the result of the CLIP_PC.

In Oracle Database 11*g* Release 1, Oracle does not provide additional functionality for updating individual points or addition of new points to a point cloud. When adding or modifying existing points, you will have to reconstruct the entire point cloud object by invoking the CREATE_PC procedure as in Listing E-5. This functionality may be added to the SDO_PC_PKG package in later releases.

Storing Triangulated Irregular Networks

A triangulated irregular network (TIN) is a simple approximation of the surface formed from a set of input points. Among the different methods for triangulation, the most popular is the Delaunay triangulation. A Delaunay triangulation tries to ensure that within the *scope*, that is, the *circumcircle*, of a triangle connecting three points there cannot be a fourth point from the input set. Consider the points in Figure E-3 (a). Instead of connecting A, B, and C as a triangle, if A, B, and D were to form a triangle, you could clearly observe that the circle circumscribing that triangle (called the *circumcircle*) also includes the point C and hence is not a Delaunay triangulation. Figure E-3 (b) shows a Delaunay triangulation for the given set of points.

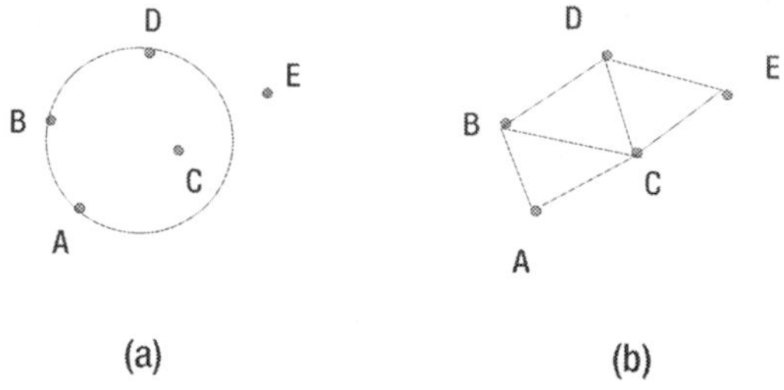

Figure E-3. *(a) Input set of points and (b) Delaunay TIN*

The SDO_TIN Data Type

Starting Oracle 11*g*, you can use the various procedures in the `SDO_TIN_PKG` package to create and query TINs[3] in an Oracle database.[4] The created TIN can be stored using the `SDO_TIN` type in Oracle (we will use the terms TIN and `SDO_TIN` interchangeably from now on). Figure E-4 shows the storage architecture for a TIN using the `SDO_TIN` type in Oracle. As shown in the figure, you can have a table, say `tin_tab`, with a column of type `SDO_TIN`. This column stores the metadata associated with the TIN. The points of the TIN are, however, divided into subsets and stored as multiple rows (in the `points` BLOB column) of a separate table, say `tin_blktab`. We refer to the table that stores the `SDO_TIN` column as the *base table* and the table that stores the TIN blocks as the *block table*. Listing E-11 and Listing E-12 show the SQL for creating the base table named `tin_tab` and a block table named `tin_blktab`. The block table is created using the columns in `MDSYS.SDO_TIN_BLK_TABLE`. Observe that in addition to storing the `points` as a BLOB column, the blocks of a TIN (in the block table) also store `triangles` information as a BLOB column.

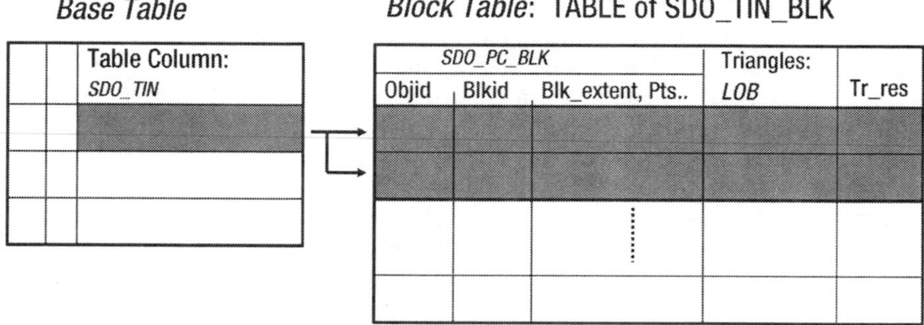

Figure E-4. *Scalable storage framework for a TIN in Oracle*

Listing E-11. *Adding an* `SDO_TIN` *Column to Store TIN Data*

```
SQL> CREATE TABLE tin_tab (tin SDO_TIN);
```

3. The created TIN will be Delaunay if no constraints such as break lines or stop lines are specified.

4. The triangulation may not be Delaunay if additional constraints such as break lines, and so on, are specified in the `CREATE_TIN` procedure. In Oracle 11*g* Release 1, these constraints are ignored.

Listing E-12. *Creating* `tin_blktab` *As the Block Table for the TIN Data*

```
SQL> CREATE TABLE tin_blktab AS SELECT * FROM MDSYS.SDO_TIN_BLK_TABLE;
```

Observe that you have to create the block table yourself, as shown in Listing E-2. You can see that we create a table `tin_blktab` to have the same fields as the table `MDSYS.SDO_TIN_BLK_TABLE`. By always creating the block table in this manner, you will not have to change your code even if Oracle changes the attributes for the block table.

■ **Note** You can create the block table directly by naming the columns and their types. But the block table should at least have the same columns as the table `MDSYS.SDO_TIN_BLK_TABLE` and can contain additional columns.

The advantages of this storage model for a TIN (which includes storing the metadata of the TIN in the base table and storing the points as multiple blocks/rows in the block table) include the following:

- No upper bound on the number of points and triangles in a TIN object (because there is no limit on the number of rows in a table).
- Efficient selection of a subset of the TIN by specifying a query window or a block (`blk_id`). The query accesses only relevant blocks for the specified query window or block.
- Efficient update of specific blocks of a TIN (not in Oracle 11.1.0.6 but will be available in subsequent releases of Oracle).
- Use of Oracle table partitioning features for the block table. You can create the block table as an Oracle-partitioned table based on `blk_id` ranges. This will extend all the features of partitioning such as manageability and parallel scans of partitions for TINs.
- Use of secure LOB structure for the points column in the block tables. Since the creation and management of the block table is in the your hands, you can alter the points column to use SecureFiles for LOB storage.[5] This will extend the performance features of Oracle SecureFiles to TINs.
- Automatic cleanup of the block table when a TIN object is deleted from the base table.
- Automatic cleanup of the block table when a base table is truncated.

Given this understanding of how a TIN is created and stored inside an Oracle database using the `SDO_TIN` data type, you can now proceed to populate the base tables with TIN objects. You can look up all manipulation functions for a TIN in the package `SDO_TIN_PKG`.

Populating a TIN

We'll now illustrate how to populate an input set of points stored in a table or view, called `INPTAB`, into a TIN (`SDO_TIN` column) in Oracle. First, Oracle stipulates that `INPTAB` has the structure shown in Listing E-13 (if it does not, you can create a view with those columns).

---

5. Please refer to the *Oracle Database SecureFiles and Large Objects Developer's Guide* to learn about this feature.

Listing E-13. *Structure of the Table Storing Input Set of Points*

```
SQL> DESC INPTAB;
 Name                                      Null?    Type
 ----------------------------------------- -------- ----------------------------
 RID                                                VARCHAR2(40)
 VAL_D1                                             NUMBER
 VAL_D2                                             NUMBER
 VAL_D3                                             NUMBER
```

The RID column is a unique identifier for a point. VAL_D1, VAL_D2, and VAL_D3 represent the ordinates for a three-dimensional point. If the total number of dimensions is N, INPTAB has to have columns of the form RID, VAL_D1,VAL_D2, . . . VAL_DN.

Tip INPTAB does not have to be a physical table. It can be an external table interface where the data is stored in a file. See the Oracle documentation for information on how to use external tables.

Note In Oracle 11*g* Release 1, to create the TIN, you need to have distinct (val_d1,val_d2) pairs in the INPTAB.

To populate a TIN object in the tin_tab table, you need to perform the following operations. Listing E-15 shows the PL/SQL block for these operations.

1. Initialize a TIN object using the SDO_TIN_PKG.INIT function. Here you specify a variety of parameters for the TIN including the following:
   - The name of the base table
   - The column in which this SDO_TIN object is being inserted
   - The block table that stores the blocks of the SDO_TIN object
   - The maximum block capacity of each TIN block
   - The extent of the SDO_TIN object specified as an SDO_GEOMETRY
   - The tolerance associated with the SDO_TIN object
   - The total number of dimensions that are stored in the SDO_TIN object

   Note that the dimensionality of the extent specifies how many dimensions are to be used for partitions (for example, if it is 2; that is, the SDO_GTYPE in extent is 2003, then the first two dimensions are used for partitioning the input point set). The total number of dimensions, on the other hand, specifies the total number that is stored with each point. In other words, this includes additional dimensions such as z values (or intensity values, and so on).
2. Insert the SDO_TIN object in the tin_tab table.
3. Insert an input set of points from the INPTAB table into the initialized TIN object using the SDO_TIN_PKG.CREATE_PC procedure. This procedure reads the points from the INPTAB table, partitions them into subsets, and inserts each subset of points into a separate row in the block table associated with the TIN. You can *optionally* specify a third parameter for a result table, RESTAB. If the result table is specified, Oracle populates it with the input set of points after augmenting each point with two additional attributes: ptn_id and point_id. The ptn_id refers to the block (blk_id) in whose points BLOB the point is stored. The point_id is the offset for the point in the points LOB. This means for the INPTAB listed in Listing E-13, the result table has to be created as in Listing E-14.

Listing E-14. *Result Table for Three-Dimensional Point Data*

```
SQL> CREATE TABLE restab (ptn_id NUMBER, point_id NUMBER,
rid VARCHAR2(24), val_d1 NUMBER, val_d2 NUMBER, val_d3 NUMBER);
```

Listing E-15 shows the PL/SQL block for populating a TIN using an input set of points. This code performs all the operations mentioned earlier: initializing a TIN object `tin`, inserting it into a table called `tin_tab`, and inserting an input point set from table `inptab` into the TIN object.

Listing E-15. *Initializing, Inserting, and Populating a TIN with an Input Set of Points*

```
SQL> -- Initialize a PointCloud object and populate it using the points in INPTAB.
DECLARE
  tin SDO_TIN;
BEGIN
  -- Initialize the TIN object.
  tin := SDO_TIN_PKG.INIT(
          'TIN_TAB', -- Table that has the SDO_TIN column defined
          'TIN',   -- Column name of the SDO_TIN object
          'TIN_BLKTAB', -- Table to store blocks of the TIN
           'blk_capacity=6000', -- max # of points per block
           SDO_GEOMETRY(2003, 8307, NULL,   -- Extent: 2 in 2003 indicates that
          -- ptn_dimensionality is 2. This means only the first 2 dimensions are
          -- used in partitioning the input point set. The index on the block table
          -- will also have a dimensionality of 2 in this case.
          --
              SDO_ELEM_INFO_ARRAY(1,1003,3),
              SDO_ORDINATE_ARRAY(-180, -90, 180, 90)
           ),
           0.00000005, -- Tolerance for TIN
           3, -- Total number of dimensions is 3; the third dimension is stored
               -- but not used for partitioning
           NULL  -- This parameter is for enabling compression but  always set to
                     -- NULL in  Oracle 11gR1;
   );

  -- Insert the TIN object  into the "base" table.
  INSERT INTO tin_tab (tin) VALUES (tin);

  -- Create the blocks for the TIN.
  SDO_TIN_PKG.CREATE_TIN(
    tin,       -- Initialized TIN object
    'INPTAB' -- Name of input table to ingest into the point cloud
    'RESTAB'     -- Name of output table that stores the points
                      -- (with addl. Columns ptn_id,pt_id)  );
END;
/
```

The code in Listing E-15 populates the blocks in the block table. You can verify that the number of points in `INPTAB` match the sum of the number of points in each block in the `tin_blktab` using the SQL shown in Listings E-16 and E-17.

Listing E-16. *Number of Points in* `INPTAB`

```
SQL>  SELECT count(*) FROM INPTAB;
```

Listing E-17. *Number of Points in Each Block of the Block Table*

```
SQL> SELECT blk_id, num_points FROM tin_blktab;
```

Caution The `sdo_tin_pkg.create_tin` procedure is a DDL operation. If you want to roll back the operation of inserting points into a point cloud object, you need to explicitly delete the point cloud object from the base table (which will implicitly clean up the corresponding entries in the block table). When applicable, use `truncate` instead of `delete`, because `truncate` is faster.

Querying a TIN

Once you have populated a TIN, you can query it by specifying a query window using the `SDO_TIN_PKG.CLIP_TIN` function. This function takes as input an `SDO_TIN` object, an `SDO_GEOMETRY` as a query window, and additional `NULL` parameters (see the documentation for details) to return a table of `MDSYS.SDO_TIN_BLK_TABLE` (that is, essentially a new block table), where the points completely intersect the query window. You can store the returned rows as a table `QRYRES`, as shown in Listing E-18.

Listing E-18. *Querying a TIN Object*

```
SQL> CREATE TABLE qryres AS SELECT * FROM MDSYS.SDO_TIN_BLK_TABLE;

-- Query
DECLARE
  inp  SDO_TIN;
BEGIN
  SELECT pc INTO inp  FROM tin_tab WHERE rownum=1;
  INSERT INTO qryres
  SELECT * FROM
    TABLE(SDO_TIN_PKG.CLIP_TIN
          (
            inp,  -- Input TIN object
            SDO_GEOMETRY(2003, 8307, NULL,
              SDO_ELEM_INFO_ARRAY(1, 1003, 3),
              SDO_ORDINATE_ARRAY(-74.1, -73.9, 39.99999,40.00001)
             ), -- QUERY
            NULL, NULL));
END;
/
```

Observe that the table `QRYRES` has the same columns as the table `MDSYS.SDO_TIN_BLK_TABLE`. This means the intersecting points and triangles are returned in the `points` BLOB and the `triangles` BLOB columns of the table. You have to read the points and the triangles into your application and unmarshall the BLOBs to extract the point and the triangle information (the LOB formats are published by Oracle). Alternately, you can convert the points and triangles in the BLOBs to an `SDO_GEOMETRY` object using the `SDO_TIN_PKG.TO_GEOMETRY` function. This function takes as input the input BLOB of points, the exact number of points in the BLOB, the input BLOB of triangles, the number of triangles in that BLOB, the index dimensionality (the dimensionality used for extent in the `SDO_TIN_PKG.INIT`), the total dimensionality of each point, and an optional `SRID` to set in the result geometry. The function returns a collection of triangles as an `SDO_GEOMETRY` object. Listing E-19 shows an example.

Listing E-19. *Get the Triangles in Each Block As a Collection* SDO_GEOMETRY

```
SQL> SELECT blk_id, SDO_TIN_PKG.TO_GEOMETRY(
                    r.points,    -- LOB containing the points
                    r.triangles,  -- LOB containing the triangles
                    r.num_points, -- # of points in the LOB
                    r.num_triangles, -- # of triangles in the LOB
                    2, -- Index dimensionality: dim value in SDO_GTYPE
                       -- of extent in SDO_TIN_PKG.INIT
                    3, -- Total dimensionality of the points in the LOB
                    8307 -- SRID
                  ) FROM  qryres r;
```

What if you just wanted the IDs of the points returned in the query and stored in the RESQRY table? Just as in the case of point clouds, you can simply use the SDO_PC_PKG.GET_PT_IDS function for this purpose. This function returns an array of numbers where each pair of numbers indicates the <ptn_id, pt_id> values for a point. You can take this information and join with the RESTAB table to obtain all attributes of all intersecting points for a given query window.

Other Manipulation Functions for TINs

Instead of using the built-in CREATE_TIN procedure, you can create your own TIN and store it in the base table and the block tables (that is, you can still utilize the SDO_TIN storage and query framework in Oracle). All you need to do is populate the relevant columns such as blk_id, num_points, blk_extent, and points and triangles BLOBs in the block table. For this, you will have to consult the Oracle documentation for the published structures for the points and triangles BLOBs.

Another common type of functionality associated with TINs is the ability *to generate and query using coarser resolution of TINs.* Oracle does not provide any functionality for generating a coarser resolution TIN from a given TIN. However, there are well-known algorithms to do that. If you generate coarser resolution TINs, you can store them in the same block table that is associated with the original TIN. The tr_res value for the coarser-resolution TIN has to be set to nonzero (0 is the default resolution for the original TIN blocks). Once you compute the coarser resolutions, you can still utilize Oracle's CLIP_TIN procedure to perform a query not just on query window but also a range on the resolution. The CLIP_TIN takes additional arguments, qry_min_res (minimum resolution level) and qry_max_res (maximum resolution level), to include in the query. Blocks that do not satisfy this resolution range are excluded from the result of the CLIP_TIN.

In Oracle 11*g* Release 1, Oracle does not provide additional functionality for updating individual points or adding new points to a TIN. When adding or modifying existing points, you will have to reconstruct the entire TIN object by invoking the CREATE_TIN procedure as in Listing E-15. Likewise, constraints such as break lines and stop lines are also not utilized in the constructed TIN. This functionality may be added to the SDO_TIN_PKG package in later releases.

Summary

Oracle Spatial provides new data types for scalable storage of point clouds and triangulated irregular networks. Each of these types is stored as multiple blocks in an associated block table. Oracle provides default routines for populating the block table using an input set of points. However, these routines can be overridden by user-defined point cloud partitioning or TIN creation routines.

Once the point cloud object or the TIN object is stored inside the Oracle storage framework, you can utilize the query functionality using the CLIP_PC or CLIP_TIN functions. These functions retrieve only relevant blocks for a query and hence provide a scalable platform for operating on these large objects. The queries can be combined with resolution parameters to support querying on multiresolution point clouds and TINs. The results of the CLIP_PC/CLIP_TIN functions can then be converted to SDO_GEOMETRY objects for display purposes in visualization tools such as MapViewer. When combined with table partitioning, the scalability can further be enhanced with the automatic use of parallel scanning on multiple partitions. In short, Oracle's SDO_PC and SDO_TIN types provide a scalable platform for storing large point sets and generating the first-level triangulated surfaces required for a three-dimensional object-modeling or city-modeling applications.

INDEX

B

D

G

J

L

M

N

P

U

Y

Z

CPSIA information can be obtained at www.ICGtesting.com
Printed in the USA
LVOW100247250412

279042LV00005B/8/P